A QUARTO
OF
MODERN LITERATURE

A QUARTO

OF MODERN

LITERATURE

ST. JOSEPH'S UNIVERSITY
PR1149.B7 1964   STX
A quarto of modern literature,

3 9353 00066 4142

Edited by

LEONARD BROWN

FIFTH EDITION

PR
1149
·B7
1964

177440

CHARLES SCRIBNER'S SONS *New York*

Copyright © 1964 Charles Scribner's Sons

Copyright 1935, 1940, 1950 © 1957 Charles Scribner's Sons; renewal copyright © 1963.

B–8.64[V]

All rights reserved. No part of this book
may be reproduced in any form without the
permission of Charles Scribner's Sons.

PRINTED IN THE UNITED STATES OF AMERICA

Library of Congress Catalog Card Number 64-16180

PUBLISHER'S PREFACE

IN planning the fifth edition of *A Quarto of Modern Literature*, we have continued to follow certain rules or principles of selection to which the continuing success of this anthology has given validity. As stated in an earlier preface, the principles are these. "We have tried to find stories, plays, poems, and articles on the one hand which have an immediate impact upon readers—and yet our final choice has been determined by the quality and likelihood of permanence of each piece. A good writer is the consciousness and the conscience of his race.

"The *Quarto* has never attempted to survey modern literature historically, and we do not attempt it in the present edition. We hope that our choices will provoke discussion and induce in the students who read the works an increasing understanding not only of literature but of human nature. It is even probable that some who read may be moved to emulate and be themselves writers."

New to this edition is a section titled "The Novel," which includes the complete texts of Edith Wharton's *Ethan Frome* and F. Scott Fitzgerald's *The Great Gatsby*. The inclusion of two novels—in addition to the usual full selection of short stories, plays, poetry, and prose—makes this edition of the *Quarto* a truly "complete" text for the course in literature. The prose section has been strengthened, we feel, by the addition of a number of selections—critical, biographical, and humorous—dealing with literary topics. Other changes include the reinsertion, in answer to numerous requests, of Jean Giraudoux's *The Madwoman of Chaillot*.

We wish to thank here those past users of the *Quarto* who have aided us in the preparation of this revision with their thoughtful and helpful suggestions, many of which have been incorporated into the present edition.

CONTENTS

PROSE

THE SHORT STORY

THE APPLE TREE

JOHN GALSWORTHY

JOHN GALSWORTHY (1867–1933) came of a Devonshire family, was educated at Harrow and for the law at Oxford, traveled widely, and at twenty-eight drifted into writing largely at the suggestion of the woman who later became his wife. After eleven years "without making a penny, or any name to speak of" he published *The Man of Property,* the first of the novels in *The Forsyte Saga,* his fictional study of British middle-class society; in the same year, 1906, *The Silver Box,* his first play, was produced. "A drama must be shaped," he tells us in *Some Platitudes Concerning Drama,* "so as to have a spire of meaning. Every grouping of life and character has its inherent moral; and the business of the dramatist is so to pose the group as to bring that moral poignantly to the light of day." He wished "to set before the public no cut-and-dried codes, but the phenomena of life and character, selected and combined, *but not distorted,* by the dramatist's outlook, set down without fear, favor, or prejudice, leaving the public to put down such poor moral as nature may afford. . . . A human being is the best plot there is," he continues, "he is organic. . . . The dramatist who hangs his characters to a plot, instead of hanging his plot to his characters, is guilty of cardinal sin. . . . Take care of character: action and dialogue will take care of themselves. . . ." His theories on the writing of fiction will be found in "A Novelist's Allegory" (*Inn of Tranquility,* 1912), and in *The Creation of Character in Literature,* 1931. Galsworthy was awarded the Order of Merit in 1929, the Nobel Prize in 1932.

"The Apple-tree, the singing, and the gold."
            —MURRAY's *Hippolytus of Euripides.*

ON their silver-wedding day Ashurst and his wife were motoring along the outskirts of the moor, intending to crown the festival by stopping the night at Torquay, where they had first met. This was the idea of Stella Ashurst, whose character contained a streak of sentiment. If she had long lost the blue-eyed, flower-like charm, the cool slim purity of face and form, the apple-blossom coloring, which had so swiftly and so oddly affected Ashurst twenty-six years ago, she was still at forty-three a comely and faithful companion, whose cheeks were faintly mottled, and whose gray-blue eyes had acquired a certain fullness.

It was she who had stopped the car where the common rose steeply to the left, and a narrow strip of larch and beech, with here and there a pine, stretched out towards the valley between the road and the first long high hill of the full moor. She was looking for a place where they might lunch, for Ashurst never looked for anything; and this, between the golden furze and the feathery green larches smelling of lemons in the last sun of April—this, with a view into the deep valley and up to the long moor heights, seemed fitting to the decisive nature of one

"The Apple Tree" (Copyright 1916, 1917 International Magazines Company; renewal copyright 1944, 1945 Hearst Magazines) is reprinted with the permission of Charles Scribner's Sons from *Five Tales* by John Galsworthy.

who sketched in water-colors, and loved romantic spots. Grasping her paint box, she got out.

"Won't this do, Frank?"

Ashurst, rather like a bearded Schiller, gray in the wings, tall, long-legged, with large remote gray eyes which sometimes filled with meaning and became almost beautiful, with nose a little to one side, and bearded lips just open—Ashurst, forty-eight, and silent, grasped the luncheon basket, and got out too.

"Oh! Look, Frank! A grave!"

By the side of the road, where the track from the top of the common crossed it at right angles and ran through a gate past the narrow wood was a thin mound of turf, six feet by one, with a moorstone to the west, and on it some one had thrown a black-thorn spray and a handful of bluebells. Ashurst looked, and the poet in him moved. At cross-roads—a suicide's grave! Poor mortals with their superstition! Whoever lay there, though, had the best of it, no clammy sepulcher among other hideous graves carved with futilities—just a rough stone, the wide sky, and wayside blessings! And, without comment, for he had learned not to be a philosopher in the bosom of his family, he strode away up on to the common, dropped the luncheon basket under a wall, spread a rug for his wife to sit on—she would turn up from her sketching when she was hungry—and took from his pocket Murray's translation of the "Hippolytus." He had soon finished reading of "The

Cyprian" and her revenge, and looked at the sky instead. And watching the white clouds so bright against the intense blue, Ashurst, on his silver-wedding day, longed for—he knew not what. Maladjusted to life—man's organism! One's mode of life might be high and scrupulous, but there was always an undercurrent of greediness, a hankering, and sense of waste. Did women have it too? Who could tell? And yet, men who gave vent to their appetites for novelty, their riotous longings for new adventures, new risks, new pleasures, these suffered, no doubt, from the reverse side of starvation, from surfeit. No getting out of it—a maladjusted animal, civilized man! There could be no garden of his choosing, of "the Apple-tree, the singing, and the gold," in the words of that lovely Greek chorus, no achievable elysium in life, or lasting haven of happiness for any man with a sense of beauty—nothing which could compare with the captured loveliness in a work of art, set down forever, so that to look on it or read was always to have the same precious sense of exaltation and restful inebriety. Life no doubt had moments with that quality of beauty, of unbidden flying rapture, but the trouble was, they lasted no longer than the span of a cloud's flight over the sun; impossible to keep them with you, as Art caught beauty and held it fast. They were fleeting as one of the glimmering or golden visions one had of the soul in nature, glimpses of its remote and brooding spirit. Here, with the sun hot on his face, a cuckoo calling from a thorn tree, and in the air the honey savor of gorse—here among the little fronds of the young fern, the starry blackthorn, while the bright clouds drifted by high above the hills and dreamy valleys—here and now was such a glimpse. But in a moment it would pass—as the face of Pan, which looks round the corner of a rock, vanishes at your stare. And suddenly he sat up. Surely there was something familiar about this view, this bit of common, that ribbon of road, the old wall behind him. While they were driving he had not been taking notice—never did; thinking of far things or of nothing—but now he saw! Twenty-six years ago, just at this time of year, from the farmhouse within half a mile of this very spot he had started for that day in Torquay whence it might be said he had never returned. And a sudden ache beset his heart; he had stumbled on just one of those past moments in his life, whose beauty and rapture he had failed to arrest, whose wings had fluttered away into the unknown; he had stumbled on a buried memory, a wild sweet time, swiftly choked and ended. And, turning on his face, he rested his chin on his hands, and stared at the short grass where the little blue milk-wort was growing. . . .

And this is what he remembered.

I

On the first of May, after their last year together at college, Frank Ashurst and his friend Robert Garton were on a tramp. They had walked that day from Brent, intending to make Chagford, but Ashurst's football knee had given out, and according to their map they had still some seven miles to go. They were sitting on a bank beside the road, where a track crossed alongside a wood, resting the knee and talking of the universe, as young men will. Both were over six feet, and thin as rails; Ashurst pale, idealistic, full of absence; Garton queer, round-the-corner, knotted, curly, like some primeval beast. Both had a literary bent; neither wore a hat. Ashurst's hair was smooth, pale, wavy, and had a way of rising on either side of his brow, as if always being flung back; Garton's was a kind of dark unfathomed mop. They had not met a soul for miles.

"My dear fellow," Garton was saying, "pity's only an effect of self-consciousness; it's a disease of the last five thousand years. The world was happier without."

Ashurst, following the clouds with his eyes, answered:

"It's the pearl in the oyster, anyway."

"My dear chap, all our modern unhappiness comes from pity. Look at animals, and Red Indians, limited to feeling their own occasional misfortunes; then look at ourselves—never free from feeling the toothaches of others. Let's get back to feeling for nobody, and have a better time."

"You'll never practice that."

Garton pensively stirred the hotch-potch of his hair.

"To attain full growth, one mustn't be squeamish. To starve oneself emotionally's a mistake. All emotion is to the good—enriches life."

"Yes, and when it runs up against chivalry?"

"Ah! That's so English! If you speak of emotion the English always think you want something physical, and are shocked. They're afraid of passion, but not of lust—oh, no!—so long as they can keep it secret."

Ashurst did not answer; he had plucked a blue floweret, and was twiddling it against the sky. A cuckoo began calling from a thorn tree. The sky, the flowers, the songs of birds! Robert was talking through his hat! And he said:

"Well, let's go on, and find some farm where we can put up." In uttering those words, he was conscious of a girl coming down from the common just above them. She was outlined against the sky, carrying a basket, and you could see that sky through the crook of her arm. And Ashurst, who saw beauty without wondering how it could advantage him, thought: 'How pretty!' The wind, blowing her dark frieze skirt against her legs, lifted her battered peacock tam-o'-shanter; her grayish blouse was worn and old, her shoes were split, her little hands rough and red, her neck browned. Her dark hair waved untidy across her broad forehead, her face was short, her upper lip short, showing a glint of teeth, her brows were straight and dark, her lashes long and dark, her nose straight; but her gray eyes were the wonder—dewy as if opened for the first time that day. She looked at Ashurst—perhaps he struck her as strange, limping along without a hat, with his large eyes on her, and his hair flung back. He could not take off what was not on his head, but put up his hand in a salute, and said:

"Can you tell us if there's a farm near here where we could stay the night? I've gone lame."

"There's only our farm near, sir." She spoke without shyness, in a pretty, soft, crisp voice.

"And where is that?"

"Down here, sir."

"Would you put us up?"

"Oh! I think we would."

"Will you show us the way?"

"Yes, sir."

He limped on, silent, and Garton took up the catechism.

"Are you a Devonshire girl?"

"No, sir."

"What then?"

"From Wales."

"Ah! I *thought* you were a Celt; so it's not your farm?"

"My aunt's, sir."

"And your uncle's?"

"He is dead."

"Who farms it, then?"

"My aunt, and my three cousins."

"But your uncle was a Devonshire man?"

"Yes, sir."

"Have you lived here long?"

"Seven years."

"And how d'you like it after Wales?"

"I don't know, sir."

"I suppose you don't remember?"

"Oh, yes! But it is different."

"I believe you!"

Ashurst broke in suddenly:

"How old are you?"

"Seventeen, sir."

"And what's your name?"

"Megan David."

"This is Robert Garton, and I am Frank Ashurst. We wanted to get on to Chagford."

"It is a pity your leg is hurting you."

Ashurst smiled, and when he smiled his face was rather beautiful.

Descending past the narrow wood, they came on the farm suddenly—a long, low, stone-built dwelling with casement windows, in a farmyard where pigs and fowls and an old mare were straying. A short steep-up grass hill behind was crowned with a few Scotch firs, and in front, an old orchard of apple-trees, just breaking into flower, stretched down to a stream and a long wild meadow. A little boy with oblique dark eyes was shepherding a pig, and by the house door stood a woman, who came towards them. The girl said:

"It is Mrs. Narracombe, my aunt."

"Mrs. Narracombe, my aunt," had a quick, dark eye, like a mother wild-duck's, and something of the same snaky turn about her neck.

"We met your niece on the road," said Ashurst; "she thought you might perhaps put us up for the night."

Mrs. Narracombe, taking them in from head to heel, answered:

"Well, I can, if you don't mind one room. Megan, get the spare room ready, and a bowl of cream. You'll be wanting tea, I suppose."

Passing through a sort of porch made by two yew trees and some flowering-currant bushes, the girl disappeared into the house, her peacock tam-o'-shanter bright athwart that rosy-pink and the dark green of the yews.

"Will you come into the parlor and rest your leg? You'll be from college, perhaps?"

"We were, but we've gone down now."

Mrs. Narracombe nodded sagely.

The parlor, brick-floored, with bare table and shiny chairs and sofa stuffed with horsehair, seemed never to have been used, it was so terribly clean. Ashurst sat down at once on the sofa, holding his lame knee between his hands, and Mrs. Narracombe gazed at him. He was the only son of a late professor of chemistry, but people found a certain lordliness in one who was often so sublimely unconscious of them.

"Is there a stream where we could bathe?"

"There's the strame at the bottom of the orchard, but sittin' down you'll not be covered!"

"How deep?"

"Well, 'tis about a foot and a half, maybe."

"Oh! That'll do fine. Which way?"

"Down the lane, through the second gate on the right, an' the pool's by the big apple-tree that stands by itself. There's trout there, if you can tickle them."

"They're more likely to tickle us!"

Mrs. Narracombe smiled. "There'll be the tea ready when you come back."

The pool, formed by the damming of a rock, had a sandy bottom; and the big apple-tree, lowest in the orchard, grew so close that its boughs almost overhung the water; it was in leaf, and all but in flower—its crimson buds just bursting. There was not room for more than one at a time in that narrow bath, and Ashurst waited his turn, rubbing his knee and gazing at the wild meadow, all rocks and thorn trees and field flowers, with a grove of beeches beyond, raised up on a flat mound. Every bough was swinging in the wind, every spring bird calling, and a slanting sunlight dappled the grass. He thought of Theocritus, and the river Cherwell, of the moon, and the maiden with the dewy eyes; of so many things that he seemed to think of nothing; and he felt absurdly happy.

II

During a late and sumptuous tea with eggs to it, cream and jam, and thin, fresh cakes touched with saffron, Garton descanted on the Celts. It was about the period of the Celtic awakening, and the discovery that there was Celtic blood about this family had excited one who believed that he was a Celt himself. Sprawling on a horsehair chair, with a hand-made cigarette dribbling from the corner of his curly lips, he had been plunging his cold pin-points of eyes into Ashurst's and praising the refinement of the Welsh. To come out of Wales into England was like the change from china to earthenware! Frank, as a d——d Englishman, had not of course perceived the exquisite refinement and emotional capacity of that Welsh girl! And, delicately stirring in the dark mat of his still wet hair, he explained how exactly she illustrated the writings of the Welsh bard Morgan-ap-Something in the twelfth century.

Ashurst, full length on the horsehair sofa, and jutting far beyond its end, smoked a deeply-colored pipe, and did not listen, thinking of the girl's face when she brought in a relay of cakes. It had been exactly like looking at a flower, or some other pretty sight in Nature—till, with a funny little shiver, she had lowered her glance and gone out, quiet as a mouse.

"Let's go to the kitchen," said Garton, "and see some more of her."

The kitchen was a white-washed room with rafters, to which were attached smoked hams; there were flower-pots on the window-sill, and guns hanging on nails, queer mugs, china and pewter, and portraits of Queen Victoria. A long, narrow table of plain wood was set with bowls and spoons, under a string of high-hung onions; two sheep-dogs and three cats lay here and there. On one side of the recessed fireplace sat two small boys, idle, and good as gold; on the other sat a stout, light-eyed, red-faced youth with hair and lashes the color of the tow he was running through the barrel of a gun; between them Mrs. Narracombe dreamily stirred some savory-scented stew in a large pot. Two other youths, oblique-eyed, dark-haired, rather sly-faced, like the two little boys, were talking together and lolling against the wall; and a short, elderly clean-shaven man in corduroys, seated in the window, was conning a battered journal. The girl Megan seemed the only active creature—drawing cider and passing with the jugs from cask to table. Seeing them thus about to eat, Garton said:

"Ah! If you'll let us, we'll come back when supper's over," and without waiting for an answer they withdrew again to the parlor. But the color in the kitchen, the warmth, the scents, and all those faces, heightened the bleakness of their shiny room, and they resumed their seats moodily.

"Regular gypsy type, those boys. There was only one Saxon—the fellow cleaning the gun. That girl is a very subtle study psychologically."

Ashurst's lips twitched. Garton seemed to him an ass just then. Subtle study! She was a wild flower. A creature it did you good to look at. Study!

Garton went on:

"Emotionally she would be wonderful. She wants awakening."

"Are you going to awaken her?"

Garton looked at him and smiled. 'How coarse and English you are!" that curly smile seemed saying.

And Ashurst puffed his pipe. Awaken her! This fool had the best opinion of himself! He threw up the window and leaned out. Dusk had gathered thick. The farm buildings and the wheel-house were all dim and bluish, the apple-trees but a blurred wilderness; the air smelled of wood smoke from the kitchen fire. One bird going to bed later than the others was uttering a half-hearted twitter, as though surprised at the darkness. From the stable came the snuffle and stamp of a feeding horse. And away over there was the loom of the moor, and away and away the shy stars which had not as yet full light, pricking white through the deep blue heavens. A quavering owl hooted. Ashurst drew a deep breath. What a night to wander out in! A padding of unshod hoofs came up the lane, and three dim, dark shapes passed—ponies on an evening march. Their heads, black and fuzzy, showed above the gate. At the tap of his pipe, and a shower of little sparks, they shied round and scampered. A bat went fluttering past, uttering its almost inaudible "chip, chip." Ashurst held out his hand; on the upturned palm he could feel the dew. Suddenly from overhead he heard little blurring boys' voices, little thumps of boots thrown down, and another voice, crisp and soft—the girl's putting them to bed, no doubt; and nine clear words: "No, Rick, you can't have the cat in bed"; then came a skirmish of giggles and gurgles, a soft slap, a laugh so low and pretty that it made him shiver a little. A blowing sound, and the glim of the candle which was fingering the dusk above, went out; silence reigned. Ashurst withdrew into the room and sat down; his knee pained him, and his soul felt gloomy.

"You go to the kitchen," he said; "I'm going to bed."

III

For Ashurst the wheel of slumber was wont to turn noiseless and slick and swift, but though he seemed sunk in sleep when his companion came up, he was really wide awake; and long after Garton, smothered in the other bed of that low-roofed room, was worshiping darkness with his upturned nose, he heard the owls. Barring the discomfort of his knee, it was not unpleasant—the cares of life did not loom large in night watches for this young man. In fact he had none; just enrolled a barrister, with literary aspirations, the world before him, no father or mother, and four hundred a year of his own. Did it matter where he went, what he did, or when he did it? His bed, too, was hard, and this preserved him from fever. He lay, sniffing the scent of the night which drifted into the low room through the open casement close to his head. Except for a definite irritation with his friend, natural when you have tramped with a man for three days, Ashurst's memories and visions that sleepless night were kindly and wistful and exciting. One vision, specially clear and unreasonable, for he had not even been conscious of noting it, was the face of the youth cleaning the gun; its intent, stolid, yet startled uplook at the kitchen doorway, quickly shifted to the girl carrying the cider jug. This red, blue-eyed, light-lashed, tow-haired face stuck as firmly in his memory as the girl's own face, so dewy and simple. But at last, in the square of darkness through the uncurtained casement, he saw day coming, and heard one hoarse and sleepy caw. Then followed silence, dead as ever, till the song of a blackbird, not properly awake, adventured into the hush. And, from staring at the framed brightening light, Ashurst fell asleep.

Next day his knee was badly swollen; the walking tour was obviously over. Garton, due back in London on the morrow, departed at midday with an ironical smile which left a scar of irritation—healed the moment his loping figure vanished round the corner of the steep lane. All day Ashurst rested his knee, in a green-painted wooden chair on the patch of grass by the yew-tree porch, where the sunlight distilled the scent of stocks and gilly-flowers, and a ghost of scent from the flowering-currant bushes. Beatifically, he smoked, dreamed, watched.

A farm in spring is all birth—young things coming out of bud and shell, and human beings watching over the process with faint excitement feeding and tending what has been born. So still the young man sat, that a mother-goose, with stately cross-footed waddle, brought her six yellow-necked gray-backed goslings to strop their little beaks against the grass blades at his feet. Now and again Mrs. Narracombe or the girl Megan would come and ask if he wanted anything, and he would smile and say: "Nothing, thanks. It's splendid here." Towards teatime they came out together, bearing a long poultice of some dark stuff in a bowl, and after a long and solemn scrutiny of his swollen knee, bound it on. When they were gone, he thought of the girl's soft "Oh!"—of her pitying eyes, and the little wrinkle in her brow. And again he felt that unreasoning irritation against his departed friend, who had talked such rot about her. When she brought out his tea, he said:

"How did you like my friend, Megan?"

She forced down her upper lip, as if afraid that to smile was not polite. "He was a funny gentleman; he made us laugh. I think he is very clever."

"What did he say to make you laugh?"

"He said I was a daughter of the bards. What are they?"

"Welsh poets, who lived hundreds of years ago."

"Why am I their daughter, please?"

"He meant that you were the sort of girl they sang about."

She wrinkled her brows. "I think he likes to joke. Am I?"

"Would you believe me, if I told you?"

"Oh, yes."

"Well, I think he was right."

She smiled.

And Ashurst thought: "You *are* a pretty thing!"

"He said, too, that Joe was a Saxon type. What would that be?"

"Which is Joe? With the blue eyes and red face?"

"Yes. My uncle's nephew."

"Not your cousin, then?"

"No."

"Well, he meant that Joe was like the men who came over to England about fourteen hundred years ago, and conquered it."

"Oh! I know about them; but is he?"

"Garton's crazy about that sort of thing; but I must say Joe does look a bit Early Saxon."

"Yes."

That "yes" tickled Ashurst. It was so crisp and graceful, so conclusive, and politely acquiescent in what was evidently Greek to her.

"He said that all the other boys were regular gypsies. He should not have said that. My aunt laughed, but she didn't like it, of course, and my cousins were angry. Uncle was a farmer—farmers are not gypsies. It is wrong to hurt people."

Ashurst wanted to take her hand and give it a squeeze, but he only answered:

"Quite right, Megan. By the way, I heard you putting the little ones to bed last night."

She flushed a little. "Please to drink your tea—it is getting cold. Shall I get you some fresh?"

"Do you ever have time to do anything for yourself?"

"Oh, yes."

"I've been watching, but I haven't seen it yet."

She wrinkled her brows in a puzzled frown, and her color deepened.

When she was gone, Ashurst thought: "Did she think I was chaffing her? I wouldn't for the world!" He was at that age when to some men "Beauty's a flower," as the poet says, and inspires in them the thoughts of chivalry. Never very conscious of his surroundings, it was some time before he was aware that the youth whom Garton had called "a Saxon type" was standing outside the stable door; and a fine bit of color he made in his soiled brown velvet-cords, muddy gaiters, and blue shirt; red-armed, red-faced, the sun turning his hair from tow to flax; immovably stolid, persistent, unsmiling he stood. Then, seeing Ashurst looking at him, he crossed the yard at that gait of the young countryman always ashamed not to be slow and heavy-dwelling on each leg, and disappeared round the end of the house towards the kitchen entrance. A chill came over Ashurst's mood. Clods! With all the good will in the world, how impossible to get on terms with them! And yet—see that girl! Her shoes were split, her hands rough; but—what was it? Was it really her Celtic blood, as Garton had said?—she was a lady born, a jewel, though probably she could do no more than just read and write!

The elderly, clean-shaven man he had seen last night in the kitchen had come into the yard with a dog, driving the cows to their milking. Ashurst saw that he was lame.

"You've got some good ones there!"

The lame man's face brightened. He had the upward look in his eyes which prolonged suffering often brings.

"Yeas; they'm praaper buties; gude milkers tu."

"I bet they are."

"'Ope as yure leg's better, zurr."

"Thank you, it's getting on."

The lame man touched his own: "I know what 'tes, meself; 'tes a main worritin' thing, the knee. I've a 'ad mine bad this ten year."

Ashurst made the sound of sympathy which comes so readily from those who have an independent income, and the lame man smiled again.

"Mustn't complain, though—they mighty near 'ad it off."

"Ho!"

"Yeas; an' compared with what 'twas, 'tis almost so gude as nu."

"They've put a bandage of splendid stuff on mine."

"The maid she picks et. She'm a gude maid wi' the flowers. There's folks zeem to know the healin' in things. My mother was a rare one for that. 'Ope as yu'll zune be better, zurr. Goo ahn, therr!"

Ashurst smiled. "Wi' the flowers!" A flower herself.

That evening, after his supper of cold duck, junket, and cider, the girl came in.

"Please, auntie says—will you try a piece of our Mayday cake?"

"If I may come to the kitchen for it."

"Oh, yes! You'll be missing your friend."

"Not I. But are you sure no one minds?"

"Who would mind? We shall be very pleased."

Ashurst rose too suddenly for his stiff knee, staggered and subsided. The girl gave a little gasp, and held out her hands. Ashurst took them, small, rough, brown; checked his impulse to put them to his lips, and let her pull him up. She came close beside him, offering her shoulder. And leaning on her he walked across the room. That shoulder seemed quite the pleasantest thing he had ever touched. But he had presence of mind enough to catch his stick out of the rack, and withdraw his hand before arriving at the kitchen.

That night he slept like a top, and woke with his knee of almost normal size. He again spent the morning in his chair on the grass patch, scribbling down verses; but in the afternoon he wandered about with the two little boys Nick and Rick. It was Saturday, so they were early home from school; quick, shy, dark little rascals of seven and six, soon talkative, for Ashurst had a way with children. By four o'clock they had shown him all their methods of destroying life, except the tickling of trout; and with breeches tucked up, lay on their stomachs over the trout stream, pretending they had this accomplishment also. They tickled nothing, of course, for their giggling and shouting scared every spotted thing away. Ashurst, on a rock at the edge of the beech clump, watched them, and listened to the cuckoos, till Nick, the elder and less persevering, came up and stood beside him.

"The gypsy bogle zets on that stone," he said.

"What gypsy bogle?"

"Dunno; never zeen 'e. Megan zays 'e zets there; an' old Jim zeed 'e once. 'E was zettin' there naight afore our pony kicked-in father's 'ead. 'E plays the viddle."

"What tune does he play?"

"Dunno."

"What's he like?"

" 'E's black. Old Jim zays 'e's all over 'air. 'E's a praaper bogle. 'E don' come only at naight." The little boy's oblique dark eyes slid round. "D'yu think 'e might want to take me away? Megan's feared of 'e."

"Has she seen him?"

"No. She's not afeared o' yu."

"I should think not. Why should she be?"

"She zays a prayer for yu."

"How do you know that, you little rascal?"

"When I was asleep, she said: 'God bless us all, an' Mr. Ashes.' I 'eard 'er whisperin'."

"You're a little ruffian to tell what you hear when you're not meant to hear it!"

The little boy was silent. Then he said aggressively:

"I can skin rabbits. Megan, she can't bear skinnin' 'em. I like blood."

"Oh! you do; you little monster!"

"What's that?"

"A creature that likes hurting others."

The little boy scowled. "They'm only dead rabbits, what us eats."

"Quite right, Nick. I beg your pardon."

"I can skin frogs, tu."

But Ashurst had become absent. "God bless us all, and Mr. Ashes!" And puzzled by that sudden inaccessibility, Nick ran back to the stream where the giggling and shouts again uprose at once.

When Megan brought his tea, he said:

"What's the gypsy bogle, Megan?"

She looked up, startled.

"He brings bad things."

"Surely you don't believe in ghosts?"

"I hope I will never see him."

"Of course you won't. There aren't such things. What old Jim saw was a pony."

"No! There are bogles in the rocks; they are the men who lived long ago."

"They aren't gypsies, anyway; those old men were dead long before gypsies came."

She said simply: "They are all bad."

"Why? If there are any, they're only wild, like the rabbits. The flowers aren't bad for being wild; the thorn trees were never planted—and you don't mind them. I shall go down at night and look for your bogle, and have a talk with him."

"Oh, no! Oh, no!"

"Oh, yes! I shall go and sit on his rock."

She clasped her hands together: "Oh, please!"

"Why! What does it matter if anything happens to me?"

She did not answer; and in a sort of pet he added:

"Well, I daresay I shan't see him, because I suppose I must be off soon."

"Soon?"

"Your aunt won't want to keep me here."

"Oh, yes! We always let lodgings in summer."

Fixing his eyes on her face, he asked:

"Would you like me to stay?"

"Yes."

"I'm going to say a prayer for *you* to-night!"

She flushed crimson, frowned, and went out of the room. He sat cursing himself, till his tea was stewed. It was as if he had hacked with his thick boots at a clump of bluebells. Why had he said such a silly thing? Was he just a towny college ass like Robert Garton, as far from understanding this girl?

IV

Ashurst spent the next week confirming the restoration of his leg, by exploration of the country within easy reach. Spring was a revelation to him this year. In a kind of intoxication he would watch the pink-white buds of some backward beech tree sprayed up in the sunlight against the deep blue sky, or the trunks and limbs of the few Scotch firs, tawny in violent light, or again on the moor, the gale-bent larches which had such a look of life when the wind streamed in their young green, above the rusty black underboughs. Or he would lie on the banks, gazing at the clusters of dog-violets, or up in the dead bracken, fingering the pink, transparent buds of the dewberry, while the cuckoos called and yaffles laughed, or a lark, from very high, dipped its beads of song. It was certainly different from any spring he had ever known, for spring was within him, not without. In the daytime he hardly saw the family; and when Megan brought in his meals she always seemed too busy in the house or among the young things in the yard to stay talking long. But in the evenings he installed himself in the window seat in the kitchen, smoking and chatting with the lame man Jim, or Mrs. Narracombe, while the girl sewed, or moved about, clearing the supper things away. And sometimes with the sensation a cat must feel when it purrs, he would become conscious that Megan's eyes

—those dew-gray eyes—were fixed on him with a sort of lingering soft look which was strangely flattering.

It was on Sunday week in the evening, when he was lying in the orchard listening to a blackbird and composing a love poem, that he heard the gate swing to, and saw the girl come running among the trees, with the red-cheeked, stolid Joe in swift pursuit. About twenty yards away the chase ended, and the two stood fronting each other, not noticing the stranger in the grass—the boy pressing on, the girl fending him off. Ashurst could see her face, angry, disturbed; and the youth's—who would have thought that red-faced yokel could look so distraught! And painfully affected by that sight, he jumped up. They saw him then. Megan dropped her hands, and shrank behind a tree-trunk; the boy gave an angry grunt, rushed at the bank, scrambled over and vanished. Ashurst went slowly up to her. She was standing quite still, biting her lip—very pretty, with her fine, dark hair blown loose about her face, and her eyes cast down.

"I beg your pardon," he said.

She gave him one upward look, from eyes much dilated; then, catching her breath, turned away. Ashurst followed.

"Megan!"

But she went on; and taking hold of her arm, he turned her gently round to him.

"Stop and speak to me."

"Why do you beg my pardon? It is not to me you should do that."

"Well, then, to Joe."

"How dare he come after me?"

"In love with you, I suppose."

She stamped her foot.

Ashurst uttered a short laugh. "Would you like me to punch his head?"

She cried with sudden passion:

"You laugh at me—you laugh at us!"

He caught hold of her hands, but she shrank back, till her passionate little face and loose dark hair were caught among the pink clusters of the apple blossom. Ashurst raised one of her imprisoned hands and put his lips to it. He felt how chivalrous he was, and superior to that clod Joe—just brushing that small, rough hand with his mouth! Her shrinking ceased suddenly; she seemed to tremble towards him. A sweet warmth overtook Ashurst from top to toe. This slim maiden, so simple and fine and pretty, was pleased, then, at the touch of his lips. And, yielding to a swift impulse, he put his arms round her, pressed her to him, and kissed her forehead. Then he was frightened—she went so pale, closing her eyes, so that the long, dark lashes lay on her pale cheeks; her hands, too, lay inert at her sides. The touch of her breast sent a shiver through him. "Megan!" he sighed out, and let her go. In the utter silence a blackbird shouted. Then the girl seized his hand, put it to her cheek, her heart, her lips, kissed it passionately, and fled away among the mossy trunks of the apple-trees, till they hid her from him.

Ashurst sat down on a twisted old tree growing almost along the ground, and, all throbbing and bewildered, gazed vacantly at the blossom which had crowned her hair—those pink buds with one white open apple star. What had he done? How had he let himself be thus stampeded by beauty—or—just the spring! He felt curiously happy, all the same; happy and triumphant, with shivers running through his limbs, and a vague alarm. This was the beginning of—what? The midges bit him, the dancing gnats tried to fly into his mouth, and all the spring around him seemed to grow more lovely and alive; the songs of the cuckoos and the blackbirds, the laughter of the yaffles, the level-slanting sunlight, the apple blossom which had crowned her head—! He got up from the old trunk and strode out of the orchard, wanting space, an open sky, to get on terms with these new sensations. He made for the moor, and from an ash tree in the hedge a magpie flew out to herald him.

Of man—at any age from five years on—who can say he has never been in love? Ashurst had loved his partners at his dancing class; loved his nursery governess; girls in school-holidays; perhaps never been quite out of love, cherishing always some more or less remote admiration. But this was different, not remote at all. Quite a new sensation; terribly delightful, bringing a sense of completed manhood. To be holding in his fingers such a wild flower, to be able to put it to his lips, and feel it tremble with delight against them! What intoxication, and—embarrassment! What to do with it—how meet her next time? His first caress had been cool, pitiful: but the next could not be, now that, by her burning little kiss on his hand, by her pressure of it to her heart, he knew that she loved him. Some natures are coarsened by love bestowed on them; others, like Ashurst's, are swayed and drawn, warmed and softened, almost exalted, by what they feel to be a sort of miracle.

And up there among the tors he was racked between the passionate desire to revel in this new sensation of spring fulfilled within him, and a vague but very real uneasiness. At one moment he gave himself up completely to his pride at having captured this pretty, trustful, dewy-eyed thing! At the next he thought with factitious solemnity: "Yes, my boy! But look out what you're doing! You know what comes of it!"

Dusk dropped down without his noticing—dusk on the carved, Assyrian-looking masses of the rocks. And the voice of Nature said: "This is a new world for you!" As when a man gets up at four o'clock and goes out into a summer morning, and beasts, birds, trees stare at him and he feels as if all had been made new.

He stayed up there for hours, till it grew cold, then groped his way down the stones and heather roots to the road, back into the lane, and came again past the wild meadow to the orchard. There he struck a match and looked at his watch. Nearly twelve! It was black and unstirring in there now, very different from the lingering, bird-befriended brightness of six hours ago! And suddenly he saw this idyll of his with the eyes of the outer world—had mental vision of Mrs. Narracombe's snake-like neck turned, her quick dark glance taking it all in, her shrewd face hardening; saw the gypsy-like cousins coarsely mocking and distrustful; Joe stolid and furious; only the lame man, Jim, with the suffering eyes, seemed tolerable to his mind. And the village pub!—the gossiping matrons he passed on his walks; and then—his own friends—Robert Garton's smile when he went off that morning ten days ago; so ironical and knowing! Disgusting! For a minute he literally hated this earthly, cynical world to which one belonged, willy-nilly. The gate where he was leaning grew gray, a sort of shimmer passed before him and spread into the bluish darkness. The moon! He could just see it over the bank behind; red, nearly round—a strange moon! And turning away, he went up the lane which smelled of the night and cow-dung and young leaves. In the straw-yard he could see the dark shapes of cattle, broken by the pale sickles of their horns, like so many thin moons, fallen ends-up. He unlatched the farm gate stealthily. All was dark in the house. Muffling his footsteps, he gained the porch, and, blotted against one of the yew trees, looked up at Megan's window. It was open. Was she sleeping, or lying awake perhaps disturbed—unhappy at his absence? An owl hooted while he stood there peering up, and the sound seemed to fill the whole night, so quiet was all else, save for the never-ending murmur of the stream running below the orchard. The cuckoos by day, and now the owls—how wonderful they voiced this troubled ecstasy within him! And suddenly he saw her at her window, looking out. He moved a little from the yew tree, and whispered: "Megan!" She drew back, vanished, reappeared, leaning far down. He stole forward on the grass patch, hit his shin against the green-painted chair, and held his breath at the sound. The pale blur of her stretched-down arm and face did not stir; he moved the chair, and noiselessly mounted it. By stretching up his arm he could just reach. Her hand held the huge key of the front door, and he clasped that burning hand with the cold key in it. He could just see her face, the

glint of teeth between her lips, her tumbled hair. She was still dressed—poor child, sitting up for him, no doubt! "Pretty Megan!" Her hot, roughened fingers clung to his; her face had a strange, lost look. To have been able to reach it—even with his hand! The owl hooted, a scent of sweet-briar crept into his nostrils. Then one of the farm dogs barked; her grasp relaxed, she shrank back.

"Good night, Megan!"

"Good night, sir!" She was gone! With a sigh he dropped back to earth, and, sitting on that chair, took off his boots. Nothing for it but to creep in and go to bed; yet for a long while he sat unmoving, his feet chilly in the dew, drunk on the memory of her lost, half-smiling face, and the clinging grip of her burning fingers, pressing the cold key into his hand.

V

He awoke feeling as if he had eaten heavily overnight, instead of having eaten nothing. And far off, unreal, seemed yesterday's romance! Yet it was a golden morning. Full spring had burst at last—in one night the "goldie-cups," as the little boys called them, seemed to have made the field their own, and from his window he could see apple blossoms covering the orchard as with a rose and white quilt. He went down almost dreading to see Megan; and yet, when not she but Mrs. Narracombe brought in his breakfast, he felt vexed and disappointed. The woman's quick eye and snaky neck seemed to have a new alacrity this morning. Had she noticed?

"So you an' the moon went walkin' last night, Mr. Ashurst! Did ye have your supper anywheres?"

Ashurst shook his head.

"We kept it for you, but I suppose you was too busy in your brain to think o' such a thing as that?"

Was she mocking him, in that voice of hers, which still kept some Welsh crispness against the invading burr of the West Country? If she knew! And at that moment he thought: "No, no; I'll clear out. I won't put myself in such a beastly false position."

But, after breakfast, the longing to see Megan began and increased with every minute, together with fear lest something should have been said to her which had spoiled everything. Sinister that she had not appeared, not given him even a glimpse of her! And the love poem, whose manufacture had been so important and absorbing yesterday afternoon under the apple-trees, now seemed so paltry that he tore it up and rolled it into pipe spills. What had he known of love, till she seized his hand and kissed it! And now—what did he not know? But to write of it seemed mere insipidity! He went up to his bedroom to get a book, and his heart began to beat violently, for she was in there making the bed. He stood in the doorway watching; and suddenly, with turbulent joy, he saw her stoop and kiss his pillow, just at the hollow made by his head last night. How let her know he had seen that pretty act of devotion? And yet if she heard him stealing away, it would be even worse. She took the pillow up, holding it as if reluctant to shake out the impress of his cheek, dropped it, and turned round.

"Megan!"

She put her hands up to her cheeks, but her eyes seemed to look right into him. He had never before realized the depth and purity and touching faithfulness in those dew-bright eyes, and he stammered:

"It was sweet of you to wait up for me last night."

She still said nothing, and he stammered on:

"I was wandering about on the moor; it was such a jolly night. I—I've just come up for a book."

Then, the kiss he had seen her give the pillow afflicted him with sudden headiness, and he went up to her. Touching her eyes with his lips, he thought with queer excitement: "I've done it! Yesterday all was sudden—anyhow; but now—I've done it!" The girl let her forehead rest against his lips, which moved downwards till they reached hers. That first real lover's kiss—strange, wonderful, still almost innocent —in which heart did it make the most disturbance?

"Come to the big apple-tree to-night, after they've gone to bed. Megan—promise!"

She whispered back: "I promise!"

Then, scared at her white face, scared at everything, he let her go, and went downstairs again. Yes! he had done it now! Accepted her love, declared his own! He went out to the green chair as devoid of a book as ever; and there he sat staring vacantly before him, triumphant and remorseful, while under his nose and behind his back the work of the farm went on. How long he had been sitting in that curious state of vacancy he had no notion when he saw Joe standing a little behind him to the right. The youth had evidently come from hard work in the fields, and stood shifting his feet, breathing loudly, his face colored like a setting sun, and his arms, below the rolled-up sleeves of his blue shirt, showing the hue and furry sheen of ripe peaches. His red lips were open, his blue eyes with their flaxen lashes stared fixedly at Ashurst, who said ironically:

"Well, Joe, anything I can do for you?"

"Yeas."

"What, then?"

"Yu can goo away from yere. Us don' want yu."

Ashurst's face, never too humble, assumed its most lordly look.

"Very good of you, but, do you know, I prefer the others should speak for themselves."

The youth moved a pace or two nearer, and the scent of his honest heat afflicted Ashurst's nostrils.

"What d'yu stay yere for?"

"Because it pleases me."

" 'Twon't please yu when I've bashed yure head in!"

"Indeed! When would you like to begin that?"

Joe answered only with the loudness of his breathing, but his eyes looked like those of a young and angry bull. Then a sort of spasm seemed to convulse his face.

"Megan don' want yu."

A rush of jealousy, of contempt, and anger with this thick, loud-breathing rustic got the better of Ashurst's self-possession; he jumped up and pushed back his chair.

"You can go to the devil!"

And as he said those simple words, he saw Megan in the doorway with a tiny brown spaniel puppy in her arms. She came up to him quickly:

"Its eyes are blue!" she said.

Joe turned away; the back of his neck was literally crimson.

Ashurst put his finger to the mouth of the little brown bullfrog of a creature in her arms. How cozy it looked against her!

"It's fond of you already! Ah! Megan, everything is fond of *you*."

"What was Joe saying to you, please?"

"Telling me to go away, because you didn't want me here."

She stamped her foot; then looked up at Ashurst. At that adoring look he felt his nerves quiver, just as if he had seen a moth scorching its wings.

"To-night!" he said. "Don't forget!"

"No." And smothering her face against the puppy's little fat, brown body, she slipped back into the house.

Ashurst wandered down the lane. At the gate of the wild meadow he came on the lame man and his cows.

"Beautiful day, Jim!"

"Ah! 'Tes brave weather for the grass. The ashes be later than th' oaks this year. 'When th' oak before th' ash——' "

Ashurst said idly: "Where were you standing when you saw the gypsy bogle, Jim?"

"It might be under that big apple-tree, as you might say."

"And you really do think it was there?"

The lame man answered cautiously:

"I shouldn't like to say rightly that 'twas there. 'Twas in my mind as 'twas there."

"What do you make of it?"

The lame man lowered his voice.

"They du zay old master, Mist' Narracombe, come o' gypsy stock. But that's tellin'. They'm a wonderful people, yu know, for claimin' their own. Maybe they knu'e was goin', and sent this feller along for company. That's what I've a-thought about it."

"What was he like?"

"'E 'ad 'air all over 'is face, an' goin' like this, he was, zame as if 'e 'ad a viddle. They zay there's no such thing as bogles, but I've a-zeen the 'air on this dog standin' up of a dark naight, when I couldn' zee nothin', meself."

"Was there a moon?"

"Yeas, very near full, but 'twas on'y just risen, gold-like be'ind them trees."

"And you think a ghost means trouble, do you?"

The lame man pushed his hat up; his aspiring eyes looked at Ashurst more earnestly than ever.

"'Tes not for me to zay that—but 'tes they bein' so unrestin'-like. There's things us don' understand, that's zartin, for zure. There's people that zee things, tu, an' others that don't never zee nothin'. Now, our Joe—yu might putt anything under 'is eyes an' 'e'd never see it; and them other boys, tu, they'm rattlin' fellers. But you take an' putt our Megan where there's suthin', she'll zee it, an' more tu, or I'm mistaken."

"She's sensitive, that's why."

"What's that?"

"I mean, she feels everything."

"Ah! She'm very lovin'-earted."

Ashurst, who felt color coming into his cheeks, held out his tobacco pouch.

"Have a fill, Jim?"

"Thank 'ee, sir. She'm one in an 'underd, I think."

"I expect so," said Ashurst shortly, and folding up his pouch, walked on.

"Lovin'-earted!" Yes! And what was he doing? What were his intentions—as they say—towards this loving-hearted girl? The thought dogged him, wandering through fields bright with buttercups, where the little red calves were feeding, and the swallows flying high. Yes, the oaks were before the ashes, brown-gold already; every tree in different stage and hue. The cuckoos and a thousand birds were singing; the little streams were very bright. The ancients believed in a golden age, in the garden of the Hesperides! . . . A queen wasp settled on his sleeve. Each queen wasp killed meant two thousand fewer wasps to thieve the apples which would grow from that blossom in the orchard; but who, with love in his heart, could kill anything on a day like this? He entered a field where a young red bull was feeding. It seemed to Ashurst that he looked like Joe. But the young bull took no notice of this visitor, a little drunk himself, perhaps, on the singing and the glamour of the golden pasture, under his short legs. Ashurst crossed out unchallenged to the hillside above the stream. From that slope a tor mounted to its crown of rocks. The ground there was covered with a mist of bluebells, and nearly a score of crab-apple trees were in full bloom. He threw himself down on the grass. The change from the buttercup glory and oak-goldened glamour of the fields to this ethereal beauty under the gray tor filled him with a sort of wonder; nothing the same, save the sound of running water and the songs of the cuckoos. He lay there a long time, watching the sunlight wheel till the crab-trees threw shadows over the bluebells, his only companions a few wild bees. He was not quite sane, thinking of that morning's kiss, and of to-night under the apple-tree. In such a spot as this, fauns and dryads surely lived; nymphs, white as the crab-apple blossom, retired within those trees; fauns, brown as the dead bracken, with pointed ears, lay in wait for them. The cuckoos were still calling when he woke, there was the sound of running water; but the sun had couched behind the tor, the hillside was cool, and some rabbits had come out. "To-night!" he thought. Just as from the earth everything was pushing up, unfolding under the soft insistent fingers of an unseen hand, so were his heart and senses being pushed, unfolded. He got up and broke off a spray from a crab-apple tree. The buds were like Megan—shell-like, rose-pink, wild, and fresh; and so, too, the opening flowers, white, and wild, and touching. He put the spray into his coat. And all the rush of the spring within him escaped in a triumphant sigh. But the rabbits scurried away.

VI

It was nearly eleven that night when Ashurst put down the pocket "Odyssey" which for half an hour he had held in his hands without reading, and slipped through the yard down to the orchard. The moon had just risen, very golden, over the hill, and like a bright, powerful, watching spirit peered through the bars of an ash tree's half-naked boughs. In among the apple-trees it was still dark, and he stood making sure of his direction, feeling the rough grass with his feet. A black mass close behind him stirred with a heavy grunting sound, and three large pigs settled down again close to each other, under the wall. He listened. There was no wind, but the stream's burbling whispering chuckle had gained twice its daytime strength. One bird, he could not tell what, cried "Pip—pip," "Pip—pip," with perfect monotony; he could hear a night-jar spinning very far off; an owl hooting. Ashurst moved a step or two, and again halted, aware of a dim living whiteness all round his head. On the dark unstirring trees innumerable flowers and buds all soft and blurred were being bewitched to life by the creeping moonlight. He had the oddest feeling of actual companionship, as if a million white moths or spirits had floated in and settled between dark sky and darker ground, and were opening and shutting their wings on a level with his eyes. In the bewildering, still, scentless beauty of that moment he almost lost memory of why he had come to the orchard. The flying glamour which had clothed the earth all day had not gone now that night had fallen, but only changed into this new form. He moved on through the thicket of stems and boughs covered with that live powdering whiteness, till he reached the big apple-tree. No mistaking that, even in the dark, nearly twice the height and size of any other, and leaning out towards the open meadows and the stream. Under the thick branches he stood still again, to listen. The same sounds exactly, and a faint grunting from the sleepy pigs. He put his hands on the dry, almost warm tree trunk, whose rough mossy surface gave forth a peaty scent at his touch. Would she come—would she? And among these quivering, haunted, moon-witched trees he was seized with doubts of everything! All was unearthly here, fit for no earthly lovers; fit only for god and goddess, faun and nymph—not for him and this little country girl. Would it not be almost a relief if she did not come? But all the time he was listening. And still that unknown bird went "Pip—pip," "Pip—pip," and there rose the busy chatter of the little trout stream, whereon the moon was flinging glances through the bars of her tree-prison. The blossom on a level with his eyes seemed to grow more living every moment, seemed with its mysterious white beauty more and more a part of his suspense. He plucked a fragment and held it close—three blossoms. Sacrilege to pluck fruit-tree blossom—soft, sacred, young blossom—and throw it away! Then suddenly he heard the gate close, the pigs stirring again and grunting; and leaning against the trunk, he pressed his hands to its mossy sides behind him, and held his breath. She might have been a spirit threading the trees, for all the noise she made! Then he saw her quite close—her dark form part of a little tree, her white face part of its blossom; so still, and peering towards him. He whispered: "Megan!" and held out his hands. She ran forward, straight to his breast. When he felt her heart beating against him, Ashurst knew to the full the sensations of chivalry and passion. Because she was not of his world, because she was so simple and young and headlong, adoring and defenseless, how could he be other than her protector in the dark! Because she was all simple Nature and beauty, as much a part of this spring night as was the living blossom,

how should he not take all that she would give him —how not fulfill the spring in her heart and his! And torn between these two emotions he clasped her close, and kissed her hair. How long they stood there without speaking he knew not. The stream went on chattering, the owls hooting, the moon kept stealing up and growing whiter; the blossom all round them and above frightened in suspense of living beauty. Their lips had sought each other's, and they did not speak. The moment speech began all would be unreal! Spring has no speech, nothing but rustling and whispering. Spring has so much more than speech in its unfolding flowers and leaves, and the coursing of its streams, and in its sweet restless seeking! And sometimes spring will come alive, and, like a mysterious Presence, stand, encircling lovers with its arms, laying on them the fingers of enchantment, so that, standing lips to lips, they forget everything but just a kiss. While her heart beat against him, and her lips quivered on his, Ashurst felt nothing but simple rapture—Destiny meant her for his arms, Love could not be flouted! But when their lips parted for breath, division began again at once. Only, passion now was so much the stronger, and he sighed:

"Oh! Megan! Why did you come?"

She looked up, hurt, amazed.

"Sir, you asked me to."

"Don't call me 'sir,' my pretty sweet."

"What should I be callin' you?"

"Frank."

"I could not. Oh, no!"

"But you love me—don't you?"

"I could not help lovin' you. I want to be with you —that's all."

"All!"

So faint that he hardly heard, she whispered:

"I shall die if I can't be with you."

Ashurst took a mighty breath.

"Come and be with me, then!"

"Oh!"

Intoxicated by the awe and rapture in that "Oh!" he went on, whispering:

"We'll go to London. I'll show you the world. And I *will* take care of you, I promise, Megan. I'll never be a brute to you!"

"If I can be with you—that is all."

He stroked her hair, and whispered on:

"To-morrow I'll go to Torquay and get some money, and get you some clothes that won't be noticed, and then we'll steal away. And when we get to London, soon perhaps, if you love me well enough, we'll be married."

He could feel her hair shiver with the shake of her head.

"Oh, no! I could not. I only want to be with you!"

Drunk on his own chivalry, Ashurst went on murmuring:

"It's I who am not good enough for you. Oh! Megan, when did you begin to love me?"

"When I saw you in the road, and you looked at me. The first night I loved you; but I never thought you would want me."

She slipped down suddenly to her knees, trying to kiss his feet.

A shiver of horror went through Ashurst; he lifted her up bodily and held her fast—too upset to speak.

She whispered: "Why won't you let me?"

"It's I who will kiss your feet!"

Her smile brought tears into his eyes. The whiteness of her moonlit face so close to his, the faint pink of her opened lips, had the living, unearthly beauty of the apple blossom.

And then, suddenly, her eyes widened and stared past him painfully; she writhed out of his arms, and whispered: "Look!"

Ashurst saw nothing but the brightened stream, the furze faintly gilded, the beech trees glistening, and behind them all the wide loom of the moonlit hill. Behind him came her frozen whisper: "The gypsy bogle!"

"Where?"

"There—by the stone—under the trees!"

Exasperated, he leapt the stream, and strode towards the beech clump. Prank of the moonlight! Nothing! In and out of the bowlders and thorn trees, muttering and cursing, yet with a kind of terror, he rushed and stumbled. Absurd! Silly! Then he went back to the apple-tree. But she was gone; he could hear a rustle, the grunting of the pigs, the sound of a gate closing. Instead of her, only this old apple-tree! He flung his arms round the trunk. What a substitute for her soft body; the rough moss against his face—what a substitute for her soft cheek; only the scent, as of the woods, a little the same! And above him, and around, the blossoms, more living, more moonlit than ever, seemed to glow and breathe.

VII

Descending from the train at Torquay station, Ashurst wandered uncertainly along the front, for he did not know this particular queen of English watering-places. Having little sense of what he had on, he was quite unconscious of being remarkable among its inhabitants, and strode along in his rough Norfolk jacket, dusty boots, and battered hat, without observing that people gazed at him rather blankly. He was seeking a branch of his London bank, and having found one, found also the first obstacle to his mood.

Did he know any one in Torquay! No. In that case, if he would wire to his bank in London, they would be happy to oblige him on receipt of the reply. That suspicious breath from the matter-of-fact world somewhat tarnished the brightness of his visions. But he sent the telegram.

Nearly opposite to the post office he saw a shop full of ladies' garments, and examined the window with strange sensations. To have to undertake the clothing of his rustic love was more than a little disturbing. He went in. A young woman came forward; she had blue eyes and a faintly puzzled forehead. Ashurst stared at her in silence.

"Yes, sir?"

"I want a dress for a young lady."

The young woman smiled. Ashurst frowned—the peculiarity of his request struck him with sudden force.

The young woman added hastily:

"What style would you like—something modish?"

"No. Simple."

"What figure would the young lady be?"

"I don't know; about two inches shorter than you, I should say."

"Could you give me her waist measurement?"

Megan's waist!

"Oh! anything usual!"

"Quite!"

While she was gone he stood disconsolately eyeing the models in the window, and suddenly it seemed to him incredible that Megan—his Megan—could ever be dressed save in the rough tweed skirt, coarse blouse, and tam-o'-shanter cap he was wont to see her in. The young woman had come back with several dresses in her arms, and Ashurst eyed her laying them against her own modish figure. There was one whose color he liked, a dove-gray, but to imagine Megan clothed in it was beyond him. The young woman went away, and brought some more. But on Ashurst there had now come a feeling of paralysis. How choose? She would want a hat too, and shoes, and gloves; and, suppose, when he had got them all, they commonized her, as Sunday clothes always commonized village folk! Why should she not travel as she was? Ah? But conspicuousness would matter; this was a serious elopement. And, staring at the young woman, he thought: "I wonder if she guesses, and thinks me a blackguard?"

"Do you mind putting aside that gray one for me?" he said desperately at last. "I can't decide now; I'll come in again this afternoon."

The young woman sighed.

"Oh! certainly. It's a very tasteful costume. I don't think you'll get anything that will suit your purpose better."

"I expect not," Ashurst murmured, and went out.

Freed again from the suspicious matter-of-factness of the world, he took a long breath, and went back to visions. In fancy he saw the trustful, pretty creature who was going to join her life to his; saw himself and her stealing forth at night, walking over the moor under the moon, he with his arm around her, and carrying her new garments, till, in some far-off wood, when dawn was coming, she would slip off her old things and put on these, and an early train at a distant station would bear them away on their honeymoon journey, till London swallowed them up, and the dreams of love came true.

"Frank Ashurst! Haven't seen you since Rugby, old chap!"

Ashurst's frown dissolved; the face, close to his own, was blue-eyed, suffused with sun—one of those faces where sun from within and without join in a sort of luster. And he answered:

"Phil Halliday, by Jove!"

"What are you doing here?"

"Oh! nothing. Just looking round, and getting some money. I'm staying on the moor."

"Are you lunching anywhere? Come and lunch with us; I'm here with my young sisters. They've had measles."

Hooked in by that friendly arm Ashurst went along, up a hill, down a hill, away out of the town, while the voice of Halliday, redolent of optimism as his face was of sun, explained how "in this moldy place the only decent things were the bathing and boating," and so on, till presently they came to a crescent of houses a little above and back from the sea, and into the center one—an hotel—made their way.

"Come up to my room and have a wash. Lunch'll be ready in a jiffy."

Ashurst contemplated his visage in a looking-glass. After his farmhouse bedroom, the comb and one spare shirt *régime* of the last fortnight, this room littered with clothes and brushes was a sort of Capua; and he thought:

"Queer—one doesn't realize—" But what—he did not quite know.

When he followed Halliday into the sitting-room for lunch, three faces, very fair and blue-eyed, were turned suddenly at the words: "This is Frank Ashurst —my young sisters."

Two were indeed young, about eleven and ten. The third was perhaps seventeen, tall and fair-haired too, with pink-and-white cheeks just touched by the sun, and eyebrows, rather darker than the hair, running a little upwards from her nose to their outer points. The voices of all three were like Halliday's, high and cheerful; they stood up straight, shook hands with a quick movement, looked at Ashurst critically, away again at once, and began to talk of what they were going to do in the afternoon. A regular Diana and attendant nymphs! After the farm this crisp, slangy, eager talk, this cool, clean, offhand refinement, was queer at first, and then so natural that what he had come from became suddenly remote. The names of the two little ones seemed to be Sabina and Freda; of the eldest, Stella.

Presently the one called Sabina turned to him and said:

"I say, will you come shrimping with us?—it's awful fun!"

Surprised by this unexpected friendliness, Ashurst murmured:

"I'm afraid I've got to get back this afternoon."

"Oh!"

"Can't you put it off?"

Ashurst turned to the new speaker, Stella, shook his head, and smiled. She was very pretty! Sabina said regretfully: "You might!" Then the talk switched off to caves and swimming.

"Can you swim far?"

"About two miles."

"Oh!"

"I say!"

"How jolly!"

The three pairs of blue eyes, fixed on him, made him conscious of his new importance. The sensation was agreeable. Halliday said:

"I say, you simply must stop and have a bathe. You'd better stay the night."

"Yes, do!"

But again Ashurst smiled and shook his head. Then suddenly he found himself being catechized about his physical achievements. He had rowed—it seemed—in his college boat, played in his college football team, won his college mile, and he rose from table a sort of hero. The two little girls insisted that he must see "their" cave, and they set forth chattering like magpies, Ashurst between them, Stella and her brother a little behind. In the cave, damp and darkish like any other cave, the great feature was a pool with possibility of creatures which might be caught and put into bottles. Sabina and Freda, who wore no stockings on their shapely brown legs, exhorted Ashurst to join them in the middle of it, and help sieve the water. He too was soon bootless and sockless. Time goes fast for one who has a sense of beauty, when there are pretty children in a pool and a young Diana on the edge, to receive with wonder anything you can catch! Ashurst never had much sense of time. It was a shock when, pulling out his watch, he saw it was well past three. No cashing his check to-day—the bank would be closed before he could get there. Watching his expression, the little girls cried out at once:

"Hurrah! Now you'll have to stay!"

Ashurst did not answer. He was seeing again Megan's face, when at breakfast he had whispered: "I'm going to Torquay, darling, to get everything; I shall be back this evening. If it's fine we can go to-night. Be ready." He was seeing again how she quivered and hung on his words. What would she think? Then he pulled himself together, conscious suddenly of the calm scrutiny of this other young girl, so tall and fair and Diana-like, at the edge of the pool, of her wondering blue eyes under those brows which slanted up a little. If they knew what was in his mind—if they knew that this very night he had meant—! Well, there would be a little sound of disgust, and he would be alone in the cave. And with a curious mixture of anger, chagrin, and shame, he put his watch back into his pocket and said abruptly:

"Yes; I'm dished for to-day."

"Hurrah! Now you can bathe with us."

It was impossible not to succumb a little to the contentment of these pretty children, to the smile on Stella's lips, to Halliday's "Ripping, old chap! I can lend you things for the night!" But again a spasm of longing and remorse throbbed through Ashurst, and he said moodily:

"I must send a wire!"

The attractions of the pool palling, they went back to the hotel. Ashurst sent his wire, addressing it to Mrs. Narracombe: "Sorry, detained for the night, back to-morrow." Surely Megan would understand that he had too much to do; and his heart grew lighter. It was a lovely afternoon, warm, the sea calm and blue, and swimming his great passion; the favor of these pretty children flattered him, the pleasure of looking at them, at Stella, at Halliday's sunny face; the slight unreality, yet extreme naturalness of it all —as of a last peep at normality before he took this plunge with Megan! He got his borrowed bathing dress, and they all set forth. Halliday and he undressed behind one rock, the three girls behind another. He was first into the sea, and at once swam out with the bravado of justifying his self-given reputation. When he turned he could see Halliday swimming along shore, and the girls flopping and dipping, and riding the little waves, in the way he was accustomed to despise, but now thought pretty and sensible, since it gave him the distinction of the only deep-water fish. But drawing near, he wondered if they would like him, a stranger, to come into their splashing group; he felt shy, approaching that slim nymph. Then Sabina summoned him to teach her to float, and between them the little girls kept him so

busy that he had no time even to notice whether Stella was accustomed to his presence, till suddenly he heard a startled sound from her. She was standing submerged to the waist, leaning a little forward, her slim white arms stretched out and pointing, her wet face puckered by the sun and an expression of fear.

"Look at Phil! Is he all right? Oh, look!"

Ashurst saw at once that Phil was not all right. He was splashing and struggling out of his depth, perhaps a hundred yards away; suddenly he gave a cry, threw up his arms, and went down. Ashurst saw the girl launch herself towards him, and crying out: "Go back, Stella! Go back!" he dashed out. He had never swum so fast, and reached Halliday just as he was coming up a second time. It was a case of cramp, but to get him in was not difficult, for he did not struggle. The girl, who had stopped where Ashurst told her to, helped as soon as he was in his depth, and once on the beach they sat down one on each side of him to rub his limbs, while the little ones stood by with scared faces. Halliday was soon smiling. It was—he said—rotten of him, absolutely rotten! If Frank would give him an arm, he could get to his clothes all right now. Ashurst gave him the arm, and as he did so caught sight of Stella's face, wet and flushed and tearful, all broken up out of its calm; and he thought: "I called her Stella! Wonder if she minded?"

While they were dressing, Halliday said quietly:

"You saved my life, old chap!"

"Rot!"

Clothed, but not quite in their right minds, they went up all together to the hotel and sat down to tea, except Halliday, who was lying down in his room. After some slices of bread and jam, Sabina said:

"I say, you know, you *are* a brick!" And Freda chimed in:

"Rather!"

Ashurst saw Stella looking down; he got up in confusion, and went to the window. From there he heard Sabina mutter: "I say, let's swear blood bond. Where's your knife, Freda?" and out of the corner of his eye he could see each of them solemnly prick herself, squeeze out a drop of blood and dabble on a bit of paper. He turned and made for the door.

"Don't be a stoat! Come back!" His arms were seized; imprisoned between the little girls he was brought back to the table. On it lay a piece of paper with an effigy drawn in blood, and the three names Stella Halliday, Sabina Halliday, Freda Halliday— also in blood, running towards it like the rays of a star. Sabina said:

"That's you. We shall have to kiss you, you know."

And Freda echoed:

"Oh! Blow—Yes!"

Before Ashurst could escape, some wettish hair dangled against his face, something like a bite descended on his nose, he felt his left arm pinched, and other teeth softly searching his cheek. Then he was released, and Freda said:

"Now, Stella."

Ashurst, red and rigid, looked across the table at a red and rigid Stella. Sabina giggled; Freda cried:

"Buck up—it spoils everything!"

A queer, ashamed eagerness shot through Ashurst; then he said quietly:

"Shut up, you little demons!"

Again Sabina giggled.

"Well, then, she can kiss her hand, and you can put it against your nose. It *is* on one side!"

To his amazement the girl did kiss her hand and stretch it out. Solemnly he took that cool, slim hand and laid it to his cheek. The two little girls broke into clapping, and Freda said:

"Now, then, we shall have to save your life at any time; that's settled. Can I have another cup, Stella, not so beastly weak?"

Tea was resumed, and Ashurst, folding up the paper, put it in his pocket. The talk turned on the advantages of measles, tangerine oranges, honey in a spoon, no lessons, and so forth. Ashurst listened, silent, exchanging friendly looks with Stella, whose face was again of its normal sun-touched pink and white. It was soothing to be so taken to the heart of this jolly family, fascinating to watch their faces. And after tea, while the two little girls pressed seaweed, he talked to Stella in the window seat and looked at her water-color sketches. The whole thing was like a pleasurable dream; time and incident hung up, importance and reality suspended. To-morrow he would go back to Megan, with nothing of all this left save the paper with the blood of these children, in his pocket. Children! Stella was not quite that—as old as Megan! Her talk—quick, rather hard and shy, yet friendly—seemed to flourish on his silences, and about her there was something cool and virginal—a maiden in a bower. At dinner, to which Halliday, who had swallowed too much sea water, did not come, Sabina said:

"I'm going to call you Frank."

Freda echoed:

"Frank, Frank, Franky."

Ashurst grinned and bowed.

"Every time Stella calls you Mr. Ashurst, she's got to pay a forfeit. It's ridiculous."

Ashurst looked at Stella, who grew slowly red. Sabina giggled; Freda cried:

"She's 'smoking'—'smoking!'—Yah!"

Ashurst reached out to right and left, and grasped some fair hair in each hand.

"Look here," he said, "you two! Leave Stella alone, or I'll tie you together!"

Freda gurgled:

"Ouch! You *are* a beast!"

Sabina murmured cautiously:

"*You* call *her* Stella, you see!"

"Why shouldn't I? It's a jolly name!"

"All right; we give you leave to!"

Ashurst released the hair. Stella! What would she call him—after this? But she called him nothing; till at bed-time he said, deliberately:

"Good night, Stella!"

"Good night, Mr.—Good night, Frank! It *was* jolly of you, you know!"

"Oh—that! Bosh!"

Her quick, straight handshake tightened suddenly, and as suddenly, became slack.

Ashurst stood motionless in the empty sitting-room. Only last night, under the apple-tree and the living blossoms, he had held Megan to him, kissing her eyes and lips. And he gasped, swept by that rush of remembrance. To-night it should have begun—his life with her who only wanted to be with him! And now, twenty-four hours and more must pass, because—of not looking at his watch! Why had he made friends with this family of innocents just when he was saying good-by to innocence, and all the rest of it? "But I mean to marry her," he thought; "I told her so!"

He took a candle, lighted it, and went to his bed-room, which was next to Halliday's. His friend's voice called as he was passing:

"Is that you, old chap? I say, come in."

He was sitting up in bed, smoking a pipe and reading.

"Sit down a bit."

Ashurst sat down by the open window.

"I've been thinking about this afternoon, you know," said Halliday rather suddenly. "They say you go through all your past. I didn't. I suppose I wasn't far enough gone."

"What did you think of?"

Halliday was silent for a little, then said quietly:

"Well, I did think of one thing—rather odd—of a girl at Cambridge that I might have—you know; I was glad I hadn't got her on my mind. Anyhow, old chap, I owe it to you that I'm here; I should have been in the big dark by now. No more bed, or baccy; no more anything. I say, what d'you suppose happens to us?"

Ashurst murmured:

"Go out like flames, I expect."

"Phew!"

"We may flicker, and cling about a bit, perhaps."

"H'm! I think that's rather gloomy. I say, I hope my young sisters have been decent to you?"

"Awfully decent."

Halliday put his pipe down, crossed his hands behind his neck, and turned his face towards the window.

"They're not bad kids!" he said.

Watching his friend, lying there, with that smile, and the candle-light on his face, Ashurst shuddered. Quite true! He might have been lying there with no smile, with all that sunny look gone out forever! He might not have been lying there at all, but "sanded" at the bottom of the sea, waiting for resurrection on the—ninth day, was it? And that smile of Halliday's seemed to him suddenly something wonderful, as if in it were all the difference between life and death—the little flame—the all! He got up, and said softly:

"Well, you ought to sleep, I expect. Shall I blow out?"

Halliday caught his hand.

"I can't say it, you know; but it must be rotten to be dead. Good night, old boy!"

Stirred and moved, Ashurst squeezed the hand, and went downstairs. The hall door was still open, and he passed out on to the lawn before the Crescent. The stars were bright in a very dark blue sky, and by their light some lilacs had that mysterious color of flowers by night which no one can describe. Ashurst pressed his face against a spray; and before his closed eyes Megan started up, with the tiny brown spaniel pup against her breast. "I thought of a girl that I might have—you know. I was glad I hadn't got her on my mind!" He jerked his head away from the lilac, and began pacing up and down over the grass, a gray phantom coming to substance for a moment in the light from the lamp at either end. He was with her again under the living, breathing whiteness of the blossom, the stream chattering by, the moon glinting steel-blue on the bathing-pool; back in the rapture of his kisses on her upturned face of innocence and humble passion, back in the suspense and beauty of that pagan night. He stood still once more in the shadow of the lilacs. Here the sea, not the stream, was Night's voice; the sea with its sigh and rustle; no little bird, no owl, no night-jar called or spun; but a piano tinkled, and the white houses cut the sky with solid curve, and the scent from the lilacs filled the air. A window of the hotel, high up, was lighted; he saw a shadow move across the blind. And most queer sensations stirred within him, a sort of churning, and twining, and turning of a single emotion on itself, as though spring and love, bewildered and confused, seeking the way, were baffled. This girl, who had called him Frank, whose hand had given his that sudden little clutch, this girl so cool and pure—what would *she* think of such wild, unlawful loving? He sank down on the grass, sitting there cross-legged,

with his back to the house, motionless as some carved Buddha. Was he really going to break through innocence, and steal? Sniff the scent out of a wild flower, and—perhaps—throw it away? "Of a girl at Cambridge that I might have—you know!" He put his hands to the grass, one on each side, palms downwards, and pressed; it was just warm still—the grass, barely moist, soft and firm and friendly. "What am I going to do?" he thought. Perhaps Megan was at her window, looking out at the blossom, thinking of him! Poor little Megan! "Why not?" he thought. "I love her! But do I—really love her? or do I only want her because she is so pretty, and loves me? What am I going to do?" The piano tinkled on, the stars winked; and Ashurst gazed out before him at the dark sea, as if spellbound. He got up at last, cramped and rather chilly. There was no longer light in any window. And he went in to bed.

VIII

Out of a deep and dreamless sleep he was awakened by the sound of thumping on the door. A shrill voice called:

"Hi! Breakfast's ready."

He jumped up. Where was he—? Ah!

He found them already eating marmalade, and sat down in the empty place between Stella and Sabina, who, after watching him a little, said:

"I say, do buck up; we're going to start at half-past nine."

"We're going to Berry Head, old chap; you *must* come!"

Ashurst thought: "Come! Impossible. I shall be getting things and going back." He looked at Stella. She said quickly:

"Do come!"

Sabina chimed in:

"It'll be no fun without you."

Freda got up and stood behind his chair.

"You've got to come, or else I'll pull your hair!"

Ashurst thought: "Well—one day more—to think it over! One day more!" And he said:

"All right! You needn't tweak my mane!"

"Hurrah!"

At the station he wrote a second telegram to the farm, and then—tore it up; he could not have explained why. From Brixham they drove in a very little wagonette. There, squeezed between Sabina and Freda, with his knees touching Stella's, they played "Up Jenkins"; and the gloom he was feeling gave way to frolic. In this one day more to think it over, he did not want to think! They ran races, wrestled, paddled—for to-day nobody wanted to bathe—they sang catches, played games, and ate all they had brought. The little girls fell asleep against him on the way back, and his knees still touched Stella's in the wagonette. It seemed incredible that thirty hours ago he had never set eyes on any of those three flaxen heads. In the train he talked to Stella of poetry, discovering her favorites, and telling her his own with a pleasing sense of superiority; till suddenly she said, rather low:

"Phil says you don't believe in a future life, Frank. I think that's dreadful."

Disconcerted, Ashurst muttered:

"I don't either believe or not believe—I simply don't know."

She said quickly:

"I couldn't bear that. What would be the use of living?"

Watching the frown of those pretty oblique brows, Ashurst answered:

"I don't believe in believing things because one wants to."

"But why should one *wish* to live again, if one isn't going to?"

And she looked full at him.

He did not want to hurt her, but an itch to dominate pushed him on to say:

"While one's alive one naturally wants to go on living forever; that's part of being alive. But it probably isn't anything more."

"Don't you believe in the Bible at all, then?"

Ashurst thought: "Now I shall really hurt her!"

"I believe in the Sermon on the Mount, because it's beautiful and good for all time."

"But don't you believe Christ was divine?"

He shook his head.

She turned her face quickly to the window, and there sprang into his mind Megan's prayer, repeated by little Nick: "God bless us all, and Mr. Ashes!" Who else would ever say a prayer for him, like her who at this moment must be waiting—waiting to see him come down the lane? And he thought suddenly: "What a scoundrel I am!"

All that evening this thought kept coming back; but, as is not unusual, each time with less poignancy, till it seemed almost a matter of course to be a scoundrel. And—strange!—he did not know whether he was a scoundrel if he meant to go back to Megan, or if he did not mean to go back to her.

They played cards till the children were sent off to bed; then Stella went to the piano. From over on the window seat, where it was nearly dark, Ashurst watched her between the candles—that fair head on the long, white neck bending to the movement of her hands. She played fluently, without much expression; but what a picture she made, the faint golden radiance, a sort of angelic atmosphere—hovering about

her! Who could have passionate thought or wild desires in the presence of that swaying, white-clothed girl with the seraphic head? She played a thing of Schumann's called "*Warum?*" Then Halliday brought out a flute, and the spell was broken. After this they made Ashurst sing, Stella playing him accompaniments from a book of Schumann songs, till, in the middle of "*Ich grolle nicht,*" two small figures clad in blue dressing-gowns crept in and tried to conceal themselves beneath the piano. The evening broke up in confusion, and what Sabina called "a splendid rag."

That night Ashurst hardly slept at all. He was thinking, tossing and turning. The intense domestic intimacy of these last two days, the strength of this Halliday atmosphere, seemed to ring him round, and make the farm and Megan—even Megan—seem unreal. Had he really made love to her—really promised to take her away to live with him? He must have been bewitched by the spring, the night, the apple blossom! The notion that he was going to make her his mistress—that simple child not yet eighteen—now filled him with a sort of horror, even while it still stung and whipped his blood. He muttered to himself: "It's awful, what I've done—awful!" And the sound of Schumann's music throbbed and mingled with his fevered thoughts, and he saw again Stella's cool, white, fair-haired figure and bending neck, the queer, angelic radiance about her. "I must have been—I must be—mad!" he thought. "What came into me? Poor little Megan!" "God bless us all, and Mr. Ashes!" "I want to be with you—only to be with you!" And burying his face in his pillow, he smothered down a fit of sobbing. Not to go back was awful! To go back—more awful still!

Emotion, when you are young, and give real vent to it, loses its power of torture. And he fell asleep, thinking: "What was it—a few kisses—all forgotten in a month!"

Next morning he got his check cashed, but avoided the shop of the dove-gray dress like the plague; and, instead, bought himself some necessaries. He spent the whole day in a queer mood, cherishing a kind of sullenness against himself. Instead of the hankering of the last two days, he felt nothing but a blank—all passionate longing gone, as if quenched in that outburst of tears. After tea Stella put a book down beside him, and said shyly:

"Have you read that, Frank?"

It was Farrar's "Life of Christ." Ashurst smiled. Her anxiety about his beliefs seemed to him comic, but touching. Infectious, too, perhaps, for he began to have an itch to justify himself, if not to convert her. And in the evening, when the children and Halliday were mending their shrimping nets, he said:

"At the back of orthodox religion, so far as I can see, there's always the idea of reward—what you can get for being good; a kind of begging for favors. I think it all starts in fear."

She was sitting on the sofa making reefer knots with a bit of string. She looked up quickly:

"I think it's much deeper than that."

Ashurst felt again that wish to dominate.

"You think so," he said; "but wanting the *quid pro quo* is about the deepest thing in all of us! It's jolly hard to get to the bottom of it!"

She wrinkled her brows in a puzzled frown.

"I don't think I understand."

He went on obstinately:

"Well, think, and see if the most religious people aren't those who feel that this life doesn't give them all they want. I believe in being good because to be good is good in itself."

"Then you do believe in being good?"

How pretty she looked now—it was easy to be good with her! And he nodded and said:

"I say, show me how to make that knot!"

With her fingers touching his, in maneuvering the bit of string he felt soothed and happy. And when he went to bed he willfully kept his thoughts on her, wrapping himself in her fair, cool sisterly radiance, as in some garment of protection.

Next day he found they had arranged to go by train to Totness, and picnic at Berry Pomeroy Castle. Still in that resolute oblivion of the past, he took his place with them in the landau beside Halliday, back to the horses. And, then, along the sea front, nearly at the turning to the railway station, his heart almost leaped into his mouth. Megan—Megan herself!—was walking on the far pathway, in her old skirt and jacket and her tam-o'-shanter, looking up into the faces of the passers-by. Instinctively he threw his hand up for cover, then made a feint of clearing dust out of his eyes; but between his fingers he could see her still, moving, not with her free country step, but wavering, lost-looking, pitiful—like some little dog which has missed its master and does not know whether to run on, to run back—where to run. How had she come like this?—what excuse had she found to get away?—what did she hope for? But with every turn of the wheels bearing him away from her, his heart revolted and cried to him to stop them, to get out, and go to her! When the landau turned the corner to the station he could stand it no more, and opening the carriage door, muttered: "I've forgotten something! Go on—don't wait for me! I'll join you at the castle by the next train!" He jumped, stumbled, spun round, recovered his balance, and walked forward, while the carriage with the astonished Hallidays rolled on.

From the corner he could only just see Megan, a long way ahead now. He ran a few steps, checked himself, and dropped into a walk. With each step nearer to her, further from the Hallidays, he walked more and more slowly. How did it alter anything—this sight of her? How make the going to her, and that which must come of it, less ugly? For there was no hiding it—since he had met the Hallidays he had become gradually sure that he would not marry Megan. It would only be a wild love-time, a troubled, remorseful, difficult time—and then—well, then he would get tired, just because she gave him everything, was so simple, and so trustful, so dewy. And new—wears off! The little spot of faded color, her tam-o'-shanter cap, wavered on far in front of him; she was looking up into every face, and at the house windows. Had any man ever such a cruel moment to go through? Whatever he did, he felt he would be a beast. And he uttered a groan which made a nurse-maid turn and stare. He saw Megan stop and lean against the sea-wall, looking at the sea; and he too stopped. Quite likely she had never seen the sea before, and even in her distress could not resist that sight. "Yes—she's seen nothing," he thought; "everything's before her. And just for a few weeks' passion, I shall be cutting her life to ribbons. I'd better go and hang myself rather than do it!" And suddenly he seemed to see Stella's calm eyes looking into his, the wave of fluffy hair on her forehead stirred by the wind. Ah! it would be madness, would mean giving up all that he respected, and his own self-respect. He turned and walked quickly back towards the station. But memory of that poor, bewildered little figure, those anxious eyes searching the passers-by, smote him too hard again, and once more he turned towards the sea. The cap was no longer visible; that little spot of color had vanished in the stream of the noon promenaders. And impelled by the passion of longing, the dearth which comes on one when life seems to be whirling something out of reach, he hurried forward. She was nowhere to be seen; for half an hour he looked for her; then on the beach flung himself face downward in the sand. To find her again he knew he had only to go to the station and wait till she returned from her fruitless quest, to take her train home; or to take train himself and go back to the farm, so that she found him there when she returned. But he lay inert in the sand, among the indifferent groups of children with their spades and buckets. Pity at her little figure wandering, seeking, was well-nigh merged in the spring-running of his blood; for it was all wild feeling now—the chivalrous part, what there had been of it, was gone. He wanted her again, wanted her kisses, her soft, little body, her abandonment, all her quick, warm, pagan emotion;

wanted the wonderful feeling of that night under the moon-lit apple boughs; wanted it all with a horrible intensity, as the faun wants the nymph. The quick chatter of the little bright trout-stream, the dazzle of the buttercups, the rocks of the old "wild men"; the calling of the cuckoos and yaffles, the hooting of the owls; and the red moon peeping out of the velvet dark at the living whiteness of the blossom; and her face just out of reach at the window, lost in its love-look; and her heart against his, her lips answering his, under the apple-tree—all this besieged him. Yet he lay inert. What was it which struggled against pity and this feverish longing, and kept him there paralyzed in the warm sand? Three flaxen heads—a fair face with friendly blue-gray eyes, a slim hand pressing his, a quick voice speaking his name—"So you do believe in being good?" Yes, and a sort of atmosphere as of some old walled-in English garden, with pinks, and cornflowers, and roses, and scents of lavender and lilac—cool and fair, untouched, almost holy—all that he had been brought up to feel was clean and good. And suddenly he thought: "She might come along the front again and see me!" and he got up and made his way to the rock at the far end of the beach. There, with the spray biting into his face, he could think more coolly. To go back to the farm and love Megan out in the woods, among the rocks, with everything around wild and fitting—that, he knew, was impossible, utterly. To transplant her to a great town, to keep, in some little flat or rooms, one who belonged so wholly to Nature—the poet in him shrank from it. His passion would be a mere sensuous revel, soon gone; in London, her very simplicity, her lack of all intellectual quality, would make her his secret plaything—nothing else. The longer he sat on the rock, with his feet dangling over a greenish pool from which the sea was ebbing, the more clearly he saw this; but it was as if her arms and all of her were slipping slowly, slowly down from him, into the pool, to be carried away out to sea; and her face looking up, her lost face with beseeching eyes, and dark, wet hair—possessed, haunted, tortured him! He got up at last, scaled the low rock-cliff, and made his way down into a sheltered cove. Perhaps in the sea he could get back his control—lose his fever! And stripping off his clothes, he swam out. He wanted to tire himself so that nothing mattered, and swam recklessly, fast and far; then suddenly, for no reason, felt afraid. Suppose he could not reach shore again—suppose the current set him out—or he got cramps, like Halliday! He turned to swim in. The red cliffs looked a long way off. If he were drowned they would find his clothes. The Hallidays would know; but Megan perhaps never—they took no newspaper at the farm. And

Phil Halliday's words came back to him again: "A girl at Cambridge I might have— Glad I haven't got her on my mind!" And in that moment of unreasoning fear he vowed he would not have her on his mind. Then his fear left him; he swam in easily enough, dried himself in the sun, and put on his clothes. His heart felt sore, but no longer ached; his body cool and refreshed.

When one is as young as Ashurst, pity is not a violent emotion. And, back in the Hallidays' sitting-room, eating a ravenous tea, he felt much like a man recovered from fever. Everything seemed new and clear; the tea, the buttered toast, and jam tasted absurdly good; tobacco had never smelt so nice. And walking up and down the empty room, he stopped here and there to touch or look. He took up Stella's work-basket, fingered the cotton reels and a gayly colored plait of sewing silks, smelt at the little bag filled with wood-roffe she kept among them. He sat down at the piano, playing tunes with one finger, thinking: "To-night she'll play; I shall watch her while she's playing; it does me good to watch her." He took up the book, which still lay where she had placed it beside him, and tried to read. But Megan's little, sad figure began to come back at once, and he got up and leaned in the window, listening to the thrushes in the Crescent gardens, gazing at the sea, dreamy and blue below the trees. A servant came in and cleared the tea away, and he still stood, inhaling the evening air, trying not to think. Then he saw the Hallidays coming through the gate of the Crescent, Stella a little in front of Phil and the children, with their baskets, and instinctively he drew back. His heart, too sore and discomfited, shrank from this encounter, yet wanted its friendly solace—bore a grudge against this influence, yet craved its cool innocence, and the pleasure of watching Stella's face. From against the wall behind the piano he saw her come in and stand looking a little blank as though disappointed; then she saw him and smiled, a swift, brilliant smile which warmed yet irritated Ashurst.

"You never came after us, Frank."

"No; I found I couldn't."

"Look! We picked such lovely late violets!" She held out a bunch. Ashurst put his nose to them, and there stirred within him vague longings, chilled instantly by a vision of Megan's anxious face lifted to the faces of the passers-by.

He said shortly: "How jolly!" and turned away. He went up to his room, and, avoiding the children, who were coming up the stairs, threw himself on his bed, and lay there with his arms crossed over his face. Now that he felt the die really cast, and Megan given up, he hated himself, and almost hated the Hallidays and their atmosphere of healthy, happy

English homes. Why should they have chanced here, to drive away first love—to show him that he was going to be no better than a common seducer? What right had Stella, with her fair, shy beauty, to make him know for certain that he would never marry Megan; and, tarnishing it all, bring him such bitterness of regretful longing and such pity? Megan would be back by now, worn out by her miserable seeking—poor little thing!—expecting, perhaps, to find him there when she reached home. Ashurst bit at his sleeve, to stifle a groan of remorseful longing. He went to dinner glum and silent, and his mood threw a dinge even over the children. It was a melancholy, rather ill-tempered evening, for they were all tired; several times he caught Stella looking at him with a hurt, puzzled expression, and this pleased his evil mood. He slept miserably; got up quite early, and wandered out. He went down to the beach. Alone there with the serene, the blue, the sunlit sea, his heart relaxed a little. Conceited fool—to think that Megan would take it so hard! In a week or two she would almost have forgotten! And he—well, he would have the reward of virtue! A good young man! If Stella knew, she would give him her blessing for resisting that devil she believed in; and he uttered a hard laugh. But slowly the peace and beauty of sea and sky, the flight of the lonely seagulls, made him feel ashamed. He bathed, and turned homewards.

In the Crescent gardens Stella herself was sitting on a camp stool, sketching. He stole up close behind. How fair and pretty she was, bent diligently, holding up her brush, measuring, wrinkling her brows.

He said gently:

"Sorry I was such a beast last night, Stella."

She turned round, startled, flushed very pink, and said in her quick way:

"It's all right. I knew there was something. Between friends it doesn't matter, does it?"

Ashurst answered:

"Between friends—and we are, aren't we?"

She looked up at him, nodded vehemently, and her upper teeth gleamed again in that swift, brilliant smile.

Three days later he went back to London, traveling with the Hallidays. He had not written to the farm. What was there he could say?

On the last day of April in the following year he and Stella were married. . . .

Such were Ashurst's memories, sitting against the wall among the gorse, on his silver-wedding day. At this very spot, where he had laid out the lunch, Megan must have stood outlined against the sky when he had first caught sight of her. Of all queer coincidences! And there moved in him a longing to go down and see again the farm and the orchard, and the meadow of the gypsy bogle. It would not take long; Stella would be an hour yet, perhaps.

How well he remembered it all—the little crowning group of pine trees, the steep-up grass hill behind! He paused at the farm gate. The low stone house, the yew-tree porch, the flowering currants—not changed a bit; even the old green chair was out there on the grass under the window, where he had reached up to her that night to take the key. Then he turned down the lane, and stood leaning on the orchard gate—gray skeleton of a gate, as then. A black pig even was wandering in there among the trees. Was it true that twenty-six years had passed, or had he dreamed and awakened to find Megan waiting for him by the big apple-tree? Unconsciously he put up his hand to his grizzled beard and brought himself back to reality. Opening the gate, he made his way down through the docks and nettles till he came to the edge, and the old apple-tree itself. Unchanged! A little more of the gray-green lichen, a dead branch or two, and for the rest it might have been only last night that he had embraced that mossy trunk after Megan's flight and inhaled its woody savor, while above his head the moonlit blossom had seemed to breathe and live. In that early spring a few buds were showing already; the blackbirds shouting their songs, a cuckoo calling, the sunlight bright and warm. Incredibly the same—the chattering trout-stream, the narrow pool he had lain in every morning, splashing the water over his flanks and chest; and out there in the wild meadow the beech clump and the stone where the gypsy bogle was supposed to sit. And an ache for lost youth, a hankering, a sense of wasted love and sweetness, gripped Ashurst by the throat. Surely, on this earth of such wild beauty, one was meant to hold rapture to one's heart, as this earth and sky held it! And yet, one could not!

He went to the edge of the stream, and, looking down at the little pool, thought: "Youth and spring! What has become of them all, I wonder?" And then, in sudden fear of having this memory jarred by human encounter, he went back to the lane, and pensively retraced his steps to the cross-roads.

Beside the car an old, gray-bearded laborer was leaning on a stick, talking to the chauffeur. He broke off at once, as though guilty of disrespect, and, touching his hat, prepared to limp on down the lane.

Ashurst pointed to the narrow green mound. "Can you tell me what this is?"

The old fellow stopped; on his face had come a look as though he were thinking: "You've come to the right shop, mister!"

" 'Tes a grave," he said.

"But why out here?"

The old man smiled. "That's a tale, as yu may say. An' not the first time as I've a-told et—there's plenty folks asks 'bout that bit o' turf. 'Maid's Grave' us calls et, 'ereabouts."

Ashurst held out his pouch. "Have a fill?"

The old man touched his hat again, and slowly filled an old clay pipe. His eyes, looking upward out of a mass of wrinkles and hair, were still quite bright.

"If yu don' mind, zurr, I'll zet down—my leg's 'urtin' a bit to-day." And he sat down on the mound of turf.

"There's always a vlower on this grave. An' 'tain't so very lonesome, neither; brave lot o' folks goes by now, in they new motor cars an' things—not as 'twas in th' old days. She've a-got company up 'ere. 'Twas a poor soul killed 'erself."

"I see!" said Ashurst. "Cross-roads burial. I didn't know that custom was kept up."

"Ah! but 'twas a main long time ago. Us 'ad a parson as was very God-fearin' then. Let me see, I've 'ad my pension six year come Michaelmas, an' I were just on fifty when 't 'appened. There's none livin' knows more about et than what I du. She belonged close 'ere; same farm as where I used to work along o' Mrs. Narracombe—'tes Nick Narracombe's now; I dus a bit for 'im still, odd times."

Ashurst, who was leaning against the gate, lighting his pipe, left his curved hands before his face for long after the flame of the match had gone out.

"Yes?" he said, and to himself his voice sounded hoarse and queer.

"She was one in an 'underd, poor maid! I puts a vlower 'ere every time I passes. Pretty maid an' gude maid she was, though they wouldn't burry 'er up tu th' church, nor where she wanted to be burried neither." The old laborer paused, and put his hairy, twisted hand flat down on the turf beside the bluebells.

"Yes?" said Ashurst.

"In a manner of speakin'," the old man went on, "I think as 'twas a love-story—though there's no one never knu for zartin. Yu can't tell what's in a maid's 'ead—but that's wot I think about it." He drew his hand along the turf. "I was fond o' that maid—don' know as there was any one as wasn' fond of 'er. But she was tu lovin'-'earted—that's where 'twas, I think." He looked up. And Ashurst, whose lips were trembling in the cover of his beard, murmured again: "Yes?"

"'Twas in the spring, 'bout now as't might be, or a little later—blossom time—an' we 'ad one o' they young college gentlemen stayin' at the farm—nice feller tu, with 'is 'ead in the air. I liked 'e very well, an' I never see nothin' between 'em, but to my thinkin' 'e turned the maid's fancy." The old man took the pipe out of his mouth, spat, and went on:

"Yu see, 'e went away sudden one day, an' never come back. They got 'is knapsack and bits o' things down there still. That's what stuck in my mind—'is never sendin' for 'em. 'Is name was Ashes, or somethin' like that."

"Yes?" said Ashurst once more.

The old man licked his lips.

"'Er never said nothin', but from that day 'er went kind of dazed lukin'; didn' seem rightly therr at all. I never knu a 'uman creature so changed in me life—never. There was another young feller at the farm—Joe Biddaford 'is name wer', that was praaperly sweet on 'er, tu; I guess 'e used to plague 'er wi' 'is attentions. She got to luke quite wild. I'd zee her sometimes of an avenin' when I was bringin' up the calves; ther' she'd stand in th' orchard, under the big appletree, lukin' straight before 'er. 'Well,' I used t' think, 'I dunno what 'tes that's the matter wi' yu, but yu'm lukin' pitiful, that yu be!'"

The old man relit his pipe, and sucked at it reflectively.

"Yes?" said Ashurst.

"I remembers one day I said to 'er: 'What's the matter, Megan?'—'er name was Megan David, she come from Wales same as 'er aunt, ol' Missis Narracombe. 'Yu'm frettin' about something,' I says. 'No, Jim,' she says, 'I'm not frettin'.' 'Yes, yu be!' I says. 'No,' she says, and tu tears cam' rollin' out. 'Yu'm cryin'—what's that, then?' I says. She puts 'er 'and over 'er 'eart: 'It 'urts me,' she says; 'but 'twill sune be better,' she says. 'But if anything shude 'appen to me, Jim, I wants to be buried under this 'ere appletree.' I laughed. 'What's goin' to 'appen to yu?' I says: 'don't 'ee be fulish.' 'No,' she says, 'I won't be fulish.' Well, I know what maids are, an' I never thought no more about et, till tu days arter that, 'bout six in the avenin' I was comin' up wi' the calves, when I see somethin' dark lyin' in the strame, close to that big apple-tree. I says to meself: 'Is that a pig—funny place for a pig to get to!' an' I goes up to et, an' I see what 'twas."

The old man stopped: his eyes, turned upward, had a bright, suffering look.

"'Twas the maid, in a little narrer pool ther' that's made by the stoppin' of a rock—where I see the young gentleman bathin' once or twice. 'Er was lyin' on 'er face in the watter. There was a plant o' goldiecups growin' out o' the stone just above 'er 'ead. An' when I come to luke at 'er face, 'twas luvly, butiful, so calm's a baby's—wonderful butiful et wus. When the doctor saw 'er, 'e said: ''Er culdn' never a-done it in that little bit o' watter if 'er 'adn't a-been in an extarsy.' Ah! an' judgin' from 'er face, that was just 'ow she was. Et made me cry praaper—butiful et was! 'Twas June then, but she'd a-found a little bit of apple blossom left over somewheres, and stuck et in 'er 'air. That's why I thinks 'er must a-been in an extarsy, to go to et gay, like that. Why! there wasn't more than a fute and 'arf o' watter. But I tell 'ee one thing—that meadder's 'arnted; I knu et, an' she knu et; an' no one'll persuade me as 'tesn't. I told 'em what she said to me 'bout bein' buried under th' apple-tree. But I think that turned 'em—made et luke tu much 's ef she'd 'ad it in 'er mind deliberate; an' so they buried 'er up 'ere. Parson we 'ad then was very particular, 'e was."

Again the old man drew his hand over the turf.

" 'Tes wonderful, et seems," he added slowly, "what maids 'll du for love. She 'ad a lovin' 'eart; I guess 'twas broken. But us never *knu* nothin'!"

He looked up as if for approval of his story, but Ashurst had walked past him as if he were not there.

Up on the top of the hill, beyond where he had spread the lunch, over, out of sight, he lay down on his face. So had his virtue been rewarded, and "the Cyprian," goddess of love, taken her revenge! And before his eyes, dim with tears, came Megan's face with the sprig of apple blossoms in her dark, wet hair. 'What did I do that was wrong?' he thought. 'What did I do?' But he could not answer. Spring, with its rush of passion, its flowers and song—the spring in his heart and Megan's! Was it just Love seeking a victim! The Greek was right, then—the words of the "Hippolytus" as true to-day!

> *"For mad is the heart of Love,*
> *And gold the gleam of his wing;*
> *And all to the spell thereof*
> *Bend when he makes his spring.*
> *All life that is wild and young*
> *In mountain and wave and stream,*
> *All that of earth is sprung,*
> *Or breathes in the red sunbeam;*
> *Yea, and Mankind. O'er all a royal throne*
> *Cyprian, Cyprian, is thine alone!"*

The Greek was right! Megan! Poor little Megan—coming over the hill! Megan under the old apple-tree waiting and looking! Megan dead, with beauty printed on her! . . .

A voice said:

"Oh, there you are! Look."

Ashurst rose, took his wife's sketch, and stared at it in silence.

"Is the foreground right, Frank?"

"Yes."

"But there's something wanting, isn't there?"

Ashurst nodded. Wanting? The apple-tree, the singing, and the gold!

THE SECRET SHARER

JOSEPH CONRAD

JOSEPH CONRAD (1857–1924) was born Jósef Teodor Konrad Korzeniowski in Russian Poland. He went to sea before he was twenty in a French vessel, shifted to the English merchant service, learned English by reading newspapers and eventually passed the examinations for a master's command. At thirty-seven, after twenty years at sea, he retired to England, broken in health, and with the sympathetic encouragement of John Galsworthy turned to writing. Harassed by poverty, ill-health and the problem of language—it is said he thought in Polish, translated into French in his mind and then into English on paper—he nevertheless achieved a place in the very front rank of modern literature. Among his books are *Lord Jim* (1900), *Youth* (1902), *Nostromo* (1904), *Under Western Eyes* (1911), *Victory* (1915), *The Shadow Line* (1917). "Art," said Conrad in the 'Preface' to *The Nigger of the Narcissus* (1898), "may be defined as a single-minded attempt to render the highest kind of justice to the visible universe, by bringing to light the truth, manifold and one, underlying its every aspect. . . . My task which I am trying to achieve is, by the power of the written word to make you hear, to make you feel—it is, before all, to make you *see*. That—and no more, and it is everything. If I succeed, you shall find there according to your deserts: encouragement, consolation, fear, charm—all you demand—and, perhaps, also that glimpse of truth for which you have forgotten to ask."

O N my right hand there were lines of fishing-stakes resembling a mysterious system of half-submerged bamboo fences, incomprehensible in its division of the domain of tropical fishes, and crazy of aspect as if abandoned forever by some nomad tribe of fishermen now gone to the other end of the ocean; for there was no sign of human habitation as far as the eye could reach. To the left a group of barren islets, suggesting ruins of stone walls, towers, and blockhouses, had its foundations set in a blue sea that itself looked solid, so still and stable did it lie below my feet; even the track of light from the westering sun shone smoothly, without that animated glitter which tells of an imperceptible ripple. And when I turned my head to take a parting glance at the tug which had just left us anchored outside the bar, I saw the straight line of the flat shore joined to the stable sea, edge to edge, with a perfect and unmarked closeness, in one leveled floor half brown, half blue under the enormous dome of the sky. Corresponding in their insignificance to the islets of the sea, two small clumps of trees, one on each side of the only fault in the impeccable joint, marked the mouth of the river Meinam we had just left on the first preparatory stage of our homeward journey; and, far back on the inland level, a larger and loftier mass,

From *'Twixt Land and Sea* by Joseph Conrad by permission of the Trustees of the Joseph Conrad Estate and Messrs. J. M. Dent & Sons Ltd.

the grove surrounding the great Paknam pagoda, was the only thing on which the eye could rest from the vain task of exploring the monotonous sweep of the horizon. Here and there gleams as of a few scattered pieces of silver marked the windings of the great river; and on the nearest of them, just within the bar, the tug steaming right into the land became lost to my sight, hull and funnel and masts, as though the impassive earth had swallowed her up without an effort, without a tremor. My eye followed the light cloud of her smoke, now here, now there, above the plain, according to the devious curves of the stream, but always fainter and farther away, till I lost it at last behind the miter-shaped hill of the great pagoda. And then I was left alone with my ship, anchored at the head of the Gulf of Siam.

She floated at the starting-point of a long journey, very still in an immense stillness, the shadows of her spars flung far to the eastward by the setting sun. At that moment I was alone on her decks. There was not a sound in her—and around us nothing moved, nothing lived, not a canoe on the water, not a bird in the air, not a cloud in the sky. In this breathless pause at the threshold of a long passage we seemed to be measuring our fitness for a long and arduous enterprise, the appointed task of both our existences to be carried out, far from all human eyes, with only sky and sea for spectators and for judges.

There must have been some glare in the air to

interfere with one's sight, because it was only just before the sun left us that my roaming eyes made out beyond the highest ridge of the principal islet of the group something which did away with the solemnity of perfect solitude. The tide of darkness flowed on swiftly; and with tropical suddenness a swarm of stars came out above the shadowy earth, while I lingered yet, my hand resting lightly on my ship's rail as if on the shoulder of a trusted friend. But, with all that multitude of celestial bodies staring down at one, the comfort of quiet communion with her was gone for good. And there were also disturbing sounds by this time—voices, footsteps forward; the steward flitted along the main-deck, a busily ministering spirit; a hand-bell tinkled urgently under the poop-deck. . . .

I found my two officers waiting for me near the supper table, in the lighted cuddy. We sat down at once, and as I helped the chief mate, I said:

"Are you aware that there is a ship anchored inside the islands? I saw her mastheads above the ridge as the sun went down."

He raised sharply his simple face, overcharged by a terrible growth of whisker, and emitted his usual ejaculations: "Bless my soul, sir! You don't say so!"

My second mate was a round-cheeked, silent young man, grave beyond his years, I thought; but as our eyes happened to meet I detected a slight quiver on his lips. I looked down at once. It was not my part to encourage sneering on board my ship. It must be said, too, that I knew very little of my officers. In consequence of certain events of no particular significance, except to myself, I had been appointed to the command only a fortnight before. Neither did I know much of the hands forward. All these people had been together for eighteen months or so, and my position was that of the only stranger on board. I mention this because it has some bearing on what is to follow. But what I felt most was my being a stranger to the ship; and if all the truth must be told, I was somewhat of a stranger to myself. The youngest man on board (barring the second mate), and untried as yet by a position of the fullest responsibility, I was willing to take the adequacy of the others for granted. They had simply to be equal to their tasks; but I wondered how far I should turn out faithful to that ideal conception of one's own personality every man sets up for himself secretly.

Meantime the chief mate, with an almost visible effect of collaboration on the part of his round eyes and frightful whiskers, was trying to evolve a theory of the anchored ship. His dominant trait was to take all things into earnest consideration. He was of a painstaking turn of mind. As he used to say, he "liked to account to himself" for practically everything that came in his way, down to a miserable scorpion he had found in his cabin a week before. The why and the wherefore of that scorpion—how it got on board and came to select his room rather than the pantry (which was a dark place and more what a scorpion would be partial to), and how on earth it managed to drown itself in the inkwell of his writing-desk—had exercised him infinitely. The ship within the islands was much more easily accounted for; and just as we were about to rise from table he made his pronouncement. She was, he doubted not, a ship from home lately arrived. Probably she drew too much water to cross the bar except at the top of spring tides. Therefore she went into that natural harbor to wait for a few days in preference to remaining in an open roadstead.

"That's so," confirmed the second mate, suddenly, in his slightly hoarse voice. "She draws over twenty feet. She's the Liverpool ship *Sephora* with a cargo of coal. Hundred and twenty-three days from Cardiff."

We looked at him in surprise.

"The tugboat skipper told me when he came on board for your letters, sir," explained the young man. "He expects to take her up the river the day after tomorrow."

After thus overwhelming us with the extent of his information he slipped out of the cabin. The mate observed regretfully that he "could not account for that young fellow's whims." What prevented him telling us all about it at once, he wanted to know.

I detained him as he was making a move. For the last two days the crew had had plenty of hard work, and the night before they had very little sleep. I felt painfully that I—a stranger—was doing something unusual when I directed him to let all hands turn in without setting an anchor-watch. I proposed to keep on deck myself till one o'clock or thereabouts. I would get the second mate to relieve me at that hour.

"He will turn out the cook and the steward at four," I concluded, "and then give you a call. Of course at the slightest sign of any sort of wind we'll have the hands up and make a start at once."

He concealed his astonishment. "Very well, sir." Outside the cuddy he put his head in the second mate's door to inform him of my unheard-of caprice to take a five hours' anchor-watch on myself. I heard the other raise his voice incredulously—"What? The Captain himself?" Then a few more murmurs, a door closed, then another. A few moments later I went on deck.

My strangeness, which had made me sleepless, had prompted that unconventional arrangement, as if I had expected in those solitary hours of the night to get on terms with the ship of which I knew nothing, manned by men of whom I knew very little more. Fast alongside a wharf, littered like any ship in port with a tangle of unrelated things, invaded by unrelated shore people, I had hardly seen her yet properly. Now, as she lay cleared for sea, the stretch of her main-deck seemed to me very fine under the stars. Very fine, very roomy for her size, and very inviting. I descended the poop and paced the waist, my mind picturing to myself the coming passage through the Malay Archipelago, down the Indian Ocean, and up the Atlantic. All its phases were familiar enough to me, every characteristic, all the alternatives which were likely to face me on the high seas—everything! . . . except the novel responsibility of command. But I took heart from the reasonable thought that the ship was like other ships, the men like other men, and that the sea was not likely to keep any special surprises expressly for my discomfiture.

Arrived at that comforting conclusion, I bethought myself of a cigar and went below to get it. All was still down there. Everybody at the after end of the ship was sleeping profoundly. I came out again on the quarter-deck, agreeably at ease in my sleeping-suit on that warm breathless night, barefooted, a glowing cigar in my teeth, and, going forward, I was met by the profound silence of the fore end of the ship. Only as I passed the door of the forecastle I heard a deep, quiet, trustful sigh of some sleeper inside. And suddenly I rejoiced in the great security of the sea as compared with the unrest of the land, in my choice of that untempted life presenting no disquieting problems, invested with an elementary moral beauty by the absolute straightforwardness of its appeal and by the singleness of its purpose.

The riding-light in the fore-rigging burned with a clear, untroubled, as if symbolic, flame, confident and bright in the mysterious shades of the night. Passing on my way aft along the other side of the ship, I observed that the rope side-ladder, put over, no doubt, for the master of the tug when he came to fetch away our letters, had not been hauled in as it should have been. I became annoyed at this, for exactitude in small matters is the very soul of discipline. Then I reflected that I had myself peremptorily dismissed my officers from duty, and by my own act had prevented the anchor-watch being formally set and things properly attended to. I asked myself whether it was wise ever to interfere with the established routine of duties even from the kindest of motives. My action might have made me appear eccentric. Goodness only knew how that absurdly whiskered mate would "account" for my conduct,

and what the whole ship thought of that informality of their new captain. I was vexed with myself.

Not from compunction certainly, but, as it were mechanically, I proceeded to get the ladder in myself. Now a side-ladder of that sort is a light affair and comes in easily, yet my vigorous tug, which should have brought it flying on board, merely recoiled upon my body in a totally unexpected jerk. What the devil! . . . I was so astounded by the immovableness of that ladder that I remained stock-still, trying to account for it to myself like that imbecile mate of mine. In the end, of course, I put my head over the rail.

The side of the ship made an opaque belt of shadow on the darkling glassy shimmer of the sea. But I saw at once something elongated and pale floating very close to the ladder. Before I could form a guess a faint flash of phosphorescent light, which seemed to issue suddenly from the naked body of a man, flickered in the sleeping water with the elusive, silent play of summer lightning in a night sky. With a gasp I saw revealed to my stare a pair of feet, the long legs, a broad livid back immersed right up to the neck in a greenish cadaverous glow. One hand, awash, clutched the bottom rung of the ladder. He was complete but for the head. A headless corpse! The cigar dropped out of my gaping mouth with a tiny plop and a short hiss quite audible in the absolute stillness of all things under heaven. At that I suppose he raised up his face, a dimly pale oval in the shadow of the ship's side. But even then I could only barely make out down there the shape of his black-haired head. However, it was enough for the horrid, frost-bound sensation which had gripped me about the chest to pass off. The moment of vain exclamations was past, too. I only climbed on the spare spar and leaned over the rail as far as I could, to bring my eyes nearer to that mystery floating alongside.

As he hung by the ladder, like a resting swimmer, the sea-lightning played about his limbs at every stir; and he appeared in it ghastly, silvery, fish-like. He remained as mute as a fish, too. He made no motion to get out of the water, either. It was inconceivable that he should not attempt to come on board, and strangely troubling to suspect that perhaps he did not want to. And my first words were prompted by just that troubled incertitude.

"What's the matter?" I asked in my ordinary tone, speaking down to the face upturned exactly under mine.

"Cramp," it answered, no louder. Then slightly anxious, "I say, no need to call anyone."

"I was not going to," I said.

"Are you alone on deck?"

"Yes."

I had somehow the impression that he was on the point of letting go the ladder to swim away beyond my ken—mysterious as he came. But, for the moment, this being appearing as if he had risen from the bottom of the sea (it was certainly the nearest land to the ship) wanted only to know the time. I told him. And he, down there, tentatively:

"I suppose your captain's turned in?"

"I am sure he isn't," I said.

He seemed to struggle with himself, for I heard something like the low, bitter murmur of doubt. "What's the good?" His next words came out with a hesitating effort.

"Look here, my man. Could you call him out quietly?"

I thought the time had come to declare myself.

"*I* am the captain."

I heard a "By Jove!" whispered at the level of the water. The phosphorescence flashed in the swirl of the water all about his limbs, his other hand seized the ladder.

"My name's Leggatt."

The voice was calm and resolute. A good voice. The self-possession of that man had somehow induced a corresponding state in myself. It was very quietly that I remarked:

"You must be a good swimmer."

"Yes. I've been in the water practically since nine o'clock. The question for me now is whether I am to let go this ladder and go on swimming till I sink from exhaustion, or—to come on board here."

I felt this was no mere formula of desperate speech, but a real alternative in the view of a strong soul. I should have gathered from this that he was young; indeed, it is only the young who are ever confronted by such clear issues. But at the time it was pure intuition on my part. A mysterious communication was established already between us two—in the face of that silent, darkened tropical sea. I was young, too; young enough to make no comment. The man in the water began suddenly to climb up the ladder, and I hastened away from the rail to fetch some clothes.

Before entering the cabin I stood still, listening in the lobby at the foot of the stairs. A faint snore came through the closed door of the chief mate's room. The second mate's door was on the hook, but the darkness in there was absolutely soundless. He, too, was young and could sleep like a stone. Remained the steward, but he was not likely to wake up before he was called. I got a sleeping-suit out of my room and, coming back on deck, saw the naked man from the sea sitting on the main-hatch, glimmering white in the darkness, his elbows on his knees and his head in his hands. In a moment he had concealed his damp body in a sleeping-suit of the same gray-stripe pattern as the one I was wearing and followed me like my double on the poop. Together we moved right aft, barefooted, silent.

"What is it?" I asked in a deadened voice, taking the lighted lamp out of the binnacle, and raising it to his face.

"An ugly business."

He had rather regular features; a good mouth; light eyes under somewhat heavy, dark eyebrows; a smooth, square forehead; no growth on his cheeks; a small, brown mustache, and a well-shaped, round chin. His expression was concentrated, meditative, under the inspecting light of the lamp I held up to his face; such as a man thinking hard in solitude might wear. My sleeping-suit was just right for his size. A well-knit young fellow of twenty-five at most. He caught his lower lip with the edge of white, even teeth.

"Yes," I said, replacing the lamp in the binnacle. The warm, heavy tropical night closed upon his head again.

"There's a ship over there," he murmured.

"Yes, I know. The *Sephora*. Did you know of us?"

"Hadn't the slightest idea. I am the mate of her—" He paused and corrected himself. "I should say I *was*."

"Aha! Something wrong?"

"Yes. Very wrong indeed. I've killed a man."

"What do you mean? Just now?"

"No, on the passage. Weeks ago. Thirty-nine south. When I say a man—"

"Fit of temper," I suggested, confidently.

The shadowy, dark head, like mine, seemed to nod imperceptibly above the ghostly gray of my sleeping-suit. It was, in the night, as though I had been faced by my own reflection in the depths of a somber and immense mirror.

"A pretty thing to have to own up to for a Conway boy," murmured my double, distinctly.

"You're a Conway boy?"

"I am," he said, as if startled. Then, slowly . . . "Perhaps you too—"

It was so; but being a couple of years older I had left before he joined. After a quick interchange of dates a silence fell; and I thought suddenly of my absurd mate with his terrific whiskers and the "Bless my soul—you don't say so" type of intellect. My double gave me an inkling of his thoughts by saying: "My father's a parson in Norfolk. Do you see me before a judge and jury on that charge? For myself I can't see the necessity. There are fellows that an angel from heaven— And I am not that. He was one of those creatures that are just simmering all the time with a silly sort of wickedness. Miserable devils that have no business to live at all. He wouldn't do his duty and wouldn't let anybody else do theirs. But what's the good of talking! You know well enough the sort of ill-conditioned snarling cur—"

He appealed to me as if our experiences had been as identical as our clothes. And I knew well enough the pestiferous danger of such a character where there are no means of legal repression. And I knew well enough also that my double there was no homicidal ruffian. I did not think of asking him for details, and he told me the story roughly in brusque, disconnected sentences. I needed no more. I saw it all going on as though I were myself inside that other sleeping-suit.

"It happened while we were setting a reefed fore-sail, at dusk. Reefed foresail! You understand the sort of weather. The only sail we had left to keep the ship running; so you may guess what it had been like for days. Anxious sort of job, that. He gave me some of his cursed insolence at the sheet. I tell you I was overdone with this terrific weather that seemed to have no end to it. Terrific, I tell you—and a deep ship. I believe the fellow himself was half crazed with funk. It was no time for gentlemanly reproof, so I turned round and felled him like an ox. He up and at me. We closed just as an awful sea made for the ship. All hands saw it coming and took to the rigging, but I had him by the throat, and went on shaking him like a rat, the men above us yelling, 'Look out! look out!' Then a crash as if the sky had fallen on my head. They say that for over ten minutes hardly anything was to be seen of the ship—just the three masts and a bit of the forecastle head and of the poop all awash driving along in a smother of foam. It was a miracle that they found us, jammed together behind the forebitts. It's clear that I meant business, because I was holding him by the throat still when they picked us up. He was black in the face. It was too much for them. It seems they rushed us aft together, gripped as we were, screaming 'Murder!' like a lot of lunatics, and broke into the cuddy. And the ship running for her life, touch and go all the time, any minute her last in a sea fit to turn your hair gray only a-looking at it. I understand that the skipper, too, started raving like the rest of them. The man had been deprived of sleep for more than a week, and to have this sprung on him at the height of a furious gale nearly drove him out of his mind. I wonder they didn't fling me overboard after getting the carcass of their precious ship-mate out of my fingers. They had rather a job to separate us, I've been told. A sufficiently fierce story to make an old judge and a respectable jury sit up a bit. The first thing I heard when I came to myself was the maddening howling of that endless gale, and on that

the voice of the old man. He was hanging on to my bunk, staring into my face out of his sou'wester.

"'Mr. Leggatt, you have killed a man. You can act no longer as chief mate of this ship.'"

His care to subdue his voice made it sound monotonous. He rested a hand on the end of the skylight to steady himself with, and all that time did not stir a limb, so far as I could see. "Nice little tale for a quiet tea-party," he concluded in the same tone.

One of my hands, too, rested on the end of the skylight; neither did I stir a limb, so far as I knew. We stood less than a foot from each other. It occurred to me that if old "Bless my soul—you don't say so" were to put his head up the companion and catch sight of us, he would think he was seeing double, or imagine himself come upon a scene of weird witchcraft; the strange captain having a quiet confabulation by the wheel with his own gray ghost. I became very much concerned to prevent anything of the sort. I heard the other's soothing undertone.

"My father's a parson in Norfolk," it said. Evidently he had forgotten he had told me this important fact before. Truly a nice little tale.

"You had better slip down into my stateroom now," I said, moving off stealthily. My double followed my movements; our bare feet made no sound; I let him in, closed the door with care, and, after giving a call to the second mate, returned on deck for my relief.

"Not much sign of any wind yet," I remarked when he approached.

"No, sir. Not much," he assented, sleepily, in his hoarse voice, with just enough deference, no more, and barely suppressing a yawn.

"Well, that's all you have to look out for. You have got your orders."

"Yes, sir."

I paced a turn or two on the poop and saw him take up his position face forward with his elbow in the ratlines of the mizzen-rigging before I went below. The mate's faint snoring was still going on peacefully. The cuddy lamp was burning over the table on which stood a vase with flowers, a polite attention from the ship's provision merchant—the last flowers we should see for the next three months at the very least. Two bunches of bananas hung from the beam symmetrically, one on each side of the rudder-casing. Everything was as before in the ship—except that two of her captain's sleeping-suits were simultaneously in use, one motionless in the cuddy, the other keeping very still in the captain's stateroom.

It must be explained here that my cabin had the form of the capital letter L, the door being within the angle and opening into the short part of the letter. A couch was to the left, the bed-place to the right; my writing-desk and the chronometers' table faced the door. But anyone opening it, unless he stepped right inside, had no view of what I call the long (or vertical) part of the letter. It contained some lockers surmounted by a bookcase; and a few clothes, a thick jacket or two, caps, oilskin coat, and such like, hung on hooks. There was at the bottom of that part a door opening into my bath-room, which could be entered also directly from the saloon. But that way was never used.

The mysterious arrival had discovered the advantage of this particular shape. Entering my room, lighted strongly by a big bulkhead lamp swung on gimbals above my writing-desk, I did not see him anywhere till he stepped out quietly from behind the coats hung in the recessed part.

"I heard somebody moving about, and went in there at once," he whispered.

I, too, spoke under my breath.

"Nobody is likely to come in here without knocking and getting permission."

He nodded. His face was thin and the sunburn faded, as though he had been ill. And no wonder. He had been, I heard presently, kept under arrest in his cabin for nearly seven weeks. But there was nothing sickly in his eyes or in his expression. He was not a bit like me, really; yet, as we stood leaning over my bed-place, whispering side by side, with our dark heads together and our backs to the door, anybody bold enough to open it stealthily would have been treated to the uncanny sight of a double captain busy talking in whispers with his other self.

"But all this doesn't tell me how you came to hang on to our side-ladder," I inquired, in the hardly audible murmurs we used, after he had told me something more of the proceedings on board the *Sephora* once the bad weather was over.

"When we sighted Java Head I had had time to think all those matters out several times over. I had six weeks of doing nothing else, and with only an hour or so every evening for a tramp on the quarter-deck."

He whispered, his arms folded on the side of my bed-place, staring through the open port. And I could imagine perfectly the manner of this thinking out—a stubborn if not a steadfast operation; something of which I should have been perfectly incapable.

"I reckoned it would be dark before we closed with the land," he continued, so low that I had to strain my hearing, near as we were to each other, shoulder touching shoulder almost. "So I asked to speak to the old man. He always seemed very sick when he came to see me—as if he could not look me in the face. You know, that foresail saved the ship. She was

too deep to have run long under bare poles. And it was I that managed to set it for him. Anyway, he came. When I had him in my cabin—he stood by the door looking at me as if I had the halter round my neck already—I asked him right away to leave my cabin door unlocked at night while the ship was going through Sunda Straits. There would be the Java coast within two or three miles, off Angier Point. I wanted nothing more. I've had a prize for swimming my second year in the Conway."

"I can believe it," I breathed out.

"God only knows why they locked me in every night. To see some of their faces you'd have thought they were afraid I'd go about at night strangling people. Am I a murdering brute? Do I look it? By Jove! if I had been he wouldn't have trusted himself like that into my room. You'll say I might have chucked him aside and bolted out, there and then—it was dark already. Well, no. And for the same reason I wouldn't think of trying to smash the door. There would have been a rush to stop me at the noise, and I did not mean to get into a confounded scrimmage. Somebody else might have got killed—for I would not have broken out only to get chucked back, and I did not want any more of that work. He refused, looking more sick than ever. He was afraid of the men, and also of that old second mate of his who had been sailing with him for years—a gray-headed old humbug; and his steward, too, had been with him devil knows how long—seventeen years or more—a dogmatic sort of loafer who hated me like poison, just because I was the chief mate. No chief mate ever made more than one voyage in the *Sephora*, you know. Those two old chaps ran the ship. Devil only knows what the skipper wasn't afraid of (all his nerve went to pieces altogether in that hellish spell of bad weather we had)—of what the law would do to him—of his wife, perhaps. Oh, yes! she's on board. Though I don't think she would have meddled. She would have been only too glad to have me out of the ship in any way. The 'brand of Cain' business, don't you see. That's all right. I was ready enough to go off wandering on the face of the earth—and that was price enough to pay for an Abel of that sort. Anyhow, he wouldn't listen to me. 'This thing must take its course. I represent the law here.' He was shaking like a leaf. 'So you won't?' 'No!' 'Then I hope you will be able to sleep on that,' I said, and turned my back on him. 'I wonder that *you* can,' cries he, and locks the door.

"Well, after that, I couldn't. Not very well. That was three weeks ago. We have had a slow passage through the Java Sea; drifted about Carimata for ten days. When we anchored here they thought, I suppose, it was all right. The nearest land (and that's five miles) is the ship's destination; the consul would soon set about catching me; and there would have been no object in bolting to these islets there. I don't suppose there's a drop of water on them. I don't know how it was, but tonight that steward, after bringing me my supper, went out to let me eat it, and left the door unlocked. And I ate it—all there was, too. After I had finished I strolled out on the quarter-deck. I don't know that I meant to do anything. A breath of fresh air was all I wanted, I believe. Then a sudden temptation came over me. I kicked off my slippers and was in the water before I had made up my mind fairly. Somebody heard the splash and they raised an awful hullabaloo. 'He's gone! Lower the boats! He's committed suicide! No, he's swimming.' Certainly I was swimming. It's not so easy for a swimmer like me to commit suicide by drowning. I landed on the nearest islet before the boat left the ship's side. I heard them pulling about in the dark, hailing, and so on, but after a bit they gave up. Everything quieted down and the anchorage became as still as death. I sat down on a stone and began to think. I felt certain they would start searching for me at daylight. There was no place to hide on those stony things—and if there had been, what would have been the good? But now I was clear of that ship, I was not going back. So after a while I took off all my clothes, tied them up in a bundle with a stone inside, and dropped them in the deep water on the outer side of that islet. That was suicide enough for me. Let them think what they liked, but I didn't mean to drown myself. I meant to swim till I sank—but that's not the same thing. I struck out for another of these little islands, and it was from that one that I first saw your riding-light. Something to swim for. I went on easily, and on the way I came upon a flat rock a foot or two above water. In the daytime, I dare say, you might make it out with a glass from your poop. I scrambled up on it and rested myself for a bit. Then I made another start. That last spell must have been over a mile."

His whisper was getting fainter and fainter, and all the time he stared straight out through the porthole, in which there was not even a star to be seen. I had not interrupted him. There was something that made comment impossible in his narrative, or perhaps in himself; a sort of feeling, a quality, which I can't find a name for. And when he ceased, all I found was a futile whisper: "So you swam for our light?"

"Yes—straight for it. It was something to swim for. I couldn't see any stars low down because the coast was in the way, and I couldn't see the land, either. The water was like glass. One might have been swimming in a confounded thousand-feet-deep cis-

tern with no place for scrambling out anywhere; but what I didn't like was the notion of swimming round and round like a crazed bullock before I gave out; and as I didn't mean to go back . . . No. Do you see me being hauled back, stark naked, off one of these little islands by the scruff of the neck and fighting like a wild beast? Somebody would have got killed for certain, and I did not want any of that. So I went on. Then your ladder—"

"Why didn't you hail the ship?" I asked, a little louder.

He touched my shoulder lightly. Lazy footsteps came right over our heads and stopped. The second mate had crossed from the other side of the poop and might have been hanging over the rail, for all we knew.

"He couldn't hear us talking—could he?" My double breathed into my very ear, anxiously.

His anxiety was an answer, a sufficient answer, to the question I had put to him. An answer containing all the difficulty of that situation. I closed the port-hole quietly, to make sure. A louder word might have been overheard.

"Who's that?" he whispered then.

"My second mate. But I don't know much more of the fellow than you do."

And I told him a little about myself. I had been appointed to take charge while I least expected anything of the sort, not quite a fortnight ago. I didn't know either the ship or the people. Hadn't had the time in port to look about me or size anybody up. And as to the crew, all they knew was that I was appointed to take the ship home. For the rest, I was almost as much of a stranger on board as himself, I said. And at the moment I felt it most acutely. I felt that it would take very little to make me a suspect person in the eyes of the ship's company.

He had turned about meantime; and we, the two strangers in the ship, faced each other in identical attitudes.

"Your ladder—" he murmured, after a silence. "Who'd have thought of finding a ladder hanging over at night in a ship anchored out here! I felt just then a very unpleasant faintness. After the life I've been leading for nine weeks, anybody would have got out of condition. I wasn't capable of swimming round as far as your rudder-chains. And, lo and behold; there was a ladder to get hold of. After I gripped it I said to myself, 'What's the good?' When I saw a man's head looking over I thought I would swim away presently and leave him shouting—in whatever language it was. I didn't mind being looked at. I—I liked it. And then you speaking to me so quietly—as if you had expected me—made me hold on a little longer. It had been a confounded lonely time—I don't mean while swimming. I was glad to talk a little to somebody that didn't belong to the *Sephora.* As to asking for the captain, that was a mere impulse. It could have been no use, with all the ship knowing about me and the other people pretty certain to be round here in the morning. I don't know— I wanted to be seen, to talk with somebody, before I went on. I don't know what I would have said. . . . 'Fine night, isn't it?' or something of the sort."

"Do you think they will be round here presently?" I asked with some incredulity.

"Quite likely," he said, faintly.

He looked extremely haggard all of a sudden. His head rolled on his shoulders.

"H'm. We shall see then. Meantime get into that bed," I whispered. "Want help? There."

It was a rather high bed-place with a set of drawers underneath. This amazing swimmer really needed the lift I gave him by seizing his leg. He tumbled in, rolled over on his back, and flung one arm across his eyes. And then, with his face nearly hidden, he must have looked exactly as I used to look in that bed. I gazed upon my other self for a while before drawing across carefully the two green serge curtains which ran on a brass rod. I thought for a moment of pinning them together for greater safety, but I sat down on the couch, and once there I felt unwilling to rise and hunt for a pin. I would do it in a moment. I was extremely tired, in a peculiarly intimate way, by the strain of stealthiness, by the effort of whispering and the general secrecy of this excitement. It was three o'clock by now and I had been on my feet since nine, but I was not sleepy; I could not have gone to sleep. I sat there, fagged out, looking at the curtains, trying to clear my mind of the confused sensation of being in two places at once, and greatly bothered by an exasperating knocking in my head. It was a relief to discover suddenly that it was not in my head at all, but on the outside of the door. Before I could collect myself the words "Come in" were out of my mouth, and the steward entered with a tray, bringing in my morning coffee. I had slept, after all, and I was so frightened that I shouted, "This way! I am here, steward," as though he had been miles away. He put down the tray on the table next the couch and only then said, very quietly, "I can see you are here, sir." I felt him give me a keen look, but I dared not meet his eyes just then. He must have wondered why I had drawn the curtains of my bed before going to sleep on the couch. He went out, hooking the door open as usual.

I heard the crew washing decks above me. I knew I would have been told at once if there had been any wind. Calm, I thought, and I was doubly vexed. Indeed, I felt dual more than ever. The steward reappeared suddenly in the doorway. I jumped up from the couch so quickly that he gave a start.

"What do you want here?"

"Close your port, sir—they are washing decks."

"It is closed," I said, reddening.

"Very well, sir." But he did not move from the doorway and returned my stare in an extraordinary, equivocal manner for a time. Then his eyes wavered, all his expression changed, and in a voice unusually gentle, almost coaxingly:

"May I come in to take the empty cup away, sir?"

"Of course!" I turned my back on him while he popped in and out. Then I unhooked and closed the door and even pushed the bolt. This sort of thing could not go on very long. The cabin was as hot as an oven, too. I took a peep at my double, and discovered that he had not moved, his arm was still over his eyes; but his chest heaved; his hair was wet; his chin glistened with perspiration. I reached over him and opened the port.

"I must show myself on deck," I reflected.

Of course, theoretically, I could do what I liked, with no one to say nay to me within the whole circle of the horizon; but to lock my cabin door and take the key away I did not dare. Directly I put my head out of the companion I saw the group of my two officers, the second mate barefooted, the chief mate in long india-rubber boots, near the break of the poop, and the steward half-way down the poop-ladder talking to them eagerly. He happened to catch sight of me and dived, the second ran down on the main-deck shouting some order or other, and the chief mate came to meet me, touching his cap.

There was a sort of curiosity in his eye that I did not like. I don't know whether the steward had told them that I was "queer" only, or downright drunk, but I know the man meant to have a good look at me. I watched him coming with a smile which, as he got into point-blank range, took effect and froze his very whiskers. I did not give him time to open his lips.

"Square the yards by lifts and braces before the hands go to breakfast."

It was the first particular order I had given on board that ship; and I stayed on deck to see it executed, too. I had felt the need of asserting myself without loss of time. That sneering young cub got taken down a peg or two on that occasion, and I also seized the opportunity of having a good look at the face of every foremast man as they filed past me to go to the after braces. At breakfast time, eating nothing myself, I presided with such frigid dignity that the two mates were only too glad to escape from the cabin as soon as decency permitted; and all the time the dual working of my mind distracted me almost to the point of insanity. I was constantly watching myself, my secret self, as dependent on my actions as my own personality, sleeping in that bed, behind that door which faced me as I sat at the head of the table. It was very much like being mad, only it was worse because one was aware of it.

I had to shake him for a solid minute, but when at last he opened his eyes it was in the full possession of his senses, with an inquiring look.

"All's well so far," I whispered. "Now you must vanish into the bath-room."

He did so, as noiseless as a ghost, and then I rang for the steward, and facing him boldly, directed him to tidy up my stateroom while I was having my bath —"and be quick about it." As my tone admitted of no excuses, he said, "Yes, sir," and ran off to fetch his dust-pan and brushes. I took a bath and did most of my dressing, splashing, and whistling softly for the steward's edification, while the secret sharer of my life stood drawn up bolt upright in that little space, his face looking very sunken in daylight, his eyelids lowered under the stern, dark line of his eyebrows drawn together by a slight frown.

When I left him there to go back to my room the steward was finishing dusting. I sent for the mate and engaged him in some insignificant conversation. It was, as it were, trifling with the terrific character of his whiskers; but my object was to give him an opportunity for a good look at my cabin. And then I could at last shut, with a clear conscience, the door of my stateroom and get my double back into the recessed part. There was nothing else for it. He had to sit still on a small folding stool, half smothered by the heavy coats hanging there. We listened to the steward going into the bath-room out of the saloon, filling the water-bottles there, scrubbing the bath, setting things to rights, whisk, bang, clatter— out again into the saloon—turn the key—click. Such was my scheme for keeping my second self invisible. Nothing better could be contrived under the circumstances. And there we sat; I at my writing-desk ready to appear busy with some papers, he behind me out of sight of the door. It would not have been prudent to talk in daytime; and I could not have stood the excitement of that queer sense of whispering to myself. Now and then, glancing over my shoulder, I saw him far back there, sitting rigidly on the low stool, his bare feet close together, his arms folded, his head hanging on his breast—and perfectly still. Anybody would have taken him for me.

I was fascinated by it myself. Every moment I had to glance over my shoulder. I was looking at him when a voice outside the door said:

"Beg pardon, sir."

"Well!" . . . I kept my eyes on him, and so when the voice outside the door announced, "There's a ship's boat coming our way, sir," I saw him give a start—the first movement he had made for hours. But he did not raise his bowed head.

"All right. Get the ladder over."

I hesitated. Should I whisper something to him? But what? His immobility seemed to have been never disturbed. What could I tell him he did not know already? . . . Finally I went on deck.

II

The skipper of the *Sephora* had a thin red whisker all round his face, and the sort of complexion that goes with hair of that color; also the particular, rather smeary shade of blue in the eyes. He was not exactly a showy figure; his shoulders were high, his stature but middling—one leg slightly more bandy than the other. He shook hands, looking vaguely around. A spiritless tenacity was his main characteristic, I judged. I behaved with a politeness which seemed to disconcert him. Perhaps he was shy. He mumbled to me as if he were ashamed of what he was saying; gave his name (it was something like Archbold—but at this distance of years I hardly am sure), his ship's name, and a few other particulars of that sort, in the manner of a criminal making a reluctant and doleful confession. He had had terrible weather on the passage out—terrible—terrible—wife aboard, too.

By this time we were seated in the cabin and the steward brought in a tray with a bottle and glasses. "Thanks! No." Never took liquor. Would have some water, though. He drank two tumblerfuls. Terrible thirsty work. Ever since daylight had been exploring the islands round his ship.

"What was that for—fun?" I asked, with an appearance of polite interest.

"No!" He sighed. "Painful duty. "

As he persisted in his mumbling and I wanted my double to hear every word, I hit upon the notion of informing him that I regretted to say I was hard of hearing.

"Such a young man, too!" he nodded, keeping his smeary blue, unintelligent eyes fastened upon me. "What was the cause of it—some disease?" he inquired, without the least sympathy and as if he thought that, if so, I'd got no more than I deserved.

"Yes; disease," I admitted in a cheerful tone which seemed to shock him. But my point was gained, because he had to raise his voice to give me his tale. It is not worth while to record that version. It was just over two months since all this had happened, and he had thought so much about it that he seemed completely muddled as to its bearings, but still immensely impressed.

"What would you think of such a thing happening on board your own ship? I've had the *Sephora* for these fifteen years. I am a well-known shipmaster."

He was densely distressed—and perhaps I should have sympathized with him if I had been able to detach my mental vision from the unsuspected sharer of my cabin as though he were my second self. There he was on the other side of the bulkhead, four or five feet from us, no more, as we sat in the saloon. I looked politely at Captain Archbold (if that was his name), but it was the other I saw, in a gray sleeping-suit, seated on a low stool, his bare feet close together, his arms folded, and every word said between us falling into the ears of his dark head bowed on his chest.

"I have been at sea now, man and boy, for seven-and-thirty years, and I've never heard of such a thing happening in an English ship. And that it should be my ship. Wife on board, too."

I was hardly listening to him.

"Don't you think," I said, "that the heavy sea which, you told me, came aboard just then might have killed the man? I have seen the sheer weight of a sea kill a man very neatly, by simply breaking his neck."

"Good God!" he uttered, impressively, fixing his smeary blue eyes on me. "The sea! No man killed by the sea ever looked like that." He seemed positively scandalized at my suggestion. And as I gazed at him, certainly not prepared for anything original on his part, he advanced his head close to mine and thrust his tongue out at me so suddenly that I couldn't help starting back.

After scoring over my calmness in this graphic way he nodded wisely. If I had seen the sight, he assured me, I would never forget it as long as I lived. The weather was too bad to give the corpse a proper sea burial. So next day at dawn they took it up on the poop, covering its face with a bit of bunting; he read a short prayer, and then, just as it was, in its oilskins and long boots, they launched it amongst those mountainous seas that seemed ready every moment to swallow up the ship herself and the terrified lives on board of her.

"That reefed foresail saved you," I threw in.

"Under God—it did," he exclaimed fervently. "It was by a special mercy, I firmly believe, that it stood some of those hurricane squalls."

"It was the setting of that sail which—" I began.

"God's own hand in it," he interrupted me. "Nothing less could have done it. I don't mind telling you that I hardly dared give the order. It seemed impossible that we could touch anything without los-

ing it, and then our last hope would have been gone."

The terror of that gale was on him yet. I let him go on for a bit, then said, casually—as if returning to a minor subject:

"You were very anxious to give up your mate to the shore people, I believe?"

He was. To the law. His obscure tenacity on that point had in it something incomprehensible and a little awful; something, as it were, mystical, quite apart from his anxiety that he should not be suspected of "countenancing any doings of that sort." Seven-and-thirty virtuous years at sea, of which over twenty of immaculate command, and the last fifteen in the *Sephora*, seemed to have laid him under some pitiless obligation.

"And you know," he went on, groping shame-facedly amongst his feelings, "I did not engage that young fellow. His people had some interest with my owners. I was in a way forced to take him on. He looked very smart, very gentlemanly, and all that. But do you know—I never liked him, somehow. I am a plain man. You see, he wasn't exactly the sort for the chief mate of a ship like the *Sephora*."

I had become so connected in thoughts and impressions with the secret sharer of my cabin that I felt as if I, personally, were being given to understand that I, too, was not the sort that would have done for the chief mate of a ship like the *Sephora*. I had no doubt of it in my mind.

"Not at all the style of man. You understand," he insisted, superfluously, looking hard at me.

I smiled urbanely. He seemed at a loss for a while.

"I suppose I must report a suicide."

"Beg pardon?"

"Sui-cide! That's what I'll have to write to my owners directly I get in."

"Unless you manage to recover him before tomorrow," I assented, dispassionately. . . . "I mean, alive."

He mumbled something which I really did not catch, and I turned my ear to him in a puzzled manner. He fairly bawled:

"The land—I say, the mainland is at least seven miles off my anchorage."

"About that."

My lack of excitement, of curiosity, of surprise, of any sort of pronounced interest, began to arouse his distrust. But except for the felicitous pretense of deafness I had not tried to pretend anything. I had felt utterly incapable of playing the part of ignorance properly, and therefore was afraid to try. It is also certain that he had brought some ready-made suspi-cions with him, and that he viewed my politeness as a strange and unnatural phenomenon. And yet how else could I have received him? Not heartily! That was impossible for psychological reasons, which I need not state here. My only object was to keep off his inquiries. Surlily? Yes, but surliness might have provoked a point-blank question. From its novelty to him and from its nature, punctilious courtesy was the manner best calculated to restrain the man. But there was the danger of his breaking through my defense bluntly. I could not, I think, have met him by a direct lie, also for psychological (not moral) reasons. If he had only known how afraid I was of his putting my feeling of identity with the other to the test! But, strangely enough—(I thought of it only afterwards)—I believe that he was not a little disconcerted by the reverse side of that weird situation, by something in me that reminded him of the man he was seeking—suggested a mysterious similitude to the young fellow he had distrusted and disliked from the first.

However that might have been, the silence was not very prolonged. He took another oblique step.

"I reckon I had no more than a two-mile pull to your ship. Not a bit more."

"And quite enough, too, in this awful heat," I said.

Another pause full of mistrust followed. Necessity, they say, is mother of invention, but fear, too, is not barren of ingenious suggestions. And I was afraid he would ask me point-blank for news of my other self.

"Nice little saloon, isn't it?" I remarked, as if noticing for the first time the way his eyes roamed from one closed door to the other. "And very well fitted out, too. Here, for instance," I continued, reaching over the back of my seat negligently and flinging the door open, "is my bath-room."

He made an eager movement, but hardly gave it a glance. I got up, shut the door of the bath-room, and invited him to have a look round, as if I were very proud of my accommodation. He had to rise and be shown round, but he went through the business without any raptures whatever.

"And now we'll have a look at my stateroom," I declared, in a voice as loud as I dared to make it, crossing the cabin to the starboard side with purposely heavy steps.

He followed me in and gazed around. My intelligent double had vanished. I played my part.

"Very convenient—isn't it?"

"Very nice. Very comf . . ." He didn't finish and went out brusquely as if to escape from some unrighteous wiles of mine. But it was not to be. I had been too frightened not to feel vengeful; I felt I had him on the run, and I meant to keep him on the run. My polite insistence must have had something menacing in it, because he gave in suddenly. And I did not let him off a single item; mate's room, pantry,

storerooms, the very sail-locker which was also under the poop—he had to look into them all. When at last I showed him out on the quarter-deck he drew a long, spiritless sigh, and mumbled dismally that he must really be going back to his ship now. I desired my mate, who had joined us, to see to the captain's boat.

The man of whiskers gave a blast on the whistle which he used to wear hanging round his neck, and yelled, "Sephora's away!" My double down there in my cabin must have heard, and certainly could not feel more relieved than I. Four fellows came running out from somewhere forward and went over the side, while my own men, appearing on deck too, lined the rail. I escorted my visitor to the gangway ceremoniously, and nearly overdid it. He was a tenacious beast. On the very ladder he lingered, and in that unique, guiltily conscientious manner of sticking to the point:

"I say . . . you . . . you don't think that—"

I covered his voice loudly:

"Certainly not. . . . I am delighted. Good-by."

I had an idea of what he meant to say, and just saved myself by the privilege of defective hearing. He was too shaken generally to insist, but my mate, close witness of that parting, looked mystified and his face took a thoughtful cast. As I did not want to appear as if I wished to avoid all communication with my officers, he had the opportunity to address me.

"Seems a very nice man. His boat's crew told our chaps a very extraordinary story, if what I am told by the steward is true. I suppose you had it from the captain, sir?"

"Yes. I had a story from the captain."

"A very horrible affair—isn't it, sir?"

"It is."

"Beats all these tales we hear about murders in Yankee ships."

"I don't think it beats them. I don't think it resembled them in the least."

"Bless my soul—you don't say so! But of course I've no acquaintance whatever with American ships, not I, so I couldn't go against your knowledge. It's horrible enough for me. . . . But the queerest part is that those fellows seemed to have some idea the man was hidden aboard here. They had really. Did you ever hear of such a thing?"

"Preposterous—isn't it?"

We were walking to and fro athwart the quarter-deck. No one of the crew forward could be seen (the day was Sunday), and the mate pursued:

"There was some little dispute about it. Our chaps took offense. 'As if we would harbor a thing like that,' they said. 'Wouldn't you like to look for him in our coal-hole?' Quite a tiff. But they made it up in the end. I suppose he did drown himself. Don't you, sir?"

"I don't suppose anything."

"You have no doubt in the matter, sir?"

"None whatever."

I left him suddenly. I felt I was producing a bad impression, but with my double down there it was most trying to be on deck. And it was almost as trying to be below. Altogether a nerve-trying situation. But on the whole I felt less torn in two when I was with him. There was no one in the whole ship whom I dared take into my confidence. Since the hands had got to know his story, it would have been impossible to pass him off for anyone else, and an accidental discovery was to be dreaded now more than ever. . . .

The steward being engaged in laying the table for dinner, we could talk only with our eyes when I first went down. Later in the afternoon we had a cautious try at whispering. The Sunday quietness of the ship was against us; the stillness of air and water around her was against us; the elements, the men were against us—everything was against us in our secret partnership; time itself—for this could not go on forever. The very trust in Providence was, I suppose, denied to his guilt. Shall I confess that this thought cast me down very much? And as to the chapter of accidents which counts for so much in the book of success, I could only hope that it was closed. For what favorable accident could be expected?

"Did you hear everything?" were my first words as soon as we took up our position side by side, leaning over my bed-place.

He had. And the proof of it was his earnest whisper, "The man told you he hardly dared to give the order."

I understood the reference to be to that saving foresail.

"Yes. He was afraid of it being lost in the setting."

"I assure you he never gave the order. He may think he did, but he never gave it. He stood there with me on the break of the poop after the maintopsail blew away, and whimpered about our last hope—positively whimpered about it and nothing else—and the night coming on! To hear one's skipper go on like that in such weather was enough to drive any fellow out of his mind. It worked me up into a sort of desperation. I just took it into my own hands and went away from him, boiling, and— But what's the use telling you? *You* know! . . . Do you think that if I had not been pretty fierce with them I should have got the men to do anything? Not it! The bo's'n perhaps? Perhaps! It wasn't a heavy sea—it was a sea

gone mad! I suppose the end of the world will be something like that; and a man may have the heart to see it coming once and be done with it—but to have to face it day after day— I don't blame anybody. I was precious little better than the rest. Only—I was an officer of that old coal-wagon, anyhow—"

"I quite understand," I conveyed that sincere assurance into his ear. He was out of breath with whispering; I could hear him pant slightly. It was all very simple. The same strung-up force which had given twenty-four men a chance, at least, for their lives, had, in a sort of recoil, crushed an unworthy mutinous existence.

But I had no leisure to weigh the merits of the matter—footsteps in the saloon, a heavy knock. "There's enough wind to get under way with, sir." Here was the call of a new claim upon my thoughts and even upon my feelings.

"Turn the hands up," I cried through the door. "I'll be on deck directly."

I was going out to make the acquaintance of my ship. Before I left the cabin our eyes met—the eyes of the only two strangers on board. I pointed to the recessed part where the little camp-stool awaited him and laid my finger on my lips. He made a gesture—somewhat vague—a little mysterious, accompanied by a faint smile, as if of regret.

This is not the place to enlarge upon the sensations of a man who feels for the first time a ship move under his feet to his own independent word. In my case they were not unalloyed. I was not wholly alone with my command; for there was that stranger in my cabin. Or rather, I was not completely and wholly with her. Part of me was absent. That mental feeling of being in two places at once affected me physically as if the mood of secrecy had penetrated my very soul. Before an hour had elapsed since the ship had begun to move, having occasion to ask the mate (he stood by my side) to take a compass bearing of the Pagoda, I caught myself reaching up to his ear in whispers. I say I caught myself, but enough had escaped to startle the man. I can't describe it otherwise than by saying that he shied. A grave, preoccupied manner, as though he were in possession of some perplexing intelligence, did not leave him henceforth. A little later I moved away from the rail to look at the compass with such a stealthy gait that the helmsman noticed it—and I could not help noticing the unusual roundness of his eyes. These are trifling instances, though it's to no commander's advantage to be suspected of ludicrous eccentricities. But I was also more seriously affected. There are to a seamen certain words, gestures, that should in given conditions come as naturally, as instinctively as the winking of a menaced eye. A cer-

tain order should spring onto his lips without thinking; a certain sign should get itself made, so to speak,
without reflection. But all unconscious alertness had
abandoned me. I had to make an effort of will to
recall myself back (from the cabin) to the conditions
of the moment. I felt that I was appearing an irresolute commander to those people who were watching
me more or less critically.

And, besides, there were the scares. On the second
day out, for instance, coming off the deck in the
afternoon (I had straw slippers on my bare feet) I
stopped at the open pantry door and spoke to the
steward. He was doing something there with his
back to me. At the sound of my voice he nearly
jumped out of his skin, as the saying is, and incidentally broke a cup.

"What on earth's the matter with you?" I asked,
astonished.

He was extremely confused. "Beg your pardon, sir.
I made sure you were in your cabin."

"You see I wasn't."

"No, sir. I could have sworn I had heard you moving in there not a moment ago. It's most extraordinary . . . very sorry, sir."

I passed on with an inward shudder. I was so
identified with my secret double that I did not even
mention the fact in those scanty, fearful whispers we
exchanged. I suppose he had made some slight noise
of some kind or other. It would have been miraculous
if he hadn't at one time or another. And yet, haggard
as he appeared, he looked always perfectly self-
controlled, more than calm—almost invulnerable. On
my suggestion he remained almost entirely in the
bath-room, which, upon the whole, was the safest
place. There could be really no shadow of an excuse
for anyone ever wanting to go in there, once the
steward had done with it. It was a very tiny place.
Sometimes he reclined on the floor, his legs bent, his
head sustained on one elbow. At others I would find
him on the camp-stool, sitting in his gray sleeping-
suit and with his cropped dark hair like a patient,
unmoved convict. At night I would smuggle him
into my bed-place, and we would whisper together,
with the regular foot-falls of the officer of the watch
passing and repassing over our heads. It was an infinitely miserable time. It was lucky that some tins
of fine preserves were stowed in a locker in my stateroom; hard bread I could always get hold of; and so
he lived on stewed chicken, pâté de foie gras, asparagus, cooked oysters, sardines—on all sorts of abominable sham delicacies out of tins. My early morning
coffee he always drank; and it was all I dared do for
him in that respect.

Every day there was the horrible maneuvering to
go through so that my room and then the bath-room

should be done in the usual way. I came to hate the
sight of the steward, to abhor the voice of that harmless man. I felt that it was he who would bring on
the disaster of discovery. It hung like a sword over
our heads.

The fourth day out, I think (we were then working down the east side of the Gulf of Siam, tack for
tack, in light winds and smooth water)—the fourth
day, I say, of this miserable juggling with the unavoidable, as we sat at our evening meal, that man,
whose slightest movement I dreaded, after putting
down the dishes ran up on deck busily. This could
not be dangerous. Presently he came down again;
and then it appeared that he had remembered a coat
of mine which I had thrown over a rail to dry after
having been wetted in a shower which had passed
over the ship in the afternoon. Sitting stolidly at the
head of the table I became terrified at the sight of
the garment on his arm. Of course he made for my
door. There was no time to lose.

"Steward," I thundered. My nerves were so shaken
that I could not govern my voice and conceal my
agitation. This was the sort of thing that made my
terrifically whiskered mate tap his forehead with his
forefinger. I had detected him using that gesture
while talking on deck with a confidential air to the
carpenter. It was too far to hear a word, but I had
no doubt that this pantomime could only refer to the
strange new captain.

"Yes, sir," the pale-faced steward turned resignedly to me. It was this maddening course of being
shouted at, checked without rhyme or reason, arbi-
trarily chased out of my cabin, suddenly called into
it, sent flying out of his pantry on incomprehensible
errands, that accounted for the growing wretchedness of his expression.

"Where are you going with that coat?"

"To your room, sir."

"Is there another shower coming?"

"I'm sure I don't know, sir. Shall I go up again and
see, sir?"

"No! never mind."

My object was attained, as of course my other
self in there would have heard everything that
passed. During this interlude my two officers never
raised their eyes off their respective plates; but the
lip of that confounded cub, the second mate, quivered visibly.

I expected the steward to hook my coat on and
come out at once. He was very slow about it; but
I dominated my nervousness sufficiently not to shout
after him. Suddenly I became aware (it could be
heard plainly enough) that the fellow for some reason or other was opening the door of the bath-room.
It was the end. The place was literally not big

enough to swing a cat in. My voice died in my throat and I went stony all over. I expected to hear a yell of surprise and terror, and made a movement, but had not the strength to get on my legs. Everything remained still. Had my second self taken the poor wretch by the throat? I don't know what I could have done next moment if I had not seen the steward come out of my room, close the door, and then stand quietly by the sideboard.

"Saved," I thought. "But, no! Lost! Gone! He was gone!"

I laid my knife and fork down and leaned back in my chair. My head swam. After a while, when sufficiently recovered to speak in a steady voice, I instructed my mate to put the ship round at eight o'clock himself.

"I won't come on deck," I went on. "I think I'll turn in, and unless the wind shifts I don't want to be disturbed before midnight. I feel a bit seedy."

"You did look middling bad a little while ago," the chief mate remarked without showing any great concern.

They both went out, and I stared at the steward clearing the table. There was nothing to be read on that wretched man's face. But why did he avoid my eyes I asked myself. Then I thought I should like to hear the sound of his voice.

"Steward!"

"Sir!" Startled as usual.

"Where did you hang up that coat?"

"In the bath-room, sir." The usual anxious tone. "It's not quite dry yet, sir."

For some time longer I sat in the cuddy. Had my double vanished as he had come? But of his coming there was an explanation, whereas his disappearance would be inexplicable. . . . I went slowly into my dark room, shut the door, lighted the lamp, and for a time dared not turn round. When at last I did I saw him standing bolt-upright in the narrow recessed part. It would not be true to say I had a shock, but an irresistible doubt of his bodily existence flitted through my mind. Can it be, I asked myself, that he is not visible to other eyes than mine? It was like being haunted. Motionless, with a grave face, he raised his hands slightly at me in a gesture which meant clearly, "Heavens! what a narrow escape!" Narrow indeed. I think I had come creeping quietly as near insanity as any man who has not actually gone over the border. That gesture restrained me, so to speak.

The mate with the terrific whiskers was now putting the ship on the other tack. In the moment of profound silence which follows upon the hands going to their stations I heard on the poop his raised voice: "Hard alee!" and the distant shout of the order repeated on the main-deck. The sails, in that light breeze, made but a faint fluttering noise. It ceased. The ship was coming round slowly; I held my breath in the renewed stillness of expectation; one wouldn't have thought that there was a single living soul on her decks. A sudden brisk shout, "Mainsail haul!" broke the spell, and in the noisy cries and rush overhead of the men running away with the main-brace we two, down in my cabin, came together in our usual position by the bed-place.

He did not wait for my question. "I heard him fumbling here and just managed to squat myself down in the bath," he whispered to me. "The fellow only opened the door and put his arm in to hang the coat up. All the same—"

"I never thought of that," I whispered back, even more appalled than before at the closeness of the shave, and marveling at that something unyielding in his character which was carrying him through so finely. There was no agitation in his whisper. Whoever was being driven distracted, it was not he. He was sane. And the proof of his sanity was continued when he took up the whispering again.

"It would never do for me to come to life again."

It was something that a ghost might have said. But what he was alluding to was his old captain's reluctant admission of the theory of suicide. It would obviously serve his turn—if I had understood at all the view which seemed to govern the unalterable purpose of his action.

"You must maroon me as soon as ever you can get amongst these islands off the Cambodge shore," he went on.

"Maroon you! We are not living in a boy's adventure tale," I protested. His scornful whispering took me up.

"We aren't indeed! There's nothing of a boy's tale in this. But there's nothing else for it. I want no more. You don't suppose I am afraid of what can be done to me? Prison or gallows or whatever they may please. But you don't see me coming back to explain such things to an old fellow in a wig and twelve respectable tradesmen, do you? What can they know whether I am guilty or not—or of *what* I am guilty, either? That's my affair. What does the Bible say? 'Driven off the face of the earth.' Very well. I am off the face of the earth now. As I came at night so I shall go."

"Impossible!" I murmured. "You can't."

"Can't? . . . Not naked like a soul on the Day of Judgment. I shall freeze on to this sleeping-suit. The Last Day is not yet—and . . . you have understood thoroughly. Didn't you?"

I felt suddenly ashamed of myself. I may say truly that I understood—and my hesitation in letting that man swim away from my ship's side had been a mere sham sentiment, a sort of cowardice.

"It can't be done now till next night," I breathed out. "The ship is on the offshore tack and the wind may fail us."

"As long as I know that you understand," he whispered. "But of course you do. It's a great satisfaction to have got somebody to understand. You seem to have been there on purpose." And in the same whisper, as if we two whenever we talked had to say things to each other which were not fit for the world to hear, he added, "It's very wonderful."

We remained side by side talking in our secret way—but sometimes silent or just exchanging a whispered word or two at long intervals. And as usual he stared through the port. A breath of wind came now and again into our faces. The ship might have been moored in dock, so gently and on an even keel she slipped through the water, that did not murmur even at our passage, shadowy and silent like a phantom sea.

At midnight I went on deck, and to my mate's great surprise put the ship round on the other tack. His terrible whiskers flitted round me in silent criticism. I certainly should not have done it if it had been only a question of getting out of that sleepy gulf as quickly as possible. I believe he told the second mate, who relieved him, that it was a great want of judgment. The other only yawned. That intolerable cub shuffled about so sleepily and lolled against the rails in such a slack, improper fashion that I came down on him sharply.

"Aren't you properly awake yet?"

"Yes, sir! I am awake."

"Well, then, be good enough to hold yourself as if you were. And keep a look-out. If there's any current we'll be closing with some islands before daylight."

The east side of the gulf is fringed with islands, some solitary, others in groups. On the blue background of the high coast they seem to float on silvery patches of calm water, arid and gray, or dark green and rounded like clumps of evergreen bushes, with the larger ones, a mile or two long, showing the outlines of ridges, ribs of gray rock under the dank mantle of matted leafage. Unknown to trade, to travel, almost to geography, the manner of life they harbor is an unsolved secret. There must be villages —settlements of fishermen at least—on the largest of them, and some communication with the world is probably kept up by native craft. But all that forenoon, as we headed for them, fanned along by the faintest of breezes, I saw no sign of man or canoe in the field of the telescope I kept on pointing at the scattered group.

At noon I gave no orders for a change of course, and the mate's whiskers became much concerned and seemed to be offering themselves unduly to my notice. At last I said:

"I am going to stand right in. Quite in—as far as I can take her."

The stare of extreme surprise imparted an air of ferocity also to his eyes, and he looked truly terrific for a moment.

"We're not doing well in the middle of the gulf," I continued, casually. "I am going to look for the land breezes tonight."

"Bless my soul! Do you mean, sir, in the dark amongst the lot of all them islands and reefs and shoals?"

"Well—if there are any regular land breezes at all on this coast one must get close inshore to find them, mustn't one?"

"Bless my soul!" he exclaimed again under his breath. All that afternoon he wore a dreamy, contemplative appearance which in him was a mark of perplexity. After dinner I went into my stateroom as if I meant to take some rest. There we two bent our dark heads over a half-unrolled chart lying on my bed.

"There," I said. "It's got to be Koh-ring. I've been looking at it ever since sunrise. It has got two hills and a low point. It must be inhabited. And on the coast opposite there is what looks like the mouth of a biggish river—with some town, no doubt, not far up. It's the best chance for you that I can see."

"Anything. Koh-ring let it be."

He looked thoughtfully at the chart as if surveying chances and distances from a lofty height—and following with his eyes his own figure wandering on the blank land of Cochin-China, and then passing off that piece of paper clean out of sight into uncharted regions. And it was as if the ship had two captains to plan her course for her. I had been so worried and restless running up and down that I had not had the patience to dress that day. I had remained in my sleeping-suit, with straw slippers and a soft floppy hat. The closeness of the heat in the gulf had been most oppressive, and the crew were used to see me wandering in that airy attire.

"She will clear the south point as she heads now," I whispered into his ear. "Goodness only knows when, though, but certainly after dark. I'll edge her in to half a mile, as far as I may be able to judge in the dark—"

"Be careful," he murmured, warningly—and I realized suddenly that all my future, the only future for which I was fit, would perhaps go irretrievably to pieces in any mishap to my first command.

I could not stop a moment longer in the room. I

motioned him to get out of sight and made my way on the poop. That unplayful cub had the watch. I walked up and down for a while thinking things out, then beckoned him over.

"Send a couple of hands to open the two quarter-deck ports," I said, mildly.

He actually had the impudence, or else so forgot himself in his wonder at such an incomprehensible order, as to repeat:

"Open the quarter-deck ports! What for, sir?"

"The only reason you need concern yourself about is because I tell you to do so. Have them opened wide and fastened properly."

He reddened and went off, but I believe made some jeering remark to the carpenter as to the sensible practice of ventilating a ship's quarter-deck. I know he popped into the mate's cabin to impart the fact to him because the whiskers came on deck, as it were by chance, and stole glances at me from below—for signs of lunacy or drunkenness, I suppose.

A little before supper, feeling more restless than ever, I rejoined, for a moment, my second self. And to find him sitting so quietly was surprising, like something against nature, inhuman.

I developed my plan in a hurried whisper.

"I shall stand in as close as I dare and then put her round. I will presently find means to smuggle you out of here into the sail-locker, which communicates with the lobby. But there is an opening, a sort of square for hauling the sails out, which gives straight on the quarter-deck and which is never closed in fine weather, so as to give air to the sails. When the ship's way is deadened in stays and all the hands are at the main-braces you will have a clear road to slip out and get overboard through the open quarter-deck port. I've had them both fastened up. Use a rope's end to lower yourself into the water so as to avoid a splash—you know. It could be heard and cause some beastly complication."

He kept silent for a while, then whispered, "I understand."

"I won't be there to see you go," I began with an effort. "The rest . . . I only hope I have understood, too."

"You have. From first to last"—and for the first time there seemed to be a faltering, something strained in his whisper. He caught hold of my arm, but the ringing of the supper bell made me start. He didn't, though; he only released his grip.

After supper I didn't come below again till well past eight o'clock. The faint, steady breeze was loaded with dew; and the wet, darkened sails held all there was of propelling power in it. The night, clear and starry, sparkled darkly, and the opaque, lightless patches shifting slowly against the low stars were the drifting islets. On the port bow there was a big one more distant and shadowily imposing by the great space of sky it eclipsed.

On opening the door I had a back view of my very own self looking at a chart. He had come out of the recess and was standing near the table.

"Quite dark enough," I whispered.

He stepped back and leaned against my bed with a level, quiet glance. I sat on the couch. We had nothing to say to each other. Over our heads the officer of the watch moved here and there. Then I heard him move quickly. I knew what that meant. He was making for the companion; and presently his voice was outside my door.

"We are drawing in pretty fast, sir. Land looks rather close."

"Very well," I answered. "I am coming on deck directly."

I waited till he was gone out of the cuddy, then rose. My double moved too. The time had come to exchange our last whispers, for neither of us was ever to hear each other's natural voice.

"Look here!" I opened a drawer and took out three sovereigns. "Take this anyhow. I've got six and I'd give you the lot, only I must keep a little money to buy some fruit and vegetables for the crew from native boats as we go through Sunda Straits."

He shook his head.

"Take it," I urged him, whispering desperately. "No one can tell what—"

He smiled and slapped meaningly the only pocket of the sleeping-jacket. It was not safe, certainly. But I produced a large old silk handkerchief of mine, and tying the three pieces of gold in a corner, pressed it on him. He was touched, I suppose, because he took it at last and tied it quickly round his waist under the jacket, on his bare skin.

Our eyes met; several seconds elapsed, till, our glances still mingled, I extended my hand and turned the lamp out. Then I passed through the cuddy, leaving the door of my room wide open. . . . "Steward!"

He was still lingering in the pantry in the greatness of his zeal, giving a rub-up to a plated cruet stand the last thing before going to bed. Being careful not to wake up the mate, whose room was opposite, I spoke in an undertone.

He looked round anxiously. "Sir!"

"Can you get me a little hot water from the galley?"

"I am afraid, sir, the galley fire's been out for some time now."

"Go and see."

He flew up the stairs.

"Now," I whispered, loudly, into the saloon—too

loudly, perhaps, but I was afraid I couldn't make a sound. He was by my side in an instant—the double captain slipped past the stairs—through a tiny dark passage . . . a sliding door. We were in the sail-locker, scrambling on our knees over the sails. A sudden thought struck me. I saw myself wandering barefooted, bareheaded, the sun beating on my dark poll. I snatched off my floppy hat and tried hurriedly in the dark to ram it on my other self. He dodged and fended off silently. I wonder what he thought had come to me before he understood and suddenly desisted. Our hands met gropingly, lingered, united in a steady, motionless clasp for a second. . . . No word was breathed by either of us when they separated.

I was standing quietly by the pantry door when the steward returned.

"Sorry, sir. Kettle barely warm. Shall I light the spirit-lamp?"

"Never mind."

I came out on deck slowly. It was now a matter of conscience to shave the land as close as possible—for now he must go overboard whenever the ship was put in stays. Must! There could be no going back for him. After a moment I walked over to leeward and my heart flew into my mouth at the nearness of the land on the bow. Under any other circumstances I would not have held on a minute longer. The second mate had followed me anxiously.

I looked on till I felt I could command my voice.

"She will weather," I said then in a quiet tone.

"Are you going to try that, sir?" he stammered out incredulously.

I took no notice of him and raised my tone just enough to be heard by the helmsman.

"Keep her good full."

"Good full, sir."

The wind fanned my cheek, the sails slept, the world was silent. The strain of watching the dark loom of the land grow bigger and denser was too much for me. I had shut my eyes—because the ship must go closer. She must! The stillness was intolerable. Were we standing still?

When I opened my eyes the second view started my heart with a thump. The black southern hill of Koh-ring seemed to hang right over the ship like a towering fragment of the everlasting night. On that enormous mass of blackness there was not a gleam to be seen, not a sound to be heard. It was gliding irresistibly towards us and yet seemed already within reach of the hand. I saw the vague figures of the watch grouped in the waist, gazing in awed silence.

"Are you going on, sir?" inquired an unsteady voice at my elbow.

I ignored it. I had to go on.

"Keep her full. Don't check her way. That won't do now," I said, warningly.

"I can't see the sails very well," the helmsman answered me, in strange, quavering tones.

Was she close enough? Already she was, I won't say in the shadow of the land, but in the very blackness of it, already swallowed up as it were, gone too close to be recalled, gone from me altogether.

"Give the mate a call," I said to the young man who stood at my elbow as still as death. "And turn all hands up."

My tone had a borrowed loudness reverberated from the height of the land. Several voices cried out together: "We are all on deck, sir."

Then stillness again, with the great shadow gliding closer, towering higher, without a light, without a sound. Such a hush had fallen on the ship that she might have been a bark of the dead floating in slowly under the very gate of Erebus.

"My God! Where are we?"

It was the mate moaning at my elbow. He was thunderstruck, and as it were deprived of the moral support of his whiskers. He clapped his hands and absolutely cried out, "Lost!"

"Be quiet," I said, sternly.

He lowered his tone, but I saw the shadowy gesture of his despair. "What are we doing here?"

"Looking for the land wind."

He made as if to tear his hair, and addressed me recklessly.

"She will never get out. You have done it, sir. I knew it'd end in something like this. She will never weather, and you are too close now to stay. She'll drift ashore before she's round. O my God!"

I caught his arm as he was raising it to batter his poor devoted head, and shook it violently.

"She's ashore already," he wailed, trying to tear himself away.

"Is she? . . . Keep good full there!"

"Good full, sir," cried the helmsman in a frightened, thin, child-like voice.

I hadn't let go the mate's arm and went on shaking it. "Ready about, do you hear? You go forward"—shake—"and stop there"—shake—"and hold your noise"—shake—"and see these head-sheets properly overhauled"—shake, shake—shake.

And all the time I dared not look towards the land lest my heart should fail me. I released my grip at last and he ran forward as if fleeing for dear life.

I wondered what my double there in the sail-locker thought of this commotion. He was able to hear everything—and perhaps he was able to understand why, on my conscience, it had to be thus close—no less. My first order "Hard alee!" re-echoed ominously under the towering shadow of Koh-ring as if I had shouted in a mountain gorge. And then I watched the land intently. In that smooth water and light wind it was impossible to feel the ship coming-to. No! I could not feel her. And my second self was making now ready to slip out and lower himself overboard. Perhaps he was gone already . . . ?

The great black mass brooding over our very mast-heads began to pivot away from the ship's side silently. And now I forgot the secret stranger ready to depart, and remembered only that I was a total stranger to the ship. I did not know her. Would she do it? How was she to be handled?

I swung the mainyard and waited helplessly. She was perhaps stopped, and her very fate hung in the balance, with the black mass of Koh-ring like the gate of the everlasting night towering over her taff-rail. What would she do now? Had she way on her yet? I stepped to the side swiftly, and on the shadowy water I could see nothing except a faint phosphorescent flash revealing the glassy smoothness of the sleeping surface. It was impossible to tell—and I had not learned yet the feel of my ship. Was she moving? What I needed was something easily seen, a piece of paper, which I could throw overboard and watch. I had nothing on me. To run down for it I didn't dare. There was no time. All at once my strained, yearning stare distinguished a white object floating within a yard of the ship's side. White on the black water. A phosphorescent flash passed under it. What was that thing? . . . I recognized my own floppy hat. It must have fallen off his head . . . and he didn't bother. Now I had what I wanted—the saving mark for my eyes. But I hardly thought of my other self, now gone from the ship, to be hidden forever from all friendly faces, to be a fugitive and a vagabond on the earth, with no brand of the curse on his sane forehead to stay a slaying hand . . . too proud to explain.

And I watched the hat—the expression of my sudden pity for his mere flesh. It had been meant to save his homeless head from the dangers of the sun. And now—behold—it was saving the ship, by serving me for a mark to help out the ignorance of my strangeness. Ha! It was drifting forward, warning me just in time that the ship had gathered stern-way.

"Shift the helm," I said in a low voice to the seaman standing still like a statue.

The man's eyes glistened wildly in the binnacle light as he jumped round to the other side and spun round the wheel.

I walked to the break of the poop. On the over-shadowed deck all hands stood by the forebraces waiting for my order. The stars ahead seemed to be gliding from right to left. And all was so still in the world that I heard the quiet remark, "She's round," passed in a tone of intense relief between two seamen.

"Let go and haul."

The foreyards ran round with a great noise, amidst cheery cries. And now the frightful whiskers made themselves heard giving various orders. Already the ship was drawing ahead. And I was alone with her. Nothing! no one in the world should stand now between us, throwing a shadow on the way of silent knowledge and mute affection, the perfect communion of a seaman with his first command.

Walking to the taffrail, I was in time to make out, on the very edge of a darkness thrown by a towering black mass like the very gateway of Erebus—yes, I was in time to catch an evanescent glimpse of my white hat left behind to mark the spot where the secret sharer of my cabin and of my thoughts, as though he were my second self, had lowered himself into the water to take his punishment: a free man, a proud swimmer striking out for a new destiny.

THE BLUE HOTEL

STEPHEN CRANE

STEPHEN CRANE (1871–1900) was born in Newark, New Jersey, attended Lafayette College and Syracuse University, worked in New York as a reporter and later as a war correspondent in Cuba and Greece, and eventually settled in England. His most distinguished work is probably the novel, *The Red Badge of Courage* (1895).

THE Palace Hotel at Fort Romper was painted a light blue, a shade that is on the legs of a kind of heron, causing the bird to declare its position against any background. The Palace Hotel, then, was always screaming and howling in a way that made the dazzling winter landscape of Nebraska seem only a gray swampish hush. It stood alone on the prairie, and when the snow was falling the town two hundred yards away was not visible. But when the traveler alighted at the railway station he was obliged to pass the Palace Hotel before he could come upon the company of low clapboard houses which composed Fort Romper, and it was not to be thought that any traveler could pass the Palace Hotel without looking at it. Pat Scully, the proprietor, had proved himself a master of strategy when he chose his paints. It is true that on clear days, when the great transcontinental expresses, long lines of swaying Pullmans, swept through Fort Romper, passengers were overcome at the sight, and the cult that knows the brown-reds and the subdivisions of the dark greens of the East expressed shame, pity, horror, in a laugh. But to the citizens of this prairie town and to the people who would naturally stop there, Pat Scully had performed a feat. With this opulence and splendor, these creeds, classes, egotisms, that streamed through Romper on the rails day after day, they had no color in common.

As if the displayed delights of such a blue hotel were not sufficiently enticing, it was Scully's habit to go every morning and evening to meet the leisurely trains that stopped at Romper and work his seductions upon any man that he might see wavering, gripsack in hand.

One morning, when a snow-crusted engine dragged its long string of freight cars and its one passenger coach to the station, Scully performed the marvel of catching three men. One was a shaky and quick-eyed Swede, with a great shining cheap valise; one was a

tall bronzed cowboy, who was on his way to a ranch near the Dakota line; one was a little silent man from the East, who didn't look it, and didn't announce it. Scully practically made them prisoners. He was so nimble and merry and kindly that each probably felt it would be the height of brutality to try to escape. They trudged off over the creaking board sidewalks in the wake of the eager little Irishman. He wore a heavy fur cap squeezed tightly down on his head. It caused his two red ears to stick out stiffly, as if they were made of tin.

At last, Scully, elaborately, with boisterous hospitality, conducted them through the portals of the blue hotel. The room which they entered was small. It seemed to be merely a proper temple for an enormous stove, which, in the center, was humming with godlike violence. At various points on its surface the iron had become luminous and glowed yellow from the heat. Beside the stove Scully's son Johnnie was playing High-Five with an old farmer who had whiskers both gray and sandy. They were quarreling. Frequently the old farmer turned his face toward a box of sawdust—colored brown from tobacco juice —that was behind the stove, and spat with an air of great impatience and irritation. With a loud flourish of words Scully destroyed the game of cards, and bustled his son upstairs with part of the baggage of the new guests. He himself conducted them to three basins of the coldest water in the world. The cowboy and the Easterner burnished themselves fiery red with this water, until it seemed to be some kind of metal-polish. The Swede, however, merely dipped his fingers gingerly and with trepidation. It was notable that throughout this series of small ceremonies the three travelers were made to feel that Scully was very benevolent. He was conferring great favors upon them. He handed the towel from one to another with an air of philanthropic impulse.

Afterward they went to the first room, and, sitting about the stove, listened to Scully's officious clamor at his daughters, who were preparing the midday meal. They reflected in the silence of experienced

Reprinted from *Stephen Crane: An Omnibus*, edited by Robert Wooster Stallman, by permission of Alfred A. Knopf, Inc. Copyright 1952 by Alfred A. Knopf, Inc.

men who tread carefully amid new people. Nevertheless, the old farmer, stationary, invincible in his chair near the warmest part of the stove, turned his face from the sawdust-box frequently and addressed a glowing commonplace to the strangers. Usually he was answered in short but adequate sentences by either the cowboy or the Easterner. The Swede said nothing. He seemed to be occupied in making furtive estimates of each man in the room. One might have thought that he had the sense of silly suspicion which comes to guilt. He resembled a badly frightened man.

Later, at dinner, he spoke a little, addressing his conversation entirely to Scully. He volunteered that he had come from New York, where for ten years he had worked as a tailor. These facts seemed to strike Scully as fascinating, and afterward he volunteered that he had lived at Romper for fourteen years. The Swede asked about the crops and the price of labor. He seemed barely to listen to Scully's extended replies. His eyes continued to rove from man to man.

Finally, with a laugh and a wink, he said that some of these Western communities were very dangerous; and after his statement he straightened his legs under the table, tilted his head, and laughed again, loudly. It was plain that the demonstration had no meaning to the others. They looked at him wondering and in silence.

II

As the men trooped heavily back into the front room, the two little windows presented views of a turmoiling sea of snow. The huge arms of the wind were making attempts—mighty, circular, futile—to embrace the flakes as they sped. A gate-post like a still man with a blanched face stood aghast amid this profligate fury. In a hearty voice Scully announced the presence of a blizzard. The guests of the blue hotel, lighting their pipes, assented with grunts of lazy masculine contentment. No island of the sea could be exempt in the degree of this little room with its humming stove. Johnnie, son of Scully, in a tone which defined his opinion of his ability as a card-player, challenged the old farmer of both gray and sandy whiskers to a game of High-Five. The farmer agreed with a contemptuous and bitter scoff. They sat close to the stove, and squared their knees under a wide board. The cowboy and the Easterner watched the game with interest. The Swede remained near the window, aloof, but with a countenance that showed signs of an inexplicable excitement.

The play of Johnnie and the gray-beard was suddenly ended by another quarrel. The old man arose while casting a look of heated scorn at his adversary.

He slowly buttoned his coat, and then stalked with fabulous dignity from the room. In the discreet silence of all other men the Swede laughed. His laughter rang somehow childish. Men by this time had begun to look at him askance, as if they wished to inquire what ailed him.

A new game was formed jocosely. The cowboy volunteered to become the partner of Johnnie, and they all then turned to ask the Swede to throw in his lot with the little Easterner. He asked some questions about the game, and, learning that it wore many names, and that he had played it when it was under an alias, he accepted the invitation. He strode toward the men nervously, as if he expected to be assaulted. Finally, seated, he gazed from face to face and laughed shrilly. This laugh was so strange that the Easterner looked up quickly, the cowboy sat intent and with his mouth open, and Johnnie paused, holding the cards with still fingers.

Afterward there was a short silence. Then Johnnie said, "Well, let's get at it. Come on now!" They pulled their chairs forward until their knees were bunched under the board. They began to play, and their interest in the game caused the others to forget the manner of the Swede.

The cowboy was a board-whacker. Each time that he held superior cards he whanged them, one by one, with exceeding force, down upon the improvised table, and took the tricks with a glowing air of prowess and pride that sent thrills of indignation into the hearts of his opponents. A game with a board-whacker in it is sure to become intense. The countenances of the Easterner and the Swede were miserable whenever the cowboy thundered down his aces and kings, while Johnnie, his eyes gleaming with joy, chuckled and chuckled.

Because of the absorbing play none considered the strange ways of the Swede. They paid strict heed to the game. Finally, during a lull caused by a new deal, the Swede suddenly addressed Johnnie: "I suppose there have been a good many men killed in this room." The jaws of the others dropped and they looked at him.

"What in hell are you talking about?" said Johnnie.

The Swede laughed again his blatant laugh, full of a kind of false courage and defiance. "Oh, you know what I mean all right," he answered.

"I'm a liar if I do!" Johnnie protested. The card game was halted, and the men stared at the Swede. Johnnie evidently felt that as the son of the proprietor he should make a direct inquiry. "Now, what might you be drivin' at, mister?" he asked. The Swede winked at him. It was a wink full of cunning. His fingers shook on the edge of the board. "Oh, maybe you think I have been to nowheres. Maybe you think I'm a tenderfoot?"

"I don't know nothin' about you," answered Johnnie, "and I don't give a damn where you've been. All I got to say is that I don't know what you're driving at. There hain't never been nobody killed in this room."

The cowboy, who had been steadily gazing at the Swede, then spoke: "What's wrong with you, mister?"

Apparently it seemed to the Swede that he was formidably menaced. He shivered and turned white near the corners of his mouth. He sent an appealing glance in the direction of the little Easterner. During these moments he did not forget to wear his air of advanced potvalor. "They say they don't know what I mean," he remarked mockingly to the Easterner.

The latter answered after prolonged and cautious reflection. "I don't understand you," he said, impassively.

The Swede made a movement then which announced that he thought he had encountered treachery from the only quarter where he had expected sympathy, if not help. "Oh, I see you are all against me, I see——"

The cowboy was in a state of deep stupefaction. "Say," he cried, as he tumbled the deck violently down upon the board, "say, what are you gittin' at, hey?"

The Swede sprang up with the celerity of a man escaping from a snake on the floor. "I don't want to fight!" he shouted. "I don't want to fight!"

The cowboy stretched his long legs indolently and deliberately. His hands were in his pockets. He spat into the sawdust-box. "Well, who the hell thought you did?" he inquired.

The Swede backed rapidly toward a corner of the room. His hands were out protectingly in front of his chest, but he was making an obvious struggle to control his fright. "Gentlemen," he quavered, "I suppose I am going to be killed before I can leave this house! I suppose I am going to be killed before I can leave this house!" In his eyes was the dying-swan look. Through the windows could be seen the snow turning blue in the shadow of dusk. The wind tore at the house, and some loose thing beat regularly against the clapboards like a spirit tapping.

A door opened, and Scully himself entered. He paused in surprise as he noted the tragic attitude of the Swede. Then he said, "What's the matter here?"

The Swede answered him swiftly and eagerly: "These men are going to kill me."

"Kill you!" ejaculated Scully. "Kill you! What are you talkin'?"

The Swede made the gesture of a martyr.

Scully wheeled sternly upon his son. "What is this, Johnnie?"

The lad had grown sullen. "Damned if I know," he answered. "I can't make no sense to it." He began to shuffle the cards, fluttering them together with an angry snap. "He says a good many men have been killed in this room, or something like that. And he says he's goin' to be killed here too. I don't know what ails him. He's crazy, I shouldn't wonder."

Scully then looked for explanation to the cowboy, but the cowboy simply shrugged his shoulders.

"Kill you?" said Scully again to the Swede. "Kill you? Man, you're off your nut."

"Oh, I know," burst out the Swede. "I know what will happen. Yes, I'm crazy—yes. Yes, of course, I'm crazy—yes. But I know one thing—" There was a sort of sweat of misery and terror upon his face. "I know I won't get out of here alive."

The cowboy drew a deep breath, as if his mind was passing into the last stages of dissolution. "Well, I'm doggoned," he whispered to himself.

Scully wheeled suddenly and faced his son. "You've been troublin' this man!"

Johnnie's voice was loud with its burden of grievance. "Why, good Gawd, I ain't done nothin' to 'im."

The Swede broke in. "Gentlemen, do not disturb yourselves. I will leave this house. I will go away, because"—he accused them dramatically with his glance—"because I do not want to be killed."

Scully was furious with his son. "Will you tell me what is the matter, you young divil? What's the matter, anyhow? Speak out!"

"Blame it!" cried Johnnie in despair, "don't I tell you I don't know? He—he says we want to kill him, and that's all I know. I can't tell what ails him."

The Swede continued to repeat: "Never mind, Mr. Scully; never mind. I will leave this house. I will go away, because I do not wish to be killed. Yes, of course, I am crazy—yes. But I know one thing! I will go away. I will leave this house. Never mind, Mr. Scully; never mind. I will go away."

"You will not go 'way," said Scully. "You will not go 'way until I hear the reason of this business. If anybody has troubled you I will take care of him. This is my house. You are under my roof, and I will not allow any peaceable man to be troubled here." He cast a terrible eye upon Johnnie, the cowboy, and the Easterner.

"Never mind, Mr. Scully; never mind. I will go away. I do not wish to be killed." The Swede moved toward the door which opened upon the stairs. It was evidently his intention to go at once for his baggage.

"No, no," shouted Scully peremptorily; but the white-faced man slid by him and disappeared.

"Now," said Scully severely, "what does this mane?"

Johnnie and the cowboy cried together: "Why, we didn't do nothin' to 'im!"

Scully's eyes were cold. "No," he said, "you didn't?"

Johnnie swore a deep oath. "Why, this is the wildest loon I ever see. We didn't do nothin' at all. We were jest sittin' here playin' cards, and he——"

The father suddenly spoke to the Easterner, "Mr. Blanc," he asked, "what has these boys been doin'?"

The Easterner reflected again. "I didn't see anything wrong at all," he said at last, slowly.

Scully began to howl. "But what does it mane?" He stared ferociously at his son. "I have a mind to lather you for this, me boy."

Johnnie was frantic. "Well, what have I done?" he bawled at his father.

III

"I think you are tongue-tied," said Scully finally to his son, the cowboy, and the Easterner; and at the end of this scornful sentence he left the room.

Upstairs the Swede was swiftly fastening the straps of his great valise. Once his back happened to be half turned toward the door, and, hearing a noise there, he wheeled and sprang up, uttering a loud cry. Scully's wrinkled visage showed grimly in the light of the small lamp he carried. This yellow effulgence, streaming upward, colored only his prominent features, and left his eyes, for instance, in mysterious shadow. He resembled a murderer.

"Man! man!" he exclaimed, "have you gone daffy?"

"Oh, no! Oh, no!" rejoined the other. "There are people in this world who know pretty nearly as much as you do—understand?"

For a moment they stood gazing at each other. Upon the Swede's deathly pale cheeks were two spots brightly crimson and sharply edged, as if they had been carefully painted. Scully placed the light on the table and sat himself on the edge of the bed. He spoke ruminatively. "By cracky, I never heard of such a thing in my life. It's a complete muddle. I can't, for the soul of me, think how you ever got this idea into your head." Presently he lifted his eyes and asked: "And did you sure think they were going to kill you?"

The Swede scanned the old man as if he wished to see into his mind. "I did," he said at last. He obviously suspected that this answer might precipitate an outbreak. As he pulled on a strap his whole arm shook, the elbow wavering like a bit of paper.

Scully banged his hand impressively on the footboard of the bed. "Why, man, we're goin' to have a line of ilictric street-cars in this town next spring."

"'A line of electric street-cars,'" repeated the Swede, stupidly.

"And," said Scully, "there's a new railroad goin' to be built down from Broken Arm to here. Not to mintion the four churches and the smashin' big brick schoolhouse. Then there's the big factory, too. Why, in two years Romper'll be a met-tro-*pol*-is."

Having finished the preparation of his baggage, the Swede straightened himself. "Mr. Scully," he said, with sudden hardihood, "how much do I owe you?"

"You don't owe me anythin'," said the old man, angrily.

"Yes, I do," retorted the Swede. He took seventy-five cents from his pocket and tendered it to Scully; but the latter snapped his fingers in disdainful refusal. However, it happened that they both stood gazing in a strange fashion at three silver pieces on the Swede's open palm.

"I'll not take your money," said Scully at last. "Not after what's been goin' on here." Then a plan seemed to strike him. "Here," he cried, picking up his lamp and moving toward the door. "Here! Come with me a minute."

"No," said the Swede, in overwhelming alarm.

"Yes," urged the old man. "Come on! I want you to come and see a picter—just across the hall—in my room."

The Swede must have concluded that his hour was come. His jaw dropped and his teeth showed like a dead man's. He ultimately followed Scully across the corridor, but he had the step of one hung in chains.

Scully flashed the light high on the wall of his own chamber. There was revealed a ridiculous photograph of a little girl. She was leaning against a balustrade of gorgeous decoration, and the formidable bang to her hair was prominent. The figure was as graceful as an upright sled-stake, and, withal, it was of the hue of lead. "There," said Scully, tenderly, "that's the picter of my little girl that died. Her name was Carrie. She had the purtiest hair you ever saw! I was that fond of her, she——"

Turning then, he saw that the Swede was not contemplating the picture at all, but, instead, was keeping keen watch on the gloom in the rear.

"Look, man!" cried Scully, heartily. "That's the picter of my little gal that died. Her name was Carrie. And then here's the picter of my oldest boy, Michael. He's a lawyer in Lincoln, an' doin' well. I gave that boy a grand eddication, and I'm glad for it now. He's a fine boy. Look at 'im now. Ain't he bold as blazes, him there in Lincoln, an honored an' respicted gintleman! An honored and respicted gintleman," concluded Scully with a flourish. And, so saying, he smote the Swede jovially on the back.

The Swede faintly smiled.

"Now," said the old man, "there's only one more thing." He dropped suddenly to the floor and thrust his head beneath the bed. The Swede could hear his muffled voice. "I'd keep it under me piller if it wasn't for that boy Johnnie. Then there's the old woman— Where is it now? I never put it twice in the same place. Ah, now come out with you!"

Presently he backed clumsily from under the bed, dragging with him an old coat rolled into a bundle. "I've fetched him," he muttered. Kneeling on the floor, he unrolled the coat and extracted from its heart a large yellow-brown whisky-bottle.

His first maneuver was to hold the bottle up to the light. Reassured, apparently, that nobody had been tampering with it, he thrust it with a generous movement toward the Swede.

The weak-kneed Swede was about to eagerly clutch this element of strength, but he suddenly jerked his hand away and cast a look of horror upon Scully.

"Drink," said the old man affectionately. He had risen to his feet, and now stood facing the Swede.

There was a silence. Then again Scully said: "Drink!"

The Swede laughed wildly. He grabbed the bottle, put it to his mouth; and as his lips curled absurdly around the opening and his throat worked, he kept his glance, burning with hatred, upon the old man's face.

IV

After the departure of Scully the three men, with the cardboard still upon their knees, preserved for a long time an astounded silence. Then Johnnie said: "That's the doddangedest Swede I ever see."

"He ain't no Swede," said the cowboy, scornfully.

"Well, what is he then?" cried Johnnie. "What is he then?"

"It's my opinion," replied the cowboy deliberately, "he's some kind of a Dutchman." It was a venerable custom of the country to entitle as Swedes all light-haired men who spoke with a heavy tongue. In consequence the idea of the cowboy was not without its daring. "Yes, sir," he repeated. "It's my opinion this feller is some kind of a Dutchman."

"Well, he says he's a Swede, anyhow," muttered Johnnie, sulkily. He turned to the Easterner: "What do you think, Mr. Blanc?"

"Oh, I don't know," replied the Easterner.

"Well, what do you think makes him act that way?" asked the cowboy.

"Why, he's frightened." The Easterner knocked his pipe against a rim of the stove. "He's clear frightened out of his boots."

"What at?" cried Johnnie and the cowboy together.

The Easterner reflected over his answer.

"Oh, I don't know, but it seems to me this man has been reading dime novels, and he thinks he's right out in the middle of it—the shootin' and stabbin' and all."

"But," said the cowboy, deeply scandalized, "this ain't Wyoming, ner none of them places. This is Nebrasker."

"Yes," added Johnnie, "an' why don't he wait till he gits out West?"

The traveled Easterner laughed. "It isn't different there even—not in these days. But he thinks he's right in the middle of hell."

Johnnie and the cowboy mused long.

"It's awful funny," remarked Johnnie at last.

"Yes," said the cowboy. "This is a queer game. I hope we don't git snowed in, because then we'd have to stand this here man bein' around with us all the time. That wouldn't be no good."

"I wish pop would throw him out," said Johnnie.

Presently they heard a loud stamping on the stairs, accompanied by ringing jokes in the voice of old Scully, and laughter, evidently from the Swede. The men around the stove stared vacantly at each other. "Gosh!" said the cowboy. The door flew open, and old Scully, flushed and anecdotal, came into the room. He was jabbering at the Swede, who followed him, laughing bravely. It was the entry of two roisterers from a banquet hall.

"Come now," said Scully sharply to the three seated men, "move up and give us a chance at the stove." The cowboy and the Easterner obediently sidled their chairs to make room for the new-comers. Johnnie, however, simply arranged himself in a more indolent attitude, and then remained motionless.

"Come! Git over, there," said Scully.

"Plenty of room on the other side of the stove," said Johnnie.

"Do you think we want to sit in the draught?" roared the father.

But the Swede here interposed with a grandeur of confidence. "No, no. Let the boy sit where he likes," he cried in a bullying voice to the father.

"All right! All right!" said Scully, deferentially. The cowboy and the Easterner exchanged glances of wonder.

The five chairs were formed in a crescent about one side of the stove. The Swede began to talk; he talked arrogantly, profanely, angrily. Johnnie, the cowboy, and the Easterner maintained a morose silence, while old Scully appeared to be receptive and eager, breaking in constantly with sympathetic ejaculations.

Finally the Swede announced that he was thirsty. He moved in his chair, and said that he would go for a drink of water.

"I'll git it for you," cried Scully at once.

"No," said the Swede, contemptuously. "I'll get it for myself." He arose and stalked with the air of an owner off into the executive parts of the hotel.

As soon as the Swede was out of hearing Scully sprang to his feet and whispered intensely to the others: "Upstairs he thought I was tryin' to poison 'im."

"Say," said Johnnie, "this makes me sick. Why don't you throw 'im out in the snow?"

"Why, he's all right now," declared Scully. "It was only that he was from the East, and he thought this was a tough place. That's all. He's all right now."

The cowboy looked with admiration upon the Easterner. "You were straight," he said. "You were on to that there Dutchman."

"Well," said Johnnie to his father, "he may be all right now, but I don't see it. Other time he was scared, but now he's too fresh."

Scully's speech was always a combination of Irish brogue and idiom, Western twang and idiom, and scraps of curiously formal diction taken from the storybooks and newspapers. He now hurled a strange mass of language at the head of his son. "What do I keep? What do I keep? What do I keep?" he demanded, in a voice of thunder. He slapped his knee impressively, to indicate that he himself was going to make reply, and that all should heed. "I keep a hotel," he shouted. "A hotel, do you mind? A guest under my roof has sacred privileges. He is to be intimidated by none. Not one word shall he hear that would prijudice him in favor of goin' away. I'll not have it. There's no place in this here town where they can say they iver took in a guest of mine because he was afraid to stay here." He wheeled suddenly upon the cowboy and the Easterner. "Am I right?"

"Yes, Mr. Scully," said the cowboy, "I think you're right."

"Yes, Mr. Scully," said the Easterner, "I think you're right."

V

At six-o'clock supper, the Swede fizzed like a fire-wheel. He sometimes seemed on the point of bursting into riotous song, and in all his madness he was encouraged by old Scully. The Easterner was encased in reserve; the cowboy sat in wide-mouthed amazement, forgetting to eat, while Johnnie wrathily de-molished great plates of food. The daughters of the house, when they were obliged to replenish the biscuits, approached as warily as Indians, and, having succeeded in their purpose, fled with ill-concealed trepidation. The Swede domineered the whole feast, and he gave it the appearance of a cruel bacchanal. He seemed to have grown suddenly taller; he gazed, brutally disdainful, into every face. His voice rang through the room. Once when he jabbed out harpoon-fashion with his fork to pinion a biscuit, the weapon nearly impaled the hand of the Easterner, which had been stretched quietly out for the same biscuit.

After supper, as the men filed toward the other room, the Swede smote Scully ruthlessly on the shoulder. "Well, old boy, that was a good, square meal." Johnnie looked hopefully at his father; he knew that shoulder was tender from an old fall; and, indeed, it appeared for a moment as if Scully was going to flame out over the matter, but in the end he smiled a sickly smile and remained silent. The others understood from his manner that he was admitting his responsibility for the Swede's new view-point.

Johnnie, however, addressed his parent in an aside. "Why don't you license somebody to kick you downstairs?" Scully scowled darkly by way of reply.

When they were gathered about the stove, the Swede insisted on another game of High-Five. Scully gently deprecated the plan at first, but the Swede turned a wolfish glare upon him. The old man subsided, and the Swede canvassed the others. In his tone there was always a great threat. The cowboy and the Easterner both remarked indifferently that they would play. Scully said that he would presently have to go to meet the 6.58 train, and so the Swede turned menacingly upon Johnnie. For a moment their glances crossed like blades, and then Johnnie smiled and said, "Yes, I'll play."

They formed a square, with the little board on their knees. The Easterner and the Swede were again partners. As the play went on, it was noticeable that the cowboy was not board-whacking as usual. Meanwhile, Scully, near the lamp, had put on his spectacles and, with an appearance curiously like an old priest, was reading a newspaper. In time he went out to meet the 6.58 train, and, despite his precautions, a gust of polar wind whirled into the room as he opened the door. Besides scattering the cards, it chilled the players to the marrow. The Swede cursed frightfully. When Scully returned, his entrance disturbed a cozy and friendly scene. The Swede again cursed. But presently they were once more intent, their heads bent forward and their hands moving swiftly. The Swede had adopted the fashion of board-whacking.

Scully took up his paper and for a long time remained immersed in matters which were extraordinarily remote from him. The lamp burned badly, and once he stopped to adjust the wick. The newspaper, as he turned from page to page, rustled with a slow and comfortable sound. Then suddenly he heard three terrible words: "You are cheatin'!"

Such scenes often prove that there can be little of dramatic import in environment. Any room can present a tragic front; any room can be comic. This little den was now hideous as a torture-chamber. The new faces of the men themselves had changed it upon the instant. The Swede held a huge fist in front of Johnnie's face, while the latter looked steadily over it into the blazing orbs of his accuser. The Easterner had grown pallid; the cowboy's jaw had dropped in that expression of bovine amazement which was one of his important mannerisms. After the three words, the first sound in the room was made by Scully's paper as it floated forgotten to his feet. His spectacles had also fallen from his nose, but by a clutch he had saved them in air. His hand, grasping the spectacles, now remained poised awkwardly and near his shoulder. He stared at the card-players.

Probably the silence was while a second elapsed. Then, if the floor had been suddenly twitched out from under the men they could not have moved quicker. The five had projected themselves headlong toward a common point. It happened that Johnnie, in rising to hurl himself upon the Swede, had stumbled slightly because of his curiously instinctive care for the cards and the board. The loss of the moment allowed time for the arrival of Scully, and also allowed the cowboy time to give the Swede a great push which sent him staggering back. The men found tongue together, and hoarse shouts of rage, appeal, or fear burst from every throat. The cowboy pushed and jostled feverishly at the Swede, and the Easterner and Scully clung wildly to Johnnie; but through the smoky air, above the swaying bodies of the peace-compellers, the eyes of the two warriors ever sought each other in glances of challenge that were at once hot and steely.

Of course the board had been overturned, and now the whole company of cards was scattered over the floor, where the boots of the men trampled the fat and painted kings and queens as they gazed with their silly eyes at the war that was waging above them.

Scully's voice was dominating the yells. "Stop now! Stop, I say! Stop, now——"

Johnnie, as he struggled to burst through the rank formed by Scully and the Easterner, was crying, "Well, he says I cheated! He says I cheated! I won't allow no man to say I cheated! If he says I cheated, he's a——!"

The cowboy was telling the Swede, "Quit, now! Quit, d'ye hear——"

The screams of the Swede never ceased: "He did cheat! I saw him! I saw him——"

As for the Easterner, he was importuning in a voice that was not heeded: "Wait a moment, can't you? Oh, wait a moment. What's the good of a fight over a game of cards? Wait a moment——"

In this tumult no complete sentences were clear. "Cheat"—"Quit"—"He says"—these fragments pierced the uproar and rang out sharply. It was remarkable that, whereas Scully undoubtedly made the most noise, he was the least heard of any of the riotous band.

Then suddenly there was a great cessation. It was as if each man had paused for breath; and although the room was still lighted with the anger of men, it could be seen that there was no danger of immediate conflict, and at once Johnnie, shouldering his way forward, almost succeeded in confronting the Swede. "What did you say I cheated for? What did you say I cheated for? I don't cheat, and I won't let no man say I do!"

The Swede said, "I saw you! I saw you!"

"Well," cried Johnnie, "I'll fight any man what says I cheat!"

"No, you won't," said the cowboy. "Not here."

"Ah, be still, can't you?" said Scully, coming between them.

The quiet was sufficient to allow the Easterner's voice to be heard. He was repeating, "Oh, wait a moment, can't you? What's the good of a fight over a game of cards? Wait a moment!"

Johnnie, his red face appearing above his father's shoulder, hailed the Swede again. "Did you say I cheated?"

The Swede showed his teeth. "Yes."

"Then," said Johnnie, "we must fight."

"Yes, fight," roared the Swede. He was like a demoniac. "Yes, fight! I'll show you what kind of a man I am! I'll show you who you want to fight! Maybe you think I can't fight! Maybe you think I can't! I'll show you, you skin, you card-sharp! Yes, you cheated! You cheated! You cheated!"

"Well, let's go at it, then, mister," said Johnnie, coolly.

The cowboy's brow was beaded with sweat from his efforts in intercepting all sorts of raids. He turned in despair to Scully. "What are you goin' to do now?"

A change had come over the Celtic visage of the old man. He now seemed all eagerness; his eyes glowed.

"We'll let them fight," he answered, stalwartly. "I

can't put up with it any longer. I've stood this damned Swede till I'm sick. We'll let them fight."

VI

The men prepared to go out of doors. The Easterner was so nervous that he had great difficulty in getting his arms into the sleeves of his new leather coat. As the cowboy drew his fur cap down over his ears his hands trembled. In fact, Johnnie and old Scully were the only ones who displayed no agitation. These preliminaries were conducted without words.

Scully threw open the door. "Well, come on," he said. Instantly a terrific wind caused the flame of the lamp to struggle at its wick, while a puff of black smoke sprang from the chimney-top. The stove was in mid-current of the blast, and its voice swelled to equal the roar of the storm. Some of the scarred and bedabbled cards were caught up from the floor and dashed helplessly against the farther wall. The men lowered their heads and plunged into the tempest as into a sea.

No snow was falling, but great whirls and clouds of flakes, swept up from the ground by the frantic winds, were streaming southward with the speed of bullets. The covered land was blue with the sheen of an unearthly satin, and there was no other hue save where, at the low, black railway station—which seemed incredibly distant—one light gleamed like a tiny jewel. As the men floundered into a thigh-deep drift, it was known that the Swede was bawling out something. Scully went to him, put a hand on his shoulder, and projected an ear. "What's that you say?" he shouted.

"I say," bawled the Swede again, "I won't stand much show against this gang. I know you'll all pitch on me."

Scully smote him reproachfully on the arm. "Tut, man!" he yelled. The wind tore the words from Scully's lips and scattered them far alee.

"You are all a gang of—" boomed the Swede, but the storm also seized the remainder of this sentence.

Immediately turning their backs upon the wind, the men had swung around a corner to the sheltered side of the hotel. It was the function of the little house to preserve here, amid this great devastation of snow, an irregular V-shape of heavily encrusted grass, which crackled beneath the feet. One could imagine the great drifts piled against the windward side. When the party reached the comparative peace of this spot it was found that the Swede was still bellowing.

"Oh, I know what kind of a thing this is! I know you'll all pitch on me. I can't lick you all!"

Scully turned upon him panther-fashion. "You'll not have to whip all of us. You'll have to whip my son Johnnie. An' the man what troubles you durin' that time will have me to dale with."

The arrangements were swiftly made. The two men faced each other, obedient to the harsh commands of Scully, whose face, in the subtly luminous gloom, could be seen set in the austere impersonal lines that are pictured on the countenances of the Roman veterans. The Easterner's teeth were chattering, and he was hopping up and down like a mechanical toy. The cowboy stood rock-like.

The contestants had not stripped off any clothing. Each was in his ordinary attire. Their fists were up, and they eyed each other in a calm that had the elements of leonine cruelty in it.

During this pause, the Easterner's mind, like a film, took lasting impressions of three men—the iron-nerved master of the ceremony; the Swede, pale, motionless, terrible; and Johnnie, serene yet ferocious, brutish yet heroic. The entire prelude had in it a tragedy greater than the tragedy of action, and this aspect was accentuated by the long, mellow cry of the blizzard, as it sped the tumbling and wailing flakes into the black abyss of the south.

"Now!" said Scully.

The two combatants leaped forward and crashed together like bullocks. There was heard the cushioned sound of blows, and of a curse squeezing out from between the tight teeth of one.

As for the spectators, the Easterner's pent-up breath exploded from him with a pop of relief, absolute relief from the tension of the preliminaries. The cowboy bounded into the air with a yowl. Scully was immovable as from supreme amazement and fear at the fury of the fight which he himself had permitted and arranged.

For a time the encounter in the darkness was such a perplexity of flying arms that it presented no more detail than would a swiftly revolving wheel. Occasionally a face, as if illumined by a flash of light, would shine out, ghastly and marked with pink spots. A moment later, the men might have been known as shadows, if it were not for the involuntary utterance of oaths that came from them in whispers.

Suddenly a holocaust of warlike desire caught the cowboy, and he bolted forward with the speed of a broncho. "Go it, Johnnie! go it! Kill him! Kill him!"

Scully confronted him. "Kape back," he said; and by his glance the cowboy could tell that this man was Johnnie's father.

To the Easterner there was a monotony of unchangeable fighting that was an abomination. This confused mingling was eternal to his sense, which was concentrated in a longing for the end, the priceless end. Once the fighters lurched near him, and as he scrambled hastily backward he heard them breathe like men on the rack.

"Kill him, Johnnie! Kill him! Kill him! Kill him!" The cowboy's face was contorted like one of those agony masks in museums.

"Keep still," said Scully, icily.

Then there was a sudden loud grunt, incomplete, cut short, and Johnnie's body swung away from the Swede and fell with sickening heaviness to the grass. The cowboy was barely in time to prevent the mad Swede from flinging himself upon his prone adversary. "No, you don't," said the cowboy, interposing an arm. "Wait a second."

Scully was at his son's side. "Johnnie! Johnnie, me boy!" His voice had a quality of melancholy tenderness. "Johnnie! Can you go on with it?" He looked anxiously down into the bloody, pulpy face of his son.

There was a moment of silence, and then Johnnie answered in his ordinary voice, "Yes, I—it—yes."

Assisted by his father he struggled to his feet. "Wait a bit now till you git your wind," said the old man.

A few paces away the cowboy was lecturing the Swede. "No, you don't! Wait a second!"

The Easterner was plucking at Scully's sleeve. "Oh, this is enough," he pleaded. "This is enough! Let it go as it stands. This is enough!"

"Bill," said Scully, "git out of the road." The cowboy stepped aside. "Now." The combatants were actuated by a new caution as they advanced toward collision. They glared at each other, and then the Swede aimed a lightning blow that carried with it his entire weight. Johnnie was evidently half stupid from weakness, but he miraculously dodged, and his fist sent the over-balanced Swede sprawling.

The cowboy, Scully, and the Easterner burst into a cheer that was like a chorus of triumphant soldiery, but before its conclusion the Swede had scuffled agilely to his feet and come in berserk abandon at his foe. There was another perplexity of flying arms, and Johnnie's body again swung away and fell, even as a bundle might fall from a roof. The Swede instantly staggered to a little wind-waved tree and leaned upon it, breathing like an engine, while his savage and flame-lit eyes roamed from face to face as the men bent over Johnnie. There was a splendor of isolation in his situation at this time which the Easterner felt once when, lifting his eyes from the man on the ground, he beheld that mysterious and lonely figure, waiting.

"Are you any good yet, Johnnie?" asked Scully in a broken voice.

The son gasped and opened his eyes languidly. After a moment he answered, "No—I ain't—any good

—any—more." Then, from shame and bodily ill, he began to weep, the tears furrowing down through the bloodstains on his face. "He was too—too—too heavy for me."

Scully straightened and addressed the waiting figure. "Stranger," he said, evenly, "it's all up with our side." Then his voice changed into that vibrant huskiness which is commonly the tone of the most simple and deadly announcements. "Johnnie is whipped."

Without replying, the victor moved off on the route to the front door of the hotel.

The cowboy was formulating new and unspellable blasphemies. The Easterner was startled to find that they were out in a wind that seemed to come direct from the shadowed arctic floes. He heard again the wail of the snow as it was flung to its grave in the south. He knew now that all this time the cold had been sinking into him deeper and deeper, and he wondered that he had not perished. He felt indifferent to the condition of the vanquished man.

"Johnnie, can you walk?" asked Scully.

"Did I hurt—hurt him any?" asked the son.

"Can you walk, boy? Can you walk?"

Johnnie's voice was suddenly strong. There was a robust impatience in it. "I asked you whether I hurt him any!"

"Yes, yes, Johnnie," answered the cowboy, consolingly; "he's hurt a good deal."

They raised him from the ground, and as soon as he was on his feet he went tottering off, rebuffing all attempts at assistance. When the party rounded the corner they were fairly blinded by the pelting of the snow. It burned their faces like fire. The cowboy carried Johnnie through the drift to the door. As they entered, some cards again rose from the floor and beat against the wall.

The Easterner rushed to the stove. He was so profoundly chilled that he almost dared to embrace the glowing iron. The Swede was not in the room. Johnnie sank into a chair and, folding his arms on his knees, buried his face in them. Scully, warming one foot and then the other at a rim of the stove, muttered to himself with Celtic mournfulness. The cowboy had removed his fur cap, and with a dazed and rueful air he was running one hand through his tousled locks. From overhead they could hear the creaking of boards, as the Swede tramped here and there in his room.

The sad quiet was broken by the sudden flinging open of a door that led toward the kitchen. It was instantly followed by an inrush of women. They precipitated themselves upon Johnnie amid a chorus of lamentation. Before they carried their prey off to the kitchen, there to be bathed and harangued with that mixture of sympathy and abuse which is a feat of their sex, the mother straightened herself and fixed old Scully with an eye of stern reproach. "Shame be upon you, Patrick Scully!" she cried. "Your own son, too. Shame be upon you!"

"There, now! Be quiet, now!" said the old man, weakly.

"Shame be upon you, Patrick Scully!" The girls, rallying to this slogan, sniffed disdainfully in the direction of those trembling accomplices, the cowboy and the Easterner. Presently they bore Johnnie away, and left the three men to dismal reflection.

VII

"I'd like to fight this here Dutchman myself," said the cowboy, breaking a long silence.

Scully wagged his head sadly. "No, that wouldn't do. It wouldn't be right. It wouldn't be right."

"Well, why wouldn't it?" argued the cowboy. "I don't see no harm in it."

"No," answered Scully, with mournful heroism. "It wouldn't be right. It was Johnnie's fight, and now we mustn't whip the man just because he whipped Johnnie."

"Yes, that's true enough," said the cowboy; "but— he better not get fresh with me, because I couldn't stand no more of it."

"You'll not say a word to him," commanded Scully, and even then they heard the tread of the Swede on the stairs. His entrance was made theatric. He swept the door back with a bang and swaggered to the middle of the room. No one looked at him. "Well," he cried, insolently, at Scully, "I s'pose you'll tell me now how much I owe you?"

The old man remained stolid. "You don't owe me nothin'."

"Huh!" said the Swede, "huh! Don't owe 'im nothin'."

The cowboy addressed the Swede. "Stranger, I don't see how you come to be so gay around here."

Old Scully was instantly alert. "Stop!" he shouted, holding his hand forth, fingers upward. "Bill, you shut up!"

The cowboy spat carelessly into the sawdust-box. "I didn't say a word, did I?" he asked.

"Mr. Scully," called the Swede, "how much do I owe you?" It was seen that he was attired for departure, and that he had his valise in his hand.

"You don't owe me nothin'," repeated Scully in the same imperturbable way.

"Huh!" said the Swede. "I guess you're right. I guess if it was any way at all, you'd owe me somethin'. That's what I guess." He turned to the cowboy. " 'Kill him! Kill him! Kill him!' " he mimicked, and

then guffawed victoriously. " 'Kill him!' " He was convulsed with ironical humor.

But he might have been jeering the dead. The three men were immovable and silent, staring with glassy eyes at the stove.

The Swede opened the door and passed into the storm, giving one derisive glance backward at the still group.

As soon as the door was closed, Scully and the cowboy leaped to their feet and began to curse. They trampled to and fro, waving their arms and smashing into the air with their fists. "Oh, but that was a hard minute!" wailed Scully. "That was a hard minute! Him there leerin' and scoffin'! One bang at his nose was worth forty dollars to me that minute! How did you stand it, Bill?"

"How did I stand it?" cried the cowboy in a quivering voice. "How did I stand it? Oh!"

The old man burst into sudden brogue. "I'd loike to take that Swade," he wailed, "and hould 'im down on a shtone flure and bate 'im to a jelly wid a shtick!"

The cowboy groaned in sympathy. "I'd like to git him by the neck and ha-ammer him"—he brought his hand down on a chair with a noise like a pistol-shot —"hammer that there Dutchman until he couldn't tell himself from a dead coyote!"

"I'd bate 'im until he——"

"I'd show *him* some things——"

And then together they raised a yearning, fanatic cry—"Oh-o-oh! if we only could——"

"Yes!"

"Yes!"

"And then I'd——"

"O-o-oh!"

VIII

The Swede, tightly gripping his valise, tacked across the face of the storm as if he carried sails. He was following a line of little naked, gasping trees which, he knew, must mark the way of the road. His face, fresh from the pounding of Johnnie's fists, felt more pleasure than pain in the wind and the driving snow. A number of square shapes loomed upon him finally, and he knew them as the houses of the main body of the town. He found a street and made travel along it, leaning heavily upon the wind whenever, at a corner, a terrific blast caught him.

He might have been in a deserted village. We picture the world as thick with conquering and elate humanity, but here, with the bugles of the tempest pealing, it was hard to imagine a peopled earth. One viewed the existence of man then as a marvel, and conceded a glamour of wonder to these lice which were caused to cling to a whirling, fire-smitten, ice-locked, disease-stricken, space-lost bulb. The conceit of man was explained by this storm to be the very engine of life. One was a coxcomb not to die in it. However, the Swede found a saloon.

In front of it an indomitable red light was burning, and the snowflakes were made blood-color as they flew through the circumscribed territory of the lamp's shining. The Swede pushed open the door of the saloon and entered. A sanded expanse was before him, and at the end of it four men sat about a table drinking. Down one side of the room extended a radiant bar, and its guardian was leaning upon his elbows listening to the talk of the men at the table. The Swede dropped his valise upon the floor and, smiling fraternally upon the barkeeper, said, "Gimme some whisky, will you?" The man placed a bottle, a whisky-glass, and a glass of ice-thick water upon the bar. The Swede poured himself an abnormal portion of whisky and drank it in three gulps. "Pretty bad night," remarked the bartender, indifferently. He was making the pretension of blindness which is usually a distinction of his class; but it could have been seen that he was furtively studying the half-erased blood-stains on the face of the Swede. "Bad night," he said again.

"Oh, it's good enough for me," replied the Swede, hardily, as he poured himself some more whisky. The barkeeper took his coin and maneuvered it through its reception by the highly nickeled cash-machine. A bell rang; a card labeled "20 cts." had appeared.

"No," continued the Swede, "this isn't too bad weather. It's good enough for me."

"So?" murmured the barkeeper, languidly.

The copious drams made the Swede's eyes swim, and he breathed a trifle heavier. "Yes, I like this weather. I like it. It suits me." It was apparently his design to impart a deep significance to these words.

"So?" murmured the bartender again. He turned to gaze dreamily at the scroll-like birds and bird-like scrolls which had been drawn with soap upon the mirrors in back of the bar.

"Well, I guess I'll take another drink," said the Swede, presently. "Have something?"

"No, thanks; I'm not drinking'," answered the bartender. Afterward he asked, "How did you hurt your face?"

The Swede immediately began to boast loudly. "Why, in a fight. I thumped the soul out of a man down here at Scully's hotel."

The interest of the four men at the table was at last aroused.

"Who was it?" said one.

"Johnnie Scully," blustered the Swede. "Son of the man what runs it. He will be pretty near dead for some weeks, I can tell you. I made a nice thing of

him, I did. He couldn't get up. They carried him in the house. Have a drink?"

Instantly the men in some subtle way encased themselves in reserve. "No, thanks," said one. The group was of curious formation. Two were prominent local business men; one was the district attorney; and one was a professional gambler of the kind known as "square." But a scrutiny of the group would not have enabled an observer to pick the gambler from the men of more reputable pursuits. He was, in fact, a man so delicate in manner, when among people of fair class, and so judicious in his choice of victims, that in the strictly masculine part of the town's life he had come to be explicitly trusted and admired. People called him a thoroughbred. The fear and contempt with which his craft was regarded were undoubtedly the reason why his quiet dignity shone conspicuous above the quiet dignity of men who might be merely hatters, billiard-markers, or grocery clerks. Beyond an occasional unwary traveler who came by rail, this gambler was supposed to prey solely upon reckless and senile farmers, who, when flush with good crops, drove into town in all the pride and confidence of an absolutely invulnerable stupidity. Hearing at times in circuitous fashion of the despoilment of such a farmer, the important men of Romper invariably laughed in contempt of the victim, and if they thought of the wolf at all, it was with a kind of pride at the knowledge that he would never dare think of attacking their wisdom and courage. Besides, it was popular that this gambler had a real wife and two real children in a neat cottage in a suburb, where he led an exemplary home life; and when anyone even suggested a discrepancy in his character, the crowd immediately vociferated descriptions of this virtuous family circle. Then men who led exemplary home lives, and men who did not lead exemplary home lives, all subsided in a bunch, remarking that there was nothing more to be said.

However, when a restriction was placed upon him —as, for instance, when a strong clique of members of the new Pollywog Club refused to permit him, even as a spectator, to appear in the rooms of the organization—the candor and gentleness with which he accepted the judgment disarmed many of his foes and made his friends more desperately partisan. He invariably distinguished between himself and a respectable Romper man so quickly and frankly that his manner actually appeared to be a continual broadcast compliment.

And one must not forget to declare the fundamental fact of his entire position in Romper. It is irrefutable that in all affairs outside his business, in all matters that occur eternally and commonly between man and man, this thieving card-player was so generous, so just, so moral, that, in a contest, he could have put to flight the consciences of nine tenths of the citizens of Romper.

And so it happened that he was seated in this saloon with the two prominent local merchants and the district attorney.

The Swede continued to drink raw whisky, meanwhile babbling at the barkeeper and trying to induce him to indulge in potations. "Come on. Have a drink. Come on. What—no? Well, have a little one, then. By gawd, I've whipped a man tonight, and I want to celebrate. I whipped him good, too. Gentlemen," the Swede cried to the men at the table, "have a drink?"

"Ssh!" said the barkeeper.

The group at the table, although furtively attentive, had been pretending to be deep in talk, but now a man lifted his eyes toward the Swede and said, shortly, "Thanks. We don't want any more."

At this reply the Swede ruffled out his chest like a rooster. "Well," he exploded, "it seems I can't get anybody to drink with me in this town. Seems so, don't it? Well!"

"Ssh!" said the barkeeper.

"Say," snarled the Swede, "don't you try to shut me up. I won't have it. I'm a gentleman, and I want people to drink with me. And I want 'em to drink with me now. *Now*—do you understand?" He rapped the bar with his knuckles.

Years of experience had calloused the bartender. He merely grew sulky. "I hear you," he answered.

"Well," cried the Swede, "listen hard then. See those men over there? Well, they're going to drink with me, and don't you forget it. Now you watch."

"Hi!" yelled the barkeeper, "this won't do!"

"Why won't it?" demanded the Swede. He stalked over to the table, and by chance laid his hand upon the shoulder of the gambler. "How about this?" he asked wrathfully. "I asked you to drink with me."

The gambler simply twisted his head and spoke over his shoulder. "My friend, I don't know you."

"Oh, hell!" answered the Swede, "come and have a drink."

"Now, my boy," advised the gambler, kindly, "take your hand off my shoulder and go 'way and mind your own business." He was a little, slim man, and it seemed strange to hear him use this tone of heroic patronage to the burly Swede. The other men at the table said nothing.

"What! You won't drink with me, you little dude? I'll make you, then! I'll make you!" The Swede had grasped the gambler frenziedly at the throat, and was dragging him from his chair. The other men sprang up. The barkeeper dashed around the corner of his bar. There was a great tumult, and then was

seen a long blade in the hand of the gambler. It shot forward, and a human body, this citadel of virtue, wisdom, power, was pierced as easily as if it had been a melon. The Swede fell with a cry of supreme astonishment.

The prominent merchants and the district attorney must have at once tumbled out of the place backward. The bartender found himself hanging limply to the arm of a chair and gazing into the eyes of a murderer.

"Henry," said the latter, as he wiped his knife on one of the towels that hung beneath the bar rail, "you tell 'em where to find me. I'll be home, waiting for 'em." Then he vanished. A moment afterward the barkeeper was in the street dinning through the storm for help and, moreover, companionship.

The corpse of the Swede, alone in the saloon, had its eyes fixed upon a dreadful legend that dwelt atop of the cash-machine: "This registers the amount of your purchase."

IX

Months later, the cowboy was frying pork over the stove of a little ranch near the Dakota line, when there was a quick thud of hoofs outside, and presently the Easterner entered with the letters and the papers.

"Well," said the Easterner at once, "the chap that killed the Swede has got three years. Wasn't much, was it?"

"He has? Three years?" The cowboy poised his pan of pork, while he ruminated upon the news. "Three years. That ain't much."

"No. It was a light sentence," replied the Easterner as he unbuckled his spurs. "Seems there was a good deal of sympathy for him in Romper."

"If the bartender had been any good," observed the cowboy, thoughtfully, "he would have gone in and cracked that there Dutchman on the head with a bottle in the beginnin' of it and stopped all this here murderin'."

"Yes, a thousand things might have happened," said the Easterner, tartly.

The cowboy returned his pan of pork to the fire, but his philosophy continued. "It's funny, ain't it? If he hadn't said Johnnie was cheatin' he'd be alive this minute. He was an awful fool. Game played for fun, too. Not for money. I believe he was crazy."

"I feel sorry for that gambler," said the Easterner.

"Oh, so do I," said the cowboy. "He don't deserve none of it for killin' who he did."

"The Swede might not have been killed if everything had been square."

"Might not have been killed?" exclaimed the cowboy. "Everythin' square? Why, when he said that Johnnie was cheatin' and acted like such a jackass? And then in the saloon he fairly walked up to git hurt?" With these arguments the cowboy browbeat the Easterner and reduced him to rage.

"You're a fool!" cried the Easterner, viciously. "You're a bigger jackass than the Swede by a million majority. Now let me tell you one thing. Let me tell you something. Listen! Johnnie *was* cheating!"

"'Johnnie,'" said the cowboy, blankly. There was a minute of silence, and then he said, robustly, "Why, no. The game was only for fun."

"Fun or not," said the Easterner, "Johnnie was cheating. I saw him. I know it. I saw him. And I refused to stand up and be a man. I let the Swede fight it out alone. And you—you were simply puffing around the place and wanting to fight. And then old Scully himself! We are all in it! This poor gambler isn't even a noun. He is kind of an adverb. Every sin is the result of a collaboration. We, five of us, have collaborated in the murder of this Swede. Usually there are from a dozen to forty women really involved in every murder, but in this case it seems to be only five men—you, I, Johnnie, old Scully; and that fool of an unfortunate gambler came merely as a culmination, the apex of a human movement, and gets all the punishment."

The cowboy, injured and rebellious, cried out blindly into this fog of mysterious theory: "Well, I didn't do anythin', did I?"

NEIGHBOUR ROSICKY

WILLA CATHER

WILLA CATHER (1876–1947) was born in Virginia but moved at an early age to Nebraska. She said later that her first two years among the pioneering settlers of that region were, to her as a writer, the most important of her life. Educated at home before high school, she graduated from the University of Nebraska in 1895, did journalistic work and teaching in Pittsburgh, editorial work in New York, and traveled widely in this country and Europe. After 1911 she turned wholly to writing. Among her books are *O Pioneers!* (1913), *My Ántonia* (1918), *A Lost Lady* (1923), *My Mortal Enemy* (1926), *Death Comes for the Archbishop* (1927) and *Shadows on the Rock* (1931). "The higher processes of art," she said, "are all processes of simplification. . . . What I always want to do is to make the writing count for less and less and the people for more and more. I'd like the writing to be so lost in the object that it doesn't exist for the reader. . . . If [the writer] achieves anything noble, anything enduring, it must be by giving himself absolutely to his material. And this gift of sympathy is his great gift; is the fine thing in him that alone can make his work fine."

I

WHEN Doctor Burleigh told neighbour Rosicky he had a bad heart, Rosicky protested.

"So? No, I guess my heart was always pretty good. I got a little asthma, maybe. Just a awful short breath when I was pitchin' hay last summer, dat's all."

"Well, now, Rosicky, if you know more about it than I do, what did you come to me for? It's your heart that makes you short of breath, I tell you. You're sixty-five years old, and you've always worked hard, and your heart's tired. You've got to be careful from now on, and you can't do heavy work any more. You've got five boys at home to do it for you."

Reprinted from *Obscure Destinies* by Willa Cather by permission of Alfred A. Knopf, Inc. Copyright 1930, 1932 by Willa Cather.

The old farmer looked up at the doctor with a gleam of amusement in his queer, triangular-shaped eyes. His eyes were large and lively, but the lids were caught up in the middle in a curious way, so that they formed a triangle. He did not look like a sick man. His brown face was creased but not wrinkled, he had a ruddy colour in his smooth-shaven cheeks and in his lips, under his long brown moustache. His hair was thin and ragged around his ears, but very little grey. His forehead, naturally high and crossed by deep parallel lines, now ran all the way up to his pointed crown. Rosicky's face had the habit of looking interested—suggested a contented disposition and a reflective quality that was gay rather than grave. This gave him a certain detachment, the easy manner of an onlooker and observer.

"Well, I guess you ain't got no pills fur a bad

heart, Doctor Ed. I guess the only thing is fur me to git me a new one."

Doctor Burleigh swung round in his desk chair and frowned at the old farmer.

"I think if I were you I'd take a little care of the old one, Rosicky."

Rosicky shrugged. "Maybe I don't know how. I expect you mean fur me not to drink my coffee no more."

"I wouldn't, in your place. But you will do as you choose about that. I've never yet been able to separate a Bohemian from his coffee or his pipe. I've quit trying. But the sure thing is you've got to cut out farm work. You can feed the stock and do chores about the barn, but you can't do anything in the fields that makes you short of breath."

"How about shelling corn?"

"Of course not!"

Rosicky considered with puckered brows.

"I can't make my heart go no longer'n it wants to, can I, Doctor Ed?"

"I think it's good for five or six years yet, maybe more, if you'll take the strain off it. Sit around the house and help Mary. If I had a good wife like yours, I'd want to stay around the house."

His patient chuckled. "It ain't no place fur a man. I don't like no old man hanging round the kitchen too much. An' my wife, she's awful hard worker her own self."

"That's it; you can help her a little. My Lord, Rosicky, you are one of the few men I know who has a family he can get some comfort out of; happy dispositions, never quarrel among themselves, and they treat you right. I want to see you live a few years and enjoy them."

"Oh, they're good kids, all right," Rosicky assented.

The doctor wrote him a prescription and asked him how his oldest son, Rudolph, who had married in the spring, was getting on. Rudolph had struck out for himself, on rented land. "And how's Polly? I was afraid Mary mightn't like an American daughter-in-law, but it seems to be working out all right."

"Yes, she's a fine girl. Dat widder woman bring her daughters up very nice. Polly got lots of spunk, an' she got some style, too. Da's nice, for young folks to have some style." Rosicky inclined his head gallantly. His voice and his twinkly smile were an affectionate compliment to his daughter-in-law.

"It looks like a storm, and you'd better be getting home before it comes. In town in the car?" Doctor Burleigh rose.

"No, I'm in de wagon. When you got five boys, you ain't got much chance to ride round in de Ford. I ain't much for cars, noway."

"Well, it's a good road out to your place; but I don't want you bumping around in a wagon much. And never again on a hay-rake, remember!"

Rosicky placed the doctor's fee delicately behind the desk-telephone, looking the other way, as if this were an absent-minded gesture. He put on his plush cap and his corduroy jacket with a sheepskin collar, and went out.

The doctor picked up his stethoscope and frowned at it as if he were seriously annoyed with the instrument. He wished it had been telling tales about some other man's heart, some old man who didn't look the doctor in the eye so knowingly, or hold out such a warm brown hand when he said goodbye. Doctor Burleigh had been a poor boy in the country before he went away to medical school; he had known Rosicky almost ever since he could remember, and he had a deep affection for Mrs. Rosicky.

Only last winter he had had such a good breakfast at Rosicky's, and that when he needed it. He had been out all night on a long, hard confinement case at Tom Marshall's—a big rich farm where there was plenty of stock and plenty of feed and a great deal of expensive farm machinery of the newest model, and no comfort whatever. The woman had too many children and too much work, and she was no manager. When the baby was born at last, and handed over to the assisting neighbour woman, and the mother was properly attended to, Burleigh refused any breakfast in that slovenly house, and drove his buggy—the snow was too deep for a car—eight miles to Anton Rosicky's place. He didn't know another farm-house where a man could get such a warm welcome, and such good strong coffee with rich cream. No wonder the old chap didn't want to give up his coffee!

He had driven in just when the boys had come back from the barn and were washing up for breakfast. The long table, covered with a bright oilcloth, was set out with dishes waiting for them, and the warm kitchen was full of the smell of coffee and hot biscuit and sausage. Five big handsome boys, running from twenty to twelve, all with what Burleigh called natural good manners—they hadn't a bit of the painful self-consciousness he himself had to struggle with when he was a lad. One ran to put his horse away, another helped him off with his fur coat and hung it up, and Josephine, the youngest child and the only daughter, quickly set another place under her mother's direction.

With Mary, to feed creatures was the natural expression of affection—her chickens, the calves, her big hungry boys. It was a rare pleasure to feed a young man whom she seldom saw and of whom she was as proud as if he belonged to her. Some country housekeepers would have stopped to spread a white cloth over the oilcloth, to change the thick cups and plates for their best china, and the wooden-handled knives for plated ones. But not Mary.

"You must take us as you find us, Doctor Ed. I'd be glad to put out my good things for you if you was expected, but I'm glad to get you anyway at all."

He knew she was glad—she threw back her head and spoke out as if she were announcing him to the whole prairie. Rosicky hadn't said anything at all; he merely smiled his twinkling smile, put some more coal on the fire, and went into his own room to pour the doctor a little drink in a medicine glass. When they were all seated, he watched his wife's face from his end of the table and spoke to her in Czech. Then, with the instinct of politeness which seldom failed him, he turned to the doctor and said slyly: "I was just tellin' her not to ask you no questions about Mrs. Marshall till you eat some breakfast. My wife, she's terrible fur to ask questions."

The boys laughed, and so did Mary. She watched the doctor devour her biscuit and sausage, too much excited to eat anything herself. She drank her coffee and sat taking in everything about her visitor. She had known him when he was a poor country boy, and was boastfully proud of his success, always saying: "What do people go to Omaha for, to see a doctor, when we got the best one in the State right here?" If Mary liked people at all, she felt physical pleasure in the sight of them, personal exultation in any good fortune that came to them. Burleigh didn't know many women like that, but he knew she was like that.

When his hunger was satisfied, he did, of course, have to tell them about Mrs. Marshall, and he noticed what a friendly interest the boys took in the matter.

Rudolph, the oldest one (he was still living at home then), said: "The last time I was over there, she was lifting them big heavy milk-cans, and I knew she ought not to be doing it."

"Yes, Rudolph told me about that when he come home, and I said it wasn't right," Mary put in warmly. "It was all right for me to do them things up to the last, for I was terrible strong, but that woman's weakly. And do you think she'll be able to nurse it, Ed?" She sometimes forgot to give him the title she was so proud of. "And to think of your being up all night and then not able to get a decent breakfast! I don't know what's the matter with such people."

"Why, mother," said one of the boys, "if Doctor Ed had got breakfast there, we wouldn't have him here. So you ought to be glad."

"He knows I'm glad to have him, John, any time. But I'm sorry for that poor woman, how bad she'll feel the doctor had to go away in the cold without his breakfast."

"I wish I had been in practice when these were getting born." The doctor looked down the row of close-clipped heads. "I missed some good breakfasts by not being."

The boys began to laugh at their mother because she flushed so red, but she stood her ground and threw up her head. "I don't care, you wouldn't have got away from this house without breakfast. No doctor ever did. I'd have had something ready fixed that Anton could warm up for you."

The boys laughed harder than ever, and exclaimed at her: "I'll bet you would!" "She would, that!"

"Father, did you get breakfast for the doctor when we were born?"

"Yes, and he used to bring me my breakfast, too, mighty nice. I was always awful hungry!" Mary admitted with a guilty laugh.

While the boys were getting the doctor's horse, he went to the window to examine the house plants.

"What do you do to your geraniums to keep them blooming all winter, Mary? I never pass this house that from the road I don't see your windows full of flowers."

She snapped off a dark red one, and a ruffled new green leaf, and put them in his buttonhole. "There, that looks better. You look too solemn for a young man, Ed. Why don't you git married? I'm worried about you. Settin' at breakfast, I looked at you real hard, and I seen you've got some grey hairs already."

"Oh, yes! They're coming. Maybe they'd come faster if I married."

"Don't talk so. You'll ruin your health eating at the hotel. I could send your wife a nice loaf of nut bread, if you only had one. I don't like to see a young man getting grey. I'll tell you something, Ed; you make some strong black tea and keep it handy in a bowl, and every morning just brush it into your hair, an' it'll keep the grey from showin' much. That's the way I do!"

Sometimes the doctor heard gossipers in the drugstore wondering why Rosicky didn't get on faster. He was industrious, and so were his boys, but they were rather free and easy, weren't pushers, and they didn't always show good judgment. They were comfortable, they were out of debt, but they didn't get much ahead. Maybe, Doctor Burleigh reflected, people as generous and warm-hearted and affectionate as the Rosickys never got ahead much; maybe you could not enjoy your life and put it into the bank, too.

II

When Rosicky left Doctor Burleigh's office, he went into the farm-implement store to light his pipe and put on his glasses and read over the list Mary had given him. Then he went into the general merchandise place next door and stood about until the pretty girl with the plucked eyebrows, who always waited on him, was free. Those eyebrows, two thin India-ink strokes, amused him, because he remembered how they used to be. Rosicky always prolonged his shopping by a little joking; the girl knew the old fellow admired her, and she liked to chaff with him.

"Seems to me about every other week you buy ticking, Mr. Rosicky, and always the best quality," she remarked as she measured off the heavy bolt with red stripes.

"You see, my wife is always makin' goose-fedder pillows, an' de thin stuff don't hold in dem little down-fedders."

"You must have lots of pillows at your house."

"Sure. She makes quilts of dem, too. We sleeps easy. Now she's makin' a fedder quilt for my son's wife. You know Polly, that married my Rudolph. How much my bill, Miss Pearl?"

"Eight eighty-five."

"Chust make it nine, and put in some candy fur de women."

"As usual. I never did see a man buy so much candy for his wife. First thing you know, she'll be getting too fat."

"I'd like dat. I ain't much fur all dem slim women like what de style is now."

"That's one for me, I suppose, Mr. Bohunk!" Pearl sniffed and elevated her India-ink strokes.

When Rosicky went out to his wagon, it was beginning to snow—the first snow of the season, and he was glad to see it. He rattled out of town and along the highway through a wonderfully rich stretch of country, the finest farms in the county. He admired this High Prairie, as it was called, and always liked to drive through it. His own place lay in a rougher territory, where there was some clay in the soil and it was not so productive. When he bought his land, he hadn't the money to buy on High Prairie; so he told his boys, when they grumbled, that if their land hadn't some clay in it, they wouldn't own it at all. All the same, he enjoyed looking at these fine farms, as he enjoyed looking at a prize bull.

After he had gone eight miles, he came to the graveyard, which lay just at the edge of his own hay-land. There he stopped his horses and sat still on his wagon seat, looking about at the snowfall.

Over yonder on the hill he could see his own house, crouching low, with the clump of orchard behind and the windmill before, and all down the gentle hillslope the rows of pale gold cornstalks stood out against the white field. The snow was falling over the cornfield and the pasture and the hay-land, steadily, with very little wind—a nice dry snow. The graveyard had only a light wire fence about it and was all overgrown with long red grass. The fine snow, settling into this red grass and upon the few little evergreens and the headstones, looked very pretty.

It was a nice graveyard, Rosicky reflected, sort of snug and homelike, not cramped or mournful—a big sweep all round it. A man could lie down in the long grass and see the complete arch of the sky over him, hear the wagons go by; in summer the mowing-machine rattled right up to the wire fence. And it was so near home. Over there across the cornstalks his own roof and windmill looked so good to him that he promised himself to mind the doctor and take care of himself. He was awful fond of his place, he admitted. He wasn't anxious to leave it. And it was a comfort to think that he would never have to go farther than the edge of his own hayfield. The snow, falling over his barnyard and the graveyard, seemed to draw things together like. And they were all old neighbours in the graveyard, most of them friends; there was nothing to feel awkward or embarrassed about. Embarrassment was the most disagreeable feeling Rosicky knew. He didn't often have it—only with certain people whom he didn't understand at all.

Well, it was a nice snowstorm; a fine sight to see the snow falling so quietly and graciously over so much open country. On his cap and shoulders, on the horses' backs and manes, light, delicate, mysterious it fell; and with it a dry cool fragrance was released into the air. It meant rest for vegetation and men and beast, for the ground itself; a season of long nights for sleep, leisurely breakfasts, peace by the fire. This and much more went through Rosicky's mind, but he merely told himself that winter was coming, clucked to his horses, and drove on.

When he reached home, John, the youngest boy, ran out to put away his team for him, and he met Mary coming up from the outside cellar with her apron full of carrots. They went into the house together. On the table, covered with oilcloth figured with clusters of blue grapes, a place was set, and he smelled hot coffee-cake of some kind. Anton never lunched in town; he thought that extravagant, and anyhow he didn't like the food. So Mary always had something ready for him when he got home.

After he was settled in his chair, stirring his coffee

in a big cup, Mary took out of the oven a pan of *kolache* stuffed with apricots, examined them anxiously to see whether they had got too dry, put them beside his plate, and then sat down opposite him.

Rosicky asked her in Czech if she wasn't going to have any coffee.

She replied in English, as being somehow the right language for transacting business: "Now what did Doctor Ed say, Anton? You tell me just what."

"He said I was to tell you some compliments, but I forgot 'em." Rosicky's eyes twinkled.

"About you, I mean. What did he say about your asthma?"

"He says I ain't got no asthma." Rosicky took one of the little rolls in his broad brown fingers. The thickened nail of his right thumb told the story of his past.

"Well, what is the matter? And don't try to put me off."

"He don't say nothing much, only I'm a little older, and my heart ain't so good like it used to be."

Mary started and brushed her hair back from her temples with both hands as if she were a little out of her mind. From the way she glared, she might have been in a rage with him.

"He says there's something the matter with your heart? Doctor Ed says so?"

"Now don't yell at me like I was a hog in de garden, Mary. You know I always did like to hear a woman talk soft. He didn't say anything de matter wid my heart, only it ain't so young like it used to be, an' he tell me not to pitch hay or run de corn-sheller."

Mary wanted to jump up, but she sat still. She admired the way he never under any circumstances raised his voice or spoke roughly. He was city-bred, and she was country-bred; she often said she wanted her boys to have their papa's nice ways.

"You never have no pain there, do you? It's your breathing and your stomach that's been wrong. I wouldn't believe nobody but Doctor Ed about it. I guess I'll go see him myself. Didn't he give you no advice?"

"Chust to take it easy like, an' stay round de house dis winter. I guess you got some carpenter work for me to do. I kin make some new shelves for you, and I want dis long time to build a closet in de boys' room and make dem two little fellers keep dere clo'es hung up."

Rosicky drank his coffee from time to time, while he considered. His moustache was of the soft long variety and came down over his mouth like the teeth of a buggy rake over a bundle of hay. Each time he put down his cup, he ran his blue handkerchief over his lips. When he took a drink of water, he managed very neatly with the back of his hand.

Mary sat watching him intently, trying to find any change in his face. It is hard to see anyone who has become like your own body to you. Yes, his hair had got thin, and his high forehead had deep lines running from left to right. But his neck, always clean-shaved except in the busiest seasons, was not loose or baggy. It was burned a dark reddish brown, and there were deep creases in it, but it looked firm and full of blood. His cheeks had a good colour. On either side of his mouth there was a half-moon down the length of his cheek, not wrinkles, but two lines that had come there from his habitual expression. He was shorter and broader than when she married him; his back had grown broad and curved, a good deal like the shell of an old turtle, and his arms and legs were short.

He was fifteen years older than Mary, but she had hardly ever thought about it before. He was her man, and the kind of man she liked. She was rough, and he was gentle—city-bred, as she always said. They had been shipmates on a rough voyage and had stood by each other in trying times. Life had gone well with them because, at bottom, they had the same ideas about life. They agreed, without discussion, as to what was most important and what was secondary. They didn't often exchange opinions, even in Czech —it was as if they had thought the same thought together. A good deal had to be sacrificed and thrown overboard in a hard life like theirs, and they had never disagreed as to the things that could go. It had been a hard life, and a soft life, too. There wasn't anything brutal in the short, broad-backed man with the three-cornered eyes and the forehead that went on to the top of his skull. He was a city man, a gentle man, and though he had married a rough farm girl, he had never touched her without gentleness.

They had been at one accord not to hurry through life, not to be always skimping and saving. They saw their neighbours buy more land and feed more stock than they did, without discontent. Once when the creamery agent came to the Rosickys to persuade them to sell him their cream, he told them how much money the Fasslers, their nearest neighbours, had made on their cream last year.

"Yes," said Mary, "and look at them Fassler children! Pale, pinched little things, they look like skimmed milk. I had rather put some colour into my children's faces than put money into the bank."

The agent shrugged and turned to Anton.

"I guess we'll do like she says," said Rosicky.

III

Mary very soon got into town to see Doctor Ed, and then she had a talk with her boys and set a guard over Rosicky. Even John, the youngest, had his father on his mind. If Rosicky went to throw hay down from the loft, one of the boys ran up the ladder and took the fork from him. He sometimes complained that though he was getting to be an old man, he wasn't an old woman yet.

That winter he stayed in the house in the afternoons and carpentered, or sat in the chair between the window full of plants and the wooden bench where the two pails of drinking-water stood. This spot was called "Father's corner," though it was not a corner at all. He had a shelf there, where he kept his Bohemian papers and his pipes and tobacco, and his shears and needles and thread and tailor's thimble. Having been a tailor in his youth, he couldn't bear to see a woman patching at his clothes, or at the boys'. He liked tailoring, and always patched all the overalls and jackets and work shirts. Occasionally he made over a pair of pants one of the older boys had outgrown, for the little fellow.

While he sewed, he let his mind run back over his life. He had a good deal to remember, really; life in three countries. The only part of his youth he didn't like to remember was the two years he had spent in London, in Cheapside, working for a German tailor who was wretchedly poor. Those days, when he was nearly always hungry, when his clothes were dropping off him for dirt, and the sound of a strange language kept him in continual bewilderment, had left a sore spot in his mind that wouldn't bear touching.

He was twenty when he landed at Castle Garden in New York, and he had a protector who got him work in a tailor shop in Vesey Street, down near the Washington Market. He looked upon that part of his life as very happy. He became a good workman, he was industrious, and his wages were increased from time to time. He minded his own business and envied nobody's good fortune. He went to night school and learned to read English. He often did overtime work and was well paid for it, but somehow he never saved anything. He couldn't refuse a loan to a friend, and he was self-indulgent. He liked a good dinner, and a little went for beer, a little for tobacco; a good deal went to the girls. He often stood through an opera on Saturday nights; he could get standing-room for a dollar. Those were the great days of opera in New York, and it gave a fellow something to think about for the rest of the week. Rosicky had a quick ear, and a childish love of all the stage splendour; the scenery, the costumes, the ballet. He usually went with a chum, and after the performance they had beer, and maybe some oysters, somewhere. It was a fine life; for the first five years or so it satisfied him completely. He was never hungry or cold or dirty, and everything amused him: a fire, a dog fight, a

parade, a storm, a ferry ride. He thought New York the finest, richest, friendliest city in the world.

Moreover, he had what he called a happy home life. Very near the tailor shop was a small furniture factory, where an old Austrian, Loeffler, employed a few skilled men and made unusual furniture, most of it to order, for the rich German housewives uptown. The top floor of Loeffler's five-story factory was a loft, where he kept his choice lumber and stored the odd pieces of furniture left on his hands. One of the young workmen he employed was a Czech, and he and Rosicky became fast friends. They persuaded Loeffler to let them have a sleeping-room in one corner of the loft. They bought good beds and bedding and had their pick of the furniture kept up there. The loft was low-pitched, but light and airy, full of windows, and good-smelling by reason of the fine lumber put up there to season. Old Loeffler used to go down to the docks and buy wood from South America and the East from the sea captains. The young men were as foolish about their house as a bridal pair. Zichec, the young cabinet-maker, devised every sort of convenience, and Rosicky kept their clothes in order. At night and on Sundays, when the quiver of machinery underneath was still, it was the quietest place in the world, and on summer nights all the sea winds blew in. Zichec often practised on his flute in the evening. They were both fond of music and went to the opera together. Rosicky thought he wanted to live like that forever.

But as the years passed, all alike, he began to get a little restless. When spring came round, he would begin to feel fretted, and he got to drinking. He was likely to drink too much of a Saturday night. On Sunday he was languid and heavy, getting over his spree. On Monday he plunged into work again. So he never had time to figure out what ailed him, although he knew something did. When the grass turned green in Park Place, and the lilac hedge at the back of Trinity church-yard put out its blossoms, he was tormented by a longing to run away. That was why he drank too much; to get a temporary illusion of freedom and wide horizons.

Rosicky, the old Rosicky, could remember as if it were yesterday the day when the young Rosicky found out what was the matter with him. It was on a Fourth-of-July afternoon, and he was sitting in Park Place in the sun. The lower part of New York was empty. Wall Street, Liberty Street, Broadway, all empty. So much stone and asphalt with nothing going on, so many empty windows. The emptiness was intense, like the stillness in a great factory when the machinery stops and the belts and bands cease running. It was too great a change, it took all the strength out of one. Those blank buildings, without the stream of life pouring through them, were like empty jails. It struck young Rosicky that this was the trouble with big cities; they built you in from the earth itself, cemented you away from any contact with the ground. You lived in an unnatural world, like the fish in an aquarium, who were probably much more comfortable than they ever were in the sea.

On that very day he began to think seriously about the articles he had read in the Bohemian papers, describing prosperous Czech farming communities in the West. He believed he would like to go out there as a farm-hand; it was hardly possible that he could ever have land of his own. His people had always been workmen; his father and grandfather had worked in shops. His mother's parents had lived in the country, but they rented their farm and had a hard time to get along. Nobody in his family had ever owned any land—that belonged to a different station of life altogether. Anton's mother died when he was little, and he was sent into the country to her parents. He stayed with them until he was twelve, and formed those ties with the earth and the farm animals and growing things which are never made at all unless they are made early. After his grandfather died, he went back to live with his father and stepmother, but she was very hard on him, and his father helped him to get passage to London.

After that Fourth-of-July day in Park Place, the desire to return to the country never left him. To work on another man's farm would be all he asked; to see the sun rise and set and to plant things and watch them grow. He was a very simple man. He was like a tree that has not many roots, but one tap-root that goes down deep. He subscribed for a Bohemian paper printed in Chicago, then for one printed in Omaha. His mind got farther and farther west. He began to save a little money to buy his liberty. When he was thirty-five, there was a great meeting in New York of Bohemian athletic societies, and Rosicky left the tailor shop and went home with the Omaha delegates to try his fortune in another part of the world.

IV

Perhaps the fact that his own youth was well over before he began to have a family was one reason why Rosicky was so fond of his boys. He had almost a grandfather's indulgence for them. He had never had to worry about any of them—except, just now, a little about Rudolph.

On Saturday night the boys always piled into the Ford, took little Josephine, and went to town to the moving-picture show. One Saturday morning they were talking at the breakfast table about starting early that evening, so that they would have an hour or so to see the Christmas things in the stores before the show began. Rosicky looked down the table.

"I hope you boys ain't disappointed, but I want you to let me have de car tonight. Maybe some of you can go in with de neighbours."

Their faces fell. They worked hard all the week, and they were still children. A new jack-knife or a box of candy pleased the older ones as much as the little fellow.

"If you and mother are going to town," Frank said, "maybe you could take a couple of us along with you, anyway."

"No, I want to take de car down to Rudolph's, and let him an' Polly go in to de show. She don't git into town enough, an' I'm afraid she's gittin' lonesome, an' he can't afford no car yet."

That settled it. The boys were a good deal dashed. Their father took another piece of apple-cake and went on: "Maybe next Saturday night de two little fellers can go along wid dem."

"Oh, is Rudolph going to have the car every Saturday night?"

Rosicky did not reply at once; then he began to speak seriously: "Listen, boys; Polly ain't lookin' so good. I don't like to see nobody lookin' sad. It comes hard fur a town girl to be a farmer's wife. I don't want no trouble to start in Rudolph's family. When it starts, it ain't so easy to stop. An American girl don't git used to our ways all at once. I like to tell Polly she and Rudolph can have the car every Saturday night till after New Year's, if it's all right with you boys."

"Sure it's all right, papa," Mary cut in. "And it's good you thought about that. Town girls is used to more than country girls. I lay awake nights, scared she'll make Rudolph discontented with the farm."

The boys put as good a face on it as they could. They surely looked forward to their Saturday nights in town. That evening Rosicky drove the car the half mile down to Rudolph's new, bare little house.

Polly was in a short-sleeved gingham dress, clearing away the supper dishes. She was a trim, slim little thing, with blue eyes and shingled yellow hair, and her eyebrows were reduced to a mere brush-stroke, like Miss Pearl's.

"Good-evening, Mr. Rosicky. Rudolph's at the barn, I guess." She never called him father, or Mary mother. She was sensitive about having married a foreigner. She never in the world would have done it if Rudolph hadn't been such a handsome, persuasive fellow and such a gallant lover. He had graduated in her class in the high school in town, and their friendship began in the ninth grade.

Rosicky went in, though he wasn't exactly asked. "My boys ain't goin' to town tonight, an' I brought de car over fur you two to go in to de picture show."

Polly, carrying dishes to the sink, looked over her shoulder at him. "Thank you. But I'm late with my work tonight, and pretty tired. Maybe Rudolph would like to go in with you."

"Oh, I don't go to de shows! I'm too old-fashioned. You won't feel so tired after you ride in de air a ways. It's a nice clear night, an' it ain't cold. You go an' fix yourself up, Polly, an' I'll wash de dishes an' leave everything nice fur you."

Polly blushed and tossed her bob. "I couldn't let you do that, Mr. Rosicky. I wouldn't think of it."

Rosicky said nothing. He found a bib apron on a nail behind the kitchen door. He slipped it over his head and then took Polly by her two elbows and pushed her gently toward the door of her own room. "I washed up de kitchen many times for my wife, when de babies was sick or somethin'. You go an' make yourself look nice. I like you to look prettier'n any of dem town girls when you go in. De young folks must have some fun, an' I'm goin' to look out fur you, Polly."

That kind, reassuring grip on her elbows, the old man's funny bright eyes, made Polly want to drop her head on his shoulder for a second. She restrained herself, but she lingered in his grasp at the door of her room, murmuring tearfully: "You always lived in the city when you were young, didn't you? Don't you ever get lonesome out here?"

As she turned round to him, her hand fell naturally into his, and he stood holding it and smiling into her face with his peculiar, knowing, indulgent smile without a shadow of reproach in it. "Dem big cities is all right fur de rich, but dey is terrible hard for de poor."

"I don't know. Sometimes I think I'd like to take a chance. You lived in New York, didn't you?"

"An' London. Da's bigger still. I learned my trade dere. Here's Rudolph comin', you better hurry."

"Will you tell me about London sometime?"

"Maybe. Only I ain't no talker, Polly. Run an' dress yourself up."

The bedroom door closed behind her, and Rudolph came in from the outside, looking anxious. He had seen the car and was sorry any of his family should come just then. Supper hadn't been a very pleasant occasion. Halting in the doorway, he saw his father in a kitchen apron, carrying dishes to the sink. He flushed crimson and something flashed in his eye. Rosicky held up a warning finger.

"I brought de car over fur you an' Polly to go to de picture show, an' I made her let me finish here so you won't be late. You go put on a clean shirt, quick!"

"But don't the boys want the car, father?"

"Not tonight dey don't." Rosicky fumbled under his apron and found his pants pocket. He took out a silver dollar and said in a hurried whisper: "You go an' buy dat girl some ice cream an' candy tonight, like you was courtin'. She's awful good friends wid me."

Rudolph was very short of cash, but he took the money as if it hurt him. There had been a crop failure all over the county. He had more than once been sorry he'd married this year.

In a few minutes the young people came out, looking clean and a little stiff. Rosicky hurried them off, and then he took his own time with the dishes. He scoured the pots and pans and put away the milk and swept the kitchen. He put some coal in the stove and shut off the draughts, so the place would be warm for them when they got home late at night. Then he sat down and had a pipe and listened to the clock tick.

Generally speaking, marrying an American girl was certainly a risk. A Czech should marry a Czech. It was lucky that Polly was the daughter of a poor widow woman; Rudolph was proud, and if she had a prosperous family to throw up at him, they could never make it go. Polly was one of four sisters, and they all worked; one was bookkeeper in the bank, one taught music, and Polly and her younger sister had been clerks, like Miss Pearl. All four of them were musical, had pretty voices, and sang in the Methodist choir, which the eldest sister directed.

Polly missed the sociability of a store position. She missed the choir, and the company of her sisters. She didn't dislike housework, but she disliked so much of it. Rosicky was a little anxious about this pair. He was afraid Polly would grow so discontented that Rudy would quit the farm and take a factory job in Omaha. He had worked for a winter up there, two years ago, to get money to marry on. He had done very well, and they would always take him back at the stockyards. But to Rosicky that meant the end of everything for his son. To be a landless man was to be a wage-earner, a slave, all your life; to have nothing, to be nothing.

Rosicky thought he would come over and do a little carpentering for Polly after the New Year. He guessed she needed jollying. Rudolph was a serious sort of chap, serious in love and serious about his work.

Rosicky shook out his pipe and walked home across the fields. Ahead of him the lamplight shone from his kitchen windows. Suppose he were still in a tailor shop on Vesey Street, with a bunch of pale, narrow-chested sons working on machines, all coming home tired and sullen to eat supper in a kitchen that was a parlour also; with another crowded, angry family quarrelling just across the dumb-waiter shaft, and squeaking pulleys at the windows where dirty washings hung on dirty lines above a court full of old brooms and mops and ash-cans . . .

He stopped by the windmill to look up at the frosty winter stars and draw a long breath before he went inside. That kitchen with the shining windows was dear to him; but the sleeping fields and bright stars and the noble darkness were dearer still.

V

On the day before Christmas the weather set in very cold; no snow, but a bitter, biting wind that whistled and sang over the flat land and lashed one's face like fine wires. There was baking going on in the Rosicky kitchen all day, and Rosicky sat inside, making over a coat that Albert had outgrown into an overcoat for John. Mary had a big red geranium in bloom for Christmas, and a row of Jerusalem cherry trees, full of berries. It was the first year she had ever grown these; Doctor Ed brought her the seeds from Omaha when he went to some medical convention. They reminded Rosicky of plants he had seen in England; and all afternoon, as he stitched, he sat thinking about those two years in London, which his mind usually shrank from even after all this while.

He was a lad of eighteen when he dropped down into London, with no money and no connexions except the address of a cousin who was supposed to be working at a confectioner's. When he went to the pastry shop, however, he found that the cousin had gone to America. Anton tramped the streets for several days, sleeping in doorways and on the Embankment, until he was in utter despair. He knew no English, and the sound of the strange language all about him confused him. By chance he met a poor German tailor who had learned his trade in Vienna, and could speak a little Czech. This tailor, Lifschnitz, kept a repair shop in a Cheapside basement, underneath a cobbler. He didn't much need an apprentice, but he was sorry for the boy and took him in for no wages but his keep and what he could pick up. The pickings were supposed to be coppers given you when you took work home to a customer. But most of the customers called for their clothes themselves, and the coppers that came Anton's way were very few. He had, however, a place to sleep. The tailor's family lived upstairs in three rooms; a kitchen, a bedroom, where Lifschnitz and his wife and five children slept, and a living-room. Two corners of this living-room were curtained off for lodgers; in one Rosicky slept on an old horsehair sofa, with a feather quilt to wrap himself in. The other corner was rented

to a wretched, dirty boy, who was studying the violin. He actually practised there. Rosicky was dirty, too. There was no way to be anything else. Mrs. Lifschnitz got the water she cooked and washed with from a pump in a brick court, four flights down. There were bugs in the place, and multitudes of fleas, though the poor woman did the best she could. Rosicky knew she often went empty to give another potato or a spoonful of dripping to the two hungry, sad-eyed boys who lodged with her. He used to think he would never get out of there, never get a clean shirt to his back again. What would he do, he wondered, when his clothes actually dropped to pieces and the worn cloth wouldn't hold patches any longer?

It was still early when the old farmer put aside his sewing and his recollections. The sky had been a dark grey all day, with not a gleam of sun, and the light failed at four o'clock. He went to shave and change his shirt while the turkey was roasting. Rudolph and Polly were coming over for supper.

After supper they sat round in the kitchen, and the younger boys were saying how sorry they were it hadn't snowed. Everybody was sorry. They wanted a deep snow that would lie long and keep the wheat warm, and leave the ground soaked when it melted.

"Yes, sir!" Rudolph broke out fiercely; "if we have another dry year like last year, there's going to be hard times in this country."

Rosicky filled his pipe. "You boys don't know what hard times is. You don't owe nobody, you got plenty to eat an' keep warm, an' plenty water to keep clean. When you got them, you can't have it very hard."

Rudolph frowned, opened and shut his big right hand, and dropped it clenched upon his knee. "I've got to have a good deal more than that, father, or I'll quit this farming gamble. I can always make good wages railroading, or at the packing-house, and be sure of my money."

"Maybe so," his father answered dryly.

Mary, who had just come in from the pantry and was wiping her hands on the roller towel, thought Rudy and his father were getting too serious. She brought her darning-basket and sat down in the middle of the group.

"I ain't much afraid of hard times, Rudy," she said heartily. "We've had a plenty, but we've always come through. Your father wouldn't never take nothing very hard, not even hard times. I got a mind to tell you a story on him. Maybe you boys can't hardly remember the year we had that terrible hot wind, that burned everything up on the Fourth of July? All the corn an' the gardens. An' that was in the days when we didn't have alfalfa yet—I guess it wasn't invented.

"Well, that very day your father was out cultivatin'

corn, and I was here in the kitchen makin' plum preserves. We had bushels of plums that year. I noticed it was terrible hot, but it's always hot in the kitchen when you're preservin', an' I was too busy with my plums to mind. Anton come in from the field about three o'clock, an' I asked him what was the matter.

" 'Nothin',' he says, 'but it's pretty hot, an' I think I won't work no more today.' He stood round for a few minutes an' then he says: 'Ain't you near through? I want you should git up a nice supper for us tonight. It's Fourth of July.'

"I told him to git along, that I was right in the middle of preservin', but the plums would taste good on a hot biscuit. 'I'm goin' to have fried chicken, too,' he says, and he went off an' killed a couple. You three oldest boys was little fellers, playin' round outside, real hot an' sweaty, an' your father took you to the horse tank down by the windmill an' took off your clothes an' put you in. Them two box-elder trees was little then, but they made shade over the tank. Then he took off all his own clothes, an' got in with you. While he was playin' in the water with you, the Methodist preacher drove into our place to say how all the neighbours was goin' to meet at the schoolhouse that night, to pray for rain. He drove right to the windmill, of course, and there was your father and you three with no clothes on. I was in the kitchen door, an' I had to laugh, for the preacher acted like he ain't never seen a naked man before. He surely was embarrassed, an' your father couldn't git to his clothes; they was all hangin' up on the windmill to let the sweat dry out of 'em. So he laid in the tank where he was, an' put one of you boys on top of him to cover him up a little, an' talked to the preacher.

"When you got through playin' in the water, he put clean clothes on you and a clean shirt on himself, and by that time I'd begun to get supper. He says: 'It's too hot in here to eat comfortable. Let's have a picnic in the orchard. We'll eat our supper behind the mulberry hedge, under them linden trees.'

"So he carried our supper down, an' a bottle of my wild-grape wine, an' everything tasted good, I can tell you. The wind got cooler as the sun was goin' down, and it turned out pleasant, only I noticed how the leaves was curled up on the linden trees. That made me think, an' I asked your father if that hot wind all day hadn't been terrible hard on the gardens an' the corn.

" 'Corn,' he says, 'there ain't no corn.'

" 'What you talkin' about?' I said. 'Ain't we got forty acres?'

" 'We ain't got an ear,' he says, 'nor nobody else ain't got none. All the corn in this country was cooked by three o'clock today, like you'd roasted it in an oven.'

" 'You mean you won't get no crop at all?' I asked him. I couldn't believe it, after he'd worked so hard.

" 'No crop this year,' he says. 'That's why we're havin' a picnic. We might as well enjoy what we got.'

"An' that's how your father behaved, when all the neighbours was so discouraged they couldn't look you in the face. An' we enjoyed ourselves that year, poor as we was, an' our neighbours wasn't a bit better off for bein' miserable. Some of 'em grieved till they got poor digestions and couldn't relish what they did have."

The younger boys said they thought their father had the best of it. But Rudolph was thinking that, all the same, the neighbours had managed to get ahead more, in the fifteen years since that time. There must be something wrong about his father's way of doing things. He wished he knew what was going on in the back of Polly's mind. He knew she liked his father, but he knew, too, that she was afraid of something. When his mother sent over coffee-cake or prune tarts or a loaf of fresh bread, Polly seemed to regard them with a certain suspicion. When she observed to him that his brothers had nice manners, her tone implied that it was remarkable they should have. With his mother she was stiff and on her guard. Mary's hearty frankness and gusts of good humour irritated her. Polly was afraid of being unusual or conspicuous in any way, of being "ordinary," as she said!

When Mary had finished her story, Rosicky laid aside his pipe. "You boys like me to tell you about some of dem hard times I been through in London?" Warmly encouraged, he sat rubbing his forehead along the deep creases. It was bothersome to tell a long story in English (he nearly always talked to the boys in Czech), but he wanted Polly to hear this one.

"Well, you know about dat tailor shop I worked in in London? I had one Christmas dere I ain't never forgot. Times was awful bad before Christmas; de boss ain't got much work, an' have it awful hard to pay his rent. It ain't so much fun, bein' poor in a big city like London, I'll say! All de windows is full of good t'ings to eat, an' all de pushcarts in de streets is full, an' you smell 'em all de time, an' you ain't got no money—not a damn bit. I didn't mind de cold so much, though I didn't have no overcoat, chust a short jacket I'd outgrowed so it wouldn't meet on me, an' my hands was chapped raw. But I always had a good appetite, like you all know, an' de sight of dem pork pies in de windows was awful fur me!

"Day before Christmas was terrible foggy dat year, an' dat fog gits into your bones and makes you all damp like. Mrs. Lifschnitz didn't give us nothin' but a little bread an' drippin' for supper, because she was savin' to try for to give us a good dinner on Christmas Day. After supper de boss say I can go an' enjoy myself, so I went into de streets to listen to de Christmas singers. Dey sing old songs an' make very nice music, an' I run round after dem a goodways, till I got awful hungry. I t'ink maybe if I go home, I can sleep till morning an' forget my belly.

"I went into my corner real quiet, and roll up in my fedder quilt. But I ain't got my head down, till I smell somet'ing good. Seem like it git stronger an' stronger, an' I can't git to sleep noway. I can't understand dat smell. Dere was a gas light in a hall across de court, dat always shine in at my window a little. I got up an' look round. I got a little wooden box in my corner fur a stool, 'cause I ain't got no chair. I picks up dat box, and under it dere is a roast goose on a platter! I can't believe my eyes. I carry it to de window where de light comes in, an' touch it and smell it to find out, an' den I taste it to be sure. I say, I will eat chust one little bite of dat goose, so I can go to sleep, and tomorrow I won't eat none at all. But I tell you, boys, when I stop, one half of dat goose was gone!"

The narrator bowed his head, and the boys shouted. But little Josephine slipped behind his chair and kissed him on the neck beneath his ear.

"Poor little papa, I don't want him to be hungry!"

"Da's long ago, child. I ain't never been hungry since I had your mudder to cook fur me."

"Go on and tell us the rest, please," said Polly.

"Well, when I come to realize what I done, of course, I felt terrible. I felt better in de stomach, but very bad in de heart. I set on my bed wid dat platter on my knees, an' it all come to me; how hard dat poor woman save to buy dat goose, and how she get some neighbour to cook it dat got more fire, an' how she put it in my corner to keep it away from dem hungry children. Dere was a old carpet hung up to shut my corner off, an' de children wasn't allowed to go in dere. An' I know she put it in my corner because she trust me more'n she did de violin boy. I can't stand it to face her after I spoil de Christmas. So I put on my shoes and go out into de city. I tell myself I better throw myself in de river; but I guess I ain't dat kind of a boy.

"It was after twelve o'clock, an' terrible cold, an' I start out to walk about London all night. I walk along de river awhile, but dey was lots of drunks all along; men, and women too. I chust move along to keep away from de police. I git onto de Strand, an' den over to New Oxford Street, where dere was a big German restaurant on de ground floor, wid big windows all fixed up fine, an' I could see de people havin' parties inside. While I was lookin' in, two men and two ladies come out, laughin' and talkin' and feelin' happy about all dey been eatin' an' drinkin', and dey was speakin' Czech—not like de Austrians, but like de home folks talk it.

"I guess I went crazy, an' I done what I ain't never done before nor since. I went right up to dem gay people an' begun to beg dem: 'Fellow countrymen, for God's sake give me money enough to buy a goose!'

"Dey laugh, of course, but de ladies speak awful kind to me, an' dey take me back into de restaurant and give me hot coffee and cakes, an' make me tell all about how I happened to come to London, an' what I was doin' dere. Dey take my name and where I work down on paper, an' both of dem ladies give me ten shillings.

"De big market at Covent Garden ain't very far away, an' by dat time it was open. I go dere an' buy a big goose an' some pork pies, an' potatoes and onions, an' cakes an' oranges fur de children—all I could carry! When I git home, everybody is still asleep. I pile all I bought on de kitchen table, an' go in an' lay down on my bed, an' I ain't waken up till I hear dat woman scream when she come out into her kitchen. My goodness, but she was surprise'! She laugh an' cry at de same time, an' hug me and waken all de children. She ain't stop fur no breakfast; she git de Christmas dinner ready dat morning, and we all sit down an' eat all we can hold. I ain't never seen dat violin boy have all he can hold before.

"Two-t'ree days after dat, de two men come to hunt me up, an' dey ask my boss, and he give me a good report an' tell dem I was steady boy all right. One of dem Bohemians was very smart an' run a Bohemian newspaper in New York, an de' odder was a rich man, in de importing business, an' dey been travelling togedder. Dey told me how t'ings was easier in New York, an' offered to pay my passage when dey was goin' home soon on a boat. My boss say to me: 'You go. You ain't got no chance here, an' I like to see you git ahead, fur you always been a good boy to my woman, and fur dat fine Christmas dinner you give us all.' An' da's how I got to New York."

That night when Rudolph and Polly, arm in arm, were running home across the fields with the bitter wind at their backs, his heart leaped for joy when she said she thought they might have his family come over for supper on New Year's Eve. "Let's get up a nice supper, and not let your mother help at all; make her be company for once."

"That would be lovely of you, Polly," he said humbly. He was a very simple, modest boy, and he, too, felt vaguely that Polly and her sisters were more experienced and worldly than his people.

VI

The winter turned out badly for farmers. It was bitterly cold, and after the first light snows before Christmas there was no snow at all—and no rain. March was as bitter as February. On those days when the wind fairly punished the country, Rosicky sat by his window. In the fall he and the boys had put in a big wheat planting, and now the seed had frozen in the ground. All that land would have to be ploughed up and planted over again, planted in corn. It had happened before, but he was younger then, and he never worried about what had to be. He was sure of himself and of Mary; he knew they could bear what they had to bear, that they would always pull through somehow. But he was not so sure about the young ones, and he felt troubled because Rudolph and Polly were having such a hard start.

Sitting beside his flowering window while the panes rattled and the wind blew in under the door, Rosicky gave himself to reflection as he had not done since those Sundays in the loft of the furniture factory in New York, long ago. Then he was trying to find what he wanted in life for himself; now he was trying to find what he wanted for his boys, and why it was he so hungered to feel sure they would be here, working this very land, after he was gone.

They would have to work hard on the farm, and probably they would never do much more than make a living. But if he could think of them as staying here on the land, he wouldn't have to fear any great unkindness for them. Hardships, certainly; it was a hardship to have the wheat freeze in the ground when seed was so high; and to have to sell your stock because you had no feed. But there would be other years when everything came along right, and you caught up. And what you had was your own. You didn't have to choose between bosses and strikers, and go wrong either way. You didn't have to do with dishonest and cruel people. They were the only things in his experience he had found terrifying and horrible; the look in the eyes of a dishonest and crafty man, of a scheming and rapacious woman.

In the country, if you had a mean neighbour, you could keep off his land and make him keep off yours. But in the city, all the foulness and misery and brutality of your neighbours was part of your life. The worst things he had come upon in his journey through the world were human—depraved and poisonous specimens of man. To this day he could recall certain terrible faces in the London streets. There were mean people everywhere, to be sure, even in their own country town here. But they weren't tempered, hardened, sharpened, like the treacherous people in cities who live by grinding or cheating or poisoning their fellowmen. He had helped to bury two of his fellow workmen in the tailoring trade, and he was distrustful of the organized industries that see one out of the world in big cities. Here, if you were sick, you had Doctor Ed to look after you; and if you died, fat Mr. Haycock, the kindest man in the world, buried you.

It seemed to Rosicky that for good, honest boys like his, the worst they could do on the farm was better than the best they would be likely to do in the city. If he'd had a mean boy, now, one who was crooked and sharp and tried to put anything over on his brothers, then town would be the place for him. But he had no such boy. As for Rudolph, the discontented one, he would give the shirt off his back to anyone who touched his heart. What Rosicky really hoped for his boys was that they could get through the world without ever knowing much about the cruelty of human beings. "Their mother and me ain't prepared them for that," he sometimes said to himself.

These thoughts brought him back to a grateful consideration of his own case. What an escape he had had, to be sure! He, too, in his time, had had to take money for repair work from the hand of a hungry child who let it go so wistfully; because it was money due his boss. And now, in all these years, he had never had to take a cent from anyone in bitter need—never had to look at the face of a woman become like a wolf's from struggle and famine. When he thought of these things, Rosicky would put on his cap and jacket and slip down to the barn and give his work-horses a little extra oats, letting them eat it out of his hand in their slobbery fashion. It was his way of expressing what he felt, and made him chuckle with pleasure.

The spring came warm, with blue skies—but dry, dry as a bone. The boys began ploughing up the wheat-fields to plant them over in corn. Rosicky would stand at the fence corner and watch them, and the earth was so dry it blew up in clouds of brown dust that hid the horses and the sulky plough and the driver. It was a bad outlook.

The big alfalfa-field that lay between the home place and Rudolph's came up green, but Rosicky was worried because during that open windy winter a great many Russian thistle plants had blown in there and lodged. He kept asking the boys to rake them out; he was afraid their seed would root and "take the alfalfa." Rudolph said that was nonsense. The boys were working so hard planting corn, their father felt he couldn't insist about the thistles, but he set great store by that big alfalfa-field. It was a feed you could depend on—and there was some deeper reason, vague, but strong. The peculiar green of that clover woke early memories in old Rosicky, went back to something in his childhood in the Old World. When he was a little boy, he had played in fields of that strong blue-green colour.

One morning, when Rudolph had gone to town in the car, leaving a work-team idle in his barn, Rosicky went over to his son's place, put the horses to the buggy rake, and set about quietly raking up those thistles. He behaved with guilty caution, and rather enjoyed stealing a march on Doctor Ed, who was just then taking his first vacation in seven years of practice and was attending a clinic in Chicago. Rosicky got the thistles raked up, but did not stop to burn them. That would take some time, and his breath was pretty short, so he thought he had better get the horses back to the barn.

He got them into the barn and to their stalls, but the pain had come on so sharp in his chest that he didn't try to take the harness off. He started for the house, bending lower with every step. The cramp in his chest was shutting him up like a jack-knife. When he reached the windmill, he swayed and caught at the ladder. He saw Polly coming down the hill, running with the swiftness of a slim greyhound. In a flash she had her shoulder under his armpit.

"Lean on me, father, hard! Don't be afraid. We can get to the house all right."

Somehow they did, though Rosicky became blind with pain; he could keep on his legs, but he couldn't steer his course. The next thing he was conscious of was lying on Polly's bed, and Polly bending over him wringing out bath-towels in hot water and putting them on his chest. She stopped only to throw coal into the stove, and she kept the tea-kettle and the black pot going. She put these hot applications on him for nearly an hour, she told him afterward, and all that time he was drawn up stiff and blue, with the sweat pouring off him.

As the pain gradually loosed its grip, the stiffness went out of his jaws, the black circles round his eyes disappeared, and a little of his natural colour came back. When his daughter-in-law buttoned his shirt over his chest at last, he sighed.

"Da's fine, de way I feel now, Polly. It was a awful bad spell, an' I was so sorry it all come on you like it did."

Polly was flushed and excited. "Is the pain really gone? Can I leave you long enough to telephone over to your place?"

Rosicky's eyelids fluttered. "Don't telephone, Polly. It ain't no use to scare my wife. It's nice and quiet here, an' if I ain't too much trouble to you, just let me lay still till I feel like myself. I ain't got no pain now. It's nice here."

Polly bent over him and wiped the moisture from his face. "Oh, I'm so glad it's over!" she broke out impulsively. "It just broke my heart to see you suffer so, father."

Rosicky motioned her to sit down on the chair where the tea-kettle had been, and looked up at her with that lively affectionate gleam in his eyes. "You was awful good to me, I won't never forgit dat. I hate it to be sick on you like dis. Down at de barn I say to myself, dat young girl ain't had much experience in sickness, I don't want to scare her, an' maybe she's got a baby comin' or somet'ing."

Polly took his hand. He was looking at her so intently and affectionately and confidingly; his eyes seemed to caress her face, to regard it with pleasure. She frowned with her funny streaks of eyebrows, and then smiled back at him.

"I guess maybe there is something of that kind going to happen. But I haven't told anyone yet, not my mother or Rudolph. You'll be the first to know."

His hand pressed hers. She noticed that it was warm again. The twinkle in his yellow-brown eyes seemed to come nearer.

"I like mighty well to see dat little child, Polly," was all he said. Then he closed his eyes and lay half-smiling. But Polly sat still, thinking hard. She had a sudden feeling that nobody in the world, not her mother, not Rudolph, or anyone, really loved her as much as old Rosicky did. It perplexed her. She sat frowning and trying to puzzle it out. It was as if Rosicky had a special gift for loving people, something that was like an ear for music or an eye for colour. It was quiet, unobtrusive; it was merely there. You saw it in his eyes—perhaps that was why they were merry. You felt it in his hands, too. After he dropped off to sleep, she sat holding his warm, broad, flexible brown hand. She had never seen another in the least like it. She wondered if it wasn't a kind of gipsy hand, it was so alive and quick and light in its communications—very strange in a farmer. Nearly all the farmers she knew had huge lumps of fists, like mauls, or they were knotty and bony and uncomfortable-looking, with stiff fingers. But Rosicky's hand was like quick-silver, flexible, muscular, about the colour of a pale cigar, with deep, deep creases across the palm. It wasn't nervous, it wasn't a stupid lump; it was a warm brown human hand, with some cleverness in it, a great deal of generosity, and something else which Polly could only call "gipsy-like"—something nimble and lively and sure, in the way that animals are.

Polly remembered that hour long afterward; it had been like an awakening to her. It seemed to her that she had never learned so much about life from anything as from old Rosicky's hand. It brought her to herself; it communicated some direct and untranslatable message.

When she heard Rudolph coming in the car, she ran out to meet him.

"Oh, Rudy, your father's been awful sick! He raked up those thistles he's been worrying about, and afterward he could hardly get to the house. He suffered so I was afraid he was going to die."

Rudolph jumped to the ground. "Where is he now?"

"On the bed. He's asleep. I was terribly scared, because, you know, I'm so fond of your father." She slipped her arm through his and they went into the house.

That afternoon they took Rosicky home and put him to bed, though he protested that he was quite well again.

The next morning he got up and dressed and sat down to breakfast with his family. He told Mary that his coffee tasted better than usual to him, and he warned the boys not to bear any tales to Doctor Ed when he got home. After breakfast he sat down by his window to do some patching and asked Mary to thread several needles for him before she went to feed her chickens—her eyes were better than his, and her hands steadier. He lit his pipe and took up John's overalls. Mary had been watching him anxiously all morning, and as she went out of the door with her bucket of scraps, she saw that he was smiling. He was thinking, indeed, about Polly, and how he might never have known what a tender heart she had if he hadn't got sick over there. Girls nowadays didn't wear their hearts on their sleeves. But now he knew Polly would make a fine woman after the foolishness wore off. Either a woman had that sweetness at her heart or she hadn't. You couldn't always tell by the look of them; but if they had that, everything came out right in the end.

After he had taken a few stitches, the cramp began in his chest, like yesterday. He put his pipe cautiously down on the window-sill and bent over to ease the pull. No use—he had better try to get to his bed if he could. He rose and groped his way across the familiar floor, which was rising and falling like the deck of a ship. At the door he fell. When Mary came in, she found him lying there, and the moment she touched him she knew that he was gone.

Doctor Ed was away when Rosicky died, and for the first few weeks after he got home he was hard-driven. Every day he said to himself that he must get out to see that family that had lost their father. One soft, warm moonlight night in early summer he started for the farm. His mind was on other things, and not until his road ran by the graveyard did he realize that Rosicky wasn't over there on the hill where the red lamp-light shone, but here, in the moonlight. He stopped his car, shut off the engine, and sat there for a while.

A sudden hush had fallen on his soul. Everything here seemed strangely moving and significant, though signifying what, he did not know. Close by the wire fence stood Rosicky's mowing-machine, where one of the boys had been cutting hay that afternoon; his own work-horses had been going up and down there. The new-cut hay perfumed all the night air. The moonlight silvered the long, billowy grass that grew over the graves and hid the fence; the few little evergreens stood out black in it, like shadows in a pool. The sky was very blue and soft, the stars rather faint because the moon was full.

For the first time it struck Doctor Ed that this was really a beautiful graveyard. He thought of city cemeteries; acres of shrubbery and heavy stone, so arranged and lonely and unlike anything in the living world. Cities of the dead, indeed; cities of the forgotten, of the "put away." But this was open and free, this little square of long grass which the wind forever stirred. Nothing but the sky overhead, and the many-coloured fields running on until they met that sky. The horses worked here in summer; the neighbours passed on their way to town; and over yonder, in the cornfield, Rosicky's own cattle would be eating fodder as winter came on. Nothing could be more undeathlike than this place; nothing could be more right for a man who had helped to do the work of great cities and had always longed for the open country and had got to it at last. Rosicky's life seemed to him complete and beautiful.

COUNTERPARTS

JAMES JOYCE

JAMES JOYCE (1882–1941) was born and educated in Dublin. In 1904 he left Ireland and spent the remainder of his life on the Continent, chiefly in Zurich, Trieste and Paris. His books include *Dubliners* (1914), *A Portrait of the Artist as a Young Man* (1916), *Ulysses* (1922) and *Finnegans Wake* (1939). In these works he moves from short fiction in the naturalistic manner to a "stream-of-consciousness" technique in which the action is entirely inward. His books have had great influence on the younger writers of our time.

THE bell rang furiously and, when Miss Parker went to the tube, a furious voice called out in a piercing North of Ireland accent:

"Send Farrington here!"

Miss Parker returned to her machine, saying to a man who was writing at a desk:

"Mr. Alleyne wants you upstairs."

The man muttered "*Blast* him!" under his breath and pushed back his chair to stand up. When he stood up he was tall and of great bulk. He had a hanging face, dark wine-coloured, with fair eyebrows and moustache: his eyes bulged forward slightly and the whites of them were dirty. He lifted up the counter and, passing by the clients, went out of the office with a heavy step.

He went heavily upstairs until he came to the second landing, where a door bore a brass plate with the inscription *Mr. Alleyne*. Here he halted, puffing with labour and vexation, and knocked. The shrill voice cried:

"Come in!"

The man entered Mr. Alleyne's room. Simultaneously Mr. Alleyne, a little man wearing gold-rimmed glasses on a clean-shaven face, shot his head up over a pile of documents. The head itself was so pink and hairless it seemed like a large egg reposing on the papers. Mr. Alleyne did not lose a moment:

"Farrington? What is the meaning of this? Why have I always to complain of you? May I ask you why you haven't made a copy of that contract between Bodley and Kirwan? I told you it must be ready by four o'clock."

"But Mr. Shelley said, sir——"

"*Mr. Shelley said, sir.* . . . Kindly attend to what I say and not to what *Mr. Shelley says, sir*. You have always some excuse or another for shirking work. Let

From *Dubliners* by James Joyce, included in the *Portable James Joyce*. Copyright 1946, 1947 by The Viking Press, Inc. Reprinted by permission of The Viking Press, Inc., New York.

me tell you that if the contract is not copied before this evening I'll lay the matter before Mr. Crosbie. . . . Do you hear me now?"

"Yes, sir."

"Do you hear me now? . . . Ay and another little matter! I might as well be talking to the wall as talking to you. Understand once for all that you get a half an hour for your lunch and not an hour and a half. How many courses do you want, I'd like to know. . . . Do you mind me now?"

"Yes, sir."

Mr. Alleyne bent his head again upon his pile of papers. The man stared fixedly at the polished skull which directed the affairs of Crosbie & Alleyne, gauging its fragility. A spasm of rage gripped his throat for a few moments and then passed, leaving after it a sharp sensation of thirst. The man recognised the sensation and felt that he must have a good night's drinking. The middle of the month was passed and, if he could get the copy done in time, Mr. Alleyne might give him an order on the cashier. He stood still, gazing fixedly at the head upon the pile of papers. Suddenly Mr. Alleyne began to upset all the papers, searching for something. Then, as if he had been unaware of the man's presence till that moment, he shot up his head again, saying:

"Eh? Are you going to stand there all day? Upon my word, Farrington, you take things easy!"

"I was waiting to see . . ."

"Very good, you needn't wait to see. Go downstairs and do your work."

The man walked heavily towards the door and, as he went out of the room, he heard Mr. Alleyne cry after him that if the contract was not copied by evening Mr. Crosbie would hear of the matter.

He returned to his desk in the lower office and counted the sheets which remained to be copied. He took up his pen and dipped it in the ink but he continued to stare stupidly at the last words he had written: *In no case shall the said Bernard Bodley be* . . .

The evening was falling and in a few minutes they would be lighting the gas: then he could write. He felt that he must slake the thirst in his throat. He stood up from his desk and, lifting the counter as before, passed out of the office. As he was passing out the chief clerk looked at him inquiringly.

"It's all right, Mr. Shelley," said the man, pointing with his finger to indicate the objective of his journey.

The chief clerk glanced at the hat-rack, but, seeing the row complete, offered no remark. As soon as he was on the landing the man pulled a shepherd's plaid cap out of his pocket, put it on his head and ran quickly down the rickety stairs. From the street door he walked on furtively on the inner side of the path towards the corner and all at once dived into a doorway. He was now safe in the dark snug of O'Neill's shop, and, filling up the little window that looked into the bar with his inflamed face, the colour of dark wine or dark meat, he called out:

"Here, Pat, give us a g.p., like a good fellow."

The curate brought him a glass of plain porter. The man drank it at a gulp and asked for a caraway seed. He put his penny on the counter and, leaving the curate to grope for it in the gloom, retreated out of the snug as furtively as he had entered it.

Darkness, accompanied by a thick fog, was gaining upon the dusk of February and the lamps in Eustace Street had been lit. The man went up by the houses until he reached the door of the office, wondering whether he could finish his copy in time. On the stairs a moist pungent odour of perfumes saluted his nose: evidently Miss Delacour had come while he was out in O'Neill's. He crammed his cap back again into his pocket and re-entered the office, assuming an air of absent-mindedness.

"Mr. Alleyne has been calling for you," said the chief clerk severely. "Where were you?"

The man glanced at the two clients who were standing at the counter as if to intimate that their presence prevented him from answering. As the clients were both male the chief clerk allowed himself a laugh.

"I know that game," he said. "Five times in one day is a little bit. . . . Well, you better look sharp and get a copy of our correspondence in the Delacour case for Mr. Alleyne."

This address in the presence of the public, his run upstairs and the porter he had gulped down so hastily confused the man and, as he sat down at his desk to get what was required, he realised how hopeless was the task of finishing his copy of the contract before half past five. The dark damp night was coming and he longed to spend it in the bars, drinking with his friends amid the glare of gas and the clatter of glasses. He got out the Delacour correspondence and passed out of the office. He hoped Mr. Alleyne would not discover that the last two letters were missing.

The moist pungent perfume lay all the way up to Mr. Alleyne's room. Miss Delacour was a middle-aged woman of Jewish appearance. Mr. Alleyne was said to be sweet on her or on her money. She came to the office often and stayed a long time when she came. She was sitting beside his desk now in an aroma of perfumes, smoothing the handle of her umbrella and nodding the great black feather in her hat. Mr. Alleyne had swivelled his chair round to face her and thrown his right foot jauntily upon his left knee. The man put the correspondence on the desk and bowed respectfully but neither Mr. Alleyne nor Miss Delacour took any notice of his bow. Mr. Alleyne tapped a finger on the correspondence and then flicked it towards him as if to say: *That's all right: you can go.*

The man returned to the lower office and sat down again at his desk. He stared intently at the incomplete phrase: *In no case shall the said Bernard Bodley be . . .* and thought how strange it was that the last three words began with the same letter. The chief clerk began to hurry Miss Parker, saying she would never have the letters typed in time for post. The man listened to the clicking of the machine for a few minutes and then set to work to finish his copy. But his head was not clear and his mind wandered away to the glare and rattle of the public-house. It was a night for hot punches. He struggled on with his copy, but when the clock struck five he had still fourteen pages to write. Blast it! He couldn't finish it in time. He longed to execrate aloud, to bring his fist down on something violently. He was so enraged that he wrote *Bernard Bernard* instead of *Bernard Bodley* and had to begin again on a clean sheet.

He felt strong enough to clear out the whole office single-handed. His body ached to do something, to rush out and revel in violence. All the indignities of his life enraged him. . . . Could he ask the cashier privately for an advance? No, the cashier was no good, no damn good: he wouldn't give an advance. . . . He knew where he would meet the boys: Leonard and O'Halloran and Nosey Flynn. The barometer of his emotional nature was set for a spell of riot.

His imagination had so abstracted him that his name was called twice before he answered. Mr. Alleyne and Miss Delacour were standing outside the counter and all the clerks had turned round in anticipation of something. The man got up from his desk. Mr. Alleyne began a tirade of abuse, saying that two letters were missing. The man answered that he knew nothing about them, that he had made a faithful copy. The tirade continued: it was so bitter and violent that the man could hardly restrain his fist from descending upon the head of the manikin before him.

"I know nothing about any other two letters," he said stupidly.

"You—know—nothing. Of course you know nothing," said Mr. Alleyne. "Tell me," he added, glancing first for approval to the lady beside him, "do you take me for a fool? Do you think me an utter fool?"

The man glanced from the lady's face to the little egg-shaped head and back again; and, almost before he was aware of it, his tongue had found a felicitous moment:

"I don't think, sir," he said, "that that's a fair question to put to me."

There was a pause in the very breathing of the clerks. Everyone was astounded (the author of the witticism no less than his neighbours) and Miss Delacour, who was a stout amiable person, began to smile broadly. Mr. Alleyne flushed to the hue of a wild rose and his mouth twitched with a dwarf's passion. He shook his fist in the man's face till it seemed to vibrate like the knob of some electric machine:

"You impertinent ruffian! You impertinent ruffian! I'll make short work of you! Wait till you see! You'll apologise to me for your impertinence or you'll quit the office instanter! You'll quit this, I'm telling you, or you'll apologise to me!"

.   .   .   .   .   .

He stood in a doorway opposite the office watching to see if the cashier would come out alone. All the clerks passed out and finally the cashier came out with the chief clerk. It was no use trying to say a word to him when he was with the chief clerk. The man felt that his position was bad enough. He had been obliged to offer an abject apology to Mr. Alleyne for his impertinence but he knew what a hornet's nest the office would be for him. He could remember the way in which Mr. Alleyne had hounded little Peake out of the office in order to make room for his own nephew. He felt savage and thirsty and revengeful, annoyed with himself and with everyone else. Mr. Alleyne would never give him an hour's rest; his life would be a hell to him. He had made a proper fool of himself this time. Could he not keep his tongue in his cheek? But they had never pulled together from the first, he and Mr. Alleyne, ever since the day Mr. Alleyne had overheard him mimicking his North of Ireland accent to amuse Higgins and Miss Parker: that had been the beginning of it. He might have tried Higgins for the money, but sure Higgins never had anything for himself. A man with two establishments to keep up, of course he couldn't. . . .

He felt his great body again aching for the comfort of the public-house. The fog had begun to chill him and he wondered could he touch Pat in O'Neill's. He could not touch him for more than a bob—and a bob was no use. Yet he must get money somewhere or other: he had spent his last penny for the g.p. and soon it would be too late for getting money anywhere. Suddenly, as he was fingering his watch-chain, he thought of Terry Kelly's pawn-office in Fleet Street. That was the dart! Why didn't he think of it sooner?

He went through the narrow alley of Temple Bar quickly, muttering to himself that they could all go to hell because he was going to have a good night of it. The clerk in Terry Kelly's said A crown! but the consignor held out for six shillings; and in the end the six shillings was allowed him literally. He came out of the pawn-office joyfully, making a little cylinder of the coins between his thumb and fingers. In Westmoreland Street the footpaths were crowded with young men and women returning from business and ragged urchins ran here and there yelling out the names of the evening editions. The man passed through the crowd, looking on the spectacle generally with proud satisfaction and staring masterfully at the office-girls. His head was full of the noises of tram-gongs and swishing trolleys and his nose already sniffed the curling fumes of punch. As he walked on he preconsidered the terms in which he would narrate the incident to the boys:

"So, I just looked at him—coolly, you know, and looked at her. Then I looked back at him again—taking my time, you know. 'I don't think that that's a fair question to put to me,' says I."

Nosey Flynn was sitting up in his usual corner of Davy Byrne's and, when he heard the story, he stood Farrington a half-one, saying it was as smart a thing as ever he heard. Farrington stood a drink in his turn. After a while O'Halloran and Paddy Leonard came in and the story was repeated to them. O'Halloran stood tailors of malt, hot, all round and told the story of the retort he had made to the chief clerk when he was in Callan's of Frownes's Street; but, as the retort was after the manner of the liberal shepherds in the eclogues, he had to admit that it was not as clever as Farrington's retort. At this Farrington told the boys to polish off that and have another.

Just as they were naming their poisons who should come in but Higgins! Of course he had to join in with the others. The men asked him to give his version of it, and he did so with great vivacity for the sight of five small hot whiskies was very exhilarating. Everyone roared laughing when he showed the way in which Mr. Alleyne shook his fist in Farrington's face. Then he imitated Farrington, saying, "And here *was my nabs, as cool as you please,"* while Farrington looked at the company out of his heavy dirty eyes, smiling and at times drawing forth stray drops of liquor from his moustache with the aid of his lower lip.

When that round was over there was a pause. O'Halloran had money but neither of the other two seemed to have any; so the whole party left the shop somewhat regretfully. At the corner of Duke Street Higgins and Nosey Flynn bevelled off to the left while the other three turned back towards the city. Rain was drizzling down on the cold streets and, when they reached the Ballast Office, Farrington suggested the Scotch House. The bar was full of men and loud with the noise of tongues and glasses. The three men pushed past the whining match-sellers at the door and formed a little party at the corner of the counter. They began to exchange stories. Leonard introduced them to a young fellow named Weathers who was performing at the Tivoli as an acrobat and knockabout *artiste*. Farrington stood a drink all round. Weathers said he would take a small Irish and Apollinaris. Farrington, who had definite notions of what was what, asked the boys would they have an Apollinaris too; but the boys told Tim to make theirs hot. The talk became theatrical. O'Halloran stood a round and then Farrington stood another round, Weathers protesting that the hospitality was too Irish. He promised to get them in behind the scenes and introduce them to some nice girls. O'Halloran said that he and Leonard would go, but that Farrington wouldn't go because he was a married man; and Farrington's heavy dirty eyes leered at the company in token that he understood he was being chaffed. Weathers made them all have just one little tincture at his expense and promised to meet them later on at Mulligan's in Poolbeg Street.

When the Scotch House closed they went round to Mulligan's. They went into the parlour at the back and O'Halloran ordered small hot specials all round. They were all beginning to feel mellow. Farrington was just standing another round when Weathers came back. Much to Farrington's relief he drank a glass of bitter this time. Funds were getting low but they had enough to keep them going. Presently two young women with big hats and a young man in a check suit came in and sat at a table close by. Weathers saluted them and told the company that they were out of the Tivoli. Farrington's eyes wandered at every moment in the direction of one of the young women. There was something striking in her appearance. An immense scarf of peacock-blue muslin was wound round her hat and knotted in a great bow under her chin; and she wore bright yellow gloves, reaching to the elbow. Farrington gazed admiringly at the plump arm which she moved very

often and with much grace; and when, after a little time, she answered his gaze he admired still more her large dark brown eyes. The oblique staring expression in them fascinated him. She glanced at him once or twice and, when the party was leaving the room, she brushed against his chair and said *"O, pardon!"* in a London accent. He watched her leave the room in the hope that she would look back at him, but he was disappointed. He cursed his want of money and cursed all the rounds he had stood, particularly all the whiskies and Apollinaris which he had stood to Weathers. If there was one thing that he hated it was a sponge. He was so angry that he lost count of the conversation of his friends.

When Paddy Leonard called him he found that they were talking about feats of strength. Weathers was showing his biceps muscle to the company and boasting so much that the other two had called on Farrington to uphold the national honour. Farrington pulled up his sleeve accordingly and showed his biceps muscle to the company. The two arms were examined and compared and finally it was agreed to have a trial of strength. The table was cleared and the two men rested their elbows on it, clasping hands. When Paddy Leonard said *"Go!"* each was to try to bring down the other's hand on to the table. Farrington looked very serious and determined.

The trial began. After about thirty seconds Weathers brought his opponent's hand slowly down on to the table. Farrington's dark wine-coloured face flushed darker still with anger and humiliation at having been defeated by such a stripling.

"You're not to put the weight of your body behind it. Play fair," he said.

"Who's not playing fair?" said the other.

"Come on again. The two best out of three."

The trial began again. The veins stood out on Farrington's forehead, and the pallor of Weathers' complexion changed to peony. Their hands and arms trembled under the stress. After a long struggle Weathers again brought his opponent's hand slowly on to the table. There was a murmur of applause from the spectators. The curate, who was standing beside the table, nodded his red head towards the victor and said with stupid familiarity:

"Ah! that's the knack!"

"What the hell do you know about it?" said Farrington fiercely, turning on the man. "What do you put in your gab for?"

"Sh, sh!" said O'Halloran, observing the violent expression of Farrington's face. "Pony up, boys. We'll have just one little smahan more and then we'll be off."

A very sullen-faced man stood at the corner of

O'Connell Bridge waiting for the little Sandymount tram to take him home. He was full of smouldering anger and revengefulness. He felt humiliated and discontented; he did not even feel drunk; and he had only twopence in his pocket. He cursed everything. He had done for himself in the office, pawned his watch, spent all his money; and he had not even got drunk. He began to feel thirsty again and he longed to be back again in the hot reeking public-house. He had lost his reputation as a strong man, having been defeated twice by a mere boy. His heart swelled with fury and, when he thought of the woman in the big hat who had brushed against him and said *Pardon!* his fury nearly choked him.

His tram let him down at Shelbourne Road and he steered his great body along in the shadow of the wall of the barracks. He loathed returning to his home. When he went in by the side-door he found the kitchen empty and the kitchen fire nearly out. He bawled upstairs:

"Ada! Ada!"

His wife was a little sharp-faced woman who bullied her husband when he was sober and was bullied by him when he was drunk. They had five children. A little boy came running down the stairs.

"Who is that?" said the man, peering through the darkness.

"Me, pa."

"Who are you? Charlie?"

"No, pa. Tom."

"Where's your mother?"

"She's out at the chapel."

"That's right. . . . Did she think of leaving any dinner for me?"

"Yes, pa. I——"

"Light the lamp. What do you mean by having the place in darkness? Are the other children in bed?"

The man sat down heavily on one of the chairs while the little boy lit the lamp. He began to mimic his son's flat accent, saying half to himself: "*At the chapel. At the chapel, if you please!*" When the lamp was lit he banged his fist on the table and shouted:

"What's for my dinner?"

"I'm going . . . to cook it, pa," said the little boy.

The man jumped up furiously and pointed to the fire.

"On that fire! You let the fire out! By God, I'll teach you to do that again!"

He took a step to the door and seized the walking-stick which was standing behind it.

"I'll teach you to let the fire out!" he said, rolling up his sleeve in order to give his arm free play.

The little boy cried "O, pa!" and ran whimpering round the table, but the man followed him and caught him by the coat. The little boy looked about him wildly but, seeing no way of escape, fell upon his knees.

"Now, you'll let the fire out the next time!" said the man, striking at him vigorously with the stick. "Take that, you little whelp!"

The boy uttered a squeal of pain as the stick cut his thigh. He clasped his hands together in the air and his voice shook with fright.

"O, pa!" he cried. "Don't beat me, pa! And I'll . . . I'll say a *Hail Mary* for you. . . . I'll say a *Hail Mary* for you, pa, if you don't beat me. . . . I'll say a *Hail Mary*. . . ."

DEATH IN THE WOODS

SHERWOOD ANDERSON

SHERWOOD ANDERSON (1876–1941) was born in Camden, Ohio. He had little formal schooling after he was fourteen. He fought in the Spanish-American War, managed a paint factory, ultimately deserted it for writing. Among his books are *Winesburg, Ohio* (1919), *Poor White* (1920), *The Triumph of the Egg* (1921), *A Story Teller's Story* (1924), *Dark Laughter* (1925), and *Memoirs* (1942).

SHE was an old woman and lived on a farm near the town in which I lived. All country and small-town people have seen such old women, but no one

Copyright © 1926 by Eleanor Anderson. Reprinted by permission of Harold Ober Associates Incorporated.

knows much about them. Such an old woman comes into town driving an old worn-out horse or she comes afoot carrying a basket. She may own a few hens and have eggs to sell. She brings them in a basket and takes them to a grocer. There she trades them in. She gets some salt pork and some beans.

Then she gets a pound or two of sugar and some flour.

Afterwards she goes to the butcher's and asks for some dog-meat. She may spend ten or fifteen cents, but when she does she asks for something. Formerly the butchers gave liver to any one who wanted to carry it away. In our family we were always having it. Once one of my brothers got a whole cow's liver at the slaughter-house near the fairgrounds in our town. We had it until we were sick of it. It never cost a cent. I have hated the thought of it ever since.

The old farm woman got some liver and a soup-bone. She never visited with any one, and as soon as she got what she wanted she lit out for home. It made quite a load for such an old body. No one gave her a lift. People drive right down a road and never notice an old woman like that.

There was such an old woman who used to come into town past our house one Summer and Fall when I was a young boy and was sick with what was called inflammatory rheumatism. She went home later carrying a heavy pack on her back. Two or three large gaunt-looking dogs followed at her heels.

The old woman was nothing special. She was one of the nameless ones that hardly any one knows, but she got into my thoughts. I have just suddenly now, after all these years, remembered her and what happened. It is a story. Her name was Grimes, and she lived with her husband and son in a small unpainted house on the bank of a small creek four miles from town.

The husband and son were a tough lot. Although the son was but twenty-one, he had already served a term in jail. It was whispered about that the woman's husband stole horses and ran them off to some other county. Now and then, when a horse turned up missing, the man had also disappeared. No one ever caught him. Once, when I was loafing at Tom Whitehead's livery-barn, the man came there and sat on the bench in front. Two or three other men were there, but no one spoke to him. He sat for a few minutes and then got up and went away. When he was leaving he turned around and stared at the men. There was a look of defiance in his eyes. "Well, I have tried to be friendly. You don't want to talk to me. It has been so wherever I have gone in this town. If, some day, one of your fine horses turns up missing, well, then what?" He did not say anything actually. "I'd like to bust one of you on the jaw," was about what his eyes said. I remember how the look in his eyes made me shiver.

The old man belonged to a family that had had money once. His name was Jake Grimes. It all comes back clearly now. His father, John Grimes, had owned a sawmill when the country was new, and had made money. Then he got to drinking and running after women. When he died there wasn't much left.

Jake blew in the rest. Pretty soon there wasn't any more lumber to cut and his land was nearly all gone.

He got his wife off a German farmer, for whom he went to work one June day in the wheat harvest. She was a young thing then and scared to death. You see, the farmer was up to something with the girl—she was, I think, a bound girl and his wife had her suspicions. She took it out on the girl when the man wasn't around. Then, when the wife had to go off to town for supplies, the farmer got after her. She told young Jake that nothing really ever happened, but he didn't know whether to believe it or not.

He got her pretty easy himself, the first time he was out with her. He wouldn't have married her if the German farmer hadn't tried to tell him where to get off. He got her to go riding with him in his buggy one night when he was threshing on the place, and then he came for her the next Sunday night.

She managed to get out of the house without her employer's seeing, but when she was getting into the buggy he showed up. It was almost dark, and he just popped up suddenly at the horse's head. He grabbed the horse by the bridle and Jack got out his buggy-whip.

They had it out all right! The German was a tough one. Maybe he didn't care whether his wife knew or not. Jake hit him over the face and shoulders with the buggy-whip, but the horse got to acting up and he had to get out.

Then the two men went for it. The girl didn't see it. The horse started to run away and went nearly a mile down the road before the girl got him stopped. Then she managed to tie him to a tree beside the road. (I wonder how I know all this. It must have stuck in my mind from small-town tales when I was a boy.) Jake found her there after he got through with the German. She was huddled up in the buggy seat, crying, scared to death. She told Jake a lot of stuff, how the German had tried to get her, how he chased her once into the barn, how another time, when they happened to be alone in the house together, he tore her dress open clear down the front. The German, she said, might have got her that time if he hadn't heard his old woman drive in at the gate. She had been off to town for supplies. Well, she would be putting the horse in the barn. The German managed to sneak off to the fields without his wife seeing. He told the girl he would kill her if she told. What could she do? She told a lie about ripping her dress in the barn when she was feeding the stock. I remember now that she was a bound girl and did not know where her father and mother were. Maybe she did not have any father. You know what I mean.

Such bound children were often enough cruelly treated. They were children who had no parents, slaves really. There were very few orphan homes then. They were legally bound into some home. It was a matter of pure luck how it came out.

II

She married Jake and had a son and daughter, but the daughter died.

Then she settled down to feed stock. That was her job. At the German's place she had cooked the food for the German and his wife. The wife was a strong woman with big hips and worked most of the time in the fields with her husband. She fed them and fed the cows in the barn, fed the pigs, the horses and the chickens. Every moment of every day, as a young girl, was spent feeding something.

Then she married Jake Grimes and he had to be fed. She was a slight thing, and when she had been married for three or four years, and after the two children were born, her slender shoulders became stooped.

Jake always had a lot of big dogs around the house, that stood near the unused sawmill near the creek. He was always trading horses when he wasn't stealing something and had a lot of poor bony ones about. Also he kept three or four pigs and a cow. They were all pastured in the few acres left of the Grimes place and Jake did little enough work.

He went into debt for a threshing outfit and ran it for several years, but it did not pay. People did not trust him. They were afraid he would steal the grain at night. He had to go a long way off to get work and it cost too much to get there. In the Winter he hunted and cut a little firewood, to be sold in some nearby town. When the son grew up he was just like the father. They got drunk together. If there wasn't anything to eat in the house when they came home the old man gave his old woman a cut over the head. She had a few chickens of her own and had to kill one of them in a hurry. When they were all killed she wouldn't have any eggs to sell when she went to town, and then what would she do?

She had to scheme all her life about getting things fed, getting the pigs fed so they would grow fat and could be butchered in the Fall. When they were butchered her husband took most of the meat off to town and sold it. If he did not do it first the boy did. They fought sometimes and when they fought the old woman stood aside trembling.

She had got the habit of silence anyway—that was fixed. Sometimes, when she began to look old—she wasn't forty yet—and when the husband and son were both off, trading horses or drinking or hunting or stealing, she went around the house and the barnyard muttering to herself.

How was she going to get everything fed?—that was her problem. The dogs had to be fed. There wasn't enough hay in the barn for the horses and the cow. If she didn't feed the chickens how could they lay eggs? Without eggs to sell how could she get things in town, things she had to have to keep the life of the farm going? Thank heaven, she did not have to feed her husband—in a certain way. That hadn't lasted long after their marriage and after the babies came. Where he went on his long trips she did not know. Sometimes he was gone from home for weeks, and after the boy grew up they went off together.

They left everything at home for her to manage and she had no money. She knew no one. No one ever talked to her in town. When it was Winter she had to gather sticks of wood for her fire, had to try to keep the stock fed with very little grain.

The stock in the barn cried to her hungrily, the dogs followed her about. In the Winter the hens laid few enough eggs. They huddled in the corners of the barn and she kept watching them. If a hen lays an egg in the barn in the Winter and you do not find it, it freezes and breaks.

One day in Winter the old woman went off to town with a few eggs and the dogs followed her. She did not get started until nearly three o'clock and the snow was heavy. She hadn't been feeling very well for several days and so she went muttering along, scantily clad, her shoulders stooped. She had an old grain bag in which she carried her eggs, tucked away down in the bottom. There weren't many of them, but in Winter the price of eggs is up. She would get a little meat in exchange for the eggs, some salt pork, a little sugar, and some coffee perhaps. It might be the butcher would give her a piece of liver.

When she had got to town and was trading in her eggs the dogs lay by the door outside. She did pretty well, got the things she needed, more than she had hoped. Then she went to the butcher and he gave her some liver and some dog-meat.

It was the first time any one had spoken to her in a friendly way for a long time. The butcher was alone in his shop when she came in and was annoyed by the thought of such a sick-looking old woman out on such a day. It was bitter cold and the snow, that had let up during the afternoon, was falling again. The butcher said something about her husband and her son, swore at them, and the old woman stared at him, a look of mild surprise in her eyes as he talked. He said that if either the husband or the son were going to get any of the liver or the heavy bones with scraps of meat hanging to them that he had put into the grain bag, he'd see him starve first.

Starve, eh? Well, things had to be fed. Men had to

be fed, and the horses that weren't any good but maybe could be traded off, and the poor thin cow that hadn't given any milk for three months.

Horses, cows, pigs, dogs, men.

III

The old woman had to get back before darkness came if she could. The dogs followed at her heels, sniffing at the heavy grain bag she had fastened on her back. When she got to the edge of town she stopped by a fence and tied the bag on her back with a piece of rope she had carried in her dress-pocket for just that purpose. It was hard when she had to crawl over fences and once she fell over and landed in the snow. The dogs went frisking about. She had to struggle to get to her feet again, but she made it. The point of climbing over the fences was that there was a short cut over a hill and through a woods. She might have gone around by the road, but it was a mile farther that way. She was afraid she couldn't make it. And then, besides, the stock had to be fed. There was a little hay left and a little corn. Perhaps her husband and son would bring some home when they came. They had driven off in the only buggy the Grimes family had, a rickety thing, a rickety horse hitched to the buggy, two other rickety horses led by halters. They were going to trade horses, get a little money if they could. They might come home drunk. It would be well to have something in the house when they came back.

The son had an affair on with a woman at the county seat, fifteen miles away. She was a rough enough woman, a tough one. Once, in the Summer, the son had brought her to the house. Both she and the son had been drinking. Jake Grimes was away and the son and his woman ordered the old woman about like a servant. She didn't mind much; she was used to it. Whatever happened she never said anything. That was her way of getting along. She had managed that way when she was a young girl at the German's and ever since she had married Jake. That time her son brought his woman to the house they stayed all night, sleeping together just as though they were married. It hadn't shocked the old woman, not much. She had got past being shocked early in life.

With the pack on her back she went painfully along across an open field, wading in the deep snow, and got into the woods.

There was a path, but it was hard to follow. Just beyond the top of the hill, where the woods was thickest, there was a small clearing. Had some one once thought of building a house there? The clearing was as large as a building lot in town, large enough for a house and a garden. The path ran along the side of the clearing, and when she got there the old woman sat down to rest at the foot of a tree.

It was a foolish thing to do. When she got herself placed, the pack against the tree's trunk, it was nice, but what about getting up again? She worried about that for a moment and then quietly closed her eyes.

She must have slept for a time. When you are about so cold you can't get any colder. The afternoon grew a little warmer and the snow came thicker than ever. Then after a time the weather cleared. The moon even came out.

There were four Grimes dogs that had followed Mrs. Grimes into town, all tall gaunt fellows. Such men as Jake Grimes and his son always keep just such dogs. They kick and abuse them, but they stay. The Grimes dogs, in order to keep from starving, had to do a lot of foraging for themselves, and they had been at it while the old woman slept with her back to the tree at the side of the clearing. They had been chasing rabbits in the woods and in adjoining fields and in their ranging had picked up three other farm dogs.

After a time all the dogs came back to the clearing. They were excited about something. Such nights, cold and clear and with a moon, do things to dogs. It may be that some old instinct, come down from the time when they were wolves and ranged the woods in packs on Winter nights, comes back into them.

The dogs in the clearing, before the old woman, had caught two or three rabbits and their immediate hunger had been satisfied. They began to play, running in circles in the clearing. Round and round they ran, each dog's nose at the tail of the next dog. In the clearing, under the snow-laden trees and under the wintry moon they made a strange picture, running thus silently, in a circle their running had beaten in the soft snow. The dogs made no sound. They ran around and around in the circle.

It may have been that the old woman saw them doing that before she died. She may have awakened once or twice and looked at the strange sight with dim old eyes.

She wouldn't be very cold now, just drowsy. Life hangs on a long time. Perhaps the old woman was out of her head. She may have dreamed of her girl-hood at the German's, and before that, when she was a child and before her mother lit out and left her.

Her dreams couldn't have been very pleasant. Not many pleasant things had happened to her. Now and then one of the Grimes dogs left the running circle and came to stand before her. The dog thrust his face to her face. His red tongue was hanging out.

The running of the dogs may have been a kind of death ceremony. It may have been that the primitive instinct of the wolf, having been aroused in the dogs by the night and the running, made them somehow, afraid.

"Now we are no longer wolves. We are dogs, the servants of men. Keep alive, man! When man dies we become wolves again."

When one of the dogs came to where the old woman sat with her back against the tree and thrust his nose close to her face he seemed satisfied and went back to run with the pack. All the Grimes dogs did it at some time during the evening, before she died. I knew all about it afterward, when I grew to be a man, because once in a woods in Illinois, on another Winter night, I saw a pack of dogs act just like that. The dogs were waiting for me to die as they had waited for the old woman that night when I was a child, but when it happened to me I was a young man and had no intention whatever of dying.

The old woman died softly and quietly. When she was dead and when one of the Grimes dogs had come to her and had found her dead all the dogs stopped running.

They gathered about her.

Well, she was dead now. She had fed the Grimes dogs when she was alive, what about now?

There was the pack on her back, the grain bag containing the piece of salt pork, the liver the butcher had given her, the dog-meat, the soup bones. The butcher in town, having been suddenly overcome with a feeling of pity, had loaded her grain bag heavily. It had been a big haul for the old woman.

It was a big haul for the dogs now.

IV

One of the Grimes dogs sprang suddenly out from among the others and began worrying the pack on the old woman's back. Had the dogs really been wolves that one would have been the leader of the pack. What he did, all the others did.

All of them sank their teeth into the grain bag the old woman had fastened with ropes to her back.

They dragged the old woman's body out into the open clearing. The worn-out dress was quickly torn from her shoulders. When she was found, a day or two later, the dress had been torn from her body clear to the hips, but the dogs had not touched her body. They had got the meat out of the grain bag, that was all. Her body was frozen stiff when it was found, and the shoulders were so narrow and the body so slight that in death it looked like the body of some charming young girl.

Such things happened in towns of the Middle West, on farms near town, when I was a boy. A hunter out after rabbits found the old woman's body

and did not touch it. Something, the beaten round path in the little snow-covered clearing, the silence of the place, the place where the dogs had worried the body trying to pull the grain bag away or tear it open—something startled the man and he hurried off to town.

I was in Main Street with one of my brothers who was town newsboy and who was taking the afternoon papers to the stores. It was almost night.

The hunter came into a grocery and told his story. Then he went into a hardware-shop and into a drugstore. Men began to gather on the sidewalks. Then they started out along the road to the place in the woods.

My brother should have gone on about his business of distributing papers but he didn't. Every one was going to the woods. The undertaker went and the town marshal. Several men got on a dray and rode out to where the path left the road and went into the woods, but the horses weren't very sharply shod and slid about on the slippery roads. They made no better time than those of us who walked.

The town marshal was a large man whose leg had been injured in the Civil War. He carried a heavy cane and limped rapidly along the road. My brother and I followed at his heels, and as we went other men and boys joined the crowd.

It had grown dark by the time we got to where the old woman had left the road but the moon had come out. The marshal was thinking there might have been a murder. He kept asking the hunter questions. The hunter went along with his gun across his shoulders, a dog following at his heels. It isn't often a rabbit hunter has a chance to be so conspicuous. He was taking full advantage of it, leading the procession with the town marshal. "I didn't see any wounds. She was a beautiful young girl. Her face was buried in the snow. No, I didn't know her." As a matter of fact, the hunter had not looked closely at the body. He had been frightened. She might have been murdered and some one might spring out from behind a tree and murder him. In a woods, in the late afternoon, when the trees are all bare and there is white snow on the ground, when all is silent, something creepy steals over the mind and body. If something strange or uncanny has happened in the neighborhood all you think about is getting away from there as fast as you can.

The crowd of men and boys had got to where the old woman had crossed the field and went, following the marshal and the hunter, up the slight incline and into the woods.

My brother and I were silent. He had his bundle of papers in a bag slung across his shoulder. When he got back to town he would have to go on distributing his papers before he went home to supper. If I went along, as he had no doubt already determined I should, we would both be late. Either mother or our older sister would have to warm our supper.

Well, we would have something to tell. A boy did not get such a chance very often. It was lucky we just happened to go into the grocery when the hunter came in. The hunter was a country fellow. Neither of us had ever seen him before.

Now the crowd of men and boys had got to the clearing. Darkness comes quickly on such Winter nights, but the full moon made everything clear. My brother and I stood near the tree, beneath which the old woman had died.

She did not look old, lying there in that light, frozen and still. One of the men turned her over in the snow and I saw everything. My body trembled with some strange mystical feeling and so did my brother's. It might have been the cold.

Neither of us had ever seen a woman's body before. It may have been the snow, clinging to the frozen flesh, that made it look so white and lovely, so like marble. No woman had come with the party from town; but one of the men, he was the town blacksmith, took off his overcoat and spread it over her. Then he gathered her into his arms and started off to town, all the others following silently. At that time no one knew who she was.

V

I had seen everything, had seen the oval in the snow, like a miniature race-track, where the dogs had run, had seen how the men were mystified, had seen the white bare young-looking shoulders, had heard the whispered comments of the men.

The men were simply mystified. They took the body to the undertaker's, and when the blacksmith, the hunter, the marshal and several others had got inside they closed the door. If father had been there perhaps he could have got in, but we boys couldn't.

I went with my brother to distribute the rest of his papers and when we got home it was my brother who told the story.

I kept silent and went to bed early. It may have been I was not satisfied with the way he told it.

Later, in the town, I must have heard other fragments of the old woman's story. She was recognized the next day and there was an investigation.

The husband and son were found somewhere and brought to town and there was an attempt to connect them with the woman's death, but it did not work. They had perfect enough alibis.

However, the town was against them. They had to get out. Where they went I never heard.

I remember only the picture there in the forest, the men standing about, the naked girlish-looking figure, face down in the snow, the tracks made by the running dogs and the clear cold Winter sky above. White fragments of clouds were drifting across the sky. They went racing across the little open space among the trees.

The scene in the forest had become for me, without my knowing it, the foundation for the real story I am now trying to tell. The fragments, you see, had to be picked up slowly, long afterwards.

Things happened. When I was a young man I worked on the farm of a German. The hired-girl was afraid of her employer. The farmer's wife hated her.

I saw things at that place. Once later, I had a half-uncanny, mystical adventure with dogs in an Illinois forest on a clear, moon-lit Winter night. When I was a schoolboy, and on a Summer day, I went with a boy friend out along a creek some miles from town and came to the house where the old woman had lived. No one had lived in the house since her death. The doors were broken from the hinges; the window lights were all broken. As the boy and I stood in the road outside, two dogs, just roving farm dogs no doubt, came running around the corner of the house. The dogs were tall, gaunt fellows and came down to the fence and glared through at us, standing in the road.

The whole thing, the story of the old woman's death, was to me as I grew older like music heard from far off. The notes had to be picked up slowly one at a time. Something had to be understood.

The woman who died was one destined to feed animal life. Anyway, that is all she ever did. She was feeding animal life before she was born, as a child, as a young woman working on the farm of the German, after she married, when she grew old and when she died. She fed animal life in cows, in chickens, in pigs, in horses, in dogs, in men. Her daughter had died in childhood and with her one son she had no articulate relations. On the night when she died she was hurrying homeward, bearing on her body food for animal life.

She died in the clearing in the woods and even after her death continued feeding animal life.

You see it is likely that, when my brother told the story, that night when we got home and my mother and sister sat listening, I did not think he got the point. He was too young and so was I. A thing so complete has its own beauty.

I shall not try to emphasize the point. I am only explaining why I was dissatisfied then and have been ever since. I speak of that only that you may understand why I have been impelled to try to tell the simple story over again.

WHY I LIVE AT THE P.O.

EUDORA WELTY

EUDORA WELTY (1909–   ) was born in Jackson, Mississippi. She has spent most of her life in her native state, and material for much of her writing has been drawn from small-town Mississippi life. Her first short story collection, *A Curtain of Green* (1941), was ac-claimed by critics, and her succeeding books have continued to draw praise. They include *The Golden Apples* (1949), a short story collection; *The Robber Bridegroom* (1942), a novelette; *Delta Wedding* (1946) and *The Ponder Heart* (1954), novels.

I WAS getting along fine with Mama, Papa-Daddy and Uncle Rondo until my sister Stella-Rondo just separated from her husband and came back home again. Mr. Whitaker! Of course I went with Mr. Whitaker first, when he first appeared here in China Grove, taking "Pose Yourself" photos, and Stella-Rondo broke us up. Told him I was one-sided. Bigger on one side than the other, which is a de-liberate, calculated falsehood: I'm the same. Stella-Rondo is exactly twelve months to the day younger than I am and for that reason she's spoiled.

She's always had anything in the world she wanted and then she'd throw it away. Papa-Daddy gave her this gorgeous Add-a-Pearl necklace when she was eight years old and she threw it away play-ing baseball when she was nine, with only two pearls.

So as soon as she got married and moved away from home the first thing she did was separate! From Mr. Whitaker! This photographer with the popeyes she said she trusted. Came home from one of those towns up in Illinois and to our complete surprise brought this child of two.

Mama said she'd like to make her drop dead for a second. "Here you had this marvelous blonde child and never so much as wrote your mother a word about it," says Mama. "I'm thoroughly ashamed of you." But of course she wasn't.

Stella-Rondo just calmly takes off this *hat,* I wish you could see it. She says, "Why, Mama, Shirley-T.'s adopted, I can prove it."

"How?" says Mama, but all I says was, "H'm!" There I was over the hot stove, trying to stretch two chickens over five people and a completely unex-pected child into the bargain, without one moment's notice.

Copyright, 1941, by Eudora Welty. Reprinted from her volume, *A Curtain of Green and Other Stories*, by permission of Harcourt, Brace & World, Inc.

"What do you mean—'H'm!'?" says Stella-Rondo, and Mama says, "I heard that, Sister."

I said that oh, I didn't mean a thing, only that whoever Shirley-T. was, she was the spit-image of Papa-Daddy if he'd cut off his beard, which of course he'd never do in the world. Papa-Daddy's Mama's papa and sulks.

Stella-Rondo got furious! She said, "Sister, I don't need to tell you you got a lot of nerve and always did have and I'll thank you to make no future refer-ence to my adopted child whatsoever!"

"Very well," I said. "Very well, very well. Of course I noticed at once she looks like Mr. Whitaker's side too. That frown. She looks like a cross between Mr. Whitaker and Papa-Daddy."

"Well, all I can say is she isn't."

"She looks exactly like Shirley Temple to me," says Mama, but Shirley-T. just ran away from her.

So the first thing Stella-Rondo did at the table was turn Papa-Daddy against me.

"Papa-Daddy," she says. He was trying to cut up his meat. "Papa-Daddy!" I was taken completely by surprise. Papa-Daddy is about a million years old and's got this long-long beard. "Papa-Daddy, Sister says she fails to understand why you don't cut off your beard."

So Papa-Daddy l-a-y-s down his knife and fork! He's real rich. Mama says he is, he says he isn't. So he says, "Have I heard correctly? You don't under-stand why I don't cut off my beard?"

"Why," I says, "Papa-Daddy, of course I under-stand. I did not say any such of a thing, the idea!"

He says, "Hussy!"

I says, "Papa-Daddy, you know I wouldn't any more want you to cut off your beard than the man in the moon. It was the farthest thing from my mind! Stella-Rondo sat there and made that up while she was eating breast of chicken."

But he says, "So the postmistress fails to under-stand why I don't cut off my beard. Which job I got you through my influence with the government. 'Bird's nest'—is that what you call it?"

Not that it isn't the next to smallest P.O. in the entire state of Mississippi.

I says, "Oh, Papa-Daddy," I says, "I didn't say any such of a thing. I never dreamed it was a bird's nest, I have always been grateful though this is the next to smallest P.O. in the state of Mississippi, and I do not enjoy being referred to as a hussy by my own grandfather."

But Stella-Rondo says, "Yes, you did say it too. Anybody in the world could of heard you, that had ears."

"Stop right there," says Mama, looking at *me*.

So I pulled my napkin straight back through the napkin ring and left the table.

As soon as I was out of the room Mama says, "Call her back, or she'll starve to death," but Papa-Daddy says, "This is the beard I started growing on the Coast when I was fifteen years old." He would of gone on till nightfall if Shirley-T. hadn't lost the Milky Way she ate in Cairo.

So Papa-Daddy says, "I am going out and lie in the hammock, and you can all sit here and remember my words: I'll never cut off my beard as long as I live, even one inch, and I don't appreciate it in you at all." Passed right by me in the hall and went straight out and got in the hammock.

It would be a holiday. It wasn't five minutes before Uncle Rondo suddenly appeared in the hall in one of Stella-Rondo's flesh-colored kimonos, all cut on the bias, like something Mr. Whitaker probably thought was gorgeous.

"Uncle Rondo!" I says. "I didn't know who that was! Where are you going?"

"Sister," he says, "get out of my way, I'm poisoned."

"If you're poisoned stay away from Papa-Daddy," I says. "Keep out of the hammock. Papa-Daddy will certainly beat you on the head if you come within forty miles of him. He thinks I deliberately said he ought to cut off his beard after he got me the P.O., and I've told him and told him and told him, and he acts like he just don't hear me. Papa-Daddy must of gone stone deaf."

"He picked a fine day to do it then," says Uncle Rondo, and before you could say "Jack Robinson" flew out in the yard.

What he'd really done, he'd drunk another bottle of that prescription. He does it every single Fourth of July as sure as shooting, and it's horribly expensive. Then he falls over in the hammock and snores. So he insisted on zigzagging right on out to the hammock, looking like a half-wit.

Papa-Daddy woke up with this horrible yell and

right there without moving an inch he tried to turn Uncle Rondo against me. I heard every word he said. Oh, he told Uncle Rondo I didn't learn to read till I was eight years old and he didn't see how in the world I ever got the mail put up at the P.O., much less read it all, and he said if Uncle Rondo could only fathom the lengths he had gone to to get me that job! And he said on the other hand he thought Stella-Rondo had a brilliant mind and deserved credit for getting out of town. All the time he was just lying there swinging as pretty as you please and looping out his beard, and poor Uncle Rondo was *pleading* with him to slow down the hammock, it was making him as dizzy as a witch to watch it. But that's what Papa-Daddy likes about a hammock. So Uncle Rondo was too dizzy to get turned against me for the time being. He's Mama's only brother and is a good case of a one-track mind. Ask anybody. A certified pharmacist.

Just then I heard Stella-Rondo raising the upstairs window. While she was married she got this peculiar idea that it's cooler with the window shut and locked. So she has to raise the window before she can make a soul hear her outdoors.

So she raises the window and says, *"Oh!"* You would have thought she was mortally wounded.

Uncle Rondo and Papa-Daddy didn't even look up, but kept right on with what they were doing. I had to laugh.

I flew up the stairs and threw the door open! I says, "What in the wide world's the matter, Stella-Rondo? You mortally wounded?"

"No," she says, "I am not mortally wounded but I wish you would do me the favor of looking out the window there and telling me what you see."

So I shade my eyes and look out the window.

"I see the front yard," I says.

"Don't you see any human beings?" she says.

"I see Uncle Rondo trying to run Papa-Daddy out of the hammock," I says. "Nothing more. Naturally, it's so suffocating-hot in the house, with all the windows shut and locked, everybody who cares to stay in their right mind will have to go out and get in the hammock before the Fourth of July is over."

"Don't you notice anything different about Uncle Rondo?" asks Stella-Rondo.

"Why, no, except he's got on some terrible-looking flesh-colored contraption I wouldn't be found dead in, is all I can see," I says.

"Never mind, you won't be found dead in it, because it happens to be part of my trousseau, and Mr. Whitaker took several dozen photographs of me in it," says Stella-Rondo. "What on earth could Uncle Rondo *mean* by wearing part of my trousseau out in the broad open daylight without saying so much as 'Kiss my foot,' *knowing* I only got home this morn-

ing after my separation and hung my negligee up
on the bathroom door, just as nervous as I could
be?"

"I'm sure I don't know, and what do you expect
me to do about it?" I says. "Jump out the window?"

"No, I expect nothing of the kind. I simply declare that Uncle Rondo looks like a fool in it, that's
all," she says. "It makes me sick to my stomach."

"Well, he looks as good as he can," I says. "As
good as anybody in reason could." I stood up for
Uncle Rondo, please remember. And I said to Stella-
Rondo, "I think I would do well not to criticize so
freely if I were you and came home with a two-year-
old child I had never said a word about, and no
explanation whatever about my separation."

"I asked you the instant I entered this house not
to refer one more time to my adopted child, and you
gave me your word of honor you would not," was
all Stella-Rondo would say, and started pulling out
every one of her eyebrows with some cheap Kress
tweezers.

So I merely slammed the door behind me and went
down and made some green-tomato pickle. Somebody had to do it. Of course Mama had turned both
the niggers loose; she always said no earthly power
could hold one anyway on the Fourth of July, so she
wouldn't even try. It turned out that Jaypan fell in
the lake and came within a very narrow limit of
drowning.

So Mama trots in. Lifts up the lid and says, "H'm!
Not very good for your Uncle Rondo in his precari-
ous condition, I must say. Or poor little adopted
Shirley-T. Shame on you!"

That made me tired. I says, "Well, Stella-Rondo
had better thank her lucky stars it was her instead
of me came trotting in with that very peculiar-looking
child. Now if it had been me that trotted in from
Illinois and brought a peculiar-looking child of two,
I shudder to think of the reception I'd of got, much
less controlled the diet of an entire family."

"But you must remember, Sister, that you were
never married to Mr. Whitaker in the first place and
didn't go up to Illinois to live," says Mama, shaking
a spoon in my face. "If you had I would of been just
as overjoyed to see you and your little adopted girl
as I was to see Stella-Rondo, when you wound up
with your separation and came on back home."

"You would not," I says.

"Don't contradict me, I would," says Mama.

But I said she couldn't convince me though she
talked till she was blue in the face. Then I said,
"Besides, you know as well as I do that that child
is not adopted."

"She most certainly is adopted," says Mama, stiff
as a poker.

I says, "Why, Mama, Stella-Rondo had her just as

sure as anything in this world, and just too stuck up
to admit it."

"Why, Sister," said Mama. "Here I thought we
were going to have a pleasant Fourth of July, and
you start right out not believing a word your own
baby sister tells you!"

"Just like Cousin Annie Flo. Went to her grave
denying the facts of life," I remind Mama.

"I told you if you ever mentioned Auntie Flo's
name I'd slap your face," says Mama, and slaps my
face.

"All right, you wait and see," I says.

"I," says Mama, "I prefer to take my children's
word for anything when it's humanly possible." You
ought to see Mama, she weighs two hundred pounds
and has real tiny feet.

Just then something perfectly horrible occurred
to me.

"Mama," I says, "can that child talk?" I simply
had to whisper! "Mama, I wonder if that child can
be—you know—in any way? Do you realize," I says,
"that she hasn't spoken one single, solitary word to a
human being up to the minute? This is the way she
looks," I says, and I looked like this.

Well, Mama and I just stood there and stared at
each other. It was horrible!

"I remember well that Joe Whitaker frequently
drank like a fish," says Mama. "I believed to my soul
he drank *chemicals*." And without another word she
marches to the foot of the stairs and calls Stella-
Rondo.

"Stella-Rondo? O-o-o-o-o! Stella-Rondo!"

"What?" says Stella-Rondo from upstairs. Not even
the grace to get up off the bed.

"Can that child of yours talk?" asks Mama.

Stella-Rondo says, "Can she what?"

"Talk! Talk!" says Mama. "Burdyburdyburdy-
burdy!"

So Stella-Rondo yells back, "Who says she can't
talk?"

"Sister says so," says Mama.

"You didn't have to tell me, I know whose word of
honor don't mean a thing in this house," says Stella-
Rondo.

And in a minute the loudest Yankee voice I ever
heard in my life yells out, "OE'm Pop-OE the
Sailor-r-r-r Ma-a-n!" and then somebody jumps up
and down in the upstairs hall. In another second the
house would of fallen down.

"Not only talks, she can tap-dance!" calls Stella-
Rondo. "Which is more than some people I won't
name can do."

"Why, the little precious darling thing!" Mama
says, so surprised. "Just as smart as she can be!"
Starts talking baby talk right there. Then she turns
on me. "Sister, you ought to be thoroughly ashamed!

Run upstairs this instant and apologize to Stella-Rondo and Shirley-T."

"Apologize for what?" I says. "I merely wondered if the child was normal, that's all. Now that she's proved she is, why, I have nothing further to say."

But Mama just turned on her heel and flew out, furious. She ran right upstairs and hugged the baby. She believed it was adopted. Stella-Rondo hadn't done a thing but turn her against me from upstairs while I stood there helpless over the hot stove. So that made Mama, Papa-Daddy and the baby all on Stella-Rondo's side.

Next, Uncle Rondo.

I must say that Uncle Rondo had been marvelous to me at various times in the past and I was completely unprepared to be made to jump out of my skin, the way it turned out. Once Stella-Rondo did something perfectly horrible to him—broke a chain letter from Flanders Field—and he took the radio back he had given her and gave it to me. Stella-Rondo was furious! For six months we all had to call her Stella instead of Stella-Rondo, or she wouldn't answer. I always thought Uncle Rondo had all the brains of the entire family. Another time he sent me to Mammoth Cave, with all expenses paid.

But this would be the day he was drinking that prescription, the Fourth of July.

So at supper Stella-Rondo speaks up and says she thinks Uncle Rondo ought to try to eat a little something. So finally Uncle Rondo said he would try a little cold biscuits and ketchup, but that was all. So *she* brought it to him.

"Do you think it wise to disport with ketchup in Stella-Rondo's flesh-colored kimono?" I says. Trying to be considerate! If Stella-Rondo couldn't watch out for her trousseau, somebody had to.

"Any objections?" asks Uncle Rondo, just about to pour out all the ketchup.

"Don't mind what she says, Uncle Rondo," says Stella-Rondo. "Sister has been devoting this solid afternoon to sneering out my bedroom window at the way you look."

"What's that?" says Uncle Rondo. Uncle Rondo has got the most terrible temper in the world. Anything is liable to make him tear the house down if it comes at the wrong time.

So Stella-Rondo says, "Sister says, 'Uncle Rondo certainly does look like a fool in that pink kimono!' "

Do you remember who it was really said that?

Uncle Rondo spills out all the ketchup and jumps out of his chair and tears off the kimono and throws it down on the dirty floor and puts his foot on it. It had to be sent all the way to Jackson to the cleaners and re-pleated.

"So that's your opinion of your Uncle Rondo, is it?" he says. "I look like a fool, do I? Well, that's the last straw. A whole day in this house with nothing to do, and then to hear you come out with a remark like that behind my back!"

"I didn't say any such of a thing, Uncle Rondo," I says, "and I'm not saying who did, either. Why, I think you look all right. Just try to take care of yourself and not talk and eat at the same time," I says. "I think you better go lie down."

"Lie down my foot," says Uncle Rondo. I ought to of known by that he was fixing to do something perfectly horrible.

So he didn't do anything that night in the precarious state he was in—just played Casino with Mama and Stella-Rondo, and Shirley-T. and gave Shirley-T. a nickel with a head on both sides. It tickled her nearly to death, and she called him "Papa." But at 6:30 A.M. the next morning, he threw a whole five-cent package of some unused one-inch firecrackers from the store as hard as he could into my bedroom and they every one went off. Not one bad one in the string. Anybody else, there'd be one that wouldn't go off.

Well, I'm just terribly susceptible to noise of any kind, the doctor has always told me I was the most sensitive person he had ever seen in his whole life, and I was simply prostrated. I couldn't eat! People tell me they heard it as far as the cemetery, and old Aunt Jep Patterson, that had been holding her own so good, thought it was Judgment Day and she was going to meet her whole family. It's usually so quiet here.

And I'll tell you it didn't take me any longer than a minute to make up my mind what to do. There I was with the whole entire house on Stella-Rondo's side and turned against me. If I have anything at all I have pride.

So I just decided I'd go straight down to the P.O. There's plenty of room there in the back, I says to myself.

Well! I made no bones about letting the family catch on to what I was up to. I didn't try to conceal it.

The first thing they knew, I marched in where they were all playing Old Maid and pulled the electric oscillating fan out by the plug, and everything got real hot. Next I snatched the pillow I'd done the needlepoint on right off the davenport from behind Papa-Daddy. He went "Ugh!" I beat Stella-Rondo up the stairs and finally found my charm bracelet in her bureau drawer under a picture of Nelson Eddy.

"So that's the way the land lies," says Uncle Rondo. There he was, piecing on the ham. "Well, Sister, I'll be glad to donate my army cot if you got any place to set it up, providing you'll leave right this minute and let me get some peace." Uncle Rondo was in France.

"Thank you kindly for the cot and 'peace' is hardly the word I would select if I had to resort to fire-crackers at 6:30 A.M. in a young girl's bedroom," I says back to him. "And as to where I intend to go, you seem to forget my position as postmistress of China Grove, Mississippi," I says, "I've always got the P.O."

Well, that made them all sit up and take notice.

I went out front and started digging up some four-o'clocks to plant around the P.O.

"Ah-ah-ah!" says Mama, raising the window. "Those happen to be my four-o'clocks. Everything planted in that star is mine. I've never known you to make anything grow in your life."

"Very well," I says. "But I take the fern. Even you, Mama, can't stand there and deny that I'm the one watered that fern. And I happen to know where I can send in a box top and get a packet of one thousand mixed seeds, no two the same kind, free."

"Oh, where?" Mama wants to know.

But I says, "Too late. You 'tend to your house, and I'll 'tend to mine. You hear things like that all the time if you know how to listen to the radio. Perfectly marvelous offers. Get anything you want free."

So I hope to tell you I marched in and got that radio, and they could of all bit a nail in two, especially Stella-Rondo, that it used to belong to, and she well knew she couldn't get it back, I'd sue for it like a shot. And I very politely took the sewing-machine motor I helped pay the most on to give Mama for Christmas back in 1929, and a good big calendar, with the first-aid remedies on it. The thermometer and the Hawaiian ukulele certainly were rightfully mine, and I stood on the step-ladder and got all my watermelon-rind preserves and every fruit and vegetable I'd put up, every jar. Then I began to pull the tacks out of the bluebird wall vases on the archway to the dining room.

"Who told you you could have those, Miss Priss?" says Mama, fanning as hard as she could.

"I bought 'em and I'll keep track of 'em," I says. "I'll tack 'em up one on each side the post-office window, and you can see 'em when you come to ask me for your mail, if you're so dead to see 'em."

"Not I! I'll never darken the door to that post office again if I live to be a hundred," Mama says. "Ungrateful child! After all the money we spent on you at the Normal."

"Me either," says Stella-Rondo. "You can just let my mail lie there and *rot,* for all I care. I'll never come and relieve you of a single, solitary piece."

"I should worry," I says. "And who you think's going to sit down and write you all those big fat letters and postcards, by the way? Mr. Whitaker? Just because he was the only man ever dropped down in China Grove and you got him—unfairly—is he going to sit down and write you a lengthy correspondence after you come home giving no rhyme nor reason whatsoever for your separation and no explanation for the presence of that child? I may not have your brilliant mind, but I fail to see it."

So Mama says, "Sister, I've told you a thousand times that Stella-Rondo simply got homesick, and this child is far too big to be hers," and she says, "Now, why don't you all just sit down and play Casino?"

Then Shirley-T. sticks out her tongue at me in this perfectly horrible way. She has no more manners than the man in the moon. I told her she was going to cross her eyes like that some day and they'd stick.

"It's too late to stop me now," I says. "You should have tried that yesterday. I'm going to the P.O. and the only way you can possibly see me is to visit me there."

So Papa-Daddy says, "You'll never catch me setting foot in that post office, even if I should take a notion into my head to write a letter some place." He says, "I won't have you reachin' out of that little old window with a pair of shears and cuttin' off any beard of mine. I'm too smart for you!"

"We all are," says Stella-Rondo.

But I said, "If you're so smart, where's Mr. Whitaker?"

So then Uncle Rondo says, "I'll thank you from now on to stop reading all the orders I get on post-cards and telling everybody in China Grove what you think is the matter with them," but I says, "I draw my own conclusions and will continue in the future to draw them." I says, "If people want to write their inmost secrets on penny postcards, there's nothing in the wide world you can do about it, Uncle Rondo."

"And if you think we'll ever *write* another post-card you're sadly mistaken," says Mama.

"Cutting off your nose to spite your face then," I says. "But if you're all determined to have no more to do with the U. S. mail, think of this: What will Stella-Rondo do now, if she wants to tell Mr. Whitaker to come after her?"

"Wah!" says Stella-Rondo. I knew she'd cry. She had a conniption fit right there in the kitchen.

"It will be interesting to see how long she holds out," I says. "And now—I am leaving."

"Good-bye," says Uncle Rondo.

"Oh, I declare," says Mama, "to think that a family of mine should quarrel on the Fourth of July, or the day after, over Stella-Rondo leaving old Mr. Whitaker and having the sweetest little adopted child! It looks like we'd all be glad!"

"Wah!" says Stella-Rondo, and has a fresh conniption fit.

"*He* left *her*—you mark my words," I says. "That's Mr. Whitaker. I know Mr. Whitaker. After all, I knew him first. I said from the beginning he'd up and leave her. I foretold every single thing that's happened."

"Where did he go?" asks Mama.

"Probably to the North Pole, if he knows what's good for him," I says.

But Stella-Rondo just bawled and wouldn't say another word. She flew to her room and slammed the door.

"Now look what you've gone and done, Sister," says Mama. "You go apologize."

"I haven't got time, I'm leaving," I says.

"Well, what are you waiting around for?" asks Uncle Rondo.

So I just picked up the kitchen clock and started off, without saying "Kiss my foot" or anything, and never did tell Stella-Rondo good-bye.

There was a nigger girl going along on a little wagon, right in front.

"Nigger girl," I says, "come help me haul these things down the hill. I'm going to live in the post office."

Took her nine trips in her express wagon. Uncle Rondo came out on the porch and threw her a nickel.

And that's the last I've laid eyes on any of my family or my family laid eyes on me for five solid days and nights. Stella-Rondo may be telling the most horrible tales in the world about Mr. Whitaker, but I haven't heard them. As I tell everybody, I draw my own conclusions.

But oh, I like it here. It's ideal, as I've been saying. You see, I've got everything cater-cornered, the way I like it. Hear the radio? All the war news. Radio, sewing machine, book ends, ironing board and that great big piano lamp—peace, that's what I like. Butter-bean vines planted all along the front where the strings are.

Of course, there's not much mail. My family are naturally the main people in China Grove, and if they prefer to vanish from the face of the earth, for all the mail they get or the mail they write, why, I'm not going to open my mouth. Some of the folks here in town are taking up for me and some turned against me. I know which is which. There are always people who will quit buying stamps just to get on the right side of Papa-Daddy.

But here I am, and here I'll stay. I want the world to know I'm happy.

And if Stella-Rondo should come to me this minute, on bended knees, and *attempt* to explain the incidents of her life with Mr. Whitaker, I'd simply put my fingers in both my ears and refuse to listen.

THE SHORT HAPPY LIFE
OF FRANCIS MACOMBER

ERNEST HEMINGWAY

ERNEST HEMINGWAY (1899–1961) was born in Oak Park, Illinois, served with a volunteer American ambulance unit in the First World War, and was wounded on the Italian front. After the war he was identified with the literary expatriates on the Continent. During his life he traveled widely. For a time he lived in Key West, Florida, then in Cuba, and finally in Ketchum, Idaho. Among his books are *The Sun Also Rises* (1926), *A Farewell to Arms* (1929), *Death in the Afternoon* (1932), *The Fifth Column and the First Forty-Nine Stories* (1938), *For Whom the Bell Tolls* (1940), and *The Old Man and the Sea* (1952), which was cited specifically when he was awarded the Nobel Prize for Literature in 1954.

I T WAS now lunch time and they were all sitting under the double green fly of the dining tent pretending that nothing had happened.

"Will you have lime juice or lemon squash?" Macomber asked.

"I'll have a gimlet," Robert Wilson told him.

"The Short Happy Life of Francis Macomber" (Copyright 1936 Ernest Hemingway) is reprinted with the permission of Charles Scribner's Sons from *The Short Stories of Ernest Hemingway* by Ernest Hemingway.

"I'll have a gimlet too. I need something," Macomber's wife said.

"I suppose it's the thing to do," Macomber agreed. "Tell him to make three gimlets."

The mess boy had started them already, lifting the bottles out of the canvas cooling bags that sweated wet in the wind that blew through the trees that shaded the tents.

"What had I ought to give them?" Macomber asked.

"A quid would be plenty," Wilson told him. "You don't want to spoil them."

"Will the headman distribute it?"

"Absolutely."

Francis Macomber had, half an hour before, been carried to his tent from the edge of the camp in triumph on the arms and shoulders of the cook, the personal boys, the skinner and the porters. The gun-bearers had taken no part in the demonstration. When the native boys put him down at the door of his tent, he had shaken all their hands, received their congratulations, and then gone into the tent and sat on the bed until his wife came in. She did not speak to him when she came in and he left the tent at once to wash his face and hands in the portable wash basin outside and go over to the dining tent to sit in a comfortable canvas chair in the breeze and the shade.

"You've got your lion," Robert Wilson said to him, "and a damned fine one too."

Mrs. Macomber looked at Wilson quickly. She was an extremely handsome and well-kept woman of the beauty and social position which had, five years before, commanded five thousand dollars as the price of endorsing, with photographs, a beauty product which she had never used. She had been married to Francis Macomber for eleven years.

"He is a good lion, isn't he?" Macomber said. His wife looked at him now. She looked at both these men as though she had never seen them before.

One, Wilson, the white hunter, she knew she had never truly seen before. He was about middle height with sandy hair, a stubby mustache, a very red face and extremely cold blue eyes with faint white wrinkles at the corners that grooved merrily when he smiled. He smiled at her now and she looked away from his face at the way his shoulders sloped in the loose tunic he wore with the four big cartridges held in loops where the left breast pocket should have been, at his big brown hands, his old slacks, his very dirty boots and back to his red face again. She noticed where the baked red of his face stopped in a white line that marked the circle left by his Stetson hat that hung now from one of the pegs of the tent pole.

"Well, here's to the lion," Robert Wilson said. He smiled at her again and, not smiling, she looked curiously at her husband.

Francis Macomber was very tall, very well built if you did not mind that length of bone, dark, his hair cropped like an oarsman, rather thin-lipped, and was considered handsome. He was dressed in the same sort of safari clothes that Wilson wore except that his were new, he was thirty-five years old, kept himself very fit, was good at court games, had a number of big-game fishing records, and had just shown himself, very publicly, to be a coward.

"Here's to the lion," he said. "I can't ever thank you for what you did."

Margaret, his wife, looked away from him and back to Wilson.

"Let's not talk about the lion," she said.

Wilson looked over at her without smiling and now she smiled at him.

"It's been a very strange day," she said. "Hadn't you ought to put your hat on even under the canvas at noon? You told me that, you know."

"Might put it on," said Wilson.

"You know you have a very red face, Mr. Wilson," she told him and smiled again.

"Drink," said Wilson.

"I don't think so," she said. "Francis drinks a great deal, but his face is never red."

"It's red today," Macomber tried a joke.

"No," said Margaret. "It's mine that's red today. But Mr. Wilson's is always red."

"Must be racial," said Wilson. "I say, you wouldn't like to drop my beauty as a topic, would you?"

"I've just started on it."

"Let's chuck it," said Wilson.

"Conversation is going to be so difficult," Margaret said.

"Don't be silly, Margot," her husband said.

"No difficulty," Wilson said. "Got a damn fine lion."

Margot looked at them both and they both saw that she was going to cry. Wilson had seen it coming for a long time and he dreaded it. Macomber was past dreading it.

"I wish it hadn't happened. Oh, I wish it hadn't happened," she said and started for her tent. She made no noise of crying but they could see that her shoulders were shaking under the rose-colored, sun-proofed shirt she wore.

"Women upset," said Wilson to the tall man. "Amounts to nothing. Strain on the nerves and one thing'n another."

"No," said Macomber. "I suppose that I rate that for the rest of my life now."

"Nonsense. Let's have a spot of the giant killer," said Wilson. "Forget the whole thing. Nothing to it anyway."

"We might try," said Macomber. "I won't forget what you did for me though."

"Nothing," said Wilson. "All nonsense."

So they sat there in the shade where the camp was pitched under some wide-topped acacia trees with a boulder-strewn cliff behind them, and a stretch of grass that ran to the bank of a boulder-filled stream in front with forest beyond it, and drank their just-cool lime drinks and avoided one another's eyes while the boys set the table for lunch. Wilson could tell that the boys all knew about it now and when he saw Macomber's personal boy looking curiously at his master while he was putting dishes on the table he snapped at him in Swahili. The boy turned away with his face blank.

"What were you telling him?" Macomber asked.

"Nothing. Told him to look alive or I'd see he got about fifteen of the best."

"What's that? Lashes?"

"It's quite illegal," Wilson said. "You're supposed to fine them."

"Do you still have them whipped?"

"Oh, yes. They could raise a row if they chose to complain. But they don't. They prefer it to the fines."

"How strange!" said Macomber.

"Not strange, really," Wilson said. "Which would you rather do? Take a good birching or lose your pay?"

Then he felt embarrassed at asking it and before Macomber could answer he went on, "We all take a beating every day, you know, one way or another."

This was no better. "Good God," he thought. "I am a diplomat, aren't I?"

"Yes, we take a beating," said Macomber, still not looking at him. "I'm awfully sorry about that lion business. It doesn't have to go any further, does it? I mean no one will hear about it, will they?"

"You mean will I tell it at the Mathaiga Club?" Wilson looked at him now coldly. He had not expected this. So he's a bloody four-letter man as well as a bloody coward, he thought. I rather liked him too until today. But how is one to know about an American?

"No," said Wilson. "I'm a professional hunter. We never talk about our clients. You can be quite easy on that. It's supposed to be bad form to ask us not to talk though."

He had decided now that to break would be much easier. He would eat, then, by himself and could read a book with his meals. They would eat by themselves. He would see them through the safari on a very formal basis—what was it the French called it? Distinguished consideration—and it would be a damn sight easier than having to go through this emotional trash. He'd insult him and make a good clean break. Then he could read a book with his meals and he'd still be drinking their whisky. That was the phrase for it when a safari went bad. You ran into another white hunter and you asked, "How is everything going?" and he answered, "Oh, I'm still drinking their whisky," and you knew everything had gone to pot.

"I'm sorry," Macomber said and looked at him

with his American face that would stay adolescent until it became middle-aged, and Wilson noted his crew-cropped hair, fine eyes only faintly shifty, good nose, thin lips and handsome jaw. "I'm sorry I didn't realize that. There are lots of things I don't know."

So what could he do, Wilson thought. He was all ready to break it off quickly and neatly and here the beggar was apologizing after he had just insulted him. He made one more attempt. "Don't worry about me talking," he said. "I have a living to make. You know in Africa no woman ever misses her lion and no white man ever bolts."

"I bolted like a rabbit," Macomber said.

Now what in hell were you going to do about a man who talked like that, Wilson wondered.

Wilson looked at Macomber with his flat, blue, machine-gunner's eyes and the other smiled back at him. He had a pleasant smile if you did not notice how his eyes showed when he was hurt.

"Maybe I can fix it up on buffalo," he said. "We're after them next, aren't we?"

"In the morning if you like," Wilson told him. Perhaps he had been wrong. This was certainly the way to take it. You most certainly could not tell a damned thing about an American. He was all for Macomber again. If you could forget the morning. But, of course, you couldn't. The morning had been about as bad as they come.

"Here comes the Memsahib," he said. She was walking over from her tent looking refreshed and cheerful and quite lovely. She had a very perfect oval face, so perfect that you expected her to be stupid. But she wasn't stupid, Wilson thought, no, not stupid.

"How is the beautiful red-faced Mr. Wilson? Are you feeling better, Francis, my pearl?"

"Oh, much," said Macomber.

"I've dropped the whole thing," she said, sitting down at the table. "What importance is there to whether Francis is any good at killing lions? That's not his trade. That's Mr. Wilson's trade. Mr. Wilson is really very impressive killing anything. You do kill anything, don't you?"

"Oh, anything," said Wilson. "Simply anything." They are, he thought, the hardest in the world; the hardest, the cruelest, the most predatory and the most attractive and their men have softened or gone to pieces nervously as they have hardened. Or is it that they pick men they can handle? They can't know that much at the age they marry, he thought. He was grateful that he had gone through his education on American women before now because this was a very attractive one.

"We're going after buff in the morning," he told her.

"I'm coming," she said.

"No, you're not."

"Oh, yes, I am. Mayn't I, Francis?"

"Why not stay in camp?"

"Not for anything," she said. "I wouldn't miss something like today for anything."

When she left, Wilson was thinking, when she went off to cry, she seemed a hell of a fine woman. She seemed to understand, to realize, to be hurt for him and for herself and to know how things really stood. She is away for twenty minutes and now she is back, simply enamelled in that American female cruelty. They are the damnedest women. Really the damnedest.

"We'll put on another show for you tomorrow," Francis Macomber said.

"You're not coming," Wilson said.

"You're very mistaken," she told him. "And I want *so* to see you perform again. You were lovely this morning. That is if blowing things' heads off is lovely."

"Here's the lunch," said Wilson. "You're very merry, aren't you?"

"Why not? I didn't come out here to be dull."

"Well, it hasn't been dull," Wilson said. He could see the boulders in the river and the high bank beyond with the trees and he remembered the morning.

"Oh, no," she said. "It's been charming. And tomorrow. You don't know how I look forward to tomorrow."

"That's eland he's offering you," Wilson said.

"They're the big cowy things that jump like hares, aren't they?"

"I suppose that describes them," Wilson said.

"It's very good meat," Macomber said.

"Did you shoot it, Francis?" she asked.

"Yes."

"They're not dangerous, are they?"

"Only if they fall on you," Wilson told her.

"I'm so glad."

"Why not let up on the bitchery just a little, Margot," Macomber said, cutting the eland steak and putting some mashed potato, gravy and carrot on the down-turned fork that tined through the piece of meat.

"I suppose I could," she said, "since you put it so prettily."

"Tonight we'll have champagne for the lion," Wilson said. "It's a bit too hot at noon."

"Oh, the lion," Margot said. "I'd forgotten the lion!"

So, Robert Wilson thought to himself, she *is* giving him a ride, isn't she? Or do you suppose that's her idea of putting up a good show? How should a woman act when she discovers her husband is a bloody coward? She's damn cruel but they're all cruel. They govern, of course, and to govern one has to be cruel sometimes. Still, I've seen enough of their damn terrorism.

"Have some more eland," he said to her politely.

That afternoon, late, Wilson and Macomber went out in the motor car with the native driver and the two gun-bearers. Mrs. Macomber stayed in the camp. It was too hot to go out, she said, and she was going with them in the early morning. As they drove off Wilson saw her standing under the big tree, looking pretty rather than beautiful in her faintly rosy khaki, her dark hair drawn back off her forehead and gathered in a knot low on her neck, her face as fresh, he thought, as though she were in England. She waved to them as the car went off through the swale of high grass and curved around through the trees into the small hills of orchard bush.

In the orchard bush they found a herd of impala, and leaving the car they stalked one old ram with long, wide-spread horns and Macomber killed it with a very creditable shot that knocked the buck down at a good two hundred yards and sent the herd off bounding wildly and leaping over one another's back in long, leg-drawn-up leaps as unbelievable and as floating as those one makes sometimes in dreams.

"That was a good shot," Wilson said. "They're a small target."

"Is it a worth-while head?" Macomber asked.

"It's excellent," Wilson told him. "You shoot like that and you'll have no trouble."

"Do you think we'll find buffalo tomorrow?"

"There's a good chance of it. They feed out early in the morning and with luck we may catch them in the open."

"I'd like to clear away that lion business," Macomber said. "It's not very pleasant to have your wife see you do something like that."

I should think it would be even more unpleasant to do it, Wilson thought, wife or no wife, or to talk about it having done it. But he said, "I wouldn't think about that any more. Any one could be upset by his first lion. That's all over."

But that night after dinner and a whisky and soda by the fire before going to bed, as Francis Macomber lay on his cot with the mosquito bar over him and listened to the night noises it was not all over. It was neither all over nor was it beginning. It was there exactly as it happened with some parts of it indelibly emphasized and he was miserably ashamed at it. But more than shame he felt cold, hollow fear in him. The fear was still there like a cold slimy hollow in all the emptiness where once his confidence had been and it made him feel sick. It was still there with him now.

It had started the night before when he had wakened and heard the lion roaring somewhere up along the river. It was a deep sound and at the end there were sort of coughing grunts that made him seem just outside the tent, and when Francis Macomber woke in the night to hear it he was afraid. He could hear his wife breathing quietly, asleep. There was no one to tell he was afraid, nor to be afraid with him, and, lying alone, he did not know the Somali proverb that says a brave man is always frightened three times by a lion; when he first sees his track, when he first hears him roar and when he first confronts him. Then while they were eating breakfast by lantern lights out in the dining tent, before the sun was up, the lion roared again and Francis thought he was just at the edge of camp.

"Sounds like an old-timer," Robert Wilson said, looking up from his kippers and coffee. "Listen to him cough."

"Is he very close?"

"A mile or so up the stream."

"Will we see him?"

"We'll have a look."

"Does his roaring carry that far? It sounds as though he were right in camp."

"Carries a hell of a long way," said Robert Wilson. "It's strange the way it carries. Hope he's a shootable cat. The boys said there was a very big one about here."

"If I get a shot, where should I hit him," Macomber asked, "to stop him?"

"In the shoulders," Wilson said. "In the neck if you can make it. Shoot for bone. Break him down."

"I hope I can place it properly," Macomber said.

"You shoot very well," Wilson told him. "Take your time. Make sure of him. The first one in is the one that counts."

"What range will it be?"

"Can't tell. Lion has something to say about that. Won't shoot unless it's close enough so you can make sure."

"At under a hundred yards?" Macomber asked.

Wilson looked at him quickly.

"Hundred's about right. Might have to take him a bit under. Shouldn't chance a shot at much over that. A hundred's a decent range. You can hit him wherever you want at that. Here comes the Memsahib."

"Good morning," she said. "Are we going after that lion?"

"As soon as you deal with your breakfast," Wilson said. "How are you feeling?"

"Marvellous," she said. "I'm very excited."

"I'll just go and see that everything is ready," Wilson went off. As he left the lion roared again.

"Noisy beggar," Wilson said. "We'll put a stop to that."

"What's the matter, Francis?" his wife asked him.

"Nothing," Macomber said.

"Yes, there is," she said. "What are you upset about?"

"Nothing," he said.

"Tell me," she looked at him. "Don't you feel well?"

"It's that damned roaring," he said. "It's been going on all night, you know."

"Why didn't you wake me," she said. "I'd love to have heard it."

"I've got to kill the damned thing," Macomber said, miserably.

"Well, that's what you're out here for, isn't it?"

"Yes. But I'm nervous. Hearing the thing roar gets on my nerves."

"Well then, as Wilson said, kill him and stop his roaring."

"Yes, darling," said Francis Macomber. "It sounds easy, doesn't it?"

"You're not afraid, are you?"

"Of course not. But I'm nervous from hearing him roar all night."

"You'll kill him marvellously," she said. "I know you will. I'm awfully anxious to see it."

"Finish your breakfast and we'll be starting."

"It's not light yet," she said. "This is a ridiculous hour."

Just then the lion roared in a deep-chested moaning, suddenly guttural, ascending vibration that seemed to shake the air and ended in a sigh and a heavy, deep-chested grunt.

"He sounds almost here," Macomber's wife said.

"My God," said Macomber. "I hate that damned noise."

"It's very impressive."

"Impressive. It's frightful."

Robert Wilson came up then carrying his short, ugly, shockingly big-bored .505 Gibbs and grinning.

"Come on," he said. "Your gun-bearer has your Springfield and the big gun. Everything's in the car. Have your solids?"

"Yes."

"I'm ready," Mrs. Macomber said.

"Must make him stop that racket," Wilson said. "You get in front. The Memsahib can sit back here with me."

They climbed into the motor car and, in the gray first daylight, moved off up the river through the trees. Macomber opened the breech of his rifle and saw he had metal-cased bullets, shut the bolt and put the rifle on safety. He saw his hand was trembling. He felt in his pocket for more cartridges and moved his fingers over the cartridges in the loops of his tunic front. He turned back to where Wilson sat in the rear seat of the doorless, box-bodied motor car beside his wife, them both grinning with excitement, and Wilson leaned forward and whispered.

"See the birds dropping. Means the old boy has left his kill."

On the far bank of the stream Macomber could see, above the trees, vultures circling and plummeting down.

"Chances are he'll come to drink along here," Wilson whispered. "Before he goes to lay up. Keep an eye out."

They were driving slowly along the high bank of the stream which here cut deeply to its boulder-filled bed, and they wound in and out through big trees as they drove. Macomber was watching the opposite bank when he felt Wilson take hold of his arm. The car stopped.

"There he is," he heard the whisper. "Ahead and to the right. Get out and take him. He's a marvellous lion."

Macomber saw the lion now. He was standing almost broadside, his great head up and turned toward them. The early morning breeze that blew toward them was just stirring his dark mane, and the lion looked huge, silhouetted on the rise of bank in the gray morning light, his shoulders heavy, his barrel of a body bulking smoothly.

"How far is he?" asked Macomber, raising his rifle.

"About seventy-five. Get out and take him."

"Why not shoot from where I am?"

"You don't shoot them from cars," he heard Wilson saying in his ear. "Get out. He's not going to stay there all day."

Macomber stepped out of the curved opening at the side of the front seat, onto the step and down onto the ground. The lion still stood looking majestically and cooly toward this object that his eyes only showed in silhouette, bulking like some super-rhino. There was no man smell carried toward him and he watched the object, moving his great head a little from side to side. Then watching the object, not afraid, but hesitating before going down the bank to drink with such a thing opposite him, he saw a man figure detach himself from it and he turned his heavy head and swung away toward the cover of the trees as he heard a cracking crash and felt the slam of a .30—06 220-grain solid bullet that bit his flank and ripped in sudden hot scalding nausea through his stomach. He trotted, heavy, big-footed, swinging wounded full-bellied, through the trees toward the tall grass and cover, and the crash came again to go past him ripping the air apart. Then it crashed again and he left the blow as it hit his lower ribs and ripped on through, blood sudden hot and frothy in his mouth, and he galloped toward the high grass where he could crouch and not be seen and make them bring the crashing thing close enough so he could make a rush and get the man that held it.

Macomber had not thought how the lion felt as he got out of the car. He only knew his hands were shaking and as he walked away from the car it was almost impossible for him to make his legs move. They were stiff in the thighs, but he could feel the muscles fluttering. He raised the rifle, sighted on the junction of the lion's head and shoulders and pulled the trigger. Nothing happened though he pulled until he thought his finger would break. Then he knew he had the safety on and as he lowered the rifle to move the safety over he moved another frozen pace forward, and the lion seeing his silhouette now clear of the silhouette of the car, turned and started off at a trot, and, as Macomber fired, he heard a whunk that meant that the bullet was home; but the lion kept on going. Macomber shot again and every one saw the bullet throw a spout of dirt beyond the trotting lion. He shot again, remembering to lower his aim, and they all heard the bullet hit, and the lion went into a gallop and was in the tall grass before he had the bolt pushed forward.

Macomber stood there feeling sick at his stomach, his hands that held the Springfield still cocked, shaking, and his wife and Robert Wilson were standing by him. Beside him too were the two gun-bearers chattering in Wakamba.

"I hit him," Macomber said. "I hit him twice."

"You gut-shot him and you hit him somewhere forward," Wilson said without enthusiasm. The gunbearers looked very grave. They were silent now.

"You may have killed him," Wilson went on. "We'll have to wait a while before we go in to find out."

"What do you mean?"

"Let him get sick before we follow him up."

"Oh," said Macomber.

"He's a hell of a fine lion," Wilson said cheerfully. "He's gotten into a bad place though."

"Why is it bad?"

"Can't see him until you're on him."

"Oh," said Macomber.

"Come on," said Wilson. "The Memsahib can stay here in the car. We'll go to have a look at the blood spoor."

"Stay here, Margot," Macomber said to his wife. His mouth was very dry and it was hard for him to talk.

"Why?" she asked.

"Wilson says to."

"We're going to have a look," Wilson said. "You stay here. You can see even better from here."

"All right."

Wilson spoke in Swahili to the driver. He nodded and said, "Yes, Bwana."

Then they went down the steep bank and across the stream, climbing over and around the boulders and up the other bank, pulling up by some projecting roots, and along it until they found where the lion had been trotting when Macomber first shot. There was dark blood on the short grass that the gun-bearers pointed out with grass stems, and that ran away behind the river bank trees.

"What do we do?" asked Macomber.

"Not much choice," said Wilson. "We can't bring the car over. Bank's too steep. We'll let him stiffen up a bit and then you and I'll go in and have a look for him."

"Can't we set the grass on fire?" Macomber asked.

"Too green."

"Can't we send beaters?"

Wilson looked at him appraisingly. "Of course we can," he said. "But it's just a touch murderous. You see we know the lion's wounded. You can drive an unwounded lion—he'll move on ahead of a noise—but a wounded lion's going to charge. You can't see him until you're right on him. He'll make himself perfectly flat in cover you wouldn't think would hide a hare. You can't very well send boys in there to that sort of a show. Somebody bound to get mauled."

"What about the gun-bearers?"

"Oh, they'll go with us. It's their *shauri*. You see, they signed on for it. They don't look too happy though, do they?"

"I don't want to go in there," said Macomber. It was out before he knew he'd said it.

"Neither do I," said Wilson very cheerily. "Really no choice though." Then, as an afterthought, he glanced at Macomber and saw suddenly how he was trembling and the pitiful look on his face.

"You don't have to go in, of course," he said. "That's what I'm hired for, you know. That's why I'm so expensive."

"You mean you'd go in by yourself? Why not leave him there?"

Robert Wilson, whose entire occupation had been with the lion and the problem he presented, and who had not been thinking about Macomber except to note that he was rather windy, suddenly felt as though he had opened the wrong door in a hotel and seen something shameful.

"What do you mean?"

"Why not just leave him?"

"You mean pretend to ourselves he hasn't been hit?"

"No. Just drop it."

"It isn't done."

"Why not?"

"For one thing, he's certain to be suffering. For another, some one else might run onto him."

"I see."

"But you don't have to have anything to do with it."

"I'd like to," Macomber said. "I'm just scared, you know."

"I'll go ahead when we go in," Wilson said, "with Kongoni tracking You keep behind me and a little to one side. Chances are we'll hear him growl. If we see him we'll both shoot. Don't worry about anything. I'll keep you backed up. As a matter of fact, you know, perhaps you'd better not go. It might be much better. Why don't you go over and join the Memsahib while I just get it over with?"

"No, I want to go."

"All right," said Wilson. "But don't go in if you don't want to. This is my *shauri* now, you know."

"I want to go," said Macomber.

They sat under a tree and smoked.

"Want to go back and speak to the Memsahib while we're waiting?" Wilson asked.

"No."

"I'll just step back and tell her to be patient."

"Good," said Macomber. He sat there, sweating under his arms, his mouth dry, his stomach hollow feeling, wanting to find courage to tell Wilson to go on and finish off the lion without him. He could not know that Wilson was furious because he had not noticed the state he was in earlier and sent him back to his wife. While he sat there Wilson came up. "I have your big gun," he said. "Take it. We've given him time, I think. Come on."

Macomber took the big gun and Wilson said:

"Keep behind me and about five yards to the right and do exactly as I tell you." Then he spoke in Swahili to the two gun-bearers who looked the picture of gloom.

"Let's go," he said.

"Could I have a drink of water?" Macomber asked. Wilson spoke to the older gun-bearer, who wore a canteen on his belt, and the man unbuckled, unscrewed the top and handed it to Macomber, who took it noticing how heavy it seemed and how hairy and shoddy the felt covering was in his hand. He raised it to drink and looked ahead at the high grass with the flat-topped trees behind it. A breeze was blowing toward them and the grass rippled gently in the wind. He looked at the gun-bearer and he could see the gun-bearer was suffering too with fear.

Thirty-five yards into the grass the big lion lay flattened out along the ground. His ears were back and his only movement was a slight twitching up and down of his long, black-tufted tail. He had turned at bay as soon as he had reached this cover and he was sick with the wound through his full belly, and weakening with the wound through his lungs that brought a thin foamy red to his mouth each time he breathed. His flanks were wet and hot and flies were on the little openings the solid bullets had made in his tawny hide, and his big yellow eyes, narrowed with hate, looked straight ahead, only blinking when the pain came as he breathed, and his claws dug in the soft baked earth. All of him, pain, sickness, hatred and all of his remaining strength, was tightening into an absolute concentration for a rush. He could hear the men talking and he waited, gathering all of himself into this preparation for a charge as soon as the men would come into the grass. As he heard their voices his tail stiffened to twitch up and down, and, as they came into the edge of the grass, he made a coughing grunt and charged.

Kongoni, the old gun-bearer, in the lead watching the blood spoor, Wilson watching the grass for any movement, his big gun ready, the second gun-bearer looking ahead and listening, Macomber close to Wilson, his rifle cocked, they had just moved into the grass when Macomber heard the blood-choked coughing grunt, and saw the swishing rush in the grass. The next thing he knew was running; running wildly, in panic in the open, running toward the stream.

He heard the *ca-ra-wong!* of Wilson's big rifle, and again in a second a crashing *carawong!* and turning saw the lion, horrible-looking now, with half his head seeming to be gone, crawling toward Wilson in the edge of the tall grass while the red-faced man worked the bolt on the short ugly rifle and aimed carefully as another blasting *carawong!* came from the muzzle, and the crawling, heavy, yellow bulk of the lion stiffened and the huge, mutilated head slid forward and Macomber, standing by himself in the clearing where he had run, holding a loaded rifle, while two black men and a white man looked back at him in contempt, knew the lion was dead. He came toward Wilson, his tallness all seeming a naked reproach, and Wilson looked at him and said:

"Want to take pictures?"

"No," he said.

That was all any one had said until they reached the motor car. Then Wilson had said:

"Hell of a fine lion. Boys will skin him out. We might as well stay here in the shade."

Macomber's wife had not looked at him nor he at her and he had sat by her in the back seat with Wilson sitting in the front seat. Once he had reached over and taken his wife's hand without looking at her and she had removed her hand from his. Looking across the stream to where the gun-bearers were skinning out the lion he could see that she had been able to see the whole thing. While they sat there his wife had reached forward and put her hand on Wilson's shoulder. He turned and she had leaned forward over the low seat and kissed him on the mouth.

"Oh, I say," said Wilson, going redder than his natural baked color.

"Mr. Robert Wilson," she said. "The beautiful red-faced Mr. Robert Wilson."

Then she sat down beside Macomber again and looked away across the stream to where the lion lay, with uplifted, white-muscled, tendon-marked naked forearms, and white bloating belly, as the black men fleshed away the skin. Finally the gun-bearers brought the skin over, wet and heavy, and climbed in behind with it, rolling it up before they got in, and the motor car started. No one had said anything more until they were back in camp.

That was the story of the lion. Macomber did not know how the lion had felt before he started his rush, nor during it when the unbelievable smash of the .505 with a muzzle velocity of two tons had hit him in the mouth, nor what kept him coming after that, when the second ripping crash had smashed his hind quarters and he had come crawling on toward the crashing, blasting thing that had destroyed him. Wilson knew something about it and only expressed it by saying, "Damned fine lion," but Macomber did not know how Wilson felt about things either. He did not know how his wife felt except that she was through with him.

His wife had been through with him before but it never lasted. He was very wealthy, and would be much wealthier, and he knew she would not leave him ever now. That was one of the few things that he really knew. He knew about that, about motor cycles —that was earliest—about motor cars, about duck-shooting, about fishing, trout, salmon and big-sea, about sex in books, many books, too many books, about all court games, about dogs, not much about horses, about hanging on to his money, about most of the other things his world dealt in, and about his wife not leaving him. His wife had been a great beauty and she was still a great beauty in Africa, but she was not a great enough beauty any more at home to be able to leave him and better herself and she knew it and he knew it. She had missed the chance to leave him and he knew it. If he had been better with women she would probably have started to worry about him getting another new, beautiful wife; but she knew too much about him to worry about him either. Also, he had always had a great tolerance which seemed the nicest thing about him if it were not the most sinister.

All in all they were known as a comparatively happily married couple, one of those whose disruption is often rumored but never occurs, and as the society columnist put it, they were adding more than a spice of *adventure* to their much envied and ever-enduring *Romance* by a *Safari* in what was known as *Darkest Africa* until the Martin Johnsons lighted it on so many silver screens where they were pursuing *Old Simba* the lion, the buffalo, *Tembo* and the elephant and as well collecting specimens for the Museum of Natural History. This same columnist had reported them *on the verge* at least three times in the past and they had been. But they always made it up. They had a sound basis of union. Margot was too beautiful for Macomber to divorce her and Macomber had too much money for Margot ever to leave him.

It was now about three o'clock in the morning and Francis Macomber, who had been asleep a little while after he had stopped thinking about the lion, wakened and then slept again, woke suddenly, frightened in a dream of the bloody-headed lion standing over him, and listening while his heart pounded, he realized that his wife was not in the other cot in the tent. He lay awake with that knowledge for two hours.

At the end of that time his wife came into the tent, lifted her mosquito bar and crawled cozily into bed.

"Where have you been?" Macomber asked in the darkness.

"Hello," she said. "Are you awake?"

"Where have you been?"

"I just went out to get a breath of air."

"You did, like hell."

"What do you want me to say, darling?"

"Where have you been?"

"Out to get a breath of air."

"That's a new name for it. You *are* a bitch."

"Well, you're a coward."

"All right," he said. "What of it?"

"Nothing as far as I'm concerned. But please let's not talk, darling, because I'm very sleepy."

"You think that I'll take anything."

"I know you will, sweet."

"Well, I won't."

"Please, darling, let's not talk. I'm so very sleepy."

"There wasn't going to be any of that. You promised there wouldn't be."

"Well, there is now," she said sweetly.

"You said if we made this trip that there would be none of that. You promised."

"Yes, darling. That's the way I meant it to be. But the trip was spoiled yesterday. We don't have to talk about it, do we?"

"You don't wait long when you have an advantage, do you?"

"Please let's not talk. I'm so sleepy, darling."

"I'm going to talk."

"Don't mind me then, because I'm going to sleep." And she did.

At breakfast they were all three at the table before daylight and Francis Macomber found that, of all the many men that he had hated, he hated Robert Wilson the most.

"Sleep well?" Wilson asked in his throaty voice, filling a pipe.

"Did you?"

"Topping," the white hunter told him.

You bastard, thought Macomber, you insolent bastard.

So she woke him when she came in, Wilson thought, looking at them both with his flat, cold eyes. Well, why doesn't he keep his wife where she belongs? What does he think I am, a bloody plaster saint? Let him keep her where she belongs. It's his own fault.

"Do you think we'll find buffalo?" Margot asked, pushing away a dish of apricots.

"Chance of it," Wilson said and smiled at her. "Why don't you stay in camp?"

"Not for anything," she told him.

"Why not order her to stay in camp?" Wilson said to Macomber.

"You order her," said Macomber coldly.

"Let's not have any ordering, nor," turning to Macomber, "any silliness, Francis," Margot said quite pleasantly.

"Are you ready to start?" Macomber asked.

"Any time," Wilson told him. "Do you want the Memsahib to go?"

"Does it make any difference whether I do or not?"

The hell with it, thought Robert Wilson. The utter complete hell with it. So this is what it's going to be like. Well, this is what it's going to be like, then.

"Makes no difference," he said.

"You sure you wouldn't like to stay in camp with her yourself and let me go out and hunt the buffalo?" Macomber asked.

"Can't do that," said Wilson. "Wouldn't talk rot if I were you."

"I'm not talking rot. I'm disgusted."

"Bad word, disgusted."

"Francis, will you please try to speak sensibly?" his wife said.

"I speak too damned sensibly," Macomber said. "Did you ever eat such filthy food?"

"Something wrong with the food?" asked Wilson quietly.

"No more than with everything else."

"I'd pull yourself together, laddybuck," Wilson said very quietly. "There's a boy waits at table that understands a little English."

"The hell with him."

Wilson stood up and puffing on his pipe strolled away, speaking a few words in Swahili to one of the gun-bearers who was standing waiting for him. Macomber and his wife sat on at the table. He was staring at his coffee cup.

"If you make a scene I'll leave you, darling," Margot said quietly.

"No, you won't."

"You can try it and see."

"You won't leave me."

"No," she said. "I won't leave you and you'll behave yourself."

"Behave myself? That's a way to talk. Behave myself."

"Yes. Behave yourself."

"Why don't *you* try behaving?"

"I've tried it so long. So very long."

"I hate that red-faced swine," Macomber said. "I loathe the sight of him."

"He's really *very* nice."

"Oh, *shut* up," Macomber almost shouted. Just then the car came up and stopped in front of the dining tent and the driver and the two gun-bearers got out. Wilson walked over and looked at the husband and wife sitting there at the table.

"Going shooting?" he asked.

"Yes," said Macomber, standing up. "Yes."

"Better bring a woolly. It will be cool in the car," Wilson said.

"I'll get my leather jacket," Margot said.

"The boy has it," Wilson told her. He climbed into the front with the driver and Francis Macomber and his wife sat, not speaking, in the back seat.

Hope the silly beggar doesn't take a notion to blow the back of my head off, Wilson thought to himself. Women *are* a nuisance on safari.

The car was grinding down to cross the river at a pebbly ford in the gray daylight and then climbed, angling up the steep bank, where Wilson had ordered a way shovelled out the day before so they could reach the parklike wooded rolling country on the far side.

It was a good morning, Wilson thought. There was a heavy dew and as the wheels went through the grass and low bushes he could smell the odor of the crushed fronds. It was an odor like verbena and he liked this early morning smell of the dew, the crushed bracken and the look of the tree trunks showing black through the early morning mist, as the car made its way through the untracked, parklike country. He had put the two in the back seat out of his mind now and was thinking about buffalo. The buffalo that he was after stayed in the daytime in a thick swamp where it was impossible to get a shot, but in the night they fed out into an open stretch of country and if he could come between them and their swamp with the car, Macomber would have a good chance at them in the open. He did not want to hunt buff with Macomber in thick cover. He did not want to hunt buff or anything else with Macomber at all, but he was a professional hunter and he had hunted with some rare ones in his time. If they got buff today there would only be rhino to come and the poor man would have gone through his dangerous game and things might pick up. He'd have nothing more to do with the woman and Macomber would get over that too. He must have gone through plenty of that before by the look of things. Poor beggar. He must have a way of getting over it. Well, it was the poor sod's own bloody fault.

He, Robert Wilson, carried a double size cot on safari to accommodate any windfalls he might receive. He had hunted for a certain clientele, the international, fast, sporting set, where the women did not feel they were getting their money's worth unless they had shared that cot with the white hunter. He despised them when he was away from them although he liked some of them well enough at the time, but he made his living by them; and their standards were his standards as long as they were hiring him.

They were his standards in all except the shooting. He had his own standards about the killing and they could live up to them or get some one else to hunt them. He knew, too, that they all respected him for this. This Macomber was an odd one though. Damned if he wasn't. Now the wife. Well, the wife. Yes, the wife. Hm, the wife. Well he'd dropped all that. He looked around at them. Macomber sat grim and furious. Margot smiled at him. She looked younger today, more innocent and fresher and not so professionally beautiful. What's in her heart God knows, Wilson thought. She hadn't talked much last night. At that it was a pleasure to see her.

The motor car climbed up a slight rise and went on through the trees and then out into a grassy prairielike opening and kept in the shelter of the trees along the edge, the driver going slowly and Wilson looking carefully out across the prairie and all along its far side. He stopped the car and studied the opening with his field glasses. Then he motioned to the driver to go on and the car moved slowly along, the driver avoiding wart-hog holes and driving around the mud castles ants had built. Then, looking across the opening, Wilson suddenly turned and said,

"By God, there they are!"

And looking where he pointed, while the car

jumped forward and Wilson spoke in rapid Swahili to the driver, Macomber saw three huge, black animals looking almost cylindrical in their long heaviness, like big black tank cars, moving at a gallop across the far edge of the open prairie. They moved at a stiff-necked, stiff-bodied gallop and he could see the up-swept wide black horns on their heads as they galloped heads out; the heads not moving.

"They're three old bulls," Wilson said. "We'll cut them off before they get to the swamp."

The car was going a wild forty-five miles an hour across the open and as Macomber watched, the buffalo got bigger and bigger until he could see the gray, hairless, scabby look of one huge bull and how his neck was a part of his shoulders and the shiny black of his horns as he galloped a little behind the others that were strung out in that steady plunging gait; and then, the car swaying as though it had just jumped a road, they drew up close and he could see the plunging hugeness of the bull, and the dust in his sparsely haired hide, the wide boss of horn and his outstretched, wide-nostrilled muzzle, and he was raising his rifle when Wilson shouted, "Not from the car, you fool!" and he had no fear, only hatred of Wilson, while the brakes clamped on and the car skidded, plowing sideways to an almost stop and Wilson was out on one side and he on the other, stumbling as his feet hit the still speeding-by of the earth, and then he was shooting at the bull as he moved away, hearing the bullets whunk into him, emptying his rifle at him as he moved steadily away, finally remembering to get his shots forward into the shoulder, and as he fumbled to re load, he saw the bull was down. Down on his knees, his big head tossing, and seeing the other two still galloping he shot at the leader and hit him. He shot again and missed and he heard the *carawonging* roar as Wilson shot and saw the leading bull slide forward onto his nose.

"Get that other," Wilson said. "Now you're shooting!"

But the other bull was moving steadily at the same gallop and he missed, throwing a spout of dirt, and Wilson missed and the dust rose in a cloud and Wilson shouted, "Come on. He's too far!" and grabbed his arm and they were in the car again, Macomber and Wilson hanging on the sides and rocketing swayingly over the uneven ground, drawing up on the steady, plunging, heavy-necked, straight-moving gallop of the bull.

They were behind him and Macomber was filling his rifle, dropping shells onto the ground, jamming it, clearing the jam, then they were almost up with the bull when Wilson yelled "Stop," and the car skidded so that it almost swung over and Macomber fell forward onto his feet, slammed his bolt forward and fired as far forward as he could aim into the galloping, rounded black back, aimed and shot again, then again, then again, and the bullets, all of them hitting, had no effect on the buffalo that he could see. Then Wilson shot, the roar deafening him, and he could see the bull stagger. Macomber shot again, aiming carefully, and down he came, onto his knees.

"All right," Wilson said. "Nice work. That's three."

Macomber felt a drunken elation.

"How many times did you shoot?" he asked.

"Just three," Wilson said. "You killed the first bull. The biggest one. I helped you finish the other two. Afraid they might have got into cover. You had them killed. I was just mopping up a little. You shot damn well."

"Let's go to the car," said Macomber. "I want a drink."

"Got to finish off that buff first," Wilson told him. The buffalo was on his knees and he jerked his head furiously and bellowed in pig-eyed, roaring rage as they came toward him.

"Watch he doesn't get up," Wilson said. Then, "Get a little broadside and take him in the neck just behind the ear."

Macomber aimed carefully at the center of the huge, jerking, rage-driven neck and shot. At the shot the head dropped forward.

"That does it," said Wilson. "Got the spine. They're a hell of a looking thing, aren't they?"

"Let's get the drink," said Macomber. In his life he had never felt so good.

In the car Macomber's wife sat very white faced. "You were marvellous, darling," she said to Macomber. "What a ride."

"Was it rough?" Wilson asked.

"It was frightful. I've never been more frightened in my life."

"Let's all have a drink," Macomber said.

"By all means," said Wilson. "Give it to the Memsahib." She drank the neat whisky from the flask and shuddered a little when she swallowed. She handed the flask to Macomber who handed it to Wilson.

"It was frightfully exciting," she said. "It's given me a dreadful headache. I didn't know you were allowed to shoot them from cars though."

"No one shot from cars," said Wilson coldly.

"I mean chase them from cars."

"Wouldn't ordinarily," Wilson said. "Seemed sporting enough to me though while we were doing it. Taking more chance driving that way across the plain full of holes and one thing and another than hunting on foot. Buffalo could have charged us each time we shot if he liked. Gave him every chance. Wouldn't mention it to any one though. It's illegal if that's what you mean."

"It seemed very unfair to me," Margot said, "chasing those big helpless things in a motor car."

"Did it?" said Wilson.

"What would happen if they heard about it in Nairobi?"

"I'd lose my licence for one thing. Other unpleasantnesses," Wilson said, taking a drink from the flask. "I'd be out of business."

"Really?"

"Yes, really."

"Well," said Macomber, and he smiled for the first time all day. "Now she has something on you."

"You have such a pretty way of putting things, Francis," Margot Macomber said. Wilson looked at them both. If a four-letter man marries a five-letter woman, he was thinking, what number of letters would their children be? What he said was, "We lost a gun-bearer. Did you notice it?"

"My God, no," Macomber said.

"Here he comes," Wilson said. "He's all right. He must have fallen off when we left the first bull."

Approaching them was the middle-aged gunbearer, limping along in his knitted cap, khaki tunic, shorts and rubber sandals, gloomy-faced and disgusted looking. As he came up he called out to Wilson in Swahili and they all saw the change in the white hunter's face.

"What does he say?" asked Margot.

"He says the first bull got up and went into the bush," Wilson said with no expression in his voice.

"Oh," said Macomber blankly.

"Then it's going to be just like the lion," said Margot, full of anticipation.

"It's not going to be a damned bit like the lion," Wilson told her. "Did you want another drink, Macomber?"

"Thanks, yes," Macomber said. He expected the feeling he had had about the lion to come back but it did not. For the first time in his life he really felt wholly without fear. Instead of fear he had a feeling of definite elation.

"We'll go and have a look at the second bull," Wilson said. "I'll tell the driver to put the car in the shade."

"What are you going to do?" asked Margaret Macomber.

"Take a look at the buff," Wilson said.

"I'll come."

"Come along."

The three of them walked over to where the second buffalo bulked blackly in the open, head forward on the grass, the massive horns swung wide.

"He's a very good head," Wilson said. "That's close to a fifty-inch spread."

Macomber was looking at him with delight.

"He's hateful looking," said Margot. "Can't we go into the shade?"

"Of course," Wilson said. "Look," he said to Macomber, and pointed. "See that patch of bush?"

"Yes."

"That's where the first bull went in. The gunbearer said when he fell off the bull was down. He was watching us helling along and the other two buff galloping. When he looked up there was the bull up and looking at him. Gun-bearer ran like hell and the bull went off slowly into that bush."

"Can we go in after him now?" asked Macomber eagerly.

Wilson looked at him appraisingly. Damned if this isn't a strange one, he thought. Yesterday he's scared sick and today he's a ruddy fire eater.

"No, we'll give him a while."

"Let's please go into the shade," Margot said. Her face was white and she looked ill.

They made their way to the car where it stood under a single, wide-spreading tree and all climbed in.

"Chances are he's dead in there," Wilson remarked. "After a little we'll have a look."

Macomber felt a wild unreasonable happiness that he had never known before.

"By God, that was a chase," he said. "I've never felt any such feeling. Wasn't it marvellous, Margot?"

"I hated it."

"Why?"

"I hated it," she said bitterly. "I loathed it."

"You know I don't think I'd be afraid of anything again," Macomber said to Wilson. "Something happened in me after we first saw the buff and started after him. Like a dam bursting. It was pure excitement."

"Cleans out your liver," said Wilson. "Damn funny things happen to people."

Macomber's face was shining. "You know something did happen to me," he said. "I feel absolutely different."

His wife said nothing and eyed him strangely. She was sitting far back in the seat and Macomber was sitting forward talking to Wilson who turned sideways talking over the back of the front seat.

"You know, I'd like to try another lion," Macomber said. "I'm really not afraid of them now. After all, what can they do to you?"

"That's it," said Wilson. "Worst one can do is kill you. How does it go? Shakespeare. Damned good. See if I can remember. Oh, damned good. Used to quote it to myself at one time. Let's see. 'By my troth, I care not; a man can die but once; we owe God a death and let it go which way it will, he that dies this year is quit for the next.' Damned fine, eh?"

He was very embarrased, having brought out this thing he had lived by, but he had seen men come of age before and it always moved him. It was not a matter of their twenty-first birthday.

It had taken a strange chance of hunting, a sudden precipitation into action without opportunity for worrying beforehand, to bring this about with Macomber, but regardless of how it had happened it had most certainly happened. Look at the beggar now, Wilson thought. It's that some of them stay little boys so long, Wilson thought. Sometimes all their lives. Their figures stay boyish when they're fifty. The great American boy-men. Damned strange people. But he liked this Macomber now. Damned strange fellow. Probably meant the end of cuckoldry too. Well, that would be a damned good thing. Damned good thing. Beggar had probably been afraid all his life. Don't know what started it. But over now. Hadn't had time to be afraid with the buff. That and being angry too. Motor car too. Motor cars made it familiar. Be a damn fire eater now. He'd seen it in the war work the same way. More of a change than any loss of virginity. Fear gone like an operation. Something else grew in its place. Main thing a man had. Made him into a man. Women knew it too. No bloody fear.

From the far corner of the seat Margaret Macomber looked at the two of them. There was no change in Wilson. She saw Wilson as she had seen him the day before when she had first realized what his great talent was. But she saw the change in Francis Macomber now.

"Do you have that feeling of happiness about what's going to happen?" Macomber asked, still exploring his new wealth.

"You're not supposed to mention it," Wilson said, looking in the other's face. "Much more fashionable to say you're scared. Mind you, you'll be scared too, plenty of times."

"But you *have* a feeling of happiness about action to come?"

"Yes," said Wilson. "There's that. Doesn't do to talk too much about all this. Talk the whole thing away. No pleasure in anything if you mouth it up too much."

"You're both talking rot," said Margot. "Just because you've chased some helpless animals in a motor car you talk like heroes."

"Sorry," said Wilson. "I have been gassing too much." She's worried about it already, he thought.

"If you don't know what we're talking about why not keep out of it?" Macomber asked his wife.

"You've gotten awfully brave, awfully suddenly," his wife said contemptuously, but her contempt was not secure. She was very afraid of something.

Macomber laughed, a very natural hearty laugh. "You know I *have*," he said. "I really have."

"Isn't it sort of late?" Margot said bitterly. Because she had done the best she could for many years back and the way they were together now was no one person's fault.

"Not for me," said Macomber.

Margot said nothing but sat back in the corner of the seat."

"Do you think we've given him time enough?" Macomber asked Wilson cheerfully.

"We might have a look," Wilson said. "Have you any solids left?"

"The gun-bearer has some."

Wilson called in Swahili and the older gun-bearer, who was skinning out one of the heads, straightened up, pulled a box of solids out of his pocket and brought them over to Macomber, who filled his magazine and put the remaining shells in his pocket.

"You might as well shoot the Springfield," Wilson said. "You're used to it. We'll leave the Mannlicher in the car with the Memsahib. Your gun-bearer can carry your heavy gun. I've this damned cannon. Now let me tell you about them." He had saved this until the last because he did not want to worry Macomber. "When a buff comes he comes with his head high and thrust straight out. The boss of the horns covers any sort of a brain shot. The only shot is straight into the nose. The only other shot is into his chest or, if you're to one side, into the neck or the shoulders. After they've been hit once they take a hell of a lot of killing. Don't try anything fancy. Take the easiest shot there is. They've finished skinning out that head now. Should we get started?"

He called to the gun-bearers, who came up wiping their hands, and the older one got into the back.

"I'll only take Kongoni," Wilson said. "The other can watch to keep the birds away."

As the car moved slowly across the open space toward the island of brushy trees that ran in a tongue of foliage along a dry water course that cut the open swale, Macomber felt his heart pounding and his mouth was dry again, but it was excitement, not fear.

"Here's where he went in," Wilson said. Then to the gun-bearer in Swahili, "Take the blood spoor."

The car was parallel to the patch of bush. Macomber, Wilson and the gun-bearer got down. Macomber, looking back, saw his wife, with the rifle by her side, looking at him. He waved to her and she did not wave back.

The brush was very thick ahead and the ground was dry. The middle-aged gun-bearer was sweating heavily and Wilson had his hat down over his eyes and his red neck showed just ahead of Macomber. Suddenly the gun-bearer said something in Swahili to Wilson and ran forward.

"He's dead in there," Wilson said. "Good work," and he turned to grip Macomber's hand and as they shook hands, grinning at each other, the gun-bearer shouted wildly and they saw him coming out of the bush sideways, fast as a crab, and the bull coming, nose out, mouth tight closed, blood dripping, massive head straight out, coming in a charge, his little pig eyes bloodshot as he looked at them. Wilson, who was ahead, was kneeling shooting, and Macomber, as he fired, unhearing his shot in the roaring of Wilson's gun, saw fragments like slate burst from the huge boss of the horns, and the head jerked, he shot again at the wide nostrils and saw the horns jolt again and fragments fly, and he did not see Wilson now and, aiming carefully, shot again with the buffalo's huge bulk almost on him and his rifle almost level with the oncoming head, nose out, and he could see the little wicked eyes and the head started to lower and he felt a sudden white-hot, blinding flash explode inside his head and that was all he ever felt.

Wilson had ducked to one side to get in a shoulder shot. Macomber had stood solid and shot for the nose, shooting a touch high each time and hitting the heavy horns, splintering and chipping them like hitting a slate roof, and Mrs. Macomber, in the car, had shot at the buffalo with the 6.5 Mannlicher as it seemed about to gore Macomber and had hit her husband about two inches up and a little to one side of the base of his skull.

Francis Macomber lay now, face down, not two yards from where the buffalo lay on his side and his wife knelt over him with Wilson beside her.

"I wouldn't turn him over," Wilson said.

The woman was crying hysterically.

"I'd get back in the car," Wilson said. "Where's the rifle?"

She shook her head, her face contorted. The gun-bearer picked up the rifle.

"Leave it as it is," said Wilson. Then, "Go get Abdulla so that he may witness the manner of the accident."

He knelt down, took a handkerchief from his pocket, and spread it over Francis Macomber's crew-cropped head where it lay. The blood sank into the dry, loose earth.

Wilson stood up and saw the buffalo on his side, his legs out, his thinly-haired belly crawling with ticks. "Hell of a good bull," his brain registered automatically. "A good fifty inches, or better. Better." He called to the driver and told him to spread a blanket over the body and stay by it. Then he walked over to the motor car where the woman sat crying in the corner.

"That was a pretty thing to do," he said in a toneless voice. "He *would* have left you too."

"Stop it," she said.

"Of course it's an accident," he said. "I know that."

"Stop it," she said.

"Don't worry," he said. "There will be a certain amount of unpleasantness but I will have some photographs taken that will be very useful at the inquest. There's the testimony of the gun-bearers and the driver too. You're perfectly all right."

"Stop it," she said.

"There's a hell of a lot to be done," he said. "And I'll have to send a truck off to the lake to wireless for a plane to take the three of us into Nairobi. Why didn't you poison him? That's what they do in England."

"Stop it. Stop it. Stop it," the woman cried.

Wilson looked at her with his flat blue eyes.

"I'm through now," he said. "I was a little angry. I'd begun to like your husband."

"Oh, please stop it," she said. "Please, please stop it."

"That's better," Wilson said. "Please is much better. Now I'll stop."

THE BEAR

WILLIAM FAULKNER

WILLIAM FAULKNER (1897–1962) was born in New Albany, Mississippi. The novelist lived most of his life in Oxford, Mississippi, the center of the region which he has immortalized in his imaginative saga of Yoknapatawpha County, whose decadent gentlemen and "poor whites" are the subject of almost all of his fiction. His books include *The Sound and the Fury* (1929), *Sanctuary* (1931), *Light in August* (1932), *Absalom, Absalom!* (1936), *Go Down, Moses* (1942), and *Requiem for a Nun* (1951). *A Fable* (1954) and *The Reivers* (1962) were both awarded Pulitzer Prizes. In 1949 Faulkner was awarded the Nobel Prize for Literature.

HE was ten. But it had already begun, long before that day when at last he wrote his age in two figures and he saw for the first time the camp where his father and Major de Spain and old General Compson and the others spent two weeks each November and two weeks again each June. He had already inherited then, without ever having seen it, the tremendous bear with one trap-ruined foot which, in an area almost a hundred miles deep, had earned itself a name, a definite designation like a living man.

He had listened to it for years: the long legend of corncribs rifled, of shotes and grown pigs and even calves carried bodily into the woods and devoured, of traps and deadfalls overthrown and dogs mangled and slain, and shotgun and even rifle charges delivered at point-blank range and with no more effect than so many peas blown through a tube by a boy— a corridor of wreckage and destruction beginning back before he was born, through which sped, not fast but rather with the ruthless and irresistible deliberation of a locomotive, the shaggy tremendous shape.

It ran in his knowledge before he ever saw it. It looked and towered in his dreams before he even saw the unaxed woods where it left its crooked print, shaggy, huge, red-eyed, not malevolent but just big— too big for the dogs which tried to bay it, for the horses which tried to ride it down, for the men and the bullets they fired into it, too big for the very country which was its constricting scope. He seemed to see it entire with a child's complete divination before he ever laid eyes on either—the doomed wilderness whose edges were being constantly and punily gnawed at by men with axes and plows who feared it

Copyright 1942 by William Faulkner. Reprinted by permission of Random House, Inc.

because it was wilderness, men myriad and nameless even to one another in the land where the old bear had earned a name, through which ran not even a mortal animal but an anachronism, indomitable and invincible, out of an old dead time, a phantom, epitome and apotheosis of the old wild life at which the puny humans swarmed and hacked in a fury of abhorrence and fear, like pygmies about the ankles of a drowsing elephant: the old bear solitary, indomitable and alone, widowered, childless, and absolved of mortality—old Priam reft of his old wife and having outlived all his sons.

Until he was ten, each November he would watch the wagon containing the dogs and the bedding and food and guns and his father and Tennie's Jim, the Negro, and Sam Fathers, the Indian, son of a slave woman and a Chickasaw chief, depart on the road to town, to Jefferson, where Major de Spain and the others would join them. To the boy, at seven, eight, and nine, they were not going into the Big Bottom to hunt bear and deer, but to keep yearly rendezvous with the bear which they did not even intend to kill. Two weeks later they would return, with no trophy, no head and skin. He had not expected it. He had not even been afraid it would be in the wagon. He believed that even after he was ten and his father would let him go too, for those two weeks in November, he would merely make another one, along with his father and Major de Spain and General Compson and the others, the dogs which feared to bay at it and the rifles and shotguns which failed even to bleed it, in the yearly pageant of the old bear's furious immortality.

Then he heard the dogs. It was in the second week of his first time in the camp. He stood with Sam Fathers against a big oak beside the faint crossing where they had stood each dawn for nine days now, hearing the dogs. He had heard them once before, one morning last week—a murmur, sourceless, echoing through the wet woods, swelling presently into separate voices which he could recognize and call by name. He had raised and cocked the gun as Sam told him and stood motionless again while the uproar, the invisible course, swept up and past and faded; it seemed to him that he could actually see the deer, the buck, blond, smoke-colored, elongated with speed, fleeing, vanishing, the woods, the gray solitude, still ringing even when the cries of the dogs had died away.

"Now let the hammers down," Sam said.

"You knew they were not coming here too," he said.

"Yes," Sam said. "I want you to learn how to do when you didn't shoot. It's after the chance for the bear or the deer has done already come and gone that men and dogs get killed."

"Anyway," he said, "it was just a deer."

Then on the tenth morning he heard the dogs again. And he readied the too-long, too-heavy gun as Sam had taught him, before Sam even spoke. But this time it was no deer, no ringing chorus of dogs running strong on a free scent, but a moiling yapping an octave too high, with something more than indecision and even abjectness in it, not even moving very fast, taking a long time to pass completely out of hearing, leaving then somewhere in the air that echo, thin, slightly hysterical, abject, almost grieving, with no sense of a fleeing, unseen, smoke-colored, grass-eating shape ahead of it, and Sam, who had taught him first of all to cock the gun and take position where he could see everywhere and then never move again, had himself moved up beside him; he could hear Sam breathing at his shoulder, and he could see the arched curve of the old man's inhaling nostrils.

"Hah," Sam said. "Not even running. Walking."

"Old Ben!" the boy said. "But up here!" he cried. "Way up here!"

"He do it every year," Sam said. "Once. Maybe to see who in camp this time, if he can shoot or not. Whether we got the dog yet that can bay and hold him. He'll take them to the river, then he'll send them back home. We may as well go back too; see how they look when they come back to camp."

When they reached the camp the hounds were already there, ten of them crouching back under the kitchen, the boy and Sam squatting to peer back into the obscurity where they had huddled, quiet, the eyes luminous, glowing at them and vanishing, and no sound, only that effluvium of something more than dog, stronger than dog and not just animal, just beast,

because still there had been nothing in front of that abject and almost painful yapping save the solitude, the wilderness, so that when the eleventh hound came in at noon and with all the others watching—even old Uncle Ash, who called himself first a cook—Sam daubed the tattered ear and the raked shoulder with turpentine and axle grease, to the boy it was still no living creature, but the wilderness which, leaning for the moment down, had patted lightly once the hound's temerity.

"Just like a man," Sam said. "Just like folks. Put off as long as she could having to be brave, knowing all the time that sooner or later she would have to be brave to keep on living with herself, and knowing all the time beforehand what was going to happen to her when she done it."

That afternoon, himself on the one-eyed wagon mule which did not mind the smell of blood nor, as they told him, of bear, and with Sam on the other one, they rode for more than three hours through the rapid, shortening winter day. They followed no path, no trail even that he could see; almost at once they were in a country which he had never seen before. Then he knew why Sam had made him ride the mule which would not spook. The sound one stopped short and tried to whirl and bolt even as Sam got down, blowing its breath, jerking and wrenching at the rein, while Sam held it, coaxing it forward with his voice, since he could not risk tying it, drawing it forward while the boy got down from the marred one.

Then, standing beside Sam in the gloom of the dying afternoon, he looked down at the rotted overturned log, gutted and scored with claw marks and, in the wet earth beside it, the print of the enormous warped two-toed foot. He knew now what he had smelled when he peered under the kitchen where the dogs huddled. He realized for the first time that the bear which had run in his listening and loomed in his dreams since before he could remember to the contrary, and which, therefore, must have existed in the listening and dreams of his father and Major de Spain and even old General Compson, too, before they began to remember in their turn, was a mortal animal, and that if they had departed for the camp each November without any actual hope of bringing its trophy back, it was not because it could not be slain, but because so far they had had no actual hope to.

"Tomorrow," he said.

"We'll try tomorrow," Sam said. "We ain't got the dog yet."

"We've got eleven. They ran him this morning."

"It won't need but one," Sam said. "He ain't here. Maybe he ain't nowhere. The only other way will be for him to run by accident over somebody that has a gun."

"That wouldn't be me," the boy said. "It will be Walter or Major or—"

"It might," Sam said. "You watch close in the morning. Because he's smart. That's how come he has lived this long. If he gets hemmed up and has to pick out somebody to run over, he will pick out you."

"How?" the boy said. "How will he know—" He ceased. "You mean he already knows me, that I ain't never been here before, ain't had time to find out yet whether I—" He ceased again, looking at Sam, the old man whose face revealed nothing until it smiled. He said humbly, not even amazed, "It was me he was watching. I don't reckon he did need to come but once."

The next morning they left the camp three hours before daylight. They rode this time because it was too far to walk, even the dogs in the wagon; again the first gray light found him in a place which he had never seen before, where Sam had placed him and told him to stay and then departed. With the gun which was too big for him, which did not even belong to him, but to Major de Spain, and which he had fired only once—at a stump on the first day, to learn the recoil and how to reload it—he stood against a gum tree beside a little bayou whose black still water crept without movement out of a canebrake and crossed a small clearing and into cane again, where, invisible, a bird—the big woodpecker called Lord-to-God by Negroes—clattered at a dead limb.

It was a stand like any other, dissimilar only in incidentals to the one where he had stood each morning for ten days; a territory new to him, yet no less familiar than that other one which, after almost two weeks, he had come to believe he knew a little—the same solitude, the same loneliness through which human beings had merely passed without altering it, leaving no mark, no scar, which looked exactly as it must have looked when the first ancestor of Sam Fathers' Chickasaw predecessors crept into it and looked about, club or stone ax or bone arrow drawn and poised; different only because, squatting at the edge of the kitchen, he smelled the hounds huddled and cringing beneath it and saw the raked ear and shoulder of the one who, Sam said, had had to be brave once in order to live with herself, and saw yesterday in the earth beside the gutted log the print of the living foot.

He heard no dogs at all. He never did hear them. He only heard the drumming of the woodpecker stop short off and knew that the bear was looking at him. He never saw it. He did not know whether it was in front of him or behind him. He did not move, holding the useless gun, which he had not even had warning to cock and which even now he did not cock, tasting in his saliva that taint as of brass which he knew now because he had smelled it when he peered under the kitchen at the huddled dogs.

Then it was gone. As abruptly as it had ceased, the woodpecker's dry, monotonous clatter set up again, and after a while he even believed he could hear the dogs—a murmur, scarce a sound even, which he had probably been hearing for some time before he even remarked it, drifting into hearing and then out again, dying away. They came nowhere near him. If it was a bear they ran, it was another bear. It was Sam himself who came out of the cane and crossed the bayou, followed by the injured bitch of yesterday. She was almost at heel, like a bird dog, making no sound. She came and crouched against his leg, trembling, staring off into the cane.

"I didn't see him," he said. "I didn't, Sam!"

"I know it," Sam said. "He done the looking. You didn't hear him neither, did you?"

"No," the boy said. "I—"

"He's smart," Sam said. "Too smart." He looked down at the hound, trembling faintly and steadily against the boy's knee. From the raked shoulder a few drops of fresh blood oozed and clung. "Too big. We ain't got the dog yet. But maybe someday. Maybe not next time. But someday."

So I must see him, he thought. *I must look at him.* Otherwise, it seemed to him that it would go on like this forever, as it had gone on with his father and Major de Spain, who was older than his father, and even with old General Compson, who had been old enough to be a brigade commander in 1865. Otherwise, it would go on so forever, next time and next time, after and after and after. It seemed to him that he could never see the two of them, himself and the bear, shadowy in the limbo from which time emerged, becoming time; the old bear absolved of mortality and himself partaking, sharing a little of it, enough of it. And he knew now what he had smelled in the huddled dogs and tasted in his saliva. He recognized fear. *So I will have to see him,* he thought, without dread or even hope. *I will have to look at him.*

It was in June of the next year. He was eleven. They were in camp again, celebrating Major de Spain's and General Compson's birthdays. Although the one had been born in September and the other in the depth of winter and in another decade, they had met for two weeks to fish and shoot squirrels and turkey and run coons and wildcats with the dogs at night. That is, he and Boon Hoggenback and the Negroes fished and shot squirrels and ran the coons and cats, because the proved hunters, not only Major de Spain and old General Compson, who spent those two weeks sitting in a rocking chair before a tremendous iron pot of Brunswick stew, stirring and tasting, with old Ash to quarrel with about how he was making it and Tennie's Jim to pour whiskey from the demijohn into the tin dipper from which he drank it, but even the boy's father and Walter Ewell, who were still young enough, scorned such, other than shooting the wild gobblers with pistols for wagers on their marksmanship.

Or, that is, his father and the others believed he was hunting squirrels. Until the third day, he thought that Sam Fathers believed that too. Each morning he would leave the camp right after breakfast. He had his own gun now, a Christmas present. He went back to the tree beside the bayou where he had stood that morning. Using the compass which old General Compson had given him, he ranged from that point; he was teaching himself to be a better-than-fair woodsman without knowing he was doing it. On the second day he even found the gutted log where he had first seen the crooked print. It was almost completely crumbled now, healing with unbelievable speed, a passionate and almost visible relinquishment, back into the earth from which the tree had grown.

He ranged the summer woods now, green with gloom; if anything, actually dimmer than in November's gray dissolution, where, even at noon, the sun fell only in intermittent dappling upon the earth, which never completely dried out and which crawled with snakes—moccasins and water snakes and rattlers, themselves the color of the dappling gloom, so that he would not always see them until they moved, returning later and later, first day, second day, passing in the twilight of the third evening the little log pen enclosing the log stable where Sam was putting up the horses for the night.

"You ain't looked right yet," Sam said.

He stopped. For a moment he didn't answer. Then he said peacefully, in a peaceful rushing burst as when a boy's miniature dam in a little brook gives way, "All right. But how? I went to the bayou. I even found that log again. I—"

"I reckon that was all right. Likely he's been watching you. You never saw his foot?"

"I," the boy said—"I didn't—I never thought—"

"It's the gun," Sam said. He stood beside the fence, motionless—the old man, the Indian, in the battered faded overalls and the five-cent straw hat which in the Negro's race had been the badge of his enslavement and was now the regalia of his freedom. The camp—the clearing, the house, the barn and its tiny lot with which Major de Spain in his turn had scratched punily and evanescently at the wilderness —faded in the dusk, back into the immemorial darkness of the woods. *The gun,* the boy thought. *The gun.*

"Be scared," Sam said. "You can't help that. But don't be afraid. Ain't nothing in the woods going to hurt you unless you corner it, or it smells that you are afraid. A bear or a deer, too, has got to be scared of a coward the same as a brave man has got to be."

The gun, the boy thought.

"You will have to choose," Sam said.

He left the camp before daylight, long before Uncle Ash would wake in his quilts on the kitchen floor and start the fire for breakfast. He had only the compass and a stick for snakes. He could go almost a mile before he would begin to need the compass. He sat on a log, the invisible compass in his invisible hand, while the secret night sounds, fallen still at his movements, scurried again and then ceased for good, and the owls ceased and gave over to the waking of day birds, and he could see the compass. Then he went fast yet still quietly; he was becoming better and better as a woodsman, still without having yet realized it.

He jumped a doe and a fawn at sunrise, walked them out of the bed, close enough to see them—the crash of undergrowth, the white scut, the fawn scudding behind her faster than he had believed it could run. He was hunting right, upwind, as Sam had taught him; not that it mattered now. He had left the gun; of his own will and relinquishment he had accepted not a gambit, not a choice, but a condition in which not only the bear's heretofore inviolable anonymity but all the old rules and balances of hunter and hunted had been abrogated. He would not even be afraid, not even in the moment when the fear would take him completely—blood, skin, bowels, bones, memory from the long time before it became his memory—all save that thin, clear, immortal lucidity which alone differed him from this bear and from all the other bear and deer he would ever kill in the humility and pride of his skill and endurance, to which Sam had spoken when he leaned in the twilight on the lot fence yesterday.

By noon he was far beyond the little bayou, farther into the new and alien country than he had ever been. He was traveling now not only by the old, heavy, biscuit-thick silver watch which had belonged to his grandfather. When he stopped at last, it was for the first time since he had risen from the log at dawn when he could see the compass. It was far enough. He had left the camp nine hours ago; nine hours from now, dark would have already been an hour old. But he didn't think that. He thought, *All right. Yes. But what?* and stood for a moment, alien and small in the green and topless solitude, answering his own question before it had formed and ceased. It was the watch, the compass, the stick— the three lifeless mechanicals with which for nine hours he had fended the wilderness off; he hung the watch and compass carefully on a bush and leaned the stick beside them and relinquished completely to it.

He had not been going very fast for the last two or three hours. He went no faster now, since distance would not matter even if he could have gone fast. And he was trying to keep a bearing on the tree where he had left the compass, trying to complete a circle which would bring him back to it or at least intersect itself, since direction would not matter now either. But the tree was not there, and he did as Sam had schooled him—made the next circle in the opposite direction, so that the two patterns would bisect somewhere, but crossing no print of his own feet, finding the tree at last, but in the wrong place—no bush, no compass, no watch—and the tree not even the tree, because there was a down log beside it and he did what Sam Fathers had told him was the next thing and the last.

As he sat down on the log he saw the crooked print—the warped, tremendous, two-toed indentation which, even as he watched it, filled with water. As he looked up, the wilderness coalesced, solidified—the glade, the tree he sought, the bush, the watch and the compass glinting where a ray of sunshine touched them. Then he saw the bear. It did not emerge, appear; it was just there, immobile, solid, fixed in the hot dappling of the green and windless noon, not as big as he had dreamed it, but as big as he had expected it, bigger, dimensionless, against the dappled obscurity, looking at him where he sat quietly on the log and looked back at it.

Then it moved. It made no sound. It did not hurry. It crossed the glade, walking for an instant into the full glare of the sun; when it reached the other side it stopped again and looked back at him across one shoulder while his quiet breathing inhaled and exhaled three times.

Then it was gone. It didn't walk into the woods, the undergrowth. It faded, sank back into the wilderness as he had watched a fish, a huge old bass, sink and vanish into the dark depths of its pool without even any movement of its fins.

He thought, *It will be next fall.* But it was not next fall, nor the next nor the next. He was fourteen then. He had killed his buck, and Sam Fathers had marked his face with the hot blood, and in the next year he killed a bear. But even before that accolade he had become as competent in the woods as many grown men with the same experience; by his

fourteenth year he was a better woodsman than most grown men with more. There was no territory within thirty miles of the camp that he did not know— bayou, ridge, brake, landmark, tree and path. He could have led anyone to any point in it without deviation, and brought them out again. He knew the game trails that even Sam Fathers did not know; in his thirteenth year he found a buck's bedding place, and unbeknown to his father he borrowed Walter Ewell's rifle and lay in wait at dawn and killed the buck when it walked back to the bed, as Sam had told him how the old Chickasaw fathers did.

But not the old bear, although by now he knew its footprints better than he did his own, and not only the crooked one. He could see any one of the three sound ones and distinguish it from any other, and not only by its size. There were other bears within these thirty miles which left tracks almost as large, but this was more than that. If Sam Fathers had been his mentor and the back-yard rabbits and squirrels at home his kindergarten, then the wilderness the old bear ran was his college, the old male bear itself, so long unwifed and childless as to have become its own ungendered progenitor, was his alma mater. But he never saw it.

He could find the crooked print now almost whenever he liked, fifteen or ten or five miles, or sometimes nearer the camp than that. Twice while on stand during the three years he heard the dogs strike its trail by accident; on the second time they jumped it seemingly, the voices high, abject, almost human in hysteria, as on that first morning two years ago. But not the bear itself. He would remember that noon three years ago, the glade, himself and the bear fixed during that moment in the windless and dappled blaze, and it would seem to him that it had never happened, that he had dreamed that too. But it had happened. They had looked at each other, they had emerged from the wilderness old as earth, synchronized to the instant by something more than the blood that moved the flesh and bones which bore them, and touched, pledged something, affirmed, something more lasting than the frail web of bones and flesh which any accident could obliterate.

Then he saw it again. Because of the very fact that he thought of nothing else, he had forgotten to look for it. He was still hunting with Walter Ewell's rifle. He saw it cross the end of a long blow-down, a corridor where a tornado had swept, rushing through rather than over the tangle of trunks and branches as a locomotive would have, faster than he had ever believed it could move, almost as fast as a deer even, because a deer would have spent most of that time in the air, faster than he could bring the rifle sights up with it. And now he knew what had been wrong during all the three years. He sat on a log, shaking and trembling as if he had never seen the woods before nor anything that ran them, wondering with incredulous amazement how he could have forgotten the very thing which Sam Fathers had told him and which the bear itself had proved the next day and had now returned after three years to reaffirm.

And now he knew what Sam Fathers had meant about the right dog, a dog in which size would mean less than nothing. So when he returned alone in April—school was out then, so that the sons of farmers could help with the land's planting, and at last his father had granted him permission, on his promise to be back in four days—he had the dog. It was his own, a mongrel of the sort called by Negroes a fyce, a ratter, itself not much bigger than a rat and possessing that bravery which had long since stopped being courage and had become foolhardiness.

It did not take four days. Alone again, he found the trail on the first morning. It was not a stalk; it was an ambush. He timed the meeting almost as if it were an appointment with a human being. Himself holding the fyce muffled in a feed sack and Sam Fathers with two of the hounds on a piece of a plow-line rope, they lay down wind of the trail at dawn of the second morning. They were so close that the bear turned without even running, as if in surprised amazement at the shrill and frantic uproar of the released fyce, turning at bay against the trunk of a tree, on its hind feet; it seemed to the boy that it would never stop rising, taller and taller, and even the two hounds seemed to take a desperate and despairing courage from the fyce, following it as it went in.

Then he realized that the fyce was actually not going to stop. He flung, threw the gun away, and ran; when he overtook and grasped the frantically pin-wheeling little dog, it seemed to him that he was directly under the bear.

He could smell it, strong and hot and rank. Sprawling, he looked up to where it loomed and towered over him like a cloudburst and colored like a thunderclap, quite familiar, peacefully and even lucidly familiar, until he remembered: This was the way he had used to dream about it. Then it was gone. He didn't see it go. He knelt, holding the frantic fyce with both hands, hearing the abashed wailing of the hounds drawing farther and farther away, until Sam came up. He carried the gun. He laid it down quietly beside the boy and stood looking down at him.

"You've done seed him twice now with a gun in your hands," he said. "This time you couldn't have missed him."

The boy rose. He still held the fyce. Even in his arms and clear of the ground, it yapped frantically, straining and surging after the fading uproar of the two hounds like a tangle of wire springs. He was panting a little, but he was neither shaking nor trembling now.

"Neither could you!" he said. "You had the gun! Neither did you!"

"And you didn't shoot," his father said. "How close were you?"

"I don't know, sir," he said. "There was a big wood tick inside his right hind leg. I saw that. But I didn't have the gun then."

"But you didn't shoot when you had the gun," his father said. "Why?"

But he didn't answer, and his father didn't wait for him to, rising and crossing the room, across the pelt of the bear which the boy had killed two years ago and the larger one which his father had killed before he was born, to the bookcase beneath the mounted head of the boy's first buck. It was the room which his father called the office, from which all the plantation business was transacted; in it for the fourteen years of his life he had heard the best of all talking. Major de Spain would be there and sometimes old General Compson, and Walter Ewell and Boon Hoggenback and Sam Fathers and Tennie's Jim, too, were hunters, knew the woods and what ran them.

He would hear it, not talking himself but listening —the wilderness, the big woods, bigger and older than any recorded document of white man fatuous enough to believe he had bought any fragment of it or Indian ruthless enough to pretend that any fragment of it had been his to convey. It was of the men, not white nor black nor red, but men, hunters with the will and hardihood to endure and the humility and skill to survive, and the dogs and the bear and deer juxtaposed and reliefed against it, ordered and compelled by and within the wilderness in the ancient and unremitting contest by the ancient and immitigable rules which voided all regrets and brooked no quarter, the voices quiet and weighty and deliberate for retrospection and recollection and exact remembering, while he squatted in the blazing firelight as Tennie's Jim squatted, who stirred only to put more wood on the fire and to pass the bottle from one glass to another. Because the bottle was always present, so that after a while it seemed to him that those fierce instants of heart and brain and courage and wiliness and speed were concentrated and distilled into that brown liquor which not women, not boys and children, but only hunters drank, drinking not of the blood they had spilled but some condensation of the wild immortal spirit, drinking it moderately, humbly even, not with the pagan's base hope of acquiring the virtues of cunning and strength and speed, but in salute to them.

His father returned with the book and sat down again and opened it. "Listen," he said. He read the five stanzas aloud, his voice quiet and deliberate in the room where there was no fire now because it was already spring. Then he looked up. The boy watched him. "All right," his father said. "Listen." He read again, but only the second stanza this time, to the end of it, the last two lines, and closed the book and put it on the table beside him. "She cannot fade, though thou hast not thy bliss, for ever wilt thou love, and she be fair," he said.

"He's talking about a girl," the boy said.

"He had to talk about something," his father said. Then he said, "He was talking about truth. Truth doesn't change. Truth is one thing. It covers all things which touch the heart—honor and pride and pity and justice and courage and love. Do you see now?"

He didn't know. Somehow it was simpler than that. There was an old bear, fierce and ruthless, not merely just to stay alive, but with the fierce pride of liberty and freedom, proud enough of the liberty and freedom to see it threatened without fear or even alarm; nay, who at times even seemed deliberately to put that freedom and liberty in jeopardy in order to savor them, to remind his old strong bones and flesh to keep supple and quick to defend and preserve them. There was an old man, son of a Negro slave and an Indian king, inheritor on the one side of the long chronicle of a people who had learned humility through suffering, and pride through the endurance which survived the suffering and injustice, and on the other side, the chronicle of a people even longer in the land than the first, yet who no longer existed in the land at all save in the solitary brotherhood of an old Negro's alien blood and the wild and invincible spirit of an old bear. There was a boy who wished to learn humility and pride in order to become skillful and worthy in the woods, who suddenly found himself becoming so skillful so rapidly that he feared he would never become worthy because he

had not learned humility and pride, although he had tried to, until one day and as suddenly he discovered that an old man who could not have defined either had led him, as though by the hand, to that point where an old bear and a little mongrel of a dog showed him that, by possessing one thing other, he would possess them both.

And a little dog, nameless and mongrel and many-fathered, grown, yet weighing less than six pounds, saying as if to itself, "I can't be dangerous, because there's nothing much smaller than I am; I can't be fierce, because they would call it just a noise; I can't be humble, because I'm already too close to the ground to genuflect; I can't be proud, because I wouldn't be near enough to it for anyone to know who was casting the shadow, and I don't even know that I'm not going to heaven, because they have already decided that I don't possess an immortal soul. So all I can be is brave. But it's all right. I can be that, even if they still call it just noise."

That was all. It was simple, much simpler than somebody talking in a book about youth and a girl he would never need to grieve over, because he could never approach any nearer her and would never have to get any farther away. He had heard about a bear, and finally got big enough to trail it, and he trailed it four years and at last met it with a gun in his hands and he didn't shoot. Because a little dog—But he could have shot long before the little dog covered the twenty yards to where the bear waited, and Sam Fathers could have shot at any time during that interminable minute while Old Ben stood on his hind feet over them. He stopped. His father was watching him gravely across the spring-rife twilight of the room; when he spoke, his words were as quiet as the twilight, too, not loud, because they did not need to be because they would last, "Courage, and honor, and pride," his father said, "and pity, and love of justice and of liberty. They all touch the heart, and what the heart holds to becomes truth, as far as we know the truth. Do you see now?"

Sam, and Old Ben, and Nip, he thought. And himself too. He had been all right too. His father had said so. "Yes, sir," he said.

METAMORPHOSIS

FRANZ KAFKA

FRANZ KAFKA (1883–1924) was born in Prague, educated for the law at the University of Prague and worked in the workmen's compensation division of the Austrian government. This controversial figure in modern literature has described in a famous letter to his father the sense of oppression, engendered by his father's authoritarian personality, under which he lived and wrote; he suffered from tuberculosis and spent several years in sanitoriums; and on two occasions rejected marriage because of a sense of self-inadequacy. Most of his work was edited and published posthumously against his wishes by his friend Max Brod, who sees in it centrally the theme of loneliness. One of Kafka's aphorisms, however, in behalf of the justification of life, offers us another perspective: "One must not cheat anybody, not even the world of its triumph." Among Kafka's books are The Trial, The Castle, Amerika, *two volumes of diaries, and several collections of short stories, notably* The Great Wall of China.

AS Gregor Samsa awoke one morning from a troubled dream, he found himself changed in his bed to some monstrous kind of vermin.

He lay on his back, which was as hard as armor plate, and, raising his head a little, he could see the arch of his great, brown belly, divided by bowed corrugations. The bedcover was slipping helplessly off the summit of the curve, and Gregor's legs, pitiably thin compared with their former size, fluttered helplessly before his eyes.

"What has happened?" he thought. It was no dream. His room, a real man's room—though rather small—lay quiet within its four familiar walls. Over the table, where a collection of cloth samples was scattered—Samsa was a commercial traveler—hung the picture that he had recently cut from an illustrated paper and had put in a pretty gilded frame. This picture showed a lady sitting very upright, wearing a small fur hat and a fur boa; she offered to the gaze a heavy muff into which her arm was thrust up to the elbow.

Gregor looked toward the window; rain could be heard falling on the panes; the foggy weather made him sad. "How would it be if I go to sleep again for awhile and forget all this stupidity?" he thought; but it was absolutely impossible, for he was used to sleeping on the right side and in his present plight he could not get into that position. However hard he tried to throw himself violently on his side, he always turned over on his back with a little swinging movement. He tried a hundred times, closing his eyes so that he should not see the trembling of his legs, and he did not give up until he felt in his side a slight but deep pain, never before experienced.

"God!" he thought, "What a job I've chosen. Traveling day in, day out. A much more worrying occupation than working in the office! And apart from business itself, this plague of traveling: the anxieties of changing trains, the irregular, inferior meals, the ever changing faces, never to be seen again, people with whom one has no chance to be friendly. To hell with it all!" He felt a little itch above his stomach and wriggled nearer to the bed-post, dragging himself slowly on his back so that he might more easily raise his head; and he saw, just where he was itching, a few little white points, whose purpose he could not guess at; he tried to scratch the place with one of his feet but he had to draw it back quickly, for the contact made him shudder coldly.

He returned to his former position. He said to himself: "Nothing is more degrading than always to have to rise so early. A man must have his sleep. Other travelers can live like harem women. When I return to the hotel in the morning to enter my orders, I find these gentlemen still at breakfast. I'd like to see what my boss would say if I tried it; I should be sacked immediately. Who knows if that wouldn't be a good thing, after all! If I didn't hold back because of my parents, I would have given notice long ago; I would have gone to the boss and I wouldn't have minced matters. He would have fallen from his desk. That's a funny thing; to sit on a desk so as to speak to one's employees from such a height, especially when one is hard of hearing and people must come close! Still, all hope is not lost; once I have got together the money my parents owe him—that will be in about five or six years—I shall certainly do it. Then I'll take the big step! Meanwhile, I must get up, for my train goes at five."

He looked at the alarm clock which was ticking on

the chest. "My God!" he thought; it was half-past six; quarter to seven was not far off. Hadn't the alarm gone? From the bed it could be seen that the little hand was set at four, right enough; the alarm had sounded. But had he been able to sleep calmly through that furniture-shattering din? Calmly, no; his sleep had not been calm; but he had slept only the sounder for that. What should he do now?

The next train went at seven; to catch it he must hurry madly, and his collection of samples was not packed; besides, he himself did not feel at all rested nor inclined to move. And even if he did catch the train, his employer's anger was inevitable, since the firm's errand boy would have been waiting at the five o'clock train and would have notified the firm of his lapse. He was just a toady to his boss, a stupid and servile boy. Supposing Gregor pretended to be ill? But that would be very tiresome, and suspicious, too, for during the four years he had been with the firm he had never had the slightest illness. The manager would come with the Health Insurance doctor; he would reproach his parents for their son's idleness and would cut short any objections by giving the doctor's arguments that no people are sick, only idle. And would he be so far wrong, in such a case? Gregor felt in very good fettle, apart from his unnecessary need for more sleep after such a long night; he even had an unusually keen appetite.

Just as he was quickly turning these thoughts over in his mind without being able to decide to leave the bed—while the alarm clock struck a quarter to seven—he heard a cautious knock on his door, close by his bed's head.

"Gregor," someone called—it was his mother—"It is a quarter to seven. Didn't you want to catch the train?"

What a soft voice! Gregor trembled as he heard his own voice reply. It was unmistakably his former voice, but with it could be heard, as if from below, a painful whining, which only allowed the words their real shape for a moment, immediately to confuse their sound so that one wondered if one had really heard aright. Gregor would have liked to answer fully and to give an explanation but, in these circumstances, he contented himself by saying, "Yes, yes, thank you, mother. I am just getting up." No doubt the door prevented her from judging the change in Gregor's voice, for the explanation reassured his mother, who went away, shuffling in her slippers. But because of this little dialogue the other members of the family had become aware that, contrary to custom, Gregor was still in the house, and his father started to knock on one of the side doors, softly, but with his fists.

"Gregor, Gregor," he cried, "what is the matter?"

And, after a moment, in a warning tone, "Gregor! Gregor!"

At the other side door, the young man's sister softly called, "Gregor, aren't you well? Do you need anything?"

"I am getting ready," said Gregor, answering both sides and forcing himself to pronounce carefully and to separate each word with a long pause, to keep a natural voice.

His father went back to breakfast, but the sister still whispered, "Gregor, open the door, I beg you." But Gregor had no intention of answering this request; on the contrary, he complimented himself on having learned the habit of always locking his door, as if in a hotel.

He would get up quietly, without being bothered by anyone; he would dress, and above all, he would have breakfast; then would come the time to reflect, for he felt it was not in bed that a reasonable solution could be found. He recalled how often an unusual position adopted in bed had resulted in slight pains which proved imaginary as soon as he arose, and Gregor was curious to see his present hallucination gradually dissolve. As for the change in his voice, his private opinion was that it was the prelude to some serious quinsy, the occupational malady of travelers.

He had no difficulty in turning back the coverlet; he needed only to blow himself up a little, and it fell of its own accord. But beyond that he was impeded by his tremendous girth. To get up, he needed arms and hands; but he had only numerous little legs, in perpetual vibration, over which he had no control. Before he could bend one leg, he first had to stretch it out; and when at last he had performed the desired movement, all the other legs worked uncontrollably, in intensely painful agitation. "I must not stay uselessly in bed," said Gregor to himself.

To get his body out of bed, he first tried moving the hind part. But unfortunately this hind part, which he had not yet seen, and of which he could form no very precise idea, went so slowly it proved to be very difficult to move; he summoned all his strength to throw himself forward but, ill-calculating his course, he hurled himself violently against one of the bedposts, and the searing pain he felt showed that the lower part of his body was without doubt the most sensitive.

He then tried to start with the fore part of his body and cautiously turned his head toward the side of the bed. In this he succeeded quite easily, and the rest of his body, despite its weight and size, followed the direction of his head. But when his head left the bed and was hanging in mid-air, he was afraid to continue any further; if he were to fall in this position, it would be a miracle if he did not crack his head; and this was no moment to lose his senses—better to stay in bed.

But when, panting after his efforts, he again found himself stretched out just as before, when he saw his little legs struggling more wildly than ever, despairing of finding any means of bringing peace and order into this chaotic procedure, he once again realized that he absolutely could not stay in bed and that it was perfectly reasonable to sacrifice everything to the slightest chance of getting out. At the same time he did not forget that cool and wise reflection would be far better than desperate resolutions. Ordinarily, at such moments he turned his eyes to the window to gain encouragement and hope. But this day the fog prevented him from seeing the other side of the street; the window gave him neither confidence nor strength. "Seven o'clock already," he said as he listened once more to the sound of the alarm clock. "Seven o'clock already, and the fog has got no thinner!" He lay back again for a moment, breathing weakly, as though, in the complete silence, he could calmly await the return to his normal self.

Then he said, "Before a quarter past it is absolutely essential for me to be up. In any case, someone will be sent from the office to ask for me before then, for the place opens at seven." And he began to rock on his back in order to get his whole body out of bed in one movement. In this manner he would be able to protect his head by raising it sharply as he fell. His back seemed to be hard; nothing would be risked by falling on it to the floor; his only fear was that the noise of his fall, which must surely resound through the whole house, might arouse terror, or, at the very least, uneasiness. However, that would have to be risked.

When Gregor had half his body out of bed—the new method seemed more like a game than a task, for he had only to swing himself on his back—he began to think how easily he could have got up if only he had had a little assistance. Two strong people—he thought of his father and the servant girl—would have been quite enough; they would have needed only to pass their arms under his round back, raise it from the bed, quickly lean forward with their burden, and then wait carefully till he had completed the operation of settling himself on the ground, where he hoped his feet would at last find a way of working together. But even if the doors had not been closed, would it have been wise for him to call for help? At this idea, despite his misery, he could not repress a smile.

Now he had progressed so far that, by sharply accentuating his swinging movement, he felt he was nearly losing his balance; he would have to take a serious decision, for in five minutes it would be a quarter to eight—but suddenly there was a knock at the front door.

"Someone from the office," he said to himself, and he felt his blood run cold, while his little legs quickened their saraband. For a moment all was quiet.

"They're not going to the door," thought Gregor, in an access of absurd hope. But of course the maid, with a firm tread, went to the door and opened it. Gregor needed to hear only the caller's first words of greeting to know immediately who it was—the manager himself. Why was Gregor, particularly, condemned to work for a firm where the worst was suspected at the slightest inadvertence of the employees? Were the employees, without exception, all scoundrels? Was there among their number not one devoted, faithful servant, who, if it did so happen that by chance he missed a few hours work one morning, might have found himself so numbed with remorse that he just could not leave his bed? Would it not have been enough to send some apprentice to put things right—if, in any case, it was necessary to make inquiries at all—instead of the manager himself having to come, in order to let the whole innocent family know that the clearing-up of so suspicious an affair could only be entrusted to a person of his importance? These thoughts so irritated Gregor that he swung himself out of bed with all his might. This made a loud thud, but not the terrible crash that he had feared. The carpet somewhat softened the blow, and Gregor's back was more elastic than he had thought, and so his act was not accompanied by any din. Only his head had been slightly hurt. Gregor had not raised it enough, and it had been knocked in the fall. He turned over a little to rub it on the carpet, in pain and anger.

"Something fell in there just then," cried the manager, in the room on the left. Gregor tried to imagine his employer's face if such a mishap had occurred to him; for such a thing was possible, he had to admit. But, as if in brutal reply, the manager began pacing up and down in the next room, making his patent-leather boots creak.

And in the other room on the right, Gregor's sister whispered to warn her brother, "Gregor, the manager is here."

"I know," said Gregor to himself, but he dared not raise his voice enough for his sister to hear.

"Gregor," said his father in the room on the left, "the manager has come to find out why you didn't catch the early train. We don't know what to say. He wants to speak to you personally. So please open the door. I'm sure he will be kind enough to excuse the untidiness of your room."

"Good morning, good morning, Mr. Samsa," interrupted the manager, cordial and brisk.

"He is not well," said his mother to the manager, while his father went on shouting through the door. "Believe me, he is not well, sir. How else could Gregor have missed the train? The boy thinks of nothing but his work! It makes me upset to see how he never goes out after supper; do you know he's just spent a whole week here and been at home every evening! He sits down with us at the table and stays there, quietly reading the paper or studying his time-tables. His greatest indulgence is to do a little fret-work. Just lately he made a small picture frame. It was finished in two or three evenings, and you'd be surprised how pretty it is; it is hanging up in his room. As soon as Gregor opens his door, you will be able to see it. I am so glad you came, sir, because without you we would never have got Gregor to open his door, he is so obstinate; and surely he must be ill, even though he denied it this morning."

"I am just coming," said Gregor slowly and care-fully, but he continued to lie still, so as not to miss a word of the conversation.

"I can offer no other suggestion," declared the manager. "Let us only hope it is nothing serious. However, we businessmen must often—fortunately or not, as you will—get on with our jobs and ignore our little indispositions."

"Well, can the manager come in now?" asked his father impatiently, rapping on the door again.

"No," said Gregor. In the room on the left there was a painful silence; in that on the right the sister began to sob.

Why did she not go to the others? Possibly she had only just got out of bed and was not yet dressed. And why did she weep? Because he did not get up to let the manager in, because he risked losing his position, and because the boss would once more worry his parents about their old debts? These were misplaced troubles! Gregor was still there and had not the slightest intention of letting his family down. At this very moment he was stretched out on the carpet, and nobody seeing him in this state could seriously have demanded that he should let the man-ager enter his room. But it was not on account of this slight impoliteness—for which in normal times he could easily have made his excuses later—that Gregor would be dismissed. And he thought it would be more reasonable, just now, to leave him alone rather than to upset him with tears and speeches. But it was just this uncertainty which was making the others uneasy and which excused their behavior.

"Herr Samsa," now cried the manager, raising his voice, "What is the matter? You barricade yourself in your room, you don't answer yes or no, you needlessly upset your parents, and you neglect your professional duties in an unheard-of manner. I am speaking in the name of your employer and of your parents, and I beg you seriously to give us a satisfactory explanation immediately. I am astonished, astonished! I took you for a quiet, reasonable young man, and here you sud-denly give yourself airs, behaving in an absolutely fantastic manner! The head of the firm, speaking to me this morning in your absence, suggested an ex-planation which I rejected; he mentioned the samples which were entrusted to you a while ago. I gave him my word of honor that this had nothing to do with the affair, but now that I have been witness to your obstinacy, I can assure you, Herr Samsa, that it de-prives me of any wish to defend you. Your job is by no means safe! I had intended to tell you this in private but, since you oblige me to waste my time here for nothing, I see no reason for keeping quiet before your parents. I'd have you know that lately your work has been far from satisfactory; we realize, of course, that the time of the year is not propitious for big business, but you must understand, Herr Samsa, that a period with no business at all should not and can not be tolerated!"

Gregor was beside himself; in his anxiety he forgot everything else. "But, sir," he cried, "I will open the door immediately. I will open it. I felt a little ill; a slight giddiness prevented me from getting up. I am still in bed. But I feel better already. I am just get-ting up. Only a moment's patience. I am not quite so well as I thought. But I am all right, really. How can it be that illness should take one so quickly? Only yesterday I felt quite well, my parents can tell you; and then last evening I had a slight symptom. They must have noticed it. Why didn't I let them know at the office! But then, one always thinks one will be able to get rid of an illness without staying at home. Please, sir, spare my parents. The complaints you made just now are really without any foundation. No one has even suggested them before. Perhaps you have not seen the last orders I sent in. I will leave on the eight o'clock train; these few moments of rest have done me a great deal of good. Please don't stay, sir, I shall be at the office immediately; and please inform the director of what has happened and put in a good word for me."

And while Gregor hastily cried these words, scarcely realizing what he said, he had, with an ease due to his previous exertions, approached the chest of drawers, against which he now tried to raise himself. He wanted to open the door; he wanted to be seen and to speak with the manager. He was curious to know what impression he would make on these peo-ple who were so imperiously demanding his pres-ence. If he frightened them, that would be reas-suring, for he would stop being cross-questioned and be left in peace. If they took everything quietly, then he, too, need not be alarmed. And if he hurried he might still catch the eight o'clock train. The chest was polished, and Gregor slipped on it several times but, by a supreme effort, he managed to get upright. He paid no attention to the pains in his stomach, though they were hurting him. He let himself drop forward onto the top of a near-by chair and clung there with his little legs. Then, finding himself master of his body, he stayed very quiet in order to listen to what the manager had to say.

"Did you understand a word of what he said?" the manager asked the parents. "Is he trying to make fools of us?"

"Good heavens," cried the mother, already in tears. "Perhaps he is seriously ill, and here we are torturing him all this while! Grete! Grete!" she called.

"Mother!" cried the daughter from the other side. They were separated by Gregor's room.

"Fetch a doctor immediately. Gregor is ill. A doctor, quickly! Did you hear him speak?"

"It was an animal's voice," said the manager; after the cries of the women, his voice seemed curiously gentle.

"Anna, Anna!" shouted the father through the hall into the kitchen, clapping his hands. "Get a locksmith, quick!" And already the two young girls—how could his sister have dressed so soon?—ran along the corridor with rustling skirts and opened the front door. No one heard the door close; no doubt it had been left open, as is the custom in houses to which a great misfortune has come.

However, Gregor had become calmer. Doubtless they had not understood his words, though they had seemed clear enough to him, clearer, indeed, than the first time; perhaps his ears were becoming more accustomed to the sounds. But at least they were obliged to realize that his case was not normal, and they were ready, now, to help him. The assurance and resourcefulness with which the first steps had been taken comforted him considerably. He felt himself integrated into human society once again, and, without differentiating between them, he hoped for great and surprising things from the locksmith and the doctor. To clear his throat for the decisive conversation which he would have to hold soon, he coughed a little, but as quietly as possible, for he feared that even his cough might not sound human. Meanwhile, in the next room, it had become quiet. Perhaps his parents were sitting at table in a secret conference with the manager; perhaps everyone was leaning against the door, listening.

Gregor made his way slowly toward it with the chair; then he abandoned the chair and flung himself at the door, holding himself erect against the woodwork—for the bottoms of his feet secreted a sticky substance—and he rested a moment from his efforts. After this, he tried to turn the key in the lock with his mouth. Unfortunately, it seemed he had no proper teeth. How could he take hold of the key? In compensation, instead of teeth he possessed a pair of very strong mandibles and succeeded in seizing the key in the lock, regardless of the pain this caused him; a brownish liquid flowed out of his mouth, spread over the lock, and dropped to the floor.

"Listen!" said the manager in the next room. "He is just turning the key."

This was valuable encouragement for Gregor; he would have liked his father, his mother, everybody, to start calling to him, "Courage, Gregor, go on, push hard!" And, with the idea that everyone was following his efforts with passionate attention, he clutched the key with all the power of his jaws until he was nearly unconscious. Following the progress of the turning key, he twisted himself around the lock, hanging on by his mouth, and, clinging to the key, pressed it down again, whenever it slipped, with all the weight of his body. The clear click of the lock as it snapped back awoke Gregor from his momentary coma.

"I have dispensed with the locksmith," he thought, and sighed and leaned his head against the handle to open one panel of the double doors completely.

This method, the only possible one, prevented the others from seeing him for some time, even with the door open. Still erect, he had to grope his way round the door with great caution in order not to spoil his entry by falling flat on his back; so he was concentrating toward this end, with all his attention absorbed by the maneuver, when he heard the manager utter a sonorous, "Oh!" such as the roaring of the wind produces, and saw him—he was just by the door—press his hand over his open mouth and slowly stagger back as if some invisible and intensely powerful force were driving him from the spot. His mother—who, despite the presence of the manager, was standing by with her hair in curlers, still disordered by sleep—began to look at the father, clasping her hands; then she made two steps toward Gregor and fell backward into the family circle in the midst of a confusion of skirts which spread around her, while her face, falling on her breast, was concealed from sight. The father clenched his fists with a menacing air, as if to beat Gregor back into his room; then he looked around the dining room in perplexity, covered his eyes with his hand, and wept with great sobs which shook his powerful chest.

Gregor did not enter the room; he stood against the closed half of the double doors, allowing only a part of his body to be seen, while, above, he turned his head to one side to see what would happen. Meanwhile, it had grown much lighter; on either side of the street a part of the long, dark building opposite could clearly be seen—it was a hospital, with regular windows startlingly pitting its façade; it was still raining, but in great separate drops which fell to the ground, one by one. The breakfast crockery was spread all over the table, for breakfast was the most important meal of the day for Gregor's father; he would prolong it for hours while he read various newspapers. On the wall hung a photograph of Gregor in lieutenant's uniform, taken while he was in military service; he was smiling; his hand lay on the hilt of his sword. By his expression, he seemed happy to be alive; by his gesture, he appeared to command respect for his rank. The living-room door was ajar, and, as the front door was also open, the balcony and the first steps of the stairway could just be seen.

"Now," said Gregor, and he realized that he was the only one to have kept calm, "Now I will get dressed, collect my samples, and go. Will you, will you let me go? Surely you can now see, sir, that I am not obstinate, that I do mean to work; commercial traveling is tiresome, I admit, but without it I cannot live. Where are you going, sir? To the office? Yes? Will you give them a faithful account of what has happened? After all, anyone might find for a moment that they were incapable of resuming their work, but that's just a good opportunity to review the work they have been doing, and to bear in mind that, once the obstacle is removed, they will be able to return with twice the heart. I owe so much to the director, as you know very well. I have my parents and my sister to consider. I am in an awkward position, but I shall return to work. Only, please do not make things more difficult for me; they are hard enough as it is. Take my part at the office. I know only too well they don't like travelers. They think we earn our money too easily, that we lead too grand a life. I realize that the present situation doesn't encourage the removal of this prejudice; but you, sir, the manager, can judge the circumstances better than the rest of the staff, better than the director himself—though this is between ourselves—for in his executive capacity he is often easily misled by an employee's prejudice. You know quite well that the traveler, who is hardly ever in the office the whole year round, is often the victim of scandal, of a chance, undeserved complaint against which he is powerless to defend himself, for he does not even know that he is being accused; he only learns of it as he returns, exhausted, at the end of his trip, when the sad consequences of an affair, whose circumstances he can no longer recall, painfully confront him. Please, sir, don't leave

me without a word to show that you think all this at least a little reasonable."

But, at Gregor's first words, the manager had turned away and only glanced back, with snarling lips, over his trembling shoulder. During Gregor's speech, he had not stood still for a moment; instead, he had retreated furtively, step by step, toward the door—always keeping Gregor in sight—as if some secret law forbade him to leave the room. He had already reached the hall and, as he took the very last step out of the living room, one would have thought the floor was burning his shoes, so sharply did he spring. Then he stretched his hand toward the balustrade, as if some unearthly deliverance awaited him at the foot of the stairs.

Gregor realized that, if he were to keep his job, on no account must the manager be allowed to leave in this condition. Unfortunately, his parents did not realize the position very clearly; they had for so long held the idea that Gregor was settled in the firm for life and were so taken up with their present troubles that they had little thought for such a contingency. But Gregor had more foresight. The manager must be stopped, calmed, convinced, and finally won over. The future of Gregor and of his family depended on it! If only his sister were there! She had understood, she had actually begun to weep while Gregor still lay quietly on his back. And the manager, who liked women, would have listened to her; he would have let himself be guided by her; she would have closed the door and would have proved to him, in the hall, how unreasonable his terror was. But she was not there; Gregor himself must manage this affair. And without even considering whether he would ever be able to return to work, nor whether his speech had been understood, he let go of the doorpost to glide through the opening and overtake the manager (who was clutching the balustrade with both hands in a ridiculous manner), vainly sought for a foothold, and, uttering a cry, he fell, with his frail little legs crumpled beneath him.

Suddenly, for the first time that whole morning, he experienced a feeling of physical well-being; his feet were on firm ground; he noticed with joy that his legs obeyed him wonderfully and were even eager to carry him wherever he might wish. But while, under the nervous influence of his need for haste, he hesitated on the spot, not far from his mother, he saw her suddenly jump, fainting though she seemed to be, and throw her arms about with outspread fingers, crying, "Help, for God's sake, help!" She turned her head, the better to see Gregor; then, in flagrant contradiction, she began to retreat madly, having forgotten that behind her stood the table, still laden with breakfast things. She staggered against it and sat down suddenly, like one distraught, regardless of the fact that, at her elbow, the overturned coffee-pot was making a pool of coffee on the carpet.

"Mother, mother," whispered Gregor, looking up at her. The manager had quite gone out of his mind. Seeing the coffee spilling, Gregor could not prevent himself from snapping his jaws several times in the air, as if he were eating. Thereupon his mother again began to shriek and quickly jumped up from the table and fell into the arms of the father, who had rushed up behind her. But Gregor had no time to bother about them. The manager was already on the stairs; with his chin on the balustrade, he was looking back for the last time.

Gregor summoned all his courage to try to bring him back; the manager must have suspected something of the sort, for he leaped several steps at a single bound and disappeared with a cry of, "Huh!" which resounded in the hollow of the stair well. This flight had the unfortunate effect of causing Gregor's father—who till now had remained master of himself—to lose his head completely; instead of running after the manager, or at least not interfering with Gregor in his pursuit, he seized in his right hand the manager's walking stick, which had been left behind on a chair with his overcoat and hat, took up in his left a newspaper from the table, and began stamping his feet and brandishing the newspaper and the cane to drive Gregor back into his room. Gregor's prayers were unavailing, were not even understood; he had turned to his father a supplicating head, but, meek though he showed himself, his father merely stamped all the louder. In the dining room, despite the cold, the mother had opened the window wide and was leaning out as far as possible, pressing her face in her hands. A great rush of air swept the space between the room and the stairway; the curtains billowed, the papers rustled, and a few sheets flew over the carpet. But the father pursued Gregor pitilessly, whistling and whooping like a savage, and Gregor, who was not used to walking backward, progressed but slowly.

Had he been able to turn around he could have reached his room quickly, but he feared to make his father impatient by the slowness of his turning and feared also that at any moment he might receive a mortal blow on his head or on his back from this menacing stick. Soon Gregor had no choice; for he realized with terror that when he was going backward he was not master of his direction and, still fearfully watching the attitude of his father out of the corner of his eye, he began his turning movement as quickly as possible, which was really only very slowly. Perhaps his father realized his good intention for, instead of hindering this move, he guided him

from a little distance away, helping Gregor with the tip of the stick. If only he had left off that insupportable whistling! Gregor was completely losing his head. He had nearly completed his turn when, bewildered by the din, he mistook his direction and began to go back to his former position. When at last, to his great joy, he found himself facing the half-opened double doors, he discovered that his body was too big to pass through without hurt. Naturally, it never occurred to his father, in his present state, to open the other half of the double doors in order to allow Gregor to pass. He was dominated by the one fixed idea that Gregor should be made to return to his room as quickly as possible. He would never have entertained the long-winded performance which Gregor would have needed to rear up and pass inside. Gregor heard him storming behind him, no doubt to urge him through as though there were no obstacle in his path; the hubbub no longer sounded like the voice of one single father. Now was no time to play, and Gregor—come what may—hurled himself into the doorway. There he lay, jammed in a slanting position, his body raised up on one side and his flank crushed by the door jamb, whose white paint was now covered with horrible brown stains. He was caught fast and could not free himself unaided; on one side his little legs fluttered in the air, on the other they were painfully pressed under his body; then his father gave him a tremendous blow from behind with the stick. Despite the pain, this was almost a relief; he was lifted bodily into the middle of the room and fell, bleeding thickly. The door was slammed by a thrust of the stick, and then, at last, all was still.

II

It was dusk when Gregor awoke from his heavy, deathlike sleep. Even had he not been disturbed, he would doubtless soon have awakened, for he felt he had had his fill of rest and sleep; however, he seemed to have been awakened by the cautious, furtive noise of a key turning in the lock of the hall door. The reflection of the electric tramway lay dimly here and there about the ceiling and on the upper parts of the furniture, but below, where Gregor was, it was dark. Slowly he dragged himself toward the door to ascertain what had happened and fumbled around clumsily with his feelers, whose use he was at last learning to appreciate. His left side seemed to him to be one long, irritating scar, and he limped about on his double set of legs. One of his legs had been seriously injured during the morning's events—it was a miracle that only one should be hurt—and it dragged lifelessly behind.

When he reached the door, he realized what had attracted him: the smell of food. For there was a bowl of sweetened milk in which floated little pieces of bread. He could have laughed with delight, his appetite had grown so since morning; he thrust his head up to the eyes in the milk. But he drew it back quickly; his painful left side gave him some difficulty, for he could only eat by convulsing his whole body and snorting; also, he could not bear the smell of milk, which once had been his favorite drink and which his sister had no doubt prepared for this special reason. He turned from the bowl in disgust and dragged himself to the middle of the room.

The gas was lit in the dining room; he could see it through the cracks of the door. Now was the time when, ordinarily, his father would read aloud to his family from the evening paper, but this time Gregor heard nothing. Perhaps this traditional reading, which his sister always retailed to him in her conversation and in her letters, had not lapsed entirely from the customs of the household. But everywhere was still, and yet surely someone was in the room.

"What a quiet life my family has led," thought Gregor, staring before him in the darkness, and he felt very proud, for it was to him that his parents and his sister owed so placid a life in so nice a flat. What would happen now, if this peace, this satisfaction, this well-being should end in terror and disaster? In order to dissipate such gloomy thoughts, Gregor began to take a little exercise and crawled back and forth over the floor.

Once during the evening he saw the door on the left open slightly, and once it was the door on the right; someone had wished to enter but had found the task too risky. Gregor resolved to stop by the dining-room door and to entice the hesitant visitor as best he might or at least to see who it was; but the door never opened again, and Gregor waited in vain. That morning, when the door had been locked, everyone had tried to invade his room; but now that they had succeeded in opening it no one came to see him; they had even locked his doors on the outside.

Not till late was the light extinguished, and Gregor could guess that his parents and his sister had been waiting till then, for he heard them all go off on tiptoe. Now no one would come to him till the morning, and so he would have the necessary time to reflect on the ordering of his new life; but his great room, in which he was obliged to remain flat on his stomach on the floor, frightened him in a way that he could not understand—for he had lived in it for the past five years—and, with a half-involuntary action of which he was a little ashamed, he hastily slid under the couch; he soon found that here his back was a little crushed and he could not raise his head;

he only regretted that his body was too large to go entirely under the couch.

He spent the whole night there, sometimes in a half-sleep from which the pangs of hunger would wake him with a start, sometimes ruminating on his misfortune and his vague hopes, always concluding that his duty was to remain docile and to try to make things bearable for his family, whatever unpleasantness the situation might impose upon them.

Early in the morning he had a chance to test the strength of his new resolutions; it was still almost dark; his sister, already half dressed, opened the hall door and looked in curiously. She did not see Gregor at once but when she perceived him under the sofa —"Heavens, he must be somewhere; he can't have flown away!"—she was overcome by an unmanageable terror and rushed off, slamming the door. Then, repenting her gesture, she opened it again and entered on tiptoe, as if it were the room of a stranger or one seriously ill. Gregor stretched his head out from the side of the sofa and watched her. Would she notice that he had left the milk, and not from lack of appetite? Would she bring him something which suited his taste better? If she did not do so of her own accord, he would rather have died of hunger than draw her attention to these things, despite his overwhelming desire to rush out of his hiding place, to throw himself at his sister's feet, and to beg for something to eat. But suddenly the sister saw the full bowl in astonishment. A little milk had been spilled around it; using a piece of paper, she took up the bowl without touching it and carried it off to the kitchen. Gregor waited anxiously to see what she would bring him in its place and racked his brains to guess. But he had never realized to what lengths his sister's kindness would go. In order to discover her brother's likes, she brought a whole choice of eatables spread on an old newspaper. There were half-rotted stumps of vegetables, the bones of yesterday's dinner covered with a thick white sauce, a few currants and raisins, some almonds, some cheese that Gregor, a few days before, had declared uneatable, a stale loaf, a piece of salted bread and butter, and another without salt. Besides this she brought back the bowl which had become so important to Gregor. This time it was filled with water, and, guessing that her brother would not like to eat before her, she very kindly retired, closing and locking the door to show him that he might eat in peace. Now that his meal was ready, Gregor felt all his legs trembling. His wounds seemed cured, for he felt not the slightest hindrance, and he was astonished to remember that when he had been human and had cut his finger slightly only a few months ago, it had pained him for several days after.

"Have I become less sensitive?" he wondered; but already he had begun sucking at the cheese, which had suddenly and imperiously attracted him above all the other food. Gluttonously he swallowed in turn the cheese, the vegetables, and the sauce, his eyes moist with satisfaction; as to the fresh things, he wanted none of them; their smell repelled him, and, in order to eat, he separated them from the others.

When he had finished and was idly making up his mind to return to his place, his sister slowly began to turn the key in the lock to give him the signal for retreat. He was very frightened, though he was half asleep, and hurried to reach the sofa. It needed great determination to remain beneath it during the time, however short, that his sister was in the room; his heavy meal had so swollen his body that he could scarcely breathe in his retreat. Between two fits of suffocation he saw, with his eyes filled with tears, that his sister, intending no harm, was sweeping up the remains of his meal with the very things that he had not touched, as if he needed them no more; she put the refuse into a bucket, which she covered with a wooden lid and hastily carried away. Hardly had she turned the handle before Gregor struggled out from his hiding place to expand his body to its proper size.

So he was fed each day; in the morning, before his parents and the maid were awake, and in the afternoon, when lunch was over and while his parents were taking their nap and the maid had been provided with some task or other by his sister. Certainly they did not wish Gregor to die of hunger but perhaps they preferred to know nothing about his meals except by hearsay—they could not have borne to see him—perhaps, also, in order to diminish their disgust, his sister was taking pains to spare them the slightest trouble. He must realize that they, too, had their share of misfortune.

Gregor never learned what excuses they had made to rid themselves of the doctor and the locksmith, for, as no one attempted to understand him, no one, not even his sister, imagined that he could understand them. He had to be content, when she came into his room, to listen to her invoking the saints between her sighs. It was only much later, when Grete had become somewhat accustomed to the new situation—to which she never really became reconciled—that Gregor would occasionally overhear an expression which showed some kindness or allowed him to guess at such a meaning. When he had eaten all the food off the newspaper she would say, "He liked what I brought today"; at other times, when he had no appetite—and lately this had become more frequent—she would say, almost sadly, "Now he has left it all."

But even if he could learn no news directly, Gregor overheard a good deal of what was said in the dining room; as soon as he heard anyone speak, he would hurry to the most propitious door and press his whole body close against it. At first, especially, there was little conversation which did not bear more or less directly on his predicament. For two whole days, the mealtimes were given over to deliberating on the new attitude which must be maintained toward Gregor; even between meals they spoke mostly on the same theme, for now at least two members of the household always remained at home, each one fearing to remain alone and, particularly, to leave Gregor unwatched.

It was not very clear how much the maid knew of what had happened, but, on the very first day, she had fallen on her knees and begged his mother to let her go; and a quarter of an hour later she had left the house in tearful gratitude, as if her release were the greatest evidence of the kindness she had met with in the house; and of her own accord she took a long and boring oath never to reveal the secret to anyone. Now his sister and his mother had to look after the cooking; this entailed little trouble, for the appetite of the Samsa family had gone. Occasionally Gregor would hear one member of the family vainly exhorting another to eat. The reply was always the same: "Thank you, I have had enough," or some such phrase. Perhaps, also, they did not drink. Often his sister would ask her father if he would like some beer; she would cheerfully offer to fetch it, or, faced with her father's silence, she would say, to remove any scruples on his part, that the landlady could go for it, but her father would always reply with a loud, "No!" and nothing more would be said.

In the course of the very first day, the father had clearly explained their precise financial situation to his wife and daughter. From time to time he would get up from the table and hunt for some paper or account book in his Wertheim safe, which he had saved from the crash when his business had failed five years before. He could be heard opening the complicated locks of the safe and closing it again after he had taken out what he sought. Ever since he became a prisoner, nothing had given Gregor such pleasure as these financial explanations. He had always imagined that his father had been unable to save a penny from the ruins of his business; in any case, his father had never said anything to undeceive him, and Gregor had never questioned him upon the matter; he had done all he could to help his family to forget as quickly as possible the disaster which had plunged them into such despair.

He had set to work with splendid ardor; in less than no time, from being a junior clerk he had been promoted to the position of traveler, with all the benefits of such a post; and his successes were suddenly transformed into hard cash which could be spread on the table before the surprised and delighted eyes of his family. Those were happy times —they had never since recovered such a sense of delight, though Gregor now earned enough to feed the whole Samsa family. Everyone had grown accustomed to it, his family as much as himself; they took the money gratefully, he gave it willingly, but the act was accompanied by no remarkable effusiveness. Only his sister had remained particularly affectionate toward Gregor, and it was his secret plan to have her enter the conservatory next year regardless of the considerable cost of such an enterprise, which he would try to meet in some way; for, unlike him, Grete was very fond of music and wished to take up the study of the violin. This matter of the conservatory recurred often in the brief conversations between Gregor and his sister, whenever Gregor had a few days to spend with his family; they hardly ever spoke of it except as a dream impossible to realize; his parents did not much like the innocent allusions to the subject, but Gregor thought very seriously of it and had promised himself that he would solemnly announce his plan next Christmas eve.

It was ideas of this kind, ideas completely unsuited to his present situation, which now passed constantly through Gregor's mind while he held himself pressed erect against the door, listening. He would get so tired that he could no longer hear anything; then he would let himself go and allow his head to fall against the door; but he would draw it back immediately, for the slightest noise was noticed in the dining room and would be followed by an interval of silence.

"What can he be doing now?" his father would say after a moment's pause, turning, no doubt, toward the door; the interrupted conversation would only gradually be resumed.

His father was often obliged to repeat his explanations in order to recall forgotten details or to make them understood by his wife, who did not always grasp them the first time. Gregor thus learned, by what the father said, that, despite all their misfortunes, his parents had been able to save a certain amount from their former property—little enough, it is true, but it had been augmented, to some extent, by interest. Also, they had not spent all the money that Gregor, keeping only a few shillings for himself, had handed over to his family each week, enabling them to gather together a little capital. Behind his door, Gregor nodded his head in approval; he was so happy at this unexpected foresight and thrift. Doubtless, with these savings his father could have more rapidly paid off the debt he had contracted to

Gregor's employer, which would have brought nearer the date of Gregor's release; but under the circumstances it was much better that his father had acted as he had.

Unfortunately this money was not quite sufficient to enable the family to live on its interest; it would last a year, perhaps two, but no more. It was a sum which must not be touched, which must be kept for a case of urgent necessity. As for money on which to live, that would have to be earned. Now, despite his good health, the father was nevertheless an old man who had ceased to work five years before and who could not be expected to entertain any foolish hopes of getting employment; during these five years of retirement—his first holiday in a life entirely devoted to work and unsuccess—he had become very fat and moved with great difficulty. And the old mother would not be able to earn much, suffering as she did from asthma, for even now it was an effort for her to get about the house; she passed a good deal of her time each day lying on the sofa, panting and wheezing under the open window. And was the breadwinner to be the sister, who was still but a child, seventeen years old, so suited to the life she had led till then, nicely dressed, getting plenty of sleep, helping in the house, taking part in a few harmless little entertainments, and playing her violin? Whenever the conversation fell on this topic, Gregor left the door and lay on the leather sofa, whose coolness was so soothing to his body, burning as it was with anxiety and shame.

Often he lay all night, sleepless, and hearing no sound for hours on end save the creak of the leather as he turned. Or, uncomplainingly, he would push his armchair toward the window, crawl up on it, and, propped on the seat, he would lean against the window, not so much to enjoy the view as to recall the sense of release he once used to feel whenever he looked across the pavements; for now he was daily becoming more shortsighted, he could not even make out the hospital opposite, which he had cursed when he was human because he could see it all too clearly; and had he not known so well that he was living in Charlottenstrasse, a quiet but entirely urban street, he might have thought his window gave out on a desert, where the gray of the sky and the gray of the earth merged indistinguishably together. His attentive sister had only to see the armchair by the window twice to understand; from then on, each time she tidied the room she would push the armchair to the window, and would always leave its lower half open.

If only Gregor had been able to speak to his sister, to thank her for all she was doing for him, he could have borne her services easier; but as it was, they pained and embarrassed him. Grete naturally tried to hide any appearance of blame or trouble regarding the situation, and as time went on she played her part even better, but she could not prevent her brother from realizing his predicament more and more clearly. Each time she entered his room, it was terrible for Gregor. Hardly had she entered, when, despite the pains she always took to spare the others the sight of its interior, she would not even take time to shut the door but would run to the window, open it hastily with a single push, as if to escape imminent suffocation, and would stand there for a minute, however cold it might be, breathing deeply. Twice a day she terrified Gregor with this rush and clatter; he shrank trembling under the couch the whole time; he knew his sister would have spared him this had she been able to stand being in the room with him with the window shut.

One day—it must have been a month after Gregor's change, and his sister had no grounds for astonishment at his appearance—she came a little earlier than usual and found him looking out of the window, motionless and in such a position as to inspire terror. If she had not liked to enter, that would not have surprised Gregor, for his position prevented her from opening the window. But not only would she not enter; she sprang back, slammed the door, and locked it; a stranger might have thought that Gregor was lying in wait for his sister, to attack her. Naturally he hid himself under the couch immediately, but he had to wait till midday for Grete's return, and, when she did come, she appeared unusually troubled. He realized that his appearance was still disgusting to the poor girl, that it would always be so, and that she must fiercely resist her own impulse to flee the moment she caught sight of the tiniest part of Gregor's body protruding from under the sofa. To spare her this sight, he took a sheet on his back, dragged it to the sofa—a task which occupied some hours—and spread it in such a way that his sister could see nothing under the sofa, even if she stooped. Had she found this precaution unnecessary, she would have taken the sheet away, for she guessed that Gregor did not so completely shut himself away for pleasure; but she left the sheet where it lay, and Gregor, prudently parting the curtain with his head to see what impression this new arrangement had made upon his sister, thought he detected a look of gratitude in her face.

During the first fortnight his parents had not been able to bring themselves to enter his room, and he often heard them praising the zeal of his sister, whom they had regarded, so far, as a useless young girl and of whom they had often complained. But now, both his father and mother would wait quite frequently

outside Gregor's door while his sister was tidying the room, and scarcely had she come out again before they would make her tell them in detail exactly how she had found the room, what Gregor had eaten, and, in detail, what he was doing at that moment; they would ask her, too, if there were the slightest signs of improvement. His mother seemed impatient to see Gregor, but the father and sister restrained her with argument to which she listened very attentively and with which she wholly agreed. Later, however, they had to use force, and when his mother began to cry, "Let me go to Gregor! My poor boy! Don't you understand that I must see him!" Gregor thought that perhaps it would be as well if his mother did come in, not every day, of course, but perhaps once a week; she would understand things better than his sister, who was but a child, for all her courage, and had perhaps taken on such a difficult task out of childish lightheartedness.

Gregor's wish to see his mother was soon realized. Gregor avoided showing himself at the window during the day, out of consideration to his parents; but his restricted walks around the floor did not fully compensate him for this self-denial, nor could he bear to lie still for long, even during the night; he took no more pleasure in eating, and it soon became his habit to distract himself by walking—around the room, back and forth along the walls, and across the ceiling, on which he would hang; it was quite a different matter from walking across the floor. His breathing became freer, a light, swinging motion went through his body, and he felt so elated that now and then, to his own surprise, he would let himself go and fall to the floor. But by now, knowing better how to manage his body, he succeeded in rendering these falls harmless. His sister soon noticed his new pastime, for he left sticky marks here and there in his track, and Grete took it into her head to help him in his walks by removing all the furniture likely to be a hindrance, particularly the chest and the desk. Unfortunately, she was not strong enough to manage this on her own and dared not ask the help of her father; as for the maid, she certainly would have refused, for if this sixteen-year-old child had worked bravely since the former cook had left, it was on condition that she could stay continually barricaded in the kitchen, whose doors she would only open on special demand. So there was nothing else for it; Grete would have to enlist the mother's help one day when the father was away.

The mother gladly consented, but her exclamations of joy were hushed before Gregor's door. The sister first made sure that everything was in order in the room; then she allowed the mother to enter. In his great haste, Gregor had pulled the sheet down further than usual, and the many folds in which it fell gave the scene the air of a still life. This time he refrained from peeping under the sheet to spy on his mother but he was delighted to have her near.

"You may come in; he is not in sight," said his sister; and, taking her mother by the hand, she led her into the room. Then Gregor heard the two frail women struggling to remove the heavy old chest; the sister undertook the hardest part of the task, despite the warnings of her mother, who feared she might do herself some harm. It took a long time. They had been struggling with the chest for four hours when the mother declared that it might be best to leave it where it was, that it was too heavy for them, that they would not finish moving it before the father returned, and that, with the chest in the middle of the room, Gregor would be considerably impeded in his movements, and, finally, who knew whether he might not be displeased by the removal of his furniture?

The mother thought he would be; the sight of the bare walls struck cold at her heart; might Gregor not feel the same, having long grown so accustomed to the furniture, and would he not feel forsaken in his empty room? "Isn't it a fact," said the mother in a low voice—she had spoken in whispers ever since she entered the room, so that Gregor whose hiding place she had not yet discovered, might not overhear, not so much what she was saying—for she was persuaded that he could not understand—but the very sound of her voice. "Isn't it a fact that when we remove the furniture, we seem to imply that we are giving up all hope of seeing him cured and are wickedly leaving him to his fate? I think it would be better to keep the room just as it was before, so that Gregor will find nothing changed when he comes back to us and will be able the more easily to forget what has happened meanwhile."

Hearing his mother's words, Gregor realized how these two monotonous months, in the course of which nobody had addressed a word to him, must have affected his mind; he could not otherwise explain his desire for an empty room. Did he really wish to allow this warm, comfortable room with its genial furniture to be transformed into a cavern in which, in rapid and complete forgetfulness of his human past, he might exercise his right to crawl all over the walls? It seemed he was already so near to forgetting; and it had required nothing less than his mother's voice, which he had not heard for so long, to rouse him. Nothing should be removed, everything must stay as it is, he could not bear to forego the good influence of his furniture, and, if it prevented him from indulging his crazy impulses, then so much the better.

Unfortunately, his sister was not of this opinion;

she had become accustomed to assume authority over her parents where Gregor was concerned—this not without cause—and now the mother's remarks were enough to make her decide to remove not only the desk and the chest—which till now had been their only aim—but all the other furniture as well, except the indispensable sofa. This was not the result of mere childish bravado, nor the outcome of that new feeling of self-confidence which she had just acquired so unexpectedly and painfully. No, she really believed that Gregor had need of plenty of room for exercise and that, as far as she could see, he never used the furniture. Perhaps, also, the romantic character of girls of her age was partly responsible for her decision, a sentiment which strove to satisfy itself on every possible occasion and which now drove her to dramatize her brother's situation to such an extent so that she could devote herself to Gregor even more passionately than hitherto; for in a room over whose bare walls Gregor reigned alone, no one but Grete dare enter and stay.

She did not allow herself to be turned from her resolve by her mother, made irresolute by the oppressive atmosphere of the room, and who did not hesitate now to remove the chest as best she could. Gregor could bear to see the chest removed, at a pinch, but the desk must stay. And hardly had the women left the room, panting as they pushed the chest, than Gregor put out his head to examine the possibilities of making a prudent and tactful appearance. But unfortunately it was his mother who returned first, while Grete, in the side room, her arms around the chest, was rocking it from side to side without being able to settle it in position. The mother was not used to the sight of Gregor; it might give her a serious shock. Terrified, he hastened to retreat to the other end of the sofa, but he could not prevent the sheet from fluttering slightly, which immediately attracted his mother's attention. She stopped short, stood stockstill for a moment, then hurried back to Grete.

Gregor assured himself that nothing extraordinary was happening—they were merely removing a few pieces of furniture—but the coming and going of the women, their little cries, the scraping of the furniture over the floor, seemed to combine in such an excruciating din that, however much he withdrew his head, contracted his legs, and pressed himself to the ground, he had to admit that he could not bear this torture much longer. They were emptying his room, taking away from him all that he loved; they had already removed the chest in which he kept his saw and his fretwork outfit; now they were shifting his desk, which had stood so solid and fast to the floor all the time it was in use, that desk on which he had written his lessons while he was at the commercial school, at the secondary school, even at the preparatory school. However, he could no longer keep pace with their intentions, for so absent minded had he become he had almost forgotten their existence, now that fatigue had quietened them and the clatter of the weary feet could no longer be heard.

So he came out—the women were only leaning against the desk in the next room, recovering their breath—and he found himself so bewildered that he changed his direction four times; he really could not decide what he should first salvage—when suddenly he caught sight of the picture of the woman in furs which assumed tremendous importance on the bare wall; he hastily climbed up and pressed himself against the glass, which stuck to his burning belly and refreshed him delightfully. This picture, at least, which Gregor entirely covered, should not be snatched away from him by anyone. He turned his head toward the dining-room door to observe the women as they returned.

They had had but a short rest and were already coming back; Grete's arm was round her mother's waist, supporting her.

"Well, what shall we take now?" said Grete, and she looked around. Her eyes met those of Gregor on the wall. If she succeeded in keeping her presence of mind, it was only for her mother's sake, toward whom she leaned her head to prevent her from seeing anything and said, a little too quickly and with a trembling voice, "Come, wouldn't it be better to go back to the living room for a minute?" The girl's intention was clear to Gregor: she wished to put her mother in a safe place and then to drive him from the wall. Well, let her try! He lay over his picture, and he would not let it go. He would rather leap into his sister's face.

But Grete had merely disquieted her mother; now she turned, saw the gigantic brown stain spread over the wallpaper and, before she realized that it was Gregor she was seeing, she cried, "O God! O God!" in a screaming, raucous voice, fell on the sofa with outspread arms in a gesture of complete renunciation, and gave no further sign of life. "You, Gregor!" cried the sister, raising her fist and piercing Gregor with a look. It was the first word she had addressed to him directly ever since his metamorphosis. Then she ran to get some smelling salts from the dining room to rouse her mother from her swoon. Gregor decided to help—there was still time to save the picture—alas, he found he had stuck fast to the glass and had to make a violent effort to detach himself; then he hurried into the dining room as if able to give his sister some good advice, but he was obliged to content himself with remaining passively behind

her while she rummaged among the bottles, and he frightened her so terribly when she turned around that a bottle fell and broke on the floor, a splinter wounded Gregor in the face, and a corrosive medicine flowed round his feet; then Grete hastily grabbed up all the bottles she could carry and rushed in to her mother, slamming the door behind her with her foot. Now Gregor was shut out from his mother, who perhaps was nearly dead through his fault; he dared not open the door lest he drive away his sister, who must stay by his mother; so there was nothing to do but wait, and, gnawed by remorse and distress, he began to wander over the walls, the furniture, and the ceilings so rapidly that everything began to spin around him, till in despair he fell heavily on to the middle of the huge table.

A moment passed; Gregor lay stretched there, around all was still; perhaps that was a good sign. But suddenly he heard a knock. The maid was naturally barricaded in her kitchen; Grete herself must go to the door. His father had returned.

"What has happened?" were his first words; no doubt Grete's expression had explained everything.

The girl replied in a stifled voice—probably she leaned her face against her father's breast—"Mother fainted, but she is better now. Gregor has got out."

"I was waiting for that," said the father, "I told you all along, but you women will never listen."

Gregor realized by these words that his father had misunderstood Grete's brief explanation and imagined that his son had broken loose in some reprehensible way. There was no time to explain. Gregor had to find some way of pacifying his father, so he quickly crawled to the door of his room and pressed himself against it for his father to see, as he came in, how he had every intention of returning to his own room immediately and that it was not at all necessary to drive him back with violence; one had only to open the door and he would quickly withdraw.

But his father was in no mood to notice these fine points. As he entered he cried, "Ah!" in a tone at once of joy and anger; Gregor turned his head away from the door and lifted it toward his father. He was astonished. He had never imagined his father as he stood before him now; it is true that for some time now he had neglected to keep himself acquainted with the events of the house, preferring to devote himself to his new mode of existence, and he had therefore been unaware of a certain change of character in his family. And yet—and yet, was that really his father? Was it really the same man who once had lain wearily in bed when Gregor had been leaving on his journeys, who met him, on his return, in his nightshirt, seated in an armchair out of which he could not even lift himself, throwing his arms high to show

how pleased he was? Was this that same old man who, on the rare walks which the family would take together, two or three Sundays a year and on special holidays, would hobble between Gregor and his mother, while they walked slower and slower for him, as he, covered with an old coat, carefully set his stick before him and prudently worked his way forward; and yet, despite their slowness, he would be obliged to stop, whenever he wished to say anything, and call his escort back to him? How upstanding he had become since then!

Now he was wearing a blue uniform with gold buttons, without a single crease, just as you see the employees of banking houses wearing; above the big, stiff collar his double chin spread its powerful folds; under his bristly eyebrows the watchful expression of his black eyes glittered young and purposefully; his white hair, ordinarily untidy, had been carefully brushed till it shone. He threw on to the sofa his cap, ornamented with the gilded monogram of some bank, making it describe the arc of a circle across the room, and, with his hands in his trouser pockets, the long flaps of his coat turned back, he walked toward Gregor with a menacing air. He himself did not know what he was going to do; however, he raised his feet very high, and Gregor, astonished at the enormous size of the soles of his boots, took care to remain still, for he knew that, from the first day of his metamorphosis, his father had held the view that the greatest severity was the only attitude to take up toward Gregor. Then he began to beat a retreat before his father's approach, halting when the other stopped and beginning again at his father's slightest move. In this way they walked several times round the room without any decisive result; it did not even take on the appearance of a pursuit, so slow was their pace.

Gregor was provisionally keeping to the floor; he feared that if his father saw him climbing about the walls or rushing across the ceiling, he might take this maneuver for some refinement of bad behavior. However, he had to admit that he could not go on much longer in this way; in the little time his father needed to take a step, Gregor had to make a whole series of gymnastic movements and, as he had never had good lungs, he now began to pant and wheeze; he tried to recover his breath quickly in order to gather all his strength for a supreme effort, scarcely daring to open his eyes, so stupefied that he could think of no other way to safety than by pursuing his present course; he had already forgotten that the walls were at his disposal, and the carefully carved furniture, all covered with festoons of plush and lace as it was. Suddenly something flew sharply by him, fell to the ground, and rolled away. It was an apple, carelessly thrown;

a second one flew by. Paralyzed with terror, Gregor stayed still. It was useless to continue his course, now that his father had decided to bombard him. He had emptied the bowls of fruit on the sideboard, filled his pockets, and now threw apple after apple, without waiting to take aim.

These little red apples rolled about the floor as if electrified knocking against each other. One lightly-thrown apple struck Gregor's back and fell off without doing any harm, but the next one literally pierced his flesh. He tried to drag himself a little further away, as if a change of position could relieve the shattering agony he suddenly felt, but he seemed to be nailed fast to the spot and stretched his body helplessly, not knowing what to do. With his last, hopeless glance, he saw his door opened suddenly, and, in front of his sister, who was shouting at the top of her voice, his mother came running in, in her petticoat, for his sister had partly undressed her that she might breathe easier in her swoon. And his mother, who ran to the father, losing her skirts one by one, stumbled forward, thrust herself against her husband, embraced him, pressed him to her, and, with her hands clasped at the back of his neck—already Gregor could see no more—begged him to spare Gregor's life.

III

The apple which no one dared draw from Gregor's back remained embedded in his flesh as a palpable memory, and the grave wound which he now had borne for a month seemed to have reminded his father that Gregor, despite his sad and terrible change, remained none the less a member of the family and must not be treated as an enemy; on the contrary, duty demanded that disgust should be overcome and Gregor be given all possible help.

His wound had made him lose, irremediably, no doubt, much of his agility; now, merely to cross his room required a long, long time, as if he were an aged invalid; his walks across the walls could no longer be considered. But this aggravation of his state was largely compensated for, in his opinion, by the fact that now, every evening, the dining-room door was left open; for two hours he would wait for this. Lying in the darkness of his room, invisible to the diners, he could observe the whole family gathered round the table in the lamplight, and he could, by common consent, listen to all they had to say—it was much better than before.

It must be admitted that they no longer held those lively conversations of which, in former times, he had always thought with such sadness as he crept into his damp bed in some little hotel room. Most of the time, now, they discussed nothing in particular after dinner. The father would soon settle himself to doze in his armchair; the mother and daughter would bid each other be silent; the mother, leaning forward in the light, would sew at some fine needlework for a lingerie shop, and the sister, who had obtained a job as a shop assistant, would study shorthand or French in the hope of improving her position. Now and then the father would wake up and, as if he did not know that he had been asleep, would say to his wife, "How late you are sewing tonight!" and would fall off to sleep again, while the mother and sister would exchange a tired smile.

By some capricious obstinacy, the father always refused to take off his uniform, even at home; his dressing gown hung unused in the wardrobe, and he slept in his armchair in full livery, as if to keep himself always ready to carry out some order; even in his own home he seemed to await his superior's voice. Moreover, the uniform had not been new when it was issued to him and now each day it became more shabby, despite the care which the two women devoted to it; and Gregor often spent the evening staring dully at this coat, so spotted and stained, whose polished buttons always shone so brightly, and in which the old man slept, uncomfortably but peacefully.

As soon as the clock struck ten, the mother, in a low voice, tried to rouse her husband and to encourage him to go to bed, as it was impossible to get proper sleep in such a position, and he must sleep normally before returning to work at six the next morning. But, with the obstinacy which had characterized him ever since he had obtained his position at the bank, he would stay at the table although he regularly dropped off to sleep, and thus it would become more and more difficult to induce him to change his armchair for the bed. The mother and sister might insist with their little warnings; he stayed there just the same, slowly nodding his head, his eyes shut tight, and would not get up. The mother might shake him by the wrist, might whisper endearments in his ear; the daughter might abandon her work to assist her mother, but all in vain. The old man would merely sink deeper in his chair. At last the two women would have to take him under the arms to make him open his eyes; then he would look at each in turn and say, "What a life! Is this the hard-earned rest of my old days?" and, leaning on the two women, he would rise painfully, as if he were a tremendous weight, and would allow himself to be led to the door by his wife and daughter; then he would wave them off and continue alone, while the mother and sister, the one quickly throwing down her pen, the other her needle, would run after him to help.

Who in the overworked and overtired family had time to attend to Gregor, except for his most pressing needs? The household budget was ever more and more reduced; at last the maid was dismissed. In her place, a gigantic charwoman with bony features and white hair, which stood up all around her head, came, morning and evening, to do the harder work. The rest was done by the mother, over and above her interminable mending and darning. It even happened that they were obliged to sell various family trinkets which formerly had been worn proudly by the mother and sister at ceremonies and festivals, as Gregor discovered one evening when he heard them discussing the price they hoped to get. But their most persistent complaints were about this flat, which was so much larger than they needed and which had now become too expensive for the family purse; they could not leave, they said, for they could not imagine how Gregor could be moved. Alas, Gregor understood that it was not really he who was the chief obstacle to this removal, for he might easily have been transported in a large wooden box pierced with a few air holes. No, what particularly prevented the family from changing their residence was their own despair, the idea that they had been stricken by such a misfortune as had never before occurred in the family or within the circle of their acquaintances.

Of all the deprivations which the world imposes on poor people, not one had been spared them; the father took his day-time meals with the lesser employees of the bank, the mother was killing herself mending the linen of strangers, the sister ran here and there behind her counter at the customers' bidding; but the family had energy for nothing further. It seemed to poor Gregor that his wound reopened whenever his mother and sister, returning from putting the father to bed, would leave their work in disorder and bring their chairs nearer to each other, till they were sitting almost cheek to cheek; then the mother would say, pointing to Gregor's room, "Close the door, Grete," and he would once more be left in darkness, while, outside, the two women mingled their tears or, worse, sat at the table staring with dry eyes.

These days and nights brought Gregor no sleep. From time to time he thought of taking the family affairs in hand, as he once used, the very next time the door was opened; at the end of a long perspective of time he dimly saw in his mind his employer and the manager, the clerks and apprentices, the porter with his narrow ideas, two or three acquaintances from other offices, a provincial barmaid—a fleeting but dear memory—and a cashier in a hat shop, whom he had pursued earnestly but too slowly; they passed through his mind in confusion, mingled with unknown and forgotten faces; but none of them could bring help to him or his family; nothing was to be gained from them. He was pleased to be able to dismiss them from his mind but now he no longer cared what happened to his family; on the contrary, he only felt enraged because they neglected to tidy his room, and, though nothing imaginable could excite his appetite, he began making involved plans for a raid on the larder, with a view to taking such food as he had a right to, even if he was not hungry. Nowadays his sister no longer tried to guess what might please him; she made a hasty appearance twice a day, in the morning and in the afternoon, before going to her shop, and pushed a few scraps of food into the room with her foot; in the evening, without even bothering to see whether he had touched his meal or whether he had left it entirely—and this was usually the case—she would sweep up the remains with a whisk of the broom.

As for tidying up the room, which Grete now did in the evenings, it could not have been done in a more hasty manner. Great patches of dirt streaked the wall, little heaps of dust and ordure lay here and there about the floor. At first Gregor would place himself in the filthiest places whenever his sister appeared, so that this might seem a reproach to her. But he could have stayed there for weeks, and still Grete would not have altered her conduct; she saw the dirt as well as he but she had finally decided to take no further trouble. This did not prevent her from taking even more jealous care than ever to insure that no other member of the family should presume on her right to the tidying of the room.

Once the mother undertook to give Gregor's room a great cleaning which required several buckets of water, and this deluge deeply upset poor Gregor, crouched under his sofa in bitter immobility—but the mother's punishment soon came. Hardly had the sister, coming home in the evening, noticed the difference in Gregor's room, than, feeling deeply offended, she ran crying and screaming into the dining room, despite the appeal of her mother, who raised her hands in supplication; the father, who was quietly seated at table, leaped up, astonished but powerless to pacify her. Then he, too, became agitated; shouting, he began to attack the mother, on the one hand, for not leaving the care and cleaning of Gregor's room to the girl and, on the other hand, he forbade his daughter ever again to dare to clean it; the mother tried to draw the old man, quivering with anger as he was, into the bedroom; the daughter, shaken with sobs, was banging on the table with her little fists, while Gregor loudly hissed with rage to think that no one had the decency or

consideration to close the door and thus spare him the sight of all this trouble and uproar.

But even if the sister, tired out by her work in the shop, could not bother to look after Gregor as carefully as hitherto, she could still have arranged that he should not be neglected without necessarily calling on the aid of her mother, for there was always the charwoman. This old woman, whose bony frame had helped her out of worse trouble during her long life, could not really be said to feel any disgust with Gregor. Though she was not inquisitive, she had opened his door one day and had stood with her hands folded over her stomach, astonished at the sight of Gregor, who began to trot here and there in his alarm, though she had no thought of chasing him. From that day, morning and evening, the old woman never lost an opportunity of opening the door a little to peer into the room.

At first she would call Gregor to make him come out, crying in a familiar tone, "Come on, you old cockroach!" or, "Hey, look at the old cockroach!" To such invitations Gregor would not respond; instead he remained motionless beneath his sofa as if the door had not been opened. If they had only ordered the charwoman to clean his room out each day instead of allowing her to go on teasing and upsetting him! Early one morning, when heavy rain—perhaps a sign of approaching spring—beat on the roofs, Gregor was so annoyed by the old woman as she began to bait him again that he suddenly turned on her, in a somewhat cumbersome and uncertain manner, it must be admitted, but with every intention of attacking her. She was not at all frightened of him; there was a chair by the door; she took it up and brandished it, opening wide her mouth with the obvious intention of not closing it until she had brought the chair down with a crash on Gregor's back. "Ah, is that all?" she asked, seeing him return to his former position, and she quietly put the chair back in its place.

Nowadays Gregor hardly ate at all. When, by some chance, he passed by his scraps, he would amuse himself by taking a piece of food in his mouth and keeping it there for hours, usually spitting it out in the end. At first he had thought that his loss of appetite was due to the misery into which the state of his room had plunged him; no doubt this was a mistake, for he had soon become reconciled to the squalor of his surroundings. His family had got into the habit of piling into his room whatever could not be accommodated elsewhere, and this meant a great deal, now that one of the rooms had been let to three lodgers. They were very earnest and serious men; all three had thick beards—as Gregor saw one day when he was peering through a crack in the door—and they were fanatically tidy; they insisted on order, not only in their own room, but also, now that they were living here, throughout the whole household, and especially in the kitchen.

They had brought with them all that they needed, and this rendered superfluous a great many things about the house which could neither be sold nor thrown away, and which were now all stacked in Gregor's room, as were the ash bucket and the rubbish bin. Everything that seemed for the moment useless would be dumped in Gregor's room by the charwoman, who was always in a breathless hurry to get through her work; he would just have time to see a hand brandishing some unwanted utensil, and then the door would slam again. Perhaps the old woman intended to return and find the objects she so carelessly relegated here when she needed them and had time to search; or perhaps she meant to throw them all away some day, but in actual fact they stayed in the room, on the very spot where they had first fallen, so that Gregor was obliged to pick his way among the rubbish to make a place for himself —a game for which his taste began to grow, in spite of the appalling misery and fatigue which followed these peregrinations, leaving him paralyzed for hours. As the lodgers sometimes dined at home in the living room, the door of this room would be shut on certain evenings; however, Gregor no longer attached any importance to this; for some while, now, he had ceased to profit by those evenings when the family would open the door and he would remain shrinking in the darkest corner of his room, where the family could not see him.

One day the woman forgot to close the dining-room door, and it was still ajar when the lodgers came in and lit the gas. They sat down at table in the places that previously had been occupied by the father, the mother, and Gregor; each unfolded his napkin and took up his knife and fork. Soon the mother appeared in the doorway with a plate of meat; the sister followed her, carrying a dish of potatoes. When their meal had been set before them the lodgers leaned over to examine it, and the one who was seated in the middle and who appeared to have some authority over the others, cut a piece of meat as it lay on the dish to ascertain whether it was tender or whether he should send it back to the kitchen. He seemed satisfied, however, and the two women, who had been anxiously watching, gave each other a smile of relief.

The family itself lived in the kitchen. However, the father, before going into the kitchen, always came into the dining room and bowed once with his cap in his hand, then made his way around the table. The boarders rose together and murmured something in their beards. Once they were alone, they began to eat in silence. It seemed curious to Gregor that he could hear the gnashing of their teeth above all the clatter of cutlery; it was as if they wanted to prove to him that one must have real teeth in order to eat properly, and that the best mandibles in the world were but an unsatisfactory substitute. "I am hungry," thought Gregor sadly, "but not for these things. How these lodgers can eat! And in the meantime I might die, for all they care."

He could not remember hearing his sister play since the arrival of the lodgers; but this evening the sound of the violin came from the kitchen. The lodgers had just finished their meal; the middle one had brought a newspaper and had given a page to each of the others; now they all three read, leaning back in their chairs and smoking. The sound of the violin attracted their attention, and they rose and walked on tiptoe toward the hall door, where they halted and remained very close together.

Apparently they had been heard in the kitchen, for the father cried, "Does the violin upset you gentlemen? We'll stop it immediately."

"On the contrary," said the man in the middle. "Would Fräulein Samsa not like to come in and play to us here in the dining room, where it is much nicer and more comfortable?"

"Oh, thank you," said the father, as if he were the violinist.

The gentlemen walked back across the room and waited. Soon the father came in with the music stand, the mother with the sheets of music, and the sister with the violin. The sister calmly prepared to play; her parents, who had never before let their rooms, were exaggeratedly polite to the boarders and were afraid to seem presumptuous by sitting in their own chairs; the father leaned against the door, his right hand thrust between two buttons of his livery coat; but one of the gentlemen offered the mother a chair in which she finally sat, not daring to move from her corner throughout the performance.

The girl now began to play, while her father and mother, from either side, watched the movement of her hands. Attracted by the music, Gregor had crawled forward a little and had thrust his head into the room. He was no longer astonished that nowadays he had entirely lost that consideration for others, that anxiety to cause no trouble that once had been his pride. Yet never had he more reason to remain hidden, for now, because of the dirt that lay about his room, flying up at the slightest movement, he was always covered with dust and fluff, with ends of cotton and hairs, and with morsels of stale food, which stuck to his back or to his feet and which he trailed after him wherever he went; his apathy had grown too great for him to bother anymore about cleaning himself several times a day by lying on his back and rubbing himself on the carpet, as once he used to do. And this filthy state did not prevent him from crawling over the spotless floor without a moment's shame.

So far, no one had noticed him. The family was too absorbed by the music of the violin, and the lodgers, who had first stood with their hands in their pockets, very close to the music stand—which disturbed the sister a great deal as she was obliged to see their image dancing amid the notes—had at last retired toward the window, where they stood speaking together half aloud, with lowered heads, under the anxious gaze of the father, who was watching attentively. It had become only too evident that they had been deceived in their hopes of hearing some beautiful violin piece, or at least some amusing little tune; it seemed that what the girl was playing bored them and that now they only tolerated her out of politeness. By the way in which they puffed the smoke of their cigars, by the energy with which they blew it toward the ceiling through the mouth or the nose, one could guess how fidgety they were becoming. And the sister was playing so nicely. Her face leaning to one side, her glance followed the score carefully and sadly. Gregor crawled forward a little more and put his head as near as possible to the floor to meet her gaze. Could it be that he was only an animal, when music moved him so? It seemed to him to open a way toward that unknown nourishment he so longed for. He resolved to creep up to his sister and to pull at her dress to make her understand that she must come with him, for no one here would appreciate her music as much as he. He would never let her out of his room—at least, while he lived—for once, his horrible shape would serve him some useful purpose; he would be at all doors at once, repulsing intruders with his raucous breath; but his sister would not be forced to stay there; she must live with him of her own accord; she would sit by him on the sofa, hearing what he had to say; then he would tell her in confidence that he had firmly intended to send her to the Conservatory and had planned to let everyone know last Christmas—was Christmas really past?—without listening to any objections, had his misfortune not overtaken him too soon. His sister, moved by this explanation, would surely burst into tears, and Gregor, climbing up on her shoulder, would kiss her neck; this would be all the easier, for she had worn neither collar nor ribbon ever since she had been working in the shop.

"Herr Samsa," cried the middle lodger, and he pointed at Gregor, who slowly came into the room. The violin was suddenly silenced, the middle lodger turned to his friends, grinning and shaking his head, then once more he stared at Gregor. The father seemed to consider it more urgent to reassure the lodgers than to drive his son from the room, though the lodgers did not seem to be at all upset by the spectacle; in fact, Gregor seemed to amuse them more highly than did the violin. The father hurried forward and, with outstretched arms, tried to drive them into their room, hiding Gregor from them with his body. Now they began to be really upset, but it is not known whether this was on account of the father's action or because they had been living with such a monstrous neighbor as Gregor without being made aware of it. They demanded explanations, waving their arms in the air; and, fidgeting nervously with their beards, they retreated toward their own door. Meanwhile the sister had recovered from the distress that the sudden interruption of her music had caused her; after remaining a moment completely at a loss, with the violin and the bow hanging from her helpless hands, following the score with her eyes as if she were still playing, she suddenly came back to life, laid the violin in her mother's lap—the mother sat suffocating in her chair, her lungs working violently—and rushed into the next room, toward which the lodgers were rapidly retreating before Herr Samsa's onslaught. One could see how quickly, under Grete's practised hand, pillows and covers were set in order on the beds. The lodgers had not yet reached the room when their beds were already prepared, and Grete had slipped out. The father seemed so possessed by his strange fury that he had quite forgotten the respect due to lodgers.

He drove them to the door of the room, where the middle lodger suddenly came to a stop, stamping thunderously on the floor. "I wish to inform you," said this man, raising his hand and looking around for the two women, "that in view of the disgusting circumstances which govern this family and this house"—and here he spat quickly on the carpet—"I hereby immediately give up my room. Naturally, you will not get a penny for the time I have been living here; on the contrary, I am considering whether I should not claim compensation from you, damages which should easily be awarded in any court of law; it is a matter about which I shall inquire, believe me." He was silent and stared into space, as if awaiting something. Accordingly, his two friends also spoke up: "We, too, give our notice." Thereupon the gentleman in the middle seized the door handle, and they went inside. The door closed with a crash.

The father stumbled toward his chair, put his trembling hands upon the arms, and let himself drop into it; he looked exactly as if he were settling himself for his customary evening nap, but the way his head drooped heavily from side to side showed that he was thinking of something other than sleep. All this time Gregor had stayed still on the spot where he had surprised the lodgers. He felt completely paralyzed with bewilderment at the checking of his plans—perhaps, also, with weakness due to his prolonged fasting. He feared that the whole household would fall upon him immediately; he foresaw the precise moment when this catastrophe would happen, and now he waited. Even the violin did not frighten him as it fell with a clatter from the trembling fingers of his mother, who until now had held it in her lap.

"My dear parents," said his sister, who beat with her hand on the table by way of introduction. "Things cannot go on like this. Even if you do not realize it, I can see it quite clearly. I will not mention my brother's name when I speak of this monster here; I merely want to say: we must find some means of getting rid of it. We have done all that is humanly possible to care for it, to put up with it; I believe that nobody could reproach us in the least."

"She's a thousand times right," said the father. But the mother, who had not yet recovered her breath, coughed helplessly behind her hand, her eyes haggard.

The sister hurried toward her mother and held her forehead. Grete's words seemed to have made up the father's mind, for now he sat up in his armchair and fidgeted with his cap among the dishes on the table, from which the lodgers' meal had not yet been cleared; from time to time he stared at Gregor.

"We must find a way of getting rid of it," repeated the sister, now speaking only to her father, for her mother, shaken by her coughing, could hear nothing. "It will bring you both to the grave. I can see it coming. When people have to work all day, as we must, we cannot bear this eternal torture each time we come home at night. I can stand it no longer." And she wept so bitterly that her tears fell on her mother's face, who wiped them off with a mechanical movement of her hand.

"But what can we do, child?" said the father in a pitiful voice. It was surprising to see how well he understood his daughter.

The sister merely shrugged her shoulders as a sign of the perplexity which, during her tears, had replaced her former assurance.

"If he could only understand us," said the father in a half-questioning tone, but the sister, through her tears, made a violent gesture with her hand as a sign that this was not to be thought of.

"If only he could understand us," repeated the father—and he shut his eyes as he spoke, as if to show that he agreed with the sister that such a thing was quite impossible. "If only he could understand us, perhaps there would be some way of coming to an agreement. But as it is . . ."

"It must go!" cried the sister. "That's the only way out. You must get the idea out of your head that this is Gregor. We have believed that for too long, and that is the cause of all our unhappiness. How could it be Gregor? If it were really he, he would long ago have realized that he could not live with human beings and would have gone off on his own accord. I haven't a brother any longer, but we can go on living and can honor his memory. In his place we have this monster that pursues us and drives away our lodgers; perhaps it wants the whole flat to itself, to drive us out into the streets. Look, father, look!" she suddenly screamed, "it's beginning again!" And in an access of terror, which Gregor could not understand, she let go her mother so suddenly that she bounced in the seat of the armchair; it seemed as if the sister would rather sacrifice her mother than stay near Gregor; she hastily took refuge behind her father, who was very upset by her behavior and now stood up, spreading his arms to protect her.

But Gregor had no thought of frightening anyone, least of all his sister. He had merely started to turn around in order to go back to his room; but it must be realized that this looked very alarming, for his weakness obliged him to assist his difficult turning movement with his head, which he raised and lowered many times, clutching at the carpet with his mandibles. At last he ceased and stared at the family. It seemed they realized his good intentions. They were watching him in mute sadness. The mother lay in her armchair, her outstretched legs pressed tightly together, her eyes nearly closed with fatigue; the father and sister were sitting side by side, and the girl's arm was round her father's neck.

"Now, perhaps, they will let me turn," thought Gregor, and he once more set about his task. He could not repress a sigh of weariness; he was obliged to rest from time to time. However, no one hurried him; they left him entirely alone. When he had completed his turn, he immediately beat a retreat, crawling straight ahead. He was astonished at the distance which separated him from his room; he did not realize that this was due merely to his weak state and that a little before he could have covered the distance without noticing it. His family did not disturb him by a single cry, a single exclamation; but this he did not even notice, so necessary was it to concentrate all his will on getting back to his room. It was only when he had at long last reached his door that he thought of turning his head, not completely, because his neck had become very stiff, but sufficiently to reassure himself that nothing had changed behind him; only his sister was not standing up. His last look was toward his mother, who, by this time, was fast asleep.

Hardly was he in his room before the door was slammed, locked, and double bolted. So sudden was the crash that Gregor's legs gave way. It was his sister who had rushed to the door. She had stood up so as to be ready immediately and at the right moment had run forward so lightly that he had not heard her come; as she turned the key in the lock, she cried to her parents, "At last!"

"What now?" asked Gregor, looking around himself in the darkness. He soon discovered that he could not move. This did not surprise him in the least; it seemed to him much more remarkable that such frail legs had hitherto been able to bear his weight. Now he experienced a feeling of relative comfort. True, his whole body ached, but it seemed that these aches became less and less until finally they disappeared. Even the rotted apple embedded in his back hardly hurt him now; no more did the inflammation of the surrounding parts, covered with fine dust, cause him any further discomfort. He thought of his family in tender solicitude. He realized that he must go, and his opinion on this point was even more firm, if possible, than that of his sister. He lay in this state of peaceful and empty meditation till the clock struck the third morning hour. He saw the landscape grow lighter through the window; then, against his will, his head fell forward and his last feeble breath streamed from his nostrils.

When the charwoman arrived early in the morning —and though she had often been forbidden to do so, she always slammed the door so loudly in her vigor and haste that once she was in the house it was impossible to get any sleep—she did not at first notice anything unusual as she paid her customary morning visit to Gregor. She imagined that he was deliberately lying motionless in order to play the role of an "injured party," as she herself would say—she deemed him capable of such refinements; as she had a long broom in her hand, she tried to tickle him from the doorway. Meeting with little success, she grew angry; she gave him one or two hard pushes, and it was only when his body moved unresistingly before her thrusts that she became curious. She quickly realized what had happened, opened her eyes wide, and whistled in astonishment, but she did not stay in the room; she ran to the bedroom, opened the door, and loudly shouted into the darkness, "Come and look! He's stone dead! He's lying there, absolutely dead as a doornail!"

Herr and Frau Samsa sat up in their bed and tried to calm each other; the old woman had frightened them so much and they did not realize the sense of

her message immediately. But now they hastily scrambled out of bed, Herr Samsa on one side, his wife on the other; Herr Samsa put the coverlet over his shoulders, Frau Samsa ran out, clad only in her nightdress; and it was thus that they rushed into Gregor's room. Meanwhile, the dining-room door was opened—Grete had been sleeping there since the arrival of the lodgers—she was fully dressed, as if she had not slept all night, and the pallor of her face seemed to bear witness to her sleeplessness.

"Dead?" said Frau Samsa, staring at the charwoman with a questioning look, though she could see as much for herself without further examination.

"I should say so," said the charwoman, and she pushed Gregor to one side with her broom, to support her statement. Frau Samsa made a movement as if to hold back the broom, but she did not complete her gesture.

"Well," said Herr Samsa, "we can thank God for that!" He crossed himself and signed the three women to do likewise.

Grete, whose eyes had never left the corpse, said, "Look how thin he was! It was such a long time since he had eaten anything. His meals used to come out of the room just as they were taken in." And, indeed, Gregor's body was quite flat and dry; this could be seen more easily now that he was no longer supported on his legs and there was nothing to deceive one's sight.

"Come with us a moment, Grete!" said Frau Samsa with a sad smile, and Grete followed her parents into their bedroom, not without turning often to gaze at the corpse. The charwoman closed the door and opened the French windows. Despite the early hour, the fresh morning air had a certain warmth. It was already the end of March.

The three lodgers came out of their room and gazed around in astonishment for their breakfast; they had been forgotten. "Where is our breakfast?" the middle lodger petulantly demanded of the old woman. But she merely laid her finger to her mouth and signed them, with a mute and urgent gesture, to follow her into Gregor's room. So they entered and stood around Gregor's corpse, with their hands in the pockets of their rather shabby coats, in the middle of the room already bright with sunlight.

Then the bedroom door opened and Herr Samsa appeared in his uniform with his wife on one arm, his daughter on the other. All seemed to have been weeping, and from time to time Grete pressed her face against her father's arm.

"Leave my house immediately!" said Herr Samsa, and he pointed to the door, while the women still clung to his arms.

Somewhat disconcerted, the middle lodger said with a timid smile, "Whatever do you mean?"

The two others clasped their hands behind their backs and kept on rubbing their palms together, as if they were expecting some great dispute which could only end in triumph for them.

"I mean exactly what I say!" answered Herr Samsa and, in line with the two women, he marched straight at the lodger. The latter, however, stood quietly in his place, his eyes fixed on the floor, as if reconsidering what he should do.

"Well, then, we will go," he said at last, raising his eyes to Herr Samsa as if searching, in a sudden access of humility, for some slight approval of his resolution.

Herr Samsa merely nodded several times, opening his eyes very wide. Thereupon the lodger walked away with big strides and soon reached the anteroom; his two friends, who for some while had ceased wringing their hands, now bounded after him, as if afraid Herr Samsa might reach the door before them and separate them from their leader. Once they had gained the hall, they took down their hats from the pegs, grabbed their sticks from the umbrella stand, bowed silently, and left the flat.

With a suspicion which, it appears, was quite unjustified, Herr Samsa ran out onto the landing after them with the women and leaned over the balustrade to watch the three men as they slowly, but steadily, descended the interminable stairway, disappearing once as they reached a certain point on each floor, and then, after a few seconds, coming into view again. As they went farther down the staircase, so the Samsa family's interest diminished, and when they had been met and passed by a butcher's boy who came proudly up the stairs with his basket on his head, Herr Samsa and the women quickly left the landing and went indoors again with an air of relief.

They decided to spend the whole day resting; perhaps they might take a walk in the country; they had earned a respite and needed it urgently. And so they sat down to the table to write three letters of excuse: Herr Samsa to the manager of the Bank, Frau Samsa to her employer, and Grete to the head of her department at the shop. The charwoman came in while they were writing and announced that her work was done and that she was going. The three writers at first merely nodded their heads, without raising their eyes, but, as the old woman did not leave, they eventually laid down their pens and looked crossly at her.

"Well?" asked Herr Samsa. The charwoman was standing in the doorway, smiling as if she had some very good news to tell them but which she would not

impart till she had been begged to. The little ostrich feather which stood upright on her hat and which had always annoyed Herr Samsa so much ever since the old woman had entered their service, now waved lightly in all directions.

"Well, what is it?" asked Frau Samsa, toward whom the old woman had always shown so much more respect than to the others.

"Well . . ." she replied, and she laughed so much she could hardly speak for some while. "Well, you needn't worry about getting rid of that thing in there, I have fixed it already."

Frau Samsa and Grete leaned over the table as if to resume their letter-writing; Herr Samsa, noticing that the woman was about to launch forth into a detailed explanation, cut her short with a peremptory gesture of his outstretched hand. Then, prevented from speaking, she suddenly remembered that she was in a great hurry and, crying, "Goodbye, everyone," in a peevish tone, she half turned and was gone in a flash, savagely slamming the door behind her.

"This evening we must sack her," declared Herr Samsa; but neither his wife nor his daughter answered; the old woman had not been able to disturb their newly won tranquillity. They arose, went to the window, and stood there, with their arms around each other; Herr Samsa, turning toward them in his armchair, stared at them for a moment in silence. Then he cried, "Come, come, it's all past history now; you can start paying a little attention to me." The women immediately hurried to him, kissed him, and sat down to finish their letters.

Then they all left the apartment together, a thing they had been unable to do for many months past, and they boarded a tram which would take them some way into the country. There were no other passengers in the compartment, which was warm and bright in the sun. Casually leaning back in their seats, they began to discuss their future. On careful reflection, they decided that things were not nearly so bad as they might have been, for—and this was a point they had not hitherto realized—they had all three found really interesting occupations which looked even more promising in the future. They decided to effect what really should be the greatest improvement as soon as possible. That was to move from the flat they occupied at present. They would take a smaller, cheaper flat, but one more practical, and especially in a better neighborhood than the present one, which Gregor had chosen. Hearing their daughter speak in more and more lively tones, Herr and Frau Samsa noticed almost together that, during this affair, Grete had blossomed into a fine strapping girl, despite the make-up which made her cheeks look pale. They became calmer; almost unconsciously they exchanged glances; it occurred to both of them that it would soon be time for her to find a husband. And it seemed to them that their daughter's gestures were a confirmation of these new dreams of theirs, and encouragement for their good intentions, when, at the end of the journey, the girl rose before them and stretched her young body.

THE LOST BOY

THOMAS WOLFE

THOMAS WOLFE (1900–1938) was born in Asheville, North Carolina, graduated from the University of North Carolina, took his M.A. at Harvard, and taught English briefly at Washington Square College, New York University. He lived for a time in England and Europe. "A man must use the material and experience of his own life," he said, "if he is to create anything that has substantial value." The central problem for him as a writer was a sense of form, as he tells us in *The Story of a Novel* (1936). Among his books are *Look Homeward, Angel* (1929), *Of Time and the River* (1935), *From Death to Morning* (1935), and *You Can't Go Home Again* (1940). His collected letters were published in 1956.

I

LIGHT came and went and came again, the booming strokes of three o'clock beat out across the town in thronging bronze from the courthouse bell, light winds of April blew the fountain out in rainbow sheets, until the plume returned and pulsed, as Grover turned into the Square. He was a child, dark-eyed and grave, birthmarked upon his neck— a berry of warm brown—and with a gentle face, too quiet and too listening for his years. The scuffed boy's shoes, the thick-ribbed stockings gartered at the knees, the short knee pants cut straight with three small useless buttons at the side, the sailor blouse, the old cap battered out of shape, perched sideways up on top of the raven head, the old soiled canvas bag slung from the shoulder, empty now, but waiting for the crisp sheets of the afternoon—these friendly, shabby garments, shaped by Grover, uttered him. He turned and passed along the north side of the Square and in that moment saw the union of Forever and of Now.

Light came and went and came again, the great plume of the fountain pulsed and winds of April sheeted it across the Square in a rainbow gossamer of spray. The fire department horses drummed on the floors with wooden stomp, most casually, and with dry whiskings of their clean, coarse tails. The street cars ground into the Square from every portion of the compass and halted briefly like wound toys in

From *The Hills Beyond* by Thomas Wolfe. Copyright, 1937, by Maxwell Perkins as Executor. Used by permission of Harper & Row, Publishers.

their familiar quarter-hourly formula. A dray, hauled by a boneyard nag, rattled across the cobbles on the other side before his father's shop. The courthouse bell boomed out its solemn warning of immediate three, and everything was just the same as it had always been.

He saw that haggis of vexed shapes with quiet eyes —that hodgepodge of ill-sorted architectures that made up the Square, and he did not feel lost. For "Here," thought Grover, "here is the Square as it has always been—and papa's shop, the fire department and the City Hall, the fountain pulsing with its plume, the street cars coming in and halting at the quarter hour, the hardware store on the corner there, the row of old brick buildings on this side of the street, the people passing and the light that comes and changes and that always will come back again, and everything that comes and goes and changes in the Square, and yet will be the same again. And here," the boy thought, "is Grover with his paper bag. Here is old Grover, almost twelve years old. Here is the month of April, 1904. Here is the courthouse bell and three o'clock. Here is Grover on the Square that never changes. Here is Grover, caught upon this point of time."

It seemed to him that the Square, itself the accidental masonry of many years, the chance agglomeration of time and of disrupted strivings, was the center of the universe. It was for him, in his soul's picture, the earth's pivot, the granite core of changelessness, the eternal place where all things came and passed and yet abode forever and would never change.

He passed the old shack on the corner—the wooden fire-trap where S. Goldberg ran his wiener stand. Then he passed the Singer place next door, with its gleaming display of new machines. He saw them and admired them, but he felt no joy. They brought back to him the busy hum of housework and of women sewing, the intricacy of stitch and weave, the mystery of style and pattern, the memory of women bending over flashing needles, the pedaled tread, the busy whir. It was women's work: it filled him with unknown associations of dullness and of vague depression. And always, also, with a moment's twinge of horror, for his dark eye would always travel toward that needle stitching up and down so fast the eye could never follow it. And then he would remember how his mother once had told him she had driven the needle through her finger, and always, when he passed this place, he would remember it and for a moment crane his neck and turn his head away.

He passed on then, but had to stop again next door before the music store. He always had to stop by places that had shining perfect things in them. He loved hardware stores and windows full of accurate geometric tools. He loved windows full of hammers, saws, and planing boards. He liked windows full of strong new rakes and hoes, with unworn handles, of white perfect wood, and stamped hard and vivid with the maker's seal. He loved to see such things as these in the windows of hardware stores. And he would fairly gloat upon them and think that some day he would own a set himself.

Also, he always stopped before the music and piano store. It was a splendid store. And in the window was a small white dog upon his haunches, with head cocked gravely to one side, a small white dog that never moved, that never barked, that listened attentively at the flaring funnel of a horn to hear "His Master's Voice"—a horn forever silent, and a voice that never spoke. And within were many rich and shining shapes of great pianos, an air of splendor and of wealth.

And now, indeed, he *was* caught, held suspended. A waft of air, warm chocolate-laden, filled his nostrils. He tried to pass the white front of the little eight-foot shop; he paused, struggling with conscience; he could not go on. It was the little candy shop run by old Crocker and his wife. And Grover could not pass.

"Old stingy Crockers!" he thought scornfully. "I'll not go there anymore. But—" as the maddening fragrance of rich cooking chocolate touched him once again—"I'll just look in the window and see what they've got." He paused a moment, looking with his dark and quiet eyes into the window of the little candy shop. The window, spotlessly clean, was filled with trays of fresh-made candy. His eyes rested on a tray of chocolate drops. Unconsciously he licked his lips. Put one of them upon your tongue and it just melted there, like honeydew. And then the trays full of rich home-made fudge. He gazed longingly at the deep body of the chocolate fudge, reflectively at maple walnut, more critically, yet with longing, at the mints, the nougatines, and all the other dainties.

"Old stingy Crockers!" Grover muttered once again, and turned to go. "I wouldn't go in *there* again."

And yet he did not go away. "Old stingy Crockers" they might be; still they did make the best candy in town, the best, in fact, that he had ever tasted.

He looked through the window back into the little shop and saw Mrs. Crocker there. A customer had gone in and had made a purchase, and as Grover looked he saw Mrs. Crocker, with her little wrenny face, her pinched features, lean over and peer primly at the scales. She had a piece of fudge in her clean, bony, little fingers, and as Grover looked, she broke it, primly, in her little bony hands. She dropped a morsel down into the scales. They weighted down alarmingly, and her thin lips tightened. She snatched the piece of fudge out of the scales and broke it carefully once again. This time the scales wavered, went down very slowly, and came back again. Mrs. Crocker carefully put the reclaimed piece of fudge back in the tray, dumped the remainder in a paper bag, folded it and gave it to the customer, counted the money carefully and doled it out into the till, the pennies in one place, the nickels in another.

Grover stood there, looking scornfully. "Old stingy Crocker—afraid that she might give a crumb away!"

He grunted scornfully and again he turned to go. But now Mr. Crocker came out from the little partitioned place where they made all their candy, bearing a tray of fresh-made fudge in his skinny hands. Old Man Crocker rocked along the counter to the front and put it down. He really rocked along. He was a cripple. And like his wife, he was a wrenny, wizened little creature, with bony hands, thin lips, a pinched and meager face. One leg was inches shorter than the other, and on this leg there was an enormous thick-soled boot, with a kind of wooden, rocker-like arrangement, six inches high at least, to make up for the deficiency. On this wooden cradle Mr. Crocker rocked along, with a prim and apprehensive little smile, as if he were afraid he was going to lose something.

"Old stingy Crocker!" muttered Grover. "Humph! He wouldn't give you anything!"

And yet—he did not go away. He hung there curiously, peering through the window, with his dark and gentle face now focused and intent, alert and curious, flattening his nose against the glass. Unconsciously he scratched the thick-ribbed fabric of one stockinged leg with the scuffed and worn toe of his old shoe. The fresh, warm odor of the new-made fudge was delicious. It was a little maddening. Half consciously he began to fumble in one trouser pocket, and pulled out his purse, a shabby worn old black one with a twisted clasp. He opened it and prowled about inside.

What he found was not inspiring—a nickel and two pennies and—he had forgotten them—the stamps. He took the stamps out and unfolded them. There were five twos, eight ones, all that remained of the dollar-sixty-cents' worth which Reed, the pharmacist, had given him for running errands a week or two before.

"Old Crocker," Grover thought, and looked somberly at the grotesque little form as it rocked back into the shop again, around the counter, and up the other side. "Well—" again he looked indefinitely at the stamps in his hand—"he's had all the rest of them. He might as well take these."

So, soothing conscience with this sop of scorn, he went into the shop and stood looking at the trays in the glass case and finally decided. Pointing with a slightly grimy finger at the fresh-made tray of chocolate fudge, he said, "I'll take fifteen cents' worth of this, Mr. Crocker." He paused a moment, fighting with embarrassment, then he lifted his dark face and said quietly, "And please, I'll have to give you stamps again."

Mr. Crocker made no answer. He did not look at Grover. He pressed his lips together primly. He went rocking away and got the candy scoop, came back, slid open the door of the glass case, put fudge into the scoop, and, rocking to the scales, began to weigh the candy out. Grover watched him as he peered and squinted, he watched him purse and press his lips together, he saw him take a piece of fudge and break it in two parts. And then old Crocker broke two parts in two again. He weighed, he squinted, and he hovered, until it seemed to Grover that by calling *Mrs.* Crocker stingy he had been guilty of a rank injustice. But finally, to his vast relief, the job was over, the scales hung there, quivering apprehensively, upon the very hairline of nervous balance, as if even the scales were afraid that one more move from Old Man Crocker and they would be undone.

Mr. Crocker took the candy then and dumped it in a paper bag and, rocking back along the counter toward the boy, he dryly said: "Where are the stamps?" Grover gave them to him. Mr. Crocker relinquished his clawlike hold upon the bag and set it down upon the counter. Grover took the bag and dropped it in his canvas sack, and then remembered. "Mr. Crocker—" again he felt the old embarrassment that was almost like strong pain— "I gave you too much," Grover said. "There were eighteen cents in stamps. You—you can just give me three ones back."

Mr. Crocker did not answer. He was busy with his bony little hands, unfolding the stamps and flattening them out on top of the glass counter. When he had done so, he peered at them sharply for a moment, thrusting his scrawny neck forward and running his eye up and down, like a bookkeeper who totes up rows of figures.

When he had finished, he said tartly: "I don't like this kind of business. If you want candy, you should have the money for it. I'm not a post office. The next time you come in here and want anything, you'll have to pay me money for it."

Hot anger rose in Grover's throat. His olive face suffused with angry color. His tarry eyes got black and bright. He was on the verge of saying: "Then why did you take my other stamps? Why do you tell me now, when you have taken all the stamps I had, that you don't want them?"

But he was a boy, a boy of eleven years, a quiet, gentle, gravely thoughtful boy, and he had been taught how to respect his elders. So he just stood there looking with his tar-black eyes. Old Man Crocker, pursing at the mouth a little, without meeting Grover's gaze, took the stamps up in his thin, parched fingers and, turning, rocked away with them down to the till.

He took the twos and folded them and laid them in one rounded scallop, then took the ones and folded them and put them in the one next to it. Then he closed the till and started to rock off, down toward the other end. Grover, his face now quiet and grave, kept looking at him, but Mr. Crocker did not look at Grover. Instead he began to take some stamped cardboard shapes and fold them into boxes.

In a moment Grover said, "Mr. Crocker, will you give me the three ones, please?"

Mr. Crocker did not answer. He kept folding boxes, and he compressed his thin lips quickly as he did so. But Mrs. Crocker, back turned to her spouse, also folding boxes with her birdlike hands, muttered: "Hm! *I'd* give him nothing!"

Mr. Crocker looked up, looked at Grover, said, "What are you waiting for?"

"Will you give me the three ones, please?" Grover said.

"I'll give you nothing," Mr. Crocker said.

He left his work and came rocking forward along the counter. "Now you get out of here! Don't you come in here with any more of those stamps," said Mr. Crocker.

"I should like to know where he gets them—that's what *I* should like to know," said Mrs. Crocker.

She did not look up as she said these words. She inclined her head a little to the side, in Mr. Crocker's direction, and continued to fold the boxes with her bony fingers.

"You get out of here!" said Mr. Crocker. "And don't you come back here with any stamps. . . . Where did you get those stamps?" he said.

"That's just what *I've* been thinking," Mrs. Crocker said. "*I've* been thinking all along."

"You've been coming in here for the last two weeks with those stamps," said Mr. Crocker. "I don't like the look of it. Where did you get those stamps?" he said.

"That's what *I've* been thinking," said Mrs. Crocker, for a second time.

Grover had got white underneath his olive skin. His eyes had lost their luster. They looked like dull, stunned balls of tar. "From Mr. Reed," he said. "I got the stamps from Mr. Reed." Then he burst out desperately, "Mr. Crocker—Mr. Reed will tell you how I got the stamps. I did some work for Mr. Reed, he gave me those stamps two weeks ago."

"Mr. Reed," said Mrs. Crocker acidly. She did not turn her head. "I call it mighty funny."

"Mr. Crocker," Grover said, "if you'll just let me have three ones——"

"You get out of here!" cried Mr. Crocker, and he began rocking forward toward Grover. "Now don't you come in here again, boy! There's something funny about this whole business! I don't like the look of it," said Mr. Crocker. "If you can't pay as other people do, then I don't want your trade."

"Mr. Crocker," Grover said again, and underneath the olive skin his face was gray, "if you'll just let me have those three——"

"You get out of here!" Mr. Crocker cried, rocking down toward the counter's end. "If you don't get out, boy——"

"*I'd* call a policeman, that's what I'd do," Mrs. Crocker said.

Mr. Crocker rocked around the lower end of the counter. He came rocking up to Grover. "You get out," he said.

He took the boy and pushed him with his bony little hands, and Grover was sick and gray down to the hollow pit of his stomach.

"You've got to give me those three ones," he said.

"You get out of here!" shrilled Mr. Crocker. He seized the screen door, pulled it open, and pushed Grover out. "Don't you come back in here," he said, pausing for a moment, and working thinly at the lips. He turned and rocked back in the shop again. The screen door slammed behind him. Grover stood there on the pavement. And light came and went and came again into the Square.

The boy stood there, and a wagon rattled past. There were some people passing by, but Grover did not notice them. He stood there blindly, in the watches of the sun, feeling this was Time, this was the center of the universe, the granite core of changelessness, and feeling, this is Grover, this the Square, this is Now.

But something had gone out of day. He felt the overwhelming, soul-sickening guilt that all the children, all the good men of the earth, have felt since Time began. And even anger had died down, had been drowned out, in this swelling tide of guilt, and "This is the Square"—thought Grover as before— "This is Now. There is my father's shop. And all of it is as it has always been—save I."

And the Square reeled drunkenly around him, light went in blind gray motes before his eyes, the fountain sheeted out to rainbow iridescence and returned to its proud, pulsing plume again. But all the brightness had gone out of day, and "Here is the Square, and here is permanence, and here is Time—and all of it the same as it has always been, save I."

The scuffed boots of the lost boy moved and stumbled blindly. The numb feet crossed the pavement— reached the cobbled street, reached the plotted central square—the grass plots, and the flower beds, so soon to be packed with red geraniums.

"I want to be alone," thought Grover, "where I cannot go near him. . . . Oh God, I hope he never hears, that no one ever tells him——"

The plume blew out, the iridescent sheet of spray blew over him. He passed through, found the other side and crossed the street, and—"Oh God, if papa ever hears!" thought Grover, as his numb feet started up the steps into his father's shop.

He found and felt the steps—the width and thickness of old lumber twenty feet in length. He saw it all —the iron columns on his father's porch, painted with the dull anomalous black-green that all such columns in this land and weather come to; two angels, flyspecked, and the waiting stones. Beyond and all around, in the stonecutter's shop, cold shapes of white and marble, rounded stone, the languid angel with strong marble hands of love.

He went on down the aisle, the white shapes stood around him. He went on to the back of the workroom. This he knew—the little cast-iron stove in left-hand corner, caked, brown, heat-blistered, and the elbow of the long stack running out across the shop; the high and dirty window looking down across the Market Square toward Niggertown; the rude old shelves, plank-boarded, thick, the wood not smooth but pulpy, like the strong hair of an animal; upon the shelves the chisels of all sizes and a layer of stone dust; an emery wheel with pump tread; and a door that let out on the alleyway, yet the alleyway twelve feet below. Here in the room, two trestles of this coarse spiked wood upon which rested gravestones, and at one, his father at work.

The boy looked, saw the name was Creasman: saw the carved analysis of John, the symmetry of the s, the fine sentiment that was being polished off beneath the name and date: "John Creasman, November 7, 1903."

Gant looked up. He was a man of fifty-three, gaunt-visaged, mustache cropped, immensely long and tall and gaunt. He wore good dark clothes— heavy, massive—save he had no coat. He worked in shirt-sleeves with his vest on, a strong watch chain stretching across his vest, wing collar and black tie, Adam's apple, bony forehead, bony nose, light eyes, gray-green, undeep and cold, and, somehow, lonely-looking, a striped apron going up around his shoulders, and starched cuffs. And in one hand a tremendous rounded wooden mallet like a butcher's bole; and in his other hand, a strong cold chisel.

"How are you, son?"

He did not look up as he spoke. He spoke quietly, absently. He worked upon the chisel and the wooden mallet, as a jeweler might work on a watch, except that in the man and in the wooden mallet there was power too.

"What is it, son?" he said.

He moved around the table from the head, started up on "J" once again.

"Papa, I never stole the stamps," said Grover.

Gant put down the mallet, laid the chisel down. He came around the trestle.

"What?" he said.

As Grover winked his tar-black eyes, they brightened, the hot tears shot out. "I never stole the stamps," he said.

"Hey? What is this?" his father said. "What stamps?"

"That Mr. Reed gave me, when the other boy was sick and I worked there for three days. . . . And Old Man Crocker," Grover said, "he took all the stamps. And I told him Mr. Reed had given them to me. And now he owes me three ones—and Old Man Crocker says he don't believe that they were mine. He says—he says—that I must have taken them somewhere," Grover blurted out.

"The stamps that Reed gave you—hey?" the stonecutter said. "The stamps you had—" He wet his thumb upon his lips, threw back his head and slowly swung his gaze around the ceiling, then turned and strode quickly from his workshop out into the storeroom.

Almost at once he came back again, and as he passed the old gray painted-board partition of his office he cleared his throat and wet his thumb and said, "Now, I tell you——"

Then he turned and strode up toward the front again and cleared his throat and said, "I tell you now—" He wheeled about and started back, and as he came along the aisle between the marshaled rows of gravestones he said beneath his breath, "By God, now——"

He took Grover by the hand and they went out flying. Down the aisle they went by all the gravestones, past the fly-specked angels waiting there, and down the wooden steps and across the Square. The fountain pulsed, the plume blew out in sheeted iridescence, and it swept across them; an old gray horse, with a peaceful look about his torn lips, swucked up the cool mountain water from the trough as Grover and his father went across the Square, but they did not notice it.

They crossed swiftly to the other side in a direct line to the candy shop. Gant was still dressed in his long striped apron, and he was still holding Grover by the hand. He opened the screen door and stepped inside.

"Give him the stamps," Gant said.

Mr. Crocker came rocking forward behind the counter, with the prim and careful look that now was somewhat like a smile. "It was just—" he said.

"Give him the stamps," Gant said, and threw some coins down on the counter.

Mr. Crocker rocked away and got the stamps. He came rocking back. "I just didn't know—" he said.

The stonecutter took the stamps and gave them to the boy. And Mr. Crocker took the coins.

"It was just that—" Mr. Crocker began again, and smiled.

Gant cleared his throat: "You never were a father," he said. "You never knew the feelings of a father, or understood the feelings of a child; and that is why you acted as you did. But a judgment is upon you. God has cursed you. He has afflicted you. He has made you lame and childless as you are—and lame and childless, miserable as you are, you will go to your grave and be forgotten!"

And Crocker's wife kept kneading her bony little hands and said, imploringly, "Oh, no—oh don't say that, please don't say that."

The stonecutter, the breath still hoarse in him, left the store, still holding the boy tightly by the hand. Light came again into the day.

"Well, son," he said, and laid his hand on the boy's back. "Well, son," he said, "now don't you mind."

They walked across the Square, the sheeted spray of iridescent light swept out on them, the horse swizzled at the water-trough, and "Well, son," the stonecutter said.

And the old horse sloped down, ringing with his hoofs upon the cobblestones.

"Well, son," said the stonecutter once again, "be a good boy."

And he trod his own steps then with his great stride and went back again into his shop.

The lost boy stood upon the Square, hard by the porch of his father's shop.

"This is Time," thought Grover. "Here is the Square, here is my father's shop, and here am I."

And light came and went and came again—but now not quite the same as it had done before. The boy saw the pattern of familiar shapes and knew that they were just the same as they had always been. But something had gone out of day, and something had come in again. Out of the vision of those quiet eyes some brightness had gone, and into their vision had come some deeper color. He could not say, he did not know through what transforming shadows life had passed within that quarter hour. He only knew that something had been lost—something forever gained.

Just then a buggy curved out through the Square, and fastened to the rear end was a poster, and it said "St. Louis" and "Excursion" and "The Fair."

II—THE MOTHER

As we went down through Indiana—you were too young, child, to remember it—but I always think of all of you the way you looked that morning, when we went down through Indiana, going to the Fair. All of the apple trees were coming out, and it was April; it was the beginning of spring in southern Indiana and everything was getting green. Of course we don't have farms at home like those in Indiana. The children had never seen such farms as those, and I reckon, kidlike, they had to take it in.

So all of them kept running up and down the aisle —well, no, except for you and Grover. *You* were too young, Eugene. You were just three, I kept you with me. As for Grover—well, I'm going to tell you about that.

But the rest of them kept running up and down the aisle and from one window to another. They kept calling out and hollering to each other every time they saw something new. They kept trying to look out on all sides, in every way at once as if they wished they had eyes at the back of their heads. It was the first time any of them had ever been in Indiana, and I reckon that it all seemed strange and new.

And so it seemed they couldn't get enough. It seemed they never could be still. They kept running up and down and back and forth, hollering and shouting to each other, until—"I'll vow! You children! I never saw the beat of you!" I said. "The way that you keep running up and down and back and forth and never can be quiet for a minute beats all I ever saw," I said.

You see, they were excited about going to St. Louis, and so curious over everything they saw. They couldn't help it, and they wanted to see everything. But—"I'll vow!" I said. "If you children don't sit down and rest you'll be worn to a frazzle before we ever get to see St. Louis and the Fair!"

Except for Grover! He—no, sir! not him. Now, boy, I want to tell you—I've raised the lot of you—and if I do say so, there wasn't a numbskull in the lot. But *Grover!* Well, you've all grown up now, all of you have gone away, and none of you are children anymore. . . . And of course, I hope that, as the fellow says, you reached the dignity of man's estate. I suppose you have the judgment of grown men. . . . But *Grover! Grover* had it even then!

Oh, even as a child, you know—at a time when I was almost afraid to trust the rest of you out of my sight—I could depend on Grover. He could go anywhere, I could send him anywhere, and I'd always know he'd get back safe, and do exactly what I told him to!

Why, I didn't even have to tell him. You could send that child to market and tell him what you wanted, and he'd come home with *twice* as much as you could get yourself for the same money!

Now you know, I've always been considered a good trader. But *Grover!*—why, it got so finally that I wouldn't even tell him. Your papa said to me: "You'd be better off if you'd just tell him what you want and leave the rest to him. For," your papa says, "damned if I don't believe he's a better trader than you are. He gets more for the money than anyone I ever saw."

Well, I had to admit it, you know. I had to own up then. Grover, even as a child, was a far better trader than I was. . . . Why, yes, they told it on him all over town, you know. They said all of the market men, all of the farmers, knew him. They'd begin to laugh when they saw him coming—they'd say: "Look out! Here's Grover! Here's one trader you're not going to fool!"

And they were right! *That* child! I'd say, "Grover, suppose you run uptown and see if they've got anything good to *eat* today"—and I'd just wink at him, you know, but he'd know what I meant. I wouldn't let on that I *wanted* anything exactly, but I'd say, "Now it just occurs to me that some good fresh stuff may be coming in from the country, so suppose you take this dollar and just see what you can do with it."

Well, sir, that was all that was needed. The minute you told that child that you depended on his judgment, he'd have gone to the ends of the earth for you —and, let me tell you something, he wouldn't *miss*, either!

His eyes would get as black as coals—oh! the way that child would look at you, the intelligence and sense in his expression. He'd say: "Yes, *ma'am!* Now don't you worry, mama. You leave it all to me—and I'll do *good!*" said Grover.

And he'd be off like a streak of lightning and—oh Lord! As your father said to me, "I've been living in this town for almost thirty years," he said—"I've seen it grow up from a crossroads village, and I thought I knew everything there was to know about it—but that child—" your papa says—"he knows places that I never heard of!" . . . Oh, he'd go right down there to that place below your papa's shop where the draymen and the country people used to park their wagons—or he'd go down there to those old lots on Concord Street where the farmers used to keep their wagons. And, child that he was, he'd go right in among them, sir—*Grover* would!—go right in and barter with them like a grown man!

And he'd come home with things he'd bought that would make your eyes stick out. . . . Here he comes one time with another boy, dragging a great bushel basket full of ripe termaters between them. "Why, Grover!" I says. "How on earth are we ever going to use them? Why they'll go bad on us before we're half way through with them." "Well, mama," he says, "I know—" oh, just as solemn as a judge—"but they were the last the man had," he says, "and he wanted to go home, and so I got them for ten cents," he says. "They were so cheap," said Grover, "I thought it was a shame to let 'em go, and I figgered that what we couldn't eat—why," says Grover, "you could *put up!*" Well, the way he said it—so earnest and so serious— I had to laugh. "But I'll vow!" I said. "If you don't beat all!" . . . But that was *Grover!*—the way he was in *those* days! As everyone said, boy that he was, he had the sense and judgment of a grown man. . . . Child, child, I've seen you all grow up, and all of you were bright enough. There were no half-wits in *my* family. But for all-round intelligence, judgment, and general ability, Grover surpassed the whole crowd. I've never seen his equal, and everyone who knew him as a child will say the same.

So that's what I tell them now when they ask me about all of you. I have to tell the truth. I always said that *you* were smart enough, Eugene—but when they come around and brag to me about you, and about how you have got on and have a kind of name—I don't let on, you know, I just sit there and let them

talk. I don't brag on you—if *they* want to brag on you, that's *their* business. I never bragged on one of my own children in my life. When father raised us up, we were all brought up to believe that it was not good breeding to brag about your kin. "If the others want to do it," father said, "well, let *them* do it. Don't ever let on by a word or sign that you know what they are talking about. Just let *them* do the talking, and say nothing."

So when they come around and tell me all about the things *you've* done—I don't let on to them, I never say a word. Why yes!—why, here, you know—oh, along about a month or so ago, this feller comes—a well-dressed man, you know—he looked intelligent, a good substantial sort of person. He said he came from New Jersey, or somewhere up in that part of the country, and he began to ask me all sorts of questions—what you were like when you were a boy, and all such stuff as that.

I just pretended to study it all over and then I said, "Well, yes"—real serious-like, you know—"well, yes— I reckon I ought to know a little something about him. Eugene was my child, just the same as all the others were. I brought him up just the way I brought up all the others. And," I says—oh, just as solemn as you please—"he wasn't a *bad* sort of a boy. Why," I says, "up to the time that he was twelve years old he was just about the same as any other boy—a good, average, normal sort of fellow."

"Oh," he says, "But didn't you notice something? Wasn't there something kind of strange?" he says— "something different from what you noticed in the other children?"

I didn't let on, you know—I just took it all in and looked as solemn as an owl—I just pretended to study it all over, just as serious as you please.

"Why no," I says, real slow-like, after I'd studied it all over. "As I remember it, he was a good, ordinary, normal sort of boy, just like all the others."

"Yes," he says—oh, all excited-like, you know—"But didn't you notice how brilliant he was? Eugene must have been more brilliant than the rest!"

"Well, now," I says, and pretended to study that all over too. "Now let me see. . . . Yes," I says—I just looked him in the eye, as solemn as you please— "he did pretty well. . . . Well, yes," I says, "I guess he was a fairly bright sort of a boy. I never had no complaints to make of him on that score. He was bright enough," I says. "The only trouble with him was that he was lazy."

"Lazy!" he says—oh, you should have seen the look upon his face, you know—he jumped like someone had stuck a pin in him. "Lazy!" he says. "Why, you don't mean to tell me——"

"Yes," I says—oh, I never cracked a smile—"I was

telling him the same thing myself the last time that I saw him. I told him it was a mighty lucky thing for him that he had the gift of gab. Of course, he went off to college and read a lot of books, and I reckon that's where he got this flow of language they say he has. But as I said to him the last time that I saw him: 'Now look a-here,' I said. 'If you can earn your living doing a light, easy class of work like this you do,' I says, 'you're mighty lucky, because none of the rest of your people,' I says, 'had any such luck as that. They had to work hard for a living.' "

Oh, I told him, you know. I came right out with it. I made no bones about it. And I tell you what—I wish you could have seen his face. It was a study.

"Well," he says, at last, "you've got to admit this, haven't you—he was the brightest boy you had, now wasn't he?"

I just looked at him a moment. I had to tell the truth. I couldn't fool him any longer. "No," I says. "He was a good, bright boy—I got no complaint to make about him on that score—but the brightest boy I had, the one that surpassed all the rest of them in sense, and understanding, and in judgment—the best boy I had—the smartest boy I ever saw—was—well, it wasn't Eugene," I said. "It was another one."

He looked at me a moment, then he said, "Which boy was that?"

Well, I just looked at him, and smiled. I shook my head, you know. I wouldn't tell him. "I never brag about my own," I said. "You'll have to find out for yourself."

But—I'll have to tell *you*—and you know yourself, I brought the whole crowd up, I knew you all. And you can take my word for it—the best one of the lot was—*Grover!*

And when I think of Grover as he was along about that time, I always see him sitting there, so grave and earnest-like with his nose pressed to the window, as we went down through Indiana in the morning, to the Fair.

All through that morning we were going down along beside the Wabash River—the Wabash River flows through Indiana, it is the river that they wrote the song about—so all that morning we were going down along the river. And I sat with all you children gathered about me as we went down through Indiana, going to St. Louis, to the Fair.

And Grover sat there, so still and earnest-like, looking out the window, and he didn't move. He sat there like a man. He was just eleven and a half years old, but he had more sense, more judgment, and more understanding than any child I ever saw.

So here he sat beside this gentleman and looked out the window. I never knew the man—I never asked his name—but I tell you what! He was cer-

tainly a fine-looking, well-dressed, good, substantial sort of man, and I could see that he had taken a great liking to Grover. And Grover sat there looking out, and then turned to this gentleman, as grave and earnest as a grown-up man, and says, "What kind of crops grow here, sir?" Well, this gentleman threw his head back and just hah-hahed. "Well, I'll see if I can tell you," says this gentleman, and then, you know, he talked to him, they talked together, and Grover took it all in, as solemn as you please, and asked this gentleman every sort of question—what the trees were, what was growing there, how big the farms were—all sorts of questions, which this gentleman would answer, until I said: "Why, I'll vow, Grover! You shouldn't ask so many questions. You'll bother the very life out of this gentleman."

The gentleman threw his head back and laughed right out. "Now you leave that boy alone. He's all right," he said. "He doesn't bother me a bit, and if I know the answers to his questions I will answer him. And if I don't know, why, then, I'll tell him so. But he's *all right*," he said, and put his arm round Grover's shoulders. "You leave him alone. He doesn't bother me a bit."

And I can still remember how he looked that morning, with his black eyes, his black hair, and with the birthmark on his neck—so grave, so serious, so earnest-like—as he sat by the train window and watched the apple trees, the farms, the barns, the houses, and the orchards, taking it all in, I reckon, because it was strange and new to him.

It was so long ago, but when I think of it, it all comes back, as if it happened yesterday. Now all of you have either died or grown up and gone away, and nothing is the same as it was then. But all of you were there with me that morning and I guess I should remember how the others looked, but somehow I don't. Yet I can still see Grover just the way he was, the way he looked that morning when we went down through Indiana, by the river, to the Fair.

III—The Sister

Can you remember, Eugene, how Grover used to look? I mean the birthmark, the black eyes, the olive skin. The birthmark always showed because of those open sailor blouses kids used to wear. But I guess you must have been too young when Grover died. . . . I was looking at that old photograph the other day. You know the one I mean—that picture showing mama and papa and all of us children before the house on Woodson Street. *You* weren't there, Eugene. *You* didn't get in. *You* hadn't arrived when that was taken. . . . You remember how mad you used to get when we'd tell you that you were only a dishrag hanging out in Heaven when something happened?

You were the baby. That's what you get for being the baby. You don't get in the picture, do you? . . . I was looking at that old picture just the other day. There we were. And, my God, what is it all about? I mean, when you see the way we were—Daisy and Ben and Grover, Steve and all of us—and then how everyone either dies or grows up and goes away—and then—look at us now! Do you ever get to feeling funny? You know what I mean—do you ever get to feeling *queer*—when you try to figure these things out? You've been to college and you ought to know the answer—and I wish you'd tell me if you know.

My Lord, when I think sometimes of the way I used to be—the dreams I used to have. Playing the piano, practicing seven hours a day, thinking that some day I would be a great pianist. Taking singing lessons from Aunt Nell because I felt that some day I was going to have a great career in opera. . . . Can you beat it now? Can you imagine it? *Me!* In grand opera! . . . Now I want to ask you. I'd like to know.

My Lord! When I go uptown and walk down the street and see all these funny-looking little boys and girls hanging around the drug store—do you suppose any of them have ambitions the way we did? Do you suppose any of these funny-looking little girls are thinking about a big career in opera? . . . Didn't you ever see that picture of us? I was looking at it just the other day. It was made before the old house down on Woodson Street, with papa standing there in his swallow-tail, and mama there beside him—and Grover, and Ben, and Steve, and Daisy, and myself, with our feet upon our bicycles. Luke, poor kid, was only four or five. *He* didn't have a bicycle like us. But there he was. And there were all of us together.

Well, there I was, and my poor old skinny legs and long white dress, and two pigtails hanging down my back. And all the funny-looking clothes we wore, with the doo-lolley business on them. . . . But I guess you can't remember. You weren't born.

But, well, we were a right nice-looking set of people, if I do say so. And there was "86" the way it used to be, with the front porch, the grape vines, and the flower beds before the house—and "Miss Eliza" standing there by papa, with a watch charm pinned upon her waist. . . . I shouldn't laugh, but "Miss Eliza"—well, mama was a pretty woman then. Do you know what I mean? "Miss Eliza" was a right good-looking woman, and papa in his swallow-tail was a good-looking man. Do you remember how he used to get dressed up on Sunday? And how grand we thought he was? And how he let me take his money out and count it? And how rich we all thought he was? And how wonderful that dinkey little shop

on the Square looked to us? . . . Can you beat it, now? Why we thought that papa was the biggest man in town and—oh, you can't tell me! You can't tell me! He had his faults, but papa was a wonderful man. You know he was!

And there was Steve and Ben and Grover, Daisy, Luke, and me lined up there before the house with one foot on our bicycles. And I got to thinking back about it all. It all came back.

Do you remember anything about St. Louis? You were only three or four years old then, but you must remember something. . . . Do you remember how you used to bawl when I would scrub you? How you'd bawl for Grover? Poor kid, you used to yell for Grover every time I'd get you in the tub. . . . He was a sweet kid and he was crazy about you—he almost brought you up.

That year Grover was working at the Inside Inn out on the Fair Grounds. Do you remember the old Inside Inn? That big old wooden thing inside the Fair? And how I used to take you there to wait for Grover when he got through working? And old fat Billy Pelham at the newsstand—how he always used to give you a stick of chewing gum?

They were all crazy about Grover. Everybody liked him. . . . And how proud Grover was of you! Don't you remember how he used to show you off? How he used to take you around and make you talk to Billy Pelham? And Mr. Curtis at the desk? And how Grover would try to make you talk and get you to say "Grover"? And you couldn't say it—you couldn't pronounce the "r." You'd say "Gova." Have you forgotten that? You shouldn't forget *that*, because—you were a *cute* kid, then—Ho-ho-ho-ho-ho—I don't know where it's gone to, but you were a big hit in those days. . . . I tell you, boy, you were Somebody back in those days.

And I was thinking of it all the other day when I was looking at that photograph. How we used to go and meet Grover there, and how he'd take us to the Midway. Do you remember the Midway? The Snake-Eater and the Living Skeleton, the Fat Woman and the Chute-the-chute, the Scenic Railway and the Ferris Wheel? How you bawled the night we took you up on the Ferris Wheel? You yelled your head off—I tried to laugh it off, but I tell you, I was scared myself. Back in those days, that was Something. And how Grover laughed at us and told us there was no danger. . . . My Lord! poor little Grover. He wasn't quite twelve years old at the time, but he seemed so grown up to us. I was two years older, but I thought he knew it all.

It was always that way with him. Looking back now, it sometimes seems that it was Grover who brought us up. He was always looking after us, telling us what to do, bringing us something—some ice cream or some candy, something he had bought out of the poor little money he'd gotten at the Inn.

Then I got to thinking of the afternoon we sneaked away from home. Mama had gone out somewhere. And Grover and I got on the street car and went downtown. And my Lord, we thought that we were going Somewhere. In those days, that was what we called a *trip*. A ride in the street car was something to write home about in those days. . . . I hear that it's all built up around there now.

So we got on the car and rode the whole way down into the business section of St. Louis. We got out on Washington Street and walked up and down. And I tell you, boy, we thought that that was Something. Grover took me into a drug store and set me up to soda water. Then we came out and walked around some more, down to the Union Station and clear over to the river. And both of us half scared to death at what we'd done and wondering what mama would say if she found out.

We stayed down there till it was getting dark, and we passed by a lunchroom—an old one-armed joint with one-armed chairs and people sitting on stools and eating at the counter. We read all the signs to see what they had to eat and how much it cost, and I guess nothing on the menu was more than fifteen cents, but it couldn't have looked grander to us if it had been Delmonico's. So we stood there with our noses pressed against the window looking in. Two skinny little kids, both of us scared half to death, getting the thrill of a lifetime out of it. You know what I mean? And smelling everything with all our might and thinking how good it all smelled. . . . Then Grover turned to me and whispered: "Come on, Helen. Let's go in. It says fifteen cents for pork and beans. And I've got the money," Grover said. "I've got sixty cents."

I was so scared I couldn't speak. I'd never been in a place like that before. But I kept thinking, "Oh Lord, if mama should find out!" I felt as if we were committing some big crime. . . . Don't you know how it is when you're a kid? It was the thrill of a lifetime. . . . I couldn't resist. So we both went in and sat down on those high stools before the counter and ordered pork and beans and a cup of coffee. I suppose we were too frightened at what we'd done really to enjoy anything. We just gobbled it all up in a hurry, and gulped our coffee down. And I don't know whether it was the excitement—I guess the poor kid was already sick when we came in there and didn't know it. But I turned and looked at him, and he was white as death. . . . And when I asked him what was the matter, he wouldn't tell me. He was too proud. He said he was all right, but I could

see that he was sick as a dog. . . . So he paid the bill. It came to forty cents—I'll never forget *that* as long as I live. . . . And sure enough, we no more than got out the door—he hardly had time to reach the curb—before it all came up.

And the poor kid was so scared and so ashamed. And what scared him so was not that he had gotten sick, but that he had spent all that money and it had come to nothing. And mama would find out. . . . Poor kid, he just stood there looking at me and he whispered: "Oh Helen, don't tell mama. She'll be mad if she finds out." Then we hurried home, and he was still white as a sheet when we got there.

Mama was waiting for us. She looked at us—you know how "Miss Eliza" looks at you when she thinks you're been doing something that you shouldn't. Mama said, "Why, where on earth have you two children been?" I guess she was all set to lay us out. Then she took one look at Grover's face. That was enough for her. She said, "Why, child, what in the world!" She was white as a sheet herself. . . . And all that Grover said was—"Mama, I feel sick."

He was sick as a dog. He fell over on the bed, and we undressed him and mama put her hand upon his forehead and came out in the hall—she was so white you could have made a black mark on her face with chalk—and whispered to me, "Go get the doctor quick, he's burning up."

And I went chasing up the street, my pigtails flying, to Dr. Packer's house. I brought him back with me. When he came out of Grover's room he told mama what to do but I don't know if she even heard him.

Her face was white as a sheet. She looked at me and looked right through me. She never saw me. And oh, my Lord, I'll never forget the way she looked, the way my heart stopped and came up in my throat. I was only a skinny little kid of fourteen. But she looked as if she was dying right before my eyes. And I knew that if anything happened to him, she'd never get over it if she lived to be a hundred.

Poor old mama. You know, he always was her eyeballs—you know that, don't you?—not the rest of us! —no, sir! I know what I'm talking about. It always has been Grover—she always thought more of him than she did of any of the others. And—poor kid!—he was a sweet kid. I can still see him lying there, and remember how sick he was, and how scared I was! I don't know why I was so scared. All we'd done had been to sneak away from home and go into a lunchroom—but I felt guilty about the whole thing, as if it was my fault.

It all came back to me the other day when I was looking at that picture, and I thought, my God, we were two kids together, and I was only two years older than Grover was, and now I'm forty-six. . . . Can you believe it? Can you figure it out—the way we grow up and change and go away? . . . And my Lord, Grover seemed so grown-up to me. He was such a quiet kid—I guess that's why he seemed older than the rest of us.

I wonder what Grover would say now if he could see that picture. All my hopes and dreams and big ambitions have come to nothing, and it's all so long ago, as if it happened in another world. Then it comes back, as if it happened yesterday. . . . Sometimes I lie awake at night and think of all the people who have come and gone, and how everything is different from the way we thought that it would be. Then I go out on the street next day and see the faces of the people that I pass. . . . Don't they look strange to you? Don't you see something funny in people's eyes, as if all of them were puzzled about something? As if they were wondering what had happened to them since they were kids? Wondering what it is that they have lost? . . . Now am I crazy, or do you know what I mean? You've been to college, Gene, and I want you to tell me if you know the answer. Now do they look that way to you? I never noticed that look in people's eyes when I was a kid—did you?

My God, I wish I knew the answer to these things. I'd like to find out what is wrong—what has changed since then—and if we have the same queer look in our eyes, too. Does it happen to us all, to everyone? . . . Grover and Ben, Steve, Daisy, Luke, and me—all standing there before that house on Woodson Street in Altamont—there we are, and you see the way we were—and how it all gets lost. What is it, anyway, that people lose?

How is it that nothing turns out the way we thought it would be? It all gets lost until it seems that it has never happened—that it is something we dreamed somewhere. . . . You see what I mean? . . . It seems that it must be something we heard somewhere—that it happened to someone else. And then it all comes back again.

And suddenly you remember just how it was, and see again those two funny, frightened, skinny little kids with their noses pressed against the dirty window of that lunchroom thirty years ago. You remember the way it felt, the way it smelled, even the strange smell in the old pantry in that house we lived in then. And the steps before the house, the way the rooms looked. And those two little boys in sailor suits who used to ride up and down before the house on tricycles. . . . And the birthmark on Grover's neck. . . . The Inside Inn. . . . St. Louis and the Fair.

It all comes back as if it happened yesterday. And

then it goes away again, and seems farther off and stranger than if it happened in a dream.

IV—THE BROTHER

"*This* is King's Highway," the man said.

And then Eugene looked and saw that it was just a street. There were some big new buildings, a large hotel, some restaurants and "bar-grill" places of the modern kind, the livid monotone of neon lights, ceaseless traffic of motor cars—all this was new, but it was just a street. And he knew that it had always been just a street and nothing more—but somehow—well, he stood there looking at it, wondering what else he had expected to find.

The man kept looking at him with inquiry in his eyes, and Eugene asked him if the Fair had not been out this way.

"Sure, the Fair was out beyond here," the man said. "Out where the park is now. But this street you're looking for—don't you remember the name of it or nothing?" the man said.

Eugene said he thought the name of the street was Edgemont, but that he wasn't sure. Anyhow it was something like that. And he said the house was on the corner of that street and of another street.

Then the man said: "What was that other street?"

Eugene said he did not know, but that King's Highway was a block or so away, and that an interurban line ran past about half a block from where he once had lived.

"What line was this?" the man said, and stared at him.

"The interurban line," Eugene said.

Then the man stared at him again, and finally, "I don't know no interurban line," he said.

Eugene said it was a line that ran behind some houses, and that there were board fences there and grass beside the tracks. But somehow he could not say that it was summer in those days and that you could smell the ties, a wooden, tarry smell, and feel a kind of absence in the afternoon after the car had gone. He only said the interurban line was back behind somewhere between the backyards of some houses and some old board fences, and that King's Highway was a block or two away.

He did not say that King's Highway had not been a street in those days but a kind of road that wound from magic out of some dim and haunted land, and that along the way it had got mixed in with Tom the Piper's son, with hot cross buns, with all the light that came and went, and with coming down through Indiana in the morning, and the smell of engine smoke, the Union Station, and most of all with voices lost and far and long ago that said "King's Highway."

He did not say these things about King's Highway because he looked about him and he saw what King's Highway was. All he could say was that the street was near King's Highway, and was on the corner, and that the interurban trolley line was close to there. He said it was a stone house, and that there were stone steps before it, and a strip of grass. He said he thought the house had had a turret at one corner, he could not be sure.

The man looked at him again, and said, "This is King's Highway, but I never heard of any street like that."

Eugene left him then, and went on till he found the place. And so at last he turned into the street, finding the place where the two corners met, the huddled block, the turret, and the steps, and paused a moment, looking back, as if the street were Time.

For a moment he stood there, waiting—for a word, and for a door to open, for the child to come. He waited but no words were spoken; no one came.

Yet all of it was just as it had always been, except that the steps were lower, the porch less high, the strip of grass less wide, than he had thought. All the rest of it was as he had known it would be. A gray-stone front, three-storied, with a slant slate roof, the side red brick and windowed, still with the old arched entrance in the center for the doctor's use.

There was a tree in front, and a lamp post; and behind and to the side, more trees than he had known there would be. And all the slatey turret gables, all the slatey window gables, going into points, and the two arched windows, in strong stone, in the front room.

It was all so strong, so solid, and so ugly—and all so enduring and so good, the way he had remembered it, except he did not smell the tar, the hot and caulky dryness of the old cracked ties, the boards of backyard fences and the coarse and sultry grass, and absence in the afternoon when the street car had gone, and the twins, sharp-visaged in their sailor suits, pumping with furious shrillness on tricycles up and down before the house, and the feel of the hot afternoon, and the sense that everyone was absent at the Fair.

Except for this, it all was just the same; except for this and for King's Highway, which was now a street; except for this, and for the child that did not come.

It was a hot day. Darkness had come. The heat rose up and hung and sweltered like a sodden blanket in St. Louis. It was wet heat, and one knew that there would be no relief or coolness in the night. And when one tried to think of the time when the heat would go away, one said: "It cannot last. It's bound to go away," as we always say it in America.

But one did not believe it when he said it. The heat soaked down and men sweltered in it; the faces of the people were pale and greasy with the heat. And in their faces was a patient wretchedness, and one felt the kind of desolation that one feels at the end of a hot day in a great city in America—when one's home is far away, across the continent, and he thinks of all that distance, all that heat, and feels, "Oh God! but it's a big country!"

And he feels nothing but absence, absence, and the desolation of America, the loneliness and sadness of the high, hot skies, and evening coming on across the Middle West, across the sweltering and heat-sunken land, across all the lonely little towns, the farms, the fields, the oven swelter of Ohio, Kansas, Iowa, and Indiana at the close of day, and voices, casual in the heat, voices of the little stations, quiet, casual, somehow faded into that enormous vacancy and weariness of heat, of space, and of the immense, the sorrowful, the most high and awful skies.

Then he hears the engine and the wheel again, the wailing whistle and the bell, the sound of shifting in the sweltering yard, and walks the street, and walks the street, beneath the clusters of hard lights, and by the people with sagged faces, and is drowned in desolation and in no belief.

He feels the way one feels when one comes back, and knows that he should not have come, and when he sees that, after all, King's Highway is—a street; and St. Louis—the enchanted name—a big, hot, common town upon the river, sweltering in wet, dreary heat, and not quite South, and nothing else enough to make it better.

It had not been like this before. He could remember how it would get hot, and how good the heat was, and how he would lie out in the backyard on an airing mattress, and how the mattress would get hot and dry and smell like a hot mattress full of sun, and how the sun would make him want to sleep, and how, sometimes, he would go down into the basement to feel coolness, and how the cellar smelled as cellars always smell—a cool, stale smell, the smell of cobwebs and of grimy bottles. And he could remember, when you opened the door upstairs, the smell of the cellar would come up to you—cool, misty, stale and dank and dark—and how the thought of the dark cellar always filled him with a kind of numb excitement, a kind of visceral expectancy.

He could remember how it got hot in the afternoons, and how he would feel a sense of absence and vague sadness in the afternoons, when everyone had gone away. The house would seem so lonely and sometimes he would sit inside, on the second step of the hall stairs, and listen to the sound of silence and of absence in the afternoon. He could smell the oil upon the floor and on the stairs, and see the sliding doors with their brown varnish and the beady chains across the door, and thrust his hands among the beady chains, and gather them together in his arms, and let them clash, and swish with light beady swishings all around him. He could feel darkness, absence, varnished darkness, and stained light within the house, through the stained glass of the window on the stairs, through the small stained glasses by the door, stained light and absence, silence and the smell of floor oil and vague sadness in the house on a hot mid-afternoon. And all these things themselves would have a kind of life: would seem to wait attentively, to be most living and most still.

He would sit there and listen. He could hear the girl next door practice her piano lessons in the afternoon, and hear the street car coming by between the backyard fences, half a block away, and smell the dry and sultry smell of backyard fences, the smell of coarse hot grasses by the car tracks in the afternoon, the smell of tar, of dry caulked ties, the smell of bright worn flanges, and feel the loneliness of backyards in the afternoon and the sense of absence when the car was gone.

Then he would long for evening and return, the slant of light, and feet along the street, the sharp-faced twins in sailor suits upon their tricycles, the smell of supper and the sound of voices in the house again, and Grover coming from the Fair.

That is how it was when he came into the street, and found the place where the two corners met, and turned at last to see if Time was there. He passed the house: some lights were burning, the door was open, and a woman sat upon the porch. And presently he turned, came back, and stopped before the house again. The corner light fell blank upon the house. He stood looking at it, and put his foot upon the step.

Then he said to the woman who was sitting on the porch: "This house—excuse me—but could you tell me, please, who lives here in this house?"

He knew his words were strange and hollow, and he had not said what he wished to say. She stared at him a moment, puzzled.

Then she said: "I live here. Who are you looking for?"

He said, "Why, I am looking for——"

And then he stopped, because he knew he could not tell her what it was that he was looking for.

"There used to be a house—" he said.

The woman was now staring at him hard.

He said, "I think I used to live here."

She said nothing.

In a moment he continued, "I used to live here in this house," he said, "when I was a little boy."

She was silent, looking at him, then she said: "Oh.

Are you sure this was the house? Do you remember the address?"

"I have forgotten the address," he said, "but it was Edgemont Street, and it was on the corner. And I know this is the house."

"This isn't Edgemont Street," the woman said. "The name is Bates."

"Well, then, they changed the name of the street," he said, "but this is the same house. It hasn't changed."

She was silent a moment, then she nodded: "Yes. They did change the name of the street. I remember when I was a child they called it something else," she said. "But that was a long time ago. When was it that you lived here?"

"In 1904."

Again she was silent, looking at him. Then presently: "Oh. That was the year of the Fair. You were here then?"

"Yes." He now spoke rapidly, with more confidence. "My mother had the house, and we were here for seven months. And the house belonged to Dr. Packer," he went on. "We rented it from him."

"Yes," the woman said, and nodded, "this was Dr. Packer's house. He's dead now, he's been dead for many years. But this was the Packer house, all right."

"That entrance on the side," he said, "where the steps go up, that was for Dr. Packer's patients. That was the entrance to his office."

"Oh," the woman said, "I didn't know that. I've often wondered what it was. I didn't know what it was for."

"And this big room in front here," he continued, "that was the office. And there were sliding doors, and next to it, a kind of alcove for his patients——"

"Yes, the alcove is still there, only all of it has been made into one room now—and I never knew just what the alcove was for."

"And there were sliding doors on this side, too, that opened on the hall—and a stairway going up upon this side. And halfway up the stairway, at the landing, a little window of colored glass—and across the sliding doors here in the hall, a kind of curtain made of strings of beads."

She nodded, smiling. "Yes, it's just the same—we still have the sliding doors and the stained glass window on the stairs. There's no bead curtain any more," she said, "but I remember when people had them. I know what you mean."

"When we were here," he said, "we used the doctor's office for a parlor—except later on—the last month or two—and then we used it for—a bedroom."

"It is a bedroom now," she said. "I run the house— I rent rooms—all of the rooms upstairs are rented—

but I have two brothers and they sleep in this front room."

Both of them were silent for a moment, then Eugene said, "My brother stayed there too."

"In the front room?" the woman said.

He answered, "Yes."

She paused, then said: "Won't you come in? I don't believe it's changed much. Would you like to see?"

He thanked her and said he would, and he went up the steps. She opened the screen door to let him in.

Inside it was just the same—the stairs, the hallway, the sliding doors, the window of stained glass upon the stairs. And all of it was just the same, except for absence, the stained light of absence in the afternoon, and the child who once had sat there, waiting on the stairs.

It was all the same except that as a child he had sat there feeling things were *Somewhere*—and now he *knew*. He had sat there feeling that a vast and sultry river was somewhere—and now he knew! He had sat there wondering what King's Highway was, where it began, and where it ended—now he knew! He had sat there haunted by the magic word "downtown"—now he knew!—and by the street car, after it had gone—and by all things that came and went and came again, like the cloud shadows passing in a wood, that never could be captured.

And he felt that if he could only sit there on the stairs once more, in solitude and absence in the afternoon, he would be able to get it back again. Then would he be able to remember all that he had seen and been—the brief sum of himself, the universe of his four years, with all the light of Time upon it—that universe which was so short to measure, and yet so far, so endless, to remember. Then would he be able to see his own small face again, pooled in the dark mirror of the hall, and peer once more into the grave eyes of the child that he had been, and discover there in his quiet three-years' self the lone integrity of "I," knowing: "Here is the House, and here House listening; here is Absence, Absence in the afternoon; and here in this House, this Absence, is my core, my kernel—here am I!"

But as he thought it, he knew that even if he could sit here alone and get it back again, it would be gone as soon as seized, just as it had been then—first coming like the vast and drowsy rumors of the distant and enchanted Fair, then fading like cloud shadows on a hill, going like faces in a dream—coming, going, coming, possessed and held but never captured, like lost voices in the mountains long ago—and like the dark eyes and quiet face of the dark, lost boy, his brother, who, in the mysterious rhythms of his life

and work, used to come into this house, then go, and return again.

The woman took Eugene back into the house and through the hall. He told her of the pantry, told her where it was and pointed to the place, but now it was no longer there. And he told her of the backyard, and of the old board fence around the yard. But the old board fence was gone. And he told her of the carriage house, and told her it was painted red. But now there was a small garage. And the backyard was still there, but smaller than he thought, and now there was a tree.

"I did not know there was a tree," he said. "I do not remember any tree."

"Perhaps it was not there," she said. "A tree could grow in thirty years." And then they came back through the house again and paused at the sliding doors.

"And could I see this room?" he said.

She slid the doors back. They slid open smoothly, with a rolling heaviness, as they used to do. And then he saw the room again. It was the same. There was a window at the side, the two arched windows at the front, the alcove and the sliding doors, the fireplace with the tiles of mottled green, the mantel of dark mission wood, the mantel posts, a dresser and a bed, just where the dresser and the bed had been so long ago.

"Is this the room?" the woman said. "It hasn't changed?"

He told her that it was the same.

"And your brother slept here where my brothers sleep?"

"This is his room," he said.

They were silent. He turned to go, and said, "Well, thank you. I appreciate your showing me."

She said that she was glad and that it was no trouble. "And when you see your family, you can tell them that you saw the house," she said. "My name is Mrs. Bell. You can tell your mother that a Mrs. Bell has the house now. And when you see your brother, you can tell him that you saw the room he slept in, and that you found it just the same."

He told her then that his brother was dead.

The woman was silent for a moment. Then she looked at him and said: "He died here, didn't he? In this room?"

He told her that it was so.

"Well, then," she said, "I knew it. I don't know how. But when you told me he was here, I knew it."

He said nothing. In a moment the woman said, "What did he die of?"

"Typhoid."

She looked shocked and troubled, and said involuntarily, "My two brothers——"

"That was a long time ago," he said. "I don't think you need to worry now."

"Oh, I wasn't thinking about that," she said. "It was just hearing that a little boy—your brother—was—was in this room that my two brothers sleep in now——"

"Well, maybe I shouldn't have told you then. But he was a good boy—and if you'd known him you wouldn't mind."

She said nothing, and he added quickly: "Besides, he didn't stay here long. This wasn't really his room—but the night he came back with my sister he was so sick—they didn't move him."

"Oh," the woman said, "I see." And then: "Are you going to tell your mother you were here?"

"I don't think so."

"I—I wonder how she feels about this room."

"I don't know. She never speaks of it."

"Oh. . . . How old was he?"

"He was twelve."

"You must have been pretty young yourself."

"I was not quite four."

"And—you just wanted to see the room, didn't you? That's why you came back."

"Yes."

"Well—" indefinitely—"I guess you've seen it now."

"Yes, thank you."

"I guess you don't remember much about him, do you? I shouldn't think you would."

"No, not much."

The years dropped off like fallen leaves: the face came back again—the soft dark oval, the dark eyes, the soft brown berry on the neck, the raven hair, all bending down, approaching—the whole appearing to him ghostwise, intent and instant.

"Now say it—*Grover!*"

"Gova."

"No—not Gova.—*Grover!* . . . Say it!"

"Gova."

"Ah-h—you didn't say it. You said Gova. *Grover—*now say it!"

"Gova."

"Look, I tell you what I'll do if you say it right. Would you like to go down to King's Highway? Would you like Grover to set you up? All right, then. If you say Grover and say it right, I'll take you to King's Highway and set you up to ice cream. Now say it right—*Grover!*"

"Gova."

"Ah-h, you-u. You're the craziest little old boy I ever did see. Can't you even say Grover?"

"Gova."

"Ah-h, you-u. Old Tongue-Tie, that's what you are. . . . Well, come on, then, I'll set you up anyway."

It all came back, and faded, and was lost again. Eugene turned to go, and thanked the woman and said good-bye.

"Well, then, good-bye," the woman said, and they shook hands. "I'm glad if I could show you. I'm glad if—" She did not finish, and at length she said: "Well, then, that was a long time ago. You'll find everything changed now, I guess. It's all built up around here now—and way out beyond here, out beyond where the Fair Grounds used to be. I guess you'll find it changed."

They had nothing more to say. They just stood there for a moment on the steps, and then shook hands once more.

"Well, good-bye."

And again he was in the street, and found the place where the corners met, and for the last time turned to see where Time had gone.

And he knew that he would never come again, and that lost magic would not come again. Lost now was all of it—the street, the heat, King's Highway, and Tom the Piper's son, all mixed in with the vast and drowsy murmur of the Fair, and with the sense of absence in the afternoon, and the house that waited, and the child that dreamed. And out of the enchanted wood, that thicket of man's memory, Eugene knew that the dark eye and the quiet face of his friend and brother—poor child, life's stranger, and life's exile, lost like all of us, a cipher in blind mazes, long ago—the lost boy was gone forever, and would not return.

THE RED PONY I

THE GIFT

JOHN STEINBECK

JOHN STEINBECK (1902–   ) was born in Salinas, California, studied biology as a special student at Stanford and worked at many odd jobs while beginning to write. He has displayed in much of his mature work a deep sympathy with simple and deprived people, at the same time viewing their actual condition with a realistic eye. His style ranges from an almost cruel realism to the lyrical. Among his books are *Tortilla Flat* (1935), *In Dubious Battle* (1936), *Of Mice and Men* (1937), *The Long Valley* (1938), *Grapes of Wrath* (1939), which won the Pulitzer Prize, *The Moon is Down* (1942), *Cannery Row* (1945), *East of Eden* (1952), and *The Winter of our Discontent* (1961), which was mentioned when he was awarded the Nobel Prize for Literature in 1962.

A T DAYBREAK Billy Buck emerged from the bunkhouse and stood for a moment on the porch looking up at the sky. He was a broad, bandy-legged little man with a walrus mustache, with square hands; puffed and muscled on the palms. His eyes were a contemplative, watery grey and the hair which protruded from under his Stetson hat was spiky and weathered. Billy was still stuffing his shirt into his blue jeans as he stood on the porch. He unbuckled his belt and tightened it again. The belt showed, by the worn shiny places opposite each hole, the gradual increase of Billy's middle over a period of years. When he had seen to the weather, Billy cleared each nostril by holding its mate closed with his forefinger and blowing fiercely. Then he walked down to the barn, rubbing his hands together. He curried and brushed two saddle horses in the stalls, talking quietly to them all the time; and he had hardly finished when the iron triangle started ringing at the ranch house. Billy stuck the brush and curry-comb together and laid them on the rail, and went up to breakfast. His action had been so deliberate and yet so wasteless of time that he came to the house while Mrs. Tiflin was still ringing the triangle. She nodded her grey head to him and withdrew into the kitchen. Billy Buck sat down on the steps, because he was a cow-hand, and it wouldn't be fitting that he should go first into the dining-room. He heard Mr. Tiflin in the house, stamping his feet into his boots.

The high jangling note of the triangle put the boy Jody in motion. He was only a little boy, ten years old, with hair like dusty yellow grass and with shy polite grey eyes, and with a mouth that worked when he thought. The triangle picked him up out of sleep. It didn't occur to him to disobey the harsh note. He never had: no one he knew ever had. He brushed the tangled hair out of his eyes and skinned his nightgown off. In a moment he was dressed—blue chambray shirt and overalls. It was late in the summer, so of course there were no shoes to bother with. In the kitchen he waited until his mother got from in front of the sink and went back to the stove. Then he washed himself and brushed back his wet hair with his fingers. His mother turned sharply on him as he left the sink. Jody looked shyly away.

"I've got to cut your hair before long," his mother said. "Breakfast's on the table. Go on in, so Billy can come."

Jody sat at the long table which was covered with white oilcloth washed through to the fabric in some places. The fried eggs lay in rows on their platter. Jody took three eggs on his plate and followed with three thick slices of crisp bacon. He carefully scraped a spot of blood from one of the egg yolks.

Billy Buck clumped in. "That won't hurt you," Billy explained. "That's only a sign the rooster leaves."

Jody's tall stern father came in then and Jody knew from the noise on the floor that he was wearing boots, but he looked under the table anyway, to make sure. His father turned off the oil lamp over the table, for plenty of morning light now came through the windows.

Jody did not ask where his father and Billy Buck were riding that day, but he wished he might go along. His father was a disciplinarian. Jody obeyed him in everything without questions of any kind.

From *The Portable Steinbeck.* Copyright, 1937, 1943, by John Steinbeck. Reprinted by permission of The Viking Press, Inc., New York.

Now, Carl Tiflin sat down and reached for the egg platter.

"Got the cows ready to go, Billy?" he asked.

"In the lower corral," Billy said. "I could just as well take them in alone."

"Sure you could. But a man needs company. Besides your throat gets pretty dry." Carl Tiflin was jovial this morning.

Jody's mother put her head in the door. "What time do you think to be back, Carl?"

"I can't tell. I've got to see some men in Salinas. Might be gone till dark."

The eggs and coffee and big biscuits disappeared rapidly. Jody followed the two men out of the house. He watched them mount their horses and drive six old milk cows out of the corral and start over the hill toward Salinas. They were going to sell the old cows to the butcher.

When they had disappeared over the crown of the ridge Jody walked up the hill in back of the house. The dogs trotted around the house corner hunching their shoulders and grinning horribly with pleasure. Jody patted their heads—Doubletree Mutt with the big thick tail and yellow eyes, and Smasher, the shepherd, who had killed a coyote and lost an ear in doing it. Smasher's one good ear stood up higher than a collie's ear should. Billy Buck said that always happened. After the frenzied greeting the dogs lowered their noses to the ground in a businesslike way and went ahead, looking back now and then to make sure that the boy was coming. They walked up through the chicken yard and saw the quail eating with the chickens. Smasher chased the chickens a little to keep in practice in case there should ever be sheep to herd. Jody continued on through the large vegetable patch where the green corn was higher than his head. The cow-pumpkins were green and small yet. He went on to the sagebrush line where the cold spring ran out of its pipe and fell into a round wooden tub. He leaned over and drank close to the green mossy wood where the water tasted best. Then he turned and looked back on the ranch, on the low, whitewashed house girded with red geraniums, and on the long bunkhouse by the cypress tree where Billy Buck lived alone. Jody could see the great black kettle under the cypress tree. That was where the pigs were scalded. The sun was coming over the ridge now, glaring on the whitewash of the houses and barns, making the wet grass blaze softly. Behind him, in the tall sagebrush, the birds were scampering on the ground, making a great noise among the dry leaves; the squirrels piped shrilly on the side-hills. Jody looked along at the farm buildings. He felt an uncertainty in the air, a feeling of change and of loss and of the gain of new and unfamiliar things. Over

the hillside two big black buzzards sailed low to the ground and their shadows slipped smoothly and quickly ahead of them. Some animal had died in the vicinity. Jody knew it. It might be a cow or it might be the remains of a rabbit. The buzzards overlooked nothing. Jody hated them as all decent things hate them, but they could not be hurt because they made away with carrion.

After a while the boy sauntered down hill again. The dogs had long ago given him up and gone into the brush to do things in their own way. Back through the vegetable garden he went, and he paused for a moment to smash a green muskmelon with his heel, but he was not happy about it. It was a bad thing to do, he knew perfectly well. He kicked dirt over the ruined melon to conceal it.

Back at the house his mother bent over his rough hands, inspecting his fingers and nails. It did little good to start him clean to school for too many things could happen on the way. She sighed over the black cracks on his fingers, and then gave him his books and his lunch and started him on the mile walk to school. She noticed that his mouth was working a good deal this morning.

Jody started his journey. He filled his pockets with little pieces of white quartz that lay in the road, and every so often he took a shot at a bird or at some rabbit that had stayed sunning itself in the road too long. At the crossroads over the bridge he met two friends and the three of them walked to school together, making ridiculous strides and being rather silly. School had just opened two weeks before. There was still a spirit of revolt among the pupils.

It was four o'clock in the afternoon when Jody topped the hill and looked down on the ranch again. He looked for the saddle horses, but the corral was empty. His father was not back yet. He went slowly, then, toward the afternoon chores. At the ranch house, he found his mother sitting on the porch, mending socks.

"There's two doughnuts in the kitchen for you," she said. Jody slid to the kitchen, and returned with half of one of the doughnuts already eaten and his mouth full. His mother asked him what he had learned in school that day, but she didn't listen to his doughnut-muffled answer. She interrupted, "Jody, tonight see you fill the wood-box clear full. Last night you crossed the sticks and it wasn't only about half full. Lay the sticks flat tonight. And Jody, some of the hens are hiding eggs, or else the dogs are eating them. Look about in the grass and see if you can find any nests."

Jody, still eating, went out and did his chores. He saw the quail come down to eat with the chickens when he threw out the grain. For some reason his father was proud to have them come. He never allowed any shooting near the house for fear the quail might go away.

When the wood-box was full, Jody took his twenty-two rifle up to the cold spring at the brush line. He drank again and then aimed the gun at all manner of things, at rocks, at birds on the wing, at the big black pig kettle under the cypress tree, but he didn't shoot for he had no cartridges and wouldn't have until he was twelve. If his father had seen him aim the rifle in the direction of the house he would have put the cartridges off another year. Jody remembered this and did not point the rifle down the hill again. Two years was enough to wait for cartridges. Nearly all of his father's presents were given with reservations which hampered their value somewhat. It was good discipline.

The supper waited until dark for his father to return. When at last he came in with Billy Buck, Jody could smell the delicious brand on their breaths. Inwardly he rejoiced, for his father sometimes talked to him when he smelled of brandy, sometimes even told things he had done in the wild days when he was a boy.

After supper, Jody sat by the fireplace and his shy polite eyes sought the room corners, and he waited for his father to tell what it was he contained, for Jody knew he had news of some sort. But he was disappointed. His father pointed a stern finger at him.

"You'd better go to bed, Jody. I'm going to need you in the morning."

That wasn't so bad. Jody liked to do the things he had to do as long as they weren't routine things. He looked at the floor and his mouth worked out a question before he spoke it. "What are we going to do in the morning, kill a pig?" he asked softly.

"Never you mind. You better get to bed."

When the door was closed behind him, Jody heard his father and Billy Buck chuckling and he knew it was a joke of some kind. And later, when he lay in bed, trying to make words out of murmurs in the other room, he heard his father protest, "But, Ruth, I didn't give much for him."

Jody heard the hoot-owls hunting mice down by the barn, and he heard a fruit tree limb tap-tapping against the house. A cow was lowing when he went to sleep.

When the triangle sounded in the morning, Jody dressed more quickly even than usual. In the kitchen, while he washed his face and combed back his hair, his mother addressed him irritably. "Don't you go out until you get a good breakfast in you."

He went into the dining-room and sat at the long white table. He took a steaming hotcake from the platter, arranged two fried eggs on it, covered them with another hotcake and squashed the whole thing with his fork.

His father and Billy Buck came in. Jody knew from the sound of the floor that both of them were wearing flatheeled shoes, but he peered under the table to make sure. His father turned off the oil lamp, for the day had arrived, and he looked stern and disciplinary, but Billy Buck didn't look at Jody at all. He avoided the shy questioning eyes of the boy and soaked a whole piece of toast in his coffee.

Carl Tiflin said crossly, "You come with us after breakfast!"

Jody had trouble with his food then, for he felt a kind of doom in the air. After Billy had tilted his saucer and drained the coffee which had slopped into it, and had wiped his hands on his jeans, the two men stood up from the table and went out into the morning light together, and Jody respectfully followed a little behind them. He tried to keep his mind from running ahead, tried to keep it absolutely motionless.

His mother called, "Carl! Don't you let it keep him from school."

They marched past the cypress, where a singletree hung from a limb to butcher the pigs on, and past the black iron kettle, so it was not a pig killing. The sun shone over the hill and threw long, dark shadows of the trees and buildings. They crossed a stubble-field to shortcut to the barn. Jody's father unhooked the door and they went in. They had been walking toward the sun on the way down. The barn was black as night in contrast and warm from the hay and from the beasts. Jody's father moved over toward the one box stall. "Come here!" he ordered. Jody could begin to see things now. He looked into the box stall and then stepped back quickly.

A red pony colt was looking at him out of the stall. Its tense ears were forward and a light of disobedience was in its eyes. Its coat was rough and thick as an airedale's fur and its mane was long and tangled. Jody's throat collapsed in on itself and cut his breath short.

"He needs a good currying," his father said, "and if I ever hear of you not feeding him or leaving his stall dirty, I'll sell him off in a minute."

Jody couldn't bear to look at the pony's eyes any more. He gazed down at his hands for a moment, and he asked very shyly, "Mine?" No one answered him. He put his hands out toward the pony. Its grey nose came close, sniffing loudly, and then the lips drew back and the strong teeth closed on Jody's fingers. The pony shook its head up and down and seemed to laugh with amusement. Jody regarded his bruised fingers. "Well," he said with pride— "Well, I guess he can bite all right." The two men laughed, somewhat in relief. Carl Tiflin went out of the barn and walked up a sidehill to be by himself, for he was embarrassed, but Billy Buck stayed. It was easier to talk to Billy Buck. Jody asked again—"Mine?"

Billy became professional in tone. "Sure! That is, if you look out for him and break him right. I'll show you how. He's just a colt. You can't ride him for some time."

Jody put out his bruised hand again, and this time the red pony let his nose be rubbed. "I ought to have a carrot," Jody said. "Where'd we get him, Billy?"

"Bought him at a sheriff's auction," Billy explained. "A show went broke in Salinas and had debts. The sheriff was selling off their stuff."

The pony stretched out his nose and shook the forelock from his wild eyes. Jody stroked the nose a little. He said softly, "There isn't a—saddle?"

Billy Buck laughed. "I'd forgot. Come along."

In the harness room he lifted down a little saddle of red morocco leather. "It's just a show saddle," Billy Buck said disparagingly. "It isn't practical for the brush, but it was cheap at the sale."

Jody couldn't trust himself to look at the saddle either, and he couldn't speak at all. He brushed the shining red leather with his fingertips, and after a long time he said, "It'll look pretty on him though." He thought of the grandest and prettiest things he knew. "If he hasn't a name already, I think I'll call him Gabilan Mountains," he said.

Billy Buck knew how he felt. "It's a pretty long name. Why don't you just call him Gabilan? That means hawk. That would be a fine name for him." Billy felt glad. "If you will collect tail hair, I might be able to make a hair rope for you sometime. You could use it for a hackamore."

Jody wanted to go back to the box stall. "Could I lead him to school, do you think—to show the kids?"

But Billy shook his head. "He's not even halter-broke yet. We had a time getting him here. Had to almost drag him. You better be starting for school though."

"I'll bring the kids to see him here this afternoon," Jody said.

Six boys came over the hill half an hour early that afternoon, running hard, their heads down, their forearms working, their breath whistling. They swept by the house and cut across the stubble-field to the barn. And then they stood self-consciously before the pony, and then they looked at Jody with eyes in which there was a new admiration and a new respect. Before today Jody had been a boy, dressed in overalls and a blue shirt—quieter than most, even suspected of being a little cowardly. And now he was different. Out of a thousand centuries they drew the ancient admiration of the footman for the horseman. They knew instinctively that a man on a horse is spiritually as well as physically bigger than a man on foot. They knew that Jody had been miraculously lifted out of equality with them, and had been placed over them. Gabilan put his head out of the stall and sniffed them.

"Why'nt you ride him?" the boys cried. "Why'nt you braid his tail with ribbons like in the fair?" "When you going to ride him?"

Jody's courage was up. He too felt the superiority of the horseman. "He's not old enough. Nobody can ride him for a long time. I'm going to train him on the long halter. Billy Buck is going to show me how."

"Well, can't we even lead him around a little?"

"He isn't even halter-broke," Jody said. He wanted to be completely alone when he took the pony out the first time. "Come and see the saddle."

They were speechless at the red morocco saddle, completely shocked out of comment. "It isn't much use in the brush," Jody explained. "It'll look pretty on him though. Maybe I'll ride bareback when I go into the brush."

"How you going to rope a cow without a saddle horn?"

"Maybe I'll get another saddle for every day. My father might want me to help him with the stock." He let them feel the red saddle, and showed them the brass chain throat-latch on the bridle and the big brass buttons at each temple where the headstall and brow band crossed. The whole thing was too wonderful. They had to go away after a little while, and each boy, in his mind, searched among his possessions for a bribe worthy of offering a return for a ride on the red pony when the time should come.

Jody was glad when they had gone. He took brush and currycomb from the wall, took down the barrier of the box stall and stepped cautiously in. The pony's eyes glittered, and he edged around into kicking position. But Jody touched him on the shoulder and rubbed his high arched neck as he had always seen Billy Buck do, and he crooned, "So-o-o Boy," in a deep voice. The pony gradually relaxed his tenseness. Jody curried and brushed until a pile of dead hair lay in the stall and until the pony's coat had taken on a deep red shine. Each time he finished he thought it might have been done better. He braided the mane into a dozen little pigtails, and he braided the forelock, and then he undid them and brushed the hair out straight again.

Jody did not hear his mother enter the barn. She was angry when she came, but when she looked in at the pony and at Jody working over him, she felt a curious pride rise up in her. "Have you forgot the wood-box?" she asked gently. "It's not far off from dark and there's not a stick of wood in the house, and the chickens aren't fed."

Jody quickly put up his tools. "I forgot, ma'am."

"Well, after this do your chores first. Then you won't forget. I expect you'll forget lots of things now if I don't keep an eye on you."

"Can I have carrots from the garden for him, ma'am?"

She had to think about that. "Oh—I guess so, if you only take the big tough ones."

"Carrots keep the coat good," he said, and again she felt the curious rush of pride.

Jody never waited for the triangle to get him out of bed after the coming of the pony. It became his habit to creep out of bed even before his mother was awake, to slip into his clothes and go quietly to the barn to see Gabilan. In the grey quiet mornings when the land and the brush and the houses and the trees were silver-grey and black like a photograph negative, he stole toward the barn, past the sleeping stones and the sleeping cypress tree. The turkeys, roosting in the tree out of coyotes' reach, clicked drowsily. The fields glowed with a grey frost-like light and in the dew the tracks of rabbits and of field mice stood out sharply. The good dogs came stiffly out of their little houses, hackles up and deep growls in their throats. Then they caught Jody's scent, and their stiff tails rose up and waved a greeting—Doubletree Mutt with the big thick tail, and Smasher, the incipient shepherd—then went lazily back to their warm beds.

It was a strange time and mysterious journey, to Jody—an extension of a dream. When he first had the pony he liked to torture himself during the trip by thinking Gabilan would not be in his stall, and worse, would never have been there. And he had other delicious little self-induced pains. He thought how the rats had gnawed ragged holes in the red saddle, and how the mice had nibbled Gabilan's tail until it was stringy and thin. He usually ran the last little way to the barn. He unlatched the rusty hasp of the barn door and stepped in, and no matter how quietly he opened the door, Gabilan was always looking at him over the barrier of the box stall and Gabilan whinnied softly and stamped his front foot, and his eyes had big sparks of red fire in them like oakwood embers.

Sometimes, if the work horses were to be used that day, Jody found Billy Buck in the barn harnessing and currying. Billy stood with him and looked long at Gabilan and he told Jody a great many things about horses. He explained that they were terribly afraid for their feet, so that one must make a practice of lifting the legs and patting the hooves and ankles to remove their terror. He told Jody how horses love conversation. He must talk to the pony all the time, and tell him the reasons for everything. Billy wasn't sure a horse could understand everything that was said to him, but it was impossible to say how much was understood. A horse never kicked up a fuss if some one he liked explained things to him. Billy could give examples, too. He had known, for instance, a horse nearly dead beat with fatigue to perk up when told it was only a little farther to his destination. And he had known a horse paralyzed with fright to come out of it when his rider told him what it was that was frightening him. While he talked in the mornings, Billy Buck cut twenty or thirty straws into neat three-inch lengths and stuck them into his hatband. Then during the whole day, if he wanted to pick his teeth or merely to chew on something, he had only to reach up for one of them.

Jody listened carefully, for he knew and the whole country knew that Billy Buck was a fine hand with horses. Billy's own horse was a stringy cayuse with a hammer head, but he nearly always won the first prizes at the stock trials. Billy could rope a steer, take a double half-hitch about the horn with his riata, and dismount, and his horse would play the steer as an angler plays a fish, keeping a tight rope until the steer was down or beaten.

Every morning, after Jody had curried and brushed the pony, he let down the barrier of the stall, and Gabilan thrust past him and raced down the barn and into the corral. Around and around he galloped, and sometimes he jumped forward and landed on stiff legs. He stood quivering, stiff ears forward, eyes rolling so that the whites showed, pretending to be frightened. At last he walked snorting to the water-trough and buried his nose in the water up to the nostrils. Jody was proud then, for he knew that was the way to judge a horse. Poor horses only touched their lips to the water, but a fine spirited beast put his whole nose and mouth under, and only left room to breathe.

Then Jody stood and watched the pony, and he saw things he had never noticed about any other horse, the sleek, sliding flank muscles and the cords of the buttocks, which flexed like a closing fist, and the shine the sun put on the red coat. Having seen horses all his life, Jody had never looked at them very closely before. But now he noticed the moving ears which gave expression and even inflection of expression to the face. The pony talked with his ears. You could tell exactly how he felt about everything by the way his ears pointed. Sometimes they were stiff and upright and sometimes lax and sagging. They went back when he was angry or fearful, and forward when he was anxious and curious and pleased; and their exact position indicated which emotion he had.

Billy Buck kept his word. In the early fall the training began. First there was the halter-breaking, and that was the hardest because it was the first thing. Jody held a carrot and coaxed and promised and pulled on the rope. The pony set his feet like a burro when he felt the strain. But before long he learned. Jody walked all over the ranch leading him. Gradually he took to dropping the rope until the pony followed him unled wherever he went.

And then came the training on the long halter. That was slower work. Jody stood in the middle of a circle, holding the long halter. He clucked with his tongue and the pony started to walk in a big circle, held in by the long rope. He clucked again to make the pony trot, and again to make him gallop. Around and around Gabilan went thundering and enjoying it immensely. Then he called, "Whoa," and the pony stopped. It was not long until Gabilan was perfect at it. But in many ways he was a bad pony. He bit Jody in the pants and stomped on Jody's feet. Now and then his ears went back and he aimed a tremendous kick at the boy. Every time he did one of these bad things, Gabilan settled back and seemed to laugh to himself.

Billy Buck worked at the hair rope in the evenings before the fireplace. Jody collected tail hair in a bag, and he sat and watched Billy slowly constructing the rope, twisting a few hairs to make a string and rolling two strings together for a cord, and then braiding a number of cords to make the rope. Billy rolled the finished rope on the floor under his foot to make it round and hard.

The long halter work rapidly approached perfection. Jody's father, watching the pony stop and start and trot and gallop, was a little bothered by it.

"He's getting to be almost a trick pony," he complained. "I don't like trick horses. It takes all the—dignity out of a horse to make him do tricks. Why, a trick horse is kind of like an actor—no dignity, no character of his own." And his father said, "I guess you better be getting him used to the saddle pretty soon."

Jody rushed for the harness-room. For some time he had been riding the saddle on a sawhorse. He changed the stirrup length over and over, and could never get it just right. Sometimes, mounted on the sawhorse in the harness-room, with collars and hames and tugs hung all about him, Jody rode out beyond the room. He carried his rifle across the pommel. He saw the fields go flying by, and he heard the beat of the galloping hoofs.

It was a ticklish job, saddling the pony the first time. Gabilan hunched and reared and threw the saddle off before the cinch could be tightened. It had to be replaced again and again until at last the pony let it stay. And the cinching was difficult, too. Day by day Jody tightened the girth a little more until at last the pony didn't mind the saddle at all.

Then there was the bridle. Billy explained how to use a stick of licorice for a bit until Gabilan was used to having something in his mouth. Billy explained, "Of course we could force-break him to everything, but he wouldn't be as good a horse if we did. He'd always be a little bit afraid, and he wouldn't mind because he wanted to."

The first time the pony wore the bridle he whipped his head about and worked his tongue against the bit until the blood oozed from the corners of his mouth. He tried to rub the headstall off on the manger. His ears pivoted about and his eyes turned red with fear and with general rambunctiousness. Jody rejoiced, for he knew that only a mean-souled horse does not resent training.

And Jody trembled when he thought of the time when he would first sit in the saddle. The pony would probably throw him off. There was no disgrace in that. The disgrace would come if he did not get right up and mount again. Sometimes he dreamed that he lay in the dirt and cried and couldn't make himself mount again. The shame of the dream lasted until the middle of the day.

Gabilan was growing fast. Already he had lost the long-leggedness of the colt; his mane was getting longer and blacker. Under the constant currying and brushing his coat lay as smooth and gleaming as orange-red lacquer. Jody oiled the hoofs and kept them carefully trimmed so they would not crack.

The hair rope was nearly finished. Jody's father gave him an old pair of spurs and bent in the side bars and cut down the strap and took up the chainlets until they fitted. And then one day Carl Tiflin said:

"The pony's growing faster than I thought. I guess you can ride him by Thanksgiving. Think you can stick on?"

"I don't know," Jody said shyly. Thanksgiving was only three weeks off. He hoped it wouldn't rain, for rain would spot the red saddle.

Gabilan knew and liked Jody by now. He nickered when Jody came across the stubble-field, and in the pasture he came running when his master whistled for him. There was always a carrot for him every time.

Billy Buck gave him riding instructions over and over. "Now when you get up there, just grab tight with your knees and keep your hands away from the saddle, and if you get throwed, don't let that stop you. No matter how good a man is, there's always some horse can pitch him. You just climb up again before he gets to feeling smart about it. Pretty soon, he won't throw you no more, and pretty soon he *can't* throw you no more. That's the way to do it."

"I hope it don't rain before," Jody said.

"Why not? Don't want to get throwed in the mud?"

That was partly it, and also he was afraid that in the flurry of bucking Gabilan might slip and fall on him and break his leg or his hip. He had seen that happen to men before, had seen how they writhed on the ground like squashed bugs, and he was afraid of it.

He practiced on the sawhorse how he would hold the reins in his left hand and a hat in his right hand. If he kept his hands thus busy, he couldn't grab the horn if he felt himself going off. He didn't like to think of what would happen if he did grab the horn. Perhaps his father and Billy Buck would never speak to him again, they would be so ashamed. The news would get about and his mother would be ashamed too. And in the school yard—it was too awful to contemplate.

He began putting his weight in a stirrup when Gabilan was saddled, but he didn't throw his leg over the pony's back. That was forbidden until Thanksgiving.

Every afternoon he put the red saddle on the pony and cinched it tight. The pony was learning already to fill his stomach out unnaturally large while the cinching was going on, and then to let it down when the straps were fixed. Sometimes Jody led him up to the brush line and let him drink from the round green tub, and sometimes he led him up through the stubble-field to the hilltop from which it was possible to see the white town of Salinas and the geometric fields of the great valley, and the oak trees clipped by the sheep. Now and then they broke through the brush and came to little cleared circles so hedged in that the world was gone and only the sky and the circle of brush were left from the old life. Gabilan liked these trips and showed it by keeping his head very high and by quivering his nostrils with interest. When the two came back from an expedition they smelled of the sweet sage they had forced through.

Time dragged on toward Thanksgiving, but winter came fast. The clouds swept down and hung all day over the land and brushed the hilltops, and the winds blew shrilly at night. All day the dry oak leaves drifted down from the trees until they covered the ground, and yet the trees were unchanged.

Jody had wished it might not rain before Thanksgiving, but it did. The brown earth turned dark and the trees glistened. The cut ends of the stubble turned black with mildew; the haystacks grayed from exposure to the damp, and on the roofs the moss, which had been all summer as grey as lizards, turned a brilliant yellow-green. During the week of rain, Jody kept the pony in the box stall out of the dampness, except for a little time after school when he took him out for exercise and to drink at the water-trough in the upper corral. Not once did Gabilan get wet.

The wet weather continued until little new grass appeared. Jody walked to school dressed in a slicker and short rubber boots. At length one morning the sun came out brightly. Jody, at his work in the box stall, said to Billy Buck, "Maybe I'll leave Gabilan in the corral when I go to school today."

"Be good for him to be out in the sun," Billy assured him. "No animal likes to be cooped up too long. Your father and me are going back on the hill to clean the leaves out of the spring." Billy nodded and picked his teeth with one of his little straws.

"If the rain comes, though—" Jody suggested.

"Not likely to rain today. She's rained herself out." Billy pulled up his sleeves and snapped his arm bands. "If it comes on to rain—why a little rain don't hurt a horse."

"Well, if it does come on to rain, you put him in, will you, Billy? I'm scared he might get cold so I couldn't ride him when the time comes."

"Oh sure! I'll watch out for him if we get back in time. But it won't rain today."

And so Jody, when he went to school left Gabilan standing out in the corral.

Billy Buck wasn't wrong about many things. He couldn't be. But he was wrong about the weather that day, for a little after noon the clouds pushed over the hills and the rain began to pour down. Jody heard it start on the schoolhouse roof. He considered holding up one finger for permission to go to the outhouse and, once outside, running for home to put the pony in. Punishment would be prompt both at school and at home. He gave it up and took ease from Billy's assurance that rain couldn't hurt a horse. When school was finally out, he hurried home through the dark rain. The banks at the sides of the road spouted little jets of muddy water. The rain slanted and swirled under a cold and gusty wind. Jody dog-trotted home, slopping through the gravelly mud of the road.

From the top of the ridge he could see Gabilan standing miserably in the corral. The red coat was almost black, and streaked with water. He stood head down with his rump to the rain and wind. Jody arrived running and threw open the barn door and led the wet pony in by his forelock. Then he found a gunny sack and rubbed the soaked hair and rubbed the legs and ankles. Gabilan stood patiently, but he trembled in gusts like the wind.

When he had dried the pony as well as he could, Jody went up to the house and brought hot water down to the barn and soaked the grain in it. Gabilan was not very hungry. He nibbled at the hot mash, but he was not very much interested in it, and he still shivered now and then. A little steam rose from his damp back.

It was almost dark when Billy Buck and Carl Tiflin came home. "When the rain started we put up at Ben Herche's place, and the rain never let up all afternoon," Carl Tiflin explained. Jody looked reproachfully at Billy Buck and Billy felt guilty.

"You said it wouldn't rain," Jody accused him.

Billy looked away. "It's hard to tell, this time of year," he said, but his excuse was lame. He had no right to be fallible, and he knew it.

"The pony got wet, got soaked through."

"Did you dry him off?"

"I rubbed him with a sack and I gave him hot grain."

Billy nodded in agreement.

"Do you think he'll take cold, Billy?"

"A little rain never hurt anything," Billy assured him.

Jody's father joined the conversation then and lectured the boy a little. "A horse," he said, "isn't any lap-dog kind of thing." Carl Tiflin hated weakness and sickness, and he held a violent contempt for helplessness.

Jody's mother put a platter of steaks on the table and boiled potatoes and boiled squash, which clouded the room with their steam. They sat down to eat. Carl Tiflin still grumbled about weakness put into animals and men by too much coddling.

Billy Buck felt bad about his mistake. "Did you blanket him?" he asked.

"No. I couldn't find any blanket. I laid some sacks over his back."

"We'll go down and cover him up after we eat, then." Billy felt better about it then. When Jody's father had gone in to the fire and his mother was washing dishes, Billy found and lighted a lantern. He and Jody walked through the mud to the barn. The barn was dark and warm and sweet. The horses still munched their evening hay. "You hold the lantern!" Billy ordered. And he felt the pony's legs and tested the heat of the flanks. He put his cheek against the pony's grey muzzle and then he rolled up the eyelids to look at the eyeballs and he lifted the lips to see the gums, and he put his fingers inside the ears. "He

don't seem so chipper," Billy said. "I'll give him a rub-down."

Then Billy found a sack and rubbed the pony's legs violently and he rubbed the chest and the withers. Gabilan was strangely spiritless. He submitted patiently to the rubbing. At last Billy brought an old cotton comforter from the saddle-room, and threw it over the pony's back and tied it at neck and chest with string.

"Now he'll be all right in the morning," Billy said.

Jody's mother looked up when he got back to the house. "You're late up from bed," she said. She held his chin in her hard hand and brushed the tangled hair out of his eyes and she said, "Don't worry about the pony. He'll be all right. Billy's as good as any horse doctor in the country."

Jody hadn't known she could see his worry. He pulled gently away from her and knelt down in front of the fireplace until it burned his stomach. He scorched himself through and then went in to bed, but it was a hard thing to go to sleep. He awakened after what seemed a long time. The room was dark but there was a greyness in the window like that which precedes the dawn. He got up and found his overalls and searched for the legs, and then the clock in the other room struck two. He laid his clothes down and got back into bed. It was broad daylight when he awakened again. For the first time he had slept through the ringing of the triangle. He leaped up, flung on his clothes and went out of the door still buttoning his shirt. His mother looked after him for a moment and then went quietly back to her work. Her eyes were brooding and kind. Now and then her mouth smiled a little but without changing her eyes at all.

Jody ran on toward the barn. Halfway there he heard the sound he dreaded, the hollow rasping cough of a horse. He broke into a sprint then. In the barn he found Billy Buck with the pony. Billy was rubbing its legs with his strong thick hands. He looked up and smiled gaily.

"He just took a little cold," Billy said. "We'll have him out of it in a couple of days."

Jody looked at the pony's face. The eyes were half closed and the lids thick and dry. In the eye corners a crust of hard mucus stuck. Gabilan's ears hung loosely sideways and his head was low. Jody put out his hand, but the pony did not move close to it. He coughed again and his whole body constricted with the effort. A little stream of thin fluid ran from his nostrils.

Jody looked back at Billy Buck. "He's awful sick, Billy."

"Just a little cold, like I said," Billy insisted. "You

go get some breakfast and then go back to school. I'll take care of him."

"But you might have to do something else. You might leave him."

"No, I won't. I won't leave him at all. Tomorrow's Saturday. Then you can stay with him all day." Billy had failed again, and he felt badly about it. He had to cure the pony now.

Jody walked up to the house and took his place listlessly at the table. The eggs and bacon were cold and greasy, but he didn't notice it. He ate his usual amount. He didn't even ask to stay home from school. His mother pushed his hair back when she took his plate. "Billy'll take care of the pony," she assured him.

He moped through the whole day at school. He couldn't answer any questions nor read any words. He couldn't even tell anyone the pony was sick, for that might make him sicker. And when school was finally out he started home in dread. He walked slowly and let the other boys leave him. He wished he might continue walking and never arrive at the ranch.

Billy was in the barn, as he had promised, and the pony was worse. His eyes were almost closed now, and his breath whistled shrilly past an obstruction in his nose. A film covered that part of the eyes that was visible at all. It was doubtful whether the pony could see anymore. Now and then he snorted, to clear his nose, and by the action seemed to plug it tighter. Jody looked dispiritedly at the pony's coat. The hair lay rough and unkempt and seemed to have lost all of its old luster. Billy stood quietly besides the stall. Jody hated to ask, but he had to know.

"Billy, is he—is he going to get well?"

Billy put his fingers between the bars under the pony's jaw and felt about. "Feel here," he said and he guided Jody's fingers to a large lump under the jaw. "When that gets bigger, I'll open it up and then he'll get better."

Jody looked quickly away, for he had heard about that lump. "What is it the matter with him?"

Billy didn't want to answer, but he had to. He couldn't be wrong three times. "Strangles," he said shortly, "but don't you worry about that. I'll pull him out of it. I've seen them get well when they were worse than Gabilan is. I'm going to steam him now. You can help."

"Yes," Jody said miserably. He followed Billy into the grain room and watched him make the steaming bag ready. It was a long canvas nose bag with straps to go over a horse's ears. Billy filled it one-third full of bran and then he added a couple of handfuls of dried hops. On top of the dry substance he poured a little carbolic acid and a little turpentine. "I'll be mix-

ing it all up while you run to the house for a kettle of boiling water," Billy said.

When Jody came back with the steaming kettle, Billy buckled the straps over Gabilan's head and fitted the bag tightly around his nose. Then through a little hole in the side of the bag he poured the boiling water on the mixture. The pony started away as a cloud of strong steam rose up, but then the soothing fumes crept through his nose and into his lungs, and the sharp steam began to clear out the nasal passages. He breathed loudly. His legs trembled in an ague, and his eyes closed against the biting cloud. Billy poured in more water and kept the steam rising for fifteen minutes. At last he set down the kettle and took the bag from Gabilan's nose. The pony looked better. He breathed freely, and his eyes were open wider than they had been.

"See how good it makes him feel," Billy said. "Now we'll wrap him up in the blanket again. Maybe he'll be nearly well by morning."

"I'll stay with him tonight," Jody suggested.

"No. Don't you do it. I'll bring my blankets down here and put them in the hay. You can stay tomorrow and steam him if he needs it."

The evening was falling when they went to the house for their supper. Jody didn't even realize that some one else had fed the chickens and filled the wood-box. He walked up past the house to the dark brush line and took a drink of water from the tub. The spring water was so cold that it stung his mouth and drove a shiver through him. The sky above the hills was still light. He saw a hawk flying so high that it caught the sun on its breast and shone like a spark. Two blackbirds were driving him down the sky, glittering as they attacked their enemy. In the west, the clouds were moving in to rain again.

Jody's father didn't speak at all while the family ate supper, but after Billy Buck had taken his blankets and gone to sleep in the barn, Carl Tiflin built a high fire in the fireplace and told stories. He told about the wild man who ran naked through the country and had a tail and ears like a horse, and he told about the rabbit-cats of Moro Cojo that hopped into the trees for birds. He revived the famous Maxwell brothers who found a vein of gold and hid the traces of it so carefully that they could never find it again.

Jody sat with his chin in his hands; his mouth worked nervously, and his father gradually became aware that he wasn't listening very carefully. "Isn't that funny?" he asked.

Jody laughed politely and said, "Yes, sir." His father was angry and hurt, then. He didn't tell any more stories. After awhile, Jody took a lantern and went down to the barn. Billy Buck was asleep in the hay, and, except that his breath rasped a little in his lungs, the pony seemed to be much better. Jody stayed a little while, running his fingers over the red rough coat, and then he took up the lantern and went back to the house. When he was in bed his mother came into the room.

"Have you enough covers on? It's getting winter."

"Yes, ma'am."

"Well, get some rest tonight." She hesitated to go out, stood uncertainly. "The pony will be all right," she said.

Jody was tired. He went to sleep quickly and didn't awaken until dawn. The triangle sounded, and Billy Buck came up from the barn before Jody could get out of the house.

"How is he?" Jody demanded.

Billy always wolfed his breakfast. "Pretty good. I'm going to open that lump this morning. Then he'll be better maybe."

After breakfast, Billy got out his best knife, one with a needle point. He whetted the shining blade a long time on a little carborundum stone. He tried the point and the blade again and again on his calloused thumb-ball, and at last he tried it on his upper lip.

On the way to the barn, Jody noticed how the young grass was up and how the stubble was melting day by day into the new green crop of volunteer. It was a cold sunny morning.

As soon as he saw the pony, Jody knew he was worse. His eyes were closed and sealed shut with dried mucus. His head hung so low that his nose almost touched the straw of his bed. There was a little groan in each breath, a deep-seated, patient groan.

Billy lifted the weak head and made a quick slash with the knife. Jody saw the yellow pus run out. He held up the head while Billy swabbed out the wound with weak carbolic acid salve.

"Now he'll feel better," Billy assured him. "That yellow poison is what makes him sick."

Jody looked unbelieving at Billy Buck. "He's awful sick."

Billy thought a long time what to say. He nearly tossed off a careless assurance, but he saved himself in time. "Yes, he's pretty sick," he said at last. "I've seen worse ones get well. If he doesn't get pneumonia, we'll pull him through. You stay with him. If he gets worse, you can come and get me."

For a long time after Billy went away, Jody stood beside the pony, stroking him behind the ears. The pony didn't flip his head the way he had done when he was well. The groaning in his breathing was becoming more hollow.

Doubletree Mutt looked into the barn, his big tail waving provocatively, and Jody was so incensed at his health that he found a hard black clod on the floor and deliberately threw it. Doubletree Mutt went yelping away to nurse a bruised paw.

In the middle of the morning, Billy Buck came back and made another steam bag. Jody watched to see whether the pony improved this time as he had before. His breathing eased a little, but he did not raise his head.

The Saturday dragged on. Late in the afternoon Jody went to the house and brought his bedding down and made up a place to sleep in the hay. He didn't ask permission. He knew from the way his mother looked at him that she would let him do almost anything. That night he left a lantern burning on a wire over the box stall. Billy had told him to rub the pony's legs every little while.

At nine o'clock the wind sprang up and howled around the barn. And in spite of his worry, Jody grew sleepy. He got into his blankets and went to sleep, but the breathy groans of the pony sounded in his dreams. And in his sleep he heard a crashing noise which went on and on until it awakened him. The wind was rushing through the barn. He sprang up and looked down the lane of stalls. The barn door had blown open, and the pony was gone.

He caught the lantern and ran outside into the gale, and he saw Gabilan weakly shambling away into the darkness, head down, legs working slowly and mechanically. When Jody ran up and caught him by the forelock, he allowed himself to be led back and put into his stall. His groans were louder, and a fierce whistling came from his nose. Jody didn't sleep anymore then. The hissing of the pony's breath grew louder and sharper.

He was glad when Billy Buck came in at dawn. Billy looked for a time at the pony as though he had never seen him before. He felt the ears and flanks. "Jody," he said, "I've got to do something you won't want to see. You run up to the house for a while."

Jody grabbed him fiercely by the forearm. "You're not going to shoot him?"

Billy patted his hand. "No. I'm going to open a little hole in his windpipe so he can breathe. His nose is filled up. When he gets well, we'll put a little brass button in the hole for him to breathe through."

Jody couldn't have gone away if he had wanted to. It was awful to see the red hide cut, but infinitely more terrible to know it was being cut and not to see it. "I'll stay right here," he said bitterly. "You sure you got to?"

"Yes. I'm sure. If you stay, you can hold his head. If it doesn't make you sick, that is."

The fine knife came out again and was whetted again just as carefully as it had been the first time. Jody held the pony's head up and the throat taut, while Billy felt up and down for the right place. Jody sobbed once as the bright knife point disappeared into the throat. The pony plunged weakly away and then stood still, trembling violently. The blood ran thickly out and up the knife and across Billy's hand and into his shirtsleeve. The sure square hand sawed out a round hole in the flesh, and the breath came bursting out of the hole, throwing a fine spray of blood. With the rush of oxygen, the pony took a sudden strength. He lashed out with his hind feet and tried to rear, but Jody held his head down while Billy mopped the new wound with carbolic salve. It was a good job. The blood stopped flowing and the air puffed out of the hole and sucked it in regularly with a little bubbling noise.

The rain brought in by the night wind began to fall on the barn roof. Then the triangle rang for breakfast. "You go up and eat while I wait," Billy said. "We've got to keep this hole from plugging up."

Jody walked slowly out of the barn. He was too dispirited to tell Billy how the barn door had blown open and let the pony out. He emerged into the wet grey morning and sloshed up to the house, taking a perverse pleasure in splashing through all the puddles. His mother fed him and put dry clothes on. She didn't question him. She seemed to know he couldn't answer questions. But when he was ready to go back to the barn she brought him a pan of steaming meal. "Give him this," she said.

But Jody did not take the pan. He said, "He won't eat anything," and ran out of the house. At the barn, Billy showed him how to fix a ball of cotton on a stick, with which to swab out the breathing hole when it became clogged with mucus.

Jody's father walked into the barn and stood with them in front of the stall. At length he turned to the boy. "Hadn't you better come with me? I'm going to drive over the hill." Jody shook his head. "You better come on, out of this," his father insisted.

Billy turned on him angrily. "Let him alone. It's his pony, isn't it?"

Carl Tiflin walked away without saying another word. His feelings were badly hurt.

All morning Jody kept the wound open and the air passing in and out freely. At noon the pony lay wearily down on his side and stretched his nose out.

Billy came back. "If you're going to stay with him tonight, you better take a little nap," he said. Jody went absently out of the barn. The sky had cleared to a hard thin blue. Everywhere the birds were busy with worms that had come to the damp surface of the ground.

Jody walked to the brush line and sat on the edge of the mossy tub. He looked down at the house and at the old bunkhouse and at the dark cypress tree.

The place was familiar, but curiously changed. It wasn't itself anymore, but a frame for things that were happening. A cold wind blew out of the east now, signifying that the rain was over for a little while. At his feet Jody could see the little arms of new weeds spreading out over the ground. In the mud about the spring were thousands of quail tracks.

Doubletree Mutt came sideways and embarrassed up through the vegetable patch, and Jody, remembering how he had thrown the clod, put his arm about the dog's neck and kissed him on his wide black nose. Doubletree Mutt sat still, as though he knew some solemn thing was happening. His big tail slapped the ground gravely. Jody pulled a swollen tick out of Mutt's neck and popped it dead between his thumbnails. It was a nasty thing. He washed his hands in the cold spring water.

Except for the steady swish of the wind, the farm was very quiet. Jody knew his mother wouldn't mind if he didn't go in to eat his lunch. After a little while he went slowly back to the barn. Mutt crept into his own little house and whined softly to himself for a long time.

Billy Buck stood up from the box and surrendered the cotton swab. The pony still lay on his side and the wound in his throat bellowsed in and out. When Jody saw how dry and dead the hair looked, he knew at last that there was no hope for the pony. He had seen the dead hair before on dogs and on cows, and it was a sure sign. He sat heavily on the box and let down the barrier of the box stall. For a long time he kept his eyes on the moving wound, and at last he dozed, and the afternoon passed quickly. Just before dark his mother brought a deep dish of stew and left it for him and went away. Jody ate a little of it, and, when it was dark, he set the lantern on the floor by the pony's head so he could watch the wound and keep it open. And he dozed again until the night chill awakened him. The wind was blowing fiercely, bringing the north cold with it. Jody brought a blanket from his bed in the hay and wrapped himself in it. Gabilan's breathing was quiet at last; the hole in his throat moved gently. The owls flew through the hayloft, shrieking and looking for mice. Jody put his hands down on his head and slept. In his sleep he was aware that the wind had increased. He heard it slamming about the barn.

It was daylight when he awakened. The barn door had swung open. The pony was gone. He sprang up and ran out into the morning light.

The pony's tracks were plain enough, dragging through the frostlike dew on the young grass, tired tracks with little lines between them where the hoofs had dragged. They headed for the brush line halfway up the ridge. Jody broke into a run and followed them. The sun shone on the sharp white quartz that stuck through the ground here and there. As he followed the plain trail, a shadow cut across in front of him. He looked up and saw a high circle of black buzzards, and the slowly revolving circle dropped lower and lower. The solemn birds soon disappeared over the ridge. Jody ran faster then, forced on by panic and rage. The trail entered the brush at last and followed a winding route among the tall sage bushes.

At the top of the ridge Jody was winded. He paused, puffing noisily. The blood pounded in his ears. Then he saw what he was looking for. Below, in one of the little clearings in the brush, lay the red pony. In the distance, Jody could see the legs moving slowly and convulsively. And in a circle around him stood the buzzards, waiting for the moment of death they know so well.

Jody leaped forward and plunged down the hill. The wet ground muffled his steps and the brush hid him. When he arrived, it was all over. The first buzzard sat on the pony's head and its beak had just risen dripping with dark eye fluid. Jody plunged into the circle like a cat. The black brotherhood arose in a cloud, but the big one on the pony's head was too late. As it hopped along to take off, Jody caught its wing tip and pulled it down. It was nearly as big as he was. The free wing crashed into his face with the force of a club, but he hung on. The claws

fastened on his leg and the wing elbows battered his head on either side. Jody groped blindly with his free hand. His fingers found the neck of the struggling bird. The red eyes looked into his face, calm and fearless and fierce; the naked head turned from side to side. Then the beak opened and vomited a stream of putrefied fluid. Jody brought up his knee and fell on the great bird. He held the neck to the ground with one hand while his other found a piece of sharp white quartz. The first blow broke the beak sideways and black blood spurted from the twisted, leathery mouth corners. He struck again and missed. The red fearless eyes still looked at him, impersonal and unafraid and detached. He struck again and again, until the buzzard lay dead, until its head was a red pulp. He was still beating the dead bird when Billy Buck pulled him off and held him tightly to calm his shaking.

Carl Tiflin wiped the blood from the boy's face with a red bandana. Jody was limp and quiet now. His father moved the buzzard with his toe. "Jody," he explained, "the buzzard didn't kill the pony. Don't you know that?"

"I know it," Jody said wearily.

It was Billy Buck who was angry. He had lifted Jody in his arms, and had turned to carry him home. But he turned back on Carl Tiflin. " 'Course he knows it," Billy said furiously, "Jesus Christ! man, can't you see how he'd feel about it?"

OF THIS TIME, OF THAT PLACE

LIONEL TRILLING

LIONEL TRILLING (1905–   ) was born in New York City and received his education, including the doctorate in philosophy, from Columbia University. A sensitive and creative critic, and a writer of fiction as well, he has served as advisor to the editorial boards of the *Kenyon Review* and the *Partisan Review*. Among his books are *E. M. Forster* (1943), *The Liberal Imagination* (1950), *The Opposing Self* (1955), and *A Gathering of the Fugitives* (1956).

IT WAS a fine September day. By noon it would be summer again, but now it was true autumn with a touch of chill in the air. As Joseph Howe stood on the porch of the house in which he lodged, ready to leave for his first class of the year, he thought with pleasure of the long indoor days that were coming. It was a moment when he could feel glad of his profession.

On the lawn the peach tree was still in fruit and young Hilda Aiken was taking a picture of it. She

Copyright © 1960 by Lionel Trilling. Reprinted by permission of the author.

held the camera tight against her chest. She wanted the sun behind her, but she did not want her own long morning shadow in the foreground. She raised the camera, but that did not help, and she lowered it, but that made things worse. She twisted her body to the left, then to the right. In the end she had to step out of the direct line of the sun. At last she snapped the shutter and wound the film with intense care.

Howe, watching her from the porch, waited for her to finish and called good morning. She turned, startled, and almost sullenly lowered her glance. In the year Howe had lived at the Aikens', Hilda had accepted him as one of her family, but since his absence of the summer she had grown shy. Then suddenly she lifted her head and smiled at him, and the humorous smile confirmed his pleasure in the day. She picked up her bookbag and set off for school.

The handsome houses on the streets to the college were not yet fully awake, but they looked very friendly. Howe went by the Bradby house where he would be a guest this evening at the first dinner party of the year. When he had gone the length of the picket fence, the whitest in town, he turned back. Along the path there was a fine row of asters and he went through the gate and picked one for his buttonhole. The Bradbys would be pleased if they happened to see him invading their lawn and the knowledge of this made him even more comfortable.

He reached the campus as the hour was striking. The students were hurrying to their classes. He himself was in no hurry. He stopped at his dim cubicle of an office and lit a cigarette. The prospect of facing his class had suddenly presented itself to him and his hands were cold; the lawful seizure of power he was about to make seemed momentous. Waiting did not help. He put out his cigarette, picked up a pad of theme paper, and went to his classroom.

As he entered, the rattle of voices ceased, and the twenty-odd freshmen settled themselves and looked at him appraisingly. Their faces seemed gross, his heart sank at their massed impassivity, but he spoke briskly.

'My name is Howe,' he said, and turned and wrote it on the blackboard. The carelessness of the scrawl confirmed his authority. He went on, 'My office is 412 Slemp Hall, and my office-hours are Monday, Wednesday and Friday from eleven-thirty to twelve-thirty.'

He wrote, 'M., W., F., 11:30-12:30.' He said, 'I'll be very glad to see any of you at that time. Or if you can't come then, you can arrange with me for some other time.'

He turned again to the blackboard and spoke over his shoulder. 'The text for the course is Jarman's *Modern Plays*, revised edition. The Co-op has it in stock.' He wrote the name, underlined 'revised edition' and waited for it to be taken down in the new notebooks.

When the bent heads were raised again he began his speech of prospectus. 'It is hard to explain—' he said, and paused as they composed themselves. 'It is hard to explain what a course like this is intended to do. We are going to try to learn something about

modern literature and something about prose composition.'

As he spoke, his hands warmed and he was able to look directly at the class. Last year on the first day the faces had seemed just as cloddish, but as the term wore on they became gradually alive and quite likable. It did not seem possible that the same thing could happen again.

'I shall not lecture in this course,' he continued. 'Our work will be carried on by discussion and we will try to learn by an exchange of opinion. But you will soon recognize that my opinion is worth more than anyone else's here.'

He remained grave as he said it, but two boys understood and laughed. The rest took permission from them and laughed too. All Howe's private ironies protested the vulgarity of the joke, but the laughter made him feel benign and powerful.

When the little speech was finished, Howe picked up the pad of paper he had brought. He announced that they would write an extemporaneous theme. Its subject was traditional, 'Who I am and why I came to Dwight College.' By now the class was more at ease and it gave a ritualistic groan of protest. Then there was a stir as fountain pens were brought out and the writing-arms of the chairs were cleared, and the paper was passed about. At last, all the heads bent to work, and the room became still.

Howe sat idly at his desk. The sun shone through the tall clumsy windows. The cool of the morning was already passing. There was a scent of autumn and of varnish and the stillness of the room was deep and oddly touching. Now and then a student's head was raised and scratched in the old, elaborate students' pantomime that calls the teacher to witness honest intellectual effort.

Suddenly a tall boy stood within the frame of the open door. 'Is this,' he said, and thrust a large nose into a college catalogue, 'is this the meeting place of English 1A? The section instructed by Dr. Joseph Howe?'

He stood on the very sill of the door, as if refusing to enter until he was perfectly sure of all his rights. The class looked up from work, found him absurd and gave a low mocking cheer.

The teacher and the new student, with equal pointedness, ignored the disturbance. Howe nodded to the boy, who pushed his head forward and then jerked it back in a wide elaborate arc to clear his brow of a heavy lock of hair. He advanced into the room and halted before Howe, almost at attention. In a loud, clear voice he announced, 'I am Tertan, Ferdinand R., reporting at the direction of Head of Department Vincent.'

The heraldic formality of this statement brought

forth another cheer. Howe looked at the class with a sternness he could not really feel, for there was indeed something ridiculous about this boy. Under his displeased regard the rows of heads dropped to work again. Then he touched Tertan's elbow, led him up to the desk and stood so as to shield their conversation from the class.

'We are writing an extemporaneous theme,' he said. 'The subject is, "Who I am and why I came to Dwight College."'

He stripped a few sheets from the pad and offered them to the boy. Tertan hesitated and then took the paper, but he held it only tentatively. As if with the effort of making something clear, he gulped, and a slow smile fixed itself on his face. It was at once knowing and shy.

'Professor,' he said, 'to be perfectly fair to my classmates'—he made a large gesture over the room—'and to you'—he inclined his head to Howe—'this would not be for me an extemporaneous subject.'

Howe tried to understand. 'You mean you've already thought about it—you've heard we always give the same subject? That doesn't matter.'

Again the boy ducked his head and gulped. It was the gesture of one who wishes to make a difficult explanation with perfect candor. 'Sir,' he said, and made the distinction with great care, 'the topic I did not expect, but I have given much ratiocination to the subject.'

Howe smiled and said, 'I don't think that's an unfair advantage. Just go ahead and write.'

Tertan narrowed his eyes and glanced sidewise at Howe. His strange mouth smiled. Then in quizzical acceptance, he ducked his head, threw back the heavy, dank lock, dropped into a seat with a great loose noise and began to write rapidly.

The room fell silent again and Howe resumed his idleness. When the bell rang, the students who had groaned when the task had been set now groaned again because they had not finished. Howe took up the papers, and held the class while he made the first assignment. When he dismissed it, Tertan bore down on him, his slack mouth held ready for speech.

'Some professors,' he said, 'are pedants. They are Dryasdusts. However, some professors are free souls and creative spirits. Kant, Hegel and Nietzsche were all professors.' With this pronouncement he paused. 'It is my opinion,' he continued, 'that you occupy the second category.'

Howe looked at the boy in surprise and said with good-natured irony, 'With Kant, Hegel and Nietzsche?'

Not only Tertan's hand and head but his whole awkward body waved away the stupidity. 'It is the

kind and not the quantity of the kind,' he said sternly.

Rebuked, Howe said as simply and seriously as he could, 'It would be nice to think so.' He added, 'Of course I am not a professor.'

This was clearly a disappointment but Tertan met it. 'In the French sense,' he said with composure. 'Generically, a teacher.'

Suddenly he bowed. It was such a bow, Howe fancied, as a stage-director might teach an actor playing a medieval student who takes leave of Abelard—stiff, solemn, with elbows close to the body and feet together. Then, quite as suddenly, he turned and left.

A queer fish, and as soon as Howe reached his office, he sifted through the batch of themes and drew out Tertan's. The boy had filled many sheets with his unformed headlong scrawl. 'Who am I?' he had begun. 'Here, in a mundane, not to say commercialized academe, is asked the question which from time long immemorably out of mind has accreted doubts and thoughts in the psyche of man to pester him as a nuisance. Whether in St. Augustine (or Austin as sometimes called) or Miss Bashkirtsieff or Frederic Amiel or Empedocles, or in less lights of the intellect than these, this posed question has been ineluctable.'

Howe took out his pencil. He circled 'academe' and wrote 'vocab.' in the margin. He underlined 'time long immemorably out of mind' and wrote 'Diction!' But this seemed inadequate for what was wrong. He put down his pencil and read ahead to discover the principle of error in the theme. 'Today as ever, in spite of gloomy prophets of the dismal science (economics) the question is uninvalidated. Out of the starry depths of heaven hurtles this spear of query demanding to be caught on the shield of the mind ere it pierces the skull and the limbs be unstrung.'

Baffled but quite caught, Howe read on. 'Materialism, by which is meant the philosophic concept and not the moral idea, provides no aegis against the question which lies beyond the tangible (metaphysics). Existence without alloy is the question presented. Environment and heredity relegated aside, the rags and old clothes of practical life discarded, the name and the instrumentality of livelihood do not, as the prophets of the dismal science insist on in this connection, give solution to the interrogation which not from the professor merely but veritably from the cosmos is given. I think, therefore I am (cogito etc.) but who am I? Tertan I am, but what is Tertan? Of this time, of that place, of some parentage, what does it matter?'

Existence without alloy: the phrase established

itself. Howe put aside Tertan's paper and at random picked up another. 'I am Arthur J. Casebeer, Jr.,' he read. 'My father is Arthur J. Casebeer and my grandfather was Arthur J. Casebeer before him. My mother is Nina Wimble Casebeer. Both of them are college graduates and my father is in insurance. I was born in St. Louis eighteen years ago and we still make our residence there.'

Arthur J. Casebeer, who knew who he was, was less interesting than Tertan, but more coherent. Howe picked up Tertan's paper again. It was clear that none of the routine marginal comments, no 'sent. str.' or 'punct.' or 'vocab.' could cope with this torrential rhetoric. He read ahead, contenting himself with underscoring the errors against the time when he should have the necessary 'conference' with Tertan.

It was a busy and official day of cards and sheets, arrangements and small decisions, and it gave Howe pleasure. Even when it was time to attend the first of the weekly Convocations he felt the charm of the beginning of things when intention is still innocent and uncorrupted by effort. He sat among the young instructors on the platform, and joined in their humorous complaints at having to assist at the ceremony, but actually he got a clear satisfaction from the ritual of prayer, and prosy speech, and even from wearing his academic gown. And when the Convocation was over the pleasure continued as he crossed the campus, exchanging greetings with men he had not seen since the spring. They were people who did not yet, and perhaps never would, mean much to him, but in a year they had grown amiably to be part of his life. They were his fellow-townsmen.

The day had cooled again at sunset, and there was a bright chill in the September twilight. Howe carried his voluminous gown over his arm, he swung his doctoral hood by its purple neckpiece, and on his head he wore his mortarboard with its heavy gold tassel bobbing just over his eye. These were the weighty and absurd symbols of his new profession and they pleased him. At twenty-six Joseph Howe had discovered that he was neither so well off nor so bohemian as he had once thought. A small income, adequate when supplemented by a sizable cash legacy, was genteel poverty when the cash was all spent. And the literary life—the room at the Lafayette, or the small apartment without a lease, the long summers on the Cape, the long afternoons and the social evenings—began to weary him. His writing filled his mornings, and should perhaps have filled his life, yet it did not. To the amusement of his friends, and with a certain sense that he was betraying his own freedom, he had used the last of his legacy for a year at Harvard. The small but respec-

table reputation of his two volumes of verse had proved useful—he continued at Harvard on a fellowship and when he emerged as Doctor Howe he received an excellent appointment, with prospects, at Dwight.

He had his moments of fear when all that had ever been said of the dangers of the academic life had occurred to him. But after a year in which he had tested every possibility of corruption and seduction he was ready to rest easy. His third volume of verse, most of it written in his first years of teaching, was not only ampler but, he thought, better than its predecessors.

There was a clear hour before the Bradby dinner party, and Howe looked forward to it. But he was not to enjoy it, for lying with his mail on the hall table was a copy of this quarter's issue of *Life and Letters*, to which his landlord subscribed. Its severe cover announced that its editor, Frederic Woolley, had this month contributed an essay called 'Two Poets,' and Howe, picking it up, curious to see who the two poets might be, felt his own name start out at him with cabalistic power—Joseph Howe. As he continued to turn the pages his hand trembled.

Standing in the dark hall, holding the neat little magazine, Howe knew that his literary contempt for Frederic Woolley meant nothing, for he suddenly understood how he respected Woolley in the way of the world. He knew this by the trembling of his hand. And of the little world as well as the great, for although the literary groups of New York might dismiss Woolley, his name carried high authority in the academic world. At Dwight it was even a revered name, for it had been here at the college that Frederic Woolley had made the distinguished scholarly career from which he had gone on to literary journalism. In middle life he had been induced to take the editorship of *Life and Letters*, a literary monthly not widely read but heavily endowed, and in its pages he had carried on the defense of what he sometimes called the older values. He was not without wit, he had great knowledge and considerable taste, and even in the full movement of the 'new' literature he had won a certain respect for his refusal to accept it. In France, even in England, he would have been connected with a more robust tradition of conservatism, but America gave him an audience not much better than genteel. It was known in the college that to the subsidy of *Life and Letters* the Bradbys contributed a great part.

As Howe read, he saw that he was involved in nothing less than an event. When the Fifth Series of *Studies in Order and Value* came to be collected, this latest of Frederic Woolley's essays would not be merely another step in the old direction. Clearly and unmistakably, it was a turning point. All his literary life Woolley had been concerned with the relation of literature to morality, religion, and the private and delicate pieties, and he had been unalterably opposed to all that he had called 'inhuman humanitarianism.' But here, suddenly, dramatically late, he had made an about-face, turning to the public life and to the humanitarian politics he had so long despised. This was the kind of incident the histories of literature make much of. Frederic Woolley was opening for himself a new career and winning a kind of new youth. He contrasted the two poets, Thomas Wormser, who was admirable, Joseph Howe, who was almost dangerous. He spoke of the 'precious subjectivism' of Howe's verse. 'In times like ours,' he wrote, 'with millions facing penury and want, one feels that the qualities of the *tour d'ivoire* are well-nigh inhuman, nearly insulting. The *tour d'ivoire* becomes the *tour d'ivresse,* and it is not self-intoxicated poets that our people need.' The essay said more: 'The problem is one of meaning. I am not ignorant that the creed of the esoteric poets declares that a poem does not and should not *mean* anything, that it *is* something. But poetry is what the poet makes it, and if he is a true poet he makes what his society needs. And what is needed now is the tradition in which Mr. Wormser writes, the true tradition of poetry. The Howes do no harm, but they do no good when positive good is demanded of all responsible men. Or do the Howes indeed do no harm? Perhaps Plato would have said they do, that in some ways theirs is the Phrygian music that turns men's minds from the struggle. Certainly it is true that Thomas Wormser writes in the lucid Dorian mode which sends men into battle with evil.'

It was easy to understand why Woolley had chosen to praise Thomas Wormser. The long, lilting lines of *Corn Under Willows* hymned, as Woolley put it, the struggle for wheat in the Iowa fields, and expressed the real lives of real people. But why out of the dozen more notable examples he had chosen Howe's little volume as the example of 'precious subjectivism' was hard to guess. In a way it was funny, this multiplication of himself into 'the Howes.' And yet this becoming the multiform political symbol by whose creation Frederic Woolley gave the sign of a sudden new life, this use of him as a sacrifice whose blood was necessary for the rites of rejuvenation, made him feel oddly unclean.

Nor could Howe get rid of a certain practical resentment. As a poet he had a special and respectable place in the college life. But it might be another thing to be marked as the poet of a wilful and selfish obscurity.

As he walked to the Bradbys', Howe was a little tense and defensive. It seemed to him that all the world knew of the 'attack' and agreed with it. And, indeed, the Bradbys had read the essay but Professor Bradby, a kind and pretentious man, said, 'I see my old friend knocked you about a bit, my boy,' and his wife Eugenia looked at Howe with her childlike blue eyes and said, 'I shall *scold* Frederic for the untrue things he wrote about you. You aren't the least obscure.' They beamed at him. In their genial snobbery they seemed to feel that he had distinguished himself. He was the leader of Howeism. He enjoyed the dinner party as much as he had thought he would.

And in the following days, as he was more preoccupied with his duties, the incident was forgotten. His classes had ceased to be mere groups. Student after student detached himself from the mass and required or claimed a place in Howe's awareness. Of them all it was Tertan who first and most violently signaled his separate existence. A week after classes had begun Howe saw his silhouette on the frosted glass of his office door. It was motionless for a long time, perhaps stopped by the problem of whether or not to knock before entering. Howe called, 'Come in!' and Tertan entered with his shambling stride.

He stood beside the desk, silent and at attention. When Howe asked him to sit down, he responded with a gesture of head and hand, as if to say that such amenities were beside the point. Nevertheless, he did take the chair. He put his ragged, crammed briefcase between his legs. His face, which Howe now observed fully for the first time, was confusing, for it was made up of florid curves, the nose arched in the bone and voluted in the nostril, the mouth loose and soft and rather moist. Yet the face was so thin and narrow as to seem the very type of asceticism. Lashes of unusual length veiled the eyes and, indeed, it seemed as if there were a veil over the whole countenance. Before the words actually came, the face screwed itself into an attitude of preparation for them.

'You can confer with me now?' Tertan said.

'Yes, I'd be glad to. There are several things in your two themes I want to talk to you about.' Howe reached for the packet of themes on his desk and sought for Tertan's. But the boy was waving them away.

'These are done perforce,' he said. 'Under the pressure of your requirement. They are not significant; mere duties.' Again his great hand flapped vaguely to dismiss his themes. He leaned forward and gazed at his teacher.

'You are,' he said, 'a man of letters? You are a poet?' It was more declaration than question.

'I should like to think so,' Howe said.

At first Tertan accepted the answer with a show of appreciation, as though the understatement made a secret between himself and Howe. Then he chose to misunderstand. With his shrewd and disconcerting control of expression, he presented to Howe a puzzled grimace. 'What does that mean?' he said.

Howe retracted the irony. 'Yes. I am a poet.' It sounded strange to say.

'That,' Tertan said, 'is a wonder.' He corrected himself with his ducking head. 'I mean that is wonderful.'

Suddenly, he dived at the miserable briefcase between his legs, put it on his knees, and began to fumble with the catch, all intent on the difficulty it presented. Howe noted that his suit was worn thin, his shirt almost unclean. He became aware, even, of a vague and musty odor of garments worn too long in unaired rooms. Tertan conquered the lock and began to concentrate upon a search into the interior. At last he held in his hand what he was after, a torn and crumpled copy of *Life and Letters*.

'I learned it from here,' he said, holding it out.

Howe looked at him sharply, his hackles a little up. But the boy's face was not only perfectly innocent, it even shone with a conscious admiration. Apparently nothing of the import of the essay had touched him except the wonderful fact that his teacher was a 'man of letters.' Yet this seemed too stupid, and Howe, to test it, said, 'The man who wrote that doesn't think it's wonderful.'

Tertan made a moist hissing sound as he cleared his mouth of saliva. His head, oddly loose on his neck, wove a pattern of contempt in the air. 'A critic,' he said, 'who admits *prima facie* that he does not understand.' Then he said grandly, 'It is the inevitable fate.'

It was absurd, yet Howe was not only aware of the absurdity but of a tension suddenly and wonderfully relaxed. Now that the 'attack' was on the table between himself and this strange boy, and subject to the boy's funny and absolutely certain contempt, the hidden force of his feeling was revealed to him in the very moment that it vanished. All unsuspected, there had been a film over the world, a transparent but discoloring haze of danger. But he had no time to stop over the brightened aspect of things. Tertan was going on. 'I also am a man of letters. Putative.'

'You have written a good deal?' Howe meant to be no more than polite, and he was surprised at the tenderness he heard in his words.

Solemnly the boy nodded, threw back the dank lock, and sucked in a deep, anticipatory breath. 'First, a work of homiletics, which is a defense of the principles of religious optimism against the pessi-mism of Schopenhauer and the humanism of Nietzsche.'

'Humanism? Why do you call it humanism?'

'It is my nomenclature for making a deity of man,' Tertan replied negligently. 'Then three fictional works, novels. And numerous essays in science, combating materialism. Is it your duty to read these if I bring them to you?'

Howe answered simply, 'No, it isn't exactly my duty, but I shall be happy to read them.'

Tertan stood up and remained silent. He rested his bag on the chair. With a certain compunction—for it did not seem entirely proper that, of two men of letters, one should have the right to blue-pencil the other, to grade him or to question the quality of his 'sentence structure'—Howe reached for Tertan's papers. But before he could take them up, the boy suddenly made his bow-to-Abelard, the stiff inclination of the body with the hands seeming to emerge from the scholar's gown. Then he was gone.

But after his departure something was still left of him. The timbre of his curious sentences, the downright finality of so quaint a phrase as 'It is the inevitable fate' still rang in the air. Howe gave the warmth of his feeling to the new visitor who stood at the door announcing himself with a genteel clearing of the throat.

'Doctor Howe, I believe?' the student said. A large hand advanced into the room and grasped Howe's hand. 'Blackburn, sir, Theodore Blackburn, vice-president of the Student Council. A great pleasure, sir.'

Out of a pair of ruddy cheeks a pair of small eyes twinkled good-naturedly. The large face, the large body were not so much fat as beefy and suggested something 'typical'—monk, politician, or innkeeper.

Blackburn took the seat beside Howe's desk. 'I may have seemed to introduce myself in my public capacity, sir,' he said. 'But it is really as an individual that I came to see you. That is to say, as one of your students to be.'

He spoke with an English intonation and he went on, 'I was once an English major, sir.'

For a moment Howe was startled, for the roast-beef look of the boy and the manner of his speech gave a second's credibility to one sense of his statement. Then the collegiate meaning of the phrase asserted itself, but some perversity made Howe say what was not really in good taste even with so forward a student, 'Indeed? What regiment?'

Blackburn stared and then gave a little pouf-pouf of laughter. He waved the misapprehension away. '*Very* good, sir. It certainly is an ambiguous term.' He chuckled in appreciation of Howe's joke, then cleared his throat to put it aside. 'I look forward to taking your course in the romantic poets, sir,' he said earnestly. 'To me the romantic poets are the very crown of English literature.'

Howe made a dry sound, and the boy, catching some meaning in it, said, 'Little as I know them, of course. But even Shakespeare who is so dear to us of the Anglo-Saxon tradition is in a sense but the preparation for Shelley, Keats and Byron. And Wadsworth.'

Almost sorry for him, Howe dropped his eyes. With some embarrassment, for the boy was not actually his student, he said softly, 'Wordsworth.'

'Sir?'

'Wordsworth, not Wadsworth. You said Wadsworth.'

'Did I, sir?' Gravely he shook his head to rebuke himself for the error. 'Wordsworth, of course—slip of the tongue.' Then, quite in command again, he went on. 'I have a favor to ask of you, Doctor Howe. You see, I began my college course as an English major,'—he smiled—'as I said.'

'Yes?'

'But after my first year I shifted. I shifted to the social sciences. Sociology and government—I find them stimulating and very *real.*' He paused, out of respect for reality. 'But now I find that perhaps I have neglected the other side.'

'The other side?' Howe said.

'Imagination, fancy, culture. A well-rounded man.' He trailed off as if there were perfect understanding between them. 'And so, sir, I have decided to end my senior year with your course in the romantic poets.'

His voice was filled with an indulgence which Howe ignored as he said flatly and gravely, 'But that course isn't given until the spring term.'

'Yes, sir, and that is where the favor comes in. Would you let me take your romantic prose course? I can't take it for credit, sir, my program is full, but just for background it seems to me that I ought to take it. I do hope,' he concluded in a manly way, 'that you will consent.'

'Well, it's no great favor, Mr. Blackburn. You can come if you wish, though there's not much point in it if you don't do the reading.'

The bell rang for the hour and Howe got up.

'May I begin with this class, sir?' Blackburn's smile was candid and boyish.

Howe nodded carelessly and together, silently, they walked to the classroom down the hall. When they reached the door Howe stood back to let his student enter, but Blackburn moved adroitly behind him and grasped him by the arm to urge him over the threshold. They entered together with Blackburn's hand firmly on Howe's biceps, the student inducting the teacher into his own room. Howe felt a surge of temper rise in him and almost violently he disengaged his arm and walked to the desk, while Blackburn found a seat in the front row and smiled at him.

II

The question was, At whose door must the tragedy be laid?

All night the snow had fallen heavily and only now was abating in sparse little flurries. The windows were valanced high with white. It was very quiet; something of the quiet of the world had reached the class, and Howe found that everyone was glad to talk or listen. In the room there was a comfortable sense of pleasure in being human.

Casebeer believed that the blame for the tragedy rested with heredity. Picking up the book he read, 'The sins of the fathers are visited on their children.' This opinion was received with general favor. Nevertheless, Johnson ventured to say that the fault was all Pastor Manders' because the Pastor had made Mrs. Alving go back to her husband and was always hiding the truth. To this Hibbard objected with logic enough, 'Well then, it was really all her husband's fault. He *did* all the bad things.' De Witt, his face bright with an impatient idea, said that the fault was all society's. 'By society I don't mean upper-crust society,' he said. He looked around a little defiantly, taking in any members of the class who might be members of upper-crust society. 'Not in that sense. I mean the social unit.'

Howe nodded and said, 'Yes, of course.'

'If the society of the time had progressed far enough in science,' De Witt went on, 'then there would be no problem for Mr. Ibsen to write about. Captain Alving plays around a little, gives way to perfectly natural biological urges, and he gets a social disease, a venereal disease. If the disease is cured, no problem. Invent salvarsan and the disease is cured. The problem of heredity disappears and li'l Oswald just doesn't get paresis. No paresis, no problem—no problem, no play.'

This was carrying the ark into battle, and the class looked at De Witt with respectful curiosity. It was his usual way and on the whole they were sympathetic with his struggle to prove to Howe that science was better than literature. Still, there was something in his reckless manner that alienated them a little.

'Or take birth-control, for instance,' De Witt went on. 'If Mrs. Alving had some knowledge of contraception, she wouldn't have had to have li'l Oswald at all. No li'l Oswald, no play.'

The class was suddenly quieter. In the back row Stettenhover swung his great football shoulders in a righteous sulking gesture, first to the right, then to the left. He puckered his mouth ostentatiously. Intellect was always ending up by talking dirty.

Tertan's hand went up, and Howe said, 'Mr. Tertan.' The boy shambled to his feet and began his long characteristic gulp. Howe made a motion with his fingers, as small as possible, and Tertan ducked his head and smiled in apology. He sat down. The class laughed. With more than half the term gone, Tertan had not been able to remember that one did not rise to speak. He seemed unable to carry on the life of the intellect without this mark of respect for it. To Howe the boy's habit of rising seemed to accord with the formal shabbiness of his dress. He never wore the casual sweaters and jackets of his classmates. Into the free and comfortable air of the college classroom he brought the stuffy sordid strictness of some crowded, metropolitan high school.

'Speaking from one sense,' Tertan began slowly, 'there is no blame ascribable. From the sense of determinism, who can say where the blame lies? The preordained is the preordained and it cannot be said without rebellion against the universe, a palpable absurdity.'

In the back row Stettenhover slumped suddenly in his seat, his heels held out before him, making a loud, dry, disgusted sound. His body sank until his neck rested on the back of his chair. He folded his hands across his belly and looked significantly out of the window, exasperated not only with Tertan, but with Howe, with the class, with the whole system designed to encourage this kind of thing. There was a certain insolence in the movement and Howe flushed. As Tertan continued to speak, Howe stalked casually toward the window and placed himself in the line of Stettenhover's vision. He stared at the great fellow, who pretended not to see him. There was so much power in the big body, so much contempt in the Greek-athlete face under the crisp Greek-athlete curls, that Howe felt almost physical fear. But at last Stettenhover admitted him to focus and under his disapproving gaze sat up with slow indifference. His eyebrows raised high in resignation, he began to examine his hands. Howe relaxed and turned his attention back to Tertan.

'Flux of existence,' Tertan was saying, 'produces all things, so that judgment wavers. Beyond the phenomena, what? But phenomena are adumbrated and to them we are limited.'

Howe saw it for a moment as perhaps it existed in the boy's mind—the world of shadows which are cast by a great light upon a hidden reality as in the old myth of the Cave. But the little brush with Stetten-

hover had tired him, and he said irritably, 'But come to the point, Mr. Tertan.'

He said it so sharply that some of the class looked at him curiously. For three months he had gently carried Tertan through his verbosities, to the vaguely respectful surprise of the other students, who seemed to conceive that there existed between this strange classmate and their teacher some special understanding from which they were content to be excluded. Tertan looked at him mildly, and at once came brilliantly to the point. 'This is the summation of the play,' he said and took up his book and read, ' "Your poor father never found any outlet for the overmastering joy of life that was in him. And I brought no holiday into his home, either. Everything seemed to turn upon duty and I am afraid I made your poor father's home unbearable to him, Oswald." Spoken by Mrs. Alving.'

Yes that was surely the 'summation' of the play and Tertan had hit it, as he hit, deviously and eventually, the literary point of almost everything. But now, as always, he was wrapping it away from sight. 'For most mortals,' he said, 'there are only joys of biological urgings, gross and crass, such as the sensuous Captain Alving. For certain few there are the transmutations beyond these to a contemplation of the utter whole.'

Oh, the boy was mad. And suddenly the word, used in hyperbole, intended almost for the expression of exasperated admiration, became literal. Now that the word was used, it became simply apparent to Howe that Tertan was mad.

It was a monstrous word and stood like a bestial thing in the room. Yet it so completely comprehended everything that had puzzled Howe, it so arranged and explained what for three months had been perplexing him that almost at once its horror became domesticated. With this word Howe was able to understand why he had never been able to communicate to Tertan the value of a single criticism or correction of his wild, verbose themes. Their conferences had been frequent and long but had done nothing to reduce to order the splendid confusion of the boy's ideas. Yet, impossible though its expression was, Tertan's incandescent mind could always strike for a moment into some dark corner of thought.

And now it was suddenly apparent that it was not a faulty rhetoric that Howe had to contend with. With his new knowledge he looked at Tertan's face and wondered how he could have so long deceived himself. Tertan was still talking, and the class had lapsed into a kind of patient unconsciousness, a coma of respect for words which, for all that most of them knew, might be profound. Almost with a suffusion of shame, Howe believed that in some dim way the class had long ago had some intimation of Tertan's madness. He reached out as decisively as he could to seize the thread of Tertan's discourse before it should be entangled further.

'Mr. Tertan says that the blame must be put upon whoever kills the joy of living in another. We have been assuming that Captain Alving was a wholly bad man, but what if we assume that he became bad only because Mrs. Alving, when they were first married, acted toward him in the prudish way she says she did?'

It was a ticklish idea to advance to freshmen and perhaps not profitable. Not all of them were following.

'That would put the blame on Mrs. Alving herself, whom most of you admire. And she herself seems to think so.' He glanced at his watch. The hour was nearly over. 'What do you think, Mr. De Witt?'

De Witt rose to the idea; he wanted to know if society couldn't be blamed for educating Mrs. Alving's temperament in the wrong way. Casebeer was puzzled, Stettenhover continued to look at his hands until the bell rang.

Tertan, his brows louring in thought, was making as always for a private word. Howe gathered his books and papers to leave quickly. At this moment of his discovery and with the knowledge still raw, he could not engage himself with Tertan. Tertan sucked in his breath to prepare for speech and Howe made ready for the pain and confusion. But at that moment Casebeer detached himself from the group with which he had been conferring and which he seemed to represent. His constituency remained at a tactful distance. The mission involved the time of an assigned essay. Casebeer's presentation of the plea—it was based on the freshmen's heavy duties at the fraternities during Carnival Week—cut across Tertan's preparations for speech. 'And so some of us fellows thought,' Casebeer concluded with heavy solemnity, 'that we could do a better job, give our minds to it more, if we had more time.'

Tertan regarded Casebeer with mingled curiosity and revulsion. Howe not only said that he would postpone the assignment but went on to talk about the Carnival, and even drew the waiting constituency into the conversation. He was conscious of Tertan's stern and astonished stare, then of his sudden departure.

Now that the fact was clear, Howe knew that he must act on it. His course was simple enough. He must lay the case before the Dean. Yet he hesitated. His feeling for Tertan must now, certainly, be in some way invalidated. Yet could he, because of a word, hurry to assign to official and reasonable solici-

tude what had been, until this moment, so various and warm? He could at least delay and, by moving slowly, lend a poor grace to the necessary, ugly act of making his report.

It was with some notion of keeping the matter in his own hands that he went to the Dean's office to look up Tertan's records. In the outer office the Dean's secretary greeted him brightly, and at his request brought him the manila folder with the small identifying photograph pasted in the corner. She laughed. 'He was looking for the birdie in the wrong place,' she said.

Howe leaned over her shoulder to look at the picture. It was as bad as all the Dean's-office photographs were, but it differed from all that Howe had ever seen. Tertan, instead of looking into the camera, as no doubt he had been bidden, had, at the moment of exposure, turned his eyes upward. His mouth, as though conscious of the trick played on the photographer, had the sly superior look that Howe knew.

The secretary was fascinated by the picture. 'What a funny boy,' she said. 'He looks like Tartuffe!'

And so he did, with the absurd piety of the eyes and the conscious slyness of the mouth and the whole face bloated by the bad lens.

'Is he *like* that?' the secretary said.

'Like Tartuffe? No.'

From the photograph there was little enough comfort to be had. The records themselves gave no clue to madness, though they suggested sadness enough. Howe read of a father, Stanislaus Tertan, born in Budapest and trained in engineering in Berlin, once employed by the Hercules Chemical Corporation—this was one of the factories that dominated the sound end of the town—but now without employment. He read of a mother Erminie (Youngfellow) Tertan, born in Manchester, educated at a Normal School at Leeds, now housewife by profession. The family lived on Greenbriar Street which Howe knew as a row of once elegant homes near what was now the factory district. The old mansion had long ago been divided into small and primitive apartments. Of Ferdinand himself there was little to learn. He lived with his parents, had attended a Detroit high school and had transferred to the local school in his last year. His rating for intelligence, as expressed in numbers, was high, his scholastic record was remarkable, he held a college scholarship for his tuition.

Howe laid the folder on the secretary's desk. 'Did you find what you wanted to know?' she asked.

The phrases from Tertan's momentous first theme came back to him. 'Tertan I am, but what is Tertan? Of this time, of that place, of some parentage, what does it matter?'

'No, I didn't find it,' he said.

Now that he had consulted the sad, half-meaningless record he knew all the more firmly that he must not give the matter out of his own hands. He must not release Tertan to authority. Not that he anticipated from the Dean anything but the greatest kindness for Tertan. The Dean would have the experience and skill which he himself could not have. One way or another the Dean could answer the question, 'What is Tertan?' Yet this was precisely what he feared. He alone could keep alive—not forever but for a somehow important time—the question, 'What is Tertan?' He alone could keep it still a question. Some sure instinct told him that he must not surrender the question to a clean official desk in a clear official light to be dealt with, settled and closed.

He heard himself saying, 'Is the Dean busy at the moment? I'd like to see him.'

His request came thus unbidden, even forbidden, and it was one of the surprising and startling incidents of his life. Later when he reviewed the events, so disconnected in themselves, or so merely odd, of the story that unfolded for him that year, it was over this moment, on its face the least notable, that he paused longest. It was frequently to be with fear and never without a certainty of its meaning in his own knowledge of himself that he would recall this simple, routine request, and the feeling of shame and freedom it gave him as he sent everything down the official chute. In the end, of course, no matter what he did to 'protect' Tertan, he would have had to make the same request and lay the matter on the Dean's clean desk. But it would always be a landmark of his life that, at the very moment when he was rejecting the official way, he had been, without will or intention, so gladly drawn to it.

After the storm's last delicate flurry, the sun had come out. Reflected by the new snow, it filled the office with a golden light which was almost musical in the way it made all the commonplace objects of efficiency shine with a sudden sad and noble significance. And the light, now that he noticed it, made the utterance of his perverse and unwanted request even more momentous.

The secretary consulted the engagement pad. 'He'll be free any minute. Don't you want to wait in the parlor?'

She threw open the door of the large and pleasant room in which the Dean held his Committee meetings, and in which his visitors waited. It was designed with a homely elegance on the masculine side of the eighteenth-century manner. There was a small coal fire in the grate and the handsome mahogany table was strewn with books and magazines. The large windows gave on the snowy lawn, and there was such a fine width of window that the white case-ments and walls seemed at this moment but a continuation of the snow, the snow but an extension of casement and walls. The outdoors seemed taken in and made safe, the indoors seemed luxuriously freshened and expanded.

Howe sat down by the fire and lighted a cigarette. The room had its intended effect upon him. He felt comfortable and relaxed, yet nicely organized, some young diplomatic agent of the eighteenth century, the newly fledged Swift carrying out Sir William Temple's business. The rawness of Tertan's case quite vanished. He crossed his legs and reached for a magazine.

It was that famous issue of *Life and Letters* that his idle hand had found and his blood raced as he sifted through it, and the shape of his own name, Joseph Howe, sprang out at him, still cabalistic in its power. He tossed the magazine back on the table as the door of the Dean's office opened and the Dean ushered out Theodore Blackburn.

'Ah, Joseph!' the Dean said.

Blackburn said, 'Good morning, Doctor.' Howe winced at the title and caught the flicker of amusement over the Dean's face. The Dean stood with his hand high on the door-jamb and Blackburn, still in the doorway, remained standing almost under the long arm.

Howe nodded briefly to Blackburn, snubbing his eager deference. 'Can you give me a few minutes?' he said to the Dean.

'All the time you want. Come in.' Before the two men could enter the office, Blackburn claimed their attention with a long full 'er.' As they turned to him, Blackburn said, 'Can *you* give *me* a few minutes, Doctor Howe?' His eyes sparkled at the little audacity he had committed, the slightly impudent play with hierarchy. Of the three of them Blackburn kept himself the lowest, but he reminded Howe of his subaltern relation to the Dean.

'I mean, of course,' Blackburn went on easily, 'when you've finished with the Dean.'

'I'll be in my office shortly,' Howe said, turned his back on the ready 'Thank you, sir,' and followed the Dean into the inner room.

'Energetic boy,' said the Dean. 'A bit beyond himself but very energetic. Sit down.'

The Dean lighted a cigarette, leaned back in his chair, sat easy and silent for a moment, giving Howe no signal to go ahead with business. He was a young Dean, not much beyond forty, a tall handsome man with sad, ambitious eyes. He had been a Rhodes scholar. His friends looked for great things from him, and it was generally said that he had notions of education which he was not yet ready to try to put into practice.

His relaxed silence was meant as a compliment to Howe. He smiled and said, 'What's the business, Joseph?'

'Do you know Tertan—Ferdinand Tertan, a freshman?'

The Dean's cigarette was in his mouth and his hands were clasped behind his head. He did not seem to search his memory for the name. He said, 'What about him?'

Clearly the Dean knew something, and he was waiting for Howe to tell him more. Howe moved only tentatively. Now that he was doing what he had resolved not to do, he felt more guilty at having been so long deceived by Tertan and more need to be loyal to his error.

'He's a strange fellow,' he ventured. He said stubbornly, 'In a strange way he's very brilliant.' He concluded, 'But very strange.'

The springs of the Dean's swivel chair creaked as he came out of his sprawl and leaned forward to Howe. 'Do you mean he's so strange that it's something you could give a name to?'

Howe looked at him stupidly. 'What do you mean?' he said.

'What's his trouble?' the Dean said more neutrally.

'He's very brilliant, in a way. I looked him up and he has a top intelligence rating. But somehow, and it's hard to explain just how, what he says is always on the edge of sense and doesn't quite make it.'

The Dean looked at him and Howe flushed up. The Dean had surely read Woolley on the subject of 'the Howes' and the *tour d'ivresse*. Was that quick glance ironical?

The Dean picked up some papers from his desk, and Howe could see that they were in Tertan's impatient scrawl. Perhaps the little gleam in the Dean's glance had come only from putting facts together.

'He sent me this yesterday,' the Dean said. 'After an interview I had with him. I haven't been able to do more than glance at it. When you said what you did, I realized there was something wrong.'

Twisting his mouth, the Dean looked over the letter. 'You seem to be involved,' he said without looking up. 'By the way, what did you give him at mid-term?'

Flushing, setting his shoulders, Howe said firmly, 'I gave him A-minus.'

The Dean chuckled. 'Might be a good idea if some of our nicer boys went crazy—just a little.' He said, 'Well,' to conclude the matter and handed the papers to Howe. 'See if this is the same thing you've been finding. Then we can go into the matter again.'

Before the fire in the parlor, in the chair that Howe had been occupying, sat Blackburn. He sprang to his feet as Howe entered.

'I said my office, Mr. Blackburn.' Howe's voice was sharp. Then he was almost sorry for the rebuke, so clearly and naively did Blackburn seem to relish his stay in the parlor, close to authority.

'I'm in a bit of a hurry, sir,' he said, 'and I did want to be sure to speak to you, sir.'

He was really absurd, yet fifteen years from now he would have grown up to himself, to the assurance and mature beefiness. In banks, in consular offices, in brokerage firms, on the bench, more seriously affable, a little sterner, he would make use of his ability to be administered by his job. It was almost reassuring. Now he was exercising his too-great skill on Howe. 'I owe you an apology, sir,' he said.

Howe knew that he did, but he showed surprise.

'I mean, Doctor, after your having been so kind about letting me attend your class, I stopped coming.' He smiled in deprecation. 'Extracurricular activities take up so much of my time. I'm afraid I undertook more than I could perform.'

Howe had noticed the absence and had been a little irritated by it after Blackburn's elaborate plea. It was an absence that might be interpreted as a comment on the teacher. But there was only one way for him to answer. 'You've no need to apologize,' he said. 'It's wholly your affair.'

Blackburn beamed. 'I'm so glad you feel that way about it, sir. I was worried you might think I had stayed away because I was influenced by—' he stopped and lowered his eyes.

Astonished, Howe said, 'Influenced by what?'

'Well, by—' Blackburn hesitated and for answer pointed to the table on which lay the copy of *Life and Letters*. Without looking at it, he knew where to direct his hand. 'By the unfavorable publicity, sir.' He hurried on. 'And that brings me to another point, sir. I am secretary of Quill and Scroll, sir, the student literary society, and I wonder if you would address us. You could read your own poetry, sir, and defend your own point of view. It would be very interesting.'

It was truly amazing. Howe looked long and cruelly into Blackburn's face, trying to catch the secret of the mind that could have conceived this way of manipulating him, this way so daring and inept—but not entirely inept—with its malice so without malignity. The face did not yield its secret. Howe smiled broadly and said, 'Of course I don't think you were influenced by the unfavorable publicity.'

'I'm still going to take—regularly, for credit—your romantic poets course next term,' Blackburn said.

'Don't worry, my dear fellow, don't worry about it.'

Howe started to leave and Blackburn stopped him with, 'But about Quill, sir?'

'Suppose we wait until next term? I'll be less busy then.'

And Blackburn said, 'Very good, sir, and thank you.'

In his office the little encounter seemed less funny to Howe, was even in some indeterminate way disturbing. He made an effort to put it from his mind by turning to what was sure to disturb him more, the Tertan letter read in the new interpretation. He found what he had always found, the same florid leaps beyond fact and meaning, the same headlong certainty. But as his eye passed over the familiar scrawl it caught his own name, and for the second time that hour he felt the race of his blood.

'The Paraclete,' Tertan had written to the Dean, 'from a Greek word meaning to stand in place of, but going beyond the primitive idea to mean traditionally the helper, the one who comforts and assists, cannot without fundamental loss be jettisoned. Even if taken no longer in the supernatural sense, the concept remains deeply in the human consciousness inevitably. Humanitarianism is no reply, for not every man stands in the place of every other man for this other comrade's comfort. But certain are chosen out of the human race to be the consoler of some other. Of these, for example, is Joseph Barker Howe, Ph.D. Of intellects not the first yet of true intellect and lambent instructions, given to that which is intuitive and irrational, not to what is logical in the strict word, what is judged by him is of the heart and not the head. Here is one chosen, in that he chooses himself to stand in the place of another for comfort and consolation. To him more than another I give my gratitude, with all respect to our Dean who reads this, a noble man, but merely dedicated, not consecrated. But not in the aspect of the Paraclete only is Dr. Joseph Barker Howe established, for he must be the Paraclete to another aspect of himself, that which is driven and persecuted by the lack of understanding in the world at large, so that he in himself embodies the full history of man's tribulations and, overflowing upon others, notably the present writer, is the ultimate end.'

This was love. There was no escape from it. Try as Howe might to remember that Tertan was mad and all his emotions invalidated, he could not destroy the effect upon him of his student's stern, affectionate regard. He had betrayed not only a power of mind but a power of love. And, however firmly he held before his attention the fact of Tertan's madness, he could do nothing to banish the physical sensation of gratitude he felt. He had never thought of himself as 'driven and persecuted' and he did not now. But still he could not make meaningless his sensation of gratitude. The pitiable Tertan sternly pitied him, and comfort came from Tertan's never-to-be-comforted mind.

III

In an academic community, even an efficient one, official matters move slowly. The term drew to a close with no action in the case of Tertan, and Joseph Howe had to confront a curious problem. How should he grade his strange student, Tertan?

Tertan's final examination had been no different from all his other writing, and what did one 'give' such a student? De Witt must have his A, that was clear. Johnson would get a B. With Casebeer it was a question of a B-minus or a C-plus, and Stettenhover, who had been crammed by the team tutor to fill half a blue-book with his thin feminine scrawl, would have his C-minus which he would accept with mingled indifference and resentment. But with Tertan it was not so easy.

The boy was still in the college process and his name could not be omitted from the grade sheet. Yet what should a mind under suspicion of madness be graded? Until the medical verdict was given, it was for Howe to continue as Tertan's teacher and to keep his judgment pedagogical. Impossible to give him an F: he had not failed. B was for Johnson's stolid mediocrity. He could not be put on the edge of passing with Stettenhover, for he exactly did not pass. In energy and richness of intellect he was perhaps even De Witt's superior, and Howe toyed grimly with the notion of giving him an A, but that would lower the value of the A De Witt had won with his beautiful and clear, if still arrogant, mind. There was a notation which the Registrar recognized—Inc., for Incomplete, and in the horrible comedy of the situation, Howe considered that. But really only a mark of M for Mad would serve.

In his perplexity, Howe sought the Dean, but the Dean was out of town. In the end, he decided to maintain the A-minus he had given Tertan at midterm. After all, there had been no falling away from that quality. He entered it on the grade sheet with something like bravado.

Academic time moves quickly. A college year is not really a year, lacking as it does three months. And it is endlessly divided into units which, at their beginning, appear larger than they are—terms, half-terms, months, weeks. And the ultimate unit, the hour, is not really an hour, lacking as it does ten minutes. And so the new term advanced rapidly, and one day the fields about the town were all brown, cleared of even the few thin patches of snow which had lingered so long.

Howe, as he lectured on the romantic poets, became conscious of Blackburn emanating wrath. Blackburn did it well. did it with enormous dignity.

He did not stir in his seat, he kept his eyes fixed on Howe in perfect attention, but he abstained from using his notebook, there was no mistaking what he proposed to himself as an attitude. His elbow on the writing-wing of the chair, his chin on the curled fingers of his hand, he was the embodiment of intellectual indignation. He was thinking his own thoughts, would give no public offense, yet would claim his due, was not to be intimidated. Howe knew that he would present himself at the end of the hour.

Blackburn entered the office without invitation. He did not smile; there was no cajolery about him. Without invitation he sat down beside Howe's desk. He did not speak until he had taken the blue-book from his pocket. He said, 'What does this mean, sir?'

It was a sound and conservative student tactic. Said in the usual way it meant, 'How could you have so misunderstood me?' or 'What does this mean for my future in the course?' But there were none of the humbler tones in Blackburn's way of saying it.

Howe made the established reply, 'I think that's for you to tell me.'

Blackburn continued icy. 'I'm sure I can't, sir.'

There was a silence between them. Both dropped their eyes to the blue-book on the desk. On its cover Howe had penciled: 'F. This is very poor work.'

Howe picked up the blue-book. There was always the possibility of injustice. The teacher may be bored by the mass of papers and not wholly attentive. A phrase, even the student's handwriting, may irritate him unreasonably. 'Well,' said Howe, 'Let's go through it.'

He opened the first page. 'Now here: you write, "In *The Ancient Mariner,* Coleridge lives in and transports us to a honey-sweet world where all is rich and strange, a world of charm to which we can escape from the humdrum existence of our daily lives, the world of romance. Here, in this warm and honey-sweet land of charming dreams we can relax and enjoy ourselves." '

Howe lowered the paper and waited with a neutral look for Blackburn to speak. Blackburn returned the look boldly, did not speak, sat stolid and lofty. At last Howe said, speaking gently, 'Did you mean that, or were you just at a loss for something to say?'

'You imply that I was just "bluffing"?' The quotation marks hung palpable in the air about the word.

'I'd like to know. I'd prefer believing that you were bluffing to believing that you really thought this.'

Blackburn's eyebrows went up. From the height of a great and firm-based idea he looked at his teacher. He clasped the crags for a moment and then pounced, craftily, suavely. 'Do you mean, Doctor Howe, that there aren't two opinions possible?'

It was superbly done in its air of putting all of Howe's intellectual life into the balance. Howe remained patient and simple. 'Yes, many opinions are possible, but not this one. Whatever anyone believes of *The Ancient Mariner,* no one can in reason believe that it represents a—a honey-sweet world in which we can relax.'

'But that is what I *feel,* sir.'

This was well-done, too. Howe said, 'Look, Mr. Blackburn. Do you really relax with hunger and thirst, the heat and the sea-serpents, the dead men with staring eyes, Life in Death and the skeletons? Come now, Mr. Blackburn.'

Blackburn made no answer, and Howe pressed forward. 'Now, you say of Wordsworth, "Of peasant stock himself, he turned from the effete life of the salons and found in the peasant the hope of a flaming revolution which would sweep away all the old ideas. This is the subject of his best poems." '

Beaming at his teacher with youthful eagerness, Blackburn said, 'Yes, sir, a rebel, a bringer of light to suffering mankind. I see him as a kind of Prothemeus.'

'A kind of what?'

'Prothemeus, sir.'

'Think, Mr. Blackburn. We were talking about him only today and I mentioned his name a dozen times. You don't mean Prothemeus. You mean—' Howe waited, but there was no response.

'You mean Prometheus.'

Blackburn gave no assent, and Howe took the reins. 'You've done a bad job here, Mr. Blackburn, about as bad as could be done.' He saw Blackburn stiffen and his genial face harden again. 'It shows either a lack of preparation or a complete lack of understanding.' He saw Blackburn's face begin to go to pieces and he stopped.

'Oh, sir,' Blackburn burst out, 'I've never had a mark like this before, never anything below a B, never. A thing like this has never happened to me before.'

It must be true, it was a statement too easily verified. Could it be that other instructors accepted such flaunting nonsense? Howe wanted to end the interview. 'I'll set it down to lack of preparation,' he said. 'I know you're busy. That's not an excuse, but it's an explanation. Now, suppose you really prepare, and then take another quiz in two weeks. We'll forget this one and count the other.'

Blackburn squirmed with pleasure and gratitude. 'Thank you, sir. You're really very kind, very kind.'

Howe rose to conclude the visit. 'All right, then— in two weeks.'

It was that day that the Dean imparted to Howe the conclusion of the case of Tertan. It was simple and a little anti-climactic. A physician had been called in, and had said the word, given the name.

'A classic case, he called it,' the Dean said. 'Not a doubt in the world,' he said. His eyes were full of miserable pity, and he clutched at a word. 'A classic case, a classic case.' To his aid and to Howe's there came the Parthenon and the form of the Greek drama, the Aristotelian logic, Racine and the Well-Tempered Clavichord, the blueness of the Aegean and its clear sky. Classic—that is to say, without a doubt, perfect in its way, a veritable model, and, as the Dean had been told, sure to take a perfectly predictable and inevitable course to a foreknown conclusion.

It was not only pity that stood in the Dean's eyes. For a moment there was fear too. 'Terrible,' he said, 'it is simply terrible.'

Then he went on briskly. 'Naturally, we've told the boy nothing. And, naturally, we won't. His tuition's paid by his scholarship, and we'll continue him on the rolls until the end of the year. That will be kindest. After that the matter will be out of our control. We'll see, of course, that he gets into the proper hands. I'm told there will be no change, he'll go on like this, be as good as this, for four to six months. And so we'll just go along as usual.'

So Tertan continued to sit in Section 5 of English 1A, to his classmates still a figure of curiously dignified fun, symbol to most of them of the respectable but absurd intellectual life. But to his teacher he was now very different. He had not changed—he was still the greyhound casting for the scent of ideas, and Howe could see that he was still the same Tertan, but he could not feel it. What he felt as he looked at the boy sitting in his accustomed place was the hard blank of a fact. The fact itself was formidable and depressing. But what Howe was chiefly aware of was that he had permitted the metamorphosis of Tertan from person to fact.

As much as possible he avoided seeing Tertan's upraised hand and eager eye. But the fact did not know of its mere factuality, it continued its existence as if it were Tertan, hand up and eye questioning, and one day it appeared in Howe's office with a document.

'Even the spirit who lives egregiously, above the herd, must have its relations with the fellowman,' Tertan declared. He laid the document on Howe's desk. It was headed 'Quill and Scroll Society of Dwight College. Application for Membership.'

'In most ways these are crass minds,' Tertan said, touching the paper. 'Yet as a whole, bound together in their common love of letters, they transcend their intellectual lacks since it is not a paradox that the whole is greater than the sum of its parts.'

'When are the elections?' Howe asked.

'They take place tomorrow.'

'I certainly hope you will be successful.'

'Thank you. Would you wish to implement that hope?' A rather dirty finger pointed to the bottom of the sheet. 'A faculty recommender is necessary,' Tertan said stiffly, and waited.

'And you wish me to recommend you?'

'It would be an honor.'

'You may use my name.'

Tertan's finger pointed again. 'It must be a written sponsorship, signed by the sponsor.' There was a large blank space on the form under the heading, 'Opinion of Faculty Sponsor.'

This was almost another thing and Howe hesitated. Yet there was nothing else to do and he took out his fountain pen. He wrote, 'Mr. Ferdinand Tertan is marked by his intense devotion to letters and by his exceptional love of all things of the mind.' To this he signed his name, which looked bold and assertive on the white page. It disturbed him, the strange affirming power of a name. With a business-like air, Tertan whipped up the paper, folding it with decision, and put it into his pocket. He bowed and took his departure, leaving Howe with the sense of having done something oddly momentous.

And so much now seemed odd and momentous to Howe that should not have seemed so. It was odd and momentous, he felt, when he sat with Blackburn's second quiz before him, and wrote in an excessively firm hand the grade of C-minus. The paper was a clear, an indisputable failure. He was carefully and consciously committing a cowardice. Blackburn had told the truth when he had pleaded his past record. Howe had consulted it in the Dean's office. It showed no grade lower than a B-minus. A canvass of some of Blackburn's previous instructors had brought vague attestations to the adequate powers of a student imperfectly remembered, and sometimes surprise that his abilities could be questioned at all.

As he wrote the grade, Howe told himself that his cowardice sprang from an unwillingness to have more dealings with a student he disliked. He knew it was simpler than that. He knew he feared Blackburn; that was the absurd truth. And cowardice did not solve the matter after all. Blackburn, flushed with a first success, attacked at once. The minimal passing grade had not assuaged his feelings and he sat at Howe's desk and again the blue-book lay between them. Blackburn said nothing. With an enormous impudence, he was waiting for Howe to speak and explain himself.

At last Howe said sharply and rudely, 'Well?' His throat was tense and the blood was hammering in his head. His mouth was tight with anger at himself for his disturbance.

Blackburn's glance was almost baleful. 'This is impossible, sir.'

'But there it is,' Howe answered.

'Sir?' Blackburn had not caught the meaning but his tone was still haughty.

Impatiently Howe said, "There it is, plain as day. Are you here to complain again?'

'Indeed I am, sir.' There was surprise in Blackburn's voice that Howe should ask the question.

'I shouldn't complain if I were you. You did a thoroughly bad job on your first quiz. This one is a little, only a very little, better.' This was not true. If anything, it was worse.

'That might be a matter of opinion, sir.'

'It is a matter of opinion. Of my opinion.'

'Another opinion might be different, sir.'

'You really believe that?' Howe said.

'Yes.' The omission of the 'sir' was monumental.

'Whose, for example?'

'The Dean's, for example.' Then the fleshy jaw came forward a little. 'Or a certain literary critic's, for example.'

It was colossal and almost too much for Blackburn himself to handle. The solidity of his face almost crumpled under it. But he withstood his own audacity and went on. 'And the Dean's opinion might be guided by the knowledge that the person who gave me this mark is the man whom a famous critic, the most eminent judge of literature in this country, called a drunken man. The Dean might think twice about whether such a man is fit to teach Dwight students.'

Howe said in quiet admonition, 'Blackburn, you're mad,' meaning no more than to check the boy's extravagance.

But Blackburn paid no heed. He had another shot in the locker. 'And the Dean might be guided by the information, of which I have evidence, documentary evidence,'—he slapped his breast pocket twice—'that this same person personally recommended to the college literary society, the oldest in the country, that he personally recommended a student who is crazy, who threw the meeting into an uproar—a psychiatric case. The Dean might take that into account.'

Howe was never to learn the details of that 'uproar.' He had always to content himself with the dim but passionate picture which at that moment sprang into his mind, of Tertan standing on some abstract height and madly denouncing the multitude of Quill and Scroll who howled him down.

He sat quiet a moment and looked at Blackburn. The ferocity had entirely gone from the student's face. He sat regarding his teacher almost benevolently. He had played a good card and now, scarcely at all unfriendly, he was waiting to see the effect. Howe took up the blue-book and negligently sifted through it. He read a page, closed the book, struck out the C-minus and wrote an F.

'Now you may take the paper to the Dean,' he said. 'You may tell him that after reconsidering it, I lowered the grade.'

The gasp was audible. 'Oh, sir!' Blackburn cried. 'Please!' His face was agonized. 'It means my graduation, my livelihood, my future. Don't do this to me.'

'It's done already.'

Blackburn stood up. 'I spoke rashly, sir, hastily. I had no intention, no real intention, of seeing the Dean. It rests with you—entirely, entirely. I *hope* you will restore the first mark.'

'Take the matter to the Dean or not, just as you choose. The grade is what you deserve and it stands.'

Blackburn's head dropped. 'And will I be failed at mid-term, sir?'

'Of course.'

From deep out of Blackburn's great chest rose a cry of anguish. 'Oh, sir, if you want me to go down on my knees to you, I will, I will.'

Howe looked at him in amazement.

'I will, I will. On my knees, sir. This mustn't, mustn't happen.'

He spoke so literally, meaning so very truly that his knees and exactly his knees were involved and seeming to think that he was offering something of tangible value to his teacher, that Howe, whose head had become icy clear in the nonsensical drama, thought, 'The boy is mad,' and began to speculate fantastically whether something in himself attracted or developed aberration. He could see himself standing absurdly before the Dean and saying, 'I've found another. This time it's the vice-president of the Council, the manager of the debating team and secretary of Quill and Scroll.'

One more such discovery, he thought, and he himself would be discovered! And there, suddenly, Blackburn was on his knees with a thump, his huge thighs straining his trousers, his hand outstretched in a great gesture of supplication.

With a cry, Howe shoved back his swivel chair and it rolled away on its casters half across the little room. Blackburn knelt for a moment to nothing at all, then got to his feet.

Howe rose abruptly. He said, 'Blackburn, you will stop acting like an idiot. Dust your knees off, take your paper and get out. You've behaved like a fool and a malicious person. You have half a term to do a decent job. Keep your silly mouth shut and try to do it. Now get out.'

Blackburn's head was low. He raised it and there was a pious light in his eyes. 'Will you shake hands, sir?' he said. He thrust out his hand.

'I will not,' Howe said.

Head and hand sank together. Blackburn picked up his blue-book and walked to the door. He turned and said, 'Thank you, sir.' His back, as he departed, was heavy with tragedy and stateliness.

IV

After years of bad luck with the weather, the College had a perfect day for Commencement. It was wonderfully bright, the air so transparent, the wind so brisk that no one could resist talking about it.

As Howe set out for the campus he heard Hilda calling from the back yard. She called, 'Professor, professor,' and came running to him.

Howe said, 'What's this "professor" business?'

'Mother told me,' Hilda said. 'You've been promoted. And I want to take your picture.'

'Next year,' said Howe. 'I won't be a professor until next year. And you know better than to call anybody "professor." '

'It was just in fun,' Hilda said. She seemed disappointed.

'But you can take my picture if you want. I won't look much different next year.' Still, it was frightening. It might mean that he was to stay in this town all his life.

Hilda brightened. 'Can I take it in this?' she said, and touched the gown he carried over his arm.

Howe laughed. 'Yes, you can take it in this.'

'I'll get my things and meet you in front of Otis,' Hilda said. 'I have the background all picked out.'

On the campus the Commencement crowd was already large. It stood about in eager, nervous little family groups. As he crossed, Howe was greeted by a student, capped and gowned, glad of the chance to make an event for his parents by introducing one of his teachers. It was while Howe stood there chatting that he saw Tertan.

He had never seen anyone quite so alone, as though a circle had been woven about him to separate him from the gay crowd on the campus. Not that Tertan was not gay, he was the gayest of all. Three weeks had passed since Howe had last seen him, the weeks of examination, the lazy week before Commencement, and this was now a different Tertan. On his head he wore a panama hat, broadbrimmed and fine, of the shape associated with South American planters. He wore a suit of raw silk, luxurious, but yellowed with age and much too tight, and he sported a whangee cane. He walked sedately, the hat tilted at a devastating angle, the stick coming up and down in time to his measured tread. He had, Howe guessed, outfitted himself to greet the day in the clothes of that ruined father whose existence was on record in the Dean's office. Gravely and arrogantly he surveyed the scene—in it, his whole bearing seemed to say, but not of it. With his haughty step, with his flashing eye, Tertan was coming nearer. Howe did not wish to be seen. He shifted his position slightly. When he looked again, Tertan was not in sight.

The chapel clock struck the quarter hour. Howe detached himself from his chat and hurried to Otis Hall at the far end of the campus. Hilda had not yet come. He went up into the high portico and, using the glass of the door for a mirror, put on his gown, adjusted the hood on his shoulders and set the mortarboard on his head. When he came down the steps, Hilda had arrived.

Nothing could have told him more forcibly that a year had passed than the development of Hilda's photographic possessions from the box camera of the previous fall. By a strap about her neck was hung a leather case, so thick and strong, so carefully stitched and so molded to its contents that it could only hold a costly camera. The appearance was deceptive, Howe knew, for he had been present at the Aikens' pre-Christmas conference about its purchase. It was only a fairly good domestic camera. Still, it looked very impressive. Hilda carried another leather case from which she drew a collapsible tripod. Decisively she extended each of its gleaming legs and set it up on the path. She removed the camera from its case and fixed it to the tripod. In its compact efficiency the camera almost had a life of its own, but Hilda treated it with easy familiarity, looked into its eye, glanced casually at its gauges. Then from a pocket she took still another leather case and drew from it a small instrument through which she looked first at Howe, who began to feel inanimate and lost, and then at the sky. She made some adjustment on the instrument, then some adjustment on the camera. She swept the scene with her eye, found a spot and pointed the camera in its direction. She walked to the spot, stood on it and beckoned to Howe. With each new leather case, with each new instrument, and with each new adjustment she had grown in ease and now she said, 'Joe, will you stand here?'

Obediently Howe stood where he was bidden. She had yet another instrument. She took out a tape-measure on a mechanical spool. Kneeling down before Howe, she put the little metal ring of the tape under the tip of his shoe. At her request, Howe pressed it with his toe. When she had measured her distance, she nodded to Howe who released the tape. At a touch, it sprang back into the spool. 'You have to be careful if you're going to get what you want,' Hilda said. 'I don't believe in all this snap-snap-snapping,' she remarked loftily. Howe nodded in agreement, although he was beginning to think Hilda's care excessive.

Now at last the moment had come. Hilda squinted into the camera, moved the tripod slightly. She stood to the side, holding the plunger of the shutter-cable. 'Ready,' she said. 'Will you relax, Joseph, please?' Howe realized that he was standing frozen. Hilda stood poised and precise as a setter, one hand holding the little cable, the other extended with curled dainty fingers like a dancer's, as if expressing to her subject the precarious delicacy of the moment. She pressed the plunger and there was the click. At once she stirred to action, got behind the camera, turned a new exposure. 'Thank you,' she said. 'Would you stand under that tree and let me do a character study with light and shade?'

The childish absurdity of the remark restored Howe's ease. He went to the little tree. The pattern the leaves made on his gown was what Hilda was after. He had just taken a satisfactory position when he heard in the unmistakable voice, 'Ah, Doctor! Having your picture taken?'

Howe gave up the pose and turned to Blackburn who stood on the walk, his hands behind his back, a little too large for his bachelor's gown. Annoyed that Blackburn should see him posing for a character study in light and shade, Howe said irritably, 'Yes, having my picture taken.'

Blackburn beamed at Hilda. 'And the little photographer?' he said. Hilda fixed her eyes on the ground and stood closer to her brilliant and aggressive camera. Blackburn, teetering on his heels, his hands behind his back, wholly prelatical and benignly patient, was not abashed at the silence. At last Howe said, 'If you'll excuse us, Mr. Blackburn, we'll go on with the picture.'

'Go right ahead, sir. I'm running along.' But he only came closer. 'Doctor Howe,' he said fervently, 'I want to tell you how glad I am that I was able to satisfy your standards at last.'

Howe was surprised at the hard, insulting brightness of his own voice, and even Hilda looked up curiously as he said, 'Nothing you have ever done has satisfied me, and nothing you could ever do would satisfy me, Blackburn.'

With a glance at Hilda, Blackburn made a gesture as if to hush Howe—as though all his former bold malice had taken for granted a kind of understanding between himself and his teacher, a secret which must not be betrayed to a third person. 'I only meant, sir,' he said, 'that I was able to pass your course after all.'

Howe said, 'You didn't pass my course. I passed you out of my course. I passed you without even reading your paper. I wanted to be sure the college would be rid of you. And when all the grades were in and I did read your paper, I saw I was right not to have read it first.'

Blackburn presented a stricken face. 'It was very bad, sir?'

But Howe had turned away. The paper had been fantastic. The paper had been, if he wished to see it so, mad. It was at this moment that the Dean came up behind Howe and caught his arm. 'Hello, Joseph,' he said. 'We'd better be getting along, it's almost late.'

He was not a familiar man, but when he saw Blackburn, who approached to greet him, he took Blackburn's arm, too. 'Hello, Theodore,' he said. Leaning forward on Howe's arm and on Blackburn's, he said, 'Hello, Hilda dear.' Hilda replied quietly, 'Hello, Uncle George.'

Still clinging to their arms, still linking Howe and Blackburn, the Dean said, 'Another year gone, Joe, and we've turned out another crop. After you've been here a few years, you'll find it reasonably upsetting—you wonder how there can be so many graduating classes while you stay the same. But of course you don't stay the same.' Then he said, 'Well,' sharply, to dismiss the thought. He pulled Blackburn's arm and swung him around to Howe. 'Have you heard about Teddy Blackburn?' he asked. 'He has a job already, before graduation—the first man of his class to be placed.' Expectant of congratulations, Blackburn beamed at Howe. Howe remained silent.

'Isn't that good?' the Dean said. Still Howe did not answer and the Dean, puzzled and put out, turned to Hilda. 'That's a very fine-looking camera, Hilda.' She touched it with affectionate pride.

'Instruments of precision,' said a voice. 'Instruments of precision.' Of the three with joined arms, Howe was the nearest to Tertan, whose gaze took in all the scene except the smile and the nod which Howe gave him. The boy leaned on his cane. The broad-brimmed hat, canting jauntily over his eye, confused the image of his face that Howe had established, suppressed the rigid lines of the ascetic and brought out the baroque curves. It made an effect of perverse majesty.

'Instruments of precision,' said Tertan for the last time, addressing no one, making a casual comment to the universe. And it occurred to Howe that Tertan might not be referring to Hilda's equipment. The sense of the thrice-woven circle of the boy's loneliness smote him fiercely. Tertan stood in majestic jauntiness, superior to all the scene, but his isolation made Howe ache with a pity of which Tertan was more the cause than the object, so general and indiscriminate was it.

Whether in his sorrow he made some unintended movement toward Tertan which the Dean checked, or whether the suddenly tightened grip on his arm was the Dean's own sorrow and fear, he did not know. Tertan watched them in the incurious way people watch a photograph being taken, and suddenly the thought that, to the boy, it must seem that the three were posing for a picture together made Howe detach himself almost rudely from the Dean's grasp.

'I promised Hilda another picture,' he announced—needlessly, for Tertan was no longer there, he had vanished in the last sudden flux of visitors who, now that the band had struck up, were rushing nervously to find seats.

'You'd better hurry,' the Dean said. 'I'll go along, it's getting late for me.' He departed and Blackburn walked stately by his side.

Howe again took his position under the little tree which cast its shadow over his face and gown. 'Just hurry, Hilda, won't you?' he said. Hilda held the cable at arm's length, her other arm crooked and her fingers crisped. She rose on her toes and said 'Ready,' and pressed the release. 'Thank you,' she said gravely and began to dismantle her camera as he hurried off to join the procession.

IT MUST HAVE BEEN SPRING

JOHN O'HARA

JOHN O'HARA (1905–   ) burst on the literary scene in 1934 with his novel *Appointment in Samarra*, a biting realistic study of the self-styled "smart set" of a small American city. A sure ear for the cadence of American speech, an ironic view of character, and a tight and economical narrative style are displayed in all his fiction, novels and short stories alike. Among his books are *Butterfield 8* (1935), *A Rage to Live* (1949), *Ten North Frederick* (1955), *From the Terrace* (1958), and *Sermons and Soda Water* (1961). His collection of short stories *Pal Joey* (1940) was the basis for a musical comedy for which he wrote the libretto.

IT must have been one of the very first days of spring. I was wearing my boots and my new corduroy habit, and carrying my spurs in my pocket. I always carried my spurs on the way to the stable, because it was eight squares from home to the stable, and I usually had to pass a group of newsboys on the way, and when I wore the spurs they would yell at me, even my friends among them. The spurs seemed to make a difference. The newsboys were used to seeing me in riding breeches and boots or leather puttees, but when I wore the spurs they always seemed to notice it, and they would yell "Cowboy-crazy!", and once I got in a fight about it and got a tooth knocked out. It was not only because I hated what they called me. I hated their ignorance; I could not stop and explain to them that I was not cowboy-crazy, that I rode an English saddle and posted to the trot. I could not explain to a bunch of newsboys that Julia was a five-gaited mare, a full sister to Golden Firefly, and that she herself could have been shown if she hadn't had a blanket scald.

This day that I remember, which must have been

Copyright 1934 by John O'Hara. Reprinted by permission of Random House, Inc.

one of the very first days of spring, becomes clearer in my memory. I remember the sounds: the woop-woop of my new breeches each time I took a step, and the clop sound of the draught horses' hooves in the thawed ground of the streets. The draught horses were pulling wagon-loads of coal from the near-by mines up the hill, and when they got halfway up the driver would give them a rest; there would be a ratchety noise as he pulled on the brake, and then the sound of the breast chains and trace chains loosening up while the horses rested. Then presently the loud slap of the brake handle against the iron guard, and the driver yelling "Gee opp!", and then the clop sound again as the horses' hooves sank into the sloppy roadway.

My father's office was on the way to the stable, and we must have been at peace that day. Oh, I know we were, because I remember it was the first time I wore the new breeches and jacket. They had come from Philadelphia that day. At school, which was across the street from our house, I had looked out the window and there was Wanamaker's truck in front of our house, and I knew that The Things had come. Probably crates and burlap rolls containing furniture and rugs and other things that did not concern me; but also a box in which I knew would be my breeches and jacket. I went home for dinner, at noon, but there was no time for me to try on the new things until after school. Then I did hurry home and changed, because I thought I might find my father in his office if I hurried, although it would be after office hours, and I wanted him to see me in the new things.

Now, I guess my mother had telephoned him to wait, but then I only knew that when I got within two squares of the office, he came out and stood on the porch. He was standing with his legs spread apart, with his hands dug deep in his hip pockets and the skirt of his tweed coat stuck out behind like a sparrow's tail. He was wearing a gray soft hat with a black ribbon and with white piping around the edge of the brim. He was talking across the street to Mr. George McRoberts, the lawyer, and his teeth gleamed under his black mustache. He glanced in my direction and saw me and nodded, and put one foot up on the porch seat and went on talking until I got there.

I moved toward him, as always, with my eyes cast down, and I felt my riding crop getting sticky in my hand and I changed my grip on it and held the bone handle. I never could tell anything by my father's nod, whether he was pleased with me or otherwise. As I approached him, I had no way of telling whether he was pleased with me for something or annoyed because someone might have told him they had seen me smoking. I had a package of Melachrinos in my pocket, and I wanted to throw them in the Johnstons' garden, but it was too late now; I was in plain sight. He would wait until I got there, even though he might only nod again when I did, as he sometimes did.

I stood at the foot of the porch. "Hello," I said.

He did not answer me for a few seconds. Then he said, "Come up here till I have a look at you."

I went up on the porch. He looked at my boots. "Well," he said. "Did you polish them?"

"No. I had Mike do it. I charged it. It was a quarter, but you said—"

"I know. Well, you look all right. How are the breeches? You don't want to get them too tight across the knee or they'll hurt you."

I raised my knees to show him that the breeches felt all right.

"Mm-hmm," he said. And then, "Good Lord!" He took off his hat and laid it on the porch seat, and then began to tie my stock over again. I never did learn to tie it the way he wanted it, the way it should have been. Now I was terribly afraid, because he could always smell smoke—he didn't smoke himself—and I remembered I had had a cigarette at recess. But he finished tying the stock and then drew away and commenced to smile.

He called across the street to Mr. McRoberts. "Well, George. How does he look?"

"Like a million, Doctor. Regular English country squire, eh?"

"English, hell!"

"Going horseback riding?" said Mr. McRoberts to me.

"Yes," I said.

"Wonderful exercise. How about you, Doctor? You ought to be going, too."

"Me? I'm a working man. I'm going to trephine a man at four-thirty. No, this is the horseman in my family. Best horseman in Eastern Pennsylvania," said my father. He turned to me. "Where to this afternoon? See that the mare's hooves are clean and see if that nigger is bedding her the way I told him. Give her a good five-mile exercise out to Indian Run and then back the Old Road. All right."

I started to go. I went down the porch steps and we both said goodbye, and then, when I was a few steps away, he called to me to wait.

"You look fine," he said. "You really look like something. Here." He gave me a five-dollar bill. "Save it. Give it to your mother to put in the bank for you."

"Thank you," I said, and turned away, because suddenly I was crying. I went up the street to the stable with my head bent down, because I could let the tears roll right out of my eyes and down to the ground without putting my hand up to my face. I knew he was still looking.

THE NOVEL

ETHAN FROME

EDITH WHARTON

EDITH WHARTON (1862–1937) was born in New York City. Her family belonged to the aristocracy of the Atlantic seaboard, which was largely conditioned by the traditions of European culture. Her early years were lived partly in Europe, she was privately educated, and after 1906 settled in France. Her relief work for the Allies during the First World War won her the Legion of Honor from France and the Order of Leopold from Belgium. Her books include *The House of Mirth* (1905), which established her reputation, *Ethan Frome* (1911), "the book to the making of which I brought the greatest joy and the fullest ease," *The Custom of the Country* (1913), *The Age of Innocence* (1920), which won the Pulitzer Prize, several volumes of short stories, *The Writing of Fiction* (1925), and her autobiographical volume *A Backward Glance* (1934). ". . . every great novel," she said, "must first of all be based on a profound sense of moral values and then constructed with a classical unity and economy of means. . . . My last page is always latent in my first."

I HAD the story, bit by bit, from various people, and, as generally happens in such cases, each time it was a different story.

If you know Starkfield, Massachusetts, you know the post-office. If you know the post-office you must have seen Ethan Frome drive up to it, drop the reins on his hollow-backed bay and drag himself across the brick pavement to the white colonnade: and you must have asked who he was.

It was there that, several years ago, I saw him for the first time; and the sight pulled me up sharp. Even then he was the most striking figure in Starkfield, though he was but the ruin of a man. It was not so much his great height that marked him, for the "natives" were easily singled out by their lank longitude from the stockier foreign breed: it was the careless powerful look he had, in spite of a lameness checking each step like the jerk of a chain. There was something bleak and unapproachable in his face, and he was so stiffened and grizzled that I took him for an old man and was surprised to hear that he was not more than fifty-two. I had this from Harmon Gow, who had driven the stage from Bettsbridge to Starkfield in pre-trolley days and knew the chronicle of all the families on his line.

"He's looked that way ever since he had his smash-up; and that's twenty-four years ago come next February," Harmon threw out between reminiscent pauses.

The "smash-up" it was—I gathered from the same

Ethan Frome (Copyright 1911 Charles Scribner's Sons; renewal copyright 1939 Frederic R. King and Leroy King) by Edith Wharton is reprinted with the permission of Charles Scribner's Sons.

informant—which, besides drawing the red gash across Ethan Frome's forehead, had so shortened and warped his right side that it cost him a visible effort to take the few steps from his buggy to the post-office window. He used to drive in from his farm every day at about noon, and as that was my own hour for fetching my mail I often passed him in the porch or stood beside him while we waited on the motions of the distributing hand behind the grating. I noticed that though he came so punctually, he seldom received anything but a copy of the *Bettsbridge Eagle*, which he put without a glance into his sagging pocket. At intervals, however, the post-master would hand him an envelope addressed to Mrs. Zenobia—or Mrs. Zeena—Frome, and usually bearing conspicuously in the upper left-hand corner the address of some manufacturer of patent medicine and the name of his specific. These documents my neighbour would also pocket without a glance, as if too much used to them to wonder at their number and variety, and would then turn away with a silent nod to the post-master.

Every one in Starkfield knew him and gave him a greeting tempered to his own grave mien; but his taciturnity was respected and it was only on rare occasions that one of the older men of the place detained him for a word. When this happened he would listen quietly, his blue eyes on the speaker's face, and answer in so low a tone that his words never reached me; then he would climb stiffly into his buggy, gather up the reins in his left hand and drive slowly away in the direction of his farm.

"It was a pretty bad smash-up?" I questioned Harmon, looking after Frome's retreating figure, and thinking how gallantly his lean brown head, with its shock of light hair, must have sat on his strong shoulders before they were bent out of shape.

"Wust kind," my informant assented. "More'n enough to kill most men. But the Fromes are tough. Ethan'll likely touch a hundred."

"Good God!" I exclaimed. At the moment Ethan Frome, after climbing to his seat, had leaned over to assure himself of the security of a wooden box—also with a druggist's label on it—which he had placed in the back of the buggy, and I saw his face as it probably looked when he thought himself alone. "*That* man touch a hundred? He looks as if he was dead and in hell now!"

Harmon drew a slab of tobacco from his pocket, cut off a wedge and pressed it into the leather pouch of his cheek. "Guess he's been in Starkfield too many winters. Most of the smart ones get away."

"Why didn't *he?*"

"Somebody had to stay and care for the folks. There warn't ever anybody but Ethan. Fust his father—then his mother—then his wife."

"And then the smash-up?"

Harmon chuckled sardonically. "That's so. He *had* to stay then."

"I see. And since then they've had to care for him?"

Harmon thoughtfully passed his tobacco to the other cheek. "Oh, as to that: I guess it's always Ethan done the caring."

Though Harmon Gow developed the tale as far as his mental and moral reach permitted, there were perceptible gaps between his facts, and I had the sense that the deeper meaning of the story was in the gaps. But one phrase stuck in my memory and served as the nucleus about which I grouped my subsequent inferences:"Guess he's been in Starkfield too many winters."

Before my own time there was up I had learned to know what that meant. Yet I had come in the degenerate day of trolley, bicycle and rural delivery, when communication was easy between the scattered mountain villages, and the bigger towns in the valleys, such as Bettsbridge and Shadd's Falls, had libraries, theatres and Y.M.C.A. halls to which the youth of the hills could descend for recreation. But when winter shut down on Starkfield, and the village lay under a sheet of snow perpetually renewed from the pale skies, I began to see what life there— or rather its negation—must have been in Ethan Frome's young manhood.

I had been sent up by my employers on a job connected with the big power-house at Corbury Junction, and a long-drawn carpenters' strike had so delayed the work that I found myself anchored at Starkfield—the nearest habitable spot—for the best part of the winter. I chafed at first, and then, under the hypnotising effect of routine, gradually began to find a grim satisfaction in the life. During the early part of my stay I had been struck by the contrast between the vitality of the climate and the deadness of the community. Day by day, after the December snows were over, a blazing blue sky poured down torrents of light and air on the white landscape, which gave them back in an intenser glitter. One would have supposed that such an atmosphere must quicken the emotions as well as the blood; but it seemed to produce no change except that of retarding still more the sluggish pulse of Starkfield. When I had been there a little longer, and had seen this phase of crystal clearness followed by long stretches of sunless cold; when the storms of February had pitched their white tents about the devoted village and the wild cavalry of March winds had charged down to their support; I began to understand why Starkfield emerged from its six months' siege like a starved garrison capitulating without quarter. Twenty years earlier the means of resistance must have been far fewer, and the enemy in command of almost all the lines of access between the beleaguered villages; and, considering these things, I felt the sinister force of Harmon's phrase: "Most of the smart ones get away." But if that were the case, how could any combination of obstacles have hindered the flight of a man like Ethan Frome?

During my stay at Starkfield I lodged with a middle-aged widow colloquially known as Mrs. Ned Hale. Mrs. Hale's father had been the village lawyer of the previous generation, and "lawyer Varnum's house," where my landlady still lived with her mother, was the most considerable mansion in the village. It stood at one end of the main street, its classic portico and small-paned windows looking down a flagged path between Norway spruces to the slim white steeple of the Congregational church. It was clear that the Varnum fortunes were at the ebb, but the two women did what they could to preserve a decent dignity; and Mrs. Hale, in particular, had a certain wan refinement not out of keeping with her pale old-fashioned house.

In the "best parlour," with its black horse-hair and mahogany weakly illuminated by a gurgling Carcel lamp, I listened every evening to another and more delicately shaded version of the Starkfield chronicle. It was not that Mrs. Ned Hale felt, or affected, any social superiority to the people about her; it was only that the accident of a finer sensibility and a little more education had put just enough distance between herself and her neighbours to enable her to judge them with detachment. She was not unwilling to exercise this faculty, and I had great hopes of getting from her the missing facts of Ethan Frome's story, or rather such a key to his character as should co-ordinate the facts I knew. Her mind was a storehouse of innocuous anecdote, and any question about her acquaintances brought forth a volume of detail; but on the subject of Ethan Frome I found her unexpectedly reticent. There was no hint of disapproval in her reserve; I merely felt in her an insurmountable reluctance to speak of him or his affairs, a low "Yes, I knew them both . . . it was awful . . ." seeming to be the utmost concession that her distress could make to my curiosity.

So marked was the change in her manner, such depths of sad initiation did it imply, that, with some doubts as to my delicacy, I put the case anew to my village oracle, Harmon Gow; but got for my pains only an uncomprehending grunt.

"Ruth Varnum was always as nervous as a rat; and, come to think of it, she was the first one to see 'em after they was picked up. It happened right below lawyer Varnum's, down at the bend of the Corbury road, just round about the time that Ruth got engaged to Ned Hale. The young folks was all friends, and I guess she just can't bear to talk about it. She's had troubles enough of her own."

All the dwellers in Starkfield, as in more notable communities, had had troubles enough of their own to make them comparatively indifferent to those of their neighbours; and though all conceded that Ethan Frome's had been beyond the common measure, no one gave me an explanation of the look in his face which, as I persisted in thinking, neither poverty nor physical suffering could have put there. Nevertheless, I might have contented myself with the story pieced together from these hints had it not been for the provocation of Mrs. Hale's silence, and —a little later—for the accident of personal contact with the man.

On my arrival at Starkfield, Denis Eady, the rich Irish grocer, who was the proprietor of Starkfield's nearest approach to a livery stable, had entered into an agreement to send me over daily to Corbury Flats, where I had to pick up my train for the Junction. But about the middle of the winter Eady's horses fell ill of a local epidemic. The illness spread to the other Starkfield stables and for a day or two I was put to it to find a means of transport. Then Harmon Gow suggested that Ethan Frome's bay was still on his legs and that his owner might be glad to drive me over.

I stared at the suggestion. "Ethan Frome? But I've never even spoken to him. Why on earth should he put himself out for me?"

Harmon's answer surprised me still more. "I don't know as he would; but I know he wouldn't be sorry to earn a dollar."

I had been told that Frome was poor, and that the sawmill and the arid acres of his farm yielded scarcely enough to keep his household through the winter; but I had not supposed him to be in such want as Harmon's words implied, and I expressed my wonder.

"Well, matters ain't gone any too well with him," Harmon said. "When a man's been setting round like a hulk for twenty years or more, seeing things that want doing, it eats inter him, and he loses his grit. That Frome farm was always 'bout as bare's a milkpan when the cat's been round; and you know what one of them old watermills is wuth nowadays. When Ethan could sweat over 'em both from sun-up to dark he kinder choked a living out of 'em; but his folks ate up most everything, even then, and I don't see how he makes out now. Fust his father got a kick, out haying, and went soft in the brain, and gave away money like Bible texts afore he died. Then his mother got queer and dragged along for years as weak as a baby; and his wife Zeena, she's always been the greatest hand at doctoring in the county. Sickness and trouble: that's what Ethan's had his plate full up with, ever since the very first helping."

The next morning, when I looked out, I saw the hollow-backed bay between the Varnum spruces, and Ethan Frome, throwing back his worn bearskin made room for me in the sleigh at his side. After that, for a week, he drove me over every morning to Corbury Flats, and on my return in the afternoon met me again and carried me back through the icy night to Starkfield. The distance each way was barely three miles, but the old bay's pace was slow, and even with firm snow under the runners we were nearly an hour on the way. Ethan Frome drove in silence, the reins loosely held in his left hand, his brown seamed profile, under the helmet-like peak of the cap, relieved against the banks of snow like the bronze image of a hero. He never turned his face to mine, or answered, except in monosyllables, the questions I put, or such slight pleasantries as I ventured. He seemed a part of the mute melancholy landscape, an incarnation of its frozen woe, with all that was warm and sentient in him fast bound below the surface; but there was nothing unfriendly in his silence. I simply felt that he lived in a depth of moral isolation too remote for casual access, and I had the sense that his loneliness was not merely the result of his personal plight, tragic as I guessed that to be, but had in it, as Harmon Gow had hinted, the profound accumulated cold of many Starkfield winters.

Only once or twice was the distance between us bridged for a moment; and the glimpses thus gained confirmed my desire to know more. Once I happened to speak of an engineering job I had been on the previous year in Florida, and of the contrast between the winter landscape about us and that in which I had found myself the year before; and to my surprise Frome said suddenly: "Yes: I was down there once, and for a good while afterward I could call up the sight of it in winter. But now it's all snowed under."

He said no more, and I had to guess the rest from the inflection of his voice and his sharp relapse into silence.

Another day, on getting into my train at the Flats, I missed a volume of popular science—I think it was on some recent discoveries in bio-chemistry—which I had carried with me to read on the way. I thought no more about it till I got into the sleigh again that evening, and saw the book in Frome's hand.

"I found it after you were gone," he said.

I put the volume into my pocket and we dropped back into our usual silence; but as we began to crawl up the long hill from Corbury Flats to the Starkfield ridge I became aware in the dusk that he had turned his face to mine.

"There are things in that book that I didn't know the first word about," he said.

I wondered less at his words than at the queer note of resentment in his voice. He was evidently surprised and slightly aggrieved at his own ignorance.

"Does that sort of thing interest you?" I asked.

"It used to."

"There are one or two rather new things in the book: there have been some big strides lately in that particular line of research." I waited a moment for an answer that did not come; then I said: "If you'd like to look the book through I'd be glad to leave it with you."

He hesitated, and I had the impression that he felt himself about to yield to a stealing tide of inertia; then, "Thank you—I'll take it," he answered shortly.

I hoped that this incident might set up some more direct communication between us. Frome was so simple and straightforward that I was sure his curiosity about the book was based on a genuine interest in its subject. Such tastes and acquirements in a man of his condition made the contrast more poignant between his outer situation and his inner needs, and I hoped that the chance of giving expression to the latter might at least unseal his lips. But something in his past history, or in his present way of living, had apparently driven him too deeply into himself for any casual impulse to draw him back to his kind. At our next meeting he made no allusion to the book, and our intercourse seemed fated to remain as negative and one-sided as if there had been no break in his reserve.

Frome had been driving me over to the Flats for about a week when one morning I looked out of my window into a thick snow-fall. The height of the white waves massed against the garden-fence and along the wall of the church showed that the storm must have been going on all night, and that the drifts were likely to be heavy in the open. I thought it probable that my train would be delayed; but I had to be at the power-house for an hour or two that afternoon, and I decided, if Frome turned up, to push through to the Flats and wait there till my train came in. I don't know why I put it in the conditional, however, for I never doubted that Frome would appear. He was not the kind of man to be turned from his business by any commotion of the elements; and at the appointed hour his sleigh glided up through the snow like a stage-apparition behind thickening veils of gauze.

I was getting to know him too well to express either wonder or gratitude at his keeping his appointment; but I exclaimed in surprise as I saw him turn his horse in a direction opposite to that of the Corbury road.

"The railroad's blocked by a freight-train that got stuck in a drift below the Flats," he explained, as we jogged off into the stinging whiteness.

"But look here—where are you taking me, then?"

"Straight to the Junction, by the shortest way," he answered, pointing up School House Hill with his whip.

"To the Junction—in this storm? Why, it's a good ten miles!"

"The bay'll do it if you give him time. You said you had some business there this afternoon. I'll see you get there."

He said it so quietly that I could only answer: "You're doing me the biggest kind of a favour."

"That's all right," he rejoined.

Abreast of the schoolhouse the road forked, and we dipped down a lane to the left, between hemlock boughs bent inward to their trunks by the weight of the snow. I had often walked that way on Sundays, and knew that the solitary roof showing through bare branches near the bottom of the hill was that of Frome's saw-mill. It looked exanimate enough, with its idle wheel looming above the black stream dashed with yellow-white spume, and its cluster of sheds sagging under their white load. Frome did not even turn his head as we drove by, and still in silence we began to mount the next slope. About a mile farther, on a road I had never travelled, we came to an orchard of starved apple-trees writhing over a hillside among outcroppings of slate that nuzzled up through the snow like animals pushing out their noses to breathe. Beyond the orchard lay a field or two, their boundaries lost under drifts; and above the fields, huddled against the white immensities of land and sky, one of those lonely New England farm-houses that make the landscape lonelier.

"That's my place," said Frome, with a sideway jerk of his lame elbow; and in the distress and oppression of the scene I did not know what to answer. The snow had ceased, and a flash of watery sunlight exposed the house on the slope above us in all its plaintive ugliness. The black wraith of a deciduous creeper flapped from the porch, and the thin wooden walls, under their worn coat of paint, seemed to shiver in the wind that had risen with the ceasing of the snow.

"The house was bigger in my father's time: I had to take down the 'L,' a while back," Frome continued, checking with a twitch of the left rein the bay's evident intention of turning in through the broken-down gate.

I saw then that the unusually forlorn and stunted look of the house was partly due to the loss of what is known in New England as the "L": that long deep-roofed adjunct usually built at right angles to the main house, and connecting it, by way of storerooms and tool-house, with the wood-shed and cow-barn. Whether because of its symbolic sense, the image it presents of a life linked with the soil, and enclosing in itself the chief sources of warmth and nourishment, or whether merely because of the consolatory thought that it enables the dwellers in that harsh climate to get to their morning's work without facing the weather, it is certain that the "L" rather than the house itself seems to be the centre, the actual hearth-stone, of the New England farm. Perhaps this connection of ideas, which had often occurred to me in my rambles about Starkfield, caused me to hear a wistful note in Frome's words, and to see in the diminished dwelling the image of his own shrunken body.

"We're kinder side-tracked here now," he added, "but there was considerable passing before the railroad was carried through to the Flats." He roused the lagging bay with another twitch; then, as if the mere sight of the house had let me too deeply into his confidence for any farther pretence of reserve, he went on slowly: "I've always set down the worst of mother's trouble to that. When she got the rheumatism so bad she couldn't move around she used to sit up there and watch the road by the hour; and one year, when they was six months mending the Bettsbridge pike after the floods, and Harmon Gow had to bring his stage round this way, she picked up so that she used to get down to the gate most days to see him. But after the trains begun running nobody ever come by here to speak of, and mother never could get it through her head what had happened, and it preyed on her right along till she died."

As we turned into the Corbury road the snow began to fall again, cutting off our last glimpse of the house; and Frome's silence fell with it, letting down between us the old veil of reticence. This time the wind did not cease with the return of the snow. Instead, it sprang up to a gale which now and then, from a tattered sky, flung pale sweeps of sunlight over a landscape chaotically tossed. But the bay was as good as Frome's word, and we pushed on to the Junction through the wild white scene.

In the afternoon the storm held off, and the clearness in the west seemed to my inexperienced eye the pledge of a fair evening. I finished my business as quickly as possible, and we set out for Starkfield with a good chance of getting there for supper. But at sunset the clouds gathered again, bringing an earlier night, and the snow began to fall straight and steadily from a sky without wind, in a soft universal diffusion more confusing than the gusts and eddies of the morning. It seemed to be a part of the thickening darkness, to be the winter night itself descending on us layer by layer.

The small ray of Frome's lantern was soon lost in this smothering medium, in which even his sense of direction, and the bay's homing instinct, finally ceased to serve us. Two or three times some ghostly landmark sprang up to warn us that we were astray, and then was sucked back into the mist; and when we finally regained our road the old horse began to show signs of exhaustion. I felt myself to blame for having accepted Frome's offer, and after a short discussion I persuaded him to let me get out of the sleigh and walk along through the snow at the bay's side. In this way we struggled on for another mile or two, and at last reached a point where Frome, peering into what seemed to me formless night, said: "That's my gate down yonder."

The last stretch had been the hardest part of the way. The bitter cold and the heavy going had nearly knocked the wind out of me, and I could feel the horse's side ticking like a clock under my hand.

"Look here, Frome," I began, "there's no earthly use in your going any farther—" but he interrupted me: "Nor you neither. There's been about enough of this for anybody."

I understood that he was offering me a night's shelter at the farm, and without answering I turned into the gate at his side, and followed him to the barn, where I helped him to unharness and bed down the tired horse. When this was done he unhooked the lantern from the sleigh, stepped out again into the night, and called to me over his shoulder: "This way."

Far off above us a square of light trembled through the screen of snow. Staggering along in Frome's wake I floundered toward it, and in the darkness almost fell into one of the deep drifts against the front of the house. Frome scrambled up the slippery steps of the porch, digging a way through the snow with his heavily booted foot. Then he lifted his lantern, found the latch, and led the way into the house. I went after him into a low unlit passage, at the back of which a ladder-like staircase rose into obscurity. On our right a line of light marked the door of the room which had sent its ray across the night; and behind the door I heard a woman's voice droning querulously.

Frome stamped on the worn oil-cloth to shake the snow from his boots, and set down his lantern on a kitchen chair which was the only piece of furniture in the hall. Then he opened the door.

"Come in," he said; and as he spoke the droning voice grew still . . .

It was that night that I found the clue to Ethan Frome, and began to put together this vision of his story . . .

. . . . . .

I

The village lay under two feet of snow, with drifts at the windy corners. In a sky of iron the points of the Dipper hung like icicles and Orion flashed his cold fires. The moon had set, but the night was so transparent that the white house-fronts between the elms looked gray against the snow, clumps of bushes made black stains on it, and the basement windows of the church sent shafts of yellow light far across the endless undulations.

Young Ethan Frome walked at a quick pace along the deserted street, past the bank and Michael Eady's new brick store and lawyer Varnum's house with the two black Norway spruces at the gate. Opposite the Varnum gate, where the road fell away toward the Corbury valley, the church reared its slim white steeple and narrow peristyle. As the young man walked toward it the upper windows drew a black arcade along the side wall of the building, but from the lower openings, on the side where the ground sloped steeply down to the Corbury road, the light shot its long bars, illuminating many fresh furrows in the track leading to the basement door, and showing, under an adjoining shed, a line of sleighs with heavily blanketed horses.

The night was perfectly still, and the air so dry and pure that it gave little sensation of cold. The effect produced on Frome was rather of a complete absence of atmosphere, as though nothing less tenuous than ether intervened between the white earth under his feet and the metallic dome overhead. "It's like being in an exhausted receiver," he thought. Four or five years earlier he had taken a year's course at a technological college at Worcester, and dabbled in the laboratory with a friendly professor of physics; and the images supplied by that experience still cropped up, at unexpected moments, through the totally different associations of thought in which he had since been living. His father's death, and the misfortunes following it, had put a premature end to Ethan's studies; but though they had not gone far enough to be of much practical use they had fed his fancy and made him aware of huge cloudy meanings behind the daily face of things.

As he strode along through the snow the sense of such meanings glowed in his brain and mingled with the bodily flush produced by his sharp tramp. At the end of the village he paused before the darkened front of the church. He stood there a moment, breathing quickly, and looking up and down the street, in which not another figure moved. The pitch of the Corbury road, below lawyer Varnum's spruces, was the favourite coasting-ground of Starkfield, and on clear evenings the church corner rang till late with the shouts of the coasters; but to-night not a sled darkened the whiteness of the long declivity. The hush of midnight lay on the village, and all its waking life was gathered behind the church windows, from which strains of dance-music flowed with the broad bands of yellow light.

The young man, skirting the side of the building, went down the slope toward the basement door. To keep out of range of the revealing rays from within he made a circuit through the untrodden snow and gradually approached the farther angle of the basement wall. Thence, still hugging the shadow, he edged his way cautiously forward to the nearest window, holding back his straight spare body and craning his neck till he got a glimpse of the room.

Seen thus, from the pure and frosty darkness in which he stood, it seemed to be seething in a mist of heat. The metal reflectors of the gas-jets sent crude waves of light against the whitewashed walls, and the iron flanks of the stove at the end of the hall looked as though they were heaving with volcanic fires. The floor was thronged with girls and young men. Down the side wall facing the window stood a row of kitchen chairs from which the older women had just risen. By this time the music had stopped, and the musicians—a fiddler, and the young lady who played the harmonium on Sundays—were hastily refreshing themselves at one corner of the supper-table which aligned its devastated pie-dishes and ice-cream saucers on the platform at the end of the hall. The guests were preparing to leave, and the tide had already set toward the passage where coats and wraps were hung, when a young man with a sprightly foot and a shock of black hair shot into the middle of the floor and clapped his hands. The signal took instant effect. The musicians hurried to their instruments, the dancers—some already half-muffled for departure—fell into line down each side of the room, the older spectators slipped back to their chairs, and the lively young man, after diving about here and there in the throng, drew forth a girl who had already wound a cherry-coloured "fascinator" about her head, and, leading her up to the end of the floor, whirled her down its length to the bounding tune of a Virginia reel.

Frome's heart was beating fast. He had been straining for a glimpse of the dark head under the cherry-coloured scarf and it vexed him that another eye should have been quicker than his. The leader of the reel, who looked as if he had Irish blood in his veins, danced well, and his partner caught his fire. As she passed down the line, her light figure swinging from hand to hand in circles of increasing swiftness, the scarf flew off her head and stood out behind her shoulders, and Frome, at each turn, caught sight of her laughing panting lips, the cloud of dark hair about her forehead, and the dark eyes which seemed the only fixed points in a maze of flying lines.

The dancers were going faster and faster, and the musicians, to keep up with them, belaboured their instruments like jockeys lashing their mounts on the homestretch; yet it seemed to the young man at the window that the reel would never end. Now and then he turned his eyes from the girl's face to that of her partner, which, in the exhilaration of the dance, had taken on a look of almost impudent ownership. Denis Eady was the son of Michael Eady, the ambitious Irish grocer, whose suppleness and effrontery had given Starkfield its first notion of "smart" business methods, and whose new brick store testified to the success of the attempt. His son seemed likely to follow in his steps, and was meanwhile applying the same arts to the conquest of the Starkfield maidenhood. Hitherto Ethan Frome had been content to think him a mean fellow; but now he positively invited a horse-whipping. It was strange that the girl did not seem aware of it: that she could lift her rapt face to her dancer's, and drop her hands into his, without appearing to feel the offence of his look and touch.

Frome was in the habit of walking into Starkfield to fetch home his wife's cousin, Mattie Silver, on the rare evenings when some chance of amusement drew her to the village. It was his wife who had suggested, when the girl came to live with them, that such opportunities should be put in her way. Mattie Silver came from Stamford, and when she entered the Fromes' household to act as her cousin Zeena's aid it was thought best, as she came without pay, not to let her feel too sharp a contrast between the life she had left and the isolation of a Starkfield farm. But for this—as Frome sardonically reflected—it would hardly have occurred to Zeena to take any thought for the girl's amusement.

When his wife first proposed that they should give Mattie an occasional evening out he had inwardly demurred at having to do the extra two miles to the village and back after his hard day on the farm; but not long afterward he had reached the point of wishing that Starkfield might give all its nights to revelry.

Mattie Silver had lived under his roof for a year, and from early morning till they met at supper he had frequent chances of seeing her; but no moments in her company were comparable to those when, her arm in his, and her light step flying to keep time with his long stride, they walked back through the night to the farm. He had taken to the girl from the first day, when he had driven over to the Flats to meet her, and she had smiled and waved to him from the train, crying out "You must be Ethan!" as she jumped down with her bundles, while he reflected, looking over her slight person: "She don't look much on housework, but she ain't a fretter, anyhow." But it was not only that the coming to his house of a bit of hopeful young life was like the lighting of a fire on a cold hearth. The girl was more than the bright serviceable creature he had thought her. She had an eye to see and an ear to hear: he could show her things, and tell her things, and taste the bliss of feeling that all he imported left long reverberations and echoes he could wake at will.

It was during their night walks back to the farm that he felt most intensely the sweetness of this communion. He had always been more sensitive than the people about him to the appeal of natural beauty. His unfinished studies had given form to this sensibility and even in his unhappiest moments field and sky spoke to him with a deep and powerful persuasion. But hitherto the emotion had remained in him as a silent ache, veiling with sadness the beauty that evoked it. He did not even know whether any one else in the world felt as he did, or whether he was the sole victim of this mournful privilege. Then he learned that one other spirit had trembled with the same touch of wonder; that at his side, living under his roof and eating his bread, was a creature to whom he could say: "That's Orion down yonder; the big fellow to the right is Aldebaran, and the bunch of little ones—like bees swarming—they're the Pleiades . . ." or whom he could hold entranced before a ledge of granite thrusting up through the fern while he unrolled the huge panorama of the ice age, and the long dim stretches of succeeding time. The fact that admiration for his learning mingled with Mattie's wonder at what he taught was not the least part of his pleasure. And there were other sensations, less definable but more exquisite, which drew them together with a shock of silent joy: the cold red of sunset behind winter hills, the flight of cloud-flocks over slopes of golden stubble, or the intensely blue shadows of hemlocks on sunlit snow. When she said to him once: "It looks just as if it was painted!" it seemed to Ethan that the art of definition could go no farther, and that words had at last been found to utter his secret soul. . . .

As he stood in the darkness outside the church these memories came back with the poignancy of vanished things. Watching Mattie whirl down the floor from hand to hand he wondered how he could ever have thought that his dull talk interested her. To him, who was never gay but in her presence, her gaiety seemed plain proof of indifference. The face she lifted to her dancers was the same which, when she saw him, always looked like a window that has caught the sunset. He even noticed two or three gestures which, in his fatuity, he had thought she kept for him: a way of throwing her head back when she was amused, as if to taste her laugh before she let it out, and a trick of sinking her lids slowly when anything charmed or moved her.

The sight made him unhappy, and his unhappiness roused his latent fears. His wife had never shown any jealousy of Mattie, but of late she had grumbled increasingly over the house-work and found oblique ways of attracting attention to the girl's inefficiency. Zeena had always been what Starkfield called "sickly," and Frome had to admit that, if she were as ailing as she believed, she needed the help of a stronger arm than the one which lay so lightly in his during the night walks to the farm. Mattie had no natural turn for house-keeping, and her training had done nothing to remedy the defect. She was quick to learn, but forgetful and dreamy, and not disposed to take the matter seriously. Ethan had an idea that if she were to marry a man she was fond of the dormant instinct would wake, and her pies and biscuits become the pride of the county; but domesticity in the abstract did not interest her. At first she was so awkward that he could not help laughing at her; but she laughed with him and that made them better friends. He did his best to supplement her unskilled efforts, getting up earlier than usual to light the kitchen fire, carrying in the wood overnight, and neglecting the mill for the farm that he might help her about the house during the day. He even crept down on Saturday nights to scrub the kitchen floor after the women had gone to bed; and Zeena, one day, had surprised him at the churn and had turned away silently, with one of her queer looks.

Of late there had been other signs of her disfavour, as intangible but more disquieting. One cold winter morning, as he dressed in the dark, his candle flickering in the draught of the ill-fitting window, he had heard her speak from the bed behind him.

"The doctor don't want I should be left without anybody to do for me," she said in her flat whine.

He had supposed her to be asleep, and the sound of her voice had startled him, though she was given to abrupt explosions of speech after long intervals of secretive silence.

He turned and looked at her where she lay indistinctly outlined under the dark calico quilt, her high-boned face taking a grayish tinge from the whiteness of the pillow.

"Nobody to do for you?" he repeated.

"If you say you can't afford a hired girl when Mattie goes."

Frome turned away again, and taking up his razor stooped to catch the reflection of his stretched cheek in the blotched looking-glass above the wash-stand.

"Why on earth should Mattie go?"

"Well, when she gets married, I mean," his wife's drawl came from behind him.

"Oh, she'd never leave us as long as you needed her," he returned, scraping hard at his chin.

"I wouldn't ever have it said that I stood in the way of a poor girl like Mattie marrying a smart fellow like Denis Eady," Zeena answered in a tone of plaintive self-effacement.

Ethan, glaring at his face in the glass, threw his head back to draw the razor from ear to chin. His hand was steady, but the attitude was an excuse for not making an immediate reply.

"And the doctor don't want I should be left without anybody," Zeena continued. "He wanted I should speak to you about a girl he's heard about, that might come——"

Ethan laid down the razor and straightened himself with a laugh.

"Denis Eady! If that's all I guess there's no such hurry to look round for a girl."

"Well, I'd like to talk to you about it," said Zeena obstinately.

He was getting into his clothes in fumbling haste. "All right. But I haven't got the time now; I'm late as it is," he returned, holding his old silver turnip-watch to the candle.

Zeena, apparently accepting this as final, lay watching him in silence while he pulled his suspenders over his shoulders and jerked his arms into his coat; but as he went toward the door she said, suddenly and incisively, "I guess you're always late, now you shave every morning."

That thrust had frightened him more than any vague insinuations about Denis Eady. It was a fact that since Mattie Silver's coming he had taken to shaving every day; but his wife always seemed to be asleep when he left her side in the winter darkness, and he had stupidly assumed that she would not notice any change in his appearance. Once or twice in the past he had been faintly disquieted by Zenobia's way of letting things happen without seeming to remark them, and then, weeks afterward, in a casual phrase, revealing that she had all along taken her notes and drawn her inferences. Of late, however, there had been no room in his thoughts for such vague apprehensions. Zeena herself, from an oppressive reality, had faded into an insubstantial shade. All his life was lived in the sight and sound of Mattie Silver, and he could no longer conceive of its being otherwise. But now, as he stood outside the church, and saw Mattie spinning down the floor with Denis Eady, a throng of disregarded hints and menaces wove their cloud about his brain. . . .

II

As the dancers poured out of the hall Frome, drawing back behind the projecting storm-door, watched the segregation of the grotesquely muffled groups, in which a moving lantern ray now and then lit up a face flushed with food and dancing. The villagers, being afoot, were the first to climb the slope to the main street, while the country neighbours packed themselves more slowly into the sleighs under the shed.

"Ain't you riding, Mattie?" a woman's voice called back from the throng about the shed, and Ethan's heart gave a jump. From where he stood he could not see the persons coming out of the hall till they had advanced a few steps beyond the wooden sides of the storm-door; but through its cracks he heard a clear voice answer: "Mercy no! Not on such a night."

She was there, then, close to him, only a thin board between. In another moment she would step forth into the night, and his eyes, accustomed to the obscurity, would discern her as clearly as though she stood in daylight. A wave of shyness pulled him back into the dark angle of the wall, and he stood there in silence instead of making his presence known to her. It had been one of the wonders of their intercourse that from the first, she the quicker, finer, more expressive, instead of crushing him by the con-

trast, had given him something of her own ease and freedom; but now he felt as heavy and loutish as in his student days, when he had tried to "jolly" the Worcester girls at a picnic.

He hung back, and she came out alone and paused within a few yards of him. She was almost the last to leave the hall, and she stood looking uncertainly about her as if wondering why he did not show himself. Then a man's figure approached, coming so close to her that under their formless wrappings they seemed merged in one dim outline.

"Gentleman friend gone back on you? Say, Matt, that's tough! No, I wouldn't be mean enough to tell the other girls. I ain't as low-down as that." (How Frome hated his cheap banter!) "But look at here, ain't it lucky I got the old man's cutter down there waiting for us?"

Frome heard the girl's voice, gaily incredulous: "What on earth's your father's cutter doin' down there?"

"Why, waiting for me to take a ride. I got the roan colt too. I kinder knew I'd want to take a ride tonight," Eady, in his triumph, tried to put a sentimental note into his bragging voice.

The girl seemed to waver, and Frome saw her twirl the end of her scarf irresolutely about her fingers. Not for the world would he have made a sign to her, though it seemed to him that his life hung on her next gesture.

"Hold on a minute while I unhitch the colt," Denis called to her, springing toward the shed.

She stood perfectly still, looking after him, in an attitude of tranquil expectancy torturing to the hidden watcher. Frome noticed that she no longer turned her head from side to side, as though peering through the night for another figure. She let Denis Eady lead out the horse, climb into the cutter and fling back the bearskin to make room for her at his side; then, with a swift motion of flight, she turned about and darted up the slope toward the front of the church.

"Good-bye! Hope you'll have a lovely ride!" she called back to him over her shoulder.

Denis laughed, and gave the horse a cut that brought him quickly abreast of her retreating figure.

"Come along! Get in quick! It's as slippery as thunder on this turn," he cried, leaning over to reach out a hand to her.

She laughed back at him: "Good-night! I'm not getting in."

By this time they had passed beyond Frome's earshot and he could only follow the shadowy pantomime of their silhouettes as they continued to move along the crest of the slope above him. He saw Eady, after a moment, jump from the cutter and go toward the girl with the reins over one arm. The other he tried to slip through hers; but she eluded him nimbly, and Frome's heart, which had swung out over a black void, trembled back to safety. A moment later he heard the jingle of departing sleigh bells and discerned a figure advancing alone toward the empty expanse of snow before the church.

In the black shade of the Varnum spruces he caught up with her and she turned with a quick "Oh!"

"Think I'd forgotten you, Matt?" he asked with sheepish glee.

She answered seriously: "I thought maybe you couldn't come back for me."

"Couldn't? What on earth could stop me?"

"I knew Zeena wasn't feeling any too good to-day."

"Oh, she's in bed long ago." He paused, a question struggling in him. "Then you meant to walk home all alone?"

"Oh, I ain't afraid!" she laughed.

They stood together in the gloom of the spruces, an empty world glimmering about them wide and gray under the stars. He brought his question out.

"If you thought I hadn't come, why didn't you ride back with Denis Eady?"

"Why, where *were* you? How did you know? I never saw you!"

Her wonder and his laughter ran together like spring rills in a thaw. Ethan had the sense of having done something arch and ingenious. To prolong the effect he groped for a dazzling phrase, and brought out, in a growl of rapture: "Come along."

He slipped an arm through hers, as Eady had done, and fancied it was faintly pressed against her side; but neither of them moved. It was so dark under the spruces that he could barely see the shape of her head beside his shoulder. He longed to stoop his cheek and rub it against her scarf. He would have liked to stand there with her all night in the blackness. She moved forward a step or two and then paused again above the dip of the Corbury road. Its icy slope, scored by innumerable runners, looked like a mirror scratched by travellers at an inn.

"There was a whole lot of them coasting before the moon set," she said.

"Would you like to come in and coast with them some night?" he asked.

"Oh, *would* you, Ethan? It would be lovely!"

"We'll come to-morrow if there's a moon."

She lingered, pressing closer to his side. "Ned Hale and Ruth Varnum came just as *near* running into the big elm at the bottom. We were all sure they were killed." Her shiver ran down his arm. "Wouldn't it have been too awful? They're so happy!"

"Oh, Ned ain't much at steering. I guess I can take you down all right!" he said disdainfully.

He was aware that he was "talking big," like Denis Eady; but his reaction of joy had unsteadied him, and the inflection with which she had said of the engaged couple "They're so happy!" made the words sound as if she had been thinking of herself and him.

"The elm *is* dangerous, though. It ought to be cut down," she insisted.

"Would you be afraid of it, with me?"

"I told you I ain't the kind to be afraid," she tossed back, almost indifferently; and suddenly she began to walk on with a rapid step.

These alterations of mood were the despair and joy of Ethan Frome. The motions of her mind were as incalculable as the flit of a bird in the branches. The fact that he had no right to show his feelings, and thus provoke the expression of hers, made him attach a fantastic importance to every change in her look and tone. Now he thought she understood him, and feared; now he was sure she did not, and despaired. To-night the pressure of accumulated misgivings sent the scale drooping toward despair, and her indifference was the more chilling after the flush of joy into which she had plunged him by dismissing Denis Eady. He mounted School House Hill at her side and walked on in silence till they reached the lane leading to the saw-mill; then the need of some definite assurance grew too strong for him.

"You'd have found me right off if you hadn't gone back to have that last reel with Denis," he brought out awkwardly. He could not pronounce the name without a stiffening of the muscles of his throat.

"Why, Ethan, how could I tell you were there?"

"I suppose what folks say is true," he jerked out at her, instead of answering.

She stopped short, and he felt, in the darkness, that her face was lifted quickly to his. "Why, what do folks say?"

"It's natural enough you should be leaving us," he floundered on, following his thought.

"Is that what they say?" she mocked back at him; then, with a sudden drop of her sweet treble: "You mean that Zeena—ain't suited with me any more?" she faltered.

Their arms had slipped apart and they stood motionless, each seeking to distinguish the other's face.

"I know I ain't anything like as smart as I ought to be," she went on, while he vainly struggled for expression. "There's lots of things a hired girl could do that come awkward to me still—and I haven't got much strength in my arms. But if she'd only tell me I'd try. You know she hardly ever says anything, and sometimes I can see she ain't suited, and yet I don't know why." She turned on him with a sudden flash of indignation. "You'd ought to tell me, Ethan Frome —you'd ought to! Unless *you* want me to go too——"

Unless he wanted her to go too! The cry was balm to his raw wound. The iron heavens seemed to melt and rain down sweetness. Again he struggled for the all-expressive word, and again, his arm in hers, found only a deep "Come along."

They walked on in silence through the blackness of the hemlock-shaded lane, where Ethan's saw-mill gloomed through the night, and out again into the comparative clearness of the fields. On the farther side of the hemlock belt the open country rolled away before them gray and lonely under the stars. Sometimes their way led them under the shade of an overhanging bank or through the thin obscurity of a clump of leafless trees. Here and there a farmhouse stood far back among the fields, mute and cold as a grave-stone. The night was so still that they heard the frozen snow crackling under their feet. The crash of a loaded branch falling far off in the woods reverberated like a musket-shot, and once a fox barked, and Mattie shrank closer to Ethan, and quickened her steps.

At length they sighted the group of larches at Ethan's gate, and as they drew near it the sense that the walk was over brought back his words.

"Then you don't want to leave us, Matt?"

He had to stoop his head to catch her stifled whisper: "Where'd I go, if I did?"

The answer sent a pang through him but the tone suffused him with joy. He forgot what else he had meant to say and pressed her against him so closely that he seemed to feel her warmth in his veins.

"You ain't crying are you, Matt?"

"No, of course I'm not," she quavered.

They turned in at the gate and passed under the shaded knoll where, enclosed in a low fence, the Frome grave-stones slanted at crazy angles through the snow. Ethan looked at them curiously. For years that quiet company had mocked his restlessness, his desire for change and freedom. "We never got away —how should you?" seemed to be written on every headstone; and whenever he went in or out of his gate he thought with a shiver: "I shall just go on living here till I join them." But now all desire for change had vanished, and the sight of the little enclosure gave him a warm sense of continuance and stability.

"I guess we'll never let you go, Matt," he whispered, as though even the dead, lovers once, must conspire with him to keep her; and brushing by the graves, he thought: "We'll always go on living here together, and some day she'll lie there beside me."

He let the vision possess him as they climbed the hill to the house. He was never so happy with her as when he abandoned himself to these dreams. Halfway up the slope Mattie stumbled against some unseen obstruction and clutched his sleeve to steady herself. The wave of warmth that went through him was like the prolongation of his vision. For the first time he stole his arm about her, and she did not resist. They walked on as if they were floating on a summer stream.

Zeena always went to bed as soon as she had had her supper, and the shutterless windows of the house were dark. A dead cucumber-vine dangled from the porch like the crape streamer tied to the door for a death, and the thought flashed through Ethan's brain: "If it was there for Zeena—" Then he had a distinct sight of his wife lying in her bedroom asleep, her mouth slightly open, her false teeth in a tumbler by the bed. . . .

They walked around to the back of the house, between the rigid gooseberry bushes. It was Zeena's habit, when they came back late from the village, to leave the key of the kitchen door under the mat. Ethan stood before the door, his head heavy with dreams, his arm still about Mattie. "Matt—" he began, not knowing what he meant to say.

She slipped out of his hold without speaking, and he stooped down and felt for the key.

"It's not there!" he said, straightening himself with a start.

They strained their eyes at each other through the icy darkness. Such a thing had never happened before.

"Maybe she's forgotten it," Mattie said in a tremulous whisper; but both of them knew that it was not like Zeena to forget.

"It might have fallen off into the snow," Mattie continued, after a pause during which they had stood intently listening.

"It must have been pushed off, then," he rejoined in the same tone. Another wild thought tore through him. What if tramps had been there—what if . . .

Again he listened, fancying he heard a distant sound in the house; then he felt in his pocket for a match, and kneeling down, passed its light slowly over the rough edges of snow about the doorstep.

He was still kneeling when his eyes, on a level with the lower panel of the door, caught a faint ray beneath it. Who could be stirring in that silent house? He heard a step on the stairs, and again for an instant the thought of tramps tore through him. Then the door opened and he saw his wife.

Against the dark background of the kitchen she stood up tall and angular, one hand drawing a quilted counterpane to her flat breast, while the other held a lamp. The light, on a level with her chin, drew out of the darkness her puckered throat and the projecting wrist of the hand that clutched the quilt, and deepened fantastically the hollows and prominences of her high-boned face under its ring of crimping-pins. To Ethan, still in the rosy haze of his hour with Mattie, the sight came with the intense precision of the last dream before waking. He felt as if he had never before known what his wife looked like.

She drew aside without speaking, and Mattie and Ethan passed into the kitchen, which had the deadly chill of a vault after the dry cold of the night.

"Guess you forgot about us, Zeena," Ethan joked, stamping the snow from his boots.

"No. I just felt so mean I couldn't sleep."

Mattie came forward, unwinding her wraps, the colour of the cherry scarf in her fresh lips and cheeks. "I'm so sorry, Zeena! Isn't there anything I can do?"

"No; there's nothing." Zeena turned away from her. "You might 'a' shook off that snow outside," she said to her husband.

She walked out of the kitchen ahead of them and pausing in the hall raised the lamp at arm's-length, as if to light them up the stairs.

Ethan paused also, affecting to fumble for the peg on which he hung his coat and cap. The doors of the two bedrooms faced each other across the narrow upper landing, and to-night it was peculiarly repugnant to him that Mattie should see him follow Zeena.

"I guess I won't come up yet awhile," he said, turning as if to go back to the kitchen.

Zeena stopped short and looked at him. "For the land's sake—what you going to do down here?"

"I've got the mill accounts to go over."

She continued to stare at him, the flame of the unshaded lamp bringing out with microscopic cruelty the fretful lines of her face.

"At this time o' night? You'll ketch your death. The fire's out long ago."

Without answering he moved away toward the kitchen. As he did so his glance crossed Mattie's and he fancied that a fugitive warning gleamed through her lashes. The next moment they sank to her flushed cheeks and she began to mount the stairs ahead of Zeena.

"That's so. It *is* powerful cold down here," Ethan assented; and with lowered head he went up in his wife's wake, and followed her across the threshold of their room.

III

There was some hauling to be done at the lower end of the wood-lot, and Ethan was out early the next day.

The winter morning was as clear as crystal. The sunrise burned red in a pure sky, the shadows on the rim of the wood-lot were darkly blue, and beyond the white and scintillating fields patches of far-off forest hung like smoke.

It was in the early morning stillness, when his muscles were swinging to their familiar task and his lungs expanding with long draughts of mountain air, that Ethan did his clearest thinking. He and Zeena had not exchanged a word after the door of their room had closed on them. She had measured out some drops from a medicine-bottle on a chair by the bed and, after swallowing them, and wrapping her head in a piece of yellow flannel, had lain down with her face turned away. Ethan undressed hurriedly and blew out the light so that he should not see her when he took his place at her side. As he lay there he could hear Mattie moving about in her room, and her candle, sending its small ray across the landing, drew a scarcely perceptible line of light under his door. He kept his eyes fixed on the light till it vanished. Then the room grew perfectly black, and not a sound was audible but Zeena's asthmatic breathing. Ethan felt confusedly that there were many things he ought to think about but through his tingling veins and tired brain only one sensation throbbed: the warmth of Mattie's shoulder against his. Why had he not kissed her when he held her there? A few hours earlier he would not have asked himself the question. Even a few minutes earlier, when they had stood alone outside the house, he would not have dared to think of kissing her. But since he had seen her lips in the lamplight he felt that they were his.

Now, in the bright morning air, her face was still before him. It was part of the sun's red and of the pure glitter on the snow. How the girl had changed since she had come to Starkfield! He remembered what a colourless slip of a thing she had looked the day he had met her at the station. And all the first winter, how she had shivered with cold when the northerly gales shook the thin clapboards and the snow beat like hail against the loose-hung windows!

He had been afraid that she would hate the hard life, the cold and loneliness; but not a sign of discontent escaped her. Zeena took the view that Mattie was bound to make the best of Starkfield since she hadn't any other place to go to; but this did not strike Ethan as conclusive. Zeena, at any rate, did not apply the principle in her own case.

He felt all the more sorry for the girl because misfortune had, in a sense, indentured her to them. Mattie Silver was the daughter of a cousin of Zenobia Frome's, who had inflamed his clan with mingled sentiments of envy and admiration by descending from the hills of Connecticut, where he had married a Stamford girl and succeeded to her father's thriving "drug" business. Unhappily Orin Silver, a man of far-reaching aims, had died too soon to prove that the end justifies the means. His accounts revealed merely what the means had been; and these were such that it was fortunate for his wife and daughter that his books were examined only after his impressive funeral. His wife died of the disclosure, and Mattie, at twenty, was left alone to make her way on the fifty dollars obtained from the sale of her piano. For this purpose her equipment, though varied, was inadequate. She could trim a hat, make molasses candy, recite "Curfew shall not ring to-night," and play "The Lost Chord" and a pot-pourri from "Carmen." When she tried to extend the field of her activities in the direction of stenography and book-keeping her health broke down, and six months on her feet behind the counter of a department store did not tend to restore it. Her nearest relations had been induced to place their savings in her father's hands, and though, after his death, they ungrudgingly acquitted themselves of the Christian duty of returning good for evil by giving his daughter all the advice at their disposal, they could hardly be expected to supplement it by material aid. But when Zenobia's doctor recommended her looking about for some one to help her with the house-work the clan instantly saw the chance of exacting a compensation from Mattie. Zenobia, though doubtful of the girl's efficiency, was tempted by the freedom to find fault without much risk of losing her; and so Mattie came to Starkfield.

Zenobia's fault-finding was of the silent kind, but not the less penetrating for that. During the first months Ethan alternately burned with the desire to see Mattie defy her and trembled with fear of the result. Then the situation grew less strained. The pure air, and the long summer hours in the open, gave back life and elasticity to Mattie, and Zeena, with more leisure to devote to her complex ailments, grew less watchful of the girl's omissions; so that Ethan, struggling on under the burden of his barren farm and failing saw-mill, could at least imagine that peace reigned in his house.

There was really, even now, no tangible evidence to the contrary; but since the previous night a vague dread had hung on his sky-line. It was formed of Zeena's obstinate silence, of Mattie's sudden look of warning, of the memory of just such fleeting imperceptible signs as those which told him, on certain stainless mornings, that before night there would be rain.

His dread was so strong that, man-like, he sought to postpone certainty. The hauling was not over till mid-day, and as the lumber was to be delivered to Andrew Hale, the Starkfield builder, it was really easier for Ethan to send Jotham Powell, the hired man, back to the farm on foot, and drive the load down to the village himself. He had scrambled up on the logs, and was sitting astride of them, close over his shaggy grays, when, coming between him and their steaming necks, he had a vision of the warning look that Mattie had given him the night before.

"If there's going to be any trouble I want to be there," was his vague reflection, as he threw to Jotham the unexpected order to unhitch the team and lead them back to the barn.

It was a slow trudge home through the heavy fields, and when the two men entered the kitchen Mattie was lifting the coffee from the stove and Zeena was already at the table. Her husband stopped short at sight of her. Instead of her usual calico wrapper and knitted shawl she wore her best dress of brown merino, and above her thin strands of hair, which still preserved the tight undulations of the crimping-pins, rose a hard perpendicular bonnet, as to which Ethan's clearest notion was that he had to pay five dollars for it at the Bettsbridge Emporium. On the floor beside her stood his old valise and a bandbox wrapped in newspapers.

"Why, where are you going, Zeena?" he exclaimed.

"I've got my shooting pains so bad that I'm going over to Bettsbridge to spend the night with Aunt Martha Pierce and see that new doctor," she answered in a matter-of-fact tone, as if she had said she was going into the store-room to take a look at the preserves, or up to the attic to go over the blankets.

In spite of her sedentary habits such abrupt decisions were not without precedent in Zeena's history. Twice or thrice before she had suddenly packed Ethan's valise and started off to Bettsbridge, or even Springfield, to seek the advice of some new doctor, and her husband had grown to dread these expeditions because of their cost. Zeena always came back laden with expensive remedies, and her last visit to Springfield had been commemorated by her paying twenty dollars for an electric battery of which she had never been able to learn the use. But for the moment his sense of relief was so great as to preclude all other feelings. He had now no doubt that Zeena had spoken the truth in saying, the night before, that she had sat up because she felt "too mean" to sleep: her abrupt resolve to seek medical advice showed that, as usual, she was wholly absorbed in her health.

As if expecting a protest, she continued plaintively; "If you're too busy with the hauling I presume you can let Jotham Powell drive me over with the sorrel in time to ketch the train at the Flats."

Her husband hardly heard what she was saying. During the winter months there was no stage between Starkfield and Bettsbridge, and the trains which stopped at Corbury Flats were slow and infrequent. A rapid calculation showed Ethan that Zeena could not be back at the farm before the following evening. . . .

"If I'd supposed you'd 'a' made any objection to Jotham Powell's driving me over—" she began again, as though his silence had implied refusal. On the brink of departure she was always seized with a flux of words. "All I know is," she continued, "I can't go on the way I am much longer. The pains are clear away down to my ankles now, or I'd 'a' walked in to Starkfield on my own feet, sooner'n put you out, and ask Michael Eady to let me ride over on his wagon to the Flats, when he sends to meet the train that brings his groceries. I'd 'a' had two hours to wait in the station, but I'd sooner 'a' done it, even with this cold, than to have you say——"

"Of course Jotham'll drive you over," Ethan roused himself to answer. He became suddenly conscious that he was looking at Mattie while Zeena talked to him, and with an effort he turned his eyes to his wife. She sat opposite the window, and the pale light reflected from the banks of snow made her face look more than usually drawn and bloodless, sharpened the three parallel creases between ear and cheek, and drew querulous lines from her thin nose to the corners of her mouth. Though she was but seven years her husband's senior, and he was only twenty-eight, she was already an old woman.

Ethan tried to say something befitting the occasion, but there was only one thought in his mind: the fact that, for the first time since Mattie had come to live with them, Zeena was to be away for a night. He wondered if the girl were thinking of it too. . . .

He knew that Zeena must be wondering why he did not offer to drive her to the Flats and let Jotham Powell take the lumber to Starkfield, and at first he could not think of a pretext for not doing so; then he said: "I'd take you over myself, only I've got to collect the cash for the lumber."

As soon as the words were spoken he regretted them, not only because they were untrue—there being no prospect of his receiving cash payment from Hale—but also because he knew from experience the imprudence of letting Zeena think he was in funds on the eve of one of her therapeutic excursions. At the moment, however, his one desire was to avoid the long drive with her behind the ancient sorrel who never went out of a walk.

Zeena made no reply: she did not seem to hear what he had said. She had already pushed her plate aside, and was measuring out a draught from a large bottle at her elbow.

"It ain't done me a speck of good, but I guess I might as well use it up," she remarked; adding, as she pushed the empty bottle toward Mattie: "If you can get the taste out it'll do for pickles."

IV

As soon as his wife had driven off Ethan took his coat and cap from the peg. Mattie was washing up the dishes, humming one of the dance tunes of the night before. He said "So long, Matt," and she answered gaily "So long, Ethan"; and that was all.

It was warm and bright in the kitchen. The sun slanted through the south window on the girl's moving figure, on the cat dozing in a chair, and on the geraniums brought in from the door-way, where Ethan had planted them in the summer to "make a garden" for Mattie. He would have liked to linger on, watching her tidy up and then settle down to her sewing; but he wanted still more to get the hauling done and be back at the farm before night.

All the way down to the village he continued to think of his return to Mattie. The kitchen was a poor place, not "spruce" and shining as his mother had kept it in his boyhood; but it was surprising what a homelike look the mere fact of Zeena's absence gave it. And he pictured, what it would be like that evening, when he and Mattie were there after supper. For the first time they would be alone together indoors, and they would sit there, one on each side of the stove, like a married couple, he in his stocking feet and smoking his pipe, she laughing and talking in that funny way she had which was always as new to him as if he had never heard her before.

The sweetness of the picture, and the relief of knowing that his fears of "trouble" with Zeena were unfounded, sent up his spirits with a rush, and he, who was usually so silent, whistled and sang aloud as he drove through the snowy fields. There was in him a slumbering spark of sociability which the long Starkfield winters had not yet extinguished. By nature grave and inarticulate, he admired recklessness and gaiety in others and was warmed to the marrow by friendly human intercourse. At Worcester, though he had the name of keeping to himself and not being much of a hand at a good time, he had secretly gloried in being clapped on the back and hailed as "Old Ethe" or "Old Stiff"; and the cessation of such familiarities had increased the chill of his return to Starkfield.

There the silence had deepened about him year by year. Left alone, after his father's accident, to carry the burden of farm and mill, he had had no time for convivial loiterings in the village; and when his mother fell ill the loneliness of the house grew more oppressive than that of the fields. His mother had been a talker in her day, but after her "trouble" the sound of her voice was seldom heard, though she had not lost the power of speech. Sometimes, in the long winter evenings, when in desperation her son asked her why she didn't "say something," she would lift a finger and answer: "Because I'm listening"; and on stormy nights, when the loud wind was about the house, she would complain, if he spoke to her: "They're talking so out there that I can't hear you."

It was only when she drew toward her last illness, and his cousin Zenobia Pierce came over from the next village to help him nurse her, that human speech was heard again in the house. After the mortal silence of his long imprisonment Zeena's volubility was music in his ears. He felt that he might have "gone like his mother" if the sound of a new voice had not come to steady him. Zeena seemed to understand his case at a glance. She laughed at him for not knowing the simplest sick-bed duties and told him to "go right along out" and leave her to see to things. The mere fact of obeying her orders, of feeling free to go about his business again and talk with other men, restored his shaken balance and magnified his sense of what he owed her. Her efficiency shamed and dazzled him. She seemed to possess by instinct all the household wisdom that his long apprenticeship had not instilled in him. When the end came it was she who had to tell him to hitch up and go for the undertaker, and she thought it "funny" that he had not settled beforehand who was to have his mother's clothes and the sewing-machine. After the funeral, when he saw her preparing to go away, he was seized with an unreasoning dread of being left alone on the farm; and before he knew what he was doing he had asked her to stay there with him. He had often thought since that it would not have happened if his mother had died in spring instead of winter. . . .

When they married it was agreed that, as soon as he could straighten out the difficulties resulting from Mrs. Frome's long illness, they would sell the farm and saw-mill and try their luck in a large town. Ethan's love of nature did not take the form of a taste for agriculture. He had always wanted to be an engineer, and to live in towns, where there were lectures and big libraries and "fellows doing things." A slight engineering job in Florida, put in his way during his period of study at Worcester, increased his faith in his ability as well as his eagerness to see the world; and he felt sure that, with a "smart" wife like Zeena, it would not be long before he had made himself a place in it.

Zeena's native village was slightly larger and nearer to the railway than Starkfield, and she had let her husband see from the first that life on an isolated farm was not what she had expected when she married. But purchasers were slow in coming, and while he waited for them Ethan learned the impossibility of transplanting her. She chose to look down on Starkfield, but she could not have lived in a place which looked down on her. Even Bettsbridge or Shadd's Falls would not have been sufficiently aware of her, and in the greater cities which attracted Ethan she would have suffered a complete loss of identity. And within a year of their marriage she developed the "sickliness" which had since made her notable even in a community rich in pathological instances. When she came to take care of his mother she had seemed to Ethan like the very genius of health, but he soon saw that her skill as a nurse had been acquired by the absorbed observation of her own symptoms.

Then she too fell silent. Perhaps it was the inevitable effect of life on the farm, or perhaps, as she sometimes said, it was because Ethan "never listened." The charge was not wholly unfounded. When she spoke it was only to complain, and to complain of things not in his power to remedy; and to check a tendency to impatient retort he had first formed the habit of not answering her, and finally of thinking of other things while she talked. Of late, however, since he had had reasons for observing her more closely, her silence had begun to trouble him. He recalled his mother's growing taciturnity, and wondered if Zeena were also turning "queer." Women did, he knew. Zeena, who had at her fingers' ends the pathological chart of the whole region, had cited many cases of the kind while she was nursing his mother; and he himself knew of certain lonely farm-houses in the neighbourhood where stricken creatures pined, and of others where sudden tragedy had come of their presence. At times, looking at Zeena's shut face, he felt the chill of such forebodings. At other times her silence seemed deliberately assumed to conceal far-reaching intentions, mysterious conclusions drawn from suspicions and resentments impossible to guess. That supposition was even more disturbing than the other; and it was the one which had come to him the night before, when he had seen her standing in the kitchen door.

Now her departure for Bettsbridge had once more eased his mind, and all his thoughts were on the prospect of his evening with Mattie. Only one thing weighed on him, and that was his having told Zeena that he was to receive cash for the lumber. He foresaw so clearly the consequence of this imprudence that with considerable reluctance he decided to ask Andrew Hale for a small advance on his load.

When Ethan drove into Hale's yard the builder was just getting out of his sleigh.

"Hello, Ethe!" he said. "This comes handy."

Andrew Hale was a ruddy man with a big gray moustache and a stubbly double-chin unconstrained by a collar; but his scrupulously clean shirt was always fastened by a small diamond stud. This display of opulence was misleading, for though he did a fairly good business it was known that his easy-going habits and the demands of his large family frequently kept him what Starkfield called "behind." He was an old friend of Ethan's family, and his house one of the few to which Zeena occasionally went, drawn there by the fact that Mrs. Hale, in her youth, had done more "doctoring" than any other woman in Starkfield, and was still a recognized authority on symptoms and treatment.

Hale went up to the grays and patted their sweating flanks.

"Well, sir," he said, "you keep them two as if they was pets."

Ethan set about unloading the logs and when he had finished his job he pushed open the glazed door of the shed which the builder used as his office. Hale sat with his feet up on the stove, his back propped against a battered desk strewn with papers: the place, like the man, was warm, genial and untidy.

"Sit right down and thaw out," he greeted Ethan.

The latter did not know how to begin, but at length he managed to bring out his request for an advance of fifty dollars. The blood rushed to his thin skin under the sting of Hale's astonishment. It was the builder's custom to pay at the end of three months, and there was no precedent between the two men for a cash settlement.

Ethan felt that if he had pleaded an urgent need Hale might have made shift to pay him; but pride, and an instinctive prudence, kept him from resorting to this argument. After his father's death it had taken time to get his head above water, and he did not want Andrew Hale, or any one else in Starkfield, to think he was going under again. Besides, he hated lying; if he wanted the money he wanted it, and it was nobody's business to ask why. He therefore made his demand with the awkwardness of a proud man who will not admit to himself that he is stooping; and he was not much surprised at Hale's refusal.

The builder refused genially, as he did everything else: he treated the matter as something in the nature of a practical joke, and wanted to know if Ethan meditated buying a grand piano or adding a "cupolo" to his house; offering, in the latter case, to give his services free of cost.

Ethan's arts were soon exhausted, and after an embarrassed pause he wished Hale good day and opened the door of the office. As he passed out the builder suddenly called after him: "See here—you ain't in a tight place, are you?"

"Not a bit," Ethan's pride retorted before his reason had time to intervene.

"Well, that's good! Because I *am,* a shade. Fact is, I was going to ask you to give me a little extra time on that payment. Business is pretty slack, to begin with, and then I'm fixing up a little house for Ned and Ruth when they're married. I'm glad to do it for 'em, but it costs." His look appealed to Ethan for sympathy. "The young people like things nice. You know how it is yourself: it's not so long ago since you fixed up your own place for Zeena."

Ethan left the grays in Hale's stable and went about some other business in the village. As he walked away the builder's last phrase lingered in his ears, and he reflected grimly that his seven years with Zeena seemed to Starkfield "not so long."

The afternoon was drawing to an end, and here and there a lighted pane spangled the cold gray dusk and made the snow look whiter. The bitter weather had driven every one indoors and Ethan had the long rural street to himself. Suddenly he heard the brisk play of sleigh-bells and a cutter passed him, drawn by a free-going horse. Ethan recognised Michael Eady's roan colt, and young Denis Eady, in a handsome new fur cap, leaned forward and waved a greeting. "Hello, Ethe!" he shouted and spun on.

The cutter was going in the direction of the Frome farm, and Ethan's heart contracted as he listened to the dwindling bells. What more likely than that Denis Eady had heard of Zeena's departure for Betts-bridge, and was profiting by the opportunity to spend an hour with Mattie? Ethan was ashamed of the storm of jealousy in his breast. It seemed unworthy of the girl that his thoughts of her should be so violent.

He walked on to the church corner and entered the shade of the Varnum spruces, where he had stood with her the night before. As he passed into their gloom he saw an indistinct outline just ahead of him. At his approach it melted for an instant into two separate shapes and then conjoined again, and he heard a kiss, and a half-laughing "Oh!" provoked by the discovery of his presence. Again the outline hastily disunited and the Varnum gate slammed on one half while the other hurried on ahead of them. Ethan smiled at the discomfiture he had caused. What did it matter to Ned Hale and Ruth Varnum if they were caught kissing each other? Everybody in Starkfield knew they were engaged. It pleased Ethan to have surprised a pair of lovers on the spot where he and Mattie had stood with such a thirst for each other in their hearts; but he felt a pang at the thought that these two need not hide their happiness.

He fetched the grays from Hale's stable and started on his long climb back to the farm. The cold was less sharp than earlier in the day and a thick fleecy sky threatened snow for the morrow. Here and there a star pricked through, showing behind it a deep well of blue. In an hour or two the moon would push up over the ridge behind the farm, burn a gold-edged rent in the clouds, and then be swallowed by them. A mournful peace hung on the fields, as though they felt the relaxing grasp of the cold and stretched themselves in their long winter sleep.

Ethan's ears were alert for the jingle of sleigh-bells, but not a sound broke the silence of the lonely road. As he drew near the farm he saw, through the thin screen of larches at the gate, a light twinkling in the house above him. "She's up in her room," he said to himself, "fixing herself up for supper"; and he remembered Zeena's sarcastic stare when Mattie, on the evening of her arrival, had come down to supper with smoothed hair and a ribbon at her neck.

He passed by the graves on the knoll and turned his head to glance at one of the older headstones, which had interested him deeply as a boy because it bore his name.

SACRED TO THE MEMORY OF
ETHAN FROME AND ENDURANCE HIS WIFE,
WHO DWELLED TOGETHER IN PEACE
FOR FIFTY YEARS.

He used to think that fifty years sounded like a long time to live together; but now it seemed to him that they might pass in a flash. Then, with a sudden dart of irony, he wondered if, when their turn came, the same epitaph would be written over him and Zeena.

He opened the barn-door and craned his head into the obscurity, half-fearing to discover Denis Eady's roan colt in the stall beside the sorrel. But the old horse was there alone, mumbling his crib with toothless jaws, and Ethan whistled cheerfully while he bedded down the grays and shook an extra measure of oats into their mangers. His was not a tuneful throat, but harsh melodies burst from it as he locked the barn and sprang up the hill to the house. He reached the kitchen-porch and turned the door-handle; but the door did not yield to his touch.

Startled at finding it locked he rattled the handle violently; then he reflected that Mattie was alone and that it was natural she should barricade herself at nightfall. He stood in the darkness expecting to hear her step. It did not come, and after vainly strain-ing his ears he called out in a voice that shook with joy: "Hello, Matt!"

Silence answered; but in a minute or two he caught a sound on the stairs and saw a line of light above the door-frame, as he had seen it the night before. So strange was the precision with which the incidents of the previous evening were repeating themselves that he half expected, when he heard the key turn, to see his wife before him on the threshold; but the door opened, and Mattie faced him.

She stood just as Zeena had stood, a lifted lamp in her hand, against the black background of the kitchen. She held the light at the same level, and it drew out with the same distinctness her slim young throat and the brown wrist no bigger than a child's. Then, striking upward, it threw a lustrous fleck on her lips, edged her eyes with velvet shade, and laid a milky whiteness above the black curve of her brows.

She wore her usual dress of darkish stuff, and there was no bow at her neck; but through her hair she had run a streak of crimson ribbon. This tribute to the unusual transformed and glorified her. She seemed to Ethan taller, fuller, more womanly in shape and motion. She stood aside, smiling silently, while he entered, and then moved away from him with something soft and flowing in her gait. She set the lamp on the table, and he saw that it was carefully laid for supper, with fresh dough-nuts, stewed blueberries and his favourite pickles in a dish of gay red glass. A bright fire glowed in the stove and the cat lay stretched before it, watching the table with a drowsy eye.

Ethan was suffocated with the sense of well-being. He went out into the passage to hang up his coat and pull off his wet boots. When he came back Mattie had set the teapot on the table and the cat was rubbing itself persuasively against her ankles.

"Why, Puss! I nearly tripped over you," she cried, the laughter sparkling through her lashes.

Again Ethan felt a sudden twinge of jealousy. Could it be his coming that gave her such a kindled face?

"Well, Matt, any visitors?" he threw off, stooping down carelessly to examine the fastening of the stove.

She nodded and laughed "Yes, one," and he felt a blackness settling on his brows.

"Who was that?" he questioned, raising himself up to slant a glance at her beneath his scowl.

Her eyes danced with malice. "Why, Jotham Powell. He came in after he got back, and asked for a drop of coffee before he went down home."

The blackness lifted and light flooded Ethan's brain. "That's all? Well, I hope you made out to let him have it." And after a pause he felt it right to add: "I suppose he got Zeena over to the Flats all right?"

"Oh, yes; in plenty of time."

The name threw a chill between them, and they stood a moment looking sideways at each other before Mattie said with a shy laugh: "I guess it's about time for supper."

They drew their seats up to the table, and the cat, unbidden, jumped between them into Zeena's empty chair. "Oh, Puss!" said Mattie, and they laughed again.

Ethan, a moment earlier, had felt himself on the brink of eloquence; but the mention of Zeena had paralysed him. Mattie seemed to feel the contagion of his embarrassment, and sat with downcast lids, sipping her tea, while he feigned an insatiable appetite for dough-nuts and sweet pickles. At last, after casting about for an effective opening, he took a long gulp of tea, cleared his throat, and said: "Looks as if there'd be more snow."

She feigned great interest. "Is that so? Do you suppose it'll interfere with Zeena's getting back?" She flushed red as the question escaped her, and hastily set down the cup she was lifting.

Ethan reached over for another helping of pickles. "You never can tell, this time of year, it drifts so bad on the Flats." The name had benumbed him again, and once more he felt as if Zeena were in the room between them.

"Oh, Puss, you're too greedy!" Mattie cried.

The cat, unnoticed, had crept up on muffled paws from Zeena's seat to the table, and was stealthily elongating its body in the direction of the milk-jug, which stood between Ethan and Mattie. The two leaned forward at the same moment and their hands met on the handle of the jug. Mattie's hand was underneath, and Ethan kept his clasped on it a moment longer than was necessary. The cat, profiting by this unusual demonstration, tried to effect an unnoticed retreat, and in doing so backed into the pickle-dish, which fell to the floor with a crash.

Mattie, in an instant, had sprung from her chair and was down on her knees by the fragments.

"Oh, Ethan, Ethan—it's all to pieces! What will Zeena say?"

But this time his courage was up. "Well, she'll have to say it to the cat, any way!" he rejoined with a laugh, kneeling down at Mattie's side to scrape up the swimming pickles.

She lifted stricken eyes to him. "Yes, but, you see, she never meant it should be used, not even when there was company; and I had to get up on the step-ladder to reach it down from the top shelf of the china-closet, where she keeps it with all her best

things, and of course she'll want to know why I did it——"

The case was so serious that it called forth all of Ethan's latent resolution.

"She needn't know anything about it if you keep quiet. I'll get another just like it to-morrow. Where did it come from? I'll go to Shadd's Falls for it if I have to!"

"Oh, you'll never get another even there! It was a wedding present—don't you remember? It came all the way from Philadelphia, from Zeena's aunt that married the minister. That's why she wouldn't ever use it. Oh, Ethan, Ethan, what in the world shall I do?"

She began to cry, and he felt as if every one of her tears were pouring over him like burning lead. "Don't, Matt, don't—oh, *don't*" he implored her.

She struggled to her feet, and he rose and followed her helplessly while she spread out the pieces of glass on the kitchen dresser. It seemed to him as if the shattered fragments of their evening lay there.

"Here, give them to me," he said in a voice of sudden authority.

She drew aside, instinctively obeying his tone. "Oh, Ethan, what are you going to do?"

Without reply he gathered the pieces of glass into his broad palm and walked out of the kitchen to the passage. There he lit candle-end, opened the china-closet, and, reaching his long arm up to the highest shelf, laid the pieces together with such accuracy of touch that a close inspection convinced him of the impossibility of detecting from below that the dish was broken. If he glued it together the next morning months might elapse before his wife noticed what had happened, and meanwhile he might after all be able to match the dish at Shadd's Falls or Bettsbridge. Having satisfied himself that there was no risk of immediate discovery he went back to the kitchen with a lighter step, and found Mattie disconsolately removing the last scraps of pickle from the floor.

"It's all right, Matt. Come back and finish supper," he commanded her.

Completely reassured, she shone on him through tear-hung lashes, and his soul swelled with pride as he saw how his tone subdued her. She did not even ask what he had done. Except when he was steering a big log down the mountain to his mill he had never known such a thrilling sense of mastery.

V

They finished supper, and while Mattie cleared the table Ethan went to look at the cows and then took a last turn about the house. The earth lay dark under a muffled sky and the air was so still that now and then he heard a lump of snow come thumping down from a tree far off on the edge of the wood-lot.

When he returned to the kitchen Mattie had pushed up his chair to the stove and seated herself near the lamp with a bit of sewing. The scene was just as he had dreamed of it that morning. He sat down, drew his pipe from his pocket and stretched his feet to the glow. His hard day's work in the keen air made him feel at once lazy and light of mood, and he had a confused sense of being in another world, where all was warmth and harmony and time could bring no change. The only drawback to his complete well-being was the fact that he could not see Mattie from where he sat; but he was too indolent to move and after a moment he said: "Come over here and sit by the stove."

Zeena's empty rocking-chair stood facing him. Mattie rose obediently, and seated herself in it. As her young brown head detached itself against the patch-work cushion that habitually framed his wife's gaunt countenance, Ethan had a momentary shock. It was almost as if the other face, the face of the superseded woman, had obliterated that of the intruder. After a moment Mattie seemed to be affected by the same sense of constraint. She changed her position, leaning forward to bend her head above her work, so that he saw only the fore-shortened tip of her nose and the streak of red in her hair; then she slipped to her feet, saying "I can't see to sew," and went back to her chair by the lamp.

Ethan made a pretext of getting up to replenish the stove, and when he returned to his seat he pushed it sideways that he might get a view of her profile and of the lamplight falling on her hands. The cat, who had been a puzzled observer of these unusual movements, jumped up into Zeena's chair, rolled itself into a ball, and lay watching them with narrowed eyes.

Deep quiet sank on the room. The clock ticked above the dresser, a piece of charred wood fell now and then in the stove, and the faint sharp scent of the geraniums mingled with the odour of Ethan's smoke, which began to throw a blue haze about the lamp and to hang its greyish cobwebs in the shadowy corners of the room.

All constraint had vanished between the two, and they began to talk easily and simply. They spoke of everyday things, of the prospect of snow, of the next church sociable, of the loves and quarrels of Starkfield. The commonplace nature of what they said produced in Ethan an illusion of long-established intimacy which no outburst of emotion could have given, and he set his imagination adrift on the fiction that they had always spent their evenings thus and would always go on doing so . . .

"This is the night we were to have gone coasting, Matt," he said at length, with the rich sense, as he spoke, that they could go on any other night they chose, since they had all time before them.

She smiled back at him. "I guess you forgot!"

"No, I didn't forget; but it's as dark as Egypt outdoors. We might go to-morrow if there's a moon."

She laughed with pleasure, her head tilted back, the lamplight sparkling on her lips and teeth. "That would be lovely, Ethan!"

He kept his eyes fixed on her, marvelling at the way her face changed with each turn of their talk, like a wheat-field under a summer breeze. It was intoxicating to find such magic in his clumsy words, and he longed to try new ways of using it.

"Would you be scared to go down the Corbury road with me on a night like this?" he asked.

Her cheeks burned redder. "I ain't any more scared than you are!"

"Well, *I'd* be scared, then; I wouldn't do it. That's an ugly corner down by the big elm. If a fellow didn't keep his eyes open he'd go plumb into it." He luxuriated in the sense of protection and authority which his words conveyed. To prolong and intensify the feeling he added: "I guess we're well enough here."

She let her lids sink slowly, in the way he loved. "Yes, we're well enough here," she sighed.

Her tone was so sweet that he took the pipe from his mouth and drew his chair up to the table. Leaning forward, he touched the farther end of the strip of brown stuff that she was hemming. "Say, Matt," he began with a smile, "what do you think I saw under the Varnum spruces, coming along home just now? I saw a friend of yours getting kissed."

The words had been on his tongue all the evening, but now that he had spoken them they struck him as inexpressibly vulgar and out of place.

Mattie blushed to the roots of her hair and pulled her needle rapidly twice or thrice through her work, insensibly drawing the end of it away from him. "I suppose it was Ruth and Ned," she said in a low voice, as though he had suddenly touched on something grave.

Ethan had imagined that his allusion might open the way to the accepted pleasantries, and these perhaps in turn to a harmless caress, if only a mere touch on her hand. But now he felt as if her blush had set a flaming guard about her. He supposed it was his natural awkwardness that made him feel so. He knew that most young men made nothing at all of giving a pretty girl a kiss, and he remembered that the night before, when he had put his arm about

Mattie, she had not resisted. But that had been out-of-doors, under the open irresponsible night. Now, in the warm lamplit room, with all its ancient implications of conformity and order, she seemed infinitely farther away from him and more unapproachable.

To ease his constraint he said: "I suppose they'll be setting a date before long."

"Yes. I shouldn't wonder if they got married some time along in the summer." She pronounced the word *married* as if her voice caressed it. It seemed a rustling covert leading to enchanted glades. A pang shot through Ethan, and he said, twisting away from her in his chair: "It'll be your turn next, I wouldn't wonder."

She laughed a little uncertainly. "Why do you keep on saying that?"

He echoed her laugh. "I guess I do it to get used to the idea."

He drew up to the table again and she sewed on in silence, with dropped lashes, while he sat in fascinated contemplation of the way in which her hands went up and down above the strip of stuff, just as he had seen a pair of birds make short perpendicular flights over a nest they were building. At length, without turning her head or lifting her lids, she said in a low tone: "It's not because you think Zeena's got anything against me, is it?"

His former dread started up full-armed at the suggestion. "Why, what do you mean?" he stammered.

She raised distressed eyes to his, her work dropping on the table between them. "I don't know. I thought last night she seemed to have."

"I'd like to know what," he growled.

"Nobody can tell with Zeena." It was the first time they had ever spoken so openly of her attitude toward Mattie, and the repetition of the name seemed to carry it to the farther corners of the room and send it back to them in long repercussions of sound. Mattie waited, as if to give the echo time to drop, and then went on: "She hasn't said anything to *you?*"

He shook his head. "No, not a word."

She tossed the hair back from her forehead with a laugh. "I guess I'm just nervous, then. I'm not going to think about it any more."

"Oh, no—don't let's think about it, Matt!"

The sudden heat of his tone made her colour mount again, not with a rush, but gradually, delicately, like the reflection of a thought stealing slowly across her heart. She sat silent, her hands clasped on her work, and it seemed to him that a warm current flowed toward him along the strip of stuff that still lay unrolled between them. Cautiously he slid his hand palm-downward along the table till his fingertips touched the end of the stuff. A faint vibration of her lashes seemed to show that she was aware of his

gesture, and that it had sent a counter-current back to her; and she let her hands lie motionless on the other end of the strip.

As they sat thus he heard a sound behind him and turned his head. The cat had jumped from Zeena's chair to dart at a mouse in the wainscot, and as a result of the sudden movement the empty chair had set up a spectral rocking.

"She'll be rocking in it herself this time to-morrow," Ethan thought. "I've been in a dream, and this is the only evening we'll ever have together." The return to reality was as painful as the return to consciousness after taking an anæsthetic. His body and brain ached with indescribable weariness, and he could think of nothing to say or to do that should arrest the mad flight of the moments.

His alteration of mood seemed to have communicated itself to Mattie. She looked up at him languidly, as though her lids were weighted with sleep and it cost her an effort to raise them. Her glance fell on his hand, which now completely covered the end of her work and grasped it as if it were a part of herself. He saw a scarcely perceptible tremor cross her face, and without knowing what he did he stooped his head and kissed the bit of stuff in his hold. As his lips rested on it he felt it glide slowly from beneath them, and saw that Mattie had risen and was silently rolling up her work. She fastened it with a pin, and then, finding her thimble and scissors, put them with the roll of stuff into the box covered with fancy paper which he had once brought to her from Bettsbridge.

He stood up also, looking vaguely about the room. The clock above the dresser struck eleven.

"Is the fire all right?" she asked in a low voice.

He opened the door of the stove and poked aimlessly at the embers. When he raised himself again he saw that she was dragging toward the stove the old soapbox lined with carpet in which the cat made its bed. Then she recrossed the floor and lifted two of the geranium pots in her arms, moving them away from the cold window. He followed her and brought the other geraniums, the hyacinth bulbs in a cracked custard bowl and the German ivy trained over an old croquet hoop.

When these nightly duties were performed there was nothing left to do but to bring in the tin candlestick from the passage, light the candle and blow out the lamp. Ethan put the candlestick in Mattie's hand and she went out of the kitchen ahead of him, the light that she carried before her making her dark hair look like a drift of mist on the moon.

"Good-night, Matt," he said as she put her foot on the first step of the stairs.

She turned and looked at him a moment. "Good-night, Ethan," she answered, and went up.

When the door of her room had closed on her he remembered that he had not even touched her hand.

VI

The next morning at breakfast Jotham Powell was between them, and Ethan tried to hide his joy under an air of exaggerated indifference, lounging back in his chair to throw scraps to the cat, growling at the weather, and not so much as offering to help Mattie when she rose to clear away the dishes.

He did not know why he was so irrationally happy, for nothing was changed in his life or hers. He had not even touched the tip of her fingers or looked her full in the eyes. But their evening together had given him a vision of what life at her side might be, and he was glad now that he had done nothing to trouble the sweetness of the picture. He had a fancy that she knew what had restrained him . . .

There was a last load of lumber to be hauled to the village, and Jotham Powell—who did not work regularly for Ethan in winter—had "come round" to help with the job. But a wet snow, melting to sleet, had fallen in the night and turned the roads to glass. There was more wet in the air and it seemed likely to both men that the weather would "milden" toward afternoon and make the going safer. Ethan therefore proposed to his assistant that they should load the sledge at the wood-lot, as they had done on the previous morning, and put off the "teaming" to Starkfield till later in the day. This plan had the advantage of enabling him to send Jotham to the Flats after dinner to meet Zenobia, while he himself took the lumber down to the village.

He told Jotham to go out and harness up the grays, and for a moment he and Mattie had the kitchen to themselves. She had plunged the breakfast dishes into a tin dish-pan and was bending above it with her slim arms bared to the elbow, the steam from the hot water beading her forehead and tightening her rough hair into little brown rings like the tendrils on the traveller's joy.

Ethan stood looking at her, his heart in his throat. He wanted to say: "We shall never be alone again like this." Instead, he reached down his tobacco-pouch from a shelf of the dresser, put it into his pocket and said: "I guess I can make out to be home for dinner."

She answered "All right, Ethan," and he heard her singing over the dishes as he went.

As soon as the sledge was loaded he meant to send Jotham back to the farm and hurry on foot into the village to buy the glue for the pickle-dish. With ordinary luck he should have had time to carry out this plan; but everything went wrong from the start.

On the way over to the wood-lot one of the grays slipped on a glare of ice and cut his knee; and when they got him up again Jotham had to go back to the barn for a strip of rag to bind the cut. Then, when the loading finally began, a sleety rain was coming down once more, and the tree trunks were so slippery that it took twice as long as usual to lift them and get them in place on the sledge. It was what Jotham called a sour morning for work, and the horses, shivering and stamping under their wet blankets, seemed to like it as little as the men. It was long past the dinner-hour when the job was done, and Ethan had to give up going to the village because he wanted to lead the injured horse home and wash the cut himself.

He thought that by starting out again with the lumber as soon as he had finished his dinner he might get back to the farm with the glue before Jotham and the old sorrel had had time to fetch Zenobia from the Flats; but he knew the chance was a slight one. It turned on the state of the roads and on the possible lateness of the Bettsbridge train. He remembered afterward, with a grim flash of self-derision, what importance he had attached to the weighing of these probabilities . . .

As soon as dinner was over he set out again for the wood-lot, not daring to linger till Jotham Powell left. The hired man was still drying his wet feet at the stove, and Ethan could only give Mattie a quick look as he said beneath his breath: "I'll be back early."

He fancied that she nodded her comprehension; and with that scant solace he had to trudge off through the rain.

He had driven his load half-way to the village when Jotham Powell overtook him, urging the reluctant sorrel toward the Flats. "I'll have to hurry up to do it," Ethan mused, as the sleigh dropped down ahead of him over the dip of the school-house hill. He worked like ten at the unloading, and when it was over hastened on to Michael Eady's for the glue. Eady and his assistant were both "down street," and young Denis, who seldom deigned to take their place, was lounging by the stove with a knot of the golden youth of Starkfield. They hailed Ethan with ironic compliment and offers of conviviality; but no one knew where to find the glue. Ethan, consumed with the longing for a last moment alone with Mattie, hung about impatiently while Dennis made an ineffectual search in the obscurer corners of the store.

"Looks as if we were all sold out. But if you'll wait around till the old man comes along maybe he can put his hand on it."

"I'm obliged to you, but I'll try if I can get it down at Mrs. Homan's," Ethan answered, burning to be gone.

Denis's commercial instinct compelled him to aver on oath that what Eady's store could not produce would never be found at the widow Homan's; but Ethan, heedless of this boast, had already climbed to the sledge and was driving on to the rival establishment. Here, after considerable search, and sympathetic questions as to what he wanted it for, and whether ordinary flour paste wouldn't do as well if she couldn't find it, the widow Homan finally hunted down her solitary bottle of glue to its hiding-place in a medley of cough-lozenges and corset-laces.

"I hope Zeena ain't broken anything she sets store by," she called after him as he turned the grays toward home.

The fitful bursts of sleet had changed into a steady rain and the horses had heavy work even without a load behind them. Once or twice, hearing sleigh-bells, Ethan turned his head, fancying that Zeena and Jotham might overtake him; but the old sorrel was not in sight, and he set his face against the rain and urged on his ponderous pair.

The barn was empty when the horses turned into it and, after giving them the most perfunctory ministrations they had ever received from him, he strode up to the house and pushed open the kitchen door.

Mattie was there alone, as he had pictured her. She was bending over a pan on the stove; but at the sound of his step she turned with a start and sprang to him.

"See, here, Matt, I've got some stuff to mend the dish with! Let me get at it quick," he cried, waving the bottle in one hand while he put her lightly aside; but she did not seem to hear him.

"Oh, Ethan—Zeena's come," she said in a whisper, clutching his sleeve.

They stood and stared at each other, pale as culprits.

"But the sorrel's not in the barn!" Ethan stammered.

"Jotham Powell brought some goods over from the Flats for his wife, and he drove right on home with them," she explained.

He gazed blankly about the kitchen, which looked cold and squalid in the rainy winter twilight.

"How is she?" he asked, dropping his voice to Mattie's whisper.

She looked away from him uncertainly. "I don't know. She went right up to her room."

"She didn't say anything?"

"No."

Ethan let out his doubts in a low whistle and thrust the bottle back into his pocket. "Don't fret; I'll come down and mend it in the night," he said. He pulled on his wet coat again and went back to the barn to feed the grays.

While he was there Jotham Powell drove up with the sleigh, and when the horses had been attended to Ethan said to him: "You might as well come back up for a bite." He was not sorry to assure himself of Jotham's neutralising presence at the supper table, for Zeena was always "nervous" after a journey. But the hired man, though seldom loth to accept a meal not included in his wages, opened his stiff jaws to answer slowly: "I'm obliged to you, but I guess I'll go along back."

Ethan looked at him in surprise. "Better come up and dry off. Looks as if there'd be something hot for supper."

Jotham's facial muscles were unmoved by this appeal and, his vocabulary being limited, he merely repeated: "I guess I'll go along back."

To Ethan there was something vaguely ominous in this stolid rejection of free food and warmth, and he wondered what had happened on the drive to nerve Jotham to such stoicism. Perhaps Zeena had failed to see the new doctor or had not liked his counsels: Ethan knew that in such cases the first person she met was likely to be held responsible for her grievance.

When he re-entered the kitchen the lamp lit up the same scene of shining comfort as on the previous evening. The table had been as carefully laid, a clear fire glowed in the stove, the cat dozed in its warmth, and Mattie came forward carrying a plate of doughnuts.

She and Ethan looked at each other in silence; then she said, as she had said the night before: "I guess it's about time for supper."

VII

Ethan went out into the passage to hang up his wet garments. He listened for Zeena's step and, not hearing it, called her name up the stairs. She did not answer, and after a moment's hesitation he went up and opened her door. The room was almost dark, but in the obscurity he saw her sitting by the window, bolt upright, and knew by the rigidity of the outline projected against the pane that she had not taken off her travelling dress.

"Well, Zeena," he ventured from the threshold.

She did not move, and he continued: "Supper's about ready. Ain't you coming?"

She replied: "I don't feel as if I could touch a morsel."

It was the consecrated formula, and he expected it to be followed, as usual, by her rising and going down to supper. But she remained seated, and he could think of nothing more felicitous than: "I presume you're tired after the long ride."

Turning her head at this, she answered solemnly: "I'm a great deal sicker than you think."

Her words fell on his ear with a strange shock of wonder. He had often heard her pronounce them before—what if at last they were true?

He advanced a step or two into the dim room. "I hope that's not so, Zeena," he said.

She continued to gaze at him through the twilight with a mien of wan authority, as of one consciously singled out for a great fate. "I've got complications," she said.

Ethan knew the word for one of exceptional import. Almost everybody in the neighbourhood had "troubles," frankly localized and specified; but only the chosen had "complications." To have them was in itself a distinction, though it was also, in most cases, a death-warrant. People struggled on for years with "troubles," but they almost always succumbed to "complications."

Ethan's heart was jerking to and fro between two extremities of feeling, but for the moment compassion prevailed. His wife looked so hard and lonely, sitting there in the darkness with such thoughts.

"Is that what the new doctor told you?" he asked, instinctively lowering his voice.

"Yes. He says any regular doctor would want me to have an operation."

Ethan was aware that, in regard to the important question of surgical intervention, the female opinion of the neighbourhood was divided, some glorying in the prestige conferred by operations while others shunned them as indelicate. Ethan, from motives of economy, had always been glad that Zeena was of the latter faction.

In the agitation caused by the gravity of her announcement he sought a consolatory short cut. "What do you know about this doctor anyway? Nobody ever told you that before."

He saw his blunder before she could take it up; she wanted sympathy, not consolation.

"I didn't need to have anybody tell me I was losing ground every day. Everybody but you could see it. And everybody in Bettsbridge knows about Dr. Buck. He has his office in Worcester, and comes over once a fortnight to Shadd's Falls and Bettsbridge for consultations. Eliza Spears was wasting away with kidney trouble before she went to him, and now she's up and around, and singing in the choir."

"Well, I'm glad of that. You must do just what he tells you," Ethan answered sympathetically.

She was still looking at him. "I mean to," she said. He was struck by a new note in her voice. It was neither whining nor reproachful, but drily resolute.

"What does he want you should do?" he asked, with a mounting vision of fresh expenses.

"He wants I should have a hired girl. He says I oughtn't to have to do a single thing around the house."

"A hired girl?" Ethan stood transfixed.

"Yes. And Aunt Martha found me one right off. Everybody said I was lucky to get a girl to come away out here, and I agreed to give her a dollar extry to make sure. She'll be over to-morrow afternoon."

Wrath and dismay contended in Ethan. He had foreseen an immediate demand for money, but not a permanent drain on his scant resources. He no longer believed what Zeena had told him of the supposed seriousness of her state: he saw in her expedition to Bettsbridge only a plot hatched between herself and her Pierce relations to foist on him the cost of a servant; and for the moment wrath predominated.

"If you meant to engage a girl you ought to have told me before you started," he said.

"How could I tell you before I started? How did I know what Dr. Buck would say?"

"Oh, Dr. Buck—" Ethan's incredulity escaped in a short laugh. "Did Dr. Buck tell you how I was to pay her wages?"

Her voice rose furiously with his. "No, he didn't. For I'd 'a' been ashamed to tell *him* that you grudged me the money to get back my health, when I lost it nursing your own mother!"

"*You* lost your health nursing mother?"

"Yes; and my folks all told me at the time you couldn't do no less than marry me after——"

"Zeena!"

Through the obscurity which hid their faces their thoughts seemed to dart at each other like serpents shooting venom. Ethan was seized with horror of the scene and shame at his own share in it. It was as senseless and savage as a physical fight between two enemies in the darkness.

He turned to the shelf above the chimney, groped for matches and lit the one candle in the room. At first its weak flame made no impression on the shadows; then Zeena's face stood grimly out against the uncurtained pane, which had turned from gray to black.

It was the first scene of open anger between the couple in their sad seven years together, and Ethan felt as if he had lost an irretrievable advantage in descending to the level of recrimination. But the practical problem was there and had to be dealt with.

"You know I haven't got the money to pay for a girl, Zeena. You'll have to send her back: I can't do it."

"The doctor says it'll be my death if I go on slaving the way I've had to. He doesn't understand how I've stood it as long as I have."

"Slaving!—" He checked himself again. "You sha'n't lift a hand, if he says so. I'll do everything round the house myself——"

She broke in: "You're neglecting the farm enough already," and this being true, he found no answer, and left her time to add ironically: "Better send me over to the almshouse and done with it. . . . I guess there's been Fromes there afore now."

The taunt burned into him, but he let it pass. "I haven't got the money. That settles it."

There was a moment's pause in the struggle, as though the combatants were testing their weapons. Then Zeena said in a level voice: "I thought you were to get fifty dollars from Andrew Hale for that lumber."

"Andrew Hale never pays under three months." He had hardly spoken when he remembered the excuse he had made for not accompanying his wife to the station the day before; and the blood rose to his frowning brows.

"Why, you told me yesterday you'd fixed it up with him to pay cash down. You said that was why you couldn't drive me over to the Flats."

Ethan had no suppleness in deceiving. He had never before been convicted of a lie, and all the resources of evasion failed him. "I guess that was a misunderstanding," he stammered.

"You ain't got the money?"

"No."

"And you ain't going to get it?"

"No."

"Well, I couldn't know that when I engaged the girl, could I?"

"No." He paused to control his voice. "But you know it now. I'm sorry, but it can't be helped. You're a poor man's wife, Zeena; but I'll do the best I can for you."

For a while she sat motionless, as if reflecting, her arms stretched along the arms of her chair, her eyes fixed on vacancy. "Oh, I guess we'll make out," she said mildly.

The change in her tone reassured him. "Of course we will! There's a whole lot more I can do for you, and Mattie——"

Zeena, while he spoke, seemed to be following out some elaborate mental calculation. She emerged from it to say: "There'll be Mattie's board less, any-how——"

Ethan, supposing the discussion to be over, had turned to go down to supper. He stopped short, not grasping what he heard. "Mattie's board less—?" he began.

Zeena laughed. It was an odd unfamiliar sound—he did not remember ever having heard her laugh before.

"You didn't suppose I was going to keep two girls, did you? No wonder you were scared at the expense!"

He still had but a confused sense of what she was saying. From the beginning of the discussion he had instinctively avoided the mention of Mattie's name, fearing he hardly knew what: criticism, complaints, or vague allusions to the imminent probability of her marrying. But the thought of a definite rupture had never come to him, and even now could not lodge itself in his mind.

"I don't know what you mean," he said. "Mattie Silver's not a hired girl. She's your relation."

"She's a pauper that's hung onto us all after her father'd done his best to ruin us. I've kep' her here a whole year: it's somebody else's turn now."

As the shrill words shot out Ethan heard a tap on the door, which he had drawn shut when he turned back from the threshold.

"Ethan—Zeena!" Mattie's voice sounded gaily from the landing, "do you know what time it is? Supper's been ready half an hour."

Inside the room there was a moment's silence; then Zeena called out from her seat: "I'm not coming down to supper."

"Oh, I'm sorry! Aren't you well? Sha'n't I bring you up a bite of something?"

Ethan roused himself with an effort and opened the door. "Go along down, Matt. Zeena's just a little tired. I'm coming."

He heard her "All right!" and her quick step on the stairs; then he shut the door and turned back into the room. His wife's attitude was unchanged, her face inexorable, and he was seized with the despairing sense of his helplessness.

"You ain't going to do it, Zeena?"

"Do what?" she emitted between flattened lips.

"Send Mattie away—like this?"

"I never bargained to take her for life!"

He continued with rising vehemence: "You can't put her out of the house like a thief—a poor girl without friends or money. She's done her best for you and she's got no place to go to. You may forget she's your kin but everybody else'll remember it. If you do a thing like that what do you suppose folks'll say of you?"

Zeena waited a moment, as if giving him time to feel the full force of the contrast between his own excitement and her composure. Then she replied in the same smooth voice: "I know well enough what they say of my having kep' her here as long as I have."

Ethan's hand dropped from the door-knob, which he had held clenched since he had drawn the door shut on Mattie. His wife's retort was like a knife-cut across the sinews and he felt suddenly weak and powerless. He had meant to humble himself, to argue that Mattie's keep didn't cost much, after all, that he could make out to buy a stove and fix up a place in the attic for the hired girl—but Zeena's words revealed the peril of such pleadings.

"You mean to tell her she's got to go—at once?" he faltered out, in terror of letting his wife complete her sentence.

As if trying to make him see reason she replied impartially: "The girl will be over from Bettsbridge to-morrow, and I presume she's got to have somewheres to sleep."

Ethan looked at her with loathing. She was no longer the listless creature who had lived at his side in a state of sullen self-absorption, but a mysterious alien presence, an evil energy secreted from the long years of silent brooding. It was the sense of his helplessness that sharpened his antipathy. There had never been anything in her that one could appeal to; but as long as he could ignore and command he had remained indifferent. Now she had mastered him and he abhorred her. Mattie was her relation, not his: there were no means by which he could compel her to keep the girl under her roof. All the long misery of his baffled past, or his youth of failure, hardship and vain effort, rose up in his soul in bitterness and seemed to take shape before him in the woman who at every turn had barred his way. She had taken everything else from him; and now she meant to take the one thing that made up for all the others. For a moment such a flame of hate rose in him that it ran down his arm and clenched his fist against her. He took a wild step forward and then stopped.

"You're—you're not coming down?" he said in a bewildered voice.

"No. I guess I'll lay down on the bed a little while," she answered mildly; and he turned and walked out of the room.

In the kitchen Mattie was sitting by the stove, the cat curled up on her knees. She sprang to her feet as Ethan entered and carried the covered dish of meat-pie to the table.

"I hope Zeena isn't sick?" she asked.

"No."

She shone at him across the table. "Well, sit right down then. You must be starving." She uncovered the pie and pushed it over to him. So they were to have one more evening together, her happy eyes seemed to say!

He helped himself mechanically and began to eat; then disgust took him by the throat and he laid down his fork.

Mattie's tender gaze was on him and she marked the gesture.

"Why, Ethan, what's the matter? Don't it taste right?"

"Yes—it's first-rate. Only I—" He pushed his plate away, rose from his chair, and walked around the table to her side. She started up with frightened eyes.

"Ethan, there's something wrong! I *knew* there was!"

She seemed to melt against him in her terror, and he caught her in his arms, held her fast there, felt her lashes beat his cheek like netted butterflies.

"What is it—what is it?" she stammered; but he had found her lips at last and was drinking unconsciousness of everything but the joy they gave him.

She lingered a moment, caught in the same strong current; then she slipped from him and drew back a step or two, pale and troubled. Her look smote him with compunction, and he cried out, as if he saw her drowning in a dream: "You can't go, Matt! I'll never let you!"

"Go—go?" she stammered. "Must I go?"

The words went on sounding between them as though a torch of warning flew from hand to hand through a black landscape.

Ethan was overcome with shame at his lack of self-control in flinging the news at her so brutally. His head reeled and he had to support himself against the table. All the while he felt as if he were still kissing her, and yet dying of thirst for her lips.

"Ethan, what has happened! Is Zeena mad with me?"

Her cry steadied him, though it deepened his wrath and pity. "No, no," he assured her, "it's not that. But this new doctor has scared her about herself. You know she believes all they say the first time she sees them. And this one's told her she won't get well unless she lays up and don't do a thing about the house—not for months——"

He paused, his eyes wandering from her miserably. She stood silent a moment, drooping before him like a broken branch. She was so small and weak-looking that it wrung his heart; but suddenly she lifted her head and looked straight at him. "And she wants somebody handier in my place? Is that it?"

"That's what she says to-night."

"If she says it to-night she'll say it to-morrow."

Both bowed to the inexorable truth: they knew that Zeena never changed her mind, and that in her case a resolve once taken was equivalent to an act performed.

There was a long silence between them; then Mattie said in a low voice: "Don't be too sorry, Ethan."

"Oh, God—oh, God," he groaned. The glow of passion he had felt for her had melted to an aching tenderness. He saw her quick lids beating back the tears, and longed to take her in his arms and soothe her.

"You're letting your supper get cold," she admonished him with a pale gleam of gaiety.

"Oh, Matt—Matt—where'll you go to?"

Her lids sank and a tremor crossed her face. He saw that for the first time the thought of the future came to her distinctly. "I might get something to do over at Stamford," she faltered, as if knowing that he knew she had no hope.

He dropped back into his seat and hid his face in his hands. Despair seized him at the thought of her setting out alone to renew the weary quest for work. In the only place where she was known she was surrounded by indifference or animosity; and what chance had she, inexperienced and untrained, among the million bread-seekers of the cities? There came back to him miserable tales he had heard at Worcester, and the faces of girls whose lives had begun as hopefully as Mattie's. . . . It was not possible to think of such things without a revolt of his whole being. He sprang up suddenly.

"You can't go, Matt! I won't let you! She's always had her way, but I mean to have mine now——"

Mattie lifted her hand with a quick gesture, and he heard his wife's step behind him.

Zeena came into the room with her dragging down-at-the-heel step, and quietly took her accustomed seat between them.

"I felt a little mite better, and Dr. Buck says I ought to eat all I can to keep my stren'th up, even if I ain't got any appetite," she said in her flat whine, reaching across Mattie for the teapot. Her "good" dress had been replaced by the black calico and brown knitted shawl which formed her daily wear, and with them she had put on her usual face and manner. She poured out her tea, added a great deal of milk to it, helped herself largely to pie and pickles, and made the familiar gesture of adjusting her false teeth before she began to eat. The cat rubbed itself ingratiatingly against her, and she said "Good Pussy," stooped to stroke it and gave it a scrap of meat from her plate.

Ethan sat speechless, not pretending to eat, but Mattie nibbled valiantly at her food and asked Zeena one or two questions about her visit to Bettsbridge. Zeena answered in her every-day tone and, warming to the theme, regaled them with several vivid descriptions of intestinal disturbances among her friends and relatives. She looked straight at Mattie as she spoke, a faint smile deepening the vertical lines between her nose and chin.

When supper was over she rose from her seat and pressed her hand to the flat surface over the region of her heart. "That pie of yours always sets a mite heavy, Matt," she said, not ill-naturedly. She seldom abbreviated the girl's name, and when she did so it was always a sign of affability.

"I've a good mind to go and hunt up those stomach powders I got last year over in Springfield," she continued. "I ain't tried them for quite a while, and maybe they'll help the heartburn."

Mattie lifted her eyes. "Can't I get them for you, Zeena?" she ventured.

"No. They're in a place you don't know about," Zeena answered darkly, with one of her secret looks.

She went out of the kitchen and Mattie, rising, began to clear the dishes from the table. As she passed Ethan's chair their eyes met and clung together desolately. The warm still kitchen looked as peaceful as the night before. The cat had sprung to Zeena's rocking-chair, and the heat of the fire was beginning to draw out the faint sharp scent of the geraniums. Ethan dragged himself wearily to his feet.

"I'll go out and take a look round," he said, going toward the passage to get his lantern.

As he reached the door he met Zeena coming back into the room, her lips twitching with anger, a flush of excitement on her sallow face. The shawl had slipped from her shoulders and was dragging at her down-trodden heels, and in her hands she carried the fragments of the red glass pickle-dish.

"I'd like to know who done this," she said, looking sternly from Ethan to Mattie.

There was no answer, and she continued in a trembling voice: "I went to get those powders I'd put away in father's old spectacle-case, top of the china-closet, where I keep the things I set store by, so's folks sha'n't meddle with them—" Her voice broke, and two small tears hung on her lashless lids and ran slowly down her cheeks. "It takes the step-ladder to get at the top shelf, and I put Aunt Philura Maple's pickle-dish up there o' purpose when we was married, and it's never been down since, 'cept for the spring cleaning, and then I always lifted it with my own hands, so's 't it shouldn't get broke." She laid the fragments reverently on the table. "I want to know who done this," she quavered.

At the challenge Ethan turned back into the room and faced her. "I can tell you, then. The cat done it."

"The *cat?*"

"That's what I said."

She looked at him hard, and then turned her eyes to Mattie, who was carrying the dish-pan to the table.

"I'd like to know how the cat got into my china-closet," she said.

"Chasin' mice, I guess," Ethan rejoined. "There was a mouse round the kitchen all last evening."

Zeena continued to look from one to the other; then she emitted her small strange laugh. "I knew the cat was a smart cat," she said in a high voice, "but I didn't know he was smart enough to pick up the pieces of my pickle-dish and lay 'em edge to edge on the very shelf he knocked 'em off of."

Mattie suddenly drew her arms out of the steaming water. "It wasn't Ethan's fault, Zeena! The cat *did* break the dish; but I got it down from the china-closet, and I'm the one to blame for its getting broken."

Zeena stood beside the ruin of her treasure, stiffening into a stony image of resentment. "*You* got down my pickle-dish—what for?"

A bright flush flew to Mattie's cheeks. "I wanted to make the supper-table pretty," she said.

"You wanted to make the supper-table pretty; and you waited till my back was turned, and took the thing I set most store by of anything I've got, and wouldn't never use it, not even when the minister come to dinner, or Aunt Martha Pierce come over from Bettsbridge—" Zeena paused with a gasp, as if terrified by her own evocation of the sacrilege. "You're a bad girl, Mattie Silver, and I always known it. It's the way your father begun, and I was warned of it when I took you, and I tried to keep my things where you couldn't get at 'em—and now you've took from me the one I cared for most of all—" She broke off in a short spasm of sobs that passed and left her more than ever like a shape of stone.

"If I'd 'a' listened to folks, you'd 'a' gone before now, and this wouldn't 'a' happened," she said; and gathering up the bits of broken glass she went out of the room as if she carried a dead body. . . .

VIII

When Ethan was called back to the farm by his father's illness his mother gave him, for his own use, a small room behind the untenanted "best parlour." Here he had nailed up shelves for his books, built himself a box-sofa out of boards and a mattress, laid out his papers on a kitchen-table, hung on the rough plaster wall an engraving of Abraham Lincoln and a calendar with "Thoughts from the Poets," and tried, with these meagre properties to produce some likeness to the study of a "minister" who had been kind to him and lent him books when he was at Worcester. He still took refuge there in summer, but when Mattie came to live at the farm he had had to give her his stove, and consequently the room was uninhabitable for several months of the year.

To this retreat he descended as soon as the house was quiet, and Zeena's steady breathing from the bed had assured him that there was to be no sequel to the scene in the kitchen. After Zeena's departure he and Mattie had stood speechless, neither seeking to approach the other. Then the girl had returned to her task of clearing up the kitchen for the night and he had taken his lantern and gone on his usual round outside the house. The kitchen was empty when he came back to it; but his tobacco-pouch and pipe had been laid on the table, and under them was a scrap of paper torn from the back of a seedsman's catalogue, on which three words were written: "Don't trouble, Ethan."

Going into his cold dark "study" he placed the lantern on the table and, stooping to its light, read the message again and again. It was the first time that Mattie had ever written to him, and the possession of the paper gave him a strange new sense of her nearness; yet it deepened his anguish by reminding him that henceforth they would have no other way of communicating with each other. For the life of her smile, the warmth of her voice, only cold paper and dead words!

Confused motions of rebellion stormed in him. He was too young, too strong, too full of the sap of living, to submit so easily to the destruction of his hopes. Must he wear out all his years at the side of a bitter querulous woman? Other possibilities had been in him, possibilities sacrificed, one by one, to Zeena's narrow-mindedness and ignorance. And what good had come of it? She was a hundred times bitterer and more discontented than when he had married her: the one pleasure left her was to inflict pain on him. All the healthy instincts of self-defence rose up in him against such waste . . .

He bundled himself into his old coon-skin coat and lay down on the box-sofa to think. Under his cheek he felt a hard object with strange protuberances. It was a cushion which Zeena had made for him when they were engaged; the only piece of needlework he had ever seen her do. He flung it across the floor and propped his head against the wall . . .

He knew a case of a man over the mountain—a young fellow about his own age—who had escaped from just such a life of misery by going West with the girl he cared for. His wife had divorced him, and he had married the girl and prospered. Ethan had seen the couple the summer before at Shadd's Falls, where they had come to visit relatives. They had a little girl with fair curls, who wore a gold locket and was dressed like a princess. The deserted wife had not done badly either. Her husband had given her the farm and she had managed to sell it, and with that and the alimony she had started a lunch-room at Bettsbridge and bloomed into activity and importance. Ethan was fired by the thought. Why should he not leave with Mattie the next day, instead of letting her go alone? He would hide his valise under the seat of the sleigh, and Zeena would suspect nothing till she went upstairs for her afternoon nap and found a letter on the bed . . .

His impulses were still near the surface, and he sprang up, re-lit the lantern, and sat down at the table. He rummaged in the drawer for a sheet of paper, found one, and began to write.

"Zeena, I've done all I could for you, and I don't see as it's been any use. I don't blame you, nor I don't blame myself. Maybe both of us will do better separate. I'm going to try my luck West, and you can sell the farm and mill, and keep the money——"

His pen paused on the word, which brought home to him the relentless conditions of his lot. If he gave the farm and mill to Zeena what would be left him to start his own life with? Once in the West he was sure of picking up work—he would not have feared to try his chance alone. But with Mattie depending on him the case was different. And what of Zeena's fate? Farm and mill were mortgaged to the limit of their value, and even if she found a purchaser—in itself an unlikely chance—it was doubtful if she could clear a thousand dollars on the sale. Meanwhile, how could she keep the farm going? It was only by incessant labour and personal supervision that Ethan drew a meagre living from his land, and his wife, even if she were in better health than she imagined, could never carry such a burden alone.

Well, she could go back to her people, then, and see what they would do for her. It was the fate she was forcing on Mattie—why not let her try it herself? By the time she had discovered his whereabouts, and brought suit for divorce, he would probably—wherever he was—be earning enough to pay her a sufficient alimony. And the alternative was to let Mattie go forth alone, with far less hope of ultimate provision . . .

He had scattered the contents of the table-drawer in his search for a sheet of paper, and as he took up his pen his eye fell on an old copy of the *Bettsbridge Eagle*. The advertising sheet was folded uppermost, and he read the seductive words: "Trips to the West: Reduced Rates."

He drew the lantern nearer and eagerly scanned the fares; then the paper fell from his hand and he pushed aside his unfinished letter. A moment ago he had wondered what he and Mattie were to live on when they reached the West; now he saw that he had not even the money to take her there. Borrowing was out of the question: six months before he had given his only security to raise funds for necessary repairs to the mill, and he knew that without security no one

at Starkfield would lend him ten dollars. The inexorable facts closed in on him like prison-warders handcuffing a convict. There was no way out—none. He was a prisoner for life, and now his one ray of light was to be extinguished.

He crept back heavily to the sofa, stretching himself out with limbs so leaden that he felt as if they would never move again. Tears rose in his throat and slowly burned their way to his lids.

As he lay there, the window-pane that faced him, growing gradually lighter, inlaid upon the darkness a square of moon-suffused sky. A crooked tree-branch crossed it, a branch of the apple-tree under which, on summer evenings, he had sometimes found Mattie sitting when he came up from the mill. Slowly the rim of the rainy vapours caught fire and burnt away, and a pure moon swung into the blue. Ethan, rising on his elbow, watched the landscape whiten and shape itself under the sculpture of the moon. This was the night on which he was to have taken Mattie coasting, and there hung the lamp to light them! He looked out at the slopes bathed in lustre, the silver-edged darkness of the woods, the spectral purple of the hills against the sky, and it seemed as though all the beauty of the night had been poured out to mock his wretchedness . . .

He fell asleep, and when he woke the chill of the winter dawn was in the room. He felt cold and stiff and hungry, and ashamed of being hungry. He rubbed his eyes and went to the window. A red sun stood over the gray rim of the fields, behind trees that looked black and brittle. He said to himself: "This is Matt's last day," and tried to think what the place would be without her.

As he stood there he heard a step behind him and she entered.

"Oh, Ethan—were you here all night?"

She looked so small and pinched, in her poor dress, with the red scarf wound about her, and the cold light turning her paleness sallow, that Ethan stood before her without speaking.

"You must be frozen," she went on, fixing lustreless eyes on him.

He drew a step nearer. "How did you know I was here?"

"Because I heard you go down stairs again after I went to bed, and I listened all night, and you didn't come up."

All his tenderness rushed to his lips. He looked at her and said: "I'll come right along and make up the kitchen fire."

They went back to the kitchen, and he fetched the coal and kindlings and cleared out the stove for her, while she brought in the milk and the cold remains of the meat-pie. When warmth began to radiate from the stove, and the first ray of sunlight lay on the kitchen floor, Ethan's dark thoughts melted in the mellower air. The sight of Mattie going about her work as he had seen her on so many mornings made it seem impossible that she should ever cease to be a part of the scene. He said to himself that he had doubtless exaggerated the significance of Zeena's threats, and that she too, with the return of daylight, would come to a saner mood.

He went up to Mattie as she bent above the stove, and laid his hand on her arm. "I don't want you should trouble either," he said, looking down into her eyes with a smile.

She flushed up warmly and whispered back: "No, Ethan, I ain't going to trouble."

"I guess things'll straighten out," he added.

There was no answer but a quick throb of her lids, and he went on: "She ain't said anything this morning?"

"No. I haven't seen her yet."

"Don't you take any notice when you do."

With this injunction he left her and went out to the cow-barn. He saw Jotham Powell walking up the hill through the morning mist, and the familiar sight added to his growing conviction of security.

As the two men were clearing out the stalls Jotham rested on his pitch-fork to say: "Dan'l Byrne's goin' over to the Flats to-day noon, an' he c'd take Mattie's trunk along, and make it easier ridin' when I take her over in the sleigh."

Ethan looked at him blankly, and he continued: "Mis' Frome said the new girl'd be at the Flats at five, and I was to take Mattie then, so's 't she could ketch the six o'clock train for Stamford."

Ethan felt the blood drumming in his temples. He had to wait a moment before he could find voice to say: "Oh, it ain't so sure about Mattie's going——"

"That so?" said Jotham indifferently; and they went on with their work.

When they returned to the kitchen the two women were already at breakfast. Zeena had an air of unusual alertness and activity. She drank two cups of coffee and fed the cat with the scraps left in the pie-dish; then she rose from her seat and, walking over to the window, snipped two or three yellow leaves from the geraniums. "Aunt Martha's ain't got a faded leaf on 'em; but they pine away when they ain't cared for," she said reflectively. Then she turned to Jotham and asked: "What time'd you say Dan'l Byrne'd be along?"

The hired man threw a hesitating glance at Ethan. "Round about noon," he said.

Zeena turned to Mattie. "That trunk of yours is too heavy for the sleigh, and Dan'l Byrne'll be round to take it over to the Flats," she said.

"I'm much obliged to you, Zeena," said Mattie.

"I'd like to go over things with you first," Zeena continued in an unperturbed voice. "I know there's a huckabuck towel missing; and I can't make out what you done with that match-safe 't used to stand behind the stuffed owl in the parlour."

She went out, followed by Mattie, and when the men were alone Jotham said to his employer: "I guess I better let Dan'l come round, then."

Ethan finished his usual morning tasks about the house and barn; then he said to Jotham: "I'm going down to Starkfield. Tell them not to wait dinner."

The passion of rebellion had broken out in him again. That which had seemed incredible in the sober light of day had really come to pass, and he was to assist as a helpless spectator at Mattie's banishment. His manhood was humbled by the part he was compelled to play and by the thought of what Mattie must think of him. Confused impulses struggled in him as he strode along to the village. He had made up his mind to do something, but he did not know what it would be.

The early mist had vanished and the fields lay like a silver shield under the sun. It was one of the days when the glitter of winter shines through a pale haze of spring. Every yard of the road was alive with Mattie's presence, and there was hardly a branch against the sky or a tangle of brambles on the bank in which some bright shred of memory was not caught. Once, in the stillness, the call of a bird in a mountain ash was so like her laughter that his heart tightened and then grew large; and all these things made him see that something must be done at once.

Suddenly it occurred to him that Andrew Hale, who was a kind-hearted man, might be induced to reconsider his refusal and advance a small sum on the lumber if he were told that Zeena's ill-health made it necessary to hire a servant. Hale, after all, knew enough of Ethan's situation to make it possible for the latter to renew his appeal without too much loss of pride; and, moreover, how much did pride count in the ebullition of passions in his breast?

The more he considered his plan the more hopeful it seemed. If he could get Mrs. Hale's ear he felt certain of success, and with fifty dollars in his pocket nothing could keep him from Mattie . . .

His first object was to reach Starkfield before Hale had started for his work; he knew the carpenter had a job down the Corbury road and was likely to leave his house early. Ethan's long strides grew more rapid with the accelerated beat of his thoughts, and as he reached the foot of School House Hill he caught sight of Hale's sleigh in the distance. He hurried forward to meet it, but as it drew nearer he saw that it was driven by the carpenter's youngest boy and that the figure at his side, looking like a large upright cocoon in spectacles, was that of Mrs. Hale. Ethan signed to them to stop, and Mrs. Hale leaned forward, her pink wrinkles twinkling with benevolence.

"Mr. Hale? Why, yes, you'll find him down home now. He ain't going to his work this forenoon. He woke up with a touch o' lumbago, and I just made him put on one of old Dr. Kidder's plasters and set right up into the fire."

Beaming maternally on Ethan, she bent over to add: "I on'y just heard from Mr. Hale 'bout Zeena's going over to Bettsbridge to see that new doctor. I'm real sorry she's feeling so bad again! I hope he thinks he can do something for her? I don't know anybody round here's had more sickness than Zeena. I always tell Mr. Hale I don't know what she'd 'a' done if she hadn't 'a' had you to look after her; and I used to say the same thing 'bout your mother. You've had an awful mean time, Ethan Frome."

She gave him a last nod of sympathy while her son chirped to the horse; and Ethan, as she drove off, stood in the middle of the road and stared after the retreating sleigh.

It was a long time since any one had spoken to him as kindly as Mrs. Hale. Most people were either indifferent to his troubles, or disposed to think it natural that a young fellow of his age should have carried without repining the burden of three crippled lives. But Mrs. Hale had said "You've had an awful mean time, Ethan Frome," and he felt less alone with his misery. If the Hales were sorry for him they would surely respond to his appeal . . .

He started down the road toward their house, but at the end of a few yards he pulled up sharply, the blood in his face. For the first time, in the light of the words he had just heard, he saw what he was about to do. He was planning to take advantage of the Hales' sympathy to obtain money from them on false pretences. That was a plain statement of the cloudy purpose which had driven him in headlong to Starkfield.

With the sudden perception of the point to which his madness had carried him, the madness fell and he saw his life before him as it was. He was a poor man, the husband of a sickly woman, whom his desertion would leave alone and destitute; and even if he had had the heart to desert her he could have done so only by deceiving two kindly people who had pitied him.

He turned and walked slowly back to the farm.

IX

At the kitchen door Daniel Byrne sat in his sleigh behind a big-boned gray who pawed the snow and swung his long head restlessly from side to side.

Ethan went into the kitchen and found his wife by the stove. Her head was wrapped in her shawl, and she was reading a book called "Kidney Troubles And Their Cure" on which he had had to pay extra postage only a few days before.

Zeena did not move or look up when he entered, and after a moment he asked: "Where's Mattie?"

Without lifting her eyes from the page she replied: "I presume she's getting down her trunk."

The blood rushed to his face. "Getting down her trunk—alone?"

"Jotham Powell's down in the wood-lot, and Dan'l Byrne says he darsn't leave that horse," she returned.

Her husband, without stopping to hear the end of the phrase, had left the kitchen and sprung up the stairs. The door of Mattie's room was shut, and he wavered a moment on the landing. "Matt," he said in a low voice; but there was no answer, and he put his hand on the door-knob.

He had never been in her room except once, in the early summer, when he had gone there to plaster up a leak in the eaves, but he remembered exactly how everything had looked: the red and white quilt on her narrow bed, the pretty pin-cushion on the chest of drawers, and over it the enlarged photograph of her mother, in an oxydized frame, with a bunch of dyed grasses at the back. Now these and all other tokens of her presence had vanished, and the room looked as bare and comfortless as when Zeena had shown her into it on the day of her arrival. In the middle of the floor stood her trunk, and on the trunk she sat in her Sunday dress, her back turned to the door and her face in her hands. She had not heard Ethan's call because she was sobbing; and she did not hear his step till he stood close behind her and laid his hands on her shoulders.

"Matt—oh, don't—oh, *Matt!*"

She started up, lifting her wet face to his. "Ethan—I thought I wasn't ever going to see you again!"

He took her in his arms, pressing her close, and with a trembling hand smoothed away the hair from her forehead.

"Not see me again? What do you mean?"

She sobbed out: "Jotham said you told him we wasn't to wait dinner for you, and I thought——"

"You thought I meant to cut it?" he finished for her grimly.

She clung to him without answering, and he laid his lips on her hair, which was soft yet springy, like certain mosses on warm slopes, and had the faint woody fragrance of fresh sawdust in the sun.

Through the door they heard Zeena's voice calling out from below: "Dan'l Byrne says you better hurry up if you want him to take that trunk."

They drew apart with stricken faces. Words of

resistance rushed to Ethan's lips and died there. Mattie found her handkerchief and dried her eyes; then, bending down, she took hold of a handle of the trunk.

Ethan put her aside. "You let go, Matt," he ordered her.

She answered: "It takes two to coax it round the corner"; and submitting to this argument he grasped the other handle, and together they manœuvred the heavy trunk out to the landing.

"Now let go," he repeated; then he shouldered the trunk and carried it down the stairs and across the passage to the kitchen. Zeena, who had gone back to her seat by the stove, did not lift her head from her book as he passed. Mattie followed him out of the door and helped him to lift the trunk into the back of the sleigh. When it was in place they stood side by side on the doorstep watching Daniel Byrne plunge off behind his fidgety horse.

It seemed to Ethan that his heart was bound with cords which an unseen hand was tightening with every tick of the clock. Twice he opened his lips to speak to Mattie and found no breath. At length, as she turned to re-enter the house, he laid a detaining hand on her.

"I'm going to drive you over, Matt," he whispered.

She murmured back: "I think Zeena wants I should go with Jotham."

"I'm going to drive you over," he repeated; and she went into the kitchen without answering.

At dinner Ethan could not eat. If he lifted his eyes they rested on Zeena's pinched face, and the corners of her straight lips seemed to quiver away into a smile. She ate well, declaring that the mild weather made her feel better, and pressed a second helping of beans on Jotham Powell, whose wants she generally ignored.

Mattie, when the meal was over, went about her usual task of clearing the table and washing up the dishes. Zeena, after feeding the cat, had returned to her rocking-chair by the stove, and Jotham Powell, who always lingered last, reluctantly pushed back his chair and moved toward the door.

On the threshold he turned back to say to Ethan: "What time'll I come round for Mattie?"

Ethan was standing near the window, mechanically filling his pipe while he watched Mattie move to and fro. He answered: "You needn't come round; I'm going to drive her over myself."

He saw the rise of the colour in Mattie's averted cheek, and the quick lifting of Zeena's head.

"I want you should stay here this afternoon, Ethan," his wife said. "Jotham can drive Mattie over."

Mattie flung an imploring glance at him, but he repeated curtly: "I'm going to drive her over myself."

Zeena continued in the same even tone: "I wanted you should stay and fix up that stove in Mattie's room afore the girl gets here. It ain't been drawing right for nigh on a month now."

Ethan's voice rose indignantly. "If it was good enough for Mattie I guess it's good enough for a hired girl."

"That girl that's coming told me she was used to a house where they had a furnace," Zeena persisted with the same monotonous mildness.

"She'd better ha' stayed there then," he flung back at her; and turning to Mattie he added in a hard voice: "You be ready by three, Matt; I've got business at Corbury."

Jotham Powell had started for the barn, and Ethan strode down after him aflame with anger. The pulses in his temples throbbed and a fog was in his eyes. He went about his task without knowing what force directed him, or whose hands and feet were fulfilling its orders. It was not till he led out the sorrel and backed him between the shafts of the sleigh that he once more became conscious of what he was doing. As he passed the bridle over the horse's head, and wound the traces around the shafts, he remembered the day when he had made the same preparations in order to drive over and meet his wife's cousin at the Flats. It was little more than a year ago, on just such a soft afternoon, with a "feel" of spring in the air. The sorrel, turning the same big ringed eye on him, nuzzled the palm of his hand in the same way; and one by one all the days between rose up and stood before him . . .

He flung the bearskin into the sleigh, climbed to the seat, and drove up to the house. When he entered the kitchen it was empty, but Mattie's bag and shawl lay ready by the door. He went to the foot of the stairs and listened. No sound reached him from above, but presently he thought he heard some one moving about in his deserted study, and pushing open the door he saw Mattie, in her hat and jacket, standing with her back to him near the table.

She started at his approach and turning quickly, said: "Is it time?"

"What are you doing here, Matt?" he asked her.

She looked at him timidly. "I was just taking a look round—that's all," she answered, with a wavering smile.

They went back into the kitchen without speaking, and Ethan picked up her bag and shawl.

"Where's Zeena?" he asked.

"She went upstairs right after dinner. She said she had those shooting pains again, and didn't want to be disturbed."

"Didn't she say good-bye to you?"

"No. That was all she said."

Ethan, looking slowly about the kitchen, said to himself with a shudder that in a few hours he would be returning to it alone. Then the sense of unreality overcame him once more, and he could not bring himself to believe that Mattie stood there for the last time before him.

"Come on," he said almost gaily, opening the door and putting her bag into the sleigh. He sprang to his seat and bent over to tuck the rug about her as she slipped into the place at his side. "Now then, go 'long," he said, with a shake of the reins that sent the sorrel placidly jogging down the hill.

"We got lots of time for a good ride, Matt!" he cried, seeking her hand beneath the fur and pressing it in his. His face tingled and he felt dizzy, as if he had stopped in at the Starkfield saloon on a zero day for a drink.

At the gate, instead of making for Starkfield, he turned the sorrel to the right, up the Bettsbridge road. Mattie sat silent, giving no sign of surprise; but after a moment she said: "Are you going round by Shadow Pond?"

He laughed and answered: "I knew you'd know!"

She drew closer under the bearskin, so that, looking sideways around his coat-sleeve, he could just catch the tip of her nose and a blown brown wave of hair. They drove slowly up the road between fields glistening under the pale sun, and then bent to the right down a lane edged with spruce and larch. Ahead of them, a long way off, a range of hills stained by mottlings of black-forest flowed away in round white curves against the sky. The lane passed into a pine-wood with boles reddening in the afternoon sun and delicate blue shadows on the snow. As they entered it the breeze fell and a warm stillness seemed to drop from the branches with the dropping needles. Here the snow was so pure that the tiny tracks of wood-animals had left on it intricate lace-like patterns, and the bluish cones caught in its surface stood out like ornaments of bronze.

Ethan drove on in silence till they reached a part of the wood where the pines were more widely spaced; then he drew up and helped Mattie to get out of the sleigh. They passed between the aromatic trunks, the snow breaking crisply under their feet, till they came to a small sheet of water with steep wooded sides. Across its frozen surface, from the farther bank, a single hill rising against the western sun threw the long conical shadow which gave the lake its name. It was a shy secret spot, full of the same dumb melancholy that Ethan felt in his heart.

He looked up and down the little pebbly beach till his eye lit on a fallen tree-trunk half submerged in snow.

"There's where we sat at the picnic," he reminded her.

The entertainment of which he spoke was one of the few that they had taken part in together: a "church picnic" which, on a long afternoon of the preceding summer, had filled the retired place with merry-making. Mattie had begged him to go with her but he had refused. Then, toward sunset, coming down from the mountain where he had been felling timber, he had been caught by some strayed revellers and drawn into the group by the lake, where Mattie, encircled by facetious youths, and bright as a blackberry under her spreading hat, was brewing coffee over a gipsy fire. He remembered the shyness he had felt at approaching her in his uncouth clothes, and then the lighting up of her face, and the way she had broken through the group to come to him with a cup in her hand. They had sat for a few minutes on the fallen log by the pond, and she had missed her gold locket, and set the young men searching for it; and it was Ethan who had spied it in the moss . . . That was all; but all their intercourse had been made up of just such inarticulate flashes, when they seemed to come suddenly upon happiness as if they had surprised a butterfly in the winter woods . . .

"It was right there I found your locket," he said, pushing his foot into a dense tuft of blueberry bushes.

"I never saw anybody with such sharp eyes!" she answered.

She sat down on the tree-trunk in the sun and he sat down beside her.

"You were as pretty as a picture in that pink hat," he said.

She laughed with pleasure. "Oh, I guess it was the hat!" she rejoined.

They had never before avowed their inclination so openly, and Ethan, for a moment, had the illusion that he was a free man, wooing the girl he meant to marry. He looked at her hair and longed to touch it again, and to tell her that it smelt of the woods; but he had never learned to say such things.

Suddenly she rose to her feet and said: "We mustn't stay here any longer."

He continued to gaze at her vaguely, only half-roused from his dream. "There's plenty of time," he answered.

They stood looking at each other as if the eyes of each were straining to absorb and hold fast the other's image. There were things he had to say to her before they parted, but he could not say them in that place of summer memories, and he turned and followed her in silence to the sleigh. As they drove away the sun sank behind the hill and the pine-boles turned from red to gray.

By a devious track between the fields they wound

back to the Starkfield road. Under the open sky the light was still clear, with a reflection of cold red on the eastern hills. The clumps of trees in the snow seemed to draw together in ruffled lumps, like birds with their heads under their wings; and the sky, as it paled, rose higher, leaving the earth more alone.

As they turned into the Starkfield road Ethan said: "Matt, what do you mean to do?"

She did not answer at once, but at length she said: "I'll try to get a place in a store."

"You know you can't do it. The bad air and the standing all day nearly killed you before."

"I'm a lot stronger than I was before I came to Starkfield."

"And now you're going to throw away all the good it's done you!"

There seemed to be no answer to this, and again they drove on for a while without speaking. With every yard of the way some spot where they had stood, and laughed together or been silent, clutched at Ethan and dragged him back.

"Isn't there any of your father's folks could help you?"

"There isn't any of 'em I'd ask."

He lowered his voice to say: "You know there's nothing I wouldn't do for you if I could."

"I know there isn't."

"But I can't——"

She was silent, but he felt a slight tremor in the shoulder against his.

"Oh, Matt," he broke out, "if I could ha' gone with you now I'd ha' done it——"

She turned to him, pulling a scrap of paper from her breast. "Ethan—I found this," she stammered. Even in the failing light he saw it was the letter to his wife that he had begun the night before and forgotten to destroy. Through his astonishment there ran a fierce thrill of joy. "Matt—" he cried; "if I could ha' done it, would you?"

"Oh, Ethan, Ethan—what's the use?" With a sudden movement she tore the letter in shreds and sent them fluttering off into the snow.

"Tell me, Matt! Tell me!" he adjured her.

She was silent for a moment; then she said, in such a low tone that he had to stoop his head to hear her: "I used to think of it sometimes, summer nights, when the moon was so bright I couldn't sleep."

His heart reeled with the sweetness of it. "As long ago as that?"

She answered, as if the date had long been fixed for her: "The first time was at Shadow Pond."

"Was that why you gave me my coffee before the others?"

"I don't know. Did I? I was dreadfully put out

when you wouldn't go to the picnic with me; and then, when I saw you coming down the road, I thought maybe you'd gone home that way o' purpose; and that made me glad."

They were silent again. They had reached the point where the road dipped to the hollow by Ethan's mill and as they descended the darkness descended with them, dropping down like a black veil from the heavy hemlock boughs.

"I'm tied hand and foot, Matt. There isn't a thing I can do," he began again.

"You must write to me sometimes, Ethan."

"Oh, what good'll writing do? I want to put my hand out and touch you. I want to do for you and care for you. I want to be there when you're sick and when you're lonesome."

"You mustn't think but what I'll do all right."

"You won't need me, you mean? I suppose you'll marry!"

"Oh, Ethan!" she cried.

"I don't know how it is you make me feel, Matt. I'd a'most rather have you dead than that!"

"Oh, I wish I was, I wish I was!" she sobbed.

The sound of her weeping shook him out of his dark anger, and he felt ashamed.

"Don't let's talk that way," he whispered.

"Why shouldn't we, when it's true? I've been wishing it every minute of the day."

"Matt! You be quiet! Don't you say it."

"There's never anybody been good to me but you."

"Don't say that either, when I can't lift a hand for you!"

"Yes; but it's true just the same."

They had reached the top of School House Hill and Starkfield lay below them in the twilight. A cutter, mounting the road from the village, passed them by in a joyous flutter of bells, and they straightened themselves and looked ahead with rigid faces. Along the main street lights had begun to shine from the house-fronts and stray figures were turning in here and there at the gates. Ethan, with a touch of his whip, roused the sorrel to a languid trot.

As they drew near the end of the village the cries of children reached them, and they saw a knot of boys, with sleds behind them, scattering across the open space before the church.

"I guess this'll be their last coast for a day or two," Ethan said, looking up at the mild sky.

Mattie was silent, and he added: "We were to have gone down last night."

Still she did not speak and, prompted by an obscure desire to help himself and her through their miserable last hour, he went on discursively: "Ain't it funny we haven't been down together but just that once last winter?"

She answered: "It wasn't often I got down to the village."

"That's so," he said.

They had reached the crest of the Corbury road, and between the indistinct white glimmer of the church and the black curtain of the Varnum spruces the slope stretched away below them without a sled on its length. Some erratic impulse prompted Ethan to say: "How'd you like me to take you down now?"

She forced a laugh. "Why, there isn't time!"

"There's all the time we want. Come along!" His one desire now was to postpone the moment of turning the sorrel toward the Flats.

"But the girl," she faltered. "The girl'll be waiting at the station."

"Well, let her wait. You'd have to if she didn't. Come!"

The note of authority in his voice seemed to subdue her, and when he had jumped from the sleigh she let him help her out, saying only, with a vague feint of reluctance: "But there isn't a sled round anywheres."

"Yes, there is! Right over there under the spruces."

He threw the bearskin over the sorrel, who stood passively by the roadside, hanging a meditative head. Then he caught Mattie's hand and drew her after him toward the sled.

She seated herself obediently and he took his place behind her, so close that her hair brushed his face. "All right, Matt?" he called out, as if the width of the road had been between them.

She turned her head to say: "It's dreadfully dark. Are you sure you can see?"

He laughed contemptuously: "I could go down this coast with my eyes tied!" and she laughed with him, as if she liked his audacity. Nevertheless he sat still a moment, straining his eyes down the long hill, for it was the most confusing hour of the evening, the hour when the last clearness from the upper sky is merged with the rising night in a blur that disguises landmarks and falsifies distances.

"Now!" he cried.

The sled started with a bound, and they flew on through the dusk, gathering smoothness and speed as they went, with the hollow night opening out below them and the air singing by like an organ. Mattie sat perfectly still, but as they reached the bend at the foot of the hill, where the big elm thrust out a deadly elbow, he fancied that she shrank a little closer.

"Don't be scared, Matt!" he cried exultantly, as they spun safely past it and flew down the second slope; and when they reached the level ground beyond, and the speed of the sled began to slacken, he heard her give a little laugh of glee.

They sprang off and started to walk back up the hill. Ethan dragged the sled with one hand and passed the other through Mattie's arm.

"Were you scared I'd run you into the elm?" he asked with a boyish laugh.

"I told you I was never scared with you," she answered.

The strange exaltation of his mood had brought on one of his rare fits of boastfulness. "It *is* a tricky place, though. The least swerve, and we'd never ha' come up again. But I can measure distances to a hair's-breadth—always could."

She murmured: "I always say you've got the surest eye . . ."

Deep silence had fallen with the starless dusk, and they leaned on each other without speaking; but at every step of their climb Ethan said to himself: "It's the last time we'll ever walk together."

They mounted slowly to the top of the hill. When they were abreast of the church he stooped his head to her to ask: "Are you tired?" and she answered, breathing quickly: "It was splendid!"

With a pressure of his arm he guided her toward the Norway spruces. "I guess this sled must be Ned Hale's. Anyhow I'll leave it where I found it." He drew the sled up to the Varnum gate and rested it against the fence. As he raised himself he suddenly felt Mattie close to him among the shadows.

"Is this where Ned and Ruth kissed each other?" she whispered breathlessly, and flung her arms about him. Her lips, groping for his, swept over his face, and he held her fast in a rapture of surprise.

"Good-bye—good-bye," she stammered, and kissed him again.

"Oh, Matt I can't let you go!" broke from him in the same old cry.

She freed herself from his hold and he heard her sobbing. "Oh, I can't go either!" she wailed.

"Matt! What'll we do? What'll we do?"

They clung to each other's hands like children, and her body shook with desperate sobs.

Through the stillness they heard the church clock striking five.

"Oh, Ethan, it's time!" she cried.

He drew her back to him. "Time for what? You don't suppose I'm going to leave you now?"

"If I missed my train where'd I go?"

"Where are you going if you catch it?"

She stood silent, her hands lying cold and relaxed in his.

"What's the good of either of us going anywheres without the other one now?" he said.

She remained motionless, as if she had not heard him. Then she snatched her hands from his, threw her arms about his neck, and pressed a sudden drenched cheek against his face. "Ethan! Ethan! I want you to take me down again!"

"Down where?"

"The coast. Right off," she panted. "So 't we'll never come up any more."

"Matt! What on earth do you mean?"

She put her lips close against his ear to say: "Right into the big elm. You said you could. So 't we'd never have to leave each other any more."

"Why, what are you talking of? You're crazy!"

"I'm not crazy; but I will be if I leave you."

"Oh, Matt, Matt—" he groaned.

She tightened her fierce hold about his neck. Her face lay close to his face.

"Ethan, where'll I go if I leave you? I don't know how to get along alone. You said so yourself just now. Nobody but you was ever good to me. And there'll be that strange girl in the house . . . and she'll sleep in my bed, where I used to lay nights and listen to hear you come up the stairs. . . ."

The words were like fragments torn from his heart. With them came the hated vision of the house he was going back to—of the stairs he would have to go up every night, of the woman who would wait for him there. And the sweetness of Mattie's avowal, the wild wonder of knowing at last that all that had happened to him had happened to her too, made the other vision more abhorrent, the other life more intolerable to return to. . . .

Her pleadings still came to him between short sobs, but he no longer heard what she was saying. Her hat had slipped back and he was stroking her hair. He wanted to get the feeling of it into his hand, so that it would sleep there like a seed in winter. Once he found her mouth again, and they seemed to be by the pond together in the burning August sun. But his cheek touched hers, and it was cold and full of weeping, and he saw the road to the Flats under the night and heard the whistle of the train up the line.

The spruces swathed them in blackness and silence. They might have been in their coffins underground. He said to himself: "Perhaps it'll feel like this . . ." and then again: "After this I sha'n't feel anything . . ."

Suddenly he heard the old sorrel whinny across the road, and thought: "He's wondering why he doesn't get his supper . . ."

"Come," Mattie whispered, tugging at his hand.

Her sombre violence constrained him; she seemed the embodied instrument of fate. He pulled the sled out, blinking like a night-bird as he passed from the shade of the spruces into the transparent dusk of the open. The slope below them was deserted. All Starkfield was at supper, and not a figure crossed the open space before the church. The sky, swollen with the clouds that announce a thaw, hung as low as before a summer storm. He strained his eyes through the dimness, and they seemed less keen, less capable than usual.

He took his seat on the sled and Mattie instantly placed herself in front of him. Her hat had fallen into the snow and his lips were in her hair. He stretched out his legs, drove his heels into the road to keep the sled from slipping forward, and bent her head back between his hands. Then suddenly he sprang up again.

"Get up," he ordered her.

It was the tone she always heeded, but she cowered down in her seat, repeating vehemently: "No, no, no!"

"Get up!"

"Why?"

"I want to sit in front."

"No, no! How can you steer in front?"

"I don't have to. We'll follow the track."

They spoke in smothered whispers, as though the night were listening.

"Get up! Get up!" he urged her; but she kept on repeating: "Why do you want to sit in front?"

"Because I—because I want to feel you holding me," he stammered, and dragged her to her feet.

The answer seemed to satisfy her, or else she yielded to the power of his voice. He bent down, feeling in the obscurity for the glassy slide worn by preceding coasters, and placed the runners carefully between its edges. She waited while he seated himself with crossed legs in the front of the sled; then she crouched quickly down at his back and clasped her arms about him. Her breath in his neck set him shuddering again, and he almost sprang from his seat. But in a flash he remembered the alternative. She was right: this was better than parting. He leaned back and drew her mouth to his . . .

Just as they started he heard the sorrel's whinny again, and the familiar wistful call, and all the confused images it brought with it, went with him down the first reach of the road. Half-way down there was a sudden drop, then a rise, and after that another long delirious descent. As they took wing for this it seemed to him that they were flying indeed, flying far up into the cloudy night, with Starkfield immeasurably below them, falling away like a speck in space . . . Then the big elm shot up ahead, lying in wait for them at the bend of the road, and he said between his teeth: "We can fetch it; I know we can fetch it——"

As they flew toward the tree Mattie pressed her arms tighter, and her blood seemed to be in his veins. Once or twice the sled swerved a little under them. He slanted his body to keep it headed for the elm, repeating to himself again and again: "I know we can fetch it"; and little phrases she had spoken ran through his head and danced before him on the air. The big tree loomed bigger and closer, and as they bore down on it he thought: "It's waiting for us: it seems to know." But suddenly his wife's face, with twisted monstrous lineaments, thrust itself between him and his goal, and he made an instinctive movement to brush it aside. The sled swerved in response, but he righted it again, kept it straight, and drove down on the black projecting mass. There was a last instant when the air shot past him like millions of fiery wires; and then the elm . . .

The sky was still thick, but looking straight up he saw a single star, and tried vaguely to reckon whether it were Sirius, or—or— The effort tired him too much, and he closed his heavy lids and thought that he would sleep. . . . The stillness was so profound that he heard a little animal twittering somewhere near by under the snow. It made a small frightened *cheep* like a field mouse, and he wondered languidly if it were hurt. Then he understood that it must be in pain: pain so excruciating that he seemed, mysteriously, to feel it shooting through his own body. He tried in vain to roll over in the direction of the sound and stretched his left arm out across the snow. And now it was as though he felt rather than heard the twittering; it seemed to be under his palm, which rested on something soft and springy. The thought of the animal's suffering was intolerable to him and he struggled to raise himself, and could not because a rock, or some huge mass, seemed to be lying on him. But he continued to finger about cautiously with his left hand, thinking he might get hold of the little creature and help it; and all at once he knew that the soft thing he had touched was Mattie's hair and that his hand was on her face.

He dragged himself to his knees, the monstrous load on him moving with him as he moved, and his hand went over and over her face, and he felt that the twittering came from her lips . . .

He got his face down close to hers, with his ear to her mouth, and in the darkness he saw her eyes open and heard her say his name.

"Oh, Matt, I thought we'd fetched it," he moaned; and far off, up the hill, he heard the sorrel whinny, and thought: "I ought to be getting him his feed . . ."

. . . .

The querulous drone ceased as I entered Frome's kitchen, and of the two women sitting there I could not tell which had been the speaker.

One of them, on my appearing, raised her tall bony figure from her seat, not as if to welcome me—for she threw me no more than a brief glance of surprise—but

simply to set about preparing the meal which Frome's absence had delayed. A slatternly calico wrapper hung from her shoulders and the wisps of her thin gray hair were drawn away from a high forehead and fastened at the back by a broken comb. She had pale opaque eyes which revealed nothing and reflected nothing, and her narrow lips were of the same sallow colour as her face.

The other woman was much smaller and slighter. She sat huddled in an arm-chair near the stove, and when I came in she turned her head quickly toward me, without the least corresponding movement of her body. Her hair was as gray as her companion's, her face as bloodless and shrivelled, but amber-tinted, with swarthy shadows sharpening the nose and hollowing the temples. Under her shapeless dress her body kept its limp immobility, and her dark eyes had the bright witch-like stare that disease of the spine sometimes gives.

Even for that part of the country the kitchen was a poor-looking place. With the exception of the dark-eyed woman's chair, which looked like a soiled relic of luxury bought at a country auction, the furniture was of the roughest kind. Three coarse china plates and a broken-nosed milk-jug had been set on a greasy table scored with knife-cuts, and a couple of straw-bottomed chairs and a kitchen dresser of unpainted pine stood meagrely against the plaster walls.

"My, it's cold here! The fire must be 'most out," Frome said, glancing about him apologetically as he followed me in.

The tall woman, who had moved away from us toward the dresser, took no notice; but the other, from her cushioned niche, answered complainingly, in a high thin voice: "It's on'y just been made up this very minute. Zeena fell asleep and slep' ever so long, and I thought I'd be frozen stiff before I could wake her up and get her to 'tend to it."

I knew then that it was she who had been speaking when we entered.

Her companion, who was just coming back to the table with the remains of a cold mince-pie in a battered pie-dish, set down her unappetising burden without appearing to hear the accusation brought against her.

Frome stood hesitatingly before her as she advanced; then he looked at me and said: "This is my wife, Mis' Frome." After another interval he added, turning toward the figure in the arm-chair: "And this is Miss Mattie Silver . . ."

. . . .

Mrs. Hale, tender soul, had pictured me as lost in the Flats and buried under a snow-drift; and so lively was her satisfaction on seeing me safely restored to her the next morning that I felt my peril had caused me to advance several degrees in her favour.

Great was her amazement, and that of old Mrs. Varnum, on learning that Ethan Frome's old horse had carried me to and from Corbury Junction through the worst blizzard of the winter; greater still their surprise when they heard that his master had taken me in for the night.

Beneath their wondering exclamations I felt a secret curiosity to know what impressions I had received from my night in the Frome household, and divined that the best way of breaking down their reserve was to let them try to penetrate mine. I therefore confined myself to saying, in a matter-of-fact tone, that I had been received with great kindness, and that Frome had made a bed for me in a room on the ground-floor which seemed in happier days to have been fitted up as a kind of writing-room or study.

"Well," Mrs. Hale mused, "in such a storm I suppose he felt he couldn't do less than take you in—but I guess it went hard with Ethan. I don't believe but what you're the only stranger has set foot in that house for over twenty years. He's that proud he don't even like his oldest friends to go there; and I don't know as any do, any more, except myself and the doctor . . ."

"You still go there, Mrs. Hale?" I ventured.

"I used to go a good deal after the accident, when I was first married; but after awhile I got to think it made 'em feel worse to see us. And then one thing and another came, and my own troubles . . . But I generally make out to drive over there round about New Year's, and once in the summer. Only I always try to pick a day when Ethan's off somewheres. It's bad enough to see the two women sitting there—but *his* face, when he looks round that bare place, just kills me . . . You see, I can look back and call it up in his mother's day, before their troubles."

Old Mrs. Varnum, by this time, had gone up to bed, and her daughter and I were sitting alone, after supper, in the austere seclusion of the horse-hair parlour. Mrs. Hale glanced at me tentatively, as though trying to see how much footing my conjectures gave her; and I guessed that if she had kept silence till now it was because she had been waiting, through all the years, for some one who should see what she alone had seen.

I waited to let her trust in me gather strength before I said: "Yes, it's pretty bad, seeing all three of them there together."

She drew her mild brows into a frown of pain. "It was just awful from the beginning. I was here in the house when they were carried up—they laid Mattie Silver in the room you're in. She and I were great friends, and she was to have been my bride's-maid in the spring . . . When she came to I went up to her and stayed all night. They gave her things to quiet her, and she didn't know much till to'rd morning, and then all of a sudden she woke up just like herself, and looked straight at me out of her big eyes, and said . . . Oh, I don't know why I'm telling you all this," Mrs. Hale broke off, crying.

She took off her spectacles, wiped the moisture from them, and put them on again with an unsteady hand. "It got about the next day," she went on, "that Zeena Frome had sent Mattie off in a hurry because she had a hired girl coming, and the folks here could never rightly tell what she and Ethan were doing that night coasting, when they'd ought to have been on their way to the Flats to ketch the train . . . I never knew myself what Zeena thought—I don't to this day. Nobody knows Zeena's thoughts. Anyhow, when she heard o' the accident she came right in and stayed with Ethan over to the minister's, where they'd carried him. And as soon as the doctors said that Mattie could be moved, Zeena sent for her and took her back to the farm."

"And there she's been ever since?"

Mrs. Hale answered simply: "There was nowhere else for her to go"; and my heart tightened at the thought of the hard compulsions of the poor.

"Yes, there she's been," Mrs. Hale continued, "and Zeena's done for her, and done for Ethan, as good as she could. It was a miracle, considering how sick she was—but she seemed to be raised right up just when the call came to her. Not as she's ever given up doctoring, and she's had sick spells right along; but she's had the strength given her to care for those two for over twenty years, and before the accident came she thought she couldn't even care for herself."

Mrs. Hale paused a moment, and I remained silent, plunged in the vision of what her words evoked. "It's horrible for them all," I murmured.

"Yes: it's pretty bad. And they ain't any of 'em easy people either. Mattie *was*, before the accident; I never knew a sweeter nature. But she's suffered too much—that's what I always say when folks tell me how she's soured. And Zeena, she was always cranky. Not but what she bears with Mattie wonderful—I've seen that myself. But sometimes the two of them get going at each other, and then Ethan's face'd break your heart . . . When I see that, I think it's *him* that suffers most . . . anyhow it ain't Zeena, because she ain't got the time . . . It's a pity, though," Mrs. Hale ended, sighing, "that they're all shut up there'n that one kitchen. In the summertime, on pleasant days, they move Mattie into the parlour, or out in the door-yard, and that makes it easier . . .

but winters there's the fires to be thought of; and there ain't a dime to spare up at the Fromes'."

Mrs. Hale drew a deep breath, as though her memory were eased of its long burden, and she had no more to say: but suddenly an impulse of complete avowal seized her.

She took off her spectacles again, leaned toward me across the bead-work table-cover, and went on with lowered voice: "There was one day, about a week after the accident, when they all thought Mattie couldn't live. Well, I say it's a pity she *did*. I said it right out to our minister once, and he was shocked at me. Only he wasn't with me that morning when she first came to . . . And I say, if she'd ha' died, Ethan might ha' lived; and the way they are now, I don't see's there's much difference between the Fromes up at the farm and the Fromes down in the graveyard; 'cept that down there they're all quiet and the women have got to hold their tongues."

THE GREAT GATSBY

F. SCOTT FITZGERALD

F. SCOTT FITZGERALD (1896–1940) was born in St. Paul, Minnesota, entered Princeton in 1913 but left to enlist in the Army in 1917. His first novel, *This Side of Paradise* (1920), a tale of the jazz age following the First World War, was a great success. He lived for a number of years on the Riviera and in Rome. His last three years were lived in Hollywood, where he wrote for the motion pictures. *The Great Gatsby* (1925), here reprinted in its entirety, is of course Fitzgerald's most popular novel. Among his other books are *The Beautiful and Damned* (1921); *Tender Is the Night* (1934); *The Last Tycoon* (1941), an unfinished novel; *The Crack-Up* (1945) and *Afternoon of an Author* (1957), collections of his last writings; and *The Letters of F. Scott Fitzgerald* (1963).

Then wear the gold hat, if that will move her;
If you can bounce high, bounce for her too,
Till she cry "Lover, gold-hatted, high-bouncing lover,
I must have you!"
                    —THOMAS PARKE D'INVILLIERS

I

IN my younger and more vulnerable years my father gave me some advice that I've been turning over in my mind ever since.

"Whenever you feel like criticizing any one," he told me, "just remember that all the people in this world haven't had the advantages that you've had."

He didn't say any more, but we've always been unusually communicative in a reserved way, and I understood that he meant a great deal more than that. In consequence, I'm inclined to reserve all judgments, a habit that has opened up many curious natures to me and also made me the victim of not a few veteran bores. The abnormal mind is quick to detect and attach itself to this quality when it appears in a normal person, and so it came about that in college I was unjustly accused of being a politician, because I was privy to the secret griefs of wild, unknown men. Most of the confidences were unsought—frequently I have feigned sleep, preoccupation, or a hostile levity when I realized by some unmistakable sign that an intimate revelation was quivering on the horizon; for the intimate revelations of young men, or at least the terms in which they express them, are usually plagiaristic and marred by obvious suppressions. Reserving judgments is a matter of infinite hope. I am still a little afraid of missing

Copyright 1925 Charles Scribner's Sons; renewal copyright 1953 Frances Scott Fitzgerald Lanahan. Reprinted with the permission of Charles Scribner's Sons.

something if I forget that, as my father snobbishly suggested, and I snobbishly repeat, a sense of the fundamental decencies is parcelled out unequally at birth.

And, after boasting this way of my tolerance, I come to the admission that it has a limit. Conduct may be founded on the hard rock or the wet marshes, but after a certain point I don't care what it's founded on. When I came back from the East last autumn I felt that I wanted the world to be in uniform and at a sort of moral attention forever; I wanted no more riotous excursions with privileged glimpses into the human heart. Only Gatsby, the man who gives his name to this book, was exempt from my reaction—Gatsby, who represented everything for which I have an unaffected scorn. If personality is an unbroken series of successful gestures, then there was something gorgeous about him, some heightened sensitivity to the promises of life, as if he were related to one of those intricate machines that register earthquakes ten thousand miles away. This responsiveness had nothing to do with that flabby impressionability which is dignified under the name of the "creative temperament"—it was an extraordinary gift for hope, a romantic readiness such as I have never found in any other person and which it is not likely I shall ever find again. No—Gatsby turned out all right at the end; it is what preyed on Gatsby, what foul dust floated in the wake of his dreams that temporarily closed out my interest in the abortive sorrows and short-winded elations of men.

My family have been prominent, well-to-do people in this Middle Western city for three generations. The Carraways are something of a clan, and we have a tradition that we're descended from the Dukes of Buccleuch, but the actual founder of my line was my grandfather's brother, who came here in fifty-one, sent a substitute to the Civil War, and started the wholesale hardware business that my father carries on to-day.

I never saw this great-uncle, but I'm supposed to look like him—with special reference to the rather hard-boiled painting that hangs in father's office. I graduated from New Haven in 1915, just a quarter of a century after my father, and a little later I participated in that delayed Teutonic migration known as the Great War. I enjoyed the counter-raid so thoroughly that I came back restless. Instead of being the warm center of the world, the Middle West now seemed like the ragged edge of the universe—so I decided to go East and learn the bond business. Everybody I knew was in the bond business, so I supposed it could support one more single man. All my aunts and uncles talked it over as if they were choosing a prep school for me, and finally said, "Why —ye-es," with very grave, hesitant faces. Father agreed to finance me for a year, and after various delays I came East, permanently, I thought, in the spring of twenty-two.

The practical thing was to find rooms in the city, but it was a warm season, and I had just left a country of wide lawns and friendly trees, so when a young man at the office suggested that we take a house together in a commuting town, it sounded like a great idea. He found the house, a weatherbeaten cardboard bungalow at eighty a month, but at the last minute the firm ordered him to Washington, and I went out to the country alone. I had a dog—at least I had him for a few days until he ran away—and an old Dodge and a Finnish woman, who made my bed and cooked breakfast and muttered Finnish wisdom to herself over the electric stove.

It was lonely for a day or so until one morning some man, more recently arrived than I, stopped me on the road.

"How do you get to West Egg village?" he asked helplessly.

I told him. And as I walked on I was lonely no longer. I was a guide, a pathfinder, an original settler. He had casually conferred on me the freedom of the neighborhood.

And so with the sunshine and the great bursts of leaves growing on the trees, just as things grow in fast movies, I had that familiar conviction that life was beginning over again with the summer.

There was so much to read, for one thing, and so much fine health to be pulled down out of the young breath-giving air. I bought a dozen volumes on banking and credit and investment securities, and they stood on my shelf in red and gold like new money from the mint, promising to unfold the shining secrets that only Midas and Morgan and Mæcenas knew. And I had the high intention of reading many other books besides. I was rather literary in college—one year I wrote a series of very solemn and obvious editorials for the *Yale News*—and now I was going to bring back all such things into my life and become again that most limited of all specialists, the "well-rounded man." This isn't just an epigram—life is much more successfully looked at from a single window, after all.

It was a matter of chance that I should have rented a house in one of the strangest communities in North America. It was on that slender riotous island which extends itself due east of New York—and where there are, among other natural curiosities, two unusual formations of land. Twenty miles from the city a pair of enormous eggs, identical in contour and separated only by a courtesy bay, jut out into the most domesticated body of salt water in the Western hemisphere, the great wet barnyard of Long Island Sound. They are not perfect ovals—like the egg in the Columbus story, they are both crushed flat at the contact end—but their physical resemblance must be a source of perpetual confusion to the gulls that fly overhead. To the wingless a more arresting phenomenon is their dissimilarity in every particular except shape and size.

I lived at West Egg, the—well, the less fashionable of the two, though this is a most superficial tag to express the bizarre and not a little sinister contrast between them. My house was at the very tip of the egg, only fifty yards from the Sound, and squeezed between two huge places that rented for twelve or fifteen thousand a season. The one on my right was a colossal affair by any standard—it was a factual imitation of some Hôtel de Ville in Normandy, with a tower on one side, spanking new under a thin beard of raw ivy, and a marble swimming pool, and more than forty acres of lawn and garden. It was Gatsby's mansion. Or, rather, as I didn't know Mr. Gatsby, it was a mansion, inhabited by a gentleman of that name. My own house was an eyesore, but it was a small eyesore, and it had been overlooked, so I had a view of the water, a partial view of my neighbor's lawn, and the consoling proximity of millionaires—all for eighty dollars a month.

Across the courtesy bay the white palaces of fashionable East Egg glittered along the water, and the history of the summer really begins on the evening I drove over there to have dinner with the Tom Buchanans. Daisy was my second cousin once removed, and I'd known Tom in college. And just after the war I spent two days with them in Chicago.

Her husband, among various physical accomplishments, had been one of the most powerful ends that

ever played football at New Haven—a national figure
in a way, one of those men who reach such an acute
limited excellence at twenty-one that everything
afterward savors of anticlimax. His family were
enormously wealthy—even in college his freedom
with money was a matter for reproach—but now he'd
left Chicago and come East in a fashion that rather
took your breath away; for instance, he'd brought
down a string of polo ponies from Lake Forest. It
was hard to realize that a man in my own generation
was wealthy enough to do that.

Why they came East I don't know. They had spent
a year in France for no particular reason, and then
drifted here and there unrestfully wherever people
played polo and were rich together. This was a
permanent move, said Daisy over the telephone, but
I didn't believe it—I had no sight into Daisy's heart,
but I felt that Tom would drift on forever seeking,
a little wistfully, for the dramatic turbulence of
some irrecoverable football game.

And so it happened that on a warm windy evening
I drove over to East Egg to see two old friends whom
I scarcely knew at all. Their house was even more
elaborate than I expected, a cheerful red-and-white
Georgian Colonial mansion, overlooking the bay. The
lawn started at the beach and ran toward the front
door for a quarter of a mile, jumping over sun-dials
and brick walks and burning gardens—finally when it
reached the house drifting up the side in bright vines
as though from the momentum of its run. The front
was broken by a line of French windows, glowing
now with reflected gold and wide open to the warm
windy afternoon, and Tom Buchanan in riding
clothes was standing with his legs apart on the front
porch.

He had changed since his New Haven years. Now
he was a sturdy straw-haired man of thirty with a
rather hard mouth and a supercilious manner. Two
shining arrogant eyes had established dominance
over his face and gave him the appearance of always
leaning aggressively forward. Not even the effemi-
nate swank of his riding clothes could hide the
enormous power of that body—he seemed to fill those
glistening boots until he strained the top lacing, and
you could see a great pack of muscle shifting when
his shoulder moved under his thin coat. It was a
body capable of enormous leverage—a cruel body.

His speaking voice, a gruff husky tenor, added to
the impression of fractiousness he conveyed. There
was a touch of paternal contempt in it, even toward
people he liked—and there were men at New Haven
who had hated his guts.

"Now, don't think my opinion on these matters is
final," he seemed to say, "just because I'm stronger
and more of a man than you are." We were in the
same senior society, and while we were never intimate I always had the impression that he approved
of me and wanted me to like him with some harsh,
defiant wistfulness of his own.

We talked for a few minutes on the sunny porch.

"I've got a nice place here," he said, his eyes flashing about restlessly.

Turning me around by one arm, he moved a broad
flat hand along the front vista, including in its sweep
a sunken Italian garden, a half acre of deep, pungent
roses, and a snub-nosed motor-boat that bumped the
tide offshore.

"It belonged to Demaine, the oil man." He turned
me around again, politely and abruptly. "We'll go
inside."

We walked through a high hallway into a bright
rosy-colored space, fragilely bound into the house by
French windows at either end. The windows were
ajar and gleaming white against the fresh grass outside that seemed to grow a little way into the house.
A breeze blew through the room, blew curtains in
at one end and out the other like pale flags, twisting
them up toward the frosted wedding-cake of the
ceiling, and then rippled over the wine-colored rug,
making a shadow on it as wind does on the sea.

The only completely stationary object in the room
was an enormous couch on which two young women
were buoyed up as though upon an anchored bal-
loon. They were both in white, and their dresses
were rippling and fluttering as if they had just been
blown back in after a short flight around the house.
I must have stood for a few moments listening to the
whip and snap of the curtains and the groan of a
picture on the wall. Then there was a boom as Tom
Buchanan shut the rear windows and the caught
wind died out about the room, and the curtains and
the rugs and the two young women ballooned slowly
to the floor.

The younger of the two was a stranger to me. She
was extended full length at her end of the divan,
completely motionless, and with her chin raised a
little, as if she were balancing something on it which
was quite likely to fall. If she saw me out of the
corner of her eyes she gave no hint of it—indeed, I
was almost surprised into murmuring an apology for
having disturbed her by coming in.

The other girl, Daisy, made an attempt to rise—she
leaned slightly forward with a conscientious expression—then she laughed, an absurd, charming little
laugh, and I laughed too and came forward into the
room.

"I'm p-paralyzed with happiness."

She laughed again, as if she said something very
witty, and held my hand for a moment, looking up
into my face, promising that there was no one in the

world she so much wanted to see. That was a way she had. She hinted in a murmur that the surname of the balancing girl was Baker. (I've heard it said that Daisy's murmur was only to make people lean toward her; an irrelevant criticism that made it no less charming.)

At any rate, Miss Baker's lips fluttered, she nodded at me almost imperceptibly, and then quickly tipped her head back again—the object she was balancing had obviously tottered a little and given her something of a fright. Again a sort of apology arose to my lips. Almost any exhibition of complete self-sufficiency draws a stunned tribute from me.

I looked back at my cousin, who began to ask me questions in her low, thrilling voice. It was the kind of voice that the ear follows up and down, as if each speech is an arrangement of notes that will never be played again. Her face was sad and lovely with bright things in it, bright eyes and a bright passionate mouth, but there was an excitement in her voice that men who had cared for her found difficult to forget: a singing compulsion, a whispered "Listen," a promise that she had done gay, exciting things just a while since and that there were gay, exciting things hovering in the next hour.

I told her how I had stopped off in Chicago for a day on my way East, and how a dozen people had sent their love through me.

"Do they miss me?" she cried ecstatically.

"The whole town is desolate. All the cars have the left rear wheel painted black as a mourning wreath, and there's a persistent wail all night along the north shore."

"How gorgeous! Let's go back, Tom. To-morrow!" Then she added irrelevantly: "You ought to see the baby."

"I'd like to."

"She's asleep. She's three years old. Haven't you ever seen her?"

"Never."

"Well, you ought to see her. She's——"

Tom Buchanan, who had been hovering restlessly about the room, stopped and rested his hand on my shoulder.

"What you doing, Nick?"

"I'm a bond man."

"Who with?"

I told him.

"Never heard of them," he remarked decisively.

This annoyed me.

"You will," I answered shortly. "You will if you stay in the East."

"Oh, I'll stay in the East, don't you worry," he said, glancing at Daisy and then back at me, as if he were alert for something more. "I'd be a God damned fool to live anywhere else."

At this point Miss Baker said: "Absolutely!" with such suddenness that I started—it was the first word she had uttered since I came into the room. Evidently it surprised her as much as it did me, for she yawned and with a series of rapid, deft movements stood up into the room.

"I'm stiff," she complained, "I've been lying on that sofa for as long as I can remember."

"Don't look at me," Daisy retorted, "I've been trying to get you to New York all afternoon."

"No, thanks," said Miss Baker to the four cocktails just in from the pantry, "I'm absolutely in training."

Her host looked at her incredulously.

"You are!" He took down his drink as if it were a drop in the bottom of a glass. "How you ever get anything done is beyond me."

I looked at Miss Baker, wondering what it was she "got done." I enjoyed looking at her. She was a slender, small-breasted girl, with an erect carriage, which she accentuated by throwing her body backward at the shoulders like a young cadet. Her gray sun-strained eyes looked back at me with polite reciprocal curiosity out of a wan, charming, discontented face. It occurred to me now that I had seen her, or a picture of her, somewhere before.

"You live in West Egg," she remarked contemptuously. "I know somebody there."

"I don't know a single——"

"You must know Gatsby."

"Gatsby?" demanded Daisy. "What Gatsby?"

Before I could reply that he was my neighbor dinner was announced; wedging his tense arm imperatively under mine, Tom Buchanan compelled me from the room as though he were moving a checker to another square.

Slenderly, languidly, their hands set lightly on their hips, the two young women preceded us out onto a rosy-colored porch, open toward the sunset, where four candles flickered on the table in the diminished wind.

"Why *candles?*" objected Daisy, frowning. She snapped them out with her fingers. "In two weeks it'll be the longest day in the year." She looked at us all radiantly. "Do you always watch for the longest day of the year and then miss it? I always watch for the longest day in the year and then miss it."

"We ought to plan something," yawned Miss Baker, sitting down at the table as if she were getting into bed.

"All right," said Daisy. "What'll we plan?" She turned to me helplessly: "What do people plan?"

Before I could answer her eyes fastened with an awed expression on her little finger.

"Look!" she complained; "I hurt it."

We all looked—the knuckle was black and blue.

"You did it, Tom," she said accusingly. "I know you didn't mean to, but you *did* do it. That's what I get for marrying a brute of a man, a great, big, hulking physical specimen of a——"

"I hate that word hulking," objected Tom crossly, "even in kidding."

"Hulking," insisted Daisy.

Sometimes she and Miss Baker talked at once, unobtrusively and with a bantering inconsequence that was never quite chatter, that was as cool as their white dresses and their impersonal eyes in the absence of all desire. They were here, and they accepted Tom and me, making only a polite pleasant effort to entertain or to be entertained. They knew that presently dinner would be over and a little later the evening, too, would be over and casually put away. It was sharply different from the West, where an evening was hurried from phase to phase toward its close, in a continually disappointed anticipation or else in sheer nervous dread of the moment itself.

"You make me feel uncivilized, Daisy," I confessed on my second glass of corky but rather impressive claret. "Can't you talk about crops or something?"

I meant nothing in particular by this remark, but it was taken up in an unexpected way.

"Civilization's going to pieces," broke out Tom violently. "I've gotten to be a terrible pessimist about things. Have you read 'The Rise of the Colored Empires' by this man Goddard?"

"Why, no," I answered, rather surprised by his tone.

"Well, it's a fine book, and everybody ought to read it. The idea is if we don't look out the white race will be—will be utterly submerged. It's all scientific stuff; it's been proved."

"Tom's getting very profound," said Daisy, with an expression of unthoughtful sadness. "He reads deep books with long words in them. What was that word we——"

"Well, these books are all scientific," insisted Tom, glancing at her impatiently. "This fellow has worked out the whole thing. It's up to us, who are the dominant race, to watch out or these other races will have control of things."

"We've got to beat them down," whispered Daisy, winking ferociously toward the fervent sun.

"You ought to live in California—" began Miss Baker, but Tom interrupted her by shifting heavily in his chair.

"This idea is that we're Nordics. I am, and you are, and you are, and—" After an infinitesimal hesitation he included Daisy with a slight nod, and she winked at me again. "—And we've produced all the things that go to make civilization—oh, science and art, and all that. Do you see?"

There was something pathetic in his concentration, as if his complacency, more acute than of old, was not enough to him any more. When, almost immediately, the telephone rang inside and the butler left the porch Daisy seized upon the momentary interruption and leaned toward me.

"I'll tell you a family secret," she whispered enthusiastically. "It's about the butler's nose. Do you want to hear about the butler's nose?"

"That's why I came over to-night."

"Well, he wasn't always a butler; he used to be the silver polisher for some people in New York that had a silver service for two hundred people. He had to polish it from morning till night, until finally it began to affect his nose——"

"Things went from bad to worse," suggested Miss Baker.

"Yes. Things went from bad to worse, until finally he had to give up his position."

For a moment the last sunshine fell with romantic affection upon her glowing face; her voice compelled me forward breathlessly as I listened—then the glow faded, each light deserting her with lingering regret, like children leaving a pleasant street at dusk.

The butler came back and murmured something close to Tom's ear, whereupon Tom frowned, pushed back his chair, and without a word went inside. As if his absence quickened something within her, Daisy leaned forward again, her voice glowing and singing.

"I love to see you at my table, Nick. You remind me of a—of a rose, an absolute rose. Doesn't he?" She turned to Miss Baker for confirmation: "An absolute rose?"

This was untrue. I am not even faintly like a rose. She was only extemporizing, but a stirring warmth flowed from her, as if her heart was trying to come out to you concealed in one of those breathless, thrilling words. Then suddenly she threw her napkin on the table and excused herself and went into the house.

Miss Baker and I exchanged a short glance consciously devoid of meaning. I was about to speak when she sat up alertly and said "Sh!" in a warning voice. A subdued impassioned murmur was audible in the room beyond, and Miss Baker leaned forward unashamed, trying to hear. The murmur trembled on the verge of coherence, sank down, mounted excitedly, and then ceased altogether.

"This Mr. Gatsby you spoke of is my neighbor—" I said.

"Don't talk. I want to hear what happens."

"Is something happening?" I inquired innocently.

"You mean to say you don't know?" said Miss Baker, honestly surprised. "I thought everybody knew."

"I don't."

"Why—" she said hesitantly, "Tom's got some woman in New York."

"Got some woman?" I repeated blankly.

Miss Baker nodded.

"She might have the decency not to telephone him at dinner time. Don't you think?"

Almost before I had grasped her meaning there was the flutter of a dress and the crunch of leather boots, and Tom and Daisy were back at the table.

"It couldn't be helped!" cried Daisy with tense gayety.

She sat down, glanced searchingly at Miss Baker and then at me, and continued: "I looked outdoors for a minute, and it's very romantic outdoors. There's a bird on the lawn that I think must be a nightingale come over on the Cunard or White Star Line. He's singing away—" Her voice sang: "It's romantic, isn't it, Tom?"

"Very romantic," he said, and then miserably to me: "If it's light enough after dinner, I want to take you down to the stables."

The telephone rang inside, startlingly, and as Daisy shook her head decisively at Tom the subject of the stables, in fact all subjects, vanished into air. Among the broken fragments of the last five minutes at table I remember the candles being lit again, pointlessly, and I was conscious of wanting to look squarely at every one, and yet to avoid all eyes. I couldn't guess what Daisy and Tom were thinking, but I doubt if even Miss Baker, who seemed to have mastered a certain hardy scepticism, was able utterly to put this fifth guest's shrill metallic urgency out of mind. To a certain temperament the situation might have seemed intriguing—my own instinct was to telephone immediately for the police.

The horses, needless to say, were not mentioned again. Tom and Miss Baker, with several feet of twilight between them, strolled back into the library, as if to a vigil beside a perfectly tangible body, while, trying to look pleasantly interested and a little deaf, I followed Daisy around a chain of connecting verandas to the porch in front. In its deep gloom we sat down side by side on a wicker settee.

Daisy took her face in her hands as if feeling its lovely shape, and her eyes moved gradually out into the velvet dusk. I saw that turbulent emotions possessed her, so I asked what I thought would be some sedative questions about her little girl.

"We don't know each other very well, Nick," she said suddenly. "Even if we are cousins. You didn't come to my wedding."

"I wasn't back from the war."

"That's true." She hesitated. "Well, I've had a very bad time, Nick, and I'm pretty cynical about everything."

Evidently she had reason to be. I waited but she didn't say any more, and after a moment I returned rather feebly to the subject of her daughter.

"I suppose she talks, and—eats, and everything."

"Oh, yes." She looked at me absently. "Listen, Nick; let me tell you what I said when she was born. Would you like to hear?"

"Very much."

"It'll show you how I've gotten to feel about—things. Well, she was less than an hour old and Tom was God knows where. I woke up out of the ether with an utterly abandoned feeling, and asked the nurse right away if it was a boy or a girl. She told me it was a girl, and so I turned my head away and wept. 'All right,' I said, 'I'm glad it's a girl. And I hope she'll be a fool—that's the best thing a girl can be in this world, a beautiful little fool.'

"You see I think everything's terrible anyhow," she went on in a convinced way. "Everybody thinks so—the most advanced people. And I *know*. I've been everywhere and seen everything and done everything." Her eyes flashed around her in a defiant way, rather like Tom's, and she laughed with thrilling scorn. "Sophisticated—God, I'm sophisticated!"

The instant her voice broke off, ceasing to compel my attention, my belief, I felt the basic insincerity of what she had said. It made me uneasy, as though the whole evening had been a trick of some sort to exact a contributory emotion from me. I waited, and sure enough, in a moment she looked at me with an absolute smirk on her lovely face, as if she had asserted her membership in a rather distinguished secret society to which she and Tom belonged.

Inside, the crimson room bloomed with light. Tom and Miss Baker sat at either end of the long couch and she read aloud to him from *The Saturday Evening Post*—the words, murmurous and uninflected, running together in a soothing tune. The lamp-light, bright on his boots and dull on the autumn-leaf yellow of her hair, glinted along the paper as she turned a page with a flutter of slender muscles in her arms.

When we came in she held us silent for a moment with a lifted hand.

"To be continued," she said, tossing the magazine on the table, "in our very next issue."

Her body asserted itself with a restless movement of her knee, and she stood up.

"Ten o'clock," she remarked, apparently finding the time on the ceiling. "Time for this good girl to go to bed."

"Jordan's going to play in the tournament tomorrow," explained Daisy, "over at Westchester."

"Oh—you're *Jor*dan Baker."

I knew now why her face was familiar—its pleasing contemptuous expression had looked out at me from many rotogravure pictures of the sporting life at

Asheville and Hot Springs and Palm Beach. I had heard some story of her too, a critical, unpleasant story, but what it was I had forgotten long ago.

"Good night," she said softly. "Wake me at eight, won't you?"

"If you'll get up."

"I will. Good night, Mr. Carraway. See you anon."

"Of course you will," confirmed Daisy. "In fact, I think I'll arrange a marriage. Come over often, Nick, and I'll sort of—oh—fling you together. You know—lock you up accidentally in linen closets and push you out to sea in a boat, and all that sort of thing——"

"Good night," called Miss Baker from the stairs. "I haven't heard a word."

"She's a nice girl," said Tom after a moment. "They oughtn't to let her run around the country this way."

"Who oughtn't to?" inquired Daisy coldly.

"Her family."

"Her family is one aunt about a thousand years old. Besides, Nick's going to look after her, aren't you, Nick? She's going to spend lots of week-ends out here this summer. I think the home influence will be very good for her."

Daisy and Tom looked at each other for a moment in silence.

"Is she from New York?" I asked quickly.

"From Louisville. Our white girlhood was passed together there. Our beautiful white——"

"Did you give Nick a little heart-to-heart talk on the veranda?" demanded Tom suddenly.

"Did I?" She looked at me. "I can't seem to remember, but I think we talked about the Nordic race. Yes, I'm sure we did. It sort of crept up on us and first thing you know——"

"Don't believe everything you hear, Nick," he advised me.

I said lightly that I had heard nothing at all, and a few minutes later I got up to go home. They came to the door with me and stood side by side in a cheerful square of light. As I started my motor Daisy peremptorily called: "Wait!

"I forgot to ask you something, and it's important. We heard you were engaged to a girl out West."

"That's right," corroborated Tom kindly. "We heard that you were engaged."

"It's a libel. I'm too poor."

"But we heard it," insisted Daisy, surprising me by opening up again in a flower-like way. "We heard it from three people, so it must be true."

Of course I knew what they were referring to, but I wasn't even vaguely engaged. The fact that gossip had published the banns was one of the reasons I had come East. You can't stop going with an old friend on account of rumors, and on the other hand I had no intention of being rumored into marriage.

Their interest rather touched me and made them less remotely rich—nevertheless, I was confused and a little disgusted as I drove away. It seemed to me that the thing for Daisy to do was to rush out of the house, child in arms—but apparently there were no such intentions in her head. As for Tom, the fact that he "had some woman in New York" was really less surprising than that he had been depressed by a book. Something was making him nibble at the edge of stale ideas as if his sturdy physical egotism no longer nourished his peremptory heart.

Already it was deep summer on roadhouse roofs and in front of wayside garages, where new red gas-pumps sat out in pools of light, and when I reached my estate at West Egg I ran the car under its shed and sat for a while on an abandoned grass roller in the yard. The wind had blown off, leaving a loud, bright night, with wings beating in the trees and a persistent organ sound as the full bellows of the earth blew the frogs full of life. The silhouette of a moving cat wavered across the moonlight, and turning my head to watch it, I saw that I was not alone —fifty feet away a figure had emerged from the shadow of my neighbor's mansion and was standing with his hands in his pockets regarding the silver pepper of the stars. Something in his leisurely movements and the secure position of his feet upon the lawn suggested that it was Mr. Gatsby himself, come out to determine what share was his of our local heavens.

I decided to call to him. Miss Baker had mentioned him at dinner, and that would do for an introduction. But I didn't call to him, for he gave a sudden intimation that he was content to be alone—he stretched out his arms toward the dark water in a curious way, and, far as I was from him, I could have sworn he was trembling. Involuntarily I glanced seaward—and distinguished nothing except a single green light, minute and far way, that might have been the end of a dock. When I looked once more for Gatsby he had vanished, and I was alone again in the unquiet darkness.

II

About half way between West Egg and New York the motor road hastily joins the railroad and runs beside it for a quarter of a mile, so as to shrink away from a certain desolate area of land. This is a valley of ashes—a fantastic farm where ashes grow like wheat into ridges and hills and grotesque gardens; where ashes take the forms of houses and chimneys and rising smoke and, finally, with a transcendent effort, of ash-gray men who move dimly and already crumbling through the powdery air. Occasionally a line of gray cars crawls along an invisible track, gives out a ghastly creak, and comes to rest, and immediately the ash-gray men swarm up with leaden spades and stir up an impenetrable cloud, which screens their obscure operations from your sight.

But above the gray land and the spasms of bleak dust which drift endlessly over it, you perceive, after a moment, the eyes of Doctor T. J. Eckleburg. The eyes of Doctor T. J. Eckleburg are blue and gigantic —their retinas are one yard high. They look out of no face, but, instead, from a pair of enormous yellow spectacles which pass over a non-existent nose. Evidently some wild wag of an oculist set them there to fatten his practice in the borough of Queens, and then sank down himself into eternal blindness, or forgot them and moved away. But his eyes, dimmed a little by many paintless days under sun and rain, brood on over the solemn dumping ground.

The valley of ashes is bounded on one side by a small foul river, and, when the drawbridge is up to let barges through, the passengers on waiting trains can stare at the dismal scene for as long as half an hour. There is always a halt there of at least a minute, and it was because of this that I first met Tom Buchanan's mistress.

The fact that he had one was insisted upon wherever he was known. His acquaintances resented the fact that he turned up in popular restaurants with her and, leaving her at a table, sauntered about, chatting with whomsoever he knew. Though I was curious to see her, I had no desire to meet her— but I did. I went up to New York with Tom on the train one afternoon, and when we stopped by the ashheaps he jumped to his feet and, taking hold of my elbow, literally forced me from the car.

"We're getting off," he insisted. "I want you to meet my girl."

I think he'd tanked up a good deal at luncheon, and his determination to have my company bordered on violence. The supercilious assumption was that on Sunday afternoon I had nothing better to do.

I followed him over a low whitewashed railroad fence, and we walked back a hundred yards along the road under Doctor Eckleburg's persistent stare. The only building in sight was a small block of yellow brick sitting on the edge of the waste land, a sort of compact Main Street ministering to it, and contiguous to absolutely nothing. One of the three shops it contained was for rent and another was an all-night restaurant, approached by a trail of ashes; the third was a garage—*Repairs*. GEORGE B. WILSON. *Cars bought and sold.*—and I followed Tom inside.

The interior was unprosperous and bare; the only car visible was the dust-covered wreck of a Ford which crouched in a dim corner. It had occurred to me that this shadow of a garage must be a blind, and that sumptuous and romantic apartments were concealed overhead, when the proprietor himself appeared in the door of an office, wiping his hands on a piece of waste. He was a blond, spiritless man, anæmic, and faintly handsome. When he saw us a damp gleam of hope sprang into his light blue eyes.

"Hello, Wilson, old man," said Tom, slapping him jovially on the shoulder. "How's business?"

"I can't complain," answered Wilson unconvincingly. "When are you going to sell me that car?"

"Next week; I've got my man working on it now."

"Works pretty slow, don't he?"

"No, he doesn't," said Tom coldly. "And if you feel that way about it, maybe I'd better sell it somewhere else after all."

"I don't mean that," explained Wilson quickly. "I just meant——"

His voice faded off and Tom glanced impatiently around the garage. Then I heard footsteps on a stairs, and in a moment the thickish figure of a woman blocked out the light from the office door. She was in the middle thirties, and faintly stout, but she carried her surplus flesh sensuously as some women can. Her face, above a spotted dress of dark blue crêpe-de-chine, contained no facet or gleam of beauty, but there was an immediately perceptible vitality about her as if the nerves of her body were continually smouldering. She smiled slowly and, walking through her husband as if he were a ghost, shook hands with Tom, looking him flush in the eye. Then she wet her lips, and without turning around spoke to her husband in a soft, coarse voice:

"Get some chairs, why don't you, so somebody can sit down."

"Oh, sure," agreed Wilson hurriedly, and went toward the little office, mingling immediately with the cement color of the walls. A white ashen dust veiled his dark suit and his pale hair as it veiled everything in the vicinity—except his wife, who moved close to Tom.

"I want to see you," said Tom intently. "Get on the next train."

"All right."

"I'll meet you by the news-stand on the lower level."

She nodded and moved away from him just as George Wilson emerged with two chairs from his office door.

We waited for her down the road and out of sight. It was a few days before the Fourth of July, and a gray, scrawny Italian child was setting torpedoes in a row along the railroad track.

220 THE NOVEL

"Terrible place, isn't it," said Tom, exchanging a frown with Doctor Eckleburg.

"Awful."

"It does her good to get away."

"Doesn't her husband object?"

"Wilson? He thinks she goes to see her sister in New York. He's so dumb he doesn't know he's alive."

So Tom Buchanan and his girl and I went up together to New York—or not quite together, for Mrs. Wilson sat discreetly in another car. Tom deferred that much to the sensibilities of those East Eggers who might be on the train.

She had changed her dress to a brown figured muslin, which stretched tight over her rather wide hips as Tom helped her to the platform in New York. At the news-stand she bought a copy of *Town Tattle* and a moving-picture magazine, and in the station drug-store some cold cream and a small flask of perfume. Up-stairs, in the solemn echoing drive she let four taxicabs drive away before she selected a new one, lavender-colored with gray upholstery, and in this we slid out from the mass of the station into the glowing sunshine. But immediately she turned sharply from the window and, leaning forward, tapped on the front glass.

"I want to get one of those dogs," she said earnestly. "I want to get one for the apartment. They're nice to have—a dog."

We backed up to a gray old man who bore an absurd resemblance to John D. Rockefeller. In a basket swung from his neck cowered a dozen very recent puppies of an indeterminate breed.

"What kind are they?" asked Mrs. Wilson eagerly, as he came to the taxi-window.

"All kinds. What kind do you want, lady?"

"I'd like to get one of those police dogs; I don't suppose you got that kind?"

The man peered doubtfully into the basket, plunged in his hand and drew one up, wriggling, by the back of the neck.

"That's no police dog," said Tom.

"No, it's not exactly a po*lice* dog," said the man with disappointment in his voice. "It's more of an Airedale." He passed his hand over the brown washrag of a back. "Look at that coat. Some coat. That's a dog that'll never bother you with catching cold."

"I think it's cute," said Mrs. Wilson enthusiastically. "How much is it?"

"That dog?" He looked at it admiringly. "That dog will cost you ten dollars."

The Airedale—undoubtedly there was an Airedale concerned in it somewhere, though its feet were startlingly white—changed hands and settled down into Mrs. Wilson's lap, where she fondled the weatherproof coat with rapture.

"Is it a boy or a girl?" she asked delicately.

"That dog? That dog's a boy."

"It's a bitch," said Tom decisively. "Here's your money. Go and buy ten more dogs with it."

We drove over to Fifth Avenue, so warm and soft, almost pastoral, on the summer Sunday afternoon that I wouldn't have been surprised to see a great flock of white sheep turn the corner.

"Hold on," I said, "I have to leave you here."

"No, you don't," interposed Tom quickly. "Myrtle'll be hurt if you don't come up to the apartment. Won't you, Myrtle?"

"Come on," she urged. "I'll telephone my sister Catherine. She's said to be very beautiful by people who ought to know."

"Well, I'd like to, but——"

We went on, cutting back again over the Park toward the West Hundreds. At 158th Street the cab stopped at one slice in a long white cake of apartment-houses. Throwing a regal homecoming glance around the neighborhood, Mrs. Wilson gathered up her dog and her other purchases, and went haughtily in.

"I'm going to have the McKees come up," she announced as we rose in the elevator. "And, of course, I got to call up my sister, too."

The apartment was on the top floor—a small living-room, a small dining-room, a small bedroom, and a bath. The living-room was crowded to the doors with a set of tapestried furniture entirely too large for it, so that to move about was to stumble continually over scenes of ladies swinging in the gardens of Versailles. The only picture was an over-enlarged photograph, apparently a hen sitting on a blurred rock. Looked at from a distance, however, the hen resolved itself into a bonnet, and the countenance of a stout old lady beamed down into the room. Several old copies of *Town Tattle* lay on the table together with a copy of *Simon Called Peter,* and some of the small scandal magazines of Broadway. Mrs. Wilson was first concerned with the dog. A reluctant elevator-boy went for a box full of straw and some milk, to which he added on his own initiative a tin of large, hard dog-biscuits—one of which decomposed apathetically in the saucer of milk all afternoon. Meanwhile Tom brought out a bottle of whiskey from a locked bureau door.

I have been drunk just twice in my life, and the second time was that afternoon; so everything that happened has a dim, hazy cast over it, although until after eight o'clock the apartment was full of cheerful sun. Sitting on Tom's lap Mrs. Wilson called up several people on the telephone; then there were no cigarettes, and I went out to buy some at the drugstore on the corner. When I came back they had disappeared, so I sat down discreetly in the living-room and read a chapter of *Simon Called Peter*—either it was terrible stuff or the whiskey distorted things, because it didn't make any sense to me.

Just as Tom and Myrtle (after the first drink Mrs. Wilson and I called each other by our first names) reappeared, company commenced to arrive at the apartment-door.

The sister, Catherine, was a slender, worldly girl of about thirty, with a solid, sticky bob of red hair, and a complexion powdered milky white. Her eyebrows had been plucked and then drawn on again at a more rakish angle, but the efforts of nature toward the restoration of the old alignment gave a blurred air to her face. When she moved about there was an incessant clicking as innumerable pottery bracelets jingled up and down upon her arms. She came in with such a proprietary haste, and looked around so possessively at the furniture that I wondered if she lived here. But when I asked her she laughed immoderately, repeated my question aloud, and told me she lived with a girl friend at a hotel.

Mr. McKee was a pale, feminine man from the flat below. He had just shaved, for there was a white spot of lather on his cheekbone, and he was most respectful in his greeting to every one in the room. He informed me that he was in the "artistic game," and I gathered later that he was a photographer and had made the dim enlargement of Mrs. Wilson's mother which hovered like an ectoplasm on the wall. His wife was shrill, languid, handsome, and horrible. She told me with pride that her husband had photographed her a hundred and twenty-seven times since they had been married.

Mrs. Wilson had changed her costume some time before, and was now attired in an elaborate afternoon dress of cream-colored chiffon, which gave out a continual rustle as she swept about the room. With the influence of the dress her personality had also undergone a change. The intense vitality that had been so remarkable in the garage was converted into impressive hauteur. Her laughter, her gestures, her assertions became more violently affected moment by moment, and as she expanded the room grew smaller around her, until she seemed to be revolving on a noisy, creaking pivot through the smoky air.

"My dear," she told her sister in a high, mincing shout, "most of these fellas will cheat you every time. All they think of is money. I had a woman up here last week to look at my feet, and when she gave me the bill you'd of thought she had my appendicitis out."

"What was the name of the woman?" asked Mrs. McKee.

"Mrs. Eberhardt. She goes around looking at people's feet in their own homes."

"I like your dress," remarked Mrs. McKee, "I think it's adorable."

Mrs. Wilson rejected the compliment by raising her eyebrow in disdain.

"It's just a crazy old thing," she said. "I just slip it on sometimes when I don't care what I look like."

"But it looks wonderful on you, if you know what I mean," pursued Mrs. McKee. "If Chester could only get you in that pose I think he could make something of it."

We all looked in silence at Mrs. Wilson, who removed a strand of hair from over her eyes and looked back at us with a brilliant smile. Mr. McKee regarded her intently with his head on one side, and then moved his hand back and forth slowly in front of his face.

"I should change the light," he said after a moment. "I'd like to bring out the modelling of the features. And I'd try to get hold of all the back hair."

"I wouldn't think of changing the light," cried Mrs. McKee. "I think it's——"

Her husband said "*Sh!*" and we all looked at the subject again, whereupon Tom Buchanan yawned audibly and got to his feet.

"You McKees have something to drink," he said. "Get some more ice and mineral water, Myrtle, before everybody goes to sleep."

"I told that boy about the ice." Myrtle raised her eyebrows in despair at the shiftlessness of the lower orders. "These people! You have to keep after them all the time."

She looked at me and laughed pointlessly. Then she flounced over to the dog, kissed it with ecstasy, and swept into the kitchen, implying that a dozen chefs awaited her orders there.

"I've done some nice things out on Long Island," asserted Mr. McKee.

Tom looked at him blankly.

"Two of them we have framed down-stairs."

"Two what?" demanded Tom.

"Two studies. One of them I call *Montauk Point—The Gulls,* and the other I call *Montauk Point—The Sea.*"

The sister Catherine sat down beside me on the couch.

"Do you live down on Long Island, too?" she inquired.

"I live at West Egg."

"Really? I was down there at a party about a month ago. At a man named Gatsby's. Do you know him?"

"I live next door to him."

"Well, they say he's a nephew or a cousin of

Kaiser Wilhelm's. That's where all his money comes from."

"Really?"

She nodded.

"I'm scared of him. I'd hate to have him get anything on me."

This absorbing information about my neighbor was interrupted by Mrs. McKee's pointing suddenly at Catherine:

"Chester, I think you could do something with *her*," she broke out, but Mr. McKee only nodded in a bored way, and turned his attention to Tom.

"I'd like to do more work on Long Island, if I could get the entry. All I ask is that they should give me a start."

"Ask Myrtle," said Tom, breaking into a short shout of laughter as Mrs. Wilson entered with a tray. "She'll give you a letter of introduction, won't you, Myrtle?"

"Do what?" she asked, startled.

"You'll give McKee a letter of introduction to your husband, so he can do some studies of him." His lips moved silently for a moment as he invented. "*George B. Wilson at the Gasoline Pump*, or something like that."

Catherine leaned close to me and whispered in my ear:

"Neither of them can stand the person they're married to."

"Can't they?"

"Can't *stand* them." She looked at Myrtle and then at Tom. "What I say is, why go on living with them if they can't stand them? If I was them I'd get a divorce and get married to each other right away."

"Doesn't she like Wilson either?"

The answer to this was unexpected. It came from Myrtle, who had overheard the question, and it was violent and obscene.

"You see," cried Catherine triumphantly. She lowered her voice again. "It's really his wife that's keeping them apart. She's a Catholic, and they don't believe in divorce."

Daisy was not a Catholic, and I was a little shocked at the elaborateness of the lie.

"When they do get married," continued Catherine, "they're going West to live for a while until it blows over."

"It'd be more discreet to go to Europe."

"Oh, do you like Europe?" she exclaimed surprisingly. "I just got back from Monte Carlo."

"Really."

"Just last year. I went over there with another girl."

"Stay long?"

"No, we just went to Monte Carlo and back. We went by way of Marseilles. We had over twelve hundred dollars when we started, but we got gypped out of it all in two days in the private rooms. We had an awful time getting back, I can tell you. God, how I hated that town!"

The late afternoon sky boomed in the window for a moment like the blue honey of the Mediterranean —then the shrill voice of Mrs. McKee called me back into the room.

"I almost made a mistake, too," she declared vigorously. "I almost married a little kike who'd been after me for years. I knew he was below me. Everybody kept saying to me: 'Lucille, that man's 'way below you!' But if I hadn't met Chester, he'd of got me sure."

"Yes, but listen," said Myrtle Wilson, nodding her head up and down, "at least you didn't marry him."

"I know I didn't."

"Well, I married him," said Myrtle, ambiguously. "And that's the difference between your case and mine."

"Why did you, Myrtle?" demanded Catherine. "Nobody forced you to."

Myrtle considered.

"I married him because I thought he was a gentleman," she said finally. "I thought he knew something about breeding, but he wasn't fit to lick my shoe."

"You were crazy about him for a while," said Catherine.

"Crazy about him!" cried Myrtle incredulously. "Who said I was crazy about him? I never was any more crazy about him than I was about that man there."

She pointed suddenly at me, and every one looked at me accusingly. I tried to show by my expression that I had played no part in her past.

"The only *crazy* I was was when I married him. I knew right away I made a mistake. He borrowed somebody's best suit to get married in, and never even told me about it, and the man came after it one day when he was out." She looked around to see who was listening. "'Oh, is that your suit?' I said. 'This is the first I ever heard about it.' But I gave it to him and then I lay down and cried to beat the band all afternoon."

"She really ought to get away from him," resumed Catherine to me. "They've been living over that garage for eleven years. And Tom's the first sweetie she ever had."

The bottle of whiskey—a second one—was now in constant demand by all present, excepting Catherine, who "felt just as good on nothing at all." Tom rang for the janitor and sent him for some celebrated sandwiches, which were a complete supper in themselves. I wanted to get out and walk eastward toward the park through the soft twilight, but each time I tried to go I became entangled in some wild, strident argument which pulled me back, as if with ropes, into my chair. Yet high over the city our line of yellow windows must have contributed their share of human secrecy to the casual watcher in the darkening streets, and I was him too, looking up and wondering. I was within and without, simultaneously enchanted and repelled by the inexhaustible variety of life.

Myrtle pulled her chair close to mine, and suddenly her warm breath poured over me the story of her first meeting with Tom.

"It was on the two little seats facing each other that are always the last ones left on the train. I was going up to New York to see my sister and spend the night. He had on a dress suit and patent leather shoes, and I couldn't keep my eyes off him, but every time he looked at me I had to pretend to be looking at the advertisement over his head. When he came into the station he was next to me, and his white shirt-front pressed against my arm, and so I told him I'd have to call policeman, but he knew I lied. I was so excited that when I got into a taxi with him I didn't hardly know I wasn't getting into a subway train. All I kept thinking about, over and over, was 'You can't live forever; you can't live forever.'"

She turned to Mrs. McKee and the room rang full of her artificial laughter.

"My dear," she cried, "I'm going to give you this dress as soon as I'm through with it. I've got to get another one tomorrow. I'm going to make a list of all the things I've got to get. A massage and a wave, and a collar for the dog, and one of those cute little ashtrays where you touch a spring, and a wreath with a black silk bow for mother's grave that'll last all summer. I got to write down a list so I won't forget all the things I got to do."

It was nine o'clock—almost immediately afterward I looked at my watch and found it was ten. Mr. McKee was asleep on a chair with his fists clenched in his lap, like a photograph of a man of action. Taking out my handkerchief I wiped from his cheek the remains of the spot of dried lather that had worried me all the afternoon.

The little dog was sitting on the table looking with blind eyes through the smoke, and from time to time groaning faintly. People disappeared, reappeared, made plans to go somewhere, and then lost each other, searched for each other, found each other a few feet away. Some time toward midnight Tom Buchanan and Mrs. Wilson stood face to face, discussing in impassioned voices whether Mrs. Wilson had any right to mention Daisy's name.

"Daisy! Daisy! Daisy!" shouted Mrs. Wilson. "I'll say it whenever I want to! Daisy! Dai——"

Making a short deft movement, Tom Buchanan broke her nose with his open hand.

Then there were bloody towels upon the bathroom floor, and women's voices scolding, and high over the confusion a long broken wail of pain. Mr. McKee awoke from his doze and started in a daze toward the door. When he had gone halfway he turned around and stared at the scene—his wife and Catherine scolding and consoling as they stumbled here and there among the crowded furniture with articles of aid, and the despairing figure on the couch, bleeding fluently, and trying to spread a copy of *Town Tattle* over the tapestry scenes of Versailles. Then Mr. McKee turned and continued on out the door. Taking my hat from the chandelier, I followed.

"Come to lunch some day," he suggested, as we groaned down in the elevator.

"Where?"

"Anywhere."

"Keep your hands off the lever," snapped the elevator boy.

"I beg your pardon," said Mr. McKee with dignity, "I didn't know I was touching it."

"All right," I agreed, "I'll be glad to."

. . . I was standing beside his bed and he was sitting up between the sheets, clad in his underwear, with a great portfolio in his hands.

"Beauty and the Beast . . . Loneliness . . . Old Grocery Horse . . . Brook'n Bridge. . . ."

Then I was lying half asleep in the cold lower level of the Pennsylvania Station, staring at the morning *Tribune*, and waiting for the four o'clock train.

III

There was music from my neighbor's house through the summer nights. In his blue gardens men and girls came and went like moths among the whisperings and the champagne and the stars. At high tide in the afternoon I watched his guests diving from the tower of his raft, or taking the sun on the hot sand of his beach while his two motor-boats slit the waters of the Sound, drawing aquaplanes over cataracts of foam. On week-ends his Rolls-Royce became an omnibus, bearing parties to and from the city between nine in the morning and long past midnight, while his station wagon scampered like a brisk yellow bug to meet all trains. And on Mondays eight servants, including an extra gardener, toiled all day with mops and scrubbing-brushes and hammers and garden-shears, repairing the ravages of the night before.

Every Friday five crates of oranges and lemons arrived from a fruiterer in New York—every Monday these same oranges and lemons left his back door in a pyramid of pulpless halves. There was a machine in the kitchen which could extract the juice of two hundred oranges in half an hour if a little button was pressed two hundred times by a butler's thumb.

At least once a fortnight a corps of caterers came down with several hundred feet of canvas and enough colored lights to make a Christmas tree of Gatsby's enormous garden. On buffet tables, garnished with glistening hors-d'œuvre, spiced baked hams crowded against salads of harlequin designs and pastry pigs and turkeys bewitched to a dark gold. In the main hall a bar with a real brass rail was set up, and stocked with gins and liquors and with cordials so long forgotten that most of his female guests were too young to know one from another.

By seven o'clock the orchestra has arrived, no thin five-piece affair, but a whole pitful of oboes and trombones and saxophones and viols and cornets and piccolos, and low and high drums. The last swimmers have come in from the beach now and are dressing up-stairs; the cars from New York are parked five deep in the drive, and already the halls and salons and verandas are gaudy with primary colors, and hair shorn in strange new ways, and shawls beyond the dreams of Castile. The bar is in full swing, and floating rounds of cocktails permeate the garden outside, until the air is alive with chatter and laughter, and casual innuendo and introductions forgotten on the spot, and enthusiastic meetings between women who never knew each other's names.

The lights grow brighter as the earth lurches away from the sun, and now the orchestra is playing yellow cocktail music, and the opera of voices pitches a key higher. Laughter is easier minute by minute, spilled with prodigality, tipped out at a cheerful word. The groups change more swiftly, swell with new arrivals, dissolve and form in the same breath; already there are wanderers, confident girls who weave here and there among the stouter and more stable, become for a sharp, joyous moment the center of a group, and then, excited with triumph, glide on through the sea-change of faces and voices and color under the constantly changing light.

Suddenly one of these gypsies, in trembling opal, seizes a cocktail out of the air, dumps it down for courage and, moving her hands like Frisco, dances out alone on the canvas platform. A momentary hush; the orchestra leader varies his rhythm obligingly for her, and there is a burst of chatter as the erroneous news goes around that she is Gilda Gray's understudy from the *Follies*. The party has begun.

I believe that on the first night I went to Gatsby's house I was one of the few guests who had actually been invited. People were not invited—they went there. They got into automobiles which bore them out to Long Island, and somehow they ended up at Gatsby's door. Once there they were introduced by somebody who knew Gatsby, and after that they conducted themselves according to the rules of behavior associated with amusement parks. Sometimes they came and went without having met Gatsby at all, came for the party with a simplicity of heart that was its own ticket of admission.

I had been actually invited. A chauffeur in a uniform of robin's-egg blue crossed my lawn early that Saturday morning with a surprisingly formal note from his employer: the honor would be entirely Gatsby's, it said, if I would attend his "little party" that night. He had seen me several times, and had intended to call on me long before, but a peculiar combination of circumstances had prevented it—signed Jay Gatsby, in a majestic hand.

Dressed up in white flannels I went over to his lawn a little after seven, and wandered around rather ill at ease among swirls and eddies of people I didn't know—though here and there was a face I had noticed on the commuting train. I was immediately struck by the number of young Englishmen dotted about; all well dressed, all looking a little hungry, and all talking in low, earnest voices to solid and prosperous Americans. I was sure that they were selling something: bonds or insurance or automobiles. They were at least agonizingly aware of the easy money in the vicinity and convinced that it was theirs for a few words in the right key.

As soon as I arrived I made an attempt to find my host, but the two or three people of whom I asked his whereabouts stared at me in such an amazed way, and denied so vehemently any knowledge of his movements, that I slunk off in the direction of the cocktail table—the only place in the garden where a single man could linger without looking purposeless and alone.

I was on my way to get roaring drunk from sheer embarrassment when Jordan Baker came out of the house and stood at the head of the marble steps, leaning a little backward and looking with contemptuous interest down into the garden.

Welcome or not, I found it necessary to attach myself to some one before I should begin to address cordial remarks to the passers-by.

"Hello!" I roared, advancing toward her. My voice seemed unnaturally loud across the garden.

"I thought you might be here," she responded absently as I came up. "I remembered you lived next door to——"

She held my hand impersonally, as a promise that she'd take care of me in a minute, and gave ear to two girls in twin yellow dresses, who stopped at the foot of the steps.

"Hello!" they cried together. "Sorry you didn't win."

That was for the golf tournament. She had lost in the finals the week before.

"You don't know who we are," said one of the girls in yellow, "but we met you here about a month ago."

"You've dyed your hair since then," remarked Jordan, and I started, but the girls had moved casually on and her remark was addressed to the premature moon, produced like the supper, no doubt, out of a caterer's basket. With Jordan's slender golden arm resting on mine, we descended the steps and sauntered about the garden. A tray of cocktails floated at us through the twilight, and we sat down at a table with the two girls in yellow and three men, each one introduced to us as Mr. Mumble.

"Do you come to these parties often?" inquired Jordan of the girl beside her.

"The last one was the one I met you at," answered the girl, in an alert confident voice. She turned to her companion: "Wasn't it for you, Lucille?"

It was for Lucille, too.

"I like to come," Lucille said. "I never care what I do, so I always have a good time. When I was here last I tore my gown on a chair, and he asked me my name and address—inside of a week I got a package from Croirier's with a new evening gown in it."

"Did you keep it?" asked Jordan.

"Sure I did. I was going to wear it tonight, but it was too big in the bust and had to be altered. It was gas blue with lavender beads. Two hundred and sixty-five dollars."

"There's something funny about a fellow that'll do a thing like that," said the other girl eagerly. "He doesn't want any trouble with *anybody*."

"Who doesn't?" I inquired.

"Gatsby. Somebody told me——"

The two girls and Jordan leaned together confidentially.

"Somebody told me they thought he killed a man once."

A thrill passed over all of us. The three Mr. Mumbles bent forward and listened eagerly.

"I don't think it's so much *that*," argued Lucille sceptically; "it's more that he was a German spy during the war."

One of the men nodded in confirmation.

"I heard that from a man who knew all about him, grew up with him in Germany," he assured us positively.

"Oh, no," said the first girl, "it couldn't be that, because he was in the American army during the war." As our credulity switched back to her she leaned forward with enthusiasm. "You look at him sometimes when he thinks nobody's looking at him. I'll bet he killed a man."

She narrowed her eyes and shivered. Lucille shivered. We all turned and looked around for Gatsby. It was testimony to the romantic speculation he inspired that there were whispers about him from those who had found little that it was necessary to whisper about in this world.

The first supper—there would be another one after midnight—was now being served, and Jordan invited me to join her own party, who were spread around a table on the other side of the garden. There were three married couples and Jordan's escort, a persistent undergraduate given to violent innuendo, and obviously under the impression that sooner or later Jordan was going to yield him up her person to a greater or lesser degree. Instead of rambling, this party had preserved a dignified homogeneity, and assumed to itself the function of representing the staid nobility of the country-side—East Egg condescending to West Egg, and carefully on guard against its spectroscopic gayety.

"Let's get out," whispered Jordan, after a somehow wasteful and inappropriate half-hour; "this is much too polite for me."

We got up, and she explained that we were going to find the host: I had never met him, she said, and it was making me uneasy. The undergraduate nodded in a cynical, melancholy way.

The bar, where we glanced first, was crowded, but Gatsby was not there. She couldn't find him from the top of the steps, and he wasn't on the veranda. On a chance we tried an important-looking door, and walked into a high Gothic library, panelled with carved English oak, and probably transported complete from some ruin overseas.

A stout, middle-aged man, with enormous owl-eyed spectacles, was sitting somewhat drunk on the edge of a great table, staring with unsteady concentration at the shelves of books. As we entered he wheeled excitedly around and examined Jordan from head to foot.

"What do you think?" he demanded impetuously.

"About what?"

He waved his hand toward the book-shelves.

"About that. As a matter of fact you needn't bother to ascertain. I ascertained. They're real."

"The books?"

He nodded.

"Absolutely real—have pages and everything. I thought they'd be a nice durable cardboard. Matter of fact, they're absolutely real. Pages and— Here! Lemme show you."

Taking our scepticism for granted, he rushed to

the bookcases and returned with Volume One of the "Stoddard Lectures."

"See!" he cried triumphantly. "It's a bona-fide piece of printed matter. It fooled me. This fella's a regular Belasco. It's a triumph. What thoroughness! What realism! Knew when to stop, too—didn't cut the pages. But what do you want? What do you expect?"

He snatched the book from me and replaced it hastily on its shelf, muttering that if one brick was removed the whole library was liable to collapse.

"Who brought you?" he demanded. "Or did you just come? I was brought. Most people were brought."

Jordan looked at him alertly, cheerfully, without answering.

"I was brought by a woman named Roosevelt," he continued. "Mrs. Claud Roosevelt. Do you know her? I met her somewhere last night. I've been drunk for about a week now, and I thought it might sober me up to sit in a library."

"Has it?"

"A little bit, I think. I can't tell yet. I've only been here an hour. Did I tell you about the books? They're real. They're——"

"You told us."

We shook hands with him gravely and went back outdoors.

There was dancing now on the canvas in the garden; old men pushing young girls backward in eternal graceless circles, superior couples holding each other tortuously, fashionably, and keeping in the corners—and a great number of single girls dancing individualistically or relieving the orchestra for a moment of the burden of the banjo or the traps. By midnight the hilarity had increased. A celebrated tenor had sung in Italian, and a notorious contralto had sung in jazz, and between the numbers people were doing "stunts" all over the garden, while happy, vacuous bursts of laughter rose toward the summer sky. A pair of stage twins, who turned out to be the girls in yellow, did a baby act in costume, and champagne was served in glasses bigger than finger-bowls. The moon had risen higher, and floating in the Sound was a triangle of silver scales, trembling a little to the stiff, tinny drip of the banjoes on the lawn.

I was still with Jordan Baker. We were sitting at a table with a man of about my age and a rowdy little girl, who gave way upon the slightest provocation to uncontrollable laughter. I was enjoying myself now. I had taken two finger-bowls of champagne, and the scene had changed before my eyes into something significant, elemental, and profound.

At a lull in the entertainment the man looked at me and smiled.

"Your face is familiar," he said, politely. "Weren't you in the Third Division during the war?"

"Why, yes. I was in the ninth machine-gun battalion."

"I was in the Seventh Infantry until June nineteen-eighteen. I knew I'd seen you somewhere before."

We talked for a moment about some wet, gray little villages in France. Evidently he lived in this vicinity, for he told me that he had just bought a hydroplane, and was going to try it out in the morning.

"Want to go with me, old sport? Just near the shore along the Sound."

"What time?"

"Any time that suits you best."

It was on the tip of my tongue to ask his name when Jordan looked around and smiled.

"Having a gay time now?" she inquired.

"Much better." I turned again to my new acquaintance. "This is an unusual party for me. I haven't even seen the host. I live over there—" I waved my hand at the invisible hedge in the distance, "and this man Gatsby sent over his chauffeur with an invitation."

For a moment he looked at me as if he failed to understand.

"I'm Gatsby," he said suddenly.

"What!" I exclaimed. "Oh, I beg your pardon."

"I thought you knew, old sport. I'm afraid I'm not a very good host."

He smiled understandingly—much more than understandingly. It was one of those rare smiles with a quality of eternal reassurance in it, that you may come across four or five times in life. It faced—or seemed to face—the whole external world for an instant, and then concentrated on *you* with an irresistible prejudice in your favor. It understood you just as far as you wanted to be understood, believed in you as you would like to believe in yourself, and assured you that it had precisely the impression of you that, at your best, you hoped to convey. Precisely at that point it vanished—and I was looking at an elegant young roughneck, a year or two over thirty, whose elaborate formality of speech just missed being absurd. Some time before he introduced himself I'd got a strong impression that he was picking his words with care.

Almost at the moment when Mr. Gatsby identified himself, a butler hurried toward him with the information that Chicago was calling him on the wire. He excused himself with a small bow that included each of us in turn.

"If you want anything just ask for it, old sport," he urged me. "Excuse me. I will rejoin you later."

When he was gone I turned immediately to Jordan—constrained to assure her of my surprise. I had expected that Mr. Gatsby would be a florid and corpulent person in his middle years.

"Who is he?" I demanded. "Do you know?"

"He's just a man named Gatsby."

"Where is he from, I mean? And what does he do?"

"Now *you're* started on the subject," she answered with a wan smile. "Well, he told me once he was an Oxford man."

A dim background started to take shape behind him, but at her next remark it faded away.

"However, I don't believe it."

"Why not?"

"I don't know," she insisted, "I just don't think he went there."

Something in her tone reminded me of the other girl's "I think he killed a man," and had the effect of stimulating my curiosity. I would have accepted without question the information that Gatsby sprang from the swamps of Louisiana or from the lower East Side of New York. That was comprehensible. But young men didn't—at least in my provincial inexperience I believed they didn't—drift coolly out of nowhere and buy a palace on Long Island Sound.

"Anyhow, he gives large parties," said Jordan, changing the subject with an urban distaste for the concrete. "And I like large parties. They're so intimate. At small parties there isn't any privacy."

There was the boom of a bass drum, and the voice of the orchestra leader rang out suddenly above the echolalia of the garden.

"Ladies and gentlemen," he cried. "At the request of Mr. Gatsby we are going to play for you Mr. Vladimir Tostoff's latest work, which attracted so much attention at Carnegie Hall last May. If you read the papers you know there was a big sensation." He smiled with jovial condescension, and added: "Some sensation!" Whereupon everybody laughed.

"The piece is known," he concluded lustily, "as Vladimir Tostoff's *Jazz History of the World*."

The nature of Mr. Tostoff's composition eluded me, because just as it began my eyes fell on Gatsby, standing alone on the marble steps and looking from one group to another with approving eyes. His tanned skin was drawn attractively tight on his face and his short hair looked as though it were trimmed every day. I could see nothing sinister about him. I wondered if the fact that he was not drinking helped to set him off from his guests, for it seemed to me that he grew more correct as the fraternal hilarity increased. When the *Jazz History of the World* was over, girls were putting their heads on men's shoulders in a puppyish, convivial way, girls were swooning backward playfully into men's arms, even into groups, knowing that some one would arrest their falls—but no one swooned backward on Gatsby, and no French bob touched Gatsby's shoulder, and no singing quartets were formed with Gatsby's head for one link.

"I beg your pardon."

Gatsby's butler was suddenly standing beside us.

"Miss Baker?" he inquired. "I beg your pardon, but Mr. Gatsby would like to speak to you alone."

"With me?" she exclaimed in surprise.

"Yes, madame."

She got up slowly, raising her eyebrows at me in astonishment, and followed the butler toward the house. I noticed that she wore her evening-dress, all her dresses, like sports clothes—there was a jauntiness about her movements as if she had first learned to walk upon golf courses on clean, crisp mornings.

I was alone and it was almost two. For some time confused and intriguing sounds had issued from a long, many-windowed room which overhung the terrace. Eluding Jordan's undergraduate, who was now engaged in an obstetrical conversation with two chorus girls, and who implored me to join him, I went inside.

The large room was full of people. One of the girls in yellow was playing the piano, and beside her stood a tall, red-haired young lady from a famous chorus, engaged in song. She had drunk a quantity of champagne, and during the course of her song she had decided, ineptly, that everything was very, very sad—she was not only singing, she was weeping too. Whenever there was a pause in the song she filled it with gasping, broken sobs, and then took up the lyric again in a quavering soprano. The tears coursed down her cheeks—not freely, however, for when they came into contact with her heavily beaded eyelashes they assumed an inky color, and pursued the rest of their way in slow black rivulets. A humorous suggestion was made that she sing the notes on her face, whereupon she threw up her hands, sank into a chair, and went off into a deep vinous sleep.

"She had a fight with a man who says he's her husband," explained a girl at my elbow.

I looked around. Most of the remaining women were now having fights with men said to be their husbands. Even Jordan's party, the quartet from East Egg, were rent asunder by dissension. One of the men was talking with curious intensity to a young actress, and his wife, after attempting to laugh at the situation in a dignified and indifferent way, broke down entirely and resorted to flank attacks—at intervals she appeared suddenly at his side like an angry diamond, and hissed: "You promised!" into his ear.

The reluctance to go home was not confined to wayward men. The hall was at present occupied by two deplorably sober men and their highly indignant wives. The wives were sympathizing with each other in slightly raised voices.

"Whenever he sees I'm having a good time he wants to go home."

"Never heard anything so selfish in my life."

"We're always the first ones to leave."

"So are we."

"Well, we're almost the last tonight," said one of the men sheepishly. "The orchestra left half an hour ago."

In spite of this wives' agreement that such malevolence was beyond credibility, the dispute ended in a short struggle, and both wives were lifted, kicking, into the night.

As I waited for my hat in the hall the door of the library opened and Jordan Baker and Gatsby came out together. He was saying some last word to her, but the eagerness in his manner tightened abruptly into formality as several people approached him to say good-by.

Jordan's party were calling impatiently to her from the porch, but she lingered for a moment to shake hands.

"I've just heard the most amazing thing," she whispered. "How long were we in there?"

"Why, about an hour."

"It was . . . simply amazing," she repeated abstractedly. "But I swore I wouldn't tell it and here I am tantalizing you." She yawned gracefully in my face. "Please come and see me. . . . Phone book. . . . Under the name of Mrs. Sigourney Howard. . . . My aunt. . . ." She was hurrying off as she talked—her brown hand waved a jaunty salute as she melted into her party at the door.

Rather ashamed that on my first appearance I had stayed so late, I joined the last of Gatsby's guests, who were clustered around him. I wanted to explain that I'd hunted for him early in the evening and to apologize for not having known him in the garden.

"Don't mention it," he enjoined me eagerly. "Don't give it another thought, old sport." The familiar expression held no more familiarity than the hand which reassuringly brushed my shoulder. "And don't forget we're going up in the hydroplane tomorrow morning, at nine o'clock."

Then the butler, behind his shoulder:

"Philadelphia wants you on the 'phone, sir."

"All right, in a minute. Tell them I'll be right there. . . . Good night."

"Good night."

"Good night." He smiled—and suddenly there seemed to be a pleasant significance in having been among the last to go, as if he had desired it all the time. "Good night, old sport. . . . Good night."

But as I walked down the steps I saw that the evening was not quite over. Fifty feet from the door a dozen headlights illuminated a bizarre and tumultuous scene. In the ditch beside the road, right side up, but violently shorn of one wheel, rested a new coupé which had left Gatsby's drive not two minutes before. The sharp jut of a wall accounted for the detachment of the wheel, which was now getting considerable attention from half a dozen curious chauffeurs. However, as they had left their cars blocking the road, a harsh, discordant din from those in the rear had been audible for some time, and added to the already violent confusion of the scene.

A man in a long duster had dismounted from the wreck and now stood in the middle of the road, looking from the car to the tire and from the tire to the observers in a pleasant, puzzled way.

"See!" he explained. "It went in the ditch."

The fact was infinitely astonishing to him, and I recognized first the unusual quality of wonder, and then the man—it was the late patron of Gatsby's library.

"How'd it happen?"

He shrugged his shoulders.

"I know nothing whatever about mechanics," he said decisively.

"But how did it happen? Did you run into the wall?"

"Don't ask me," said Owl Eyes, washing his hands of the whole matter. "I know very little about driving—next to nothing. It happened, and that's all I know."

"Well, if you're a poor driver you oughtn't to try driving at night."

"But I wasn't even trying," he explained indignantly, "I wasn't even trying."

An awed hush fell upon the bystanders.

"Do you want to commit suicide?"

"You're lucky it was just a wheel! A bad driver and not even *trying*!"

"You don't understand," explained the criminal. "I wasn't driving. There's another man in the car."

The shock that followed this declaration found voice in a sustained "Ah-h-h!" as the door of the coupé swung slowly open. The crowd—it was now a crowd—stepped back involuntarily, and when the door had opened wide there was a ghostly pause. Then, very gradually, part by part, a pale, dangling individual stepped out of the wreck, pawing tentatively at the ground with a large uncertain dancing shoe.

Blinded by the glare of the headlights and confused by the incessant groaning of the horns, the apparition stood swaying for a moment before he perceived the man in the duster.

"Wha's matter?" he inquired calmly. "Did we run outa gas?"

"Look!"

Half a dozen fingers pointed at the amputated wheel—he stared at it for a moment, and then looked upward as though he suspected that it had dropped from the sky.

"It came off," some one explained.

He nodded.

"At first I din' notice we'd stopped."

A pause. Then, taking a long breath and straightening his shoulders, he remarked in a determined voice:

"Wonder'ff tell me where there's a gas'line station?"

At least a dozen men, some of them a little better off than he was, explained to him that wheel and car were no longer joined by any physical bond.

"Back out," he suggested after a moment. "Put her in reverse."

"But the *wheel's* off!"

He hesitated.

"No harm in trying," he said.

The caterwauling horns had reached a crescendo and I turned away and cut across the lawn toward home. I glanced back once. A wafer of a moon was shining over Gatsby's house, making the night fine as before, and surviving the laughter and the sound of his still glowing garden. A sudden emptiness seemed to flow now from the windows and the great doors, endowing with complete isolation the figure of the host, who stood on the porch, his hand up in a formal gesture of farewell.

Reading over what I have written so far, I see I have given the impression that the events of three nights several weeks apart were all that absorbed me. On the contrary, they were merely casual events in a crowded summer, and, until much later, they absorbed me infinitely less than my personal affairs.

Most of the time I worked. In the early morning the sun threw my shadow westward as I hurried down the white chasms of lower New York to the Probity Trust. I knew the other clerks and young bond-salesmen by their first names, and lunched with them in dark, crowded restaurants on little pig sausages and mashed potatoes and coffee. I even had a short affair with a girl who lived in Jersey City and worked in the accounting department, but her brother began throwing mean looks in my direction, so when she went on her vacation in July I let it blow quietly away.

I took dinner usually at the Yale Club—for some reason it was the gloomiest event of my day—and then I went upstairs to the library and studied investments and securities for a conscientious hour. There were generally a few rioters around, but they never came into the library, so it was a good place to work. After that, if the night was mellow, I strolled down Madison Avenue past the old Murray Hill Hotel, and over 33d Street to the Pennsylvania Station.

I began to like New York, the racy, adventurous feel of it at night, and the satisfaction that the constant flicker of men and women and machines gives to the restless eye. I liked to walked up Fifth Avenue and pick out romantic women from the crowd and imagine that in a few minutes I was going to enter into their lives, and no one would ever know or disapprove. Sometimes, in my mind, I followed them to their apartments on the corners of hidden streets, and they turned and smiled back at me before they faded through a door into warm darkness. At the enchanted metropolitan twilight I felt a haunting loneliness sometimes, and felt it in others—poor young clerks who loitered in front of windows waiting until it was time for a solitary restaurant dinner —young clerks in the dusk, wasting the most poignant moments of night and life.

Again at eight o'clock, when the dark lanes of the Forties were lined five deep with throbbing taxicabs, bound for the theater district, I felt a sinking in my heart. Forms leaned together in the taxis as they waited, and voices sang, and there was laughter from unheard jokes, and lighted cigarettes outlined unintelligible gestures inside. Imagining that I, too, was hurrying toward gayety and sharing their intimate excitement, I wished them well.

For a while I lost sight of Jordan Baker, and then in midsummer I found her again. At first I was flattered to go places with her, because she was a golf champion, and everyone knew her name. Then it was something more. I wasn't actually in love, but I felt a sort of tender curiosity. The bored haughty face that she turned to the world concealed something— most affectations conceal something eventually, even though they don't in the beginning—and one day I found what it was. When we were on a house-party together up in Warwick, she left a borrowed car out in the rain with the top down, and then lied about it —and suddenly I remembered the story about her that had eluded me that night at Daisy's. At her first big golf tournament there was a row that nearly reached the newspapers—a suggestion that she had moved her ball from a bad lie in the semi-final round. The thing approached the proportions of a scandal —then died away. A caddy retracted his statement, and the only other witness admitted that he might have been mistaken. The incident and the name had remained together in my mind.

Jordan Baker instinctively avoided clever, shrewd men, and now I saw that this was because she felt safer on a plane where any divergence from a code would be thought impossible. She was incurably dishonest. She wasn't able to endure being at a disadvantage and, given this unwillingness, I suppose she had begun dealing in subterfuges when she was very young in order to keep that cool, insolent smile turned to the world and yet satisfy the demands of her hard, jaunty body.

It made no difference to me. Dishonesty in a woman is a thing you never blame deeply—I was casually sorry, and then I forgot. It was on that same house-party that we had a curious conversation about driving a car. It started because she passed so close to some workman that our fender flicked a button on one man's coat.

"You're a rotten driver," I protested. "Either you ought to be more careful, or you oughtn't to drive at all."

"I am careful."

"No, you're not."

"Well, other people are," she said lightly.

"What's that got to do with it?"

"They'll keep out of my way," she insisted. "It takes two to make an accident."

"Suppose you met somebody just as careless as yourself."

"I hope I never will," she answered. "I hate careless people. That's why I like you."

Her gray, sun-strained eyes stared straight ahead, but she had deliberately shifted our relations, and for a moment I thought I loved her. But I am slow-thinking and full of interior rules that act as brakes on my desires, and I knew that first I had to get myself definitely out of that tangle back home. I'd been writing letters once a week and signing them: "Love, Nick," and all I could think of was how, when that certain girl played tennis, a faint mustache of perspiration appeared on her upper lip. Nevertheless there was a vague understanding that had to be tactfully broken off before I was free.

Every one suspects himself of at least one of the cardinal virtues, and this is mine: I am one of the few honest people that I have ever known.

IV

On Sunday morning while church bells rang in the villages alongshore, the world and its mistress returned to Gatsby's house and twinkled hilariously on his lawn.

"He's a bootlegger," said the young ladies, moving somewhere between his cocktails and his flowers. "One time he killed a man who had found out that he was nephew to Von Hindenburg and second cousin to the devil. Reach me a rose, honey, and pour me a last drop into that there crystal glass."

Once I wrote down on the empty spaces of a timetable the names of those who came to Gatsby's house that summer. It is an old timetable now, disintegrating at its folds, and headed "This schedule in effect July 5th, 1922." But I can still read the gray names, and they will give you a better impression than my generalities of those who accepted Gatsby's hospitality and paid him the subtle tribute of knowing nothing whatever about him.

From East Egg, then, came the Chester Beckers and the Leeches, and a man named Bunsen, whom I knew at Yale, and Doctor Webster Civet, who was drowned last summer up in Maine. And the Hornbeams and the Willie Voltaires, and a whole clan named Blackbuck, who always gathered in a corner and flipped up their noses like goats at whosoever came near. And the Ismays and the Chrysties (or rather Hubert Auerbach and Mr. Chrystie's wife), and Edgar Beaver, whose hair, they say, turned cotton-white one winter afternoon for no good reason at all.

Clarence Endive was from East Egg, as I remember. He came only once, in white knickerbockers, and had a fight with a bum named Etty in the garden. From farther out on the Island came the Cheadles and the O. R. P. Schraeders, and the Stonewall Jackson Abrams of Georgia, and the Fishguards and the Ripley Snells. Snell was there three days before he went to the penitentiary, so drunk out on the gravel drive that Mrs. Ulysses Swett's automobile ran over his right hand. The Dancies came, too, and S. B. Whitebait, who was well over sixty, and Maurice A. Flink, and the Hammerheads, and Beluga the tobacco importer, and Beluga's girls.

From West Egg came the Poles and the Mulreadys and Cecil Roebuck and Cecil Schoen and Gulick the State senator and Newton Orchid, who controlled Films Par Excellence, and Eckhaust and Clyde Cohen and Don S. Schwartze (the son) and Arthur McCarty, all connected with the movies in one way or another. And the Catlips and the Bembergs and G. Earl Muldoon, brother to that Muldoon who afterward strangled his wife. Da Fontano the promoter came there, and Ed Legros and James B. ("Rot-Gut") Ferret and the De Jongs and Ernest Lilly—they came to gamble, and when Ferret wandered into the garden it meant he was cleaned out and Associated Traction would have to fluctuate profitably next day.

A man named Klipspringer was there so often and

so long that he became known as "the boarder"—I doubt if he had any other home. Of theatrical people there were Gus Waize and Horace O'Donavan and Lester Myer and George Duckweed and Francis Bull. Also from New York were the Chromes and the Backhyssons and the Dennickers and Russel Betty and the Corrigans and the Kellehers and the Dewars and the Scullys and S. W. Belcher and the Smirkes and the young Quinns, divorced now, and Henry L. Palmetto, who killed himself by jumping in front of a subway train in Times Square.

Benny McClenahan arrived always with four girls. They were never quite the same ones in physical person, but they were so identical one with another that it inevitably seemed they had been there before. I have forgotten their names—Jaqueline, I think, or else Consuela, or Gloria or Judy or June, and their last names were either the melodious names of flowers and months or the sterner ones of the great American capitalists whose cousins, if pressed, they would confess themselves to be.

In addition to all these I can remember that Faustina O'Brien came there at least once and the Baedeker girls and young Brewer, who had his nose shot off in the war, and Mr. Albrucksburger and Miss Haag, his fiancée, and Ardita Fitz-Peters and Mr. P. Jewett, once head of the American Legion, and Miss Claudia Hip, with a man reputed to be her chauffeur, and a prince of something, whom we called Duke, and whose name, if I ever knew it, I have forgotten.

All these people came to Gatsby's house in the summer.

At nine o'clock, one morning late in July, Gatsby's gorgeous car lurched up the rocky drive to my door and gave out a burst of melody from its three-noted horn. It was the first time he had called on me, though I had gone to two of his parties, mounted in his hydroplane, and, at his urgent invitation, made frequent use of his beach.

"Good morning, old sport. You're having lunch with me today and I thought we'd ride up together."

He was balancing himself on the running board of his car with that resourcefulness of movement that is so peculiarly American—that comes, I suppose, with the absence of lifting work or rigid sitting in youth and, even more, with the formless grace of our nervous, sporadic games. This quality was continually breaking through his punctilious manner in the shape of restlessness. He was never quite still; there was always a tapping foot somewhere or the impatient opening and closing of a hand.

He saw me looking with admiration at his car.

"It's pretty, isn't it, old sport!" He jumped off to give me a better view. "Haven't you ever seen it before?"

I'd seen it. Everybody had seen it. It was a rich cream color, bright with nickel, swollen here and there in its monstrous length with triumphant hat-boxes and supper-boxes and tool-boxes, and terraced with a labyrinth of wind-shields that mirrored a dozen suns. Sitting down behind many layers of glass in a sort of green leather conservatory, we started to town.

I had talked with him perhaps half a dozen times in the past month and found, to my disappointment, that he had little to say. So my first impression, that he was a person of some undefined consequence, had gradually faded and he had become simply the proprietor of an elaborate road-house next door.

And then came that disconcerting ride. We hadn't reached West Egg Village before Gatsby began leaving his elegant sentences unfinished and slapping himself indecisively on the knee of his caramel-colored suit.

"Look here, old sport," he broke out surprisingly, "what's your opinion of me, anyhow?"

A little overwhelmed, I began the generalized evasions which that question deserves.

"Well, I'm going to tell you something about my life," he interrupted. "I don't want you to get a wrong idea of me from all these stories you hear."

So he was aware of the bizarre accusations that flavored conversation in his halls.

"I'll tell you God's truth." His right hand suddenly ordered divine retribution to stand by. "I am the son of some wealthy people in the Middle West—all dead now. I was brought up in America but educated at Oxford, because all my ancestors have been educated there for many years. It is a family tradition."

He looked at me sideways—and I knew why Jordan Baker had believed he was lying. He hurried the phrase "educated at Oxford," or swallowed it, or choked on it, as though it had bothered him before. And with this doubt, his whole statement fell to pieces, and I wondered if there wasn't something a little sinister about him, after all.

"What part of the Middle West?" I inquired casually.

"San Francisco."

"I see."

"My family all died and I came into a good deal of money."

His voice was solemn, as if the memory of that sudden extinction of a clan still haunted him. For a moment I suspected that he was pulling my leg, but a glance at him convinced me otherwise.

"After that I lived like a young rajah in all the capitals of Europe—Paris, Venice, Rome—collecting

jewels, chiefly rubies, hunting big game, painting a
little, things for myself only, and trying to forget
something very sad that had happened to me long
ago."

With an effort I managed to restrain my incredulous laughter. The very phrases were worn so threadbare that they evoked no image except that of a
turbaned "character" leaking sawdust at every pore
as he pursued a tiger through the Bois de Boulogne.

"Then came the war, old sport. It was a great relief, and I tried very hard to die, but I seemed to bear
an enchanted life. I accepted a commission as first
lieutenant when it began. In the Argonne Forest I
took two machine-gun detachments so far forward
that there was a half mile gap on either side of us
where the infantry couldn't advance. We stayed there
two days and two nights, a hundred and thirty men
with sixteen Lewis guns, and when the infantry
came up at last they found the insignia of three
German divisions among the piles of dead. I was
promoted to be a major, and every Allied government gave me a decoration—even Montenegro, little
Montenegro down on the Adriatic Sea!"

Little Montenegro! He lifted up the words and
nodded at them—with his smile. The smile comprehended Montenegro's troubled history and sympathized with the brave struggles of the Montenegrin
people. It appreciated fully the chain of national
circumstances which had elicited this tribute from
Montenegro's warm little heart. My incredulity was
submerged in fascination now; it was like skimming
hastily through a dozen magazines.

He reached in his pocket, and a piece of metal,
slung on a ribbon, fell into my palm.

"That's the one from Montenegro."

To my astonishment, the thing had an authentic
look. "Orderi di Danilo," ran the circular legend,
"Montenegro, Nicolas Rex."

"Turn it."

"Major Jay Gatsby," I read, "For Valour Extraordinary."

"Here's another thing I always carry. A souvenir
of Oxford days. It was taken in Trinity Quad—the
man on my left is now the Earl of Doncaster."

It was a photograph of half a dozen young men in
blazers loafing in an archway through which were
visible a host of spires. There was Gatsby, looking a
little, not much, younger—with a cricket bat in his
hand.

Then it was all true. I saw the skins of tigers flaming in his palace on the Grand Canal; I saw him
opening a chest of rubies to ease, with their crimson-
lighted depths, the gnawings of his broken heart.

"I'm going to make a big request of you today," he
said, pocketing his souvenirs with satisfaction, "so I

thought you ought to know something about me. I
didn't want you to think I was just some nobody.
You see, I usually find myself among strangers because I drift here and there trying to forget the sad
thing that happened to me." He hesitated. "You'll
hear about it this afternoon."

"At lunch?"

"No, this afternoon. I happened to find out that
you're taking Miss Baker to tea."

"Do you mean you're in love with Miss Baker?"

"No, old sport, I'm not. But Miss Baker has kindly
consented to speak to you about this matter."

I hadn't the faintest idea what "this matter" was,
but I was more annoyed than interested. I hadn't
asked Jordan to tea in order to discuss Mr. Jay
Gatsby. I was sure the request would be something
utterly fantastic, and for a moment I was sorry I'd
ever set foot upon his overpopulated lawn.

He wouldn't say another word. His correctness
grew on him as we neared the city. We passed Port
Roosevelt, where there was a glimpse of red-belted
ocean-going ships, and sped along a cobbled slum
lined with the dark, undeserted saloons of the faded-
gilt nineteenth-hundreds. Then the valley of ashes
opened out on both sides of us, and I had a glimpse
of Mrs. Wilson straining at the garage pump with
panting vitality as we went by.

With fenders spread like wings we scattered light
through half Astoria—only half, for as we twisted
among the pillars of the elevated I heard the familiar
"jug-jug-*spat!*" of a motorcycle, and a frantic policeman rode alongside.

"All right, old sport," called Gatsby. We slowed
down. Taking a white card from his wallet, he
waved it before the man's eyes.

"Right you are," agreed the policeman, tipping his
cap. "Know you next time, Mr. Gatsby. Excuse *me!*"

"What was that?" I inquired. "The picture of
Oxford?"

"I was able to do the commissioner a favor once,
and he sends me a Christmas card every year."

Over the great bridge, with the sunlight through
the girders making a constant flicker upon the moving cars, with the city rising up across the river in
white heaps and sugar lumps all built with a wish out
of non-olfactory money. The city seen from the
Queensboro Bridge is always the city seen for the
first time, in its first wild promise of all the mystery
and the beauty in the world.

A dead man passed us in a hearse heaped with
blooms, followed by two carriages with drawn blinds,
and by more cheerful carriages for friends. The
friends looked out at us with the tragic eyes and
short upper lips of southeastern Europe, and I was
glad that the sight of Gatsby's splendid car was in-

cluded in their somber holiday. As we crossed Blackwell's Island a limousine passed us, driven by a white chauffeur, in which sat three modish negroes, two bucks and a girl. I laughed aloud as the yolks of their eyeballs rolled toward us in haughty rivalry.

"Anything can happen now that we've slid over this bridge," I thought; "anything at all. . . ."

Even Gatsby could happen, without any particular wonder.

Roaring noon. In a well-fanned Forty-second Street cellar I met Gatsby for lunch. Blinking away the brightness of the street outside, my eyes picked him out obscurely in the anteroom, talking to another man.

"Mr. Carraway, this is my friend Mr. Wolfsheim."

A small, flat-nosed Jew raised his large head and regarded me with two fine growths of hair which luxuriated in either nostril. After a moment I discovered his tiny eyes in the half-darkness.

"—So I took one look at him," said Mr. Wolfsheim, shaking my hand earnestly, "and what do you think I did?"

"What?" I inquired politely.

But evidently he was not addressing me, for he dropped my hand and covered Gatsby with his expressive nose.

"I handed the money to Katspaugh and I sid: 'All right, Katspaugh, don't pay him a penny till he shuts his mouth.' He shut it then and there."

Gatsby took an arm of each of us and moved forward into the restaurant, whereupon Mr. Wolfsheim swallowed a new sentence he was starting and lapsed into a somnambulatory abstraction.

"Highballs?" asked the head waiter.

"This is a nice restaurant here," said Mr. Wolfsheim, looking at the Presbyterian nymphs on the ceiling. "But I like across the street better!"

"Yes, highballs," agreed Gatsby, and then to Mr. Wolfsheim: "It's too hot over there."

"Hot and small—yes," said Mr. Wolfsheim, "but full of memories."

"What place is that?" I asked.

"The old Metropole.

"The old Metropole," brooded Mr. Wolfsheim gloomily. "Filled with faces dead and gone. Filled with friends gone now forever. I can't forget so long as I live the night they shot Rosy Rosenthal there. It was six of us at the table, and Rosy had eat and drunk a lot all evening. When it was almost morning the waiter came up to him with a funny look and says somebody wants to speak to him outside. 'All right,' says Rosy, and begins to get up, and I pulled him down in his chair.

" 'Let the bastards come in here if they want you, Rosy, but don't you, so help me, move outside this room.'

"It was four o'clock in the morning then, and if we'd of raised the blinds we'd of seen daylight."

"Did he go?" I asked innocently.

"Sure he went." Mr. Wolfsheim's nose flashed at me indignantly. "He turned around in the door and says: 'Don't let that waiter take away my coffee!' Then he went out on the sidewalk, and they shot him three times in his full belly and drove away."

"Four of them were electrocuted," I said, remembering.

"Five, with Becker." His nostrils turned to me in an interested way. "I understand you're looking for a business gonnegtion."

The juxtaposition of these two remarks was startling. Gatsby answered for me:

"Oh, no," he exclaimed, "this isn't the man."

"No?" Mr. Wolfsheim seemed disappointed.

"This is just a friend. I told you we'd talk about that some other time."

"I beg your pardon," said Mr. Wolfsheim, "I had a wrong man."

A succulent hash arrived, and Mr. Wolfsheim, forgetting the more sentimental atmosphere of the old Metropole, began to eat with ferocious delicacy. His eyes, meanwhile, roved very slowly all around the room—he completed the arc by turning to inspect the people directly behind. I think that, except for my presence, he would have taken one short glance beneath our own table.

"Look here, old sport," said Gatsby, leaning toward me, "I'm afraid I made you a little angry this morning in the car."

There was the smile again, but this time I held out against it.

"I don't like mysteries," I answered, "and I don't understand why you won't come out frankly and tell me what you want. Why has it all got to come through Miss Baker?"

"Oh, it's nothing underhand," he assured me. "Miss Baker's a great sportswoman, you know, and she'd never do anything that wasn't all right."

Suddenly he looked at his watch, jumped up, and hurried from the room, leaving me with Mr. Wolfsheim at the table.

"He has to telephone," said Mr. Wolfsheim, following him with his eyes. "Fine fellow, isn't he? Handsome to look at and a perfect gentleman."

"Yes."

"He's an Oggsford man."

"Oh!"

"He went to Oggsford College in England. You know Oggsford College?"

"I've heard of it."

"It's one of the most famous colleges in the world."

"Have you known Gatsby for a long time?" I inquired.

"Several years," he answered in a gratified way. "I made the pleasure of his acquaintance just after the war. But I knew I had discovered a man of fine breeding after I talked with him an hour. I said to myself: 'There's the kind of man you'd like to take home and introduce to your mother and sister.'" He paused. "I see you're looking at my cuff buttons."

I hadn't been looking at them, but I did now. They were composed of oddly familiar pieces of ivory.

"Finest specimens of human molars," he informed me.

"Well!" I inspected them. "That's a very interesting idea."

"Yeah." He flipped his sleeves up under his coat. "Yeah, Gatsby's very careful about women. He would never so much as look at a friend's wife."

When the subject of this instinctive trust returned to the table and sat down Mr. Wolfsheim drank his coffee with a jerk and got to his feet.

"I have enjoyed my lunch," he said, "and I'm going to run off from you two young men before I outstay my welcome."

"Don't hurry, Meyer," said Gatsby, without enthusiasm. Mr. Wolfsheim raised his hand in a sort of benediction.

"You're very polite, but I belong to another generation," he announced solemnly. "You sit here and discuss your sports and your young ladies and your—" He supplied an imaginary noun with another wave of his hand. "As for me, I am fifty years old, and I won't impose myself on you any longer."

As he shook hands and turned away his tragic nose was trembling. I wondered if I had said anything to offend him.

"He becomes very sentimental sometimes," explained Gatsby. "This is one of his sentimental days. He's quite a character around New York—a denizen of Broadway."

"Who is he, anyhow, an actor?"

"No."

"A dentist?"

"Meyer Wolfsheim? No, he's a gambler." Gatsby hesitated, then added coolly: "He's the man who fixed the World's Series back in 1919."

"Fixed the World's Series?" I repeated.

The idea staggered me. I remembered, of course, that the World's Series had been fixed in 1919, but if I had thought of it at all I would have thought of it as a thing that merely *happened,* the end of some inevitable chain. It never occurred to me that one man could start to play with the faith of fifty million

people—with the single-mindedness of a burglar blowing a safe.

"How did he happen to do that?" I asked after a minute.

"He just saw the opportunity."

"Why isn't he in jail?"

"They can't get him, old sport. He's a smart man."

I insisted on paying the check. As the waiter brought my change I caught sight of Tom Buchanan across the crowded room.

"Come along with me for a minute," I said; "I've got to say hello to some one."

When he saw us Tom jumped up and took half a dozen steps in our direction.

"Where've you been?" he demanded eagerly. "Daisy's furious because you haven't called up."

"This is Mr. Gatsby, Mr. Buchanan."

They shook hands briefly, and a strained, unfamiliar look of embarrassment came over Gatsby's face.

"How've you been, anyhow?" demanded Tom of me. "How'd you happen to come up this far to eat?"

"I've been having lunch with Mr. Gatsby."

I turned toward Mr. Gatsby, but he was no longer there.

One October day in nineteen-seventeen——

(said Jordan Baker that afternoon, sitting up very straight on a straight chair in the tea-garden at the Plaza Hotel)

—I was walking along from one place to another, half on the sidewalks and half on the lawns. I was happier on the lawns because I had on shoes from England with rubber nobs on the soles that bit into the soft ground. I had on a new plaid skirt also that blew a little in the wind, and whenever this happened the red, white, and blue banners in front of all the houses stretched out stiff and said *tut-tut-tut-tut,* in a disapproving way.

The largest of the banners and the largest of the lawns belonged to Daisy Fay's house. She was just eighteen, two years older than me, and by far the most popular of all the young girls in Louisville. She dressed in white, and had a little white roadster, and all day long the telephone rang in her house and excited young officers from Camp Taylor demanded the privilege of monopolizing her that night. "Anyways, for an hour!"

When I came opposite her house that morning her white roadster was beside the curb, and she was sitting in it with a lieutenant I had never seen before. They were so engrossed in each other that she didn't see me until I was five feet away.

"Hello, Jordan," she called unexpectedly. "Please come here."

I was flattered that she wanted to speak to me, because of all the older girls I admired her most. She asked me if I was going to the Red Cross and make bandages. I was. Well, then, would I tell them that she couldn't come that day? The officer looked at Daisy while she was speaking, in a way that every young girl wants to be looked at some time, and because it seemed romantic to me I have remembered the incident ever since. His name was Jay Gatsby, and I didn't lay eyes on him again for over four years—even after I'd met him on Long Island I didn't realize it was the same man.

That was nineteen-seventeen. By the next year I had a few beaux myself, and I began to play in tournaments, so I didn't see Daisy very often. She went with a slightly older crowd—when she went with anyone at all. Wild rumors were circulating about her—how her mother had found her packing her bag one winter night to go to New York and say good-by to a soldier who was going overseas. She was effectually prevented, but she wasn't on speaking terms with her family for several weeks. After that she didn't play around with the soldiers any more, but only with a few flat-footed, short-sighted young men in town, who couldn't get into the army at all.

By the next autumn she was gay again, gay as ever. She had a début after the Armistice, and in February she was presumably engaged to a man from New Orleans. In June she married Tom Buchanan of Chicago, with more pomp and circumstance than Louisville ever knew before. He came down with a hundred people in four private cars, and hired a whole floor of the Muhlbach Hotel, and the day before the wedding he gave her a string of pearls valued at three hundred and fifty thousand dollars.

I was a bridesmaid. I came into her room half an hour before the bridal dinner, and found her lying on her bed as lovely as the June night in her flowered dress—and as drunk as a monkey. She had a bottle of Sauterne in one hand and a letter in the other.

" 'Gratulate me," she muttered. "Never had a drink before, but oh how I do enjoy it."

"What's the matter, Daisy?"

I was scared, I can tell you; I'd never seen a girl like that before.

"Here, deares'." She groped around in a wastebasket she had with her on the bed and pulled out the string of pearls. "Take 'em down-stairs and give 'em back to whoever they belong to. Tell 'em all Daisy's change' her mine. Say: 'Daisy's change' her mine!' "

She began to cry—she cried and cried. I rushed out and found her mother's maid, and we locked the door and got her into a cold bath. She wouldn't let

go of the letter. She took it into the tub with her and squeezed it up into a wet ball, and only let me leave it in the soap-dish when she saw that it was coming to pieces like snow.

But she didn't say another word. We gave her spirits of ammonia and put ice on her forehead and hooked her back into her dress, and half an hour later, when we walked out of the room, the pearls were around her neck and the incident was over. Next day at five o'clock she married Tom Buchanan without so much as a shiver, and started off on a three months' trip to the South Seas.

I saw them in Santa Barbara when they came back, and I thought I'd never seen a girl so mad about her husband. If he left the room for a minute she'd look around uneasily, and say: "Where's Tom gone?" and wear the most abstracted expression until she saw him coming in the door. She used to sit on the sand with his head in her lap by the hour, rubbing her fingers over his eyes and looking at him with unfathomable delight. It was touching to see them together—it made you laugh in a hushed, fascinated way. That was in August. A week after I left Santa Barbara Tom ran into a wagon on the Ventura road one night, and ripped a front wheel off his car. The girl who was with him got into the papers, too, because her arm was broken—she was one of the chambermaids in the Santa Barbara Hotel.

The next April Daisy had her little girl, and they went to France for a year. I saw them one spring in Cannes, and later in Deauville, and then they came back to Chicago to settle down. Daisy was popular in Chicago, as you know. They moved with a fast crowd, all of them young and rich and wild, but she came out with an absolutely perfect reputation. Perhaps because she doesn't drink. It's a great advantage not to drink among hard-drinking people. You can hold your tongue, and, moreover, you can time any little irregularity of your own so that everybody else is so blind that they don't see or care. Perhaps Daisy never went in for amour at all—and yet there's something in that voice of hers. . . .

Well, about six weeks ago, she heard the name Gatsby for the first time in years. It was when I asked you—do you remember?—if you knew Gatsby in West Egg. After you had gone home she came into my room and woke me up, and said: "What Gatsby?" and when I described him—I was half asleep—she said in the strangest voice that it must be the man she used to know. It wasn't until then that I connected this Gatsby with the officer in her white car.

When Jordan Baker had finished telling all this we had left the Plaza for half an hour and were driving in a victoria through Central Park. The sun had gone down behind the tall apartments of the movie stars in the West Fifties, and the clear voices of little girls, already gathered like crickets on the grass, rose through the hot twilight:

> *"I'm the Sheik of Araby.*
> *Your love belongs to me.*
> *At night when you're asleep*
> *Into your tent I'll creep——"*

"It was a strange coincidence," I said.

"But it wasn't a coincidence at all."

"Why not?"

"Gatsby bought that house so that Daisy would be just across the bay."

Then it had not been merely the stars to which he had aspired on that June night. He came alive to me, delivered suddenly from the womb of his purposeless splendor.

"He wants to know," continued Jordan, "if you'll invite Daisy to your house some afternoon and then let him come over."

The modesty of the demand shook me. He had waited five years and bought a mansion where he dispensed starlight to casual moths—so that he could "come over" some afternoon to a stranger's garden.

"Did I have to know all this before he could ask such a little thing?"

"He's afraid, he's waited so long. He thought you might be offended. You see, he's a regular tough underneath it all."

Something worried me.

"Why didn't he ask you to arrange a meeting?"

"He wants her to see his house," she explained. "And your house is right next door."

"Oh!"

"I think he half expected her to wander into one of his parties, some night," went on Jordan, "but she never did. Then he began asking people casually if they knew her, and I was the first one he found. It was that night he sent for me at his dance, and you should have heard the elaborate way he worked up to it. Of course, I immediately suggested a luncheon in New York—and I thought he'd go mad:

" 'I don't want to do anything out of the way!' he kept saying. 'I want to see her right next door.'

"When I said you were a particular friend of Tom's, he started to abandon the whole idea. He doesn't know very much about Tom, though he says he's read a Chicago paper for years just on the chance of catching a glimpse of Daisy's name."

It was dark now, and as we dipped under a little bridge I put my arm around Jordan's golden shoulder and drew her toward me and asked her to dinner. Suddenly I wasn't thinking of Daisy and Gatsby any more, but of this clean, hard, limited person, who dealt in universal scepticism, and who leaned back jauntily just within the circle of my arm. A phrase began to beat in my ears with a sort of heady excitement: "There are only the pursued, the pursuing, the busy, and the tired."

"And Daisy ought to have something in her life," murmured Jordan to me.

"Does she want to see Gatsby?"

"She's not to know about it. Gatsby doesn't want her to know. You're just supposed to invite her to tea."

We passed a barrier of dark trees, and then the façade of Fifty-ninth Street, a block of delicate pale light, beamed down into the park. Unlike Gatsby and Tom Buchanan, I had no girl whose disembodied face floated along the dark cornices and blinding signs, and so I drew up the girl beside me, tightening my arms. Her wan, scornful mouth smiled, and so I drew her up again closer, this time to my face.

V

When I came home to West Egg that night I was afraid for a moment that my house was on fire. Two o'clock and the whole corner of the peninsula was blazing with light, which fell unreal on the shrubbery and made thin elongating glints upon the roadside wires. Turning a corner, I saw that it was Gatsby's house, lit from tower to cellar.

At first I thought it was another party, a wild rout that had resolved itself into "hide-and-go-seek" or "sardines-in-the-box" with all the house thrown open to the game. But there wasn't a sound. Only wind in the trees, which blew the wires and made the lights go off and on again as if the house had winked into the darkness. As my taxi groaned away I saw Gatsby walking toward me across his lawn.

"Your place looks like the World's Fair," I said.

"Does it?" He turned his eyes toward it absently. "I have been glancing into some of the rooms. Let's go to Coney Island, old sport. In my car."

"It's too late."

"Well, suppose we take a plunge in the swimming-pool? I haven't made use of it all summer."

"I've got to go to bed."

"All right."

He waited, looking at me with suppressed eagerness.

"I talked with Miss Baker," I said after a moment. "I'm going to call up Daisy tomorrow and invite her over here to tea."

"Oh, that's all right," he said carelessly. "I don't want to put you to any trouble."

"What day would suit you?"

"What day would suit *you?*" he corrected me

quickly. "I don't want to put you to any trouble, you see."

"How about the day after tomorrow?"

He considered for a moment. Then, with reluctance:

"I want to get the grass cut," he said.

We both looked at the grass—there was a sharp line where my ragged lawn ended and the darker, well-kept expanse of his began. I suspected that he meant my grass.

"There's another little thing," he said uncertainly, and hesitated.

"Would you rather put it off for a few days?" I asked.

"Oh, it isn't about that. At least—" He fumbled with a series of beginnings. "Why, I thought—why, look here, old sport, you don't make much money, do you?"

"Not very much."

This seemed to reassure him and he continued more confidently.

"I thought you didn't, if you'll pardon my—you see, I carry on a little business on the side, a sort of side line, you understand. And I thought that if you don't make very much— You're selling bonds, aren't you, old sport?"

"Trying to."

"Well, this would interest you. It wouldn't take up much of your time and you might pick up a nice bit of money. It happens to be a rather confidential sort of thing."

I realize now that under different circumstances that conversation might have been one of the crises of my life. But, because the offer was obviously and tactlessly for a service to be rendered, I had no choice except to cut him off there.

"I've got my hands full," I said. "I'm much obliged but I couldn't take on any more work."

"You wouldn't have to do any business with Wolfsheim." Evidently he thought that I was shying away from the "gonnegtion" mentioned at lunch, but I assured him he was wrong. He waited a moment longer, hoping I'd begin a conversation, but I was too absorbed to be responsive, so he went unwillingly home.

The evening had made me light-headed and happy; I think I walked into a deep sleep as I entered my front door. So I don't know whether or not Gatsby went to Coney Island, or for how many hours he "glanced into rooms" while his house blazed gaudily on. I called up Daisy from the office next morning, and invited her to come to tea.

"Don't bring Tom," I warned her.

"What?"

"Don't bring Tom."

"Who is 'Tom'?" she asked innocently.

The day agreed upon was pouring rain. At eleven o'clock a man in a raincoat, dragging a lawn-mower, tapped at my front door and said that Mr. Gatsby had sent him over to cut my grass. This reminded me that I had forgotten to tell my Finn to come back, so I drove into West Egg Village to search for her among soggy whitewashed alleys and to buy some cups and lemons and flowers.

The flowers were unnecessary, for at two o'clock a greenhouse arrived from Gatsby's, with innumerable receptacles to contain it. An hour later the front door opened nervously, and Gatsby, in a white flannel suit, silver shirt, and gold-colored tie, hurried in. He was pale, and there were dark signs of sleeplessness beneath his eyes.

"Is everything all right?" he asked immediately.

"The grass looks fine, if that's what you mean."

"What grass?" he inquired blankly. "Oh, the grass in the yard." He looked out the window at it, but, judging from his expression, I don't believe he saw a thing.

"Looks very good," he remarked vaguely. "One of the papers said they thought the rain would stop about four. I think it was *The Journal*. Have you got everything you need in the shape of—of tea?"

I took him into the pantry, where he looked a little reproachfully at the Finn. Together we scrutinized the twelve lemon cakes from the delicatessen shop.

"Will they do?" I asked.

"Of course, of course! They're fine!" and he added hollowly, ". . . old sport."

The rain cooled about half-past three to a damp mist, through which occasional thin drops swam like dew. Gatsby looked with vacant eyes through a copy of Clay's *Economics*, starting at the Finnish tread that shook the kitchen floor, and peering toward the bleared windows from time to time as if a series of invisible but alarming happenings were taking place outside. Finally he got up and informed me, in an uncertain voice, that he was going home.

"Why's that?"

"Nobody's coming to tea. It's too late!" He looked at his watch as if there was some pressing demand on his time elsewhere. "I can't wait all day."

"Don't be silly; it's just two minutes to four."

He sat down miserably, as if I had pushed him, and simultaneously there was the sound of a motor turning into my lane. We both jumped up, and, a little harrowed myself, I went out into the yard.

Under the dripping bare lilac-trees a large open car was coming up the drive. It stopped. Daisy's face, tipped sideways beneath a three-cornered lavender hat, looked out at me with a bright ecstatic smile.

"Is this absolutely where you live, my dearest one?"

The exhilarating ripple of her voice was a wild tonic in the rain. I had to follow the sound of it for a moment, up and down, with my ear alone, before any words came through. A damp streak of hair lay like a dash of blue paint across her cheek, and her hand was wet with glistening drops as I took it to help her from the car.

"Are you in love with me," she said low in my ear, "or why did I have to come alone?"

"That's the secret of Castle Rackrent. Tell your chauffeur to go far away and spend an hour."

"Come back in an hour, Ferdie." Then in a grave murmur: "His name is Ferdie."

"Does the gasoline affect his nose?"

"I don't think so," she said innocently. "Why?"

We went in. To my overwhelming surprise the living-room was deserted.

"Well, that's funny," I exclaimed.

"What's funny?"

She turned her head as there was a light dignified knocking at the front door. I went out and opened it. Gatsby, pale as death, with his hands plunged like weights in his coat pockets, was standing in a puddle of water glaring tragically into my eyes.

With his hands still in his coat pockets he stalked by me into the hall, turned sharply as if he were on a wire, and disappeared into the living-room. It wasn't a bit funny. Aware of the loud beating of my own heart I pulled the door to against the increasing rain.

For half a minute there wasn't a sound. Then from the living-room I heard a sort of choking murmur and part of a laugh, followed by Daisy's voice on a clear artificial note:

"I certainly am awfully glad to see you again."

A pause; it endured horribly. I had nothing to do in the hall, so I went into the room.

Gatsby, his hands still in his pockets, was reclining against the mantelpiece in a strained counterfeit of perfect ease, even of boredom. His head leaned back so far that it rested against the face of a defunct mantelpiece clock, and from this position his distraught eyes stared down at Daisy, who was sitting, frightened but graceful, on the edge of a stiff chair.

"We've met before," muttered Gatsby. His eyes glanced momentarily at me, and his lips parted with an abortive attempt at a laugh. Luckily the clock took this moment to tilt dangerously at the pressure of his head, whereupon he turned and caught it with trembling fingers and set it back in place. Then he sat down, rigidly, his elbow on the arm of the sofa and his chin in his hand.

"I'm sorry about the clock," he said.

My own face had now assumed a deep tropical burn. I couldn't muster up a single commonplace out of the thousand in my head.

"It's an old clock," I told them idiotically.

I think we all believed for a moment that it had smashed in pieces on the floor.

"We haven't met for many years," said Daisy, her voice as matter-of-fact as it could ever be.

"Five years next November."

The automatic quality of Gatsby's answer set us all back at least another minute. I had them both on their feet with the desperate suggestion that they help me make tea in the kitchen when the demoniac Finn brought it in on a tray.

Amid the welcome confusion of cups and cakes a certain physical decency established itself. Gatsby got himself into a shadow and, while Daisy and I talked, looked conscientiously from one to the other of us with tense, unhappy eyes. However, as calmness wasn't an end in itself, I made an excuse at the first possible moment, and got to my feet.

"Where are you going?" demanded Gatsby in immediate alarm.

"I'll be back."

"I've got to speak to you about something before you go."

He followed me wildly into the kitchen, closed the door, and whispered: "Oh, God!" in a miserable way.

"What's the matter?"

"This is a terrible mistake," he said, shaking his head from side to side, "a terrible, terrible mistake."

"You're just embarrassed, that's all," and luckily I added: "Daisy's embarrassed too."

"She's embarrassed?" he repeated incredulously.

"Just as much as you are."

"Don't talk so loud."

"You're acting like a little boy," I broke out impatiently. "Not only that, but you're rude. Daisy's sitting in there all alone."

He raised his hand to stop my words, looked at me with unforgettable reproach, and, opening the door cautiously, went back into the other room.

I walked out the back way—just as Gatsby had when he had made his nervous circuit of the house half an hour before—and ran for a huge black knotted tree, whose massed leaves made a fabric against the rain. Once more it was pouring, and my irregular lawn, well-shaved by Gatsby's gardener, abounded in small muddy swamps and prehistoric marshes. There was nothing to look at from under the tree except Gatsby's enormous house, so I stared at it, like Kant at his church steeple, for half an hour. A brewer had built it early in the "period" craze, a decade before, and there was a story that he'd agreed to pay five years' taxes on all the neighboring cottages if the owners would have their roofs thatched with straw. Perhaps their refusal took the heart out of his plan to Found a Family—he went into an immediate decline. His children sold his house with the black wreath still on the door. Americans, while occasionally willing to be serfs, have always been obstinate about being peasantry.

After half an hour, the sun shone again, and the grocer's automobile rounded Gatsby's drive with the raw material for his servants' dinner—I felt sure he wouldn't eat a spoonful. A maid began opening the upper windows of his house, appeared momentarily in each, and, leaning from a large central bay, spat meditatively into the garden. It was time I went back. While the rain continued it had seemed like the murmur of their voices, rising and swelling a little now and then with gusts of emotion. But in the new silence I felt that silence had fallen within the house too.

I went in—after making every possible noise in the kitchen, short of pushing over the stove—but I don't believe they heard a sound. They were sitting at either end of the couch, looking at each other as if some question had been asked, or was in the air, and every vestige of embarrassment was gone. Daisy's face was smeared with tears, and when I came in she jumped up and began wiping at it with her handkerchief before a mirror. But there was a change in Gatsby that was simply confounding. He literally glowed; without a word or a gesture of exultation a new well-being radiated from him and filled the little room.

"Oh, hello, old sport," he said, as if he hadn't seen me for years. I thought for a moment he was going to shake hands.

"It's stopped raining."

"Has it?" When he realized what I was talking about, that there were twinkle-bells of sunshine in the room, he smiled like a weather man, like an ecstatic patron of recurrent light, and repeated the news to Daisy. "What do you think of that? It's stopped raining."

"I'm glad, Jay." Her throat, full of aching, grieving beauty, told only of her unexpected joy.

"I want you and Daisy to come over to my house," he said, "I'd like to show her around."

"You're sure you want me to come?"

"Absolutely, old sport."

Daisy went up-stairs to wash her face—too late I thought with humiliation of my towels—while Gatsby and I waited on the lawn.

"My house looks well, doesn't it?" he demanded. "See how the whole front of it catches the light."

I agreed that it was splendid.

"Yes." His eyes went over it, every arched door and square tower. "It took me just three years to earn the money that bought it."

"I thought you inherited your money."

"I did, old sport," he said automatically, "but I lost most of it in the big panic—the panic of the war."

I think he hardly knew what he was saying, for when I asked him what business he was in he answered: "That's my affair," before he realized that it wasn't an appropriate reply.

"Oh, I've been in several things," he corrected himself. "I was in the drug business and then I was in the oil business. But I'm not in either one now." He looked at me with more attention. "Do you mean you've been thinking over what I proposed the other night?"

Before I could answer, Daisy came out of the house and two rows of brass buttons on her dress gleamed in the sunlight.

"That huge place *there?*" she cried pointing.

"Do you like it?"

"I love it, but I don't see how you live there all alone."

"I keep it always full of interesting people, night and day. People who do interesting things. Celebrated people."

Instead of taking the short cut along the Sound we went down to the road and entered by the big postern. With enchanting murmurs Daisy admired this aspect or that of the feudal silhouette against the sky, admired the gardens, the sparkling odor of jonquils and the frothy odor of hawthorn and plum blossoms and the pale gold odor of kiss-me-at-the-gate. It was strange to reach the marble steps and find no stir of bright dresses in and out of the door, and hear no sound but bird voices in the trees.

And inside, as we wandered through Marie Antoinette music-rooms and Restoration salons, I felt that there were guests concealed behind every couch and table, under orders to be breathlessly silent until we had passed through. As Gatsby closed the door of "the Merton College Library" I could have sworn I heard the owl-eyed man break into ghostly laughter.

We went upstairs, through period bedrooms swathed in rose and lavender silk and vivid with new flowers, through dressing-rooms and poolrooms, and bathrooms, with sunken baths—intruding into one chamber where a dishevelled man in pajamas was doing liver exercises on the floor. It was Mr. Klipspringer, the "boarder." I had seen him wandering hungrily about the beach that morning. Finally we came to Gatsby's own apartment, a bedroom and a bath, and an Adam study, where we sat down and drank a glass of some Chartreuse he took from a cupboard in the wall.

He hadn't once ceased looking at Daisy, and I think he revalued everything in his house according to the measure of response it drew from her well-loved eyes. Sometimes, too, he stared around at his possessions in a dazed way, as though in her actual and astounding presence none of it was any longer real. Once he nearly toppled down a flight of stairs.

His bedroom was the simplest room of all—except where the dresser was garnished with a toilet set of pure dull gold. Daisy took the brush with delight, and smoothed her hair, whereupon Gatsby sat down and shaded his eyes and began to laugh.

"It's the funniest thing, old sport," he said hilariously. "I can't—when I try to——"

He had passed visibly through two states and was entering upon a third. After his embarrassment and his unreasoning joy he was consumed with wonder at her presence. He had been full of the idea so long, dreamed it right through to the end, waited with his teeth set, so to speak, at an inconceivable pitch of intensity. Now, in the reaction, he was running down like an overwound clock.

Recovering himself in a minute he opened for us two hulking patent cabinets which held his massed suits and dressing-gowns and ties, and his shirts, piled like bricks in stacks a dozen high.

"I've got a man in England who buys me clothes. He sends over a selection of things at the beginning of each season, spring and fall."

He took out a pile of shirts and began throwing them, one by one, before us, shirts of sheer linen and thick silk and fine flannel, which lost their folds as they fell and covered the table in many-colored disarray. While we admired he brought more and the soft rich heap mounted higher—shirts with stripes and scrolls and plaids in coral and apple-green and lavender and faint orange, with monograms of Indian blue. Suddenly, with a strained sound, Daisy bent her head into the shirts and began to cry stormily.

"They're such beautiful shirts," she sobbed, her voice muffled in the thick folds. "It makes me sad because I've never seen such—such beautiful shirts before."

After the house, we were to see the grounds and the swimming-pool, and the hydroplane and the midsummer flowers—but outside Gatsby's window it began to rain again, so we stood in a row looking at the corrugated surface of the Sound.

"If it wasn't for the mist we could see your home across the bay," said Gatsby. "You always have a green light that burns all night at the end of your dock."

Daisy put her arm through his abruptly, but he seemed absorbed in what he had just said. Possibly it had occurred to him that the colossal significance of that light had now vanished forever. Compared to the great distance that had separated him from Daisy it had seemed very near to her, almost touching her. It had seemed as close as a star to the moon. Now it was again a green light on a dock. His count of enchanted objects had diminished by one.

I began to walk about the room, examining various indefinite objects in the half darkness. A large photograph of an elderly man in yachting costume attracted me, hung on the wall over his desk.

"Who's this?"

"That? That's Mr. Dan Cody, old sport."

The name sounded faintly familiar.

"He's dead now. He used to be my best friend years ago."

There was a small picture of Gatsby, also in yachting costume, on the bureau—Gatsby with his head thrown back defiantly—taken apparently when he was about eighteen.

"I adore it," exclaimed Daisy. "The pompadour! You never told me you had a pompadour—or a yacht."

"Look at this," said Gatsby quickly. "Here's a lot of clippings—about you."

They stood side by side examining it. I was going to ask to see the rubies when the phone rang, and Gatsby took up the receiver.

"Yes. . . . Well, I can't talk now. . . . I can't talk now, old sport. . . . I said a *small* town. . . . He must know what a small town is. . . . Well, he's no use to us if Detroit is his idea of a small town. . . ."

He rang off.

"Come here *quick!*" cried Daisy at the window.

The rain was still falling, but the darkness had parted in the west, and there was a pink and golden billow of foamy clouds above the sea.

"Look at that," she whispered, and then after a moment: "I'd like to just get one of those pink clouds and put you in it and push you around."

I tried to go then, but they wouldn't hear of it; perhaps my presence made them feel more satisfactorily alone.

"I know what we'll do," said Gatsby, "we'll have Klipspringer play the piano."

He went out of the room calling "Ewing!" and returned in a few minutes accompanied by an embarrassed, slightly worn young man, with shell-rimmed glasses and scanty blond hair. He was now decently clothed in a sport shirt, open at the neck, sneakers, and duck trousers of a nebulous hue.

"Did we interrupt your exercises?" inquired Daisy politely.

"I was asleep," cried Mr. Klipspringer, in a spasm

of embarrassment. "That is, I'd *been* asleep. Then I got up. . . ."

"Klipspringer plays the piano," said Gatsby, cutting him off. "Don't you, Ewing, old sport?"

"I don't play well. I don't—I hardly play at all. I'm all out of prac——"

"We'll go downstairs," interrupted Gatsby. He flipped a switch. The gray windows disappeared as the house glowed full of light.

In the music-room Gatsby turned on a solitary lamp beside the piano. He lit Daisy's cigarette from a trembling match, and sat down with her on a couch far across the room, where there was no light save what the gleaming floor bounced in from the hall.

When Klipspringer had played *The Love Nest* he turned around on the bench and searched unhappily for Gatsby in the gloom.

"I'm all out of practice, you see. I told you I couldn't play. I'm all out of prac——"

"Don't talk so much, old sport," commanded Gatsby. "Play!"

> *"In the morning,*
> *In the evening,*
> *Ain't we got fun——"*

Outside the wind was loud and there was a faint flow of thunder along the Sound. All the lights were going on in West Egg now; the electric trains, men-carrying, were plunging home through the rain from New York. It was the hour of a profound human change, and excitement was generating on the air

> *"One thing's sure and nothing's surer*
> *The rich get richer and the poor get—children.*
> *In the meantime,*
> *In between time——"*

As I went over to say good-by I saw that the expression of bewilderment had come back into Gatsby's face, as though a faint doubt had occurred to him as to the quality of his present happiness. Almost five years! There must have been moments even that afternoon when Daisy tumbled short of his dreams—not through her own fault, but because of the colossal vitality of his illusion. It had gone beyond her, beyond everything. He had thrown himself into it with a creative passion, adding to it all the time, decking it out with every bright feather that drifted his way. No amount of fire or freshness can challenge what a man will store up in his ghostly heart.

As I watched him he adjusted himself a little, visibly. His hand took hold of hers, and as she said something low in his ear he turned toward her with a rush of emotion. I think that voice held him most, with its fluctuating, feverish warmth, because it

couldn't be over-dreamed—that voice was a deathless song.

They had forgotten me, but Daisy glanced up and held out her hand; Gatsby didn't know me now at all. I looked once more at them and they looked back at me, remotely, possessed by intense life. Then I went out of the room and down the marble steps into the rain, leaving them there together.

VI

About this time an ambitous young reporter from New York arrived one morning at Gatsby's door and asked him if he had anything to say.

"Anything to say about what?" inquired Gatsby politely.

"Why—any statement to give out."

It transpired after a confused five minutes that the man had heard Gatsby's name around his office in a connection which he either wouldn't reveal or didn't fully understand. This was his day off and with laudable initiative he had hurried out "to see."

It was a random shot, and yet the reporter's instinct was right. Gatsby's notoriety, spread about by the hundreds who had accepted his hospitality and so become authorities upon his past, had increased all summer until he fell just short of being news. Contemporary legends such as the "underground pipe-line to Canada" attached themselves to him, and there was one persistent story that he didn't live in a house at all, but in a boat that looked like a house and was moved secretly up and down the Long Island shore. Just why these inventions were a source of satisfaction to James Gatz of North Dakota isn't easy to say.

James Gatz—that was really, or at least legally, his name. He had changed it at the age of seventeen and at the specific moment that witnessed the beginning of his career—when he saw Dan Cody's yacht drop anchor over the most insidious flat on Lake Superior. It was James Gatz who had been loafing along the beach that afternoon in a torn green jersey and a pair of canvas pants, but it was already Jay Gatsby who borrowed a rowboat, pulled out to the *Tuolomee,* and informed Cody that a wind might catch him and break him up in half an hour.

I suppose he'd had the name ready for a long time, even then. His parents were shiftless and unsuccessful farm people—his imagination had never really accepted them as his parents at all. The truth was that Jay Gatsby of West Egg, Long Island, sprang from his Platonic conception of himself. He was a son of God—a phrase which, if it means anything, means just that—and he must be about His Father's business, the service of a vast, vulgar, and meretricious beauty. So he invented just the sort of

Jay Gatsby that a seventeen-year-old boy would be likely to invent, and to this conception he was faithful to the end.

For over a year he had been beating his way along the south shore of Lake Superior as a clam-digger and a salmon-fisher or in any other capacity that brought him food and bed. His brown, hardening body lived naturally through the half-fierce, half-lazy work of the bracing days. He knew women early, and since they spoiled him he became contemptuous of them, of young virgins because they were ignorant, of the others because they were hysterical about things which in his overwhelming self-absorption he took for granted.

But his heart was in a constant, turbulent riot. The most grotesque and fantastic conceits haunted him in his bed at night. A universe of ineffable gaudiness spun itself out in his brain while the clock ticked on the washstand and the moon soaked with wet light his tangled clothes upon the floor. Each night he added to the pattern of his fancies until drowsiness closed down upon some vivid scene with an oblivious embrace. For a while these reveries provided an outlet for his imagination; they were a satisfactory hint of the unreality of reality, a promise that the rock of the world was founded securely on a fairy's wing.

An instinct toward his future glory had led him, some months before, to the small Lutheran college of St. Olaf in southern Minnesota. He stayed there two weeks, dismayed at its ferocious indifference to the drums of his destiny, to destiny itself, and despising the janitor's work with which he was to pay his way through. Then he drifted back to Lake Superior, and he was still searching for something to do on the day that Dan Cody's yacht dropped anchor in the shallows alongshore.

Cody was fifty years old then, a product of the Nevada silver fields, of the Yukon, of every rush for metal since seventy-five. The transactions in Montana copper that made him many times a millionaire found him physically robust but on the verge of soft-mindedness, and, suspecting this, an infinite number of women tried to separate him from his money. The none too savory ramifications by which Ella Kaye, the newspaper woman, played Madame de Maintenon to his weakness and sent him to sea in a yacht, were common knowledge to the turgid sub-journalism of 1902. He had been coasting along all too hospitable shores for five years when he turned up as James Gatz's destiny in Little Girl Bay.

To young Gatz, resting on his oars and looking up at the railed deck, that yacht represented all the beauty and glamour in the world. I suppose he smiled at Cody—he had probably discovered that people liked him when he smiled. At any rate Cody asked him a few questions (one of them elicited the brand new name) and found that he was quick and extravagantly ambitious. A few days later he took him to Duluth and bought him a blue coat, six pairs of white duck trousers, and a yachting cap. And when the *Tuolomee* left for the West Indies and the Barbary Coast Gatsby left too.

He was employed in a vague personal capacity—while he remained with Cody he was in turn steward, mate, skipper, secretary, and even jailor, for Dan Cody sober knew what lavish doings Dan Cody drunk might soon be about, and he provided for such contingencies by reposing more and more trust in Gatsby. The arrangement lasted five years, during which the boat went three times around the Continent. It might have lasted indefinitely except for the fact that Ella Kaye came on board one night in Boston and a week later Dan Cody inhospitably died.

I remember the portrait of him up in Gatsby's bedroom, a gray, florid man with a hard, empty face —the pioneer debauchee, who during one phase of American life brought back to the Eastern seaboard the savage violence of the frontier brothel and saloon. It was indirectly due to Cody that Gatsby drank so little. Sometimes in the course of gay parties women used to rub champagne into his hair; for himself he formed the habit of letting liquor alone.

And it was from Cody that he inherited money—a legacy of twenty-five thousand dollars. He didn't get it. He never understood the legal device that was used against him, but what remained of the millions went intact to Ella Kaye. He was left with his singularly appropriate education; the vague contour of Jay Gatsby had filled out to the substantiality of a man.

He told me all this very much later, but I've put it down here with the idea of exploding those first wild rumors about his antecedents, which weren't even faintly true. Moreover he told it to me at a time of confusion, when I had reached the point of believing everything and nothing about him. So I take advantage of this short halt, while Gatsby, so to speak, caught his breath, to clear this set of misconceptions away.

It was a halt, too, in my association with his affairs. For several weeks I didn't see him or hear his voice on the phone—mostly I was in New York, trotting around with Jordan and trying to ingratiate myself with her senile aunt—but finally I went over to his house one Sunday afternoon. I hadn't been there two minutes when somebody brought Tom Buchanan in for a drink. I was startled, naturally, but the really surprising thing was that it hadn't happened before.

They were a party of three on horseback—Tom and a man named Sloane and a pretty woman in a brown riding-habit, who had been there previously.

"I'm delighted to see you," said Gatsby, standing on his porch. "I'm delighted that you dropped in."

As though they cared!

"Sit right down. Have a cigarette or a cigar." He walked around the room quickly, ringing bells. "I'll have something to drink for you in just a minute."

He was profoundly affected by the fact that Tom was there. But he would be uneasy anyhow until he had given them something, realizing in a vague way that that was all they came for. Mr. Sloane wanted nothing. A lemonade? No, thanks. A little champagne? Nothing at all, thanks. . . . I'm sorry——

"Did you have a nice ride?"

"Very good roads around here."

"I suppose the automobiles——"

"Yeah."

Moved by an irresistible impulse, Gatsby turned to Tom, who had accepted the introduction as a stranger.

"I believe we've met somewhere before, Mr. Buchanan."

"Oh, yes," said Tom, gruffly polite, but obviously not remembering. "So we did. I remember very well."

"About two weeks ago."

"That's right. You were with Nick here."

"I know your wife," continued Gatsby, almost aggressively.

"That so?"

Tom turned to me.

"You live near here, Nick?"

"Next door."

"That so?"

Mr. Sloane didn't enter into the conversation, but lounged back haughtily in his chair; the woman said nothing either—until unexpectedly, after two highballs, she became cordial.

"We'll all come over to your next party, Mr. Gatsby," she suggested. "What do you say?"

"Certainly; I'd be delighted to have you."

"Be ver' nice," said Mr. Sloane, without gratitude. "Well—think ought to be starting home."

"Please don't hurry," Gatsby urged them. He had control of himself now, and he wanted to see more of Tom. "Why don't you—why don't you stay for supper? I wouldn't be surprised if some other people dropped in from New York."

"You come to supper with *me*," said the lady enthusiastically. "Both of you."

This included me. Mr. Sloane got to his feet.

"Come along," he said—but to her only.

"I mean it," she insisted. "I'd love to have you. Lots of room."

Gatsby looked at me questioningly. He wanted to go, and he didn't see that Mr. Sloane had determined he shouldn't.

"I'm afraid I won't be able to," I said.

"Well, you come," she urged, concentrating on Gatsby.

Mr. Sloane murmured something close to her ear.

"We won't be late if we start now," she insisted aloud.

"I haven't got a horse," said Gatsby. "I used to ride in the army, but I've never bought a horse. I'll have to follow you in my car. Excuse me for just a minute."

The rest of us walked out on the porch, where Sloane and the lady began an impassioned conversation aside.

"My God, I believe the man's coming," said Tom. "Doesn't he know she doesn't want him?"

"She says she does want him."

"She has a big dinner party and he won't know a soul there." He frowned. "I wonder where in the devil he met Daisy. By God, I may be old-fashioned in my ideas, but women run around too much these days to suit me. They meet all kinds of crazy fish."

Suddenly Mr. Sloane and the lady walked down the steps and mounted their horses.

"Come on," said Mr. Sloane to Tom, "we're late. We've got to go." And then to me: "Tell him we couldn't wait, will you?"

Tom and I shook hands, the rest of us exchanged a cool nod, and they trotted quickly down the drive, disappearing under the August foliage just as Gatsby, with hat and light overcoat in hand, came out the front door.

Tom was evidently perturbed at Daisy's running around alone, for on the following Saturday night he came with her to Gatsby's party. Perhaps his presence gave the evening its peculiar quality of oppressiveness—it stands out in my memory from Gatsby's other parties that summer. There were the same people, or at least the same sort of people, the same profusion of champagne, the same many-colored, many-keyed commotion, but I felt an unpleasantness in the air, a pervading harshness that hadn't been there before. Or perhaps I had merely grown used to it, grown to accept West Egg as a world complete in itself, with its own standards and its own great figures, second to nothing because it had no consciousness of being so, and now I was looking at it again, through Daisy's eyes. It is invariably saddening to look through new eyes at things upon which you have expended your own powers of adjustment.

They arrived at twilight, and, as we strolled out among the sparkling hundreds, Daisy's voice was playing murmurous tricks in her throat.

"These things excite me *so*," she whispered. "If you want to kiss me any time during the evening, Nick, just let me know and I'll be glad to arrange it for you. Just mention my name. Or present a green card. I'm giving out green——"

"Look around," suggested Gatsby.

"I'm looking around. I'm having a marvellous——"

"You must see the faces of many people you've heard about."

Tom's arrogant eyes roamed the crowd.

"We don't go around very much," he said; "in fact, I was just thinking I don't know a soul here."

"Perhaps you know that lady," Gatsby indicated a gorgeous, scarcely human orchid of a woman who sat in state under a white-plum tree. Tom and Daisy stared, with that peculiarly unreal feeling that accompanies the recognition of a hitherto ghostly celebrity of the movies.

"She's lovely," said Daisy.

"The man bending over her is her director."

He took them ceremoniously from group to group:

"Mrs. Buchanan . . . and Mr. Buchanan—" After an instant's hesitation he added: "the polo player."

"Oh, no," objected Tom quickly, "not me."

But evidently the sound of it pleased Gatsby, for Tom remained "the polo player" for the rest of the evening.

"I've never met so many celebrities," Daisy exclaimed. "I liked that man—what was his name?—with the sort of blue nose."

Gatsby identified him, adding that he was a small producer.

"Well, I liked him anyhow."

"I'd a little rather not be the polo player," said Tom pleasantly, "I'd rather look at all these famous people in—in oblivion."

Daisy and Gatsby danced. I remember being surprised by his graceful, conservative fox-trot—I had never seen him dance before. Then they sauntered over to my house and sat on the steps for half an hour, while at her request I remained watchfully in the garden. "In case there's a fire or a flood," she explained, "or any act of God."

Tom appeared from his oblivion as we were sitting down to supper together. "Do you mind if I eat with some people over there?" he said. "A fellow's getting off some funny stuff."

"Go ahead," answered Daisy genially, "and if you want to take down any addresses here's my little gold pencil." . . . She looked around after a moment and told me the girl was "common but pretty," and

I knew that except for the half-hour she'd been alone with Gatsby she wasn't having a good time.

We were at a particularly tipsy table. That was my fault—Gatsby had been called to the phone, and I'd enjoyed these same people only two weeks before. But what had amused me then turned septic on the air now.

"How do you feel, Miss Baedeker?"

The girl addressed was trying, unsuccessfully, to slump against my shoulder. At this inquiry she sat up and opened her eyes.

"Wha'?"

A massive and lethargic woman, who had been urging Daisy to play golf with her at the local club to-morrow, spoke in Miss Baedeker's defence:

"Oh, she's all right now. When she's had five or six cocktails she always starts screaming like that. I tell her she ought to leave it alone."

"I do leave it alone," affirmed the accused hollowly.

"We heard you yelling, so I said to Doc Civet here: 'There's somebody that needs your help, Doc.'"

"She's much obliged, I'm sure," said another friend, without gratitude, "but you got her dress all wet when you stuck her head in the pool."

"Anything I hate is to get my head stuck in a pool," mumbled Miss Baedeker. "They almost drowned me once over in New Jersey."

"Then you ought to leave it alone," countered Doctor Civet.

"Speak for yourself!" cried Miss Baedeker violently. "Your hand shakes. I wouldn't let you operate on me!"

It was like that. Almost the last thing I remember was standing with Daisy and watching the moving-picture director and his Star. They were still under the white-plum tree and their faces were touching except for a pale, thin ray of moonlight between. It occurred to me that he had been very slowly bending toward her all evening to attain this proximity, and even while I watched I saw him stoop one ultimate degree and kiss at her cheek.

"I like her," said Daisy, "I think she's lovely."

But the rest offended her—and inarguably, because it wasn't a gesture but an emotion. She was appalled by West Egg, this unprecedented "place" that Broadway had begotten upon a Long Island fishing village —appalled by its raw vigor that chafed under the old euphemisms and by the too obtrusive fate that herded its inhabitants along a short-cut from nothing to nothing. She saw something awful in the very simplicity she failed to understand.

I sat on the front steps with them while they waited for their car. It was dark here in front; only the bright door sent ten square feet of light volleying out into the soft black morning. Sometimes a shadow moved against a dressing-room blind above, gave way to another shadow, an indefinite procession of shadows, who rouged and powdered in an invisible glass.

"Who is this Gatsby anyhow?" demanded Tom suddenly. "Some big bootlegger?"

"Where'd you hear that?" I inquired.

"I didn't hear it. I imagined it. A lot of these newly rich people are just big bootleggers, you know."

"Not Gatsby," I said shortly.

He was silent for a moment. The pebbles of the drive crunched under his feet.

"Well, he certainly must have strained himself to get this menagerie together."

A breeze stirred the gray haze of Daisy's fur collar.

"At least they're more interesting than the people we know," she said with an effort.

"You didn't look so interested."

"Well, I was."

Tom laughed and turned to me.

"Did you notice Daisy's face when that girl asked her to put her under a cold shower?"

Daisy began to sing with the music in a husky, rhythmic whisper, bringing out a meaning in each word that it had never had before and would never have again. When the melody rose, her voice broke up sweetly, following it, in a way contralto voices have, and each change tipped out a little of her warm human magic upon the air.

"Lots of people come who haven't been invited," she said suddenly. "That girl hadn't been invited. They simply force their way in and he's too polite to object."

"I'd like to know who he is and what he does," insisted Tom. "And I think I'll make a point of finding out."

"I can tell you right now," she answered. "He owned some drug-stores, a lot of drug-stores. He built them up himself."

The dilatory limousine came rolling up the drive.

"Good night, Nick," said Daisy.

Her glance left me and sought the lighted top of the steps, where *Three O'Clock in the Morning*, a neat, sad little waltz of that year, was drifting out the open door. After all, in the very casualness of Gatsby's party there were romantic possibilities totally absent from her world. What was it up there in the song that seemed to be calling her back inside? What would happen now in the dim, incalculable hours? Perhaps some unbelievable guest would arrive, a person infinitely rare and to be marvelled at, some authentically radiant young girl who with one fresh glance at Gatsby, one moment of magical en-

counter, would blot out those five years of unwavering devotion.

I stayed late that night, Gatsby asked me to wait until he was free, and I lingered in the garden until the inevitable swimming party had run up, chilled and exalted, from the black beach, until the lights were extinguished in the guest-rooms overhead. When he came down the steps at last the tanned skin was drawn unusually tight on his face, and his eyes were bright and tired.

"She didn't like it," he said immediately.

"Of course she did."

"She didn't like it," he insisted. "She didn't have a good time."

He was silent, and I guessed at his unutterable depression.

"I feel far away from her," he said. "It's hard to make her understand."

"You mean about the dance?"

"The dance?" He dismissed all the dances he had given with a snap of his fingers. "Old sport, the dance is unimportant."

He wanted nothing less of Daisy than that she should go to Tom and say: "I never loved you." After she had obliterated four years with that sentence they could decide upon the more practical measures to be taken. One of them was that, after she was free, they were to go back to Louisville and be married from her house—just as if it were five years ago.

"And she doesn't understand," he said. "She used to be able to understand. We'd sit for hours——"

He broke off and began to walk up and down a desolate path of fruit rinds and discarded favors and crushed flowers.

"I wouldn't ask too much of her," I ventured. "You can't repeat the past."

"Can't repeat the past?" he cried incredulously. "Why of course you can!"

He looked around him wildly, as if the past were lurking here in the shadow of his house, just out of reach of his hand.

"I'm going to fix everything just the way it was before," he said, nodding determinedly. "She'll see."

He talked a lot about the past, and I gathered that he wanted to recover something, some idea of himself perhaps, that had gone into loving Daisy. His life had been confused and disordered since then, but if he could once return to a certain starting place and go over it all slowly, he could find out what that thing was. . . .

. . . One autumn night, five years before, they had been walking down the street when the leaves were falling, and they came to a place where there were no trees and the sidewalk was white with moonlight. They stopped here and turned toward each other. Now it was a cool night with that mysterious excitement in it which comes at the two changes of the year. The quiet lights in the houses were humming out into the darkness and there was a stir and bustle among the stars. Out of the corner of his eye Gatsby saw that the blocks of the sidewalks really formed a ladder and mounted to a secret place above the trees—he could climb to it, if he climbed alone, and once there he could suck on the pap of life, gulp down the incomparable milk of wonder.

His heart beat faster and faster as Daisy's white face came up to his own. He knew that when he kissed this girl, and forever wed his unutterable visions to her perishable breath, his mind would never romp again like the mind of God. So he waited, listening for a moment longer to the tuning-fork that had been struck upon a star. Then he kissed her. At his lips' touch she blossomed for him like a flower and the incarnation was complete.

Through all he said, even through his appalling sentimentality, I was reminded of something—an elusive rhythm, a fragment of lost words, that I had heard somewhere a long time ago. For a moment a phrase tried to take shape in my mouth and my lips parted like a dumb man's, as though there was more struggling upon them than a wisp of startled air. But they made no sound, and what I had almost remembered was uncommunicable forever.

VII

It was when curiosity about Gatsby was at its highest that the lights in his house failed to go on one Saturday night—and, as obscurely as it had begun, his career as Trimalchio was over. Only gradually did I become aware that the automobiles which turned expectantly into his drive stayed for just a minute and then drove sulkily away. Wondering if he were sick I went over to find out—an unfamiliar butler with a villainous face squinted at me suspiciously from the door.

"Is Mr. Gatsby sick?"

"Nope." After a pause he added "sir" in a dilatory, grudging way.

"I hadn't seen him around, and I was rather worried. Tell him Mr. Carraway came over."

"Who?" he demanded rudely.

"Carraway."

"Carraway. All right, I'll tell him."

Abruptly he slammed the door.

My Finn informed me that Gatsby had dismissed every servant in his house a week ago and replaced them with half a dozen others, who never went into West Egg Village to be bribed by the tradesmen, but ordered moderate supplies over the telephone. The grocery boy reported that the kitchen looked like a pigsty, and the general opinion in the village was that the new people weren't servants at all.

Next day Gatsby called me on the phone.

"Going away?" I inquired.

"No, old sport."

"I hear you fired all your servants."

"I wanted somebody who wouldn't gossip. Daisy comes over quite often—in the afternoons."

So the whole caravansary had fallen in like a card house at the disapproval in her eyes.

"They're some people Wolfsheim wanted to do something for. They're all brothers and sisters. They used to run a small hotel."

"I see."

He was calling up at Daisy's request—would I come to lunch at her house to-morrow? Miss Baker would be there. Half an hour later Daisy herself telephoned and seemed relieved to find that I was coming. Something was up. And yet I couldn't believe that they would choose this occasion for a scene—especially for the rather harrowing scene that Gatsby had outlined in the garden.

The next day was broiling, almost the last, certainly the warmest, of the summer. As my train emerged from the tunnel into sunlight, only the hot whistles of the National Biscuit Company broke the simmering hush at noon. The straw seats of the car hovered on the edge of combustion; the woman next to me perspired delicately for a while into her white shirtwaist, and then, as her newspaper dampened under her fingers, lapsed despairingly into deep heat with a desolate cry. Her pocket-book slapped to the floor.

"Oh, my!" she gasped.

I picked it up with a weary bend and handed it back to her, holding it at arm's length and by the extreme tip of the corners to indicate that I had no designs upon it—but every one near by, including the woman, suspected me just the same.

"Hot!" said the conductor to familiar faces. "Some weather! . . . Hot! . . . Hot! . . . Hot! . . . Is it hot enough for you? Is it hot? Is it . . . ?"

My commutation ticket came back to me with a dark stain from his hand. That any one should care in this heat whose flushed lips he kissed, whose head made damp the pajama pocket over his heart!

. . . Through the hall of the Buchanans' house blew a faint wind, carrying the sound of the telephone bell out to Gatsby and me as we waited at the door.

"The master's body!" roared the butler into the mouthpiece. "I'm sorry, madame, but we can't furnish it—it's far too hot to touch this noon!"

What he really said was: "Yes . . . Yes . . . I'll see."

He set down the receiver and came toward us, glistening slightly, to take our stiff straw hats.

"Madame expects you in the salon!" he cried, needlessly indicating the direction. In this heat every extra gesture was an affront to the common store of life.

The room, shadowed well with awnings, was dark and cool. Daisy and Jordan lay upon an enormous couch, like silver idols weighing down their own white dresses against the singing breeze of the fans.

"We can't move," they said together.

Jordan's fingers, powdered white over their tan, rested for a moment in mine.

"And Mr. Thomas Buchanan, the athlete?" I inquired.

Simultaneously I heard his voice, gruff, muffled, husky, at the hall telephone.

Gatsby stood in the centre of the crimson carpet and gazed around with fascinated eyes. Daisy watched him and laughed, her sweet, exciting laugh; a tiny gust of powder rose from her bosom into the air.

"The rumor is," whispered Jordan, "that that's Tom's girl on the telephone."

We were silent. The voice in the hall rose high with annoyance: "Very well, then, I won't sell you the car at all. . . . I'm under no obligations to you at all . . . and as for your bothering me about it at lunch time, I won't stand that at all!"

"Holding down the receiver," said Daisy cynically.

"No, he's not," I assured her. "It's a bona-fide deal. I happen to know about it."

Tom flung open the door, blocked out its space for a moment with his thick body, and hurried into the room.

"Mr. Gatsby!" He put out his broad, flat hand with well-concealed dislike. "I'm glad to see you, sir. . . . Nick. . . ."

"Make us a cold drink," cried Daisy.

As he left the room again she got up and went over to Gatsby and pulled his face down, kissing him on the mouth.

"You know I love you," she murmured.

"You forget there's a lady present," said Jordan.

Daisy looked around doubtfully.

"You kiss Nick too."

"What a low, vulgar girl!"

"I don't care!" cried Daisy, and began to clog on the brick fireplace. Then she remembered the heat and sat down guiltily on the couch just as a freshly laundered nurse leading a little girl came into the room.

"Bles-sed pre-cious," she crooned, holding out her arms. "Come to your own mother that loves you."

The child, relinquished by the nurse, rushed across the room and rooted shyly into her mother's dress.

"The bles-sed pre-cious! Did mother get powder on your old yellowy hair? Stand up now, and say—How-de-do."

Gatsby and I in turn leaned down and took the small reluctant hand. Afterward he kept looking at the child with surprise. I don't think he had ever really believed in its existence before.

"I got dressed before luncheon," said the child, turning eagerly to Daisy.

"That's because your mother wanted to show you off." Her face bent into the single wrinkle of the small white neck. "You dream, you. You absolute little dream."

"Yes," admitted the child calmly. "Aunt Jordan's got on a white dress too."

"How do you like mother's friends?" Daisy turned her around so that she faced Gatsby. "Do you think they're pretty?"

"Where's Daddy?"

"She doesn't look like her father," explained Daisy. "She looks like me. She's got my hair and shape of the face."

Daisy sat back upon the couch. The nurse took a step forward and held out her hand.

"Come, Penny."

"Good-by, sweetheart!"

With a reluctant backward glance the well-disciplined child held to her nurse's hand and was pulled out the door, just as Tom came back, preceding four gin rickeys that clicked full of ice.

Gatsby took up his drink.

"They certainly look cool," he said, with visible tension.

We drank in long, greedy swallows.

"I read somewhere that the sun's getting hotter every year," said Tom genially. "It seems that pretty soon the earth's going to fall into the sun—or wait a minute—it's just the opposite—the sun's getting colder every year.

"Come outside," he suggested to Gatsby, "I'd like you to have a look at the place."

I went with them out to the veranda. On the green Sound, stagnant in the heat, one small sail crawled slowly toward the fresher sea. Gatsby's eyes followed it momentarily; he raised his hand and pointed across the bay.

"I'm right across from you."

"So you are."

Our eyes lifted over the rose-beds and the hot lawn and the weedy refuse of the dog-days along-shore. Slowly the white wings of the boat moved against the blue cool limit of the sky. Ahead lay the scalloped ocean and the abounding blessed isles.

"There's sport for you," said Tom, nodding. "I'd like to be out there with him for about an hour."

We had luncheon in the dining-room, darkened too against the heat, and drank down nervous gayety with the cold ale.

"What'll we do with ourselves this afternoon?" cried Daisy, "and the day after that, and the next thirty years?"

"Don't be morbid," Jordan said. "Life starts all over again when it gets crisp in the fall."

"But it's so hot," insisted Daisy, on the verge of tears, "and everything's so confused. Let's all go to town!"

Her voice struggled on through the heat, beating against it, molding its senselessness into forms.

"I've heard of making a garage out of a stable," Tom was saying to Gatsby, "but I'm the first man who ever made a stable out of a garage."

"Who wants to go to town?" demanded Daisy insistently. Gatsby's eyes floated toward her. "Ah," she cried, "you look so cool."

Their eyes met, and they stared together at each other, alone in space. With an effort she glanced down at the table.

"You always look so cool," she repeated.

She had told him that she loved him, and Tom Buchanan saw. He was astounded. His mouth opened a little, and he looked at Gatsby, and then back at Daisy as if he had just recognized her as some one he knew a long time ago.

"You resemble the advertisement of the man," she went on innocently. "You know the advertisement of the man——"

"All right," broke in Tom quickly, "I'm perfectly willing to go to town. Come on—we're all going to town."

He got up, his eyes still flashing between Gatsby and his wife. No one moved.

"Come on!" His temper cracked a little. "What's the matter, anyhow? If we're going to town, let's start."

His hand, trembling with his effort at self-control, bore to his lips the last of his glass of ale. Daisy's voice got us to our feet and out on to the blazing gravel drive.

"Are we just going to go?" she objected. "Like this? Aren't we going to let any one smoke a cigarette first?"

"Everybody smoked all through lunch."

"Oh, let's have fun," she begged him. "It's too hot to fuss."

He didn't answer.

"Have it your own way," she said. "Come on, Jordan."

They went upstairs to get ready while we three men stood there shuffling the hot pebbles with our feet. A silver curve of the moon hovered already in the western sky. Gatsby started to speak, changed his mind, but not before Tom wheeled and faced him expectantly.

"Have you got your stables here?" asked Gatsby with an effort.

"About a quarter of a mile down the road."

"Oh."

A pause.

"I don't see the idea of going to town," broke out Tom savagely. "Women get these notions in their heads——"

"Shall we take anything to drink?" called Daisy from an upper window.

"I'll get some whiskey," answered Tom. He went inside.

Gatsby turned to me rigidly:

"I can't say anything in his house, old sport."

"She's got an indiscreet voice," I remarked. "It's full of—" I hesitated.

"Her voice is full of money," he said suddenly.

That was it. I'd never understood before. It was full of money—that was the inexhaustible charm that rose and fell in it, the jingle of it, the cymbals' song of it. . . . High in a white palace the king's daughter, the golden girl. . . .

Tom came out of the house wrapping a quart bottle in a towel, followed by Daisy and Jordan wearing small tight hats of metallic cloth and carrying light capes over their arms.

"Shall we all go in my car?" suggested Gatsby. He felt the hot, green leather of the seat. "I ought to have left it in the shade."

"Is it standard shift?" demanded Tom.

"Yes."

"Well, you take my coupé and let me drive your car to town."

The suggestion was distasteful to Gatsby.

"I don't think there's much gas," he objected.

"Plenty of gas," said Tom boisterously. He looked at the gauge. "And if it runs out I can stop at a drug-store. You can buy anything at a drug-store nowadays."

A pause followed this apparently pointless remark. Daisy looked at Tom frowning, and an indefinable expression, at once definitely unfamiliar and vaguely recognizable, as if I had only heard it described in words, passed over Gatsby's face.

"Come on, Daisy," said Tom, pressing her with his hand toward Gatsby's car. "I'll take you in this circus wagon."

He opened the door, but she moved out from the circle of his arm.

"You take Nick and Jordan. We'll follow you in the coupé."

She walked close to Gatsby, touching his coat with her hand. Jordan and Tom and I got into the front seat of Gatsby's car, Tom pushed the unfamiliar gears tentatively, and we shot off into the oppressive heat, leaving them out of sight behind.

"Did you see that?" demanded Tom.

"See what?"

He looked at me keenly, realizing that Jordan and I must have known all along.

"You think I'm pretty dumb, don't you?" he suggested. "Perhaps I am, but I have a—almost a second sight, sometimes, that tells me what to do. Maybe you don't believe that, but science——"

He paused. The immediate contingency overtook him, pulled him back from the edge of the theoretical abyss.

"I've made a small investigation of this fellow," he continued. "I could have gone deeper if I'd known——"

"Do you mean you've been to a medium?" inquired Jordan humorously.

"What?" Confused, he stared at us as we laughed. "A medium?"

"About Gatsby."

"About Gatsby! No, I haven't. I said I'd been making a small investigation of his past."

"And you found he was an Oxford man," said Jordan helpfully.

"An Oxford man!" He was incredulous. "Like hell he is! He wears a pink suit."

"Nevertheless he's an Oxford man."

"Oxford, New Mexico," snorted Tom contemptuously, "or something like that."

"Listen, Tom. If you're such a snob, why did you invite him to lunch?" demanded Jordan crossly.

"Daisy invited him; she knew him before we were married—God knows where!"

We were all irritable now with the fading ale, and aware of it we drove for a while in silence. Then as Doctor T. J. Eckleburg's faded eyes came into sight down the road, I remembered Gatsby's caution about gasoline.

"We've got enough to get us to town," said Tom.

"But there's a garage right here," objected Jordan. "I don't want to get stalled in this baking heat."

Tom threw on both brakes impatiently, and we slid to an abrupt dusty stop under Wilson's sign. After a moment the proprietor emerged from the interior of his establishment and gazed hollow-eyed at the car.

"Let's have some gas!" cried Tom roughly. "What do you think we stopped for—to admire the view?"

"I'm sick," said Wilson without moving. "Been sick all day."

"What's the matter?"

"I'm all run down."

"Well, shall I help myself?" Tom demanded. "You sounded well enough on the phone."

With an effort Wilson left the shade and support of the doorway and, breathing hard, unscrewed the cap of the tank. In the sunlight his face was green.

"I didn't mean to interrupt your lunch," he said. "But I need money pretty bad, and I was wondering what you were going to do with your old car."

"How do you like this one?" inquired Tom. "I bought it last week."

"It's a nice yellow one," said Wilson, as he strained at the handle.

"Like to buy it?"

"Big chance," Wilson smiled faintly. "No, but I could make some money on the other."

"What do you want money for, all of a sudden?"

"I've been here too long. I want to get away. My wife and I want to go West."

"Your wife does," exclaimed Tom, startled.

"She's been talking about it for ten years." He rested for a moment against the pump, shading his eyes. "And now she's going whether she wants to or not. I'm going to get her away."

The coupé flashed by us with a flurry of dust and the flash of a waving hand.

"What do I owe you?" demanded Tom harshly.

"I just got wised up to something funny the last two days," remarked Wilson. "That's why I want to get away. That's why I been bothering you about the car."

"What do I owe you?"

"Dollar twenty."

The relentless beating heat was beginning to confuse me and I had a bad moment there before I realized that so far his suspicions hadn't alighted on Tom. He had discovered that Myrtle had some sort of life apart from him in another world, and the shock had made him physically sick. I stared at him and then at Tom, who had made a parallel discovery less than an hour before—and it occurred to me that there was no difference between men, in intelligence or race, so profound as the difference between the sick and the well. Wilson was so sick that he looked guilty, unforgivably guilty—as if he just got some poor girl with child.

"I'll let you have that car," said Tom. "I'll send it over to-morrow afternoon."

That locality was always vaguely disquieting, even in the broad glare of afternoon, and now I turned my head as though I had been warned of something behind. Over the ashheaps the giant eyes of Doctor T. J. Eckleburg kept their vigil, but I perceived, after a moment, that the other eyes were regarding us with peculiar intensity from less than twenty feet away.

In one of the windows over the garage the curtains had been moved aside a little, and Myrtle Wilson was peering down at the car. So engrossed was she that she had no consciousness of being observed, and one emotion after another crept into her face like objects into a slowly developing picture. Her expression was curiously familiar—it was an expression I had often seen on women's faces, but on Myrtle Wilson's face it seemed purposeless and inexplicable until I realized that her eyes, wide with jealous terror, were fixed not on Tom, but on Jordan Baker, whom she took to be his wife.

There is no confusion like the confusion of a simple mind, and as we drove away Tom was feeling the hot whips of panic. His wife and his mistress, until an hour ago secure and inviolate, were slipping precipitately from his control. Instinct made him step on the accelerator with the double purpose of overtaking Daisy and leaving Wilson behind, and we sped along toward Astoria at fifty miles an hour, until, among the spidery girders of the elevated, we came in sight of the easy-going blue coupé.

"Those big movies around Fiftieth Street are cool," suggested Jordan. "I love New York on summer afternoons when every one's away. There's something very sensuous about it—overripe, as if all sorts of funny fruits were going to fall into your hands."

The word "sensuous" had the effect of further disquieting Tom, but before he could invent a protest the coupé came to a stop, and Daisy signalled us to draw up alongside.

"Where are we going?" she cried.

"How about the movies?"

"It's so hot," she complained. "You go. We'll ride around and meet you after." With an effort her wit rose faintly, "We'll meet you on some corner. I'll be the man smoking two cigarettes."

"We can't argue about it here," Tom said impatiently, as a truck gave out a cursing whistle behind us. "You follow me to the south side of Central Park, in front of the Plaza."

Several times he turned his head and looked back for their car, and if the traffic delayed them he slowed up until they came into sight. I think he was afraid they would dart down a side street and out of his life forever.

But they didn't. And we all took the less explicable step of engaging the parlor of a suite in the Plaza Hotel.

The prolonged and tumultuous argument that ended by herding us into that room eludes me, though I have a sharp physical memory that, in the course of it, my underwear kept climbing like a damp snake around my legs and intermittent beads of sweat raced cool across my back. The notion originated with Daisy's suggestion that we hire five bathrooms and take cold baths, and then assumed more tangible form as "a place to have a mint julep." Each of us said over and over that it was a "crazy idea"—we all talked at once to a baffled clerk and thought, or pretended to think, that we were being very funny . . .

The room was large and stifling, and, though it was already four o'clock, opening the windows admitted only a gust of hot shrubbery from the Park. Daisy went to the mirror and stood with her back to us, fixing her hair.

"It's a swell suite," whispered Jordan respectfully, and every one laughed.

"Open another window," commanded Daisy, without turning around.

"There aren't any more."

"Well, we'd better telephone for an axe——"

"The thing to do is to forget about the heat," said Tom impatiently. "You make it ten times worse by crabbing about it."

He unrolled the bottle of whiskey from the towel and put it on the table.

"Why not let her alone, old sport?" remarked Gatsby. "You're the one that wanted to come to town."

There was a moment of silence. The telephone book slipped from its nail and splashed to the floor, whereupon Jordan whispered, "Excuse me"—but this time no one laughed.

"I'll pick it up," I offered.

"I've got it." Gatsby examined the parted string, muttered "Hum!" in an interested way, and tossed the book on a chair.

"That's a great expression of yours, isn't it?" said Tom sharply.

"What is?"

"All this 'old sport' business. Where'd you pick that up?"

"Now see here, Tom," said Daisy, turning around from the mirror, "if you're going to make personal remarks I won't stay here a minute. Call up and order some ice for the mint julep."

As Tom took up the receiver the compressed heat exploded into sound and we were listening to the portentous chords of Mendelssohn's Wedding March from the ballroom below.

"Imagine marrying anybody in this heat!" cried Jordan dismally.

"Still—I was married in the middle of June," Daisy remembered, "Louisville in June! Somebody fainted. Who was it fainted, Tom?"

"Biloxi," he answered shortly.

"A man named Biloxi. 'Blocks' Biloxi, and he made boxes—that's a fact—and he was from Biloxi, Tennessee."

"They carried him into my house," appended Jordan, "because we lived just two doors from the church. And he stayed three weeks, until Daddy told him he had to get out. The day after he left Daddy died." After a moment she added as if she might have sounded irreverent, "There wasn't any connection."

"I used to know a Bill Biloxi from Memphis," I remarked.

"That was his cousin. I knew his whole family history before he left. He gave me an aluminum putter that I use today."

The music had died down as the ceremony began and now a long cheer floated in at the window, followed by intermittent cries of "Yea—ea—ea!" and finally by a burst of jazz as the dancing began.

"We're getting old," said Daisy. "If we were young we'd rise and dance."

"Remember Biloxi," Jordan warned her. "Where'd you know him, Tom?"

"Biloxi?" He concentrated with an effort. "I didn't know him. He was a friend of Daisy's."

"He was not," she denied. "I'd never seen him before. He came down in the private car."

"Well, he said he knew you. He said he was raised in Louisville. Asa Bird brought him around at the last minute and asked if we had room for him."

Jordan smiled.

"He was probably bumming his way home. He told me he was president of your class at Yale."

Tom and I looked at each other blankly.

"Biloxi?"

"First place, we didn't have any president——"

Gatsby's foot beat a short, restless tattoo and Tom eyed him suddenly.

"By the way, Mr. Gatsby, I understand you're an Oxford man."

"Not exactly."

"Oh, yes, I understand you went to Oxford."

"Yes—I went there."

A pause. Then Tom's voice, incredulous and insulting:

"You must have gone there about the time Biloxi went to New Haven."

Another pause. A waiter knocked and came in with crushed mint and ice, but the silence was unbroken by his "thank you" and the soft closing of the door. This tremendous detail was to be cleared up at last.

"I told you I went there," said Gatsby.

"I heard you, but I'd like to know when."

"It was in nineteen-nineteen. I only stayed five months. That's why I can't really call myself an Oxford man."

Tom glanced around to see if we mirrored his unbelief. But we were all looking at Gatsby.

"It was an opportunity they gave to some of the officers after the Armistice," he continued. "We could go to any of the universities in England or France."

I wanted to get up and slap him on the back. I had one of those renewals of complete faith in him that I'd experienced before.

Daisy rose, smiling faintly, and went to the table.

"Open the whiskey, Tom," she ordered, "and I'll make you a mint julep. Then you won't seem so stupid to yourself. . . . Look at the mint!"

"Wait a minute," snapped Tom, "I want to ask Mr. Gatsby one more question."

"Go on," Gatsby said politely.

"What kind of a row are you trying to cause in my house anyhow?"

They were out in the open at last and Gatsby was content.

"He isn't causing a row," Daisy looked desperately from one to the other. "You're causing a row. Please have a little self-control."

"Self-control!" repeated Tom incredulously. "I suppose the latest thing is to sit back and let Mr. Nobody from Nowhere make love to your wife. Well, if that's the idea you can count me out. . . . Nowadays people begin by sneering at family life and family institutions, and next they'll throw everything overboard and have intermarriage between black and white."

Flushed with his impassioned gibberish, he saw himself standing alone on the last barrier of civilization.

"We're all white here," murmured Jordan.

"I know I'm not very popular. I don't give big parties. I suppose you've got to make your house into a pigsty in order to have any friends—in the modern world."

Angry as I was, as we all were, I was tempted to laugh whenever he opened his mouth. The transition from libertine to prig was so complete.

"I've got something to tell *you*, old sport—" began Gatsby. But Daisy guessed at his intention.

"Please don't!" she interrupted helplessly. "Please let's all go home. Why don't we all go home?"

"That's a good idea." I got up. "Come on, Tom. Nobody wants a drink."

"I want to know what Mr. Gatsby has to tell me."

"Your wife doesn't love you," said Gatsby. "She's never loved you. She loves me."

"You must be crazy!" exclaimed Tom automatically.

Gatsby sprang to his feet, vivid with excitement.

"She never loved you, do you hear?" he cried. "She only married you because I was poor and she was tired of waiting for me. It was a terrible mistake, but in her heart she never loved any one except me!"

At this point Jordan and I tried to go, but Tom and Gatsby insisted with competitive firmness that we remain—as though neither of them had anything to conceal and it would be a privilege to partake vicariously of their emotions.

"Sit down, Daisy," Tom's voice groped unsuccessfully for the paternal note. "What's been going on? I want to hear all about it."

"I told you what's been going on," said Gatsby. "Going on for five years—and you didn't know."

Tom turned to Daisy sharply.

"You've been seeing this fellow for five years?"

"Not seeing," said Gatsby. "No, we couldn't meet. But both of us loved each other all that time, old sport, and you didn't know. I used to laugh sometimes"—but there was no laughter in his eyes—"to think that you didn't know."

"Oh—that's all." Tom tapped his thick fingers together like a clergyman and leaned back in his chair.

"You're crazy!" he exploded. "I can't speak about what happened five years ago, because I didn't know Daisy then—and I'll be damned if I see how you got within a mile of her unless you brought the groceries to the back door. But all the rest of that's a God damned lie. Daisy loved me when she married me and she loves me now."

"No," said Gatsby, shaking his head.

"She does, though. The trouble is that sometimes she gets foolish ideas in her head and doesn't know what she's doing." He nodded sagely. "And what's more, I love Daisy too. Once in a while I go off on a spree and make a fool of myself, but I always come back, and in my heart I love her all the time."

"You're revolting," said Daisy. She turned to me, and her voice, dropping an octave lower, filled the room with thrilling scorn: "Do you know why we left Chicago? I'm surprised that they didn't treat you to the story of that little spree."

Gatsby walked over and stood beside her.

"Daisy, that's all over now," he said earnestly. "It doesn't matter any more. Just tell him the truth—that you never loved him—and it's all wiped out forever."

She looked at him blindly. "Why—how could I love him—possibly?"

"You never loved him."

She hesitated. Her eyes fell on Jordan and me with a sort of appeal, as though she realized at last what she was doing—and as though she had never, all along, intended doing anything at all. But it was done now. It was too late.

"I never loved him," she said, with perceptible reluctance.

"Not at Kapiolani?" demanded Tom suddenly.

"No."

From the ballroom beneath, muffled and suffocating chords were drifting up on hot waves of air.

"Not that day I carried you down from the Punch Bowl to keep your shoes dry?" There was a husky tenderness in his tone. . . . "Daisy?"

"Please don't." Her voice was cold, but the rancor was gone from it. She looked at Gatsby. "There, Jay," she said—but her hand as she tried to light a cigarette was trembling. Suddenly she threw the cigarette and the burning match on the carpet.

"Oh, you want too much!" she cried to Gatsby. "I love you now—isn't that enough? I can't help what's past." She began to sob helplessly. "I did love him once—but I loved you too."

Gatsby's eyes opened and closed.

"You loved me too?" he repeated.

"Even that's a lie," said Tom savagely. "She didn't know you were alive. Why—there're things between Daisy and me that you'll never know, things that neither of us can ever forget."

The words seemed to bite physically into Gatsby.

"I want to speak to Daisy alone," he insisted. "She's all excited now——"

"Even alone I can't say I never loved Tom," she admitted in a pitiful voice. "It wouldn't be true."

"Of course it wouldn't," agreed Tom.

She turned to her husband.

"As if it mattered to you," she said.

"Of course it matters. I'm going to take better care of you from now on."

"You don't understand," said Gatsby, with a touch of panic. "You're not going to take care of her any more."

"I'm not?" Tom opened his eyes wide and laughed. He could afford to control himself now. "Why's that?"

"Daisy's leaving you."

"Nonsense."

"I am, though," she said with a visible effort.

"She's not leaving me!" Tom's words suddenly leaned down over Gatsby. "Certainly not for a common swindler who'd have to steal the ring he put on her finger."

"I won't stand this!" cried Daisy. "Oh, please let's get out."

"Who are you, anyhow?" broke out Tom. "You're one of that bunch that hangs around with Meyer Wolfsheim—that much I happen to know. I've made a little investigation into your affairs—and I'll carry it further to-morrow."

"You can suit yourself about that, old sport," said Gatsby steadily.

"I found out what your 'drug-stores' were." He turned to us and spoke rapidly. "He and this Wolfsheim bought up a lot of side-street drug-stores here and in Chicago and sold grain alcohol over the counter. That's one of his little stunts. I picked him for a bootlegger the first time I saw him, and I wasn't far wrong."

"What about it?" said Gatsby politely. "I guess your friend Walter Chase wasn't too proud to come in on it."

"And you left him in the lurch, didn't you? You let him go to jail for a month over in New Jersey. God! You ought to hear Walter on the subject of *you*."

"He came to us dead broke. He was very glad to pick up some money, old sport."

"Don't you call me 'old sport'!" cried Tom. Gatsby said nothing. "Walter could have you up on the betting laws too, but Wolfsheim scared him into shutting his mouth."

That unfamiliar yet recognizable look was back again in Gatsby's face.

"That drug-store business was just small change," continued Tom slowly, "but you've got something on now that Walter's afraid to tell me about."

I glanced at Daisy, who was staring terrified between Gatsby and her husband, and at Jordan, who had begun to balance an invisible but absorbing object on the tip of her chin. Then I turned back to Gatsby—and was startled at his expression. He looked—and this is said in all contempt for the babbled slander of his garden—as if he had "killed a man." For a moment the set of his face could be described in just that fantastic way.

It passed, and he began to talk excitedly to Daisy, denying everything, defending his name against accusations that had not been made. But with every word she was drawing further and further into herself, so he gave that up, and only the dead dream fought on as the afternoon slipped away, trying to touch what was no longer tangible, struggling unhappily, undespairingly, toward that lost voice across the room.

The voice begged again to go.

"*Please*, Tom! I can't stand this any more."

Her frightened eyes told that whatever intentions, whatever courage she had had, were definitely gone.

"You two start on home, Daisy," said Tom. "In Mr. Gatsby's car."

She looked at Tom, alarmed now, but he insisted with magnanimous scorn.

"Go on. He won't annoy you. I think he realizes that his presumptuous little flirtation is over."

They were gone, without a word, snapped out, made accidental, isolated, like ghosts, even from our pity.

After a moment Tom got up and began wrapping the unopened bottle of whiskey in the towel.

"Want any of this stuff? Jordan? . . . Nick?"

I didn't answer.

"Nick?" He asked again.

"What?"

"Want any?"

"No . . . I just remembered that today's my birthday."

I was thirty. Before me stretched the portentous, menacing road of a new decade.

It was seven o'clock when we got into the coupé with him and started for Long Island. Tom talked incessantly, exulting and laughing, but his voice was as remote from Jordan and me as the foreign clamor on the sidewalk or the tumult of the elevated overhead. Human sympathy has its limits, and we were content to let all their tragic arguments fade with the city lights behind. Thirty—the promise of a decade of loneliness, a thinning list of single men to know, a thinning briefcase of enthusiasm, thinning hair. But there was Jordan beside me, who, unlike Daisy, was too wise ever to carry well-forgotten dreams from age to age. As we passed over the dark bridge her wan face fell lazily against my coat's shoulder and the formidable stroke of thirty died away with the reassuring pressure of her hand.

So we drove on toward death through the cooling twilight.

The young Greek, Michaelis, who ran the coffee joint beside the ashheaps was the principal witness at the inquest. He had slept through the heat until after five, when he strolled over to the garage, and found George Wilson sick in his office—really sick, pale as his own pale hair and shaking all over. Michaelis advised him to go to bed, but Wilson refused, saying that he'd miss a lot of business if he did. While his neighbor was trying to persuade him a violent racket broke out overhead.

"I've got my wife locked in up there," explained Wilson calmly. "She's going to stay there till the day after to-morrow, and then we're going to move away."

Michaelis was astonished; they had been neighbors for four years, and Wilson had never seemed faintly capable of such a statement. Generally he was one of these worn-out men: when he wasn't working, he sat on a chair in the doorway and stared at the people and the cars that passed along the road. When any one spoke to him he invariably laughed in an agreeable, colorless way. He was his wife's man and not his own.

So naturally Michaelis tried to find out what had happened, but Wilson wouldn't say a word—instead he began to throw curious, suspicious glances at his visitor and ask him what he'd been doing at certain times on certain days. Just as the latter was getting uneasy, some workmen came past the door bound for his restaurant, and Michaelis took the opportunity to get away, intending to come back later. But he didn't. He supposed he forgot to, that's all. When he came outside again, a little after seven, he was reminded of the conversation because he heard Mrs. Wilson's voice, loud and scolding, down-stairs in the garage.

"Beat me!" he heard her cry. "Throw me down and beat me, you dirty little coward!"

A moment later she rushed out into the dusk, waving her hands and shouting—before he could move from his door the business was over.

The "death car" as the newspapers called it, didn't stop; it came out of the gathering darkness, wavered tragically for a moment, and then disappeared around the next bend. Michaelis wasn't even sure of its color—he told the first policeman that it was light green. The other car, the one going toward New York, came to rest a hundred yards beyond, and its driver hurried back to where Myrtle Wilson, her life violently extinguished, knelt in the road and mingled her thick dark blood with the dust.

Michaelis and this man reached her first, but when they had torn open her shirtwaist, still damp with perspiration, they saw that her left breast was swinging loose like a flap, and there was no need to listen for the heart beneath. The mouth was wide open and ripped at the corners, as though she had choked a little in giving up the tremendous vitality she had stored so long.

We saw the three or four automobiles and the crowd when we were still some distance away.

"Wreck!" said Tom. "That's good. Wilson'll have a little business at last."

He slowed down, but still without any intention of stopping, until, as we came nearer, the hushed, intent faces of the people at the garage door made him automatically put on the brakes.

"We'll take a look," he said doubtfully, "just a look."

I became aware now of a hollow, wailing sound which issued incessantly from the garage, a sound which as we got out of the coupé and walked toward the door resolved itself into the words "Oh, my God!" uttered over and over in a gasping moan.

"There's some bad trouble here," said Tom excitedly.

He reached up on tiptoes and peered over a circle

of heads into the garage, which was lit only by a yellow light in a swinging wire basket overhead. Then he made a harsh sound in his throat, and with a violent thrusting movement of his powerful arms pushed his way through.

The circle closed up again with a running murmur of expostulation; it was a minute before I could see anything at all. Then new arrivals deranged the line, and Jordan and I were pushed suddenly inside.

Myrtle Wilson's body, wrapped in a blanket, and then in another blanket, as though she suffered from a chill in the hot night, lay on a work-table by the wall, and Tom, with his back to us, was bending over it, motionless. Next to him stood a motorcycle policeman taking down names with much sweat and correction in a little book. At first I couldn't find the source of the high, groaning words that echoed clamorously through the bare garage—then I saw Wilson standing on the raised threshold of his office, swaying back and forth and holding to the doorposts with both hands. Some man was talking to him in a low voice and attempting, from time to time, to lay a hand on his shoulder, but Wilson neither heard nor saw. His eyes would drop slowly from the swinging light to the laden table by the wall, and then jerk back to the light again, and he gave out incessantly his high, horrible call:

"Oh, my Ga-od! Oh, my Ga-od! Oh, Ga-od! Oh, my Ga-od!"

Presently Tom lifted his head with a jerk and, after staring around the garage with glazed eyes, addressed a mumbled incoherent remark to the policeman.

"M–a–v–" the policeman was saying, "–o——"

"No, r—" corrected the man, "M–a–v–r–o——"

"Listen to me!" muttered Tom fiercely.

"r" said the policeman, "o——"

"g——"

"g—" He looked up as Tom's broad hand fell sharply on his shoulder. "What you want, fella?"

"What happened?—that's what I want to know."

"Auto hit her. Ins'antly killed."

"Instantly killed," repeated Tom, staring.

"She ran out ina road. Son-of-a-bitch didn't even stopus car."

"There was two cars," said Michaelis, "one comin', one goin', see?"

"Going where?" asked the policeman keenly.

"One goin' each way. Well, she"—his hand rose toward the blankets but stopped half way and fell to his side—"she ran out there an' the one comin' from N'York knock right into her, goin' thirty or forty miles an hour."

"What's the name of this place here?" demanded the officer.

"Hasn't got any name."

A pale well-dressed negro stepped near.

"It was a yellow car," he said, "big yellow car. New."

"See the accident?" asked the policeman.

"No, but the car passed me down the road, going faster'n forty. Going fifty, sixty."

"Come here and let's have your name. Look out now. I want to get his name."

Some words of this conversation must have reached Wilson, swaying in the office door, for suddenly a new theme found voice among his gasping cries:

"You don't have to tell me what kind of car it was! I know what kind of car it was!"

Watching Tom, I saw the wad of muscle back of his shoulder tighten under his coat. He walked quickly over to Wilson and, standing in front of him, seized him firmly by the upper arms.

"You've got to pull yourself together," he said with soothing gruffness.

Wilson's eyes fell upon Tom; he started up on his tiptoes and then would have collapsed to his knees had not Tom held him upright.

"Listen," said Tom, shaking him a little. "I just got here a minute ago, from New York. I was bringing you that coupé we've been talking about. That yellow car I was driving this afternoon wasn't mine —do you hear? I haven't seen it all afternoon."

Only the negro and I were near enough to hear what he said, but the policeman caught something in the tone and looked over with truculent eyes.

"What's all that?" he demanded.

"I'm a friend of his." Tom turned his head but kept his hands firm on Wilson's body. "He says he knows the car that did it. . . . It was a yellow car."

Some dim impulse moved the policeman to look suspiciously at Tom.

"And what color's your car?"

"It's a blue car, a coupé."

"We've come straight from New York," I said.

Someone who had been driving a little behind us confirmed this, and the policeman turned away.

"Now, if you'll let me have that name again correct——"

Picking up Wilson like a doll, Tom carried him into the office, set him down in a chair, and came back.

"If somebody'll come here and sit with him," he snapped authoritatively. He watched while the two men standing closest glanced at each other and went unwillingly into the room. Then Tom shut the door on them and came down the single step, his eyes avoiding the table. As he passed close to me he whispered: "Let's get out."

Self-consciously, with his authoritative arms breaking the way, we pushed through the still gathering crowd, passing a hurried doctor, case in hand, who had been sent for in wild hope half an hour ago.

Tom drove slowly until we were beyond the bend —then his foot came down hard, and the coupé raced along through the night. In a little while I heard a low husky sob, and saw that the tears were overflowing down his face.

"The God damned coward!" he whimpered. "He didn't even stop his car."

The Buchanans' house floated suddenly toward us through the dark rustling trees. Tom stopped beside the porch and looked up at the second floor, where two windows bloomed with light among the vines.

"Daisy's home," he said. As we got out of the car he glanced at me and frowned slightly.

"I ought to have dropped you in West Egg, Nick. There's nothing we can do to-night."

A change had come over him, and he spoke gravely, and with decision. As we walked across the moonlight gravel to the porch he disposed of the situation in a few brisk phrases.

"I'll telephone for a taxi to take you home, and while you're waiting you and Jordan better go in the kitchen and have them get you some supper—if you want any." He opened the door. "Come in."

"No, thanks. But I'd be glad if you'd order me the taxi. I'll wait outside."

Jordan put her hand on my arm.

"Won't you come in, Nick?"

"No, thanks."

I was feeling a little sick and I wanted to be alone. But Jordan lingered for a moment more.

"It's only half-past nine," she said.

I'd be damned if I'd go in; I'd had enough of all of them for one day, and suddenly that included Jordan too. She must have seen something of this in my expression, for she turned abruptly away and ran up the porch steps into the house. I sat down for a few minutes with my head in my hands, until I heard the phone taken up inside and the butler's voice calling a taxi. Then I walked slowly down the drive away from the house, intending to wait by the gate.

I hadn't gone twenty yards when I heard my name and Gatsby stepped from between two bushes into the path. I must have felt pretty weird by that time, because I could think of nothing except the luminosity of his pink suit under the moon.

"What are you doing?" I inquired.

"Just standing here, old sport."

Somehow, that seemed a despicable occupation. For all I knew he was going to rob the house in a moment; I wouldn't have been surprised to see sinister faces, the faces of "Wolfsheim's people," behind him in the dark shrubbery.

"Did you see any trouble on the road?" he asked after a minute.

"Yes."

He hesitated.

"Was she killed?"

"Yes."

"I thought so; I told Daisy I thought so. It's better that the shock should all come at once. She stood it pretty well."

He spoke as if Daisy's reaction was the only thing that mattered.

"I got to West Egg by a side road," he went on, "and left the car in my garage. I don't think anybody saw us, but of course I can't be sure."

I disliked him so much by this time that I didn't find it necessary to tell him he was wrong.

"Who was the woman?" he inquired.

"Her name was Wilson. Her husband owns the garage. How the devil did it happen?"

"Well, I tried to swing the wheel—" He broke off, and suddenly I guessed at the truth.

"Was Daisy driving?"

"Yes," he said after a moment, "but of course I'll say I was. You see, when we left New York she was very nervous and she thought it would steady her to drive—and this woman rushed out at us just as we were passing a car coming the other way. It all happened in a minute, but it seemed to me that she wanted to speak to us, thought we were somebody she knew. Well, first Daisy turned away from the woman toward the other car, and then she lost her nerve and turned back. The second my hand reached the wheel I felt the shock—it must have killed her instantly."

"It ripped her open——"

"Don't tell me, old sport." He winced. "Anyhow—Daisy stepped on it. I tried to make her stop, but she couldn't, so I pulled on the emergency brake. Then she fell over into my lap and I drove on.

"She'll be all right tomorrow," he said presently. "I'm just going to wait here and see if he tries to bother her about that unpleasantness this afternoon. She's locked herself into her room, and if he tries any brutality she's going to turn the light out and on again."

"He won't touch her," I said. "He's not thinking about her."

"I don't trust him, old sport."

"How long are you going to wait?"

"All night, if necessary. Anyhow, till they all go to bed."

A new point of view occurred to me. Suppose Tom found out that Daisy had been driving. He might think he saw a connection in it—he might think anything. I looked at the house; there were two or three bright windows downstairs and the pink glow from Daisy's room on the second floor.

"You wait here," I said. "I'll see if there's any sign of a commotion."

I walked back along the border of the lawn, traversed the gravel softly, and tiptoed up the veranda steps. The drawing-room curtains were open, and I saw that the room was empty. Crossing the porch where we had dined that June night three months before, I came to a small rectangle of light which I guessed was the pantry window. The blind was drawn, but I found a rift at the sill.

Daisy and Tom were sitting opposite each other at the kitchen table, with a plate of cold fried chicken between them, and two bottles of ale. He was talking intently across the table at her, and in his earnestness his hand had fallen upon and covered her own. Once in a while she looked up at him and nodded in agreement.

They weren't happy, and neither of them had touched the chicken or the ale—and yet they weren't unhappy either. There was an unmistakable air of natural intimacy about the picture, and anybody would have said that they were conspiring together.

As I tiptoed from the porch I heard my taxi feeling its way along the dark road toward the house. Gatsby was waiting where I had left him in the drive.

"It is all quiet up there?" he asked anxiously.

"Yes, it's all quiet." I hesitated. "You'd better come home and get some sleep."

He shook his head.

"I want to wait here till Daisy goes to bed. Good night, old sport."

He put his hands in his coat pockets and turned back eagerly to his scrutiny of the house, as though my presence marred the sacredness of the vigil. So I walked away and left him standing there in the moonlight—watching over nothing.

VIII

I couldn't sleep all night; a fog-horn was groaning incessantly on the Sound, and I tossed half-sick between grotesque reality and savage, frightening dreams. Toward dawn I heard a taxi go up Gatsby's drive, and immediately I jumped out of bed and began to dress—I felt that I had something to tell him, something to warn him about, and morning would be too late.

Crossing his lawn, I saw that his front door was still open and he was leaning against a table in the hall, heavy with dejection or sleep.

"Nothing happened," he said wanly. "I waited,

and about four o'clock she came to the window and stood there for a minute and then turned out the light."

His house had never seemed so enormous to me as it did that night when we hunted through the great rooms for cigarettes. We pushed aside curtains that were like pavilions, and felt over innumerable feet of dark wall for electric light switches—once I tumbled with a sort of splash upon the keys of a ghostly piano. There was an inexplicable amount of dust everywhere, and the rooms were musty, as though they hadn't been aired for many days. I found the humidor on an unfamiliar table, with two stale, dry cigarettes inside. Throwing open the French windows of the drawing-room, we sat smoking out into the darkness.

"You ought to go away," I said. "It's pretty certain they'll trace your car."

"Go away *now*, old sport?"

"Go to Atlantic City for a week, or up to Montreal."

He wouldn't consider it. He couldn't possibly leave Daisy until he knew what she was going to do. He was clutching at some last hope and I couldn't bear to shake him free.

It was this night that he told me the strange story of his youth with Dan Cody—told it to me because "Jay Gatsby" had broken up like glass against Tom's hard malice, and the long secret extravaganza was played out. I think that he would have acknowledged anything now, without reserve, but he wanted to talk about Daisy.

She was the first "nice" girl he had ever known. In various unrevealed capacities he had come in contact with such people, but always with indiscernible barbed wire between. He found her excitingly desirable. He went to her house, at first with other officers from Camp Taylor, then alone. It amazed him—he had never been in such a beautiful house before. But what gave it an air of breathless intensity was that Daisy lived there—it was as casual a thing to her as his tent out at camp was to him. There was a ripe mystery about it, a hint of bedrooms upstairs more beautiful and cool than other bedrooms, of gay and radiant activities taking place through its corridors, and of romances that were not musty and laid away already in lavender, but fresh and breathing and redolent of this year's shining motor-cars and of dances whose flowers were scarcely withered. It excited him, too, that many men had already loved Daisy—it increased her value in his eyes. He felt their presence all about the house, pervading the air with the shades and echoes of still vibrant emotions.

But he knew that he was in Daisy's house by a colossal accident. However glorious might be his future as Jay Gatsby, he was at present a penniless young man without a past, and at any moment the invisible cloak of his uniform might slip from his shoulders. So he made the most of his time. He took what he could get, ravenously and unscrupulously—eventually he took Daisy one still October night, took her because he had no real right to touch her hand.

He might have despised himself, for he had certainly taken her under false pretenses. I don't mean that he had traded on his phantom millions, but he had deliberately given Daisy a sense of security; he let her believe that he was a person from much the same stratum as herself—that he was fully able to take care of her. As a matter of fact, he had no such facilities—he had no comfortable family standing behind him, and he was liable at the whim of an impersonal government to be blown anywhere about the world.

But he didn't despise himself and it didn't turn out as he had imagined. He had intended, probably, to take what he could and go—but now he found that he had committed himself to the following of a grail. He knew that Daisy was extraordinary, but he didn't realize just how extraordinary a "nice" girl could be. She vanished into her rich house, into her rich, full life, leaving Gatsby—nothing. He felt married to her, that was all.

When they met again, two days later, it was Gatsby who was breathless, who was, somehow, betrayed. Her porch was bright with the bought luxury of star-shine; the wicker of the settee squeaked fashionably as she turned toward him and he kissed her curious and lovely mouth. She had caught a cold, and it made her voice huskier and more charming than ever, and Gatsby was overwhelmingly aware of the youth and mystery that wealth imprisons and preserves, of the freshness of many clothes, and of Daisy, gleaming like silver, safe and proud above the hot struggles of the poor.

"I can't describe to you how surprised I was to find out I loved her, old sport. I even hoped for a while that she'd throw me over, but she didn't, because she was in love with me too. She thought I knew a lot because I knew different things from her . . . Well, there I was, 'way off my ambitions, getting deeper in love every minute, and all of a sudden I didn't care. What was the use of doing great things if I could have a better time telling her what I was going to do?"

On the last afternoon before he went abroad, he sat with Daisy in his arms for a long, silent time. It was a cold fall day, with fire in the room and her cheeks flushed. Now and then she moved and he changed his arm a little, and once he kissed her dark shining hair. The afternoon had made them tranquil for a while, as if to give them a deep memory for the long parting the next day promised. They had never been closer in their month of love, nor communicated more profoundly one with another, than when she brushed silent lips against his coat's shoulder or when he touched the end of her fingers, gently, as though she were asleep.

He did extraordinarily well in the war. He was a captain before he went to the front, and following the Argonne battles he got his majority and the command of the divisional machine-guns. After the Armistice he tried frantically to get home, but some complication or misunderstanding sent him to Oxford instead. He was worried now—there was a quality of nervous despair in Daisy's letters. She didn't see why he couldn't come. She was feeling the pressure of the world outside, and she wanted to see him and feel his presence beside her and be reassured that she was doing the right thing after all.

For Daisy was young and her artificial world was redolent of orchids and pleasant, cheerful snobbery and orchestras which set the rhythm of the year, summing up the sadness and suggestiveness of life in new tunes. All night the saxophones wailed the hopeless comment of the *Beale Street Blues* while a hundred pairs of golden and silver slippers shuffled the shining dust. At the gray tea hour there were always rooms that throbbed incessantly with this low, sweet fever, while fresh faces drifted here and there like rose petals blown by the sad horns around the floor.

Through this twilight universe Daisy began to move again with the season; suddenly she was again keeping half a dozen dates a day with half a dozen men, and drowsing asleep at dawn with the beads and chiffon of an evening dress tangled among dying orchids on the floor beside her bed. And all the time something within her was crying for a decision. She wanted her life shaped now, immediately—and the decision must be made by some force—of love, of money, of unquestionable practicality—that was close at hand.

That force took shape in the middle of spring with the arrival of Tom Buchanan. There was a wholesome bulkiness about his person and his position, and Daisy was flattered. Doubtless there was a certain struggle and a certain relief. The letter reached Gatsby while he was still at Oxford.

It was dawn now on Long Island and we went about opening the rest of the windows downstairs, filling the house with gray-turning, gold-turning light. The shadow of a tree fell abruptly across the

dew and ghostly birds began to sing among the blue leaves. There was a slow, pleasant movement in the air, scarcely a wind, promising a cool, lovely day.

"I don't think she ever loved him," Gatsby turned around from a window and looked at me challengingly. "You must remember, old sport, she was very excited this afternoon. He told her those things in a way that frightened her—that made it look as if I was some kind of cheap sharper. And the result was she hardly knew what she was saying."

He sat down gloomily.

"Of course she might have loved him just for a minute, when they were first married—and loved me more even then, do you see?"

Suddenly he came out with a curious remark.

"In any case," he said, "it was just personal."

What could you make of that, except to suspect some intensity in his conception of the affair that couldn't be measured?

He came back from France when Tom and Daisy were still on their wedding trip, and made a miserable but irresistible journey to Louisville on the last of his army pay. He stayed there a week, walking the streets where their footsteps had clicked together through the November night and revisiting the out-of-the-way places to which they had driven in her white car. Just as Daisy's house had always seemed to him more mysterious and gay than other houses, so his idea of the city itself, even though she was gone from it, was pervaded with a melancholy beauty.

He left feeling that if he had searched harder, he might have found her—that he was leaving her behind. The day-coach—he was penniless now—was hot. He went out to the open vestibule and sat down on a folding-chair, and the station slid away and the backs of unfamiliar buildings moved by. Then out into the spring fields, where a yellow trolley raced them for a minute with the people in it who might once have seen the pale magic of her face along the casual street.

The track curved and now it was going away from the sun, which, as it sank lower, seemed to spread itself in benediction over the vanishing city where she had drawn her breath. He stretched out his hand desperately as if to snatch only a wisp of air, to save a fragment of the spot that she had made lovely for him. But it was all going by too fast now for his blurred eyes and he knew that he had lost that part of it, the freshest and the best, forever.

It was nine o'clock when we finished breakfast and went out on the porch. The night had made a sharp difference in the weather and there was an autumn flavor in the air. The gardener, the last one of

Gatsby's former servants, came to the foot of the steps.

"I'm going to drain the pool today, Mr. Gatsby. Leaves'll start falling pretty soon, and then there's always trouble with the pipes."

"Don't do it today," Gatsby answered. He turned to me apologetically. "You know, old sport, I've never used that pool all summer?"

I looked at my watch and stood up.

"Twelve minutes to my train."

I didn't want to go to the city. I wasn't worth a decent stroke of work, but it was more than that—I didn't want to leave Gatsby. I missed that train, and then another, before I could get myself away.

"I'll call you up," I said finally.

"Do, old sport."

"I'll call you about noon."

We walked slowly down the steps.

"I suppose Daisy'll call too." He looked at me anxiously, as if he hoped I'd corroborate this.

"I suppose so."

"Well, good-by."

We shook hands and I started away. Just before I reached the hedge I remembered something and turned around.

"They're a rotten crowd," I shouted across the lawn. "You're worth the whole damn bunch put together."

I've always been glad I said that. It was the only compliment I ever gave him, because I disapproved of him from beginning to end. First he nodded politely, and then his face broke into that radiant and understanding smile, as if we'd been in ecstatic cahoots on that fact all the time. His gorgeous pink rag of a suit made a bright spot of color against the white steps, and I thought of the night when I first came to his ancestral home, three months before. The lawn and drive had been crowded with the faces of those who guessed at his corruption—and he had stood on those steps, concealing his incorruptible dream, as he waved them good-by.

I thanked him for his hospitality. We were always thanking him for that—I and the others.

"Good-by," I called. "I enjoyed breakfast, Gatsby."

Up in the city, I tried for a while to list the quotations on an interminable amount of stock, then I fell asleep in my swivel-chair. Just before noon the phone woke me, and I started up with sweat breaking out on my forehead. It was Jordan Baker; she often called me up at this hour because the uncertainty of her own movements between hotels and clubs and private houses made her hard to find in any other way. Usually her voice came over the wire as something fresh and cool, as if a divot from a green golf-links had come sailing in at the office window, but this morning it seemed harsh and dry.

"I've left Daisy's house," she said. "I'm at Hempstead, and I'm going down to Southampton this afternoon."

Probably it had been tactful to leave Daisy's house, but the act annoyed me, and her next remark made me rigid.

"You weren't so nice to me last night."

"How could it have mattered then?"

Silence for a moment. Then:

"However—I want to see you."

"I want to see you, too."

"Suppose I don't go to Southampton, and come into town this afternoon?"

"No—I don't think this afternoon."

"Very well."

"It's impossible this afternoon. Various——"

We talked like that for a while, and then abruptly we weren't talking any longer. I don't know which of us hung up with a sharp click, but I know I didn't care. I couldn't have talked to her across a tea-table that day if I never talked to her again in this world.

I called Gatsby's house a few minutes later, but the line was busy. I tried four times; finally an exasperated central told me the wire was being kept open for long distance from Detroit. Taking out my time-table, I drew a small circle around the three-fifty train. Then I leaned back in my chair and tried to think. It was just noon.

When I passed the ashheaps on the train that morning I had crossed deliberately to the other side of the car. I supposed there'd be a curious crowd around there all day with little boys searching for dark spots in the dust, and some garrulous man telling over and over what had happened, until it became less and less real even to him and he could tell it no longer, and Myrtle Wilson's tragic achievement was forgotten. Now I want to go back a little and tell what happened at the garage after we left there the night before.

They had difficulty in locating the sister, Catherine. She must have broken her rule against drinking that night, for when she arrived she was stupid with liquor and unable to understand that the ambulance had already gone to Flushing. When they convinced her of this, she immediately fainted, as if that was the intolerable part of the affair. Someone, kind or curious, took her in his car and drove her in the wake of her sister's body.

Until long after midnight a changing crowd lapped up against the front of the garage, while George Wilson rocked himself back and forth on the couch inside. For a while the door of the office was open, and every one who came into the garage glanced irresistibly through it. Finally some one said it was a shame, and closed the door. Michaelis and several other men were with him; first, four or five men, later two or three men. Still later Michaelis had to ask the last stranger to wait there fifteen minutes longer, while he went back to his own place and made a pot of coffee. After that, he stayed there alone with Wilson until dawn.

About three o'clock the quality of Wilson's incoherent muttering changed—he grew quieter and began to talk about the yellow car. He announced that he had a way of finding out whom the yellow car belonged to, and then he blurted out that a couple of months ago his wife had come from the city with her face bruised and her nose swollen.

But when he heard himself say this, he flinched and began to cry "Oh, my God!" again in his groaning voice. Michaelis made a clumsy attempt to distract him.

"How long have you been married, George? Come on there, try and sit still a minute and answer my question. How long have you been married?"

"Twelve years."

"Ever had any children? Come on, George, sit still —I asked you a question. Did you ever have any children?"

The hard brown beetles kept thudding against the dull light, and whenever Michaelis heard a car go tearing along the road outside it sounded to him like the car that hadn't stopped a few hours before. He didn't like to go into the garage, because the work bench was stained where the body had been lying, so he moved uncomfortably around the office—he knew every object in it before morning—and from time to time sat down beside Wilson trying to keep him more quiet.

"Have you got a church you go to sometimes, George? Maybe even if you haven't been there for a long time? Maybe I could call up the church and get a priest to come over and he could talk to you, see?"

"Don't belong to any."

"You ought to have a church, George, for times like this. You must have gone to church once. Didn't you get married in a church? Listen, George, listen to me. Didn't you get married in a church?"

"That was a long time ago."

The effort of answering broke the rhythm of his rocking—for a moment he was silent. Then the same half-knowing, half-bewildered look came back into his faded eyes.

"Look in the drawer there," he said, pointing at the desk.

"Which drawer?"

"That drawer—that one."

Michaelis opened the drawer nearest his hand. There was nothing in it but a small, expensive dog-leash, made of leather and braided silver. It was apparently new.

"This?" he inquired, holding it up.

Wilson stared and nodded.

"I found it yesterday afternoon. She tried to tell me about it, but I knew it was something funny."

"You mean your wife bought it?"

"She had it wrapped in tissue paper on her bureau."

Michaelis didn't see anything odd in that, and he gave Wilson a dozen reasons why his wife might have bought the dog-leash. But conceivably Wilson had heard some of these same explanations before, from Myrtle, because he began saying "Oh, my God!" again in a whisper—his comforter left several explanations in the air.

"Then he killed her," said Wilson. His mouth dropped open suddenly.

"Who did?"

"I have a way of finding out."

"You're morbid, George," said his friend. "This has been a strain to you and you don't know what you're saying. You'd better try and sit quiet till morning."

"He murdered her."

"It was an accident, George."

Wilson shook his head. His eyes narrowed and his mouth widened slightly with the ghost of a superior "Hm!"

"I know," he said definitely, "I'm one of these trusting fellas and I don't think any harm to nobody, but when I get to know a thing I know it. It was the man in that car. She ran out to speak to him and he wouldn't stop."

Michaelis had seen this too, but it hadn't occurred to him that there was any special significance in it. He believed that Mrs. Wilson had been running away from her husband, rather than trying to stop any particular car.

"How could she of been like that?"

"She's a deep one," said Wilson, as if that answered the question. "Ah-h-h——"

He began to rock again, and Michaelis stood twisting the leash in his hand.

"Maybe you got some friend that I could telephone for, George?"

This was a forlorn hope—he was almost sure that Wilson had no friend: there was not enough of him for his wife. He was glad a little later when he noticed a change in the room, a blue quickening by the window, and realized that dawn wasn't far off. About five o'clock it was blue enough outside to snap off the light.

Wilson's glazed eyes turned out to the ashheaps, where small gray clouds took on fantastic shapes and scurried here and there in the faint dawn wind.

"I spoke to her," he muttered, after a long silence. "I told her she might fool me but she couldn't fool God. I took her to the window"—with an effort he got up and walked to the rear window and leaned with his face pressed against it—"and I said 'God knows what you've been doing, everything you've been doing. You may fool me, but you can't fool God!'"

Standing behind him, Michaelis saw with a shock that he was looking at the eyes of Doctor T. J. Eckleburg, which had just emerged, pale and enormous, from the dissolving night.

"God sees everything," repeated Wilson.

"That's an advertisement," Michaelis assured him. Something made him turn away from the window and look back into the room. But Wilson stood there a long time, his face close to the window pane, nodding into the twilight.

By six o'clock Michaelis was worn out, and grateful for the sound of a car stopping outside. It was one of the watchers of the night before who had promised to come back, so he cooked breakfast for three, which he and the other man ate together. Wilson was quieter now, and Michaelis went home to sleep; when he awoke four hours later and hurried back to the garage, Wilson was gone.

His movements—he was on foot all the time—were afterward traced to Port Roosevelt and then to Gad's Hill, where he bought a sandwich that he didn't eat, and a cup of coffee. He must have been tired and walking slowly, for he didn't reach Gad's Hill until noon. Thus far there was no difficulty in accounting for his time—there were boys who had seen a man "acting sort of crazy," and motorists at whom he stared oddly from the side of the road. Then for three hours he disappeared from view. The police, on the strength of what he said to Michaelis, that he "had a way of finding out," supposed that he spent that time going from garage to garage thereabout, inquiring for a yellow car. On the other hand, no garage man who had seen him ever came forward, and perhaps he had an easier, surer way of finding out what he wanted to know. By half-past two he was in West Egg, where he asked some one the way to Gatsby's house. So by that time he knew Gatsby's name.

At two o'clock Gatsby put on his bathing-suit and left word with the butler that if any one phoned word was to be brought to him at the pool. He stopped at the garage for a pneumatic mattress that had amused his guests during the summer, and the chauffeur helped him pump it up. Then he gave instructions that the open car wasn't to be taken out under any circumstances—and this was strange, because the front right fender needed repair.

Gatsby shouldered the mattress and started for the pool. Once he stopped and shifted it a little, and the chauffeur asked him if he needed help, but he shook his head and in a moment disappeared among the yellowing trees.

No telephone message arrived, but the butler went without his sleep and waited for it until four o'clock—until long after there was any one to give it to if it came. I have an idea that Gatsby himself didn't believe it would come, and perhaps he no longer cared. If that was true he must have felt that he had lost the old warm world, paid a high price for living too long with a single dream. He must have looked up at an unfamiliar sky through frightening leaves and shivered as he found what a grotesque thing a rose is and how raw the sunlight was upon the scarcely created grass. A new world, material without being real, where poor ghosts, breathing dreams like air, drifted fortuitously about . . . like that ashen, fantastic figure gliding toward him through the amorphous trees.

The chauffeur—he was one of Wolfsheim's protégés—heard the shots—afterward he could only say that he hadn't thought anything much about them. I drove from the station directly to Gatsby's house and my rushing anxiously up the front steps was the first thing that alarmed any one. But they knew then, I firmly believe. With scarcely a word said, four of us, the chauffeur, butler, gardener, and I, hurried down to the pool.

There was a faint, barely perceptible movement of the water as the fresh flow from one end urged its way toward the drain at the other. With little ripples that were hardly the shadows of waves, the laden mattress moved irregularly down the pool. A small gust of wind that scarcely corrugated the surface was enough to disturb its accidental course with its accidental burden. The touch of a cluster of leaves revolved it slowly, tracing, like the leg of transit, a thin red circle in the water.

It was after we started with Gatsby toward the house that the gardener saw Wilson's body a little way off in the grass, and the holocaust was complete.

IX

After two years I remember the rest of that day, and that night and the next day, only as an endless drill of police and photographers and newspaper men in and out of Gatsby's front door. A rope stretched across the main gate and a policeman by it kept out the curious, but little boys soon discovered that they could enter through my yard, and there were always a few of them clustered open-mouthed about the pool. Some one with a positive manner, perhaps a detective, used the expression "madman" as he bent over Wilson's body that afternoon, and the adventitious authority of his voice set the key for the newspaper reports next morning.

Most of those reports were a nightmare—grotesque, circumstantial, eager, and untrue. When Michaelis's testimony at the inquest brought to light Wilson's suspicions of his wife I thought the whole tale would shortly be served up in racy pasquinade—but Catherine, who might have said anything, didn't say a word. She showed a surprising amount of character about it too—looked at the coroner with determined eyes under that corrected brow of hers, and swore that her sister had never seen Gatsby, that her sister was completely happy with her husband, that her sister had been into no mischief whatever. She convinced herself of it, and cried into her handkerchief, as if the very suggestion was more than she could endure. So Wilson was reduced to a man "deranged by grief" in order that the case might remain in its simplest form. And it rested there.

But all this part of it seemed remote and unessential. I found myself on Gatsby's side, and alone. From the moment I telephoned news of the catastrophe to West Egg Village, every surmise about him, and every practical question, was referred to me. At first I was surprised and confused; then, as he lay in his house and didn't move or breathe or speak, hour upon hour, it grew upon me that I was responsible, because no one else was interested—interested, I mean, with that intense personal interest to which every one has some vague right at the end.

I called up Daisy half an hour after we found him, called her instinctively and without hesitation. But she and Tom had gone away early that afternoon, and taken baggage with them.

"Left no address?"

"No."

"Say when they'd be back?"

"No."

"Any idea where they are? How I could reach them?"

"I don't know. Can't say."

I wanted to get somebody for him. I wanted to go into the room where he lay and reassure him: "I'll get somebody for you, Gatsby. Don't worry. Just trust me and I'll get somebody for you——"

Meyer Wolfsheim's name wasn't in the phone book. The butler gave me his office address on Broad-way, and I called Information, but by the time I had the number it was long after five, and no one answered the phone.

"Will you ring again?"

"I've rung them three times."

"It's very important."

"Sorry. I'm afraid no one's there."

I went back to the drawing-room and thought for an instant that they were chance visitors, all these official people who suddenly filled it. But, as they drew back the sheet and looked at Gatsby with unmoved eyes, his protest continued in my brain:

"Look here, old sport, you've got to get somebody for me. You've got to try hard. I can't go through this alone."

Some one started to ask me questions, but I broke away and going upstairs looked hastily through the unlocked parts of his desk—he'd never told me definitely that his parents were dead. But there was nothing—only the picture of Dan Cody, a token of forgotten violence, staring down from the wall.

Next morning I sent the butler to New York with a letter to Wolfsheim, which asked for information and urged him to come out on the next train. That request seemed superfluous when I wrote it. I was sure he'd start when he saw the newspapers, just as I was sure there'd be a wire from Daisy before noon—but neither a wire nor Mr. Wolfsheim arrived; no one arrived except more police and photographers and newspaper men. When the butler brought back Wolfsheim's answer I began to have a feeling of defiance, of scornful solidarity between Gatsby and me against them all.

Dear Mr. Carraway. This has been one of the most terrible shocks of my life to me I hardly can believe it that it is true at all. Such a mad act as that man did should make us all think. I cannot come down now as I am tied up in some very important business and cannot get mixed up in this thing now. If there is anything I can do a little later let me know in a letter by Edgar. I hardly know where I am when I hear about a thing like this and am completely knocked down and out.

  Yours truly

  MEYER WOLFSHEIM

and then hasty addenda beneath:

Let me know about the funeral etc do not know his family at all.

When the phone rang that afternoon and Long Distance said Chicago was calling I thought this would be Daisy at last. But the connection came through as a man's voice, very thin and far away.

"This is Slagle speaking . . ."

"Yes?" The name was unfamiliar.

"Hell of a note, isn't it? Get my wire?"

"There haven't been any wires."

"Young Parke's in trouble," he said rapidly. "They picked him up when he handed the bonds over the counter. They got a circular from New York giving 'em the numbers just five minutes before. What d'you know about that, hey? You never can tell in these hick towns——"

"Hello!" I interrupted breathlessly. "Look here—this isn't Mr. Gatsby. Mr. Gatsby's dead."

There was a long silence on the other end of the wire, followed by an exclamation . . . then a quick squawk as the connection was broken.

I think it was on the third day that a telegram signed Henry C. Gatz arrived from a town in Minnesota. It said only that the sender was leaving immediately and to postpone the funeral until he came.

It was Gatsby's father, a solemn old man, very helpless and dismayed, bundled up in a long cheap ulster against the warm September day. His eyes leaked continuously with excitement, and when I took the bag and umbrella from his hands he began to pull so incessantly at his sparse gray beard that I had difficulty in getting off his coat. He was on the point of collapse, so I took him into the music room and made him sit down while I sent for something to eat. But he wouldn't eat, and the glass of milk spilled from his trembling hand.

"I saw it in the Chicago newspaper," he said. "It was all in the Chicago newspaper. I started right away."

"I didn't know how to reach you."

His eyes, seeing nothing, moved ceaselessly about the room.

"It was a madman," he said. "He must have been mad."

"Wouldn't you like some coffee?" I urged him.

"I don't want anything. I'm all right now, Mr. ——"

"Carraway."

"Well, I'm all right now. Where have they got Jimmy?"

I took him into the drawing-room, where his son lay, and left him there. Some little boys had come up on the steps and were looking into the hall; when I told them who had arrived, they went reluctantly away.

After a little while Mr. Gatz opened the door and came out, his mouth ajar, his face flushed slightly, his eyes leaking isolated and unpunctual tears. He had reached an age where death no longer has the quality of ghastly surprise, and when he looked around him now for the first time and saw the height and splendor of the hall and the great rooms opening out from

it into other rooms, his grief began to be mixed with an awed pride. I helped him to a bedroom upstairs; while he took off his coat and vest I told him that all arrangements had been deferred until he came.

"I didn't know what you'd want, Mr. Gatsby——"

"Gatz is my name."

"—Mr. Gatz. I thought you might want to take the body West."

He shook his head.

"Jimmy always liked it better down East. He rose up to his position in the East. Were you a friend of my boy's, Mr. ——?"

"We were close friends."

"He had a big future before him, you know. He was only a young man, but he had a lot of brain power here."

He touched his head impressively, and I nodded.

"If he'd of lived, he'd of been a great man. A man like James J. Hill. He'd of helped build up the country."

"That's true," I said, uncomfortably.

He fumbled at the embroidered coverlet, trying to take it from the bed, and lay down stiffly—was instantly asleep.

That night an obviously frightened person called up, and demanded to know who I was before he would give his name.

"This is Mr. Carraway," I said.

"Oh!" He sounded relieved. "This is Klipspringer."

I was relieved too, for that seemed to promise another friend at Gatsby's grave. I didn't want it to be in the papers and draw a sight-seeing crowd, so I'd been calling up a few people myself. They were hard to find.

"The funeral's tomorrow," I said. "Three o'clock, here at the house. I wish you'd tell anybody who'd be interested."

"Oh, I will," he broke out hastily. "Of course I'm not likely to see anybody, but if I do."

His tone made me suspicious.

"Of course you'll be there yourself."

"Well, I'll certainly try. What I called up about is——"

"Wait a minute," I interrupted. "How about saying you'll come?"

"Well, the fact is—the truth of the matter is that I'm staying with some people up here in Greenwich, and they rather expect me to be with them tomorrow. In fact, there's a sort of picnic or something. Of course I'll do my very best to get away."

I ejaculated an unrestrained "Huh!" and he must have heard me, for he went on nervously:

"What I called up about was a pair of shoes I left there. I wonder if it'd be too much trouble to have the butler send them on. You see, they're tennis shoes, and I'm sort of helpless without them. My address is care of B. F.——"

I didn't hear the rest of the name, because I hung up the receiver.

After that I felt a certain shame for Gatsby—one gentleman to whom I telephoned implied that he had got what he deserved. However, that was my fault, for he was one of those who used to sneer most bitterly at Gatsby on the courage of Gatsby's liquor, and I should have known better than to call him.

The morning of the funeral I went up to New York to see Meyer Wolfsheim; I couldn't seem to reach him any other way. The door that I pushed open, on the advice of an elevator boy, was marked "The Swastika Holding Company," and at first there didn't seem to be any one inside. But when I'd shouted "hello" several times in vain, an argument broke out behind a partition, and presently a lovely Jewess appeared at an interior door and scrutinized me with black hostile eyes.

"Nobody's in," she said. "Mr. Wolfsheim's gone to Chicago."

The first part of this was obviously untrue, for some one had begun to whistle "The Rosary," tunelessly, inside.

"Please say that Mr. Carraway wants to see him."

"I can't get him back from Chicago, can I?"

At this moment a voice, unmistakably Wolfsheim's, called "Stella!" from the other side of the door.

"Leave your name on the desk," she said quickly. "I'll give it to him when he gets back."

"But I know he's there."

She took a step toward me and began to slide her hands indignantly up and down her hips.

"You young men think you can force your way in here any time," she scolded. "We're getting sickantired of it. When I say he's in Chicago, he's in Chicago."

I mentioned Gatsby.

"Oh-h!" She looked at me over again. "Will you just— What was your name?"

She vanished. In a moment Meyer Wolfsheim stood solemnly in the doorway, holding out both hands. He drew me into his office, remarking in a reverent voice that it was a sad time for all of us, and offered me a cigar.

"My memory goes back to when first I met him," he said. "A young major just out of the army and covered over with medals he got in the war. He was so hard up he had to keep on wearing his uniform because he couldn't buy some regular clothes. First time I saw him was when he come into Winebrenner's poolroom at Forty-third Street and asked for a

job. He hadn't eat anything for a couple of days. 'Come on have some lunch with me,' I sid. He ate more than four dollars' worth of food in half an hour."

"Did you start him in business?" I inquired.

"Start him! I made him."

"Oh."

"I raised him up out of nothing, right out of the gutter. I saw right away he was a fine-appearing, gentlemanly young man, and when he told me he was an Oggsford I knew I could use him good. I got him to join up in the American Legion and he used to stand high there. Right off he did some work for a client of mine up to Albany. We were so thick like that in everything"—he held up two bulbous fingers—"always together."

I wondered if this partnership had included the World's Series transaction in 1919.

"Now he's dead," I said after a moment. "You were his closest friend, so I know you'll want to come to his funeral this afternoon."

"I'd like to come."

"Well, come then."

The hair in his nostrils quivered slightly, and as he shook his head his eyes filled with tears.

"I can't do it—I can't get mixed up in it," he said.

"There's nothing to get mixed up in. It's all over now."

"When a man gets killed I never like to get mixed up in it in any way. I keep out. When I was a young man it was different—if a friend of mine died, no matter how, I stuck with them to the end. You may think that's sentimental, but I mean it—to the bitter end."

I saw that for some reason of his own he was determined not to come, so I stood up.

"Are you a college man?" he inquired suddenly.

For a moment I thought he was going to suggest a "gonnegtion," but he only nodded and shook my hand.

"Let us learn to show our friendship for a man when he is alive and not after he is dead," he suggested. "After that my own rule is to let everything alone."

When I left his office the sky had turned dark and I got back to West Egg in a drizzle. After changing my clothes I went next door and found Mr. Gatz walking up and down excitedly in the hall. His pride in his son and in his son's possessions was continually increasing and now he had something to show me.

"Jimmy sent me this picture." He took out his wallet with trembling fingers. "Look there."

It was a photograph of the house, cracked in the corners and dirty with many hands. He pointed out every detail to me eagerly. "Look there!" and then sought admiration from my eyes. He had shown it so often that I think it was more real to him now than the house itself.

"Jimmy sent it to me. I think it's a very pretty picture. It shows up well."

"Very well. Had you seen him lately?"

"He come out to see me two years ago and bought me the house I live in now. Of course we was broke up when he run off from home, but I see now there was a reason for it. He knew he had a big future in front of him. And ever since he made a success he was very generous with me."

He seemed reluctant to put away the picture, held it for another minute, lingeringly, before my eyes. Then he returned the wallet and pulled from his pocket a ragged old copy of a book called *Hopalong Cassidy*.

"Look here, this is a book he had when he was a boy. It just shows you."

He opened it at the back cover and turned it around for me to see. On the last fly-leaf was printed the word SCHEDULE, and the date September 12, 1906. And underneath:

Rise from bed	6.00	A.M.
Dumbbell exercise and wall-scaling	6.15–6.30	"
Study electricity, etc.	7.15–8.15	"
Work	8.30–4.30	P.M.
Baseball and sports	4.30–5.00	"
Practice elocution, poise and how		
to attain it	5.00–6.00	"
Study needed inventions	7.00–9.00	"

GENERAL RESOLVES

No wasting time at Shafters or [a name, indecipherable]
No more smoking or chewing.
Bath every other day
Read one improving book or magazine per week
Save $5.00 [crossed out] $3.00 per week
Be better to parents

"I come across this book by accident," said the old man. "It just shows you, don't it?"

"It just shows you."

"Jimmy was bound to get ahead. He always had some resolves like this or something. Do you notice what he's got about improving his mind? He was always great for that. He told me I et like a hog once, and I beat him for it."

He was reluctant to close the book, reading each item aloud and then looking eagerly at me. I think he rather expected me to copy down the list for my own use.

A little before three the Lutheran minister arrived from Flushing, and I began to look involuntarily out the windows for other cars. So did Gatsby's father. And as the time passed and the servants came in and stood waiting in the hall, his eyes began to blink anxiously, and he spoke of the rain in a worried, uncertain way. The minister glanced several times at his watch, so I took him aside and asked him to wait for half an hour. But it wasn't any use. Nobody came.

About five o'clock our procession of three cars reached the cemetery and stopped in a thick drizzle beside the gate—first a motor hearse, horribly black and wet, then Mr. Gatz and the minister and I in the limousine, and a little later four or five servants and the postman from West Egg, in Gatsby's station wagon, all wet to the skin. As we started through the gate into the cemetery I heard a car stop and then the sound of some one splashing after us over the soggy ground. I looked around. It was the man with owl-eyed glasses whom I had found marvelling over Gatsby's books in the library one night three months before.

I'd never seen him since then. I don't know how he knew about the funeral, or even his name. The rain poured down his thick glasses, and he took them off and wiped them to see the protecting canvas unrolled from Gatsby's grave.

I tried to think about Gatsby then for a moment, but he was already too far away, and I could only remember, without resentment, that Daisy hadn't sent a message or a flower. Dimly I heard some one murmur "Blessed are the dead that the rain falls on," and then the owl-eyed man said "Amen to that," in a brave voice.

We straggled down quickly through the rain to the cars. Owl-eyes spoke to me by the gate.

"I couldn't get to the house," he remarked.

"Neither could anybody else."

"Go on!" He started. "Why, my God! they used to go there by the hundreds."

He took off his glasses and wiped them again, outside and in.

"The poor son-of-a-bitch," he said.

One of my most vivid memories is of coming back West from prep school and later from college at Christmas time. Those who went farther than Chicago would gather in the old dim Union Station at six o'clock of a December evening, with a few Chicago friends, already caught up into their own holiday gayeties, to bid them a hasty good-by. I remember the fur coats of the girls returning from Miss This-or-That's and the chatter of frozen breath and the hands waving overhead as we caught sight of old acquaintances, and the matchings of invitations:

"Are you going to the Ordways'? the Herseys'? the Schultzes'?" and the long green tickets clasped tight in our gloved hands. And last the murky yellow cars of the Chicago, Milwaukee & St. Paul railroad looking cheerful as Christmas itself on the tracks beside the gate.

When we pulled out into the winter night and the real snow, our snow, began to stretch out beside us and twinkle against the windows, and the dim lights of small Wisconsin stations moved by, a sharp wild brace came suddenly into the air. We drew in deep breaths of it as we walked back from dinner through the cold vestibules, unutterably aware of our identity with this country for one strange hour, before we melted indistinguishably into it again.

That's my Middle West—not the wheat or the prairies or the lost Swede towns, but the thrilling returning trains of my youth, and the street lamps and sleigh bells in the frosty dark and the shadows of holly wreaths thrown by lighted windows on the snow. I am part of that, a little solemn with the feel of those long winters, a little complacent from growing up in the Carraway house in a city where dwellings are still called through decades by a family's name. I see now that this has been a story of the West, after all—Tom and Gatsby, Daisy and Jordan and I, were all Westerners, and perhaps we possessed some deficiency in common which made us subtly unadaptable to Eastern life.

Even when the East excited me most, even when I was most keenly aware of its superiority to the bored, sprawling, swollen towns beyond the Ohio, with their interminable inquisitions which spared only the children and the very old—even then it had always for me a quality of distortion. West Egg, especially, still figures in my more fantastic dreams. I see it as a night scene by El Greco: a hundred houses, at once conventional and grotesque, crouching under a sullen, overhanging sky and a lustreless moon. In the foreground four solemn men in dress suits are walking along the sidewalk with a stretcher on which lies a drunken woman in a white evening dress. Her hand, which dangles over the side, sparkles cold with jewels. Gravely the men turn in at a house—the wrong house. But no one knows the woman's name, and no one cares.

After Gatsby's death the East was haunted for me like that, distorted beyond my eyes' power of correction. So when the blue smoke of brittle leaves was in the air and the wind blew the wet laundry stiff on the line I decided to come back home.

There was one thing to be done before I left, an awkward, unpleasant thing that perhaps had better have been let alone. But I wanted to leave things in order and not just trust that obliging and indifferent sea to sweep my refuse away. I saw Jordan Baker and talked over and around what had happened to us together, and what had happened afterward to me, and she lay perfectly still, listening, in a big chair.

She was dressed to play golf, and I remember thinking she looked like a good illustration, her chin raised a little jauntily, her hair the color of an autumn leaf, her face the same brown tint as the fingerless glove on her knee. When I had finished she told me without comment that she was engaged to another man. I doubted that, though there were several she could have married at a nod of her head, but I pretended to be surprised. For just a minute I wondered if I wasn't making a mistake, then I thought it all over again quickly and got up to say good-by.

"Nevertheless you did throw me over," said Jordan suddenly. "You threw me over on the telephone. I don't give a damn about you now, but it was a new experience for me, and I felt a little dizzy for a while."

We shook hands.

"Oh, and do you remember"—she added—"a conversation we had once about driving a car?"

"Why—not exactly."

"You said a bad driver was only safe until she met another bad driver? Well, I met another bad driver, didn't I? I mean it was careless of me to make such a wrong guess. I thought you were rather an honest, straightforward person. I thought it was your secret pride."

"I'm thirty," I said. "I'm five years too old to lie to myself and call it honor."

She didn't answer. Angry, and half in love with her, and tremendously sorry, I turned away.

One afternoon late in October I saw Tom Buchanan. He was walking ahead of me along Fifth Avenue in his alert, aggressive way, his hands out a little from his body as if to fight off interference, his head moving sharply here and there, adapting itself to his restless eyes. Just as I slowed up to avoid overtaking him he stopped and began frowning into the windows of a jewelry store. Suddenly he saw me and walked back, holding out his hand.

"What's the matter, Nick? Do you object to shaking hands with me?"

"Yes. You know what I think of you."

"You're crazy, Nick," he said quickly. "Crazy as hell. I don't know what's the matter with you."

"Tom," I inquired, "what did you say to Wilson that afternoon?"

He stared at me without a word, and I knew I

had guessed right about those missing hours. I started to turn away, but he took a step after me and grabbed my arm.

"I told him the truth," he said. "He came to the door while we were getting ready to leave, and when I sent down word that we weren't in he tried to force his way upstairs. He was crazy enough to kill me if I hadn't told him who owned the car. His hand was on a revolver in his pocket every minute he was in the house—" He broke off defiantly. "What if I did tell him? That fellow had it coming to him. He threw dust into your eyes just like he did in Daisy's, but he was a tough one. He ran over Myrtle like you'd run over a dog and never even stopped his car."

There was nothing I could say, except the one unutterable fact that it wasn't true.

"And if you think I didn't have my share of suffering—look here, when I went to give up that flat and saw that damn box of dog biscuits sitting there on the side-board, I sat down and cried like a baby. By God it was awful——"

I couldn't forgive him or like him, but I saw that what he had done was, to him, entirely justified. It was all very careless and confused. They were careless people, Tom and Daisy—they smashed up things and creatures and then retreated back into their money or their vast carelessness, or whatever it was that kept them together, and let other people clean up the mess they had made. . . .

I shook hands with him; it seemed silly not to, for I felt suddenly as though I were talking to a child. Then he went into the jewelry store to buy a pearl necklace—or perhaps only a pair of cuff buttons—rid of my provincial squeamishness forever.

Gatsby's house was still empty when I left—the grass on his lawn had grown as long as mine. One of the taxi drivers in the village never took a fare past the entrance gate without stopping for a minute and pointing inside; perhaps it was he who drove Daisy and Gatsby over to East Egg the night of the accident, and perhaps he had made a story about it all his own. I didn't want to hear it and I avoided him when I got off the train.

I spent my Saturday nights in New York because those gleaming, dazzling parties of his were with me so vividly that I could still hear the music and the laughter, faint and incessant, from his garden, and the cars going up and down his drive. One night I did hear a material car there, and saw its lights stop at his front steps. But I didn't investigate. Probably it was some final guest who had been away at the ends of the earth and didn't know that the party was over.

On the last night, with my trunk packed and my car sold to the grocer, I went over and looked at that huge incoherent failure of a house once more. On the white steps an obscene word, scrawled by some boy with a piece of brick, stood out clearly in the moonlight, and I erased it, drawing my shoe raspingly along the stone. Then I wandered down to the beach and sprawled out on the sand.

Most of the big shore places were closed now and there were hardly any lights except the shadowy, moving glow of a ferryboat across the Sound. And as the moon rose higher the inessential houses began to melt away until gradually I became aware of the old island here that flowered once for Dutch sailors' eyes —a fresh, green breast of the new world. Its vanished trees, the trees that had made way for Gatsby's house, had once pandered in whispers to the last and greatest of all human dreams; for a transitory enchanted moment man must have held his breath in the presence of this continent, compelled into an æsthetic contemplation he neither understood nor desired, face to face for the last time in history with something commensurate to his capacity for wonder.

And as I sat there brooding on the old, unknown world, I thought of Gatsby's wonder when he first picked out the green light at the end of Daisy's dock. He had come a long way to this blue lawn, and his dream must have seemed so close that he could hardly fail to grasp it. He did not know that it was already behind him, somewhere back in that vast obscurity beyond the city, where the dark fields of the republic rolled on under the night.

Gatsby believed in the green light, the orgiastic future that year by year recedes before us. It eluded us then, but that's no matter—tomorrow we will run faster, stretch out our arms farther. . . . And one fine morning——

So we beat on, boats against the current, borne back ceaselessly into the past.

DRAMA

PYGMALION

GEORGE BERNARD SHAW

GEORGE BERNARD SHAW (1856–1950) was born in Dublin of Protestant stock. In 1876 after an irregular education he moved to London where he read incessantly and continued his study of music. Converted to Socialism in 1882, his early works were propaganda novels, none of them successful. At the same time, he was writing book reviews and music criticism for a living and pouring forth pamphlets and the spoken word in the interest of the Fabian Society. Inspired by the work of Ibsen, Shaw began his career as a dramatist with *Widowers' Houses* (1892). In 1897 *The Devil's Disciple,* a brilliant success, encouraged him to give up journalism and devote all his time to writing for the theater. Shaw's work and personality cannot be summed up in a few words. His dramas were designed as vehicles for his ideas which he was careful also to expound in long and sharply written "Prefaces" to the published plays. On most occasions he seemed deliberately to take the unpopular side of public questions and for more than sixty years outraged his conventional contemporaries. A witty English critic once described him as "Shelley in a beard" which may not have been too far from the truth. Among his principal dramas are *Candida* (first produced 1895), *Man and Superman* (produced 1903), *Pygmalion* (produced 1913), *Back to Methuselah* (produced 1922), *Saint Joan* (produced 1923), *The Apple Cart* (1929), *On the Rocks* (1933), and *Geneva* (1938).

PREFACE TO PYGMALION

A PROFESSOR OF PHONETICS

As WILL be seen later on, Pygmalion needs, not a preface, but a sequel, which I have supplied in its due place.

The English have no respect for their language, and will not teach their children to speak it. They cannot spell it because they have nothing to spell it with but an old foreign alphabet of which only the consonants—and not all of them—have any agreed speech value. Consequently no man can teach himself what it should sound like from reading it; and it is impossible for an Englishman to open his mouth without making some other Englishman despise him. Most European languages are now accessible in black and white to foreigners: English and French are not thus accessible even to Englishmen and Frenchmen. The reformer we need most today is an energetic enthusiast: that is why I have made such a one the hero of a popular play.

There have been heroes of that kind crying in the wilderness for many years past. When I became interested in the subject towards the end of the eighteen-seventies, the illustrious Alexander Melville Bell, the

Copyright © 1916, 1930, 1942, by George Bernard Shaw. Copyright renewed 1944 by George Bernard Shaw. Reprinted by permission of Dodd, Mead and Company, Inc., The Public Trustee and The Society of Authors.

inventor of Visible Speech, had emigrated to Canada, where his son invented the telephone; but Alexander J. Ellis was still a London Patriarch, with an impressive head always covered by a velvet skull cap, for which he would apologize to public meetings in a very courtly manner. He and Tito Pagliardini, another phonetic veteran, were men whom it was impossible to dislike. Henry Sweet, then a young man, lacked their sweetness of character: he was about as conciliatory to conventional mortals as Ibsen or Samuel Butler. His great ability as a phonetician (he was, I think, the best of them all at his job) would have entitled him to high official recognition, and perhaps enabled him to popularize his subject, but for his Satanic contempt for all academic dignitaries and persons in general who thought more of Greek than of phonetics. Once, in the days when the Imperial Institute rose in South Kensington, and Joseph Chamberlain was booming the Empire, I induced the editor of a leading monthly review to commission an article from Sweet on the imperial importance of his subject. When it arrived, it contained nothing but a savagely derisive attack on a professor of language and literature whose chair Sweet regarded as proper to a phonetic expert only. The article, being libellous, had to be returned as impossible; and I had to renounce my dream of dragging its author into the limelight. When I met him afterwards, for the first time for many years, I found to my astonishment that he, who had been a quite tolerably presentable young man, had actually managed by sheer scorn to alter his personal appearance until he had become a sort of walking repudiation of Oxford and all its traditions. It must have been largely in his own despite that he was squeezed into something called a Readership of phonetics there. The future of phonetics rests probably with his pupils, who all swore by him; but nothing could bring the man himself into any sort of compliance with the university to which he nevertheless clung by divine right in an intensely Oxonian way. I daresay his papers, if he has left any, include some satires that may be published without too destructive results fifty years hence. He was, I believe, not in the least an ill-natured man: very much the opposite, I should say; but he would not suffer fools gladly; and to him all scholars who were not rabid phoneticians were fools.

Those who knew him will recognize in my third act the allusion to the Current Shorthand in which he used to write postcards. It may be acquired from a four and sixpenny manual published by the Clarendon Press. The postcards which Mrs. Higgins describes are such as I have received from Sweet. I would decipher a sound which a cockney would represent by *zerr*, and a Frenchman by *seu*, and then write demanding with some heat what on earth it meant. Sweet, with boundless contempt for my stupidity, would reply that it not only meant but obviously was the word Result, as no other word containing that sound, and capable of making sense with the context, existed in any language spoken on earth. That less expert mortals should require fuller indications was beyond Sweet's patience. Therefore, though the whole point of his Current Shorthand is that it can express every sound in the language perfectly, vowels as well as consonants, and that your hand has to make no stroke except the easy and current ones with which you write m, n, and u, l, p, and q, scribbling them at whatever angle comes easiest to you, his unfortunate determination to make this remarkable and quite legible script serve also as a shorthand reduced it in his own practice to the most inscrutable of cryptograms. His true objective was the provision of a full, accurate, legible script for our language; but he was led past that by his contempt for the popular Pitman system of shorthand, which he called the Pitfall system. The triumph of Pitman was a triumph of business organization: there was a weekly paper to persuade you to learn Pitman: there were cheap textbooks and exercise books and transcripts of speeches for you to copy, and schools where experienced teachers coached you up to the necessary proficiency.

Sweet could not organize his market in that fashion. He might as well have been the Sybil who tore up the leaves of prophecy that nobody would attend to. The four and sixpenny manual, mostly in his lithographed handwriting, that was never vulgarly advertized, may perhaps some day be taken up by a syndicate and pushed upon the public as The Times pushed the Encyclopædia Britannica; but until then it will certainly not prevail against Pitman. I have bought three copies of it during my lifetime; and I am informed by the publishers that its cloistered existence is still a steady and healthy one. I actually learned the system two several times; and yet the shorthand in which I am writing these lines is Pitman's. And the reason is, that my secretary cannot transcribe Sweet, having been perforce taught in the schools of Pitman. In America I could use the commercially organized Gregg shorthand, which has taken a hint from Sweet by making its letters writable (current, Sweet would have called them) instead of having to be geometrically drawn like Pitman's; but all these systems, including Sweet's, are spoilt by making them available for verbatim reporting, in which complete and exact spelling and word division are impossible. A complete and exact phonetic script is neither practicable nor necessary for ordinary use; but if we enlarge our alphabet to the Russian size, and make our spelling as phonetic as Spanish, the advance will be prodigious.

Pygmalion Higgins is not a portrait of Sweet, to whom the adventure of Eliza Doolittle would have been impossible; still, as will be seen, there are touches of Sweet in the play. With Higgins's physique and temperament Sweet might have set the Thames on fire. As it was, he impressed himself professionally on Europe to an extent that made his comparative personal obscurity, and the failure of Oxford to do justice to his eminence, a puzzle to foreign specialists in his subject. I do not blame Oxford, because I think Oxford is quite right in demanding a certain social amenity from its nurslings (heaven knows it is not exorbitant in its requirement!); for although I well know how hard it is for a man of genius with a seriously underrated subject to maintain serene and kindly relations with the men who underrate it, and who keep all the best places for less important subjects which they profess without originality and sometimes without much capacity for them, still, if he overwhelms them with wrath and disdain, he cannot expect them to heap honors on him.

Of the later generations of phoneticians I know little. Among them towered Robert Bridges, to whom perhaps Higgins may owe his Miltonic sympathies, though here again I must disclaim all portraiture. But if the play makes the public aware that there are such people as phoneticians, and that they are among the most important people in England at present, it will serve its turn.

I wish to boast that Pygmalion has been an extremely successful play, both on stage and screen, all over Europe and North America as well as at home. It is so intensely and deliberately didactic, and its subject is esteemed so dry, that I delight in throwing it at the heads of the wiseacres who repeat the parrot cry that art should never be didactic. It goes to prove my contention that great art can never be anything else.

Finally, and for the encouragement of people troubled with accents that cut them off from all high employment, I may add that the change wrought by Professor Higgins in the flower-girl is neither impossible nor uncommon. The modern concierge's daughter who fulfills her ambition by playing the Queen of Spain in Ruy Blas at the Théâtre Français is only one of many thousands of men and women who have sloughed off their native dialects and acquired a new tongue. Our West End shop assistants and domestic servants are bilingual. But the thing has to be done scientifically, or the last state of the aspirant may be worse than the first. An honest slum dialect is more tolerable than the attempts of phonetically untaught persons to imitate the plutocracy. Ambitious flower-girls who read this play must not imagine that they can pass themselves off as fine ladies by untutored imitation. They must learn their alphabet over again, and differently, from a phonetic expert. Imitation will only make them ridiculous.

NOTE FOR TECHNICIANS. A complete representation of the play as printed in this edition is technically possible only on the cinema screen or on stages furnished with exceptionally elaborate machinery. For ordinary theatrical use the scenes separated by rows of asterisks are to be omitted. In the dialogue an e upside down indicates the indefinite vowel, sometimes called obscure or neutral, for which, though it is one of the commonest sounds in English speech, our wretched alphabet has no letter.

ACT I

London at 11.15 p.m. Torrents of heavy summer rain. Cab whistles blowing frantically in all directions. Pedestrians running for shelter into the portico of St. Paul's church (not Wren's cathedral but Inigo Jones's church in Covent Garden vegetable market), among them a lady and her daughter in evening dress. All are peering out gloomily at the rain, except one man with his back turned to the rest, wholly preoccupied with a notebook in which he is writing.
The church clock strikes the first quarter.

THE DAUGHTER [*in the space between the central pillars, close to the one on her left*] I'm getting chilled to the bone. What can Freddy be doing all this time? He's been gone twenty minutes.

THE MOTHER [*on her daughter's right*] Not so long. But he ought to have got us a cab by this.

A BYSTANDER [*on the lady's right*] He wont get no cab not until half-past eleven, missus, when they come back after dropping their theatre fares.

THE MOTHER. But we must have a cab. We cant stand here until half-past eleven. It's too bad.

THE BYSTANDER. Well, it ain't my fault, missus.

THE DAUGHTER. If Freddy had a bit of gumption, he would have got one at the theatre door.

THE MOTHER. What could he have done, poor boy?

THE DAUGHTER. Other people got cabs. Why couldnt he?

[FREDDY *rushes in out of the rain from the Southampton Street side, and comes between them closing a dripping umbrella. He is a young man of twenty, in evening dress, very wet round the ankles.*]

THE DAUGHTER. Well, havnt you got a cab?

FREDDY. Theres not one to be had for love or money.

THE MOTHER. Oh, Freddy, there must be one. You cant have tried.

THE DAUGHTER. It's too tiresome. Do you expect us to go and get one ourselves?

FREDDY. I tell you theyre all engaged. The rain was so sudden: nobody was prepared; and everybody had to take a cab. Ive been to Charing Cross one way and nearly to Ludgate Circus the other; and they were all engaged.

THE MOTHER. Did you try Trafalgar Square?

FREDDY. There wasn't one at Trafalgar Square.

THE DAUGHTER. Did you try?

FREDDY. I tried as far as Charing Cross Station. Did you expect me to walk to Hammersmith?

THE MOTHER. You really are very helpless, Freddy. Go again; and dont come back until you have found a cab.

FREDDY. I shall simply get soaked for nothing.

THE DAUGHTER. And what about us? Are we to stay

here all night in this draught, with next to nothing on? You selfish pig—

FREDDY. Oh, very well: I'll go, I'll go. [*He opens his umbrella and dashes off Strandwards, but comes into collision with a flower girl who is hurrying in for shelter, knocking her basket out of her hands. A blinding flash of lightning, followed instantly by a rattling peal of thunder, orchestrates the incident*].

THE FLOWER GIRL. Nah then, Freddy: look wh' y' gowin, deah.

FREDDY. Sorry [*he rushes off*].

THE FLOWER GIRL [*picking up her scattered flowers and replacing them in the basket*] Theres menners f' yer! Tɔ-oo banches o voylets trod into the mad. [*She sits down on the plinth of the column, sorting her flowers, on the lady's right. She is not at all a romantic figure. She is perhaps eighteen, perhaps twenty, hardly older. She wears a little sailor hat of black straw that has long been exposed to the dust and soot of London and has seldom if ever been brushed. Her hair needs washing rather badly: its mousy color can hardly be natural. She wears a shoddy black coat that reaches nearly to her knees and is shaped to her waist. She has a brown skirt with a coarse apron. Her boots are much the worse for wear. She is no doubt as clean as she can afford to be; but compared to the ladies she is very dirty. Her features are no worse than theirs; but their condition leaves something to be desired; and she needs the services of a dentist*].

THE MOTHER. How do you know that my son's name is Freddy, pray?

THE FLOWER GIRL. Ow, eez yɔ-ooa san, is e? Wal, fewd dan y' dɔ-ooty bawmz a mather should, eed now bettern to spawl a pore gel's flahrzn than ran awy athaht pyin. Will ye-oo py me f'them? [*Here, with apologies, this desperate attempt to represent her dialect without a phonetic alphabet must be abandoned as unintelligible outside London*].

THE DAUGHTER. Do nothing of the sort, mother. The idea!

THE MOTHER. Please allow me, Clara. Have you any pennies?

THE DAUGHTER. No. Ive nothing smaller than sixpence.

THE FLOWER GIRL [*hopefully*] I can give you change for a tanner, kind lady.

THE MOTHER [*to* CLARA] Give it to me. [CLARA *parts reluctantly.*] Now [*to the girl*] This is for your flowers.

THE FLOWER GIRL. Thank you kindly, lady.

THE DAUGHTER. Make her give you the change. These things are only a penny a bunch.

THE MOTHER. Do hold your tongue, Clara. [*To the girl*] You can keep the change.

THE FLOWER GIRL. Oh, thank you, lady.

THE MOTHER. Now tell me how you know that young gentleman's name.

THE FLOWER GIRL. I didnt.

THE MOTHER. I heard you call him by it. Dont try to deceive me.

THE FLOWER GIRL [*protesting*] Who's trying to deceive you? I called him Freddy or Charlie same as you might yourself if you was talking to a stranger and wished to be pleasant.

THE DAUGHTER. Sixpence thrown away! Really, mamma, you might have spared Freddy that. [*She retreats in disgust behind the pillar*].

[*An elderly gentleman of the amiable military type rushes into the shelter, and closes a dripping umbrella. He is in the same plight as* FREDDY, *very wet about the ankles. He is in evening dress, with a light overcoat. He takes the place left vacant by the daughter.*]

THE GENTLEMAN. Phew!

THE MOTHER [*to the gentleman*] Oh, sir, is there any sign of its stopping?

THE GENTLEMAN. I'm afraid not. It started worse than ever about two minutes ago [*he goes to the plinth beside the flower girl; puts up his foot on it; and stoops to turn down his trouser ends*].

THE MOTHER. Oh dear! [*She retires sadly and joins her daughter*].

THE FLOWER GIRL [*taking advantage of the military gentleman's proximity to establish friendly relations with him*] If it's worse, it's a sign it's nearly over. So cheer up, Captain; and buy a flower off a poor girl.

THE GENTLEMAN. I'm sorry. I havnt any change.

THE FLOWER GIRL. I can give you change, Captain.

THE GENTLEMAN. For a sovereign? Ive nothing less.

THE FLOWER GIRL. Garn! Oh do buy a flower off me, Captain. I can change half-a-crown. Take this for tuppence.

THE GENTLEMAN. Now dont be troublesome: theres a good girl. [*Trying his pockets*] I really havnt any change—Stop: heres three hapence, if thats any use to you [*he retreats to the other pillar*].

THE FLOWER GIRL [*disappointed, but thinking three half-pence better than nothing*] Thank you, sir.

THE BYSTANDER [*to the girl*] You be careful: give him a flower for it. Theres a bloke here behind taking down every blessed word youre saying. [*All turn to the man who is taking notes*].

THE FLOWER GIRL [*springing up terrified*] I aint done nothing wrong by speaking to the gentleman. Ive a right to sell flowers if I keep off the kerb. [*Hysterically*] I'm a respectable girl: so help me, I never spoke to him except to ask him to buy a flower off me.

General hubbub, mostly sympathetic to the flower girl, but deprecating her excessive sensibility. Cries of Dont start hollerin. Who's hurting you? Nobody's going to touch you. Whats the good of fussing? Steady on. Easy easy, etc., *come from the elderly staid spectators, who pat her comfortingly. Less patient ones bid her shut her head, or ask her roughly what is wrong with her. A remoter group, not knowing what the matter is, crowd in and increase the noise with question and answer:* Whats the row? What-she do? Where is he? A tec taking her down. What! him? Yes: him over there: Took money off the gentleman, etc.

THE FLOWER GIRL [*breaking through them to the gentleman, crying wildly*] Oh, sir, dont let him charge me. You dunno what it means to me. Theyll take away my character and drive me on the streets for speaking to gentlemen. They—

THE NOTE TAKER [*coming forward on her right, the rest crowding after him*] There! there! there! there! who's hurting you, you silly girl? What do you take me for?

THE BYSTANDER. It's aw rawt: e's a genleman: look at his bɔ-oots. [*Explaining to the note taker*] She thought you was a copper's nark, sir.

THE NOTE TAKER [*with quick interest*] Whats a copper's nark?

THE BYSTANDER [*inapt at definition*] It's a—well, it's a copper's nark, as you might say. What else would you call it? A sort of informer.

THE FLOWER GIRL [*still hysterical*] I take my Bible oath I never said a word—

THE NOTE TAKER [*overbearing but good-humored*] Oh, shut up, shut up. Do I look like a policeman?

THE FLOWER GIRL [*far from reassured*] Then what did you take down my words for? How do I know whether you took me down right? You just shew me what youve wrote about me. [*The note taker opens his book and holds it steadily under her nose, though the pressure of the mob trying to read it over his shoulders would upset a weaker man*]. Whats that? That aint proper writing. I cant read that.

THE NOTE TAKER. I can. [*Reads, reproducing her pronunciation exactly*] "Cheer ap, Keptin; n' baw ya flahr orf a pore gel."

THE FLOWER GIRL [*much distressed*] It's because I called him Captain. I meant no harm. [*To the gentleman*] Oh, sir, dont let him lay a charge agen me for a word like that. You—

THE GENTLEMAN. Charge! I make no charge. [*To the note taker*] Really, sir, if you are a detective, you need not begin protecting me against molestation by young women until I ask you. Anybody could see that the girl meant no harm.

THE BYSTANDERS GENERALLY [*demonstrating against police espionage*] Course they could. What business is it of yours? You mind your own affairs. He wants promotion, he does. Taking down people's words! Girl never said a word to him. What harm if she did? Nice thing a girl cant shelter from the rain without being insulted, etc., etc., etc. [*She is conducted by the more sympathetic demonstrators back to her plinth, where she resumes her seat and struggles with her emotion*].

THE BYSTANDER. He aint a tec. He's a bloming busybody: thats what he is. I tell you, look at his bɔ-oots.

THE NOTE TAKER [*turning on him genially*] And how are all your people down at Selsey?

THE BYSTANDER [*suspiciously*] Who told you my people come from Selsey?

THE NOTE TAKER. Never you mind. They did. [*To the girl*] How do you come to be up so far east? You were born in Lisson Grove.

THE FLOWER GIRL [*appalled*] Oh, what harm is there in my leaving Lisson Grove? It wasnt fit for a pig to live in; and I had to pay four-and-six a week. [*In tears*] Oh, boo—hoo—oo—

THE NOTE TAKER. Live where you like; but stop that noise.

THE GENTLEMAN [*to the girl*] Come, come! he cant touch you: you have a right to live where you please.

A SARCASTIC BYSTANDER [*thrusting himself between the note taker and the gentleman*] Park Lane, for instance. I'd like to go into the Housing Question with you, I would.

THE FLOWER GIRL [*subsiding into a brooding melancholy over her basket, and talking very low-spiritedly to herself*] I'm a good girl, I am.

THE SARCASTIC BYSTANDER [*not attending to her*] Do you know where I come from?

THE NOTE TAKER [*promptly*] Hoxton.

[*Titterings. Popular interest in the note taker's performance increases*].

THE SARCASTIC ONE [*amazed*] Well, who said I didnt? Bly me! you know everything, you do.

THE FLOWER GIRL [*still nursing her sense of injury*] Aint no call to meddle with me, he aint.

THE BYSTANDER [*to her*] Of course he aint. Dont you stand it from him. [*To the note taker*] See here: what call have you to know about people what never offered to meddle with you?

THE FLOWER GIRL. Let him say what he likes. I dont want to have no truck with him.

THE BYSTANDER. You take us for dirt under your feet, dont you? Catch you taking liberties with a gentleman!

THE SARCASTIC BYSTANDER. Yes: tell him where he come from if you want to go fortune-telling.

THE NOTE TAKER. Cheltenham, Harrow, Cambridge, and India.

THE GENTLEMAN. Quite right.

[*Great laughter. Reaction in the note taker's favor. Exclamations of* He knows all about it. Told him proper. Hear him tell the toff where he come from? *etc.*].

THE GENTLEMAN. May I ask, sir, do you do this for your living at a music hall?

THE NOTE TAKER. I've thought of that. Perhaps I shall some day.

[*The rain has stopped; and the persons on the outside of the crowd begin to drop off*].

THE FLOWER GIRL [*resenting the reaction*] He's no gentleman, he aint, to interfere with a poor girl.

THE DAUGHTER [*out of patience, pushing her way rudely to the front and displacing the gentleman, who politely retires to the other side of the pillar*] What on earth is Freddy doing? I shall get pneumownia if I stay in this draught any longer.

THE NOTE TAKER [*to himself, hastily making a note of her pronunciation of "monia"*] Earlscourt.

THE DAUGHTER [*violently*] Will you please keep your impertinent remarks to yourself.

THE NOTE TAKER. Did I say that out loud? I didnt mean to. I beg your pardon. Your mother's Epsom, unmistakeably.

THE MOTHER [*advancing between the daughter and the note taker*] How very curious! I was brought up in Largelady Park, near Epsom.

THE NOTE TAKER [*uproariously amused*] Ha! ha! What a devil of a name! Excuse me. [*To the daughter*] You want a cab, do you?

THE DAUGHTER. Dont dare speak to me.

THE MOTHER. Oh please, please, Clara. [*Her daughter repudiates her with an angry shrug and retires haughtily*] We should be so grateful to you, sir, if you found us a cab. [*The note taker produces a whistle*] Oh, thank you. [*She joins her daughter*].

[*The note taker blows a piercing blast*].

THE SARCASTIC BYSTANDER. There! I knowed he was a plainclothes copper.

THE BYSTANDER. That aint a police whistle: thats a sporting whistle.

THE FLOWER GIRL [*still preoccupied with her wounded feelings*] He's no right to take away my character. My character is the same to me as any lady's.

THE NOTE TAKER. I dont know whether youve noticed it; but the rain stopped about two minutes ago.

THE BYSTANDER. So it has. Why didn't you say so before? and us losing our time listening to your silliness! [*He walks off towards the Strand*].

THE SARCASTIC BYSTANDER. I can tell where you come from. You come from Anwell. Go back there.

THE NOTE TAKER [*helpfully*] Hanwell.

THE SARCASTIC BYSTANDER [*affecting great distinction of speech*] Thenk you, teacher. Haw haw! So long [*he touches his hat with mock respect and strolls off*].

THE FLOWER GIRL. Frightening people like that! How would he like it himself?

THE MOTHER. It's quite fine now, Clara. We can walk to a motor bus. Come. [*She gathers her skirts above her ankles and hurries off towards the Strand*].

THE DAUGHTER. But the cab—[*her mother is out of hearing*]. Oh, how tiresome! [*She follows angrily*].

[*All the rest have gone except the note taker, the gentleman, and the flower girl, who sits arranging her basket, and still pitying herself in murmurs*].

THE FLOWER GIRL. Poor girl! Hard enough for her to live without being worrited and chivied.

THE GENTLEMAN [*returning to his former place on the note taker's left*] How do you do it, if I may ask?

THE NOTE TAKER. Simply phonetics. The science of speech. Thats my profession: also my hobby. Happy is the man who can make a living by his hobby! You can spot an Irishman or a Yorkshireman by his brogue. *I* can place any man within six miles. I can place him within two miles in London. Sometimes within two streets.

THE FLOWER GIRL. Ought to be ashamed of himself, unmanly coward!

THE GENTLEMAN. But is there a living in that?

THE NOTE TAKER. Oh yes. Quite a fat one. This is an age of upstarts. Men begin in Kentish Town with £80 a year, and end in Park Lane with a hundred thousand. They want to drop Kentish Town; but they give themselves away every time they open their mouths. Now I can teach them—

THE FLOWER GIRL. Let him mind his own business and leave a poor girl—

THE NOTE TAKER [*explosively*] Woman: cease this detestable boohooing instantly; or else seek the shelter of some other place of worship.

THE FLOWER GIRL [*with feeble defiance*] Ive a right to be here if I like, same as you.

THE NOTE TAKER. A woman who utters such depressing and disgusting sounds has no right to be anywhere—no right to live. Remember that you are a human being with a soul and the divine gift of articulate speech: that your native language is the language of Shakespear and Milton and The Bible; and dont sit there crooning like a bilious pigeon.

THE FLOWER GIRL [*quite overwhelmed, looking up*

at him in mingled wonder and deprecation without daring to raise her head] Ah-ah-ah-ow-ow-ow-oo!

THE NOTE TAKER [*whipping out his book*] Heavens! what a sound! [*He writes; then holds out the book and reads, reproducing her vowels exactly*] Ah-ah-ah-ow-ow-ow-oo!

THE FLOWER GIRL [*tickled by the performance, and laughing in spite of herself*] Garn!

THE NOTE TAKER. You see this creature with her kerbstone English: the English that will keep her in the gutter to the end of her days. Well, sir, in three months I could pass that girl off as a duchess at an ambassador's garden party. I could even get her a place as lady's maid or shop assistant, which requires better English.

THE FLOWER GIRL. What's that you say?

THE NOTE TAKER. Yes, you squashed cabbage leaf, you disgrace to the noble architecture of these columns, you incarnate insult to the English language: I could pass you off as the Queen of Sheba. [*To the Gentleman*] Can you believe that?

THE GENTLEMAN. Of course I can. I am myself a student of Indian dialects; and—

THE NOTE TAKER [*eagerly*] Are you? Do you know Colonel Pickering, the author of Spoken Sanscrit?

THE GENTLEMAN. I am Colonel Pickering. Who are you?

THE NOTE TAKER. Henry Higgins, author of Higgins's Universal Alphabet.

PICKERING [*with enthusiasm*] I came from India to meet you.

HIGGINS. I was going to India to meet you.

PICKERING. Where do you live?

HIGGINS. 27A Wimpole Street. Come and see me tomorrow.

PICKERING. I'm at the Carlton. Come with me now and lets have a jaw over some supper.

HIGGINS. Right you are.

THE FLOWER GIRL [*to* PICKERING, *as he passes her*] Buy a flower, kind gentleman. I'm short for my lodging.

PICKERING. I really havnt any change. I'm sorry [*he goes away*].

HIGGINS [*shocked at the girl's mendacity*] Liar. You said you could change half-a-crown.

THE FLOWER GIRL [*rising in desperation*] You ought to be stuffed with nails, you ought. [*Flinging the basket at his feet*] Take the whole blooming basket for sixpence.

[*The church clock strikes the second quarter*].

HIGGINS [*hearing in it the voice of God, rebuking him for his Pharisaic want of charity to the poor girl*] A reminder. [*He raises his hat solemnly; then throws a handful of money into the basket and follows* PICKERING].

THE FLOWER GIRL [*picking up a half-crown*] Ah-ow-ooh! [*Picking up a couple of florins*] Aaah-ow-ooh! [*Picking up several coins*] Aaaaah-ow-ooh! [*Picking up a half-sovereign*] Aaaaaaaaaaaah-ow-ooh!!!

FREDDY [*springing out of a taxicab*] Got one at last. Hallo! [*To the girl*] Where are the two ladies that were here?

THE FLOWER GIRL. They walked to the bus when the rain stopped.

FREDDY. And left me with a cab on my hands! Damnation!

THE FLOWER GIRL [*with grandeur*] Never mind, young man. I'm going home in a taxi. [*She sails off to the cab. The driver puts his hand behind him and holds the door firmly shut against her. Quite understanding his mistrust, she shews him her handful of money.*] A taxi fare aint no object to me, Charlie. [*He grins and opens the door*]. Here. What about the basket?

THE TAXIMAN. Give it here. Tuppence extra.

LIZA. No: I dont want nobody to see it. [*She crushes it into the cab and gets in, continuing the conversation through the window*] Goodbye, Freddy.

FREDDY [*dazedly raising his hat*] Goodbye.

TAXIMAN. Where to?

LIZA. Bucknam Pellis [Buckingham Palace].

TAXIMAN. What d'ye mean—Bucknam Pellis?

LIZA. Dont you know where it is? In the Green Park, where the King lives. Goodbye, Freddy. Dont let me keep you standing there. Goodbye.

FREDDY. Goodbye. [*He goes*].

TAXIMAN. Here? Whats this about Bucknam Pellis? What business have you at Bucknam Pellis?

LIZA. Of course I havnt none. But I wasn't going to let him know that. You drive me home.

TAXIMAN. And wheres home?

LIZA. Angel Court, Drury Lane, next Meiklejohn's oil shop.

TAXIMAN. That sounds more like it, Judy. [*He drives off*].

* * * * *

Let us follow the taxi to the entrance to Angel Court, a narrow little archway between two shops, one of them Meiklejohn's oil shop. When it stops there, Eliza gets out, dragging her basket with her.

LIZA. How much?

TAXIMAN [*indicating the taximeter*] Cant you read? A shilling.

LIZA. A shilling for two minutes!!

TAXIMAN. Two minutes or ten: it's all the same.

LIZA. Well, I dont call it right.

TAXIMAN. Ever been in a taxi before?

LIZA [*with dignity*] Hundreds and thousands of times, young man.

TAXIMAN [*laughing at her*] Good for you, Judy. Keep the shilling, darling, with best love from all at home. Good luck! [*He drives off*].

LIZA [*humiliated*] Impidence!

[*She picks up the basket and trudges up the alley with it to her lodging: a small room with very old wall paper hanging loose in the damp places. A broken pane in the window is mended with paper. A portrait of a popular actor and a fashion plate of ladies' dresses, all wildly beyond poor* ELIZA*'s means, both torn from newspapers, are pinned up on the wall. A birdcage hangs in the window; but its tenant died long ago: it remains as a memorial only*].

[*These are the only visible luxuries: the rest is the irreducible minimum of poverty's needs: a wretched bed heaped with all sorts of coverings that have any warmth in them, a draped packing case with a basin and jug on it and a little looking glass over it, a chair and table, the refuse of some suburban kitchen, and an American alarum clock on the shelf above the unused fireplace: the whole lighted with a gas lamp with a penny in the slot meter. Rent: four shillings a week*].

Here Eliza, chronically weary, but too excited to go to bed, sits, counting her new riches and dreaming and planning what to do with them, until the gas goes out, when she enjoys for the first time the sensation of being able to put in another penny without grudging it. This prodigal mood does not extinguish her gnawing sense of the need for economy sufficiently to prevent her from calculating that she can dream and plan in bed more cheaply and warmly than sitting up without a fire. So she takes off her shawl and skirt and adds them to the miscellaneous bedclothes. Then she kicks off her shoes and gets into bed without any further change.

ACT II

Next day at 11 a.m. HIGGINS*'s laboratory in Wimpole Street. It is a room on the first floor, looking on the street, and was meant for the drawing room. The double doors are in the middle of the back wall; and persons entering find in the corner to their right two tall file cabinets at right angles to one another against the walls. In this corner stands a flat writing-table, on which are a phonograph, a laryngoscope, a row of tiny organ pipes with a bellows, a set of lamp chimneys for singing flames with burners attached to a gas plug in the wall by an indiarubber tube, several tuning-forks of different sizes, a life-size image of half a human head, shewing in section the vocal organs, and a box containing a supply of wax cylinders for the phonograph.*

Further down the room, on the same side, is a fireplace, with a comfortable leather-covered easy-chair at the side of the hearth nearest the door, and a coal-scuttle. There is a clock on the mantlepiece. Between the fireplace and the phonograph table is a stand for newspapers.

On the other side of the central door, to the left of the visitor, is a cabinet of shallow drawers. On it is a telephone and the telephone directory. The corner beyond, and most of the side wall, is occupied by a grand piano, with the keyboard at the end furthest from the door, and a bench for the players extending the full length of the keyboard. On the piano is a dessert dish heaped with fruit and sweets, mostly chocolates.

The middle of the room is clear. Besides the easy-chair, the piano bench, and two chairs at the phonograph table, there is one stray chair. It stands near the fireplace. On the walls, engravings: mostly Piranesis and mezzotint portraits. No paintings.

PICKERING *is seated at the table, putting down some cards and a tuning-fork which he has been using.* HIGGINS *is standing up near him, closing two or three file drawers which are hanging out. He appears in the morning light as a robust, vital, appetizing sort of man of forty or thereabouts, dressed in a professional-looking black frock-coat with a white linen collar and black silk tie. He is of energetic, scientific type, heartily, even violently interested in everything that can be studied as a scientific subject, and careless about himself and other people, including their feelings. He is, in fact, but for his years and size, rather like a very impetuous baby "taking notice" eagerly and loudly, and requiring almost as much watching to keep him out of unintended mischief. His manner varies from genial bullying when he is in a good humor to stormy petulance when anything goes wrong; but he is so entirely frank and void of malice that he remains likeable even in his least reasonable moments.*

HIGGINS [*as he shuts the last drawer*] Well, I think thats the whole show.

PICKERING. It's really amazing. I havnt taken half of it in, you know.

HIGGINS. Would you like to go over any of it again?

PICKERING [*rising and coming to the fireplace, where he plants himself with his back to the fire*] No, thank you: not now. I'm quite done up for this morning.

HIGGINS [*following him, and standing beside him on his left*] Tired of listening to sounds?

PICKERING. Yes. It's a fearful strain. I rather fancied myself because I can pronounce twenty-four distinct vowel sounds; but your hundred and thirty beat me. I cant hear a bit of difference between most of them.

HIGGINS [*chuckling, and going over to the piano to eat sweets*] Oh, that comes with practice. You hear no difference at first; but you keep on listening, and presently you find theyre all as different as A from B. [MRS. PEARCE *looks in: she is* HIGGINS's *housekeeper*]. Whats the matter?

MRS. PEARCE [*hesitating, evidently perplexed*] A young woman asks to see you, sir.

HIGGINS. A young woman! What does she want?

MRS. PEARCE. Well, sir, she says youll be glad to see her when you know what she's come about. She's quite a common girl, sir. Very common indeed. I should have sent her away, only I thought perhaps you wanted her to talk into your machines. I hope Ive not done wrong; but really you see such queer people sometimes—youll excuse me, I'm sure, sir—

HIGGINS. Oh, thats all right, Mrs. Pearce. Has she an interesting accent?

MRS. PEARCE. Oh, something dreadful, sir, really. I dont know how you can take an interest in it.

HIGGINS [*to* PICKERING] Lets have her up. Shew her up, Mrs. Pearce [*he rushes across to his working table and picks out a cylinder to use on the phonograph*].

MRS. PEARCE [*only half resigned to it*] Very well, sir. It's for you to say. [*She goes downstairs*].

HIGGINS. This is rather a bit of luck. I'll shew you how I make records. We'll set her talking; and I'll take it down first in Bell's Visible Speech; then in broad Romic; and then we'll get her on the phonograph so that you can turn her on as often as you like with the written transcript before you.

MRS. PEARCE [*returning*] This is the young woman, sir.

[*The flower girl enters in state. She has a hat with three ostrich feathers, orange, sky-blue, and red. She has a nearly clean apron, and the shoddy coat has been tidied a little. The pathos of this deplorable figure, with its innocent vanity and consequential air, touches* PICKERING, *who has already straightened himself in the presence of* MRS. PEARCE. *But as to* HIGGINS, *the only distinction he makes between men and women is that when he is neither bullying nor exclaiming to the heavens against some feather-weight cross, he coaxes women as a child coaxes its nurse when it wants to get anything out of her*].

HIGGINS [*brusquely, recognizing her with unconcealed disappointment, and at once, babylike, making an intolerable grievance of it*] Why, this is the girl I jotted down last night. She's no use: I've got all the records I want of the Lisson Grove lingo; and I'm not going to waste another cylinder on it. [*To the girl*] Be off with you: I dont want you.

THE FLOWER GIRL. Dont you be so saucy. You aint heard what I come for yet. [*To* MRS. PEARCE, *who is waiting at the door for further instructions*] Did you tell him I come in a taxi?

MRS. PEARCE. Nonsense, girl! what do you think a gentleman like Mr. Higgins cares what you came in?

THE FLOWER GIRL. Oh, we are proud! He aint above giving lessons, not him: I heard him say so. Well, I aint come here to ask for any compliment; and if my money's not good enough I can go elsewhere.

HIGGINS. Good enough for what?

THE FLOWER GIRL. Good enough for ya-oo. Now you know, dont you? I've come to have lessons, I am. And to pay for em ta-oo: make no mistake.

HIGGINS [*stupent*] Well!!! [*Recovering his breath with a gasp*] What do you expect me to say to you?

THE FLOWER GIRL. Well, if you was a gentleman, you might ask me to sit down, I think. Dont I tell you I'm bringing you business?

HIGGINS. Pickering: shall we ask this baggage to sit down, or shall we throw her out of the window?

THE FLOWER GIRL [*running away in terror to the piano, where she turns at bay*] Ah-ah-oh-ow-ow-ow-oo! [*Wounded and whimpering*] I wont be called a baggage when Ive offered to pay like any lady.

[*Motionless, the two men stare at her from the other side of the room, amazed*].

PICKERING [*gently*] But what is it you want?

THE FLOWER GIRL. I want to be a lady in a flower shop stead of sellin at the corner of Tottenham Court Road. But they wont take me unless I can talk more genteel. He said he could teach me. Well, here I am ready to pay him—not asking any favor—and he treats me zif I was dirt.

MRS. PEARCE. How can you be such a foolish ignorant girl as to think you could afford to pay Mr. Higgins?

THE FLOWER GIRL. Why shouldnt I? I know what lessons cost as well as you do; and I'm ready to pay.

HIGGINS. How much?

THE FLOWER GIRL [*coming back to him, triumphant*] Now youre talking! I thought youd come off it when you saw a chance of getting back a bit of what you chucked at me last night. [*Confidentially*] Youd had a drop in, hadnt you?

HIGGINS [*peremptorily*] Sit down.

THE FLOWER GIRL. Oh, if youre going to make a compliment of it—

HIGGINS [*thundering at her*] Sit down.

MRS. PEARCE [*severely*] Sit down, girl. Do as youre told.

THE FLOWER GIRL. Ah-ah-ah-ow-ow-oo! [*She stands, half rebellious, half bewildered*].

PICKERING [*very courteous*] Wont you sit down? [*He places the stray chair near the hearthrug between himself and* HIGGINS.]

LIZA [*coyly*] Dont mind if I do. [*She sits down.* PICKERING *returns to the hearthrug*].

HIGGINS. Whats your name?

THE FLOWER GIRL. Liza Doolittle.

HIGGINS [*declaiming gravely*]

> Eliza, Elizabeth, Betsy and Bess,
> They went to the woods to get a bird's nes':

PICKERING. They found a nest with four eggs in it:

HIGGINS. They took one apiece, and left three in it.

[*They laugh heartily at their own fun*].

LIZA. Oh, dont be silly.

MRS. PEARCE [*placing herself behind* ELIZA's *chair*] You mustnt speak to the gentleman like that.

LIZA. Well, why wont he speak sensible to me?

HIGGINS. Come back to business. How much do you propose to pay me for the lessons?

LIZA. Oh, I know whats right. A lady friend of mine gets French lessons for eighteenpence an hour from a real French gentleman. Well, you wouldnt have the face to ask me the same for teaching me my own language as you would for French; so I wont give more than a shilling. Take it or leave it.

HIGGINS [*walking up and down the room, rattling his keys and his cash in his pockets*] You know, Pickering, if you consider a shilling, not as a simple shilling, but as a percentage of this girl's income, it works out as fully equivalent to sixty or seventy guineas from a millionaire.

PICKERING. How so?

HIGGINS. Figure it out. A millionaire has about £150 a day. She earns about half-a-crown.

LIZA [*haughtily*] Who told you I only—

HIGGINS [*continuing*] She offers me two-fifths of her day's income for a lesson. Two-fifths of a millionaire's income for a day would be somewhere about £60. It's handsome. By George, it's enormous! it's the biggest offer I ever had.

LIZA [*rising, terrified*] Sixty pounds! What are you talking about? I never offered you sixty pounds. Where would I get—

HIGGINS. Hold your tongue.

LIZA [*weeping*] But I aint got sixty pounds. Oh—

MRS. PEARCE. Dont cry, you silly girl. Sit down. Nobody is going to touch your money.

HIGGINS. Somebody is going to touch you, with a broomstick, if you dont stop snivelling. Sit down.

LIZA [*obeying slowly*] Ah-ah-ah-ow-oo-o! One would think you was my father.

HIGGINS. If I decide to teach you, I'll be worse than two fathers to you. Here [*he offers her his silk handkerchief*]!

LIZA. Whats this for?

HIGGINS. To wipe your eyes. To wipe any part of your face that feels moist. Remember: thats your handkerchief; and thats your sleeve. Dont mistake the one for the other if you wish to become a lady in a shop.

[LIZA, *utterly bewildered, stares helplessly at him*].

MRS. PEARCE. It's no use talking to her like that, Mr. Higgins: she doesnt understand you. Besides, youre quite wrong: she doesnt do it that way at all [*she takes the handkerchief*].

LIZA [*snatching it*] Here! You give me that handkerchief. He gev it to me, not to you.

PICKERING [*laughing*] He did. I think it must be regarded as her property, Mrs. Pearce.

MRS. PEARCE [*resigning herself*] Serve you right, Mr. Higgins.

PICKERING. Higgins: I'm interested. What about the ambassador's garden party? I'll say youre the greatest teacher alive if you make that good. I'll bet you all the expenses of the experiment you cant do it. And I'll pay for the lessons.

LIZA. Oh, you are real good. Thank you, Captain.

HIGGINS [*tempted, looking at her*] It's almost irresistible. She's so deliciously low—so horribly dirty—

LIZA [*protesting extremely*] Ah-ah-ah-ah-ow-ow-oo-oo!!! I aint dirty: I washed my face and hands afore I come, I did.

PICKERING. Youre certainly not going to turn her head with flattery, Higgins.

MRS. PEARCE [*uneasy*] Oh, dont say that, sir: theres more ways than one of turning a girl's head; and nobody can do it better than Mr. Higgins, though he may not always mean it. I do hope, sir, you wont encourage him to do anything foolish.

HIGGINS [*becoming excited as the idea grows on him*] What is life but a series of inspired follies? The difficulty is to find them to do. Never lose a chance: it doesnt come every day. I shall make a duchess of this draggletailed guttersnipe.

LIZA [*strongly deprecating this view of her*] Ah-ah-ah-ow-ow-oo!

HIGGINS [*carried away*] Yes: in six months—in three if she has a good ear and a quick tongue—I'll take her anywhere and pass her off as anything. We'll start today: now! this moment! Take her away and clean her, Mrs. Pearce. Monkey Brand, if it wont come off any other way. Is there a good fire in the kitchen?

MRS. PEARCE [*protesting*] Yes; but—

HIGGINS [*storming on*] Take all her clothes off and burn them. Ring up Whitely or somebody for new ones. Wrap her up in brown paper til they come.

LIZA. Youre no gentleman, youre not, to talk of such things. I'm a good girl, I am; and I know what the like of you are, I do.

HIGGINS. We want none of your Lisson Grove prudery here, young woman. Youve got to learn to behave like a duchess. Take her away, Mrs. Pearce. If she gives you any trouble, wallop her.

LIZA [*springing up and running between* PICKERING *and* MRS. PEARCE *for protection*] No! I'll call the police, I will.

MRS. PEARCE. But Ive no place to put her.

HIGGINS. Put her in the dustbin.

LIZA. Ah-ah-ah-ow-ow-oo!

PICKERING. Oh come, Higgins! be reasonable.

MRS. PEARCE [*resolutely*] You must be reasonable, Mr. Higgins: really you must. You cant walk over everybody like this.

[HIGGINS, *thus scolded, subsides. The hurricane is succeeded by a zephyr of amiable surprise*].

HIGGINS [*with professional exquisiteness of modulation*] I walk over everybody! My dear Mrs. Pearce, my dear Pickering, I never had the slightest intention of walking over anyone. All I propose is that we should be kind to this poor girl. We must help her to prepare and fit herself for her new station in life. If I did not express myself clearly it was because I did not wish to hurt her delicacy, or yours.

[LIZA, *reassured, steals back to her chair*].

MRS. PEARCE [*to* PICKERING] Well, did you ever hear anything like that, sir?

PICKERING [*laughing heartily*] Never, Mrs. Pearce: never.

HIGGINS [*patiently*] Whats the matter?

MRS. PEARCE. Well, the matter is, sir, that you cant take a girl up like that as if you were picking up a pebble on the beach.

HIGGINS. Why not?

MRS. PEARCE. Why not! But you dont know anything about her. What about her parents? She may be married.

LIZA. Garn!

HIGGINS. There! As the girl very properly says, Garn! Married indeed! Dont you know that a woman of that class looks a worn out drudge of fifty a year after she's married?

LIZA. Whood marry me?

HIGGINS [*suddenly resorting to the most thrilling beautiful low tones in his best elocutionary style*] By George, Eliza, the streets will be strewn with the bodies of men shooting themselves for your sake before Ive done with you.

MRS. PEARCE. Nonsense, sir. You mustnt talk like that to her.

LIZA [*rising and squaring herself determinedly*] I'm going away. He's off his chump, he is. I dont want no balmies teaching me.

HIGGINS [*wounded in his tenderest point by her insensibility to his elocution*] Oh, indeed! I'm mad, am I? Very well, Mrs. Pearce: you neednt order the new clothes for her. Throw her out.

LIZA [*whimpering*] Nah-ow. You got no right to touch me.

MRS. PEARCE. You see now what comes of being saucy. [*Indicating the door*] This way, please.

LIZA [*almost in tears*] I didnt want no clothes. I wouldnt have taken them [*she throws away the handkerchief*]. I can buy my own clothes.

HIGGINS [*deftly retrieving the handkerchief and intercepting her on her reluctant way to the door*] Youre an ungrateful wicked girl. This is my return for offering to take you out of the gutter and dress you beautifully and make a lady of you.

MRS. PEARCE. Stop, Mr. Higgins. I wont allow it. It's you that are wicked. Go home to your parents, girl; and tell them to take better care of you.

LIZA. I aint got no parents. They told me I was big enough to earn my own living and turned me out.

MRS. PEARCE. Wheres your mother?

LIZA. I aint got no mother. Her that turned me out was my sixth stepmother. But I done without them. And I'm a good girl, I am.

HIGGINS. Very well, then, what on earth is all this fuss about? The girl doesnt belong to anybody—is no use to anybody but me. [*He goes to* MRS. PEARCE *and begins coaxing*]. You can adopt her, Mrs. Pearce: I'm sure a daughter would be a great amusement to you. Now dont make any more fuss. Take her downstairs; and—

MRS. PEARCE. But whats to become of her? Is she to be paid anything? Do be sensible, sir.

HIGGINS. Oh, pay her whatever is necessary: put it down in the housekeeping book. [*Impatiently*] What on earth will she want with money? She'll have her food and her clothes. She'll only drink if you give her money.

LIZA [*turning on him*] Oh you are a brute. It's a lie: nobody ever saw the sign of liquor on me. [*To* PICKERING] Oh, sir: youre a gentleman: dont let him speak to me like that.

PICKERING [*in good-humored remonstrance*] Does it occur to you, Higgins, that the girl has some feelings?

HIGGINS [*looking critically at her*] Oh no, I dont

think so. Not any feelings that we need bother about. [*Cheerily*] Have you, Eliza?

LIZA. I got my feelings same as anyone else.

HIGGINS [*to* PICKERING, *reflectively*] You see the difficulty?

PICKERING. Eh? What difficulty?

HIGGINS. To get her to talk grammar. The mere pronunciation is easy enough.

LIZA. I don't want to talk grammar. I want to talk like a lady in a flower-shop.

MRS. PEARCE. Will you please keep to the point, Mr. Higgins. I want to know on what terms the girl is to be here. Is she to have any wages? And what is to become of her when youve finished your teaching? You must look ahead a little.

HIGGINS [*impatiently*] Whats to become of her if I leave her in the gutter? Tell me that, Mrs. Pearce.

MRS. PEARCE. Thats her own business, not yours, Mr. Higgins.

HIGGINS. Well, when Ive done with her, we can throw her back into the gutter; and then it will be her own business again; so thats all right.

LIZA. Oh, youve no feeling heart in you: you dont care for nothing but yourself. [*She rises and takes the floor resolutely*]. Here! Ive had enough of this. I'm going [*making for the door*]. You ought to be ashamed of yourself, you ought.

HIGGINS [*snatching a chocolate cream from the piano, his eyes suddenly beginning to twinkle with mischief*] Have some chocolates, Eliza.

LIZA [*halting, tempted*] How do I know what might be in them? Ive heard of girls being drugged by the like of you.

[HIGGINS *whips out his penknife; cuts a chocolate in two; puts one half into his mouth and bolts it; and offers her the other half.*]

HIGGINS. Pledge of good faith, Eliza. I eat one half: you eat the other. [LIZA *opens her mouth to retort: he pops the half chocolate into it*]. You shall have boxes of them, barrels of them, every day. You shall live on them. Eh?

LIZA [*who has disposed of the chocolate after being nearly choked by it*] I wouldnt have ate it, only I'm too ladylike to take it out of my mouth.

HIGGINS. Listen, Eliza. I think you said you came in a taxi.

LIZA. Well, what if I did? Ive as good a right to take a taxi as anyone else.

HIGGINS. You have, Eliza; and in future you shall have as many taxis as you want. You shall go up and down and round the town in a taxi every day. Think of that, Eliza.

MRS. PEARCE. Mr. Higgins: youre tempting the girl. It's not right. She should think of the future.

HIGGINS. At her age! Nonsense! Time enough to think of the future when you havnt any future to think of. No, Eliza: do as this lady does: think of other people's futures; but never think of your own. Think of chocolates, and taxis, and gold, and diamonds.

LIZA. No: I dont want no gold and no diamonds. I'm a good girl, I am. [*She sits down again, with an attempt at dignity*].

HIGGINS. You shall remain so, Eliza, under the care of Mrs. Pearce. And you shall marry an officer in the Guards, with a beautiful moustache: the son of a marquis, who will disinherit him for marrying you, but will relent when he sees your beauty and goodness—

PICKERING. Excuse me, Higgins; but I really must interfere. Mrs. Pearce is quite right. If this girl is to put herself in your hands for six months for an experiment in teaching, she must understand thoroughly what she's doing.

HIGGINS. How can she? She's incapable of understanding anything. Besides, do any of us understand what we are doing? If we did, would we ever do it?

PICKERING. Very clever, Higgins; but not to the present point. [*To* ELIZA] Miss Doolittle—

LIZA [*overwhelmed*] Ah-ah-ow-oo!

HIGGINS. There! Thats all youll get out of Eliza. Ah-ah-ow-oo! No use explaining. As a military man you ought to know that. Give her her orders: thats enough for her. Eliza: you are to live here for the next six months, learning how to speak beautifully, like a lady in a florist's shop. If youre good and do whatever youre told, you shall sleep in a proper bedroom, and have lots to eat, and money to buy chocolates and take rides in taxis. If youre naughty and idle you will sleep in the back kitchen among the black beetles, and be walloped by Mrs. Pearce with a broomstick. At the end of six months you shall go to Buckingham Palace in a carriage, beautifully dressed. If the King finds out youre not a lady, you will be taken by the police to the Tower of London, where your head will be cut off as a warning to other presumptuous flower girls. If you are not found out, you shall have a present of seven-and-sixpence to start life with as a lady in a shop. If you refuse this offer you will be a most ungrateful wicked girl; and the angels will weep for you. [*To* PICKERING] Now are you satisfied, Pickering? [*To* MRS. PEARCE] Can I put it more plainly and fairly, Mrs. Pearce?

MRS. PEARCE [*patiently*] I think youd better let me speak to the girl properly in private. I dont know that I can take charge of her or consent to the arrangement at all. Of course I know you dont mean her any harm; but when you get what you call interested in people's accents, you never think or care what may happen to them or you. Come with me, Eliza.

HIGGINS. Thats all right. Thank you, Mrs. Pearce. Bundle her off to the bath-room.

LIZA [*rising reluctantly and suspiciously*] Youre a great bully, you are. I wont stay here if I dont like. I wont let nobody wallop me. I never asked to go to Bucknam Palace, I didnt. I was never in trouble with the police, not me. I'm a good girl—

MRS. PEARCE. Dont answer back, girl. You dont understand the gentleman. Come with me. [*She leads the way to the door, and holds it open for* ELIZA].

LIZA [*as she goes out*] Well, what I say is right. I wont go near the King, not if I'm going to have my head cut off. If I'd known what I was letting myself in for, I wouldnt have come here. I always been a good girl; and I never offered to say a word to him; and I dont owe him nothing; and I dont care; and I wont be put upon; and I have my feelings the same as anyone else—

[MRS. PEARCE *shuts the door; and* ELIZA's *plaints are no longer audible*].

* * * * *

Eliza is taken upstairs to the third floor greatly to her surprise; for she expected to be taken down to the scullery. There Mrs. Pearce opens a door and takes her into a spare bedroom.

MRS. PEARCE. I will have to put you here. This will be your bedroom.

LIZA. O-h, I couldnt sleep here, missus. It's too good for the likes of me. I should be afraid to touch anything. I aint a duchess yet, you know.

MRS. PEARCE. You have got to make yourself as clean as the room: then you wont be afraid of it. And you must call me Mrs. Pearce, not missus. [*She throws open the door of the dressingroom, now modernized as a bathroom*].

LIZA. Gawd! whats this? Is this where you wash clothes? Funny sort of copper I call it.

MRS. PEARCE. It is not a copper. This is where we wash ourselves, Eliza, and where I am going to wash you.

LIZA. You expect me to get into that and wet myself all over! Not me. I should catch my death. I knew a woman did it every Saturday night; and she died of it.

MRS. PEARCE. Mr. Higgins has the gentlemen's bathroom downstairs; and he has a bath every morning, in cold water.

LIZA. Ugh! He's made of iron, that man.

MRS. PEARCE. If you are to sit with him and the Colonel and be taught you will have to do the same. They wont like the smell of you if you dont. But you can have the water as hot as you like. There are two taps: hot and cold.

LIZA [*weeping*] I couldnt. I dursnt. Its not natural: it would kill me. Ive never had a bath in my life: not what youd call a proper one.

MRS. PEARCE. Well, dont you want to be clean and sweet and decent, like a lady? You know you cant be a nice girl inside if youre a dirty slut outside.

LIZA. Boohoo!!!!

MRS. PEARCE. Now stop crying and go back into your room and take off all your clothes. Then wrap yourself in this [*Taking down a gown from its peg and handing it to her*] and come back to me. I will get the bath ready.

LIZA [*all tears*] I cant. I wont. I'm not used to it. Ive never took off all my clothes before. It's not right: it's not decent.

MRS. PEARCE. Nonsense, child. Dont you take off all your clothes every night when you go to bed?

LIZA [*amazed*] No. Why should I? I should catch my death. Of course I take off my skirt.

MRS. PEARCE. Do you mean that you sleep in the underclothes you wear in the daytime?

LIZA. What else have I to sleep in?

MRS. PEARCE. You will never do that again as long as you live here. I will get you a proper nightdress.

LIZA. Do you mean change into cold things and lie awake shivering half the night? You want to kill me, you do.

MRS. PEARCE. I want to change you from a frowzy slut to a clean respectable girl fit to sit with the gentlemen in the study. Are you going to trust me and do what I tell you or be thrown out and sent back to your flower basket?

LIZA. But you dont know what the cold is to me. You dont know how I dread it.

MRS. PEARCE. Your bed won't be cold here: I will put a hot water bottle in it. [*Pushing her into the bedroom*] Off with you and undress.

LIZA. Oh, if only I'd known what a dreadful thing it is to be clean I'd never have come. I didnt know when I was well off. I—[MRS. PEARCE *pushes her through the door, but leaves it partly open lest her prisoner should take to flight*].

[MRS. PEARCE *puts on a pair of white rubber sleeves, and fills the bath, mixing hot and cold, and testing the result with the bath thermometer. She perfumes it with a handful of bath salts and adds a palmful of mustard. She then takes a formidable looking long handled scrubbing brush and soaps it profusely with a ball of scented soap*].

[ELIZA *comes back with nothing on but the bath gown huddled tightly round her, a piteous spectacle of abject terror*].

MRS. PEARCE. Now come along. Take that thing off.

LIZA. Oh I couldnt, Mrs. Pearce: I reely couldnt. I never done such a thing.

MRS. PEARCE. Nonsense. Here: step in and tell me whether its hot enough for you.

LIZA. Ah-oo! Ah-oo! It's too hot.

MRS. PEARCE [deftly snatching the gown away and throwing ELIZA down on her back] It wont hurt you. [She sets to work with the scrubbing brush].

[ELIZA's screams are heartrending].

* * * * *

Meanwhile the Colonel has been having it out with Higgins about Eliza. Pickering has come from the hearth to the chair and seated himself astride of it with his arms on the back to cross-examine him.

PICKERING. Excuse the straight question, Higgins. Are you a man of good character where women are concerned?

HIGGINS [moodily] Have you ever met a man of good character where women are concerned?

PICKERING. Yes: very frequently.

HIGGINS [dogmatically, lifting himself on his hands to the level of the piano, and sitting on it with a bounce] Well, I havnt. I find that the moment I let a woman make friends with me, she becomes jealous, exacting, suspicious, and a damned nuisance. I find that the moment I let myself make friends with a woman, I become selfish and tyrannical. Women upset everything. When you let them into your life, you find that the woman is driving at one thing and youre driving at another.

PICKERING. At what, for example?

HIGGINS [coming off the piano restlessly] Oh, Lord knows! I suppose the woman wants to live her own life; and the man wants to live his; and each tries to drag the other on to the wrong track. One wants to go north and the other south; and the result is that both have to go east, though they both hate the east wind. [He sits down on the bench at the keyboard]. So here I am, a confirmed old bachelor, and likely to remain so.

PICKERING [rising and standing over him gravely] Come, Higgins! You know what I mean. If I'm to be in this business I shall feel responsible for that girl. I hope it's understood that no advantage is to be taken of her position.

HIGGINS. What! That thing! Sacred, I assure you. [Rising to explain] You see, she'll be a pupil; and teaching would be impossible unless pupils were sacred. Ive taught scores of American millionairesses how to speak English: the best looking women in the world. I'm seasoned. They might as well be blocks of wood. I might as well be a block of wood. It's—

[MRS. PEARCE opens the door. She has ELIZA's hat in her hand. PICKERING retires to the easy-chair at the hearth and sits down].

HIGGINS [eagerly] Well, Mrs. Pearce: is it all right?

MRS. PEARCE [at the door] I just wish to trouble you with a word, if I may, Mr. Higgins.

HIGGINS. Yes, certainly. Come in. [She comes forward]. Dont burn that, Mrs. Pearce. I'll keep it as a curiosity. [He takes the hat].

MRS. PEARCE. Handle it carefully, sir, please. I had to promise her not to burn it; but I had better put it in the oven for a while.

HIGGINS [putting it down hastily on the piano] Oh! thank you. Well, what have you to say to me?

PICKERING. Am I in the way?

MRS. PEARCE. Not in the least, sir. Mr. Higgins: will you please be very particular what you say before the girl?

HIGGINS [sternly] Of course. I'm always particular about what I say. Why do you say this to me?

MRS. PEARCE [unmoved] No, sir: youre not at all particular when youve mislaid anything or when you get a little impatient. Now it doesnt matter before me: I'm used to it. But you really must not swear before the girl.

HIGGINS [indignantly] I swear! [Most emphatically] I never swear. I detest the habit. What the devil do you mean?

MRS. PEARCE [stolidly] Thats what I mean, sir. You swear a great deal too much. I dont mind your damning and blasting, and what the devil and where the devil and who the devil—

HIGGINS. Mrs. Pearce: this language from your lips! Really!

MRS. PEARCE [not to be put off]—but there is a certain word I must ask you not to use. The girl used it herself when she began to enjoy the bath. It begins with the same letter as bath. She knows no better: she learnt it at her mother's knee. But she must not hear it from your lips.

HIGGINS [loftily] I cannot charge myself with having ever uttered it, Mrs. Pearce. [She looks at him steadfastly. He adds, hiding an uneasy conscience with a judicial air] Except perhaps in a moment of extreme and justifiable excitement.

MRS. PEARCE. Only this morning, sir, you applied it to your boots, to the butter, and to the brown bread.

HIGGINS. Oh, that! Mere alliteration, Mrs. Pearce, natural to a poet.

MRS. PEARCE. Well, sir, whatever you choose to call it, I beg you not to let the girl hear you repeat it.

HIGGINS. Oh, very well, very well. Is that all?

MRS. PEARCE. No, sir. We shall have to be very particular with this girl as to personal cleanliness.

HIGGINS. Certainly. Quite right. Most important.

MRS. PEARCE. I mean not to be slovenly about her dress or untidy in leaving things about.

HIGGINS [*going to her solemnly*] Just so. I intended to call your attention to that. [*He passes on to PICKERING, who is enjoying the conversation immensely*]. It is these little things that matter, Pickering. Take care of the pence and the pounds will take care of themselves is as true of personal habits as of money. [*He comes to anchor on the hearthrug, with the air of a man in an unassailable position*].

MRS. PEARCE. Yes, sir. Then might I ask you not to come down to breakfast in your dressing-gown, or at any rate not to use it as a napkin to the extent you do, sir. And if you would be so good as not to eat everything off the same plate, and to remember not to put the porridge saucepan out of your hand on the clean tablecloth, it would be a better example to the girl. You know you nearly choked yourself with a fishbone in a jam only last week.

HIGGINS [*routed from the hearthrug and drifting back to the piano*] I may do these things sometimes in absence of mind; but surely I dont do them habitually. [*Angrily*] By the way: my dressing-gown smells most damnably of benzine.

MRS. PEARCE. No doubt it does, Mr. Higgins. But if you will wipe your fingers—

HIGGINS [*yelling*] Oh very well, very well: I'll wipe them in my hair in future.

MRS. PEARCE. I hope youre not offended, Mr. Higgins.

HIGGINS [*shocked at finding himself thought capable of an unamiable sentiment*] Not at all, not at all. Youre quite right, Mrs. Pearce: I shall be particularly careful before the girl. Is that all?

MRS. PEARCE. No, sir. Might she use some of those Japanese dresses you brought from abroad? I really cant put her back into her old things.

HIGGINS. Certainly. Anything you like. Is that all?

MRS. PEARCE. Thank you, sir. Thats all. [*She goes out*].

HIGGINS. You know, Pickering, that woman has the most extraordinary ideas about me. Here I am, a shy, diffident sort of man. Ive never been able to feel really grown-up and tremendous, like other chaps. And yet she's firmly persuaded that I'm an arbitrary overbearing bossing kind of person. I cant account for it.

[MRS. PEARCE *returns*].

MRS. PEARCE. If you please, sir, the trouble's beginning already. Theres a dustman downstairs, Alfred Doolittle, wants to see you. He says you have his daughter here.

PICKERING [*rising*] Phew! I say!

HIGGINS [*promptly*] Send the blackguard up.

MRS. PEARCE. Oh, very well, sir. [*She goes out*].

PICKERING. He may not be a blackguard, Higgins.

HIGGINS. Nonsense. Of course he's a blackguard.

PICKERING. Whether he is or not, I'm afraid we shall have some trouble with him.

HIGGINS [*confidently*] Oh no: I think not. If theres any trouble he shall have it with me, not I with him. And we are sure to get something interesting out of him.

PICKERING. About the girl?

HIGGINS. No. I mean his dialect.

PICKERING. Oh!

MRS. PEARCE [*at the door*] Doolittle, sir. [*She admits* DOOLITTLE *and retires*].

[ALFRED *is an elderly but vigorous dustman, clad in the costume of his profession, including a hat with a back brim covering his neck and shoulders. He has well marked and rather interesting features, and seems equally free from fear and conscience. He has a remarkably expressive voice, the result of a habit of giving vent to his feelings without reserve. His present pose is that of wounded honor and stern resolution*].

DOOLITTLE [*at the door, uncertain which of the two gentlemen is his man*] Professor Iggins?

HIGGINS. Here. Good morning. Sit down.

DOOLITTLE. Morning, Governor. [*He sits down magisterially*] I come about a very serious matter, Governor.

HIGGINS [*to* PICKERING] Brought up in Hounslow. Mother Welsh, I should think. [DOOLITTLE *opens his mouth, amazed.* HIGGINS *continues*] What do you want, Doolittle?

DOOLITTLE [*menacingly*] I want my daughter: thats what I want. See?

HIGGINS. Of course you do. Youre her father, arnt you? You dont suppose anyone else wants her, do you? I'm glad to see you have some spark of family feeling left. She's upstairs. Take her away at once.

DOOLITTLE [*rising, fearfully taken aback*] What!

HIGGINS. Take her away. Do you suppose I'm going to keep your daughter for you?

DOOLITTLE [*remonstrating*] Now, now, look here, Governor. Is this reasonable? Is it fairity to take advantage of a man like this? The girl belongs to me. You got her. Where do I come in? [*He sits down again*].

HIGGINS. Your daughter had the audacity to come to my house and ask me to teach her how to speak properly so that she could get a place in a flowershop. This gentleman and my housekeeper have been here all the time. [*Bullying him*] How dare you come here and attempt to blackmail me? You sent her here on purpose.

DOOLITTLE [*protesting*] No, Governor.

HIGGINS. You must have. How else could you possibly know that she is here?

DOOLITTLE. Don't take a man up like that, Governor.

HIGGINS. The police shall take you up. This is a plant—a plot to extort money by threats. I shall telephone for the police [*he goes resolutely to the telephone and opens the directory*].

DOOLITTLE. Have I asked you for a brass farthing? I leave it to the gentleman here: have I said a word about money?

HIGGINS [*throwing the book aside and marching down on* DOOLITTLE *with a poser*] What else did you come for?

DOOLITTLE [*sweetly*] Well, what would a man come for? Be human, Governor.

HIGGINS [*disarmed*] Alfred: did you put her up to it?

DOOLITTLE. So help me, Governor, I never did. I take my Bible oath I aint seen the girl these two months past.

HIGGINS. Then how did you know she was here?

DOOLITTLE ["*most musical, most melancholy*"] I'll tell you, Governor, if youll only let me get a word in. I'm willing to tell you. I'm wanting to tell you. I'm waiting to tell you.

HIGGINS. Pickering: this chap has a certain natural gift of rhetoric. Observe the rhythm of his native woodnotes wild. "I'm willing to tell you: I'm wanting to tell you: I'm waiting to tell you." Sentimental rhetoric! thats the Welsh strain in him. It also accounts for his mendacity and dishonesty.

PICKERING. Oh, please, Higgins: I'm west country myself. [*To* DOOLITTLE] How did you know the girl was here if you didnt send her?

DOOLITTLE. It was like this, Governor. The girl took a boy in the taxi to give him a jaunt. Son of her landlady, he is. He hung about on the chance of her giving him another ride home. Well, she sent him back for her luggage when she heard you was willing for her to stop here. I met the boy at the corner of Long Acre and Endell Street.

HIGGINS. Public house. Yes?

DOOLITTLE. The poor man's club, Governor: why shouldnt I?

PICKERING. Do let him tell his story, Higgins.

DOOLITTLE. He told me what was up. And I ask you, what was my feelings and my duty as a father? I says to the boy, "You bring me the luggage," I says—

PICKERING. Why didnt you go for it yourself?

DOOLITTLE. Landlady wouldnt have trusted me with it, Governor. She's that kind of woman: you know. I had to give the boy a penny afore he trusted me with it, the little swine. I brought it to her just

to oblige you like, and make myself agreeable. Thats all.

HIGGINS. How much luggage?

DOOLITTLE. Musical instrument, Governor. A few pictures, a trifle of jewelry, and a bird-cage. She said she didnt want no clothes. What was I to think from that, Governor? I ask you as a parent what was I to think?

HIGGINS. So you came to rescue her from worse than death, eh?

DOOLITTLE [*appreciatively: relieved at being so well understood*] Just so, Governor. Thats right.

PICKERING. But why did you bring her luggage if you intended to take her away?

DOOLITTLE. Have I said a word about taking her away? Have I now?

HIGGINS [*determinedly*] Youre going to take her away, double quick. [*He crosses to the hearth and rings the bell*].

DOOLITTLE [*rising*] No, Governor. Dont say that. I'm not the man to stand in my girl's light. Heres a career opening for her, as you might say; and—

[MRS. PEARCE *opens the door and awaits orders*].

HIGGINS. Mrs. Pearce: this is Eliza's father. He has come to take her away. Give her to him. [*He goes back to the piano, with an air of washing his hands of the whole affair*].

DOOLITTLE. No. This is a misunderstanding. Listen here—

MRS. PEARCE. He cant take her away, Mr. Higgins: how can he? You told me to burn her clothes.

DOOLITTLE. Thats right. I cant carry the girl through the streets like a blooming monkey, can I? I put it to you.

HIGGINS. You have put it to me that you want your daughter. Take your daughter. If she has no clothes go out and buy her some.

DOOLITTLE [*desperate*] Wheres the clothes she come in? Did I burn them or did your missus here?

MRS. PEARCE. I am the housekeeper, if you please. I have sent for some clothes for your girl. When they come you can take her away. You can wait in the kitchen. This way, please.

[DOOLITTLE, *much troubled, accompanies her to the door; then hesitates; finally turns confidentially to* HIGGINS].

DOOLITTLE. Listen here, Governor. You and me is men of the world, aint we?

HIGGINS. Oh! Men of the world, are we? Youd better go, Mrs. Pearce.

MRS. PEARCE. I think so, indeed, sir. [*She goes, with dignity*].

PICKERING. The floor is yours, Mr. Doolittle.

DOOLITTLE [*to* PICKERING] I thank you, Governor.

[*To* HIGGINS, *who takes refuge on the piano bench, a little overwhelmed by the proximity of his visitor; for* DOOLITTLE *has a professional flavour of dust about him*]. Well, the truth is, I've taken a sort of fancy to you, Governor; and if you want the girl, I'm not so set on having her back home again but what I might be open to an arrangement. Regarded in the light of a young woman, she's a fine handsome girl. As a daughter she's not worth her keep; and so I tell you straight. All I ask is my rights as a father; and youre the last man alive to expect me to let her go for nothing; for I can see youre one of the straight sort, Governor. Well, whats a five-pound note to you? and whats Eliza to me? [*He turns to his chair and sits down judicially*].

PICKERING. I think you ought to know, Doolittle, that Mr. Higgins's intentions are entirely honorable.

DOOLITTLE. Course they are, Governor. If I thought they wasn't, I'd ask fifty.

HIGGINS [*revolted*] Do you mean to say that you would sell your daughter for £50?

DOOLITTLE. Not in a general way I would; but to oblige a gentleman like you I'd do a good deal, I do assure you.

PICKERING. Have you no morals, man?

DOOLITTLE [*unabashed*] Cant afford them, Governor. Neither could you if you was as poor as me. Not that I mean any harm, you know. But if Liza is going to have a bit out of this, why not me too?

HIGGINS [*troubled*] I dont know what to do, Pickering. There can be no question that as a matter of morals it's a positive crime to give this chap a farthing. And yet I feel a sort of rough justice in his claim.

DOOLITTLE. Thats it, Governor. Thats all I say. A father's heart, as it were.

PICKERING. Well, I know the feeling; but really it seems hardly right—

DOOLITTLE. Dont say that, Governor. Dont look at it that way. What am I, Governors both? I ask you, what am I? I'm one of the undeserving poor: thats what I am. Think of what that means to a man. It means that he's up agen middle class morality all the time. If theres anything going, and I put in for a bit of it, it's always the same story: "Youre undeserving; so you cant have it." But my needs is as great as the most deserving widow's that ever got money out of six different charities in one week for the death of the same husband. I dont need less than a deserving man: I need more. I dont eat less hearty than him; and I drink a lot more. I want a bit of amusement, cause I'm a thinking man. I want cheerfulness and a song and a band when I feel low. Well, they charge me just the same for everything as they charge the deserving. What is middle class morality? Just an

excuse for never giving me anything. Therefore, I ask you, as two gentlemen, not to play that game on me. I'm playing straight with you. I aint pretending to be deserving. I'm undeserving; and I mean to go on being undeserving. I like it; and thats the truth. Will you take advantage of a man's nature to do him out of the price of his own daughter what he's brought up and fed and clothed by the sweat of his brow until she's growed big enough to be interesting to you two gentlemen? Is five pounds unreasonable? I put it to you; and I leave it to you.

HIGGINS [*rising, and going over to* PICKERING] Pickering: if we were to take this man in hand for three months, he could choose between a seat in the Cabinet and a popular pulpit in Wales.

PICKERING. What do you say to that, Doolittle?

DOOLITTLE. Not me, Governor, thank you kindly. Ive heard all the preachers and all the prime ministers—for I'm a thinking man and game for politics or religion or social reform same as all the other amusements—and I tell you it's a dog's life any way you look at it. Undeserving poverty is my line. Taking one station in society with another, it's—it's—well, it's the only one that has any ginger in it, to my taste.

HIGGINS. I suppose we must give him a fiver.

PICKERING. He'll make a bad use of it, I'm afraid.

DOOLITTLE. Not me, Governor, so help me I wont. Dont you be afraid that I'll save it and spare it and live idle on it. There wont be a penny of it left by Monday: I'll have to go to work same as if I'd never had it. It wont pauperize me, you bet. Just one good spree for myself and the missus, giving pleasure to ourselves and employment to others, and satisfaction to you to think it's not been throwed away. You couldnt spend it better.

HIGGINS [*taking out his pocket book and coming between* DOOLITTLE *and the piano*] This is irresistible. Lets give him ten. [*He offers two notes to the dustman*].

DOOLITTLE. No, Governor. She wouldnt have the heart to spend ten; and perhaps I shouldnt neither. Ten pounds is a lot of money: it makes a man feel prudent like; and then goodbye to happiness. You give me what I ask you, Governor: not a penny more, and not a penny less.

PICKERING. Why dont you marry that missus of yours? I rather draw the line at encouraging that sort of immorality.

DOOLITTLE. Tell her so, Governor: tell her so. *I'm* willing. It's me that suffers by it. Ive no hold on her. I got to be agreeable to her. I got to give her presents. I got to buy her clothes something sinful. I'm a slave to that woman, Governor, just because I'm not her lawful husband. And she knows it too.

Catch her marrying me! Take my advice, Governor: marry Eliza while she's young and dont know no better. If you dont you'll be sorry for it after. If you do, she'll be sorry for it after; but better her than you, because youre a man, and she's only a woman and dont know how to be happy anyhow.

HIGGINS. Pickering: if we listen to this man another minute, we shall have no convictions left. [*To* DOOLITTLE] Five pounds I think you said.

DOOLITTLE. Thank you kindly, Governor.

HIGGINS. Youre sure you wont take ten?

DOOLITTLE. Not now. Another time, Governor.

HIGGINS [*handing him a five-pound note*] Here you are.

DOOLITTLE. Thank you, Governor. Good morning. [*He hurries to the door, anxious to get away with his booty. When he opens it he is confronted with a dainty and exquisitely clean young Japanese lady in a simple blue cotton kimono printed cunningly with small white jasmine blossoms.* MRS. PEARCE *is with her. He gets out of her way deferentially and apologizes*]. Beg pardon, miss.

THE JAPANESE LADY. Garn! Dont you know your own daughter?

DOOLITTLE [*exclaiming*] Bly me! it's Eliza!
HIGGINS [*simul-*] Whats that? This!
PICKERING [*taneously*] By Jove!

LIZA. Dont I look silly?

HIGGINS. Silly?

MRS. PEARCE [*at the door*] Now, Mr. Higgins, please dont say anything to make the girl conceited about herself.

HIGGINS [*conscientiously*] Oh! Quite right, Mrs. Pearce. [*To* ELIZA] Yes: damned silly.

MRS. PEARCE. Please, sir.

HIGGINS [*correcting himself*] I mean extremely silly.

LIZA. I should look all right with my hat on. [*She takes up her hat; puts it on; and walks across the room to the fireplace with a fashionable air*].

HIGGINS. A new fashion, by George! And it ought to look horrible!

DOOLITTLE [*with fatherly pride*] Well, I never thought she'd clean up as good looking as that, Governor. She's a credit to me, aint she?

LIZA. I tell you, it's easy to clean up here. Hot and cold water on tap, just as much as you like, there is. Woolly towels, there is; and a towel horse so hot, it burns your fingers. Soft brushes to scrub yourself, and a wooden bowl of soap smelling like primroses. Now I know why ladies is so clean. Washing's a treat for them. Wish they could see what it is for the like of me!

HIGGINS. I'm glad the bathroom met with your approval.

LIZA. It didnt: not all of it; and I dont care who hears me say it. Mrs. Pearce knows.

HIGGINS. What was wrong, Mrs. Pearce?

MRS. PEARCE [*blandly*] Oh, nothing, sir. It doesnt matter.

LIZA. I had a good mind to break it. I didnt know which way to look. But I hung a towel over it, I did.

HIGGINS. Over what?

MRS. PEARCE. Over the looking-glass, sir.

HIGGINS. Doolittle: you have brought your daughter up too strictly.

DOOLITTLE. Me! I never brought her up at all, except to give her a lick of a strap now and again. Dont put it on me, Governor. She aint accustomed to it, you see: thats all. But she'll soon pick up your free-and-easy ways.

LIZA. I'm a good girl, I am; and I wont pick up no free-and-easy ways.

HIGGINS. Eliza: if you say again that youre a good girl, your father shall take you home.

LIZA. Not him. You dont know my father. All he come here for was to touch you for some money to get drunk on.

DOOLITTLE. Well, what else would I want money for? To put into the plate in church, I suppose. [*She puts out her tongue at him. He is so incensed by this that* PICKERING *presently finds it necessary to step between them*]. Dont you give me none of your lip; and dont let me hear you giving this gentleman any of it neither, or youll hear from me about it. See?

HIGGINS. Have you any further advice to give her before you go, Doolittle? Your blessing, for instance.

DOOLITTLE. No, Governor: I aint such a mug as to put up my children to all I know myself. Hard enough to hold them in without that. If you want Eliza's mind improved, Governor, you do it yourself with a strap. So long, gentlemen. [*He turns to go*].

HIGGINS [*impressively*] Stop. Youll come regularly to see your daughter. It's your duty, you know. My brother is a clergyman; and he could help you in your talks with her.

DOOLITTLE [*evasively*] Certainly, I'll come, Governor. Not just this week, because I have a job at a distance. But later on you may depend on me. Afternoon, gentlemen. Afternoon, maam. [*He touches his hat to* MRS. PEARCE, *who disdains the salutation and goes out. He winks at* HIGGINS, *thinking him probably a fellow-sufferer from* MRS. PEARCE's *difficult disposition, and follows her*].

LIZA. Dont you believe the old liar. He'd as soon you set a bulldog on him as a clergyman. You wont see him again in a hurry.

HIGGINS. I dont want to, Eliza. Do you?

LIZA. Not me. I dont want never to see him again,

I dont. He's a disgrace to me, he is, collecting dust, instead of working at his trade.

PICKERING. What is his trade, Eliza?

LIZA. Talking money out of other people's pockets into his own. His proper trade's a navvy; and he works at it sometimes too—for exercise—and earns good money at it. Aint you going to call me Miss Doolittle any more?

PICKERING. I beg your pardon, Miss Doolittle. It was a slip of the tongue.

LIZA. Oh, I dont mind; only it sounded so genteel. I should just like to take a taxi to the corner of Tottenham Court Road and get out there and tell it to wait for me, just to put the girls in their place a bit. I wouldnt speak to them, you know.

PICKERING. Better wait til we get you something really fashionable.

HIGGINS. Besides, you shouldnt cut your old friends now that you have risen in the world. Thats what we call snobbery.

LIZA. You dont call the like of them my friends now, I should hope. Theyve took it out of me often enough with their ridicule when they had the chance; and now I mean to get a bit of my own back. But if I'm to have fashionable clothes, I'll wait. I should like to have some. Mrs. Pearce says youre going to give me some to wear in bed at night different to what I wear in the daytime; but it do seem a waste of money when you could get something to shew. Besides, I never could fancy changing into cold things on a winter night.

MRS. PEARCE [*coming back*] Now, Eliza. The new things have come for you to try on.

LIZA. Ah-ow-oo-ooh! [*She rushes out*].

MRS. PEARCE [*following her*] Oh, dont rush about like that, girl. [*She shuts the door behind her*].

HIGGINS. Pickering: we have taken on a stiff job.

PICKERING [*with conviction*] Higgins: we have.

* * * * *

There seems to be some curiosity as to what Higgins's lessons to Eliza were like. Well, here is a sample: the first one.

Picture Eliza, in her new clothes, and feeling her inside put out of step by a lunch, dinner, and breakfast of a kind to which it is unaccustomed, seated with Higgins and the Colonel in the study, feeling like a hospital out-patient at a first encounter with the doctors.

Higgins, constitutionally unable to sit still, discomposes her still more by striding restlessly about. But for the reassuring presence and quietude of her friend the Colonel she would run for her life, even back to Drury Lane.

HIGGINS. Say your alphabet.

LIZA. I know my alphabet. Do you think I know nothing? I dont need to be taught like a child.

HIGGINS [*thundering*] Say your alphabet.

PICKERING. Say it, Miss Doolittle. You will understand presently. Do what he tells you; and let him teach you in his own way.

LIZA. Oh well, if you put it like that—Ahyee, bɔyee, cɔyee, dɔyee—

HIGGINS [*with the roar of a wounded lion*] Stop. Listen to this, Pickering. This is what we pay for as elementary education. This unfortunate animal has been locked up for nine years in school at our expense to teach her to speak and read the language of Shakespear and Milton. And the result is Ahyee, Bɔyee, Cɔ-yee, Dɔyee. [*To* ELIZA] Say, A, B, C, D.

LIZA [*almost in tears*] But I'm sayin it. Ahyee, Bɔyee, Cɔyee—

HIGGINS. Stop. Say a cup of tea.

LIZA. A cappɔtɔ-ee.

HIGGINS. Put your tongue forward until it squeezes against the top of your lower teeth. Now say cup.

LIZA. C-c-c—I cant. C-Cup.

PICKERING. Good. Splendid, Miss Doolittle.

HIGGINS. By Jupiter, she's done it the first shot. Pickering: we shall make a duchess of her. [*To* ELIZA] Now do you think you could possibly say tea? Not tɔ-yee, mind: if you ever say bɔ-yee cɔ-yee dɔ-yee again you shall be dragged round the room three times by the hair of your head. [*Fortissimo*] T, T, T, T.

LIZA. [*weeping*] I cant hear no difference cep that it sounds more genteel-like when you say it.

HIGGINS. Well, if you can hear that difference, what the devil are you crying for? Pickering: give her a chocolate.

PICKERING. No, no. Never mind crying a little, Miss Doolittle: you are doing very well; and the lessons wont hurt. I promise you I wont let him drag you round the room by your hair.

HIGGINS. Be off with you to Mrs. Pearce and tell her about it. Think about it. Try to do it by yourself: and keep your tongue well forward in your mouth instead of trying to roll it up and swallow it. Another lesson at half-past four this afternoon. Away with you.

[ELIZA, *still sobbing, rushes from the room*].

And that is the sort of ordeal poor Eliza has to go through for months before we meet her again on her first appearance in London society of the professional class.

ACT III

It is MRS. HIGGINS's *at-home day. Nobody has yet arrived. Her drawing room, in a flat on Chelsea Embankment, has three windows looking on the river; and the ceiling is not so lofty as it would be in an older house of the same pretension. The windows are open, giving access to a balcony with flowers in pots. If you stand with your face to the windows, you have the fireplace on your left and the door in the right-hand wall close to the corner nearest the windows.*

MRS. HIGGINS *was brought up on Morris and Burne Jones; and her room, which is very unlike her son's room in Wimpole Street, is not crowded with furniture and little tables and nicknacks. In the middle of the room there is a big ottoman; and this, with the carpet, the Morris wall-papers, and the Morris chintz window curtains and brocade covers of the otto-man and its cushions, supply all the ornament, and are much too handsome to be hidden by odds and ends of useless things. A few good oil-paintings from the exhibitions in the Grosvenor Gallery thirty years ago (the Burne Jones, not the Whistler side of them) are on the walls. The only landscape is a Cecil Lawson on the scale of a Rubens. There is a portrait of* MRS. HIGGINS *as she was when she defied the fashion in her youth in one of the beautiful Rossettian cos-tumes which, when caricatured by people who did not understand, led to the absurdities of popular estheticism in the eighteen-seventies.*

In the corner diagonally opposite the door MRS. HIGGINS, *now over sixty and long past taking the trouble to dress out of the fashion, sits writ-ing at an elegantly simple writing-table with a bell button within reach of her hand. There is a Chippendale chair further back in the room be-tween her and the window nearest her side. At the other side of the room, further forward, is an Elizabethan chair roughly carved in the taste of Inigo Jones. On the same side a piano in a decorated case. The corner between the fire-place and the window is occupied by a divan cushioned in Morris chintz.*

It is between four and five in the afternoon.

The door is opened violently; and HIGGINS *enters with his hat on.*

MRS. HIGGINS [*dismayed*] Henry! [*Scolding him*] What are you doing here today? It is my at-home day: you promised not to come. [*As he bends to kiss her, she takes his hat off, and presents it to him*].

HIGGINS. Oh bother! [*He throws the hat down on the table*].

MRS. HIGGINS. Go home at once.

HIGGINS [*kissing her*] I know, mother. I came on purpose.

MRS. HIGGINS. But you mustnt. I'm serious, Henry.

You offend all my friends: they stop coming when-ever they meet you.

HIGGINS. Nonsense! I know I have no small talk; but people dont mind. [*He sits on the settee*].

MRS. HIGGINS. Oh! dont they? Small talk indeed! What about your large talk? Really, dear, you mustnt stay.

HIGGINS. I must. Ive a job for you. A phonetic job.

MRS. HIGGINS. No use, dear. I'm sorry; but I cant get round your vowels; and though I like to get pretty postcards in your patent shorthand, I always have to read the copies in ordinary writing you so thoughtfully send me.

HIGGINS. Well, this isnt a phonetic job.

MRS. HIGGINS. You said it was.

HIGGINS. Not your part of it. Ive picked up a girl.

MRS. HIGGINS. Does that mean that some girl has picked you up?

HIGGINS. Not at all. I dont mean a love affair.

MRS. HIGGINS. What a pity!

HIGGINS. Why?

MRS. HIGGINS. Well, you never fall in love with anyone under forty-five. When will you discover that there are some rather nice-looking young women about?

HIGGINS. Oh, I cant be bothered with young women. My idea of a lovable woman is somebody as like you as possible. I shall never get into the way of seriously liking young women: some habits lie too deep to be changed. [*Rising abruptly and walking about, jingling his money and his keys in his trouser pockets*] Besides, theyre all idiots.

MRS. HIGGINS. Do you know what you would do if you really loved me, Henry?

HIGGINS. Oh bother! What? Marry, I suppose.

MRS. HIGGINS. No. Stop fidgeting and take your hands out of your pockets. [*With a gesture of despair, he obeys and sits down again*]. Thats a good boy. Now tell me about the girl.

HIGGINS. She's coming to see you.

MRS. HIGGINS. I dont remember asking her.

HIGGINS. You didnt. *I* asked her. If youd known her you wouldnt have asked her.

MRS. HIGGINS. Indeed! Why?

HIGGINS. Well, it's like this. She's a common flower girl. I picked her off the kerbstone.

MRS. HIGGINS. And invited her to my at-home!

HIGGINS [*rising and coming to her to coax her*] Oh, thatll be all right. Ive taught her to speak properly; and she has strict orders as to her behavior. She's to keep to two subjects: the weather and everybody's health—Fine day and How do you do, you know—and not to let herself go on things in general. That will be safe.

MRS. HIGGINS. Safe! To talk about our health! about our insides! perhaps about our outsides! How could you be so silly, Henry?

HIGGINS [*impatiently*] Well, she must talk about something. [*He controls himself and sits down again*]. Oh, she'll be all right: dont you fuss. Pickering is in it with me. Ive a sort of bet on that I'll pass her off as a duchess in six months. I started on her some months ago; and she's getting on like a house on fire. I shall win my bet. She has a quick ear; and she's easier to teach than my middle-class pupils because she's had to learn a complete new language. She talks English almost as you talk French.

MRS. HIGGINS. Thats satisfactory, at all events.

HIGGINS. Well, it is and it isnt.

MRS. HIGGINS. What does that mean?

HIGGINS. You see, Ive got her pronunciation all right; but you have to consider not only how a girl pronounces, but what she pronounces; and that's where—

[*They are interrupted by the parlor-maid, announcing guests*].

THE PARLOR-MAID. Mrs. and Miss Eynsford Hill. [*She withdraws*].

HIGGINS. Oh Lord! [*He rises; snatches his hat from the table; and makes for the door; but before he reaches it his mother introduces him*].

[MRS. *and* MISS EYNSFORD HILL *are the mother and daughter who sheltered from the rain in Covent Garden. The mother is well bred, quiet, and has the habitual anxiety of straitened means. The daughter has acquired a gay air of being very much at home in society: the bravado of genteel poverty*].

MRS. EYNSFORD HILL [*to* MRS. HIGGINS] How do you do? [*They shake hands*].

MISS EYNSFORD HILL. How d'you do? [*She shakes*].

MRS. HIGGINS [*introducing*] My son Henry.

MRS. EYNSFORD HILL. Your celebrated son! I have so longed to meet you, Professor Higgins.

HIGGINS [*glumly, making no movement in her direction*] Delighted. [*He backs against the piano and bows brusquely*].

MISS EYNSFORD HILL [*going to him with confident familiarity*] How do you do?

HIGGINS [*staring at her*] Ive seen you before somewhere. I havnt the ghost of a notion where; but Ive heard your voice. [*Drearily*] It doesnt matter. Youd better sit down.

MRS. HIGGINS. I'm sorry to say that my celebrated son has no manners. You mustnt mind him.

MISS EYNSFORD HILL [*gaily*] I don't. [*She sits in the Elizabethan chair*].

MRS. EYNSFORD HILL [*a little bewildered*] Not at all. [*She sits on the ottoman between her daughter and MRS. HIGGINS, who has turned her chair away from the writing-table*].

HIGGINS. Oh, have I been rude? I didnt mean to be.

[*He goes to the central window, through which, with his back to the company, he contemplates the river and the flowers in Battersea Park on the opposite bank as if they were a frozen desert*].

[*The parlor-maid returns, ushering in* PICKERING].

THE PARLOR-MAID. Colonel Pickering. [*She withdraws*].

PICKERING. How do you do, Mrs. Higgins?

MRS. HIGGINS. So glad youve come. Do you know Mrs. Eynsford Hill—Miss Eynsford Hill? [*Exchange of bows. The Colonel brings the Chippendale chair a little forward between* MRS. HILL *and* MRS. HIGGINS, *and sits down*].

PICKERING. Has Henry told you what weve come for?

HIGGINS [*over his shoulder*] We were interrupted: damn it!

MRS. HIGGINS. Oh Henry, Henry, really!

MRS. EYNSFORD HILL [*half rising*] Are we in the way?

MRS. HIGGINS [*Rising and making her sit down again*] No, no. You couldnt have come more fortunately: we want you to meet a friend of ours.

HIGGINS [*turning hopefully*] Yes, by George! We want two or three people. You'll do as well as anybody else.

[*The parlor-maid returns, ushering* FREDDY].

THE PARLOR-MAID. Mr. Eynsford Hill.

HIGGINS [*almost audibly, past endurance*] God of Heaven! another of them.

FREDDY [*shaking hands with* MRS. HIGGINS] Ahdedo?

MRS. HIGGINS. Very good of you to come. [*Introducing*] Colonel Pickering.

FREDDY [*bowing*] Ahdedo?

MRS. HIGGINS. I dont think you know my son, Professor Higgins.

FREDDY [*going to* HIGGINS] Ahdedo?

HIGGINS [*looking at him much as if he were a pickpocket*] I'll take my oath Ive met you before somewhere. Where was it?

FREDDY. I dont think so.

HIGGINS [*resignedly*] It dont matter, anyhow. Sit down.

[*He shakes* FREDDY'S *hand, and almost slings him on to the ottoman with his face to the window; then comes round to the other side of it*].

HIGGINS. Well, here we are, anyhow! [*He sits down on the ottoman next* MRS. EYNSFORD HILL, *on her left*]

And now, what the devil are we going to talk about until Eliza comes?

MRS. HIGGINS. Henry: you are the life and soul of the Royal Society's soirées; but really youre rather trying on more commonplace occasions.

HIGGINS. Am I? Very sorry. [*Beaming suddenly*] I suppose I am, you know. [*Uproariously*] Ha, ha!

MISS EYNSFORD HILL [*who considers* HIGGINS *quite eligible matrimonially*] I sympathize. *I* havnt any small talk. If people would only be frank and say what they really think!

HIGGINS [*relapsing into gloom*] Lord forbid!

MRS. EYNSFORD HILL [*taking up her daughter's cue*] But why?

HIGGINS. What they think they ought to think is bad enough, Lord knows; but what they really think would break up the whole show. Do you suppose it would be really agreeable if I were to come out now with what *I* really think?

MISS EYNSFORD HILL [*gaily*] Is it so very cynical?

HIGGINS. Cynical! Who the dickens said it was cynical? I mean it wouldnt be decent.

MRS. EYNSFORD HILL [*seriously*] Oh! I'm sure you dont mean that, Mr. Higgins.

HIGGINS. You see, we're all savages, more or less. We're supposed to be civilized and cultured—to know all about poetry and philosophy and art and science, and so on; but how many of us know even the meanings of these names? [*To* MISS HILL] What do you know of poetry? [*To* MRS. HILL] What do you know of science? [*Indicating* FREDDY] What does he know of art or science or anything else? What the devil do you imagine I know of philosophy?

MRS. HIGGINS [*warningly*] Or of manners, Henry?

THE PARLOR-MAID [*opening the door*] Miss Doolittle. [*She withdraws*].

HIGGINS [*rising hastily and running to* MRS. HIGGINS] Here she is, mother. [*He stands on tiptoe and makes signs over his mother's head to* ELIZA *to indicate to her which lady is her hostess*].

[ELIZA, *who is exquisitely dressed, produces an impression of such remarkable distinction and beauty as she enters that they all rise, quite fluttered. Guided by* HIGGINS'S *signals, she comes to* MRS. HIGGINS *with studied grace*].

LIZA [*speaking with pedantic correctness of pronunciation and great beauty of tone*] How do you do, Mrs. Higgins? [*She gasps slightly in making sure of the H in* HIGGINS, *but is quite successful*]. Mr. Higgins told me I might come.

MRS. HIGGINS [*cordially*] Quite right: I'm very glad indeed to see you.

PICKERING. How do you do, Miss Doolittle?

LIZA [*shaking hands with him*] Colonel Pickering, is it not?

MRS. EYNSFORD HILL. I feel sure we have met before, Miss Doolittle. I remember your eyes.

LIZA. How do you do? [*She sits down on the ottoman gracefully in the place just left vacant by* HIGGINS].

MRS. EYNSFORD HILL [*introducing*] My daughter Clara.

LIZA. How do you do?

CLARA [*impulsively*] How do you do? [*She sits down on the ottoman beside* ELIZA, *devouring her with her eyes*].

FREDDY [*coming to their side of the ottoman*] Ive certainly had the pleasure.

MRS. EYNSFORD HILL [*introducing*] My son Freddy.

LIZA. How do you do?

[FREDDY *bows and sits down in the Elizabethan chair, infatuated*].

HIGGINS [*suddenly*] By George, yes: it all comes back to me! [*They stare at him*]. Covent Garden! [*Lamentably*] What a damned thing!

MRS. HIGGINS. Henry, please! [*He is about to sit on the edge of the table*] Dont sit on my writing-table: youll break it.

HIGGINS [*sulkily*] Sorry.

[*He goes to the divan, stumbling into the fender and over the fire-irons on his way; extricating himself with muttered imprecations; and finishing his disastrous journey by throwing himself so impatiently on the divan that he almost breaks it.* MRS. HIGGINS *looks at him, but controls herself and says nothing*].

[*A long and painful pause ensues*].

MRS. HIGGINS [*at last, conversationally*] Will it rain, do you think?

LIZA. The shallow depression in the west of these islands is likely to move slowly in an easterly direction. There are no indications of any great change in the barometrical situation.

FREDDY. Ha! ha! how awfully funny!

LIZA. What is wrong with that, young man? I bet I got it right.

FREDDY. Killing!

MRS. EYNSFORD HILL. I'm sure I hope it wont turn cold. Theres so much influenza about. It runs right through our whole family regularly every spring.

LIZA [*darkly*] My aunt died of influenza: so they said.

MRS. EYNSFORD HILL [*clicks her tongue sympathetically*]!!!

LIZA [*in the same tragic tone*] But it's my belief they done the old woman in.

MRS. HIGGINS [*puzzled*] Done her in?

LIZA. Y-e-e-e-es, Lord love you! Why should she die of influenza? She come through diphtheria right enough the year before. I saw her with my own eyes.

Fairly blue with it, she was. They all thought she was dead; but my father he kept ladling gin down her throat til she came to so sudden that she bit the bowl off the spoon.

MRS. EYNSFORD HILL [*startled*] Dear me!

LIZA [*piling up the indictment*] What call would a woman with that strength in her have to die of influenza? What become of her new straw hat that should have come to me? Somebody pinched it; and what I say is, them as pinched it done her in.

MRS. EYNSFORD HILL. What does doing her in mean?

HIGGINS [*hastily*] Oh, thats the new small talk. To do a person in means to kill them.

MRS. EYNSFORD HILL [*to* ELIZA, *horrified*] You surely dont believe that your aunt was killed?

LIZA. Do I not! Them she lived with would have killed her for a hat-pin, let alone a hat.

MRS. EYNSFORD HILL. But it cant have been right for your father to pour spirits down her throat like that. It might have killed her.

LIZA. Not her. Gin was mother's milk to her. Besides, he'd poured so much down his own throat that he knew the good of it.

MRS. EYNSFORD HILL. Do you mean that he drank?

LIZA. Drank! My word! Something chronic.

MRS. EYNSFORD HILL. How dreadful for you!

LIZA. Not a bit. It never did him no harm what I could see. But then he did not keep it up regular. [*Cheerfully*] On the burst, as you might say, from time to time. And always more agreeable when he had a drop in. When he was out of work, my mother used to give him fourpence and tell him to go out and not come back until he'd drunk himself cheerful and loving-like. Theres lots of women has to make their husbands drunk to make them fit to live with. [*Now quite at her ease*] You see, it's like this. If a man has a bit of conscience, it always takes him when he's sober; and then it makes him low-spirited. A drop of booze just takes that off and makes him happy. [*To* FREDDY, *who is in convulsions of suppressed laughter*] Here! What are you sniggering at?

FREDDY. The new small talk. You do it so awfully well.

LIZA. If I was doing it proper, what was you laughing at? [*To* HIGGINS] Have I said anything I oughtnt?

MRS. HIGGINS [*interposing*] Not at all, Miss Doolittle.

LIZA. Well, thats a mercy, anyhow. [*Expansively*] What I always say is—

HIGGINS [*rising and looking at his watch*] Ahem!

LIZA [*looking round at him; taking the hint; and rising*] Well: I must go. [*They all rise.* FREDDY *goes to the door*]. So pleased to have met you. Goodbye. [*She shakes hands with* MRS. HIGGINS].

MRS. HIGGINS. Goodbye.

LIZA. Goodbye, Colonel Pickering.

PICKERING. Goodbye, Miss Doolittle. [*They shake hands*].

LIZA [*nodding to the others*] Goodbye, all.

FREDDY [*opening the door for her*] Are you walking across the Park, Miss Doolittle? If so—

LIZA [*with perfectly elegant diction*] Walk! Not bloody likely. [*Sensation*]. I am going in a taxi. [*She goes out*].

[PICKERING *gasps and sits down.* FREDDY *goes out on the balcony to catch another glimpse of* ELIZA].

MRS. EYNSFORD HILL [*suffering from shock*] Well, I really cant get used to the new ways.

CLARA [*throwing herself discontentedly into the Elizabethan chair*] Oh, it's all right, mamma, quite right. People will think we never go anywhere or see anybody if you are so old-fashioned.

MRS. EYNSFORD HILL. I daresay I am very old-fashioned; but I do hope you wont begin using that expression, Clara. I have got accustomed to hear you talking about men as rotters, and calling everything filthy and beastly; though I do think it horrible and unladylike. But this last is really too much. Dont you think so, Colonel Pickering?

PICKERING. Dont ask me. Ive been away in India for several years; and manners have changed so much that I sometimes dont know whether I'm at a respectable dinnertable or in a ship's forecastle.

CLARA. It's all a matter of habit. Theres no right or wrong in it. Nobody means anything by it. And it's so quaint, and gives such a smart emphasis to things that are not in themselves very witty. I find the new small talk delightful and quite innocent.

MRS. EYNSFORD HILL [*rising*] Well, after that, I think it's time for us to go.

[PICKERING *and* HIGGINS *rise*].

CLARA [*rising*] Oh yes: we have three at-homes to go to still. Goodbye, Mrs. Higgins. Goodbye, Colonel Pickering. Goodbye, Professor Higgins.

HIGGINS [*coming grimly at her from the divan, and accompanying her to the door*] Goodbye. Be sure you try on that small talk at the three at-homes. Dont be nervous about it. Pitch it in strong.

CLARA [*all smiles*] I will. Goodbye. Such nonsense, all this early Victorian prudery!

HIGGINS [*tempting her*] Such damned nonsense!

CLARA. Such bloody nonsense!

MRS. EYNSFORD HILL [*convulsively*] Clara!

CLARA. Ha! ha! [*She goes out radiant, conscious of being thoroughly up to date, and is heard descending the stairs in a stream of silvery laughter*].

FREDDY [*to the heavens at large*] Well, I ask you—

[*He gives it up, and comes to* MRS. HIGGINS]. Goodbye.

MRS. HIGGINS [*shaking hands*] Goodbye. Would you like to meet Miss Doolittle again?

FREDDY [*eagerly*] Yes, I should, most awfully.

MRS. HIGGINS. Well, you know my days.

FREDDY. Yes, Thanks awfully. Goodbye. [*He goes out*].

MRS. EYNSFORD HILL. Goodbye, Mr. Higgins.

HIGGINS. Goodbye. Goodbye.

MRS. EYNSFORD HILL [*to* PICKERING] It's no use. I shall never be able to bring myself to use that word.

PICKERING. Dont. It's not compulsory, you know. Youll get on quite well without it.

MRS. EYNSFORD HILL. Only, Clara is so down on me if I am not positively reeking with the latest slang. Goodbye.

PICKERING. Goodbye [*They shake hands*].

MRS. EYNSFORD HILL [*to* MRS. HIGGINS] You mustnt mind Clara. [PICKERING, *catching from her lowered tone that this is not meant for him to hear, discreetly joins* HIGGINS *at the window*]. We're so poor! and she gets so few parties, poor child! She doesnt quite know. [MRS. HIGGINS, *seeing that her eyes are moist, takes her hand sympathetically and goes with her to the door*]. But the boy is nice. Dont you think so?

MRS. HIGGINS. Oh, quite nice. I shall always be delighted to see him.

MRS. EYNSFORD HILL. Thank you, dear. Goodbye. [*She goes out*].

HIGGINS [*eagerly*] Well? Is Eliza presentable [*he swoops on his mother and drags her to the ottoman, where she sits down in* ELIZA's *place with her son on her left*]?

[PICKERING *returns to his chair on her right*].

MRS. HIGGINS. You silly boy, of course she's not presentable. She's a triumph of your art and of her dressmaker's; but if you suppose for a moment that she doesn't give herself away in every sentence she utters, you must be perfectly cracked about her.

PICKERING. But dont you think something might be done? I mean something to eliminate the sanguinary element from her conversation.

MRS. HIGGINS. Not as long as she is in Henry's hands.

HIGGINS [*aggrieved*] Do you mean that my language is improper?

MRS. HIGGINS. No, dearest: it would be quite proper —say on a canal barge; but it would not be proper for her at a garden party.

HIGGINS [*deeply injured*] Well I must say—

PICKERING [*interrupting him*] Come, Higgins: you must learn to know yourself. I havent heard such language as yours since we used to review the volunteers in Hyde Park twenty years ago.

HIGGINS [*sulkily*] Oh, well, if you say so, I suppose I dont always talk like a bishop.

MRS. HIGGINS [*quieting* HENRY *with a touch*] Colonel Pickering: will you tell me what is the exact state of things in Wimpole Street?

PICKERING [*cheerfully: as if this completely changed the subject*] Well, I have come to live there with Henry. We work together at my Indian Dialects; and we think it more convenient—

MRS. HIGGINS. Quite so. I know all about that: it's an excellent arrangement. But where does this girl live?

HIGGINS. With us, of course. Where should she live?

MRS. HIGGINS. But on what terms? Is she a servant? If not, what is she?

PICKERING [*slowly*] I think I know what you mean, Mrs. Higgins.

HIGGINS. Well, dash me if *I* do! Ive had to work at the girl every day for months to get her to her present pitch. Besides, she's useful. She knows where my things are, and remembers my appointments and so forth.

MRS. HIGGINS. How does your housekeeper get on with her?

HIGGINS. Mrs. Pearce? Oh, she's jolly glad to get so much taken off her hands; for before Eliza came, she used to have to find things and remind me of my appointments. But she's got some silly bee in her bonnet about Eliza. She keeps saying "You dont think, sir": doesnt she, Pick?

PICKERING. Yes: thats the formula. "You dont think, sir." Thats the end of every conversation about Eliza.

HIGGINS. As if I ever stop thinking about the girl and her confounded vowels and consonants. I'm worn out, thinking about her, and watching her lips and her teeth and her tongue, not to mention her soul, which is the quaintest of the lot.

MRS. HIGGINS. You certainly are a pretty pair of babies, playing with your live doll.

HIGGINS. Playing! The hardest job I ever tackled: make no mistake about that, mother. But you have no idea how frightfully interesting it is to take a human being and change her into a quite different human being by creating a new speech for her. It's filling up the deepest gulf that separates class from class and soul from soul.

PICKERING [*drawing his chair closer to* MRS. HIGGINS *and bending over to her eagerly*] Yes: it's enormously interesting. I assure you, Mrs. Higgins, we take Eliza very seriously. Every week—every day almost—there is some new change. [*Closer again*] We keep records of every stage—dozens of gramophone disks and photographs—

HIGGINS [*assailing her at the other ear*] Yes, by

George: it's the most absorbing experiment I ever tackled. She regularly fills our lives up: doesnt she, Pick?

PICKERING. We're always talking Eliza.

HIGGINS. Teaching Eliza.

PICKERING. Dressing Eliza.

MRS. HIGGINS. What!

HIGGINS. Inventing new Elizas.

HIGGINS.		
	[*speaking together*]	You know, she has the most extraordinary quickness of ear:
PICKERING.		I assure you, my dear Mrs. Higgins, that girl
HIGGINS.		just like a parrot. Ive tried her with every
PICKERING.		is a genius. She can play the piano quite beautifully.
HIGGINS.		possible sort of sound that a human being can make—
PICKERING.		We have taken her to classical concerts and to music
HIGGINS.		Continental dialects, African dialects, Hottentot
PICKERING.		halls; and it's all the same to her: she plays everything
HIGGINS.		clicks, things it took me years to get hold of; and
PICKERING.		she hears right off when she comes home, whether it's
HIGGINS.		she picks them up like a shot, right away, as if she had
PICKERING.		Beethoven and Brahms or Lehar and Lionel Monckton;
HIGGINS.		been at it all her life.
PICKERING.		though six months ago, she'd never as much as touched a piano—

MRS. HIGGINS [*putting her fingers in her ears, as they are by this time shouting one another down with an intolerable noise*] Sh-sh-sh—sh! [*They stop*].

PICKERING. I beg your pardon. [*He draws his chair back apologetically*].

HIGGINS. Sorry. When Pickering starts shouting nobody can get a word in edgeways.

MRS. HIGGINS. Be quiet, Henry. Colonel Pickering: dont you realize that when Eliza walked in Wimpole Street, something walked in with her?

PICKERING. Her father did. But Henry soon got rid of him.

MRS. HIGGINS. It would have been more to the point if her mother had. But as her mother didnt something else did.

PICKERING. But what?

MRS. HIGGINS [*unconsciously dating herself by the word*] A problem.

PICKERING. Oh, I see. The problem of how to pass her off as a lady.

HIGGINS. I'll solve that problem. Ive half solved it already.

MRS. HIGGINS. No, you two infinitely stupid male creatures: the problem of what is to be done with her afterwards.

HIGGINS. I dont see anything in that. She can go her own way, with all the advantages I have given her.

MRS. HIGGINS. The advantages of that poor woman who was here just now! The manners and habits that disqualify a fine lady from earning her own living without giving her a fine lady's income! Is that what you mean?

PICKERING [*indulgently, being rather bored*] Oh, that will be all right, Mrs. Higgins. [*He rises to go*].

HIGGINS [*rising also*] We'll find her some light employment.

PICKERING. She's happy enough. Dont you worry about her. Goodbye. [*He shakes hands as if he were consoling a frightened child, and makes for the door*].

HIGGINS. Anyhow, theres no good bothering now. The thing's done. Goodbye, mother. [*He kisses her, and follows* PICKERING].

PICKERING [*turning for a final consolation*] There are plenty of openings. We'll do whats right. Goodbye.

HIGGINS [*to* PICKERING *as they go out together*] Lets take her to the Shakespear exhibition at Earls Court.

PICKERING. Yes: lets. Her remarks will be delicious.

HIGGINS. She'll mimic all the people for us when we get home.

PICKERING. Ripping. [*Both are heard laughing as they go downstairs*].

MRS. HIGGINS [*rises with an impatient bounce, and returns to her work at the writing-table. She sweeps a litter of disarranged papers out of the way; snatches a sheet of paper from her stationery case; and tries resolutely to write. At the third time she gives it up;*

flings down her pen; grips the table angrily and exclaims] Oh, men! men!! men!!!

* * * * *

Clearly Eliza will not pass as a duchess yet; and Higgins's bet remains unwon. But the six months are not yet exhausted; and just in time Eliza does actually pass as a princess. For a glimpse of how she did it imagine an Embassy in London one summer evening after dark. The hall door has an awning and a carpet across the sidewalk to the kerb, because a grand reception is in progress. A small crowd is lined up to see the guests arrive.

A Rolls-Royce car drives up. Pickering in evening dress, with medals and orders, alights, and hands out Eliza, in opera cloak, evening dress, diamonds, fan, flowers and all accessories. Higgins follows. The car drives off; and the three go up the steps and into the house, the door opening for them as they approach.

Inside the house they find themselves in a spacious hall from which the grand staircase rises. On the left are the arrangements for the gentlemen's cloaks. The male guests are depositing their hats and wraps there.

On the right is a door leading to the ladies' cloakroom. Ladies are going in cloaked and coming out in splendor. Pickering whispers to Eliza and points out the ladies' room. She goes into it. Higgins and Pickering take off their overcoats and take tickets for them from the attendant.

One of the guests, occupied in the same way, has his back turned. Having taken his ticket, he turns round and reveals himself as an important looking young man with an astonishingly hairy face. He has an enormous moustache, flowing out into luxuriant whiskers. Waves of hair cluster on his brow. His hair is cropped closely at the back, and glows with oil. Otherwise he is very smart. He wears several worthless orders. He is evidently a foreigner, guessable as a whiskered Pandour from Hungary; but in spite of the ferocity of his moustache he is amiable and genially voluble.

Recognizing Higgins, he flings his arms wide apart and approaches him enthusiastically.

WHISKERS. Maestro, maestro [*he embraces* HIGGINS *and kisses him on both cheeks*]. You remember me?

HIGGINS. No I dont. Who the devil are you?

WHISKERS. I am your pupil: your first pupil, your best and greatest pupil. I am little Nepommuck, the marvellous boy. I have made your name famous throughout Europe. You teach me phonetic. You cannot forget ME.

HIGGINS. Why dont you shave?

NEPOMMUCK. I have not your imposing appearance, your chin, your brow. Nobody notice me when I shave. Now I am famous: they call me Hairy Faced Dick.

HIGGINS. And what are you doing here among all these swells?

NEPOMMUCK. I am interpreter. I speak 32 languages. I am indispensable at these international parties. You are great cockney specialist: you place a man anywhere in London the moment he open his mouth. I place any man in Europe.

[*A footman hurries down the grand staircase and comes to* NEPOMMUCK].

FOOTMAN. You are wanted upstairs. Her Excellency cannot understand the Greek gentleman.

NEPOMMUCK. Thank you, yes, immediately.

[*The footman goes and is lost in the crowd*].

NEPOMMUCK [*to* HIGGINS] This Greek diplomatist pretends he cannot speak nor understand English. He cannot deceive me. He is the son of a Clerkenwell watchmaker. He speaks English so villainously that he dare not utter a word of it without betraying his origin. I help him to pretend; but I make him pay through the nose. I make them all pay. Ha ha! [*He hurries upstairs*].

PICKERING. Is this fellow really an expert? Can he find out Eliza and blackmail her?

HIGGINS. We shall see. If he finds her out I lose my bet.

[ELIZA *comes from the cloakroom and joins them*].

PICKERING. Well, Eliza, now for it. Are you ready?

LIZA. Are you nervous, Colonel?

PICKERING. Frightfully. I feel exactly as I felt before my first battle. It's the first time that frightens.

LIZA. It is not the first time for me, Colonel. I have done this fifty times—hundreds of times—in my little piggery in Angel Court in my day-dreams. I am in a dream now. Promise me not to let Professor Higgins wake me; for if he does I shall forget everything and talk as I used to in Drury Lane.

PICKERING. Not a word, Higgins. [*To* ELIZA] Now, ready?

LIZA. Ready.

PICKERING. Go.

[*They mount the stairs,* HIGGINS *last.* PICKERING *whispers to the footman on the first landing*].

FIRST LANDING FOOTMAN. Miss Doolittle, Colonel Pickering, Professor Higgins.

SECOND LANDING FOOTMAN. Miss Doolittle, Colonel Pickering, Professor Higgins.

[*At the top of the staircase the Ambassador and his wife, with* NEPOMMUCK *at her elbow, are receiving*].

HOSTESS [*taking* ELIZA's *hand*] How d'ye do?

HOST [*same play*] How d'ye do? How d'ye do, Pickering?

LIZA [*with a beautiful gravity that awes her hostess*] How do you do? [*She passes on to the drawing-room*].

HOSTESS. Is that your adopted daughter, Colonel Pickering? She will make a sensation.

PICKERING. Most kind of you to invite her for me. [*He passes on*].

HOSTESS [*to* NEPOMMUCK] Find out all about her.

NEPOMMUCK [*bowing*] Excellency—[*he goes into the crowd*].

HOST. How d'ye do, Higgins? You have a rival here tonight. He introduced himself as your pupil. Is he any good?

HIGGINS. He can learn a language in a fortnight—knows dozens of them. A sure mark of a fool. As a phonetician, no good whatever.

HOSTESS. How d'ye do, Professor?

HIGGINS. How do you do? Fearful bore for you this sort of thing. Forgive my part in it. [*He passes on*].

In the drawingroom and its suite of salons the reception is in full swing. Eliza passes through. She is so intent on her ordeal that she walks like a somnambulist in a desert instead of a débutante in a fashionable crowd. They stop talking to look at her, admiring her dress, her jewels, and her strangely attractive self. Some of the younger ones at the back stand on their chairs to see.

The Host and Hostess come in from the staircase and mingle with their guests. Higgins, gloomy and contemptuous of the whole business, comes into the group where they are chatting.

HOSTESS. Ah, here is Professor Higgins: he will tell us. Tell us all about the wonderful young lady, Professor.

HIGGINS [*almost morosely*] What wonderful young lady?

HOSTESS. You know very well. They tell me there has been nothing like her in London since people stood on their chairs to look at Mrs. Langtry.

[NEPOMMUCK *joins the group, full of news*].

HOSTESS. Ah, here you are at last, Nepommuck. Have you found out all about the Doolittle lady?

NEPOMMUCK. I have found out all about her. She is a fraud.

HOSTESS. A fraud! Oh no.

NEPOMMUCK. YES, yes. She cannot deceive me. Her name cannot be Doolittle.

HIGGINS. Why?

NEPOMMUCK. Because Doolittle is an English name. And she is not English.

HOSTESS. Oh, nonsense! She speaks English perfectly.

NEPOMMUCK. Too perfectly. Can you shew me any English woman who speaks English as it should be spoken? Only foreigners who have been taught to speak it speak it well.

HOSTESS. Certainly she terrified me by the way she said How d'ye do. I had a schoolmistress who talked like that; and I was mortally afraid of her. But if she is not English what is she?

NEPOMMUCK. Hungarian.

ALL THE REST. Hungarian!

NEPOMMUCK. Hungarian. And of royal blood. I am Hungarian. My blood is royal.

HIGGINS. Did you speak to her in Hungarian?

NEPOMMUCK. I did. She was very clever. She said "Please speak to me in English: I do not understand French." French! She pretend not to know the difference between Hungarian and French. Impossible: she knows both.

HIGGINS. And the blood royal? How did you find that out?

NEPOMMUCK. Instinct, maestro, instinct. Only the Magyar races can produce that air of the divine right, those resolute eyes. She is a princess.

HOST. What do you say, Professor?

HIGGINS. I say an ordinary London girl out of the gutter and taught to speak by an expert. I place her in Drury Lane.

NEPOMMUCK. Ha ha ha! Oh, maestro, maestro, you are mad on the subject of cockney dialects. The London gutter is the whole world for you.

HIGGINS [*to the Hostess*] What does your Excellency say?

HOSTESS. Oh, of course I agree with Nepommuck. She must be a princess at least.

HOST. Not necessarily legitimate, of course. Morganatic perhaps. But that is undoubtedly her class.

HIGGINS. I stick to my opinion.

HOSTESS. Oh, you are incorrigible.

[*The group breaks up, leaving* HIGGINS *isolated.* PICKERING *joins him*].

PICKERING. Where is Eliza? We must keep an eye on her.

[ELIZA *joins them*].

LIZA. I dont think I can bear much more. The people all stare so at me. An old lady has just told me that I speak exactly like Queen Victoria. I am sorry if I have lost your bet. I have done my best; but nothing can make me the same as these people.

PICKERING. You have not lost it, my dear. You have won it ten times over.

HIGGINS. Let us get out of this. I have had enough of chattering to these fools.

PICKERING. Eliza is tired; and I am hungry. Let us clear out and have supper somewhere.

ACT IV

The Wimpole Street laboratory. Midnight. Nobody in the room. The clock on the mantelpiece strikes twelve. The fire is not alight: it is a summer night.

Presently HIGGINS *and* PICKERING *are heard on the stairs.*

HIGGINS [*calling down to* PICKERING] I say, Pick: lock up, will you? I shant be going out again.

PICKERING. Right. Can Mrs. Pearce go to bed? We dont want anything more, do we?

HIGGINS. Lord, no!

[ELIZA *opens the door and is seen on the lighted landing in all the finery in which she has just won* HIGGINS's *bet for him. She comes to the hearth, and switches on the electric lights there. She is tired: her pallor contrasts strongly with her dark eyes and hair; and her expression is almost tragic. She takes off her cloak; puts her fan and gloves on the piano; and sits down on the bench, brooding and silent.* HIGGINS, *in evening dress, with overcoat and hat, comes in, carrying a smoking jacket which he has picked up downstairs. He takes off the hat and overcoat; throws them carelessly on the newspaper stand; disposes of his coat in the same way; puts on the smoking jacket; and throws himself wearily into the easy-chair at the hearth.* PICKERING, *similarly attired, comes in. He also takes off his hat and overcoat, and is about to throw them on* HIGGINS's *when he hesitates*].

PICKERING. I say: Mrs. Pearce will row if we leave these things lying about in the drawing room.

HIGGINS. Oh, chuck them over the bannisters into the hall. She'll find them there in the morning and put them away all right. She'll think we were drunk.

PICKERING. We are, slightly. Are there any letters?

HIGGINS. I didnt look. [PICKERING *takes the overcoats and hats and goes downstairs.* HIGGINS *begins half singing half yawning an air from* La Fanciulla del Golden West. *Suddenly he stops and exclaims*] I wonder where the devil my slippers are!

[ELIZA *looks at him darkly; then rises suddenly and leaves the room.*

HIGGINS *yawns again, and resumes his song.*

PICKERING *returns, with the contents of the letter-box in his hand*].

PICKERING. Only circulars, and this coroneted billet-doux for you. [*He throws the circulars into the fender, and posts himself on the hearth-rug, with his back to the grate*].

HIGGINS [*glancing at the billet-doux*] Money-lender. [*He throws the letter after the circulars*].

[ELIZA *returns with a pair of large down-at-heel slippers. She places them on the carpet before* HIGGINS, *and sits as before without a word*].

HIGGINS [*yawning again*] Oh Lord! What an evening! What a crew! What a silly tomfoolery! [*He raises his shoe to unlace it, and catches sight of the slippers. He stops unlacing and looks at them as if they had appeared there of their own accord*]. Oh! theyre there, are they?

PICKERING [*stretching himself*] Well, I feel a bit tired. It's been a long day. The garden party, a dinner party, and the reception! Rather too much of a good thing. But youve won your bet, Higgins. Eliza did the trick, and something to spare, eh?

HIGGINS [*fervently*] Thank God it's over!

[ELIZA *flinches violently; but they take no notice of her; and she recovers herself and sits stonily as before*].

PICKERING. Were you nervous at the garden party? I was. Eliza didnt seem a bit nervous.

HIGGINS. Oh, she wasnt nervous. I knew she'd be all right. No: it's the strain of putting the job through all these months that has told on me. It was interesting enough at first, while we were at the phonetics; but after that I got deadly sick of it. If I hadnt backed myself to do it I should have chucked the whole thing up two months ago. It was a silly notion: the whole thing has been a bore.

PICKERING. Oh come! the garden party was frightfully exciting. My heart began beating like anything.

HIGGINS. Yes, for the first three minutes. But when I saw we were going to win hands down, I felt like a bear in a cage, hanging about doing nothing. The dinner was worse: sitting gorging there for over an hour, with nobody but a damned fool of a fashionable woman to talk to! I tell you, Pickering, never again for me. No more artificial duchesses. The whole thing has been simple purgatory.

PICKERING. Youve never been broken in properly to the social routine. [*Strolling over to the piano*] I rather enjoy dipping into it occasionally myself: it makes me feel young again. Anyhow, it was a great success: an immense success. I was quite frightened once or twice because Eliza was doing it so well. You see, lots of the real people cant do it at all: theyre such fools that they think style comes by nature to people in their position; and so they never learn. Theres always something professional about doing a thing superlatively well.

HIGGINS. Yes: thats what drives me mad: the silly people dont know their own silly business. [*Rising*] However, it's over and done with; and now I can go to bed at last without dreading tomorrow.

[ELIZA's *beauty becomes murderous*].

PICKERING. I think I shall turn in too. Still, it's been

a great occasion: a triumph for you. Goodnight. [*He goes*].

HIGGINS [*following him*] Goodnight. [*Over his shoulder, at the door*] Put out the lights, Eliza; and tell Mrs. Pearce not to make coffee for me in the morning: I'll take tea. [*He goes out*].

[ELIZA *tries to control herself and feel indifferent as she rises and walks across to the hearth to switch off the lights. By the time she gets there she is on the point of screaming. She sits down in* HIGGINS's *chair and holds on hard to the arms. Finally she gives way and flings herself furiously on the floor, raging*].

HIGGINS [*in despairing wrath outside*] What the devil have I done with my slippers? [*He appears at the door*].

LIZA [*snatching up the slippers, and hurling them at him one after the other with all her force*] There are your slippers. And there. Take your slippers; and may you never have a day's luck with them!

HIGGINS [*astounded*] What on earth—! [*He comes to her*]. Whats the matter? Get up. [*He pulls her up*]. Anything wrong?

LIZA [*breathless*] Nothing wrong—with you. Ive won your bet for you, havnt I? Thats enough for you. *I* dont matter, I suppose.

HIGGINS. You won my bet! You! Presumptuous insect! *I* won it. What did you throw those slippers at me for?

LIZA. Because I wanted to smash your face. I'd like to kill you, you selfish brute. Why didnt you leave me where you picked me out of—in the gutter? You thank God it's all over, and that now you can throw me back again there, do you? [*She crisps her fingers frantically*].

HIGGINS [*looking at her in cool wonder*] The creature is nervous, after all.

LIZA [*gives a suffocated scream of fury, and instinctively darts her nails at his face*]!!

HIGGINS [*catching her wrists*] Ah! would you? Claws in, you cat. How dare you shew your temper to me? Sit down and be quiet. [*He throws her roughly into the easy-chair*].

LIZA [*crushed by superior strength and weight*] Whats to become of me? Whats to become of me?

HIGGINS. How the devil do I know whats to become of you? What does it matter what becomes of you?

LIZA. You dont care. I know you dont care. You wouldnt care if I was dead. I'm nothing to you—not so much as them slippers.

HIGGINS [*thundering*] Those slippers.

LIZA [*with bitter submission*] Those slippers. I didnt think it made any difference now.

[*A pause.* ELIZA *hopeless and crushed.* HIGGINS *a little uneasy.*]

HIGGINS [*in his loftiest manner*] Why have you begun going on like this? May I ask whether you complain of your treatment here?

LIZA. No.

HIGGINS. Has anybody behaved badly to you? Colonel Pickering? Mrs. Pearce? Any of the servants?

LIZA. No.

HIGGINS. I presume you dont pretend that *I* have treated you badly?

LIZA. No.

HIGGINS. I am glad to hear it. [*He moderates his tone*]. Perhaps youre tired after the strain of the day. Will you have a glass of champagne? [*He moves towards the door*].

LIZA. No. [*Recollecting her manners*] Thank you.

HIGGINS [*good-humored again*] This has been coming on you for some days. I suppose it was natural for you to be anxious about the garden party. But thats all over now. [*He pats her kindly on the shoulder. She writhes*]. Theres nothing more to worry about.

LIZA. No. Nothing more for you to worry about. [*She suddenly rises and gets away from him by going to the piano bench, where she sits and hides her face.*] Oh God! I wish I was dead.

HIGGINS [*staring after her in sincere surprise*] Why? In heaven's name, why? [*Reasonably, going to her*] Listen to me, Eliza. All this irritation is purely subjective.

LIZA. I dont understand. I'm too ignorant.

HIGGINS. It's only imagination. Low spirits and nothing else. Nobody's hurting you. Nothing's wrong. You go to bed like a good girl and sleep it off. Have a little cry and say your prayers: that will make you comfortable.

LIZA. I heard your prayers. "Thank God it's all over!"

HIGGINS [*impatiently*] Well, dont you thank God it's all over? Now you are free and can do what you like.

LIZA [*pulling herself together in desperation*] What am I fit for? What have you left me fit for? Where am I to go? What am I to do? Whats to become of me?

HIGGINS [*enlightened, but not at all impressed*] Oh, thats whats worrying you, is it? [*He thrusts his hands into his pockets, and walks about in his usual manner, rattling the contents of his pockets, as if condescending to a trivial subject out of pure kindness*]. I shouldnt bother about it if I were you. I should imagine you wont have much difficulty in settling yourself somewhere or other, though I hadnt quite realized that you were going away. [*She looks quickly at him: he does not look at her, but examines the dessert stand on the piano and decides that he will eat an apple*]. You might marry, you know. [*He *bites a large piece out of the apple and munches it noisily*]. You see, Eliza, all men are not confirmed old bachelors like me and the Colonel. Most men are the marrying sort (poor devils!); and youre not bad-looking: it's quite a pleasure to look at you sometimes—not now, of course, because youre crying and looking as ugly as the very devil; but when youre all right and quite yourself, youre what I should call attractive. That is, to the people in the marrying line, you understand. You go to bed and have a good nice rest; and then get up and look at yourself in the glass; and you wont feel so cheap.

> [ELIZA *again looks at him, speechless, and does not stir.*
>
> *The look is quite lost on him: he eats his apple with a dreamy expression of happiness, as it is quite a good one*].

HIGGINS [*a genial afterthought occurring to him*] I daresay my mother could find some chap or other who would do very well.

LIZA. We were above that at the corner of Tottenham Court Road.

HIGGINS [*waking up*] What do you mean?

LIZA. I sold flowers. I didnt sell myself. Now youve made a lady of me I'm not fit to sell anything else. I wish youd left me where you found me.

HIGGINS [*slinging the core of the apple decisively into the grate*] Tosh, Eliza. Dont you insult human relations by dragging all this cant about buying and selling into it. You neednt marry the fellow if you dont like him.

LIZA. What else am I to do?

HIGGINS. Oh, lots of thing. What about your old idea of a florist's shop? Pickering could set you up in one: he has lots of money. [*Chuckling*] He'll have to pay for all those togs you have been wearing today; and that, with the hire of the jewellery, will make a big hole in two hundred pounds. Why, six months ago you would have thought it the millennium to have a flower shop of your own. Come! youll be all right. I must clear off to bed: I'm devilish sleepy. By the way, I came down for something: I forget what it was.

LIZA. Your slippers.

HIGGINS. Oh yes, of course. You shied them at me. [*He picks them up, and is going out when she rises and speaks to him*].

LIZA. Before you go, sir—

HIGGINS [*dropping the slippers in his surprise at her calling him Sir*] Eh?

LIZA. Do my clothes belong to me or to Colonel Pickering?

HIGGINS [*coming back into the room as if her question were the very climax of unreason*] What the devi', use would they be to Pickering?

LIZA. He might want them for the next girl you pick up to experiment on.

HIGGINS [*shocked and hurt*] Is that the way you feel towards us?

LIZA. I dont want to hear anything more about that. All I want to know is whether anything belongs to me. My own clothes were burnt.

HIGGINS. But what does it matter? Why need you start bothering about that in the middle of the night?

LIZA. I want to know what I may take away with me. I dont want to be accused of stealing.

HIGGINS [*now deeply wounded*] Stealing! You shouldnt have said that, Eliza. That shews a want of feeling.

LIZA. I'm sorry. I'm only a common ignorant girl; and in my station I have to be careful. There cant be any feelings between the like of you and the like of me. Please will you tell me what belongs to me and what doesnt?

HIGGINS [*very sulky*] You may take the whole damned houseful if you like. Except the jewels. Theyre hired. Will that satisfy you? [*He turns on his heel and is about to go in extreme dudgeon*].

LIZA [*drinking in his emotion like nectar, and nagging him to provoke a further supply*] Stop, please. [*She takes off her jewels*]. Will you take these to your room and keep them safe? I dont want to run the risk of their being missing.

HIGGINS [*furious*] Hand them over. [*She puts them into his hands*]. If these belonged to me instead of to the jeweller, I'd ram them down your ungrateful throat. [*He perfunctorily thrusts them into his pockets, unconsciously decorating himself with the protruding ends of the chains*].

LIZA [*taking a ring off*] This ring isnt the jeweller's: it's the one you bought me in Brighton. I dont want it now. [HIGGINS *dashes the ring violently into the fireplace, and turns on her so threateningly that she crouches over the piano with her hands over her face, and exclaims*] Dont you hit me.

HIGGINS. Hit you! You infamous creature, how dare you accuse me of such a thing? It is you who have hit me. You have wounded me to the heart.

LIZA [*thrilling with hidden joy*] I'm glad. Ive got a little of my own back, anyhow.

HIGGINS [*with dignity, in his finest professional style*] You have caused me to lose my temper: a thing that has hardly ever happened to me before. I prefer to say nothing more tonight. I am going to bed.

LIZA [*pertly*] Youd better leave a note for Mrs. Pearce about the coffee; for she wont be told by me.

HIGGINS [*formally*] Damn Mrs. Pearce; and damn the coffee; and damn you; and [*wildly*] damn my own folly in having lavished my hard-earned knowledge and the treasure of my regard and intimacy on a heartless guttersnipe. [*He goes out with impressive decorum, and spoils it by slamming the door savagely*].

> [ELIZA *goes down on her knees on the hearthrug to look for the ring. When she finds it she considers for a moment what to do with it. Finally she flings it down on the dessert stand and goes upstairs in a tearing rage*].

* * * * *

The furniture of Eliza's room has been increased by a big wardrobe and a sumptuous dressing-table. She comes in and switches on the electric light. She goes to the wardrobe; opens it; and pulls out a walking dress, a hat, and a pair of shoes, which she throws on the bed. She takes off her evening dress and shoes; then takes a padded hanger from the wardrobe; adjusts it carefully in the evening dress; and hangs it in the wardrobe, which she shuts with a slam. She puts on her walking shoes, her walking dress, and hat. She takes her wrist watch from the dressing-table and fastens it on. She pulls on her gloves; takes her vanity bag; and looks into it to see that her purse is there before hanging it on her wrist. She makes for the door. Every movement expresses her furious resolution.

She takes a last look at herself in the glass.

She suddenly puts out her tongue at herself; then leaves the room, switching off the electric light at the door.

Meanwhile, in the street outside, Freddy Eynsford Hill, lovelorn, is gazing up at the second floor, in which one of the windows is still lighted.

FREDDY. Goodnight, darling, darling, darling.

> [ELIZA *comes out, giving the door a considerable bang behind her*].

LIZA. Whatever are you doing here?

FREDDY. Nothing. I spend most of my nights here. It's the only place where I'm happy. Dont laugh at me, Miss Doolittle.

LIZA. Dont you call me Miss Doolittle, do you hear? Liza's good enough for me. [*She breaks down and grabs him by the shoulders*] Freddy: you dont think I'm a heartless guttersnipe, do you?

FREDDY. Oh no, no, darling: how can you imagine such a thing? You are the loveliest, dearest—

> [*He loses all self-control and smothers her with kisses. She, hungry for comfort, responds. They stand there in one another's arms*].
> [*An elderly police constable arrives*].

CONSTABLE [*scandalized*] Now then! Now then!! Now then!!!

> [*They release one another hastily*].

FREDDY. Sorry, constable. Weve only just become engaged.

> [*They run away*].

The constable shakes his head, reflecting on his own courtship and on the vanity of human hopes. He moves off in the opposite direction with slow professional steps.

The flight of the lovers takes them to Cavendish Square. There they halt to consider their next move.

LIZA [*out of breath*] He didnt half give me a fright, that copper. But you answered him proper.

FREDDY. I hope I havent taken you out of your way. Where were you going?

LIZA. To the river.

FREDDY. What for?

LIZA. To make a hole in it.

FREDDY [*horrified*] Eliza, darling. What do you mean? What's the matter?

LIZA. Never mind. It doesnt matter now. There's nobody in the world now but you and me, is there?

FREDDY. Not a soul.

> [*They indulge in another embrace, and are again surprised by a much younger constable*].

SECOND CONSTABLE. Now then, you two! What's this? Where do you think you are? Move along here, double quick.

FREDDY. As you say, sir, double quick.

They run away again, and are in Hanover Square before they stop for another conference.

FREDDY. I had no idea the police were so devilishly prudish.

LIZA. It's their business to hunt girls off the streets.

FREDDY. We must go somewhere. We cant wander about the streets all night.

LIZA. Cant we? I think it'd be lovely to wander about for ever.

FREDDY. Oh, darling.

> [*They embrace again, oblivious of the arrival of a crawling taxi. It stops*].

TAXIMAN. Can I drive you and the lady anywhere, sir?

> [*They start asunder*].

LIZA. Oh, Freddy, a taxi. The very thing.

FREDDY. But, damn it, I've no money.

LIZA. I have plenty. The Colonel thinks you should never go out without ten pounds in your pocket. Listen. We'll drive about all night; and in the morning I'll call on old Mrs. Higgins and ask her what I ought to do. I'll tell you all about it in the cab. And the police wont touch us there.

FREDDY. Righto! Ripping. [*To the Taximan*] Wimbledon Common. [*They drive off*].

ACT V

MRS. HIGGINS's *drawing room. She is at her writing-table. As before. The parlormaid comes in.*

THE PARLORMAID [*at the door*] Mr. Henry, maam, is downstairs with Colonel Pickering.

MRS. HIGGINS. Well, shew them up.

THE PARLORMAID. Theyre using the telephone, maam. Telephoning to the police, I think.

MRS. HIGGINS. What!

THE PARLORMAID [*coming further in and lowering her voice*] Mr. Henry is in a state, maam. I thought I'd better tell you.

MRS. HIGGINS. If you had told me that Mr. Henry was not in a state it would have been more surprising. Tell them to come up when theyve finished with the police. I suppose he's lost something.

THE PARLORMAID. Yes, maam [*going*].

MRS. HIGGINS. Go upstairs and tell Miss Doolittle that Mr. Henry and the Colonel are here. Ask her not to come down til I send for her.

THE PARLORMAID. Yes, maam.

[HIGGINS *bursts in. He is, as the parlormaid has said, in a state*].

HIGGINS. Look here, mother: heres a confounded thing!

MRS. HIGGINS. Yes, dear. Good morning. [*He checks his impatience and kisses her, whilst the parlormaid goes out*]. What is it?

HIGGINS. Eliza's bolted.

MRS. HIGGINS [*calmly continuing her writing*] You must have frightened her.

HIGGINS. Frightened her! nonsense! She was left last night, as usual, to turn out the lights and all that; and instead of going to bed she changed her clothes and went right off: her bed wasnt slept in. She came in a cab for her things before seven this morning; and that fool Mrs. Pearce let her have them without telling me a word about it. What am I to do?

MRS. HIGGINS. Do without, I'm afraid, Henry. The girl has a perfect right to leave if she chooses.

HIGGINS [*wandering distractedly across the room*] But I cant find anything. I dont know what appointments Ive got. I'm—[PICKERING *comes in.* MRS. HIGGINS *puts down her pen and turns away from the writing-table*].

PICKERING [*shaking hands*] Good morning, Mrs. Higgins. Has Henry told you? [*He sits down on the ottoman*].

HIGGINS. What does that ass of an inspector say? Have you offered a reward?

MRS. HIGGINS [*rising in indignant amazement*] You dont mean to say you have set the police after Eliza.

HIGGINS. Of course. What are the police for? What else could we do? [*He sits in the Elizabethan chair*].

PICKERING. The inspector made a lot of difficulties. I really think he suspected us of some improper purpose.

MRS. HIGGINS. Well, of course he did. What right have you to go to the police and give the girl's name as if she were a thief, or a lost umbrella, or something? Really! [*She sits down again, deeply vexed*].

HIGGINS. But we want to find her.

PICKERING. We cant let her go like this, you know, Mrs. Higgins. What were we to do?

MRS. HIGGINS. You have no more sense, either of you, than two children. Why—

[*The parlormaid comes in and breaks off the conversation*].

THE PARLORMAID. Mr. Henry: a gentleman wants to see you very particular. He's been sent on from Wimpole Street.

HIGGINS. Oh, bother! I cant see anyone now. Who is it?

THE PARLORMAID. A Mr. Doolittle, sir.

PICKERING. Doolittle! Do you mean the dustman?

THE PARLORMAID. Dustman! Oh no, sir: a gentleman.

HIGGINS [*springing up excitedly*] By George, Pick, it's some relative of hers that she's gone to. Somebody we know nothing about. [*To the parlormaid*] Send him up, quick.

THE PARLORMAID. Yes, sir. [*She goes*].

HIGGINS [*eagerly, going to his mother*] Genteel relatives! now we shall hear something. [*He sits down in the Chippendale chair*].

MRS. HIGGINS. Do you know any of her people?

PICKERING. Only her father: the fellow we told you about.

THE PARLORMAID [*announcing*] Mr. Doolittle. [*She withdraws*].

[DOOLITTLE *enters. He is resplendently dressed as for a fashionable wedding, and might, in fact, be the bridegroom. A flower in his buttonhole, a dazzling silk hat, and patent leather shoes complete the effect. He is too concerned with the business he has come on to notice* MRS. HIGGINS. *He walks straight to* HIGGINS, *and accosts him with vehement reproach*].

DOOLITTLE [*indicating his own person*] See here! Do you see this? You done this.

HIGGINS. Done what, man?

DOOLITTLE. This, I tell you. Look at it. Look at this hat. Look at this coat.

PICKERING. Has Eliza been buying you clothes?

DOOLITTLE. Eliza! not she. Why would she buy me clothes?

MRS. HIGGINS. Good morning, Mr. Doolittle. Wont you sit down?

DOOLITTLE [*taken aback as he becomes conscious*

that he has forgotten his hostess] Asking your pardon, maam. [*He approaches her and shakes her proffered hand*]. Thank you. [*He sits down on the ottoman, on* PICKERING'S *right*]. I am that full of what has happened to me that I cant think of anything else.

HIGGINS. What the dickens has happened to you?

DOOLITTLE. I shouldnt mind if it had only happened to me: anything might happen to anybody and nobody to blame but Providence, as you might say. But this is something that you done to me: yes, you, Enry Iggins.

HIGGINS. Have you found Eliza?

DOOLITTLE. Have you lost her?

HIGGINS. Yes.

DOOLITTLE. You have all the luck, you have. I aint found her; but she'll find me quick enough now after what you done to me.

MRS. HIGGINS. But what has my son done to you, Mr. Doolittle?

DOOLITTLE. Done to me! Ruined me. Destroyed my happiness. Tied me up and delivered me into the hands of middle class morality.

HIGGINS [*rising intolerantly and standing over* DOOLITTLE] Youre raving. Youre drunk. Youre mad. I gave you five pounds. After that I had two conversations with you, at half-a-crown an hour. Ive never seen you since.

DOOLITTLE. Oh! Drunk am I? Mad am I? Tell me this. Did you or did you not write a letter to an old blighter in America that was giving five millions to found Moral Reform Societies all over the world, and that wanted you to invent a universal language for him?

HIGGINS. What! Ezra D. Wannafeller! He's dead. [*He sits down again carelessly*].

DOOLITTLE. Yes: he's dead; and I'm done for. Now did you or did you not write a letter to him to say that the most original moralist at present in England, to the best of your knowledge, was Alfred Doolittle, a common dustman?

HIGGINS. Oh, after your first visit I remember making some silly joke of the kind.

DOOLITTLE. Ah! you may well call it a silly joke. It put the lid on me right enough. Just give him the chance he wanted to shew that Americans is not like us: that they reckonize and respect merit in every class of life, however humble. Them words is in his blooming will, in which, Henry Higgins, thanks to your silly joking, he leaves me a share in his Pre-digested Cheese Trust worth four thousand a year on condition that I lecture for his Wannafeller Moral Reform World League as often as they ask me up to six times a year.

HIGGINS. The devil he does! Whew! [*Brightening suddenly*] What a lark!

PICKERING. A safe thing for you, Doolittle. They wont ask you twice.

DOOLITTLE. It aint the lecturing I mind. I'll lecture them blue in the face, I will, and not turn a hair. It's making a gentleman of me that I object to. Who asked him to make a gentleman of me? I was happy. I was free. I touched pretty nigh everybody for money when I wanted it, same as I touched you, Enry Iggins. Now I am worrited; tied neck and heels; and everybody touches me for money. It's a fine thing for you, says my solicitor. Is it? says I. You mean it's a good thing for you, I says. When I was a poor man and had a solicitor once when they found a pram in the dust cart, he got me off, and got shut of me and got me shut of him as quick as he could. Same with the doctors: used to shove me out of the hospital before I could hardly stand on my legs, and nothing to pay. Now they finds out that I'm not a healthy man and cant live unless they looks after me twice a day. In the house I'm not let do a hand's turn for myself: somebody else must do it and touch me for it. A year ago I hadnt a relative in the world except two or three that wouldnt speak to me. Now Ive fifty, and not a decent week's wages among the lot of them. I have to live for others and not for myself: that middle class morality. You talk of losing Eliza. Dont you be anxious: I bet she's on my doorstep by this: she that could support herself easy by selling flowers if I wasnt respectable. And the next one to touch me will be you, Enry Iggins. I'll have to learn to speak middle class language from you, instead of speaking proper English. Thats where youll come in; and I daresay thats what you done it for.

MRS. HIGGINS. But, my dear Mr. Doolittle, you need not suffer all this if you are really in earnest. Nobody can force you to accept this bequest. You can repudiate it. Isnt that so, Colonel Pickering?

PICKERING. I believe so.

DOOLITTLE [*softening his manner in deference to her sex*] Thats the tragedy of it, maam. It's easy to say chuck it; but I havnt the nerve. Which of us has? We're all intimidated. Intimidated, maam: thats what we are. What is there for me if I chuck it but the workhouse in my old age? I have to dye my hair already to keep my job as a dustman. If I was one of the deserving poor, and had put by a bit, I could chuck it; but then why should I, acause the deserving poor might as well be millionaires for all the happiness they ever has. They dont know what happiness is. But I, as one of the undeserving poor, have nothing between me and the pauper's uniform but this here blasted four thousand a year that shoves me into the middle class. (Excuse the expression, maam; youd use it yourself if you had my provocation.) Theyve got you every way you turn: it's a choice between the Skilly of the workhouse and the Char Bydis of the middle class; and I havnt the nerve for the workhouse. Intimidated: thats what I am. Broke. Bought up. Happier men than me will call for my dust, and touch me for their tip; and I'll look on helpless, and envy them. And thats what your son has brought me to. [*He is overcome by emotion*].

MRS. HIGGINS. Well, I'm very glad youre not going to do anything foolish, Mr. Doolittle. For this solves the problem of Eliza's future. You can provide for her now.

DOOLITTLE [*with melancholy resignation*] Yes, maam: I'm expected to provide for everyone now, out of four thousand a year.

HIGGINS [*jumping up*] Nonsense! he cant provide for her. He shant provide for her. She doesnt belong to him. I paid him five pounds for her. Doolittle: either youre an honest man or a rogue.

DOOLITTLE [*tolerantly*] A little of both, Henry, like the rest of us: a little of both.

HIGGINS. Well, you took that money for the girl; and you have no right to take her as well.

MRS. HIGGINS. Henry: dont be absurd. If you want to know where Eliza is, she is upstairs.

HIGGINS [*amazed*] Upstairs!!! Then I shall jolly soon fetch her downstairs. [*He makes resolutely for the door*].

MRS. HIGGINS [*rising and following him*] Be quiet, Henry. Sit down.

HIGGINS. I—

MRS. HIGGINS. Sit down, dear; and listen to me.

HIGGINS. Oh very well, very well, very well. [*He throws himself ungraciously on the ottoman, with his face towards the windows*]. But I think you might have told us this half an hour ago.

MRS. HIGGINS. Eliza came to me this morning. She told me of the brutal way you two treated her.

HIGGINS [*bounding up again*] What!

PICKERING [*rising also*] My dear Mrs. Higgins, she's been telling you stories. We didnt treat her brutally. We hardly said a word to her; and we parted on particularly good terms. [*Turning on HIGGINS*] Higgins: did you bully her after I went to bed?

HIGGINS. Just the other way about. She threw my slippers in my face. She behaved in the most outrageous way. I never gave her the slightest provocation. The slippers came bang into my face the moment I entered the room—before I had uttered a word. And used perfectly awful language.

PICKERING [*astonished*] But why? What did we do to her?

MRS. HIGGINS. I think I know pretty well what you did. The girl is naturally rather affectionate, I think. Isnt she, Mr. Doolittle?

DOOLITTLE. Very tender-hearted, maam. Takes after me.

MRS. HIGGINS. Just so. She had become attached to you both. She worked very hard for you, Henry. I dont think you quite realize what anything in the nature of brain work means to a girl of her class. Well, it seems that when the great day of trial came, and she did this wonderful thing for you without making a single mistake, you two sat there and never said a word to her, but talked together of how glad you were that it was all over and how you had been bored with the whole thing. And then you were surprised because she threw your slippers at you! *I* should have thrown the fire-irons at you.

HIGGINS. We said nothing except that we were tired and wanted to go to bed. Did we, Pick?

PICKERING [*shrugging his shoulders*] That was all.

MRS. HIGGINS [*ironically*] Quite sure?

PICKERING. Absolutely. Really, that was all.

MRS. HIGGINS. You didnt thank her, or pet her, or admire her, or tell her how splendid she'd been.

HIGGINS [*impatiently*] But she knew all about that. We didnt make speeches to her, if thats what you mean.

PICKERING [*conscience stricken*] Perhaps we were a little inconsiderate. Is she very angry?

MRS. HIGGINS [*returning to her place at the writing-table*] Well, I'm afraid she wont go back to Wimpole Street, especially now that Mr. Doolittle is able to keep up the position you have thrust on her; but she says she is quite willing to meet you on friendly terms and to let bygones be bygones.

HIGGINS [*furious*] Is she, by George? Ho!

MRS. HIGGINS. If you promise to behave yourself, Henry, I'll ask her to come down. If not, go home; for you have taken up quite enough of my time.

HIGGINS. Oh, all right. Very well. Pick: you behave yourself. Let us put on our best Sunday manners for this creature that we picked out of the mud. [*He flings himself sulkily into the Elizabethan chair*].

DOOLITTLE [*remonstrating*] Now, now, Enry Iggins! Have some consideration for my feelings as a middle class man.

MRS. HIGGINS. Remember your promise, Henry. [*She presses the bell-button on the writing-table*]. Mr. Doolittle: will you be so good as to step out on the balcony for a moment. I dont want Eliza to have the shock of your news until she has made it up with these two gentlemen. Would you mind?

DOOLITTLE. As you wish, lady. Anything to help Henry to keep her off my hands. [*He disappears through the window*].

[*The parlormaid answers the bell. PICKERING sits down in DOOLITTLE's place*].

MRS. HIGGINS. Ask Miss Doolittle to come down, please.

THE PARLORMAID. Yes, maam. [*She goes out*].

MRS. HIGGINS. Now, Henry: be good.

HIGGINS. I am behaving myself perfectly.

PICKERING. He is doing his best, Mrs. Higgins.

[*A pause.* HIGGINS *throws back his head; stretches out his legs; and begins to whistle*].

MRS. HIGGINS. Henry, dearest, you dont look at all nice in that attitude.

HIGGINS [*pulling himself together*] I was not trying to look nice, mother.

MRS. HIGGINS. It doesnt matter, dear. I only wanted to make you speak.

HIGGINS. Why?

MRS. HIGGINS. Because you cant speak and whistle at the same time.

[HIGGINS *groans. Another very trying pause*].

HIGGINS [*springing up, out of patience*] Where the devil is that girl? Are we to wait here all day?

[ELIZA *enters, sunny, self-possessed, and giving a staggeringly convincing exhibition of ease of manner. She carries a little workbasket, and is very much at home.* PICKERING *is too much taken aback to rise*].

LIZA. How do you do, Professor Higgins? Are you quite well?

HIGGINS [*choking*] Am I— [*He can say no more*].

LIZA. But of course you are: you are never ill. So glad to see you again, Colonel Pickering. [*He rises hastily; and they shake hands*]. Quite chilly this morning, isnt it? [*She sits down on his left. He sits beside her*].

HIGGINS. Dont you dare try this game on me. I taught it to you; and it doesnt take me in. Get up and come home; and dont be a fool.

[ELIZA *takes a piece of needlework from her basket, and begins to stitch at it, without taking the least notice of this outburst*].

MRS. HIGGINS. Very nicely put, indeed, Henry. No woman could resist such an invitation.

HIGGINS. You let her alone, mother. Let her speak for herself. You will jolly soon see whether she has an idea that I havnt put into her head or a word that I havnt put into her mouth. I tell you I have created this thing out of the squashed cabbage leaves of Covent Garden; and now she pretends to play the fine lady with me.

MRS. HIGGINS [*placidly*] Yes, dear; but youll sit down, wont you?

[HIGGINS *sits down again, savagely*].

LIZA [*to* PICKERING, *taking no apparent notice of* HIGGINS, *and working away deftly*] Will you drop me altogether now that the experiment is over, Colonel Pickering?

PICKERING. Oh dont. You mustnt think of it as an experiment. It shocks me, somehow.

LIZA. Oh, I'm only a squashed cabbage leaf—

PICKERING [*impulsively*] No.

LIZA [*continuing quietly*]—but I owe so much to you that I should be very unhappy if you forgot me.

PICKERING. It's very kind of you to say so, Miss Doolittle.

LIZA. It's not because you paid for my dresses. I know you are generous to everybody with money. But it was from you that I learnt really nice manners; and that is what makes one a lady, isnt it? You see it was so very difficult for me with the example of Professor Higgins always before me. I was brought up to be just like him, unable to control myself, and using bad language on the slightest provocation. And I should never have known that ladies and gentlemen didnt behave like that if you hadnt been there.

HIGGINS. Well!!

PICKERING. Oh, thats only his way, you know. He doesnt mean it.

LIZA. Oh, *I* didnt mean it either, when I was a flower girl. It was only my way. But you see I did it; and thats what makes the difference after all.

PICKERING. No doubt. Still, he taught you to speak; and I couldnt have done that, you know.

LIZA [*trivially*] Of course: that is his profession.

HIGGINS. Damnation!

LIZA [*continuing*] It was just like learning to dance in the fashionable way: there was nothing more than that in it. But do you know what began my real education?

PICKERING. What?

LIZA [*stopping her work for a moment*] Your calling me Miss Doolittle that day when I first came to Wimpole Street. That was the beginning of self-respect for me. [*She resumes her stitching*] And there were a hundred little things you never noticed, because they came naturally to you. Things about standing up and taking off your hat and opening doors—

PICKERING. Oh, that was nothing.

LIZA. Yes: things that shewed you thought and felt about me as if I were something better than a scullery-maid; though of course I know you would have been just the same to a scullery-maid if she had been let into the drawing room. You never took off your boots in the dining room when I was there.

PICKERING. You mustnt mind that. Higgins takes off his boots all over the place.

LIZA. I know. I am not blaming him. It is his way, isnt it? But it made such a difference to me that you didnt do it. You see, really and truly, apart from the things anyone can pick up (the dressing and the proper way of speaking, and so on), the difference between a lady and a flower girl is not how she behaves, but how she's treated. I shall always be a flower girl to Professor Higgins, because he always treats me as a flower girl, and always will; but I know I can be a lady to you, because you always treat me as a lady, and always will.

MRS. HIGGINS. Please dont grind your teeth, Henry.

PICKERING. Well, this is really very nice of you, Miss Doolittle.

LIZA. I should like you to call me Eliza, now, if you would.

PICKERING. Thank you. Eliza, of course.

LIZA. And I should like Professor Higgins to call me Miss Doolittle.

HIGGINS. I'll see you damned first.

MRS. HIGGINS. Henry! Henry!

PICKERING [*laughing*] Why dont you slang back at him? Dont stand it. It would do him a lot of good.

LIZA. I cant. I could have done it once; but now I cant go back to it. You told me, you know, that when a child is brought to a foreign country, it picks up the language in a few weeks, and forgets its own. Well, I am a child in your country. I have forgotten my own language, and can speak nothing but yours. Thats the real break-off with the corner of Tottenham Court Road. Leaving Wimpole Street finishes it.

PICKERING [*much alarmed*] Oh! but youre coming back to Wimpole Street, arnt you? Youll forgive Higgins?

HIGGINS [*rising*] Forgive! Will she, by George! Let her go. Let her find out how she can get on without us. She will relapse into the gutter in three weeks without me at her elbow.

[DOOLITTLE *appears at the centre window. With a look of dignified reproach at* HIGGINS, *he comes slowly and silently to his daughter, who, with her back to the window, is unconscious of his approach*].

PICKERING. He's incorrigible, Eliza. You wont relapse, will you?

LIZA. No: not now. Never again. I have learnt my lesson. I dont believe I could utter one of the old sounds if I tried. [DOOLITTLE *touches her on the left shoulder. She drops her work, losing her self-possession utterly at the spectacle of her father's splendor*] A-a-a-a-ah-ow-ooh!

HIGGINS [*with a crow of triumph*] Aha! Just so. A-a-a-ahowooh! A-a-a-ahowooh! A-a-a-ahowooh! Victory! Victory! [*He throws himself on the divan, folding his arms, and spraddling arrogantly*].

DOOLITTLE. Can you blame the girl? Dont look at me like that, Eliza. It aint my fault. Ive come into some money.

LIZA. You must have touched a millionaire this time, dad.

DOOLITTLE. I have. But I'm dressed something special today. I'm going to St. George's, Hanover Square. Your stepmother is going to marry me.

LIZA [*angrily*] Youre going to let yourself down to marry that low common woman!

PICKERING [*quietly*] He ought to, Eliza. [*To* DOOLITTLE] Why has she changed her mind?

DOOLITTLE [*sadly*] Intimidated, Governor. Intimidated. Middle class morality claims its victim. Wont you put on your hat, Liza, and come and see me turned off?

LIZA. If the Colonel says I must, I—I'll [*almost sobbing*] I'll demean myself. And get insulted for my pains, like enough.

DOOLITTLE. Dont be afraid: she never comes to words with anyone now, poor woman! respectability has broke all the spirit out of her.

PICKERING [*squeezing* ELIZA's *elbow gently*] Be kind to them, Eliza. Make the best of it.

LIZA [*forcing a little smile for him through her vexation*] Oh well, just to shew theres no ill feeling. I'll be back in a moment. [*She goes out*].

DOOLITTLE [*sitting down beside* PICKERING] I feel uncommon nervous about the ceremony, Colonel. I wish youd come and see me through it.

PICKERING. But youve been through it before, man. You were married to Eliza's mother.

DOOLITTLE. Who told you that, Colonel?

PICKERING. Well, nobody told me. But I concluded —naturally—

DOOLITTLE. No: that aint the natural way, Colonel: it's only the middle class way. My way was always the undeserving way. But dont say nothing to Eliza. She dont know: I always had a delicacy about telling her.

PICKERING. Quite right. We'll leave it so, if you dont mind.

DOOLITTLE. And youll come to the church, Colonel, and put me through straight?

PICKERING. With pleasure. As far as a bachelor can.

MRS. HIGGINS. May I come, Mr. Doolittle? I should be very sorry to miss your wedding.

DOOLITTLE. I should indeed be honored by your condescension, maam; and my poor old woman would take it as a tremenjous compliment. She's been very low, thinking of the happy days that are no more.

MRS. HIGGINS [*rising*] I'll order the carriage and get ready. [*The men rise, except* HIGGINS]. I shant be more than fifteen minutes. [*As she goes to the door* ELIZA *comes in, hatted and buttoning her gloves*]. I'm going to the church to see your father married, Eliza. You had better come in the brougham with me. Colonel Pickering can go on with the bridegroom.

[MRS. HIGGINS *goes out.* ELIZA *comes to the middle of the room between the centre window and the ottoman.* PICKERING *joins her*].

DOOLITTLE. Bridegroom. What a word! It makes a man realize his position, somehow. [*He takes up his hat and goes towards the door*].

PICKERING. Before I go, Eliza, do forgive Higgins and come back to us.

LIZA. I dont think dad would allow me. Would you, dad?

DOOLITTLE [*sad but magnanimous*] They played you off very cunning, Eliza, them two sportsmen. If it had been only one of them, you could have nailed him. But you see, there was two; and one of them chaperoned the other, as you might say. [*To* PICKERING] It was artful of you, Colonel; but I bear no malice: I should have done the same myself. I been the victim of one woman after another all my life, and I dont grudge you two getting the better of Liza. I shant interfere. It's time for us to go, Colonel. So long, Henry. See you in St. George's, Eliza. [*He goes out*].

PICKERING [*coaxing*] Do stay with us, Eliza. [*He follows* DOOLITTLE].

[ELIZA *goes out on the balcony to avoid being alone with* HIGGINS. *He rises and joins her there. She immediately comes back into the room and makes for the door; but he goes along the balcony and gets his back to the door before she reaches it*].

HIGGINS. Well, Eliza, youve had a bit of your own back, as you call it. Have you had enough? and are you going to be reasonable? Or do you want any more?

LIZA. You want me back only to pick up your slippers and put up with your tempers and fetch and carry for you.

HIGGINS. I havnt said I wanted you back at all.

LIZA. Oh, indeed. Then what are we talking about?

HIGGINS. About you, not about me. If you come back I shall treat you just as I have always treated you. I cant change my nature; and I dont intend to change my manners. My manners are exactly the same as Colonel Pickering's.

LIZA. Thats not true. He treats a flower girl as if she was a duchess.

HIGGINS. And I treat a duchess as if she was a flower girl.

LIZA. I see [*She turns away composedly, and sits on the ottoman, facing the window*]. The same to everybody.

HIGGINS. Just so.

LIZA. Like father.

HIGGINS [*grinning, a little taken down*] Without accepting the comparison at all points, Eliza, it's quite true that your father is not a snob, and that he will be quite at home in any station of life to which his eccentric destiny may call him. [*Seriously*] The great secret, Eliza, is not having bad manners or good manner or any other particular sort of manners, but having the same manner for all human souls: in short, behaving as if you were in Heaven, where there are no third-class carriages, and one soul is as good as another.

LIZA. Amen. You are a born preacher.

HIGGINS [*irritated*] The question is not whether I treat you rudely, but whether you ever heard me treat anyone else better.

LIZA [*with sudden sincerity*] I dont care how you treat me. I dont mind your swearing at me. I shouldnt mind a black eye: Ive had one before this. But [*standing up and facing him*] I wont be passed over.

HIGGINS. Then get out of my way; for I wont stop for you. You talk about me as if I were a motor bus.

LIZA. So you are a motor bus: all bounce and go, and no consideration for anyone. But I can do without you: dont think I cant.

HIGGINS. I know you can. I told you you could.

LIZA [*wounded, getting away from him to the other side of the ottoman with her face to the hearth*] I know you did, you brute. You wanted to get rid of me.

HIGGINS. Liar.

LIZA. Thank you. [*She sits down with dignity*].

HIGGINS. You never asked yourself, I suppose, whether *I* could do without you.

LIZA [*earnestly*] Dont you try to get round me. You'll have to do without me.

HIGGINS [*arrogant*] I can do without anybody. I have my own soul: my own spark of divine fire. But [*with sudden humility*] I shall miss you, Eliza. [*He sits down near her on the ottoman*] I have learnt something from your idiotic notions: I confess that humbly and gratefully. And I have grown accustomed to your voice and appearance. I like them, rather.

LIZA. Well, you have both of them on your gramophone and in your book of photographs. When you feel lonely without me, you can turn the machine on. It's got no feelings to hurt.

HIGGINS. I cant turn your soul on. Leave me those feelings; and you can take away the voice and the face. They are not you.

LIZA. Oh, you are a devil. You can twist the heart in a girl as easy as some could twist her arms to hurt her. Mrs. Pearce warned me. Time and again she has wanted to leave you; and you always got round her at the last minute. And you dont care a bit for her. And you dont care a bit for me.

HIGGINS. I care for life, for humanity; and you are

a part of it that has come my way and been built into my house. What more can you or anyone ask?

LIZA. I wont care for anybody that doesnt care for me.

HIGGINS. Commercial principles, Eliza. Like [*reproducing her Covent Garden pronunciation with professional exactness*] s'yollin voylets [selling violets], isnt it?

LIZA. Dont sneer at me. It's mean to sneer at me.

HIGGINS. I have never sneered in my life. Sneering doesnt become either the human face or the human soul. I am expressing my righteous contempt for Commercialism. I dont and wont trade in affection. You call me a brute because you couldnt buy a claim on me by fetching my slippers and finding my spectacles. You were a fool: I think a woman fetching a man's slippers is a disgusting sight: did I ever fetch your slippers? I think a good deal more of you for throwing them in my face. No use slaving for me and then saying you want to be cared for: who cares for a slave? If you come back, come back for the sake of good fellowship; for youll get nothing else. Youve had a thousand times as much out of me as I have out of you; and if you dare to set up your little dog's tricks of fetching and carrying slippers against my creation of a Duchess Eliza, I'll slam the door in your silly face.

LIZA. What did you do it for if you didnt care for me?

HIGGINS [*heartily*] Why, because it was my job.

LIZA. You never thought of the trouble it would make for me.

HIGGINS. Would the world ever have been made if its maker had been afraid of making trouble? Making life means making trouble. Theres only one way of escaping trouble; and thats killing things. Cowards, you notice, are always shrieking to have troublesome people killed.

LIZA. I'm no preacher: I dont notice things like that. I notice that you dont notice me.

HIGGINS [*jumping up and walking about intolerantly*] Eliza: youre an idiot. I waste the treasures of my Miltonic mind by spreading them before you. Once for all, understand that I go my way and do my work without caring twopence what happens to either of us. I am not intimidated, like your father and your stepmother. So you can come back or go to the devil: which you please.

LIZA. What am I to come back for?

HIGGINS [*bouncing up on his knees on the ottoman and leaning over it to her*] For the fun of it. Thats why I took you on.

LIZA [*with averted face*] And you may throw me out tomorrow if I dont do everything you want me to?

HIGGINS. Yes; and you may walk out tomorrow if I dont do everything you want me to.

LIZA. And live with my stepmother?

HIGGINS. Yes, or sell flowers.

LIZA. Oh! if I only could go back to my flower basket! I should be independent of both you and father and all the world! Why did you take my independence from me? Why did I give it up? I'm a slave now, for all my fine clothes.

HIGGINS. Not a bit. I'll adopt you as my daughter and settle money on you if you like. Or would you rather marry Pickering?

LIZA [*looking fiercely round at him*] I wouldnt marry you if you asked me; and youre nearer my age than what he is.

HIGGINS [*gently*] Than he is: not "than what he is."

LIZA [*losing her temper and rising*] I'll talk as I like. Youre not my teacher now.

HIGGINS [*reflectively*] I dont suppose Pickering would, though. He's as confirmed an old bachelor as I am.

LIZA. Thats not what I want; and dont you think it. I've always had chaps enough wanting me that way. Freddy Hill writes to me twice and three times a day, sheets and sheets.

HIGGINS [*disagreeably surprised*] Damn his impudence! [*He recoils and finds himself sitting on his heels.*]

LIZA. He has a right to if he likes, poor lad. And he does love me.

HIGGINS [*getting off the ottoman*] You have no right to encourage him.

LIZA. Every girl has a right to be loved.

HIGGINS. What! By fools like that?

LIZA. Freddy's not a fool. And if he's weak and poor and wants me, may be he'd make me happier than my betters that bully me and dont want me.

HIGGINS. Can he make anything of you? Thats the point.

LIZA. Perhaps I could make something of him. But I never thought of us making anything of one another; and you never think of anything else. I only want to be natural.

HIGGINS. In short, you want me to be as infatuated about you as Freddy? Is that it?

LIZA. No I dont. Thats not the sort of feeling I want from you. And dont you be too sure of yourself or of me. I could have been a bad girl if I'd liked. Ive seen more of some things than you, for all your learning. Girls like me can drag gentlemen down to make love to them easy enough. And they wish each other dead the next minute.

HIGGINS. Of course they do. Then what in thunder are we quarrelling about?

LIZA [*much troubled*] I want a little kindness. I

know I'm a common ignorant girl, and you a book-learned gentleman; but I'm not dirt under your feet. What I done [*correcting herself*] what I did was not for the dresses and the taxis: I did it because we were pleasant together and I come—came—to care for you; not to want you to make love to me, and not forgetting the difference between us, but more friendly like.

HIGGINS. Well, of course. Thats just how I feel. And how Pickering feels. Eliza: youre a fool.

LIZA. Thats not a proper answer to give me [*she sinks on the chair at the writing-table in tears*].

HIGGINS. It's all youll get until you stop being a common idiot. If youre going to be a lady, youll have to give up feeling neglected if the men you know dont spend half their time snivelling over you and the other half giving you black eyes. If you cant stand the coldness of my sort of life, and the strain of it, go back to the gutter. Work til youre more a brute than a human being; and then cuddle and squabble and drink til you fall asleep. Oh, it's a fine life, the life of the gutter. It's real: it's warm: it's violent: you can feel it through the thickest skin: you can taste it and smell it without any training or any work. Not like Science and Literature and Classical Music and Philosophy and Art. You find me cold, unfeeling, selfish, dont you? Very well: be off with you to the sort of people you like. Marry some sentimental hog or other with lots of money, and a thick pair of lips to kiss you with and a thick pair of boots to kick you with. If you cant appreciate what youve got, youd better get what you can appreciate.

LIZA [*desperate*] Oh, you are a cruel tyrant. I cant talk to you: you turn everything against me: I'm always in the wrong. But you know very well all the time that youre nothing but a bully. You know I cant go back to the gutter, as you call it, and that I have no real friends in the world but you and the Colonel. You know well I couldnt bear to live with a low common man after you two; and it's wicked and cruel of you to insult me by pretending I could. You think I must go back to Wimpole Street because I have nowhere else to go but father's. But dont you be too sure that you have me under your feet to be trampled on and talked down. I'll marry Freddy, I will, as soon as I'm able to support him.

HIGGINS [*thunderstruck*] Freddy!!! that young fool! That poor devil who couldnt get a job as an errand boy even if he had the guts to try for it! Woman: do you not understand that I have made you a consort for a king?

LIZA. Freddy loves me: that makes him king enough for me. I dont want him to work: he wasnt brought up to it as I was. I'll go and be a teacher.

HIGGINS. Whatll you teach, in heaven's name?

LIZA. What you taught me. I'll teach phonetics.

HIGGINS. Ha! ha! ha!

LIZA. I'll offer myself as an assistant to that hairy-faced Hungarian.

HIGGINS [*rising in a fury*] What! That imposter! that humbug! that toadying ignoramus! Teach him my methods! my discoveries! You take one step in his direction and I'll wring your neck. [*He lays hands on her*]. Do you hear?

LIZA [*defiantly non-resistant*] Wring away. What do I care? I knew youd strike me some day. [*He lets her go, stamping with rage at having forgotten himself, and recoils so hastily that he stumbles back into his seat on the ottoman*]. Aha! Now I know how to deal with you. What a fool I was not to think of it before! You cant take away the knowledge you gave me. You said I had a finer ear than you. And I can be civil and kind to people, which is more than you can. Aha! [*purposely dropping her aitches to annoy him*] Thats done you, Enry Iggins, it az. Now I dont care that [*snapping her fingers*] for your bullying and your big talk. I'll advertize it in the papers that your duchess is only a flower girl that you taught, and that she'll teach anybody to be a duchess just the same in six months for a thousand guineas. Oh, when I think of myself crawling under your feet and being trampled on and called names, when all the time I had only to lift up my finger to be as good as you, I could just kick myself.

HIGGINS [*wondering at her*] You damned impudent slut, you! But it's better than snivelling; better than fetching slippers and finding spectacles, isnt it? [*Rising*] By George, Eliza, I said I'd make a woman of you; and I have. I like you like this.

LIZA. Yes: you turn round and make up to me now that I'm not afraid of you, and can do without you.

HIGGINS. Of course I do, you little fool. Five minutes ago you were like a millstone round my neck. Now youre a tower of strength: a consort battleship. You and I and Pickering will be three old bachelors instead of only two men and a silly girl.

[MRS. HIGGINS *returns, dressed for the wedding.* ELIZA *instantly becomes cool and elegant*].

MRS. HIGGINS. The carriage is waiting, Eliza. Are you ready?

LIZA. Quite. Is the Professor coming?

MRS. HIGGINS. Certainly not. He cant behave himself in church. He makes remarks out loud all the time on the clergyman's pronunciation.

LIZA. Then I shall not see you again, Professor. Goodbye. [*She goes to the door*].

MRS. HIGGINS [*coming to* HIGGINS] Goodbye, dear.

HIGGINS. Goodbye, mother. [*He is about to kiss her, when he recollects something*]. Oh, by the way, Eliza, order a ham and a Stilton cheese, will you? And buy me a pair of reindeer gloves, number eights, and a tie to match that new suit of mine. You can choose the color. [*His cheerful, careless, vigorous voice shews that he is incorrigible*].

LIZA [*disdainfully*] Number eights are too small for you if you want them lined with lamb's wool. You have three new ties that you have forgotten in the drawer of your washstand. Colonel Pickering prefers double Gloucester to Stilton; and you dont notice the difference. I telephoned Mrs. Pearce this morning not to forget the ham. What you are to do without me I cannot imagine. [*She sweeps out*].

MRS. HIGGINS. I'm afraid youve spoilt that girl, Henry. I should be uneasy about you and her if she were less fond of Colonel Pickering.

HIGGINS. Pickering! Nonsense: she's going to marry Freddy. Ha ha! Freddy! Freddy!! Ha ha ha ha ha!!!! [*He roars with laughter as the play ends*].

The rest of the story need not be shewn in action, and indeed, would hardly need telling if our imaginations were not so enfeebled by their lazy dependence on the ready-mades and reach-me-downs of the rag-shop in which Romance keeps its stock of "happy endings" to misfit all stories. Now, the history of Eliza Doolitle, though called a romance because the transfiguration it records seems exceedingly improbable, is common enough. Such transfigurations have been achieved by hundreds of resolutely ambitious young women since Nell Gwynne set them the example by playing queens and fascinating kings in the theatre in which she began by selling oranges. Nevertheless, people in all directions have assumed, for no other reason than that she became the heroine of a romance, that she must have married the hero of it. This is unbearable, not only because her little drama, if acted on such a thoughtless assumption, must be spoiled, but because the true sequel is patent to anyone with a sense of human nature in general, and of feminine instinct in particular.

Eliza, in telling Higgins she would not marry him if he asked her, was not coquetting: she was announcing a well-considered decision. When a bachelor interests, and dominates, and teaches, and becomes important to a spinster, as Higgins with Eliza, she always, if she has character enough to be capable of it, considers very seriously indeed whether she will play for becoming that bachelor's wife, especially if he is so little interested in marriage that a determined and devoted woman might capture him if she set herself resolutely to do it. Her decision will depend a good deal on whether she is really free to choose; and that, again, will depend on her age and income. If she is at the end of her youth, and has no security for her livelihood, she will marry him because she must marry anybody who will provide for her. But at Eliza's age a good-looking girl does not feel that pressure: she feels free to pick and choose. She is therefore guided by her instinct in the matter. Eliza's instinct tells her not to marry Higgins. It does not tell her to give him up. It is not in the slightest doubt as to his remaining one of the strongest personal interests in her life. It would be very sorely strained if there was another woman likely to supplant her with him. But as she feels sure of him on that last point, she has no doubt at all as to her course, and would not have any, even if the difference of twenty years in age, which seems so great to youth, did not exist between them.

As our own instincts are not appealed to by her conclusion, let us see whether we cannot discover some reason in it. When Higgins excused his indifference to young women on the ground that they had an irresistible rival in his mother, he gave the clue to his inveterate old-bachelordom. The case is uncommon only to the extent that remarkable mothers are uncommon. If an imaginative boy has a sufficiently rich mother who has intelligence, personal grace, dignity of character without harshness, and a cultivated sense of the best art of her time to enable her to make her house beautiful, she sets a standard for him against which very few women can struggle, besides effecting for him a disengagement of his affections, his sense of beauty, and his idealism from his specifically sexual impulses. This makes him a standing puzzle to the huge number of uncultivated people who have been brought up in tasteless homes by commonplace or disagreeable parents, and to whom, consequently, literature, painting, sculpture, music, and affectionate personal relations come as modes of sex if they come at all. The word passion means nothing else to them; and that Higgins could have a passion for phonetics and idealize his mother instead of Eliza, would seem to them absurd and unnatural. Nevertheless, when we look round and see that hardly anyone is too ugly or disagreeable to find a wife or a husband if he or she wants one, whilst many old maids and bachelors are above the average in quality and culture, we cannot help suspecting that the disentanglement of sex from the associations with which it is so commonly confused, a disentanglement which persons of genius achieve by sheer intellectual analysis, is sometimes produced or aided by parental fascination.

Now, though Eliza was incapable of thus explaining to herself Higgins's formidable powers of resistance to the charm that prostrated Freddy at the first glance, she was instinctively aware that she could never obtain a complete grip of him, or come between him and his mother (the first necessity of the married woman). To put it shortly, she knew that for some mysterious reason he had not the makings of a married man in him, according to her conception of a husband as one to whom she would be his nearest and fondest and warmest interest. Even had there been no mother-rival, she would still have refused to accept an interest in herself that was secondary to philosophic interests. Had Mrs. Higgins died, there would still have been Milton and the Universal Alphabet. Landor's remark that to those who have the greatest power of loving, love is a secondary affair, would not have recommended Landor to Eliza. Put that along with her resentment of Higgins's domineering superiority, and her mistrust of his coaxing cleverness in getting round her and evading her wrath when he had gone too far with his impetuous bullying, and you will see that Eliza's instinct had good grounds for warning her not to marry her Pygmalion.

And now, whom did Eliza marry? For if Higgins was a predestinate old bachelor, she was most certainly not a predestinate old maid. Well, that can be told very shortly to those who have not guessed it from the indications she has herself given them.

Almost immediately after Eliza is stung into proclaiming her considered determination not to marry Higgins, she mentions the fact that young Mr. Frederick Eynsford Hill is pouring out his love for her daily through the post. Now Freddy is young, practically twenty years younger than Higgins: he is a gentleman (or, as Eliza would qualify him, a toff), and speaks like one. He is nicely dressed, is treated by the Colonel as an equal, loves her unaffectedly, and is not her master, nor ever likely to dominate her in spite of his advantage of social standing. Eliza has no use for the foolish romantic tradition that all women love to be mastered, if not actually bullied and beaten. "When you go to women" says Nietzsche "take your whip with you." Sensible despots have never confined that precaution to women: they have taken their whips with them when they have dealt with men, and been slavishly idealized by the men over whom they have flourished the whip much more than by women. No doubt there are slavish women as well as slavish men; and women, like men, admire those that are stronger than themselves. But to admire a strong person and to live under that strong person's thumb are two different things. The weak may not be admired and hero-worshipped; but they are by no means disliked or shunned; and they never seem to have the least difficulty in marrying people who are too good for them. They may fail in emergencies; but life is not one long emergency: it is mostly a string of situations for which no exceptional strength is needed, and with which even rather weak

people can cope if they have a stronger partner to help them out. Accordingly, it is a truth everywhere in evidence that strong people, masculine or feminine, not only do not marry stronger people, but do not shew any preference for them in selecting their friends. When a lion meets another with a louder roar "the first lion thinks the last a bore." The man or woman who feels strong enough for two, seeks for every other quality in a partner than strength.

The converse is also true. Weak people want to marry strong people who do not frighten them too much; and this often leads them to make the mistake we describe metaphorically as "biting off more than they can chew." They want too much for too little; and when the bargain is unreasonable beyond all bearing, the union becomes impossible: it ends in the weaker party being either discarded or borne as a cross, which is worse. People who are not only weak, but silly or obtuse as well, are often in these difficulties.

This being the state of human affairs, what is Eliza fairly sure to do when she is placed between Freddy and Higgins? Will she look forward to a lifetime of fetching Higgins's slippers or to a lifetime of Freddy fetching hers? There can be no doubt about the answer. Unless Freddy is biologically repulsive to her, and Higgins biologically attractive to a degree that overwhelms all her other instincts, she will, if she marries either of them, marry Freddy.

And that is just what Eliza did.

Complications ensued; but they were economic, not romantic. Freddy had no money and no occupation. His mother's jointure, a last relic of the opulence of Largelady Park, had enabled her to struggle along in Earlscourt with an air of gentility, but not to procure any serious secondary education for her children, much less give the boy a profession. A clerkship at thirty shillings a week was beneath Freddy's dignity, and extremely distasteful to him besides. His prospects consisted of a hope that if he kept up appearances somebody would do something for him. The something appeared vaguely to his imagination as a private secretaryship or a sinecure of some sort. To his mother it perhaps appeared as a marriage to some lady of means who could not resist her boy's niceness. Fancy her feelings when he married a flower girl who had become disclassed under extraordinary circumstances which were now notorious!

It is true that Eliza's situation did not seem wholly ineligible. Her father, though formerly a dustman, and now fantastically disclassed, had become extremely popular in the smartest society by a social talent which triumphed over every prejudice and every disadvantage. Rejected by the middle class, which he loathed, he had shot up at once into the highest circles by his wit, his dustmanship (which he carried like a banner), and his Nietzschean transcendence of good and evil. At intimate ducal dinners he sat on the right hand of the Duchess; and in country houses he smoked in the pantry and was made much of by the butler when he was not feeding in the dining room and being consulted by cabinet ministers. But he found it almost as hard to do all this on four thousand a year as Mrs. Eynsford Hill to live in Earlscourt on an income so pitiably smaller that I have not the heart to disclose its exact figure. He absolutely refused to add the last straw to his burden by contributing to Eliza's support.

Thus Freddy and Eliza, now Mr. and Mrs. Eynsford Hill, would have spent a penniless honeymoon but for a wedding present of £500 from the Colonel to Eliza. It lasted a long time because Freddy did not know how to spend money, never having had any to spend, and Eliza, socially trained by a pair of old bachelors, wore her clothes as long as they held together and looked pretty, without the least regard to their being many months out of fashion. Still, £500 will not last two young people for ever; and they both knew, and Eliza felt as well, that they must shift for themselves in the end. She could quarter herself on Wimpole Street because it had come to be her home; but she was quite aware that she ought not to quarter Freddy there, and that it would not be good for his character if she did.

Not that the Wimpole Street bachelors objected. When she consulted them, Higgins declined to be bothered about her housing problem when that solution was so simple. Eliza's desire to have Freddy in the house with her seemed of no more importance than if she had wanted an extra piece of bedroom furniture. Pleas as to Freddy's character, and the moral obligation on him to earn his own living, were lost on Higgins. He denied that Freddy had any character, and declared that if he tried to do any useful work some competent person would have the trouble of undoing it: a procedure involving a net loss to the community, and great unhappiness to Freddy himself, who was obviously intended by Nature for such light work as amusing Eliza, which, Higgins declared, was a much more useful and honorable occupation than working in the city. When Eliza referred again to her project of teaching phonetics, Higgins abated not a jot of his violent opposition to it. He said she was not within ten years of being qualified to meddle with his pet subject; and as it was evident that the Colonel agreed with him, she felt she could not go against them in this grave matter, and that she had no right, without Higgins's consent, to exploit the knowledge he had given her; for his knowledge seemed to her as much his private

property as his watch: Eliza was no communist. Besides, she was superstitiously devoted to them both, more entirely and frankly after her marriage than before it.

It was the Colonel who finally solved the problem, which had cost him much perplexed cogitation. He one day asked Eliza, rather shyly, whether she had quite given up her notion of keeping a flower shop. She replied that she had thought of it, but had put it out of her head, because the Colonel had said, that day at Mrs. Higgins's, that it would never do. The Colonel confessed that when he said that, he had not quite recovered from the dazzling impression of the day before. They broke the matter to Higgins that evening. The sole comment vouchsafed by him very nearly led to a serious quarrel with Eliza. It was to the effect that she would have in Freddy an ideal errand boy.

Freddy himself was next sounded on the subject. He said he had been thinking of a shop himself; though it had presented itself to his pennilessness as a small place in which Eliza should sell tobacco at one counter whilst he sold newspapers at the opposite one. But he agreed that it would be extraordinarily jolly to go early every morning with Eliza to Covent Garden and buy flowers on the scene of their first meeting: a sentiment which earned him many kisses from his wife. He added that he had always been afraid to propose anything of the sort, because Clara would make an awful row about a step that must damage her matrimonial chances, and his mother could not be expected to like it after clinging for so many years to that step of the social ladder on which retail trade is impossible.

This difficulty was removed by an event highly unexpected by Freddy's mother. Clara, in the course of her incursions into those artistic circles which were the highest within her reach, discovered that her conversational qualifications were expected to include a grounding in the novels of Mr. H. G. Wells. She borrowed them in various directions so energetically that she swallowed them all within two months. The result was a conversion of a kind quite common today. A modern Acts of the Apostles would fill fifty whole Bibles if anyone were capable of writing it.

Poor Clara, who appeared to Higgins and his mother as a disagreeable and ridiculous person, and to her own mother as in some inexplicable way a social failure, had never seen herself in either light; for, though to some extent ridiculed and mimicked in West Kensington like everybody else there, she was accepted as a rational and normal—or shall we say inevitable?—sort of human being. At worst they called her The Pusher; but to them no more than to herself had it ever occurred that she was pushing the air, and pushing it in a wrong direction. Still, she was not happy. She was growing desperate. Her one asset, the fact that her mother was what the Epsom greengrocer called a carriage lady, had no exchange value, apparently. It had prevented her from getting educated because the only education she could have afforded was education with the Earlscourt greengrocer's daughter. It had led her to seek the society of her mother's class; and that class simply would not have her, because she was much poorer than the greengrocer, and, far from being able to afford a maid, could not afford even a housemaid, and had to scrape along at home with an illiberally treated general servant. Under such circumstances nothing could give her an air of being a genuine product of Largelady Park. And yet its tradition made her regard a marriage with anyone within her reach as an unbearable humiliation. Commercial people and professional people in a small way were odious to her. She ran after painters and novelists; but she did not charm them; and her bold attempts to pick up and practise artistic and literary talk irritated them. She was, in short, an utter failure, an ignorant, incompetent, pretentious, unwelcome, penniless, useless little snob; and though she did not admit these disqualifications (for nobody ever faces unpleasant truths of this kind until the possibility of a way out dawns on them) she felt their effects too keenly to be satisfied with her position.

Clara had a startling eyeopener when, on being suddenly wakened to enthusiasm by a girl of her own age who dazzled her and produced in her a gushing desire to take her for a model, and gain her friendship, she discovered that this exquisite apparition had graduated from the gutter in a few months time. It shook her so violently, that when Mr. H. G. Wells lifted her on the point of his puissant pen, and placed her at the angle of view from which the life she was leading and the society to which she clung appeared in its true relation to real human needs and worthy social structure, he effected a conversion and a conviction of sin comparable to the most sensational feats of General Booth or Gypsy Smith. Clara's snobbery went bang. Life suddenly began to move with her. Without knowing how or why, she began to make friends and enemies. Some of the acquaintances to whom she had been a tedious or indifferent or ridiculous affliction, dropped her: others became cordial. To her amazement she found that some "quite nice" people were saturated with Wells, and that this accessibility to ideas was the secret of their niceness. People she had thought deeply religious, and had tried to conciliate on that tack with disastrous results, suddenly took an interest in her, and revealed a hostility to conventional religion which she had never conceived possible except among the most desperate

characters. They made her read Galsworthy; and Galsworthy exposed the vanity of Largelady Park and finished her. It exasperated her to think that the dungeon in which she had languished for so many unhappy years had been unlocked all the time, and that the impulses she had so carefully struggled with and stifled for the sake of keeping well with society, were precisely those by which alone she could have come into any sort of sincere human contact. In the radiance of these discoveries, and the tumult of their reaction, she made a fool of herself as freely and conspicuously as when she so rashly adopted Eliza's expletive in Mrs. Higgins's drawing room; for the new-born Wellsian had to find her bearings almost as ridiculously as a baby; but nobody hates a baby for its ineptitudes, or thinks the worse of it for trying to eat the matches; and Clara lost no friends by her follies. They laughed at her to her face this time; and she had to defend herself and fight it out as best she could.

When Freddy paid a visit to Earlscourt (which he never did when he could possibly help it) to make the desolating announcement that he and his Eliza were thinking of blackening the Largelady scutcheon by opening a shop, he found the little household already convulsed by a prior announcement from Clara that she also was going to work in an old furniture shop in Dover Street, which had been started by a fellow Wellsian. This appointment Clara owed, after all, to her old social accomplishment of Push. She had made up her mind that, cost what it might, she would see Mr. Wells in the flesh; and she had achieved her end at a garden party. She had better luck than so rash an enterprise deserved. Mr. Wells came up to her expectations. Age had not withered him, nor could custom stale his infinite variety in half an hour. His pleasant neatness and compactness, his small hands and feet, his teeming ready brain, his unaffected accessibility, and a certain fine apprehensiveness which stamped him as susceptible from his topmost hair to his tipmost toe, proved irresistible. Clara talked of nothing else for weeks and weeks afterwards. And as she happened to talk to the lady of the furniture shop, and that lady also desired above all things to know Mr. Wells and sell pretty things to him, she offered Clara a job on the chance of achieving that end through her.

And so it came about that Eliza's luck held, and the expected opposition to the flower shop melted away. The shop is in the arcade of a railway station not very far from the Victoria and Albert Museum; and if you live in that neighbourhood you may go there any day and buy a buttonhole from Eliza.

Now here is a last opportunity for romance. Would you not like to be assured that the shop was an immense success, thanks to Eliza's charms and her early business experience in Covent Garden? Alas! the truth is the truth: the shop did not pay for a long time, simply because Eliza and her Freddy did not know how to keep it. True, Eliza had not to begin at the very beginning: she knew the names and prices of the cheaper flowers; and her elation was unbounded when she found that Freddy, like all youths educated at cheap, pretentious, and thoroughly inefficient schools, knew a little Latin. It was very little, but enough to make him appear to her a Porson or Bentley, and to put him at his ease with botanical nomenclature. Unfortunately he knew nothing else; and Eliza, though she could count money up to eighteen shillings or so, and had acquired a certain familiarity with the language of Milton from her struggles to qualify herself for winning Higgins's bet, could not write out a bill without utterly disgracing the establishment. Freddy's power of stating in Latin that Balbus built a wall and that Gaul was divided into three parts did not carry with it the slightest knowledge of accounts or business: Colonel Pickering had to explain to him what a cheque book and a bank account meant. And the pair were by no means easily teachable. Freddy backed up Eliza in her obstinate refusal to believe that they could save money by engaging a bookkeeper with some knowledge of the business. How, they argued, could you possibly save money by going to extra expense when you already could not make both ends meet? But the Colonel, after making the ends meet over and over again, at last gently insisted; and Eliza, humbled to the dust by having to beg from him so often, and stung by the uproarious derision of Higgins, to whom the notion of Freddy succeeding at anything was a joke that never palled, grasped the fact that business, like phonetics, has to be learned.

On the piteous spectacle of the pair spending their evenings in shorthand schools and polytechnic classes, learning bookkeeping and typewriting with incipient junior clerks, male and female, from the elementary schools, let me not dwell. There were even classes at the London School of Economics, and a humble personal appeal to the director of that institution to recommend a course bearing on the flower business. He, being a humorist, explained to them the method of the celebrated Dickensian essay on Chinese Metaphysics by the gentleman who read an article on China and an article on Metaphysics and combined the information. He suggested that they should combine the London School with Kew Gardens. Eliza, to whom the procedure of the Dickensian gentleman seemed perfectly correct (as in fact it was) and not in the least funny (which was only her ignorance), took the advice with entire gravity. But the effort that

cost her the deepest humiliation was a request to Higgins, whose pet artistic fancy, next to Milton's verse, was caligraphy, and who himself wrote a most beautiful Italian hand, that he would teach her to write. He declared that she was congenitally incapable of forming a single letter worthy of the least of Milton's words; but she persisted; and again he suddenly threw himself into the task of teaching her with a combination of stormy intensity, concentrated patience, and occasional bursts of interesting disquisition on the beauty and nobility, the august mission and destiny, of human handwriting. Eliza ended by acquiring an extremely uncommercial script which was a positive extension of her personal beauty, and spending three times as much on stationery as anyone else because certain qualities and shapes on paper became indispensable to her. She could not even address an envelope in the usual way because it made the margins all wrong.

Their commercial schooldays were a period of disgrace and despair for the young couple. They seemed to be learning nothing about flower shops. At last they gave it up as hopeless, and shook the dust of the shorthand schools, and the polytechnics, and the London School of Economics from their feet for ever. Besides, the business was in some mysterious way beginning to take care of itself. They had somehow forgotten their objections to employing other people. They came to the conclusion that their own way was the best, and that they had really a remarkable talent for business. The Colonel, who had been compelled for some years to keep a sufficient sum on current account at his bankers to make up their deficits, found that the provision was unnecessary: the young people were prospering. It is true that there was not quite fair play between them and their competitors in trade. Their week-ends in the country cost them nothing, and saved them the price of their Sunday dinners; for the motor car was the Colonel's; and he and Higgins paid the hotel bills. Mr. F. Hill, florist and greengrocer (they soon discovered that there was money in asparagus; and asparagus led to other vegetables), had an air which stamped the business as classy; and in private life he was still Frederick Eynsford Hill, Esquire. Not that there was any swank about him: nobody but Eliza knew that he had been christened Frederick Challoner. Eliza herself swanked like anything.

That is all. That is how it has turned out. It is astonishing how much Eliza still manages to meddle in the housekeeping at Wimpole Street in spite of the shop and her own family. And it is notable that though she never nags her husband, and frankly loves the Colonel as if she were his favorite daughter, she has never got out of the habit of nagging Higgins that was established on the fatal night when she won his bet for him. She snaps his head off on the faintest provocation, or on none. He no longer dares to tease her by assuming an abysmal inferiority of Freddy's mind to his own. He storms and bullies and derides; but she stands up to him so ruthlessly that the Colonel has to ask her from time to time to be kinder to Higgins; and it is the only request of his that brings a mulish expression into her face. Nothing but some emergency or calamity great enough to break down all likes and dislikes, and throw them both back on their common humanity—and may they be spared any such trial!—will ever alter this. She knows that Higgins does not need her, just as her father did not need her. The very scrupulousness with which he told her that day that he had become used to having her there, and dependent on her for all sorts of little services, and that he should miss her if she went away (it would never have occurred to Freddy or the Colonel to say anything of the sort) deepens her inner certainty that she is "no more to him than them slippers"; yet she has a sense, too, that his indifference is deeper than the infatuation of commoner souls. She is immensely interested in him. She has even secret mischievous moments in which she wishes she could get him alone, on a desert island, away from all ties and with nobody else in the world to consider, and just drag him off his pedestal and see him making love like any common man. We all have private imaginations of that sort. But when it comes to business, to the life that she really leads as distinguished from the life of dreams and fancies, she likes Freddy and she likes the Colonel; and she does not like Higgins and Mr. Doolittle. Galatea never does quite like Pygmalion: his relation to her is too godlike to be altogether agreeable.

THE MADWOMAN OF CHAILLOT

JEAN GIRAUDOUX

JEAN GIRAUDOUX (1882–1944) was born in Bellac, Haute-Vienne, graduated with highest honors from the Ecole Normale Supérieure, passed the examinations for diplomatic service at the Quai d'Orsay, saw active service in the First World War, and with the peace resumed his duties as a diplomat. He began his career in literature as a short story writer and novelist; however after the production of his enormously successful play *Siegfried* (1928), Giraudoux turned his attention primarily to the theater. Of his plays, *Amphitryon 38* (1929), *The Enchanted* (1933), *Tiger at the Gates* (1935), *Ondine* (1939) and *The Madwoman of Chaillot* (1945) are probably the best known to audiences in this country.

CHARACTERS

THE WAITER.
THE LITTLE MAN.
THE PROSPECTOR.
THE PRESIDENT.
THE BARON.
THERESE.
THE STREET SINGER.
THE FLOWER GIRL.
THE RAGPICKER.
PAULETTE.
THE DEAF-MUTE.
IRMA.
THE SHOE-LACE PEDDLER.
THE BROKER.
THE STREET JUGGLER.
COUNTESS AURELIA, *Madwoman of Chaillot.*

THE DOORMAN.
DR. JADIN.
THE POLICEMAN.
PIERRE.
THE SERGEANT.
THE SEWER-MAN.
MME. CONSTANCE, *Madwoman of Passy.*
MLLE. GABRIELLE, *Madwoman of St. Sulpice.*
MME. JOSEPHINE, *Madwoman of La Concorde.*
THE PRESIDENTS.
THE PROSPECTORS.
THE PRESS AGENTS.
THE LADIES.
THE ADOLPHE BERTAUTS.

Copyright 1947 by Maurice Valency. Reprinted by permission of Random House, Inc.

SCENES

ACT ONE: *The Café Terrace of* Chez Francis.
ACT TWO: *The Countess' Cellar—21 Rue de Chaillot.*

ACT I

SCENE: *The café terrace at* Chez Francis, *on the Place de l'Alma in Paris. The Alma is in the stately quarter of Paris known as Chaillot, between the Champs Élysées and the Seine, across the river from the Eiffel Tower.*

Chez Francis has several rows of tables set out under its awning, and, as it is lunch time, a good many of them are occupied. At a table, downstage, a somewhat obvious BLONDE *with ravishing legs is sipping a vermouth-cassis and trying hard to engage the attention of* THE PROSPECTOR, *who sits at an adjacent table taking little sips of water and rolling them over his tongue with the air of a connoisseur. Downstage right, in front of the tables on the sidewalk, is the usual Paris bench, a stout and uncomfortable affair provided by the municipality for the benefit of those who prefer to sit without drinking. A* POLICEMAN *lounges about, keeping the peace without unnecessary exertion.*

TIME: *It is a little before noon in the Spring of next year.*

AT RISE: THE PRESIDENT *and* THE BARON *enter with importance, and are ushered to a front table by* THE WAITER.

THE PRESIDENT. Baron, sit down. This is a historic occasion. It must be properly celebrated. The waiter is going to bring out my special port.

THE BARON. Splendid.

THE PRESIDENT. [*Offers his cigar case.*] Cigar? My private brand.

THE BARON. Thank you. You know, this all gives me the feeling of one of those enchanted mornings in the *Arabian Nights* when thieves foregather in the market place. Thieves—pashas . . .

[*He sniffs the cigar judiciously, and begins lighting it.*]

THE PRESIDENT. [*Chuckles.*] Tell me about yourself.

THE BARON. Well, where shall I begin?

[THE STREET SINGER *enters. He takes off a battered black felt with a flourish and begins singing an ancient mazurka.*]

THE STREET SINGER. [*Sings.*]
    "Do you hear, Mademoiselle,
      Those musicians of hell?"

THE PRESIDENT. Waiter! Get rid of that man.

THE WAITER. He is singing *La Belle Polonaise*.

THE PRESIDENT. I didn't ask for the program. I asked you to get rid of him. [THE WAITER *doesn't budge.* THE SINGER *goes by himself.*] As you were saying, Baron . . . ?

THE BARON. Well, until I was fifty . . . [THE FLOWER GIRL *enters through the café door, center.*]

my life was relatively uncomplicated. It consisted of selling off one by one the various estates left me by my father. Three years ago, I parted with my last farm. Two years ago, I lost my last mistress. And now—all that is left me is . . .

THE FLOWER GIRL. [*To* THE BARON.] Violets, sir?

THE PRESIDENT. Run along.

[THE FLOWER GIRL *moves on.*]

THE BARON. [*Staring after her.*] So that, in short, all I have left now is my name.

THE PRESIDENT. Your name is precisely the name we need on our board of directors.

THE BARON. [*With an inclination of his head.*] Very flattering.

THE PRESIDENT. You will understand when I tell you that mine has been a very different experience. I came up from the bottom. My mother spent most of her life bent over a washtub in order to send me to school. I'm eternally grateful to her, of course, but I must confess that I no longer remember her face. It was no doubt beautiful—but when I try to recall it, I see only the part she invariably showed me—her rear.

THE BARON. Very touching.

THE PRESIDENT. When I was thrown out of school for the fifth and last time, I decided to find out for myself what makes the world go round. I ran errands for an editor, a movie star, a financier. . . . I began to understand a little what life is. Then, one day, in the subway, I saw a face. . . . My rise in life dates from that day.

THE BARON. Really?

THE PRESIDENT. One look at that face, and I knew. One look at mine, and he knew. And so I made my first thousand—passing a boxful of counterfeit notes. A year later, I saw another such face. It got me a nice berth in the narcotics business. Since then, all I do is to look out for such faces. And now here I am —president of eleven corporations, director of fifty-two companies, and, beginning today, chairman of the board of the international combine in which you have been so good as to accept a post. [THE RAGPICKER *passes, sees something under* THE PRESIDENT's *table, and stoops to pick it up.*] Looking for something?

THE RAGPICKER. Did you drop this?

THE PRESIDENT. I never drop anything.

THE RAGPICKER. Then this hundred-franc note isn't yours?

THE PRESIDENT. Give it here.

[THE RAGPICKER *gives him the note, and goes out.*]

THE BARON. Are you sure it's yours?

THE PRESIDENT. All hundred-franc notes, Baron, are mine.

THE BARON. Mr. President, there's something I've

been wanting to ask you. What exactly is the purpose of our new company? Or is that an indiscreet question . . . ?

THE PRESIDENT. Indiscreet? Not a bit. Merely unusual. As far as I know, you're the first member of a board of directors ever to ask such a question.

THE BARON. Do we plan to exploit a commodity? A utility?

THE PRESIDENT. My dear sir, I haven't the faintest idea.

THE BARON. But if you don't know—who does?

THE PRESIDENT. Nobody. And at the moment, it's becoming just a trifle embarrassing. Yes, my dear Baron, since we are now close business associates, I must confess that for the time being we're in a little trouble.

THE BARON. I was afraid of that. The stock issue isn't going well?

THE PRESIDENT. No, no—on the contrary. The stock issue is going beautifully. Yesterday morning at ten o'clock we offered 500,000 shares to the general public. By 10:05 they were all snapped up at par. By 10:20, when the police finally arrived, our offices were a shambles. . . . Windows smashed—doors torn off their hinges—you never saw anything so beautiful in your life! And this morning our stock is being quoted over the counter at 124 with no sellers, and the orders are still pouring in.

THE BARON. But in that case—what is the trouble?

THE PRESIDENT. The trouble is we have a tremendous capital, and not the slightest idea of what to do with it.

THE BARON. You mean all those people are fighting to buy stock in a company that has no object?

THE PRESIDENT. My dear Baron, do you imagine that when a subscriber buys a share of stock, he has any idea of getting behind a counter or digging a ditch? A stock certificate is not a tool, like a shovel, or a commodity, like a pound of cheese. What we sell a customer is not a share in a business, but a view of the Elysian Fields. A financier is a creative artist. Our function is to stimulate the imagination. We are poets!

THE BARON. But in order to stimulate the imagination, don't you need some field of activity?

THE PRESIDENT. Not at all. What you need for that is a name. A name that will stir the pulse like a trumpet call, set the brain awhirl like a movie star, inspire reverence like a cathedral. *United General International Consolidated!* Of course that's been used. That's what a corporation needs.

THE BARON. And do we have such a name?

THE PRESIDENT. So far we have only a blank space. In that blank space a name must be printed. This name must be a masterpiece. And if I seem a little nervous today, it's because—somehow—I've racked my brains, but it hasn't come to me. Oho! Look at that! Just like the answer to a prayer . . . ! [THE BARON *turns and stares in the direction of* THE PROSPECTOR.] You see? There's one. And what a beauty!

THE BARON. You mean that girl?

THE PRESIDENT. No, no, not the girl. That face. You see . . . ? The one that's drinking water.

THE BARON. You call that a face? That's a tombstone.

THE PRESIDENT. It's a milestone. It's a signpost. But is it pointing the way to steel, or wheat, or phosphates? That's what we have to find out. Ah! He sees me. He understands. He will be over.

THE BARON. And when he comes . . . ?

THE PRESIDENT. He will tell me what to do.

THE BARON. You mean business is done this way? You mean, you would trust a stranger with a matter of this importance?

THE PRESIDENT. Baron, I trust neither my wife, nor my daughter, nor my closest friend. My confidential secretary has no idea where I live. But a face like that I would trust with my inmost secrets. Though we have never laid eyes on each other before, that man and I know each other to the depths of our souls. He's no stranger—he's my brother, he's myself. You'll see. He'll be over in a minute. [THE DEAF-MUTE *enters and passes slowly among the tables, placing a small envelope before each customer. He comes to* THE PRESIDENT'S *table.*] What is this anyway? A conspiracy? We don't want your envelopes. Take them away. [THE DEAF-MUTE *makes a short but pointed speech in sign language.*] Waiter, what the devil's he saying?

THE WAITER. Only Irma understands him.

THE PRESIDENT. Irma? Who's Irma?

THE WAITER. [*Calls.*] Irma! It's the waitress inside, sir. Irma!

[IRMA *comes out. She is twenty. She has the face and figure of an angel.*]

IRMA. Yes?

THE WAITER. These gentlemen would . . .

THE PRESIDENT. Tell this fellow to get out of here, for God's sake! [THE DEAF-MUTE *makes another manual oration.*] What's he trying to say, anyway?

IRMA. He says it's an exceptionally beautiful morning, sir. . . .

THE PRESIDENT. Who asked him?

IRMA. But, he says, it was nicer before the gentleman stuck his face in it.

THE PRESIDENT. Call the manager!

[IRMA *shrugs. She goes back into the restaurant.* THE DEAF-MUTE *walks off, left. Meanwhile a* SHOELACE PEDDLER *has arrived.*]

PEDDLER. Shoelaces? Postcards?

THE BARON. I think I could use a shoelace.

THE PRESIDENT. No, no . . .

PEDDLER. Black? Tan?

THE BARON. [*Showing his shoes.*] What would you recommend?

PEDDLER. Anybody's guess.

THE BARON. Well, give me one of each.

THE PRESIDENT. [*Putting a hand on* THE BARON's *arm.*] Baron, although I am your chairman, I have no authority over your personal life—none, that is, except to fix the amount of your director's fees, and eventually to assign a motor car for your use. Therefore, I am asking you, as a personal favor to me, not to purchase anything from this fellow.

THE BARON. How can I resist so gracious a request? [THE PEDDLER *shrugs, and passes on.*] But I really don't understand. . . . What difference would it make?

THE PRESIDENT. Look here, Baron. Now that you're with us, you must understand that between this irresponsible riff-raff and us there is an impenetrable barrier. *We* have no dealings whatever with *them*.

THE BARON. But without us, the poor devil will starve.

THE PRESIDENT. No, he won't. He expects nothing from us. He has a clientele of his own. He sells shoelaces exclusively to those who have no shoes. Just as the necktie peddler sells only to those who wear no shirts. And that's why these street hawkers can afford to be insolent, disrespectful, and independent. They don't need us. They have a world of their own. Ah! My broker. Splendid. He's beaming.

[THE BROKER *walks up and grasps* THE PRESIDENT's *hand with enthusiasm.*]

THE BROKER. Mr. President! My heartiest congratulations! What a day! What a day!

[THE STREET JUGGLER *appears, right. He removes his coat, folds it carefully, and puts it on the bench. Then he opens a suitcase, from which he extracts a number of colored clubs.*]

THE PRESIDENT. [*Presenting* THE BROKER.] Baron Tommard, of our Board of Directors. My broker. [THE BROKER *bows. So does* THE JUGGLER. THE BROKER *sits down and signals for a drink.* THE JUGGLER *prepares to juggle.*] What's happened?

THE BROKER. Listen to this. Ten o'clock this morning. The market opens. [*As he speaks,* THE JUGGLER *provides a visual counterpart to* THE BROKER's *lines, his clubs rising and falling in rhythm to* THE BROKER's *words.*] Half million shares issued at par, par value a hundred, quoted on the curb at 124 and we start buying at 126, 127, 129—and it's going up—up—up— [THE JUGGLER's *clubs rise higher and higher.*] —132 —133—138—141—141—141—141 . . .

THE BARON. May I ask . . . ?

THE PRESIDENT. No, no—any explanation would only confuse you.

THE BROKER. Ten forty-five we start selling short on rumors of a Communist plot; market bearish. . . . 141—138—133—132—and it's down—down—down—102—and we start buying back at 93. Eleven o'clock, rumors denied—95—98—101—106—124—141—and by 11:30 we've got it all back—net profit three and a half million francs.

THE PRESIDENT. Classical. Pure. [THE JUGGLER *bows again. A* LITTLE MAN *leans over from a near-by table, listening intently, and trembling with excitement.*] And how many shares do we reserve to each member of the board?

THE BROKER. Fifty, as agreed.

THE PRESIDENT. Bit stingy, don't you think?

THE BROKER. All right—three thousand.

THE PRESIDENT. That's a little better. [*To* THE BARON.] You get the idea?

THE BARON. I'm beginning to get it.

THE BROKER. And now we come to the exciting part . . . [THE JUGGLER *prepares to juggle with balls of fire.*] Listen carefully: With 35 percent of our funded capital under Section 32 I buy 50,000 United at 36 which I immediately reconvert into 32,000 National Amalgamated two's preferred which I set up as collateral on 150,000 General Consols which I deposit against a credit of fifteen billion to buy Eastern Hennequin which I immediately turn into Argentine wheat realizing 136 percent of the original investment which naturally accrues as capital gain and not as corporate income thus saving twelve millions in taxes, and at once convert the 25 percent cotton reserve into lignite, and as our people swing into action in London and New York, I beat up the price on greige goods from 26 to 92—114—203—306 —— [THE JUGGLER *by now is juggling his fireballs in the sky. The balls no longer return to his hands.*] 404 . . .

[THE LITTLE MAN *can stand no more. He rushes over and dumps a sackful of money on the table.*]

THE LITTLE MAN. Here—take it—please, take it!

THE BROKER. [*Frigidly.*] Who is this man? What is this money?

THE LITTLE MAN. It's my life's savings. Every cent. I put it all in your hands.

THE BROKER. Can't you see we're busy?

THE LITTLE MAN. But I beg you . . . It's my only chance . . . Please don't turn me away.

THE BROKER. Oh, all right. [*He sweeps the money into his pocket.*] Well?

THE LITTLE MAN. I thought—perhaps you'd give me a little receipt. . . .

THE PRESIDENT. My dear man, people like us don't give receipts for money. We take them.

THE LITTLE MAN. Oh, pardon. Of course. I was

confused. Here it is. [*Scribbles a receipt.*] Thank you—thank you—thank you.

[*He rushes off joyfully.* THE STREET SINGER *reappears.*]

THE STREET SINGER. [*Sings.*]
"Do you hear, Mademoiselle,
Those musicians of hell?"

THE PRESIDENT. What, again? Why does he keep repeating those two lines like a parrot?

THE WAITER. What else can he do? He doesn't know any more and the song's been out of print for years.

THE BARON. Couldn't he sing a song he knows?

THE WAITER. He likes this one. He hopes if he keeps singing the beginning someone will turn up to teach him the end.

THE PRESIDENT. Tell him to move on. We don't know the song.

[THE PROFESSOR *strolls by, swinging his cane. He overhears.*]

THE PROFESSOR. [*Stops and addresses* THE PRESIDENT *politely.*] Nor do I, my dear sir. Nor do I. And yet, I'm in exactly the same predicament. I remember just two lines of my favorite song, as a child. A mazurka also, in case you're interested. . . .

THE PRESIDENT. I'm not.

THE PROFESSOR. Why is it, I wonder, that one always forgets the words of a mazurka? I suppose they just get lost in that damnable rhythm. All I remember is: [*He sings.*]
"From England to Spain
I have drunk, it was bliss . . ."

THE STREET SINGER. [*Walks over, and picks up the tune.*]
"Red wine and champagne
And many a kiss."

THE PROFESSOR. Oh, God! It all comes back to me . . . ! [*He sings.*]
"Red lips and white hands I have known
Where the nightingales dwell. . . ."

THE PRESIDENT. [*Holding his hands to his ears.*] Please—please . . .

THE STREET SINGER.
"And to each one I've whispered, 'My own,'
And to each one, I've murmured: 'Farewell.'"

THE PRESIDENT. Farewell. Farewell.

THE STREET SINGER. }
THE PROFESSOR.   } [*Duo.*]
"But there's one I shall never forget. . . ."

THE PRESIDENT. This isn't a café. It's a circus!

[*The two go off, still singing:* "There is one that's engraved in my heart." THE PROSPECTOR *gets up slowly and walks toward* THE PRESIDENT's *table. He looks down without a word.*

There is a tense silence.]

THE PROSPECTOR. Well?

THE PRESIDENT. I need a name.

THE PROSPECTOR. [*Nods, with complete comprehension.*] I need fifty thousand.

THE PRESIDENT. For a corporation.

THE PROSPECTOR. For a woman.

THE PRESIDENT. Immediately.

THE PROSPECTOR. Before evening.

THE PRESIDENT. Something . . .

THE PROSPECTOR. Unusual?

THE PRESIDENT. Something . . .

THE PROSPECTOR. Provocative?

THE PRESIDENT. Something . . .

THE PROSPECTOR. Practical.

THE PRESIDENT. Yes.

THE PROSPECTOR. Fifty thousand. Cash.

THE PRESIDENT. I'm listening.

THE PROSPECTOR. *International Substrate of Paris, Inc.*

THE PRESIDENT. [*Snaps his fingers.*] That's it! [*To* THE BROKER.] Pay him off. [THE BROKER *pays with* THE LITTLE MAN's *money.*] Now—what does it mean?

THE PROSPECTOR. It means what it says. I'm a prospector.

THE PRESIDENT. [*Rises.*] A prospector! Allow me to shake your hand. Baron. You are in the presence of one of nature's noblemen. Shake his hand. This is Baron Tommard. [*They shake hands.*] It is this man, my dear Baron, who smells out in the bowels of the earth those deposits of metal or liquid on which can be founded the only social unit of which our age is capable—the corporation. Sit down, please. [*They all sit.*] And now that we have a name . . .

THE PROSPECTOR. You need a property.

THE PRESIDENT. Precisely.

THE PROSPECTOR. I have one.

THE PRESIDENT. A claim?

THE PROSPECTOR. Terrific.

THE PRESIDENT. Foreign?

THE PROSPECTOR. French.

THE BARON. In Indo-China?

THE BROKER. Morocco?

THE PRESIDENT. In France?

THE PROSPECTOR. [*Matter of fact.*] In Paris.

THE PRESIDENT. In Paris? You've been prospecting in Paris?

THE BARON. For women, no doubt.

THE PRESIDENT. For art?

THE BROKER. For gold?

THE PROSPECTOR. Oil.

THE BROKER. He's crazy.

THE PRESIDENT. Sh! He's inspired.

THE PROSPECTOR. You think I'm crazy. Well, they thought Columbus was crazy.

THE BARON. Oil in Paris?

THE BROKER. But how is it possible?

THE PROSPECTOR. It's not only possible. It's certain.

THE PRESIDENT. Tell us.

THE PROSPECTOR. You don't know, my dear sir, what treasures Paris conceals. Paris is the least prospected place in the world. We've gone over the rest of the planet with a fine-tooth comb. But has anyone ever thought of looking for oil in Paris? Nobody. Before me, that is.

THE PRESIDENT. Genius!

THE PROSPECTOR. No. Just a practical man. I use my head.

THE BARON. But why has nobody ever thought of this before?

THE PROSPECTOR. The treasures of the earth, my dear sir, are not easy to find nor to get at. They are invariably guarded by dragons. Doubtless there is some reason for this. For once we've dug out and consumed the internal ballast of the planet, the chances are it will shoot off on some irresponsible tangent and smash itself up in the sky. Well, that's the risk we take. Anyway, that's not my business. A prospector has enough to worry about.

THE BARON. I know—snakes—tarantulas—fleas . . .

THE PROSPECTOR. Worse than that, sir. Civilization.

THE PRESIDENT. Does that annoy you?

THE PROSPECTOR. Civilization gets in our way all the time. In the first place, it covers the earth with cities and towns which are damned awkward to dig up when you want to see what's underneath. It's not only the real-estate people—you can always do business with them—it's human sentimentality. How do you do business with that?

THE PRESIDENT. I see what you mean.

THE PROSPECTOR. They say that where we pass, nothing ever grows again. What of it? Is a park any better than a coal mine? What's a mountain got that a slag pile hasn't? What would you rather have in your garden—an almond tree or an oil well?

THE PRESIDENT. Well . . .

THE PROSPECTOR. Exactly. But what's the use of arguing with these fools? Imagine the choicest place you ever saw for an excavation, and what do they put there? A playground for children! Civilization!

THE PRESIDENT. Just show us the point where you want to start digging. We'll do the rest. Even if it's in the middle of the Louvre. Where's the oil?

THE PROSPECTOR. Perhaps you think it's easy to make an accurate fix in an area like Paris where everything conspires to put you off the scent? Women —perfume—flowers—history. You can talk all you like about geology, but an oil deposit, gentlemen, has to be smelled out. I have a good nose. I go further. I have a phenomenal nose. But the minute I get the right whiff—the minute I'm on the scent—a fragrance rises from what I take to be the spiritual deposits of the past—and I'm completely at sea. Now take this very point, for example, this very spot.

THE BARON. You mean—right here in Chaillot?

THE PROSPECTOR. Right under here.

THE PRESIDENT. Good heavens!

[He looks under his chair.]

THE PROSPECTOR. It's taken me months to locate this spot.

THE BARON. But what in the world makes you think . . . ?

THE PROSPECTOR. Do you know this place, Baron?

THE BARON. Well, I've been sitting here for thirty years.

THE PROSPECTOR. Did you ever taste the water?

THE BARON. The water! Good God, no!

THE PROSPECTOR. It's plain to see that you are no prospector! A prospector, Baron, is addicted to water as a drunkard to wine. Water, gentlemen, is the one substance from which the earth can conceal nothing. It sucks out its innermost secrets and brings them to our very lips. Well—beginning at Notre Dame, where I first caught the scent of oil three months ago, I worked my way across Paris, glassful by glassful, sampling the water, until at last I came to this café. And here—just two days ago—I took a sip. My heart began to thump. Was it possible that I was deceived? I took another, a third, a fourth, a fifth. I was trembling like a leaf. But there was no mistake. Each time that I drank, my taste-buds thrilled to the most exquisite flavor known to a prospector—the flavor of — [With utmost lyricism.] petroleum!

THE PRESIDENT. Waiter! Some water and four glasses. Hurry. This round, gentlemen, is on me. And as a toast—I shall propose International Substrate of Paris, Incorporated. [THE WAITER brings a decanter and the glasses. THE PRESIDENT pours out the water amid profound silence. They taste it with the air of connoisseurs savoring something that has never before passed human lips. Then they look at each other doubtfully. THE PROSPECTOR pours himself a second glass and drinks it off.] Well . . .

THE BROKER. Ye-es . . .

THE BARON. Mm . . .

THE PROSPECTOR. Get it?

THE BARON. Tastes queer.

THE PROSPECTOR. That's it. To the unpracticed palate it tastes queer. But to the taste-buds of the expert—ah!

THE BARON. Still, there's one thing I don't quite understand . . .

THE PROSPECTOR. Yes?

THE BARON. This café doesn't have its own well, does it?

THE PROSPECTOR. Of course not. This is Paris water.

THE BROKER. Then why should it taste different here than anywhere else?

THE PROSPECTOR. Because, my dear sir, the pipes that carry this water pass deep through the earth, and the earth just here is soaked with oil, and this oil permeates the pores of the iron and flavors the water it carries. Ever so little, yes—but quite enough to betray its presence to the sensitive tongue of the specialist.

THE BARON. I see.

THE PROSPECTOR. I don't say everyone is capable of tasting it. No. But I—I can detect the presence of oil in water that has passed within fifteen miles of a deposit. Under special circumstances, twenty.

THE PRESIDENT. Phenomenal!

THE PROSPECTOR. And so here I am with the greatest discovery of the age on my hands—but the blasted authorities won't let me drill a single well unless I show them the oil! Now how can I show them the oil unless they let me dig? Completely stymied! Eh?

THE PRESIDENT. What? A man like you?

THE PROSPECTOR. That's what they think. That's what they want. Have you noticed the strange glamor of the women this morning? And the quality of the sunshine? And this extraordinary convocation of vagabonds buzzing about protectively like bees around a hive? Do you know why it is? Because they know. It's a plot to distract us, to turn us from our purpose. Well, let them try. I know there's oil here. And I'm going to dig it up, even if I . . . [He smiles.] Shall I tell you my little plan?

THE PRESIDENT. By all means.

THE PROSPECTOR. Well . . . For heaven's sake, what's that?

[At this point, the MADWOMAN enters. She is dressed in the grand fashion of 1885, a taffeta skirt with an immense train—which she has gathered up by means of a clothespin—ancient button shoes, and a hat in the style of Marie Antoinette. She wears a lorgnette on a chain, and an enormous cameo pin at her throat. In her hand she carries a small basket. She walks in with great dignity, extracts a dinner bell from the bosom of her dress, and rings it sharply. IRMA appears.]

COUNTESS. Are my bones ready, Irma?

IRMA. There won't be much today, Countess. We had broilers. Can you wait? While the gentleman inside finishes eating?

COUNTESS. And my gizzard?

IRMA. I'll try to get it away from him.

COUNTESS. If he eats my gizzard, save me the giblets. They will do for the tomcat that lives under the bridge. He likes a few giblets now and again.

IRMA. Yes, Countess.

[IRMA goes back into the café. The COUNTESS takes a few steps and stops in front of THE PRESIDENT's table. She examines him with undisguised disapproval.]

THE PRESIDENT. Waiter. Ask that woman to move on.

THE WAITER. Sorry, sir. This is her café.

THE PRESIDENT. Is she the manager of the café?

THE WAITER. She's the Madwoman of Chaillot.

THE PRESIDENT. A Madwoman? She's mad?

THE WAITER. Who says she's mad?

THE PRESIDENT. You just said so yourself.

THE WAITER. Look, sir. You asked me who she was. And I told you. What's mad about her? She's the Madwoman of Chaillot.

THE PRESIDENT. Call a policeman.

[The COUNTESS whistles through her fingers. At once, THE DOORMAN runs out of the café. He has three scarves in his hands.]

COUNTESS. Have you found it? My feather boa?

THE DOORMAN. Not yet, Countess. Three scarves. But no boa.

COUNTESS. It's five years since I lost it. Surely you've had time to find it.

THE DOORMAN. Take one of these, Countess. Nobody's claimed them.

COUNTESS. A boa like that doesn't vanish, you know. A feather boa nine feet long!

THE DOORMAN. How about this blue one?

COUNTESS. With my pink ruffle and my green veil? You're joking! Let me see the yellow. [She tries it on.] How does it look?

THE DOORMAN. Terrific.

[With a magnificent gesture, she flings the scarf about her, upsetting THE PRESIDENT's glass and drenching his trousers with water. She stalks off without a glance at him.]

THE PRESIDENT. Waiter! I'm making a complaint.

THE WAITER. Against whom?

THE PRESIDENT. Against her! Against you! The whole gang of you! That singer! That shoelace peddler! That female lunatic! Or whatever you call her!

THE BARON. Calm yourself, Mr. President. . . .

THE PRESIDENT. I'll do nothing of the sort! Baron, the first thing we have to do is to get rid of these people! Good heavens, look at them! Every size, shape, color, and period of history imaginable. It's utter anarchy! I tell you, sir, the only safeguard of order and discipline in the modern world is a standardized worker with interchangeable parts. That would solve the entire problem of management. Here, the manager . . . And there—one composite drudge grunting and sweating all over the world. Just we two. Ah, how beautiful! How easy on the eyes! How restful for the conscience!

THE BARON. Yes, yes—of course.

THE PRESIDENT. Order. Symmetry. Balance. But instead of that, what? Here in Chaillot, the very citadel of management, these insolent phantoms of the past come to beard us with their raffish individualism—with the right of the voiceless to sing, of the dumb to make speeches, of trousers to have no seats and bosoms to have dinner bells!

THE BARON. But, after all, do these people matter?

THE PRESIDENT. My dear sir, wherever the poor are happy, and the servants are proud, and the mad are respected, our power is at an end. Look at that! That waiter! That madwoman! That flower girl! Do I get that sort of service? And suppose that I—president of twelve corporations and ten times a millionaire—were to stick a gladiolus in my buttonhole and start yelling— [*He tinkles his spoon in a glass violently, yelling.*] Are my bones ready, Irma?

THE BARON. [*Reprovingly.*] Mr. President . . .

[*People at the adjoining tables turn and stare with raised eyebrows.* THE WAITER *starts to come over.*]

THE PRESIDENT. You see? Now.

THE PROSPECTOR. We were discussing my plan.

THE PRESIDENT. Ah yes, your plan. [*He glances in the direction of the* MADWOMAN's *table.*] Careful—she's looking at us.

THE PROSPECTOR. Do you know what a bomb is?

THE PRESIDENT. I'm told they explode.

THE PROSPECTOR. Exactly. You see that white building across the river. Do you happen to know what that is?

THE PRESIDENT. I do not.

THE PROSPECTOR. That's the office of the City Architect. That man has stubbornly refused to give me a permit to drill for oil anywhere within the limits of the city of Paris. I've tried everything with him—influence, bribes, threats. He says I'm crazy. And now . . .

THE PRESIDENT. Oh, my God! What is this one trying to sell us?

[*A little* OLD MAN *enters left, and doffs his hat politely. He is somewhat ostentatiously respectable—gloved, pomaded, and carefully dressed, with a white handkerchief peeping out of his breast pocket.*]

DR. JADIN. Nothing but health, sir. Or rather the health of the feet. But remember—as the foot goes, so goes the man. May I present myself . . . ? Dr. Gaspard Jadin, French Navy, retired. Former specialist in the extraction of ticks and chiggers. At present specializing in the extraction of bunions and corns. In case of sudden emergency, Martial the waiter will furnish my home address. My office is here, second row, third table, week days, twelve to five. Thank you very much. [*He sits at his table.*]

THE WAITER. Your vermouth, Doctor?

DR. JADIN. My vermouth. My vermouths. How are your gallstones today, Martial?

THE WAITER. Fine. Fine. They rattle like anything.

DR. JADIN. Splendid. [*He spies the* COUNTESS.] Good morning, Countess. How's the floating kidney? Still afloat? [*She nods graciously.*] Splendid. Splendid. So long as it floats, it can't sink.

THE PRESIDENT. This is impossible! Let's go somewhere else.

THE PROSPECTOR. No. It's nearly noon.

THE PRESIDENT. Yes. It is. Five to twelve.

THE PROSPECTOR. In five minutes' time you're going to see that City Architect blown up, building and all —boom!

THE BROKER. Are you serious?

THE PROSPECTOR. That imbecile has no one to blame but himself. Yesterday noon, he got my ultimatum—he's had twenty-four hours to think it over. No permit? All right. Within two minutes my agent is going to drop a little package in his coal bin. And three minutes after that, precisely at noon . . .

THE BARON. You prospectors certainly use modern methods.

THE PROSPECTOR. The method may be modern. But the idea is old. To get at the treasure, it has always been necessary to slay the dragon. I guarantee that after this, the City Architect will be more reasonable. The new one, I mean.

THE PRESIDENT. Don't you think we're sitting a little close for comfort?

THE PROSPECTOR. Oh no, no. Don't worry. And, above all, don't stare. We may be watched. [*A clock strikes.*] Why, that's noon. Something's wrong! Good God! What's this? [*A* POLICEMAN *staggers in bearing a lifeless body on his shoulders in the manner prescribed as "The Fireman's Lift."*] It's Pierre! My agent! [*He walks over with affected nonchalance.*] I say, Officer, what's that you've got?

THE POLICEMAN. Drowned man.

[*He puts him down on the bench.*]

THE WAITER. He's not drowned. His clothes are dry. He's been slugged.

THE POLICEMAN. Slugged is also correct. He was just jumping off the bridge when I came along and pulled him back. I slugged him, naturally, so he wouldn't drag me under. Life Saving Manual, Rule 5: "In cases where there is danger of being dragged under, it is necessary to render the subject unconscious by means of a sharp blow." He's had that.

[*He loosens the clothes and begins applying artificial respiration.*]

THE PROSPECTOR. The stupid idiot! What the devil did he do with the bomb? That's what comes of employing amateurs!

THE PRESIDENT. You don't think he'll give you away?

THE PROSPECTOR. Don't worry. [*He walks over to* THE POLICEMAN.] Say, what do you think you're doing?

THE POLICEMAN. Lifesaving. Artificial respiration. First aid to the drowning.

THE PROSPECTOR. But he's not drowning.

THE POLICEMAN. But he thinks he is.

THE PROSPECTOR. You'll never bring him round that way, my friend. That's meant for people who drown in water. It's no good at all for those who drown without water.

THE POLICEMAN. What am I supposed to do? I've just been sworn in. It's my first day on the beat. I can't afford to get in trouble. I've got to go by the book.

THE PROSPECTOR. Perfectly simple. Take him back to the bridge where you found him and throw him in. Then you can save his life and you'll get a medal. This way, you'll only get fined for slugging an innocent man.

THE POLICEMAN. What do you mean, innocent? He was just going to jump when I grabbed him.

THE PROSPECTOR. Have you any proof of that?

THE POLICEMAN. Well, I saw him.

THE PROSPECTOR. Written proof? Witnesses?

THE POLICEMAN. No, but . . .

THE PROSPECTOR. Then don't waste time arguing. You're in trouble. Quick—before anybody notices—throw him in and dive after him. It's the only way out.

THE POLICEMAN. But I don't swim.

THE PRESIDENT. You'll learn how on the way down. Before you were born, did you know how to breathe?

THE POLICEMAN. [*Convinced.*] All right. Here we go. [*He starts lifting the body.*]

DR. JADIN. One moment, please. I don't like to interfere, but it's my professional duty to point out that medical science has definitely established the fact of intra-uterine respiration. Consequently, this policeman, even before he was born, knew not only how to breathe but also how to cough, hiccup, and belch.

THE PRESIDENT. Suppose he did—how does it concern you?

DR. JADIN. On the other hand, medical science has never established the fact of intra-uterine swimming or diving. Under the circumstances, we are forced to the opinion, Officer, that if you dive in you will probably drown.

THE POLICEMAN. You think so?

THE PROSPECTOR. Who asked you for an opinion?

THE PRESIDENT. Pay no attention to that quack, Officer.

DR. JADIN. Quack, sir?

THE PROSPECTOR. This is not a medical matter. It's a legal problem. The officer has made a grave error. He's new. We're trying to help him.

THE BROKER. He's probably afraid of the water.

THE POLICEMAN. Nothing of the sort. Officially, I'm afraid of nothing. But I always follow doctor's orders.

DR. JADIN. You see, Officer, when a child is born . . .

THE PROSPECTOR. Now, what does he care about when a child is born? He's got a dying man on his hands. . . . Officer, if you want my advice . . .

THE POLICEMAN. It so happens, I care a lot about when a child is born. It's part of my duty to aid and assist any woman in childbirth or labor.

THE PRESIDENT. Can you imagine!

THE POLICEMAN. Is it true, Doctor, what they say, that when you have twins, the first born is considered to be the youngest?

DR. JADIN. Quite correct. And what's more, if the twins happen to be born at midnight on December 31st, the older is a whole year younger. He does his military service a year later. That's why you have to keep your eyes open. And that's the reason why a queen always gives birth before witnesses. . . .

THE POLICEMAN. God! The things a policeman is supposed to know! Doctor, what does it mean, if when I get up in the morning sometimes . . .

THE PROSPECTOR. [*Nudging* THE PRESIDENT *meaningfully.*] The old woman . . .

THE BROKER. Come on, Baron.

THE PRESIDENT. I think we'd better all run along.

THE PROSPECTOR. Leave him to me.

THE PRESIDENT. I'll see you later.

[THE PRESIDENT *steals off with* THE BROKER *and* THE BARON.]

THE POLICEMAN. [*Still in conference with* DR. JADIN.] But what's really worrying me, Doctor, is this—don't you think it's a bit risky for a man to marry after forty-five?

[THE BROKER *runs in breathlessly.*]

THE BROKER. Officer! Officer!

THE POLICEMAN. What's the trouble?

THE BROKER. Quick! Two women are calling for help—on the sidewalk—Avenue Wilson!

THE POLICEMAN. Two women at once? Standing up or lying down?

THE BROKER. You'd better go and see. Quick!

THE PROSPECTOR. You'd better take the Doctor with you.

THE POLICEMAN. Come along, Doctor, come along. . . . [*Pointing to* PIERRE.] Tell him to wait till I get back. Come along, Doctor.

[*He runs out,* THE DOCTOR *following.* THE PROSPECTOR *moves over toward* PIERRE, *but* IRMA *crosses in front of him and takes the boy's hand.*]

IRMA. How beautiful he is! Is he dead, Martial?

THE WAITER. [*Handing her a pocket mirror.*] Hold this mirror to his mouth. If it clouds over . . .

IRMA. It clouds over.

THE WAITER. He's alive.

[*He holds out his hand for the mirror.*]

IRMA. Just a sec—— [*She rubs it clean and looks at herself intently. Before handing it back, she fixes her hair and applies her lipstick. Meanwhile* THE PROSPECTOR *tries to get around the other side, but the* COUNTESS' *eagle eye drives him off. He shrugs his shoulders and exits with* THE BARON.] Oh, look—he's opening his eyes!

[PIERRE *opens his eyes, stares intently at* IRMA *and closes them again with the expression of a man who is among the angels.*]

PIERRE. [*Murmurs.*] Oh! How beautiful!

VOICE. [*From within the café.*] Irma!

IRMA. Coming. Coming.

[*She goes in, not without a certain reluctance. The* COUNTESS *at once takes her place on the bench, and also the young man's hand.* PIERRE *sits up suddenly, and finds himself staring, not at* IRMA, *but into the very peculiar face of the* COUNTESS. *His expression changes.*]

COUNTESS. You're looking at my iris? Isn't it beautiful?

PIERRE. Very.

[*He drops back, exhausted.*]

COUNTESS. The Sergeant was good enough to say it becomes me. But I no longer trust his taste. Yesterday, the flower girl gave me a lily, and he said it didn't suit me.

PIERRE. [*Weakly.*] It's beautiful.

COUNTESS. He'll be very happy to know that you agree with him. He's really quite sensitive. [*She calls.*] Sergeant!

PIERRE. No, please—don't call the police.

COUNTESS. But I must. I think I hurt his feelings.

PIERRE. Let me go, Madame.

COUNTESS. No, no. Stay where you are. Sergeant!

[PIERRE *struggles weakly to get up.*]

PIERRE. Please let me go.

COUNTESS. I'll do nothing of the sort. When you let someone go, you never see him again. I let Charlotte Mazumet go. I never saw her again.

PIERRE. Oh, my head.

COUNTESS. I let Adolphe Bertaut go. And I was holding him. And I never saw him again.

PIERRE. Oh, God!

COUNTESS. Except once. Thirty years later. In the market. He had changed a great deal—he didn't know me. He sneaked a melon from right under my nose, the only good one of the year. Ah, here we are. Sergeant!

[THE POLICE SERGEANT *comes in with importance.*]

THE SERGEANT. I'm in a hurry, Countess.

COUNTESS. With regard to the iris. This young man agrees with you. He says it suits me.

THE SERGEANT. [*Going.*] There's a man drowning in the Seine.

COUNTESS. He's not drowning in the Seine. He's drowning here. Because I'm holding him tight—as I should have held Adolphe Bertaut. But if I let him go, I'm sure he will go and drown in the Seine. He's a lot better looking than Adolphe Bertaut, wouldn't you say? [PIERRE *sighs deeply.*]

THE SERGEANT. How would I know?

COUNTESS. I've shown you his photograph. The one with the bicycle.

THE SERGEANT. Oh, yes. The one with the harelip.

COUNTESS. I've told you a hundred times! Adolphe Bertaut had no harelip. That was a scratch in the negative. [THE SERGEANT *takes out his notebook and pencil.*] What are you doing?

THE SERGEANT. I am taking down the drowned man's name, given name, and date of birth.

COUNTESS. You think that's going to stop him from jumping in the river? Don't be silly, Sergeant. Put that book away and try to console him.

THE SERGEANT. I should try and console him?

COUNTESS. When people want to die, it is your job as a guardian of the state to speak out in praise of life. Not mine.

THE SERGEANT. I should speak out in praise of life?

COUNTESS. I assume you have some motive for interfering with people's attempts to kill each other, and rob each other, and run each other over? If you believe that life has some value, tell him what it is. Go on.

THE SERGEANT. Well, all right. Now look, young man . . .

COUNTESS. His name is Roderick.

PIERRE. My name is not Roderick.

COUNTESS. Yes, it is. It's noon. At noon all men become Roderick.

THE SERGEANT. Except Adolphe Bertaut.

COUNTESS. In the days of Adolphe Bertaut, we were forced to change the men when we got tired of their names. Nowadays, we're more practical—each hour on the hour all names are automatically changed. The men remain the same. But you're not here to discuss Adolphe Bertaut, Sergeant. You're here to convince the young man that life is worth living.

PIERRE. It isn't.

THE SERGEANT. Quiet. Now then—what was the idea of jumping off the bridge, anyway?

COUNTESS. The idea was to land in the river. Roderick doesn't seem to be at all confused about that.

THE SERGEANT. Now how can I convince anybody that life is worth living if you keep interrupting all the time?

COUNTESS. I'll be quiet.

THE SERGEANT. First of all, Mr. Roderick, you have to realize that suicide is a crime against the state. And why is it a crime against the state? Because every time anybody commits suicide, that means one soldier less for the army, one taxpayer less for the . . .

COUNTESS. Sergeant, isn't there something about life that you really enjoy?

THE SERGEANT. That I enjoy?

COUNTESS. Well, surely in all these years, you must have found something worth living for. Some secret pleasure, or passion. Don't blush. Tell him about it.

THE SERGEANT. Who's blushing? Well, naturally, yes—I have my passions—like everybody else. The fact is, since you ask me—I love—to play—casino. And if the gentleman would like to join me, by and by when I go off duty, we can sit down to a nice little game in the back room with a nice cold glass of beer. If he wants to kill an hour, that is.

COUNTESS. He doesn't want to kill an hour. He wants to kill himself. Well? Is that all the police force has to offer by way of earthly bliss?

THE SERGEANT. Huh? You mean—— [*He jerks a thumb in the direction of the pretty* BLONDE, *who has just been joined by a* BRUNETTE *of the same stamp.*] Paulette?

[*The young man groans.*]

COUNTESS. You're not earning your salary, Sergeant. I defy anybody to stop dying on your account.

THE SERGEANT. Go ahead, if you can do any better. But you won't find it easy.

COUNTESS. Oh, this is not a desperate case at all. A young man who has just fallen in love with someone who has fallen in love with him!

PIERRE. She hasn't. How could she?

COUNTESS. Oh, yes, she has. She was holding your hand, just as I'm holding it, when all of a sudden . . . Did you ever know Marshal Canrobert's niece?

THE SERGEANT. How could he know Marshal Canrobert's niece?

COUNTESS. Lots of people knew her—when she was alive. [PIERRE *begins to struggle energetically.*] No, no, Roderick—stop—stop!

THE SERGEANT. You see? You won't do any better than I did.

COUNTESS. No? Let's bet. I'll bet my iris against one of your gold buttons. Right?—Roderick, I know very well why you tried to drown yourself in the river.

PIERRE. You don't at all.

COUNTESS. It's because that Prospector wanted you to commit a horrible crime.

PIERRE. How did you know that?

COUNTESS. He stole my boa, and now he wants you to kill me.

PIERRE. Not exactly.

COUNTESS. It wouldn't be the first time they've tried it. But I'm not so easy to get rid of, my boy, oh, no . . . Because . . .

[THE DOORMAN *rides in on his bicycle. He winks at* THE SERGEANT, *who has now seated himself while* THE WAITER *serves him a beer.*]

THE DOORMAN. Take it easy, Sergeant.

THE SERGEANT. I'm busy saving a drowning man.

COUNTESS. They can't kill me because—I have no desire to die.

PIERRE. You're fortunate.

COUNTESS. To be alive is to be fortunate, Roderick. Of course, in the morning, when you first awake, it does not always seem so very gay. When you take your hair out of the drawer, and your teeth out of the glass, you are apt to feel a little out of place in this world. Especially if you've just been dreaming that you're a little girl on a pony looking for strawberries in the woods. But all you need to feel the call of life once more is a letter in your mail giving you your schedule for the day—your mending, your shopping, that letter to your grandmother that you never seem to get around to. And so, when you've washed your face in rosewater, and powdered it—not with this awful rice-powder they sell nowadays, which does nothing for the skin, but with a cake of pure white starch—and put on your pins, your rings, your brooches, bracelets, earrings, and pearls—in short, when you are dressed for your morning coffee—and have had a good look at yourself—not in the glass, naturally—it lies—but in the side of the brass gong that once belonged to Admiral Courbet—then, Roderick, then you're armed, you're strong, you're ready—you can begin again.

[PIERRE *is listening now intently. There are tears in his eyes.*]

PIERRE. Oh, Madame . . . ! Oh, Madame . . . !

COUNTESS. After that, everything is pure delight. First the morning paper. Not, of course, these current sheets full of lies and vulgarity. I always read the *Gaulois*, the issue of March 22, 1903. It's by far the best. It has some delightful scandal, some excellent fashion notes, and, of course, the last-minute bulletin on the death of Leonide Leblanc. She used to live next door, poor woman, and when I learn of her death every morning, it gives me quite a shock. I'd gladly lend you my copy, but it's in tatters.

THE SERGEANT. Couldn't we find him a copy in some library?

COUNTESS. I doubt it. And so, when you've taken your fruit salts—not in water, naturally—no matter what they say, it's water that gives you gas—but with a bit of spiced cake—then in sunlight or rain, Chaillot calls. It is time to dress for your morning walk. This takes much longer, of course—without a maid, impossible to do it under an hour, what with your corset, corset-cover, and drawers, all of which lace or button in the back. I asked Madame Lanvin, a while ago, to fit the drawers with zippers. She was quite charming, but she declined. She thought it would spoil the style.

[THE DEAF-MUTE *comes in.*]

THE WAITER. I know a place where they put zippers on anything.

[THE RAGPICKER *enters.*]

COUNTESS. I think Lanvin knows best. But I really manage very well, Martial. What I do now is, I lace them up in front, then twist them around to the back. It's quite simple, really. Then you choose a lorgnette, and then the usual fruitless search for the feather boa that the prospector stole—I know it was he: he didn't dare look me in the eye—and then all you need is a rubber band to slip around your parasol —I lost the catch the day I struck the cat that was stalking the pigeon—it was worth it—ah, that day I earned my wages!

THE RAGPICKER. Countess, if you can use it, I found a nice umbrella catch the other day with a cat's eye in it.

COUNTESS. Thank you, Ragpicker. They say those eyes sometimes come to life and fill with tears. I'd be afraid . . .

PIERRE. Go on, Madame, go on . . .

COUNTESS. Ah! So life is beginning to interest you, is it? You see how beautiful it is?

PIERRE. What a fool I've been!

COUNTESS. Then, Roderick, I begin my rounds. I have my cats to feed, my dogs to pet, my plants to water. I have to see what the evil ones are up to in the district—those who hate people, those who hate plants, those who hate animals. I watch them sneaking off in the morning to put on their disguises—to the baths, to the beauty parlors, to the barbers. But they can't deceive me. And when they come out again with blonde hair and false whiskers, to pull up my flowers and poison my dogs, I'm there, and I'm ready. All you have to do to break their power is to cut across their path from the left. That isn't always easy. Vice moves swiftly. But I have a good long stride and I generally manage. . . . Right, my friends? [THE WAITER *and* THE RAGPICKER *nod their heads with evident approval.*] Yes, the flowers have been marvelous this year. And the butcher's dog on the Rue Bizet, in spite of that wretch that tried to poison him, is friskier than ever. . . .

THE SERGEANT. That dog had better look out. He has no license.

COUNTESS. He doesn't seem to feel the need for one.

THE RAGPICKER. The Duchess de la Rochefoucauld's whippet is getting awfully thin. . . .

COUNTESS. What can I do? She bought that dog full grown from a kennel where they didn't know his right name. A dog without his right name is bound to get thin.

THE RAGPICKER. I've got a friend who knows a lot about dogs—an Arab . . .

COUNTESS. Ask him to call on the Duchess. She receives Thursdays, five to seven. You see, then, Roderick. That's life. Does it appeal to you now!

PIERRE. It seems marvelous.

COUNTESS. Ah, Sergeant. My button. [THE SERGEANT *gives her his button and goes off. At this point* THE PROSPECTOR *enters.*] That's only the morning. Wait till I tell you about the afternoon!

THE PROSPECTOR. All right, Pierre. Come along now.

PIERRE. I'm perfectly all right here.

THE PROSPECTOR. I said, come along now.

PIERRE. [*To the* COUNTESS.] I'd better go, Madame.

COUNTESS. No.

PIERRE. It's no use. Please let go my hand.

THE PROSPECTOR. Madame, will you oblige me by letting my friend go?

COUNTESS. I will not oblige you in any way.

THE PROSPECTOR. All right. Then I'll oblige you . . . !

[*He tries to push her away. She catches up a soda-water siphon and squirts it in his face.*]

PIERRE. Countess . . .

COUNTESS. Stay where you are. This man isn't going to take you away. In the first place, I shall need you in a few minutes to take me home. I'm all alone here and I'm very easily frightened.

[THE PROSPECTOR *makes a second attempt to drag* PIERRE *away. The* COUNTESS *cracks him over the skull with the siphon. They join battle. The* COUNTESS *whistles.* THE DOORMAN *comes, then the other* VAGABONDS, *and lastly* THE POLICE SERGEANT.]

THE PROSPECTOR. Officer! Arrest this woman!

THE SERGEANT. What's the trouble here?

THE PROSPECTOR. She refuses to let this man go.

THE SERGEANT. Why should she?

THE PROSPECTOR. It's against the law for a woman to detain a man on the street.

IRMA. Suppose it's her son whom she's found again after twenty years?

THE RAGPICKER. [*Gallantly.*] Or her long-lost brother? The Countess is not so old.

THE PROSPECTOR. Officer, this is a clear case of disorderly conduct.

[THE DEAF-MUTE *interrupts with frantic signals.*]

COUNTESS. Irma, what is the Deaf-Mute saying?

IRMA. [*Interpreting*]. The young man is in danger of his life. He mustn't go with him.

THE PROSPECTOR. What does he know?

IRMA. He knows everything.

THE PROSPECTOR. Officer, I'll have to take your number.

COUNTESS. Take his number. It's 2133. It adds up to nine. It will bring you luck.

THE SERGEANT. Countess, between ourselves, what are you holding him for, anyway?

COUNTESS. I'm holding him because it's very pleasant to hold him. I've never really held anybody before, and I'm making the most of it. And because so long as *I* hold him, he's free.

THE PROSPECTOR. Pierre, I'm giving you fair warning. . . .

COUNTESS. And I'm holding him because Irma wants me to hold him. Because if I let him go, it will break her heart.

IRMA. Oh, Countess!

THE SERGEANT. [*To* THE PROSPECTOR.] All right, you—move on. Nobody's holding you. You're blocking traffic. Move on.

THE PROSPECTOR. [*Menacingly.*] I have your number. [*And murderously, to* PIERRE.] You'll regret this, Pierre.

[*Exit* PROSPECTOR.]

PIERRE. Thank you, Countess.

COUNTESS. They're blackmailing you, are they? [PIERRE *nods.*] What have you done? Murdered somebody?

PIERRE. No.

COUNTESS. Stolen something?

PIERRE. No.

COUNTESS. What then?

PIERRE. I forged a signature.

COUNTESS. Whose signature?

PIERRE. My father's. To a note.

COUNTESS. And this man has the paper, I suppose?

PIERRE. He promised to tear it up, if I did what he wanted. But I couldn't do it.

COUNTESS. But the man is mad! Does he really want to destroy the whole neighborhood?

PIERRE. He wants to destroy the whole city.

COUNTESS. [*Laughs.*] Fantastic.

PIERRE. It's not funny, Countess. He can do it. He's mad, but he's powerful, and he has friends. Their machines are already drawn up and waiting. In three months' time you may see the city covered by a forest of derricks and drills.

COUNTESS. But what are they looking for? Have they lost something?

PIERRE. They're looking for oil. They're convinced that Paris is sitting on a lake of oil.

COUNTESS. Suppose it is. What harm does it do?

PIERRE. They want to bring the oil to the surface, Countess.

COUNTESS. [*Laughs.*] How silly! Is that a reason to destroy a city? What do they want with this oil?

PIERRE. They want to make war, Countess.

COUNTESS. Oh, dear, let's forget about these horrible men. The world is beautiful. It's happy. That's how God made it. No man can change it.

THE WAITER. Ah, Countess, if you only knew . . .

COUNTESS. If I only knew what?

THE WAITER. Shall we tell her now? Shall we tell her?

COUNTESS. What is it you are hiding from me?

THE RAGPICKER. Nothing, Countess. It's you who are hiding.

THE WAITER. You tell her. You've been a pitchman. You can talk.

ALL. Tell her. Tell her. Tell her.

COUNTESS. You're frightening me, my friends. Go on. I'm listening.

THE RAGPICKER. Countess, there was a time when old clothes were as good as new—in fact, they were better. Because when people wore clothes, they gave something to them. You may not believe it, but right this minute, the highest-priced shops in Paris are selling clothes that were thrown away thirty years ago. They're selling them for new. That's how good they were.

COUNTESS. Well?

THE RAGPICKER. Countess, there was a time when garbage was a pleasure. A garbage can was not what it is now. If it smelled a little strange, it was because it was a little confused—there was everything there —sardines, cologne, iodine, roses. An amateur might jump to a wrong conclusion. But to a professional—it was the smell of God's plenty.

COUNTESS. Well?

THE RAGPICKER. Countess, the world has changed.

COUNTESS. Nonsense. How could it change? People are the same, I hope.

THE RAGPICKER. No, Countess. The people are not the same. The people are different. There's been an invasion. An infiltration. From another planet. The world is not beautiful any more. It's not happy.

COUNTESS. Not happy? Is that true? Why didn't you tell me this before?

THE RAGPICKER. Because you live in a dream, Countess. And we don't like to disturb you.

COUNTESS. But how could it have happened?

THE RAGPICKER. Countess, there was a time when you could walk around Paris, and all the people you met were just like yourself. A little cleaner, maybe, or dirtier, perhaps, or angry, or smiling—but you knew them. They were you. Well, Countess, twenty years ago, one day, on the street, I saw a face in the crowd. A face, you might say, without a face. The eyes—empty. The expression—not human. Not a human face. It saw me staring, and when it looked back at me with its gelatine eyes, I shuddered. Because I knew that to make room for this one, one of us must have left the earth. A while after, I saw another. And another. And since then, I've seen hundreds come in—yes—thousands.

COUNTESS. Describe them to me.

THE RAGPICKER. You've seen them yourself, Countess. Their clothes don't wrinkle. Their hats don't come off. When they talk, they don't look at you. They don't perspire.

COUNTESS. Have they wives? Have they children?

THE RAGPICKER. They buy the models out of shop windows, furs and all. They animate them by a secret process. Then they marry them. Naturally, they don't have children.

COUNTESS. What work do they do?

THE RAGPICKER. They don't do any work. Whenever they meet, they whisper, and then they pass each other thousand-franc notes. You see them standing on the corner by the Stock Exchange. You see them at auctions—in the back. They never raise a finger—they just stand there. In theater lobbies, by the box office—they never go inside. They don't do anything, but wherever you see them, things are not the same. I remember well the time when a cabbage could sell itself just by being a cabbage. Nowadays it's no good being a cabbage—unless you have an agent and pay him a commission. Nothing is free any more to sell itself or give itself away. These days, Countess, every cabbage has its pimp.

COUNTESS. I can't believe that.

THE RAGPICKER. Countess, little by little, the pimps have taken over the world. They don't do anything, they don't make anything—they just stand there and take their cut. It makes a difference. Look at the shop-keepers. Do you ever see one smiling at a customer any more? Certainly not. Their smiles are strictly for the pimps. The butcher has to smile at the meat-pimp, the florist at the rose-pimp, the grocer at the fresh-fruit-and-vegetable pimp. It's all organized down to the slightest detail. A pimp for birdseed. A pimp for fishfood. That's why the cost of living keeps going up all the time. You buy a glass of beer—it costs twice as much as it used to. Why? 10 per cent for the glass-pimp, 10 per cent for the beer-pimp, 20 per cent for the glass-of-beer-pimp—that's where our money goes. Personally, I prefer the old-fashioned type. Some of those men at least were loved by the women they sold. But what feelings can a pimp arouse in a leg of lamb? Pardon my language, Irma.

COUNTESS. It's all right. She doesn't understand it.

THE RAGPICKER. So now you know, Countess, why the world is no longer happy. We are the last of the free people of the earth. You saw them looking us over today. Tomorrow, the street-singer will start paying the song-pimp, and the garbage-pimp will be after me. I tell you, Countess, we're finished. It's the end of free enterprise in this world!

COUNTESS. Is this true, Roderick?

PIERRE. I'm afraid it's true.

COUNTESS. Did you know about this, Irma?

IRMA. All I know is the doorman says that faith is dead.

THE DOORMAN. I've stopped taking bets over the phone.

THE JUGGLER. The very air is different, Countess. You can't trust it any more. If I throw my torches up too high, they go out.

THE RAGPICKER. The sky-pimp puts them out.

THE FLOWER GIRL. My flowers don't last over night now. They wilt.

THE JUGGLER. Have you noticed, the pigeons don't fly any more?

THE RAGPICKER. They can't afford to. They walk.

COUNTESS. They're a lot of fools and so are you! You should have told me at once! How can you bear to live in a world where there is unhappiness? Where a man is not his own master? Are you cowards? All we have to do is to get rid of these men.

PIERRE. How can we get rid of them? They're too strong.

[THE SERGEANT walks up again.]

COUNTESS. [Smiling.] The Sergeant will help us

THE SERGEANT. Who? Me?

IRMA. There are a great many of them, Countess.

The Deaf-Mute knows them all. They employed him once, years ago, because he was deaf. [THE DEAF-MUTE *wigwags a short speech*.] They fired him because he wasn't blind. [*Another flash of sign language*.] They're all connected like the parts of a machine.

COUNTESS. So much the better. We shall drive the whole machine into a ditch.

THE SERGEANT. It's not that easy, Countess. You never catch these birds napping. They change before your very eyes. I remember when I was in the detectives. . . . You catch a president; pfft! he turns into a trustee. You catch him as trustee, and pfft! he's not a trustee—he's an honorary vice-chairman. You catch a Senator dead to rights: he becomes Minister of Justice. You get after the Minister of Justice—he is Chief of Police. And there you are—no longer in the detectives.

PIERRE. He's right, Countess. They have all the power. And all the money. And they're greedy for more.

COUNTESS. They're greedy? Ah, then, my friends, they're lost. If they're greedy, they're stupid. If they're greedy—don't worry, I know exactly what to do. Roderick, by tonight you will be an honest man. And, Juggler, your torches will stay lit. And your beer will flow freely again, Martial. And the world will be saved. Let's get to work.

THE RAGPICKER. What are you going to do?

COUNTESS. Have you any kerosene in the house, Irma?

IRMA. Yes. Would you like some?

COUNTESS. I want just a little. In a dirty bottle. With a little mud. And some mange-cure, if you have it. [*To* THE DEAF-MUTE.] Deaf-Mute! Take a letter. [IRMA *interprets in sign language. To* THE SINGER.] Singer, go and find Madame Constance.

[IRMA *and* THE WAITER *go into the café*.]

THE STREET SINGER. Yes, Countess.

COUNTESS. Ask her to be at my house by two o'clock. I'll be waiting for her in the cellar. You may tell her we have to discuss the future of humanity. That's sure to bring her.

THE STREET SINGER. Yes, Countess.

COUNTESS. And ask her to bring Mademoiselle Gabrielle and Madame Josephine with her. Do you know how to get in to speak to Madame Constance? You ring twice, and then meow three times like a cat. Do you know how to meow?

THE STREET SINGER. I'm better at barking.

COUNTESS. Better practise meowing on the way. Incidentally, I think Madame Constance knows all the verses of your mazurka. Remind me to ask her.

THE STREET SINGER. Yes, Countess. [*Exit*.]

[IRMA *comes in. She is shaking the oily concoction in a little perfume vial, which she now hands the* COUNTESS.]

IRMA. Here you are, Countess.

COUNTESS. Thanks, Irma. [*She assumes a presidential manner*.] Deaf-Mute! Ready?

[IRMA *interprets in sign language.* THE WAITER *has brought out a portfolio of letter paper and placed it on a table.* THE DEAF-MUTE *sits down before it, and prepares to write*.]

IRMA. [*Speaking for* THE DEAF-MUTE.] I'm ready.

COUNTESS. My dear Mr.—— What's his name?

[IRMA *wigwags the question to* THE DEAF-MUTE, *who answers in the same manner. It is all done so deftly that it is as if* THE DEAF-MUTE *were actually speaking*.]

IRMA. They are all called Mr. President.

COUNTESS. My dear Mr. President: I have personally verified the existence of a spontaneous outcrop of oil in the cellar of Number 21 Rue de Chaillot, which is at present occupied by a dignified person of unstable mentality. [*The* COUNTESS *grins knowingly*.] This explains why, fortunately for us, the discovery has so long been kept secret. If you should wish to verify the existence of this outcrop for yourself, you may call at the above address at three P.M. today. I am herewith enclosing a sample so that you may judge the quality and consistency of the crude. Yours very truly. Roderick, can you sign the prospector's name?

PIERRE. You wish me to?

COUNTESS. One forgery wipes out the other.

[PIERRE *signs the letter.* THE DEAF-MUTE *types the address on an envelope*.]

IRMA. Who is to deliver this?

COUNTESS. The Doorman, of course. On his bicycle. And as soon as you have delivered it, run over to the Prospector's office. Leave word that the President expects to see him at my house at three.

THE DOORMAN. Yes, Countess.

COUNTESS. I shall leave you now. I have many pressing things to do. Among others, I must press my red gown.

THE RAGPICKER. But this only takes care of two of them, Countess.

COUNTESS. Didn't the Deaf-Mute say they are all connected like the works of a machine?

IRMA. Yes.

COUNTESS. Then, if one comes, the rest will follow. And we shall have them all. My boa, please.

THE DOORMAN. The one that's stolen, Countess?

COUNTESS. Naturally. The one the Prospector stole.

THE DOORMAN. It hasn't turned up yet, Countess. But someone has left an ermine collar.

COUNTESS. Real ermine?

THE DOORMAN. Looks like it.

COUNTESS. Ermine and iris were made for each other. Let me see it.

THE DOORMAN. Yes, Countess.

[*Exit* DOORMAN.]

COUNTESS. Roderick, you shall escort me. You still look pale. I have some old Chartreuse at home. I always take a glass each year. Last year I forgot. You shall have it.

PIERRE. If there is anything I can do, Countess . . . ?

COUNTESS. There is a great deal you can do. There are all the things that need to be done in a room that no man has been in for twenty years. You can untwist the cord on the blind and let in a little sunshine for a change. You can take the mirror off the wardrobe door, and deliver me once and for all from the old harpy that lives in the mirror. You can let the mouse out of the trap. I'm tired of feeding it. [*To her friends.*] Each man to his post. See you later, my friends. [THE DOORMAN *puts the ermine collar around her shoulders.*] Thank you, my boy. It's rabbit. [*One o'clock strikes.*] Your arm, Valentine.

PIERRE. Valentine?

COUNTESS. It's just struck one. At one, all men become Valentine.

PIERRE. [*He offers his arm.*] Permit me.

COUNTESS. Or Valentino. It's obviously far from the same, isn't it, Irma? But they have that much choice.

[*She sweeps out majestically with* PIERRE. *The others disperse. All but* IRMA.]

IRMA. [*Clearing off the table.*] I hate ugliness. I love beauty. I hate meanness. I adore kindness. It may not seem so grand to some to be a waitress in Paris. I love it. A waitress meets all sorts of people. She observes life. I hate to be alone. I love people. But I have never said I love you to a man. Men try to make me say it. They put their arms around me—I pretend I don't see it. They pinch me—I pretend I don't feel it. They kiss me—I pretend I don't know it. They take me out in the evening and make me drink—but I'm careful, I never say it. If they don't like it, they can leave me alone. Because when I say I love you to Him, He will know just by looking in my eyes that many have held me and pinched me and kissed me, but I have never said I love you to anyone in the world before. Never. No. [*Looking off in the direction in which* PIERRE *has gone, she whispers softly:*] I love you.

VOICE. [*From within the café.*] Irma!

IRMA. Coming. [*Exits.*]

CURTAIN

ACT II

SCENE: *The cellar of the* COUNTESS' *house. An ancient vault set deep in the ground, with walls of solid masonry, part brick and part great ashlars, mossy and sweating. A staircase of medieval pattern is built into the thickness of the wall, and leads up to the street level from a landing halfway down. In the corners of the cellar are piled casks, packing cases, bird cages, and other odds and ends—the accumulation of centuries— the whole effect utterly fantastic.*

In the center of the vast underground room, some furniture has been arranged to give an impression of a sitting-room of the 1890's. There is a venerable chaise-longue piled with cushions that once were gay, three armchairs, a table with an oil lamp and a bowl of flowers, a shaggy rug. It is two P.M., the same day.

AT RISE: *The* COUNTESS *is sitting over a bit of mending, in one of the armchairs.* IRMA *appears on the landing and calls down.*

IRMA. Countess! The Sewer-Man is here.

COUNTESS. Thank goodness, Irma. Send him down. [THE SEWER-MAN *enters. He carries his hip-boots in his hand.*] How do you do, Mr. Sewer-Man? [THE SEWER-MAN *bows.*] But why do you have your boots in your hand instead of on your feet?

THE SEWER-MAN. Etiquette, Countess. Etiquette.

COUNTESS. How very American! I'm told that Americans nowadays apologize for their gloves if they happen to take one's hand. As if the skin of a human were nicer to touch than the skin of a sheep! And particularly if they have sweaty hands . . . !

THE SEWER-MAN. My feet never sweat, Countess.

COUNTESS. How very nice! But please don't stand on ceremony here. Put your boots on. Put them on.

THE SEWER-MAN. [*Complying.*] Thanks very much, Countess.

COUNTESS. [*While he draws on his boots.*] I'm sure you must have a very poor opinion of the upper world, from what you see of it. The way people throw their filth into your territory is absolutely scandalous! I burn all my refuse, and I scatter the ashes. All I ever throw in the drain is flowers. Did you happen to see a lily float by this morning? Mine. But perhaps you didn't notice?

THE SEWER-MAN. We notice a lot more down there, Countess, than you might think. You'd be surprised the things we notice. There's lots of things come along that were obviously intended for us—little gifts, you might call them—sometimes a brand-new shaving brush—sometimes, *The Brothers Karamazov.*

. . . Thanks for the lily, Countess. A very sweet thought.

COUNTESS. Tomorrow you shall have this iris. But now, let's come to the point. I have two questions to ask you.

THE SEWER-MAN. Yes, Countess?

COUNTESS. First—and this has nothing to do with our problem—it's just something that has been troubling me. . . . Tell me, is it true that the sewer-men of Paris have a king?

THE SEWER-MAN. Oh, now, Countess, that's another of those fairy tales out of the Sunday supplements. It just seems those writers can't keep their minds off the sewers! It fascinates them. They keep thinking of us moving around in our underground canals like gondoliers in Venice, and it sends them into a fever of romance! The things they say about us! They say we have a race of girls down there who never see the light of day! It's completely fantastic! The girls naturally come out—every Christmas and Easter. And orgies by torchlight with gondolas and guitars! With troops of rats that dance as they follow the piper! What nonsense! The rats are not allowed to dance. No, no, no. Of course we have no king. Down in the sewers, you'll find nothing but good Republicans.

COUNTESS. And no queen?

THE SEWER-MAN. No. We may run a beauty contest down there once in a while. Or crown a mermaid Queen of the May. But no queen what you'd call a queen. And, as for these swimming races they talk so much about . . . possibly once in a while—in the summer—in the dog days . . .

COUNTESS. I believe you. I believe you. And now tell me. Do you remember that night I found you here in my cellar—looking very pale and strange—you were half-dead as a matter of fact—and I gave you some brandy. . . .

THE SEWER-MAN. Yes, Countess.

COUNTESS. That night you promised if ever I should need it—you would tell me the secret of this room.

THE SEWER-MAN. The secret of the moving stone?

COUNTESS. I need it now.

THE SEWER-MAN. Only the King of the Sewer-Men knows this secret.

COUNTESS. I'm sure of it. I know most secrets, of course. As a matter of fact, I have three magic words that will open any door that words can open. I have tried them all—in various tones of voice. They don't seem to work. And this is a matter of life and death.

THE SEWER-MAN. Look, Countess.

[He locates a brick in the masonry, and pushes it. A huge block of stone slowly pivots and uncovers a trap from which a circular staircase winds into the bowels of the earth.]

COUNTESS. Good heavens! Where do those stairs lead?

THE SEWER-MAN. Nowhere.

COUNTESS. But they must go somewhere.

THE SEWER-MAN. They just go down.

COUNTESS. Let's go and see.

THE SEWER-MAN. No, Countess. Never again. That time you found me, I had a pretty close shave. I kept going down and around, and down and around for an hour, a year—I don't know. There's no end to it, Countess. Once you start you can't stop. . . . Your head begins to turn—you're lost. No—once you start down, there's no coming up.

COUNTESS. You came up.

THE SEWER-MAN. I—I am a special case. Besides, I had my tools, my ropes. And I stopped in time.

COUNTESS. You could have screamed—shouted.

THE SEWER-MAN. You could fire off a cannon.

COUNTESS. Who could have built a thing like this?

THE SEWER-MAN. Paris is old, you know. Paris is very old.

COUNTESS. You don't suppose, by any chance, there is oil down there?

THE SEWER-MAN. There's only death down there.

COUNTESS. I should have preferred a little oil too —or a vein of gold—or emeralds. You're quite sure there is nothing?

THE SEWER-MAN. Not even rats.

COUNTESS. How does one lower this stone?

THE SEWER-MAN. Simple. To open, you press here. And to close it, you push there. [He presses the brick. The stone descends.] Now there's two of us in the world that know it.

COUNTESS. I won't remember long. Is it all right if I repeat my magic words while I press it?

THE SEWER-MAN. It's bound to help.

[IRMA enters.]

IRMA. Countess, Madame Constance and Mademoiselle Gabrielle are here.

COUNTESS. Show them down, Irma. Thank you very much, Mr. Sewer-Man.

THE SEWER-MAN. Like that story about the steam laundry that's supposed to be running day and night in my sewer . . . I can assure you. . . .

COUNTESS. [Edging him toward the door.] Thank you very much.

THE SEWER-MAN. Pure imagination! They never work nights.

[He goes off, bowing graciously. CONSTANCE, the Madwoman of Passy, and GABRIELLE, the Madwoman of St. Sulpice, come down daintily. CONSTANCE is all in white. She wears an *enormous hat graced with ostrich plumes, and a lavender veil.* GABRIELLE *is costumed with the affected simplicity of the 1880's. She is atrociously made up in a remorseless parody of blushing innocence, and she minces down the stairs with macabre coyness.*]

CONSTANCE. Aurelia! Don't tell us they've found your feather boa?

GABRIELLE. You don't mean Adolphe Bertaut has proposed at last! I knew he would.

COUNTESS. How are you, Constance? [*She shouts.*] How are you, Gabrielle?

GABRIELLE. You needn't shout today, my dear. It's Wednesday. Wednesdays, I hear perfectly.

CONSTANCE. It's Thursday.

GABRIELLE. Oh, dear. Well, never mind. I'm going to make an exception just this once.

CONSTANCE. [*To an imaginary dog who has stopped on the landing.*] Come along, Dickie. Come along. And stop barking. What a racket you're making! Come on, darling—we've come to see the longest boa and the handsomest man in Paris. Come on.

COUNTESS. Constance, it's not a question of my boa today. Nor of poor Adolphe. It's a question of the future of the human race.

CONSTANCE. You think it has a future?

COUNTESS. Please don't make silly jokes. Sit down and listen to me. Today we must make a decision which may alter the fate of the world.

CONSTANCE. Couldn't we do it tomorrow? I want to wash my slippers. Now, Dickie—please!

COUNTESS. We haven't a moment to waste. Where is Josephine? Well, we'd best have our tea, and the moment Josephine comes . . .

GABRIELLE. Josephine is sitting on her bench in front of the palace waiting for President Wilson to come out. She says she's sorry, but she positively must see him today.

CONSTANCE. Dickie!

COUNTESS. What a pity! [*She gets the tea things from the side table, pours tea and serves cake and honey.*] I wish she were here to help us. She has a first-class brain.

CONSTANCE. Go ahead, dear. We're listening. [*To* DICKIE.] What is it, Dickie? You want to sit in Aunt Aurelia's lap. All right, darling. Go on. Jump, Dickie.

COUNTESS. Constance, we love you, as you know. And we love Dickie. But this is a serious matter. So let's stop being childish for once.

CONSTANCE. And what does that mean, if you please?

COUNTESS. It means Dickie. You know perfectly well that we love him and fuss over him just as if he were still alive. He's a sacred memory and we wouldn't hurt his feelings for the world. But please

don't plump him in my lap when I'm settling the future of mankind. His basket is in the corner—he knows where it is, and he can just go and sit in it.

CONSTANCE. So you're against Dickie too! You too!

COUNTESS. Constance! I'm not in the least against Dickie! I adore Dickie. But you know as well as I that Dickie is only a convention with us. It's a beautiful convention—but it doesn't have to bark all the time. Besides, it's you that spoil him. The time you went to visit your niece and left him with me, we got on marvelously together. He didn't bark, he didn't tear things, he didn't even eat. But when you're with him, one can pay attention to nothing else. I'm not going to take Dickie in my lap at a solemn moment like this, no, not for anything in the world. And that's that!

GABRIELLE. [*Very sweetly.*] Constance, dear, I don't mind taking him in my lap. He loves to sit in my lap, don't you, darling?

CONSTANCE. Kindly stop putting on angelic airs, Gabrielle. I know you very well. You're much too sweet to be sincere. There's plenty of times that I make believe that Dickie is here, when really I've left him home, and you cuddle and pet him just the same.

GABRIELLE. I adore animals.

CONSTANCE. If you adore animals, you shouldn't pet them when they're not there. It's a form of hypocrisy.

COUNTESS. Now, Constance, Gabrielle has as much right as you . . .

CONSTANCE. Gabrielle has no right to do what she does. Do you know what she does? She invites *people* to come to tea with us. *People* whom we know nothing about. *People* who exist only in her imagination.

COUNTESS. You think that's not an existence?

GABRIELLE. I don't invite them at all. They come by themselves. What can I do?

CONSTANCE. You might introduce us.

COUNTESS. If you think they're only imaginary, there's no point in your meeting them, is there?

CONSTANCE. Of course they're imaginary. But who likes to have imaginary people staring at one? Especially strangers.

GABRIELLE. Oh, they're really very nice. . . .

CONSTANCE. Tell me just one thing, Gabrielle—are they here now?

COUNTESS. Am I to be allowed to speak? Or is this going to be the same as the argument about inoculating Josephine's cat, when we didn't get to the subject at all?

CONSTANCE. Never! Never! Never! I'll never give my consent to that. [*To* DICKIE.] I'll never do a thing like that to you, Dickie sweet. . . . Oh, no! Oh, no!

[*She begins to weep softly.*]

COUNTESS. Good heavens! Now we have her in tears. What an impossible creature! With the fate of humanity hanging in the balance! All right, all right, stop crying. I'll take him in my lap. Come, Dickie, Dickie.

CONSTANCE. No. He won't go now. Oh, how can you be so cruel? Don't you suppose I know about Dickie? Don't you think I'd rather have him here alive and woolly and frisking around the way he used to? You have your Adolphe. Gabrielle has her birds. But I have only Dickie. Do you think I'd be so silly about him if it wasn't that it's only by pretending that he's here all the time that I get him to come sometimes, really? Next time I won't bring him!

COUNTESS. Now let's not get ourselves worked up over nothing. Come here, Dickie. . . . Irma is going to take you for a nice walk. [*She rings her bell.*] Irma!

[IRMA *appears on the landing.*]

CONSTANCE. No. He doesn't want to go. Besides I didn't bring him today. So there!

COUNTESS. Very well, then. Irma, make sure the door is locked.

IRMA. Yes, Countess. [IRMA *exits.*]

CONSTANCE. What do you mean? Why locked? Who's coming?

COUNTESS. If you'd let me get a word in, you'd know by now. A terrible thing has happened. This morning, this very morning, exactly at noon . . .

CONSTANCE. [*Thrilled.*] Oh, how exciting!

COUNTESS. Be quiet. This morning, exactly at noon, thanks to a young man who drowned himself in the Seine . . . Oh, yes, while I think of it—do you know a mazurka called *La Belle Polonaise?*

CONSTANCE. Yes, Aurelia.

COUNTESS. Could you sing it now? This very minute?

CONSTANCE. Yes, Aurelia.

COUNTESS. All of it?

CONSTANCE. Yes, Aurelia. But who's interrupting now, Aurelia?

COUNTESS. You're right. Well, this morning, exactly at noon, I discovered a horrible plot. There is a group of men who intend to tear down the whole city!

CONSTANCE. Is that all?

GABRIELLE. But I don't understand, Aurelia. Why should men want to tear down the city? It was they themselves who put it up.

COUNTESS. You are so innocent, my poor Gabrielle. There are people in the world who want to destroy everything. They have the fever of destruction. Even when they pretend that they're building, it is only in order to destroy. When they put up a new building, they quietly knock down two old ones. They build cities so that they can destroy the countryside. They destroy space with telephones and time with airplanes. Humanity is now dedicated to the task of universal destruction. I am speaking, of course, primarily of the male sex.

GABRIELLE. [*Shocked.*] Oh . . . !

CONSTANCE. Aurelia! Must you talk sex in front of Gabrielle?

COUNTESS. There *are* two sexes.

CONSTANCE. Gabrielle is a virgin, Aurelia!

COUNTESS. Oh, she can't be as innocent as all that. She keeps canaries.

GABRIELLE. I think you're being very cruel about men, Aurelia. Men are big and beautiful, and as loyal as dogs. I preferred not to marry, it's true. But I hear excellent reports from friends who have had an opportunity to observe them closely.

COUNTESS. My poor darling! You are still living in a dream. But one day, you will wake up as I have, and then you will see what is happening in the world. The tide has turned, my dear. Men are changing back into beasts. They know it. They no longer try to hide it. There was once such a thing as manners. I remember a time when the hungriest was the one who took the longest to pick up his fork. The one with the broadest grin was the one who needed most to go to the . . . It was such fun to keep them grinning like that for hours. But now they no longer pretend. Just look at them—snuffling their soup like pigs, tearing their meat like tigers, crunching their lettuce like crocodiles! A man doesn't take your hand nowadays. He gives you his paw.

CONSTANCE. Would that trouble you so much if they turned into animals? Personally, I think it's a good idea.

GABRIELLE. Oh, I'd love to see them like that. They'd be sweet.

CONSTANCE. It might be the salvation of the human race.

COUNTESS. [*To* CONSTANCE.] You'd make a fine rabbit, wouldn't you?

CONSTANCE. I?

COUNTESS. Naturally. You don't think it's only the men who are changing? You change along with them. Husbands and wives together. We're all one race, you know.

CONSTANCE. You think so? And why would my poor husband have to be a rabbit if he were alive?

COUNTESS. Remember his front teeth? When he nibbled his celery?

CONSTANCE. I'm happy to say, I remember absolutely nothing about him. All I remember on that subject is the time that Father Lacordaire tried to kiss me in the park.

COUNTESS. Yes, yes, of course.

CONSTANCE. And what does that mean, if you please, "Yes, yes, of course"?

COUNTESS. Constance, just this once, look us in the eye and tell us truly—did that really happen or did you read about it in a book?

CONSTANCE. Now I'm being insulted!

COUNTESS. We promise you faithfully that we'll believe it all over again afterwards, won't we, Gabrielle? But tell us the truth this once.

CONSTANCE. How dare you question my memories? Suppose I said your pearls were false!

COUNTESS. They were.

CONSTANCE. I'm not asking what they were. I'm asking what they are. Are they false or are they real?

COUNTESS. Everyone knows that little by little, as one wears pearls, they become real.

CONSTANCE. And isn't it exactly the same with memories?

COUNTESS. Now do not let us waste time. I must go on.

CONSTANCE. I think Gabrielle is perfectly right about men. There are still plenty who haven't changed a bit. There's an old Senator who bows to Gabrielle every day when he passes her in front of the palace. And he takes off his hat each time.

GABRIELLE. That's perfectly true, Aurelia. He's always pushing an empty baby carriage, and he always stops and bows.

COUNTESS. Don't be taken in, Gabrielle. It's all make-believe. And all we can expect from these make-believe men is itself make-believe. They give us face powder made of stones, sausages made of sawdust, shirts made of glass, stockings made of milk. It's all a vulgar pretense. And if that is the case, imagine what passes, these days, for virtue, sincerity, generosity, and love! I warn you, Gabrielle, don't let this Senator with the empty baby carriage pull the wool over your eyes.

GABRIELLE. He's really the soul of courtesy. He seems very correct.

COUNTESS. Those are the worst. Gabrielle, beware! He'll make you put on black riding boots, while he dances the can-can around you, singing God knows what filth at the top of his voice. The very thought makes one's blood run cold!

GABRIELLE. You think that's what he has in mind?

COUNTESS. Of course. Men have lost all sense of decency. They are all equally disgusting. Just look at them in the evening, sitting at their tables in the café, working away in unison with their toothpicks, hour after hour, digging up roast beef, veal, onion . . .

CONSTANCE. They don't harm anyone that way.

COUNTESS. Then why do you barricade your door, and make your friends meow before you let them come up? Incidentally, we must make an interesting sight, Gabrielle and I, yowling together on your doorstep like a couple of tomcats!

CONSTANCE. There's no need at all for you to yowl together. One would be quite enough. And you know perfectly well why I have to do it. It's because there are murderers.

COUNTESS. I don't quite see what prevents murderers from meowing like anybody else. But why are there murderers?

CONSTANCE. Why? Because there are thieves.

COUNTESS. And why are there thieves? Why is there almost nothing but thieves?

CONSTANCE. Because they worship money. Because money is king.

COUNTESS. Ah—now we've come to it. Because we live in the reign of the Golden Calf. Did you realize that, Gabrielle? Men now publicly worship the Golden Calf!

GABRIELLE. How awful! Have the authorities been notified?

COUNTESS. The authorities do it themselves, Gabrielle.

GABRIELLE. Oh! Has anyone talked to the bishop?

COUNTESS. Nowadays only money talks to the bishop. And so you see why I asked you to come here today. The world has gone out of its mind. Unless we do something, humanity is doomed! Constance, have you any suggestions?

CONSTANCE. I know what I always do in a case like this. . . .

COUNTESS. You write to the Prime Minister.

CONSTANCE. He always does what I tell him.

COUNTESS. Does he ever answer your letters?

CONSTANCE. He knows I prefer him not to. It might excite gossip. Besides, I don't always write. Sometimes I wire. The time I told him about the Archbishop's frigidaire, it was by wire. And they sent a new one the very next day.

COUNTESS. There was probably a commission in it for someone. And what do you suggest, Gabrielle?

CONSTANCE. Now, how can she tell you until she's consulted her voices?

GABRIELLE. I could go right home and consult them, and we could meet again after dinner.

COUNTESS. There's no time for that. Besides, your voices are not real voices.

GABRIELLE. [Furious.] How dare you say a thing like that?

COUNTESS. Where do your voices come from? Still from your sewing-machine?

GABRIELLE. Not at all. They've passed into my hot-water bottle. And it's much nicer that way. They don't chatter any more. They gurgle. But they haven't been a bit nice to me lately. Last night they kept telling me to let my canaries out. "Let them out. Let them out. Let them out."

CONSTANCE. Did you?

GABRIELLE. I opened the cage. They wouldn't go.

COUNTESS. I don't call that *voices*. Objects talk—everyone knows that. It's the principle of the phonograph. But to ask a hot-water bottle for advice is silly. What does a hot-water bottle know? No, all we have to consult here is our own judgment.

CONSTANCE. Very well then, tell us what you have decided. Since you're asking our opinion, you've doubtless made up your mind.

COUNTESS. Yes, I've thought the whole thing out. All I really needed to discover was the source of the infection. Today I found it.

CONSTANCE. Where?

COUNTESS. You'll see soon enough. I've baited a trap. In just a few minutes, the rats will be here.

GABRIELLE. [*In alarm.*] Rats!

COUNTESS. Don't be alarmed. They're still in human form.

GABRIELLE. Heavens! What are you going to do with them?

COUNTESS. That's just the question. Suppose I get these wicked men all here at once—in my cellar—have I the right to exterminate them?

GABRIELLE. To kill them?

[COUNTESS *nods.*]

CONSTANCE. That's not a question for us. You'll have to ask Father Bridet.

COUNTESS. I have asked him. Yes. One day, in confession, I told him frankly that I had a secret desire to destroy all wicked people. He said: "By all means, my child. And when you're ready to go into action, I'll lend you the jawbone of an ass."

CONSTANCE. That's just talk. You get him to put that in writing.

GABRIELLE. What's your scheme, Aurelia?

COUNTESS. That's a secret.

CONSTANCE. It's not so easy to kill them. Let's say you had a tank full of vitriol all ready for them. You could never get them to walk into it. There's nothing so stubborn as a man when you want him to do something.

COUNTESS. Leave that to me.

CONSTANCE. But if they're killed, they're bound to be missed, and then we'll be fined. They fine you for every little thing these days.

COUNTESS. They won't be missed.

GABRIELLE. I wish Josephine were here. Her sister's husband was a lawyer. She knows all about these things.

COUNTESS. Do you miss a cold when it's gone? Or the germs that caused it? When the world feels well again, do you think it will regret its illness? No, it will stretch itself joyfully, and it will smile—that's all.

CONSTANCE. Just a moment! Gabrielle, are they here now? Yes or no?

COUNTESS. What's the matter with you now?

CONSTANCE. I'm simply asking Gabrielle if her friends are in the room or not. I have a right to know.

GABRIELLE. I'm not allowed to say.

CONSTANCE. I know very well they are. I'm sure of it. Otherwise you wouldn't be making faces.

COUNTESS. May I ask what difference it makes to you if her friends are in the room?

CONSTANCE. Just this: If they're here, I'm not going to say another word! I'm certainly not going to commit myself in a matter involving the death sentence in the presence of third parties, whether they exist or not.

GABRIELLE. That's not being very nice to my guests, is it?

COUNTESS. Constance, you must be mad! Or are you so stupid as to think that just because we're alone, there's nobody with us? Do you consider us so boring or repulsive that of all the millions of beings, imaginary or otherwise, who are prowling about in space, there's not one who might possibly enjoy spending a little time with us? On the contrary, my dear—my house is full of guests always. They know that here they have a place in the universe where they can come when they're lonely and be sure of a welcome. For my part, I'm delighted to have them.

GABRIELLE. Thank you, Aurelia.

CONSTANCE. You know perfectly well, Aurelia . . .

COUNTESS. I know perfectly well that at this moment the whole universe is listening to us—and that every word we say echoes to the remotest star. To pretend otherwise is the sheerest hypocrisy.

CONSTANCE. Then why do you insult me in front of everybody? I'm not mean. I'm shy. I feel timid about giving an opinion in front of such a crowd. Furthermore, if you think I'm so bad and so stupid, why did you invite me, in the first place?

COUNTESS. I'll tell you. And I'll tell you why, disagreeable as you are, I always give you the biggest piece of cake and my best honey. It's because when you come there's always someone with you—and I don't mean Dickie—I mean someone who resembles you like a sister, only she's young and lovely, and she sits modestly to one side and smiles at me tenderly all the time you're bickering and quarreling, and never says a word. That's the Constance to whom I give the cake that you gobble, and it's because of her that you're here today, and it's her vote that I'm asking you to cast in this crucial moment. And not yours, which is of no importance whatever.

CONSTANCE. I'm leaving.

COUNTESS. Be so good as to sit down. I can't let her go yet.

CONSTANCE. [*Crossing toward the stairs.*] No. This is too much. I'm taking her with me. [IRMA *enters.*]

IRMA. Madame Josephine.

COUNTESS. Thank heaven!

GABRIELLE. We're saved.

[JOSEPHINE, *the Madwoman of La Concorde, sweeps in majestically in a get-up somewhere between the regal and the priestly.*]

JOSEPHINE. My dear friends, today once again, I waited for President Wilson—but he didn't come out.

COUNTESS. You'll have to wait quite a while longer before he does. He's been dead since 1924.

JOSEPHINE. I have plenty of time.

COUNTESS. In anyone else, Josephine, these extravagances might seem a little childish. But a person of your judgment doubtless has her reasons for wanting to talk to a man to whom no one would listen when he was alive. We have a legal problem for you. Suppose you had all the world's criminals here in this room. And suppose you had a way of getting rid of them forever. Would you have the right to do it?

JOSEPHINE. Why not?

COUNTESS. Exactly my point.

GABRIELLE. But, Josephine, so many people!

JOSEPHINE. *De minimis non curat lex!* [1] The more there are, the more legal it is. It's impersonal. It's even military. It's the cardinal principle of battle— you get all your enemies in one place, and you kill them all together at one time. Because if you had to track them down one by one in their houses and offices, you'd get tired, and sooner or later you'd stop. I believe your idea is very practical, Aurelia. I can't imagine why we never thought of it before.

GABRIELLE. Well, if you think it's all right to do it. . . .

JOSEPHINE. By all means. Your criminals have had a fair trial, I suppose?

COUNTESS. Trial?

JOSEPHINE. Certainly. You can't kill anybody without a trial. That's elementary. "No man shall be deprived of his life, liberty, and property without due process of law."

COUNTESS. They deprive us of ours.

JOSEPHINE. That's not the point. You're not accused of anything. Every accused—man, woman or child—has the right to defend himself at the bar of justice. Even animals. Before the Deluge, you will recall, the Lord permitted Noah to speak in defense of his fellow mortals. He evidently stuttered. You know the result. On the other hand, Captain Dreyfus

was not only innocent—he was defended by a marvelous orator. The result was precisely the same. So you see, in having a trial, you run no risk whatever.

COUNTESS. But if I give them the slightest cause for suspicion—I'll lose them.

JOSEPHINE. There's a simple procedure prescribed in such cases. You can summon the defendants by calling them three times—mentally, if you like. If they don't appear, the court may designate an attorney who will represent them. This attorney can then argue their case to the court, *in absentia,* and a judgment can then be rendered, *in contumacio.*

COUNTESS. But I don't know any attorneys. And we have only ten minutes.

GABRIELLE. Hurry, Josephine, hurry!

JOSEPHINE. In case of emergency, it is permissible for the court to order the first passer-by to act as attorney for the defense. A defense is like a baptism. Absolutely indispensable, but you don't have to know anything to do it. Ask Irma to get you somebody. Anybody.

COUNTESS. The Deaf-Mute?

JOSEPHINE. Well—that's getting it down a bit fine. That might be questionable on appeal.

COUNTESS. [*Calls.*] Irma! What about the Police Sergeant?

JOSEPHINE. He won't do. He's under oath to the state. [IRMA *appears.*]

IRMA. Yes, Countess?

COUNTESS. Who's out there, Irma?

IRMA. All our friends, Countess. There's the Ragpicker and . . .

COUNTESS. Send down the Ragpicker.

CONSTANCE. Do you think it's wise to have all those millionaires represented by a ragpicker?

JOSEPHINE. It's a first-rate choice. Criminals are always represented by their opposites. Murderers, by someone who obviously wouldn't hurt a fly. Rapists, by a member of the League for Decency. Experience shows it's the only way to get an acquittal.

COUNTESS. But we must not have an acquittal. That would mean the end of the world!

JOSEPHINE. Justice is justice, my dear.

[THE RAGPICKER *comes down, with a stately air. Behind him, on the landing, appear the other* VAGABONDS.]

THE RAGPICKER. Greetings, Countess. Greetings, ladies. My most sincere compliments.

COUNTESS. Has Irma told you . . . ?

THE RAGPICKER. She said something about a trial.

COUNTESS. You have been appointed attorney for the defense.

THE RAGPICKER. Terribly flattered, I'm sure.

COUNTESS. You realize, don't you, how much depends on the outcome of this trial?

[1] The law ignores trifles.

JOSEPHINE. Do you know the defendants well enough to undertake the case?

THE RAGPICKER. I know them to the bottom of their souls. I go through their garbage every day.

CONSTANCE. And what do you find there?

THE RAGPICKER. Mostly flowers.

GABRIELLE. It's true, you know, the rich are always surrounded with flowers.

CONSTANCE. How beautiful!

COUNTESS. Are you trying to prejudice the court?

THE RAGPICKER. Oh no, Countess, no.

COUNTESS. We want a completely impartial defense.

THE RAGPICKER. Of course, Countess, of course. Permit me to make a suggestion.

COUNTESS. Will you preside, Josephine?

THE RAGPICKER. Instead of speaking as attorney, suppose you let me speak directly as defendant. It will be more convincing, and I can get into it more.

JOSEPHINE. Excellent idea. Motion granted.

COUNTESS. We don't want you to be too convincing, remember.

THE RAGPICKER. Impartial, Countess, impartial.

JOSEPHINE. Well? Have you prepared your case?

THE RAGPICKER. How rich am I?

JOSEPHINE. Millions. Billions.

THE RAGPICKER. How did I get them? Theft? Murder? Embezzlement?

COUNTESS. Most likely.

THE RAGPICKER. Do I have a wife? A mistress?

COUNTESS. Everything.

THE RAGPICKER. All right. I'm ready.

GABRIELLE. Will you have some tea?

THE RAGPICKER. Is that good?

CONSTANCE. Very good for the voice. The Russians drink nothing but tea. And they talk like anything.

THE RAGPICKER. All right. Tea.

JOSEPHINE. [*To the* VAGABONDS.] Come in. Come in. All of you. You may take places. The trial is public. [*The* VAGABONDS *dispose themselves on the steps and elsewhere.*] Your bell, if you please, Aurelia.

COUNTESS. But what if I should need to ring for Irma?

JOSEPHINE. Irma will sit here, next to me. If you need her, she can ring for herself. [*To the* POLICE SERGEANT *and* THE POLICEMAN.] Conduct the accused to the bar. [*The* OFFICERS *conduct* THE RAGPICKER *to a bar improvised with a rocking chair and a packing case marked* "Fragile." THE RAGPICKER *mounts the box. She rings the bell.*] The court is now in session. [*All sit.*] Counsel for the defense, you may take the oath.

THE RAGPICKER. I swear to tell the truth, the whole truth, and nothing but the truth, so help me God.

JOSEPHINE. Nonsense! You're not a witness. You're an attorney. It's your duty to lie, conceal and distort everything, and slander everybody.

THE RAGPICKER. All right. I swear to lie, conceal and distort everything, and slander everybody.

[JOSEPHINE *rings stridently.*]

JOSEPHINE. Quiet! Begin.

THE RAGPICKER. May it please the honorable, august, and elegant Court . . .

JOSEPHINE. Flattery will get you nowhere. That will do. The defense has been heard. Cross-examination.

COUNTESS. Mr. President . . .

THE RAGPICKER. [*Bowing with dignity.*] Madame.

COUNTESS. Do you know what you are charged with?

THE RAGPICKER. I can't for the life of me imagine. My life is an open book. My ways are known to all. I am a pillar of the church and the sole support of the Opera. My hands are spotless.

COUNTESS. What an atrocious lie! Just look at them!

CONSTANCE. You don't have to insult the man. He's only lying to please you.

COUNTESS. Be quiet, Constance! You don't get the idea at all. [*To* THE RAGPICKER.] You are charged with the crime of worshipping money.

THE RAGPICKER. Worshipping money? Me?

JOSEPHINE. Do you plead guilty or not guilty? Which is it?

THE RAGPICKER. Why, Your Honor . . .

JOSEPHINE. Yes or no?

THE RAGPICKER. Yes or no? No! I don't worship money, Countess. Heavens, no! Money worships me. It adores me. It won't let me alone. It's damned embarrassing, I can tell you.

JOSEPHINE. Kindly watch your language.

COUNTESS. Defendant, tell the Court how you came by your money.

THE RAGPICKER. The first time money came to me, I was a mere boy, a little golden-haired child in the bosom of my dear family. It came to me suddenly in the guise of a gold brick which, in my innocence, I picked out of a garbage can one day while playing. I was horrified, as you can imagine. I immediately tried to get rid of it by swapping it for a little run-down one-track railroad which, to my consternation, at once sold itself for a hundred times its value. In a desperate effort to get rid of this money, I began to buy things. I bought the Northern Refineries, the Galeries Lafayette, and the Schneider-Creusot Munition Works. And now I'm stuck with them. It's a horrible fate—but I'm resigned to it. I don't ask for your sympathy, I don't ask for your pity—all I ask for is a little common human understanding. . . . [*He begins to cry.*]

COUNTESS. I object. This wretch is trying to play on the emotions of the Court.

JOSEPHINE. The Court has no emotions.

THE RAGPICKER. Everyone knows that the poor have no one but themselves to blame for their poverty. It's only just that they should suffer the consequences. But how is it the fault of the rich if they're rich?

COUNTESS. Dry your tears. You're deceiving nobody. If, as you say, you're ashamed of your money, why is it you hold onto it with such a death-grip?

THE RAGPICKER. Me?

PEDDLER. You never part with a franc!

THE JUGGLER. You wouldn't even give the poor Deaf-Mute a sou!

THE RAGPICKER. Me, hold onto money? What slander! What injustice! What a thing to say to me in the presence of this honorable, august and elegant Court! I spend all my time trying to spend my money. If I have tan shoes, I buy black ones. If I have a bicycle, I buy a motor car. If I have a wife, I buy . . .

JOSEPHINE. [*Rings.*] Order!

THE RAGPICKER. I dispatch a plane to Java for a bouquet of flowers. I send a steamer to Egypt for a basket of figs. I send a special representative to New York to fetch me an ice-cream cone. And if it's not just exactly right, back it goes. But no matter what I do, I can't get rid of my money! If I play a hundred to one shot, the horse comes in by twenty lengths. If I throw a diamond in the Seine, it turns up in the trout they serve me for lunch. Ten diamonds—ten trout. Well, now, do you suppose I can get rid of forty millions giving a sou to a deaf-mute? Is it even worth the effort?

CONSTANCE. He's right.

THE RAGPICKER. Ah! You see, my dear? At last, there is somebody who understands me! Somebody who is not only beautiful, but extraordinarily sensitive and intelligent.

COUNTESS. I object!

JOSEPHINE. Overruled!

THE RAGPICKER. I should be delighted to send you some flowers, Miss—directly I'm acquitted. What flowers do you prefer?

CONSTANCE. Roses.

THE RAGPICKER. You shall have a bale every morning for the next five years. Money means nothing to me.

CONSTANCE. And amaryllis.

THE RAGPICKER. I'll make a note of the name. [*In his best lyrical style.*] The lady understands, ladies and gentlemen. The lady is no fool. She's been

around and she knows what's what. If I gave the Deaf-Mute a franc, twenty francs, twenty million francs—I still wouldn't make a dent in the forty times a thousand million francs that I'm afflicted with! Right, little lady?

CONSTANCE. Right.

JOSEPHINE. Proceed.

THE RAGPICKER. Like on the Stock Exchange. If *you* buy a stock, it sinks at once like a plummet. But if *I* buy a stock, it turns around and soars like an eagle. If I buy it at 33 . . .

PEDDLER. It goes up to a thousand.

THE RAGPICKER. It goes to twenty thousand! That's how I bought my twelve chateaux, my twenty villas, my 234 farms. That's how I endow the Opera and keep my twelve ballerinas.

THE FLOWER GIRL. I hope every one of them deceives you every moment of the day!

THE RAGPICKER. How can they deceive me? Suppose they try to deceive me with the male chorus, the general director, the assistant electrician or the English horn—I own them all, body and soul. It would be like deceiving me with my big toe.

CONSTANCE. Don't listen, Gabrielle.

GABRIELLE. Listen to what?

THE RAGPICKER. No. I am incapable of jealousy. I have all the women—or I can have them, which is the same thing. I get the thin ones with caviar—the fat ones with pearls . . .

COUNTESS. So you think there are no women with morals?

THE RAGPICKER. I mix morals with mink—delicious combination. I drip pearls into protests. I adorn resistance with rubies. My touch is jeweled; my smile, a motor car. What woman can withstand me? I lift my little finger—and do they fall?—Like leaves in autumn—like tin cans from a second-story window.

CONSTANCE. That's going a little too far!

COUNTESS. You see where money leads.

THE RAGPICKER. Of course. When you have no money, nobody trusts you, nobody believes you, nobody likes you. Because to have money is to be virtuous, honest, beautiful, and witty. And to be without is to be ugly and boring and stupid and useless.

COUNTESS. One last question. Suppose you find this oil you're looking for. What do you propose to do with it?

THE RAGPICKER. I propose to make war! I propose to conquer the world!

COUNTESS. You have heard the defense, such as it is. I demand a verdict of guilty.

THE RAGPICKER. What are you talking about? Guilty? I? I am never guilty!

JOSEPHINE. I order you to keep quiet.

THE RAGPICKER. I am never quiet!

JOSEPHINE. Quiet, in the name of the law!

THE RAGPICKER. I am the law. When I speak, that is the law. When I present my backside, it is etiquette to smile and to apply the lips respectfully. It is more than etiquette—it is a cherished national privilege, guaranteed by the Constitution.

JOSEPHINE. That's contempt of court. The trial is over.

COUNTESS. And the verdict?

ALL. Guilty!

JOSEPHINE. Guilty as charged.

COUNTESS. Then I have full authority to carry out the sentence?

ALL. Yes!

COUNTESS. I can do what I like with them?

ALL. Yes!

COUNTESS. I have the right to exterminate them?

ALL. Yes!

JOSEPHINE. Court adjourned!

COUNTESS. [*To* THE RAGPICKER.] Congratulations, Ragpicker. A marvelous defense. Absolutely impartial.

THE RAGPICKER. Had I known a little before, I could have done better. I could have prepared a little speech, like the time I used to sell the Miracle Spot Remover. . . .

JOSEPHINE. No need for that. You did very well, extempore. The likeness was striking and the style reminiscent of Clemenceau. I predict a brilliant future for you. Good-bye, Aurelia. I'll take our little Gabrielle home.

[JOSEPHINE *and* GABRIELLE *start up the stairs.*]

CONSTANCE. I'm going to walk along the river. [*To* DICKIE.] Oh! So here you are. And your ear all bloody! Dickie! Have you been fighting again? Oh, dear . . . !

COUNTESS. [*To* THE RAGPICKER.] See that she gets home all right, won't you? She loses everything on the way. And in the queerest places. Her prayer book in the butcher shop. And her corset in church.

THE RAGPICKER. [*Bowing and offering his arm.*] Permit me, Madame.

THE STREET SINGER. Oh, Countess— my mazurka. Remember?

COUNTESS. Oh, yes. Constance, wait a moment. [*To* THE SINGER.] Well? Begin.

THE STREET SINGER. [*Sings.*]
"Do you hear, Mademoiselle,
Those musicians of hell?"

CONSTANCE. Why, of course, it's *La Belle Polonaise.* . . . [*She sings.*]
"From Poland to France
Comes this marvelous dance,
So gracious,

Audacious,
Will you foot it, perchance?"

THE STREET SINGER. I'm saved!

JOSEPHINE. [*Reappearing at the head of the stairs.*]
"Now my arm I entwine
Round these contours divine,
So pure, so impassioned,
Which Cupid has fashioned. . . ."

GABRIELLE. [*Reappearing also, she sings a quartet with the others.*]
"Come, let's dance the mazurka, that devilish measure,
'Tis a joy that's reserved to the gods for their pleasure—
Let's gallop, let's hop,
With never a stop,
My blonde Polish miss,
Let our heads spin and turn
As the dance-floor we spurn—
There was never such pleasure as this!"

[*All except the* COUNTESS *and* IRMA *exit, dancing.*]

IRMA. It's time for your afternoon nap.

COUNTESS. But suppose they come, Irma!

IRMA. I'll watch out for them.

COUNTESS. Thank you, Irma. I *am* tired. [*She smiles.*] Did you ever see a trial end more happily in your life?

IRMA. Lie down and close your eyes a moment.

[THE COUNTESS *stretches out on the chaise-longue and shuts her eyes.* IRMA *tiptoes out. In a moment,* PIERRE *comes down softly, the feather boa in his hands. He stands over the chaise-longue, looking tenderly down at the sleeping woman, then kneels beside her and takes her hand.*]

COUNTESS. [*Without opening her eyes.*] Is it you, Adolphe Bertaut?

PIERRE. It's only Pierre.

COUNTESS. Don't lie to me, Adolphe Bertaut. These are your hands. Why do you complicate things always? Say that it's you.

PIERRE. Yes. It is I.

COUNTESS. Would it cost you so much to call me Aurelia.

PIERRE. It's I, Aurelia.

COUNTESS. Why did you leave me, Adolphe Bertaut? Was she so very lovely, this Georgette of yours?

PIERRE. No. You are a thousand times lovelier.

COUNTESS. But she was clever.

PIERRE. She was stupid.

COUNTESS. It was her soul, then, that drew you? When you looked into her eyes, you saw a vision of heaven, perhaps?

PIERRE. I saw nothing.

COUNTESS. That's how it is with men. They love you because you are beautiful and clever and soulful—and at the first opportunity they leave you for someone who is plain and dull and soulless. But why does it have to be like that, Adolphe Bertaut? Why?

PIERRE. Why, Aurelia?

COUNTESS. I know very well she wasn't rich. Because when I saw you that time at the grocer's, and you snatched the only good melon from right under my nose, your cuffs, my poor friend, were badly frayed. . . .

PIERRE. Yes. She was poor.

COUNTESS. "Was" poor? Is she dead, then? If it's because she's dead that you've come back to me—then, no. Go away. I will not take their leavings from the dead. I refuse to inherit you. . . .

PIERRE. She's quite well.

COUNTESS. Your hands are still the same, Adolphe Bertaut. Your touch is young and firm. Because it's the only part of you that has stayed with me. The rest of you is pretty far gone, I'm afraid. I can see why you'd rather not come near me when my eyes are open. It's thoughtful of you.

PIERRE. Yes. I've aged.

COUNTESS. Not I. I am young because I haven't had to live down my youth, like you. I have it with me still, as fresh and beautiful as ever. But when you walk now in the park at Colombes with Georgette, I'm sure . . .

PIERRE. There is no longer a park at Colombes.

COUNTESS. Is there a park still at St. Cloud? Is there a park at Versailles? I've never gone back to see. But I think, if they could move, those trees would have walked away in disgust the day you went there with Georgette. . . .

PIERRE. They did. Not many are left.

COUNTESS. You take her also, I suppose, to hear *Denise?*

PIERRE. No one hears *Denise* any more.

COUNTESS. It was on the way home from *Denise,* Adolphe Bertaut, that I first took your arm. Because it was windy and it was late. I have never set foot in that street again. I go the other way round. It's not easy, in the winter, when there's ice. One is quite apt to fall. I often do.

PIERRE. Oh, my darling—forgive me.

COUNTESS. No, never. I will never forgive you. It was very bad taste to take her to the very places where we'd been together.

PIERRE. All the same, I swear, Aurelia . . .

COUNTESS. Don't swear. I know what you did. You gave her the same flowers. You bought her the same chocolates. But has she any left? No. I have all your flowers still. I have twelve chocolates. No, I will never forgive you as long as I live.

PIERRE. I always loved you, Aurelia.

COUNTESS. You "loved" me? Then you too are dead, Adolphe Bertaut?

PIERRE. No. I love you. I shall always love you, Aurelia.

COUNTESS. Yes. I know. That much I've always known. I knew it the moment you went away, Adolphe, and I knew that nothing could ever change it. Georgette is in his arms now—yes. But he loves me. Tonight he's taken Georgette to hear *Denise*—yes. But he loves me . . . I know it. You never loved her. Do you think I believed for one moment that absurd story about her running off with the osteopath? Of course not. Since you didn't love her, obviously she stayed with you. And, after that, when she came back, and I heard about her going off with the surveyor—I knew that couldn't be true, either. You'll never get rid of her, Adolphe Bertaut—never. Because you don't love her.

PIERRE. I need your pity, Aurelia. I need your love. Don't forget me. . . .

COUNTESS. Farewell, Adolphe Bertaut. Farewell. Let go my hand, and give it to little Pierre. [PIERRE *lets go her hand, and after a moment takes it again. The* COUNTESS *opens her eyes.*] Pierre? Ah, it's you. Has he gone?

PIERRE. Yes, Countess.

COUNTESS. I didn't hear him go. Oh, he knows how to make a quick exit, that one. [*She sees the boa.*] Good heavens! Wherever did you find it?

PIERRE. In the wardrobe, Countess. When I took off the mirror.

COUNTESS. Was there a purple felt shopping bag with it?

PIERRE. Yes, Countess.

COUNTESS. And a little child's sewing box?

PIERRE. No, Countess.

COUNTESS. Oh, they're frightened now. They're trembling for their lives. You see what they're up to? They're quietly putting back all the things they have stolen. I never open that wardrobe, of course, on account of the old woman in the mirror. But I have sharp eyes. I don't need to open it to see what's in it. Up to this morning, that wardrobe was empty. And now—you see? But, dear me, how stupid they are! The one thing I really miss is my little sewing box. It's something they stole from me when I was a child. They haven't put it back? You're quite sure?

PIERRE. What was it like?

COUNTESS. Green cardboard with paper lace and gold stamping. I got it for Christmas when I was seven. They stole it the very next day. I cried my eyes out every time I thought of it—until I was eight.

PIERRE. It's not there, Countess.

COUNTESS. The thimble was gilt. I swore I'd never use any other. Look at my poor fingers. . . .

PIERRE. They've kept the thimble too.

COUNTESS. Splendid! Then I'm under no obligation to be merciful. Put the boa around my neck, Pierre. I want them to see me wearing it. They'll think it's a real boa.

[IRMA *runs in excitedly.*]

IRMA. Here they come, Countess! You were right —it's a procession. The street is full of limousines and taxis!

COUNTESS. I will receive them. [*As* PIERRE *hesitates to leave her.*] Don't worry. There's nothing to be frightened of. [PIERRE *goes out.*] Irma, did you remember to stir the kerosene into the water?

IRMA. Yes, Countess. Here it is.

COUNTESS. [*Looking critically at the bottle.*] You might as well pour in what's left of the tea. [IRMA *shakes up the liquid.*] Don't forget, I'm supposed to be deaf. I want to hear what they're thinking.

IRMA. Yes, Countess.

COUNTESS. [*Putting the finishing touches to her make-up.*] I don't have to be merciful—but, after all, I do want to be just. . . .

[IRMA *goes up to the landing and exits. As soon as she is alone, the* COUNTESS *presses the brick, and the trap door opens. There is a confused sound of auto horns in the street above, and the noise of an approaching crowd.*]

IRMA. [*Offstage.*] Yes, Mr. President. Come in, Mr. President. You're expected, Mr. President. This way, Mr. President. [*The* PRESIDENTS *come down, led by* THE PRESIDENT. *They all look alike, are dressed alike, and all have long cigars.*] The Countess is quite deaf, gentlemen. You'll have to shout. [*She announces.*] The presidents of the boards of directors!

THE PRESIDENT. I had a premonition, Madame, when I saw you this morning, that we should meet again. [*The* COUNTESS *smiles vaguely. He continues, a tone louder.*] I want to thank you for your trust. You may place yourself in our hands with complete confidence.

SECOND PRESIDENT. Louder. The old trot can't hear you.

THE PRESIDENT. I have a letter here, Madame, in which . . .

SECOND PRESIDENT. Louder. Louder.

THIRD PRESIDENT. [*Shouting.*] Is it true that you've located . . . ? [*The* COUNTESS *stares at him blankly. He shouts at the top of his voice.*] Oil? [*The* COUNTESS *nods with a smile, and points down.* THE PRESIDENT *produces a legal paper and a fountain pen.*] Sign here.

COUNTESS. What is it? I haven't my glasses.

THE PRESIDENT. Your contract. [*He offers the pen.*]

COUNTESS. Thank you.

SECOND PRESIDENT. [*Normal voice.*] What is it?

THIRD PRESIDENT. Waiver of all rights. [*He takes it back signed.*] Thank you. [*He hands it to the* SECOND PRESIDENT.] Witness. [*The* SECOND PRESIDENT *witnesses it.* THE PRESIDENT *passes it on to the* THIRD PRESIDENT.] Notarize. [*The paper is notarized.* THE PRESIDENT *turns to the* COUNTESS *and shouts.*] My congratulations. And now, Madame—— [*He produces a gold brick wrapped in tissue paper.*] If you'll show us the well, this package is yours.

COUNTESS. What is it?

THE PRESIDENT. Pure gold. Twenty-four karat. For you.

COUNTESS. Thank you very much. [*She takes it.*] It's heavy.

SECOND PRESIDENT. Are you going to give her that?

THE PRESIDENT. Don't worry. We'll pick it up again on the way out. [*He shouts at the* COUNTESS, *pointing at the trap door.*] Is this the way?

COUNTESS. That's the way.

[*The* SECOND PRESIDENT *tries to slip in first.* THE PRESIDENT *pulls him back.*]

THE PRESIDENT. Just a minute, Mr. President. After me, if you don't mind. And watch those cigars. It's oil, you know.

[*But as he is about to descend, the* COUNTESS *steps forward.*]

COUNTESS. Just one moment . . .

THE PRESIDENT. Yes?

COUNTESS. Did any of you happen to bring along a little sewing box?

THE PRESIDENT. Sewing box? [*He pulls back another impatient* PRESIDENT.] Take it easy.

COUNTESS. Or a little gold thimble?

THE PRESIDENT. Not me.

PRESIDENTS. Not us.

COUNTESS. What a pity!

THE PRESIDENT. Can we go down now?

COUNTESS. Yes. You may go down now. Watch your step!

[*They hurry down eagerly. When they have quite disappeared,* IRMA *appears on the landing and announces the next echelon.*]

IRMA. Countess, the Prospectors.

COUNTESS. Heavens! Are there more than one?

IRMA. There's a whole delegation.

COUNTESS. Send them down.

[THE PROSPECTOR *comes in, following his nose.*]

IRMA. Come in, please.

THE PROSPECTOR. [*Sniffing the air like a bloodhound.*] I smell something. . . . Who's that?

IRMA. The Countess. She is very deaf.

THE PROSPECTOR. Good.

[*The* PROSPECTORS *also look alike. Sharp clothes, Western hats, and long noses. They crowd down the stairs after* THE PROSPECTOR, *sniffing in unison.* THE PROSPECTOR *is especially talented. He casts about on the scent until it leads him to the decanter on the table. He pours himself a glass, drinks it off, and belches with much satisfaction. The others join him at once, and follow his example. They all belch in unison.*]

PROSPECTORS. Oil?

THE PROSPECTOR. Oil!

COUNTESS. Oil.

THE PROSPECTOR. Traces? Puddles?

COUNTESS. Pools. Gushers.

SECOND PROSPECTOR. Characteristic odor?

[*He sniffs.*]

THE PROSPECTOR. Chanel Number 5. Nectar! Undoubtedly—the finest—rarest! [*He drinks.*] Sixty gravity crude: straight gasoline! [*To the* COUNTESS.] How found? By blast? Drill?

COUNTESS. By finger.

THE PROSPECTOR. [*Whipping out a document.*] Sign here, please.

COUNTESS. What is it?

THE PROSPECTOR. Agreement for dividing the profits. . . . [*The* COUNTESS *signs.*]

SECOND PROSPECTOR. [*To* FIRST PROSPECTOR.] What is it?

THE PROSPECTOR. [*Pocketing the paper.*] Application to enter a lunatic asylum. Down there?

COUNTESS. Down there.

[*The* PROSPECTORS *go down, sniffing.* IRMA *enters.*]

IRMA. The gentlemen of the press are here.

COUNTESS. The rest of the machine! Show them in.

IRMA. The Public Relations Counsellors! [*They enter, all shapes and sizes, all in blue pin-striped suits and black homburg hats.*] The Countess is very deaf, gentlemen. You'll have to shout!

FIRST PRESS AGENT. You don't say—— Delighted to make the acquaintance of so charming and beautiful a lady. . . .

SECOND PRESS AGENT. Louder. She can't hear you.

FIRST PRESS AGENT. What a face! [*Shouts.*] Madame, we are the press. You know our power. We fix all values. We set all standards. Your entire future depends on us.

COUNTESS. How do you do?

FIRST PRESS AGENT. What will we charge the old trull? The usual thirty?

SECOND PRESS AGENT. Forty.

THIRD PRESS AGENT. Sixty.

FIRST PRESS AGENT. All right—seventy-five. [*He fills in a form and offers it to the* COUNTESS.] Sign here, Countess. This contract really gives you a break.

COUNTESS. That is the entrance.

FIRST PRESS AGENT. Entrance to what?

COUNTESS. The oil well.

FIRST PRESS AGENT. Oh, we don't need to see that, Madame.

COUNTESS. Don't need to see it?

FIRST PRESS AGENT. No, no—we don't have to see it to write about it. We can imagine it. An oil well is an oil well. "That's oil we know on earth, and oil we need to know." [*He bows.*]

COUNTESS. But if you don't see it, how can you be sure the oil is there?

FIRST PRESS AGENT. If it's there, well and good. If it's not, by the time we get through, it will be. You underestimate the creative aspect of our profession, Madame. [*The* COUNTESS *shakes her head, handing back the papers.*] I warn you, if you insist on rubbing our noses in this oil, it will cost you 10 per cent extra.

COUNTESS. It's worth it.

[*She signs. They cross toward the trap door.*]

SECOND PRESS AGENT. [*Descending.*] You see, Madame, we of the press can refuse a lady nothing.

THIRD PRESS AGENT. Especially, such a lady.

[THIRD PRESS AGENT *starts going down.*]

SECOND PRESS AGENT. [*Going down. Gallantly.*] It's plain to see, Madame, that even fountains of oil have their nymphs. . . . I can use that somewhere That's copy!

[THE PRESS AGENTS *go down. As he disappears, the* FIRST PRESS AGENT *steals the gold brick and blows a kiss gallantly to the* COUNTESS, *who blows one back. There is a high-pitched chatter offstage, and* IRMA *comes in, trying hard to hold back* THREE WOMEN *who pay no attention to her whatever. These* WOMEN *are tall, slender, and as soulless as if they were molded of wax. They march down the steps, erect and abstracted like animated window models, but chattering incessantly.*]

IRMA. But, ladies, please—you have no business here—you are not expected. [*To the* COUNTESS.] There are some strange ladies coming. . . .

COUNTESS. Show them in, Irma. [*The* WOMEN *come down, without taking the slightest interest in their surroundings.*] Who are you?

FIRST WOMAN. Madame, we are the most powerful pressure group in the world.

SECOND WOMAN. We are the ultimate dynamic.

THIRD WOMAN. The mainspring of all combinations.

FIRST WOMAN. Nothing succeeds without our assistance. Is that the well, Madame?

COUNTESS. That is the well.

FIRST WOMAN. Put out your cigarettes, girls. We don't want any explosions. Not with my brand-new eyelashes.

[*They go down, still chattering. The* COUNTESS *crosses to the wall to close the trap. As she does so, there is a commotion on the landing.*]

IRMA. Countess . . .

[*A* MAN *rushes in breathlessly.*]

MAN. Just a minute! Just a minute!

[*He rushes for the trap door.*]

COUNTESS. Wait! Who are you?

MAN. I'm in a hurry. Excuse me. It's my only chance! [*He rushes down.*]

COUNTESS. But . . . [*But he is gone. She shrugs her shoulders, and presses the brick. The trap closes. She rings the bell for* IRMA.] My gold brick! Why, they've stolen my gold brick! [*She moves toward the trap. It is now closed.*] Well, let them take their god with them.

[IRMA *enters and sees with astonishment that the stage is empty of all but the* COUNTESS. *Little by little, the scene is suffused with light, faint at first, but increasing as if the very walls were glowing with the quiet radiance of universal joy. Only around the closed trap a shadow lingers.*]

IRMA. But what's happened? They've gone! They've vanished!

COUNTESS. They've evaporated, Irma. They were wicked. Wickedness evaporates.

[PIERRE *enters. He is followed by the* VAGA-BONDS, *all of them. The new radiance of the world is now very perceptible. It glows from their faces.*]

PIERRE. Oh, Countess . . . !

THE WAITER. Countess, everything's changed. Now you can breathe again. Now you can see.

PIERRE. The air is pure! The sky is clear!

IRMA. Life is beautiful again.

THE RAGPICKER. [*Rushes in.*] Countess—the pigeons! The pigeons are flying!

THE FLOWER GIRL. They don't have to walk any more.

THE RAGPICKER. They're flying. . . . The air is like crystal. And young grass is sprouting on the pavements.

COUNTESS. Is it possible?

IRMA. [*Interpreting for* THE DEAF-MUTE.] Now, Juggler, you can throw your fireballs up as high as you please—they won't go out.

THE SERGEANT. On the street, utter strangers are shaking hands, they don't know why, and offering each other almond bars!

COUNTESS. Oh, my friends . . .

THE WAITER. Countess, we thank you. . . .

[*They go on talking with happy and animated gestures, but we no longer hear them, for their words blend into a strain of unearthly music which seems to thrill from the uttermost confines of the universe. And out of this music comes a voice.*]

FIRST VOICE. Countess . . .

[*Only the* COUNTESS *hears it. She turns from the group of* VAGABONDS *in wonder.*]

SECOND VOICE. Countess . . .

THIRD VOICE. Countess . . .

[*As she looks up in rapture, the* FIRST VOICE *speaks again.*]

FIRST VOICE. Countess, we thank you. We are the friends of animals.

SECOND VOICE. We are the friends of people.

THIRD VOICE. We are the friends of friendship.

FIRST VOICE. You have freed us!

SECOND VOICE. From now on, there will be no hungry cats. . . .

THIRD VOICE. And we shall tell the Duchess her dog's right name!

[*The* VOICES *fade off. And now another group of voices is heard.*]

FIRST VOICE. Countess, we thank you. We are the friends of flowers.

SECOND VOICE. From now on, every plant in Paris will be watered. . . .

THIRD VOICE. And the sewers will be fragrant with jasmine!

[*These voices, too, are silent. For an instant, the stage is vibrant with music. Then* THE DEAF-MUTE *speaks, and his voice is the most beautiful of all.*]

THE DEAF-MUTE. Sadness flies on the wings of the morning, and out of the heart of darkness comes the light.

[*Suddenly a group of figures detaches itself from the shadows. These are exactly similar in face and figure and in dress. They are shabby in the fashion of 1900 and their cuffs are badly frayed. Each bears in his hand a ripe melon.*]

FIRST ADOLPHE BERTAUT. Countess, we thank you. We, too, are freed at last. We are the Adolphe Bertauts of the world.

SECOND ADOLPHE BERTAUT. We are no longer timid.

THIRD ADOLPHE BERTAUT. We are no longer weak.

FIRST ADOLPHE BERTAUT. From this day on, we shall hold fast to what we love. For your sake, henceforth, we shall be handsome, and our cuffs forever immaculate and new. Countess, we bring you this melon and with it our hearts . . . ! [*They all kneel.*] Will you do us the honor to be our wife?

COUNTESS. [*Sadly.*] Too late! Too late! [*She waves them aside. They take up their melons sadly and vanish. The voices of the* VAGABONDS *are heard again, and the music dies.*] Too late! Too late!

PIERRE. Too late, Countess?

IRMA. Too late for what?

COUNTESS. I say that it's too late for them. On the twenty-fourth of May, 1881, the most beautiful Easter in the memory of man, it was not too late. And on the fifth of September, 1887, the day they caught the trout and broiled it on the open fire by the brook at Villeneuve, it was not too late. And it was even not too late for them on the twenty-first of August, 1897, the day the Czar visited Paris with his guard. But they did nothing and they said nothing, and now—kiss each other, you two, this very instant!

IRMA. You mean . . . ?

PIERRE. You mean . . . ?

IRMA. But, Countess . . .

COUNTESS. It's three hours since you've met and known and loved each other. Kiss each other quickly. [PIERRE *hesitates.*] Look at him. He hesitates. He trembles. Happiness frightens him. . . . How like a man! Oh, Irma, kiss him, kiss him! If two people who love each other let a single instant wedge itself between them, it grows—it becomes a month, a year, a century; it becomes too late. Kiss him, Irma, kiss him while there is time, or in a moment his hair will be white and there will be another madwoman in Paris! Oh, make her kiss him, all of you! [*They kiss.*] Bravo! Oh, if only you'd had the courage to do that thirty years ago, how different I would be today! Dear Deaf-Mute, be still—your words dazzle our eyes! And Irma is too busy to translate for you. [*They kiss once more.*] Well, there we are. The world is safe. And you see how simple it all was? Nothing is ever so wrong in this world that a sensible woman can't set it right in the course of an afternoon. Only, the next time, don't wait until things begin to look black. The minute you notice anything, tell me at once.

THE RAGPICKER. We will, Countess. We will.

COUNTESS. [*Puts on her hat. Her tone becomes businesslike.*] Irma. My bones. My gizzard.

IRMA. I have them ready, Countess.

COUNTESS. Good. [*She puts the bones into her basket and starts for the stairs.*] Well, let's get on to more important things. Four o'clock. My poor cats must be starved. What a bore for them if humanity had to be saved every afternoon. They don't think much of it, as it is.

CURTAIN

THE GLASS MENAGERIE

TENNESSEE WILLIAMS

TENNESSEE (THOMAS LANIER) WILLIAMS (1914–   ) was born in Columbus, Mississippi. He graduated from the University of Iowa in 1938. *The Glass Menagerie* (1945) won the New York Drama Critics' Circle Award as the best play of that year. The author is said to consider it an expression of what he has to say "that is nice about people." Since its production, he has written among other plays, *A Streetcar Named Desire* (produced 1947 and the winner of the Pulitzer Prize and other awards), *Summer and Smoke* (1948), *The Rose Tattoo* (1951), *Cat On A Hot Tin Roof* (1955), and *The Night of the Iguana* (1961). The power of Williams' work and the range of his technical ability are immediately obvious to the playgoer, and although he chooses to write of shadowy people, his dramatic handling of his materials is clear-cut and theater-wise.

CHARACTERS

AMANDA WINGFIELD, *the mother.*
> *A little woman of great but confused vitality clinging frantically to another time and place. Her characterization must be carefully created, not copied from type. She is not paranoiac, but her life is paranoia. There is much to admire in* AMANDA, *and as much to love and pity as there is to laugh at. Certainly she has endurance and a kind of heroism, and though her foolishness makes her unwittingly cruel at times, there is tenderness in her slight person.*

LAURA WINGFIELD, *her daughter.*
> AMANDA, *having failed to establish contact with reality, continues to live vitally in her illusions, but* LAURA'S *situation is even graver. A childhood illness has left her crippled, one leg slightly shorter than the other, and held in a brace. This defect need not be more than suggested on the stage. Stemming from this,* LAURA'S *separation increases till she is like a piece of her own glass collection, too exquisitely fragile to move from the shelf.*

TOM WINGFIELD, *her son, and the narrator of the play.*
> *A poet with a job in a warehouse. His nature is not remorseless, but to escape from a trap he has to act without pity.*

JIM O'CONNOR, *the gentleman caller.*
> *A nice, ordinary, young man.*

SCENE

An Alley in St. Louis

PART I. Preparation for a Gentleman Caller.
PART II. The Gentleman calls.
> *Time: Now and the Past.*

PRODUCTION NOTES

BEING a "memory play," *The Glass Menagerie* can be presented with unusual freedom of convention. Because of its considerably delicate or tenuous material, atmospheric touches and subtleties of direction play a particularly important part. Expressionism and all other unconventional techniques in drama have only one valid aim, and that is a closer approach to truth. When a play employs unconventional techniques, it is not, or certainly shouldn't be, trying to escape its responsibility of dealing with reality, or interpreting experience, but is actually or should be attempting to find a closer approach, a more penetrating and vivid expression of things as they are. The straight realistic play with its genuine frigidaire and authentic ice-cubes, its characters that speak exactly as its audience speaks, corresponds to the academic landscape and has the same virtue of a photographic likeness. Everyone should know nowadays the unimportance of the photographic in art: that truth, life, or reality is an organic thing which the poetic imagination can represent or suggest, in essence, only through transformation, through changing into other forms than those which were merely present in appearance.

These remarks are not meant as a preface only to this particular play. They have to do with a conception of a new, plastic theatre which must take the

Copyright 1945 by Tennessee Williams and Edwina D. Williams. Reprinted by permission of Random House, Inc.

place of the exhausted theatre of realistic conventions if the theatre is to resume vitality as a part of our culture.

THE SCREEN DEVICE

There is *only one important difference between the original and acting versions of the play* and that is the *omission* in the latter of the device which I tentatively included in my *original* script. This device was the use of a screen on which were projected magic-lantern slides bearing images or titles. I do not regret the omission of this device from the Broadway production. The extraordinary power of Miss Taylor's performance made it suitable to have the utmost simplicity in the physical production. But I think it may be interesting to some readers to see how this device was conceived. So I am putting it into the published manuscript. These images and legends, projected from behind, were cast on a section of wall between the front-room and dining-room areas, which should be indistinguishable from the rest when not in use.

The purpose of this will probably be apparent. It is to give accent to certain values in each scene. Each scene contains a particular point (or several) which is structurally the most important. In an episodic play, such as this, the basic structure or narrative line may be obscured from the audience; the effect may seem fragmentary rather than architectural. This may not be the fault of the play so much as a lack of attention in the audience. The legend or image upon the screen will strengthen the effect of what is merely allusion in the writing and allow the primary point to be made more simply and lightly than if the entire responsibility were on the spoken lines. Aside from this structural value, I think the screen will have a definite emotional appeal, less definable but just as important. An imaginative producer or director may invent many other uses for this device than those indicated in the present script. In fact the possibilities of the device seem much larger to me than the instance of this play can possibly utilize.

THE MUSIC

Another extra-literary accent in this play is provided by the use of music. A single recurring tune, "The Glass Menagerie," is used to give emotional emphasis to suitable passages. This tune is like circus music, not when you are on the grounds or in the immediate vicinity of the parade, but when you are at some distance and very likely thinking of something else. It seems under those circumstances to continue almost interminably and it weaves in and out of your preoccupied consciousness; then it is the lightest, most delicate music in the world and perhaps the saddest. It expresses the surface vivacity of life with the underlying strain of immutable and inexpressible sorrow. When you look at a piece of delicately spun glass you think of two things: how beautiful it is and how easily it can be broken. Both of those ideas should be woven into the recurring tune, which dips in and out of the play as if it were carried on a wind that changes. It serves as a thread of connection and allusion between the narrator with his separate point in time and space and the subject of his story. Between each episode it returns as reference to the emotion, nostalgia, which is the first condition of the play. It is primarily Laura's music and therefore comes out most clearly when the play focuses upon her and the lovely fragility of glass which is her image.

THE LIGHTING

The lighting in the play is not realistic. In keeping with the atmosphere of memory, the stage is dim. Shafts of light are focused on selected areas or actors, sometimes in contradistinction to what is the apparent center. For instance, in the quarrel scene between Tom and Amanda, in which Laura has no active part, the clearest pool of light is on her figure. This is also true of the supper scene, when her silent figure on the sofa should remain the visual center. The light upon Laura should be distinct from the others, having a peculiar pristine clarity such as light used in early religious portraits of female saints or madonnas. A certain correspondence to light in religious paintings, such as El Greco's, where the figures are radiant in atmosphere that is relatively dusky, could be effectively used throughout the play. (It will also permit a more effective use of the screen.) A free, imaginative use of light can be of enormous value in giving a mobile, plastic quality to plays of a more or less static nature.

T. W.

SCENE I

The Wingfield apartment is in the rear of the building, one of those vast hive-like conglomerations of cellular living-units that flower as warty growths in overcrowded urban centers of lower middle-class population and are symptomatic of the impulse of this largest and fundamentally enslaved section of American society to avoid fluidity and differentiation and to exist and

function as one interfused mass of automatism.
The apartment faces an alley and is entered by a
fire-escape, a structure whose name is a touch of
accidental poetic truth, for all of these huge
buildings are always burning with the slow and
implacable fires of human desperation. The fire-
escape is included in the set—that is, the landing
of it and steps descending from it.
The scene is memory and is therefore nonreal-
istic. Memory takes a lot of poetic license. It
omits some details; others are exaggerated, ac-
cording to the emotional value of the articles it
touches, for memory is seated predominantly in
the heart. The interior is therefore rather dim
and poetic.
At the rise of the curtain, the audience is faced
with the dark, grim rear wall of the Wingfield
tenement. This building, which runs parallel to
the footlights, is flanked on both sides by dark,
narrow alleys which run into murky canyons of
tangled clotheslines, garbage cans, and the sin-
ister lattice-work of neighboring fire-escapes. It
is up and down these side alleys that exterior
entrances and exits are made, during the play.
At the end of TOM's *opening commentary, the*
dark tenement wall slowly reveals (by means of
a transparency) the interior of the ground floor
Wingfield apartment.
Downstage is the living room, which also serves
as a sleeping room for LAURA, *the sofa unfolding*
to make her bed. Upstage, center, and divided
by a wide arch or second proscenium with trans-
parent faded portieres (or second curtain), is
the dining room. In an old-fashioned what-not
in the living room are seen scores of transparent
glass animals. A blown-up photograph of the
father hangs on the wall of the living room, fac-
ing the audience, to the left of the archway. It
is the face of a very handsome young man in a
doughboy's First World War cap. He is gallantly
smiling, ineluctably smiling, as if to say, "I will
be smiling forever."
The audience hears and sees the opening scene
in the dining room through both the transparent
fourth wall of the building and the transparent
gauze portieres of the dining-room arch. It is
during this revealing scene that the fourth wall
slowly ascends, out of sight. This transparent ex-
terior wall is not brought down again until the
very end of the play, during TOM's *final speech.*
The narrator is an undisguised convention of
the play. He takes whatever license with dra-
matic convention is convenient to his purposes.
[TOM *enters dressed as a merchant sailor from*
alley, stage left, and strolls across the front of

the stage to the fire-escape. There he stops and
lights a cigarette. He addresses the audience.]

TOM. Yes, I have tricks in my pocket, I have things
up my sleeve. But I am the opposite of a stage
magician. He gives you illusion that has the appearance of truth. I give you truth in the pleasant disguise of illusion.

To begin with, I turn back time. I reverse it to that
quaint period, the thirties, when the huge middle
class of America was matriculating in a school for
the blind. Their eyes had failed them, or they had
failed their eyes, and so they were having their
fingers pressed forcibly down on the fiery Braille
alphabet of a dissolving economy.

In Spain there was revolution. Here there was only
shouting and confusion.

In Spain there was Guernica. Here there were disturbances of labor, sometimes pretty violent, in otherwise peaceful cities such as Chicago, Cleveland,
Saint Louis . . .

This is the social background of the play. [*Music.*]

The play is memory.

Being a memory play, it is dimly lighted, it is
sentimental, it is not realistic.

In memory everything seems to happen to music.
That explains the fiddle in the wings.

I am the narrator of the play, and also a character
in it.

The other characters are my mother, Amanda, my
sister, Laura, and a gentleman caller who appears
in the final scenes.

He is the most realistic character in the play, being
an emissary from a world of reality that we were
somehow set apart from.

But since I have a poet's weakness for symbols, I
am using this character also as a symbol; he is the
long delayed but always expected something that we
live for.

There is a fifth character in the play who doesn't
appear except in this larger-than-life-size photograph
over the mantel.

This is our father who left us a long time ago.

He was a telephone man who fell in love with long
distances; he gave up his job with the telephone company and skipped the light fantastic out of town . . .

The last we heard of him was a picture post-card
from Mazatlan, on the Pacific coast of Mexico, containing a message of two words——

"Hello—— Good-bye!" and no address.

I think the rest of the play will explain itself. . . .

[AMANDA's *voice becomes audible through the*
portieres. LEGEND ON SCREEN: "OÙ SONT LES
NEIGES?" *He divides the portieres and enters*
the upstage area. AMANDA *and* LAURA *are*
seated at a drop-leaf table. Eating is indicated

by gestures without food or utensils. AMANDA *faces the audience.* TOM *and* LAURA *are seated in profile. The interior has lit up softly and through the scrim we see* AMANDA *and* LAURA *seated at the table in the upstage area.*]

AMANDA [*calling*]. Tom?

TOM. Yes. Mother.

AMANDA. We can't say grace until you come to the table!

TOM. Coming, Mother.

[*He bows slightly and withdraws, reappearing a few moments later in his place at the table.*]

AMANDA [*to her son*]. Honey, don't *push* with your *fingers*. If you have to push with something, the thing to push with is a crust of bread. And chew—chew! Animals have sections in their stomachs which enable them to digest food without mastication, but human beings are supposed to chew their food before they swallow it down. Eat food leisurely, son, and really enjoy it. A well-cooked meal has lots of delicate flavors that have to be held in the mouth for appreciation. So chew your food and give your salivary glands a chance to function!

[TOM *deliberately lays his imaginary fork down and pushes his chair back from the table.*]

TOM. I haven't enjoyed one bite of this dinner because of your constant directions on how to eat it. It's you that make me rush through meals with your hawk-like attention to every bite I take. Sickening—spoils my appetite—all this discussion of—animals' secretion—salivary glands—mastication!

AMANDA [*lightly*]. Temperament like a Metropolitan star! [*He rises and crosses downstage.*] You're not excused from the table.

TOM. I'm getting a cigarette.

AMANDA. You smoke too much. [LAURA *rises.*]

LAURA. I'll bring in the blanc mange.

[*He remains standing with his cigarette by the portieres during the following.*]

AMANDA [*rising*]. No, sister, no, sister—you be the lady this time and I'll be the darky.

LAURA. I'm already up.

AMANDA. Resume your seat, little sister—I want you to stay fresh and pretty—for gentlemen callers!

LAURA. I'm not expecting any gentlemen callers.

AMANDA. [*Crossing out to kitchenette. Airily.*] Sometimes they come when they are least expected! Why, I remember one Sunday afternoon in Blue Mountain—[*Enters kitchenette.*]

TOM. I know what's coming!

LAURA. Yes. But let her tell it.

TOM. Again?

LAURA. She loves to tell it.

[AMANDA *returns with bowl of desert.*]

AMANDA. One Sunday afternoon in Blue Mountain—your mother received—*seventeen!*—gentlemen callers! Why, sometimes there weren't chairs enough to accommodate them all. We had to send the nigger over to bring in folding chairs from the parish house.

TOM [*remaining at portieres*]. How did you entertain those gentlemen callers?

AMANDA. I understood the art of conversation!

TOM. I bet you could talk.

AMANDA. Girls in those days *knew* how to talk, I can tell you.

TOM. Yes?

[IMAGE: AMANDA AS A GIRL ON A PORCH, GREETING CALLERS.]

AMANDA. They knew how to entertain their gentlemen callers. It wasn't enough for a girl to be possessed of a pretty face and a graceful figure—although I wasn't slighted in either respect. She also needed to have a nimble wit and a tongue to meet all occasions.

TOM. What did you talk about?

AMANDA. Things of importance going on in the world! Never anything coarse or common or vulgar. [*She addresses* TOM *as though he were seated in the vacant chair at the table though he remains by portieres. He plays this scene as though he held the book.*] My callers were gentlemen—all! Among my callers were some of the most prominent young planters of the Mississippi Delta—planters and sons of planters! [TOM *motions for music and a spot of light on* AMANDA. *Her eyes lift, her face glows, her voice becomes rich and elegiac.* SCREEN LEGEND: "OÙ SONT LES NEIGES?"]

There was young Champ Laughlin, who later became vice-president of the Delta Planters Bank.

Hadley Stevenson, who was drowned in Moon Lake and left his widow one hundred and fifty thousand in Government bonds.

There were the Cutrere brothers, Wesley and Bates. Bates was one of my bright particular beaux! He got in a quarrel with that wild Wainwright boy. They shot it out on the floor of Moon Lake Casino. Bates was shot through the stomach. Died in the ambulance on his way to Memphis. His widow was also well-provided for, came into eight or ten thousand acres, that's all. She married him on the rebound—never loved her—carried my picture on him the night he died!

And there was that boy that every girl in the Delta had set her cap for! That beautiful, brilliant young Fitzhugh boy from Greene County!

TOM. What did he leave his widow?

AMANDA. He never married! Gracious, you talk as though all of my old admirers had turned up their toes to the daisies!

TOM. Isn't this the first you've mentioned that still survives?

AMANDA. That Fitzhugh boy went North and made a fortune—came to be known as the Wolf of Wall Street! He had the Midas touch, whatever he touched turned to gold!

And I could have been Mrs. Duncan J. Fitzhugh, mind you! But—I picked your *father!*

LAURA [*rising*]. Mother, let me clear the table.

AMANDA. No, dear, you go in front and study your typewriter chart. Or practice your shorthand a little. Stay fresh and pretty!—It's almost time for our gentlemen callers to start arriving. [*She flounces girlishly toward the kitchenette.*] How many do you suppose we're going to entertain this afternoon?

[TOM *throws down the paper and jumps up with a groan.*]

LAURA [*alone in the dining room*]. I don't believe we're going to receive any, Mother.

AMANDA [*reappearing, airily*]. What? No one—not one? You must be joking! [LAURA *nervously echoes her laugh. She slips in a fugitive manner through the half-open portieres and draws them gently behind her. A shaft of very clear light is thrown on her face against the faded tapestry of the curtains.* MUSIC: "THE GLASS MENAGERIE" UNDER FAINTLY. *Lightly.*] Not one gentleman caller? It can't be true! There must be a flood, there must have been a tornado!

LAURA. It isn't a flood, it's not a tornado, Mother. I'm just not popular like you were in Blue Mountain. . . . [TOM *utters another groan.* LAURA *glances at him with a faint, apologetic smile. Her voice catching a little.*] Mother's afraid I'm going to be an old maid.

THE SCENE DIMS OUT WITH "GLASS MENAGERIE" MUSIC

SCENE II

LEGEND: "LAURA, HAVEN'T YOU EVER LIKED SOME BOY?"

On the dark stage the screen is lighted with the image of blue roses.

Gradually LAURA's *figure becomes apparent and the screen goes out. The music subsides.*

LAURA *is seated in the delicate ivory chair at the small claw-foot table.*

She wears a dress of soft violet material for a kimono—her hair tied back from her forehead with a ribbon.

She is washing and polishing her collection of glass.

[AMANDA *appears on the fire-escape steps. At the sound of her ascent,* LAURA *catches her breath, thrusts the bowl of ornaments away and*

seats herself stiffly before the diagram of the typewriter keyboard as though it held her spellbound.

Something has happened to AMANDA. *It is written in her face as she climbs to the landing: a look that is grim and hopeless and a little absurd.*

She has on one of those cheap or imitation velvety-looking cloth coats with imitation fur collar. Her hat is five or six years old, one of those dreadful cloche hats that were worn in the late twenties, and she is clasping an enormous black patent-leather pocketbook with nickel clasps and initials. This is her full-dress outfit, the one she usually wears to the D.A.R.

Before entering she looks through the door.

She purses her lips, opens her eyes very wide, rolls them upward and shakes her head.

Then she slowly lets herself in the door. Seeing her mother's expression LAURA *touches her lips with a nervous gesture.*]

LAURA. Hello, Mother, I was——

[*She makes a nervous gesture toward the chart on the wall.* AMANDA *leans against the shut door and stares at* LAURA *with a martyred look.*]

AMANDA. Deception? Deception?

[*She slowly removes her hat and gloves, continuing the sweet suffering stare. She lets the hat and gloves fall on the floor—a bit of acting.*]

LAURA [*shakily*]. How was the D.A.R. meeting? [AMANDA *slowly opens her purse and removes a dainty white handkerchief which she shakes out delicately and delicately touches to her lips and nostrils.*] Didn't you go to the D.A.R. meeting, Mother?

AMANDA [*faintly, almost inaudibly*]—No.—No [*then more forcibly*]. I did not have the strength—to go to the D.A.R. In fact, I did not have the courage! I wanted to find a hole in the ground and hide myself in it forever!

[*She crosses slowly to the wall and removes the diagram of the typewriter keyboard. She holds it in front of her for a second, staring at it sweetly and sorrowfully—then bites her lips and tears it in two pieces.*]

LAURA [*faintly*]. Why did you do that, Mother? [AMANDA *repeats the same procedure with the chart of the Gregg Alphabet.*] Why are you——

AMANDA. Why? Why? How old are you, Laura?

LAURA. Mother, you know my age.

AMANDA. I thought that you were an adult; it seems that I was mistaken.

[*She crosses slowly to the sofa and sinks down and stares at* LAURA.]

LAURA. Please don't stare at me, Mother.

[AMANDA *closes her eyes and lowers her head. Count ten.*]

AMANDA. What are we going to do, what is going to become of us, what is the future? [*Count ten.*]

LAURA. Has something happened, Mother? [AMANDA *draws a long breath and takes out the handkerchief again. Dabbing process.*] Mother, has—something happened?

AMANDA. I'll be all right in a minute, I'm just bewildered— [*Count five.*] —by life. . . .

LAURA. Mother, I wish that you would tell me what's happened!

AMANDA. As you know, I was supposed to be inducted into my office at the D.A.R. this afternoon. [IMAGE: A SWARM OF TYPEWRITERS.] But I stopped off at Rubicam's Business College to speak to your teachers about your having a cold and ask them what progress they thought you were making down there.

LAURA. Oh. . . .

AMANDA. I went to the typing instructor and introduced myself as your mother. She didn't know who you were. Wingfield, she said. We don't have any such student enrolled at the school!

I assured her she did, that you had been going to classes since early in January.

"I wonder," she said, "if you could be talking about that terribly shy little girl who dropped out of school after only a few days' attendance?"

"No," I said, "Laura, my daughter, has been going to school every day for the past six weeks!"

"Excuse me," she said. She took the attendance book out and there was your name, unmistakably printed, and all the dates you were absent until they decided that you had dropped out of school.

I still said, "No, there must have been some mistake! There must have been some mix-up in the records!"

And she said, "No—I remember her perfectly now. Her hands shook so that she couldn't hit the right keys! The first time we gave a speed-test, she broke down completely—was sick at the stomach and almost had to be carried into the wash-room! After that morning she never showed up any more. We phoned the house but never got any answer"—while I was working at Famous and Barr, I suppose, demonstrating those—— Oh!

I felt so weak I could barely keep on my feet!

I had to sit down while they got me a glass of water!

Fifty dollars' tuition, all of our plans—my hopes and ambitions for you—just gone up the spout, just gone up the spout like that.

[LAURA *draws a long breath and gets awkwardly to her feet. She crosses to the victrola and winds it up.*]

What are you doing?

LAURA. Oh!

[*She releases the handle and returns to her seat.*]

AMANDA. Laura, where have you been going when you've gone out pretending that you were going to business college?

LAURA. I've just been going out walking.

AMANDA. That's not true.

LAURA. It is. I just went walking.

AMANDA. Walking? Walking? In winter? Deliberately courting pneumonia in that light coat? Where did you walk to, Laura?

LAURA. All sorts of places—mostly in the park.

AMANDA. Even after you'd started catching that cold?

LAURA. It was the lesser of two evils, Mother. [IMAGE: WINTER SCENE IN PARK.] I couldn't go back up. I—threw up—on the floor!

AMANDA. From half past seven till after five every day you mean to tell me you walked around the park, because you wanted to make me think that you were still going to Rubicam's Business College?

LAURA. It wasn't as bad as it sounds. I went inside places to get warmed up.

AMANDA. Inside where?

LAURA. I went in the art museum and the birdhouses at the Zoo. I visited the penguins every day! Sometimes I did without lunch and went to the movies. Lately I've been spending most of my afternoons in the Jewel-box, that big glass house where they raise the tropical flowers.

AMANDA. You did all this to deceive me, just for deception? [LAURA *looks down.*] Why?

LAURA. Mother, when you're disappointed, you get that awful suffering look on your face, like the picture of Jesus' mother in the museum!

AMANDA. Hush!

LAURA. I couldn't face it.

[*Pause. A whisper of strings.* LEGEND: "THE CRUST OF HUMILITY."]

AMANDA [*hopelessly fingering the huge pocketbook*]. So what are we going to do the rest of our lives? Stay home and watch the parades go by? Amuse ourselves with the glass menagerie, darling? Eternally play those worn-out phonograph records your father left as a painful reminder of him?

We won't have a business career—we've given that up because it gave us nervous indigestion! [*Laughs wearily.*] What is there left but dependency all our lives? I know so well what becomes of unmarried women who aren't prepared to occupy a position. I've seen such pitiful cases in the South—barely tolerated spinsters living upon the grudging patronage of sister's husband or brother's wife!—stuck away in some little mouse-trap of a room—encouraged by one in-law to visit another—little birdlike women without any nest—eating the crust of humility all their life!

Is that the future that we've mapped out for ourselves?

I swear it's the only alternative I can think of!

It isn't a very pleasant alternative, is it?

Of course—some girls *do marry.* [LAURA *twists her hands nervously.*]

Haven't you ever liked some boy?

LAURA. Yes. I liked one once. [*Rises.*] I came across his picture a while ago.

AMANDA [*with some interest*]. He gave you his picture?

LAURA. No, it's in the year-book.

AMANDA [*disappointed*]. Oh—a high-school boy.

[SCREEN IMAGE: JIM AS HIGH-SCHOOL HERO BEARING A SILVER CUP.]

LAURA. Yes. His name was Jim. [LAURA *lifts the heavy annual from the claw-foot table.*] Here he is in *The Pirates of Penzance.*

AMANDA [*absently*]. The what?

LAURA. The operetta the senior class put on. He had a wonderful voice and we sat across the aisle from each other Mondays, Wednesdays, and Fridays in the Aud. Here he is with the silver cup for debating! See his grin?

AMANDA [*absently*]. He must have had a jolly disposition.

LAURA. He used to call me—Blue Roses. [IMAGE: BLUE ROSES.]

AMANDA. Why did he call you such a name as that?

LAURA. When I had that attack of pleurosis—he asked me what was the matter when I came back. I said pleurosis—he thought that I said Blue Roses! So that's what he always called me after that. Whenever he saw me, he'd holler, "Hello, Blue Roses!" I didn't care for the girl that he went out with. Emily Meisenbach. Emily was the best-dressed girl at Soldan. She never struck me, though, as being sincere . . . It says in the Personal Section—they're engaged. That's—six years ago! They must be married by now.

AMANDA. Girls that aren't cut out for business careers usually wind up married to some nice man. [*Gets up with a spark of revival.*] Sister, that's what you'll do!

[LAURA *utters a startled, doubtful laugh. She reaches quickly for a piece of glass.*]

LAURA. But, Mother——

AMANDA. Yes? [*Crossing to photograph.*]

LAURA [*in a tone of frightened apology*]. I'm—crippled! [IMAGE: SCREEN.]

AMANDA. Nonsense! Laura, I've told you never, never to use that word. Why, you're not crippled, you just have a little defect—hardly noticeable, even! When people have some slight disadvantage like that, they cultivate other things to make up for it—develop charm—and vivacity—and—*charm!* That's all you have to do! [*She turns again to the photograph.*] One thing your father had *plenty of*—was *charm!*

[TOM *motions to the fiddle in the wings.*]

THE SCENE FADES OUT WITH MUSIC

SCENE III

[LEGEND ON SCREEN: "AFTER THE FIASCO——" TOM *speaks from the fire-escape landing.*]

TOM. After the fiasco at Rubicam's Business College, the idea of getting a gentleman caller for Laura began to play a more and more important part in Mother's calculations.

It became an obsession. Like some archetype of the universal unconscious, the image of the gentleman caller haunted our small apartment. . .

[IMAGE: YOUNG MAN AT DOOR WITH FLOWERS.]

An evening at home rarely passed without some allusion to this image, this spectre, this hope. . . .

Even when he wasn't mentioned, his presence hung in Mother's preoccupied look and in my sister's frightened, apologetic manner—hung like a sentence passed upon the Wingfields!

Mother was a woman of action as well as words.

She began to take logical steps in the planned direction.

Late that winter and in the early spring—realizing that extra money would be needed to properly feather the nest and plume the bird—she conducted a vigorous campaign on the telephone, roping in subscribers to one of those magazines for matrons called *The Home-maker's Companion,* the type of journal that features the serialized sublimations of ladies of letters who think in terms of delicate cup-like breasts, slim, tapering waists, rich, creamy thighs, eyes like wood-smoke in autumn, fingers that soothe and caress like strains of music, bodies as powerful as Etruscan sculpture.

[SCREEN IMAGE: GLAMOR MAGAZINE COVER. AMANDA *enters with phone on long extension cord. She is spotted in the dim stage.*]

AMANDA. Ida Scott? This is Amanda Wingfield! We *missed* you at the D.A.R. last Monday!

I said to myself: She's probably suffering with that sinus condition! How is that sinus condition?

Horrors! Heaven have mercy!—You're a Christian martyr, yes, that's what you are, a Christian martyr!

Well, I just now happened to notice that your subscription to the *Companion's* about to expire! Yes, it expires with the next issue, honey!—just when that wonderful new serial by Bessie Mae Hopper is getting off to such an exciting start. Oh, honey, it's something that you can't miss! You remember how *Gone With the Wind* took everybody by storm? You simply couldn't go out if you hadn't read it. All everybody *talked* was Scarlett O'Hara. Well, this is a book that critics already compare to *Gone With the Wind.* It's the *Gone With the Wind* of the post-World War generation!—What?—Burning?—Oh, honey, don't let them burn, go take a look in the oven and I'll hold the wire! Heavens—I think she's hung up!

DIM OUT

[LEGEND ON SCREEN: "YOU THINK I'M IN LOVE WITH CONTINENTAL SHOEMAKERS?" *Before the stage is lighted the violent voices of* TOM *and* AMANDA *are heard. They are quarreling behind the portieres. In front of them stands* LAURA *with clenched hands and panicky expression. A clear pool of light on her figure throughout this scene.*]

TOM. What in Christ's name am I——

AMANDA [*shrilly*]. Don't you use that——

TOM. Supposed to do!

AMANDA. Expression! Not in my——

TOM. Ohhh!

AMANDA. Presence! Have you gone out of your senses?

TOM. I have, that's true, *driven* out!

AMANDA. What is the matter with you, you—big—big—IDIOT!

TOM. Look!—I've got *no thing,* no single thing——

AMANDA. Lower your voice!

TOM. In my life here that I can call my OWN! Everything is——

AMANDA. Stop that shouting!

TOM. Yesterday you confiscated my books! You had the nerve to——

AMANDA. I took that horrible novel back to the library—yes! That hideous book by that insane Mr. Lawrence. [TOM *laughs wildly.*] I cannot control the output of diseased minds or people who cater to them—[TOM *laughs still more wildly.*] BUT I WON'T ALLOW SUCH FILTH BROUGHT INTO MY HOUSE! No, no, no, no, no!

TOM. House, house! Who pays rent on it, who makes a slave of himself to——

AMANDA [*fairly screeching*]. Don't you DARE to——

TOM. No, no, I mustn't say things! *I've* got to just——

AMANDA. Let me tell you——

TOM. I don't want to hear any more!

[*He tears the portieres open. The upstage area is lit with a turgid smoky red glow.* AMANDA'S *hair is in metal curlers and she wears a very old bathrobe, much too large for her slight figure, a relic of the faithless Mr. Wingfield. An upright typewriter and a wild disarray of manuscripts is on the drop-leaf table. The quarrel was probably precipitated by* AMANDA'S *interruption of his creative labor. A chair lying overthrown on the floor. Their gesticulating shadows are cast on the ceiling by the fiery glow.*]

AMANDA. You *will* hear more, you——

TOM. No, I won't hear more, I'm going out!

AMANDA. You come right back in——

TOM. Out, out, out! Because I'm——

AMANDA. Come back here, Tom Wingfield! I'm not through talking to you!

TOM. Oh go——

LAURA [*desperately*]—Tom!

AMANDA. You're going to listen, and no more insolence from you! I'm at the end of my patience! [*He comes back toward her.*]

TOM. What do you think I'm at? Aren't I supposed to have any patience to reach the end of, Mother? I know, I know. It seems unimportant to you, what I'm *doing*—what I *want* to do—having a little *difference* between them! You don't think that——

AMANDA. I think you've been doing things that you're ashamed of. That's why you act like this. I don't believe that you go every night to the movies. Nobody goes to the movies night after night. Nobody in their right minds goes to the movies as often as you pretend to. People don't go to the movies at nearly midnight, and movies don't let out at two A.M. Come in stumbling. Muttering to yourself like a maniac! You get three hours' sleep and then go to work. Oh, I can picture the way you're doing down there. Moping, doping, because you're in no condition.

TOM [*wildly*]. No, I'm in no condition!

AMANDA. What right have you got to jeopardize your job? Jeopardize the security of us all? How do you think we'd manage if you were——

TOM. Listen! You think I'm crazy *about the warehouse?* [*He bends fiercely toward her slight figure.*] You think I'm in love with the Continental Shoemakers? You think I want to spend fifty-five *years* down there in that—*celotex interior!* with—*fluorescent —tubes!* Look! I'd rather somebody picked up a crowbar and battered out my brains—than go back mornings! I *go!* Every time you come in yelling that God damn *"Rise and Shine!" "Rise and Shine!"* I say to myself, "How *lucky dead* people are!" But I get up.

I *go!* For sixty-five dollars a month I give up all that I dream of doing and being *ever!* And you say self—*self's* all I ever think of. Why, listen, if self is what I thought of, Mother, I'd be where he is—GONE! [*Pointing to father's picture.*] As far as the system of transportation reaches! [*He starts past her. She grabs his arm.*] Don't grab at me, Mother!

AMANDA. Where are you going?

TOM. I'm going to the *movies!*

AMANDA. I don't believe that lie!

TOM. [*Crouching toward her, overtowering her tiny figure. She backs away, gasping.*] I'm going to opium dens! Yes, opium dens, dens of vice and criminals' hang-outs, Mother. I've joined the Hogan gang, I'm a hired assassin, I carry a tommy-gun in a violin case! I run a string of cat-houses in the Valley! They call me Killer, Killer Wingfield, I'm leading a double-life: a simple, honest warehouse worker by day, by night a dynamic *czar* of the *underworld, Mother.* I go to gambling casinos, I spin away fortunes on the roulette table! I wear a patch over one eye and a false mustache; sometimes I put on green whiskers. On those occasions they call me—*El Diablo!* Oh, I could tell you things to make you sleepless! My enemies plan to dynamite this place. They're going to blow us all sky-high some night! I'll be glad, very happy, and so will you! You'll go up, up on a broomstick, over Blue Mountain with seventeen gentlemen callers! You ugly—babbling old—witch. . . .

[*He goes through a series of violent, clumsy movements, seizing his overcoat, lunging to the door, pulling it fiercely open. The* WOMEN *watch him, aghast. His arm catches in the sleeve of the coat as he struggles to pull it on. For a moment he is pinioned by the bulky garment. With an outraged groan he tears the coat off again, splitting the shoulder of it, and hurls it across the room. It strikes against the shelf of* LAURA's *glass collection, there is a tinkle of shattering glass.* LAURA *cries out as if wounded.* MUSIC. LEGEND: "THE GLASS MENAGERIE."*]

LAURA [*shrilly*]. My glass!—menagerie. . . .

[*She covers her face and turns away. But* AMANDA *is still stunned and stupefied by the "ugly witch" so that she barely notices this occurrence. Now she recovers her speech.*]

AMANDA [*in an awful voice*]. I won't speak to you—until you apologize!

[*She crosses through portieres and draws them together behind her.* TOM *is left with* LAURA. LAURA *clings weakly to the mantel with her face averted.* TOM *stares at her stupidly for a moment. Then he crosses to shelf. Drops awkwardly on his knees to collect the fallen glass, glancing at* LAURA *as if he would speak but couldn't.*]

"THE GLASS MENAGERIE" *steals in as*
THE SCENE DIMS OUT

SCENE IV

The interior is dark. Faint light in the alley. A deep-voiced bell in a church is tolling the hour of five as the scene commences. [TOM *appears at the top of the alley. After each solemn boom of the bell in the tower, he shakes a little noise-maker or rattle as if to express the tiny spasm of man in contrast to the sustained power and dignity of the Almighty. This and the unsteadiness of his advance make it evident that he has been drinking.*

As he climbs the few steps to the fire-escape landing, light steals up inside.

LAURA *appears in night-dress, observing* TOM's *empty bed in the front room.*

TOM *fishes in his pockets for door-key, removing a motley assortment of articles in the search, including a perfect shower of movie-ticket stubs and an empty bottle. At last he finds the key, but just as he is about to insert it, it slips from his fingers. He strikes a match and crouches below the door.*]

TOM [*bitterly*]. One crack—and it falls through!

[LAURA *opens the door.*]

LAURA. Tom! Tom, what are you doing?

TOM. Looking for a door-key.

LAURA. Where have you been all this time?

TOM. I have been to the movies.

LAURA. All this time at the movies?

TOM. There was a very long program. There was a Garbo picture and a Mickey Mouse and a travelogue and a newsreel and a preview of coming attractions. And there was an organ solo and a collection for the milk-fund—simultaneously—which ended up in a terrible fight between a fat lady and an usher!

LAURA [*innocently*]. Did you have to stay through everything?

TOM. Of course! And, oh, I forgot! There was a big stage show! The headliner on this stage show was Malvolio the Magician. He performed wonderful tricks, many of them, such as pouring water back and forth between pitchers. First it turned to wine and then it turned to beer and then it turned to whiskey. I know it was whiskey it finally turned into because he needed somebody to come up out of the audience to help him, and I came up—both shows! It was Kentucky Straight Bourbon. A very generous fellow, he gave souvenirs. [*He pulls from his back pocket a shimmering rainbow-colored scarf.*] He gave me this. This is his magic scarf. You can have it, Laura. You wave it over a canary cage and you get a bowl of gold-fish. You wave it over the gold-fish bowl and they fly away canaries. . . . But the wonderfullest trick of all was the coffin trick. We nailed him into a coffin and he got out of the coffin without removing one nail. [*He has come inside.*] There is a trick that would come in handy for me—get me out of this 2 by 4 situation!

 [*Flops onto bed and starts removing shoes.*]
 LAURA. Tom—Shhh!
 TOM. What're you shushing me for?
 LAURA. You'll wake up Mother.
 TOM. Goody, goody! Pay 'er back for all those "Rise an' Shines." [*Lies down, groaning.*] You know it don't take much intelligence to get yourself into a nailed-up coffin, Laura. But who in hell ever got himself out of one without removing one nail?

 [*As if in answer, the father's grinning photograph lights up.*]

SCENE DIMS OUT

 [*Immediately following: The church bell is heard striking six. At the sixth stroke the alarm clock goes off in* AMANDA'S *room, and after a few moments we hear her calling: "Rise and Shine! Rise and Shine! Laura, go tell your brother to rise and shine!"*]
 TOM [*sitting up slowly*]. I'll rise—but I won't shine. [*The light increases.*]
 AMANDA. Laura, tell your brother his coffee is ready. [LAURA *slips into front room.*]
 LAURA. Tom!—It's nearly seven. Don't make Mother nervous. [*He stares at her stupidly. Beseechingly.*] Tom, speak to Mother this morning. Make up with her, apologize, speak to her!
 TOM. She won't to me. It's her that started not speaking.
 LAURA. If you just say you're sorry she'll start speaking.
 TOM. Her not speaking—is that such a tragedy?
 LAURA. Please—please!
 AMANDA [*calling from kitchenette*]. Laura, are you going to do what I asked you to do, or do I have to get dressed and go out myself?
 LAURA. Going, going—soon as I get on my coat! [*She pulls on a shapeless felt hat with nervous, jerky movement, pleadingly glancing at* TOM. *Rushes awkwardly for coat. The coat is one of* AMANDA'S, *inaccurately made-over, the sleeves too short for* LAURA.] Butter and what else?
 AMANDA [*entering upstage*]. Just butter. Tell them to charge it.

 LAURA. Mother, they make such faces when I do that.
 AMANDA. Sticks and stones can break our bones, but the expression on Mr. Garfinkel's face won't harm us! Tell your brother his coffee is getting cold.
 LAURA [*at door*]. Do what I asked you, will you, will you, Tom?
 [*He looks sullenly away.*]
 AMANDA. Laura, go now or just don't go at all!
 LAURA [*rushing out*]. Going—going!
 [*A second later she cries out.* TOM *springs up and crosses to door.* AMANDA *rushes anxiously in.* TOM *opens the door.*]
 TOM. Laura?
 LAURA. I'm all right. I slipped, but I'm all right.
 AMANDA [*peering anxiously after her*]. If anyone breaks a leg on those fire-escape steps, the landlord ought to be sued for every cent he possesses!
 [*She shuts door. Remembers she isn't speaking and returns to other room. As* TOM *enters listlessly for his coffee, she turns her back to him and stands rigidly facing the window on the gloomy gray vault of the areaway. Its light on her face with its aged but childish features is cruelly sharp, satirical as a Daumier print.* MUSIC UNDER: "AVE MARIA." TOM *glances sheepishly but sullenly at her averted figure and slumps at the table. The coffee is scalding hot; he sips it and gasps and spits it back in the cup. At his gasp,* AMANDA *catches her breath and half turns. Then catches herself and turns back to window.* TOM *blows on his coffee, glancing sidewise at his mother. She clears her throat.* TOM *clears his. He starts to rise. Sinks back down again, scratches his head, clears his throat again.* AMANDA *coughs.* TOM *raises his cup in both hands to blow on it, his eyes staring over the rim of it at his mother for several moments. Then he slowly sets the cup down and awkwardly and hesitantly rises from the chair.*]
 TOM [*hoarsely*]. Mother. I—I apologize, Mother. [AMANDA *draws a quick, shuddering breath. Her face works grotesquely. She breaks into childlike tears.*] I'm sorry for what I said, for everything that I said, I didn't mean it.
 AMANDA [*sobbingly*]. My devotion has made me a witch and so I make myself hateful to my children!
 TOM. *No,* you *don't.*
 AMANDA. I worry so much, don't sleep, it makes me nervous!
 TOM [*gently*]. I understand that.
 AMANDA. I've had to put up a solitary battle all these years. But you're my righthand bower! Don't fall down, don't fail!

TOM [*gently*]. I'll try, Mother.

AMANDA [*with great enthusiasm*]. Try and you will SUCCEED! [*The notion makes her breathless.*] Why, you—you're just *full* of natural endowments! Both of my children—they're *unusual* children! Don't you think I know it? I'm so—*proud*! Happy and—feel I've —so much to be thankful for but—— Promise me one thing, son!

TOM. What, Mother?

AMANDA. Promise, son, you'll—never be a drunkard!

TOM [*turns to her, grinning*]. I will never be a drunkard, Mother.

AMANDA. That's what frightened me so, that you'd be drinking! Eat a bowl of Purina!

TOM. Just coffee, Mother.

AMANDA. Shredded wheat biscuit?

TOM. No. No, Mother, just coffee.

AMANDA. You can't put in a day's work on an empty stomach. You've got ten minutes—don't gulp! Drinking too-hot liquids makes cancer of the stomach. . . . Put cream in.

TOM. No, thank you.

AMANDA. To cool it.

TOM. No! No, thank you, I want it black.

AMANDA. I know, but it's not good for you. We have to do all that we can to build ourselves up. In these trying times we live in, all that we have to cling to is—each other. . . . That's why it's so important to—— Tom, I—— I sent out your sister so I could discuss something with you. If you hadn't spoken I would have spoken to you.

[*Sits down.*]

TOM [*gently*]. What is it, Mother, that you want to discuss?

AMANDA. *Laura!*

[TOM *puts his cup down slowly.* LEGEND ON SCREEN: "LAURA." MUSIC: "THE GLASS MENAGERIE."]

TOM. —Oh.—Laura . . .

AMANDA [*touching his sleeve*]. You know how Laura is. So quiet but—still water runs deep! She notices things and I think she—broods about them. [TOM *looks up.*] A few days ago I came in and she was crying.

TOM. What about?

AMANDA. You.

TOM. Me?

AMANDA. She has an idea that you're not happy here.

TOM. What gave her that idea?

AMANDA. What gives her any idea? However, you do act strangely. I—I'm not criticizing, understand *that*! I know your ambitions do not lie in the warehouse, that like everybody in the whole wide world

—you've had to—make sacrifices, but—Tom—Tom— life's not easy, it calls for—Spartan endurance! There's so many things in my heart that I cannot describe to you! I've never told you but I—*loved* your father. . . .

TOM [*gently*]. I know that, Mother.

AMANDA. And you—when I see you taking after his ways! Staying out late—and—well, you *had* been drinking the night you were in that—terrifying condition! Laura says that you hate the apartment and that you go out nights to get away from it! Is that true, Tom?

TOM. No. You say there's so much in your heart that you can't describe to me. That's true of me, too. There's so much in my heart that I can't describe to *you*! So let's respect each other's——

AMANDA. But why—*why*, Tom—are you always so *restless*? Where do you *go* to, nights?

TOM. I—go to the movies.

AMANDA. Why do you go to the movies so much, Tom?

TOM. I go to the movies because—I like adventure. Adventure is something I don't have much of at work, so I go to the movies.

AMANDA. But, Tom, you go to the movies *entirely* too *much*!

TOM. I like a lot of adventure.

[AMANDA *looks baffled, then hurt. As the familiar inquisition resumes he becomes hard and impatient again.* AMANDA *slips back into her querulous attitude toward him.* IMAGE ON SCREEN: SAILING VESSEL WITH JOLLY ROGER.]

AMANDA. Most young men find adventure in their careers.

TOM. Then most young men are not employed in a warehouse.

AMANDA. The world is full of young men employed in warehouses and offices and factories.

TOM. Do all of them find adventure in their careers?

AMANDA. They do or they do without it! Not everybody has a craze for adventure.

TOM. Man is by instinct a lover, a hunter, a fighter, and none of those instincts are given much play at the warehouse!

AMANDA. Man is by instinct! Don't quote instinct to me! Instinct is something that people have got away from! It belongs to animals! Christian adults don't want it!

TOM. What do Christian adults want, then, Mother?

AMANDA. Superior things! Things of the mind and the spirit! Only animals have to satisfy instincts! Surely your aims are somewhat higher than theirs! Than monkeys—pigs——

TOM. I reckon they're not.

AMANDA. You're joking. However, that isn't what I wanted to discuss.

TOM [*rising*]. I haven't much time.

AMANDA [*pushing his shoulders*]. Sit down.

TOM. You want me to punch in red at the warehouse, Mother?

AMANDA. You have five minutes. I want to talk about Laura.

[LEGEND: "PLANS AND PROVISIONS."]

TOM. All right! What about Laura?

AMANDA. We have to be making some plans and provisions for her. She's older than you, two years, and nothing has happened. She just drifts along doing nothing. It frightens me terribly how she just drifts along.

TOM. I guess she's the type that people call home girls.

AMANDA. There's no such type, and if there is, it's a pity! That is unless the home is hers, with a husband!

TOM. What?

AMANDA. Oh, I can see the handwriting on the wall as plain as I see the nose in front of my face! It's terrifying!

More and more you remind me of your father! He was out all hours without explanation!—Then *left!* Good-bye!

And me with the bag to hold. I saw that letter you got from the Merchant Marine. I know what you're dreaming of. I'm not standing here blindfolded.

Very well, then. Then *do* it!

But not till there's somebody to take your place.

TOM. What do you mean?

AMANDA. I mean that as soon as Laura has got somebody to take care of her, married, a home of her own, independent—why, then you'll be free to go wherever you please, on land, on sea, whichever way the wind blows you!

But until that time you've got to look out for your sister. I don't say me because I'm old and don't matter! I say for your sister because she's young and dependent.

I put her in business college—a dismal failure! Frightened her so it made her sick at the stomach.

I took her over to the Young People's League at the church. Another fiasco. She spoke to nobody, nobody spoke to her. Now all she does is fool with those pieces of glass and play those worn-out records. What kind of a life is that for a girl to lead?

TOM. What can I do about it?

AMANDA. Overcome selfishness!

Self, self, self is all that you ever think of! [TOM *springs up and crosses to get his coat. It is ugly and bulky. He pulls on a cap with earmuffs.*] Where is your muffler? Put your wool muffler on! [*He snatches it angrily from the closet and tosses it around his neck and pulls both ends tight.*] Tom! I haven't said what I had in mind to ask you.

TOM. I'm too late to——

AMANDA [*Catching his arm—very importunately. Then shyly.*] Down at the warehouse, aren't there some—nice young men?

TOM. No!

AMANDA. There *must* be—*some* . . .

TOM. Mother—— [*gesture*]

AMANDA. Find out one that's clean-living—doesn't drink and—ask him out for sister!

TOM. What?

AMANDA. For *sister!* To *meet!* Get *acquainted!*

TOM [*stamping to door*]. Oh, my go-osh!

AMANDA. Will you? [*He opens door. Imploringly.*] Will you? [*He starts down.*] Will you? *Will* you, dear?

TOM [*calling back*]. YES!

[AMANDA *closes the door hesitantly and with a troubled but faintly hopeful expression.*

SCREEN IMAGE: GLAMOR MAGAZINE COVER. *Spot* AMANDA *at phone.*]

AMANDA. Ella Cartwright? This is Amanda Wingfield!

How are you, honey?

How is that kidney condition? [*Count five.*]

Horrors! [*Count five.*]

You're a Christian martyr, yes, honey, that's what you are, a Christian martyr!

Well, I just now happened to notice in my little red book that your subscription to the *Companion* has just run out! I knew that you wouldn't want to miss out on the wonderful serial starting in this new issue. It's by Bessie Mae Hopper, the first thing she's written since *Honeymoon for Three.*

Wasn't that a strange and interesting story? Well, this one is even lovelier, I believe. It has a sophisticated, society background. It's all about the horsey set on Long Island!

FADE OUT

SCENE V

LEGEND ON SCREEN: "ANNUNCIATION." *Fade with music.*

It is early dusk of a spring evening. Supper has just been finished in the Wingfield apartment. AMANDA *and* LAURA *in light-colored dresses are removing dishes from the table, in the upstage area, which is shadowy, their movements formalized almost as a dance or ritual, their moving forms as pale and silent as moths.*

[TOM, *in white shirt and trousers, rises from the table and crosses toward the fire-escape.*]

AMANDA [*as he passes her*]. Son, will you do me a favor?

TOM. What?

AMANDA. Comb your hair! You look so pretty when your hair is combed! [TOM *slouches on sofa with evening paper. Enormous caption "Franco Triumphs."*] There is only one respect in which I would like you to emulate your father.

TOM. What respect is that?

AMANDA. The care he always took of his appearance. He never allowed himself to look untidy. [*He throws down the paper and crosses to fire-escape.*] Where are you going?

TOM. I'm going out to smoke.

AMANDA. You smoke too much. A pack a day at fifteen cents a pack. How much would that amount to in a month? Thirty times fifteen is how much, Tom? Figure it out and you will be astounded at what you could save. Enough to give you a night-school course in accounting at Washington U! Just think what a wonderful thing that would be for you, Son!

[TOM *is unmoved by the thought.*]

TOM. I'd rather smoke.

[*He steps out on landing, letting the screen door slam.*]

AMANDA [*sharply*]. I know! That's the tragedy of it. . . .

[*Alone, she turns to look at her husband's picture.* DANCE MUSIC: "ALL THE WORLD IS WAITING FOR THE SUNRISE!"]

TOM [*to the audience*]. Across the alley from us was the Paradise Dance Hall. On evenings in spring the windows and doors were open and the music came outdoors. Sometimes the lights were turned out except for a large glass sphere that hung from the ceiling. It would turn slowly about and filter the dusk with delicate rainbow colors. Then the orchestra played a waltz or a tango, something that had a slow and sensuous rhythm. Couples would come outside, to the relative privacy of the alley. You could see them kissing behind ash-pits and telephone poles.

This was the compensation for lives that passed like mine, without any change or adventure.

Adventure and change were imminent in this year. They were waiting around the corner for all these kids.

Suspended in the mist over Berchtesgaden, caught in the folds of Chamberlain's umbrella——

In Spain there was Guernica!

But here there was only hot swing music and liquor, dance halls, bars, and movies, and sex that hung in the gloom like a chandelier and flooded the world with brief, deceptive rainbows. . . .

All the world was waiting for bombardments!

[AMANDA *turns from the picture and comes outside.*]

AMANDA [*sighing*]. A fire-escape landing's a poor excuse for a porch. [*She spreads a newspaper on a step and sits down, gracefully and demurely as if she were settling into a swing on a Mississippi veranda.*] What are you looking at?

TOM. The moon.

AMANDA. Is there a moon this evening?

TOM. It's rising over Garfinkel's Delicatessen.

AMANDA. So it is! A little silver slipper of a moon. Have you made a wish on it yet?

TOM. Um-hum.

AMANDA. What did you wish for?

TOM. That's a secret.

AMANDA. A secret, huh? Well, I won't tell mine either. I will be just as mysterious as you.

TOM. I bet I can guess what yours is.

AMANDA. Is my head so transparent?

TOM. You're not a sphinx.

AMANDA. No, I don't have secrets. I'll tell you what I wished for on the moon. Success and happiness for my precious children! I wish for that whenever there's a moon, and when there isn't a moon, I wish for it, too.

TOM. I thought perhaps you wished for a gentleman caller.

AMANDA. Why do you say that?

TOM. Don't you remember asking me to fetch one?

AMANDA. I remember suggesting that it would be nice for your sister if you brought home some nice young man from the warehouse. I think that I've made that suggestion more than once.

TOM. Yes, you have made it repeatedly.

AMANDA. Well?

TOM. We are going to have one.

AMANDA. *What?*

TOM. A gentleman caller!

[*The annunciation is celebrated with music.* AMANDA *rises.* IMAGE ON SCREEN: CALLER WITH BOUQUET.]

AMANDA. You mean you have asked some nice young man to come over?

TOM. Yep. I've asked him to dinner.

AMANDA. You really did?

TOM. I did!

AMANDA. You did, and did he—*accept?*

TOM. He did!

AMANDA. Well, well—well, well! That's—lovely!

TOM. I thought that you would be pleased.

AMANDA. It's definite, then?

TOM. Very definite.

AMANDA. Soon?

TOM. Very soon.

AMANDA. For heaven's sake, stop putting on and tell me some things, will you?

TOM. What things do you want me to tell you?

AMANDA. *Naturally* I would like to know when he's *coming*!

TOM. He's coming tomorrow.

AMANDA. *Tomorrow?*

TOM. Yep. Tomorrow.

AMANDA. But, Tom!

TOM. Yes, Mother?

AMANDA. Tomorrow gives me no time!

TOM. Time for what?

AMANDA. Preparations! Why didn't you phone me at once, as soon as you asked him, the minute that he accepted? Then, don't you see, I could have been getting ready!

TOM. You don't have to make any fuss.

AMANDA. Oh, Tom, Tom, Tom, of course I have to make a fuss! I want things nice, not sloppy! Not thrown together. I'll certainly have to do some fast thinking, won't I?

TOM. I don't see why you have to think at all.

AMANDA. You just don't know. We can't have a gentleman caller in a pig-sty! All my wedding silver has to be polished, the monogrammed table linen ought to be laundered! The windows have to be washed and fresh curtains put up. And how about clothes? We have to *wear* something, don't we?

TOM. Mother, this boy is no one to make a fuss over!

AMANDA. Do you realize he's the first young man we've introduced to your sister?

It's terrible, dreadful, disgraceful that poor little sister has never received a single gentleman caller! Tom, come inside!

[*She opens the screen door.*]

TOM. What for?

AMANDA. I want to ask you some things.

TOM. If you're going to make such a fuss, I'll call it off, I'll tell him not to come!

AMANDA. You certainly won't do anything of the kind. Nothing offends people worse than broken engagements. It simply means I'll have to work like a Turk! We won't be brilliant, but we will pass inspection. Come on inside. [TOM *follows, groaning.*] Sit down.

TOM. Any particular place you would like me to sit?

AMANDA. Thank heavens I've got that new sofa! I'm also making payments on a floor lamp I'll have sent out! And put the chintz covers on, they'll brighten things up! Of course I'd hoped to have these walls repapered. . . . What is the young man's name?

TOM. His name is O'Connor.

AMANDA. That, of course, means fish—tomorrow is Friday! I'll have that salmon loaf—with Durkee's dressing! What does he do? He works at the warehouse?

TOM. Of course! How else would I——

AMANDA. Tom, he—doesn't drink?

TOM. Why do you ask me that?

AMANDA. Your father *did!*

TOM. Don't get started on that!

AMANDA. He *does* drink, then?

TOM. Not that I know of!

AMANDA. Make sure, be certain! The last thing I want for my daughter's a boy who drinks!

TOM. Aren't you being a little bit premature? Mr. O'Connor has not yet appeared on the scene!

AMANDA. But will tomorrow. To meet your sister, and what do I know about his character? Nothing! Old maids are better off than wives of drunkards!

TOM. Oh, my God!

AMANDA. Be still!

TOM [*leaning forward to whisper*]. Lots of fellows meet girls whom they don't marry!

AMANDA. Oh, talk sensibly, Tom—and don't be sarcastic! [*She has gotten a hairbrush.*]

TOM. What are you doing?

AMANDA. I'm brushing that cow-lick down! What is this young man's position at the warehouse?

TOM [*submitting grimly to the brush and the interrogation*]. This young man's position is that of a shipping clerk, Mother.

AMANDA. Sounds to me like a fairly responsible job, the sort of a job *you* would be in if you just had more *get-up*.

What is his salary? Have you any idea?

TOM. I would judge it to be approximately eighty-five dollars a month.

AMANDA. Well—not princely, but——

TOM. Twenty more than I make.

AMANDA. Yes, how well I know! But for a family man, eighty-five dollars a month is not much more than you can just get by on. . . .

TOM. Yes, but Mr. O'Connor is not a family man.

AMANDA. He might be, mightn't he? Some time in the future?

TOM. I see. Plans and provisions.

AMANDA. You are the only young man that I know of who ignores the fact that the future becomes the present, the present the past, and the past turns into everlasting regret if you don't plan for it!

TOM. I will think that over and see what I can make of it.

AMANDA. Don't be supercilious with your mother! Tell me some more about this—what do you call him?

TOM. James D. O'Connor. The D. is for Delaney.

AMANDA. Irish on *both* sides! *Gracious!* And doesn't drink?

TOM. Shall I call him up and ask him right this minute?

AMANDA. The only way to find out about those things is to make discreet inquiries at the proper moment. When I was a girl in Blue Mountain and it was suspected that a young man drank, the girl whose attentions he had been receiving, if any girl *was*, would sometimes speak to the minister of his church, or rather her father would if her father was living, and sort of feel him out on the young man's character. That is the way such things are discreetly handled to keep a young woman from making a tragic mistake!

TOM. Then how did you happen to make a tragic mistake?

AMANDA. That innocent look of your father's had everyone fooled!

He *smiled*—the world was *enchanted!*

No girl can do worse than put herself at the mercy of a handsome appearance!

I hope that Mr. O'Connor is not too good-looking.

TOM. No, he's not too good-looking. He's covered with freckles and hasn't too much of a nose.

AMANDA. He's not right-down homely, though?

TOM. Not right-down homely. Just medium homely, I'd say.

AMANDA. Character's what to look for in a man.

TOM. That's what I've always said, Mother.

AMANDA. You've never said anything of the kind and I suspect you would never give it a thought.

TOM. Don't be so suspicious of me.

AMANDA. At least I hope he's the type that's up and coming.

TOM. I think he really goes in for self-improvement.

AMANDA. What reason have you to think so?

TOM. He goes to night school.

AMANDA [*beaming*]. Splendid! What does he do, I mean study?

TOM. Radio engineering and public speaking!

AMANDA. Then he has visions of being advanced in the world!

Any young man who studies public speaking is aiming to have an executive job some day!

And radio engineering? A thing for the future!

Both of these facts are very illuminating. Those are the sort of things that a mother should know concerning any young man who comes to call on her daughter. Seriously or—not.

TOM. One little warning. He doesn't know about Laura. I didn't let on that we had dark ulterior motives. I just said, why don't you come and have dinner with us? He said okay and that was the whole conversation.

AMANDA. I bet it was! You're eloquent as an oyster.

However, he'll know about Laura when he gets here. When he sees how lovely and sweet and pretty she is, he'll thank his lucky stars he was asked to dinner.

TOM. Mother, you mustn't expect too much of Laura.

AMANDA. What do you mean?

TOM. Laura seems all those things to you and me because she's ours and we love her. We don't even notice she's crippled any more.

AMANDA. Don't say crippled! You know that I never allow that word to be used!

TOM. But face facts, Mother. She is and—that's not all——

AMANDA. What do you mean "not all"?

TOM. Laura is very different from other girls.

AMANDA. I think the difference is all to her advantage.

TOM. Not quite all—in the eyes of others—strangers—she's terribly shy and lives in a world of her own and those things make her seem a little peculiar to people outside the house.

AMANDA. Don't say peculiar.

TOM. Face the facts. She is.

[THE DANCE-HALL MUSIC CHANGES TO A TANGO THAT HAS A MINOR AND SOMEWHAT OMINOUS TONE.]

AMANDA. In what way is she peculiar—may I ask?

TOM [*gently*]. She lives in a world of her own—a world of—little glass ornaments, Mother. . . . [*Gets up.* AMANDA *remains holding brush, looking at him, troubled.*] She plays old phonograph records and—that's about all——

[*He glances at himself in the mirror and crosses to door.*]

AMANDA [*sharply*]. Where are you going?

TOM. I'm going to the movies.

[*Out screen door.*]

AMANDA. Not to the movies, every night to the movies! [*Follows quickly to screen door.*] I don't believe you always go to the movies! [*He is gone.* AMANDA *looks worriedly after him for a moment. Then vitality and optimism return and she turns from the door. Crossing to portieres.*] Laura! Laura!

[LAURA *answers from kitchenette.*]

LAURA. Yes, Mother.

AMANDA. Let those dishes go and come in front! [LAURA *appears with dish towel. Gaily.*] Laura, come here and make a wish on the moon!

[SCREEN IMAGE: MOON.]

LAURA [*entering*]. Moon—moon?

AMANDA. A little silver slipper of a moon.

Look over your left shoulder, Laura, and make a wish!

[LAURA *looks faintly puzzled as if called out of sleep.* AMANDA *seizes her shoulders and turns her at an angle by the door.*]

Now!

Now, darling, *wish!*

LAURA. What shall I wish for, Mother?

AMANDA [*Her voice trembling and her eyes suddenly filling with tears*]. Happiness! Good fortune!

[*The violin rises and the stage dims out.*]

CURTAIN

SCENE VI

[IMAGE: HIGH-SCHOOL HERO.]

TOM. And so the following evening I brought Jim home to dinner. I had known Jim slightly in high school. In high school Jim was a hero. He had tremendous Irish good nature and vitality with the scrubbed and polished look of white chinaware. He seemed to move in a continual spotlight. He was a star in basketball, captain of the debating club, president of the senior class and the glee club and he sang the male lead in the annual light operas. He was always running or bounding, never just walking. He seemed always at the point of defeating the law of gravity. He was shooting with such velocity through his adolescence that you would logically expect him to arrive at nothing short of the White House by the time he was thirty. But Jim apparently ran into more interference after his graduation from Soldan. His speed had definitely slowed. Six years after he left high school he was holding a job that wasn't much better than mine.

[IMAGE: CLERK.]

He was the only one at the warehouse with whom I was on friendly terms. I was valuable to him as someone who could remember his former glory, who had seen him win basketball games and the silver cup in debating. He knew of my secret practice of retiring to a cabinet of the wash-room to work on poems when business was slack in the warehouse. He called me Shakespeare. And while the other boys in the warehouse regarded me with suspicious hostility, Jim took a humorous attitude toward me. Gradually his attitude affected the others; their hostility wore off and they also began to smile at me as people smile at an oddly fashioned dog who trots across their path at some distance.

I knew that Jim and Laura had known each other at Soldan, and I had heard Laura speak admiringly of his voice. I didn't know if Jim remembered her or not. In high school Laura had been as unobtrusive as Jim had been astonishing. If he did remember Laura, it was not as my sister, for when I asked him to dinner, he grinned and said, "You know, Shakespeare, I never thought of you as having folks!"

He was about to discover that I did. . . .

[LIGHT UP STAGE. LEGEND ON SCREEN: "THE ACCENT OF A COMING FOOT." *Friday evening. It is about five o'clock of a late spring evening which comes "scattering poems in the sky." A delicate lemony light is in the Wingfield apartment.* AMANDA *has worked like a Turk in preparation for the gentleman caller. The results are astonishing. The new floor lamp with its rose-silk shade is in place, a colored paper lantern conceals the broken light fixture in the ceiling, new billowing white curtains are at the windows, chintz covers are on chairs and sofa, a pair of new sofa pillows make their initial appearance. Open boxes and tissue paper are scattered on the floor.* LAURA *stands in the middle with lifted arms while* AMANDA *crouches before her, adjusting the hem of the new dress, devout and ritualistic. The dress is colored and designed by memory. The arrangement of* LAURA's *hair is changed; it is softer and more becoming. A fragile, unearthly prettiness has come out in* LAURA: *she is like a piece of translucent glass touched by light, given a momentary radiance, not actual, not lasting.*]

AMANDA [*impatiently*]. Why are you trembling?

LAURA. Mother, you've made me so nervous!

AMANDA. How have I made you nervous?

LAURA. By all this fuss! You make it seem so important!

AMANDA. I don't understand you, Laura. You couldn't be satisfied with just sitting home, and yet whenever I try to arange something for you, you seem to resist it. [*She gets up.*]

Now take a look at yourself.

No, wait! Wait just a moment—I have an idea!

LAURA. What is it now?

[AMANDA *produces two powder puffs which she wraps in handkerchiefs and stuffs in* LAURA's *bosom.*]

LAURA. Mother, what are you doing?

AMANDA. They call them "Gay Deceivers"!

LAURA. I won't wear them!

AMANDA. You will!

LAURA. Why should I?

AMANDA. Because, to be painfully honest, your chest is flat.

LAURA. You make it seem like we were setting a trap.

AMANDA. All pretty girls are a trap, a pretty trap, and men expect them to be.

[LEGEND: "A PRETTY TRAP."]

Now look at yourself, young lady. This is the prettiest you will ever be!

I've got to fix myself now! You're going to be surprised by your mother's appearance!

[*She crosses through portieres, humming gaily.* LAURA *moves slowly to the long mirror and stares solemnly at herself. A wind blows the white curtains inward in a slow, graceful motion and with a faint, sorrowful sighing.*]

AMANDA [*off stage*]. It isn't dark enough yet.

[LAURA *turns slowly before the mirror with a troubled look.* LEGEND ON SCREEN: "THIS IS MY SISTER: CELEBRATE HER WITH STRINGS!" MUSIC.]

AMANDA [*laughing, off*]. I'm going to show you something. I'm going to make a spectacular appearance!

LAURA. What is it, Mother?

AMANDA. Possess your soul in patience—you will see!

Something I've resurrected from that old trunk! Styles haven't changed so terribly much after all. . . .

[*She parts the portieres.*]

Now just look at your mother!

[*She wears a girlish frock of yellowed voile with a blue silk sash. She carries a bunch of jonquils—the legend of her youth is nearly revived. Feverishly.*]

This is the dress in which I led the cotillion. Won the cakewalk twice at Sunset Hill, wore one spring to the Governor's ball in Jackson!

See how I sashayed around the ballroom, Laura?

[*She raises her skirt and does a mincing step around the room.*]

I wore it on Sundays for my gentlemen callers! I had it on the day I met your father——

I had malaria fever all that spring. The change of climate from East Tennessee to the Delta—weakened resistance—I had a little temperature all the time— not enough to be serious—just enough to make me restless and giddy!—Invitations poured in—parties all over the Delta!—"Stay in bed," said Mother, "you have fever!"—but I just wouldn't.—I took quinine but kept on going, going!—Evenings, dances!—Afternoons, long, long rides! Picnics—lovely!—So lovely, that country in May.—All lacy with dogwood, literally flooded with jonquils!—That was the spring I had the craze for jonquils. Jonquils became an absolute obsession. Mother said, "Honey, there's no more room for jonquils." And still I kept on bringing in more jonquils. Whenever, wherever I saw them, I'd say, "Stop! Stop! I see jonquils!" I made the young men help me gather the jonquils! It was a joke, Amanda and her jonquils! Finally there were no more vases to hold them; every available space was filled with jonquils. No vases to hold them? All right, I'll hold them myself! And then I—— [*she stops in front of the picture.* MUSIC.] met your father!

Malaria fever and jonquils and then—this—boy. . . .

[*She switches on the rose-colored lamp.*]

I hope they get here before it starts to rain.

[*She crosses upstage and places the jonquils in bowl on table.*]

I gave your brother a little extra change so he and Mr. O'Connor could take the service car home.

LAURA [*with altered look*]. What did you say his name was?

AMANDA. O'Connor.

LAURA. What is his first name?

AMANDA. I don't remember. Oh, yes, I do. It was— Jim.

[LAURA *sways slightly and catches hold of a chair.* LEGEND ON SCREEN: "NOT JIM!"]

LAURA [*faintly*]. Not—Jim!

AMANDA. Yes, that was it, it was Jim! I've never known a Jim that wasn't nice!

[MUSIC: OMINOUS.]

LAURA. Are you sure his name is Jim O'Connor?

AMANDA. Yes. Why?

LAURA. Is he the one that Tom used to know in high school?

AMANDA. He didn't say so. I think he just got to know him at the warehouse.

LAURA. There was a Jim O'Connor we both knew in high school—— [*then, with effort*] If that is the one that Tom is bringing to dinner—you'll have to excuse me, I won't come to the table.

AMANDA. What sort of nonsense is this?

LAURA. You asked me once if I'd ever liked a boy. Don't you remember I showed you this boy's picture?

AMANDA. You mean the boy you showed me in the year book?

LAURA. Yes, that boy.

AMANDA. Laura, Laura, were you in love with that boy?

LAURA. I don't know, Mother. All I know is I couldn't sit at the table if it was him!

AMANDA. It won't be him! It isn't the least bit likely. But whether it is or not, you will come to the table. You will not be excused.

LAURA. I'll have to be, Mother.

AMANDA. I don't intend to humor your silliness, Laura. I've had too much from you and your brother, both!

So just sit down and compose yourself till they come. Tom has forgotten his key so you'll have to let them in, when they arrive.

LAURA [*panicky*]. Oh, Mother—*you* answer the door!

AMANDA [*lightly*]. I'll be in the kitchen—busy!

LAURA. Oh, Mother, please answer the door, don't make me do it!

AMANDA [*crossing into kitchenette*]. I've got to fix the dressing for the salmon. Fuss, fuss—silliness!—over a gentleman caller!

[*Door swings shut.* LAURA *is left alone.* LEGEND: "TERROR!" *She utters a low moan and turns off the lamp—sits stiffly on the edge of the sofa, knotting her fingers together.* LEGEND ON SCREEN: "THE OPENING OF A DOOR!" TOM *and* JIM *appear on the fire-escape steps and climb to landing. Hearing their approach,* LAURA *rises with a panicky gesture. She retreats to the portieres. The doorbell.* LAURA *catches her breath and touches her throat. Low drums.*]

AMANDA [*calling*]. Laura, sweetheart! The door!

[LAURA *stares at it without moving.*]

JIM. I think we just beat the rain.

TOM. Uh-huh.

[*He rings again, nervously.* JIM *whistles and fishes for a cigarette.*]

AMANDA [*very, very gaily*]. Laura, that is your brother and Mr. O'Connor! Will you let them in, darling?

[LAURA *crosses toward kitchenette door.*]

LAURA [*breathlessly*]. Mother—you go to the door!

[AMANDA *steps out of kitchenette and stares furiously at* LAURA. *She points imperiously at the door.*]

LAURA. Please, please!

AMANDA [*in a fierce whisper*]. What is the matter with you, you silly thing?

LAURA [*desperately*]. Please, you answer it, *please!*

AMANDA. I told you I wasn't going to humor you, Laura. Why have you chosen this moment to lose your mind?

LAURA. Please, please, please, you go!

AMANDA. You'll have to go to the door because I can't!

LAURA [*despairingly*]. I can't either!

AMANDA. Why?

LAURA. I'm *sick!*

AMANDA. I'm sick, too—of your nonsense! Why can't you and your brother be normal people? Fantastic whims and behavior!

[TOM *gives a long ring.*]

Preposterous goings on! Can you give me one reason— [*calls out lyrically*] COMING! JUST ONE SEC-OND!—why you should be afraid to open a door? Now you answer it, Laura!

LAURA. Oh, oh, oh . . .

[*She returns through the portieres. Darts to the victrola and winds it frantically and turns it on.*]

AMANDA. Laura Wingfield, you march right to that door!

LAURA. Yes—yes, Mother!

[*A faraway, scratchy rendition of "Dardanella" softens the air and gives her strength to move through it. She slips to the door and draws it cautiously open.* TOM *enters with the caller,* JIM O'CONNOR.]

TOM. Laura, this is Jim. Jim, this is my sister, Laura.

JIM [*stepping inside*]. I didn't know that Shakespeare had a sister!

LAURA [*retreating stiff and trembling from the door*]. How—how do you do?

JIM [*heartily extending his hand*]. Okay!

[LAURA *touches it hesitantly with hers.*]

JIM. Your hand's *cold,* Laura!

LAURA. Yes, well—I've been playing the victrola. . . .

JIM. Must have been playing classical music on it! You ought to play a little hot swing music to warm you up!

LAURA. Excuse me—I haven't finished playing the victrola. . . .

[*She turns awkwardly and hurries into the front room. She pauses a second by the victrola. Then catches her breath and darts through the portieres like a frightened deer.*]

JIM [*grinning*]. What was the matter?

TOM. Oh—with Laura? Laura is—terribly shy.

JIM. Shy, huh? It's unusual to meet a shy girl nowadays. I don't believe you ever mentioned you had a sister.

TOM. Well, now you know. I have one. Here is the *Post Dispatch.* You want a piece of it?

JIM. Uh-huh.

TOM. What piece? The comics?

JIM. Sports! [*glances at it*] Ole Dizzy Dean is on his bad behavior.

TOM [*disinterest*]. Yeah?

[*Lights cigarette and crosses back to fire-escape door.*]

JIM. Where are *you* going?

TOM. I'm going out on the terrace.

JIM [*Goes after him.*] You know, Shakespeare—I'm going to sell you a bill of goods!

TOM. What goods!

JIM. A course I'm taking.

TOM. Huh?

JIM. In public speaking! You and me, we're not the warehouse type.

TOM. Thanks—that's good news.

But what has public speaking got to do with it?

JIM. It fits you for—executive positions!

TOM. Awww.

JIM. I tell you it's done a helluva lot for me. [IMAGE: EXECUTIVE AT DESK.]

TOM. In what respect?

JIM. In every! Ask yourself what is the difference between you an' me and men in the office down front? Brains?—No!—Ability?—No! Then what? Just one little thing——

TOM. What is that one little thing?

JIM. Primarily it amounts to—social poise! Being able to square up to people and hold your own on any social level!

AMANDA [*off stage*]. Tom?

TOM. Yes, Mother?

AMANDA. Is that you and Mr. O'Connor?

TOM. Yes, Mother.

AMANDA. Well, you just make yourselves comfortable in there.

TOM. Yes, Mother.

AMANDA. Ask Mr. O'Connor if he would like to wash his hands.

JIM. Aw, no—no—thank you—I took care of that at the warehouse. Tom——

TOM. Yes?

JIM. Mr. Mendoza was speaking to me about you.

TOM. Favorably?

JIM. What do you think?

TOM. Well——

JIM. You're going to be out of a job if you don't wake up.

TOM. I am waking up——

JIM. You show no signs.

TOM. The signs are interior.

[IMAGE ON SCREEN: THE SAILING VESSEL WITH JOLLY ROGER AGAIN.]

TOM. I'm planning to change. [*He leans over the rail speaking with quiet exhilaration. The incandescent marquees and signs of the first-run movie houses light his face from across the alley. He looks like a voyager.*] I'm right at the point of committing myself to a future that doesn't include the warehouse and Mr. Mendoza or even a night-school course in public speaking.

JIM. What are you gassing about?

TOM. I'm tired of the movies.

JIM. Movies!

TOM. Yes, movies! Look at them—— [*A wave toward the marvels of Grand Avenue.*] All of those glamorous people—having adventures—hogging it all, gobbling the whole thing up! You know what happens? People go to the *movies* instead of *moving!* Hollywood characters are supposed to have all the adventures for everybody in America, with everybody in America sits in a dark room and watches them have them! Yes, until there's a war. That's when

adventure becomes available to the masses! *Everyone's* dish, not only Gable's! Then the people in the dark room come out of the dark room to have some adventures themselves— Goody, goody!—It's our turn now, to go to the South Sea Islands—to make a safari —to be exotic, far-off!—But I'm not patient. I don't want to wait till then. I'm tired of the *movies* and I am *about* to *move!*

JIM [*incredulously*]. Move?

TOM. Yes.

JIM. When?

TOM. Soon!

JIM. Where? Where?

[THEME THREE MUSIC SEEMS TO ANSWER THE QUESTION, WHILE TOM THINKS IT OVER. HE SEARCHES AMONG HIS POCKETS.]

TOM. I'm starting to boil inside. I know I seem dreamy, but inside—well, I'm boiling!—Whenever I pick up a shoe, I shudder a little thinking how short life is and what I am doing!—Whatever that means, I know it doesn't mean shoes—except as something to wear on a traveler's feet! [*Finds paper.*] Look——

JIM. What?

TOM. I'm a member.

JIM [*reading*]. The Union of Merchant Seamen.

TOM. I paid my dues this month, instead of the light bill.

JIM. You will regret it when they turn the lights off.

TOM. I won't be here.

JIM. How about your mother?

TOM. I'm like my father. The bastard son of a bastard! See how he grins? And he's been absent going on sixteen years!

JIM. You're just talking, you drip. How does your mother feel about it?

TOM. Shhh!—Here comes Mother! Mother is not acquainted with my plans!

AMANDA [*Enters portieres*]. Where are you all?

TOM. On the terrace, Mother.

[*They start inside. She advances to them.* TOM *is distinctly shocked at her appearance. Even* JIM *blinks a little. He is making his first contact with girlish Southern vivacity and in spite of the night-school course in public speaking is somewhat thrown off the beam by the unexpected outlay of social charm. Certain responses are attempted by* JIM *but are swept aside by* AMANDA'S *gay laughter and chatter.* TOM *is embarrassed but after the first shock* JIM *reacts very warmly. Grins and chuckles, is altogether won over.* IMAGE: AMANDA AS A GIRL.]

AMANDA [*Coyly smiling, shaking her girlish ringlets*]. Well, well, well, so this is Mr. O'Connor. Introductions entirely unnecessary. I've heard so much about you from my boy. I finally said to him, Tom—good gracious!—why don't you bring this paragon to supper? I'd like to meet this nice young man at the warehouse!—Instead of just hearing him sing your praises so much!

I don't know why my son is so standoffish—that's not Southern behavior!

Let's sit down and—I think we could stand a little more air in here! Tom, leave the door open. I felt a nice fresh breeze a moment ago. Where has it gone to?

Mmm, so warm already! And not quite summer, even. We're going to burn up when summer really gets started.

However, we're having—we're having a very light supper. I think light things are better fo' this time of year. The same as light clothes are. Light clothes an' light food are what warm weather calls fo'. You know our blood gets so thick during th' winter—it takes a while fo' us to *adjust* ou'selves!—when the season changes . . .

It's come so quick this year. I wasn't prepared. All of a sudden—heavens! Already summer!—I ran to the trunk an' pulled out this light dress— Terribly old! Historical almost! But feels so good—so good an' co-ol, y'know. . . .

TOM. Mother——

AMANDA. Yes, honey?

TOM. How about—supper?

AMANDA. Honey, you go ask Sister if supper is ready! You know that Sister is in full charge of supper!

Tell her you hungry boys are waiting for it. [*To* JIM.]

Have you met Laura?

JIM. She——

AMANDA. Let you in? Oh, good, you've met already! It's rare for a girl as sweet an' pretty as Laura to be domestic! But Laura is, thank heavens, not only pretty but also very domestic. I'm not at all. I never was a bit. I never could make a thing but angel-food cake. Well, in the South we had so many servants. Gone, gone, gone. All vestige of gracious living! Gone completely! I wasn't prepared for what the future brought me. All of my gentlemen callers were sons of planters and so of course I assumed that I would be married to one and raise my family on a large piece of land with plenty of servants. But man proposes—and women accepts the proposal!—To vary that old, old saying a little bit—I married no planter! I married a man who worked for the telephone company!—That gallantly smiling gentleman over there! [*Points to the picture.*] A telephone man who—fell in love with long-distance!—Now he travels and I don't even know where!—But what am I going on for about my—tribulations?

Tell me yours—I hope you don't have any!

Tom?

TOM [*returning*]. Yes, Mother?

AMANDA. Is supper nearly ready?

TOM. It looks to me like supper is on the table.

AMANDA. Let me look—— [*She rises prettily and looks through portieres.*] Oh, lovely!—But where is Sister?

TOM. Laura is not feeling well and she says that she thinks she'd better not come to the table.

AMANDA. What?—Nonsense!—Laura? Oh, Laura!

LAURA [*off stage, faintly*]. Yes, Mother.

AMANDA. You really must come to the table. We won't be seated until you come to the table!

Come in, Mr. O'Connor. You sit over there, and I'll——

Laura? Laura Wingfield!

You're keeping us waiting, honey! We can't say grace until you come to the table!

[*The back door is pushed weakly open and* LAURA *comes in. She is obviously quite faint, her lips trembling, her eyes wide and staring. She moves unsteadily toward the table.* LEGEND: "TERROR!" *Outside a summer storm is coming abruptly. The white curtains billow inward at the windows and there is a sorrowful murmur and deep blue dusk.* LAURA *suddenly stumbles—she catches at a chair with a faint moan.*]

TOM. Laura!

AMANDA. Laura!

[*There is a clap of thunder.* LEGEND: "AH!" *Despairingly.*]

Why, Laura, you *are* sick, darling! Tom, help your sister into the living room, dear!

Sit in the living room, Laura—rest on the sofa.

Well! [*to the gentleman caller*]

Standing over the hot stove made her ill!—I told her that it was just too warm this evening, but——

[TOM *comes back in.* LAURA *is on the sofa.*]

Is Laura all right now?

TOM. Yes.

AMANDA. What *is* that? Rain? A nice cool rain has come up!

[*She gives the gentleman caller a frightened look.*]

I think we may—have grace—now . . . [TOM *looks at her stupidly.*]

Tom, honey—you say grace!

TOM. Oh . . .

"For these and all thy mercies——

[*They bow their heads,* AMANDA *stealing a nervous glance at* JIM. *In the living room*

LAURA, *stretched on the sofa, clenches her hand to her lips, to hold back a shuddering sob.*]
God's Holy Name be praised"——

SCENE VII

LEGEND: "A SOUVENIR."

Half an hour later. Dinner is just being finished in the upstage area which is concealed by the drawn portieres.

As the curtain rises LAURA *is still huddled upon the sofa, her feet drawn under her, her head resting on a pale blue pillow, her eyes wide and mysteriously watchful. The new floor lamp with its shade of rose-colored silk gives a soft, becoming light to her face, bringing out the fragile, unearthly prettiness which usually escapes attention. There is a steady murmur of rain, but it is slackening and stops soon after the scene begins; the air outside becomes pale and luminous as the moon breaks out.*

A moment after the curtain rises, the lights in both rooms flicker and go out.

JIM. Hey, there, Mr. Light Bulb!

[AMANDA *laughs nervously.* LEGEND: "SUSPENSION OF A PUBLIC SERVICE."]

AMANDA. Where was Moses when the lights went out? Ha-ha. Do you know the answer to that one, Mr. O'Connor?

JIM. No, Ma'am, what's the answer?

AMANDA. In the dark! [JIM *laughs appreciatively.*] Everybody sit still. I'll light the candles. Isn't it lucky we have them on the table? Where's a match? Which of you gentlemen can provide a match?

JIM. Here.

AMANDA. Thank you, sir.

JIM. Not at all, Ma'am!

AMANDA. I guess the fuse has burnt out. Mr. O'Connor, can you tell a burnt-out fuse? I know I can't and Tom is a total loss when it comes to mechanics.

[SOUND: GETTING UP: VOICES RECEDE A LITTLE TO KITCHENETTE.]

Oh, be careful you don't bump into something. We don't want our gentleman caller to break his neck. Now wouldn't that be a fine howdy-do?

JIM. Ha-ha!

Where is the fuse-box?

AMANDA. Right here next to the stove. Can you see anything?

JIM. Just a minute.

AMANDA. Isn't electricity a mysterious thing?

Wasn't it Benjamin Franklin who tied a key to a kite?

We live in such a mysterious universe, don't we? Some people say that science clears up all the mysteries for us. In my opinion it only creates more!

Have you found it yet?

JIM. No, Ma'am. All these fuses look okay to me.

AMANDA. Tom!

TOM. Yes, Mother?

AMANDA. That light bill I gave you several days ago. The one I told you we got the notices about?

[LEGEND: "HA!"]

TOM. Oh.—Yeah.

AMANDA. You didn't neglect to pay it by any chance?

TOM. Why, I——

AMANDA. Didn't! I might have known it!

JIM. Shakespeare probably wrote a poem on that light bill, Mrs. Wingfield.

AMANDA. I might have known better than to trust him with it! There's such a high price for negligence in this world!

JIM. Maybe the poem will win a ten-dollar prize.

AMANDA. We'll just have to spend the remainder of the evening in the nineteenth century, before Mr. Edison made the Mazda lamp!

JIM. Candlelight is my favorite kind of light.

AMANDA. That shows you're romantic! But that's no excuse for Tom.

Well, we got through dinner. Very considerate of them to let us get through dinner before they plunged us into everlasting darkness, wasn't it, Mr. O'Connor?

JIM. Ha-ha!

AMANDA. Tom, as a penalty for your carelessness you can help me with the dishes.

JIM. Let me give you a hand.

AMANDA. Indeed you will not!

JIM. I ought to be good for something.

AMANDA. Good for something? [*Her tone is rhapsodic.*]

YOU? Why, Mr. O'Connor, nobody, *nobody's* given me this much entertainment in years—as you have!

JIM. Aw, now, Mrs. Wingfield!

AMANDA. I'm not exaggerating, not one bit! But Sister is all by her lonesome. You go keep her company in the parlor!

I'll give you this lovely old candelabrum that used to be on the altar at the Church of the Heavenly Rest. It was melted a little out of shape when the church burnt down. Lightning struck it one spring. Gypsy Jones was holding a revival at the time and he intimated that the church was destroyed because the Episcopalians gave card parties.

JIM. Ha-ha.

AMANDA. And how about you coaxing Sister to drink a little wine? I think it would be good for her! Can you carry both at once?

JIM. Sure. I'm Superman!

AMANDA. Now, Thomas, get into this apron!

[*The door of kitchenette swings closed on* AMANDA's *gay laughter; the flickering light approaches the portieres.* LAURA *sits up nervously as he enters. Her speech at first is low and breathless from the almost intolerable strain of being alone with a stranger.* [THE LEGEND: "I DON'T SUPPOSE YOU REMEMBER ME AT ALL!"] *In her first speeches in this scene, before* JIM's *warmth overcomes her paralyzing shyness,* LAURA's *voice is thin and breathless as though she has just run up a steep flight of stairs.* JIM's *attitude is gently humorous. In playing this scene it should be stressed that while the incident is apparently unimportant, it is to* LAURA *the climax of her secret life.*]

JIM. Hello, there, Laura.

LAURA [*faintly*]. Hello. [*She clears her throat.*]

JIM. How are you feeling now? Better?

LAURA. Yes. Yes, thank you.

JIM. This is for you. A little dandelion wine.

[*He extends it toward her with extravagant gallantry.*]

LAURA. Thank you.

JIM. Drink it—but don't get drunk!

[*He laughs heartily.* LAURA *takes the glass uncertainly, laughs shyly.*]

Where shall I set the candles?

LAURA. Oh—oh, anywhere . . .

JIM. How about here on the floor? Any objections?

LAURA. No.

JIM. I'll spread a newspaper under to catch the drippings. I like to sit on the floor. Mind if I do?

LAURA. Oh, no.

JIM. Give me a pillow?

LAURA. What?

JIM. A pillow!

LAURA. Oh . . . [*Hands him one quickly.*]

JIM. How about you? Don't you like to sit on the floor?

LAURA. Oh—yes.

JIM. Why don't you, then?

LAURA. I—will.

JIM. Take a pillow! [LAURA *does. Sits on the other sire of the candelabrum.* JIM *crosses his legs and smiles engagingly at her.*] I can't hardly see you sitting way over there.

LAURA. I can—see you.

JIM. I know, but that's not fair; I'm in the limelight. [LAURA *moves her pillow closer.*] Good! Now I can see you! Comfortable?

LAURA. Yes.

JIM. So am I. Comfortable as a cow! Will you have some gum?

LAURA. No, thank you.

JIM. I think that I will indulge, with your permission. [*Musingly unwraps it and holds it up.*] Think of the fortune made by the guy that invented the first piece of chewing gum. Amazing, huh? The Wrigley Building is one of the sights of Chicago.—I saw it summer before last when I went up to the Century of Progress. Did you take in the Century of Progress?

LAURA. No, I didn't.

JIM. Well, it was quite a wonderful exposition. What impressed me most was the Hall of Science. Gives you an idea of what the future will be in America, even more wonderful than the present time is! [*Pause. Smiling at her.*] Your brother tells me you're shy. Is that right, Laura?

LAURA. I—don't know.

JIM. I judge you to be an old-fashioned type of girl. Well, I think that's a pretty good type to be. Hope you don't think I'm being too personal—do you?

LAURA [*hastily, out of embarrassment*]. I believe I *will* take a piece of gum, if you—don't mind [*clearing her throat*]. Mr. O'Connor, have you—kept up with your singing?

JIM. Singing? Me?

LAURA. Yes. I remember what a beautiful voice you had.

JIM. When did you hear me sing? [VOICE OFF STAGE IN THE PAUSE.]

VOICE [*off stage*].

O blow, ye winds, heigh-ho,
A-roving I will go!
I'm off to my love
With a boxing glove—
Ten thousand miles away!

JIM. You say you've heard me sing?

LAURA. Oh, yes! Yes, very often . . . I—don't suppose—you remember me—at all?

JIM [*smiling doubtfully*]. You know I have an idea I've seen you before. I had that idea soon as you opened the door. It seemed almost like I was about to remember your name. But the name that I started to call you—wasn't a name! And so I stopped myself before I said it.

LAURA. Wasn't it—Blue Roses?

JIM. [*Springs up. Grinning.*] Blue Roses!—My gosh, yes—Blue Roses!

That's what I had on my tongue when you opened the door!

Isn't it funny what tricks your memory plays? I didn't connect you with high school somehow or other.

But that's where it was; it was high school. I didn't even know you were Shakespeare's sister!

Gosh, I'm sorry.

LAURA. I didn't expect you to. You—barely knew me!

JIM. But we did have a speaking acquaintance, huh?

LAURA. Yes, we—spoke to each other.

JIM. When did you recognize me?

LAURA. Oh, right away!

JIM. Soon as I came in the door?

LAURA. When I heard your name I thought it was probably you. I knew that Tom used to know you a little in high school. So when you came in the door——

Well, then I was—sure.

JIM. Why didn't you *say* something, then?

LAURA [*breathlessly*]. I didn't know what to say, I was—too surprised!

JIM. For goodness' sake! You know this sure is funny!

LAURA. Yes! Yes, isn't it, though . . .

JIM. Didn't we have a class in something together?

LAURA. Yes, we did.

JIM. What class was that?

LAURA. It was—singing—Chorus!

JIM. Aw!

LAURA. I sat across the aisle from you in the Aud.

JIM. Aw.

LAURA. Mondays, Wednesdays, and Fridays.

JIM. Now I remember—you always came in late.

LAURA. Yes, it was so hard for me, getting upstairs. I had that brace on my leg—it clumped so loud!

JIM. I never heard any clumping.

LAURA [*wincing at the recollection*]. To me it sounded like—thunder!

JIM. Well, well, I never even noticed.

LAURA. And everybody was seated before I came in. I had to walk in front of all those people. My seat was in the back row. I had to go clumping all the way up the aisle with everyone watching!

JIM. You shouldn't have been self-conscious.

LAURA. I know, but I was. It was always such a relief when the singing started.

JIM. Aw, yes, I've placed you now! I used to call you Blue Roses. How was it that I got started calling you that?

LAURA. I was out of school a little while with pleurosis. When I came back you asked me what was the matter. I said I had pleurosis—you thought I said Blue Roses. That's what you always called me after that!

JIM. I hope you didn't mind.

LAURA. Oh, no—I liked it. You see, I wasn't acquainted with many—people. . . .

JIM. As I remember you sort of stuck by yourself.

LAURA. I—I—never have had much luck at—making friends.

JIM. I don't see why you wouldn't.

LAURA. Well, I—started out badly.

JIM. You mean being——

LAURA. Yes, it sort of—stood between me——

JIM. You shouldn't have let it!

LAURA. I know, but it did, and——

JIM. You were shy with people!

LAURA. I tried not to be but never could——

JIM. Overcome it?

LAURA. No, I—I never could!

JIM. I guess being shy is something you have to work out of kind of gradually.

LAURA [*sorrowfully*]. Yes—I guess it——

JIM. Takes time!

LAURA. Yes——

JIM. People are not so dreadful when you know them. That's what you have to remember! And everybody has problems, not just you, but practically everybody has got some problems.

You think of yourself as having the only problems, as being the only one who is disappointed. But just look around you and you will see lots of people as disappointed as you are. For instance, I hoped when I was going to high school that I would be further along at this time, six years later, than I am now—— You remember that wonderful write-up I had in *The Torch*?

LAURA. Yes! [*She rises and crosses to table.*]

JIM. It said I was bound to succeed in anything I went into! [LAURA *returns with the annual.*] Holy Jeez! *The Torch!*

[*He accepts it reverently. They smile across it with mutual wonder.* LAURA *crouches beside him and they begin to turn through it.* LAURA's *shyness is dissolving in his warmth.*]

LAURA. Here you are in *The Pirates of Penzance!*

JIM [*wistfully*]. I sang the baritone lead in that operetta.

LAURA [*raptly*]. So *beautifully!*

JIM [*protesting*]. Aw——

LAURA. Yes, yes—beautifully—beautifully!

JIM. You heard me?

LAURA. All three times!

JIM. No!

LAURA. Yes!

JIM. All three performances?

LAURA [*looking down*]. Yes.

JIM. Why?

LAURA. I—wanted to ask you to—autograph my program.

JIM. Why didn't you ask me to?

LAURA. You were always surrounded by your own friends so much that I never had a chance to.

JIM. You should have just——

LAURA. Well, I—thought you might think I was——

JIM. Thought I might think you was—what?

LAURA. Oh——

JIM [*with reflective relish*]. I was beleaguered by females in those days.

LAURA. You were terribly popular!

JIM. Yeah——

LAURA. You had such a—friendly way——

JIM. I was spoiled in high school.

LAURA. Everybody—liked you!

JIM. Including you?

LAURA. I—yes, I—I did, too——

[*She gently closes the book in her lap.*]

JIM. Well, well, well!—Give me that program, Laura. [*She hands it to him. He signs it with a flourish.*] There you are—better late than never!

LAURA. Oh, I—what a—surprise!

JIM. My signature isn't worth very much right now.

But some day—maybe—it will increase in value!

Being disappointed is one thing and being discouraged is something else. I am disappointed but I am not discouraged.

I'm twenty-three years old.

How old are you?

LAURA. I'll be twenty-four in June.

JIM. That's not old age!

LAURA. No, but——

JIM. You finished high school?

LAURA [*with difficulty*]. I didn't go back.

JIM. You mean you dropped out?

LAURA. I made bad grades in my final examinations. [*She rises and replaces the book and the program. Her voice strained.*] How is—Emily Meisenbach getting along?

JIM. Oh, that kraut-head!

LAURA. Why do you call her that?

JIM. That's what she was.

LAURA. You're not still—going with her?

JIM. I never see her.

LAURA. It said in the Personal Section that you were—engaged!

JIM. I know, but I wasn't impressed by that—propaganda!

LAURA. It wasn't—the truth?

JIM. Only in Emily's optimistic opinion!

LAURA. Oh——

[LEGEND: "WHAT HAVE YOU DONE SINCE HIGH SCHOOL?" JIM *lights a cigarette and leans indolently back on his elbows smiling at* LAURA *with a warmth and charm which lights her inwardly with altar candles. She remains by the table and turns in her hands a piece of glass to cover her tumult.*]

JIM [*after several reflective puffs on a cigarette*]. What have you done since high school? [*She seems not to hear him.*] Huh? [LAURA *looks up.*] I said what have you done since high school, Laura?

LAURA. Nothing much.

JIM. You must have been doing something these six long years.

LAURA. Yes.

JIM. Well, then, such as what?

LAURA. I took a business course at business college——

JIM. How did that work out?

LAURA. Well, not very—well—I had to drop out, it gave me—indigestion—— [JIM *laughs gently.*]

JIM. What are you doing now?

LAURA. I don't do anything—much. Oh, please don't think I sit around doing nothing! My glass collection takes up a good deal of time. Glass is something you have to take good care of.

JIM. What did you say—about glass?

LAURA. Collection I said—I have one——

[*She clears her throat and turns away again, acutely shy.*]

JIM [*abruptly*]. You know what I judge to be the trouble with you?

Inferiority complex! Know what that is? That's what they call it when someone low-rates himself!

I understand it because I had it, too. Although my case was not so aggravated as yours seems to be. I had it until I took up public speaking, developed my voice, and learned that I had an aptitude for science. Before that time I never thought of myself as being outstanding in any way whatsoever!

Now I've never made a regular study of it, but I have a friend who says I can analyze people better than doctors that make a profession of it. I don't claim that to be necessarily true, but I can sure guess a person's psychology, Laura! [*Takes out his gum.*] Excuse me, Laura. I always take it out when the flavor is gone. I'll use this scrap of paper to wrap it in. I know how it is to get it stuck on a shoe.

Yep—that's what I judge to be your principal trouble. A lack of confidence in yourself as a person. You don't have the proper amount of faith in yourself. I'm basing that fact on a number of your remarks and also on certain observations I've made. For instance that clumping you thought was so awful in high school. You say that you even dreaded to walk into class. You see what you did? You dropped out of school, you gave up an education because of a clump, which as far as I know was practically non-existent! A little physical defect is what you have. Hardly noticeable even! Magnified thousands of times by imagination!

You know what my strong advice to you is? Think of yourself as *superior* in some way!

LAURA. In what way would I think?

JIM. Why, man alive, Laura! Just look about you a little. What do you see? A world full of common people! All of 'em born and all of 'em going to die!

Which of them has one-tenth of your good points? Or mine? Or anyone else's, as far as that goes—— Gosh!

Everybody excels in some one thing. Some in many!

[*Unconsciously glances at himself in the mirror.*]

All you've got to do is discover in *what!*

Take me, for instance.

[*He adjusts his tie at the mirror.*]

My interest happens to lie in electro-dynamics. I'm taking a course in radio engineering at night school, Laura, on top of a fairly responsible job at the warehouse. I'm taking that course and studying public speaking.

LAURA. Ohhhh.

JIM. Because I believe in the future of television! [*Turning back to her.*]

I wish to be ready to go up right along with it. Therefore I'm planning to get in on the ground floor. In fact I've already made the right connections and all that remains is for the industry itself to get under way! Full steam—— [*His eyes are starry.*] Knowledge—Zzzzzzzp! Money—Zzzzzzp!—Power! That's the cycle democracy is built on!

[*His attitude is convincingly dynamic.* LAURA *stares at him, even her shyness eclipsed in her absolute wonder. He suddenly grins.*]

I guess you think I think a lot of myself!

LAURA. No—o-o-o, I——

JIM. Now how about you? Isn't there something you take more interest in than anything else?

LAURA. Well, I do—as I said—have my—glass collection——

[*A peal of girlish laughter from the kitchen.*]

JIM. I'm not right sure I know what you're talking about.

What kind of glass is it?

LAURA. Little articles of it, they're ornaments mostly!

Most of them are little animals made out of glass, the tiniest little animals in the world. Mother calls them a glass menagerie!

Here's an example of one, if you'd like to see it!

This one is one of the oldest. It's nearly thirteen.

[MUSIC: "THE GLASS MENAGERIE." *He stretches out his hand.*]

Oh, be careful—if you breathe, it breaks!

JIM. I'd better not take it. I'm pretty clumsy with things.

LAURA. Go on, I trust you with him! [*Places it in his palm.*]

There now—you're holding him gently!

Hold him over the light, he loves the light! You see how the light shines through him?

JIM. It sure does shine!

LAURA. I shouldn't be partial, but he is my favorite one.

JIM. What kind of a thing is this one supposed to be?

LAURA. Haven't you noticed the single horn on his forehead?

JIM. A unicorn, huh?

LAURA. Mmm-hmmm!

JIM. Unicorns, aren't they extinct in the modern world?

LAURA. I know!

JIM. Poor little fellow, he must feel sort of lonesome.

LAURA [*smiling*]. Well, if he does he doesn't complain about it. He stays on a shelf with some horses that don't have horns and all of them seem to get along nicely together.

JIM. How do you know?

LAURA [*lightly*]. I haven't heard any arguments among them!

JIM [*grinning*]. No arguments, huh? Well, that's a pretty good sign!

Where shall I set him?

LAURA. Put him on the table. They all like a change of scenery once in a while!

JIM [*stretching*]. Well, well, well, well—— Look how big my shadow is when I stretch!

LAURA. Oh, oh, yes—it stretches across the ceiling!

JIM [*crossing to door*]. I think it's stopped raining. [*Opens fire-escape door.*] Where does the music come from?

LAURA. From the Paradise Dance Hall across the alley.

JIM. How about cutting the rug a little, Miss Wingfield?

LAURA. Oh, I——

JIM. Or is your program filled up? Let me have a look at it. [*Grasps imaginary card.*] Why, every dance is taken! I'll just have to scratch some out. [WALTZ MUSIC: "LA GOLONDRINA."] Ahh, a waltz!

[*He executes some sweeping turns by himself then holds his arms toward* LAURA.]

LAURA [*breathlessly*]. I—can't dance!

JIM. There you go, that inferiority stuff!

LAURA. I've never danced in my life!

JIM. Come on, try!

LAURA. Oh, but I'd step on you!

JIM. I'm not made out of glass.

LAURA. How—how—how do we start?

JIM. Just leave it to me. You hold your arms out a little.

LAURA. Like this?

JIM. A little bit higher. Right. Now don't tighten up, that's the main thing about it—relax.

LAURA [laughing breathlessly]. It's hard not to.

JIM. Okay.

LAURA. I'm afraid you can't budge me.

JIM. What do you bet I can't? [He swings her into motion.]

LAURA. Goodness, yes, you can!

JIM. Let yourself go, now, Laura, just let yourself go.

LAURA. I'm——

JIM. Come on!

LAURA. Trying!

JIM. Not so stiff—— Easy does it!

LAURA. I know but I'm——

JIM. Loosen th' backbone! There now, that's a lot better.

LAURA. Am I?

JIM. Lots, lots better!

[He moves her about the room in a clumsy waltz.]

LAURA. Oh, my!

JIM. Ha-ha!

LAURA. Oh, my goodness!

JIM. Ha-ha-ha! [They suddenly bump into the table. JIM stops.] What did we hit on?

LAURA. Table.

JIM. Did something fall off it? I think——

LAURA. Yes.

JIM. I hope that it wasn't the little glass horse with the horn!

LAURA. Yes.

JIM. Aw, aw, aw. Is it broken?

LAURA. Now it is just like all the other horses.

JIM. It's lost its——

LAURA. Horn!

It doesn't matter. Maybe it's a blessing in disguise.

JIM. You'll never forgive me. I bet that was your favorite piece of glass.

LAURA. I don't have favorites much. It's no tragedy, Freckles. Glass breaks so easily. No matter how careful you are. The traffic jars the shelves and things fall off them.

JIM. Still I'm awfully sorry that I was the cause.

LAURA [smiling]. I'll just imagine he had an operation.

The horn was removed to make him feel less—freakish! [They both laugh.]

Now he will feel more at home with the other horses, the ones that don't have horns . . .

JIM. Ha-ha, that's very funny! [Suddenly serious.]

I'm glad to see that you have a sense of humor.

You know—you're—well—very different!

Surprisingly different from anyone else I know!

[His voice becomes soft and hesitant with a genuine feeling.]

Do you mind me telling you that? [LAURA is abashed beyond speech.]

I mean it in a nice way . . . [LAURA nods shyly, looking away.]

You make me feel sort of—I don't know how to put it!

I'm usually pretty good at expressing things, but——

This is something that I don't know how to say!

[LAURA touches her throat and clears it—turns the broken unicorn in her hands. Even softer.]

Has anyone ever told you that you were pretty?

[PAUSE: MUSIC. LAURA looks up slowly, with wonder, and shakes her head.]

Well, you are! In a very different way from anyone else.

And all the nicer because of the difference, too.

[His voice becomes low and husky. LAURA turns away, nearly faint with the novelty of her emotions.]

I wish that you were my sister. I'd teach you to have some confidence in yourself. The different people are not like other people, but being different is nothing to be ashamed of. Because other people are not such wonderful people. They're one hundred times one thousand. You're one times one! They walk all over the earth. You just stay here. They're common as—weeds, but—you—well, you're—Blue Roses!

[IMAGE ON SCREEN: BLUE ROSES. MUSIC CHANGES.]

LAURA. But blue is wrong for—roses . . .

JIM. It's right for you!—You're—pretty!

LAURA. In what respect am I pretty?

JIM. In all respects—believe me! Your eyes—your hair—are pretty! Your hands are pretty! [He catches hold of her hand.]

You think I'm making this up because I'm invited to dinner and have to be nice. Oh, I could do that! I could put on an act for you, Laura, and say lots of things without being very sincere. But this time I am. I'm talking to you sincerely. I happened to notice you had this inferiority complex that keeps you from feeling comfortable with people. Somebody needs to build your confidence up and make you proud instead of shy and turning away and—blushing——

Somebody—ought to——

Ought to—*kiss* you, Laura!

[*His hand slips slowly up her arm to her shoulder.* MUSIC SWELLS TUMULTUOUSLY. *He suddenly turns her about and kisses her on the lips. When he releases her,* LAURA *sinks on the sofa with a bright, dazed look.* JIM *backs away and fishes in his pocket for a cigarette.* LEGEND ON SCREEN: "SOUVENIR."]

Stumble-john!

[*He lights the cigarette, avoiding her look. There is a peal of girlish laughter from* AMANDA *in the kitchen.* LAURA *slowly raises and opens her hand. It still contains the little broken glass animal. She looks at it with a tender, bewildered expression.*]

Stumble-john!

I shouldn't have done that—— That was way off the beam.

You don't smoke, do you?

[*She looks up, smiling, not hearing the question. He sits beside her a little gingerly. She looks at him speechlessly—waiting. He coughs decorously and moves a little farther aside as he considers the situation and senses her feelings, dimly, with perturbation. Gently.*]

Would you—care for a—mint?

[*She doesn't seem to hear him but her look grows brighter even.*]

Peppermint—Life-Saver?

My pocket's a regular drug store—wherever I go . . .

[*He pops a mint in his mouth. Then gulps and decides to make a clean breast of it. He speaks slowly and gingerly.*]

Laura, you know, if I had a sister like you, I'd do the same thing as Tom. I'd bring out fellows and—introduce her to them. The right type of boys of a type to—appreciate her.

Only—well—he made a mistake about me.

Maybe I've got no call to be saying this. That may not have been the idea in having me over. But what if it was?

There's nothing wrong about that. The only trouble is that in my case—I'm not in a situation to—do the right thing.

I can't take down your number and say I'll phone.

I can't call up next week and—ask for a date.

I thought I had better explain the situation in case you—misunderstood it and—hurt your feelings. . . .

[*Pause. Slowly, very slowly,* LAURA'S *look changes, her eyes returning slowly from his to the ornament in her palm.* AMANDA *utters another gay laugh in the kitchen.*]

LAURA [*faintly*]. You—won't—call again?

JIM. No, Laura, I can't. [*He rises from the sofa.*]

As I was just explaining, I've—got strings on me.

Laura, I've—been going steady!

I go out all of the time with a girl named Betty. She's a home-girl like you, and Catholic, and Irish, and in a great many ways we—get along fine.

I met her last summer on a moonlight boat trip up the river to Alton, on the *Majestic.*

Well—right away from the start it was—love!

[LEGEND: LOVE! LAURA *sways slightly forward and grips the arm of the sofa. He fails to notice, now enrapt in his own comfortable being.*]

Being in love has made a new man of me!

[*Leaning stiffly forward, clutching the arm of the sofa,* LAURA *struggles visibly with her storm. But* JIM *is oblivious; she is a long way off.*]

The power of love is really pretty tremendous!

Love is something that—changes the whole world, Laura!

[*The storm abates a little and* LAURA *leans back. He notices her again.*]

It happened that Betty's aunt took sick; she got a wire and had to go to Centralia. So Tom—when he asked me to dinner—I naturally just accepted the invitation, not knowing that you—that he—that I—— [*He stops awkwardly.*]

Huh—I'm a stumble-john!

[*He flops back on the sofa. The holy candles in the altar of* LAURA'S *face have been snuffed out. There is a look of almost infinite desolation.* JIM *glances at her uneasily.*]

I wish that you would—say something. [*She bites her lip which was trembling and then bravely smiles. She opens her hand again on the broken glass ornament. Then she gently takes his hand and raises it level with her own. She carefully places the unicorn in the palm of his hand, then pushes his fingers closed upon it.*] What are you—doing that for? You want me to have him?—Laura? [*She nods.*] What for?

LAURA. A—souvenir . . .

[*She rises unsteadily and crouches beside the victrola to wind it up.* LEGEND ON SCREEN: "THINGS HAVE A WAY OF TURNING OUT SO BADLY!" OR IMAGE: "GENTLEMAN CALLER WAVING GOOD-BYE!—GAILY." *At this moment* AMANDA *rushes brightly back in the front room. She bears a pitcher of fruit punch in an old-fashioned cut-glass pitcher and a plate of macaroons. The plate has a gold border and poppies painted on it.*]

AMANDA. Well, well, well! Isn't the air delightful after the shower?

I've made you children a little liquid refreshment. [*Turns gaily to the gentleman caller.*]

Jim, do you know that song about lemonade?

"Lemonade, lemonade
 Made in the shade and stirred with a spade——
 Good enough for any old maid!"

JIM [*uneasily*]. Ha-ha! No—I never heard it.

AMANDA. Why, Laura! You look so serious!

JIM. We were having a serious conversation.

AMANDA. Good! Now you're better acquainted!

JIM [*uncertainly*]. Ha-ha! Yes.

AMANDA. You modern young people are much more serious-minded than my generation. I was so gay as a girl!

JIM. You haven't changed, Mrs. Wingfield.

AMANDA. Tonight I'm rejuvenated! The gaiety of the occasion, Mr. O'Connor!

> [*She tosses her head with a pearl of laughter. Spills lemonade.*]

Oooo! I'm baptizing myself!

JIM. Here—let me——

AMANDA [*setting the pitcher down*]. There now. I discovered we had some maraschino cherries. I dumped them in, juice and all!

JIM. You shouldn't have gone to that trouble, Mrs. Wingfield.

AMANDA. Trouble, trouble? Why, it was loads of fun!

Didn't you hear me cutting up in the kitchen? I bet your ears were burning! I told Tom how outdone with him I was for keeping you to himself so long a time! He should have brought you over much, much sooner! Well, now that you've found your way, I want you to be a very frequent caller! Not just occasional but all the time.

Oh, we're going to have a lot of gay times together! I see them coming!

Mmm, just breathe that air! So fresh, and the moon's so pretty!

I'll skip back out—I know where my place is when young folks are having a—serious conversation!

JIM. Oh, don't go out, Mrs. Wingfield. The fact of the matter is I've got to be going.

AMANDA. Going, now? You're joking! Why, it's only the shank of the evening, Mr. O'Connor!

JIM. Well, you know how it is.

AMANDA. You mean you're a young workingman and have to keep workingmen's hours. We'll let you off early tonight. But only on the condition that next time you stay later.

What's the best night for you? Isn't Saturday night the best night for you workingmen?

JIM. I have a couple of time-clocks to punch, Mrs. Wingfield. One at morning, another one at night!

AMANDA. My, but you *are* ambitious! You work at night, too?

JIM. No, Ma'am, not work but—Betty!

> [*He crosses deliberately to pick up his hat. The band at the Paradise Dance Hall goes into a tender waltz.*]

AMANDA. Betty? Betty? Who's—Betty?

> [*There is an ominous cracking sound in the sky.*]

JIM. Oh, just a girl. The girl I go steady with!

> [*He smiles charmingly. The sky falls.* LEGEND: "THE SKY FALLS."]

AMANDA [*a long-drawn exhalation*]. Ohhhh . . . Is it a serious romance, Mr. O'Connor?

JIM. We're going to be married the second Sunday in June.

AMANDA. Ohhhh—how nice!

Tom didn't mention that you were engaged to be married.

JIM. The cat's not out of the bag at the warehouse yet.

You know how they are. They call you Romeo and stuff like that.

> [*He stops at the oval mirror to put on his hat. He carefully shapes the brim and the crown to give a discreetly dashing effect.*]

It's been a wonderful evening, Mrs. Wingfield. I guess this is what they mean by Southern hospitality.

AMANDA. It really wasn't anything at all.

JIM. I hope it don't seem like I'm rushing off. But I promised Betty I'd pick her up at the Wabash depot, an' by the time I get my jalopy down there her train'll be in. Some women are pretty upset if you keep 'em waiting.

AMANDA. Yes, I know—— The tyranny of women! [*Extends her hand.*]

Good-bye, Mr. O'Connor.

I wish you luck—and happiness—and success! All three of them, and so does Laura! —Don't you, Laura?

LAURA. Yes!

JIM [*taking her hand*]. Good-bye, Laura. I'm certainly going to treasure that souvenir. And don't you forget the good advice I gave you. [*Raises his voice to a cheery shout.*]

So long, Shakespeare!

Thanks again, ladies—— Good night!

> [*He grins and ducks jauntily out. Still bravely grimacing,* AMANDA *closes the door on the gentleman caller. Then she turns back to the room with a puzzled expression. She and* LAURA *don't dare to face each other.* LAURA *crouches beside the victrola to wind it.*]

AMANDA [*faintly*]. Things have a way of turning out so badly.

I don't believe that I would play the victrola.

Well, well—well——

Our gentleman caller was engaged to be married! Tom!

TOM [*from back*]. Yes, Mother?

AMANDA. Come in here a minute. I want to tell you something awfully funny.

TOM [*enters with macaroon and a glass of the lemonade*]. Has the gentleman caller gotten away already?

AMANDA. The gentleman caller has made an early departure.

What a wonderful joke you played on us!

TOM. How do you mean?

AMANDA. You didn't mention that he was engaged to be married.

TOM. Jim? Engaged?

AMANDA. That's what he just informed us.

TOM. I'll be jiggered! I didn't know about that.

AMANDA. That seems very peculiar.

TOM. What's peculiar about it?

AMANDA. Didn't you call him your best friend down at the warehouse?

TOM. He is, but how did I know?

AMANDA. It seems extremely peculiar that you wouldn't know your best friend was going to be married!

TOM. The warehouse is where I work, not where I know things about people!

AMANDA. You don't know things anywhere! You live in a dream; you manufacture illusions! [*He crosses to the door.*]

Where are you going?

TOM. I'm going to the movies.

AMANDA. That's right, now that you've had us make such fools of ourselves. The effort, the preparations, all the expense! The new floor lamp, the rug, the clothes for Laura! All for what? To entertain some other girl's fiancé!

Go to the movies, go! Don't think about us, a mother deserted, an unmarried sister who's crippled and has no job! Don't let anything interfere with your selfish pleasure!

Just go, go, go—to the movies!

TOM. All right, I will! The more you shout about my selfishness to me the quicker I'll go, and I won't go to the movies!

AMANDA. Go, then! Then go to the moon—you selfish dreamer!

[TOM *smashes his glass on the floor. He plunges out on the fire-escape, slamming the door.* LAURA *screams—cut off by door. Dance-hall music up.* TOM *goes to the rail and grips it desperately, lifting his face in the chill white moonlight penetrating the narrow abyss of the alley.* LEGEND ON SCREEN: "AND SO GOOD-BYE . . ." TOM's *closing speech is timed with the interior pantomime. The interior scene is played as though viewed through soundproof glass.* AMANDA *appears to be making a comforting speech to* LAURA *who is huddled upon the sofa. Now that we cannot hear the mother's speech, her silliness is gone and she has dignity and tragic beauty.* LAURA's *dark hair hides her face until at the end of the speech she lifts it to smile at her mother.* AMANDA's *gestures are slow and graceful, almost dance-like, as she comforts the daughter. At the end of her speech she glances a moment at the father's picture—then withdraws through the portieres. At close of* TOM's *speech,* LAURA *blows out the candles, ending the play.*]

TOM. I didn't go to the moon, I went much further —for time is the longest distance between two places——

Not long after that I was fired for writing a poem on the lid of a shoe-box.

I left Saint Louis. I descended the steps of this fire-escape for the last time and followed from then on, in my father's footsteps, attempting to find in motion what was lost in space——

I traveled around a great deal. The cities swept about me like dead leaves, leaves that were brightly colored but torn away from the branches.

I would have stopped, but I was pursued by something.

It always came upon me unawares, taking me altogether by surprise. Perhaps it was a familiar bit of music. Perhaps it was only a piece of transparent glass——

Perhaps I am walking along a street at night, in some strange city, before I have found companions. I pass the lighted window of a shop where perfume is sold. The window is filled with pieces of colored glass, tiny transparent bottles in delicate colors, like bits of a shattered rainbow.

Then all at once my sister touches my shoulder. I turn around and look into her eyes . . .

Oh, Laura, Laura, I tried to leave you behind me, but I am more faithful than I intended to be!

I reach for a cigarette, I cross the street, I run into the movies or a bar, I buy a drink, I speak to the nearest stranger—anything that can blow your candles out! [LAURA *bends over the candles.*]—for nowadays the world is lit by lightning! Blow out your candles, Laura—and so good-bye. . . . [*She blows the candles out.*]

THE SCENE DISSOLVES

DEATH OF A SALESMAN

ARTHUR MILLER

ARTHUR MILLER (1915–   ) was born in New York City, and graduated from the University of Michigan. In 1936 he won Michigan's Avery Hopwood Prize for drama, and in 1938 the Theatre Guild National Award. His work includes the novel *Focus* (1945), the play *All My Sons* (1947), which won the New York Drama Critics' Circle Award, and *Death of a Salesman* (1949), the recipient of many awards, among them that of the Critics' Circle and the Pulitzer Prize. His *A Memory of Two Mondays* and *A View From the Bridge*, two one-act dramas, were performed together on Broadway in 1955. His view of tragic drama is expressed in the essay "Tragedy and the Common Man" (see page 537).

CAST

(in order of appearance)

WILLY LOMAN.

LINDA.

BIFF.

HAPPY.

BERNARD.

THE WOMAN.

CHARLEY.

UNCLE BEN.

HOWARD WAGNER.

JENNY.

STANLEY.

MISS FORSYTHE.

LETTA.

The action takes place in Willy Loman's house and yard and in various places he visits in the New York and Boston of today.

Throughout the play, in the stage directions, left and right mean stage left and stage right.

ACT I

A melody is heard, played upon a flute. It is small and fine, telling of grass and trees and the horizon. The curtain rises. Before us is the Salesman's house. We are aware of towering, angular shapes behind it, surrounding it on all sides. Only the blue light of the sky falls upon the house and forestage; the surrounding area shows an angry glow of orange. As more light appears, we see a solid vault of apartment houses around the small, fragile-seeming home. An air of the

Copyright, 1949, by Arthur Miller. Reprinted by permission of The Viking Press, Inc. All rights reserved: no public or private performance of the play, professional or amateur, may be given; no film, radio or television use or public reading, without authorization from the author's representative, MCA Artists, Ltd., 598 Madison Ave., New York 22. For permission to reprint excerpts from the play, address The Viking Press, Inc., 625 Madison Ave., New York 22.

dream clings to the place, a dream rising out of reality. The kitchen at center seems actual enough, for there is a kitchen table with three chairs, and a refrigerator. But no other fixtures are seen. At the back of the kitchen there is a draped entrance, which leads to the living-room. To the right of the kitchen, on a level raised two feet, is a bedroom furnished only with a brass bedstead and a straight chair. On a shelf over the bed a silver athletic trophy stands. A window opens onto the apartment house at the side. Behind the kitchen, on a level raised six and a half feet, is the boys' bedroom, at present barely visible. Two beds are dimly seen, and at the back of the room a dormer window. (This bedroom is above the unseen living-room.) At the left a stairway curves up to it from the kitchen. The entire setting is wholly or, in some places, partially transparent. The roof-line of the house is one-dimensional; under and over it we see the apartment buildings. Before the house lies an *apron, curving beyond the forestage into the orchestra. This forward area serves as the back yard as well as the locale of all* WILLY's *imaginings and of his city scenes. Whenever the action is in the present the actors observe the imaginary wall-lines, entering the house only through its door at the left. But in the scenes of the past these boundaries are broken, and characters enter or leave a room by stepping "through" a wall onto the forestage.*

[*From the right,* WILLY LOMAN, *the Salesman, enters, carrying two large sample cases. The flute plays on. He hears but is not aware of it. He is past sixty years of age, dressed quietly. Even as he crosses the stage to the doorway of the house, his exhaustion is apparent. He unlocks the door, comes into the kitchen, and thankfully lets his burden down, feeling the soreness of his palms. A word-sigh escapes his lips—it might be "Oh, boy, oh, boy." He closes the door, then carries his cases out into the living-room through the draped kitchen doorway.* LINDA, *his wife, has stirred in her bed at the right. She gets out and puts on a robe, listening. Most often jovial, she has developed an iron repression of her exceptions to* WILLY's *behavior—she more than loves him, she admires him, as though his mercurial nature, his temper, his massive dreams and little cruelties, served her only as sharp reminders of the turbulent longings which she shares but lacks the temperament to utter and follow to their end.*]

LINDA. [*Hearing* WILLY *outside the bedroom, calls with some trepidation.*] Willy!

WILLY. It's all right. I came back.

LINDA. Why? What happened? [*Slight pause.*] Did something happen, Willy?

WILLY. No, nothing happened.

LINDA. You didn't smash the car, did you?

WILLY. [*With casual irritation.*] I said nothing happened. Didn't you hear me?

LINDA. Don't you feel well?

WILLY. I'm tired to the death. [*The flute has faded away. He sits on the bed beside her, a little numb.*] I couldn't make it. I just couldn't make it, Linda.

LINDA. [*Very carefully, delicately.*] Where were you all day? You look terrible.

WILLY. I got as far as a little above Yonkers. I stopped for a cup of coffee. Maybe it was the coffee.

LINDA. What?

WILLY. [*After a pause.*] I suddenly couldn't drive any more. The car kept going off onto the shoulder, y'know?

LINDA. [*Helpfully.*] Oh. Maybe it was the steering again. I don't think Angelo knows the Studebaker.

WILLY. No, it's me. Suddenly I realize I'm goin' sixty miles an hour and I don't remember the last five minutes. I'm—I can't seem to—keep my mind to it.

LINDA. Maybe it's your glasses. You never went for your new glasses.

WILLY. No, I see everything. I came back ten miles an hour. It took me nearly four hours from Yonkers.

LINDA. [*Resigned.*] Well, you'll just have to take a rest, Willy, you can't continue this way.

WILLY. I just got back from Florida.

LINDA. But you didn't rest your mind. Your mind is overactive, and the mind is what counts, dear.

WILLY. I'll start out in the morning. Maybe I'll feel better in the morning. [*She is taking off his shoes.*] These goddam arch supports are killing me.

LINDA. Take an aspirin. Should I get you an aspirin? It'll soothe you.

WILLY. [*With wonder.*] I was driving along, you understand? And I was fine. I was fine. I was even observing the scenery. You can imagine, me looking at scenery, on the road every week of my life. But it's so beautiful up there, Linda, the trees are so thick, and the sun is warm. I opened the windshield and just let the warm air bathe over me. And then all of a sudden I'm goin' off the road! I'm tellin' ya, I absolutely forgot I was driving. If I'd've gone the other way over the white line I might've killed somebody. So I went on again—and five minutes later I'm dreamin' again, and I nearly—— [*He presses two fingers against his eyes.*] I have such thoughts, I have such strange thoughts.

LINDA. Willy, dear. Talk to them again. There's no reason why you can't work in New York.

WILLY. They don't need me in New York. I'm the New England man. I'm vital in New England.

LINDA. But you're sixty years old. They can't expect you to keep traveling every week.

WILLY. I'll have to send a wire to Portland. I'm supposed to see Brown and Morrison tomorrow morning at ten o'clock to show the line. Goddammit, I could sell them! [*He starts putting on his jacket.*]

LINDA. [*Taking the jacket from him.*] Why don't you go down to the place tomorrow and tell Howard you've simply got to work in New York? You're too accommodating, dear.

WILLY. If old man Wagner was alive I'd a been in charge of New York now! That man was a prince, he was a masterful man. But that boy of his, that Howard, he don't appreciate. When I went north the first time, the Wagner Company didn't know where New England was!

LINDA. Why don't you tell those things to Howard, dear?

WILLY. [*Encouraged.*] I will, I definitely will. Is there any cheese?

LINDA. I'll make you a sandwich.

WILLY. No, go to sleep. I'll take some milk. I'll be up right away. The boys in?

LINDA. They're sleeping. Happy took Biff on a date tonight.

WILLY. [*Interested.*] That so?

LINDA. It was so nice to see them shaving together, one behind the other, in the bathroom. And going out together. You notice? The whole house smells of shaving lotion.

WILLY. Figure it out. Work a lifetime to pay off a house. You finally own it, and there's nobody to live in it.

LINDA. Well, dear, life is a casting off. It's always that way.

WILLY. No, no, some people—some people accomplish something. Did Biff say anything after I went this morning?

LINDA. You shouldn't have criticized him, Willy, especially after he just got off the train. You mustn't lose your temper with him.

WILLY. When the hell did I lose my temper? I simply asked him if he was making any money. Is that a criticism?

LINDA. But, dear, how could he make any money?

WILLY. [*Worried and angered.*] There's such an undercurrent in him. He became a moody man. Did he apologize when I left this morning?

LINDA. He was crestfallen, Willy. You know how he admires you. I think if he finds himself, then you'll both be happier and not fight any more.

WILLY. How can he find himself on a farm? Is that a life? A farmhand? In the beginning, when he was young, I thought, well, a young man, it's good for him to tramp around, take a lot of different jobs. But it's more than ten years now and he has yet to make thirty-five dollars a week!

LINDA. He's finding himself, Willy.

WILLY. Not finding yourself at the age of thirty-four is a disgrace!

LINDA. Shh!

WILLY. The trouble is he's lazy, goddammit!

LINDA. Willy, please!

WILLY. Biff is a lazy bum!

LINDA. They're sleeping. Get something to eat. Go on down.

WILLY. Why did he come home? I would like to know what brought him home.

LINDA. I don't know. I think he's still lost, Willy. I think he's very lost.

WILLY. Biff Loman is lost. In the greatest country in the world a young man with such—personal attractiveness, gets lost. And such a hard worker. There's one thing about Biff—he's not lazy.

LINDA. Never.

WILLY. [*With pity and resolve.*] I'll see him in the morning; I'll have a nice talk with him. I'll get him a job selling. He could be big in no time. My God! Remember how they used to follow him around in high school? When he smiled at one of them their faces lit up. When he walked down the street . . .

[*He loses himself in reminiscences.*]

LINDA. [*Trying to bring him out of it.*] Willy, dear, I got a new kind of American-type cheese today. It's whipped.

WILLY. Why do you get American when I like Swiss?

LINDA. I just thought you'd like a change——

WILLY. I don't want a change! I want Swiss cheese. Why am I always being contradicted?

LINDA. [*With a covering laugh.*] I thought it would be a surprise.

WILLY. Why don't you open a window in here, for God's sake?

LINDA. [*With infinite patience.*] They're all open, dear.

WILLY. The way they boxed us in here. Bricks and windows, windows and bricks.

LINDA. We should've bought the land next door.

WILLY. The street is lined with cars. There's not a breath of fresh air in the neighborhood. The grass don't grow any more, you can't raise a carrot in the back yard. They should've had a law against apartment houses. Remember those two beautiful elm trees out there? When I and Biff hung the swing between them?

LINDA. Yeah, like being a million miles from the city.

WILLY. They should've arrested the builder for cutting those down. They massacred the neighborhood. [*Lost.*] More and more I think of those days, Linda. This time of year it was lilac and wisteria. And then the peonies would come out, and the daffodils. What fragrance in this room!

LINDA. Well, after all, people had to move somewhere.

WILLY. No, there's more people now.

LINDA. I don't think there's more people. I think——

WILLY. There's more people! That's what's ruining this country! Population is getting out of control. The competition is maddening! Smell the stink from that apartment house! And another one on the other side . . . How can they whip cheese?

[*On* WILLY's *last line,* BIFF *and* HAPPY *raise themselves up in their beds, listening.*]

LINDA. Go down, try it. And be quiet.

WILLY. [*Turning to* LINDA, *guilty.*] You're not worried about me, are you, sweetheart?

BIFF. What's the matter?

HAPPY. Listen!

LINDA. You've got too much on the ball to worry about.

WILLY. You're my foundation and my support, Linda.

LINDA. Just try to relax, dear. You make mountains out of molehills.

WILLY. I won't fight with him any more. If he wants to go back to Texas, let him go.

LINDA. He'll find his way.

WILLY. Sure. Certain men just don't get started till later in life. Like Thomas Edison, I think. Or B. F. Goodrich. One of them was deaf. [*He starts for the bedroom doorway.*] I'll put my money on Biff.

LINDA. And Willy—if it's warm Sunday we'll drive in the country. And we'll open the windshield, and take lunch.

WILLY. No, the windshields don't open on the new cars.

LINDA. But you opened it today.

WILLY. Me? I didn't. [*He stops.*] Now isn't that peculiar! Isn't that a remarkable——

[*He breaks off in amazement and fright as the flute is heard distantly.*]

LINDA. What, darling?

WILLY. That is the most remarkable thing.

LINDA. What, dear?

WILLY. I was thinking of the Chevvy. [*Slight pause.*] Nineteen twenty-eight . . . when I had that red Chevvy—— [*Breaks off.*] That funny? I coulda sworn I was driving that Chevvy today.

LINDA. Well, that's nothing. Something must've reminded you.

WILLY. Remarkable. Ts. Remember those days? The way Biff used to simonize that car? The dealer refused to believe there was eighty thousand miles on it. [*He shakes his head.*] Heh! [*To* LINDA.] Close your eyes, I'll be right up.

[*He walks out of the bedroom.*]

HAPPY. [*To* BIFF.] Jesus, maybe he smashed up the car again!

LINDA. [*Calling after* WILLY.] Be careful on the stairs, dear! The cheese is on the middle shelf!

[*She turns, goes over to the bed, takes his jacket, and goes out of the bedroom. Light has risen on the boys' room. Unseen,* WILLY *is heard talking to himself, "Eighty thousand miles," and a little laugh.* BIFF *gets out of bed, comes downstage a bit, and stands attentively.* BIFF *is two years older than his brother* HAPPY, *well built, but in these days bears a worn air and seems less self-assured. He has succeeded less, and his dreams are stronger and less acceptable than* HAPPY'S. HAPPY *is tall, powerfully made. Sexuality is like a visible color on him, or a scent that many women have dis-*

covered. He, like his brother, is lost, but in a different way, for he has never allowed himself to turn his face toward defeat and is thus more confused and hard-skinned, although seemingly more content.]

HAPPY. [*Getting out of bed.*] He's going to get his license taken away if he keeps that up. I'm getting nervous about him, y'know, Biff?

BIFF. His eyes are going.

HAPPY. No, I've driven with him. He sees all right. He just doesn't keep his mind on it. I drove into the city with him last week. He stops at a green light and then it turns red and he goes. [*He laughs.*]

BIFF. Maybe he's color-blind.

HAPPY. Pop? Why he's got the finest eye for color in the business. You know that.

BIFF. [*Sitting down on his bed.*] I'm going to sleep.

HAPPY. You're not still sour on Dad, are you, Biff?

BIFF. He's all right, I guess.

WILLY. [*Underneath them, in the living-room.*] Yes, sir, eighty thousand miles—eighty-two thousand!

BIFF. You smoking?

HAPPY. [*Holding out a pack of cigarettes.*] Want one?

BIFF. [*Taking a cigarette.*] I can never sleep when I smell it.

WILLY. What a simonizing job, heh!

HAPPY. [*With deep sentiment.*] Funny, Biff, y'know? Us sleeping in here again? The old beds. [*He pats his bed affectionately.*] All the talk that went across those two beds, huh? Our whole lives.

BIFF. Yeah. Lotta dreams and plans.

HAPPY. [*With a deep and masculine laugh.*] About five hundred women would like to know what was said in this room. [*They share a soft laugh.*]

BIFF. Remember that big Betsy something—what the hell was her name—over on Bushwick Avenue?

HAPPY. [*Combing his hair.*] With the collie dog!

BIFF. That's the one. I got you in there, remember?

HAPPY. Yeah, that was my first time—I think. Boy, there was a pig! [*They laugh, almost crudely.*] You taught me everything I know about women. Don't forget that.

BIFF. I bet you forgot how bashful you used to be. Especially with girls.

HAPPY. Oh, I still am, Biff.

BIFF. Oh, go on.

HAPPY. I just control it, that's all. I think I got less bashful and you got more so. What happened, Biff? Where's the old humor, the old confidence? [*He shakes* BIFF's *knee.* BIFF *gets up and moves restlessly about the room.*] What's the matter?

BIFF. Why does Dad mock me all the time?

HAPPY. He's not mocking you, he——

BIFF. Everything I say there's a twist of mockery on his face. I can't get near him.

HAPPY. He just wants you to make good, that's all. I wanted to talk to you about Dad for a long time, Biff. Something's—happening to him. He—talks to himself.

BIFF. I noticed that this morning. But he always mumbled.

HAPPY. But not so noticeable. It got so embarrassing I sent him to Florida. And you know something? Most of the time he's talking to you.

BIFF. What's he say about me?

HAPPY. I can't make it out.

BIFF. What's he say about me?

HAPPY. I think the fact that you're not settled, that you're still kind of up in the air . . .

BIFF. There's one or two other things depressing him, Happy.

HAPPY. What do you mean?

BIFF. Never mind. Just don't lay it all to me.

HAPPY. But I think if you just got started—I mean —is there any future for you out there?

BIFF. I tell ya, Hap, I don't know what the future is. I don't know—what I'm supposed to want.

HAPPY. What do you mean?

BIFF. Well, I spent six or seven years after high school trying to work myself up. Shipping clerk, salesman, business of one kind or another. And it's a measly manner of existence. To get on that subway on the hot mornings in summer. To devote your whole life to keeping stock, or making phone calls, or selling or buying. To suffer fifty weeks of the year for the sake of a two-week vacation, when all you really desire is to be outdoors, with your shirt off. And always to have to get ahead of the next fella. And still—that's how you build a future.

HAPPY. Well, you really enjoy it on a farm? Are you content out there?

BIFF. [With rising agitation.] Hap, I've had twenty or thirty different kinds of jobs since I left home before the war, and it always turns out the same. I just realized it lately. In Nebraska when I herded cattle, and the Dakotas, and Arizona, and now in Texas. It's why I came home now, I guess, because I realized it. This farm I work on, it's spring there now, see? And they've got about fifteen new colts. There's nothing more inspiring or—beautiful than the sight of a mare and a new colt. And it's cool there now, see? Texas is cool now, and it's spring. And whenever spring comes to where I am, I suddenly get the feeling, my God, I'm not gettin' anywhere! What the hell am I doing, playing around with horses, twenty-eight dollars a week! I'm thirty-four years old, I oughta be makin' my future. That's when I come running home. And now, I get here, and I don't know what to do with myself. [After a pause.] I've always made a point of not wasting my life, and everytime I come back here I know that all I've done is to waste my life.

HAPPY. You're a poet, you know that, Biff? You're a—you're an idealist!

BIFF. No. I'm mixed up very bad. Maybe I oughta get married. Maybe I oughta get stuck into something. Maybe that's my trouble. I'm like a boy. I'm not married, I'm not in business, I just—I'm like a boy. Are you content, Hap? You're a success, aren't you? Are you content?

HAPPY. Hell, no!

BIFF. Why? You're making money, aren't you?

HAPPY. [Moving about with energy, expressiveness.] All I can do now is wait for the merchandise manager to die. And suppose I get to be merchandise manager? He's a good friend of mine, and he just built a terrific estate on Long Island. And he lived there about two months and sold it, and now he's building another one. He can't enjoy it once it's finished. And I know that's just what I would do. I don't know what the hell I'm workin' for. Sometimes I sit in my apartment—all alone. And I think of the rent I'm paying. And it's crazy. But then, it's what I always wanted. My own apartment, a car, and plenty of women. And still, goddammit, I'm lonely.

BIFF. [With enthusiasm.] Listen, why don't you come out West with me?

HAPPY. You and I, heh?

BIFF. Sure, maybe we could buy a ranch. Raise cattle, use our muscles. Men built like we are should be working out in the open.

HAPPY. [Avidly.] The Loman Brothers, heh?

BIFF. [With vast affection.] Sure, we'd be known all over the counties!

HAPPY. [Enthralled.] That's what I dream about, Biff. Sometimes I want to just rip my clothes off in the middle of the store and outbox that goddam merchandise manager. I mean I can outbox, outrun, and outlift anybody in that store, and I have to take orders from those common, petty sons-of-bitches till I can't stand it any more.

BIFF. I'm tellin' you, kid, if you were with me I'd be happy out there.

HAPPY. [Enthused.] See, Biff, everybody around me is so false that I'm constantly lowering my ideals . . .

BIFF. Baby, together we'd stand up for one another, we'd have someone to trust.

HAPPY. If I were around you——

BIFF. Hap, the trouble is we weren't brought up to grub for money. I don't know how to do it.

HAPPY. Neither can I!

BIFF. Then let's go!

HAPPY. The only thing is—what can you make out there?

BIFF. But look at your friend. Builds an estate and then hasn't the peace of mind to live in it.

HAPPY. Yeah, but when he walks into the store the waves part in front of him. That's fifty-two thousand dollars a year coming through the revolving door, and I got more in my pinky finger than he's got in his head.

BIFF. Yeah, but you just said——

HAPPY. I gotta show some of those pompous, self-important executives over there that Hap Loman can make the grade. I want to walk into the store the way he walks in. Then I'll go with you, Biff. We'll be together yet, I swear. But take those two we had tonight. Now weren't they gorgeous creatures?

BIFF. Yeah, yeah, most gorgeous I've had in years.

HAPPY. I get that any time I want, Biff. Whenever I feel disgusted. The only trouble is, it gets like bowling or something. I just keep knockin' them over and it doesn't mean anything. You still run around a lot?

BIFF. Naa. I'd like to find a girl—steady, somebody with substance.

HAPPY. That's what I long for.

BIFF. Go on! You'd never come home.

HAPPY. I would! Somebody with character, with resistance! Like Mom, y'know? You're gonna call me a bastard when I tell you this. That girl Charlotte I was with tonight is engaged to be married in five weeks. [*He tries on his new hat.*]

BIFF. No kiddin'!

HAPPY. Sure, the guy's in line for the vice-presidency of the store. I don't know what gets into me, maybe I just have an overdeveloped sense of competition or something, but I went and ruined her, and furthermore I can't get rid of her. And he's the third executive I've done that to. Isn't that a crummy characteristic? And to top it all, I go to their weddings! [*Indignantly, but laughing.*] Like I'm not supposed to take bribes. Manufacturers offer me a hundred-dollar bill now and then to throw an order their way. You know how honest I am, but it's like this girl, see. I hate myself for it. Because I don't want the girl, and, still, I take it and—I love it!

BIFF. Let's go to sleep.

HAPPY. I guess we didn't settle anything, heh?

BIFF. I just got one idea that I think I'm going to try.

HAPPY. What's that?

BIFF. Remember Bill Oliver?

HAPPY. Sure, Oliver is very big now. You want to work for him again?

BIFF No, but when I quit he said something to me.

He put his arm on my shoulder, and he said, "Biff, if you ever need anything, come to me."

HAPPY. I remember that. That sounds good.

BIFF. I think I'll go to see him. If I could get ten thousand or even seven or eight thousand dollars I could buy a beautiful ranch.

HAPPY. I bet he'd back you. 'Cause he thought highly of you, Biff. I mean, they all do. You're well liked, Biff. That's why I say to come back here, and we both have the apartment. And I'm tellin' you, Biff, any babe you want . . .

BIFF. No, with a ranch I could do the work I like and still be something. I just wonder, though. I wonder if Oliver still thinks I stole that carton of basketballs.

HAPPY. Oh, he probably forgot that long ago. It's almost ten years. You're too sensitive. Anyway, he didn't really fire you.

BIFF. Well, I think he was going to. I think that's why I quit. I was never sure whether he knew or not. I know he thought the world of me, though. I was the only one he'd let lock up the place.

WILLY. [*Below.*] You gonna wash the engine, Biff?

HAPPY. Shh!

[BIFF *looks at* HAPPY, *who is gazing down, listening.* WILLY *is mumbling in the parlor.*]

HAPPY. You hear that?

[*They listen.* WILLY *laughs warmly.*]

BIFF. [*Growing angry.*] Doesn't he know Mom can hear that?

WILLY. Don't get your sweater dirty, Biff!

[*A look of pain crosses* BIFF's *face.*]

HAPPY. Isn't that terrible? Don't leave again, will you? You'll find a job here. You gotta stick around. I don't know what to do about him, it's getting embarrassing.

WILLY. What a simonizing job!

BIFF. Mom's hearing that!

WILLY. No kiddin', Biff, you got a date? Wonderful!

HAPPY. Go on to sleep. But talk to him in the morning, will you?

BIFF. [*Reluctantly getting into bed.*] With her in the house. Brother!

HAPPY. [*Getting into bed.*] I wish you'd have a good talk with him.

[*The light on their room begins to fade.*]

BIFF. [*To himself in bed.*] That selfish, stupid . . .

HAPPY. Sh . . . Sleep, Biff.

[*Their light is out. Well before they have finished speaking,* WILLY's *form is dimly seen below in the darkened kitchen. He opens the refrigerator, searches in there, and takes out a bottle of milk. The apartment houses are fading out, and the entire house and sur-*

roundings become covered with leaves. Music insinuates itself as the leaves appear.]

WILLY. Just wanna be careful with those girls, Biff, that's all. Don't make any promises. No promises of any kind. Because a girl, y'know, they always believe what you tell 'em, and you're very young, Biff; you're too young to be talking seriously to girls.

[*Light rises on the kitchen.* WILLY, *talking, shuts the refrigerator door and comes downstage to the kitchen table. He pours milk into a glass. He is totally immersed in himself, smiling faintly.*]

WILLY. Too young entirely, Biff. You want to watch your schooling first. Then when you're all set, there'll be plenty of girls for a boy like you. [*He smiles broadly at a kitchen chair.*] That so? The girls pay for you? [*He laughs.*] Boy, you must really be makin' a hit.

[WILLY *is gradually addressing—psysically—a point offstage, speaking through the wall of the kitchen, and his voice has been rising in volume to that of a normal conversation.*]

WILLY. I been wondering why you polish the car so careful. Ha! Don't leave the hubcaps, boys. Get the chamois to the hubcaps. Happy, use newspaper on the windows, it's the easiest thing. Show him how to do it, Biff! You see, Happy? Pad it up, use it like a pad. That's it, that's it, good work. You're doin' all right, Hap. [*He pauses, then nods in approbation for a few seconds, then looks upward.*] Biff, first thing we gotta do when we get time is clip that big branch over the house. Afraid it's gonna fall in a storm and hit the roof. Tell you what. We get a rope and sling her around, and then we climb up there with a couple of saws and take her down. Soon as you finish the car, boys, I wanna see ya. I got a surprise for you, boys.

BIFF. [*Offstage.*] Whatta ya got, Dad?

WILLY. No, you finish first. Never leave a job till you're finished—remember that. [*Looking toward the "big trees."*] Biff, up in Albany I saw a beautiful hammock. I think I'll buy it next trip, and we'll hang it right between those two elms. Wouldn't that be something? Just swingin' there under those branches. Boy, that would be . . .

[YOUNG BIFF *and* YOUNG HAPPY *appear from the direction* WILLY *was addressing.* HAPPY *carries rags and a pail of water.* BIFF, *wearing a sweater with a block "S," carries a football.*]

BIFF. [*Pointing in the direction of the car offstage.*] How's that, Pop, professional?

WILLY. Terrific. Terrific job, boys. Good work, Biff.

HAPPY. Where's the surprise, Pop?

WILLY. In the back seat of the car.

HAPPY. Boy! [*He runs off.*]

BIFF. What is it, Dad? Tell me, what'd you buy?

WILLY. [*Laughing, cuffs him.*] Never mind, something I want you to have.

BIFF. [*Turns and starts off.*] What is it, Hap?

HAPPY. [*Offstage.*] It's a punching bag!

BIFF. Oh, Pop!

WILLY. It's got Gene Tunney's signature on it!

[HAPPY *runs onstage with a punching bag.*]

BIFF. Gee, how'd you know we wanted a punching bag?

WILLY. Well, it's the finest thing for the timing.

HAPPY. [*Lies down on his back and pedals with his feet.*] I'm losing weight, you notice, Pop?

WILLY. [*To* HAPPY.] Jumping rope is good too.

BIFF. Did you see the new football I got?

WILLY. [*Examining the ball.*] Where'd you get a new ball?

BIFF. The coach told me to practice my passing.

WILLY. That so? And he gave you the ball, heh?

BIFF. Well, I borrowed it from the locker room.

[*He laughs confidentially.*]

WILLY. [*Laughing with him at the theft.*] I want you to return that.

HAPPY. I told you he wouldn't like it!

BIFF. [*Angrily.*] Well, I'm bringing it back!

WILLY. [*Stopping the incipient argument, to* HAPPY.] Sure, he's gotta practice with a regulation ball, doesn't he? [*To* BIFF.] Coach'll probably congratulate you on your initiative!

BIFF. Oh, he keeps congratulating my initiative all the time, Pop.

WILLY. That's because he likes you. If somebody else took that ball there'd be an uproar. So what's the report, boys, what's the report?

BIFF. Where'd you go this time, Dad? Gee, we were lonesome for you.

WILLY. [*Pleased, puts an arm around each boy and they come down to the apron.*] Lonesome, heh?

BIFF. Missed you every minute.

WILLY. Don't say? Tell you a secret, boys. Don't breathe it to a soul. Someday I'll have my own business, and I'll never have to leave home any more.

HAPPY. Like Uncle Charley, heh?

WILLY. Bigger than Uncle Charley! Because Charley is not—liked. He's liked, but he's not—well liked.

BIFF. Where'd you go this time, Dad?

WILLY. Well, I got on the road, and I went north to Providence. Met the Mayor.

BIFF. The Mayor of Providence!

WILLY. He was sitting in the hotel lobby.

BIFF. What'd he say?

WILLY. He said, "Morning!" And I said, "You got a fine city here, Mayor." And then he had coffee with me. And then I went to Waterbury. Waterbury is a fine city. Big clock city, the famous Waterbury clock. Sold a nice bill there. And then Boston—Boston is the cradle of the Revolution. A fine city. And a couple of other towns in Mass., and on to Portland and Bangor and straight home!

BIFF. Gee, I'd love to go with you some time, Dad.

WILLY. Soon as summer comes.

HAPPY. Promise?

WILLY. You and Hap and I, and I'll show you all the towns. America is full of beautiful towns and fine, upstanding people. And they know me, boys, they know me up and down New England. The finest people. And when I bring you fellas up, there'll be open sesame for all of us, 'cause one thing, boys: I have friends. I can park my car in any street in New England, and the cops protect it like their own. This summer, heh?

BIFF *and* HAPPY. [*Together.*] Yeah! You bet!

WILLY. We'll take our bathing suits.

HAPPY. We'll carry your bags, Pop!

WILLY. Oh, won't that be something! Me comin' into the Boston stores with you boys carryin' my bags. What a sensation!

[BIFF *is prancing around, practicing passing the ball.*]

WILLY. You nervous, Biff, about the game?

BIFF. Not if you're gonna be there.

WILLY. What do they say about you in school, now that they made you captain?

HAPPY. There's a crowd of girls behind him every-time the classes change.

BIFF. [*Taking* WILLY's *hand.*] This Saturday, Pop, this Saturday—just for you, I'm going to break through for a touchdown.

HAPPY. You're supposed to pass.

BIFF. I'm takin' one play for Pop. You watch me, Pop, and when I take off my helmet, that means I'm breakin' out. Then you watch me crash through that line!

WILLY. [*Kisses* BIFF.] Oh, wait'll I tell this in Boston!

[BERNARD *enters in knickers. He is younger than* BIFF, *earnest and loyal, a worried boy.*]

BERNARD. Biff, where are you? You're supposed to study with me today.

WILLY. Hey, looka Bernard. What're you lookin' so anemic about, Bernard?

BERNARD. He's gotta study, Uncle Willy. He's got Regents next week.

HAPPY. [*Tauntingly, spinning* BERNARD *around.*] Let's box, Bernard!

BERNARD. Biff! [*He gets away from* HAPPY.] Listen, Biff, I heard Mr. Birnbaum say that if you don't start studyin' math he's gonna flunk you, and you won't graduate. I heard him!

WILLY. You better study with him, Biff. Go ahead now.

BERNARD. I heard him!

BIFF. Oh, Pop, you didn't see my sneakers!

[*He holds up a foot for* WILLY *to look at.*]

WILLY. Hey, that's a beautiful job of printing!

BERNARD. [*Wiping his glasses.*] Just because he printed University of Virginia on his sneakers doesn't mean they've got to graduate him, Uncle Willy!

WILLY. [*Angrily.*] What're you talking about? With scholarships to three universities, they're gonna flunk him?

BERNARD. But I heard Mr. Birnbaum say——

WILLY. Don't be a pest, Bernard! [*To his boys.*] What an anemic!

BERNARD. Okay, I'm waiting for you in my house, Biff.

[BERNARD *goes off. The* LOMANS *laugh.*]

WILLY. Bernard is not well liked, is he?

BIFF. He's liked, but he's not well liked.

HAPPY. That's right, Pop.

WILLY. That's just what I mean. Bernard can get the best marks in school, y'understand, but when he gets out in the business world, y'understand, you are going to be five times ahead of him. That's why I thank Almighty God you're both built like Adonises. Because the man who makes an appearance in the business world, the man who creates personal interest, is the man who gets ahead. Be liked and you will never want. You take me, for instance. I never have to wait in line to see a buyer. "Willy Loman is here!" That's all they have to know, and I go right through.

BIFF. Did you knock them dead, Pop?

WILLY. Knocked 'em cold in Providence, slaughtered 'em in Boston.

HAPPY. [*On his back, pedaling again.*] I'm losing weight; you notice, Pop?

[LINDA *enters, as of old, a ribbon in her hair, carrying a basket of washing.*]

LINDA. [*With youthful energy.*] Hello, dear!

WILLY. Sweetheart!

LINDA. How'd the Chevvy run?

WILLY. Chevrolet, Linda, is the greatest car ever built. [*To the boys.*] Since when do you let your mother carry wash up the stairs?

BIFF. Grab hold there, boy!

HAPPY. Where to, Mom?

LINDA. Hang them up on the line. And you better go down to your friends, Biff. The cellar is full of boys. They don't know what to do with themselves.

BIFF. Ah, when Pop comes home they can wait!

WILLY. [*Laughs appreciatively.*] You better go down and tell them what to do, Biff.

BIFF. I think I'll have them sweep out the furnace room.

WILLY. Good work, Biff.

BIFF. [*Goes through wall-line of kitchen to doorway at back and calls down.*] Fellas! Everybody sweep out the furnace room! I'll be right down!

VOICES. All right! Okay, Biff.

BIFF. George and Sam and Frank, come out back! We're hangin' up the wash! Come on, Hap, on the double!

[*He and* HAPPY *carry out the basket.*]

LINDA. The way they obey him!

WILLY. Well, that's training, the training. I'm tellin' you, I was sellin' thousands and thousands, but I had to come home.

LINDA. Oh, the whole block'll be at that game. Did you sell anything?

WILLY. I did five hundred gross in Providence and seven hundred gross in Boston.

LINDA. No! Wait a minute, I've got a pencil. [*She pulls pencil and paper out of her apron pocket.*] That makes your commission . . . Two hundred—my God! Two hundred and twelve dollars!

WILLY. Well, I didn't figure it yet, but . . .

LINDA. How much did you do?

WILLY. Well, I—I did—about a hundred and eighty gross in Providence. Well, no—it came to—roughly two hundred gross on the whole trip.

LINDA. [*Without hesitation.*] Two hundred gross. That's . . . [*She figures.*]

WILLY. The trouble was that three of the stores were half closed for inventory in Boston. Otherwise I woulda broke records.

LINDA. Well, it makes seventy dollars and some pennies. That's very good.

WILLY. What do we owe?

LINDA. Well on the first there's sixteen dollars on the refrigerator——

WILLY. Why sixteen?

LINDA. Well, the fan belt broke, so it was a dollar eighty.

WILLY. But it's brand new.

LINDA. Well, the man said that's the way it is. Till they work themselves in, y'know.

[*They move through the wall-line into the kitchen.*]

WILLY. I hope we didn't get stuck on that machine.

LINDA. They got the biggest ads of any of them!

WILLY. I know, it's a fine machine. What else?

LINDA. Well, there's nine-sixty for the washing machine. And for the vacuum cleaner there's three and a half due on the fifteenth. Then the roof; you got twenty-one dollars remaining.

WILLY. It don't leak, does it?

LINDA. No, they did a wonderful job. Then you owe Frank for the carburetor.

WILLY. I'm not going to pay that man! That goddam Chevrolet, they ought to prohibit the manufacture of that car!

LINDA. Well, you owe him three and a half. And odds and ends, comes to around a hundred and twenty dollars by the fifteenth.

WILLY. A hundred and twenty dollars! My God, if business don't pick up I don't know what I'm gonna do!

LINDA. Well, next week you'll do better.

WILLY. Oh, I'll knock 'em dead next week. I'll go to Hartford. I'm very well liked in Hartford. You know, the trouble is, Linda, people don't seem to take to me. [*They move onto the forestage.*]

LINDA. Oh, don't be foolish.

WILLY. I know it when I walk in. They seem to laugh at me.

LINDA. Why? Why would they laugh at you? Don't talk that way, Willy.

[WILLY *moves to the edge of the stage.* LINDA *goes into the kitchen and starts to darn stockings.*]

WILLY. I don't know the reason for it, but they just pass me by. I'm not noticed.

LINDA. But you're doing wonderful, dear. You're making seventy to a hundred dollars a week.

WILLY. But I gotta be at it ten, twelve hours a day. Other men—I don't know—they do it easier. I don't know why—I can't stop myself—I talk too much. A man oughta come in with a few words. One thing about Charley. He's a man of few words, and they respect him.

LINDA. You don't talk too much, you're just lively.

WILLY. [*Smiling.*] Well, I figure, what the hell, life is short, a couple of jokes. [*To himself.*] I joke too much! [*The smile goes.*]

LINDA. Why? You're——

WILLY. I'm fat. I'm very—foolish to look at, Linda. I didn't tell you, but Christmas time I happened to be calling on F. H. Stewarts', and a salesman I know, as I was going in to see the buyer I heard him say something about—walrus. And I—I cracked him right across the face. I won't take that. I simply will not take that. But they do laugh at me. I know that.

LINDA. Darling . . .

WILLY. I gotta overcome it. I know I gotta overcome it. I'm not dressing to advantage, maybe.

LINDA. Willy, darling, you're the handsomest man in the world——

WILLY. Oh, no, Linda.

LINDA. To me you are. [*Slight pause.*] The handsomest.

[*From the darkness is heard the laughter of a woman.* WILLY *doesn't turn to it, but it continues through* LINDA's *lines.*]

LINDA. And the boys, Willy. Few men are idolized by their children the way you are.

[*Music is heard as behind a scrim, to the left of of the house,* THE WOMAN, *dimly seen, is dressing.*]

WILLY. [*With great feeling.*] You're the best there is, Linda, you're a pal, you know that? On the road— on the road I want to grab you sometimes and just kiss the life outa you.

[*The laughter is loud now, and he moves into a brightening area at the left, where* THE WOMAN *has come from behind the scrim and is standing, putting on her hat, looking into a "mirror" and laughing.*]

WILLY. 'Cause I get so lonely—especially when business is bad and there's nobody to talk to. I get the feeling that I'll never sell anything again, that I won't make a living for you, or a business, a business for the boys. [*He talks through* THE WOMAN's *subsiding laughter;* THE WOMAN *primps at the "mirror."*] There's so much I want to make for——

THE WOMAN. Me? You didn't make me, Willy. I picked you.

WILLY. [*Pleased.*] You picked me?

THE WOMAN. [*Who is quite proper-looking,* WILLY's *age.*] I did. I've been sitting at that desk watching all the salesmen go by, day in, day out. But you've got such a sense of humor, and we do have such a good time together, don't we?

WILLY. Sure, sure. [*He takes her in his arms.*] Why do you have to go now?

THE WOMAN. It's two o'clock . . .

WILLY. No, come on in! [*He pulls her.*]

THE WOMAN. . . . my sisters'll be scandalized. When'll you be back?

WILLY. Oh, two weeks about. Will you come up again?

THE WOMAN. Sure thing. You do make me laugh. It's good for me. [*She squeezes his arm, kisses him.*] And I think you're a wonderful man.

WILLY. You picked me, heh?

THE WOMAN. Sure. Because you're so sweet. And such a kidder.

WILLY. Well, I'll see you next time I'm in Boston.

THE WOMAN. I'll put you right through to the buyers.

WILLY. [*Slapping her bottom.*] Right. Well, bottoms up!

THE WOMAN. [*Slaps him gently and laughs.*] You just kill me, Willy. [*He suddenly grabs her and kisses her roughly.*] You kill me. And thanks for the stockings. I love a lot of stockings. Well, good night.

WILLY. Good night. And keep your pores open!

THE WOMAN. Oh, Willy!

[THE WOMAN *bursts out laughing, and* LINDA's *laughter blends in.* THE WOMAN *disappears into the dark. Now the area at the kitchen table brightens.* LINDA *is sitting where she was at the kitchen table, but now is mending a pair of her silk stockings.*]

LINDA. You are, Willy. The handsomest man. You've got no reason to feel that——

WILLY. [*Coming out of* THE WOMAN's *dimming area and going over to* LINDA.] I'll make it all up to you, Linda, I'll——

LINDA. There's nothing to make up, dear. You're doing fine, better than——

WILLY. [*Noticing her mending.*] What's that?

LINDA. Just mending my stockings. They're so expensive——

WILLY. [*Angrily, taking them from her.*] I won't have you mending stockings in this house! Now throw them out!

[LINDA *puts the stockings in her pocket.*]

BERNARD. [*Entering on the run.*] Where is he? If he doesn't study!

WILLY. [*Moving to the forestage, with great agitation.*] You'll give him the answers!

BERNARD. I do, but I can't on a Regents! That's a state exam! They're liable to arrest me!

WILLY. Where is he? I'll whip him, I'll whip him!

LINDA. And he'd better give back that football, Willy, it's not nice.

WILLY. Biff! Where is he? Why is he taking everything?

LINDA. He's too rough with the girls, Willy. All the mothers are afraid of him!

WILLY. I'll whip him!

BERNARD. He's driving the car without a license!

[THE WOMAN's *laugh is heard.*]

WILLY. Shut up!

LINDA. All the mothers——

WILLY. Shut up!

BERNARD. [*Backing quietly away and out.*] Mr. Birnbaum says he's stuck up.

WILLY. Get outa here!

BERNARD. If he doesn't buckle down he'll flunk math! [*He goes off.*]

LINDA. He's right, Willy, you've gotta——

WILLY. [*Exploding at her.*] There's nothing the matter with him! You want him to be a worm like Bernard? He's got spirit, personality . . .

[*As he speaks,* LINDA, *almost in tears, exits into the living-room.* WILLY *is alone in the kitchen, wilting and staring. The leaves are gone. It is night again, and the apartment houses look down from behind.*]

WILLY. Loaded with it. Loaded! What is he stealing? He's giving it back, isn't he? Why is he stealing?

What did I tell him? I never in my life told him anything but decent things.

[HAPPY *in pajamas has come down the stairs;* WILLY *suddenly becomes aware of* HAPPY'S *presence.*]

HAPPY. Let's go now, come on.

WILLY. [*Sitting down at the kitchen table.*] Huh! Why did she have to wax the floors herself? Everytime she waxes the floors she keels over. She knows that!

HAPPY. Shh! Take it easy. What brought you back tonight?

WILLY. I got an awful scare. Nearly hit a kid in Yonkers. God! Why didn't I go to Alaska with my brother Ben that time! Ben! That man was a genius, that man was success incarnate! What a mistake! He begged me to go.

HAPPY. Well, there's no use in——

WILLY. You guys! There was a man started with the clothes on his back and ended up with diamond mines!

HAPPY. Boy, someday I'd like to know how he did it.

WILLY. What's the mystery? The man knew what he wanted and went out and got it! Walked into a jungle, and comes out the age of twenty-one, and he's rich! The world is an oyster, but you don't crack it open on a mattress!

HAPPY. Pop, I told you I'm gonna retire you for life.

WILLY. You'll retire me for life on seventy goddam dollars a week? And your women and your car and your apartment, and you'll retire me for life! Christ's sake, I couldn't get past Yonkers today! Where are you guys, where are you? The woods are burning! I can't drive a car!

[CHARLEY *has appeared in the doorway. He is a large man, slow of speech, laconic, immovable. In all he says, despite what he says, there is pity, and, now, trepidation. He has a robe over pajamas, slippers on his feet. He enters the kitchen.*]

CHARLEY. Everything all right?

HAPPY. Yeah, Charley, everything's . . .

WILLY. What's the matter?

CHARLEY. I heard some noise. I thought something happened. Can't we do something about the walls? You sneeze in here, and in my house hats blow off.

HAPPY. Let's go to bed, Dad. Come on.

[CHARLEY *signals to* HAPPY *to go.*]

WILLY. You go ahead. I'm not tired at the moment.

HAPPY. [*To* WILLY.] Take it easy, huh?

[*He exits.*]

WILLY. What're you doin' up?

CHARLEY. [*Sitting down at the kitchen table opposite* WILLY.] Couldn't sleep good. I had a heartburn.

WILLY. Well, you don't know how to eat.

CHARLEY. I eat with my mouth.

WILLY. No, you're ignorant. You gotta know about vitamins and things like that.

CHARLEY. Come on, let's shoot. Tire you out a little.

WILLY. [*Hesitantly.*] All right. You got cards?

CHARLEY. [*Taking a deck from his pocket.*] Yeah, I got them. Someplace. What is it with those vitamins?

WILLY. [*Dealing.*] They build up your bones. Chemistry.

CHARLEY. Yeah, but there's no bones in a heartburn.

WILLY. What are you talkin' about? Do you know the first thing about it?

CHARLEY. Don't get insulted.

WILLY. Don't talk about something you don't know anything about.

[*They are playing. Pause.*]

CHARLEY. What're you doin' home?

WILLY. A little trouble with the car.

CHARLEY. Oh. [*Pause.*] I'd like to take a trip to California.

WILLY. Don't say.

CHARLEY. You want a job?

WILLY. I got a job; I told you that. [*After a slight pause.*] What the hell are you offering me a job for?

CHARLEY. Don't get insulted.

WILLY. Don't insult me.

CHARLEY. I don't see no sense in it. You don't have to go on this way.

WILLY. I got a good job. [*Slight pause.*] What do you keep comin' in here for?

CHARLEY. You want me to go?

WILLY. [*After a pause, withering.*] I can't understand it. He's going back to Texas again. What the hell is that?

CHARLEY. Let him go.

WILLY. I got nothin' to give him, Charley. I'm clean, I'm clean.

CHARLEY. He won't starve. None a them starve. Forget about him.

WILLY. Then what have I got to remember?

CHARLEY. You take it too hard. To hell with it. When a deposit bottle is broken you don't get your nickel back.

WILLY. That's easy enough for you to say.

CHARLEY. That ain't easy for me to say.

WILLY. Did you see the ceiling I put up in the living-room?

CHARLEY. Yeah, that's a piece of work. To put up a ceiling is a mystery to me. How do you do it?

WILLY. What's the difference?

CHARLEY. Well, talk about it.

WILLY. You gonna put up a ceiling?

CHARLEY. How could I put up a ceiling?

WILLY. Then what the hell are you bothering me for?

CHARLEY. You're insulted again.

WILLY. A man who can't handle tools is not a man. You're disgusting.

CHARLEY. Don't call me disgusting, Willy.

[UNCLE BEN, *carrying a valise and an umbrella, enters the forestage from around the right corner of the house. He is a stolid man, in his sixties, with a mustache and an authoritative air. He is utterly certain of his destiny, and there is an aura of far places about him. He enters exactly as* WILLY *speaks.*]

WILLY. I'm getting awfully tired, Ben.

[BEN'S *music is heard.* BEN *looks around at everything.*]

CHARLEY. Good, keep playing; you'll sleep better. Did you call me Ben?

[BEN *looks at his watch.*]

WILLY. That's funny. For a second there you reminded me of my brother Ben.

BEN. I only have a few minutes.

[*He strolls, inspecting the place.* WILLY *and* CHARLEY *continue playing.*]

CHARLEY. You never heard from him again, heh? Since that time?

WILLY. Didn't Linda tell you? Couple of weeks ago we got a letter from his wife in Africa. He died.

CHARLEY. That so.

BEN. [*Chuckling.*] So this is Brooklyn, eh?

CHARLEY. Maybe you're in for some of his money.

WILLY. Naa, he had seven sons. There's just one opportunity I had with that man . . .

BEN. I must make a train, William. There are several properties I'm looking at in Alaska.

WILLY. Sure, sure! If I'd gone with him to Alaska that time, everything would've been totally different.

CHARLEY. Go on, you'd froze to death up there.

WILLY. What're you talking about?

BEN. Opportunity is tremendous in Alaska, William. Surprised you're not up there.

WILLY. Sure, tremendous.

CHARLEY. Heh?

WILLY. There was the only man I ever met who knew the answers.

CHARLEY. Who?

BEN. How are you all?

WILLY. [*Taking a pot, smiling.*] Fine, fine.

CHARLEY. Pretty sharp tonight.

BEN. Is Mother living with you?

WILLY. No, she died a long time ago.

CHARLEY. Who?

BEN. That's too bad. Fine specimen of a lady, Mother.

WILLY. [*To* CHARLEY.] Heh?

BEN. I'd hoped to see the old girl.

CHARLEY. Who died?

BEN. Heard anything from Father, have you?

WILLY. [*Unnerved.*] What do you mean, who died?

CHARLEY. [*Taking a pot.*] What're you talkin' about?

BEN. [*Looking at his watch.*] William, it's half-past eight!

WILLY. [*As though to dispel his confusion he angrily stops* CHARLEY'S *hand.*] That's my build!

CHARLEY. I put the ace——

WILLY. If you don't know how to play the game I'm not gonna throw my money away on you!

CHARLEY. [*Rising.*] It was my ace, for God's sake!

WILLY. I'm through, I'm through!

BEN. When did Mother die?

WILLY. Long ago. Since the beginning you never knew how to play cards.

CHARLEY. [*Picks up the cards and goes to the door.*] All right! Next time I'll bring a deck with five aces.

WILLY. I don't play that kind of game!

CHARLEY. [*Turning to him.*] You ought to be ashamed of yourself!

WILLY. Yeah?

CHARLEY. Yeah! [*He goes out.*]

WILLY. [*Slamming the door after him.*] Ignoramus!

BEN. [*As* WILLY *comes toward him through the wall-line of the kitchen.*] So you're William.

WILLY. [*Shaking* BEN'S *hand.*] Ben! I've been waiting for you so long! What's the answer? How did you do it?

BEN. Oh, there's a story in that.

[LINDA *enters the forestage, as of old, carrying the wash basket.*]

LINDA. Is this Ben?

BEN. [*Gallantly.*] How do you do, my dear.

LINDA. Where've you been all these years? Willy's always wondered why you——

WILLY. [*Pulling* BEN *away from her impatiently.*] Where is Dad? Didn't you follow him? How did you get started?

BEN. Well, I don't know how much you remember.

WILLY. Well, I was just a baby, of course, only three or four years old——

BEN. Three years and eleven months.

WILLY. What a memory, Ben!

BEN. I have many enterprises, William, and I have never kept books.

WILLY. I remember I was sitting under the wagon in—was it Nebraska?

BEN. It was South Dakota, and I gave you a bunch of wild flowers.

WILLY. I remember you walking away down some open road.

BEN. [*Laughing.*] I was going to find Father in Alaska.

WILLY. Where is he?

BEN. At that age I had a very faulty view of geography, William. I discovered after a few days that I was heading due south; so instead of Alaska, I ended up in Africa.

LINDA. Africa!

WILLY. The Gold Coast!

BEN. Principally diamond mines.

LINDA. Diamond mines!

BEN. Yes, my dear. But I've only a few minutes——

WILLY. No! Boys! Boys! [YOUNG BIFF *and* HAPPY *appear.*] Listen to this. This is your Uncle Ben, a great man! Tell my boys, Ben!

BEN. Why, boys, when I was seventeen I walked into the jungle, and when I was twenty-one I walked out. [*He laughs.*] And by God I was rich.

WILLY. [*To the boys.*] You see what I been talking about? The greatest things can happen!

BEN. [*Glancing at his watch.*] I have an appointment in Ketchikan Tuesday week.

WILLY. No, Ben! Please tell about Dad. I want my boys to hear. I want them to know the kind of stock they spring from. All I remember is a man with a big beard, and I was in Mamma's lap, sitting around a fire, and some kind of high music.

BEN. His flute. He played the flute.

WILLY. Sure, the flute, that's right!

[*New music is heard, a high, rollicking tune.*]

BEN. Father was a very great and a very wild-hearted man. We would start in Boston, and he'd toss the whole family into the wagon, and then he'd drive the team right across the country; through Ohio, and Indiana, Michigan, Illinois, and all the Western states. And we'd stop in the towns and sell the flutes that he'd made on the way. Great inventor, Father. With one gadget he made more in a week than a man like you could make in a lifetime.

WILLY. That's just the way I'm bringing them up, Ben—rugged, well liked, all-around.

BEN. Yeah? [*To* BIFF.] Hit that, boy—hard as you can. [*He pounds his stomach.*]

BIFF. Oh, no, sir!

BEN. [*Taking boxing stance.*] Come on, get to me! [*He laughs.*]

WILLY. Go to it, Biff! Go ahead, show him!

BIFF. Okay! [*He cocks his fists and starts in.*]

LINDA. [*To* WILLY.] Why must he fight, dear?

BEN. [*Sparring with* BIFF.] Good boy! Good boy!

WILLY. How's that, Ben, heh?

HAPPY. Give him the left, Biff!

LINDA. Why are you fighting?

BEN. Good boy!

[*Suddenly comes in, trips* BIFF, *and stands over him, the point of his umbrella poised over* BIFF's *eye.*]

LINDA. Look out, Biff!

BIFF. Gee!

BEN. [*Patting* BIFF's *knee.*] Never fight fair with a stranger, boy. You'll never get out of the jungle that way. [*Taking* LINDA's *hand and bowing.*] It was an honor and a pleasure to meet you, Linda.

LINDA. [*Withdrawing her hand coldly, frightened.*] Have a nice—trip.

BEN [*To* WILLY.] And good luck with your—what do you do?

WILLY. Selling.

BEN. Yes. Well . . .

[*He raises his hand in farewell to all.*]

WILLY. No, Ben, I don't want you to think . . . [*He takes* BEN's *arm to show him.*] It's Brooklyn, I know, but we hunt too.

BEN. Really, now.

WILLY. Oh, sure, there's snakes and rabbits and—that's why I moved out here. Why, Biff can fell any one of these trees in no time! Boys! Go right over to where they're building the apartment house and get some sand. We're gonna rebuild the entire front stoop right now! Watch this, Ben!

BIFF. Yes, sir! On the double, Hap!

HAPPY. [*As he and* BIFF *run off.*] I lost weight, Pop, you notice?

[CHARLEY *enters in knickers, even before the boys are gone.*]

CHARLEY. Listen, if they steal any more from that building the watchman'll put the cops on them!

LINDA. [*To* WILLY.] Don't let Biff . . . [BEN *laughs lustily.*]

WILLY. You shoulda seen the lumber they brought home last week. At least a dozen six-by-tens worth all kinds of money.

CHARLEY. Listen, if that watchman——

WILLY. I gave them hell, understand. But I got a couple of fearless characters there.

CHARLEY. Willy, the jails are full of fearless characters.

BEN. [*Clapping* WILLY *on the back, with a laugh at* CHARLEY.] And the stock exchange, friend!

WILLY. [*Joining in* BEN's *laughter.*] Where are the rest of your pants?

CHARLEY. My wife bought them.

WILLY. Now all you need is a golf club and you can go upstairs and go to sleep. [*To* BEN.] Great athlete! Between him and his son Bernard they can't hammer a nail!

BERNARD. [*Rushing in.*] The watchman's chasing Biff!

WILLY. [*Angrily.*] Shut up! He's not stealing anything!

LINDA. [*Alarmed, hurrying off left.*] Where is he? Biff, dear! [*She exits.*]

WILLY. [*Moving toward the left, away from* BEN.] There's nothing wrong. What's the matter with you?

BEN. Nervy boy. Good!

WILLY. [*Laughing.*] Oh, nerves of iron, that Biff!

CHARLEY. Don't know what it is. My New England man comes back and he's bleedin', they murdered him up there.

WILLY. It's contacts, Charley, I got important contacts!

CHARLEY. [*Sarcastically.*] Glad to hear it, Willy. Come in later; we'll shoot a little casino. I'll take some of your Portland money. [*He laughs at* WILLY *and exits.*]

WILLY. [*Turning to* BEN.] Business is bad, it's murderous. But not for me, of course.

BEN. I'll stop by on my way back to Africa.

WILLY. [*Longingly.*] Can't you stay a few days? You're just what I need, Ben, because I—I have a fine position here, but I—well, Dad left when I was such a baby and I never had a chance to talk to him and I still feel—kind of temporary about myself.

BEN. I'll be late for my train.

[*They are at opposite ends of the stage.*]

WILLY. Ben, my boys—can't we talk? They'd go into the jaws of hell for me, see, but I——

BEN. William, you're being first-rate with your boys. Outstanding, manly chaps!

WILLY. [*Hanging on to his words.*] Oh, Ben, that's good to hear! Because sometimes I'm afraid that I'm not teaching them the right kind of—— Ben, how should I teach them?

BEN. [*Giving great weight to each word, and with a certain vicious audacity.*] William, when I walked into the jungle, I was seventeen. When I walked out I was twenty-one. And, by God, I was rich!

[*He goes off into darkness around the right corner of the house.*]

WILLY. . . . was rich! That's just the spirit I want to imbue them with! To walk into a jungle! I was right! I was right! I was right!

[BEN *is gone, but* WILLY *is still speaking to him as* LINDA, *in nightgown and robe, enters the kitchen, glances around for* WILLY, *then goes to the door of the house, looks out and sees him. Comes down to his left. He looks at her.*]

LINDA. Willy, dear? Willy?

WILLY. I was right!

LINDA. Did you have some cheese? [*He can't answer.*] It's very late, darling. Come to bed, heh?

WILLY. [*Looking straight up.*] Gotta break your neck to see a star in this yard.

LINDA. You coming in?

WILLY. Whatever happened to that diamond watch fob? Remember? When Ben came from Africa that time? Didn't he give me a watch fob with a diamond in it?

LINDA. You pawned it, dear. Twelve, thirteen years ago. For Biff's radio correspondence course.

WILLY. Gee, that was a beautiful thing. I'll take a walk.

LINDA. But you're in your slippers.

WILLY. [*Starting to go around the house at the left.*] I was right! I was! [*Half to* LINDA, *as he goes, shaking his head.*] What a man! There was a man worth talking to. I was right!

LINDA. [*Calling after* WILLY.] But in your slippers, Willy!

[WILLY *is almost gone when* BIFF, *in his pajamas, comes down the stairs and enters the kitchen.*]

BIFF. What is he doing out there?

LINDA. Sh!

BIFF. God Almighty, Mom, how long has he been doing this?

LINDA. Don't, he'll hear you.

BIFF. What the hell is the matter with him?

LINDA. It'll pass by morning.

BIFF. Shouldn't we do anything?

LINDA. Oh, my dear, you should do a lot of things, but there's nothing to do, so go to sleep.

[HAPPY *comes down the stairs and sits on the steps.*]

HAPPY. I never heard him so loud, Mom.

LINDA. Well, come around more often; you'll hear him.

[*She sits down at the table and mends the lining of* WILLY's *jacket.*]

BIFF. Why didn't you ever write me about this, Mom?

LINDA. How would I write to you? For over three months you had no address.

BIFF. I was on the move. But you know I thought of you all the time. You know that, don't you, pal?

LINDA. I know, dear, I know. But he likes to have a letter. Just to know that there's still a possibility for better things.

BIFF. He's not like this all the time, is he?

LINDA. It's when you come home he's always the worst.

BIFF. When I come home?

LINDA. When you write you're coming, he's all smiles, and talks about the future, and—he's just wonderful. And then the closer you seem to come, the more shaky he gets, and then, by the time you get here, he's arguing, and he seems angry at you. I think it's just that maybe he can't bring himself to—to open up to you. Why are you so hateful to each other? Why is that?

BIFF. [*Evasively.*] I'm not hateful, Mom.

LINDA. But you no sooner come in the door than you're fighting!

BIFF. I don't know why. I mean to change. I'm tryin', Mom, you understand?

LINDA. Are you home to stay now?

BIFF. I don't know. I want to look around, see what's doin'.

LINDA. Biff, you can't look around all your life, can you?

BIFF. I just can't take hold, Mom. I can't take hold of some kind of a life.

LINDA. Biff, a man is not a bird, to come and go with the springtime.

BIFF. Your hair . . . [*He touches her hair.*] Your hair got so gray.

LINDA. Oh, it's been gray since you were in high school. I just stopped dyeing it, that's all.

BIFF. Dye it again, will ya? I don't want my pal looking old. [*He smiles.*]

LINDA. You're such a boy! You think you can go away for a year and . . . You've got to get it into your head now that one day you'll knock on this door and there'll be strange people here——

BIFF. What are you talking about? You're not even sixty, Mom.

LINDA. But what about your father?

BIFF. [*Lamely.*] Well, I meant him too.

HAPPY. He admires Pop.

LINDA. Biff, dear, if you don't have any feeling for him, then you can't have any feeling for me.

BIFF. Sure I can, Mom.

LINDA. No. You can't come just to see me, because I love him. [*With a threat, but only a threat, of tears.*] He's the dearest man in the world to me, and I won't have anyone making him feel unwanted and low and blue. You've got to make up your mind now, darling, there's no leeway any more. Either he's your father and you pay him that respect, or else you're not to come here. I know he's not easy to get along with—nobody knows that better than me—but . . .

WILLY. [*From the left, with a laugh.*] Hey, hey, Biffo!

BIFF. [*Starting to go out after* WILLY.] What the hell is the matter with him? [HAPPY *stops him.*]

LINDA. Don't—don't go near him!

BIFF. Stop making excuses for him! He always, always wiped the floor with you. Never had an ounce of respect for you.

HAPPY. He's always had respect for——

BIFF. What the hell do you know about it?

HAPPY. [*Surlily.*] Just don't call him crazy!

BIFF. He's got no character—— Charley wouldn't do this. Not in his own house—spewing out that vomit from his mind.

HAPPY. Charley never had to cope with what he's got to.

BIFF. People are worse off than Willy Loman. Believe me, I've seen them!

LINDA. Then make Charley your father, Biff. You can't do that, can you? I don't say he's a great man. Willy Loman never made a lot of money. His name was never in the paper. He's not the finest character that ever lived. But he's a human being, and a terrible thing is happening to him. So attention must be paid. He's not to be allowed to fall into his grave like an old dog. Attention, attention must be finally paid to such a person. You called him crazy——

BIFF. I didn't mean——

LINDA. No, a lot of people think he's lost his balance. But you don't have to be very smart to know what his trouble is. The man is exhausted.

HAPPY. Sure!

LINDA. A small man can be just as exhausted as a great man. He works for a company thirty-six years this March, opens up unheard-of territories to their trademark, and now in his old age they take his salary away.

HAPPY. [*Indignantly.*] I didn't know that, Mom.

LINDA. You never asked, my dear! Now that you get your spending money some place else you don't trouble your mind with him.

HAPPY. But I gave you money last——

LINDA. Christmas time, fifty dollars! To fix the hot water it cost ninety-seven fifty! For five weeks he's been on straight commission, like a beginner, an unknown!

BIFF. Those ungrateful bastards!

LINDA. Are they any worse than his sons? When he brought them business, when he was young, they were glad to see him. But now his old friends, the old buyers that loved him so and always found some order to hand him in a pinch—they're all dead, retired. He used to be able to make six, seven calls a day in Boston. Now he takes his valises out of the car and puts them back and takes them out again and he's exhausted. Instead of walking he talks now. He drives seven hundred miles, and when he gets there no one knows him any more, no one welcomes him. And what goes through a man's mind, driving seven hundred miles home without having earned a cent? Why shouldn't he talk to himself? Why? When he has to go to Charley to borrow fifty dollars a week and pretend to me that it's his pay? How long can that go on? How long? You see what I'm sitting here and waiting for? And you tell me he has no character? The man who never worked a day but for your benefit? When does he get the medal for that? Is this his reward—to turn around at the age of sixty-three and find his sons, who he loved better than his life, one a philandering bum——

HAPPY. Mom!

LINDA. That's all you are, my baby! [*To* BIFF.] And you! What happened to the love you had for him? You were such pals! How you used to talk to him on the phone every night! How lonely he was till he could come home to you!

BIFF. All right, Mom. I'll live here in my room, and I'll get a job. I'll keep away from him, that's all.

LINDA. No, Biff. You can't stay here and fight all the time.

BIFF. He threw me out of this house, remember that.

LINDA. Why did he do that? I never knew why.

BIFF. Because I know he's a fake and he doesn't like anybody around who knows!

LINDA. Why a fake? In what way? What do you mean?

BIFF. Just don't lay it all at my feet. It's between me and him—that's all I have to say. I'll chip in from now on. He'll settle for half my pay check. He'll be all right. I'm going to bed. [*He starts for the stairs.*]

LINDA. He won't be all right.

BIFF. [*Turning on the stairs, furiously.*] I hate this city and I'll stay here. Now what do you want?

LINDA. He's dying, Biff.

[HAPPY *turns quickly to her, shocked.*]

BIFF. [*After a pause.*] Why is he dying?

LINDA. He's been trying to kill himself.

BIFF. [*With great horror.*] How.

LINDA. I live from day to day.

BIFF. What're you talking about?

LINDA. Remember I wrote you that he smashed up the car again? In February?

BIFF. Well?

LINDA. The insurance inspector came. He said that they have evidence. That all these accidents in the last year—weren't—weren't—accidents.

HAPPY. How can they tell that? That's a lie.

LINDA. It seems there's a woman . . .

[*She takes a breath as*

⎧ BIFF. [*Sharply but contained.*] What
⎨ woman . . .
⎩ LINDA. [*Simultaneously*] . . . and this
woman . . .

LINDA. What?

BIFF. Nothing. Go ahead.

LINDA. What did you say?

BIFF. Nothing. I just said what woman?

HAPPY. What about her?

LINDA. Well, it seems she was walking down the road and saw his car. She says that he wasn't driving fast at all, and that he didn't skid. She says he came to that little bridge, and then deliberately smashed into the railing, and it was only the shallowness of the water that saved him.

BIFF. Oh, no, he probably just fell asleep again.

LINDA. I don't think he fell asleep.

BIFF. Why not?

LINDA. Last month . . . [*With great difficulty.*] Oh, boys, it's so hard to say a thing like this! He's just a big stupid man to you, but I tell you there's more good in him than in many other people. [*She chokes, wipes her eyes.*] I was looking for a fuse. The lights blew out, and I went down the cellar. And behind the fuse box—it happened to fall out—was a length of rubber pipe—just short.

HAPPY. No kidding?

LINDA. There's a little attachment on the end of it. I knew right away. And sure enough, on the bottom of the water heater there's a new little nipple on the gas pipe.

HAPPY. [*Angrily.*] That—jerk.

BIFF. Did you have it taken off?

LINDA. I'm—I'm ashamed to. How can I mention it to him? Every day I go down and take away that little rubber pipe. But, when he comes home, I put it back where it was. How can I insult him that way? I don't know what to do. I live from day to day, boys. I tell you, I know every thought in his mind. It sounds so old-fashioned and silly, but I tell you he put his whole life into you and you've turned your backs on him. [*She is bent over in the chair, weeping, her face in her hands.*] Biff, I swear to God! Biff, his life is in your hands!

HAPPY. [*To* BIFF.] How do you like that damned fool!

BIFF. [*Kissing her.*] All right, pal, all right. It's all settled now. I've been remiss. I know that, Mom. But now I'll stay, and I swear to you, I'll apply myself. [*Kneeling in front of her, in a fever of self-reproach.*] It's just—you see, Mom, I don't fit in business. Not that I won't try. I'll try, and I'll make good.

HAPPY. Sure you will. The trouble with you in business was you never tried to please people.

BIFF. I know, I——

HAPPY. Like when you worked for Harrison's. Bob Harrison said you were tops, and then you go and do some damn fool thing like whistling whole songs in the elevator like a comedian.

BIFF. [*Against* HAPPY.] So what? I like to whistle sometimes.

HAPPY. You don't raise a guy to a responsible job who whistles in the elevator!

LINDA. Well, don't argue about it now.

HAPPY. Like when you'd go off and swim in the middle of the day instead of taking the line around.

BIFF. [*His resentment rising.*] Well, don't you run off? You take off sometimes, don't you? On a nice summer day?

HAPPY. Yeah, but I cover myself!

LINDA. Boys!

HAPPY. If I'm going to take a fade the boss can call any number where I'm supposed to be and they'll swear to him that I just left. I'll tell you something that I hate to say, Biff, but in the business world some of them think you're crazy.

BIFF. [*Angered.*] Screw the business world!

HAPPY. All right, screw it! Great, but cover yourself!

LINDA. Hap, Hap!

BIFF. I don't care what they think! They've laughed at Dad for years, and you know why? Because we don't belong in this nuthouse of a city! We should be mixing cement on some open plain, or—or carpenters. A carpenter is allowed to whistle!

[WILLY *walks in from the entrance of the house, at left.*]

WILLY. Even your grandfather was better than a carpenter. [*Pause. They watch him.*] You never grew up. Bernard does not whistle in the elevator, I assure you.

BIFF. [*As though to laugh* WILLY *out of it.*] Yeah, but you do, Pop.

WILLY. I never in my life whistled in an elevator! And who in the business world thinks I'm crazy?

BIFF. I didn't mean it like that, Pop. Now don't make a whole thing out of it, will ya?

WILLY. Go back to the West! Be a carpenter, a cowboy, enjoy yourself!

LINDA. Willy, he was just saying——

WILLY. I heard what he said!

HAPPY. [*Trying to quiet* WILLY.] Hey, Pop, come on now . . .

WILLY. [*Continuing over* HAPPY's *line.*] They laugh at me, heh? Go to Filene's, go to the Hub, go to Slattery's, Boston. Call out the name Willy Loman and see what happens! Big shot!

BIFF. All right, Pop.

WILLY. Big!

BIFF. All right!

WILLY. Why do you always insult me?

BIFF. I didn't say a word. [*To* LINDA.] Did I say a word?

LINDA. He didn't say anything, Willy.

WILLY. [*Going to the doorway of the living-room.*] All right, good night, good night.

LINDA. Willy, dear, he just decided . . .

WILLY. [*To* BIFF.] If you get tired hanging around tomorrow, paint the ceiling I put up in the living-room.

BIFF. I'm leaving early tomorrow.

HAPPY. He's going to see Bill Oliver, Pop.

WILLY. [*Interestedly.*] Oliver? For what?

BIFF. [*With reserve, but trying, trying.*] He always said he'd stake me. I'd like to go into business, so maybe I can take him up on it.

LINDA. Isn't that wonderful?

WILLY. Don't interrupt. What's wonderful about it? There's fifty men in the City of New York who'd stake him. [*To* BIFF.] Sporting goods?

BIFF. I guess so. I know something about it and——

WILLY. He knows something about it! You know sporting goods better than Spalding, for God's sake! How much is he giving you?

BIFF. I don't know, I didn't even see him yet, but——

WILLY. Then what're you talkin' about?

BIFF. [*Getting angry.*] Well, all I said was I'm gonna see him, that's all!

WILLY. [*Turning away.*] Ah, you're counting your chickens again.

BIFF. [*Starting left for the stairs.*] Oh, Jesus, I'm going to sleep!

WILLY. [*Calling after him.*] Don't curse in this house!

BIFF. [*Turning.*] Since when did you get so clean?

HAPPY. [*Trying to stop them.*] Wait a . . .

WILLY. Don't use that language to me! I won't have it!

HAPPY. [*Grabbing* BIFF, *shouts.*] Wait a minute! I got an idea. I got a feasible idea. Come here, Biff, let's talk this over now, let's talk some sense here. When I was down in Florida last time, I thought of a great idea to sell sporting goods. It just came back to me. You and I, Biff—we have a line, the Loman Line. We train a couple of weeks, and put on a couple of exhibitions, see?

WILLY. That's an idea!

HAPPY. Wait! We form two basketball teams, see? Two water-polo teams. We play each other. It's a million dollars' worth of publicity. Two brothers, see? The Loman Brothers. Displays in the Royal Palms— all the hotels. And banners over the ring and the basketball court: "Loman Brothers." Baby, we could sell sporting goods!

WILLY. That is a one-million-dollar idea!

LINDA. Marvelous!

BIFF. I'm in great shape as far as that's concerned.

HAPPY. And the beauty of it is, Biff, it wouldn't be like a business. We'd be out playin' ball again . . .

BIFF. [*Enthused.*] Yeah, that's . . .

WILLY. Million-dollar . . .

HAPPY. And you wouldn't get fed up with it, Biff.

It'd be the family again. There'd be the old honor, and comradeship, and if you wanted to go off for a swim or somethin'—well, you'd do it! Without some smart cooky gettin' up ahead of you!

WILLY. Lick the world! You guys together could absolutely lick the civilized world.

BIFF. I'll see Oliver tomorrow. Hap, if we could work that out . . .

LINDA. Maybe things are beginning to——

WILLY. [*Wildly enthused, to* LINDA.] Stop interrupting! [*To* BIFF.] But don't wear sport jacket and slacks when you see Oliver.

BIFF. No, I'll——

WILLY. A business suit, and talk as little as possible, and don't crack any jokes.

BIFF. He did like me. Always liked me.

LINDA. He loved you!

WILLY. [*To* LINDA.] Will you stop! [*To* BIFF.] Walk in very serious. You are not applying for a boy's job. Money is to pass. Be quiet, fine, and serious. Everybody likes a kidder, but nobody lends him money.

HAPPY. I'll try to get some myself, Biff. I'm sure I can.

WILLY. I see great things for you kids, I think your troubles are over. But remember, start big and you'll end big. Ask for fifteen. How much you gonna ask for?

BIFF. Gee, I don't know——

WILLY. And don't say "Gee." "Gee" is a boy's word. A man walking in for fifteen thousand dollars does not say "Gee!"

BIFF. Ten, I think, would be top, though.

WILLY. Don't be so modest. You always started too low. Walk in with a big laugh. Don't look worried. Start off with a couple of your good stories to lighten things up. It's not what you say, it's how you say it—because personality always wins the day.

LINDA. Oliver always thought the highest of him——

WILLY. Will you let me talk?

BIFF. Don't yell at her, Pop, will ya?

WILLY. [*Angrily.*] I was talking, wasn't I?

BIFF. I don't like you yelling at her all the time, and I'm tellin' you, that's all.

WILLY. What're you, takin' over this house?

LINDA. Willy——

WILLY. [*Turning on her.*] Don't take his side all the time, goddammit!

BIFF. [*Furiously.*] Stop yelling at her!

WILLY. [*Suddenly pulling on his cheek, beaten-down, guilt-ridden.*] Give my best to Bill Oliver—he may remember me.

[*He exits through the living-room doorway.*]

LINDA. [*Her voice subdued.*] What'd you have to start that for? [BIFF *turns away.*] You see how sweet he was as soon as you talked hopefully? [*She goes over to* BIFF.] Come up and say good night to him. Don't let him go to bed that way.

HAPPY. Come on, Biff, let's buck him up.

LINDA. Please, dear. Just say good night. It takes so little to make him happy. Come. [*She goes through the living-room doorway, calling upstairs from within the living-room.*] Your pajamas are hanging in the bathroom, Willy!

HAPPY. [*Looking toward where* LINDA *went out.*] What a woman! They broke the mold when they made her. You know that, Biff?

BIFF. He's off salary. My God, working on commission!

HAPPY. Well, let's face it: he's no hot-shot selling man. Except that sometimes, you have to admit, he's a sweet personality.

BIFF. [*Deciding.*] Lend me ten bucks, will ya? I want to buy some new ties.

HAPPY. I'll take you to a place I know. Beautiful stuff. Wear one of my striped shirts tomorrow.

BIFF. She got gray. Mom got awful old. Gee, I'm gonna go in to Oliver tomorrow and knock him for a——

HAPPY. Come on up. Tell that to Dad. Let's give him a whirl. Come on.

BIFF. [*Steamed up.*] You know, with ten thousand bucks, boy!

HAPPY. [*As they go into the living-room.*] That's the talk, Biff, that's the first time I've heard the old confidence out of you! [*From within the living-room, fading off.*] You're gonna live with me, kid, and any babe you want just say the word . . .

[*The last lines are hardly heard. They are mounting the stairs to their parents' bedroom.*]

LINDA. [*Entering her bedroom and addressing* WILLY, *who is in the bathroom. She is straightening the bed for him.*] Can you do anything about the shower? It drips.

WILLY. [*From the bathroom.*] All of a sudden everything falls to pieces! Goddam plumbing, oughta be sued, those people. I hardly finished putting it in and the thing . . . [*His words rumble off.*]

LINDA. I'm just wondering if Oliver will remember him. You think he might?

WILLY. [*Coming out of the bathroom in his pajamas.*] Remember him? What's the matter with you, you crazy? If he'd've stayed with Oliver he'd be on top by now! Wait'll Oliver gets a look at him. You don't know the average caliber any more. The average young man today—— [*He is getting into bed.*] is got a caliber of zero. Greatest thing in the world for him was to bum around.

BIFF *and* HAPPY *enter the bedroom. Slight pause.*]

WILLY. [*Stops short, looking at* BIFF.] Glad to hear it, boy.

HAPPY. He wanted to say good night to you, sport.

WILLY. [*To* BIFF.] Yeah. Knock him dead, boy. What'd you want to tell me?

BIFF. Just take it easy, Pop. Good night. [*He turns to go.*]

WILLY. [*Unable to resist.*] And if anything falls off the desk while you're talking to him—like a package or something—don't you pick it up. They have office boys for that.

LINDA. I'll make a big breakfast——

WILLY. Will you let me finish? [*To* BIFF.] Tell him you were in the business in the West. Not farm work.

BIFF. All right, Dad.

LINDA. I think everything——

WILLY. [*Going right through her speech.*] And don't undersell yourself. No less than fifteen thousand dollars.

BIFF. [*Unable to bear him.*] Okay. Good night, Mom. [*He starts moving.*]

WILLY. Because you got a greatness in you, Biff; remember that. You got all kinds a greatness . . .

[*He lies back, exhausted.* BIFF *walks out.*]

LINDA. [*Calling after* BIFF.] Sleep well, darling!

HAPPY. I'm gonna get married, Mom. I wanted to tell you.

LINDA. Go to sleep, dear.

HAPPY. [*Going.*] I just wanted to tell you.

WILLY. Keep up the good work. [HAPPY *exits.*] God . . . remember that Ebbets Field game? The championship of the city?

LINDA. Just rest. Should I sing to you?

WILLY. Yeah. Sing to me. [LINDA *hums a soft lullaby.*] When that team came out—he was the tallest, remember?

LINDA. Oh, yes. And in gold.

[BIFF *enters the darkened kitchen, takes a cigarette, and leaves the house. He comes downstage into a golden pool of light. He smokes, staring at the night.*]

WILLY. Like a young god. Hercules—something like that. And the sun, the sun all around him. Remember how he waved to me? Right up from the field, with the representatives of three colleges standing by? And the buyers I brought, and the cheers when he came out—Loman, Loman, Loman! God Almighty, he'll be great yet. A star like that, magnificent, can never really fade away!

[*The light on* WILLY *is fading. The gas heater begins to glow through the kitchen wall, near the stairs, a blue flame beneath red coils.*]

LINDA. [*Timidly.*] Willy dear, what has he got against you?

WILLY. I'm so tired. Don't talk any more.

[BIFF *slowly returns to the kitchen. He stops, stares toward the heater.*]

LINDA. Will you ask Howard to let you work in New York?

WILLY. First thing in the morning. Everything'll be all right.

[BIFF *reaches behind the heater and draws out a length of rubber tubing. He is horrified and turns his head toward* WILLY's *room, still dimly lit, from which the strains of* LINDA's *desperate but monotonous humming rise.*]

WILLY. [*Staring through the window into the moonlight.*] Gee, look at the moon moving between the buildings!

[BIFF *wraps the tubing around his hand and quickly goes up the stairs.*]

CURTAIN

ACT II

Music is heard, gay and bright. The curtain rises as the music fades away. [WILLY, *in shirt sleeves, is sitting at the kitchen table, sipping coffee, his hat in his lap.* LINDA *is filling his cup when she can.*]

WILLY. Wonderful coffee. Meal in itself.

LINDA. Can I make you some eggs?

WILLY. No. Take a breath.

LINDA. You look so rested, dear.

WILLY. I slept like a dead one. First time in months. Imagine, sleeping till ten on a Tuesday morning. Boys left nice and early, heh?

LINDA. They were out of here by eight o'clock.

WILLY. Good work!

LINDA. It was so thrilling to see them leaving together. I can't get over the shaving lotion in this house!

WILLY. [*Smiling.*] Mmm——

LINDA. Biff was very changed this morning. His whole attitude seemed to be hopeful. He couldn't wait to get downtown to see Oliver.

WILLY. He's heading for a change. There's no question, there simply are certain men that take longer to get—solidified. How did he dress?

LINDA. His blue suit. He's so handsome in that suit. He could be a—anything in that suit!

[WILLY *gets up from the table.* LINDA *holds his jacket for him.*]

WILLY. There's no question, no question at all. Gee, on the way home tonight I'd like to buy some seeds.

LINDA. [*Laughing.*[That'd be wonderful. But not enough sun gets back there. Nothing'll grow any more.

WILLY. You wait, kid, before it's all over we're gonna get a little place out in the country, and I'll raise some vegetables, a couple of chickens . . .

LINDA. You'll do it yet, dear.

[WILLY *walks out of his jacket.* LINDA *follows him.*]

WILLY. And they'll get married, and come for a weekend. I'd build a little guest house. 'Cause I got so many fine tools, all I'd need would be a little lumber and some peace of mind.

LINDA. [*Joyfully.*] I sewed the lining . . .

WILLY. I could build two guest houses, so they'd both come. Did he decide how much he's going to ask Oliver for?

LINDA. [*Getting him into the jacket.*] He didn't mention it but I imagine ten or fifteen thousand. You going to talk to Howard today?

WILLY. Yeah. I'll put it to him straight and simple. He'll just have to take me off the road.

LINDA. And, Willy, don't forget to ask for a little advance, because we've got the insurance premium. It's the grace period now.

WILLY. That's a hundred . . . ?

LINDA. A hundred and eight, sixty-eight. Because we're a little short again.

WILLY. Why are we short?

LINDA. Well, you had the motor job on the car . . .

WILLY. That goddam Studebaker.

LINDA. And you got one more payment on the refrigerator . . .

WILLY. But it just broke again!

LINDA. Well, it's old, dear.

WILLY. I told you we should've bought a well-advertised machine. Charley bought a General Electric and it's twenty years old and it's still good, that son-of-a-bitch.

LINDA. But, Willy——

WILLY. Whoever heard of a Hastings refrigerator? Once in my life I would like to own something outright before it's broken! I'm always in a race with the junkyard! I just finished paying for the car and it's on its last legs. The refrigerator consumes belts like a goddam maniac. They time those things. They time them so when you've finally paid for them, they're used up.

LINDA. [*Buttoning up his jacket as he unbuttons it.*] All told, about two hundred dollars would carry us, dear. But that includes the last payment on the mortgage. After this payment, Willy, the house belongs to us.

WILLY. It's twenty-five years!

LINDA. Biff was nine years old when we bought it.

WILLY. Well, that's a great thing. To weather a twenty-five year mortgage is——

LINDA. It's an accomplishment.

WILLY. All the cement, the lumber, the reconstruction I put in this house! There ain't a crack to be found in it any more.

LINDA. Well, it served its purpose.

WILLY. What purpose? Some stranger'll come along, move in, and that's that. If only Biff would take this house, and raise a family . . . [*He starts to go.*] Good-by, I'm late.

LINDA. [*Suddenly remembering.*] Oh, I forgot! You're supposed to meet them for dinner.

WILLY. Me?

LINDA. At Frank's Chop House on Forty-eighth near Sixth Avenue.

WILLY. Is that so! How about you?

LINDA. No, just the three of you. They're gonna blow you to a big meal!

WILLY. Don't say! Who thought of that?

LINDA. Biff came to me this morning, Willy, and he said, "Tell Dad, we want to blow him to a big meal." Be there six o'clock. You and your two boys are going to have dinner.

WILLY. Gee whiz! That's really somethin'. I'm gonna knock Howard for a loop, kid. I'll get an advance, and I'll come home with a New York job. Goddammit, now I'm gonna do it!

LINDA. Oh, that's the spirit, Willy!

WILLY. I will never get behind a wheel the rest of my life!

LINDA. It's changing, Willy, I can feel it changing!

WILLY. Beyond a question. G'by, I'm late.

[*He starts to go again.*]

LINDA. [*Calling after him as she runs to the kitchen table for a handkerchief.*] You got your glasses?

WILLY. [*Feels for them, then comes back in.*] Yeah, yeah, got my glasses.

LINDA. [*Giving him the handkerchief.*] And a handkerchief.

WILLY. Yeah, handkerchief.

LINDA. And your saccharine?

WILLY. Yeah, my saccharine.

LINDA. Be careful on the subway stairs.

[*She kisses him, and a silk stocking is seen hanging from her hand.* WILLY *notices it.*]

WILLY. Will you stop mending stockings? At least while I'm in the house. It gets me nervous. I can't tell you. Please.

[LINDA *hides the stocking in her hand as she follows* WILLY *across the forestage in front of the house.*]

LINDA. Remember, Frank's Chop House.

WILLY. [*Passing the apron.*] Maybe beets would grow out there.

LINDA. [*Laughing.*] But you tried so many times.

WILLY. Yeah. Well, don't work hard today.

[*He disappears around the right corner of the house.*]

LINDA. Be careful!

[*As* WILLY *vanishes,* LINDA *waves to him. Suddenly the phone rings. She runs across the stage and into the kitchen and lifts it.*]

LINDA. Hello? Oh, Biff! I'm so glad you called, I just . . . Yes, sure, I just told him. Yes, he'll be there for dinner at six o'clock, I didn't forget. Listen, I was just dying to tell you. You know that little rubber pipe I told you about? That he connected to the gas heater? I finally decided to go down the cellar this morning and take it away and destroy it. But it's gone! Imagine? He took it away himself; it isn't there! [*She listens.*] When? Oh, then you took it. Oh —nothing, it's just that I'd hoped he'd taken it away himself. Oh, I'm not worried, darling, because this morning he left in such high spirits, it was like the old days! I'm not afraid any more. Did Mr. Oliver see you? . . . Well, you wait there then. And make a nice impression on him, darling. Just don't perspire too much before you see him. And have a nice time with Dad. He may have big news too! . . . That's right, a New York job. And be sweet to him tonight, dear. Be loving to him. Because he's only a little boat looking for a harbor. [*She is trembling with sorrow and joy.*] Oh, that's wonderful, Biff, you'll save his life. Thanks, darling. Just put your arm around him when he comes into the restaurant. Give him a smile. That's the boy . . . Good-by, dear. . . . You got your comb? . . . That's fine. Good-by, Biff dear.

[*In the middle of her speech,* HOWARD WAGNER, *thirty-six, wheels on a small typewriter table on which is a wire-recording machine and proceeds to plug it in. This is on the left forestage. Light slowly fades on* LINDA *as it rises on* HOWARD. HOWARD *is intent on threading the machine and only glances over his shoulder as* WILLY *appears.*]

WILLY. Pst! Pst!

HOWARD. Hello, Willy, come in.

WILLY. Like to have a little talk with you, Howard.

HOWARD. Sorry to keep you waiting. I'll be with you in a minute.

WILLY. What's that, Howard?

HOWARD. Didn't you ever see one of these? Wire recorder.

WILLY. Oh. Can we talk a minute?

HOWARD. Records things. Just got delivery yesterday. Been driving me crazy, the most terrific machine I ever saw in my life. I was up all night with it.

WILLY. What do you do with it?

HOWARD. I bought it for dictation, but you can do anything with it. Listen to this. I had it home last night. Listen to what I picked up. The first one is my daughter. Get this. [*He flicks the switch and "Roll out the Barrel" is heard being whistled.*] Listen to that kid whistle.

WILLY. That is lifelike, isn't it?

HOWARD. Seven years old. Get that tone.

WILLY. Ts, ts. Like to ask a little favor if you . . .

[*The whistling breaks off, and the voice of* HOWARD's *daughter is heard.*]

HIS DAUGHTER. "Now you, Daddy."

HOWARD. She's crazy for me! [*Again the same song is whistled.*] That's me! Ha! [*He winks.*]

WILLY. You're very good!

[*The whistling breaks off again. The machine runs silent for a moment.*]

HOWARD. Sh! Get this now, this is my son.

HIS SON. "The capital of Alabama is Montgomery; the capital of Arizona is Phoenix; the capital of Arkansas is Little Rock; the capital of California is Sacramento . . ." [*And on, and on.*]

HOWARD. [*Holding up five fingers.*] Five years old, Willy!

WILLY. He'll make an announcer some day!

HIS SON. [*Continuing.*] "The capital . . ."

HOWARD. Get that—alphabetical order! [*The machine breaks off suddenly.*] Wait a minute. The maid kicked the plug out.

WILLY. It certainly is a——

HOWARD. Sh, for God's sake!

HIS SON. "It's nine o'clock, Bulova watch time. So I have to go to sleep."

WILLY. That really is——

HOWARD. Wait a minute! The next is my wife. [*They wait.*]

HOWARD's VOICE. "Go on, say something." [*Pause.*] "Well, you gonna talk?"

HIS WIFE. "I can't think of anything."

HOWARD's VOICE. "Well, talk—it's turning."

HIS WIFE. [*Shyly, beaten.*] "Hello." [*Silence.*] "Oh, Howard, I can't talk into this . . ."

HOWARD. [*Snapping the machine off.*] That was my wife.

WILLY. That is a wonderful machine. Can we——

HOWARD. I tell you, Willy, I'm gonna take my camera, and my bandsaw, and all my hobbies, and out they go. This is the most fascinating relaxation I ever found.

WILLY. I think I'll get one myself.

HOWARD. Sure, they're only a hundred and a half. You can't do without it. Supposing you wanna hear Jack Benny, see? But you can't be at home at that hour. So you tell the maid to turn the radio on when

Jack Benny comes on, and this automatically goes on with the radio . . .

WILLY. And when you come home you . . .

HOWARD. You can come home twelve o'clock, one o'clock, any time you like, and you get yourself a Coke and sit yourself down, throw the switch, and there's Jack Benny's program in the middle of the night!

WILLY. I'm definitely going to get one. Because lots of time I'm on the road, and I think to myself, what I must be missing on the radio!

HOWARD. Don't you have a radio in the car?

WILLY. Well, yeah, but who ever thinks of turning it on?

HOWARD. Say, aren't you supposed to be in Boston?

WILLY. That's what I want to talk to you about, Howard. You got a minute?

[*He draws a chair in from the wing.*]

HOWARD. What happened? What're you doing here?

WILLY. Well . . .

HOWARD. You didn't crack up again, did you?

WILLY. Oh, no. No . . .

HOWARD. Geez, you had me worried there for a minute. What's the trouble?

WILLY. Well, tell you the truth, Howard. I've come to the decision that I'd rather not travel any more.

HOWARD. Not travel! Well, what'll you do?

WILLY. Remember, Christmas time, when you had the party here? You said you'd try to think of some spot for me here in town.

HOWARD. With us?

WILLY. Well, sure.

HOWARD. Oh, yeah, yeah. I remember. Well, I couldn't think of anything for you, Willy.

WILLY. I tell ya, Howard. The kids are all grown up, y'know. I don't need much any more. If I could take home—well, sixty-five dollars a week, I could swing it.

HOWARD. Yeah, but Willy, see I——

WILLY. I tell ya why, Howard. Speaking frankly and between the two of us, y'know—I'm just a little tired.

HOWARD. Oh, I could understand that, Willy. But you're a road man, Willy, and we do a road business. We've only got a half-dozen salesmen on the floor here.

WILLY. God knows, Howard, I never asked a favor of any man. I was with the firm when your father used to carry you in here in his arms.

HOWARD. I know that, Willy, but——

WILLY. Your father came to me the day you were born and asked me what I thought of the name of Howard, may he rest in peace.

HOWARD. I appreciate that, Willy, but there just is no spot here for you. If I had a spot I'd slam you right in, but I just don't have a single solitary spot.

[*He looks for his lighter.* WILLY *has picked it up and gives it to him. Pause.*]

WILLY. [*With increasing anger.*] Howard, all I need to set my table is fifty dollars a week.

HOWARD. But where am I going to put you, kid?

WILLY. Look, it isn't a question of whether I can sell merchandise, is it?

HOWARD. No, but it's a business, kid, and everybody's gotta pull his own weight.

WILLY. [*Desperately.*] Just let me tell you a story, Howard——

HOWARD. 'Cause you gotta admit, business is business.

WILLY. [*Angrily.*] Business is definitely business, but just listen for a minute. You don't understand this. When I was a boy—eighteen, nineteen—I was already on the road. And there was a question in my mind as to whether selling had a future for me. Because in those days I had a yearning to go to Alaska. See, there were three gold strikes in one month in Alaska, and I felt like going out. Just for the ride, you might say.

HOWARD. [*Barely interested.*] Don't say.

WILLY. Oh, yeah, my father lived many years in Alaska. He was an adventurous man. We've got quite a little streak of self-reliance in our family. I thought I'd go out with my older brother and try to locate him, and maybe settle in the North with the old man. And I was almost decided to go, when I met a salesman in the Parker House. His name was Dave Singleman. And he was eighty-four years old, and he'd drummed merchandise in thirty-one states. And old Dave, he'd go up to his room, y'understand, put on his green velvet slippers—I'll never forget—and pick up his phone and call the buyers, and without ever leaving his room, at the age of eighty-four, he made his living. And when I saw that, I realized that selling was the greatest career a man could want. 'Cause what could be more satisfying than to be able to go, at the age of eighty-four, into twenty or thirty different cities, and pick up a phone, and be remembered and loved and helped by so many different people? Do you know? when he died—and by the way he died the death of a salesman, in his green velvet slippers in the smoker of the New York, New Haven and Hartford, going into Boston—when he died, hundreds of salesmen and buyers were at his funeral. Things were sad on a lotta trains for months after that. [*He stands up.* HOWARD *has not looked at him.*] In those days there was personality in it, Howard. There was respect, and comradeship, and gratitude in it. Today, it's all cut and dried, and there's no chance for bringing friendship to bear—or personality. You see what I mean? They don't know me any more.

HOWARD. [*Moving away, to the right.*] That's just the thing, Willy.

WILLY. If I had forty dollars a week—that's all I'd need. Forty dollars, Howard.

HOWARD. Kid, I can't take blood from a stone, I——

WILLY. [*Desperation is on him now.*] Howard, the year Al Smith was nominated, your father came to me and——

HOWARD. [*Starting to go off.*] I've got to see some people, kid.

WILLY. [*Stopping him.*] I'm talking about your father! There were promises made across this desk! You mustn't tell me you've got people to see—I put thirty-four years into this firm, Howard, and now I can't pay my insurance! You can't eat the orange and throw the peel away—a man is not a piece of fruit! [*After a pause.*] Now pay attention. Your father—in 1928 I had a big year. I averaged a hundred and seventy dollars a week in commissions.

HOWARD. [*Impatiently.*] Now, Willy, you never averaged——

WILLY. [*Banging his hand on the desk.*] I averaged a hundred and seventy dollars a week in the year of 1928! And your father came to me—or rather, I was in the office here—it was right over this desk—and he put his hand on my shoulder——

HOWARD. [*Getting up.*] You'll have to excuse me, Willy; I gotta see some people. Pull yourself together. [*Going out.*] I'll be back in a little while.

[*On* HOWARD'S *exit, the light on his chair grows very bright and strange.*]

WILLY. Pull myself together! What the hell did I say to him? My God, I was yelling at him! How could I! [WILLY *breaks off, staring at the light, which occupies the chair, animating it. He approaches this chair, standing across the desk from it.*] Frank, Frank, don't you remember what you told me that time? How you put your hand on my shoulder, and Frank . . .

[*He leans on the desk and as he speaks the dead man's name he accidentally switches on the recorder, and instantly.*]

HOWARD'S SON. ". . . of New York is Albany. The capital of Ohio is Cincinnati, the capital of Rhode Island is . . ." [*The recitation continues.*]

WILLY. [*Leaping away with fright, shouting.*] Ha! Howard! Howard! Howard!

HOWARD. [*Rushing in.*] What happened?

WILLY. [*Pointing at the machine, which continues nasally, childishly, with the capital cities.*] Shut it off! Shut it off!

HOWARD. [*Pulling the plug out.*] Look, Willy . . .

WILLY. [*Pressing his hands to his eyes.*] I gotta get myself some coffee. I'll get some coffee . . .

[WILLY *starts to walk out.* HOWARD *stops him.*]

HOWARD. [*Rolling up the cord.*] Willy, look . . .

WILLY. I'll go to Boston.

HOWARD. Willy, you can't go to Boston for us.

WILLY. Why can't I go?

HOWARD. I don't want you to represent us. I've been meaning to tell you for a long time now.

WILLY. Howard, are you firing me?

HOWARD. I think you need a good long rest, Willy.

WILLY. Howard——

HOWARD. And when you feel better, come back, and we'll see if we can work something out.

WILLY. But I gotta earn money, Howard. I'm in no position to——

HOWARD. Where are your sons? Why don't your sons give you a hand?

WILLY. They're working on a very big deal.

HOWARD. This is no time for false pride, Willy. You go to your sons and you tell them that you're tired. You've got two great boys, haven't you?

WILLY. Oh, no question, no question, but in the meantime . . .

HOWARD. Then that's that, heh?

WILLY. All right, I'll go to Boston tomorrow.

HOWARD. No, no.

WILLY. I can't throw myself on my sons. I'm not a cripple!

HOWARD. Look, kid, I'm busy this morning.

WILLY. [*Grasping* HOWARD'S *arm.*] Howard, you've got to let me go to Boston!

HOWARD. [*Hard, keeping himself under control.*] I've got a line of people to see this morning. Sit down, take five minutes, and pull yourself together, and then go home, will ya? I need the office, Willy. [*He starts to go, turns, remembering the recorder, starts to push off the table holding the recorder.*] Oh, yeah. Whenever you can this week, stop by and drop off the samples. You'll feel better, Willy, and then come back and we'll talk. Pull yourself together, kid, there's people outside.

[HOWARD *exits, pushing the table off left.* WILLY *stares into space, exhausted. Now the music is heard—*BEN'S *music—first distantly, then closer, closer. As* WILLY *speaks,* BEN *enters from the right. He carries valise and umbrella.*]

WILLY. Oh, Ben, how did you do it? What is the answer? Did you wind up the Alaska deal already?

BEN. Doesn't take much time if you know what you're doing. Just a short business trip. Boarding ship in an hour. Wanted to say good-by.

WILLY. Ben, I've got to talk to you.

BEN. [*Glancing at his watch.*] Haven't the time, William.

WILLY. [*Crossing the apron to* BEN.] Ben, nothing's working out. I don't know what to do.

BEN. Now, look here, William. I've bought timberland in Alaska and I need a man to look after things for me.

WILLY. God, timberland! Me and my boys in those grand outdoors!

BEN. You've a new continent at your doorstep, William. Get out of these cities; they're full of talk and time payments and courts of law. Screw on your fists and you can fight for a fortune up there.

WILLY. Yes, yes! Linda, Linda!

[LINDA *enters as of old, with the wash.*]

LINDA. Oh, you're back?

BEN. I haven't much time.

WILLY. No, wait! Linda, he's got a proposition for me in Alaska.

LINDA. But you've got—— [*To* BEN.] He's got a beautiful job here.

WILLY. But in Alaska, kid, I could——

LINDA. You're doing well enough, Willy!

BEN. [*To* LINDA.] Enough for what, my dear?

LINDA. [*Frightened of* BEN *and angry at him.*] Don't say those things to him! Enough to be happy right here, right now. [*To* WILLY, *while* BEN *laughs.*] Why must everybody conquer the world? You're well liked, and the boys love you, and someday—[*To* BEN.]—why, old man Wagner told him just the other day that if he keeps it up he'll be a member of the firm, didn't he, Willy?

WILLY. Sure, sure. I am building something with this firm, Ben, and if a man is building something he must be on the right track, mustn't he?

BEN. What are you building? Lay your hand on it. Where is it?

WILLY. [*Hesitantly.*] That's true, Linda, there's nothing.

LINDA. Why? [*To* BEN.] There's a man eighty-four years old——

WILLY. That's right, Ben, that's right. When I look at that man I say, what is there to worry about?

BEN. Bah!

WILLY. It's true, Ben. All he has to do is go into any city, pick up the phone, and he's making his living and you know why?

BEN. [*Picking up his valise.*] I've got to go.

WILLY. [*Holding* BEN *back.*] Look at this boy!

[BIFF, *in his high school sweater, enters carrying suitcase.* HAPPY *carries* BIFF's *shoulder guards, gold helmet, and football pants.*]

WILLY. Without a penny to his name, three great universities are begging for him, and from there the sky's the limit, because it's not what you do, Ben. It's who you know and the smile on your face! It's contacts, Ben, contacts! The whole wealth of Alaska passes over the lunch table at the Commodore Hotel, and that's the wonder, the wonder of this country, that a man can end with diamonds here on the basis of being liked! [*He turns to* BIFF.] And that's why when you get out on that field today it's important. Because thousands of people will be rooting for you and loving you. [*To* BEN, *who has again begun to leave.*] And Ben! when he walks into a business office his name will sound out like a bell and all the doors will open to him! I've seen it, Ben, I've seen it a thousand times! You can't feel it with your hand like timber, but it's there!

BEN. Good-by, William.

WILLY. Ben, am I right? Don't you think I'm right? I value your advice.

BEN. There's a new continent at your doorstep, William. You could walk out rich. Rich! [*He is gone.*]

WILLY. We'll do it here, Ben! You hear me? We're gonna do it here!

[YOUNG BERNARD *rushes in. The gay music of the* BOYS *is heard.*]

BERNARD. Oh, gee, I was afraid you left already!

WILLY. Why? What time is it?

BERNARD. It's half-past one!

WILLY. Well, come on, everybody! Ebbets Field next stop! Where's the pennants?

[*He rushes through the wall-line of the kitchen and out into the living-room.*]

LINDA. [*To* BIFF.] Did you pack fresh underwear?

BIFF. [*Who has been limbering up.*] I want to go!

BERNARD. Biff, I'm carrying your helmet, ain't I?

HAPPY. No, I'm carrying the helmet.

BERNARD. Oh, Biff, you promised me.

HAPPY. I'm carrying the helmet.

BERNARD. How am I going to get in the locker room?

LINDA. Let him carry the shoulder guards.

[*She puts her coat and hat on in the kitchen.*]

BERNARD. Can I, Biff? 'Cause I told everybody I'm going to be in the locker room.

HAPPY. In Ebbets Field it's the clubhouse.

BERNARD. I meant the clubhouse. Biff!

HAPPY. Biff!

BIFF. [*Grandly, after a slight pause.*] Let him carry the shoulder guards.

HAPPY. [*As he gives* BERNARD *the shoulder guards.*] Stay close to us now.

[WILLY *rushes in with the pennants.*]

WILLY. [*Handing them out.*] Everybody wave when Biff comes out on the field. [HAPPY *and* BERNARD *run off.*] You set now, boy?

[*The music has died away.*]

BIFF. Ready to go, Pop. Every muscle is ready.

WILLY. [*At the edge of the apron.*] You realize what this means?

BIFF. That's right, Pop.

WILLY. [*Feeling BIFF's muscles.*] You're comin' home this afternoon captain of the All-Scholastic Championship Team of the City of New York.

BIFF. I got it, Pop. And remember, pal, when I take off my helmet, that touchdown is for you.

WILLY. Let's go! [*He is starting out, with his arm around BIFF, when CHARLEY enters, as of old, in knickers.*] I got no room for you, Charley.

CHARLEY. Room? For what?

WILLY. In the car.

CHARLEY. You goin' for a ride? I wanted to shoot some casino.

WILLY. [*Furiously.*] Casino! [*Incredulously.*] Don't you realize what today is?

LINDA. Oh, he knows, Willy. He's just kidding you.

WILLY. That's nothing to kid about!

CHARLEY. No, Linda, what's goin' on?

LINDA. He's playing in Ebbets Field.

CHARLEY. Baseball in this weather?

WILLY. Don't talk to him. Come on, come on! [*He is pushing them out.*]

CHARLEY. Wait a minute, didn't you hear the news?

WILLY. What?

CHARLEY. Don't you listen to the radio? Ebbets Field just blew up.

WILLY. You go to hell! [*CHARLEY laughs. Pushing them out.*] Come on, come on! We're late.

CHARLEY. [*As they go.*] Knock a homer, Biff, knock a homer!

WILLY. [*The last to leave, turning to CHARLEY.*] I don't think that was funny, Charley. This is the greatest day of his life.

CHARLEY. Willy, when are you going to grow up?

WILLY. Yeah, heh? When this game is over, Charley, you'll be laughing out of the other side of your face. They'll be calling him another Red Grange. Twenty-five thousand a year.

CHARLEY. [*Kidding.*] Is that so?

WILLY. Yeah, that's so.

CHARLEY. Well, then, I'm sorry, Willy. But tell me something.

WILLY. What?

CHARLEY. Who is Red Grange?

WILLY. Put up your hands. Goddam you, put up your hands!

[*CHARLEY, chuckling, shakes his head and walks away, around the left corner of the stage. WILLY follows him. The music rises to a mocking frenzy.*]

WILLY. Who the hell do you think you are, better than everybody else? You don't know everything, you big, ignorant, stupid . . . Put up your hands!

[*Light rises, on the right side of the forestage, on a small table in the reception room of CHARLEY's office. Traffic sounds are heard. BERNARD, now mature, sits whistling to himself. A pair of tennis rackets and an overnight bag are on the floor beside him.*]

WILLY. [*Offstage.*] What are you walking away for? Don't walk away! If you're going to say something say it to my face! I know you laugh at me behind my back. You'll laugh out of the other side of your goddam face after this game. Touchdown! Touchdown! Eighty thousand people! Touchdown! Right between the goal posts.

[*BERNARD is a quiet, earnest, but self-assured young man. WILLY's voice is coming from right upstage now. BERNARD lowers his feet off the table and listens. JENNY, his father's secretary, enters.*]

JENNY. [*Distressed.*] Say, Bernard, will you go out in the hall?

BERNARD. What is that noise? Who is it?

JENNY. Mr. Loman. He just got off the elevator.

BERNARD. [*Getting up.*] Who's he arguing with?

JENNY. Nobody. There's nobody with him. I can't deal with him any more, and your father gets all upset everytime he comes. I've got a lot of typing to do, and your father's waiting to sign it. Will you see him?

WILLY. [*Entering.*] Touchdown! Touch—— [*He sees JENNY*] Jenny, Jenny, good to see you. How're ya? Workin'? Or still honest?

JENNY. Fine. How've you been feeling?

WILLY. Not much any more, Jenny. Ha, ha! [*He is surprised to see the rackets.*]

BERNARD. Hello, Uncle Willy.

WILLY. [*Almost shocked.*] Bernard! Well, look who's here!

[*He comes quickly, guiltily, to BERNARD and warmly shakes his hand.*]

BERNARD. How are you? Good to see you.

WILLY. What are you doing here?

BERNARD. Oh, just stopped by to see Pop. Get off my feet till my train leaves. I'm going to Washington in a few minutes.

WILLY. Is he in?

BERNARD. Yes, he's in his office with the accountant. Sit down.

WILLY. [*Sitting down.*] What're you going to do in Washington?

BERNARD. Oh, just a case I've got there, Willy.

WILLY. That so? [*Indicating the rackets.*] You going to play tennis there?

BERNARD. I'm staying with a friend who's got a court.

WILLY. Don't say. His own tennis court. Must be fine people, I bet.

BERNARD. They are, very nice. Dad tells me Biff's in town.

WILLY. [*With a big smile.*] Yeah, Biff's in. Working on a very big deal, Bernard.

BERNARD. What's Biff doing?

WILLY. Well, he's been doing very big things in the West. But he decided to establish himself here. Very big. We're having dinner. Did I hear your wife had a boy?

BERNARD. That's right. Our second.

WILLY. Two boys! What do you know!

BERNARD. What kind of a deal has Biff got?

WILLY. Well, Bill Oliver—very big sporting-goods man—he wants Biff very badly. Called him in from the West. Long distance, carte blanche, special deliveries. Your friends have their own private tennis court?

BERNARD. You still with the old firm, Willy?

WILLY. [*After a pause.*] I'm—I'm overjoyed to see how you made the grade, Bernard, overjoyed. It's an encouraging thing to see a young man really—really—— Looks very good for Biff—very—— [*He breaks off, then.*] Bernard—— [*He is so full of emotion, he breaks off again.*]

BERNARD. What is it, Willy?

WILLY. [*Small and alone.*] What—what's the secret?

BERNARD. What secret?

WILLY. How—how did you? Why didn't he ever catch on?

BERNARD. I wouldn't know that, Willy.

WILLY. [*Confidentially, desperately.*] You were his friend, his boyhood friend. There's something I don't understand about it. His life ended after that Ebbets Field game. From the age of seventeen nothing good ever happened to him.

BERNARD. He never trained himself for anything.

WILLY. But he did, he did. After high school he took so many correspondence courses. Radio mechanics; television; God knows what, and never made the slightest mark.

BERNARD. [*Taking off his glasses.*] Willy, do you want to talk candidly?

WILLY. [*Rising, faces* BERNARD.] I regard you as a very brilliant man, Bernard. I value your advice.

BERNARD. Oh, the hell with the advice, Willy. I couldn't advise you. There's just one thing I've always wanted to ask you. When he was supposed to graduate, and the math teacher flunked him——

WILLY. Oh, that son-of-a-bitch ruined his life.

BERNARD. Yeah, but, Willy, all he had to do was go to summer school and make up that subject.

WILLY. That's right, that's right.

BERNARD. Did you tell him not to go to summer school?

WILLY. Me? I begged him to go. I ordered him to go!

BERNARD. Then why wouldn't he go?

WILLY. Why? Why! Bernard, that question has been trailing me like a ghost for the last fifteen years. He flunked the subject, and laid down and died like a hammer hit him!

BERNARD. Take it easy, kid.

WILLY. Let me talk to you—I got nobody to talk to. Bernard, Bernard, was it my fault? Y'see? It keeps going around in my mind, maybe I did something to him. I got nothing to give him.

BERNARD. Don't take it so hard.

WILLY. Why did he lay down? What is the story there? You were his friend!

BERNARD. Willy, I remember, it was June, and our grades came out. And he'd flunked math.

WILLY. That son-of-a-bitch!

BERNARD. No, it wasn't right then. Biff just got very angry, I remember, and he was ready to enroll in summer school.

WILLY. [*Surprised.*] He was?

BERNARD. He wasn't beaten by it at all. But then, Willy, he disappeared from the block for almost a month. And I got the idea that he'd gone up to New England to see you. Did he have a talk with you then? [WILLY *stares in silence.*]

BERNARD. Willy?

WILLY. [*With a strong edge of resentment in his voice.*] Yeah, he came to Boston. What about it?

BERNARD. Well, just that when he came back—I'll never forget this, it always mystifies me. Because I'd thought so well of Biff, even though he'd always taken advantage of me. I loved him, Willy, y'know? And he came back after that month and took his sneakers—remember those sneakers with "University of Virginia" printed on them? He was so proud of those, wore them every day. And he took them down in the cellar, and burned them up in the furnace. We had a fist fight. It lasted at least half an hour. Just the two of us, punching each other down cellar, and crying right through it. I've often thought of how strange it was that I knew he'd given up his life. What happened in Boston, Willy?

[WILLY *looks at him as at an intruder.*]

BERNARD. I just bring it up because you asked me.

WILLY. [*Angrily.*] Nothing. What do you mean, "What happened?" What's that got to do with anything?

BERNARD. Well, don't get sore.

WILLY. What are you trying to do, blame it on me? If a boy lays down is that my fault?

BERNARD. Now, Willy, don't get——

WILLY. Well, don't–don't talk to me that way! What does that mean, "What happened?"

[CHARLEY *enters. He is in his vest, and he carries a bottle of bourbon.*]

CHARLEY. Hey, you're going to miss that train. [*He waves the bottle.*]

BERNARD. Yeah, I'm going. [*He takes the bottle.*] Thanks, Pop. [*He picks up his rackets and bag.*] Good-by, Willy, and don't worry about it. You know, "If at first you don't succeed . . ."

WILLY. Yes, I believe in that.

BERNARD. But sometimes, Willy, it's better for a man just to walk away.

WILLY. Walk away?

BERNARD. That's right.

WILLY. But if you can't walk away?

BERNARD. [*After a slight pause.*] I guess that's when it's tough. [*Extending his hand.*] Good-by, Willy.

WILLY. [*Shaking* BERNARD's *hand.*] Good-by, boy.

CHARLEY. [*An arm on* BERNARD's *shoulder.*] How do you like this kid? Gonna argue a case in front of the Supreme Court.

BERNARD. [*Protesting.*] Pop!

WILLY. [*Genuinely shocked, pained, and happy.*] No! The Supreme Court!

BERNARD. I gotta run. 'By, Dad!

CHARLEY. Knock 'em dead, Bernard! [BERNARD *goes off.*]

WILLY. [*As* CHARLEY *takes out his wallet.*] The Supreme Court! And he didn't even mention it!

CHARLEY. [*Counting out money on the desk.*] He don't have to—he's gonna do it.

WILLY. And you never told him what to do, did you? You never took any interest in him.

CHARLEY. My salvation is that I never took any interest in anything. There's some money–fifty dollars. I got an accountant inside.

WILLY. Charley, look . . . [*With difficulty.*] I got my insurance to pay. If you can manage it–I need a hundred and ten dollars.

[CHARLEY *doesn't reply for a moment; merely stops moving.*]

WILLY. I'd draw it from my bank but Linda would know, and I . . .

CHARLEY. Sit down, Willy.

WILLY. [*Moving toward the chair.*] I'm keeping an account of everything, remember. I'll pay every penny back. [*He sits.*]

CHARLEY. Now listen to me, Willy.

WILLY. I want you to know I appreciate . . .

CHARLEY. [*Sitting down on the table.*] Willy, what're you doin'? What the hell is goin' on in your head?

WILLY. Why? I'm simply . . .

CHARLEY. I offered you a job. You can make fifty dollars a week. And I won't send you on the road.

WILLY. I've got a job.

CHARLEY. Without pay? What kind of a job is a job without pay? [*He rises.*] Now, look, kid, enough is enough. I'm no genius but I know when I'm being insulted.

WILLY. Insulted!

CHARLEY. Why don't you want to work for me?

WILLY. What's the matter with you? I've got a job.

CHARLEY. Then what're you walkin' in here every week for?

WILLY. [*Getting up.*] Well, if you don't want me to walk in here——

CHARLEY. I am offering you a job.

WILLY. I don't want your goddam job!

CHARLEY. When the hell are you going to grow up?

WILLY. [*Furiously.*] You big ignoramus, if you say that to me again I'll rap you one! I don't care how big you are! [*He's ready to fight. Pause.*]

CHARLEY. [*Kindly, going to him.*] How much do you need, Willy?

WILLY. Charley, I'm strapped. I'm strapped. I don't know what to do. I was just fired.

CHARLEY. Howard fired you?

WILLY. That snotnose. Imagine that? I named him. I named him Howard.

CHARLEY. Willy, when're you gonna realize that them things don't mean anything? You named him Howard, but you can't sell that. The only thing you got in this world is what you can sell. And the funny thing is that you're a salesman, and you don't know that.

WILLY. I've always tried to think otherwise, I guess. I always felt that if a man was impressive, and well liked, that nothing——

CHARLEY. Why must everybody like you? Who liked J. P. Morgan? Was he impressive? In a Turkish bath he'd look like a butcher. But with his pockets on he was very well liked. Now listen, Willy, I know you don't like me, and nobody can say I'm in love with you, but I'll give you a job because—just for the hell of it, put it that way. Now what do you say?

WILLY. I—I just can't work for you, Charley.

CHARLEY. What're you, jealous of me?

WILLY. I can't work for you, that's all, don't ask me why.

CHARLEY. [*Angered, takes out more bills.*] You been jealous of me all your life, you damned fool! Here, pay your insurance.

[*He puts the money in* WILLY's *hand.*]

WILLY. I'm keeping strict accounts.

CHARLEY. I've got some work to do. Take care of yourself. And pay your insurance.

WILLY. [*Moving to the right.*] Funny, y'know? After all the highways, and the trains, and the appointments, and the years, you end up worth more dead than alive.

CHARLEY. Willy, nobody's worth nothin' dead. [*After a slight pause.*] Did you hear what I said?

[WILLY *stands still, dreaming.*]

CHARLEY. Willy!

WILLY. Apologize to Bernard for me when you see him. I didn't mean to argue with him. He's a fine boy. They're all fine boys, and they'll end up big—all of them. Someday they'll all play tennis together. Wish me luck, Charley. He saw Bill Oliver today.

CHARLEY. Good luck.

WILLY. [*On the verge of tears.*] Charley, you're the only friend I got. Isn't that a remarkable thing? [*He goes out.*]

CHARLEY. Jesus!

[CHARLEY *stares after him a moment and follows. All light blacks out. Suddenly raucous music is heard, and a red glow rises behind the screen at right.* STANLEY, *a young waiter, appears, carrying a table, followed by* HAPPY, *who is carrying two chairs.*]

STANLEY. [*Putting the table down.*] That's all right, Mr. Loman, I can handle it myself.

[*He turns and takes the chairs from* HAPPY *and places them at the table.*]

HAPPY. [*Glancing around.*] Oh, this is better.

STANLEY. Sure, in the front there you're in the middle of all kinds a noise. Whenever you got a party, Mr. Loman, you just tell me and I'll put you back here. Y'know, there's a lotta people they don't like it private, because when they go out they like to see a lotta action around them because they're sick and tired to stay in the house by theirself. But I know you, you ain't from Hackensack. You know what I mean?

HAPPY. [*Sitting down.*] So how's it coming, Stanley?

STANLEY. Ah, it's a dog's life. I only wish during the war they'd a took me in the Army. I coulda been dead by now.

HAPPY. My brother's back, Stanley.

STANLEY. Oh, he come back, heh? From the Far West.

HAPPY. Yeah, big cattle man, my brother, so treat him right. And my father's coming too.

STANLEY. Oh, your father too.

HAPPY. You got a couple of nice lobsters?

STANLEY. Hundred per cent, big.

HAPPY. I want them with the claws.

STANLEY. Don't worry, I don't give you no mice. [HAPPY *laughs.*] How about some wine? It'll put a head on the meal.

HAPPY. No. You remember, Stanley, that recipe I brought you from overseas? With the champagne in it?

STANLEY. Oh, year, sure. I still got it tacked up yet in the kitchen. But that'll have to cost a buck apiece anyways.

HAPPY. That's all right.

STANLEY. What'd you, hit a number or somethin'?

HAPPY. No, it's a little celebration. My brother is—I think he pulled off a big deal today. I think we're going into business together.

STANLEY. Great! That's the best for you. Because a family business, you know what I mean?—that's the best.

HAPPY. That's what I think.

STANLEY. 'Cause what's the difference? Somebody steals? It's in the family. Know what I mean? [*Sotto voce.*] Like this bartender here. The boss is goin' crazy what kinda leak he's got in the cash register. You put it in but it don't come out.

HAPPY. [*Raising his head.*] Sh!

STANLEY. What?

HAPPY. You notice I wasn't lookin' right or left, was I?

STANLEY. No.

HAPPY. And my eyes are closed.

STANLEY. So what's the——?

HAPPY. Strudel's comin'.

STANLEY. [*Catching on, looks around.*] Ah, no, there's no——

[*He breaks off as a furred, lavishly dressed* GIRL *enters and sits at the next table. Both follow her with their eyes.*]

STANLEY. Geez, how'd ya know?

HAPPY. I got radar or something. [*Staring directly at her profile.*] Oooooooo . . . Stanley.

STANLEY. I think that's for you, Mr. Loman.

HAPPY. Look at that mouth. Oh, God. And the binoculars.

STANLEY. Geez, you got a life, Mr. Loman.

HAPPY. Wait on her.

STANLEY. [*Going to the* GIRL's *table.*] Would you like a menu, ma'am?

GIRL. I'm expecting someone, but I'd like a——

HAPPY. Why don't you bring her—excuse me, miss, do you mind? I sell champagne, and I'd like you to try my brand. Bring her a champagne, Stanley.

GIRL. That's awfully nice of you.

HAPPY. Don't mention it. It's all company money. [*He laughs.*]

GIRL. That's a charming product to be selling, isn't it?

HAPPY. Oh, gets to be like everything else. Selling is selling, y'know.

GIRL. I suppose.

HAPPY. You don't happen to sell, do you?

GIRL. No, I don't sell.

HAPPY. Would you object to a compliment from a stranger? You ought to be on a magazine cover.

GIRL. [*Looking at him a little archly.*] I have been.

[STANLEY *comes in with a glass of champagne.*]

HAPPY. What'd I say before, Stanley? You see? She's a cover girl.

STANLEY. Oh, I could see, I could see.

HAPPY. [*To the* GIRL.] What magazine?

GIRL. Oh, a lot of them. [*She takes the drink.*] Thank you.

HAPPY. You know what they say in France, don't you? "Champagne is the drink of the complexion"—— Hya, Biff!

[BIFF *has entered and sits with* HAPPY.]

BIFF. Hello, kid. Sorry I'm late.

HAPPY. I just got here. Uh, Miss—?

GIRL. Forsythe.

HAPPY. Miss Forsythe, this is my brother.

BIFF. Is Dad here?

HAPPY. His name is Biff. You might've heard of him. Great football player.

GIRL. Really? What team?

HAPPY. Are you familiar with football?

GIRL. No, I'm afraid I'm not.

HAPPY. Biff is quarterback with the New York Giants.

GIRL. Well, that is nice, isn't it? [*She drinks.*]

HAPPY. Good health.

GIRL. I'm happy to meet you.

HAPPY. That's my name: Hap. It's really Harold, but at West Point they called me Happy.

GIRL. [*Now really impressed.*] Oh, I see. How do you do? [*She turns her profile.*]

BIFF. Isn't Dad coming?

HAPPY. You want her?

BIFF. Oh, I could never make that.

HAPPY. I remember the time that idea would never come into your head. Where's the old confidence, Biff?

BIFF. I just saw Oliver——

HAPPY. Wait a minute. I've got to see that old confidence again. Do you want her? She's on call.

BIFF. Oh, no. [*He turns to look at the* GIRL.]

HAPPY. I'm telling you. Watch this. [*Turning to the* GIRL.] Honey? [*She turns to him.*] Are you busy?

GIRL. Well, I am . . . but I could make a phone call.

HAPPY. Do that, will you, honey? And see if you can get a friend. We'll be here for a while. Biff is one of the greatest football players in the country.

GIRL. [*Standing up.*] Well, I'm certainly happy to meet you.

HAPPY. Come back soon.

GIRL. I'll try.

HAPPY. Don't try, honey, try hard.

[*The* GIRL *exits.* STANLEY *follows, shaking his head in bewildered admiration.*]

HAPPY. Isn't that a shame now? A beautiful girl like that? That's why I can't get married. There's not a good woman in a thousand. New York is loaded with them, kid!

BIFF. Hap, look——

HAPPY. I told you she was on call!

BIFF. [*Strangely unnerved.*] Cut it out will ya? I want to say something to you.

HAPPY. Did you see Oliver?

BIFF. I saw him all right. Now look, I want to tell Dad a couple of things and I want you to help me.

HAPPY. What? Is he going to back you?

BIFF. Are you crazy? You're out of your goddam head, you know that?

HAPPY. Why? What happened?

BIFF. [*Breathlessly.*] I did a terrible thing today, Hap. It's been the strangest day I ever went through. I'm all numb, I swear.

HAPPY. You mean he wouldn't see you?

BIFF. Well, I waited six hours for him, see? All day. Kept sending my name in. Even tried to date his secretary so she'd get me to him, but no soap.

HAPPY. Because you're not showin' the old confidence, Biff. He remembered you, didn't he?

BIFF. [*Stopping* HAPPY *with a gesture.*] Finally, about five o'clock, he comes out. Didn't remember who I was or anything. I felt like such an idiot, Hap.

HAPPY. Did you tell him my Florida idea?

BIFF. He walked away. I saw him for one minute. I got so mad I could've torn the walls down! How the hell did I ever get the idea I was a salesman there? I even believed myself that I'd been a salesman for him! And then he gave me one look and—I realized what a ridiculous lie my whole life has been! We've been talking a dream for fifteen years. I was a shipping clerk.

HAPPY. What'd you do?

BIFF. [*With great tension and wonder.*] Well, he left, see. And the secretary went out. I was all alone in the waiting-room. I don't know what came over me, Hap. The next thing I know I'm in his office—paneled walls, everything. I can't explain it. I—Hap, I took his fountain pen.

HAPPY. Geez, did he catch you?

BIFF. I ran out. I ran down all eleven flights. I ran and ran and ran.

HAPPY. That was an awful dumb—what'd you do that for?

BIFF. [*Agonized.*] I don't know, I just—wanted to take something, I don't know. You gotta help me, Hap; I'm gonna tell Pop.

HAPPY. You crazy? What for?

BIFF. Hap, he's got to understand that I'm not the man somebody lends that kind of money to. He thinks I've been spiting him all these years and it's eating him up.

HAPPY. That's just it. You tell him something nice.

BIFF. I can't.

HAPPY. Say you got a lunch date with Oliver tomorrow.

BIFF. So what do I do tomorrow?

HAPPY. You leave the house tomorrow and come back at night and say Oliver is thinking it over. And he thinks it over for a couple of weeks, and gradually it fades away and nobody's the worse.

BIFF. But it'll go on forever!

HAPPY. Dad is never so happy as when he's looking forward to something!

[WILLY *enters.*]

HAPPY. Hello, scout!

WILLY. Gee, I haven't been here in years!

[STANLEY has followed WILLY *in and sets a chair for him.* STANLEY *starts off but* HAPPY *stops him.*]

HAPPY. Stanley!

[STANLEY *stands by, waiting for an order.*]

BIFF. [*Going to* WILLY *with guilt, as to an invalid.*] Sit down, Pop. You want a drink?

WILLY. Sure, I don't mind.

BIFF. Let's get a load on.

WILLY. You look worried.

BIFF. N-no. [*To* STANLEY.] Scotch all around. Make it doubles.

STANLEY. Doubles, right. [*He goes.*]

WILLY. You had a couple already, didn't you?

BIFF. Just a couple, yeah.

WILLY. Well, what happened, boy? [*Nodding affirmatively, with a smile.*] Everything go all right?

BIFF. [*Takes a breath, then reaches out and grasps* WILLY's *hand.*] Pal . . . [*He is smiling bravely, and* WILLY *is smiling too.*] I had an experience today.

HAPPY. Terrific, Pop.

WILLY. That so? What happened?

BIFF. [*High, slightly alcoholic, above the earth.*] I'm going to tell you everything from first to last. It's been a strange day. [*Silence. He looks around, composes himself as best he can, but his breath keeps breaking the rhythm of his voice.*] I had to wait quite a while for him, and——

WILLY. Oliver?

BIFF. Yeah, Oliver. All day, as a matter of cold fact. And a lot of—instances—facts, Pop, facts about

my life came back to me. Who was it, Pop? Who ever said I was a salesman with Oliver?

WILLY. Well, you were.

BIFF. No, Dad, I was a shipping clerk.

WILLY. But you were practically——

BIFF. [*With determination.*] Dad, I don't know who said it first, but I was never a salesman for Bill Oliver.

WILLY. What're you talking about?

BIFF. Let's hold on to the facts tonight, Pop. We're not going to get anywhere bullin' around. I was a shipping clerk.

WILLY. [*Angrily.*] All right, now listen to me——

BIFF. Why don't you let me finish?

WILLY. I'm not interested in stories about the past or any crap of that kind because the woods are burning, boys, you understand? There's a big blaze going on all around. I was fired today.

BIFF. [*Shocked.*] How could you be?

WILLY. I was fired, and I'm looking for a little good news to tell your mother, because the woman has waited and the woman has suffered. The gist of it is that I haven't got a story left in my head, Biff. So don't give me a lecture about facts and aspects. I am not interested. Now what've you got to say to me?

[STANLEY *enters with three drinks. They wait until he leaves.*]

WILLY. Did you see Oliver?

BIFF. Jesus, Dad!

WILLY. You mean you didn't go up there?

HAPPY. Sure he went up there.

BIFF. I did. I—saw him. How could they fire you?

WILLY. [*On the edge of his chair.*] What kind of welcome did he give you?

BIFF. He won't even let you work on commission?

WILLY. I'm out! [*Driving.*] So tell me, he gave you a warm welcome?

HAPPY. Sure, Pop, sure!

BIFF. [*Driven.*] Well, it was kind of——

WILLY. I was wondering if he'd remember you. [*To* HAPPY.] Imagine, man doesn't see him for ten, twelve years and gives him that kind of a welcome!

HAPPY. Damn right!

BIFF. [*Trying to return to the offensive.*] Pop, look——

WILLY. You know why he remembered you, don't you? Because you impressed him in those days.

BIFF. Let's talk quietly and get this down to the facts, huh?

WILLY. [*As though* BIFF *had been interrupting.*] Well, what happened? It's great news, Biff. Did he take you into his office or'd you talk in the waiting-room?

BIFF. Well, he came in, see, and——

WILLY. [*With a big smile.*] What'd he say? Betcha he threw his arm around you.

BIFF. Well, he kinda——

WILLY. He's a fine man. [*To* HAPPY.] Very hard man to see, y'know.

HAPPY. [*Agreeing.*] Oh, I know.

WILLY. [*To* BIFF.] Is that where you had the drinks?

BIFF. Yeah, he gave me a couple of—no, no!

HAPPY. [*Cutting in.*] He told him my Florida idea.

WILLY. Don't interrupt. [*To* BIFF.] How'd he react to the Florida idea?

BIFF. Dad, will you give me a minute to explain?

WILLY. I've been waiting for you to explain since I sat down here! What happened? He took you into his office and what?

BIFF. Well—I talked. And—and he listened, see.

WILLY. Famous for the way he listens, y'know. What was his answer?

BIFF. His answer was—— [*He breaks off, suddenly angry.*] Dad, you're not letting me tell you what I want to tell you!

WILLY. [*Accusing, angered.*] You didn't see him, did you?

BIFF. I did see him!

WILLY. What'd you insult him or something? You insulted him, didn't you?

BIFF. Listen, will you let me out of it, will you just let me out of it!

HAPPY. What the hell!

WILLY. Tell me what happened!

BIFF. [*To* HAPPY.] I can't talk to him!

[*A single trumpet note jars the ear. The light of green leaves stains the house, which holds the air of night and a dream.* YOUNG BERNARD *enters and knocks on the door of the house.*]

YOUNG BERNARD. [*Frantically.*] Mrs. Loman, Mrs. Loman!

HAPPY. Tell him what happened!

BIFF. [*To* HAPPY.] Shut up and leave me alone!

WILLY. No, no! You had to go and flunk math!

BIFF. What math? What're you talking about?

YOUNG BERNARD. Mrs. Loman, Mrs. Loman!

[LINDA *appears in the house, as of old.*]

WILLY. [*Wildly.*] Math, math, math!

BIFF. Take it easy, Pop!

YOUNG BERNARD. Mrs. Loman!

WILLY. [*Furiously.*] If you hadn't flunked you'd've been set by now!

BIFF. Now, look, I'm gonna tell you what happened, and you're going to listen to me.

YOUNG BERNARD. Mrs. Loman!

BIFF. I waited six hours——

HAPPY. What the hell are you saying?

BIFF. I kept sending in my name but he wouldn't see me. So finally he . . .

[*He continues unheard as light fades low on the restaurant.*]

YOUNG BERNARD. Biff flunked math!

LINDA. No!

YOUNG BERNARD. Birnbaum flunked him! They won't graduate him!

LINDA. But they have to. He's gotta go to the university. Where is he? Biff! Biff!

YOUNG BERNARD. No, he left. He went to Grand Central.

LINDA. Grand—— You mean he went to Boston!

YOUNG BERNARD. Is Uncle Willy in Boston?

LINDA. Oh, maybe Willy can talk to the teacher. Oh, the poor, poor boy!

[*Light on house area snaps out.*]

BIFF. [*At the table, now audible, holding up a gold fountain pen.*] . . . so I'm washed up with Oliver, you understand? Are you listening to me?

WILLY. [*At a loss.*] Yeah, sure. If you hadn't flunked——

BIFF. Flunked what? What're you talking about?

WILLY. Don't blame everything on me! I didn't flunk math—you did! What pen?

HAPPY. That was awful dumb, Biff, a pen like that is worth——

WILLY. [*Seeing the pen for the first time.*] You took Oliver's pen?

BIFF. [*Weakening.*] Dad, I just explained it to you.

WILLY. You stole Bill Oliver's fountain pen!

BIFF. I didn't exactly steal it! That's just what I've been explaining to you!

HAPPY. He had it in his hand and just then Oliver walked in, so he got nervous and stuck it in his pocket!

WILLY. My God, Biff!

BIFF. I never intended to do it, Dad!

OPERATOR'S VOICE. Standish Arms, good evening!

WILLY. [*Shouting.*] I'm not in my room!

BIFF. [*Frightened.*] Dad, what's the matter?

[*He and* HAPPY *stand up.*]

OPERATOR. Ringing Mr. Loman for you!

WILLY. I'm not there, stop it!

BIFF. [*Horrified, gets down on one knee before* WILLY.] Dad, I'll make good, I'll make good. [WILLY *tries to get to his feet.* BIFF *holds him down.*] Sit down now.

WILLY. No, you're no good, you're no good for anything.

BIFF. I am, Dad; I'll find something else, you understand? Now don't worry about anything. [*He holds up* WILLY's *face.*] Talk to me, Dad.

OPERATOR. Mr. Loman does not answer. Shall I page him?

WILLY. [*Attempting to stand, as though to rush and silence the* OPERATOR.] No, no, no!

HAPPY. He'll strike something, Pop.

WILLY. No, no . . .

BIFF. [*Desperately, standing over* WILLY.] Pop, listen! Listen to me! I'm telling you something good. Oliver talked to his partner about the Florida idea. You listening? He—he talked to his partner, and he came to me . . . I'm going to be all right, you hear? Dad, listen to me, he said it was just a question of the amount!

WILLY. Then you . . . got it?

HAPPY. He's gonna be terrific, Pop!

WILLY. [*Trying to stand.*] Then you got it, haven't you? You got it! You got it!

BIFF. [*Agonized, holds* WILLY *down.*] No, no. Look, Pop. I'm supposed to have lunch with them tomorrow. I'm just telling you this so you'll know that I can still make an impression, Pop. And I'll make good somewhere, but I can't go tomorrow, see?

WILLY. Why not? You simply——

BIFF. But the pen, Pop!

WILLY. You give it to him and tell him it was an oversight!

HAPPY. Sure, have lunch tomorrow!

BIFF. I can't say that——

WILLY. You were doing a crossword puzzle and accidentally used his pen!

BIFF. Listen, kid, I took those balls years ago, now I walk in with his fountain pen? That clinches it, don't you see? I can't face him like that! I'll try elsewhere.

PAGE'S VOICE. Paging Mr. Loman!

WILLY. Don't you want to be anything?

BIFF. Pop, how can I go back?

WILLY. You don't want to be anything, is that what's behind it?

BIFF. [*Now angry at* WILLY *for not crediting his sympathy.*] Don't take it that way! You think it was easy walking into that office after what I'd done to him? A team of horses couldn't have dragged me back to Bill Oliver!

WILLY. Then why'd you go?

BIFF. Why did I go? Why did I go! Look at you! Look at what's become of you!

[*Off left,* THE WOMAN *laughs.*]

WILLY. Biff, you're going to go to that lunch tomorrow, or——

BIFF. I can't go. I've got no appointment!

HAPPY. Biff, for . . . !

WILLY. Are you spiting me?

BIFF. Don't take it that way! Goddammit!

WILLY. [*Strikes* BIFF *and falters away from the table.*] You rotten little louse! Are you spiting me?

THE WOMAN. Someone's at the door, Willy!

BIFF. I'm no good, can't you see what I am?

HAPPY. [*Separating them.*] Hey, you're in a restaurant! Now cut it out, both of you! [*The* GIRLS *enter.*] Hello, girls, sit down. [THE WOMAN *laughs, off left.*]

MISS FORSYTHE. I guess we might as well. This is Letta.

THE WOMAN. Willy, are you going to wake up?

BIFF. [*Ignoring* WILLY.] How're ya, miss, sit down. What do you drink?

MISS FORSYTHE. Letta might not be able to stay long.

LETTA. I gotta get up very early tomorrow. I got jury duty. I'm so excited! Were you fellows ever on a jury?

BIFF. No, but I been in front of them! [*The* GIRLS *laugh.*] This is my father.

LETTA. Isn't he cute? Sit down with us, Pop.

HAPPY. Sit him down, Biff!

BIFF. [*Going to him.*] Come on, slugger, drink us under the table. To hell with it! Come on, sit down, pal.

[*On* BIFF's *last insistence,* WILLY *is about to sit.*]

THE WOMAN. [*Now urgently.*] Willy, are you going to answer the door!

[THE WOMAN's *call pulls* WILLY *back. He starts right, befuddled.*]

BIFF. Hey, where are you going?

WILLY. Open the door.

BIFF. The door?

WILLY. The washroom . . . the door . . . where's the door?

BIFF. [*Leading* WILLY *to the left.*] Just go straight down. [WILLY *moves left.*]

THE WOMAN. Willy, Willy, are you going to get up, get up, get up, get up? [WILLY *exits left.*]

LETTA. I think it's sweet you bring your daddy along.

MISS FORSYTHE. Oh, he isn't really your father!

BIFF. [*At left, turning to her resentfully.*] Miss Forsythe, you've just seen a prince walk by. A fine, troubled prince. A hard-working, unappreciated prince. A pal, you understand? A good companion. Always for his boys.

LETTA. That's so sweet.

HAPPY. Well, girls, what's the program? We're wasting time. Come on, Biff. Gather round. Where would you like to go?

BIFF. Why don't you do something for him?

HAPPY. Me!

BIFF. Don't you give a damn for him, Hap?

HAPPY. What're you talking about? I'm the one who——

BIFF. I sense it, you don't give a good goddam about him. [*He takes the rolled-up hose from his*

pocket and puts it on the table in front of HAPPY.]
Look what I found in the cellar, for Christ's sake.
How can you bear to let it go on?

HAPPY. Me? Who goes away? Who runs off and——

BIFF. Yeah, but he doesn't mean anything to you.
You could help him—I can't! Don't you understand
what I'm talking about? He's going to kill himself,
don't you know that?

HAPPY. Don't I know it! Me!

BIFF. Hap, help him! Jesus . . . help him . . .
Help me, help me, I can't bear to look at his face!

[*Ready to weep, he hurries out, up right.*]

HAPPY. [*Staring after him.*] Where are going?

MISS FORSYTHE. What's he so mad about?

HAPPY. Come on, girls, we'll catch up with him.

MISS FORSYTHE. [*As* HAPPY *pushes her out.*] Say,
I don't like that temper of his!

HAPPY. He's just a little overstrung, he'll be all
right!

WILLY. [*Off left, as* THE WOMAN *laughs.*] Don't
answer! Don't answer!

LETTA. Don't you want to tell your father——

HAPPY. No, that's not my father. He's just a guy.
Come on, we'll catch Biff, and, honey, we're going
to paint this town! Stanley, where's the check! Hey,
Stanley!

[*They exit.* STANLEY *looks toward left.*]

STANLEY. [*Calling to* HAPPY *indignantly.*] Mr.
Loman! Mr. Loman!

[STANLEY *picks up a chair and follows them off.
Knocking is heard off left.* THE WOMAN *enters.
laughing.* WILLY *follows her. She is in a black
slip; he is buttoning his shirt. Raw, sensuous
music accompanies their speech.*]

WILLY. Will you stop laughing? Will you stop?

THE WOMAN. Aren't you going to answer the door?
He'll wake the whole hotel.

WILLY. I'm not expecting anybody.

THE WOMAN. Whyn't you have another drink,
honey, and stop being so damn self-centered?

WILLY. I'm so lonely.

THE WOMAN. You know you ruined me, Willy?
From now on, whenever you come to the office, I'll
see that you go right through to the buyers. No
waiting at my desk any more, Willy. You ruined me.

WILLY. That's nice of you to say that.

THE WOMAN. Gee, you are self-centered! Why so
sad! You are the saddest, self-centeredest soul I ever
did see-saw. [*She laughs. He kisses her.*] Come on
inside, drummer boy. It's silly to be dressing in the
middle of the night. [*As knocking is heard.*] Aren't
you going to answer the door?

WILLY. They're knocking on the wrong door.

THE WOMAN. But I felt the knocking. And he
heard us talking in here. Maybe the hotel's on fire!

WILLY. [*His terror rising.*] It's a mistake.

THE WOMAN. Then tell him to go away!

WILLY. There's nobody there.

THE WOMAN. It's getting on my nerves, Willy.
There's somebody standing out there and it's getting
on my nerves!

WILLY. [*Pushing her away from him.*] All right,
stay in the bathroom here, and don't come out. I
think there's a law in Massachusetts about it, so
don't come out. It may be that new room clerk. He
looked very mean. So don't come out. It's a mistake,
there's no fire.

[*The knocking is heard again. He takes a few
steps away from her, and she vanishes into
the wing. The light follows him, and now he
is facing* YOUNG BIFF, *who carries a suitcase.*
BIFF *steps toward him. The music is gone.*]

BIFF. Why didn't you answer?

WILLY. Biff! What are you doing in Boston?

BIFF. Why didn't you answer? I've been knocking
for five minutes; I called you on the phone——

WILLY. I just heard you. I was in the bathroom and
had the door shut. Did anything happen home?

BIFF. Dad—I let you down.

WILLY. What do you mean?

BIFF. Dad . . .

WILLY. Biffo, what's this about? [*Putting his arm
around* BIFF.] Come on, let's go downstairs and get
you a malted.

BIFF. Dad, I flunked math.

WILLY. Not for the term?

BIFF. The term. I haven't got enough credits to
graduate.

WILLY. You mean to say Bernard wouldn't give you
the answers?

BIFF. He did, he tried, but I only got a sixty-one.

WILLY. And they wouldn't give you four points?

BIFF. Birnbaum refused absolutely. I begged him,
Pop, but he won't give me those points. You gotta
talk to him before they close the school. Because if
he saw the kind of man you are, and you just talked
to him in your way, I'm sure he'd come through for
me. The class came right before practice, see, and I
didn't go enough. Would you talk to him? He'd like
you, Pop. You know the way you could talk.

WILLY. You're on. We'll drive right back.

BIFF. Oh, Dad, good work! I'm sure he'll change
it for you!

WILLY. Go downstairs and tell the clerk I'm
checkin' out. Go right down.

BIFF. Yes, sir! See, the reason he hates me, Pop—
one day he was late for class so I got up at the
blackboard and imitated him. I crossed my eyes and
talked with a lithp.

WILLY. [*Laughing.*] You did? The kids like it?

BIFF. They nearly died laughing!

WILLY. Yeah? What'd you do?

BIFF. The thquare root of thixthy twee is . . . [WILLY *bursts out laughing;* BIFF *joins him.*] And in the middle of it he walked in!

[WILLY *laughs and* THE WOMAN *joins in offstage.*]

WILLY. [*Without hesitation.*] Hurry downstairs and——

BIFF. Somebody in there?

WILLY. No, that was next door.

[THE WOMAN *laughs offstage.*]

BIFF. Somebody got in your bathroom!

WILLY. No, it's the next room, there's a party——

THE WOMAN. [*Enters, laughing. She lisps this.*] Can I come in? There's something in the bathtub, Willy, and it's moving!

[WILLY *looks at* BIFF, *who is staring openmouthed and horrified at* THE WOMAN.]

WILLY. Ah—you better go back to your room. They must be finished painting by now. They're painting her room so I let her take a shower here. Go back, go back . . . [*He pushes her.*]

THE WOMAN. [*Resisting.*] But I've got to get dressed, Willy, I can't——

WILLY. Get out of here! Go back, go back . . . [*Suddenly striving for the ordinary.*] This is Miss Francis, Biff, she's a buyer. They're painting her room. Go back, Miss Francis, go back . . .

THE WOMAN. But my clothes, I can't go out naked in the hall!

WILLY. [*Pushing her offstage.*] Get outa here! Go back, go back!

[BIFF *slowly sits down on his suitcase as the argument continues offstage.*]

THE WOMAN. Where's my stockings? You promised me stockings, Willy!

WILLY. I have no stockings here!

THE WOMAN. You had two boxes of size nine sheers for me, and I want them!

WILLY. Here, for God's sake, will you get outa here!

THE WOMAN. [*Enters holding a box of stockings.*] I just hope there's nobody in the hall. That's all I hope. [*To* BIFF.] Are you football or baseball?

BIFF. Football.

THE WOMAN. [*Angry, humiliated.*] That's me too. G'night.

[*She snatches her clothes from* WILLY, *and walks out.*]

WILLY. [*After a pause.*] Well, better get going. I want to get to the school first thing in the morning. Get my suits out of the closet. I'll get my valise. [BIFF *doesn't move.*] What's the matter? [BIFF *remains motionless, tears falling.*] She's a buyer. Buys for J. H. Simmons. She lives down the hall—they're painting. You don't imagine—— [*He breaks off. After a pause.*] Now listen, pal, she's just a buyer. She sees merchandise in her room and they have to keep it looking just so . . . [*Pause. Assuming command.*] All right, get my suits. [BIFF *doesn't move.*] Now stop crying and do as I say. I gave you an order. Biff, I gave you an order! Is that what you do when I give you an order? How dare you cry! [*Putting his arm around* BIFF.] Now look, Biff, when you grow up you'll understand about these things. You mustn't—you mustn't overemphasize a thing like this. I'll see Birnbaum first thing in the morning.

BIFF. Never mind.

WILLY. [*Getting down beside* BIFF.] Never mind! He's going to give you those points. I'll see to it.

BIFF. He wouldn't listen to you.

WILLY. He certainly will listen to me. You need those points for the U. of Virginia.

BIFF. I'm not going there.

WILLY. Heh? If I can't get him to change that mark you'll make it up in summer school. You've got all summer to——

BIFF. [*His weeping breaking from him.*] Dad . . .

WILLY. [*Infected by it.*] Oh, my boy . . .

BIFF. Dad . . .

WILLY. She's nothing to me, Biff. I was lonely, I was terribly lonely.

BIFF. You—you gave her Mama's stockings!

[*His tears break through and he rises to go.*]

WILLY. [*Grabbing for* BIFF.] I gave you an order!

BIFF. Don't touch me, you—liar!

WILLY. Apologize for that!

BIFF. You fake! You phony little fake! You fake!

[*Overcome, he turns quickly and weeping fully goes out with his suitcase.* WILLY *is left on the floor on his knees.*]

WILLY. I gave you an order! Biff, come back here or I'll beat you! Come back here! I'll whip you!

[STANLEY *comes quickly in from the right and stands in front of* WILLY.]

WILLY. [*Shouts at* STANLEY.] I gave you an order . . .

STANLEY. Hey, let's pick it up, pick it up, Mr. Loman. [*He helps* WILLY *to his feet.*] Your boys left with the chippies. They said they'll see you home.

[*A second waiter watches some distance away.*]

WILLY. But we were supposed to have dinner together.

[*Music is heard,* WILLY's *theme.*]

STANLEY. Can you make it?

WILLY. I'll—sure, I can make it. [*Suddenly concerned about his clothes.*] Do I—I look all right?

STANLEY. Sure, you look all right.

[*He flicks a speck off* WILLY's *lapel.*]

WILLY. Here—here's a dollar.

STANLEY. Oh, your son paid me. It's all right.

WILLY. [*Putting it in* STANLEY's *hand.*] No, take it. You're a good boy.

STANLEY. Oh, no, you don't have to . . .

WILLY. Here—here's some more, I don't need it any more. [*After a slight pause.*] Tell me—is there a seed store in the neighborhood?

STANLEY. Seeds? You mean like to plant?

[*As* WILLY *turns,* STANLEY *slips the money back into his jacket pocket.*]

WILLY. Yes. Carrots, peas . . .

STANLEY. Well, there's hardware stores on Sixth Avenue, but it may be too late now.

WILLY. [*Anxiously.*] Oh, I'd better hurry. I've got to get some seeds. [*He starts off to the right.*] I've got to get some seeds, right away. Nothing's planted. I don't have a thing in the ground.

[WILLY *hurries out as the light goes down.* STANLEY *moves over to the right after him, watches him off. The other waiter has been staring at* WILLY.]

STANLEY. [*To the waiter.*] Well, whatta you looking at?

[*The waiter picks up the chairs and moves off right.* STANLEY *takes the table and follows him. The light fades on this area. There is a long pause, the sound of the flute coming over. The light gradually rises on the kitchen, which is empty.* HAPPY *appears at the door of the house, followed by* BIFF. HAPPY *is carrying a large bunch of long-stemmed roses. He enters the kitchen, looks around for* LINDA. *Not seeing her, he turns to* BIFF, *who is just outside the house door, and makes a gesture with his hands, indicating "Not here, I guess." He looks into the living-room and freezes. Inside,* LINDA, *unseen, is seated,* WILLY's *coat on her lap. She rises ominously and quietly and moves toward* HAPPY, *who backs up into the kitchen, afraid.*]

HAPPY. Hey, what're you doing up? [LINDA *says nothing but moves toward him implacably.*] Where's Pop? [*He keeps backing to the right, and now* LINDA *is in full view in the doorway to the living-room.*] Is he sleeping?

LINDA. Where were you?

HAPPY. [*Trying to laugh it off.*] We met two girls, Mom, very fine types. Here, we brought you some flowers. [*Offering them to her.*] Put them in your room, Ma.

[*She knocks them to the floor at* BIFF's *feet. He has now come inside and closed the door behind him. She stares at* BIFF, *silent.*]

HAPPY. Now what'd you do that for? Mom, I want you to have some flowers——

LINDA. [*Cutting* HAPPY *off, violently to* BIFF.] Don't you care whether he lives or dies?

HAPPY. [*Going to the stairs.*] Come upstairs, Biff.

BIFF. [*With a flare of disgust, to* HAPPY.] Go away from me! [*To* LINDA.] What do you mean, lives or dies? Nobody's dying around here, pal.

LINDA. Get out of my sight! Get out of here!

BIFF. I wanna see the boss.

LINDA. You're not going near him!

BIFF. Where is he?

[*He moves into the living-room and* LINDA *follows.*]

LINDA. [*Shouting after* BIFF.] You invite him for dinner. He looks forward to it all day— [BIFF *appears in his parents' bedroom, looks around, and exits.*] —and then you desert him there. There's no stranger you'd do that to!

HAPPY. Why? He had a swell time with us. Listen, when I— [LINDA *comes back into the kitchen.*] —desert him I hope I don't outlive the day!

LINDA. Get out of here!

HAPPY. Now look, Mom . . .

LINDA. Did you have to go to women tonight? You and your lousy rotten whores!

[BIFF *re-enters the kitchen.*]

HAPPY. Mom, all we did was follow Biff around trying to cheer him up! [*To* BIFF.] Boy, what a night you gave me!

LINDA. Get out of here, both of you, don't come back! I don't want you tormenting him any more. Go on now, get your things together! [*To* BIFF.] You can sleep in his apartment. [*She starts to pick up the flowers and stops herself.*] Pick up this stuff, I'm not your maid any more. Pick it up, you bum, you!

[HAPPY *turns his back to her in refusal.* BIFF *slowly moves over and gets down on his knees, picking up the flowers.*]

LINDA. You're a pair of animals! Not one, not another living soul would have had the cruelty to walk out on that man in a restaurant!

BIFF. [*Not looking at her.*] Is that what he said?

LINDA. He didn't have to say anything. He was so humiliated he nearly limped when he came in.

HAPPY. But, Mom, he had a great time with us——

BIFF. [*Cutting him off violently.*] Shut up!

[*Without another word,* HAPPY *goes upstairs.*]

LINDA. You! You didn't even go in to see if he was all right!

BIFF. [*Still on the floor in front of* LINDA, *the flowers in his hand; with self-loathing.*] No. Didn't. Didn't do a damned thing. How do you like that, heh? Left him babbling in a toilet.

LINDA. You louse. You . . .

BIFF. Now you hit it on the nose! [*He gets up, throws the flowers in the wastebasket.*] The scum of the earth, and you're looking at him!

LINDA. Get out of here!

BIFF. I gotta talk to the boss, Mom. Where is he?

LINDA. You're not going near him. Get out of this house!

BIFF [*With absolute assurance, determination.*] No. We're gonna have an abrupt conversation, him and me.

LINDA. You're not talking to him!

[*Hammering is heard from outside the house, off right.* BIFF *turns toward the noise.*]

LINDA. [*Suddenly pleading.*] Will you please leave him alone?

BIFF. What's he doing out there?

LINDA. He's planting the garden!

BIFF. [*Quietly.*] Now? Oh, my God!

[BIFF *moves outside,* LINDA *following. The light dies down on them and comes up on the center of the apron as* WILLY *walks into it. He is carrying a flashlight, a hoe, and a handful of seed packets. He raps the top of the hoe sharply to fix it firmly, and then moves to the left, measuring off the distance with his foot. He holds the flashlight to look at the seed packets, reading off the instructions. He is in the blue of night.*]

WILLY. Carrots . . . quarter-inch apart. Rows . . . one-foot rows. [*He measures it off.*] One foot. [*He puts down a package and measures off.*] Beets. [*He puts down another package and measures again.*] Lettuce. [*He reads the package, puts it down.*] One foot—— [*He breaks off as* BEN *appears at the right and moves slowly down to him.*] What a proposition, ts, ts. Terrific, terrific. 'Cause she's suffered, Ben, the woman has suffered. You understand me? A man can't go out the way he came in, Ben, a man has got to add up to something. You can't, you can't—— [BEN *moves toward him as though to interrupt.*] You gotta consider, now. Don't answer so quick. Remember, it's a guaranteed twenty-thousand-dollar proposition. Now look, Ben, I want you to go through the ins and outs of this thing with me. I've got nobody to talk to, Ben, and the woman has suffered, you hear me?

BEN. [*Standing still, considering.*] What's the proposition?

WILLY. It's twenty thousand dollars on the barrelhead. Guaranteed, gilt-edged, you understand?

BEN. You don't want to make a fool of yourself. They might not honor the policy.

WILLY. How can they dare refuse? Didn't I work like a coolie to meet every premium on the nose? And now they don't pay off? Impossible!

BEN. It's called a cowardly thing, William.

WILLY. Why? Does it take more guts to stand here the rest of my life ringing up a zero?

BEN. [*Yielding.*] That's a point, William. [*He moves, thinking, turns.*] And twenty thousand—that *is* something one can feel with the hand, it is there.

WILLY. [*Now assured, with rising power.*] Oh, Ben, that's the whole beauty of it! I see it like a diamond, shining in the dark, hard and rough, that I can pick up and touch in my hand. Not like—like an appointment! This would not be another damned-fool appointment, Ben, and it changes all the aspects. Because he thinks I'm nothing, see, and so he spites me. But the funeral—— [*Straightening up.*] Ben, that funeral will be massive! They'll come from Maine, Massachusetts, Vermont, New Hampshire! All the old-timers with the strange license plates—that boy will be thunder-struck, Ben, because he never realized—I am known! Rhode Island, New York, New Jersey—— I am known, Ben, and he'll see it with his eyes once and for all. He'll see what I am, Ben! He's in for a shock, that boy!

BEN. [*Coming down to the edge of the garden.*] He'll call you a coward.

WILLY. [*Suddenly fearful.*] No, that would be terrible.

BEN. Yes. And a damned fool.

WILLY. No, no, he mustn't; I won't have that! [*He is broken and desperate.*]

BEN. He'll hate you, William.

[*The gay music of the* BOYS *is heard.*]

WILLY. Oh, Ben, how do we get back to all the great times? Used to be so full of light, and comradeship, the sleigh-riding in winter, and the ruddiness on his cheeks. And always some kind of good news coming up, always something nice coming up ahead. And never even let me carry the valises in the house, and simonizing, simonizing that little red car! Why, why can't I give him something and not have him hate me?

BEN. Let me think about it. [*He glances at his watch.*] I still have a little time. Remarkable proposition, but you've got to be sure you're not making a fool of yourself.

[BEN *drifts off upstage and goes out of sight.* BIFF *comes down from the left.*]

WILLY. [*Suddenly conscious of* BIFF, *turns and looks up at him, then begins picking up the packages of seeds in confusion.*] Where the hell is that seed? [*Indignantly.*] You can't see nothing out here! They boxed in the whole goddam neighborhood!

BIFF. There are people all around here. Don't you realize that?

WILLY. I'm busy. Don't bother me.

BIFF. [*Taking the hoe from* WILLY.] I'm saying

good-by to you, Pop. [WILLY *looks at him, silent, unable to move.*] I'm not coming back any more.

WILLY. You're not going to see Oliver tomorrow?

BIFF. I've got no appointment, Dad.

WILLY. He put his arm around you, and you've got no appointment?

BIFF. Pop, get this now, will you? Everytime I've left it's been a fight that sent me out of here. Today I realized something about myself and I tried to explain it to you and I—I think I'm just not smart enough to make any sense out of it for you. To hell with whose fault it is or anything like that. [*He takes* WILLY's *arm.*] Let's just wrap it up, heh? Come on in; we'll tell Mom.

[*He gently tries to pull* WILLY *to left.*]

WILLY. [*Frozen, immobile, with guilt in his voice.*] No, I don't want to see her.

BIFF. Come on!

[*He pulls again, and* WILLY *tries to pull away.*]

WILLY. [*Highly nervous.*] No, no, I don't want to see her.

BIFF. [*Tries to look into* WILLY's *face, as if to find the answer there.*] Why don't you want to see her?

WILLY. [*More harshly now.*] Don't bother me, will you?

BIFF. What do you mean, you don't want to see her? You don't want them calling you yellow, do you? This isn't your fault; it's me, I'm a bum. Now come inside! [WILLY *strains to get away.*] Did you hear what I said to you?

[WILLY *pulls away and quickly goes by himself into the house.* BIFF *follows.*]

LINDA. [*To* WILLY.] Did you plant, dear?

BIFF. [*At the door, to* LINDA.] All right, we had it out. I'm going and I'm not writing any more.

LINDA. [*Going to* WILLY *in the kitchen.*] I think that's the best way, dear. 'Cause there's no use drawing it out; you'll just never get along. [WILLY *doesn't respond.*]

BIFF. People ask where I am and what I'm doing, you don't know, and you don't care. That way it'll be off your mind and you can start brightening up again. All right? That clears it, doesn't it? [WILLY *is silent, and* BIFF *goes to him.*] You gonna wish me luck, scout? [*He extends his hand.*] What do you say?

LINDA. Shake his hand, Willy.

WILLY. [*Turning to her, seething with hurt.*] There's no necessity to mention the pen at all, y'know.

BIFF. [*Gently.*] I've got no appointment, Dad.

WILLY. [*Erupting fiercely.*] He put his arm around . . . ?

BIFF. Dad, you're never going to see what I am, so

what's the use of arguing? If I strike oil I'll send you a check. Meantime forget I'm alive.

WILLY. [*To* LINDA.] Spite, see?

BIFF. Shake hands, Dad.

WILLY. Not my hand.

BIFF. I was hoping not to go this way.

WILLY. Well, this is the way you're going. Good-by.

[BIFF *looks at him a moment, then turns sharply and goes to the stairs.*]

WILLY. [*Stops him with.*] May you rot in hell if you leave this house!

BIFF. [*Turning.*] Exactly what is it that you want from me?

WILLY. I want you to know, on the train, in the mountains, in the valleys, wherever you go, that you cut down your life for spite!

BIFF. No, no.

WILLY. Spite, spite, is the word of your undoing! And when you're down and out, remember what did it. When you're rotting somewhere beside the railroad tracks, remember, and don't you dare blame it on me!

BIFF. I'm not blaming it on you!

WILLY. I won't take the rap for this, you hear?

[HAPPY *comes down the stairs and stands on the bottom step, watching.*]

BIFF. That's just what I'm telling you!

WILLY. [*Sinking into a chair at the table, with full accusation.*] You're trying to put a knife in me—don't think I don't know what you're doing!

BIFF. All right, phony! Then let's lay it on the line.

[*He whips the rubber tube out of his pocket and puts it on the table.*]

HAPPY. You crazy——

LINDA. Biff!

[*She moves to grab the hose, but* BIFF *holds it down with his hand.*]

BIFF. Leave it there! Don't move it!

WILLY. [*Not looking at it.*] What is that?

BIFF. You know goddam well what that is.

WILLY. [*Caged, wanting to escape.*] I never saw that.

BIFF. You saw it. The mice didn't bring it into the cellar! What is this supposed to do, make a hero out of you? This supposed to make me sorry for you?

WILLY. Never heard of it.

BIFF. There'll be no pity for you, you hear it? No pity!

WILLY. [*To* LINDA.] You hear the spite!

BIFF. No, you're going to hear the truth—what you are and what I am!

LINDA. Stop it!

WILLY. Spite!

HAPPY. [*Coming down toward* BIFF.] You cut it now!

BIFF. [*To* HAPPY.] The man don't know who we are! The man is gonna know! [*To* WILLY.] We never told the truth for ten minutes in this house!

HAPPY. We always told the truth!

BIFF. [*Turning on him.*] You big blow, are you the assistant buyer? You're one of the two assistants to the assistant, aren't you?

HAPPY. Well, I'm practically——

BIFF. You're practically full of it! We all are! And I'm through with it. [*To* WILLY.] Now hear this, Willy, this is me.

WILLY. I know you!

BIFF. You know why I had no address for three months? I stole a suit in Kansas City and I was in jail. [*To* LINDA, *who is sobbing.*] Stop crying. I'm through with it.

[LINDA *turns away from them, her hands covering her face.*]

WILLY. I suppose that's my fault!

BIFF. I stole myself out of every good job since high school!

WILLY. And whose fault is that?

BIFF. And I never got anywhere because you blew me so full of hot air I could never stand taking orders from anybody! That's whose fault it is!

WILLY. I hear that!

LINDA. Don't, Biff!

BIFF. It's goddam time you heard that! I had to be boss big shot in two weeks, and I'm through with it!

WILLY. Then hang yourself! For spite, hang yourself!

BIFF. No! Nobody's hanging himself, Willy! I ran down eleven flights with a pen in my hand today. And suddenly I stopped, you hear me? And in the middle of that office building, do you hear this? I stopped in the middle of that building and I saw—the sky. I saw the things that I love in this world. The work and the food and time to sit and smoke. And I looked at the pen and said to myself, what the hell am I grabbing this for? Why am I trying to become what I don't want to be? What am I doing in an office, making a contemptuous, begging fool of myself, when all I want is out there, waiting for me the minute I say I know who I am! Why can't I say that, Willy?

[*He tries to make* WILLY *face him, but* WILLY *pulls away and moves to the left.*]

WILLY. [*With hatred, threateningly.*] The door of your life is wide open!

BIFF. Pop! I'm a dime a dozen, and so are you!

WILLY. [*Turning on him now in an uncontrolled outburst.*] I am not a dime a dozen! I am Willy Loman, and you are Biff Loman!

[BIFF *starts for* WILLY, *but is blocked by* HAPPY. *In his fury,* BIFF *seems on the verge of attacking his father.*]

BIFF. I am not a leader of men, Willy, and neither are you. You were never anything but a hard-working drummer who landed in the ash can like all the rest of them! I'm one dollar an hour, Willy! I tried seven states and couldn't raise it. A buck an hour! Do you gather my meaning? I'm not bringing home any prizes any more, and you're going to stop waiting for me to bring them home!

WILLY. [*Directly to* BIFF.] You vengeful, spiteful mut!

[BIFF *breaks from* HAPPY. WILLY, *in fright, starts up the stairs.* BIFF *grabs him.*]

BIFF. [*At the peak of his fury.*] Pop, I'm nothing! I'm nothing, Pop. Can't you understand that? There's no spite in it any more. I'm just what I am, that's all.

[BIFF'S *fury has spent itself, and he breaks down, sobbing, holding on to* WILLY, *who dumbly fumbles for* BIFF'S *face.*]

WILLY. [*Astonished.*] What're you doing? What're you doing? [*To* LINDA.] Why is he crying?

BIFF. [*Crying, broken.*] Will you let me go, for Christ's sake? Will you take that phony dream and burn it before something happens? [*Struggling to contain himself, he pulls away and moves to the stairs.*] I'll go in the morning. Put him—put him to bed.

[*Exhausted,* BIFF *moves up the stairs to his room.*]

WILLY. [*After a long pause, astonished, elevated.*] Isn't that—isn't that remarkable? Biff—he likes me!

LINDA. He loves you, Willy!

HAPPY. [*Deeply moved.*] Always did, Pop.

WILLY. Oh, Biff! [*Staring wildly.*] He cried! Cried to me. [*He is choking with his love, and now cries out his promise.*] That boy—that boy is going to be magnificent!

[BEN *appears in the light just outside the kitchen.*]

BEN. Yes, outstanding, with twenty thousand behind him.

LINDA. [*Sensing the racing of his mind, fearfully, carefully.*] Now come to bed, Willy. It's all settled now.

WILLY. [*Finding it difficult not to rush out of the house.*] Yes, we'll sleep. Come on. Go to sleep, Hap.

BEN. And it does take a great kind of a man to crack the jungle.

[*In accents of dread,* BEN'S *idyllic music starts up.*]

HAPPY. [*His arm around* LINDA.] I'm getting married, Pop, don't forget it. I'm changing everything.

I'm gonna run that department before the year is up. You'll see, Mom. [*He kisses her.*]

BEN. The jungle is dark but full of diamonds, Willy.

[WILLY *turns, moves, listening to* BEN.]

LINDA. Be good. You're both good boys, just act that way, that's all.

HAPPY. 'Night, Pop. [*He goes upstairs.*]

LINDA. [*To* WILLY.] Come, dear.

BEN. [*With greater force.*] One must go in to fetch a diamond out.

WILLY. [*To* LINDA, *as he moves slowly along the edge of the kitchen, toward the door.*] I just want to get settled down, Linda. Let me sit alone for a little.

LINDA. [*Almost uttering her fear.*] I want you upstairs.

WILLY. [*Taking her in his arms.*] In a few minutes, Linda. I couldn't sleep right now. Go on, you look awful tired. [*He kisses her.*]

BEN. Not like an appointment at all. A diamond is rough and hard to the touch.

WILLY. Go on now. I'll be right up.

LINDA. I think this is the only way, Willy.

WILLY. Sure, it's the best thing.

BEN. Best thing!

WILLY. The only way. Everything is gonna be— go on, kid, get to bed. You look so tired.

LINDA. Come right up.

WILLY. Two minutes.

[LINDA *goes into the living-room, then reappears in her bedroom.* WILLY *moves just outside the kitchen door.*]

WILLY. Loves me. [*Wonderingly.*] Always loved me. Isn't that a remarkable thing? Ben, he'll worship me for it!

BEN. [*With promise.*] It's dark there, but full of diamonds.

WILLY. Can you imagine that magnificence with twenty thousand dollars in his pocket?

LINDA. [*Calling from her room.*] Willy! Come up!

WILLY. [*Calling into the kitchen.*] Yes! Yes. Coming! It's very smart, you realize that, don't you, sweetheart? Even Ben sees it. I gotta go, baby. 'By! 'By! [*Going over to* BEN, *almost dancing.*] Imagine? When the mail comes he'll be ahead of Bernard again!

BEN. A perfect proposition all around.

WILLY. Did you see how he cried to me? Oh, if I could kiss him, Ben!

BEN. Time, William, time!

WILLY. Oh, Ben, I always knew one way or another we were gonna make it, Biff and I!

BEN. [*Looking at his watch.*] The boat. We'll be late.

[*He moves slowly off into the darkness.*]

WILLY. [*Elegiacally, turning to the house.*] Now when you kick off, boy, I want a seventy-yard boot, and get right down the field under the ball, and when you hit, hit low and hit hard, because it's important, boy. [*He swings around and faces the audience.*] There's all kinds of important people in the stands, and the first thing you know . . . [*Suddenly realizing he is alone.*] Ben! Ben, where do I . . . ? [*He makes a sudden movement of search.*] Ben, how do I . . . ?

LINDA. [*Calling.*] Willy, you coming up?

WILLY. [*Uttering a gasp of fear, whirling about as if to quiet her.*] Sh! [*He turns around as if to find his way; sounds, faces, voices, seem to be swarming in upon him and he flicks at them, crying.*] Sh! Sh! [*Suddenly music, faint and high, stops him. It rises in intensity, almost to an unbearable scream. He goes up and down on his toes, and rushes off around the house.*] Shhh!

LINDA. Willy?

[*There is no answer.* LINDA *waits.* BIFF *gets up off his bed. He is still in his clothes.* HAPPY *sits up.* BIFF *stands listening.*]

LINDA. [*With real fear.*] Willy, answer me! Willy!

[*There is the sound of a car starting and moving away at full speed.*]

LINDA. No!

BIFF. [*Rushing down the stairs.*] Pop!

[*As the car speeds off, the music crashes down in a frenzy of sound, which becomes the soft pulsation of a single cello string.* BIFF *slowly returns to his bedroom. He and* HAPPY *gravely don their jackets.* LINDA *slowly walks out of her room. The music has developed into a dead march. The leaves of day are appearing over everything.* CHARLEY *and* BERNARD, *somberly dressed, appear and knock on the kitchen door.* BIFF *and* HAPPY *slowly descend the stairs to the kitchen as* CHARLEY *and* BERNARD *enter. All stop a moment when* LINDA, *in clothes of mourning, bearing a little bunch of roses, comes through the draped doorway into the kitchen. She goes to* CHARLEY *and takes his arm. Now all move toward the audience, through the wall-line of the kitchen. At the limit of the apron,* LINDA *lays down the flowers, kneels, and sits back on her heels. All stare down at the grave.*]

REQUIEM

CHARLEY. It's getting dark, Linda.

[LINDA *doesn't react. She stares at the grave.*]

BIFF. How about it, Mom? Better get some rest, heh? They'll be closing the gate soon.

[LINDA *makes no move. Pause.*]

HAPPY. [*Deeply angered.*] He had no right to do that. There was no necessity for it. We would've helped him.

CHARLEY. [*Grunting.*] Hmmm.

BIFF. Come along, Mom.

LINDA. Why didn't anybody come?

CHARLEY. It was a very nice funeral.

LINDA. But where are all the people he knew? Maybe they blame him.

CHARLEY. Naa. It's a rough world, Linda. They wouldn't blame him.

LINDA. I can't understand it. At this time especially. First time in thirty-five years we were just about free and clear. He only needed a little salary. He was even finished with the dentist.

CHARLEY. No man only needs a little salary.

LINDA. I can't understand it.

BIFF. There were a lot of nice days. When he'd come home from a trip; or on Sundays, making the stoop; finishing the cellar; putting on the new porch; when he built the extra bathroom; and put up the garage. You know something, Charley, there's more of him in that front stoop than in all the sales he ever made.

CHARLEY. Yeah. He was a happy man with a batch of cement.

LINDA. He was so wonderful with his hands.

BIFF. He had the wrong dreams. All, all, wrong.

HAPPY. [*Almost ready to fight* BIFF.] Don't say that!

BIFF. He never knew who he was.

CHARLEY. [*Stopping* HAPPY's *movement and reply. To* BIFF.] Nobody dast blame this man. You don't understand: Willy was a salesman. And for a salesman, there is no rock bottom to the life. He don't put a bolt to a nut, he don't tell you the law or give you medicine. He's a man way out there in the blue, riding on a smile and a shoeshine. And when they start not smiling back—that's an earthquake. And then you get yourself a couple of spots on your hat, and you're finished. Nobody dast blame this man. A salesman is got to dream, boy. It comes with the territory.

BIFF. Charley, the man didn't know who he was.

HAPPY. [*Infuriated.*] Don't say that!

BIFF. Why don't you come with me, Happy?

HAPPY. I'm not licked that easily. I'm staying right in this city, and I'm gonna beat this racket! [*He looks at* BIFF, *his chin set.*] The Loman Brothers!

BIFF. I know who I am, kid.

HAPPY. All right, boy. I'm gonna show you and everybody else that Willy Loman did not die in vain. He had a good dream. It's the only dream you can have—to come out number-one man. He fought it out here, and this is where I'm gonna win it for him.

BIFF. [*With a hopeless glance at* HAPPY, *bends toward his mother.*] Let's go, Mom.

LINDA. I'll be with you in a minute. Go on, Charley. [*He hesitates.*] I want to, just for a minute. I never had a chance to say good-by.

[CHARLEY *moves away, followed by* HAPPY. BIFF *remains a slight distance up and left of* LINDA. *She sits there, summoning herself. The flute begins, not far away, playing behind her speech.*]

LINDA. Forgive me, dear. I can't cry. I don't know what it is, but I can't cry. I don't understand it. Why did you ever do that? Help me, Willy, I can't cry. It seems to me that you're just on another trip. I keep expecting you. Willy, dear, I can't cry. Why did you do it? I search and search and I search, and I can't understand it, Willy. I made the last payment on the house today. Today, dear. And there'll be nobody home. [*A sob rises in her throat.*] We're free and clear. [*Sobbing more fully, released.*] We're free. [BIFF *comes slowly toward her.*] We're free . . . We're free . . .

[BIFF *lifts her to her feet and moves out up right with her in his arms.* LINDA *sobs quietly.* BERNARD *and* CHARLEY *come together and follow them, followed by* HAPPY. *Only the music of the flute is left on the darkening stage as over the house the hard towers of the apartment buildings rise into sharp focus, and*

THE CURTAIN FALLS

POETRY

THOMAS HARDY

THOMAS HARDY (1840–1928) was born in Dorsetshire, desultorily educated, worked as an architect's apprentice for six years and turned definitely to writing in 1865. Charges of pessimism brought against his novels led him to give his attention chiefly to poetry after 1896. Eventually he was the recipient of many awards and honors. His books include the novels *Far From the Madding Crowd* (1874), *The Return of the Native* (1878), *The Mayor of Casterbridge* (1886), *Tess of the D'Urbervilles* (1891) and *Jude the Obscure* (1896). *Collected Poems of Thomas Hardy* appeared in 1919, and was followed by *The Poetical Works of Thomas Hardy 1920–1924* and *Winter Words in Various Moods and Metres* (1928). "The road to a true philosophy of life," Hardy said, "seems to lie in humbly recording diverse readings of its phenomena as they are forced upon us by chance and change."

NEW YEAR'S EVE

"I have finished another year," said God,
  "In gray, green, white and brown;
I have strewn the leaf upon the sod,
Sealed up the worm within the clod,
  And let the last sun down."

"And what's the good of it?" I said,
  "What reasons made you call
From formless void this earth we tread,
When nine-and-ninety can be read
  Why nought should be at all?

"Yea, Sire; why shaped you us, 'who in
  This tabernacle groan'—
If ever a joy be found herein,
Such joy no man had wished to win
  If he had never known!"

Then he: "My labors—logicless—
  You may explain; not I:
Sense-sealed I have wrought, without a guess
That I evolved a Consciousness
  To ask for reasons why.

"Strange that ephemeral creatures who
  By my own ordering are,
Should see the shortness of my view,
Use ethic tests I never knew,
  Or made provision for!"

He sank to raptness as of yore,
  And opening New Year's Day

The selections by Hardy are from *Collected Poems by Thomas Hardy.* Copyright, 1925, by The Macmillan Company. Used with the permission of The Macmillan Company, Macmillan & Co. Ltd., London, and The Macmillan Company of Canada Limited.

Wove it by rote as theretofore,
And went on working evermore
  In his unweeting way.

THE OXEN

Christmas Eve, and twelve of the clock,
  "Now they are all on their knees,"
An elder said as we sat in a flock
  By the embers in hearthside ease.

We pictured the meek mild creatures where
  They dwelt in their strawy pen,
Nor did it occur to one of us there
  To doubt they were kneeling then.

So fair a fancy few would weave
  In these years! Yet, I feel,
If someone said on Christmas Eve,
  "Come; see the oxen kneel

"In the lonely barton by yonder coomb
  Our childhood used to know,"
I should go with him in the gloom,
  Hoping it might be so.

THE DARKLING THRUSH

I leant upon a coppice gate
  When Frost was spectre-gray,
And Winter's dregs made desolate
  The weakening eye of day.
The tangled bine-stems scored the sky
  Like strings from broken lyres,
And all mankind that haunted nigh
  Had sought their household fires.

The land's sharp features seemed to be
   The Century's corpse outleant;
His crypt the cloudy canopy,
   The wind his death-lament.
The ancient pulse of germ and birth
   Was shrunken hard and dry,
And every spirit upon earth
   Seemed fervourless as I.

At once a voice burst forth among
   The bleak twigs overhead
In a full-hearted evensong
   Of joy unlimited;
An aged thrush, frail, gaunt and small,
   In blast-beruffled plume,
Had chosen thus to fling his soul
   Upon the growing gloom.

So little cause for carolings
   Of such ecstatic sound
Was written on terrestrial things
   Afar or nigh around,
That I could think there trembled through
   His happy good-night air
Some blessed Hope, whereof he knew
   And I was unaware.

IN TIME OF "THE BREAKING OF NATIONS"

I

Only a man harrowing clods
   In a slow silent walk
With an old horse that stumbles and nods
   Half asleep as they stalk.

II

Only thin smoke without flame
   From the heaps of couch-grass;
Yet this will go onward the same
   Though Dynasties pass.

III

Yonder a maid and her wight
   Come whispering by:
War's annals will cloud into night
   Ere their story die.

THE CONVERGENCE OF THE TWAIN

(Lines on the loss of the "Titanic")

I

In a solitude of the sea
Deep from human vanity,
And the Pride of Life that planned her, stilly couches
   she.

II

Steel chambers, late the pyres
Of her salamandrine fires,
Cold currents thrid, and turn to rhythmic tidal lyres.

III

Over the mirrors meant
To glass the opulent
The sea-worm crawls—grotesque, slimed, dumb,
   indifferent.

IV

Jewels in joy designed
To ravish the sensuous mind
Lie lightless, all their sparkles bleared and black and
   blind.

V

Dim moon-eyed fishes near
Gaze at the gilded gear
And query: "What does this vaingloriousness down
   here?"

VI

Well: while was fashioning
This creature of cleaving wing,
The Immanent Will that stirs and urges everything

VII

Prepared a sinister mate
For her—so gaily great—
A Shape of Ice, for the time far and dissociate.

VIII

And as the smart ship grew
In stature, grace, and hue,
In shadowy silent distance grew the Iceberg too.

IX

Alien they seemed to be;
No mortal eye could see
The intimate welding of their later history,

X

Or sign that they were bent
By paths coincident
On being anon twin halves of one august event,

XI

Till the Spinner of the Years
Said "Now!" And each one hears
And consummation comes, and jars two hemispheres.

A. E. HOUSMAN

A. E. HOUSMAN (1859–1936) was born in Worcestershire, educated at Oxford, worked in the Government Patent Office for ten years, and taught Latin at University College, London, and later at Cambridge. *A Shropshire Lad* was published in 1896, *Last Poems* in 1922, *The Name and Nature of Poetry* in 1933, and the posthumous volume *More Poems* in 1936.

IS MY TEAM PLOWING

"Is my team plowing,
    That I was used to drive
And hear the harness jingle
    When I was man alive?"

Aye, the horses trample,
    The harness jingles now;
No change though you lie under
    The land you used to plow.

"Is football playing
    Along the river shore,
With lads to chase the leather,
    Now I stand up no more?"

Aye, the ball is flying,
    The lads play heart and soul;
The goal stands up, the keeper
    Stands up to keep the goal.

"Is my girl happy,
    That I thought hard to leave,

And has she tired of weeping
    As she lies down at eve?"

Aye, she lies down lightly,
    She lies not down to weep:
Your girl is well contented.
    Be still, my lad, and sleep.

"Is my friend hearty,
    Now I am thin and pine;
And has he found to sleep in
    A better bed than mine?"

Aye, lad, I lie easy,
    I lie as lads would choose;
I cheer a dead man's sweetheart.
    Never ask me whose.

COULD MAN BE DRUNK FOR EVER

Could man be drunk for ever
    With liquor, love, or fights,
Lief should I rouse at morning
    And lief lie down of nights.

But men at whiles are sober
    And think by fits and starts,
And if they think, they fasten
    Their hands upon their hearts.

The selections by Housman are from *The Collected Poems of A. E. Housman.* Copyright, 1940, by Henry Holt and Company, Inc. Reprinted by permission of Henry Holt and Company, Inc. and the Society of Authors as the Literary Representative of the Trustees of the estate of the late A. E. Housman, and Messrs. Jonathan Cape, Ltd., publishers of A. E. Housman's *Collected Poems.*

WHEN I WAS
ONE-AND-TWENTY

When I was one-and-twenty
  I heard a wise man say,
"Give crowns and pounds and guineas
  But not your heart away;
Give pearls away and rubies
  But keep your fancy free."
But I was one-and-twenty,
  No use to talk to me.

When I was one-and-twenty
  I heard him say again,
"The heart out of the bosom
  Was never given in vain;
'Tis paid with sighs a-plenty
  And sold for endless rue."
And I am two-and-twenty,
  And oh, 'tis true, 'tis true.

THE CHESTNUT CASTS
HIS FLAMBEAUX

The chestnut casts his flambeaux, and the flowers
  Stream from the hawthorn on the wind away,
The doors clap to, the pane is blind with showers.
  Pass me the can, lad; there's an end of May.

There's one spoilt spring to scant our mortal lot,
  One season ruined of our little store.
May will be fine next year as like as not:
  Oh ay, but then we shall be twenty-four.

We for a certainty are not the first
  Have sat in taverns while the tempest hurled
Their hopeful plans to emptiness, and cursed
  Whatever brute and blackguard made the world.

It is in truth iniquity on high
  To cheat our sentenced souls of aught they crave,
And mar the merriment as you and I
  Fare on our long fool's-errand to the grave.

Iniquity it is; but pass the can.
  My lad, no pair of kings our mothers bore;
Our only portion is the estate of man:
  We want the moon, but we shall get no more.

If here today the cloud of thunder lours
  Tomorrow it will hie on far behests;
The flesh will grieve on other bones than ours
  Soon, and the soul will mourn in other breasts.

The troubles of our proud and angry dust
  Are from eternity, and shall not fail.
Bear them we can, and if we can we must.
  Shoulder the sky, my lad, and drink your ale.

EPILOGUE

"Terence, this is stupid stuff;
You eat your victuals fast enough;
There can't be much amiss, 'tis clear,
To see the rate you drink your beer.
But oh, good Lord, the verse you make,
It gives a chap the belly-ache.
The cow, the old cow, she is dead;
It sleeps well, the hornèd head:
We poor lads, 'tis our turn now
To hear such tunes as killed the cow.
Pretty friendship 'tis to rhyme
Your friends to death before their time
Moping melancholy mad:
Come, pipe a tune to dance to, lad."

Why, if 'tis dancing you would be,
There's brisker pipes than poetry.
Say, for what were hop-yards meant,
Or why was Burton built on Trent?
Oh, many a peer of England brews
Livelier liquor than the Muse,
And malt does more than Milton can
To justify God's ways to man.
Ale, man, ale's the stuff to drink
For fellows whom it hurts to think:
Look into the pewter pot
To see the world as the world's not.
And faith, 'tis pleasant till 'tis past:
The mischief is that 'twill not last.
Oh, I have been to Ludlow fair
And left my necktie God knows where,
And carried half way home, or near,
Pints and quarts of Ludlow beer:
Then the world seemed none so bad,
And I myself a sterling lad;
And down in lovely muck I've lain,
Happy till I woke again.
Then I saw the morning sky:
Heigho, the tale was all a lie;
The world, it was the old world yet,
I was I, my things were wet,
And nothing new remained to do
But begin the game anew.

Therefore, since the world has still
Much good, but much less good than ill,
And while the sun and moon endure

Luck's a chance, but trouble's sure,
I'd face it as a wise man would,
And train for ill and not for good.
'Tis true, the stuff I bring for sale
Is not so brisk a brew as ale:
Out of a stem that scored the hand
I wrung it in a weary land.
But take it: if the smack is sour,
The better for the embittered hour;
It should do good to heart and head
When your soul is in my soul's stead;
And I will friend you, if I may,
In the dark and cloudy day.

There was a king reigned in the East:
There, when kings will sit to feast,

They get their fill before they think
With poisoned meat and poisoned drink.
He gathered all that springs to birth
From the many-venomed earth;
First a little, thence to more,
He sampled all her killing store;
And easy, smiling, seasoned sound,
Sate the king when healths went round.
They put arsenic in his meat
And stared aghast to watch him eat;
They poured strychnine in his cup
And shook to see him drink it up:
They shook, they stared as white's their shirt.
Them it was their poison hurt.
—I tell the tale that I heard told.
Mithridates, he died old.

EDWIN ARLINGTON ROBINSON

EDWIN ARLINGTON ROBINSON (1869–1935) was born in Maine, attended Harvard for two years and was appointed by President Theodore Roosevelt to a position in the Customs House in 1905. After 1910 he devoted himself entirely to writing. He spent many summers at the MacDowell Colony. He won the Pulitzer Prize in 1922, 1925 and 1928. His final *Collected Poems* was published in 1937. To the charge brought against his early poetry that he viewed the world as a prison house, he replied: "The world is not a prison house but a kind of spiritual kindergarten, where millions of bewildered infants are trying to spell God with the wrong blocks."

MINIVER CHEEVY [1]

Miniver Cheevy, child of scorn,
  Grew lean while he assailed the seasons;
He wept that he was ever born,
  And he had reasons.

Miniver loved the days of old
  When swords were bright and steeds were
    prancing;
The vision of a warrior bold
  Would set him dancing.

Miniver sighed for what was not,
  And dreamed, and rested from his labors;
He dreamed of Thebes and Camelot,
  And Priam's neighbors.

[1] From *The Town Down the River* by Edwin Arlington Robinson; copyright 1910 by Charles Scribner's Sons, 1938 by Ruth Nivison. Reprinted by permission of the publishers.

Miniver mourned the ripe renown
  That made so many a name so fragrant;
He mourned Romance, now on the town,
  And Art, a vagrant.

Miniver loved the Medici,
  Albeit he had never seen one;
He would have sinned incessantly
  Could he have been one.

Miniver cursed the commonplace
  And eyed a khaki suit with loathing;
He missed the medieval grace
  Of iron clothing.

Miniver scorned the gold he sought,
  But sore annoyed was he without it;
Miniver thought, and thought, and thought,
  And thought about it.

Miniver Cheevy, born too late,
  Scratched his head and kept on thinking;
Miniver coughed, and called it fate,
  And kept on drinking.

MR. FLOOD'S PARTY[2]

Old Eben Flood, climbing alone one night
Over the hill between the town below
And the forsaken upland hermitage
That held as much as he should ever know
On earth again of home, paused warily.
The road was his with not a native near;
And Eben, having leisure, said aloud,
For no man else in Tilbury Town to hear:

"Well, Mr. Flood, we have the harvest moon
Again, and we may not have many more;
The bird is on the wing, the poet says,
And you and I have said it here before.
Drink to the bird." He raised up to the light
The jug that he had gone so far to fill,
And answered huskily: "Well, Mr. Flood,
Since you propose it, I believe I will."

Alone, as if enduring to the end
A valiant armor of scarred hopes outworn,
He stood there in the middle of the road
Like Roland's ghost winding a silent horn.
Below him, in the town among the trees,
Where friends of other days had honored him,
A phantom salutation of the dead
Rang thinly till old Eben's eyes were dim.

Then, as a mother lays her sleeping child
Down tenderly, fearing it may awake,
He set the jug down slowly at his feet
With trembling care, knowing that most things break;
And only when assured that on firm earth
It stood, as the uncertain lives of men
Assuredly did not, he paced away,
And with his hand extended paused again:

"Well, Mr. Flood, we have not met like this
In a long time; and many a change has come
To both of us, I fear, since last it was
We had a drop together. Welcome home!"
Convivially returning with himself,
Again he raised the jug up to the light;
And with an acquiescent quaver said:
"Well, Mr. Flood, if you insist, I might.

"Only a very little, Mr. Flood—
For auld lang syne. No more, sir; that will do."
So, for the time, apparently it did,
And Eben evidently thought so too;
For soon amid the silver loneliness

Of night he lifted up his voice and sang,
Secure, with only two moons listening,
Until the whole harmonious landscape rang—

"For auld lang syne." The weary throat gave out,
The last word wavered; and the song being done,
He raised again the jug regretfully
And shook his head, and was again alone.
There was not much that was ahead of him,
And there was nothing in the town below—
Where strangers would have shut the many doors
That many friends had opened long ago.

LUKE HAVERGAL[3]

Go to the western gate, Luke Havergal,
There where the vines cling crimson on the wall,
And in the twilight wait for what will come.
The leaves will whisper there of her, and some,
Like flying words, will strike you as they fall;
But go, and if you listen, she will call.
Go to the western gate, Luke Havergal—
Luke Havergal.

No, there is not a dawn in eastern skies
To rift the fiery night that's in your eyes;
But there, where western glooms are gathering,
The dark will end the dark, if anything:
God slays himself with every leaf that flies,
And hell is more than half of paradise.
No, there is not a dawn in eastern skies—
In eastern skies.

Out of a grave I come to tell you this,
Out of a grave I come to quench the kiss
That flames upon your forehead with a glow
That blinds you to the way that you must go.
Yes, there is yet one way to where she is,
Bitter, but one that faith may never miss.
Out of a grave I come to tell you this—
To tell you this.

There is the western gate, Luke Havergal,
There are the crimson leaves upon the wall.
Go, for the winds are tearing them away,—
Nor think to riddle the dead words they say,
Nor any more to feel them as they fall;
But go, and if you trust her she will call.
There is the western gate, Luke Havergal—
Luke Havergal.

---

[2] From *Collected Poems* by permission of The Macmillan Company.

[3] "Luke Havergal" is reprinted with the permission of Charles Scribner's Sons from *The Children of Night* by Edwin Arlington Robinson (1897).

JOHN MASEFIELD

JOHN MASEFIELD (1878–   ) was born in Herefordshire, shipped on several voyages as a seaman in the merchant marine, and in 1897, stimulated by reading Chaucer, began to write. He served with the Red Cross during the First World War. In 1930 he was made Poet Laureate of England and received the Order of Merit in 1935. His books include the prose sketch *Gallipoli* (1916) and *Collected Poems* (1935).

ON GROWING OLD

Be with me, Beauty, for the fire is dying;
My dog and I are old, too old for roving;
Man, whose young passion sets the spindrift flying,
Is soon too lame to march, too cold for loving.
I take the book and gather to the fire,
Turning old yellow leaves; minute by minute,
The clock ticks to my heart; a withered wire
Moves a thin ghost of music in the spinet.
I cannot sail your seas, I cannot wander
Your cornland, nor your hill-land nor your valleys,
Ever again, nor share the battle yonder

A selection from *Enslaved.* Copyright 1920, 1948 by John Masefield. Used with the permission of The Macmillan Company.

Where the young knight the broken squadron rallies.
Only stay quiet while my mind remembers
The beauty of fire from the beauty of embers.

Beauty, have pity, for the strong have power,
The rich their wealth, the beautiful their grace,
Summer of man its sunlight and its flower,
Spring time of man all April in a face.
Only, as in the jostling in the Strand,
Where the mob thrusts or loiters or is loud
The beggar with the saucer in his hand
Asks only a penny from the passing crowd,
So, from this glittering world with all its fashion,
Its fire and play of men, its stir, its march,
Let me have wisdom, Beauty, wisdom and passion,
Bread to the soul, rain where the summers parch.
Give me but these, and though the darkness close
Even the night will blossom as the rose.

WALTER DE LA MARE

WALTER DE LA MARE (1873–1956) was born in Kent. He worked in a London office until 1906 when a book of his poems won a governmental grant of a hundred pounds a year, which enabled him thereafter to devote his time to writing. He has written many books, both prose and poetry.

THE LISTENERS

'Is there anybody there?' said the Traveller,
Knocking on the moonlit door;
And his horse in the silence champed the grasses
Of the forest's ferny floor:
And a bird flew up out of a turret,
Above the Traveller's head:
And he smote upon the door again a second time;
'Is there anybody there?' he said.

From *Collected Poems, 1901–1918*, Vol. II, by Walter de la Mare. Copyright, 1920, by Henry Holt and Company, Inc. Copyright, 1948, by Walter de la Mare. By permission of the publishers.

But no one descended to the Traveller;
No head from the leaf-fringed sill
Leaned over and looked into his grey eyes,
Where he stood perplexed and still.
But only a host of phantom listeners
That dwelt in the lone house then
Stood listening in the quiet of the moonlight
To that voice from the world of men:
Stood thronging the faint moonbeams on the dark
stair,
That goes down to the empty hall,
Hearkening in an air stirred and shaken
By the lonely Traveller's call.
And he felt in his heart their strangeness,
Their stillness answering his cry,

While his horse moved, cropping the dark turf,
  'Neath the starred and leafy sky;
For he suddenly smote on the door, even
  Louder, and lifted his head:—
'Tell them I came, and no one answered,
  That I kept my word,' he said.
Never the least stir made the listeners,
  Though every word he spake

Fell echoing through the shadowiness of the still
  house
  From the one man left awake:
Aye, they heard his foot upon the stirrup,
  And the sound of iron on stone,
And how the silence surged softly backward,
  When the plunging hoofs were gone.

ROBERT FROST

ROBERT FROST (1874–1963) was born in San Francisco but was taken at the age of ten to New England. He attended Dartmouth and Harvard briefly, but gave most of his time to teaching in country schools, farming and writing. In 1912 he went to England, where his first two books of poems were published. He returned to New England in 1915. A prolific writer, he won Pulitzer Prizes four times for his poetry. He was associated with a number of colleges and universities from time to time as professor or poet in residence, including Amherst, Michigan and the Bread Loaf School of English. Speaking of the "figure a poem makes," he said: "It begins in delight, it inclines to the impulse, it assumes direction with the first line laid down, it runs a course of lucky events, and ends in a clarification of life—not necessarily a great clarification, such as sects and cults are founded on, but in a momentary stay against confusion."

THE TUFT OF FLOWERS

I went to turn the grass once after one
Who mowed it in the dew before the sun.

The dew was gone that made his blade so keen
Before I came to view the leveled scene.

I looked for him behind an isle of trees;
I listened for his whetstone on the breeze.

But he had gone his way, the grass all mown,
And I must be, as he had been,—alone,

"As all must be," I said within my heart,
"Whether they work together or apart."

But as I said it, swift there passed me by
On noiseless wings a bewildered butterfly,

Seeking with memories grown dim over night
Some resting flower of yesterday's delight.

The selections by Frost are from *Complete Poems of Robert Frost.* Copyright, 1930, 1949, by Henry Holt and Company, Inc. Copyright, 1936, 1948, by Robert Frost. By permission of the publishers.

And once I marked his flight go round and round,
As where some flower lay withering on the ground.

And then he flew as far as eye could see,
And then on tremulous wings came back to me.

I thought of questions that have no reply,
And would have turned to toss the grass to dry;

But he turned first, and led my eye to look
At a tall tuft of flowers beside a brook,

A leaping tongue of bloom the scythe had spared
Beside a reedy brook the scythe had bared.

I left my place to know them by their name,
Finding them butterfly-weed when I came.

The mower in the dew had loved them thus,
By leaving them to flourish, not for us,

Nor yet to draw one thought of ours to him,
But from sheer morning gladness at the brim.

The butterfly and I had lit upon,
Nevertheless, a message from the dawn,

That made me hear the wakening birds around,
And hear his long scythe whispering to the ground,

And feel a spirit kindred to my own;
So that henceforth I worked no more alone;

But glad with him, I worked as with his aid,
And weary, sought at noon with him the shade;

And dreaming, as it were, held brotherly speech
With one whose thought I had not hoped to reach.

"Men work together," I told him from the heart,
"Whether they work together or apart."

MENDING WALL

Something there is that doesn't love a wall,
That sends the frozen ground-swell under it,
And spills the upper boulders in the sun;
And makes gaps even two can pass abreast.
The work of hunters is another thing:
I have come after them and made repair
Where they have left not one stone on a stone,
But they would have the rabbit out of hiding,
To please the yelping dogs. The gaps I mean,
No one has seen them made or heard them made,
But at spring mending-time we find them there.
I let my neighbor know beyond the hill;
And on a day we meet to walk the line
And set the wall between us once again.
We keep the wall between us as we go.
To each the boulders that have fallen to each.
And some are loaves and some so nearly balls
We have to use a spell to make them balance:
"Stay where you are until our backs are turned!"
We wear our fingers rough with handling them.
Oh, just another kind of outdoor game,
One on a side. It comes to little more:
There where it is we do not need the wall:
He is all pine and I am apple-orchard.
My apple trees will never get across
And eat the cones under his pines, I tell him.
He only says, "Good fences make good neighbors."
Spring is the mischief in me, and I wonder
If I could put a notion in his head:
"*Why* do they make good neighbors? Isn't it
Where there are cows? But here there are no cows.
Before I built a wall I'd ask to know
What I was walling in or walling out,
And to whom I was like to give offense.
Something there is that doesn't love a wall,
That wants it down!" I could say "elves" to him,
But it's not elves exactly, and I'd rather
He said it for himself. I see him there,
Bringing a stone grasped firmly by the top
In each hand, like an old-stone savage armed.

He moves in darkness, as it seems to me,
Not of woods only and the shade of trees.
He will not go behind his father's saying,
And he likes having thought of it so well
He says again, "Good fences make good neighbors."

TWO TRAMPS IN MUD TIME

Out of the mud two strangers came
And caught me splitting wood in the yard.
And one of them put me off my aim
By hailing cheerily "Hit them hard!"
I knew pretty well why he dropped behind
And let the other go on a way.
I knew pretty well what he had in mind:
He wanted to take my job for pay.

Good blocks of beech it was I split,
As large around as the chopping block;
And every piece I squarely hit
Fell splinterless as a cloven rock.
The blows that a life of self-control
Spares to strike for the common good
That day, giving a loose to my soul,
I spent on the unimportant wood.

The sun was warm but the wind was chill.
You know how it is with an April day
When the sun is out and the wind is still,
You're one month on in the middle of May.
But if you so much as dare to speak,
A cloud comes over the sunlit arch,
A wind comes off a frozen peak,
And you're two months back in the middle of March.

A bluebird comes tenderly up to alight
And fronts the wind to unruffle a plume,
His song so pitched as not to excite
A single flower as yet to bloom.
It is snowing a flake: and he half knew
Winter was only playing possum.
Except in color he isn't blue,
But he wouldn't advise a thing to blossom.

The water for which we may have to look
In summertime with a witching-wand,
In every wheelrut's now a brook,
In every print of a hoof a pond.
Be glad of water, but don't forget
The lurking frost in the earth beneath
That will steal forth after the sun is set
And show on the water its crystal teeth.

The time when most I loved my task
These two must make me love it more
By coming with what they came to ask.
You'd think I never had felt before
The weight of an ax-head poised aloft,
The grip on earth of outspread feet,
The life of muscles rocking soft
And smooth and moist in vernal heat.

Out of the woods two hulking tramps
(From sleeping God knows where last night,
But not long since in the lumber camps).
They thought all chopping was theirs of right.
Men of the woods and lumberjacks,
They judged me by their appropriate tool.
Except as a fellow handled an ax,
They had no way of knowing a fool.

Nothing on either side was said.
They knew they had but to stay their stay
And all their logic would fill my head:
As that I had no right to play
With what was another man's work for gain.
My right might be love but theirs was need.
And where the two exist in twain
Theirs was the better right—agreed.

But yield who will to their separation,
My object in living is to unite
My avocation and my vocation
As my two eyes make one in sight.
Only where love and need are one,
And the work is play for mortal stakes,
Is the deed ever really done
For Heaven and the future's sakes.

STOPPING BY WOODS
ON A SNOWY EVENING

Whose woods these are I think I know.
His house is in the village though;
He will not see me stopping here
To watch his woods fill up with snow.

My little horse must think it queer
To stop without a farmhouse near
Between the woods and frozen lake
The darkest evening of the year.

He gives his harness bells a shake
To ask if there is some mistake.
The only other sound's the sweep
Of easy wind and downy flake.

The woods are lovely, dark and deep,
But I have promises to keep,
And miles to go before I sleep,
And miles to go before I sleep.

ACQUAINTED WITH THE
NIGHT

I have been one acquainted with the night.
I have walked out in rain—and back in rain.
I have outwalked the furthest city light.

I have looked down the saddest city lane.
I have passed by the watchman on his beat
And dropped my eyes, unwilling to explain.

I have stood still and stopped the sound of feet
When far away an interrupted cry
Came over houses from another street,

But not to call me back or say good-bye;
And further still at an unearthly height,
One luminary clock against the sky

Proclaimed the time was neither wrong nor right.
I have been one acquainted with the night.

THE DEATH OF THE
HIRED MAN

Mary sat musing on the lamp-flame at the table
Waiting for Warren. When she heard his step,
She ran on tip-toe down the darkened passage
To meet him in the doorway with the news
And put him on his guard. "Silas is back."
She pushed him outward with her through the door
And shut it after her. "Be kind," she said.
She took the market things from Warren's arms
And set them on the porch, then drew him down
To sit beside her on the wooden steps.

"When was I ever anything but kind to him?
But I'll not have the fellow back," he said.
"I told him so last haying, didn't I?
'If he left then,' I said, 'that ended it.'
What good is he? Who else will harbor him
At his age for the little he can do?
What help he is there's no depending on.
Off he goes always when I need him most.
'He thinks he ought to earn a little pay,
Enough at least to buy tobacco with,
So he won't have to beg and be beholden.'
'All right,' I say, 'I can't afford to pay

Any fixed wages, though I wish I could.'
'Someone else can.' 'Then someone else will have to.'
I shouldn't mind his bettering himself
If that was what it was. You can be certain,
When he begins like that, there's someone at him
Trying to coax him off with pocket-money,—
In haying time, when any help is scarce.
In winter he comes back to us. I'm done."

"Sh! not so loud: he'll hear you," Mary said.

"I want him to: he'll have to soon or late."

"He's worn out. He's asleep beside the stove.
When I came up from Rowe's I found him here,
Huddled against the barn-door fast asleep,
A miserable sight, and frightening, too—
You needn't smile—I didn't recognize him—
I wasn't looking for him—and he's changed.
Wait till you see."

          "Where did you say he'd been?"

"He didn't say. I dragged him to the house,
And gave him tea and tried to make him smoke.
I tried to make him talk about his travels.
Nothing would do: he just kept nodding off."

"What did he say? Did he say anything?"

"But little."

          "Anything? Mary, confess
He said he'd come to ditch the meadow for me."

"Warren!"

          "But did he? I just want to know."

"Of course he did. What would you have him say?
Surely you wouldn't grudge the poor old man
Some humble way to save his self-respect.
He added, if you really care to know,
He meant to clear the upper pasture, too.
That sounds like something you have heard before?
Warren, I wish you could have heard the way
He jumbled everything. I stopped to look
Two or three times—he made me feel so queer—
To see if he was talking in his sleep.
He ran on Harold Wilson—you remember—
The boy you had in haying four years since.
He's finished school, and teaching in his college.
Silas declares you'll have to get him back.
He says they two will make a team for work.
Between them they will lay this farm as smooth!

The way he mixed that in with other things.
He thinks young Wilson a likely lad, though daft
On education—you know how they fought
All through July under the blazing sun,
Silas up on the cart to build the load,
Harold along beside to pitch it on."

"Yes, I took care to keep well out of earshot."

"Well, those days trouble Silas like a dream.
You wouldn't think they would. How some things
          linger!
Harold's young college boy's assurance piqued
          him.
After so many years he still keeps finding
Good arguments he sees he might have used.
I sympathize. I know just how it feels
To think of the right thing to say too late.
Harold's associated in his mind with Latin.
He asked me what I thought of Harold's saying
He studied Latin like the violin
Because he liked it—that an argument!
He said he couldn't make the boy believe
He could find water with a hazel prong—
Which showed how much good school had ever done
          him.
He wanted to go over that. But most of all
He thinks if he could have another chance
To teach him how to build a load of hay—"

"I know, that's Silas' one accomplishment.
He bundles every forkful in its place,
And tags and numbers it for future reference,
So he can find and easily dislodge it
In the unloading. Silas does that well.
He takes it out in bunches like big birds' nests.
You never see him standing on the hay
He's trying to lift, straining to lift himself."

"He thinks if he could teach him that, he'd be
Some good perhaps to someone in the world.
He hates to see a boy the fool of books.
Poor Silas, so concerned for other folk,
And nothing to look backward to with pride,
And nothing to look forward to with hope,
So now and never any different."

Part of a moon was falling down the west,
Dragging the whole sky with it to the hills.
Its light poured softly in her lap. She saw
And spread her apron to it. She put out her
          hand
Among the harp-like morning-glory strings,
Taut with the dew from garden bed to eaves,

As if she played unheard the tenderness
That wrought on him beside her in the night.
"Warren," she said, "he has come home to die:
You needn't be afraid he'll leave you this time."

"Home," he mocked gently.

     "Yes, what else but home?
It all depends on what you mean by home.
Of course he's nothing to us, anymore
Than was the hound that came a stranger to us
Out of the woods, worn out upon the trail."

"Home is the place where, when you have to go
  there,
They have to take you in."

    "I should have called it
Something you somehow haven't to deserve."
Warren leaned out and took a step or two,
Picked up a little stick, and brought it back
And broke it in his hand and tossed it by.
"Silas has better claims on us, you think,
Than on his brother? Thirteen little miles
As the road winds would bring him to his door.
Silas has walked that far no doubt today.
Why didn't he go there? His brother's rich,
A somebody—director in the bank."

"He never told us that."

    "We know it though."

"I think his brother ought to help, of course.
I'll see to that if there is need. He ought of right
To take him in, and might be willing to—
He may be better than appearances.
But have some pity on Silas. Do you think
If he'd had any pride in claiming kin
Or anything he looked for from his brother,
He'd keep so still about him all this time?"

"I wonder what's between them."

    "I can tell you.
Silas is what he is—we wouldn't mind him—
But just the kind that kinsfolk can't abide.
He never did a thing so very bad.
He don't know why he isn't quite as good
As anyone. He won't be made ashamed
To please his brother, worthless though he is."

"I can't think Si ever hurt anyone."

"No, but he hurt my heart the way he lay
And rolled his old head on that sharp-edged chair-
  back.
He wouldn't let me put him on the lounge.
You must go in and see what you can do.
I made the bed up for him there tonight.
You'll be surprised at him—how much he's broken.
His working days are done; I'm sure of it."

"I'd not be in a hurry to say that."

"I haven't been. Go, look, see for yourself.
But, Warren, please remember how it is:
He's come to help you ditch the meadow.
He has a plan. You mustn't laugh at him.
He may not speak of it, and then he may.
I'll sit and see if that small sailing cloud
Will hit or miss the moon."

    It hit the moon.
Then there was three there, making a dim row,
The moon, the little silver cloud, and she.

Warren returned—too soon, it seemed to her,
Slipped to her side, caught up her hand and waited.

"Warren," she questioned.

    "Dead," was all he answered.

CARL SANDBURG

CARL SANDBURG (1878–   ) was born in Illinois, worked at manual labor throughout the midwest, volunteered for the Spanish-American War and eventually graduated from Lombard College in 1902. After graduation he worked principally as a reporter for various newspapers. His books include *Chicago Poems* (1916), *Cornhuskers* (1918), *Smoke and Steel* (1920), *Slabs of the Sunburnt West* (1922) and *The People, Yes* (1936). His biography of Lincoln, *The Prairie Years* (1926) and *The War Years* (1939), won the Pulitzer Prize in 1940, and his collected *Poems* received the Pulitzer award in 1950.

FOUR PRELUDES ON PLAYTHINGS OF THE WIND[1]

"The past is a bucket of ashes."

I

The woman named To-morrow
sits with a hairpin in her teeth
and takes her time
and does her hair the way she wants it
and fastens at last the last braid and coil
and puts the hairpin where it belongs
and turns and drawls: Well, what of it?
My grandmother, Yesterday, is gone.
What of it? Let the dead be dead.

II

The doors were cedar
and the panels strips of gold
and the girls were golden girls
and the panels read and the girls chanted:
   We are the greatest city,
   the greatest nation:
   nothing like us ever was.

The doors are twisted on broken hinges.
Sheets of rain swish through on the wind
   where the golden girls ran and the panels read:
   We are the greatest city,
   the greatest nation:
   nothing like us ever was.

III

It has happened before.
Strong men put up a city and got
   a nation together,

And paid singers to sing and women
   to warble: We are the greatest city,
   the greatest nation:
   nothing like us ever was.

And while the singers sang
and the strong men listened
and paid the singers well
and felt good about it all,
   there were rats and lizards who listened
   . . . and the only listeners left now
   . . . are . . . the rats . . . and the lizards.

And there are black crows
crying, "Caw, caw,"
bringing mud and sticks
building a nest
   over the words carved
   on the doors where the panels were cedar
   and the strips on the panels were gold
   and the golden girls came singing:
   We are the greatest city,
   the greatest nation:
   nothing like us ever was.

The only singers now are crows crying, "Caw, caw,"
And the sheets of rain whine in the wind and doorways.
And the only listeners now are . . . the rats . . . and the lizards.

IV

The feet of the rats
scribble on the doorsills;
the hieroglyphs of the rat footprints
chatter the pedigrees of the rats
and babble of the blood
and gabble of the breed
of the grandfathers and the great-grandfathers
of the rats.

[1] From *Smoke and Steel* by Carl Sandburg, copyright, 1920, by Harcourt, Brace & World, Inc.; renewed 1948, by Carl Sandburg. Reprinted by permission of the publishers.

And the wind shifts
and the dust on a doorsill shifts
and even the writing of the rat footprints
tells us nothing, nothing at all
about the greatest city, the greatest nation
where the strong men listened
and the women warbled: Nothing like us ever was.

COOL TOMBS[2]

When Abraham Lincoln was shoveled into the tombs,
he forgot the copperheads and the assassin . . . in
the dust, in the cool tombs.

And Ulysses Grant lost all thought of con men and
Wall Street, cash and collateral turned ashes . . .
in the dust, in the cool tombs.

Pocahontas' body, lovely as a poplar, sweet as a red
haw in November or a pawpaw in May, did she
wonder? does she remember? . . . in the dust, in
the cool tombs?

Take any streetful of people buying clothes and groceries, cheering a hero or throwing confetti and
blowing tin horns . . . tell me if the lovers are
losers . . . tell me if any get more than the lovers
. . . in the dust . . . in the cool tombs.

HAZE[3]

Keep a red heart of memories
Under the great grey rain sheds of the sky,
Under the open sun and the yellow gloaming embers.
Remember all pay days of lilacs and songbirds;
All starlights of cool memories on storm paths.

Out of this prairie rise the faces of dead men.
They speak to me. I cannot tell you what they say.

Other faces rise on the prairie.
    They are unborn. The future.

Yesterday and to-morrow cross and mix on the skyline
The two are lost in a purple haze. One forgets.
    One waits.

[2] From *Cornhuskers* by Carl Sandburg. Copyright,
1918, by Henry Holt and Company. Copyright, 1946, by
Carl Sandburg. By permission of the publishers.

[3] From *Smoke and Steel* by Carl Sandburg, copyright,
1920, by Harcourt, Brace & World, Inc.; renewed 1948,
by Carl Sandburg. Reprinted by permission of the publishers.

In the yellow dust of sunsets, in the meadows of vermilion eight o'clock June nights . . . the dead
men and the unborn children speak to me . . .
I cannot tell you what they say . . . you listen
and you know.

I don't care who you are, man:
I know a woman is looking for you,
And her soul is a corn-tassel kissing a south-west wind.

(The farm-boy whose face is the colour of brick-dust,
is calling the cows; he will form the letter X with
crossed streams of milk from the teats; he will beat
a tattoo on the bottom of a tin pail with X's of
milk.)

I don't care who you are, man:
I know sons and daughters looking for you,
And they are grey dust working toward star paths
And you see them from a garret window when you
laugh
At your luck and murmur, 'I don't care.'

I don't care who you are, woman:
I know a man is looking for you,
And his soul is a south-west wind kissing a corn-
tassel.

(The kitchen girl on the farm is throwing oats to the
chickens and the buff of their feathers says hello
to the sunset's late maroon.)

I don't care who you are, woman:
I know sons and daughters looking for you
And they are next year's wheat or the year after
hidden in the dark loam.

My love is a yellow-hammer spinning circles in Ohio,
Indiana. My love is a redbird shooting flights in
straight lines in Kentucky and Tennessee. My love
is an early robin flaming an ember of copper on
her shoulders in March and April. My love is a
greybird living in the eaves of a Michigan house
all winter. Why is my love always a crying thing
of wings?

On the Indiana dunes, in the Mississippi marshes, I
have asked: Is it only a fishbone on the beach?
Is it only a dog's jaw or a horse's skull whitening in
the sun? Is the red heart of man only ashes? Is the
flame of it all a white light switched off and the
power house wires cut?

Why do the prairie roses answer every summer? Why
do the changing repeating rains come back out of

the salt sea wind-blown? Why do the stars keep
their tracks? Why do the cradles of the sky rock
new babies?

THE PEOPLE WILL
LIVE ON [4]

The people will live on.
The learning and blundering people will live on.
They will be tricked and sold and again sold
And go back to the nourishing earth for rootholds,
The people so peculiar in renewal and comeback,
You can't laugh off their capacity to take it.
The mammoth rests between his cyclonic dramas.

The people so often sleepy, weary, enigmatic,
is a vast huddle with many units saying:

"I earn my living.
I make enough to get by
and it takes all my time.
If I had more time
I could do more for myself
and maybe for others.
I could read and study
and talk things over
and find out about things.
It takes time.
I wish I had the time."

The people is tragic and comic two-face: hero and
hoodlum: phantom and gorilla twisting to moan
with a gargoyle mouth: "They buy me and sell me
. . . it's a game . . . sometime I'll break loose . . ."

Once having marched
Over the margins of animal necessity,
Over the grim line of sheer subsistence
Then man came
To the deeper rituals of his bones,
To the lights lighter than any bones,
To the time for thinking things over,
To the dance, the song, the story,
Or the hours given over to dreaming,
Once having so marched.

[4] From *The People, Yes* by Carl Sandburg, copyright,
1936, by Harcourt, Brace & World, Inc. and reprinted
with their permission.

Between the finite limitations of the five senses
and the endless yearnings of man for the beyond
the people hold to the humdrum bidding of work and
food
while reaching out when it comes their way
for lights beyond the prison of the five senses,
for keepsakes lasting beyond any hunger or death.
This reaching is alive.
The panderers and liars have violated and smutted it.
Yet this reaching is alive yet
for lights and keepsakes.

The people know the salt of the sea
and the strength of the winds
lashing the corners of the earth.
The people take the earth
as a tomb of rest and a cradle of hope.
Who else speaks for the Family of Man?
They are in tune and step
with constellations of universal law.

The people is a polychrome,
a spectrum and a prism
held in a moving monolith,
a console organ of changing themes,
a clavilux of color poems
wherein the sea offers fog
and the fog moves off in rain
and the Labrador sunset shortens
to a nocturne of clear stars
serene over the shot spray
of northern lights.
The steel mill sky is alive.
The fire breaks white and zigzag
shot on a gun-metal gloaming.
Man is a long time coming.
Man will yet win.
Brother may yet line up with brother:

This old anvil laughs at many broken hammers.
There are men who can't be bought.
The fireborn are at home in fire.
The stars make no noise.
You can't hinder the wind from blowing.
Time is a great teacher.
Who can live without hope?

In the darkness with a great bundle of grief the
people march.
In the night, and overhead a shovel of stars for keeps,
the people march:
"Where to? what next?"

JOHN HALL WHEELOCK

JOHN HALL WHEELOCK (1886–   ) is an outstanding poet in the American tradition. His *Poems Old and New* (1956) is a gathering of all the poems he considers representative of his sensitive and disciplined art. Other recent books include *The Gardener and Other Poems* (1961) and *What Is Poetry?* (1963), an examination of the nature of poetry.

WOOD-THRUSH[1]

Behind the wild-bird's throat
An Eden, more remote
Than Adam knew of, lies—
The primal paradise
Lost, yet forever here,
From that wild syrinx cries
Into the listening ear,
The labyrinthine heart,
A longing, a regret,
In which it has no part.
Where the young leaves are met
In overarching green
Soft winds stir and divide,
Where shadows cloud and throng
The coverts in between,
That early bud of song
Opens its petals wide,
Becomes a three-fold star
Of voices twined and blent,
Happy and innocent,
Within whose singing are
Troy lost and Hector slain,
Judas and Golgotha,
The longing and the pain,
Sorrows of old that were
And joy come back again
From ages earlier,
Before joy's course was run,
Before time's bounds were set—
The fountains of the sun
Are in that twining jet
Of song, so clear, so cool.
While the false heart raves on,
For longing, like a fool,
The quiet voice is gone:
The song, inept to save,
Happy and innocent,
Falls silent as the grave,
Closing the door upon
Those half-remembered things—
Only the silence sings
On, and forever on.

NIGHT THOUGHTS IN AGE[2]

Light, that out of the west looked back once more
Through lids of cloud, has closed a sleepy eye;
The heaven of stars bends over me its silence,
A harp through which the wind of time still whispers
Music some hand has hushed but left there trembling—
Conceits of an aging man who lies awake
Under familiar rafters, in this leafy
Bird-singing, haunted, green, ancestral spot
Where time has made such music! For often now,
In this belovèd country whose coastal shores
Look seaward, without limit, to the south—
Land of flung spume and spray, sea-winds and -voices,
Where the gull rides the gale on equal wing,
With motionless body and downward-bending head,
Where, in mid-summer days, offshore, the dolphin
Hurdles the water with arching leap and plunge—
I meditate, lying awake, alone,
On the sea's voice and time's receding music,
Felt ebbing in the heart and shrunken vein—
How time, that takes us all, will at the last,
In taking us, take the whole world we are dreaming:
Sun, wind and sea, whisper of rain at night,
The young, hollow-cheeked moon, the clouds of evening
Drifting in a great solitude—all these
Shall time take away, surely, and the face
From which the eyes of love look out at us
In this brief world, this horror-haunted kingdom
Of beauty and of longing and of terror,
Of phantoms and illusion, of appearance
And disappearance—magic of leger-de-main,
Trick of the prestidigitator's wand—
The huge phantasmagoria we are dreaming:
This shall time take from us, and take forever,
When we are taken by that receding music.
O marvel of things, fabulous dream, too soon,
Too soon will the wild blood cry out and death
Quell, with one blow, the inscrutable fantasy!

[1] Copyright 1952 by John Hall Wheelock. Reprinted from *Poems Old and New* by John Hall Wheelock with the permission of Charles Scribner's Sons.

[2] Copyright 1955 by John Hall Wheelock. Reprinted from *Poems Old and New* by John Hall Wheelock with the permission of Charles Scribner's Sons. This poem was originally published in *The New Yorker*.

Shall prayer change this? Youth is the hour for prayer,
That has so much to pray for; a man's life,
Lived howsoever, is a long reconcilement
To the high, lonely, unforgiving truth,
Which will not change for his or any prayer,
Now or hereafter: in that reconcilement
Lies all of wisdom. Age is the hour for praise,
Praise that is joy, praise that is acquiescence,
Praise that is adoration and gratitude
For all that has been given and not been given.
Night flows on. The wind, that all night through
Quickened the treetops with a breath of ocean,
Veers inland, falls away, and the sea's voice,
Learned in lost childhood, a remembered music,
By day or night, through love, through sleep, through
    dream,
Still breathing its perpetual benediction,

Has dwindled to a sigh. By the west window,
In the soft dark the leaves of the sycamore
Stir gently, rustle, and are still, are listening
To a silence that is music. The old house
Is full of ghosts, dear ghosts on stair and landing,
Ghosts in chamber and hall; garden and walk
Are marvellous with ghosts, where so much love
Dwelt for a little while and made such music,
Before it too was taken by the tide
That takes us all, of time's receding music.
Oh, all is music! All has been turned to music!
All that is vanished has been turned to music!
And these familiar rafters, that have known
The child, the young man and the man, now shelter
The aging man who lies here, listening, listening—
All night, in a half dream, I have lain here listening.

EZRA POUND

EZRA POUND (1885–   ) was born in Idaho, educated at Hamilton College and the University of Pennsylvania and went to Europe in 1907, where for decades he was active and influential in modern literary circles. In 1946 he was brought to this country to stand trial for treason because of his radio broadcasts for the Italian Government during the Second World War, but was judged mentally irresponsible by a group of doctors and placed in an institution, from which he was released in 1958. Among his books are *Personae* (1926), *Selected Poems,* with an introduction by T. S. Eliot (1928), and the collected *Cantos* (1948), for the last group of which, *The Pisan Cantos,* he was awarded the Bollingen Prize in 1949.

THE RIVER-MERCHANT'S WIFE:[1] A LETTER

While my hair was still cut straight across my
    forehead
I played about the front gate, pulling flowers.
You came by on bamboo stilts, playing horse,
You walked about my seat, playing with blue plums.
And we went on living in the village of Chokan:
Two small people, without dislike or suspicion.

At fourteen I married My Lord you.
I never laughed, being bashful.
Lowering my head, I looked at the wall.
Called to, a thousand times, I never looked back.

At fifteen I stopped scowling,
I desired my dust to be mingled with yours

[1] From *Personae,* copyright 1926, 1954 by Ezra Pound.
Reprinted with the permission of New Directions.

For ever and for ever and for ever.
Why should I climb the look out?

At sixteen you departed,
You went into far Ku-to-yen, by the river of swirling
    eddies,
And you have been gone five months.
The monkeys make sorrowful noise overhead.

You dragged your feet when you went out.
By the gate now, the moss is grown, the different
    mosses,
Too deep to clear them away!
The leaves fall early this autumn, in wind.
The paired butterflies are already yellow with August
Over the grass in the West garden;
They hurt me. I grow older.

If you are coming down through the narrows of the
    river Kiang,
Please let me know beforehand,
And I will come out to meet you
        As far as Cho-fu-Sa.
                    By Rihaku

CANTO I²

And then went down to the ship,
Set keel to breakers, forth on the godly sea, and
We set up mast and sail on that swart ship,
Bore sheep aboard her, and our bodies also
Heavy with weeping, and winds from sternward
Bore us out onward with bellying canvas,
Circe's this craft, the trim-coifed goddess.
Then sat we amidships, wind jamming the tiller,
Thus with stretched sail, we went over sea till day's
    end.
Sun to his slumber, shadows o'er all the ocean,
Came we then to the bounds of deepest water,
To the Kimmerian lands, and peopled cities
Covered with close-webbed mist, unpierced ever
With glitter of sun-ray
Nor with stars stretched, nor looking back from
    heaven
Swartest night stretched over wretched men there.
The ocean flowing backward, came we then to the
    place
Aforesaid by Circe.
Here did they rites, Perimeds and Eurylochus,
And drawing sword from my hip
I dug the ell-square pitkin;
Poured we libations unto each the dead,
First mead and then sweet wine, water mixed with
    white flour.
Then prayed I many a prayer to the sickly death's-
    heads;
As set in Ithaca, sterile bulls of the best
For sacrifice, heaping the pyre with goods,
A sheep to Tiresias only, black and a bell-sheep.
Dark blood flowed in the fosse,
Souls out of Erebus, cadaverous dead, of brides
Of youths and of the old who had borne much;
Souls stained with recent tears, girls tender,
Men many, mauled with bronze lance heads,
Battle spoil, bearing yet dreory arms,
These many crowded about me; with shouting,
Pallor upon me, cried to my men for more beasts;
Slaughtered the herds, sheep slain of bronze;
Poured ointment, cried to the gods,
To Pluto the strong, and praised Proserpine;

² Reprinted with the permission of New Directions.

Unsheathed the narrow sword,
I sat to keep off the impetuous impotent dead,
Till I should hear Tiresias.
But first Elpenor came, our friend Elpenor,
Unburied, cast on the wide earth,
Limbs that we left in the house of Circe,
Unwept, unwrapped in sepulcher, since toils urged
    other.
Pitiful spirit. And I cried in hurried speech:
"Elpenor, how art thou come to this dark coast?
"Cam'st thou afoot, outstripping seamen?"
        And he in heavy speech:
"Ill fate and abundant wine. I slept in Circe's ingle.
"Going down the long ladder unguarded,
"I fell against the buttress,
"Shattered the nape-nerve, the soul sought Avernus.
"But thou, O King, I bid remember me, unwept,
    unburied,
"Heap up mine arms, be tomb by sea-bord, and
    inscribed:
"'A man of no fortune and with a name to come.'
"And set my oar up, that I swung mid fellows."

And Anticlea came, whom I beat off, and then
    Tiresias Theban,
Holding his golden wand, knew me, and spoke first:
"A second time? why? man of ill star,
"Facing the sunless dead and this joyless region?
"Stand from the fosse, leave me my bloody bever
"For soothsay."
        And I stepped back,
And he strong with the blood, said then: "Odysseus
"Shalt return through spiteful Neptune, over dark
    seas,
"Lose all companions." And then Anticlea came.
Lie quiet Divus. I mean, that is Andreas Divus,
In officina Wecheli, 1538, out of Homer.
And he sailed, by Sirens and thence outward and
    away
And unto Circe.
        Venerandam,
In the Cretan's phrase, with the golden crown,
    Aphrodite,
Cypri munimenta sortita est, mirthful, oricalchi, with
    golden
Girdles and breast bands thou with dark eyelids
Bearing the golden bough of Argicida.

D. H. LAWRENCE (1885–1930) was born in Nottinghamshire, educated at the local school, taught briefly, then turned to writing. He traveled widely and restlessly during the latter part of his life, being at different times in Sicily, India, Australia, New Mexico and Mexico as well as England and Europe. His books include the novels *Sons and Lovers* (1913), *Women in Love* (1920), and the censored *Lady Chatterley's Lover* (1928), *Selected Poems* (1948), and many volumes of short stories, essays and travel sketches. His letters were edited by Aldous Huxley. "The essential quality of poetry," Lawrence said, "is that it makes a new effort of attention, and 'discovers' a new world within the known world. . . . One realm we have never conquered: the pure present . . . the immediate, instant self. . . . [In] free verse we look for the insurgent naked throb of the instant moment. . . . It does not want to get anywhere. It just takes place."

WE ARE TRANSMITTERS[1]

As we live, we are transmitters of life.
And when we fail to transmit life, life fails to flow
    through us.
That is part of the mystery of sex, it is a flow onwards.
Sexless people transmit nothing.

And if, as we work, we can transmit life into our
    work,
life, still more life rushes into us to compensate, to be
    ready
and we ripple with life through the days.

Even if it is a woman making an apple dumpling, or
    a man a stool,
if life goes into the pudding, good is the pudding
good is the stool,
content is the woman, with fresh life rippling in to
    her,
content is the man.

Give, and it shall be given unto you
is still the truth about life.
But giving life is not so easy.
It doesn't mean handing it out to some mean fool, or
    letting the living dead eat you up.
It means kindling the life-quality where it was not,
even if it's only in the whiteness of a washed pocket-
    handkerchief.

SNAKE[2]

A snake came to my water-trough
On a hot, hot day, and I in pyjamas for the heat,
To drink there.

[1] Reprinted from *The Complete Poems of D. H. Lawrence* by permission of Laurence Pollinger Limited and the Estate of the Late Mrs. Frieda Lawrence.
[2] From *Collected Poems* by D. H. Lawrence. Copyright, 1929, by Jonathan Cape and Harrison Smith, Inc. Reprinted by permission of The Viking Press, Inc.

In the deep, strange-scented shade of the great dark
    carob-tree
I came down the steps with my pitcher
And must wait, must stand and wait, for there he was
    at the trough before me.

He reached down from a fissure in the earth-wall in
    the gloom
And trailed his yellow-brown slackness soft-bellied
    down, over the edge of the stone trough
And rested his throat upon the stone bottom,
And where the water had dripped from the tap, in a
    small clearness,
He sipped with his straight mouth,
Softly drank through his straight gums, into his slack
    long body,
Silently.
Someone was before me at my water-trough,
And I, like a second comer, waiting.

He lifted his head from his drinking, as cattle do,
And looked at me vaguely, as drinking cattle do,
And flickered his two-forked tongue from his lips,
    and mused a moment,
And stooped and drank a little more,
Being earth-brown, earth-golden from the burning
    burning bowels of the earth
On the day of Sicilian July, with Etna smoking.

The voice of my education said to me
He must be killed,
For in Sicily the black, black snakes are innocent, the
    gold are venomous.

And voices in me said, If you were a man
You would take a stick and break him now, and finish
    him off.

But must I confess how I liked him,
How glad I was he had come like a guest in quiet, to
    drink at my water trough

And depart peaceful, pacified, and thankless,
Into the burning bowels of this earth?

Was it cowardice, that I dared not kill him?
Was it perversity that I longed to talk to him?
Was it humility, to feel so honoured?
I felt so honoured.

And yet those voices:
If you were not afraid, you would kill him!
And truly I was afraid, I was most afraid,
But even so, honoured still more
That he should seek my hospitality
From out the dark door of the secret earth.

He drank enough
And lifted his head, dreamily, as one who has
    drunken,
And flickered his tongue like a forked night on the
    air, so black,
Seeming to lick his lips,
And looked around like a god, unseeing, into the air,
And slowly turned his head,
And slowly, very slowly, as if thrice adream,
Proceeded to draw his slow length curving round
And climb again the broken bank of my wall-face.

And as he put his head into that dreadful hole,
And as he slowly drew up, snake-easing his shoulders,
    and entered farther,
A sort of horror, a sort of protest against his with-
    drawing into that horrid black hole,
Deliberately going into the blackness, and slowly
    drawing himself after,
Overcame me now his back was turned.

I looked round, I put down my pitcher,
I picked up a clumsy log
And threw it at the water-trough with a clatter.

I think it did not hit him,
But suddenly that part of him that was left behind
    convulsed in undignified haste,
Writhed like lightning, and was gone
Into the black hole, the earth-lipped fissure in the
    wall-front,
At which, in the intense still noon, I stared with fas-
    cination.

And immediately I regretted it.
I thought how paltry, how vulgar, what a mean act!
I despised myself and the voices of my accursed hu-
    man education.

And I thought of the albatross,
And I wished he would come back, my snake.

For he seemed to me again like a king,
Like a king in exile, uncrowned in the underworld,
Now due to be crowned again.
And so, I missed my chance with one of the lords
Of life.
And I have something to expiate;
A pettiness.

BAVARIAN GENTIANS[3]

Not every man has gentians in his house
In soft September, at slow, sad Michaelmas.

Bavarian gentians, tall and dark, but dark
Darkening the day-time torch-like with the smoking
    blueness of Pluto's gloom,
Ribbed hellish flowers erect, with their blaze of dark-
    ness spread blue
Blown into points, by the heavy white draught of the
    day.

Torch-flowers of the blue-smoking darkness, Pluto's
    dark-blue blaze
Black lamps from the halls of Dio, smoking dark blue
Giving off darkness, blue darkness, upon Demeter's
    yellow-pale day

Reach me a gentian, give me a torch!
Let me guide myself with the blue, forked torch of
    a flower
Down the darker and darker stairs, where blue is
    darkened on blueness
Down the way Persephone goes, just now, in first-
    frosted September
To the sightless realm where darkness is married to
    dark
And Persephone herself is but a voice, as a bride
A gloom invisible enfolded in the deeper dark
Of the arms of Pluto as he ravishes her once again
And pierces her once more with his passion of the
    utter dark.
Among the splendour of the black-blue torches, shed-
    ding fathomless darkness on the nuptials.

Give me a flower on a tall stem, and three dark
    flames,
For I will go to the wedding, and be wedding-guest
At the marriage of the living dark.

[3] From *Last Poems* by D. H. Lawrence. Copyright,
1933, by Frieda Lawrence. Reprinted by permission of
The Viking Press, Inc., New York.

WILLIAM BUTLER YEATS (1865–1939) was born in Ireland and educated in London and Dublin. His early poems were romantic in feeling, but he soon grew absorbed in the lore of pre-Christian Ireland. His work from about 1895 up to 1918 shows this influence in subject and manner of expression. A little after 1900, with J. M. Synge and Lady Gregory he assumed leadership of the literary "Renaissance" in Ireland and began to write for the Irish national theatre. His contributions to his country's culture were recognized by his choice as one of the first Senators of the Irish Free State. After 1918, his lifelong interest in the occult exerted marked influence on his plays and poetry. He was awarded the Nobel Prize for Literature in 1923 and, at his death, was regarded as one of the leading poets writing in the English language. *Autobiographies* was published in 1926, *Collected Poems* in 1933 and *Last Poems and Plays* in 1940.

THE WILD SWANS AT COOLE

The trees are in their autumn beauty,
The woodland paths are dry,
Under the October twilight the water
Mirrors a still sky;
Upon the brimming water among the stones
Are nine-and-fifty swans.

The nineteenth autumn has come upon me
Since I first made my count;
I saw, before I had well finished,
All suddenly mount
And scatter wheeling in great broken rings
Upon their clamorous wings.

I have looked upon those brilliant creatures,
And now my heart is sore.
All's changed since I, hearing at twilight,
The first time on this shore,
The bell-beat of their wings above my head,
Trod with a lighter tread.

Unwearied still, lover by lover,
They paddle in the cold,
Companionable streams or climb the air;
Their hearts have not grown old;
Passion or conquest, wander where they will,
Attend upon them still.

But now they drift on the still water
Mysterious, beautiful;

The selections by Yeats are reprinted from *Collected Poems of W. B. Yeats* with the permission of The Macmillan Company of New York, Mrs. W. B. Yeats, and The Macmillan Company of Canada.

Among what rushes will they build,
By what lake's edge or pool
Delight men's eyes when I awake some day
To find they have flown away?

THE LAMENTATION OF THE OLD PENSIONER

Although I shelter from the rain
Under a broken tree
My chair was nearest to the fire
In every company
That talked of love or politics
Ere Time transfigured me.

Though lads are making pikes again
For some conspiracy,
And crazy rascals rage their fill
At human tyranny;
My contemplations are of Time
That has transfigured me.

There's not a woman turns her face
Upon a broken tree,
And yet the beauties that I loved
Are in my memory;
I spit into the face of Time
That has transfigured me.

LEDA AND THE SWAN

A sudden blow: the great wings beating still
Above the staggering girl, her thighs caressed
By the dark webs, her nape caught in his bill,
He holds her helpless breast upon his breast.

How can those terrified vague fingers push
The feathered glory from her loosening thighs?
And how can body, laid in that white rush,
But feel the strange heart beating where it lies?

A shudder in the loins engenders there
The broken wall, the burning roof and tower
And Agamemnon dead.
                            Being so caught up,
So mastered by the brute blood of the air,
Did she put on his knowledge with his power
Before the indifferent beak could let her drop?

A PRAYER FOR MY DAUGHTER

Once more the storm is howling, and half hid
Under this cradle-hood and coverlid
My child sleeps on. There is no obstacle
But Gregory's wood and one bare hill
Whereby the haystack-and-roof-levelling wind,
Bred on the Atlantic, can be stayed;
And for an hour I have walked and prayed
Because of the great gloom that is in my mind.

I have walked and prayed for this young child an hour
And heard the sea-wind scream upon the tower,
And under the arches of the bridge, and scream
In the elms above the flooded stream;
Imagining in excited reverie
That the future years had come,
Dancing to a frenzied drum,
Out of the murderous innocence of the sea.

May she be granted beauty and yet not
Beauty to make a stranger's eye distraught,
Or hers before a looking-glass, for such,
Being made beautiful overmuch,
Consider beauty a sufficient end,
Lose natural kindness and may be
The heart-revealing intimacy
That chooses right, and never find a friend.

Helen being chosen found life flat and dull
And later had much trouble from a fool,
While that great Queen, that rose out of the spray,
Being fatherless could have her way,
Yet chose a bandy-legged smith for man.
It's certain that fine women eat
A crazy salad with their meat,
Whereby the Horn of Plenty is undone.

In courtesy I'd have her chiefly learned;
Hearts are not had as a gift, but hearts are earned
By those that are not entirely beautiful;
Yet many, that have played the fool
For beauty's very self, has charm made wise,
And many a poor man that has roved,
Loved and thought himself beloved,
From a glad kindness cannot take his eyes.

May she become a flourishing hidden tree
That all her thoughts may like the linnet be,
And have no business but dispensing round
Their magnanimities of sound,
Nor but in merriment begin a chase,
Nor but in merriment a quarrel.
Oh, may she live like some green laurel
Rooted in one dear perpetual place.

My mind, because the minds that I have loved,
The sort of beauty that I have approved,
Prosper but little, has dried up of late,
Yet knows that to be choked with hate
May well be of all evil chances chief.
If there's no hatred in a mind
Assault and battery of the wind
Can never tear the linnet from the leaf.

An intellectual hatred is the worst,
So let her think opinions are accursed.
Have I not seen the loveliest woman born
Out of the mouth of Plenty's horn,
Because of her opinionated mind
Barter that horn and every good
By quiet natures understood
For an old bellows full of angry wind?

Considering that, all hatred driven hence,
The soul recovers radical innocence
And learns at last that it is self-delighting,
Self-appeasing, self-affrighting,
And that its own sweet will is heaven's will;
She can, though every face should scowl
And every windy quarter howl
Or every bellows burst, be happy still.

And may her bridegroom bring her to a house
Where all's accustomed, ceremonious;
For arrogance and hatred are the wares
Peddled in the thoroughfares.
How but in custom and in ceremony
Are innocence and beauty born?
Ceremony's a name for the rich horn,
And custom for the spreading laurel tree.

SAILING TO BYZANTIUM

That is no country for old men. The young
In one another's arms, birds in the trees
(Those dying generations) at their song,
The salmon-falls, the mackerel-crowded seas,
Fish, flesh, or fowl, commend all summer long
Whatever is begotten, born, and dies.
Caught in that sensual music, all neglect
Monuments of unaging intellect.

An aged man is but a paltry thing,
A tattered coat upon a stick, unless
Soul clap its hands and sing, and louder sing
For every tatter in its mortal dress;
Nor is there singing school but studying
Monuments of its own magnificence;

And therefore I have sailed the seas and come
To the holy city of Byzantium.

O sages, standing in God's holy fire
As in the gold mosaic of a wall,
Come from the holy fire, perne in a gyre,
And be the singing-masters of my soul.
Consume my heart away—sick with desire
And fastened to a dying animal
It knows not what it is—and gather me
Into the artifice of eternity.

Once out of nature I shall never take
My bodily form from any natural thing,
But such a form as Grecian goldsmiths make
Of hammered gold and gold enamelling
To keep a drowsy emperor awake;
Or set upon a golden bough to sing
To lords and ladies of Byzantium
Of what is past, or passing, or to come.

GERARD MANLEY HOPKINS

GERARD MANLEY HOPKINS (1844–1889) was educated at Oxford. He entered the Catholic Church in 1866, and the Jesuit Order in 1868. His poems were first collected and published, posthumously, by his friend Robert Bridges in 1918. In the second and more nearly complete edition of the *Poems* (1930), an "Author's Preface," taken from one of his notebooks, explains his theory of poetry. His work is notable for its technical innovations, and for the rhythmic device which he called Sprung Rhythm. His work has had a great influence on today's poets.

GOD'S GRANDEUR

The world is charged with the grandeur of God.
　It will flame out, like shining from shook foil;
　It gathers to a greatness, like the ooze of oil
Crushed. Why do men then now not reck his rod?
Generations have trod, have trod, have trod;
　And all is seared with trade; bleared, smeared with
　　toil;
　And wears man's smudge and shares man's smell:
　　the soil
Is bare now, nor can foot feel, being shod.

And for all this, nature is never spent;
　There lives the dearest freshness deep down
　　things;
And though the last lights off the black West went
　Oh, morning, at the brown brink eastward,
　　springs—
Because the Holy Ghost over the bent

World broods with warm breast and with ah!
　bright wings.

THE WINDHOVER:

TO CHRIST OUR LORD

I caught this morning morning's minion, kingdom of
　daylight's dauphin, dapple-dawn-drawn Falcon,
　　in his riding
　Of the rolling level underneath him steady air,
　　and striding
High there, how he rung upon the rein of a wimpling
　　wing
In his ecstasy! then off, off forth on swing,
　As a skate's heel sweeps smooth on a bow-bend:
　　the hurl and gliding
　Rebuffed the big wind. My heart in hiding
Stirred for a bird,—the achieve of, the mastery of the
　　thing!

The selections by Hopkins are reprinted with the permission of the Oxford University Press, England.

Brute beauty and valor and act, oh, air, pride, plume,
    here
    Buckle! And the fire that breaks from thee then, a
    billion
Times told lovelier, more dangerous, O my chevalier!

    No wonder of it: sheer plod makes plough down
    silion
Shine, and blue-bleak embers, ah my dear,
    Fall, gall themselves, and gash gold-vermilion.

PIED BEAUTY

Glory be to God for dappled things—
    For skies of couple-colour as a brinded cow;
        For rose-moles all in stipple upon trout that
        swim;
Fresh-firecoal chestnut-falls; finches wings;
    Landscape plotted and pieced—fold, fallow, and
        plough;
        And áll trádes, their gear and tackle and trim.

All things counter, original, spare, strange;
    Whatever is fickle, freckled (who knows how?)
        With swift, slow; sweet, sour; adazzle, dim;
He fathers-forth whose beauty is past change:
            Praise him.

THE LEADEN ECHO AND
THE GOLDEN ECHO

(*Maidens' Song From St. Winefred's Well*)

THE LEADEN ECHO

How to kéep—is there ány any, is there none such,
    nowhere known some, bow or brooch or braid or
    brace,
    láce, latch or catch or key to keep
Back beauty, keep it, beauty, beauty, beauty, . . .
    from vanishing away?
O is there no frowning of these wrinkles, rankèd
    wrinkles deep,
Dówn? no waving off of these most mournful mes-
    sengers,
        still messengers, sad and stealing messengers of
        grey?
No there's none, there's none, O no there's none,
Nor can you long be, what you now are, called fair,

Do what you may do, what, do what you may,
And wisdom is early to despair:
Be beginning; since, no, nothing can be done
To keep at bay
Age and age's evils, hoar hair,
Ruck and wrinkle, drooping, dying, death's worst,
    winding sheets, tombs and worms and tumbling
    to decay;
So be beginning, be beginning to despair.
O there's none; no no no there's none:
Be beginning to despair, to despair,
Despair, despair, despair, despair.

THE GOLDEN ECHO

        Spare!
There ís one, yes I have one (Hush there!);
Only not within seeing of the sun,
Not within the singeing of the strong sun,
Tall sun's tingeing, or treacherous the tainting of the
    earth's air,
Somewhere elsewhere there is ah well where! one,
Óne. Yes I can tell such a key, I do know such a
    place,
Where whatever's prized and passes of us, everything
    that's fresh and fast flying of us, seems to us sweet
    of us and swiftly away with, done away with,
    undone,
Undone, done with, soon done with, and yet dearly
    and dangerously sweet
Of us, the wimpled-water-dimpled, not-by-morning-
    matchèd face,
The flower of beauty, fleece of beauty, too too apt to,
    ah! to fleet,
Never fleets móre, fastened with the tenderest
    truth
To its own best being and its loveliness of youth: it is
    an ever-lastingness of, O it is an all youth!
Come then, your ways and airs and looks, locks,
    maiden gear, gallantry and gaiety and grace,
Winning ways, airs innocent, maiden manners, sweet
    looks, loose locks, long locks, lovelocks, gaygear,
    going gallant, girlgrace—
Resign them, sign them, seal them, send them, motion
    them with breath,
And with sighs soaring, soaring síghs deliver
Them; beauty-in-the-ghost, deliver it, early now,
    long before death
Give beauty back, beauty, beauty, beauty, back to
    God, beauty's self and beauty's giver.
See; not a hair is, not an eyelash, not the least lash
    lost; every hair
Is, hair of the head, numbered.
Nay, what we had lighthanded left in surly the mere
    mould

Will have waked and have waxed and have walked
   with the wind whatwhile we slept,
This side, that side hurling a heavyheaded hundred-
   fold
Whatwhile we, while we slumbered.
O then, weary then why should we tread? O why are
   we so haggard at the heart, so care-coiled, care-
   killed, so fagged, so fashed, so cogged, so cumbered,
When the thing we freely fórfeit is kept with fonder
   a care,
Fonder a care kept than we could have kept it, kept
Far with fonder a care (and we, we should have lost
   it)
   finer, fonder
A care kept.—Where kept? Do but tell us where kept,
   where.—
Yonder.—What high as that! We follow, now we
   follow.
   —Yonder, yes yonder, yonder,
Yonder.

FELIX RANDAL

Felix Randal the farrier, O he is dead then? my duty
   all ended,

Who have watched his mould of man, big-boned and
   hardy—handsome
Pining, pining, till time when reason rambled in it
   and some
Fatal four disorders, fleshed there, all contended?

Sickness broke him. Impatient he cursed at first, but
   mended
Being anointed and all; though a heavenlier heart began some
Months earlier, since I had our sweet reprieve and
   ransom
Tendered to him. Ah well, God rest him all road ever
   he offended!

This seeing the sick endears them to us, us too it
   endears.
My tongue had taught thee comfort, touch had
   quenched thy tears,
Thy tears that touched my heart, child, Felix, poor
   Felix Randal;

How far from then forethought of, all thy more
   boisterous years,
When thou at the random grim forge, powerful
   amidst peers,
Didst fettle for the great grey drayhorse his bright
   and battering sandal!

T. S. ELIOT

T. S. ELIOT (1888–   ) was born in St. Louis, took his M.A. at Harvard in 1906, studied at the Sorbonne, again at Harvard, and finally at Oxford. He remained in England and in 1927 became a British citizen. The early work contained in his *Poems* (1920), and *The Waste Land* (1922) brought about his acceptance as one of the leading modern poets. This phase of his work expresses a scholar's despair at the triviality and moral decay of modern civilization. Subsequent to 1928, his acceptance of Anglo-Catholicism as a faith has given his work a posi- tive religious aspect. Among his books are *The Sacred Wood* (1921), *For Lancelot Andrewes* (1929), *Selected Essays 1917–1932*, *The Use of Poetry and the Use of Criticism* (1933), *After Strange Gods* (1934), *Collected Poems 1909–1935* (1936), and *Four Quartets* (1943). In recent years his main interest has been with drama. His most notable plays are *Murder in the Cathedral* (1935), *The Cocktail Party* (1949) and *The Confidential Clerk* (1954). In 1948, he was awarded the Nobel Prize for Literature.

ANIMULA

'Issues from the hand of God, the simple soul'
To a flat world of changing lights and noise,
To light, dark, dry or damp, chilly or warm;

The selections by Eliot are from *Collected Poems 1909–1935* by T. S. Eliot. Copyright, 1936, by Harcourt, Brace & World, Inc. Reprinted with the permission of Harcourt, Brace & World, Inc. and Faber and Faber Limited.

Moving between the legs of tables and of chairs,
Rising or falling, grasping at kisses and toys,
Advancing boldly, sudden to take alarm,
Retreating to the corner of arm and knee,
Eager to be reassured, taking pleasure
In the fragrant brilliance of the Christmas tree,
Pleasure in the wind, the sunlight and the sea;
Studies the sunlit pattern on the floor
And running stags around a silver tray;
Confounds the actual and the fanciful,

Content with playing-cards and kings and queens,
What the fairies do and what the servants say.
The heavy burden of the growing soul
Perplexes and offends more, day by day;
Week by week, offends and perplexes more
With the imperatives of 'is and seems'
And may and may not, desire and control.
The pain of living and the drug of dreams
Curl up the small soul in the window seat
Behind the *Encyclopaedia Britannica*.
Issues from the hand of time the simple soul
Irresolute and selfish, misshapen, lame,
Unable to fare forward or retreat,
Fearing the warm reality, the offered good,
Denying the importunity of the blood,
Shadow of its own shadows, spectre in its own
    gloom,
Leaving disordered papers in a dusty room;
Living first in the silence after the viaticum.

Pray for Guiterriez, avid of speed and power,
For Boudin, blown to pieces,
For this one who made a great fortune,
And that one who went his own way.
Pray for Floret, by the boarhound slain between the
    yew trees,
Pray for us now and at the hour of our birth.

THE LOVE SONG OF
J. ALFRED PRUFROCK

*S'io credesse che mia risposta fosse
A persona che mai tornasse al mondo,
Questa fiamma staria senza piu scosse.
Ma perciocche giammai di questo fondo
Non torno vivi alcun, s'i'odo il vero,
Senza tema d'infamia ti rispondo.*[1]

Let us go then, you and I,
When the evening is spread out against the sky
Like a patient etherised upon a table;
Let us go, through certain half-deserted streets,
The muttering retreats
Of restless nights in one-night cheap hotels
And sawdust restaurants with oyster-shells:
Streets that follow like a tedious argument
Of insidious intent

[1] If I believed that my answer might belong
To anyone who ever returned to the world,
This flame would leap no more.
But since, however, from these depths
No one ever returns alive, if I know the truth,
Then without fear of infamy I answer you.
                    Dante, *Inferno*, xxvii, 61–66.

To lead you to an overwhelming question . . .
Oh, do not ask, "What is it?"
Let us go and make our visit.

In the room the women come and go
Talking of Michelangelo

The yellow fog that rubs its back upon the window-
    panes,
The yellow smoke that rubs its muzzle on the
    window-panes
Licked its tongue into the corners of the evening,
Lingered upon the pools that stand in drains,
Let fall upon its back the soot that falls from
    chimneys,
Slipped by the terrace, made a sudden leap,
And seeing that it was a soft October night,
Curled once about the house, and fell asleep.

And indeed there will be time
For the yellow smoke that slides along the street,
Rubbing its back upon the window-panes;
There will be time, there will be time
To prepare a face to meet the faces that you meet;
There will be time to murder and create,
And time for all the works and days of hands
That lift and drop a question on your plate;
Time for you and time for me,
And time yet for a hundred indecisions,
And for a hundred visions and revisions,
Before the taking of a toast and tea.

In the room the women come and go
Talking of Michelangelo.

And indeed there will be time
To wonder, "Do I dare?" and, "Do I dare?"
Time to turn back and descend the stair,
With a bald spot in the middle of my hair—
(They will say: "How his hair is growing thin!")
My morning coat, my collar mounting firmly to the
    chin,
My necktie rich and modest, but asserted by a simple
    pin—
(They will say: "But how his arms and legs are
    thin!")
Do I dare
Disturb the universe?
In a minute there is time
For decisions and revisions which a minute will
    reverse.

For I have known them all already, known them all:
Have known the evenings, mornings, afternoons,
I have measured out my life with coffee spoons;

I know the voices dying with a dying fall
Beneath the music from a farther room.
    So how should I presume?

And I have known the eyes already, known them all—
The eyes that fix you in a formulated phrase,
And when I am formulated, sprawling on a pin,
When I am pinned and wriggling on the wall,
Then how should I begin
To spit out all the butt-ends of my days and ways?
    And how should I presume?

And I have known the arms already, known them
    all—
Arms that are braceleted and white and bare
(But in the lamplight, downed with light brown
    hair!)
Is it perfume from a dress
That makes me so digress?
Arms that lie along a table, or wrap about a shawl.
    And should I then presume?
    And how should I begin?

*   *   *   *   *

Shall I say, I have gone at dusk through narrow
    streets
And watched the smoke that rises from the pipes
Of lonely men in shirt-sleeves, leaning out of win-
    dows? . . .

I should have been a pair of ragged claws
Scuttling across the floors of silent seas.

*   *   *   *   *

And the afternoon, the evening, sleeps so peacefully!
Smoothed by long fingers,
Asleep . . . tired . . . or it malingers,
Stretched on the floor, here beside you and me.
Should I, after tea and cakes and ices,
Have the strength to force the moment to its crisis?
But though I have wept and fasted, wept and prayed,
Though I have seen my head (grown slightly bald)
    brought in upon a platter,
I am no prophet—and here's no great matter;
I have seen the moment of my greatness flicker
And I have seen the eternal Footman hold my coat,
    and snicker,
And in short, I was afraid.

And would it have been worth it, after all,
After the cups, the marmalade, the tea,
Among the porcelain, among some talk of you and
    me,

Would it have been worth while,
To have bitten off the matter with a smile,
To have squeezed the universe into a ball
To roll it toward some overwhelming question,
To say: "I am Lazarus, come from the dead,
Come back to tell you all, I shall tell you all"—
If one, settling a pillow by her head,
    Should say: "That is not what I meant at all;
    That is not it, at all."

And would it have been worth it, after all,
Would it have been worth while,
After the sunsets and the dooryards and the sprinkled
    streets,
After the novels, after the teacups, after the skirts
    that trail along the floor—
And this, and so much more?—
It is impossible to say just what I mean!
But as if a magic lantern threw the nerves in patterns
    on a screen:
Would it have been worth while
If one, settling a pillow or throwing off a shawl,
And turning toward the window, should say:
    "That is not it at all,
    That is not what I meant, at all."

*   *   *   *   *

No! I am not Prince Hamlet, nor was meant to be;
Am an attendant lord, one that will do
To swell a progress, start a scene or two,
Advise the prince; no doubt, an easy tool,
Deferential, glad to be of use,
Politic, cautious, and meticulous;
Full of high sentence, but a bit obtuse;
At times, indeed, almost ridiculous—
Almost, at times, the Fool.
I grow old . . . I grow old . . .
I shall wear the bottoms of my trousers rolled.

Shall I part my hair behind? Do I dare to eat a
    peach?
I shall wear white flannel trousers, and walk upon the
    beach.
I have heard the mermaids singing, each to each.

I do not think that they will sing to me.

I have seen them riding seaward on the waves
Combing the white hair of the waves blown back
When the wind blows the water white and black.
We have lingered in the chambers of the sea
By sea-girls wreathed with seaweed red and brown
Till human voices wake us, and we drown.

THE HOLLOW MEN

A penny for the Old Guy

I

We are the hollow men
We are the stuffed men
Leaning together
Headpiece filled with straw. Alas!
Our dried voices, when
We whisper together
Are quiet and meaningless
As wind in dry grass
Or rats' feet over broken glass
In our dry cellar.

Shape without form, shade without color,
Paralyzed force, gesture without motion;

Those who have crossed
With direct eyes, to death's other Kingdom
Remember us—if at all—not as lost
Violent souls, but only
As the hollow men
The stuffed men.

II

Eyes I dare not meet in dreams
In death's dream kingdom
These do not appear:
There, the eyes are
Sunlight on a broken column
There, is a tree swinging
And voices are
In the wind's singing
More distant and more solemn
Than a fading star.

Let me be no nearer
In death's dream kingdom
Let me also wear
Such deliberate disguises
Rat's skin, crowskin, crossed staves
In a field
Behaving as the wind behaves
No nearer—

Not that final meeting
In the twilight kingdom.

III

This is the dead land
This is cactus land

Here the stone images
Are raised, here they receive
The supplication of a dead man's hand
Under the twinkle of a fading star.

Is it like this
In death's other kingdom
Waking alone
At the hour when we are
Trembling with tenderness
Lips that would kiss
Form prayers to broken stone.

IV

The eyes are not here
There are no eyes here
In this valley of dying stars
In this hollow valley
This broken jaw of our lost kingdoms

In this last of meeting places
We grope together
And avoid speech
Gathered on this beach of the tumid river

Sightless, unless
The eyes reappear
As the perpetual star
Multifoliate rose
Of death's twilight kingdom
The hope only
Of empty men.

V

Here we go round the prickly pear
Prickly pear prickly pear
Here we go round the prickly pear
At five o'clock in the morning.

Between the idea
And the reality
Between the motion
And the act
Falls the Shadow
                              For Thine is the Kingdom

Between the conception
And the creation
Between the emotion
And the response
Falls the Shadow
                              Life is very long

Between the desire
And the spasm
Between the potency
And the existence
Between the essence
And the descent
Falls the Shadow
                    For Thine is the Kingdom

For Thine is
Life is
For Thine is the

This is the way the world ends
This is the way the world ends
This is the way the world ends
Not with a bang but a whimper.

GERONTION

Thou hast nor youth nor age
But as it were an after dinner sleep
Dreaming of both.

Here I am, an old man in a dry month,
Being read to by a boy, waiting for rain.
I was neither at the hot gates
Nor fought in the warm rain
Nor knee deep in the salt marsh, heaving a cutlass,
Bitten by flies, fought.
My house is a decayed house,
And the jew squats on the window sill, the owner,
Spawned in some estaminet of Antwerp,
Blistered in Brussels, patched and peeled in London.
The goat coughs at night in the field overhead;
Rocks, moss, stonecrop, iron, merds.
The woman keeps the kitchen, makes tea,
Sneezes at evening, poking the peevish gutter.
                              I an old man,
A dull head among windy spaces.

Signs are taken for wonders. "We would see a
    sign!"
The word within a word, unable to speak a word,
Swaddled with darkness. In the juvescence of the
    year
Came Christ the tiger
In depraved May, dogwood and chestnut, flowering
    judas,
To be eaten, to be divided, to be drunk
Among whispers; by Mr. Silvero
With caressing hands, at Limoges
Who walked all night in the next room:

By Hakagawa, bowing among the Titians;
By Madame de Tornquist, in the dark room
Shifting the candles; Fräulein von Kulp
Who turned in the hall, one hand on the door.
    Vacant shuttles
Weave the wind. I have no ghosts,
An old man in a draughty house
Under a windy knob.

After such knowledge, what forgiveness? Think now
History has many cunning passages, contrived
    corridors
And issues, deceives with whispering ambitions,
Guides us by vanities. Think now
She gives when our attention is distracted
And what she gives, gives with such supple con-
    fusions
That the giving famishes the craving. Gives too late
What's not believed in, or if still believed,
In memory only, reconsidered passion. Gives too soon
Into weak hands, what's thought can be dispensed
    with
Till the refusal propagates a fear. Think
Neither fear nor courage saves us. Unnatural vices
Are fathered by our heroism. Virtues
Are forced upon us by our impudent crimes.
These tears are shaken from the wrath-bearing tree.

The tiger springs in the new year. Us he devours.
    Think at last
We have not reached conclusion, when I
Stiffen in a rented house. Think at last
I have not made this show purposelessly
And it is not by any concitation
Of the backward devils.
I would meet you upon this honestly.
I that was near your heart was removed therefrom
To lose beauty in terror, terror in inquisition.
I have lost my passion: why should I need to keep it
Since what is kept must be adulterated?
I have lost my sight, smell, hearing, taste, and touch:
How should I use them for your closer contact?

These with a thousand small deliberations
Protract the profit of their chilled delirium,
Excite the membrane, when the sense has cooled,
With pungent sauces, multiply variety
In a wilderness of mirrors. What will the spider do,
Suspend its operations, will the weevil
Delay? De Bailhache, Fresca, Mrs. Cammel, whirled
Beyond the circuit of the shuddering Bear
In fractured atoms. Gull against the wind, in the
    windy straits
Of Belle Isle, or running on the Horn,
White feathers in the snow, the Gulf claims,

And an old man driven by the Trades
To a sleepy corner.
　　　　　　Tenants of the house,
Thoughts of a dry brain in a dry season.

DIFFICULTIES OF A STATESMAN

CRY what shall I cry?
All flesh is grass: comprehending
The Companions of the Bath, the Knights of the
　　British Empire, the Cavaliers,
O Cavaliers! of the Legion of Honour,
The Order of the Black Eagle (1st and 2nd class),
And the Order of the Rising Sun.
Cry cry what shall I cry?
The first thing to do is to form the committees:
The consultative councils, the standing committees,
One secretary will do for several committees.
What shall I cry?
Arthur Edward Cyril Parker is appointed telephone
　　operator
At a salary of one pound ten a week rising by annual
　　increments of five shillings
To two pounds ten a week; with a bonus of thirty
　　shillings at Christmas
And one week's leave a year.
A committee has been appointed to nominate a com-
　　mission of engineers
To consider the Water Supply.
A committee is appointed
For Public Works, chiefly the question of rebuilding
　　the fortifications.
A commission is appointed
To confer with a Volscian commission
About perpetual peace: the fletchers and javelin-
　　makers and smiths
Have appointed a joint committee to protest against
　　the reduction of orders.
Meanwhile the guards shake dice on the marches
And the frogs (O Mantuan) croak in the marshes.

Fireflies flare against the faint sheet lightning
What shall I cry?
Mother mother
Here is the row of family portraits, dingy busts, all
　　looking remarkably Roman,
Remarkably like each other, lit up successively by
　　the flare
Of a sweaty torchbearer, yawning.
O hidden under the . . . Hidden under the . . .
Where the dove's foot rested and locked for a
　　moment,
A still moment, repose of noon, set under the upper
　　branches of noon's widest tree
Under the breast feather stirred by the small wind
　　after noon
There the cyclamen spreads its wings, there the
　　clematis droops over the lintel
O mother (not among these busts, all correctly
　　inscribed)
I a tired head among these heads
Necks strong to bear them
Noses strong to break the wind
Mother
May we not be some time, almost now, together,
If the mactations, immolations, oblations, impetra-
　　tions,
Are now observed
May we not be
O hidden
Hidden in the stillness of noon, in the silent croaking
　　night.
Come with the sweep of the little bat's wing, with
　　the small flare of the firefly or lightning bug,
"Rising and falling, crowned with dust," the small
　　creatures,
The small creatures chirp thinly through the dust,
　　through the night.
O mother
What shall I cry?
We demand a committee, a representative com-
　　mittee, a committee of investigation
　　　　RESIGN　　RESIGN　　RESIGN

E. E. CUMMINGS (1894–1962) was born in Cambridge, Massachusetts, took his M.A. at Harvard in 1916 and in the following year went overseas as an ambulance driver for the Allies. There he was briefly imprisoned by the French because of a misunderstanding in an espionage case, but was eventually sent home. *The Enormous Room* (1922) is a narrative of this experience. His other books include *Eimi* (1933), *1 × 1* (1944), *Poems: 1923–1954*, and *95 Poems* (1958).

O SWEET SPONTANEOUS EARTH[1]

O sweet spontaneous
earth how often have
the
doting

    fingers of
prurient philosophers pinched
and
poked

thee
, has the naughty thumb
of science prodded
thy

    beauty   . how
often have religions taken
thee upon their scraggy knees
squeezing and

buffeting thee that thou mightest conceive
gods
    (but
true

to the incomparable
couch of death thy
rhythmic
lover

    thou answerest

them only with

       spring)

[1] From *Poems 1923–1954.* Published by Harcourt, Brace & World, Inc. Copyright, 1923, 1951, by E. E. Cummings.

THE HOURS RISE UP PUTTING OFF STARS[2]

the hours rise up putting off stars and it is
dawn
into the street of the sky light walks scattering poems

on earth a candle is
extinguished   the city
wakes
with a song upon her
mouth having death in her eyes

and it is dawn
the world
goes forth to murder dreams. . . .

i see in the street where strong
men are digging bread
and i see the brutal faces of
people contented hideous hopeless cruel happy

and it is day,

in the mirror
i see a frail
man
dreaming
dreams
dreams in the mirror

and it
is dusk   on earth

a candle is lighted
and it is dark.
the people are in their houses
the frail man is in his bed
the city

sleeps with death upon her mouth having a song in
    her eyes
the hours descend,
putting on stars. . . .
in the street of the sky night walks scattering poems

[2] *Op. cit.*

ANYONE LIVED IN A PRETTY HOW TOWN[3]

anyone lived in a pretty how town
(with up so floating many bells down)
spring summer autumn winter
he sang his didn't he danced his did.

Women and men (both little and small)
cared for anyone not at all
they sowed their isn't they reaped their same
sun moon stars rain

children guessed (but only a few
and down they forgot as up they grew
autumn winter spring summer)
that noone loved him more by more

when by now and tree by leaf
she laughed his joy she cried his grief

bird by snow and stir by still
anyone's any was all to her

someones married their everyones
laughed their cryings and did their dance
(sleep wake hope and then) they
said their nevers they slept their dream

stars rain sun moon
(and only the snow can begin to explain
how children are apt to forget to remember
with up so floating many bells down)

one day anyone died i guess
(and noone stooped to kiss his face)
busy folk buried them side by side
little by little and was by was

all by all and deep by deep
and more by more they dream their sleep
noone and anyone earth by april
wish by spirit and if by yes.

Women and men (both dong and ding)
summer autumn winter spring
reaped their sowing and went their came
sun moon stars rain

[3] From *Poems 1923–1954*. Published by Harcourt, Brace & World, Inc. Copyright, 1940, by E. E. Cummings.

ROBINSON JEFFERS

ROBINSON JEFFERS (1887–1962) was born in Pittsburgh, lived for several years in Europe as a child, graduated from Occidental College in 1905, studied further at the University of Southern California and the University of Zurich, and after receiving a legacy in 1914 settled in Carmel, California, and devoted himself to writing. His books include *Roan Stallion, Tamar and Other Poems* (1925), *Dear Judas* (1929), *Selected Poetry of Robinson Jeffers* (1938), *Be Angry at the Sun* (1941), *The Double Axe* (1948), and *Hungerfield* (1954). "Poetry," he has said, "must concern itself with (relatively) permanent things . . . (In) the Monterey coast mountains . . . for the first time in my life I could see people living—amid magnificent unspoiled scenery—essentially as they did in the Idyls or the Sagas, or in Homer's Ithaca. Here was life purged of its ephemeral accretions. Men were riding after cattle, or plowing the headland, hovered by white sea-gulls, as they have done for thousands of years and will for thousands of years to come . . . unencumbered by the mass of poetically irrelevant details and complexities that make a civilization."

HURT HAWKS[1]

I

The broken pillar of the wing jags from the clotted
    shoulder,
The wing trails like a banner in defeat,
No more to use the sky forever but live with famine

And pain a few days: cat nor coyote
Will shorten the week of waiting for death, there is
    game without talons.
He stands under the oak-bush and waits
The lame feet of salvation; at night he remembers
    freedom
And flies in a dream, the dawns ruin it.

He is strong and pain is worse to the strong, in-
    capacity is worse.

[1] From *Cawdor* by Robinson Jeffers. Copyright renewed 1956 by Robinson Jeffers. Reprinted by permission of Random House, Inc.

The curs of the day come and torment him
At distance, no one but death the redeemer will
    humble that head,
The intrepid readiness, the terrible eyes.
The wild God of the world is sometimes merciful to
    those
That ask mercy, not often to the arrogant.
You do not know him, you communal people, or you
    have forgotten him;
Intemperate and savage, the hawk remembers him;
Beautiful and wild, the hawks, and men that are
    dying, remember him.

II

I'd sooner, except the penalties, kill a man than a
    hawk; but the great redtail
Had nothing left but unable misery
From the bone too shattered for mending, the wing
    that trailed under his talons when he moved.
We had fed him six weeks, I gave him freedom,
He wandered over the foreland hill and returned in
    the evening, asking for death,
Not like a beggar, still eyed with the old
Implacable arrogance. I gave him the lead gift in the
    twilight. What fell was relaxed,
Owl-downy, soft feminine feathers; but what
Soared: the fierce rush: the night-herons by the
    flooded river cried fear at its rising
Before it was quite unsheathed from reality.

THE BLOODY SIRE [2]

It is not bad. Let them play.
Let the guns bark and the bombing-plane
Speak his prodigious blasphemies.
It is not bad, it is high time,
Stark violence is still the sire of all the world's
    values.

What but the wolf's tooth whittled so fine
The fleet limbs of the antelope?
What but fear winged the birds, and hunger
Jeweled with such eyes the great goshawk's head?
Violence has been the sire of all the world's values.

Who would remember Helen's face
Lacking the terrible halo of spears?
Who formed Christ but Herod and Caesar,
The cruel and bloody victories of Caesar?
Violence, the bloody sire of all the world's values.

Never weep, let them play,
Old violence is not too old to beget new values.

[2] From *Be Angry at the Sun* by Robinson Jeffers. Copyright 1941 by Robinson Jeffers. Reprinted by permission of Random House, Inc.

THE PURSE-SEINE [3]

Our sardine fishermen work at night in the dark of
    the moon; daylight or moonlight
They could not tell where to spread the net, unable
    to see the phosphorescence of the shoals of fish.
They work northward from Monterey, coasting Santa
    Cruz; off New Year's Point or off Pigeon Point
The look-out man will see some lakes of milk-color
    light on the sea's night-purple; he points, and
    the helmsman
Turns the dark prow, the motorboat circles the
    gleaming shoal and drifts out her seine-net.
    They close the circle
And purse the bottom of the net, then with great
    labor haul it in.

                  I cannot tell you
How beautiful the scene is, and a little terrible, then,
    when the crowded fish
Know they are caught, and wildly beat from one wall
    to the other of their closing destiny the phospho-
    rescent
Water to a pool of flame, each beautiful slender body
    sheeted with flame, like a live rocket
A comet's tail wake of clear yellow flame; while out-
    side the narrowing
Floats and cordage of the net great sea-lions come up
    to watch, sighing in the dark; the vast walls of
    night
Stand erect to the stars.

                Lately I was looking from a night mountain-
    top
On a wide city, the colored splendor, galaxies of
    light: how could I help but recall the seine-
    net
Gathering the luminous fish? I cannot tell you how
    beautiful the city appeared, and a little terrible.
I thought, We have geared the machines and locked
    all together into interdependence; we have built
    the great cities; now
There is no escape. We have gathered vast popula-
    tions incapable of free survival, insulated
From the strong earth, each person in himself help-
    less, on all dependent. The circle is closed, and
    the net
Is being hauled in. They hardly feel the cords draw-
    ing, yet they shine already. The inevitable
    mass-disasters
Will not come in our time nor in our children's, but
    we and our children

[3] From *Such Counsels You Gave Me* by Robinson Jeffers. Copyright 1937 by Random House, Inc. Reprinted by permission of Random House, Inc.

Must watch the net draw narrower, government take
    all powers—or revolution, and the new govern-
    ment
Take more than all, add to kept bodies kept souls—or
    anarchy, the mass-disasters.

            These things are Progress;
Do you marvel our verse is troubled or frowning,
    while it keeps its reason? Or it lets go, lets the
    mood flow
In the manner of the recent young men into mere
    hysteria, splintered gleams, crackled laughter.
    But they are quite wrong.
There is no reason for amazement: surely one always
    knew that cultures decay, and life's end is
    death.

SHINE,
PERISHING REPUBLIC[4]

While this America settles in the mould of its
    vulgarity, heavily thickening to empire,

[4] From *Roan Stallion, Tamar and Other Poems*. Copyright renewed 1953 by Robinson Jeffers. Reprinted by
permission of Random House, Inc.

And protest, only a bubble in the molten mass, pops
    and sighs out, and the mass hardens,

I sadly smiling remember that the flower fades to
    make fruit, the fruit rots to make earth.
Out of the mother; and through the spring exultances,
    ripeness and decadence; and home to the
    mother.

You making haste haste on decay: not blameworthy;
    life is good, be it stubbornly long or suddenly
A mortal splendor: Meteors are not needed less than
    mountains: shine, perishing republic.

But for my children, I would have them keep their
    distance from the thickening center; corruption
Never has been compulsory, when the cities lie at the
    monster's feet there are left the mountains.

And boys, be in nothing so moderate as in love of
    man, a clever servant, insufferable master.
There is the trap that catches noblest spirits, that
    caught—they say—God, when he walked on
    earth.

WILLIAM CARLOS WILLIAMS

WILLIAM CARLOS WILLIAMS (1883–1963) was born in Rutherford, New Jersey, graduated in medicine from the University of Pennsylvania, and was a practicing physician for over
forty years. Among his books are *In the American Grain* (1925), *White Mule* (1937), *Life
Along the Passaic River* (1938), *The Complete Collected Poems of William Carlos Williams
1906–1938, Paterson* (5 vols., 1946–1958), *Collected Later Poems* (1950), *The Desert Music
and Others Poems* (1954), and *Selected Essays* (1954).

GULLS

My townspeople, beyond in the great world,
are many with whom it were far more
profitable for me to live than here with you.
These whirr about me calling, calling!
and for my own part I answer them, loud as I can,
but they, being free, pass!
I remain! Therefore, listen!
For you will not soon have another singer.

    The selections by Williams are from *The Collected
Earlier Poems* by William Carlos Williams. Copyright
1938, 1951 by William Carlos Williams and reprinted by
permission of the publisher, New Directions.

First I say this: You have seen
the strange birds, have you not, that sometimes
rest upon our river in winter?
Let them cause you to think well then of the
    storms
that drive many to shelter. These things
do not happen without reason.

And the next thing I say is this:
I saw an eagle once circling against the clouds
over one of our principal churches—
Easter, it was—a beautiful day!—:
three gulls came from above the river
and crossed slowly seaward!
Oh, I know you have your own hymns, I have heard
    them—

and because I knew they invoked some great
    protector
I could not be angry with you, no matter
how much they outraged true music—

You see, it is not necessary for us to leap
    at each other,
and, as I told you, in the end
the gulls moved seaward very quietly.

TRACT

I will teach you my townspeople
how to perform a funeral—
for you have it over a troop
of artists—
unless one should scour the world—
you have the ground sense necessary.

See! the hearse leads.
I begin with a design for a hearse.
For Christ's sake not black—
nor white either—and not polished!
Let it be weathered—like a farm wagon—
with gilt wheels (this could be
applied fresh at small expense)
or no wheels at all:
a rough dray to drag over the ground.

Knock the glass out!
My God—glass, my townspeople!
For what purpose? Is it for the dead
to look out or for us to see
how well he is housed or to see
the flowers or the lack of them—
or what?
To keep the rain and snow from him?
He will have a heavier rain soon:
pebbles and dirt and what not.
Let there be no glass—
and no upholstery! phew!
and no little brass rollers
and small easy wheels on the bottom—
my townspeople what are you thinking of!
A rough plain hearse then
with gilt wheels and no top at all.
On this the coffin lies
by its own weight.

No wreaths please—
especially no hot-house flowers.
Some common memento is better,
something he prized and is known by:
his old clothes—a few books perhaps—

God knows what! You realize
how we are about these things,
my townspeople—
something will be found—anything—
even flowers if he had come to that.
So much for the hearse.

For heaven's sake though see to the driver!
Take off the silk hat! In fact
that's no place at all for him
up there unceremoniously
dragging our friend out to his own dignity!
Bring him down—bring him down!
Low and inconspicuous! I'd not have him ride
on the wagon at all—damn him—
the undertaker's understrapper!
Let him hold the reins
and walk at the side
and inconspicuously too!
Then briefly as to yourselves:
Walk behind—as they do in France,
seventh class, or if you ride
Hell take curtains! Go with some show
of inconvenience; sit openly—
to the weather as to grief.
Or do you think you can shut grief in?
What—from us? We who have perhaps
nothing to lose? Share with us
share with us—it will be money
in your pockets.
                    Go now
I think you are ready.

THE BULL

It is in captivity—
ringed, haltered, chained
to a drag
the bull is godlike

Unlike the cows
he lives alone, nozzles
the sweet grass gingerly
to pass the time away

He kneels, lies down
and stretching out
a foreleg licks himself
about the hoof

then stays
with half-closed eyes,
Olympian commentary on
the bright passage of days.

—The round sun
smooths his lacquer
through
the glossy pinetrees

his substance hard
as ivory or glass—

through which the wind
yet plays—
   Milkless

he nods
the hair between his horns
and eyes matted
with hyacinthine curls

MARIANNE MOORE

MARIANNE MOORE (1887–) is an individual metrical experimenter whose witty, ironic verses have long had the respect of her fellow poets. Born in St. Louis, Missouri, she was educated at Bryn Mawr. Her *Collected Poems* were published in 1951 and received the Pulitzer Prize in 1952. Her most recent works are *Like a Bulwark* (1956) and *O To Be a Dragon* (1959).

POETRY

I, too, dislike it: there are things that are important
 beyond all this fiddle.
Reading it, however, with a perfect contempt for it,
 one discovers in
it after all, a place for the genuine.
 Hands that can grasp, eyes
 that can dilate, hair that can rise
  if it must, these things are important not
   because a

high-sounding interpretation can be put upon them
  but because they are
 useful. When they become so derivative as to
 become unintelligible,
the same thing may be said for all of us, that we
 do not admire what
 we cannot understand: the bat
  holding on upside down or in quest of something to

eat, elephants pushing, a wild horse taking a roll,
 a tireless wolf under
a tree, the immovable critic twitching his skin like
 a horse that feels a flea, the base-
ball fan, the statistician—
 nor is it valid
  to discriminate against 'business documents
   and

school-books'; all these phenomena are important.
 One must make a distinction
 however: when dragged into prominence by half
 poets, the result is not poetry,
 nor till the poets among us can be
  'literalists of
  the imagination'—above
   insolence and triviality and can present

for inspection, imaginary gardens with real toads in
 them, shall we have
 it. In the meantime, if you demand on the one
 hand,
 the raw material of poetry in
  all its rawness and
  that which is on the other hand
   genuine, then you are interested in poetry.

From *Collected Poems* by Marianne Moore. Used with the permission of The Macmillan Company.

WALLACE STEVENS (1879–1955) was born in Reading, Pennsylvania, educated at Harvard, practiced law for a number of years and was in the insurance business in Connecticut. His books include *Harmonium* (1923), *Ideas of Order* (1935), *The Man With the Blue Guitar and Other Poems* (1937), *Notes Toward a Supreme Fiction* (1942), *Transport to Summer* (1947) and *Collected Poems* (1954), which won the National Book Award and the Pulitzer Prize in 1955.

THE PALTRY NUDE STARTS ON A SPRING VOYAGE[1]

But not on a shell, she starts,
Archaic, for the sea.
But on the first-found weed
She scuds the glitters,
Noiselessly, like one more wave.

She too is discontent
And would have purple stuff upon her arms,
Tired of the salty harbors,
Eager for the brine and bellowing
Of the high interiors of the sea.

The wind speeds her,
Blowing upon her hands
And watery back.
She touches the clouds, where she goes
In the circle of her traverse of the sea.

Yet this is meagre play
In the scurry and water-shine,
As her heels foam—
Not as when the goldener nude
Of a later day

Will go, like the centre of sea-green pomp,
In an intenser calm,
Scullion of fate,
Across the spick torrent, ceaselessly,
Upon her irretrievable way.

ANATOMY OF MONOTONY[2]

I

If from the earth we came, it was an earth
That bore us as a part of all the things
It breeds and that was lewder than it is.

Our nature is her nature. Hence it comes,
Since by our nature we grow old, earth grows
The same. We parallel the mother's death.
She walks an autumn ampler than the wind
Cries up for us and colder than the frost
Pricks in our spirits at the summer's end,
And over the bare spaces of our skies
She sees a barer sky that does not bend.

II

The body walks forth naked in the sun
And, out of tenderness or grief, the sun
Gives comfort, so that other bodies come,
Twinning our phantasy and our device,
And apt in versatile motion, touch and sound
To make the body covetous in desire
Of the still finer, more implacable chords.
So be it. Yet the spaciousness and light
In which the body walks and is deceived,
Falls from that fatal and that barer sky,
And this the spirit sees and is aggrieved.

PETER QUINCE AT THE CLAVIER[3]

I

Just as my fingers on these keys
Make music, so the selfsame sounds
On my spirit make a music, too.

Music is feeling, then, not sound;
And thus it is that what I feel,
Here in this room, desiring you,

Thinking of your blue-shadowed silk,
Is music. It is like the strain
Waked in the elders by Susanna.

Of a green evening, clear and warm,
She bathed in her still garden, while
The red-eyed elders watching, felt

[1] Reprinted from *The Collected Poems of Wallace Stevens* by permission of Alfred A. Knopf, Inc. Copyright, 1931, 1954, by Wallace Stevens.
[2] *Op. cit.*
[3] *Op cit.*

The basses of their beings throb
In witching chords, and their thin blood
Pulse pizzicati of Hosanna.

II

In the green water, clear and warm,
Susanna lay.

She searched
The touch of springs,
And found
Concealed imaginings.
She sighed,
For so much melody.

Upon the bank, she stood
In the cool
Of spent emotions.
She felt, among the leaves,
The dew
Of old devotions.

She walked upon the grass,
Still quavering.
The winds were like her maids,
On timid feet,
Fetching her woven scarves,
Yet wavering.

A breath upon her hand
Muted the night.
She turned—
A cymbal crashed,
And roaring horns.

III

Soon, with a noise like tambourines,
Came her attendant Byzantines.

They wondered why Susanna cried
Against the elders by her side;

And as they whispered, the refrain
Was like a willow swept by rain.
Anon, their lamps' uplifted flame
Revealed Susanna and her shame.

And then, the simpering Byzantines
Fled, with a noise like tambourines.

IV

Beauty is momentary in the mind—
The fitful tracing of a portal;
But in the flesh it is immortal.

The body dies; the body's beauty lives.
So evenings die, in their green going,
A wave, interminably flowing.
So gardens die, their meek breath scenting
The cowl of winter, done repenting.
So maidens die, to the auroral
Celebration of a maiden's choral.

Susanna's music touched the bawdy strings
Of those white elders; but, escaping,
Left only Death's ironic scraping.
Now, in its immortality, it plays
On the clear viol of her memory,
And makes a constant sacrament of praise.

SAD STRAINS OF A GAY WALTZ[4]

The truth is that there comes a time
When we can mourn no more over music
That is so much motionless sound.

There comes a time when the waltz
Is no longer a mode of desire, a mode
Of revealing desire and is empty of shadows.

Too many waltzes have ended. And then
There's that mountain-minded Hoon,
For whom desire was never that of the waltz,

Who found all form and order in solitude,
For whom the shapes were never the figures of men.
Now, for him, his forms have vanished.

There is order in neither sea nor sun.
The shapes have lost their glistening.
There are these sudden mobs of men,

These sudden clouds of faces and arms,
An immense suppression, freed,
These voices crying without knowing for what,

Except to be happy, without knowing how,
Imposing forms they cannot describe,
Requiring order beyond their speech.

Too many waltzes have ended. Yet the shapes
For which the voices cry, these, too, may be
Modes of desire, modes of revealing desire.

Too many waltzes—The epic of disbelief
Blares oftener and soon, will soon be constant.
Some harmonious skeptic soon in a skeptical music

[4] Reprinted from *The Collected Poems of Wallace Stevens* by permission of Alfred A. Knopf, Inc. Copyright, 1935, 1936, 1954, by Wallace Stevens.

Will unite these figures of men and their shapes
Will glisten again with motion, the music
Will be motion and full of shadows.

RE-STATEMENT OF
ROMANCE [5]

The night knows nothing of the chants of night.
It is what it is as I am what I am:
And in perceiving this I best perceive myself

[5] *Op. cit.*

And you. Only we two may interchange
Each in the other what each has to give.
Only we two are one, not you and night,

Nor night and I, but you and I, alone,
So much alone, so deeply by ourselves,
So far beyond the casual solitudes,

That night is only the background of our selves,
Supremely true each to its separate self,
In the pale light that each upon the other throws.

HART CRANE

HART CRANE (1899–1932) was born in Ohio. With high school his education became intermittent and sporadic, and for years he worked at various jobs in order to support himself while finding his way as a writer. He traveled in this country, Cuba, Europe and Mexico. "The poet's concern," he said, "must be, as always, self-discipline toward a formal integration of experience. For poetry is an architectural art, based not on Evolution or the idea of progress, but on the articulation of the contemporary human consciousness *sub specie æternitatis*. . . ." His *Collected Poems* was published in 1933.

THE RIVER
(from *The Bridge*)

*. . . and past
the din and
slogans of
the year—*

Stick your patent name on a signboard
brother—all over—going west—
young man
Tintex—Japalac—Certain-teed
Overalls ads
and lands sakes! under the new
playbill ripped
in the guaranteed corner—see Bert Williams what?
Minstrels when you steal a chicken just
save me the wing for if it isn't
Erie it ain't for miles around a
Mazda—and the telegraphic night coming on Thomas

a Ediford—and whistling down the tracks
a headlight rushing with the sound—can you
imagine—while an EXPRESS makes time like
SCIENCE—COMMERCE and the HOLYGHOST
RADIO ROARS IN EVERY HOME WE HAVE THE
NORTHPOLE WALLSTREET AND VIRGINBIRTH

The selections by Crane are from *The Collected Poems of Hart Crane* by Hart Crane. By permission of Liveright, Publishers, N.Y. Copyright © R, 1961, by Liveright Publishing Corp.

WITHOUT STONES OR WIRES OR EVEN RUNning
brooks connecting ears and no more sermons
windows flashing roar
Breathtaking—as you like it . . . eh?

So the 20th Century—so
whizzed the Limited—roared by and left
three men, still hungry on the tracks, ploddingly
watching the tail lights wizen and converge,
slipping gimleted and neatly out of sight.

The last bear, shot drinking in the
Dakotas

*to those
whose
addresses are
never near*

Loped under wires that span the
mountain stream.
Keen instruments, strung to a vast
precision
Bind town to town and
dream to ticking dream.
But some men take their liquor
slow—and count
—Though they'll confess
no rosary nor clue—
The river's minute by the far brook's year.
Under a world of whistles, wires and steam
Caboose-like they go ruminating through
Ohio, Indiana—blind baggage—

To Cheyenne tagging . . . Maybe Kalamazoo.
Time's rendings, time's blendings they construe
As final reckonings of fire and snow;
Strange bird-wit, like the elemental gist
Of unwalled winds they offer, singing low
My Old Kentucky Home and *Casey Jones*,
Some Sunny Day. I heard a road-gang chanting so
And afterwards, who had a colt's eyes—one said,
"Jesus! Oh I remember watermelon days!" And sped
High in a cloud of merriment, recalled
"—And when my Aunt Sally Simpson smiled," he
    drawled—
"It was almost Louisiana, long ago."

"There's no place like Booneville though, Buddy,"
One said, excising a last burr from his vest,
"—For early trouting." Then peering in the can,
"—But I kept on the tracks." Possessed, resigned,
He trod the fire down pensively and grinned,
Spreading dry shingles of a beard. . . .

                    Behind
My father's cannery works I used to see
Rail-squatters ranged in nomad raillery,
The ancient men—wifeless or runaway
Hobo-trekkers that forever search
An empire wilderness of freight and rails.
Each seemed a child, like me, on a loose perch,
Holding to childhood like some termless play.
John, Jake or Charley, hopping the slow freight
—Memphis to Tallahassee—riding the rods,
Blind fists of nothing, humpty-dumpty clods.

Yet they touch something like a key perhaps.
From pole to pole across the hills, the states
—They know a body under the wide rain;
Youngsters with eyes like fjords, old reprobates
              With racetrack jargon,—
but who have   dotting immensity
touched her,   They lurk across her,
knowing her   knowing her yonder breast
without name   Snow-silvered, sumac-stained
              or smoky blue—
Is past the valley-sleepers, south or west.
—As I have trod the rumorous midnights, too,

And past the circuit of the lamp's thin flame
(O Nights that brought me to her body bare!)
Have dreamed beyond the print that bound her
    name.
Trains sounding the long blizzards out—I heard
Wail into distances I knew were hers.

Papooses crying on the wind's long mane
Screamed redskin dynasties that fled the brain,

—Dead echoes! But I knew her body there,
Time like a serpent down her shoulder, dark,
And space, an eaglet's wing, laid on her hair.

Under the Ozarks, domed by Iron Mountain,
The old gods of the rain lie wrapped in pools
           Where eyeless fish curvet
nor the   a sunken fountain
myths of her And re-descend with corn
fathers . . .   from querulous crows.
Such pilferings make up their timeless eatage,
Propitiate them for their timber torn
By iron, iron—always the iron dealt cleavage!
They doze now, below axe and powder horn.

And Pullman breakfasters glide glistening steel
From tunnel into field—iron strides the dew—
Straddles the hill, a dance of wheel on wheel.
You have a half-hour's wait at Siskiyou,
Or stay the night and take the next train through.
Southward, near Cairo passing, you can see
The Ohio merging,—borne down Tennessee;
And if it's summer and the sun's in dusk
Maybe the breeze will lift the River's musk
—As though the waters breathed that you might
    know
Memphis Johnny, Steamboat Bill, Missouri Joe,
Oh, lean from the window, if the train slows down,
As though you touched hands with some ancient
    clown.
—A little while gaze absently below
And hum *Deep River* with them while they go.

Yes, turn again and sniff once more—look see,
O Sheriff, Brakeman and Authority—
Hitch up your pants and crunch another quid,
For you, too, feed the River timelessly.
And few evade full measure of their fate;
Always they smile out eerily what they seem.
I could believe he joked at heaven's gate—
Dan Midland—jolted from the cold brake-beam.

Down, down—born pioneers in time's despite,
Grimed tributaries to an ancient flow—
They win no frontier by their wayward plight,
But drift in stillness, as from Jordan's brow.

You will not hear it as the sea; even stone
Is not more hushed by gravity . . . But slow,
As loth to take more tribute—sliding prone
Like one whose eyes were buried long ago

The River, spreading, flows—and spends your dream
What are you, lost within this tideless spell?
You are your father's father, and the stream—

A liquid theme that floating niggers swell.
Damp tonnage and alluvial march of days—
Nights turbid, vascular with silted shale
And roots surrendered down of moraine clays:
The Mississippi drinks the farthest dale.

O quarrying passion, undertowed sunlight!
The basalt surface drags a jungle grace
Ochreous and lynx-barred in lengthening might;
Patience! and you shall reach the biding place!

Over De Soto's bones the freighted floors
Throb past the City storied of three thrones.
Down two more turns the Mississippi pours
(Anon tall ironsides up from salt lagoons)

And flows within itself, heaps itself free.
All fades but one thin skyline 'round . . . Ahead
No embrace opens but the stinging sea;
The River lifts itself from its long bed,

Poised wholly on its dream, a mustard glow
Tortured with history, its one will—flow!
—The Passion spreads in wide tongues, choked and
      slow,
Meeting the Gulf, hosannas silently below.

AT MELVILLE'S TOMB

Often beneath the wave, wide from this ledge
The dice of drowned men's bones he saw bequeath
An embassy. Their numbers as he watched,
Beat on the dusty shore and were obscured.

And wrecks passed without sound of bells,
The calyx of death's bounty giving back
A scattered chapter, livid hieroglyph,
The portent wound in corridors of shells.

Then in the circuit calm of one vast coil,
Its lashings charmed and malice reconciled,
Frosted eyes there were that lifted altars;
And silent answers crept across the stars.

Compass, quadrant and sextant contrive
No farther tides . . . High in the azure steeps
Monody shall not wake the mariner.
This fabulous shadow only the sea keeps.

THE AIR PLANT

GRAND CAYMAN

This tuft that thrives on saline nothingness,
Inverted octopus with heavenward arms
Thrust parching from a palm-bole hard by the cove—
A bird almost—of almost bird alarms,

Is pulmonary to the wind that jars
Its tentacles, horrific in their lurch.
The lizard's throat, held bloated for a fly,
Balloons but warily from this throbbing perch.

The needles and hack-saws of cactus bleed
A milk of earth when stricken off the stalk;
But this,—defenseless, thornless, sheds no blood,
Almost no shadow—but the air's thin talk.

Angelic Dynamo! Ventriloquist of the Blue!
While beachward creeps the shark-swept Spanish
      Main
By what conjunctions do the winds appoint
Its apotheosis, at last—the hurricane!

THE BROKEN TOWER

The bell-rope that gathers God at dawn
Dispatches me as though I dropped down the knell
Of a spent day—to wander the cathedral lawn
From pit to crucifix, feet chill on steps from hell.

Have you not heard, have you not seen that corps
Of shadows in the tower, whose shoulders sway
Antiphonal carillons launched before
The stars are caught and hived in the sun's ray?

The bells, I say, the bells break down their tower;
And swing I know not where. Their tongues engrave
Membrane through marrow, my long-scattered score
Of broken intervals. . . . And I, their sexton slave!

Oval encyclicals in canyons heaping
The impasse high with choir. Banked voices slain!
Pagodas, campaniles with reveilles outleaping—
O terraced echoes prostrate on the plain. . . .

And so it was I entered the broken world
To trace the visionary company of love, its voice
An instant in the wind (I know not whither hurled)
But not for long to hold each desperate choice.

My word I poured. But was it cognate, scored
Of that tribunal monarch of the air
Whose thigh embronzes earth, strikes crystal Word
In wounds pledged once to hope—cleft to despair?

The steep encroachments of my blood left me
No answer (could blood hold such a lofty tower
As flings the question true?)—or is it she
Whose sweet mortality stirs latent power?—

And though whose pulse I hear, counting the strokes
My veins recall and add, revived and sure
The angelus of wars my chest evokes:
What I hold healed, original now, and pure . . .

And builds, within, a tower that is not stone
(Not stone can jacket heaven)—but slip

Of pebbles—visible wings of silence sown
In azure circles, widening as they dip

The matrix of the heart, lift down the eye
That shrines the quiet lake and swells a tower . . .
The commodious, tall decorum of that sky
Unseals her earth, and lifts love in its shower.

ARCHIBALD MacLEISH

ARCHIBALD MACLEISH (1892–   ) was born in Illinois, educated at Yale and Harvard, served in the Field Artillery during the First World War and lived abroad from 1923 to 1928. Later he worked on *Fortune* magazine. He was Librarian of Congress (1939–1944), an official of the Office of War Information and of the Department of State, and served as chairman of the American delegation to the first general conference of UNESCO. He is now Boylston Professor of Rhetoric at Harvard. He has won three Pulitzer Prizes: in 1933, for *Conquistador;* in 1953, for his *Collected Poems: 1917–1952;* and in 1959, for *J.B.,* a verse drama.

ARS POETICA

A poem should be palpable and mute
As a globed fruit

Dumb
As old medallions to the thumb

Silent as the sleeve-worn stone
Of casement ledges where the moss has grown—

A poem should be wordless
As the flight of birds

* * * * *

A poem should be motionless in time
As the moon climbs

Leaving, as the moon releases
Twig by twig the night-entangled trees,

Leaving, as the moon behind the winter leaves,
Memory by memory the mind—

A poem should be motionless in time
As the moon climbs

* * * * *

A poem should be equal to:
Not true

The selections by MacLeish are from *Poems, 1924–1933, by Archibald MacLeish,* and reprinted by permission of and arrangement with Houghton Mifflin Company, the authorized publishers.

For all the history of grief
An empty doorway and a maple leaf

For love
The leaning grasses and two lights above the sea—

A poem should not mean
But be

LANDSCAPE AS A NUDE

She lies on her left side her flank golden:
Her hair is burned black with the strong sun:
The scent of her hair is of rain in the dust on her
   shoulders:
She has brown breasts and the mouth of no other
   country:

Ah she is beautiful here in the sun where she lies:
She is not like the soft girls naked in vineyards
Nor the soft naked girls of the English islands
Where the rain comes in with the surf on an east
   wind:

Hers is the west wind and the sunlight: the west
Wind is the long clean wind of the continents—
The wind turning with earth: the wind descending
Steadily out of the evening and following on:

The wind here where she lies is west: the trees
Oak ironwood cottonwood hickory: standing in
Great groves they roll on the wind as the sea would:
The grasses of Iowa Illinois Indiana

Run with the plunge of the wind as a wave tumbling:

Under her knees there is no green lawn of the
    Florentines:
Under her dusty knees is the corn stubble:
Her belly is flecked with the flickering light of the
    corn:
She lies on her left side her flank golden:
Her hair is burned black with the strong sun:
The scent of her hair is of dust and of smoke on her
    shoulders:
She has brown breasts and the mouth of no other
    country:

YOU, ANDREW MARVELL

And here face down beneath the sun
And here upon earth's noonward height
To feel the always coming on
The always rising of the night

To feel creep up the curving east
The earthy chill of dusk and slow
Upon those under lands the vast
And ever climbing shadow grow

And strange at Ecbatan the trees
Take leaf by leaf the evening strange
The flooding dark about their knees
The mountains over Persia change

And now at Kermanshah the gate
Dark empty and the withered grass
And through the twilight now the late
Few travelers in the westward pass

And Baghdad darken and the bridge
Across the silent river gone
And through Arabia the edge
Of evening widen and steal on

And deepen on Palmyra's street
The wheel rut in the ruined stone
And Lebanon fade out and Crete
High through the clouds and overblown

And over Sicily the air
Still flashing with the landward gulls
And loom and slowly disappear
The sails above the shadowy hulls

And Spain go under and the shore
Of Africa the gilded sand
And evening vanish and no more
That low pale light across that land

Nor now the long light on the sea

And here face downward in the sun
To feel how swift how secretly
The shadow of the night comes on . . .

KENNETH FEARING

KENNETH FEARING (1902–1961) was born in Chicago and educated at the University of
Wisconsin. He worked for various newspapers and magazines. Collected Poems was published
in 1940, Afternoon of a Pawnbroker in 1943, New and Selected Poems in 1956.

PORTRAIT[1]

The clear brown eyes, kindly and alert, with 20-20
vision, give confident regard to the passing world
through R. K. Lampert & Company lenses framed in
gold
    his soul, however, is all his own
        Arndt Brothers necktie and hat (with
        feather) supply a touch of youth

With his soul his own, he drives, drives, chats and
    drives the second and third bicuspids, lower

[1] From New and Selected Poems by Kenneth Fearing,
published by Indiana University Press.

right, replaced by bridgework, while two
incisors have porcelain crowns

(Render unto federal, state, and city Caesar, but
not unto time
    render nothing unto time until Amalgamated
    Death serves final notice, in proper form

The vault is ready
    the will has been drawn by Clagget, Clagget,
Clagget & Brown
        the policies are adequate, Confidential's best,
        reimbursing for disability, partial or com-
        plete, with double indemnity should the end
        be a pure and simple accident)

Nothing unto time
   nothing unto change
      nothing unto fate
         nothing unto you, and nothing unto me,
         or to any other known or unknown party
         or parties, living or deceased

But Mercury shoes, with special arch supports, take
much of the wear and tear
   on the course, a custombuilt driver corrects a
   tendency to slice
      love's ravages have been repaired (it was a
      textbook case) by Drs. Schultz, Lightner,
      Mannheim, and Goode
         while all of it is enclosed in excellent
         tweed, with Mr. Baumer's personal atten-
         tion to the shoulders and the waist

And all of it now roving, chatting amiably through
space in a Plymouth 6
   with his soul (his own) at peace, soothed by
   Walter Lippmann, and sustained by Haig &
   Haig.

TRAVELOGUE IN A
SHOOTING-GALLERY[2]

There is a jungle, there is a jungle, there is a vast,
   vivid, wild, wild, marvelous, marvelous, marvelous jungle,
Open to the public during business hours,
A jungle not very far from an Automat, between a
   hat store there, and a radio shop.

There, there, whether it rains, or it snows, or it
   shines,
Under the hot, blazing, cloudless, tropical neon
   skies that the management always arranges
   there,
Rows and rows of marching ducks, dozens and
   dozens and dozens of ducks, move steadily
   along on smoothly-oiled ballbearing feet,
Ducks as big as telephone books, slow and fearless
   and out of this world,
While lines and lines of lions, lions, rabbits, panthers,
   elephants, crocodiles, zebras, apes,
Filled with jungle hunger and jungle rage and jungle
   love,
Stalk their prey on endless, endless rotary belts
   through never-ending forests, and burning
   deserts, and limitless veldts,

[2] From *Afternoon of a Pawnbroker and Other Poems.*
Copyright, 1943, by Kenneth Fearing. Reprinted by permission of Harcourt, Brace & World, Inc.

To the sound of tom-toms, equipped with silencers,
   beaten by thousands of savages hidden there.

And there it is that all the big game hunters go,
   there the traders and the explorers come,
Leanfaced men with windswept eyes who arrive by
   streetcar, auto or subway, taxi or on foot, street-
   car or bus,
And they nod, and they say, and they need no more:
"There . . . there . . .
There they come and there they go."

And weighing machines, in this civilized jungle, will
   read your soul like an open book, for a penny at
   a time, and tell you all,
There, there, where smoking is permitted,
In a jungle that lies, like a rainbow's end, at the very
   end of every trail,
There, in the only jungle in the whole wide world
   where ducks are waiting for streetcars,
And hunters can be psychoanalyzed, while they
   smoke and wait for ducks.

AMERICAN RHAPSODY
(2)[3]

First you bite your fingernails. And then you comb
   your hair again. And then you wait. And wait.
(They say, you know, that first you lie. And then you
   steal, they say. And then, they say, you kill.)

Then the doorbell rings. Then Peg drops in. And Bill.
   And Jane. And Doc.
And first you talk, and smoke, and hear the news and
   have a drink. Then you walk down the stairs.
And you dine, then, and go to a show after that,
   perhaps, and after that a night spot, and after
   that come home again, and climb the stairs
   again, and again go to bed.

But first Peg argues, and Doc replies. First you dance
   the same dance and you drink the same drink
   you always drank before.
And the piano builds a roof of notes above the world.
And the trumpet weaves a dome of music through
   space. And the drum makes a ceiling over space
   and time and night.
And then the table-wit. And then the check. Then
   home again to bed.
But first, the stairs

[3] From *New and Selected Poems* by Kenneth Fearing,
published by Indiana University Press.

And do you now, baby, as you climb the stairs, do
    you still feel as you felt back there?
Do you feel again as you felt this morning? And the
    night before? And the night before that?
(They say, you know, that first you hear voices. And
    then you have visions, they say. Then, they say,
    you kick and scream and rave.)
Or do you feel: What is one more night in a lifetime
    of nights?
What is one more death, or friendship, or divorce
    out of two, or three? Or four? Or five?
One more face among so many, many faces, one more
    life among so many million lives?

But first, baby, as you climb and count the stairs
    (and they total the same) did you, sometime or
    somewhere, have a different idea?
Is this, baby, what you were born to feel, and do,
    and be?

REQUIEM [4]

Will they stop
    will they stand there for a moment, perhaps before
    some shop where you have gone so many times
    stand with the same blue sky above them and
    the stones, so often walked, beneath

[4] *Op. cit.*

Will it be a day like this
    as though there could be such a day again

And will their own concerns still be about the same
    and will the feeling still be this that you have felt
    so many times
      will they meet and stop and speak, one per-
      plexed and one aloof

Saying: Have you heard
    have you heard
      have you heard about the death

Yes, choosing the words, tragic, yes, a shock
    one who had so much of this, they will say, a life
    so filled with that
      then will one say that the days are growing
      crisp again, the other that the leaves are turning
        and will they say goodbye, goodbye, you
        must look me up sometime, goodbye
          then turn and go, each of them thinking,
          and yet, and yet

Each feeling, if it were I, instead, would that be all
    each wondering, suddenly alone, if that is all, in
    fact
And will that be all
    on a day like this, with motors streaming through
    the fresh parks, the streets alive with casual people
    and everywhere, on all of it, the brightness of the
    sun.

W. H. AUDEN

W. H. AUDEN (1907–   ) was born in York, England, and educated at Oxford. In 1939
he moved to the United States and became an American citizen. His more recent work displays his present concern with philosophy and religion, as opposed to his youthful enthusiasm
for left-wing politics, although he continues to experiment fruitfully with verse forms. His
books include *Collected Poems* (1945); *The Age of Anxiety* (1947), which won the Pulitzer
Prize in 1948; *Nones* (1951); *The Shield of Achilles* (1955); and *Homage to Clio* (1960).

MUSÉE DES BEAUX
ARTS [1]

About suffering they were never wrong,
The Old Masters: how well they understood
Its human position; how it takes place

[1] From *Another Time* (Random House, Inc.) by W. H.
Auden, copyright 1940 by W. H. Auden, and from *Col-
lected Shorter Poems 1930–1944* (Faber & Faber, Ltd.).
Reprinted by permission of the publishers.

While someone else is eating or opening a window or
    just walking dully along;
How, when the aged are reverently, passionately
    waiting
For the miraculous birth, there always must be
Children who did not specially want it to happen,
    skating
On a pond at the edge of the wood:
They never forgot
That even the dreadful martyrdom must run its
    course

Anyhow in a corner, some untidy spot
Where the dogs go on with their doggy life and the
     torturer's horse
Scratches its innocent behind on a tree.

In Breughel's *Icarus*, for instance: how everything
     turns away
Quite leisurely from the disaster; the ploughman
     may
Have heard the splash, the forsaken cry,
But for him it was not an important failure; the sun
     shone
As it had to on the white legs disappearing into the
     green
Water; and the expensive delicate ship that must
     have seen
Something amazing, a boy falling out of the sky,
Had somewhere to get to and sailed calmly on.

IN MEMORY OF
W. B. YEATS[2]

I

He disappeared in the dead of winter:
The brooks were frozen, the air-ports almost deserted,
And snow disfigured the public statues;
The mercury sank in the mouth of the dying day.
O all the instruments agree
The day of his death was a dark cold day.
Far from his illness
The wolves ran on through the evergreen forests,
The peasant river was untempted by the fashionable
     quays;
By mourning tongues
The death of the poet was kept from his poems.

But for him it was his last afternoon as himself,
An afternoon of nurses and rumors;
The provinces of his body revolted,
The current of his feeling failed: he became his
     admirers.

Now he is scattered among a hundred cities
And wholly given over to unfamiliar affections;
To find his happiness in another kind of wood
And be punished under a foreign code of conscience.
The words of a dead man
Are modified in the guts of the living.

[2] From *Another Time* (Random House, Inc.) by W. H.
Auden, copyright 1940 by W. H. Auden, and from *Col-
lected Shorter Poems 1930–1944* (Faber & Faber, Ltd.).
Reprinted by permission of the publishers.

But in the importance and noise of to-morrow
When the brokers are roaring like beasts on the floor
     of the Bourse,
And the poor have the sufferings to which they are
     fairly accustomed,
And each in the cell of himself is almost convinced
     of his freedom;
A few thousand will think of this day
As one thinks of a day when one did something
     slightly unusual.

O all the instruments agree
The day of his death was a dark cold day.

II

You were silly like us: your gift survived it all;
The parish of rich women, physical decay,
Yourself; mad Ireland hurt you into poetry.
Now Ireland has her madness and her weather still,
For poetry makes nothing happen: it survives
In the valley of its saying where executives
Would never want to tamper; it flows south
From ranches of isolation and the busy griefs,
Raw towns that we believe and die in; it survives,
A way of happening, a mouth.

III

Earth, receive an honored guest;
William Yeats is laid to rest:
Let the Irish vessel lie
Emptied of its poetry.

Time that is intolerant
Of the brave and innocent,
And indifferent in a week
To a beautiful physique,

Worships language and forgives
Everyone by whom it lives;
Pardons cowardice, conceit,
Lays its honors at their feet.

Time that with this strange excuse
Pardoned Kipling and his views,
And will pardon Paul Claudel,
Pardons him for writing well.

In the nightmare of the dark
All the dogs of Europe bark,
And the living nations wait,
Each sequestered in its hate;

Intellectual disgrace
Stares from every human face,

And the seas of pity lie
Locked and frozen in each eye.

Follow, poet, follow right
To the bottom of the night,
With your unconstraining voice
Still persuade us to rejoice;

With the farming of a verse
Make a vineyard of the curse,
Sing of human unsuccess
In a rapture of distress;

In the deserts of the heart
Let the healing fountain start,
In the prison of his days
Teach the free man how to praise.

CASINO [3]

Only the hands are living; to the wheel attracted,
Are moved as deer trek desperately towards a creek
  Through the dust and scrub of the desert, or gently
  As sunflowers turn to the light.

And, as the night takes up the cries of feverish
    children,
The cravings of lions in dens, the loves of dons,
  Gathers them all and remains the night, the
  Great room is full of their prayers

To the last feast of isolation self-invited
They flock, and in the rite of disbelief are joined;
  From numbers all their stars are recreated,
  The enchanted, the world, the sad.

Without, the rivers flow among the wholly living,
Quite near their trysts; and the mountains part them;
    and the bird
  Deep in the greens and moistures of summer
  Sings towards their work.

But here no nymph comes naked to the youngest
    shepherd;
The fountain is deserted; the laurel will not grow;
  The labyrinth is safe but endless, and broken
  Is Ariadne's thread.

As deeper in these hands is grooved their fortune:
    "Lucky

[3] From *The Collected Poetry of W. H. Auden* (Random House, Inc.), copyright 1945 by W. H. Auden, and from *Collected Shorter Poems 1930–1944* (Faber & Faber, Ltd.).

Were few, and it is possible that none was loved;
  And what was godlike in this generation
  Was never to be born."

LAW LIKE LOVE [4]

Law, say the gardeners, is the sun,
Law is the one
All gardeners obey
Tomorrow, yesterday, today.

Law is the wisdom of the old
The impotent grandfathers shrilly scold;
The grandchildren put out a treble tongue,
Law is the senses of the young.

Law, says the priest with a priestly look,
Expounding to an unpriestly people,
Law is the words in my priestly book,
Law is my pulpit and my steeple.

Law, says the judge as he looks down his nose,
Speaking clearly and most severely,
Law is as I've told you before,
Law is as you know I suppose,
Law is but let me explain it once more,
Law is the Law.

Yet law-abiding scholars write;
Law is neither wrong nor right,
Law is only crimes
Punished by places and by times,
Law is the clothes men wear
Anytime, anywhere,
Law is Good-morning and Good-night.

Others say, Law is our Fate;
Others say, Law is our State;
Others say, others say
Law is no more
Law has gone away.

And always the loud angry crowd
Very angry and very loud
Law is We,
And always the soft idiot softly Me.

If we, dear, know we know no more
Than they about the law,
If I no more than you
Know what we should and should not do
Except that all agree
Gladly or miserably

[4] *Op. cit.*

That the law is
And that all know this,
If therefore thinking it absurd
To identify Law with some other word.
Unlike so many men
I cannot say Law is again,
No more than they can we suppress
The universal wish to guess
Or slip out of our own position
Into an unconcerned condition.
Although I can at least confine
Your vanity and mine
To stating timidly
A timid similarity
We shall boast anyway:
Like love I say.

Like love we don't know where or why
Like love we can't compel or fly
Like love we often weep
Like love we seldom keep.

THE UNKNOWN CITIZEN[5]

*(TO JS/07/M/378
This Marble Monument
Is Erected by the State)*

He was found by the Bureau of Statistics to be
One against whom there was no official complaint,
And all the reports on his conduct agree
That in the modern sense of an old-fashioned word,
    he was a saint,

[5] From *Another Time* (Random House, Inc.) by W. H.
Auden, copyright 1940 by W. H. Auden, and from *Collected Shorter Poems 1930–1944* (Faber & Faber, Ltd.).
Reprinted by permission of the publishers.

For in everything he did he served the Greater Community.
Except for the War till the day he retired
He worked in a factory and never got fired,
But satisfied his employers, Fudge Motors Inc.
Yet he wasn't a scab or odd in his views,
For his Union reports that he paid his dues,
(Our report on his Union shows it was sound)
And our Social Psychology workers found
That he was popular with his mates and liked a drink.
The Press are convinced that he bought a paper every day
And that his reactions to advertisements were normal in every way.
Policies taken out in his name prove that he was fully insured,
And his Health-card shows he was once in hospital but left it cured.
Both Producers Research and High-Grade Living declare
He was fully sensible to the advantages of the Instalment Plan
And had everything necessary to the Modern Man,
A phonograph, a radio, a car and a frigidaire.
Our researchers into Public Opinion are content
That he held the proper opinions for the time of year;
When there was peace, he was for peace; when there was war, he went.
He was married and added five children to the population,
Which our Eugenist says was the right number for a parent of his generation,
And our teachers report that he never interfered with their education.
Was he free? Was he happy? The question is absurd:
Had anything been wrong, we should certainly have heard.

STEPHEN SPENDER (1909–   ) was born in England, educated at Oxford, and has traveled extensively on the Continent and in the United States. His poetry will be found in *Collected Poems: 1928–1953* (1954); he has also written two volumes of criticism, *The Destructive Element* (1935) and *The Making of a Poem* (1955).

THE EXPRESS[1]

After the first powerful plain manifesto
The black statement of pistons, without more fuss
But gliding like a queen, she leaves the station.
Without bowing and with restrained unconcern
She passes the houses which humbly crowd outside,
The gasworks and at last the heavy page
Of death, printed by gravestones in the cemetery.
Beyond the town there lies the open country
Where, gathering speed, she acquires mystery,
The luminous self-possession of ships on ocean.
It is now she begins to sing—at first quite low
Then loud, and at last with a jazzy madness—
The song of her whistle screaming at curves,
Of deafening tunnels, brakes, innumerable bolts.
And always light, aerial, underneath
Goes the elate metre of her wheels.
Steaming through metal landscape on her lines
She plunges new eras of wild happiness
Where speed throws up strange shapes, broad curves
And parallels clean like the steel of guns.
At last, further than Edinburgh, or Rome,
Beyond the crest of the world, she reaches night
Where only a low streamline brightness
Of phosphorus on the tossing hills is white.
Ah, like a comet through flame she moves entranced
Wrapt in her music no bird song, no, nor bough
Breaking with honey buds, shall ever equal.

I THINK CONTINUALLY OF THOSE WHO WERE TRULY GREAT[2]

I think continually of those who were truly great.
Who, from the womb, remembered the soul's history
Through corridors of light where the hours are suns
Endless and singing. Whose lovely ambition
Was that their lips, still touched with fire,

Should tell of the Spirit clothed from head to foot in song.
And who hoarded from the Spring branches
The desires falling across their bodies like blossoms.

What is precious is never to forget
The essential delight of the blood drawn from ageless springs
Breaking through rocks in worlds before our earth.
Never to deny its pleasure in the morning simple light
Nor its grave evening demand for love.
Never to allow gradually the traffic to smother
With noise and fog the flowering of the spirit.

Near the snow, near the sun, in the highest fields
See how these names are fêted by the waving grass
And by the streamers of white cloud
And whispers of wind in the listening sky.
The names of those who in their lives fought for life
Who wore at their hearts the fire's centre.
Born of the sun they travelled a short while towards the sun,
And left the vivid air signed with their honour.

ULTIMA RATIO REGUM[3]

The guns spell money's ultimate reason
In letters of lead on the spring hillside.
But the boy lying dead under the olive trees
Was too young and too silly
To have been notable to their important eye.
He was a better target for a kiss.

When he lived, tall factory hooters never summoned him.
Nor did restaurant plate-glass doors revolve to wave him in.
His name never appeared in the papers.
The world maintained its traditional wall
Round the dead with their gold sunk deep as a well,

[1] From *Poems* (Random House, Inc.) by Stephen Spender, copyright, 1934, by Modern Library, and from *Collected Poems* (Faber & Faber, Ltd.). Reprinted by permission of the publishers.
[2] *Op. cit.*

[3] From *The Still Centre* (Random House, Inc.), copyright, 1942, by Stephen Spender, and from *Collected Poems* (Faber & Faber, Ltd.). Reprinted by permission of the publishers.

Whilst his life, intangible as a Stock Exchange ru-
mour, drifted outside.

O too lightly he threw down his cap
One day when the breeze threw petals from the trees.
The unflowering wall sprouted with guns,
Machine-gun anger quickly scythed the grasses;
Flags and leaves fell from hands and branches;
The tweed cap rotted in the nettles.

Consider his life which was valueless
In terms of employment, hotel ledgers, news files.
Consider. One bullet in ten thousand kills a man.
Ask. Was so much expenditure justified
On the death of one so young and so silly
Lying under the olive trees, O world, O death?

NOT PALACES, AN ERA'S CROWN[4]

Not palaces, an era's crown
Where the mind dwells, intrigues, rests;
The architectural gold-leaved flower
From people ordered like a single mind,

[4] From *Poems* (Random House, Inc.) by Stephen
Spender, copyright, 1934, by Modern Library, and from
Collected Poems (Faber & Faber, Ltd.). Reprinted by
permission of the publishers.

I build. This only what I tell:
It is too late for rare accumulation
For family pride, for beauty's filtered dusts;
I say, stamping the words with emphasis,
Drink from here energy and only energy,
As from the electric charge of a battery,
To will this Time's change.
Eye, gazelle, delicate wanderer,
Drinker of horizon's fluid line,
Ear that suspends on a chord
The spirit drinking timelessness;
Touch, love, all senses,
Leave your gardens, your singing feasts,
Your dreams of suns circling before our sun,
Of heaven after our world.
Instead, watch images of flashing brass
That strike the outward sense, the polished will
Flag of our purpose which the wind engraves.
No spirit seek here rest. But this: No man
Shall hunger: Man shall spend equally.
Our goal which we compel: Man shall be man.

—That program of the antique Satan
Bristling with guns on the indented page
With battleship towering from hilly waves:
For what? Drive of a ruining purpose
Destroying all but its age-long exploiters.
Our program like this, yet opposite,
Death to the killers, bringing light to life.

DYLAN THOMAS

DYLAN THOMAS (1914–1953) was born in Wales and educated at the Swansea Grammar
School. By the late 1930's his rare lyric gifts had won him recognition as one of England's
finest contemporary poets. His *Collected Poems* appeared in 1953 and *Under Milk Wood* in
1954. Some of his prose sketches and essays have been gathered and published in *Quite Early
One Morning* (1954) and *A Prospect of the Sea* (1955).

THE FORCE THAT THROUGH THE GREEN FUSE DRIVES THE FLOWER

The force that through the green fuse drives the
flower
Drives my green age; that blasts the roots of trees
Is my destroyer.

The selections by Thomas are from *The Collected
Poems of Dylan Thomas.* Copyright 1953 by Dylan
Thomas. Reprinted by permission of New Directions.

And I am dumb to tell the crooked rose
My youth is bent by the same wintry fever.

The force that drives the water through the rocks
Drives my red blood; that dries the mouthing streams
Turns mine to wax.
And I am dumb to mouth unto my veins
How at the mountain spring the same mouth sucks.

The hand that whirls the water in the pool
Stirs the quicksand; that ropes the blowing wind
Hauls my shroud sail.
And I am dumb to tell the hanging man
How of my clay is made the hangman's lime.

The lips of time leech to the fountain head;
Love drips and gathers, but the fallen blood
Shall calm her sores.
And I am dumb to tell a weather's wind
How time has ticked a heaven round the stars.
And I am dumb to tell the lover's tomb
How at my sheet goes the same crooked worm.

AMONG THOSE KILLED IN THE DAWN RAID WAS A MAN AGED ONE HUNDRED

When the morning was waking over the war
He put on his clothes and stepped out and he died,
The locks yawned loose and a blast blew them wide,
He dropped where he loved on the burst pavement
    stone
And the funeral grains of the slaughtered floor.
Tell his street on its back he stopped a sun
And the craters of his eyes grew springshoots and fire
When all the keys shot from the locks, and rang.

Dig no more for the chains of his grey haired heart.
The heavenly ambulance drawn by a wound
Assembling waits for the spades' ring on the cage.
O keep his bones away from that common cart,
The morning is flying on the wings of his age
And a hundred storks perch on the sun's right hand.

IN MY CRAFT OR SULLEN ART

In my craft or sullen art
Exercised in the still night
When only the moon rages
And the lovers lie abed
With all their griefs in their arms,
I labour by singing light
Not for ambition or bread
Or the strut and trade of charms
On the ivory stages
But for the common wages
Of their most secret heart.
Not for the proud man apart
From the raging moon I write
On these spindrift pages
Not for the towering dead
With their nightingales and psalms
But for the lovers, their arms
Round the griefs of the ages,
Who pay no praise or wages
Nor heed my craft or art.

POEM IN OCTOBER

It was my thirtieth year to heaven
Woke to my hearing from harbour and neighbour
    wood
    And the mussel pooled and the heron
        Priested shore
        The morning beckon
With water praying and call of seagull and rook
And the knock of sailing boats on the net webbed
    wall
    Myself to set foot
        That second
    In the still sleeping town and set forth.
    My birthday began with the water-
Birds and the birds of the winged trees flying my
    name
    Above the farms and the white horses
        And I rose
        In rainy autumn
And walked abroad in a shower of all my days.
High tide and the heron dived when I took the road
    Over the border
        And the gates
    Of the town closed as the town awoke.

    A springful of larks in a rolling
Cloud and the roadside bushes brimming with whis-
    tling
    Blackbirds and the sun of October
        Summery
        On the hill's shoulder,
Here were fond climates and sweet singers suddenly
Come in the morning where I wandered and listened
    To the rain wringing
        Wind blow cold
    In the wood faraway under me.

    Pale rain over the dwindling harbour
And over the sea wet church the size of a snail
    With its horns through mist and the castle
        Brown as owls,
        But all the gardens
Of spring and summer were blooming in the tall tales
Beyond the border and under the lark full cloud.
    There could I marvel
        My birthday
    Away but the weather turned around.

    It turned away from the blithe country
And down the other air and the blue altered sky
    Streamed again a wonder of summer
        With apples
        Pears and red currants

And I saw in the turning so clearly a child's
Forgotten mornings when he walked with his mother
    Through the parables
      Of sun light
    And the legends of the green chapels

    And the twice told fields of infancy
That his tears burned my cheeks and his heart moved
      in mine.
    These were the woods the river and sea
      Where a boy
    In the listening
Summertime of the dead whispered the truth of his
      joy
To the trees and the stones and the fish in the tide.
    And the mystery
      Sang alive
    Still in the water and singing birds.

    And there could I marvel my birthday
Away but the weather turned around. And the true
    Joy of the long dead child sang burning
      In the sun.
    It was my thirtieth
Year to heaven stood there then in the summer noon
Though the town below lay leaved with October
      blood.
    O may my heart's truth
      Still be sung
On this high hill in a year's turning.

FERN HILL

Now as I was young and easy under the apple boughs
About the lilting house and happy as the grass was
    green,
    The night above the dingle starry,
      Time let me hail and climb
    Golden in the heydays of his eyes,
And honoured among wagons I was prince of the
    apple towns
And once below a time I lordly had the trees and
    leaves
    Trail with daisies and barley
    Down the rivers of the windfall light.

And as I was green and carefree, famous among the
    barns
About the happy yard and singing as the farm was
    home,
    In the sun that is young once only,
      Time let me play and be
    Golden in the mercy of his means,

And green and golden I was huntsman and herdsman,
    the calves
Sang to my horn, the foxes on the hills barked clear
    and cold,
    And the sabbath rang slowly
In the pebbles of the holy streams.

All the sun long it was running, it was lovely, the
    hay-
Fields high as the house, the tunes from the chim-
    neys, it was air
    And playing, lovely and watery
      And fire green as grass.
    And nightly under the simple stars
As I rode to sleep the owls were bearing the farm
    away,
All the moon long I heard, blessed among stables, the
    night-jars
    Flying with the ricks, and the horses
      Flashing into the dark.

And then to awake, and the farm, like a wanderer
    white
With the dew, come back, the cock on his shoulder:
    it was all
    Shining, it was Adam and maiden,
      The sky gathered again
    And the sun grew round that very day.
So it must have been after the birth of the simple
    light
In the first, spinning place, the spellbound horses
    walking warm
    Out of the whinnying green stable
    On to the fields of praise.

And honoured among foxes and pheasants by the gay
    house
Under the new made clouds and happy as the heart
    was long,
    In the sun born over and over,
      I ran my heedless ways,
    My wishes raced through the house-high hay
And nothing I cared, at my sky blue trades, that
    time allows
In all his tuneful turning so few and such morning
    songs
    Before the children green and golden

    Follow him out of grace,
Nothing I cared, in the lamb white days, that time
    would take me
Up to the swallow thronged loft by the shadow of my
    hand,
    In the moon that is always rising,

Nor that riding to sleep
I should hear him fly with the high fields
And wake to the farm forever fled from the childless
land.

Oh as I was young and easy in the mercy of his
means,
Time held me green and dying
Though I sang in my chains like the sea.

RICHARD EBERHART

RICHARD EBERHART (1904–   ) was born in Minnesota and educated at Dartmouth, Cambridge (as a Rhodes scholar), and at Harvard. His books include *A Bravery of Earth* (1930), *Poems, New and Selected* (1944), *Burr Oaks* (1947), *Brotherhood of Men* (1949), *Selected Poems* (1951), and *Collected Poems, 1930–1960* (1960).

IF I COULD ONLY LIVE AT THE PITCH THAT IS NEAR MADNESS[1]

If I could only live at the pitch that is near madness
When everything is as it was in my childhood
Violet, vivid, and of infinite possibility:
That the sun and the moon broke over my head.

Then I cast time out of the trees and fields,
Then I stood immaculate in the Ego;
Then I eyed the world with all delight,
Reality was the perfection of my sight.

And time has big handles on the hands,
Fields and trees a way of being themselves.
I saw battalions of the race of mankind
Standing stolid, demanding a moral answer.

I gave the moral answer and I died
And into a realm of complexity came
Where nothing is possible but necessity
And the truth wailing there like a red babe.

NEW HAMPSHIRE, FEBRUARY[2]

Nature had made them hide in crevices,
Two wasps so cold they looked like bark.
Why I do not know, but I took them
And I put them
In a metal pan, both day and dark.

Like God touching his finger to Adam
I felt, and thought of Michelangelo,
For whenever I breathed on them,
The slightest breath,
They leaped, and preened as if to go.

My breath controlled them always quite.
More sensitive than electric sparks
They came into life
Or they withdrew to ice,
While I watched, suspending remarks.

Then one in a blind career got out,
And fell to the kitchen floor. I
Crushed him with my cold ski boot,
By accident. The other
Had not the wit to try or die.

And so the other is still my pet.
The moral of this is plain.
But I will shirk it.
You will not like it. And
God does not live to explain.

SEALS, TERNS, TIME[3]

The seals at play off Western Isle
In the loose flowing of the summer tide
And burden of our strange estate—

Resting on the oar and lolling on the sea,
I saw their curious images,
Hypnotic, sympathetic eyes

[1] From *Selected Poems* by Richard Eberhart. Used by permission of Oxford University Press, Inc. and Messrs. Clarke, Irwin and Company of Toronto, Canada.
[2] *Op. cit.*

[3] From *Undercliff: Poems 1946–1953* by Richard Eberhart. Used by permission of Oxford University Press, Inc. and Messrs. Clarke, Irwin and Company of Toronto, Canada.

As the deep elapses of the soul.
O ancient blood, O blurred kind forms
That rise and peer from elemental water:

I loll upon the oar, I think upon the day,
Drawn by strong, by the animal soft bonds
Back to a dim pre-history;

While off the point of Jagged Light
In hundreds, gracefully, the fork-tailed terns
Draw swift esprits across the sky.

Their aspirations dip in mine,
The quick order of their changing spirit,
More freedom than the eye can see.

Resting lightly on the oarlocks,
Pondering, and balanced on the sea,
A gauze and spindrift of the world,

I am in compulsion hid and thwarted,
Pulled back in the mammal water,
Enticed to the release of the sky.

RANDALL JARRELL

RANDALL JARRELL (1914–   ) was born in Nashville, Tennessee and was educated at
Vanderbilt University. Since then he has distinguished himself as poet, critic, novelist, and
teacher. His books of poetry include *Blood for a Stranger* (1942), *Little Friend, Little
Friend* (1945), *Selected Poems* (1955), and *The Woman at the Washington Zoo* (1960).
Some of his critical essays have been collected in *Poetry and the Age* (1953; see selection
on page 546) and in *A Sad Heart at the Supermarket* (1961).

90 NORTH

At home, in my flannel gown, like a bear to its floe,
I clambered to bed; up the globe's impossible sides
I sailed all night—till at last, with my black beard,
My furs and my dogs, I stood at the northern pole.

There in the childish night my companions lay
    frozen,
The stiff furs knocked at my starveling throat,
And I gave my great sigh: the flakes came huddling,
Were they really my end? In the darkness I turned
    to my rest.

—Here, the flag snaps in the glare and silence
Of the unbroken ice. I stand here,
The dogs bark, my beard is black, and I stare
At the North Pole . . .
                    And now what? Why, go back.

Turn as I please, my step is to the south.
The world—my world spins on this final point

From *Blood for a Stranger* by Randall Jarrell, copyright, 1942, by Harcourt, Brace & World, Inc. and used
with their permission.

Of cold and wretchedness: all lines, all winds
End in this whirlpool I at last discover.

And it is meaningless. In the child's bed
After the night's voyage, in that warm world
Where people work and suffer for the end
That crowns the pain—in that Cloud-Cuckoo-Land

I reached my North and it had meaning.
Here at the actual pole of my existence,
Where all that I have done is meaningless,
Where I die or live by accident alone—

Where, living or dying, I am still alone;
Here where North, the night, the berg of death
Crowd to me out of the ignorant darkness,
I see at last that all the knowledge

I wrung from the darkness—that the darkness flung
    me—
Is worthless as ignorance: nothing comes from
    nothing,
The darkness from the darkness. Pain comes from the
    darkness
And we call it wisdom. It is pain.

HOWARD NEMEROV

HOWARD NEMEROV (1920–   ) was born in New York City and educated at Harvard. During the war he served as a fighter pilot with the Royal Canadian Air Force and later with the USAAF; he now teaches at Bennington College. A frequent contributor to many leading literary magazines, he is the author of four works of fiction and five volumes of poetry: *The Image and the Law* (1947), *Guide to the Ruins* (1950), *The Salt Garden* (1955), *Mirrors and Windows* (1958), and *New and Selected Poems* (1960).

THE SALT GARDEN

I

A good house, and ground whereon
With an amateur's toil
Both lawn and garden have been won
From a difficult, shallow soil
That, now inland, was once the shore
And once, maybe, the ocean floor.
Much patience, and some sweat,
Have made the garden green,
And even green the lawn.
Turnip and bean and violet
In a decent order set,
Grow, flourish and are gone;
Even the ruins of stalk and shell,
The vine when it goes brown,
Look civil and die well.
Sometimes in the late afternoon
I sit out with my wife,
Watching the work that we have done
Bend in the salt wind,
And think that here our life
Might be a long and happy one;
Though restless over the sand
The ocean's wrinkled green
Maneuvers in its sleep,
And I despise what I had planned,
Every work of the hand
For what can man keep?

II

Restless, rising at dawn,
I saw the great gull come from the mist
To stand upon the lawn.
And there he shook his savage wing
To quiet, and stood like a high priest
Bird-masked, mantled in grey.

The selections by Nemerov are from *The Salt Garden* by Howard Nemerov. Copyright 1951, 1952 by Howard Nemerov; by permission of Little, Brown & Co.

Before his fierce austerity
My thought bowed down, imagining
The wild sea lanes he wandered by
And the wild waters where he slept
Still as a candle in the crypt.
Noble, and not courteous,
He stared upon my green concerns,
Then, like a merchant prince
Come to some poor province,
Who, looking all about, discerns
No spice, no treasure house,
Nothing that can be made
Delightful to his haughty trade,
And so spreads out his sail,
Leaving to savage men
Their miserable regimen;
So did he rise, making a gale
About him by his wings,
And fought his huge freight into air
And vanished seaward with a cry—
A strange tongue but the tone clear.
He faded from my troubled eye
There where the ghostly sun
Came from the mist.
                          When he was gone
I turned back to the house
And thought of wife, of child,
And of my garden and my lawn
Serene in the wet dawn;
And thought that image of the wild
Wave where it beats the air
Had come, brutal, mysterious,
To teach the tenant gardener,
Green fellow of this paradise,
Where his salt dream lies.

THE GOOSE FISH

On the long shore, lit by the moon
To show them properly alone,
Two lovers suddenly embraced
So that their shadows were as one.
The ordinary night was graced

For them by the swift tide of blood
That silently they took at flood,
And for a little time they prized
　　　Themselves emparadised.

Then, as if shaken by stage-fright
Beneath the hard moon's bony light,
They stood together on the sand
Embarrassed in each other's sight
But still conspiring hand in hand,
Until they saw, there underfoot,
As though the world had found them out,
The goose fish turning up, though dead,
　　　His hugely grinning head.

There in the china light he lay,
Most ancient and corrupt and grey.
They hesitated at his smile,
Wondering what it seemed to say
To lovers who a little while
Before had thought to understand,
By violence upon the sand,

The only way that could be known
　　　To make a world their own.

It was a wide and moony grin
Together peaceful and obscene;
They knew not what he would express,
So finished a comedian
He might mean failure or success,
But took it for an emblem of
Their sudden, new and guilty love
To be observed by, when they kissed,
　　　That rigid optimist.

So he became their patriarch,
Dreadfully mild in the half-dark.
His throat that the sand seemed to choke,
His picket teeth, these left their mark
But never did explain the joke
That so amused him, lying there
While the moon went down to disappear
Along the still and tilted track
　　　That bears the zodiac.

HYAM PLUTZIK

HYAM PLUTZIK (1911–1962) was born in Brooklyn, New York and was educated at Trinity College and Yale University Graduate School. He received the Yale University Poetry Prize in 1933 and again in 1941. His work has been much praised by leading critics of poetry for its strength both in thought and expression. Among his published works are *Death at the Purple Rim* (1941), *Aspects of Proteus* (1949), and *Horatio, A Poem* (1961).

AN EQUATION

for instance: $y-xa+mx^2(a^2+1)=0$

Coil upon coil, the grave serpent holds
Its implacable strict pose, under a light
Like marble. The artist's damnation, the rat of time,
Cannot gnaw this form, nor event touch it with age.
Before it was, it existed, creating the mind
Which created it, out of itself. It will dissolve
Into itself, though in another language.
Its changes are not in change, nor its times in time.

And the coiled serpent quivering under a light
Crueler than marble, unwinds slowly, altering

The selections by Plutzik are from *Aspects of Proteus* by Hyam Plutzik. Copyright, 1949, by Hyam Plutzik. Reprinted by permission of Harper & Row, Publishers.

Deliberate the great convolutions, a dancer,
A mime on the brilliant stage. The sudden movement,
Swifter than creases of lightning, renews a statue:
There by its skin a snake rears beaten in copper.

It will not acknowledge the incense on your altars,
Nor hear at night in your room the weeping. . . .

THE BEGETTING OF CAIN

Longing at twilight the lovesick Adam saw
The belly of Eve upon the golden straw
Of Paradise, under the limb of the Tree.
He thought that none was near, but there were three
Who were upon the mortal grass that dusk,
Under the wispy cloud, breathing the musk
Of the young world. Creature of pointed ear,
Of the cleft hoof and the tight-mouthed sneer,
The other passed, wound round within his thought.
And Adam in his mounting passion caught

The white shoulders of that woman there. . . .
All were engulfed—these two, the birds of the air,
The burrowers of the earth, by the quenchless mind
Roaming insatiate on that lowland, blind
In its lonely hunger, lusting to make all things
One with itself. Brief as the flutter of wings

Was his mastery, though ranging through world and void
To the dusk-star shining. But all, all were destroyed:
The two on the odorous earth in the garden there;
The beasts, the birds in the nest, the fireflies in the air.

KARL SHAPIRO

KARL SHAPIRO (1913–   ) was born in Baltimore, Maryland and educated at the University of Virginia and Johns Hopkins University. A poet in the intellectual tradition, like Eliot and Auden, his work is a combination of insight and metrical subtlety; he is also a master of the dramatic lyric. Among his books are *Person, Place and Thing* (1942); *V-Letter* (1944), which was awarded a Pulitzer Prize; *Trial of a Poet* (1947); and *Poems of a Jew* (1958).

ADAM AND EVE

I

THE SICKNESS OF ADAM

In the beginning, at every step, he turned
As if by instinct to the East to praise
The nature of things. Now every path was learned
He lost the lifted, almost flower-like gaze

Of a temple dancer. He began to walk
Slowly, like one accustomed to be alone.
He found himself lost in the field of talk;
Thinking became a garden of its own.

In it were new things: words he had never said,
Beasts he had never seen and knew were not
In the true garden, terrors, and tears shed
Under a tree by him, for some new thought.

And the first anger. Once he flung a staff
At softly coupling sheep and struck the ram.
It broke away. And God heard Adam laugh
And for his laughter made the creature lame.

And wanderlust. He stood upon the Wall
To search the unfinished countries lying wide
And waste, where not a living thing could crawl,
And yet he would descend, as if to hide.

His thought drew down the guardian at the gate,
To whom man said, 'What danger am I in?'
And the angel, hurt in spirit, seemed to hate
The wingless thing that worried after sin,

From *Poems 1940–1953* by Karl Shapiro, copyright 1951 by Karl Shapiro. Reprinted by permission of Random House, Inc.

For it said nothing but marvelously unfurled
Its wings and arched them shimmering overhead,
Which must have been the signal from the world
That the first season of our life was dead.

Adam fell down with labor in his bones,
And God approached him in the cool of day
And said, 'This sickness in your skeleton
Is longing. I will remove it from your clay.'

He said also, 'I made you strike the sheep.'
It began to rain and God sat down beside
The sinking man. When he was fast asleep
He wet his right hand deep in Adam's side

And drew the graceful rib out of his breast.
Far off, the latent streams began to flow
And birds flew out of Paradise to nest
On earth. Sadly the angel watched them go.

II

THE RECOGNITION OF EVE

Whatever it was she had so fiercely fought
Had fled back to the sky, but still she lay
With arms outspread, awaiting its assault,
Staring up through the branches of the tree,
The fig tree. Then she drew a shuddering breath
And turned her head instinctively his way.
She had fought birth as dying men fight death.

Her sigh awakened him. He turned and saw
A body swollen, as though formed of fruits,
White as the flesh of fishes, soft and raw.
He hoped she was another of the brutes
So he crawled over and looked into her eyes,

The human wells that pool all absolutes.
It was like looking into double skies.

And when she spoke the first word (it was *thou*)
He was terror-stricken, but she raised her hand
And touched his wound where it was fading now,
For he must feel the place to understand.
Then he recalled the longing that had torn
His side, and while he watched it whitely mend,
He felt it stab him suddenly like a thorn.

He thought the woman had hurt him. Was it she
Or the same sickness seeking to return;
Or was there any difference, the pain set free
And she who seized him now as hard as iron?
Her fingers bit his body. She looked old
And involuted, like the newly-born.
He let her hurt him till she loosed her hold.

Then she forgot him and she wearily stood
And went in search of water through the grove.
Adam could see her wandering through the wood,
Studying her footsteps as her body wove
In light and out of light. She found a pool
And there he followed shyly to observe.
She was already turning beautiful.

III

THE KISS

The first kiss was with stumbling fingertips.
Their bodies grazed each other as if by chance
And touched and untouched in a kind of dance.
Second, they found out touching with their lips.

Some obscure angel, pausing on his course,
Shed such a brightness on the face of Eve
That Adam in grief was ready to believe
He had lost her love. The third kiss was by force.

Their lips formed foreign, unimagined oaths
When speaking of the Tree of Guilt. So wide
Their mouths, they drank each other from inside.
A gland of honey burst within their throats.

But something rustling hideously overhead,
They jumped up from the fourth caress and hid.

IV

THE TREE OF GUILT

Why, on her way to the oracle of Love,
Did she not even glance up at the Tree

Of Life, that giant with the whitish cast
And glinting leaves and berries of dull gray,
As though covered with mold? But who would taste
The medicine of immortality,
And who would 'be as God'? And in what way?

So she came breathless to the lowlier one
And like a priestess of the cult she knelt,
Holding her breasts in token for a sign,
And prayed the spirit of the burdened bough
That the great power of the tree be seen
And lift itself out of the Tree of Guilt
Where it had hidden in the leaves till now.

Or did she know already? Had the peacock
Rattling its quills, glancing its thousand eyes
At her, the iridescence of the dove,
Stench of the he-goat, everything that joins
Told her the mystery? It was not enough,
So from the tree the snake began to rise
And dropt its head and pointed at her loins.

She fell and hid her face and still she saw
The spirit of the tree emerge and slip
Into the open sky until it stood
Straight as a standing-stone, and spilled its seed.
And all the seed were serpents of the good.
Again he seized the snake and from its lip
It spat the venomous evil of the deed.

And it was over. But the woman lay
Stricken with what she knew, ripe in her thought
Like a fresh apple fallen from the limb
And rotten, like a fruit that lies too long.
This way she rose, ripe-rotten in her prime
And spurned the cold thing coiled against her foot
And called her husband, in a kind of song.

V

THE CONFESSION

As on the first day her first word was *thou*.
He waited while she said, 'Thou art the tree.'
And while she said, almost accusingly,
Looking at nothing, 'Thou art the fruit I took.'
She seemed smaller by inches as she spoke,
And Adam wondering touched her hair and shook,
Half understanding. He answered softly, 'How?'

And for the third time, in the third way, Eve:
'The tree that rises from the middle part
Of the garden.' And almost tenderly, 'Thou art
The garden. *We*.' Then she was overcome,
And Adam coldly, lest he should succumb

To pity, standing at the edge of doom,
Comforted her like one about to leave.

She sensed departure and she stood aside
Smiling and bitter. But he asked again,
'How did you eat? With what thing did you sin?'
And Eve with body slackened and uncouth,
'Under the tree I took the fruit of truth
From an angel. I ate it with my other mouth.'
And saying so, she did not know she lied.

It was the man who suddenly released
From doubt, wept in the woman's heavy arms,
Those double serpents, subtly winding forms
That climb and drop about the manly boughs;
And dry with weeping, fiery and aroused,
Fell on her face to slake his terrible thirst
And bore her body earthward like a beast.

VI

SHAME

The hard blood falls back in the manly fount,
The soft door closes under Venus' mount,
The ovoid moon moves to the Garden's side
And dawn comes, but the lovers have not died.
They have not died but they have fallen apart
In sleep, like equal halves of the same heart.

How to teach shame? How to teach nakedness
To the already naked? How to express
Nudity? How to open innocent eyes
And separate the innocent from the wise?
And how to re-establish the guilty tree
In infinite gardens of humanity?

By marring the image, by the black device
Of the goat-god, by the clown of Paradise,
By fruits of cloth and by the navel's bud,
By itching tendrils and by strings of blood,
By ugliness, by the shadow of our fear,
By ridicule, by the fig-leaf patch of hair.

Whiter than tombs, whiter than whitest clay,
Exposed beneath the whitening eye of day,

They awoke and saw the covering that reveals.
They thought they were changing into animals.
Like animals they bellowed terrible cries
And clutched each other, hiding each other's eyes.

VII

EXILE

The one who gave the warning with his wings,
Still doubting them, held out the sword of flame
Against the Tree of Whiteness as they came
Angrily, slowly by, like exiled kings,

And watched them at the broken-open gate
Stare in the distance long and overlong,
And then, like peasants, pitiful and strong,
Take the first step toward earth and hesitate.

For Adam raised his head and called aloud,
'My Father, who has made the garden pall,
Giving me all things and then taking all,
Who with your opposite nature has endowed

Woman, give us your hand for our descent.
Needing us greatly, even in our disgrace,
Guide us, for gladly do we leave this place
For our own land and wished-for banishment.'

But woman prayed, 'Guide us to Paradise.'
Around them slunk the uneasy animals,
Strangely excited, uttering coughs and growls,
And bounded down into the wild abyss.

And overhead the last migrating birds,
Then empty sky. And when the two had gone
A slow half-dozen steps across the stone,
The angel came and stood among the shards

And called them, as though joyously, by name.
They turned in dark amazement and beheld
Eden ablaze with fires of red and gold,
The garden dressed for dying in cold flame,

And it was autumn, and the present world.

ROBERT LOWELL (1917–   ), a member of the famous literary family that includes Amy Lowell and James Russell Lowell, was born in Boston and educated at Harvard University and Kenyon College. *Lord Weary's Castle* (1946), which won a Pulitzer Prize, and *The Mills of the Kavanaughs* (1951) established his position as a leading poet of his generation. More recent works are *Life Studies* (1959), an autobiography in verse and prose, and *Imitations* (1961), a collection of translated poetry.

THE DRUNKEN FISHERMAN[1]

Wallowing in this bloody sty,
I cast for fish that pleased my eye
(Truly Jehovah's bow suspends
No pots of gold to weight its ends);
Only the blood-mouthed rainbow trout
Rose to my bait. They flopped about
My canvas creel until the moth
Corrupted its unstable cloth.

A calendar to tell the day;
A handkerchief to wave away
The gnats; a couch unstuffed with storm
Pouching a bottle in one arm;
A whiskey bottle full of worms;
And bedroom slacks: are these fit terms
To mete the worm whose molten rage
Boils in the belly of old age?

Once fishing was a rabbit's foot—
O wind blow cold, O wind blow hot,
Let suns stay in or suns step out:
Life danced a jig on the sperm-whale's spout—
The fisher's fluent and obscene
Catches kept his conscience clean.
Children, the raging memory drools
Over the glory of past pools.

Now the hot river, ebbing, hauls
Its bloody waters into holes;
A grain of sand inside my shoe
Mimics the moon that might undo
Man and Creation too; remorse
Stinking, has puddled up its source;
Here tantrums thrash to a whale's rage.
This is the pot-hole of old age.

Is there no way to cast my hook
Out of this dynamited brook?
The Fisher's sons must cast about
When shallow waters peter out.
I will catch Christ with a greased worm,
And when the Prince of Darkness stalks
My bloodstream to its Stygian term . . .
On water the Man-Fisher walks.

AS A PLANE TREE BY THE WATER[2]

Darkness has called to darkness, and disgrace
Elbows about our windows in this planned
Babel of Boston where our money talks
And multiplies the darkness of a land
Of preparation where the Virgin walks
And roses spiral her enamelled face
Or fall to splinters on unwatered streets.
Our Lady of Babylon, go by, go by,
I was once the apple of your eye;
Flies, flies are on the plane tree, on the streets.

The flies, the flies, the flies of Babylon
Buzz in my ear-drums while the devil's long
Dirge of the people detonates the hour
For floating cities where his golden tongue
Enchants the masons of the Babel Tower
To raise tomorrow's city to the sun
That never sets upon these hell-fire streets
Of Boston, where the sunlight is a sword
Striking at the withholder of the Lord:
Flies, flies are on the plane tree, on the streets.

Flies strike the miraculous waters of the iced
Atlantic and the eyes of Bernadette
Who saw Our Lady standing in the cave
At Massabielle, saw her so squarely that
Her vision put out reason's eyes. The grave
Is open-mouthed and swallowed up in Christ.

[1] From *Lord Weary's Castle*, copyright, 1944, 1946, by Robert Lowell. Reprinted by permission of Harcourt, Brace & World, Inc.

[2] *Op. cit.*

O walls of Jericho! And all the streets
To our Atlantic wall are singing: "Sing,
Sing for the resurrection of the King."
Flies, flies are on the plane tree, on the streets.

FALLING ASLEEP
OVER THE AENEID [3]

The sun is blue and scarlet on my page,
And *yuck-a, yuck-a, yuck-a, yuck-a,* rage
The yellowhammers mating. Yellow fire
Blankets the captives dancing on their pyre,
And the scorched lictor screams and drops his rod.
Trojans are singing to their drunken God,
Ares. Their helmets catch on fire. Their files
Clank by the body of my comrade—miles
Of filings! Now the scythe-wheeled chariot rolls
Before their lances long as vaulting poles,
And I stand up and heil the thousand men,
Who carry Pallas to the bird-priest. Then
The bird-priest groans, and as his birds foretold,
I greet the body, lip to lip. I hold
The sword that Dido used. It tries to speak,
A bird with Dido's sworded breast. Its beak
Clangs and ejaculates the Punic word
I hear the bird-priest chirping like a bird.
I groan a little. "Who am I, and why?"
It asks, a boy's face, though its arrow-eye
Is working from its socket. "Brother, try,
O Child of Aphrodite, try to die:
To die is life." His harlots hang his bed
With feathers of his long-tailed birds. His head
Is yawning like a person. The plumes blow;
The beard and eyebrows ruffle. Face of snow,
You are the flower that country girls have caught,
A wild bee-pillaged honey-suckle brought
To the returning bridegroom—the design
Has not yet left it, and the petals shine;
The earth, its mother, has, at last, no help:
It is itself. The broken-winded yelp
Of my Phoenician hounds, that fills the brush
With snapping twigs and flying, cannot flush
The ghost of Pallas. But I take his pall,
Stiff with its gold and purple, and recall
How Dido hugged it to her, while she toiled,

[3] Copyright, 1948, by Robert Lowell. Reprinted from his volume *The Mills of the Kavanaughs* by permission of Harcourt, Brace & World, Inc.

Laughing—her golden threads, a serpent coiled
In cypress. Now I lay it like a sheet;
It clinks and settles down upon his feet,
The careless yellow hair that seemed to burn
Beforehand. Left foot, right foot—as they turn,
More pyres are rising: armored horses, bronze,
And gagged Italians, who must file by ones
Across the bitter river, when my thumb
Tightens into their wind-pipes. The beaks drum;
Their headman's cow-horned death's-head bites its
      tongue,
And stiffens, as it eyes the hero slung
Inside his feathered hammock on the crossed
Staves of the eagles that we winged. Our cost
Is nothing to the lovers, whoring Mars
And Venus, father's lover. Now his car's
Plumage is ready, and my marshals fetch
His squire, Acoetes, white with age, to hitch
Aethon, the hero's charger, and its ears
Prick, and it steps and steps, and stately tears
Lather its teeth; and then the harlots bring
The hero's charms and baton—but the King,
Vain-glorious Turnus, carried off the rest.
"I was myself, but Ares thought it best
The way it happened." At the end of time,
He sets his spear, as my descendants climb
The knees of Father Time, his beard of scalps,
His scythe, the arc of steel that crowns the Alps.
The elephants of Carthage hold those snows,
Turms of Numidian horse unsling their bows,
The flaming turkey-feathered arrows swarm
Beyond the Alps. "Pallas," I raise my arm
And shout, "Brother, eternal health. Farewell
Forever." Church is over, and its bell
Frightens the yellowhammers, as I wake
And watch the whitecaps wrinkle up the lake.
Mother's great-aunt, who died when I was eight,
Stands by our parlor sabre. "Boy, it's late.
Vergil must keep the Sabbath." Eighty years!
It all comes back. My Uncle Charles appears.
Blue-capped and bird-like. Phillips Brooks and Grant
Are frowning at his coffin, and my aunt,
Hearing his colored volunteers parade
Through Concord, laughs, and tells her English maid
To clip his yellow nostril hairs, and fold
His colors on him. . . . It is I, I hold
His sword to keep from falling, for the dust
On the stuffed birds is breathless, for the bust
Of young Augustus weighs on Vergil's shelf:
It scowls into my glasses at itself.

PROSE

ENDED: 400 YEAR BOOM

WALTER PRESCOTT WEBB

REFLECTIONS ON THE AGE OF THE FRONTIER

WALTER P. WEBB (1888–1963) was a Texan. Since 1918 he taught at the University of Texas, taking time out to lecture at London University and to serve as Harmsworth Professor of American History at Oxford. *The Great Plains* (1931), *The Texas Rangers* (1935), and *The Great Frontier* (1952) are among his books; the titles indicate the special interest he had in the westward movement of the people of the United States. He was no mere chronicler, however; history had immediate relevance for him, and valuable lessons for its readers.

IT IS difficult to discuss the frontier with an American audience because the literate American assumes that he knows what you are going to say in advance. It is difficult to expound the subject to a foreign audience for the opposite reason: the foreigner knows little about the subject, and because he cannot see that it touches his life, he is pretty indifferent to it. My purpose here is to show the American a phase of the frontier which he has not yet considered, and show the European that the frontier has for more than four centuries affected his life and well-being most profoundly.

The concept of the frontier as a factor in history was developed in the United States and has been applied primarily to American history. Though the word appears in similar form in nearly all European languages, it has a meaning and a set of connotations in the United States entirely different from those which obtain elsewhere. As used in Europe, it means the boundary between two nations and it is represented on the map by a thin line. That line is one to approach with caution, equipped with passports and permits. It is a place to stop at or to pass at national peril—"the sharp edge of sovereignty."

In America the word frontier is hardly used to indicate the nation's limits. No American would refer to the line separating the United States from Canada or from Mexico as a "frontier." The American concept holds that the frontier lies *within,* and not at the edge of the country—not a line to stop at, but an area inviting entrance. In Europe the frontier is stationary and permanent; in America it was (note the past tense) transient and temporal. It is this American idea which we shall be concerned with, and which we shall apply to the enormous region that may be called the Great Frontier.

From *Harper's Magazine,* October, 1951, by permission of the author's estate. The idea set forth in this article was expanded into a book, *The Great Frontier,* published by Houghton Mifflin in 1953.

The American concept of a moving frontier can be applied where a civilized people is advancing into a wilderness, an unsettled area, or one sparsely populated by primitive people. It was the sort of land into which the Boers moved in South Africa, the English in Australia, and the Americans and Canadians in their progress westward across North America. Likewise it was the land into which the Spaniards moved earlier in the New World. The frontier movement is an invasion of a land assumed to be vacant, as distinguished from an invasion of an occupied or civilized country. In view of the fact that from 1500 to about 1900 the European peoples were taking such lands on just such terms, it seems strange that the concept of the frontier as a force in human affairs should have hitherto been considered an American phenomenon. Actually the process was Western-world-wide.

It is not strange that the expanded concept of the frontier should have had its origin in America because here history and circumstance conspired to present the frontier factor in clear outline. The American experience with home-making in the wilderness began very early, and went on continuously because the Americans were virtually sole proprietors of an unsettled and contiguous territory of enormous extent. Always, for some three centuries, to the west of the settlements there stretched an empty country inviting entrance, luring the venturesome toward the sunset. Of the immediately adjacent territory the United States usually had undisputed possession. When no foreign power contended for it, it did not present a problem of sovereignty, and movement into it was predominately civilian, not military. The territory was adjacent to the settled area, and the journey there did not involve a sea voyage, a long trek, or any considerable outlay of capital. The settlers were citizens moving into territory owned by the nation. It was understood on all sides that the status of the individual as a citizen was unchanged, and that within a short time the new territory would automatically become a state in the Union with rights no different from those of the oldest member.

The absence of the military, the proximity of the new land to the old, the ease of migration, and the absence of any attempt on the part of the government to regulate or control the process made the American situation the last word in simplicity, so simple that it might seem to be chaotic. In these respects the movement of the American people into the frontier was unlike the movement of people from European nations into their equivalent frontier, and no doubt the simplicity of the American process explains why the historic force of the frontier was discovered first in the American context. Yet the American frontier was but a fragment of the Great Frontier, and the American process was but an example—the simplest and clearest, it is true—of a parallel but more complex development that was going on wherever European people were appropriating lands in the New Worlds.

Since America led the way in evolving the frontier process, and leads the world in the study of that process, we have no choice but to examine the American experience and to note briefly how scholars came to attend it as a field of study. American historians assume that the frontier process began with the English settlement at Jamestown in 1607, and the year 1890 is usually taken to mark the date when there was no more frontier available, when the new land was no longer new. There may be some quibbling about the dates, but they do bracket the three centuries of American frontier experience and experimentation.

It was the magnitude and the unbroken continuity of the experience that gave the frontier major importance in American life. It made no difference what other tasks the Americans had on their hands at a given time, there was the additional, ever-present one of moving into and settling new country. They did it while they fought for independence, before and after; they did it while they hammered out the principles of a democratic government shaped to the needs of frontiersmen; and they did not cease doing it in the period of civil strife. They never reached the limits of the vacancy they owned before they acquired another vacancy, by purchase, by treaty, by conquest, and in every case the frontiersmen infiltrated the country before the nation acquired it. Like locusts they swarmed, always to the west, and only the Pacific Ocean stopped them. Here in this movement beat the deep overtone of a nation's destiny, and to it all kept step unconsciously.

To say that the people were unconscious of the force that moved them, and of the medium in which they moved, is to state a fact which is easy to prove but hard to explain. It may be said that they were emotionally aware of the frontier long before they were intellectually cognizant of it. People could not have as their main task for three centuries working with raw land without getting its dirt under their nails and deep into their skins. The effects were everywhere, in democratic government, in boisterous politics, in exploitative agriculture, in mobility of population, in disregard for conventions, in rude manners, and in unbridled optimism. Though these effects were present everywhere they were not understood anywhere by the people who felt and reflected them. The frontier still lacked its philosopher, the thinker who could view the whole dramatic experience and tell what was its meaning. This philosopher arrived three years after the experience ended and told the American people that from the beginning the American frontier had been the dominant force, the determining factor, in their history thus far.

This hypothesis was presented to the American Historical Association in a paper entitled "The Significance of the Frontier in American History." The date was 1893 and the author was a young and then little-known historian. That paper made Frederick Jackson Turner a scholar with honor in his own country; it altered the whole course of American historical scholarship, and it is recognized as the most influential single piece of historical writing ever done in the United States. The key to his thesis is found in this sentence: "The existence of an area of free land, its continuous recession, and the advance of American settlement westward, explain American development." The general acceptance of this frontier hypothesis, and the fame of its author, came about because the people in America were emotionally prepared to understand this rationalization and explanation of their own long experience. Turner's pupils—many of whom became disciples—flocked to the diggings and have worked out in every cove and valley the rich vein which he uncovered, but not one of them, not even the master himself, took the next step to point out or at least to emphasize that the American frontier was but a small fragment of the Great Frontier. On that Great Frontier was also an area of free land; it was in continuous recession; and the advance of European settlement into it should explain the development of Western civilization in modern times just as the American advance explains American development.

II

What happened in America was but a detail in a much greater phenomenon, the interaction between

European civilization and the vast raw lands into which it moved. An effort will be made here to portray the whole frontier, to suggest how it affected the life and institutions of Western civilization throughout the modern period; and as a basis for this exposition four propositions are submitted for consideration:

(1) Europe had a frontier more than a century before the United States was settled.

(2) Europe's frontier was much greater than that of the United States, or of any other one nation; it was the greatest of all time.

(3) The frontier of Europe was almost, if not quite, as important in determining the life and institutions of modern Europe as the frontier of America was in shaping the course of American history. Without the frontier modern Europe would have been so different from what it became that it could hardly be considered modern at all. This is almost equivalent to saying that the frontier made Europe modern.

(4) The close of the Great Frontier may mark the end of an epoch in Western civilization just as the close of the American frontier is often said to have marked the end of the first phase of American history. If the close of the Great Frontier does mark the end of an age, the modern age, then the institutions designed to function in a society dominated largely by frontier forces will find themselves under severe strain.

If we conceive of western Europe as a unified, densely populated region with a common culture and civilization—which it has long had basically—and if we see the frontier also as a unit, a vast and vacant land without culture, we are in position to view the interaction between the two as a simple but gigantic operation extending over more than four centuries, a process that may appear to be the drama of modern civilization.

To emphasize the unity of western Europe, and at the same time set it off in sharp contrast to its opposite, the frontier, we may call it the Metropolis. Metropolis is a good name, implying what Europe really was, a cultural center holding within it everything pertaining to Western civilization. Prior to 1500 the Metropolis comprised all the "known" world save Asia, which was but vaguely known. Its area was approximately 3,750,000 square miles, and its population is estimated to have been about 100 million people.

There is no need to elaborate the conditions under which these people lived, but it should be remembered that by modern standards the society was a static one with well-defined classes. The population pressed hard on the means of subsistence. There was not much food, practically no money, and very little

freedom. What is more important, there was practically no means of escape for those people living in this closed world. The idea of progress had not been born. Heaven alone, which could be reached only through the portals of death, offered any hope to the masses of the Metropolis.

Then came the miracle that was to change everything, the emancipator bearing rich gifts of land and more land, of gold and silver, of new foods for every empty belly and new clothing stuffs for every half-naked back. Europe, the Metropolis, knocked on the door of the Great Frontier, and when the door was opened it was seen to be golden, for within there was undreamed-of treasure, enough to make the whole Metropolis rich. The long quest of a half-starved people had at last been rewarded with success beyond comprehension.

Columbus has been accepted as the symbol, as the key that unlocked the golden door to a new world, but we know that he was only one of a group of curious investigators, Portuguese, Spanish, English, Dutch, and Scandinavian, men of the Metropolis and not of one country. Within a brief period, as history is told, Columbus and his prying associates pulled back the curtains of ignorance and revealed to the Metropolis three new continents, a large part of a fourth, and thousands of islands in oceans hitherto hardly known. They brought all of these—continents, oceans, and islands—and deposited them as a free gift at the feet of the impoverished Metropolis.

The Metropolis had a new piece of property and the frontier had a new owner. The Metropolitans were naturally curious about their property, and quite naturally began to ask questions about it. How big is it? Who lives on it? What is its inherent worth? What can *I* get out of it? They learned that the frontier had an area five or six times that of Europe; that it was practically vacant, occupied by a few primitive inhabitants whose rights need not be respected; that its inherent worth could only be guessed at. As to what can *I* get out of it?, the answer came in time clear and strong: You can get everything you want from gold and silver to furs and foods, and in any quantity you want, provided only that you are willing to venture and work! And more faintly came the small voice, hardly audible: Something all of you can get as a by-product is some measure of freedom.

The Metropolitans decided to accept the gifts. Instantly the divisions in Europe were projected into the frontier as each little European power that could man a ship seized a section of the frontier bigger than itself and tried to fight all the others off. Each nation wanted it all. The result was a series of wars lasting from 1689 to 1763 and from these wars England,

France, and Spain emerged as chief owners of the frontier world. Their success was more apparent than real, for a spirit of freedom had been nurtured in the distant lands, and in less than fifty years England had lost her chief prize while Spain and France had lost practically everything.

But their loss, like their previous gain, was more apparent than real. True, by 1820 the Metropolis had lost title to most of the new land, but it had not lost something more precious than title—namely, the beneficent effects that the frontier exerted on the older countries. The political separation of most of North and South America relieved the Metropolis of responsibility and onerous obligations, but it did not cut off the abundance of profits. Europe continued to share in the riches and the opportunity that the opening of the golden door had made visible.

III

What was the essential character of the frontier? Was the direct force it exerted spiritual, intellectual, or was it material? The frontier was basically a vast body of wealth without proprietors. It was an empty land more than five times the size of western Europe, a land whose resources had not been exploited. Its first impact was mainly economic. Bathed in and invigorated by a flood of wealth, the Metropolis began to seethe with economic excitement.

With all the ships coming and going, the wharves of Europe were piled high with strange goods, the tables were set with exotic foods of delightful flavors, and new-minted coins of gold and silver rattled in the coffers of the market place. The boom began when Columbus returned from his first voyage, and it continued at an ever-accelerating pace until the frontier that fed it was no more. Assuming that the frontier closed about 1890, it may be said that the boom lasted approximately four hundred years. It lasted so long that it came to be considered the normal state, a fallacious assumption for any boom. It is conceivable that this boom has given the peculiar character to modern history, to what we call Western civilization.

Assuming that there was such a boom and that it lasted four hundred years, it follows that a set of institutions, economic, political, and social, would in that time evolve to meet the needs of the world in boom. Insofar as they were designed to meet peculiar conditions, these institutions would be specialized boomward. It is accepted that a set of institutions has developed since 1500, and we speak of them as modern to distinguish them from medieval institutions. Therefore we may well inquire whether our modern institutions—economic, political, and social, consti-

tuting the superstructure of Western civilization—are founded on boom conditions.

The factors involved, though of gigantic magnitude, are simple in nature and in their relation one to another. They are the old familiar ones of population, land, and capital. With the opening of the Great Frontier, land and capital rose out of all proportion to population, of those to share it, and therefore conditions were highly favorable to general prosperity and a boom. What we are really concerned with is an *excess* of land and an *excess* of capital for division among a relatively *fixed* number of people. The population did increase, but not until the nineteenth century did the extra population compare with the extra land and capital that had been long available.

For example, in 1500 the Metropolis had a population of 100 million people crowded into an area of 3,750,000 square miles. The population density for the entire Metropolis was 26.7 persons per square mile. For each person there was available about twenty-four acres, a ratio that changed little from 1300 to 1650. The opening of the frontier upset the whole situation by destroying the balance that had been struck between land and man. A land excess of nearly 20 million square miles became available to the same number of people, reducing population density to less than five, increasing the average area per individual to 148 acres instead of 24.

Capital may be considered in two forms, as gold and silver and as capital goods or commodities. The Metropolis was short of both forms of wealth throughout the medieval period, and the dearth of coin prior to the discoveries was most critical. It has been estimated that the total amount of gold and silver in Europe in 1492 was less than 200 million dollars, less than two dollars per person. Certainly there was not enough to serve the needs of exchange, which was carried on by barter, or to give rise to erudite theories of money economy. Then very suddenly the whole money situation changed.

By 1500 the Spaniards had cracked the treasure houses of the Great Frontier and set a stream of gold and silver flowing into the Metropolis, a stream that continued without abatement for 150 years, and that still continues. This flood of precious metals changed all the relations existing between man and money, between gold and a bushel of wheat or a *fanega* of barley. That changed relationship wrought the price revolution because temporarily—so fast did the metals come—there was more money than things, and so prices rose to the modern level. This new money was a powerful stimulus to the quest for more, and set the whole Metropolis into the frenzy of daring and adventure which gave character to the modern age.

Since our concern here is with the excess of wealth over population, we may examine with interest the rise in the quantity of gold and silver. Taking the 200 million dollars of 1492 as a base, we find that by 1600 the amount had increased eightfold, by 1700 it had risen nearly twentyfold, by 1800 it stood at thirty-sevenfold, and by 1900 at a hundred-and-four-fold over what was on hand when the frontier was opened. Obviously this increase of precious metals was out of all proportion to the increase in population. If we grant that an excess of money makes a boom, then here in this new treasure was the stuff a boom needed. It is safe to say that out of each $100 worth of precious metals produced in the world since 1493, not less than $85 have been supplied by the frontier countries and not more than $15 by the Metropolis, including Asia. The bearing of these facts on the rise of a money economy, of modern capitalism, is something for the economists to think about.

The spectacular influx of precious metals should not obscure the fact that they constituted but the initial wave of wealth rolling into the Metropolis from the Great Frontier. Wave followed wave in endless succession in the form of material things, and each deposit left the Metropolis richer than before. Unfortunately the quantity of material goods cannot be measured, but we know it was enormous. South America sent coffee, Africa, cocoa, and the West Indies sent sugar to sweeten them. Strange and flavorsome fruits came from the tropics. From primeval forests came ship timbers, pitch, and tar with which to build the fleets for merchants and warriors. North America sent furs for the rich and cotton for the poor so that all could have more than one garment. The potato, adapted to the Metropolis, became second to bread as the staff of life. The New World gave Indian corn or maize, and the rich lands on which to grow it, and in time hides and beef came from the plains and pampas of two continents. Everywhere in Europe from the royal palace to the humble cottage men smoked American tobacco and under its soothing influence dreamed of far countries, wealth, and adventure. Scientists brought home strange plants and herbs and made plant experiment stations in scores of European gardens. In South America they found the bark of a tree from which quinine was derived to cure malaria and another plant which they sent to the East Indies to establish the rubber industry. No, it is not possible to measure the amount of goods flowing into Europe, but it can be said that the Great Frontier hung for centuries like the horn of plenty over the Metropolis and emptied out on it an avalanche of wealth.

At this point let us turn to the growth of population, the number of people who in a rough sense shared the excess of land and of precious metals. As stated above the population in 1500 stood at about 100 million, and it did not increase appreciably before 1650. All the people of European origin, whether in the Metropolis or in the Great Frontier, had a little more than doubled by 1800. Not until the nineteenth century was the increase rapid. By 1850 the increase was more than threefold, by 1900 more than fivefold, but in 1940 population had increased eightfold over that of 1500. The significant fact is that between 1500 and 1850 the quantity of both land and capital stood high out of all proportion to the quantity of population. Equally significant, and somewhat disturbing, is the fact that the excess of land incident to opening the frontier disappeared in the world census of 1930. By 1940 the enlarged Western world was more crowded than the small world of Europe was in 1500. It was the observation of this fact which led Dean Inge to remark in 1938 that "the house is full." Much earlier William Graham Sumner commented on the man-land ratio: "It is this ratio of population to land which determines what are the possibilities of human development or the limits of what man can attain in civilization and comfort." To put the matter in another way, if the boom rested on a four-century excess of land over population, the land base of the boom disappeared in 1930.

The boom hypothesis of modern history may be summed up by stating that with the tapping of the resources of the Great Frontier there came into the possession of the Metropolis a body of wealth consisting of land, precious metals, and commodities out of all proportion to the number of people. . . .

IV

If the opening of the Great Frontier did precipitate a boom in Western civilization, the effects on human ideas and institutions must have been profound and far-reaching. In general such a boom would hasten the passing away of the ideas and institutions of a static culture and the sure appearance of others adapted to a dynamic and prospering society. There is no doubt that medieval society was breaking up at the time of the discoveries, that men's minds had been sharpened by their intellectual exercises, and that their spirits had been stirred by doubt. The thinkers were restless and inquiring, but what they lacked was room in which to try out their innovations, and a fresh and uncluttered soil in which some of their new ideas could take hold and grow. Their desires had to be matched with opportunity before they could realize on their aspirations, however laudable. The frontier offered them the room and the opportunity. It did not necessarily originate ideas, but it acted as a relentless sifter, letting some pass and rejecting others. Those that the frontier favored prospered, and finally matured into institutions; those it did not favor became recessive, dormant, and many institutions based on these ideas withered away. Feudal tenure, selfdom, barter, primogeniture, and the notion that the world was a no-good place in which to live are examples of things untenable in the presence of the frontier.

Since we are dealing with the modern age, it would be very helpful if we could discover what it emphasized most. Where was the chief accent of modernity? What has been its focus? *Who* has held the spotlight on the stage of history since 1500? There can be little doubt, though there may be enough to start an argument, that the answer to all these questions is: the Individual. It is he who has been emphasized, accented; it is on him that the spotlight has focused; it is his importance that has been magnified. He is—or was—the common denominator of modern times, and an examination of any strictly modern institution such as democracy or capitalism will reveal an individual at the core, trying to rule himself in one case and make some money in the other. Not God nor the devil nor the state, but the ordinary man has been the favorite child of modern history.

Did the Great Frontier, which was his contemporary, have any part in giving the individual his main chance, the triple opportunity of ruling himself, enriching himself, and saving his own soul on his own hook? These three freedoms were institutionalized in Protestantism, capitalism, and democracy—whose basic assumption is that they exist for the individual, and that the individual must be free in order to make them work. The desire for freedom men surely have always had, but in the old Metropolis conditions prevailed which made freedom impossible. Everywhere in Europe the individual was surrounded by institutions which, whether by design or not, kept him unfree. He was walled in by man-made regulations which controlled him from baptism to extreme unction.

Then the golden door of the Great Frontier opened, and a way of escape lay before him. He moved out from the Metropolis to land on a distant shore, in America, Australia, South Africa. Here in the wild and empty land there was not a single institution; man had left them, albeit temporarily, far behind. Regardless of what befell him later, for an instant he was free of all the restrictions that society had put upon him. In short, he had escaped his human masters only to find himself in the presence of another, a less picayunish one.

The character of the new master, before whom he stood stripped of his institutions, was so in contrast with that of the old one as to defy comparison. Man stood naked in the presence of nature. On this subject, Alexander von Humboldt said, "In the Old World, nations and the distinction of their civilization form the principal point in the picture; in the New World, man and his production almost disappear amidst the stupendous display of wild and gigantic nature." The outstanding qualities of wild and gigantic nature are its impersonality and impassiveness. Nature broods over man, casts its mysterious spells, but it never intervenes for or against him. It gives no orders, issues no proclamations, has no prisons, no privileges; it knows nothing of vengeance or mercy. Before nature all men are free and equal.

The important point is that the abstract man we have been following did not have to *win* his freedom. It was imposed upon him and he could not escape it. Being caught in the trap of freedom, his task was to adjust himself to it and to devise procedures which would be more convenient for living in such a state. His first task was to govern himself, for self-government is what freedom imposes.

Of course there was not just one man on the frontier. In a short time the woods were full of them, all trained in the same school. As the years went by, they formed the habits of freedom, cherished it; and when a distant government tried to take from them that to which they had grown accustomed, they resisted, and their resistance was called the American Revolution. The American frontiersmen did not fight England to gain freedom, but to preserve it and have it officially recognized by the Metropolis. "Your nation," wrote Herman Melville, "enjoyed no little independence before your declaration declared it." Whence came this independence? Not from parliaments or kings or legislative assemblies, but from the conditions, the room, the space, and the natural wealth amidst which they lived. "The land was ours," writes Robert Frost, "before we were the land's."

The other institution that magnified the importance of the individual was capitalism, an economic system under which each person undertakes to enrich himself by his own effort. It is only in the presence of great abundance that such a free-for-all system of wealth-getting can long operate. There must be present enough wealth to go around to make such an economy practicable. We have seen that the tapping of the frontier furnished just this condition, a superabundance of land, of gold and silver, and of commodities which made the principle of *laissez faire* tenable. In the frontier the embryonic capitalists of the sixteenth and seventeenth centuries hit a magnificent windfall which set them up in business by demonstrating that the game of wealth-getting was both interesting and profitable. For four hundred years, to paraphrase Bernard DeVoto, "men stumbled over fortunes looking for cows." Free homesteads in Kansas, free gold claims in California, and free grass on the Great Plains are examples of windfalls coming at the tag end of the frontier period, windfalls which come no more. In the larger sense the Great Frontier was a windfall for Europe.

There is an unpleasant logic inherent in the frontier boom hypothesis of modern history. We come to it with the reluctance that men always have when they come to the end of a boom. They look back on the grand opportunities they had, they remember the excitement and adventure of it, they tot up their accounts and hope for another chance. Western civilization today stands facing a closed frontier, and in this sense it faces a unique situation in modern times.

If we grant the boom, we must concede that the institutions we have, such as democracy and capitalism, were boom-born; we must also admit that the individual, this cherished darling of modern history, attained his glory in an abnormal period when there was enough room to give him freedom and enough wealth to give him independence. The future of the individual, of democracy and capitalism, and of many other modern institutions are deeply involved in this logic, and the lights are burning late in the capitals of the Western world where grave men are trying to determine what that future will be.

Meantime less thoughtful people speak of new frontiers, though nothing comparable to the Great Frontier has yet been found. The business man sees a business frontier in the customers he has not yet reached; the missionary sees a religious frontier among the souls he has not yet saved; the social worker sees a human frontier among the suffering people whose woes he has not yet alleviated; the educator of a sort sees the ignorance he is trying to dispel as a frontier to be taken; and the scientists permit us to believe that they are uncovering the real thing in a scientific frontier. But as yet no Columbus has come in from these voyages and announced: "Gentlemen, there is your frontier!" The best they do is to say that it is out beyond, that if you work hard enough and have faith enough, and put in a little money, you will surely find it. If you watch these peddlers of substitute frontiers, you will find that nearly every one wants you to buy something, give something, or believe in something. They want you to be a frontier for them. Unlike Columbus, they bring no continents and no oceans, no gold or silver or grass or forest to you.

I should like to make it clear that mankind is really searching for a new frontier which we once had and did not prize, and the longer we had it, the less we valued it; but now that we have lost it, we have a great pain in the heart, and we are always trying to get it back again. It seems to me that historians and all thoughtful persons are bound by their obligation to say that there is no new frontier in sight comparable in magnitude or importance to the one that is lost. They should point out the diversity and heterogeneity, not to say the absurdity, of so-called new frontiers. They are all fallacies, these new frontiers, and they are pernicious in proportion to their plausibility and respectability. The scientists themselves should join in disabusing the public as to what science can be expected to do. It can do much, but, to paraphrase Isaiah Bowman, it is not likely soon to find a new world or make the one we have much bigger than it is. If the frontier is gone, we should have the courage and honesty to recognize the fact, cease to cry for what we have lost, and devote our energy to finding the solutions to the problems now facing a frontierless society. And when the age we now call modern is modern no longer, and requires a new name, we may appropriately call it the Age of the Frontier, and leave it to its place in history.

THE PHILOSOPHER

W. SOMERSET MAUGHAM

W. SOMERSET MAUGHAM (1874–   ) is the dean of British writers of fiction. His novels include *Of Human Bondage* (1915), *The Moon and Sixpence* (1919), and *Cakes and Ale* (1930); he has written successful plays, and many of his short stories have been adapted for the stage and the motion pictures. His curiosity about men and life has led him to travel widely and to philosophize, as in this piece, over the alien cultures he has observed.

IT was surprising to find so vast a city in a spot that seemed to me so remote. From its battlemented gate towards sunset you could see the snowy mountains of Tibet. It was so populous that you could walk at ease only on the walls and it took a rapid walker three hours to complete their circuit. There was no railway within a thousand miles and the river on which it stood was so shallow that only junks of light burden could safely navigate it. Five days in a sampan were needed to reach the Upper Yangtze. For an uneasy moment you asked yourself whether trains and steamships were as necessary to the conduct of life as we who use them every day consider; for here a million persons throve, married, begat their kind, and died; here a million persons were busily occupied with commerce, art, and thought.

And here lived a philosopher of repute the desire to see whom had been to me one of the incentives of a somewhat arduous journey. He was the greatest authority in China on the Confucian learning. He was said to speak English and German with facility. He had been for many years secretary to one of the Empress Dowager's greatest viceroys, but he lived now in retirement. On certain days in the week, however, all through the year he opened his doors to such as sought after knowledge, and discoursed on the teaching of Confucius. He had a body of disciples, but it was small, since the students for the most part preferred to his modest dwelling and his severe exhortations the sumptuous buildings of the foreign university and the useful science of the barbarians: with him this was mentioned only to be scornfully dismissed. From all I heard of him I concluded that he was a man of character.

When I announced my wish to meet this distinguished person my host immediately offered to

arrange a meeting; but the days passed and nothing happened. I made inquiries and my host shrugged his shoulders.

"I sent him a chit and told him to come along," he said. "I don't know why he hasn't turned up. He's a cross-grained old fellow."

I did not think it was proper to approach a philosopher in so cavalier a fashion and I was hardly surprised that he had ignored a summons such as this. I caused a letter to be sent asking in the politest terms I could devise whether he would allow me to call upon him and within two hours received an answer making an appointment for the following morning at ten o'clock.

I was carried in a chair. The way seemed interminable. I went through crowded streets and through streets deserted till I came at last to one, silent and empty, in which at a small door in a long white wall my bearers set down my chair. One of them knocked, and after a considerable time a judas was opened; dark eyes looked through; there was a brief colloquy; and finally I was admitted. A youth, pallid of face, wizened, and poorly dressed, motioned me to follow him. I did not know if he was a servant or a pupil of the great man. I passed through a shabby yard and was led into a long, low room sparsely furnished with an American roll-top desk, a couple of blackwood chairs and two little Chinese tables. Against the walls were shelves on which were a great number of books: most of them, of course, were Chinese, but there were many, philosophical and scientific works, in English, French, and German; and there were hundreds of unbound copies of learned reviews. Where books did not take up the wall space hung scrolls on which in various calligraphies were written, I suppose, Confucian quotations. There was no carpet on the floor. It was a cold, bare, and comfortless chamber. Its sombreness was relieved only by a yellow chrysanthemum which stood by itself on the desk in a long vase.

I waited for some time and the youth who had shown me in brought a pot of tea, two cups, and a tin

"The Philosopher" by W. Somerset Maugham, copyright 1922 by McClure Publishing Co. From the book *On a Chinese Screen* by W. Somerset Maugham. Reprinted by permission of the author, Doubleday & Company, Inc., and William Heinemann Ltd.

of Virginian cigarettes. As he went out the philosopher entered. I hastened to express my sense of the honour he did me in allowing me to visit him. He waved me to a chair and poured out the tea.

"I am flattered that you wished to see me," he returned. "Your countrymen deal only with coolies and with compradores; they think every Chinese must be one or the other."

I ventured to protest. But I had not caught his point. He leaned back in his chair and looked at me with an expression of mockery.

"They think they have but to beckon and we must come."

I saw then that my friend's unfortunate communication still rankled. I did not quite know how to reply. I murmured something complimentary.

He was an old man, tall, with a thin grey queue, and bright, large eyes under which were heavy bags. His teeth were broken and discoloured. He was exceedingly thin, and his hands, fine and small, were withered and claw-like. I had been told that he was an opium-smoker. He was very shabbily dressed in a black gown, a little black cap, both much the worse for wear, and dark-grey trousers gartered at the ankle. He was watching. He did not quite know what attitude to take up, and he had the manner of a man who was on his guard. Of course the philosopher occupies a royal place among those who concern themselves with the things of the spirit and we have the authority of Benjamin Disraeli that royalty must be treated with abundant flattery. I seized my trowel. Presently I was conscious of a certain relaxation in his demeanour. He was like a man who was all set and rigid to have his photograph taken, but hearing the shutter click lets himself go and eases into his natural self. He showed me his books.

"I took the Ph. D. in Berlin, you know," he said. "And afterwards I studied for some time in Oxford. But the English, if you will allow me to say so, have no great aptitude for philosophy."

Though he put the remark apologetically it was evident that he was not displeased to say a slightly disagreeable thing.

"We have had philosophers who have not been without influence in the world of thought," I suggested.

"Hume and Berkeley? The philosophers who taught at Oxford when I was there were anxious not to offend their theological colleagues. They would not follow their thought to its logical consequences in case they should jeopardise their position in university society."

"Have you studied the modern developments of philosophy in America?" I asked.

"Are you speaking of Pragmatism? It is the last refuge of those who want to believe the incredible. I have more use for American petroleum than for American philosophy."

His judgments were tart. We sat down once more and drank another cup of tea. He began to talk with fluency. He spoke a somewhat formal but an idiomatic English. Now and then he helped himself out with a German phrase. So far as it was possible for a man of that stubborn character to be influenced he had been influenced by Germany. The method and the industry of the Germans had deeply impressed him and their philosophical acumen was patent to him when a laborious professor published in a learned magazine an essay on one of his own writings.

"I have written twenty books," he said. "And that is the only notice that has ever been taken of me in a European publication."

But his study of Western philosophy had only served in the end to satisfy him that wisdom after all was to be found within the limits of the Confucian canon. He accepted its philosophy with conviction. It answered the needs of his spirit with a completeness which made all foreign learning seem vain. I was interested in this because it bore out an opinion of mine that philosophy is an affair of character rather than of logic: the philosopher believes not according to evidence, but according to his own temperament; and his thinking merely serves to make reasonable what his instinct regards as true. If Confucianism gained so firm a hold on the Chinese it is because it explained and expressed them as no other system of thought could do.

My host lit a cigarette. His voice at first had been thin and tired, but as he grew interested in what he said it gained volume. He talked vehemently. There was in him none of the repose of the sage. He was a polemist and a fighter. He loathed the modern cry for individualism. For him society was the unit, and the family the foundation of society. He upheld the old China and the old school, monarchy, and the rigid canon of Confucius. He grew violent and bitter as he spoke of the students, fresh from foreign universities, who with sacrilegious hands tore down the oldest civilisation in the world.

"But you, do you know what you are doing?" he exclaimed. "What is the reason for which you deem yourselves our betters? Have you excelled us in arts or letters? Have our thinkers been less profound than yours? Has our civilisation been less elaborate, less complicated, less refined than yours? Why, when you lived in caves and clothed yourselves with skins we were a cultured people. Do you know that we tried an experiment which is unique in the history of the world? We sought to rule this great country not by force, but by wisdom. And for centuries we succeeded. Then why does the white man despise the yellow? Shall I tell you? Because he has invented the machine-gun. That is your superiority. We are a defenceless horde and you can blow us into eternity. You have shattered the dream of our philosophers that the world could be governed by the power of law and order. And now you are teaching our young men your secret. You have thrust your hideous inventions upon us. Do you not know that we have a genius for mechanics? Do you not know that there are in this country four hundred millions of the most practical and industrious people in the world? Do you think it will take us long to learn? And what will become of your superiority when the yellow man can make as good guns as the white and fire them as straight? You have appealed to the machine-gun and by the machine-gun shall you be judged."

But at that moment we were interrupted. A little girl came softly in and nestled close up to the old gentleman. She stared at me with curious eyes. He told me that she was his youngest child. He put his arms round her and with a murmur of caressing words kissed her fondly. She wore a black coat and trousers that barely reaches her ankles, and she had a long pig-tail hanging down her back. She was born on the day the revolution was brought to a successful issue by the abdication of the Emperor.

"I thought she heralded the Spring of a new era," he said. "She was but the last flower of this great nation's Fall."

From a drawer in his roll-top desk he took a few cash and, handing them to her, sent her away.

"You see that I wear a queue," he said, taking it in his hands. "It is a symbol. I am the last representative of the old China."

He talked to me, more gently now, of how philosophers in long past days wandered from State to State with their disciples, teaching all who were worthy to learn. Kings called them to their councils and made them rulers of cities. His erudition was great and his eloquent phrases gave a multi-coloured vitality to the incidents he related to me of the history of his country. I could not help thinking him a somewhat pathetic figure. He felt in himself the capacity to administer the state, but there was no king to entrust him with office; he had vast stores of learning which he was eager to impart to the great band of students that his soul hankered after, and there came to listen but a few, wretched, half-starved, and obtuse provincials.

Once or twice discretion had made me suggest that I should take my leave, but he had been unwilling to let me go. Now at last I was obliged to. I rose. He held my hand.

"I should like to give you something as a recollection of your visit to the last philosopher in China, but I am a poor man and I do not know what I can give you that would be worthy of your acceptance."

I protested that the recollection of my visit was in itself a priceless gift. He smiled.

"Men have short memories in these degenerate days and I should like to give you something more substantial. I would give you one of my books, but you cannot read Chinese."

He looked at me with an amicable perplexity. I had an inspiration.

"Give me a sample of your calligraphy," I said.

"Would you like that?" He smiled. "In my youth I was considered to wield the brush in a manner that was not entirely despicable."

He sat down at his desk, took a fair sheet of paper, and placed it before him. He poured a few drops of water on a stone, rubbed the ink stick in it, and took his brush. With a free movement of the arm he began to write. And as I watched him I remembered with not a little amusement something else which had been told me of him. It appeared that the old gentleman, whenever he could scrape a little money together, spent it wantonly in the streets inhabited by ladies to describe whom a euphemism is generally used. His eldest son, a person of standing in the city, was vexed and humiliated by the scandal of this behaviour; and only his strong sense of filial duty prevented him from reproaching the libertine with severity. I dare say that to a son such looseness would be disconcerting, but the student of human nature could look upon it with equanimity. Philosophers are apt to elaborate their theories in the study, forming conclusions upon life which they know only at second hand, and it has seemed to me often that their works would have a more definite significance if they had exposed themselves to the vicissitudes which befall the common run of men. I was prepared to regard the old gentleman's dalliance in hidden places with leniency. Perhaps he sought but to elucidate the most inscrutable of human illusions.

He finished. To dry the ink he scattered a little ash on the paper and rising handed it to me.

"What have you written?" I asked.

I thought there was a slightly malicious gleam in his eyes.

"I have ventured to offer you two little poems of my own."

"I did not know you were a poet."

"When China was still an uncivilised country," he retorted with sarcasm, "all educated men could write verse at least with elegance."

I took the paper and looked at the Chinese characters. They made an agreeable pattern upon it.

"Won't you also give me a translation?"

"*Traduttore—traditore*," he answered. "You cannot expect me to betray myself. Ask one of your English friends. Those who know most about China know nothing, but you will at least find one who is competent to give you a rendering of a few rough and simple lines."

I bade him farewell, and with great politeness he showed me to my chair. When I had the opportunity I gave the poems to a sinologue of my acquaintance, and here is the version he made.[1] I confess that, doubtless unreasonably, I was somewhat taken aback when I read it.

You loved me not: your voice was sweet;
Your eyes were full of laughter; your hands were tender.

[1] I owe it to the kindness of my friend Mr. P. W. Davidson.

And then you loved me: your voice was bitter;
Your eyes were full of tears; your hands were cruel.
Sad, sad that love should make you
Unlovable.

————

I craved the years would quickly pass
  That you might lose
The brightness of your eyes, the peach-blossom of your
    skin,
And all the cruel splendour of your youth.
  Then I alone would love you
  And you at last would care.

The envious years have passed full soon
  And you have lost
The brightness of your eyes, the peach-bloom of your skin,
And all the charming splendour of your youth.
    Alas, I do not love you
  And I care not if you care.

THE MOZO

D. H. LAWRENCE

This vivid picture of Indian life and character is an example of good writing about travel and strange places, for its unspoken comment is as important to the total effect as its elements of description. For a note on D. H. Lawrence, see page 435.

ROSALINO really goes with the house, though he has been in service here only two months. When we went to look at the place, we saw him lurking in the patio, and glancing furtively under his brows. He is not one of the erect, bantam little Indians that stare with a black, incomprehensible, but somewhat defiant stare. It may be Rosalino has a distant strain of other Indian blood, not Zapotec. Or it may be he is only a bit different. The difference lies in a certain sensitiveness and aloneness, as if he were a mother's boy. The way he drops his head and looks sideways under his black lashes, apprehensive, apprehending, feeling his way, as it were. Not the bold male glare of most of the Indians, who seem as if they had never, never had mothers at all.

The Aztec gods and goddesses are, as far as we have known anything about them, an unlovely and unlovable lot. In their myths there is no grace or charm, no poetry. Only this perpetual grudge, grudge, grudging, one god grudging another, the gods grudging men their existence, and men grudg-

From *Mornings in Mexico* by D. H. Lawrence. Copyright 1927 by Alfred A. Knopf, Inc. Reprinted by permission of Alfred A. Knopf, Inc.

ing the animals. The goddess of love is goddess of dirt and prostitution, a dirt-eater, a horror, without a touch of tenderness. If the god wants to make love to her, she has to sprawl down in front of him, blatant and accessible.

And then, after all, when she conceives and brings forth, what is it she produces? What is the infant-god she tenderly bears? Guess, all ye people, joyful and triumphant!

You never could.

It is a stone knife.

It is a razor-edged knife of blackish-green flint, the knife of all knives, the veritable Paraclete of knives. It is the sacrificial knife with which the priest makes a gash in his victim's breast, before he tears out the heart, to hold it smoking to the sun. And the Sun, the Sun behind the sun, is supposed to suck the smoking heart greedily with insatiable appetite.

This, then, is a pretty Christmas Eve. Lo, the goddess is gone to bed, to bring forth her child. Lo! ye people, await the birth of the saviour, the wife of a god is about to become a mother.

Tarumm-tarah! Tarumm-tarah! blow the trumpets. The child is born. Unto us a son is given. Bring him forth, lay him on a tender cushion. Show him, then, to all the people. See! See! See him upon the cushion, tenderly new-born and reposing! Ah, "qué bonito!" Oh, what a nice, blackish, smooth, keen, stone knife!

And to this day, most of the Mexican Indian women seem to bring forth stone knives. Look at them, these sons of incomprehensible mothers, with their black eyes like flints, and their stiff little bodies as taut and as keen as knives of obsidian. Take care they don't rip you up.

Our Rosalino is an exception. He drops his shoulders just a little. He is a bit bigger, also, than the average Indian down here. He must be about five feet four inches. And he hasn't got the big, obsidian, glaring eyes. His eyes are smaller, blacker, like the quick black eyes of the lizard. They don't look at one with the obsidian stare. They are just a bit aware that there is another being, unknown, at the other end of the glance. Hence he drops his head with a little apprehension, screening himself as if he were vulnerable.

Usually, these people have no correspondence with one at all. To them a white man or white woman is a sort of phenomenon, just as a monkey is a sort of phenomenon; something to watch, and wonder at, and laugh at, but not to be taken on one's own plane.

Now the white man is a sort of extraordinary white monkey that, by cunning, has learnt lots of semi-magical secrets of the universe, and made himself boss of the show. Imagine a race of big white monkeys got up in fantastic clothes, and able to kill a man by hissing at him; able to leap through the air in great hops, covering a mile in each leap; able to transmit his thoughts by a moment's effort of concentration to some great white monkey or monkeyess, a thousand miles away: and you have, from our point of view, something of the picture that the Indian has of us.

The white monkey has curious tricks. He knows, for example, the time. Now to a Mexican, and an Indian, time is a vague, foggy reality. There are only three times: en la mañana, en la tarde, en la noche: in the morning, in the afternoon, in the night. There is even no midday, and no evening.

But to the white monkey, horrible to relate, there are exact spots of time, such as five o'clock, half-past nine. The day is a horrible puzzle of exact spots of time.

The same with distance: horrible invisible distances called two miles, ten miles. To the Indians, there is near and far, and very near and very far. There is two days or one day. But two miles are as good as twenty to him, for he goes entirely by his feeling. If a certain two miles feels far to him, then it

is far, it is muy lejos! But if a certain twenty miles *feels* near and familiar, then it is not far. Oh, no, it is just a little distance. And he will let you set off in the evening, for night to overtake you in the wilderness, without a qualm. It is not far.

But the white man has a horrible, truly horrible monkey-like passion for invisible exactitudes. Mañana, to the native, may mean tomorrow, three days hence, six months hence, and never. There are no fixed points in life, save birth, and death, and the fiestas. The fixed points of birth and death evaporate spontaneously into vagueness. And the priests fix the fiestas. From time immemorial priests have fixed the fiestas, the festivals of the gods, and men have had no more to do with time. What should men have to do with time?

The same with money. These centavos and these pesos, what do they mean, after all? Little discs that have no charm. The natives insist on reckoning in invisible coins, coins that don't exist here, like reales or pesetas. If you buy two eggs for a real, you have to pay twelve and a half centavos. Since also half a centavo doesn't exist, you or the vendor forfeit the non-existent.

The same with honesty, the *meum* and the *tuum*. The white man has a horrible way of remembering, even to a centavo, even to a thimbleful of mescal. Horrible! The Indian, it seems to me, is not naturally dishonest. He is not naturally avaricious, has not even any innate cupidity. In this he is unlike the old people of the Mediterranean, to whom possessions have a mystic meaning, and a silver coin a mystic white halo, a *lueur* of magic.

To the real Mexican, no! He doesn't care. He doesn't even *like* keeping money. His deep instinct is to spend it at once, so that he needn't have it. He doesn't really want to keep anything, not even his wife and children. Nothing that he has to be responsible for. Strip, strip, strip away the past and the future, leave the naked moment of the present disentangled. Strip away memory, strip away forethought and care; leave the moment, stark and sharp and without consciousness, like the obsidian knife. The before and the after are the stuff of consciousness. The instant moment is forever keen with a razor-edge of oblivion, like the knife of sacrifice.

But the great white monkey has got hold of the keys of the world, and the black-eyed Mexican has to serve the great white monkey, in order to live. He has to learn the tricks of the white monkey-show: time of the day, coin of money, machines that start at a second, work that is meaningless and yet is paid for with exactitude, in exact coin. A whole existence of monkey-tricks and monkey-virtues. The strange monkey-virtue of charity, the white monkeys nosing round to *help*, to *save!* Could any trick be more un-natural? Yet it is one of the tricks of the great white monkey.

If an Indian is poor, he says to another: I have no food; give me to eat. Then the other hands the hungry one a couple of tortillas. That is natural. But when the white monkeys come round, they peer at the house, at the woman, at the children. They say: Your child is sick. Si, Señor. What have you done for it?—Nothing. What is to be done?—You must make a poultice. I will show you how.

Well, it was very amusing, this making hot dough to dab on the baby. Like plastering a house with mud. But why do it twice? Twice is not amusing. The child will die. Well, then, it will be in Paradise. How nice for it! That's just what God wants of it, that it shall be a cheerful little angel among the roses of Paradise. What could be better?

How tedious of the white monkey coming with the trick of salvation, to rub oil on the baby, and put poultices on it, and make you give it medicine in a spoon at morning, noon, and night. Why morning and noon and night? Why not just anytime, any-when? It will die tomorrow if you don't do these things today! But tomorrow is another day, and it is not dead now, so if it dies at another time, it must be because the other times are out of hand.

Oh, the tedious, exacting white monkeys, with their yesterdays and todays and tomorrows! Tomorrow is always another day, and yesterday is part of the encircling never. Why think outside the moment? And inside the moment one does not think. So why pretend to think? It is one of the white-monkey tricks. He is a clever monkey. But he is ugly, and he has nasty white flesh. We are not ugly, with screwed-up faces, and we have good warm-brown flesh. If we have to work for the white monkey, we don't care. His tricks are half-amusing. And one may as well amuse oneself that way as any other. So long as one is amused.

So long as the devil does not rouse in us, seeing the white monkeys forever mechanically bossing, with their incessant tick-tack of work. Seeing them get the work out of us, the sweat, the money, and then taking the very land from us, the very oil and metal out of our soil.

They do it! They do it all the time. Because they can't help it. Because grasshoppers can but hop, and ants can carry little sticks, and white monkeys can go tick-tack, tick-tack, do this, do that, time to work, time to eat, time to drink, time to sleep, time to walk, time to ride, time to wash, time to look dirty, tick-tack, tick-tack, time, time, time, time! time! Oh, cut off his nose and make him swallow it.

For the *moment* is as changeless as an obsidian knife, and the heart of the Indian is keen as the moment that divides past from future, and sacrifices them both.

To Rosalino, too, the white monkey-tricks are amusing. He is ready to work for the white monkeys, to learn some of their tricks, their monkey-speech of Spanish, their tick-tack ways. He works for four pesos a month, and his food: a few tortillas. Four pesos are two American dollars: about nine shillings. He owns two cotton shirts, two pairs of calico pantaloons, two blouses, one of pink cotton, one of darkish flannel-ette, and a pair of sandals. Also, his straw hat that he has curled up to look very jaunty, and a rather old, factory-made, rather cheap shawl, or plaid rug with fringe. *Et præterea nihil.*

His duty is to rise in the morning and sweep the street in front of the house, and water it. Then he sweeps and waters the broad, brick-tiled verandahs, and flicks the chairs with a sort of duster made of fluffy reeds. After which he walks behind the cook—she is very superior, had a Spanish grandfather, and Rosalino must address her as Señora—carrying the basket to market. Returned from the market, he sweeps the whole of the patio, gathers up the leaves and refuse, fills the pannier-basket, hitches it up on to his shoulders, and holds it by a band across his forehead, and thus, a beast of burden, goes out to deposit the garbage at the side of one of the little roads leading out of the city. Every *little* road leaves the town between heaps of garbage, an avenue of garbage blistering in the sun.

Returning, Rosalino waters the whole of the garden and sprinkles the whole of the patio. This takes most of the morning. In the afternoon, he sits without much to do. If the wind has blown or the day was hot, he starts again at about three o'clock, sweeping up leaves, and sprinkling everywhere with an old watering-can.

Then he retreats to the entrance-way, the Zaguán, which, with its big doors and its cobbled track, is big enough to admit an ox-wagon. The Zaguán is his home: just the doorway. In one corner is a low wooden bench about four feet long and eighteen inches wide. On this he screws up and sleeps, in his clothes as he is, wrapped in the old sarape.

But this is anticipating. In the obscurity of the Zaguán he sits and pores, pores, pores over a school-book, learning to read and write. He can read a bit, and write a bit. He filled a large sheet of foolscap with writing: quite nice. But I found out that what he had written was a Spanish poem, a love-poem, with no *puedo olvidar* and *voy a cortar*—the rose, of course. He had written the thing straight ahead, without verse-lines or capitals or punctuation at all, just a vast string of words, a whole foolscap sheet full. When I read a few lines aloud, he writhed and laughed in an agony of confused feelings. And of what he had written he understood a small, small amount, parrot-wise, from the top of his head. Actually it meant just words, sound, noise, to him: noise called Castellano, Castilian. Exactly like a parrot.

From seven to eight he goes to the night-school, to cover a bit more of the foolscap. He has been going for two years. If he goes two years more he will perhaps really be able to read and write six intelligible sentences: but only Spanish, which is as foreign to him as Hindustani would be to an English farmboy. Then if he can speak his quantum of Spanish, and read it and write it to a very uncertain extent, he will return to his village two days' journey on foot into the hills, and then, in time, he may even rise to be an *alcalde*, or headman of the village, responsible to the Government. If he were alcalde he would get a little salary. But far more important to him is the glory: being able to boss.

He has a *paisano*, a fellow-countryman, to sleep with him in the Zaguán, to guard the doors. Whoever gets into the house or patio must get through these big doors. There is no other entrance, not even a needle's eye. The windows to the street are heavily barred. Each house is its own small fortress. Ours is a double square, the trees and flowers in the first square, with the two wings of the house. And in the second patio, the chickens, pigeons, guinea-pigs, and the big heavy earthenware dish or tub, called an *apaxtle*, in which all the servants can bathe themselves, like chickens in a saucer.

By half-past nine at night Rosalino is lying on his little bench, screwed up, wrapped in his shawl, his sandals, called huaraches, on the floor. Usually he takes off his huaraches when he goes to bed. That is all his preparation. In another corner, wrapped up, head and all, like a mummy in his thin old blanket, the paisano, another lad of about twenty, lies asleep on the cold stones. And at an altitude of five thousand feet, the nights can be cold.

Usually everybody is in by half-past nine in our very quiet house. If not, you may thunder at the big doors. It is hard to wake Rosalino. You have to go close to him, and call. That will wake him. But don't touch him. That would startle him terribly. No one is touched unawares, except to be robbed or murdered.

"Rosalino! están tocando!"—"Rosalino! they are knocking!"

At last there starts up a strange, glaring, utterly lost Rosalino. Perhaps he just has enough wit to pull the door-catch. One wonders where he was, and what he was, in his sleep, he starts up so strange and wild and lost.

The first time he had anything to do for me was when the van was to come to carry the bit of furniture to the house. There was Aurelio, the dwarf *mozo* of our friends, and Rosalino, and the man who drove the wagon. But there *should* have been also a *cargador*—a porter. "Help them," said I to Rosalino. "You give a hand to help." But he winced away, muttering, "No quiero!—I don't want to."

The fellow, I thought to myself, is a fool. He thinks it's not his job, and perhaps he is afraid of smashing the furniture. Nothing to be done but to leave him alone.

We settled in, and Rosalino seemed to like doing things for us. He liked learning his monkey-tricks from the white monkeys. And since we started feeding him from our own meals, and for the first time in his life he had real soups, meat-stews, or a fried egg, he loved to do things in the kitchen. He would come with sparkling black eyes: "Hé comido el caldo. Grazias!"—"I have eaten the soup. Thank you."—And he would give a strange, excited little yelp of a laugh.

Came the day when we walked to Huayapa, on the Sunday, and he was very thrilled. But at night, in the evening when we got home, he lay mute on his bench—not that he was really tired. The Indian gloom, which settles on them like a black marsh-fog, had settled on him. He did not bring in the water—let me carry it by myself.

Monday morning, the same black, reptilian gloom, and a sense of hatred. He hated us. This was a bit flabbergasting, because he had been so thrilled and happy the day before. But the revulsion had come. He didn't forgive himself for having felt free and happy with us. He had eaten what we had eaten, hard-boiled eggs and sardine sandwiches and cheese; he had drunk out of the orange-peel *taza*, which delighted him so much. He had had a bottle of *gazoosa*, fizz, with us, on the way home, in San Felipe.

And now, the reaction. The flint knife. He had been happy, *therefore* we were scheming to take another advantage of him. We had some devilish white-monkey trick up our sleeve; we wanted to get at his *soul*, no doubt, and do it the white monkey's damage. We wanted to get at his heart, did we? But his heart was an obsidian knife.

He hated us, and gave off a black steam of hate, that filled the patio and made one feel sick. He did not come to the kitchen, he did not carry the water. Leave him alone.

At lunch-time on Monday he said he wanted to leave. Why? He said he wanted to go back to his village.

Very well. He was to wait just a few days, till another mozo was found.

At this a glance of pure, reptilian hate from his black eyes.

He sat motionless on his bench all the afternoon, in the Indian stupor of gloom and profound hate. In the evening, he cheered up a little and said he would stay on, at least till Easter.

Tuesday morning. More stupor and gloom and hate. He wanted to go back to his village at once. All right! No one wanted to keep him against his will. Another mozo would be found at once.

He went off in the numb stupor of gloom and hate, a very potent hate that could affect one in the pit of one's stomach with nausea.

Tuesday afternoon, and he thought he would stay.

Wednesday morning, and he wanted to go.

Very good. Enquiries made; another mozo was coming on Friday morning. It was settled.

Thursday was fiesta. Wednesday, therefore, we would go to market, the Niña—that is the mistress— myself, and Rosalino with the basket. He loved to go to market with the patrones. We would give him money and send him off to bargain for oranges, pitahayas, potatoes, eggs, a chicken, and so forth. This he simply loved to do. It put him into a temper to see us buying without bargaining and paying ghastly prices.

He bargained away, silent almost, muttering darkly. It took him a long time, but he had far greater success than even Natividad, the cook. And he came back in triumph, with much stuff and little money spent.

So again that afternoon, he was staying on. The spell was wearing off.

The Indians on the hills have a heavy, intense sort of attachment to their villages; Rosalino had not been out of the little city for two years. Suddenly finding himself in Huayapa, a real Indian hill-village, the black Indian gloom of nostalgia must have made a crack in his spirits. But he had been perfectly cheerful—perhaps too cheerful—till we got home.

Again, the Señorita had taken a photograph of him. They are all crazy to have their photographs taken. I had given him an envelope and a stamp, to send a photograph to his mother. Because in his village he had a widow mother, a brother, and a married sister. The family owned a bit of land, with orange-trees. The best oranges come from the hills, where it is cooler. Seeing the photograph, the mother, who had completely forgotten her son, as far as any keen remembering goes, suddenly, like a cracker going off inside her, wanted him: at that very moment. So she sent an urgent message.

But already it was Wednesday afternoon. Arrived a little fellow in white clothes, smiling hard. It was the brother from the hills. Now, we thought, Rosalino will have someone to walk back with. On Friday, after the fiesta, he would go.

Thursday, he escorted us with the basket to the fiesta. He bargained for flowers, and for a sarape which he didn't get, for a carved *jícara* which he did get, and for a number of toys. He and the Niña and the Señorita ate a great wafer of a pancake with sweet stuff on it. The basket grew heavy. The brother appeared, to carry the hen and the extra things. Bliss.

He was perfectly happy again. He didn't want to go on Friday; he didn't want to go at all. He wanted to stay with us and come with us to England when we went home.

So, another trip to the friend, the Mexican, who had found us the other mozo. Now to put off the other boy again: but then, they are like that.

And the Mexican, who had known Rosalino when he first came down from the hills and could speak no Spanish, told us another thing about him.

In the last revolution—a year ago—the revolutionaries of the winning side wanted more soldiers from the hills. The alcalde of the hill-village was told to pick out young men and send them down to the barracks in the city. Rosalino was among the chosen.

But Rosalino refused, said again, "No quiero!" He is one of those, like myself, who have a horror of serving in a mass of men, or even of being mixed up with a mass of men. He obstinately refused. Whereupon the recruiting soldiers beat him with the butt of their rifles till he lay unconscious, apparently dead.

Then, because they wanted him at once, and he would now be no good for some time, with his injured back, they left him, to get the revolution over without him.

This explains his fear of furniture-carrying, and his fear of being "caught."

Yet that little Aurelio, the friend's mozo, who is not above four feet six in height, a tiny fellow, fared even worse. He, too, is from the hills. In his village, a cousin of his gave some information to the *losing* side of the revolution. The cousin wisely disappeared.

But in the city, the winning side seized Aurelio, since he was the *cousin* of the delinquent. In spite of the fact that he was the faithful mozo of a foreign resident, he was flung into prison. Prisoners in prison are not fed. Either friends or relatives bring them food, or they go very, very thin. Aurelio had a married sister in town, but *she* was afraid to go to the prison, lest she and her husband should be seized. The master, then, sent his new mozo twice a day to the prison with a basket; the huge, huge prison for this little town of a few thousands.

Meanwhile the master struggled and struggled with the "authorities"—friends of the people—for Aurelio's release. Nothing to be done.

One day the new mozo arrived at the prison with the basket, to find no Aurelio. A friendly soldier gave the message Aurelio had left. "Adiós a mi patrón. Me llevan." Oh, fatal words: "Me llevan"—They are taking me off. The master rushed to the train: it had gone, with the dwarf, plucky little mozo, into the void.

Months later, Aurelio reappeared. He was in rags, haggard, and his dark throat was swollen up to the ears. He had been taken off, two hundred miles into Vera Cruz State. He had been hung up by the neck, with a fixed knot, and left hanging for hours. Why? To make the cousin come and save his relative: put his own neck into a running noose. To make the absolutely innocent fellow confess: what? Everybody knew he was innocent. At any rate, to teach everybody better next time. Oh, brotherly teaching!

Aurelio escaped, and took to the mountains. Sturdy little dwarf of a fellow, he made his way back, begging tortillas at the villages, and arrived, haggard, with a great swollen neck, to find his master waiting, and another "party" in power. More friends of the people.

Tomorrow is another day. The master nursed Aurelio well, and Aurelio is a strong, if tiny, fellow, with big, brilliant black eyes that for the moment will trust a foreigner, but none of his own people. A dwarf in stature, but perfectly made, and very strong. And very intelligent, far more quick and intelligent than Rosalino.

Is it any wonder that Aurelio and Rosalino, when they see the soldiers with guns on their shoulders marching towards the prison with some blanched prisoner between them—and one sees it every few days—stand and gaze in a blank kind of horror, and look at the patrón, to see if there is any refuge?

Not to be *caught!* Not to be *caught!* It must have been the prevailing motive of Indian-Mexico life since long before Montezuma marched his prisoners to sacrifice.

SHOOTING AN ELEPHANT

GEORGE ORWELL

GEORGE ORWELL is the pseudonym of Eric Blair (1903–1950) who was born in Bengal, India. After a public school education in England, he served as an officer with the Indian Imperial Police in Burma. Returning to Europe, he lived for a while, and partly by choice, in extreme poverty, and wrote a book about it, *Down and Out in Paris and London* (1933). In 1936, he volunteered in a Loyalist brigade in the Spanish Civil War; his *Homage to Catalonia* (1938) is a diary of his experiences and a statement of his profound disillusionment with Communism and all totalitarian states. Other books are *Burmese Days* (1934), *Animal Farm* (1945), and *Shooting an Elephant* (1950). His book best-known to American readers is the prophetic satire on totalitarian regimentation and de-humanization, *1984* (1949).

IN Moulmein, in Lower Burma, I was hated by large numbers of people—the only time in my life that I have been important enough for this to happen to me. I was sub-divisional police officer of the town, and in an aimless, petty kind of way anti-European feeling was very bitter. No one had the guts to raise a riot, but if a European woman went through the bazaars alone somebody would probably spit betel juice over her dress. As a police officer I was an obvious target and was baited whenever it seemed safe to do so. When a nimble Burman tripped me up on the

From *Shooting an Elephant and Other Essays* by George Orwell. Copyright, 1945, 1946, 1949, 1950, by Sonia Brownell Orwell. Reprinted by permission of Harcourt, Brace and Company, Inc., and Martin Secker and Warburg Ltd., publishers.

football field and the referee (another Burman) looked the other way, the crowd yelled with hideous laughter. This happened more than once. In the end the sneering yellow faces of young men that met me everywhere, the insults hooted after me when I was at a safe distance, got badly on my nerves. The young Buddhist priests were the worst of all. There were several thousands of them in the town and none of them seemed to have anything to do except stand on street corners and jeer at Europeans.

All this was perplexing and upsetting. For at that time I had already made up my mind that imperialism was an evil thing and the sooner I chucked up my job and got out of it the better. Theoretically—and secretly, of course—I was all for the Burmese and all against their oppressors, the British. As for the job

I was doing, I hated it more bitterly than I can perhaps make clear. In a job like that you see the dirty work of Empire at close quarters. The wretched prisoners huddling in the stinking cages of the lock-ups, the grey, cowed faces of the long-term convicts, the scarred buttocks of the men who had been flogged with bamboos—all these oppressed me with an intolerable sense of guilt. But I could get nothing into perspective. I was young and ill-educated and I had had to think out my problems in the utter silence that is imposed on every Englishman in the East. I did not even know that the British Empire is dying, still less did I know that it is a great deal better than the younger empires that are going to supplant it. All I knew was that I was stuck between my hatred of the empire I served and my rage against the evil-spirited little beasts who tried to make my job impossible. With one part of my mind I thought of the British Raj as an unbreakable tyranny, as something clamped down, in *saecula saeculorum*, upon the will of prostrate peoples; with another part I thought that the greatest joy in the world would be to drive a bayonet into a Buddhist's priest's guts. Feelings like these are the normal by-products of imperialism; ask any Anglo-Indian official, if you can catch him off duty.

One day something happened which in a roundabout way was enlightening. It was a tiny incident in itself, but it gave me a better glimpse than I had had before of the real nature of imperialism—the real motives for which despotic governments act. Early one morning the sub-inspector at a police station the other end of the town rang me up on the 'phone and said that an elephant was ravaging the bazaar. Would I please come and do something about it? I did not know what I could do, but I wanted to see what was happening and I got on to a pony and started out. I took my rifle, an old .44 Winchester and much too small to kill an elephant, but I thought the noise might be useful *in terrorem*. Various Burmans stopped me on the way and told me about the elephant's doings. It was not, of course, a wild elephant, but a tame one which had gone "must." It had been chained up, as tame elephants always are when their attack of "must" is due, but on the previous night it had broken its chain and escaped. Its mahout, the only person who could manage it when it was in that state, had set out in pursuit, but had taken the wrong direction and was now twelve hours' journey away, and in the morning the elephant had suddenly reappeared in the town. The Burmese population had no weapons and were quite helpless against it. It had already destroyed somebody's bamboo hut, killed a cow and raided some fruit-stalls and devoured the stock; also it had met the municipal rubbish van and, when the driver jumped out and took to his heels, had turned the van over and inflicted violences upon it.

The Burmese sub-inspector and some Indian constables were waiting for me in the quarter where the elephant had been seen. It was a very poor quarter, a labyrinth of squalid bamboo huts, thatched with palm-leaf, winding all over a steep hillside. I remember that it was a cloudy, stuffy morning at the beginning of the rains. We began questioning the people as to where the elephant had gone and, as usual, failed to get any definite information. That is invariably the case in the East; a story always sounds clear enough at a distance, but the nearer you get to the scene of events the vaguer it becomes. Some of the people said that the elephant had gone in one direction, some said that he had gone in another, some professed not even to have heard of any elephant. I had almost made up my mind that the whole story was a pack of lies, when we heard yells a little distance away. There was a loud, scandalized cry of "Go away, child! Go away this instant!" and an old woman with a switch in her hand came round the corner of a hut, violently shooing away a crowd of naked children. Some more women followed, clicking their tongues and exclaiming; evidently there was something that the children ought not to have seen. I rounded the hut and saw a man's dead body sprawling in the mud. He was an Indian, a black Dravidian coolie, almost naked, and he could not have been dead many minutes. The people said that the elephant had come suddenly upon him round the corner of the hut, caught him with its trunk, put its foot on his back and ground him into the earth. This was the rainy season and the ground was soft, and his face had scored a trench a foot deep and a couple of yards long. He was lying on his belly with arms crucified and head sharply twisted to one side. His face was coated with mud, the eyes wide open, the teeth bared and grinning with an expression of unendurable agony. (Never tell me, by the way, that the dead look peaceful. Most of the corpses I have seen looked devilish.) The friction of the great beast's foot had stripped the skin from his back as neatly as one skins a rabbit. As soon as I saw the dead man I sent an orderly to a friend's house nearby to borrow an elephant rifle. I had already sent back the pony, not wanting it to go mad with fright and throw me if it smelt the elephant.

The orderly came back in a few minutes with a rifle and five cartridges, and meanwhile some Burmans had arrived and told us that the elephant was in the paddy fields below, only a few hundred yards away. As I started forward practically the whole population of the quarter flocked out of the houses and followed me. They had seen the rifle and were all shouting excitedly that I was going to shoot the elephant. They had not shown much interest in the elephant when he was merely ravaging their homes, but it was different now that he was going to be shot. It was a bit of fun to them, as it would be to an English crowd; besides they wanted the meat. It made me vaguely uneasy. I had no intention of shooting the elephant—I had merely sent for the rifle to defend myself if necessary—and it is always unnerving to have a crowd following you. I marched down the hill, looking and feeling a fool, with the rifle over my shoulder and an ever-growing army of people jostling at my heels. At the bottom, when you got away from the huts, there was a metalled road and beyond that a miry waste of paddy fields a thousand yards across, not yet ploughed but soggy from the first rains and dotted with coarse grass. The elephant was standing eight yards from the road, his left side towards us. He took not the slightest notice of the crowd's approach. He was tearing up bunches of grass, beating them against his knees to clean them and stuffing them into his mouth.

I had halted on the road. As soon as I saw the elephant I knew with perfect certainty that I ought not to shoot him. It is a serious matter to shoot a working elephant—it is comparable to destroying a huge and costly piece of machinery—and obviously one ought not to do it if it can possibly be avoided. And at that distance, peacefully eating, the elephant looked no more dangerous than a cow. I thought then and I think now that his attack of "must" was already passing off; in which case he would merely wander harmlessly about until the mahout came back and caught him. Moreover, I did not in the least want to shoot him. I decided that I would watch him for a little while to make sure that he did not turn savage again, and then go home.

But at that moment I glanced round at the crowd that had followed me. It was an immense crowd, two thousand at the least and growing every minute. It blocked the road for a long distance on either side. I looked at the sea of yellow faces above the garish clothes—faces all happy and excited over this bit of fun, all certain that the elephant was going to be shot. They were watching me as they would watch a conjurer about to perform a trick. They did not like me, but with the magical rifle in my hands I was momentarily worth watching. And suddenly I realized that I should have to shoot the elephant after all. The people expected it of me and I had got to do it; I could feel their two thousand wills pressing me forward, irresistibly. And it was at this moment, as I stood there with the rifle in my hands, that I first grasped the hollowness, the futility of the white

man's dominion in the East. Here was I, the white man with his gun, standing in front of the unarmed native crowd—seemingly the leading actor of the piece; but in reality I was only an absurd puppet pushed to and fro by the will of those yellow faces behind. I perceived in this moment that when the white man turns tyrant it is his own freedom that he destroys. He becomes a sort of hollow, posing dummy, the conventionalized figure of a sahib. For it is the condition of his rule that he shall spend his life in trying to impress the "natives," and so in every crisis he has got to do what the "natives" expect of him. He wears a mask, and his face grows to fit it. I had got to shoot the elephant. I had committed myself to doing it when I sent for the rifle. A sahib has got to act like a sahib; he has got to appear resolute, to know his own mind and do definite things. To come all that way, rifle in hand, with two thousand people marching at my heels, and then to trail feebly away, having done nothing—no, that was impossible. The crowd would laugh at me. And my whole life, every white man's life in the East, was one long struggle not to be laughed at.

But I did not want to shoot the elephant. I watched him beating his bunch of grass against his knees, with that preoccupied grandmotherly air that elephants have. It seemed to me that it would be murder to shoot him. At that age I was not squeamish about killing animals, but I had never shot an elephant and never wanted to. (Somehow it always seems worse to kill a *large* animal.) Besides, there was the beast's owner to be considered. Alive, the elephant was worth at least a hundred pounds; dead, he would only be worth the value of his tusks, five pounds, possibly. But I had got to act quickly. I turned to some experienced-looking Burmans who had been there when we arrived, and asked them how the elephant had been behaving. They all said the same thing: he took no notice of you if you left him alone, but he might charge if you went too close to him.

It was perfectly clear to me what I ought to do. I ought to walk up to within, say, twenty-five yards of the elephant and test his behavior. If he charged, I could shoot; if he took no notice of me, it would be safe to leave him until the mahout came back. But also I knew that I was going to do no such thing. I was a poor shot with a rifle and the ground was soft mud into which one would sink at every step. If the elephant charged and I missed him, I should have about as much chance as a toad under a steam-roller. But even then I was not thinking particularly of my own skin, only of the watchful yellow faces behind. For at that moment, with the crowd watching me, I was not afraid in the ordinary sense, as I would have been if I had been alone. A white man mustn't be frightened in front of "natives"; and so, in general, he isn't frightened. The sole thought in my mind was that if anything went wrong those two thousand Burmans would see me pursued, caught, trampled on and reduced to a grinning corpse like that Indian up the hill. And if that happened it was quite probable that some of them would laugh. That would never do. There was only one alternative. I shoved the cartridges into the magazine and lay down on the road to get a better aim.

The crowd grew very still, and a deep, low, happy sigh, as of people who see the theatre curtain go up at last, breathed from innumerable throats. They were going to have their bit of fun after all. The rifle was a beautiful German thing with cross-hair sights. I did not then know that in shooting an elephant one would shoot to cut an imaginary bar running from ear-hole to ear-hole. I ought therefore, as the elephant was sideways on, to have aimed straight at his ear-hole; actually I aimed several inches in front of this, thinking the brain would be further forward.

When I pulled the trigger I did not hear the bang or feel the kick—one never does when a shot goes home—but I heard the devilish roar of glee that went up from the crowd. In that instant, in too short a time, one would have thought, even for the bullet to get there, a mysterious, terrible change had come over the elephant. He neither stirred nor fell, but every line of his body had altered. He looked suddenly stricken, shrunken, immensely old, as though the frightful impact of the bullet had paralysed him without knocking him down. At last, after what seemed a long time—it might have been five seconds, I dare say—he sagged flabbily to his knees. His mouth slobbered. An enormous senility seemed to have settled upon him. One could have imagined him thousands of years old. I fired again into the same spot. At the second shot he did not collapse but climbed with desperate slowness to his feet and stood weakly upright, with legs sagging and head drooping. I fired a third time. That was the shot that did for him. You could see the agony of it jolt his whole body and knock the last remnant of strength from his legs. But in falling he seemed for a moment to rise, for as his hind legs collapsed beneath him he seemed to tower upwards like a huge rock toppling, his trunk reaching skywards like a tree. He trumpeted, for the first and only time. And then down he came, his belly towards me, with a crash that seemed to shake the ground even where I lay.

I got up. The Burmans were already racing past me across the mud. It was obvious that the elephant would never rise again, but he was not dead. He was breathing very rhythmically with long rattling gasps, his great mound of a side painfully rising and falling. His mouth was wide open—I could see far down into caverns of pale pink throat. I waited a long time for him to die, but his breathing did not weaken. Finally I fired my two remaining shots into the spot where I thought his heart must be. The thick blood welled out of him like red velvet, but still he did not die. His body did not even jerk when the shots hit him, the tortured breathing continued without a pause. He was dying, very slowly and in great agony, but in some world remote from me where not even a bullet could damage him further. I felt that I had got to put an end to that dreadful noise. It seemed dreadful to see the great beast lying there, powerless to move and yet powerless to die, and not even to be able to finish him. I sent back for my small rifle and poured shot after shot into his heart and down his throat. They seemed to make no impression. The tortured gasps continued as steadily as the ticking of a clock.

In the end I could not stand it any longer and went away. I heard later that it took him half an hour to die. Burmans were bringing dahs and baskets even before I left, and I was told they had stripped his body almost to the bones by the afternoon.

Afterwards, of course, there were endless discussions about the shooting of the elephant. The owner was furious, but he was only an Indian and could do nothing. Besides, legally I had done the right thing, for a mad elephant has to be killed, like a mad dog, if its owner fails to control it. Among the Europeans opinion was divided. The older men said I was right, the younger men said it was a damn shame to shoot an elephant for killing a coolie, because an elephant was worth more than any damn Coringhee coolie. And afterwards I was very glad that the coolie had been killed; it put me legally in the right and it gave me a sufficient pretext for shooting the elephant. I often wondered whether any of the others grasped that I had done it solely to avoid looking a fool.

R. M. S. TITANIC

HANSON W. BALDWIN

HANSON W. BALDWIN (1903–   ) was born in Baltimore and graduated from the United States Naval Academy in 1924. He resigned from active service in the Navy in 1927 and after experience as reporter on the Baltimore *Sun* became military and naval correspondent for the New York *Times* in 1929 and military editor in 1942. He has written many articles and books on military affairs.

"R.M.S. Titanic" is a straightforward and telling narrative of disaster reconstructed from personal and official records. With no word of interpretation or direct expression of emotion the carefully selected details convey both feeling and judgment and recreate a moving event in the past.

THE White Star liner *Titanic,* largest ship the world had ever known, sailed from Southampton on her maiden voyage to New York on April 10, 1912. The paint on her strakes was fair and bright; she was fresh from Harland and Wolff's Belfast yards, strong in the strength of her forty-six thousand tons of steel, bent, hammered, shaped and riveted through the three years of her slow birth.

There was little fuss and fanfare at her sailing; her sister-ship, the *Olympic*—slightly smaller than the *Titanic*—had been in service for some months and to her had gone the thunder of the cheers.

But the *Titanic* needed no whistling steamers or shouting crowds to call attention to her superlative qualities. Her bulk dwarfed the ships near her as longshoremen singled up her mooring lines and cast off the turns of heavy rope from the dock bollards. She was not only the largest ship afloat, but was believed to be the safest. Carlisle, her builder, had given her double bottoms and had divided her hull into sixteen water-tight compartments, which made her, men thought, unsinkable. She had been built to be and had been described as a gigantic lifeboat. Her designers' dreams of a triple-screw giant, a luxurious, floating hotel, which could speed to New York at twenty-three knots, had been carefully translated from blue prints and mold loft lines at the Belfast yards into a living reality.

The *Titanic's* sailing from Southampton, though quiet, was not wholly uneventful. As the liner moved slowly toward the end of her dock that April day, the surge of her passing sucked away from the quay the steamer *New York,* moored just to seaward of the *Titanic's* berth. There were sharp cracks as the manila mooring lines of the *New York* parted under the strain. The frayed ropes writhed and whistled

Reprinted by permission of Willis Kingsley Wing. Copyright © 1933 Harper & Row, Publishers Incorporated; renewed 1961.

through the air and snapped down among the waving crowd on the pier; the *New York* swung toward the *Titanic's* bow, was checked and dragged back to the dock barely in time to avert a collision. Seamen muttered, thought it an ominous start.

Past Spithead and the Isle of Wight the *Titanic* steamed. She called at Cherbourg at dusk and then laid her course for Queenstown. At 1:30 P.M. on Thursday, April 11, she stood out of Queenstown harbor, screaming gulls soaring in her wake, with 2,201 persons—men, women, and children—aboard.

Occupying the Empire bedrooms and Georgian suites of the first-class accommodations were many well-known men and women—Colonel John Jacob Astor and his young bride; Major Archibald Butt, military aide to President Taft, and his friend, Frank D. Millet, the painter; John B. Thayer, vice-president of the Pennsylvania Railroad, and Charles M. Hayes, president of the Grand Trunk Railway of Canada; W. T. Stead, the English journalist; Jacques Futrelle, French novelist; H. B. Harris, theatrical manager, and Mrs. Harris; Mr. and Mrs. Isidor Straus; and J. Bruce Ismay, chairman and managing director of the White Star line.

Down in the plain wooden cabins of the steerage class were 706 immigrants to the land of promise, and trimly stowed in the great holds was a cargo valued at $420,000: oak beams, sponges, wine, calabashes, and an odd miscellany of the common and the rare.

The *Titanic* took her departure on Fastnet Light and, heading into the night, laid her course for New York. She was due at Quarantine the following Wednesday morning.

Sunday dawned fair and clear. The *Titanic* steamed smoothly toward the west, faint streamers of brownish smoke trailing from her funnels. The purser held services in the saloon in the morning; on the steerage deck aft the immigrants were playing games and a Scotsman was puffing "The Campbells Are Coming" on his bagpipes in the midst of the uproar.

At 9 A.M. a message from the steamer *Caronia* sputtered into the wireless shack:

Captain, *Titanic*—Westbound steamers report bergs growlers and field ice in 42 degrees N. to 51 degrees W. 12th April.

Compliments—
Barr.

It was cold in the afternoon; the sun was brilliant, but the *Titanic,* her screws turning over at 75 revolutions per minute, was approaching the Banks.

In the Marconi cabin Second Operator Harold Bride, ear-phones clamped on his head, was figuring accounts; he did not stop to answer when he heard MWL, Continental Morse for the nearby Leyland liner, *Californian,* calling the *Titanic.* The *Californian* had some message about three icebergs; he didn't bother then to take it down. About 1:42 P.M. the rasping spark of those days spoke again across the water. It was the *Baltic,* calling the *Titanic,* warning her of ice on the steamer track. Bride took the message down and sent it up to the bridge. The officer-of-the-deck glanced at it; sent it to the bearded master of the *Titanic,* Captain E. C. Smith, a veteran of the White Star service. It was lunch time then; the Captain, walking along the promenade deck, saw Mr. Ismay, stopped, and handed him the message without comment. Ismay read it, stuffed it in his pocket, told two ladies about the icebergs, and resumed his walk. Later, about 7:15 P.M., the Captain requested the return of the message in order to post it in the chart room for the information of officers.

Dinner that night in the Jacobean dining room was gay. It was bitter on deck, but the night was calm and fine; the sky was moonless but studded with stars twinkling coldly in the clear air.

After dinner some of the second-class passengers gathered in the saloon, where the Reverend Mr. Carter conducted a "hymn sing-song." It was almost ten o'clock and the stewards were waiting with biscuits and coffee as the group sang:

"O, hear us when we cry to Thee
For those in peril on the sea."

On the bridge Second Officer Lightoller—short, stocky, efficient—was relieved at ten o'clock by First Officer Murdoch. Lightoller had talked with other officers about the proximity of ice; at least five wireless ice warnings had reached the ship; lookouts had

been cautioned to be alert; captains and officers expected to reach the field at any time after 9:30 P.M. At 22 knots, its speed unslackened, the *Titanic* plowed on through the night.

Lightoller left the darkened bridge to his relief and turned in. Captain Smith went to his cabin. The steerage was long since quiet; in the first and second cabins lights were going out; voices were growing still, people were asleep. Murdoch paced back and forth on the bridge, peering out over the dark water, glancing now and then at the compass in front of Quartermaster Hichens at the wheel.

In the crow's nest, Lookout Frederick Fleet and his partner, Leigh, gazed down at the water, still and unruffled in the dim, starlit darkness. Behind and below them the ship, a white shadow with here and there a last winking light; ahead of them a dark and silent and cold ocean.

There was a sudden clang. "Dong-dong. Dong-dong. Dong-dong. Dong!" The metal clapper of the great ship's bell struck out 11:30. Mindful of the warnings, Fleet strained his eyes, searching the darkness for the dreaded ice. But there were only the stars and the sea.

In the wireless room, where Phillips, first operator, had relieved Bride, the buzz of the *Californian's* set again crackled into the ear-phones:

Californian: "Say, old man, we are stuck here, surrounded by ice."
Titanic: "Shut up, shut up; keep out. I am talking to Cape Race; you are jamming my signals."

Then, a few minutes later—about 11:40 . . .

II

Out of the dark she came, a vast, dim, white, monstrous shape, directly in the *Titanic's* path. For a moment Fleet doubted his eyes. But she was a deadly reality, this ghastly *thing.* Frantically, Fleet struck three bells—*something dead ahead.* He snatched the telephone and called the bridge:

"Iceberg! Right ahead!"

The First Officer heard but did not stop to acknowledge the message.

"Hard-a-starboard!"

Hichens strained at the wheel; the bow swung slowly to port. The monster was almost upon them now.

Murdoch leaped to the engine-room telegraph. Bells clanged. Far below in the engine-room those bells struck the first warning. Danger! The indicators on the dial faces swung round to "Stop!" Then "Full speed astern!" Frantically the engineers turned great valve wheels; answered the bridge bells. . . .

There was a slight shock, a brief scraping, a small list to port. Shell ice—slabs and chunks of it—fell on the foredeck. Slowly the *Titanic* stopped.

Captain Smith hurried out of his cabin.

"What has the ship struck?"

Murdoch answered, "An iceberg, sir. I hard-a-starboarded and reversed the engines, and I was going to hard-a-port around it, but she was too close. I could not do any more. I have closed the water-tight doors."

Fourth Officer Boxhall, other officers, the carpenter, came to the bridge. The Captain sent Boxhall and the carpenter below to ascertain the damage.

A few lights switched on in the first and second cabins; sleepy passengers peered through porthole glass; some casually asked the stewards:

"Why have we stopped?"

"I don't know, sir, but I don't suppose it is anything much."

In the smoking room a quorum of gamblers and their prey were still sitting round a poker table; the usual crowd of kibitzers looked on. They had felt the slight jar of the collision and had seen an eighty-foot ice mountain glide by the smoking room windows, but the night was calm and clear, the *Titanic* was "unsinkable"; they hadn't bothered to go on deck.

But far below, in the warren of passages on the starboard side forward, in the forward holds and boiler rooms, men could see that the *Titanic's* hurt was mortal. In No. 6 boiler room, where the red glow from the furnaces lighted up the naked, sweaty chests of coal-blackened firemen, water was pouring through a great gash about two feet above the floor plates. This was no slow leak; the ship was open to the sea; in ten minutes there were eight feet of water in No. 6. Long before then the stokers had raked the flaming fires out of the furnaces and had scrambled through the water-tight doors into No. 5 or had climbed up the long steel ladders to safety. When Boxhall looked at the mailroom in No. 3 hold, twenty-four feet above the keel, the mailbags were already floating about in the slushing water. In No. 5 boiler room a stream of water spurted into an empty bunker. All six compartments forward of No. 4 were open to the sea; in ten seconds the iceberg's jagged claw had ripped a three-hundred-foot slash in the bottom of the great *Titanic.*

Reports came to the bridge; Ismay in dressing gown ran out on deck in the cold, still starlit night, climbed up the bridge ladder.

"What has happened?"

Captain Smith: "We have struck ice."

"Do you think she is seriously damaged?"

Captain Smith: "I'm afraid she is."

Ismay went below and passed Chief Engineer William Bell fresh from an inspection of the damaged compartments. Bell corroborated the Captain's statement; hurried back down the glistening steel ladders to his duty. Man after man followed him—Thomas Andrews, one of the ship's designers, Archie Frost, the builder's chief engineer, and his twenty assistants —men who had no posts of duty in the engine-room but whose traditions called them there.

On deck, in corridor and stateroom, life flowed again. Men, women and children awoke and questioned; orders were given to uncover the lifeboats; water rose into the firemen's quarters; half-dressed stokers streamed up on deck. But the passengers— most of them—did not know that the *Titanic* was sinking. The shock of the collision had been so slight that some were not awakened by it; the *Titanic* was so huge that she must be unsinkable; the night was too calm, too beautiful, to think of death at sea.

Captain Smith half ran to the door of the radio shack. Bride, partly dressed, eyes dulled with sleep, was standing behind Phillips, waiting.

"Send the call for assistance."

The blue spark danced: "CQD—CQD—CQD—CQ—"

Miles away Marconi men heard. Cape Race heard it, and the steamships *La Provence* and *Mt. Temple.*

The sea was surging into the *Titanic's* hold. At 12:20 the water burst into the seamen's quarters through a collapsed fore and aft wooden bulkhead. Pumps strained in the engine-rooms—men and machinery making a futile fight against the sea. Steadily the water rose.

The boats were swung out—slowly; for the deck-hands were late in reaching their stations, there had been no boat drill, and many of the crew did not know to what boats they were assigned. Orders were shouted; the safety valves had lifted, and steam was blowing off in a great rushing roar. In the chart house Fourth Officer Boxhall bent above a chart, working rapidly with pencil and dividers.

12:25 A.M. Boxhall's position is sent out to a fleet of vessels: "Come at once; we have struck a berg."

To the Cunarder *Carpathia* (Arthur Henry Rostron, Master, New York to Liverpool, fifty-eight miles away): "It's a CQD, old man. Position 41-46 N.; 50-14 W."

The blue spark dancing: "Sinking; cannot hear for noise of steam."

12:30 A.M. The word is passed: "Women and children in the boats." Stewards finish waking their passengers below; life-preservers are tied on; some men smile at the precaution. "The *Titanic* is unsinkable." The *Mt. Temple* starts for the *Titanic*; the *Carpathia* with a double-watch in her stokeholds, radios, "Coming hard." The CQD changes the course of many ships—but not of one; the operator of the *Californian*, nearby, has just put down his ear-phones and turned in.

The CQD flashes over land and sea from Cape Race to New York; newspaper city rooms leap to life and presses whir.

On the *Titanic,* water creeps over the bulkhead between Nos. 5 and 6 firerooms. She is going down by the head; the engineers—fighting a losing battle—are forced back foot by foot by the rising water. Down the promenade deck, Happy Jock Hume, the bandsman, runs with his instrument.

12:45 A.M. Murdoch, in charge on the starboard side, eyes tragic, but calm and cool, orders boat No. 7 lowered. The women hang back; they want no boat-ride on an ice-strewn sea; the *Titanic* is unsinkable. The men encourage them, explain that this is just a precautionary measure: "We'll see you again at breakfast." There is little confusion; passengers stream slowly to the boat deck. In the steerage the immigrants chatter excitedly.

A sudden sharp hiss—a streaked flare against the night; Boxhall sends a rocket toward the sky. It explodes, and a parachute of white stars lights up the icy sea. "God! Rockets!" The band plays ragtime.

No. 8 is lowered, and No. 5. Ismay, still in dressing gown, calls for women and children, handles lines, stumbles in the way of an officer, is told to "get the hell out of here." Third Officer Pitman takes charge of No. 5; as he swings into the boat Murdoch grasps his hand. "Good-by and good luck, old man."

No. 6 goes over the side. There are only twenty-eight people in a lifeboat with a capacity of sixty-five.

A light stabs from the bridge; Boxhall is calling in Morse flashes, again and again, to a strange ship stopped in the ice jam five to ten miles away. Another rocket drops its shower of sparks above the ice-strewn sea and the dying ship.

1:00 A.M. Slowly the water creeps higher; the fore ports of the *Titanic* are dipping into the sea. Rope squeaks through blocks; lifeboats drop jerkily seaward. Through the shouting on the decks comes the sound of the band playing ragtime.

The "Millionaires' Special" leaves the ship—boat No. 1, with a capacity of forty people, carries only Sir Cosmo and Lady Duff Gordon and ten others. Aft, the frightened immigrants mill and jostle and rush for a boat. An officer's fist flies out; three shots are fired in the air, and the panic is quelled. . . . Four Chinese sneak unseen into a boat and hide in its bottom.

1:20 A.M. Water is coming into No. 4 boiler room. Stokers slice and shovel as water laps about their ankles—steam for the dynamos, steam for the dancing spark! As the water rises, great ash hoes rake the flaming coals from the furnaces. Safety valves pop; the stokers retreat aft, and the water-tight doors clang shut behind them.

The rockets fling their splendor toward the stars. The boats are more heavily loaded now, for the passengers know the *Titanic* is sinking. Women cling and sob. The great screws aft are rising clear of the sea. Half-filled boats are ordered to come alongside the cargo ports and take on more passengers, but the ports are never opened—and the boats are never filled. Others pull for the steamer's light miles away but never reach it; the lights disappear, the unknown ship steams off.

The water rises and the band plays ragtime.

1:30 A.M. Lightoller is getting the port boats off; Murdoch the starboard. As one boat is lowered into the sea a boat officer fires his gun along the ship's side to stop a rush from the lower decks. A woman tries to take her Great Dane into a boat with her; she is refused and steps out of the boat to die with her dog. Millet's "little smile which played on his lips all through the voyage" plays no more; his lips are grim, but he waves good-by and brings wraps for the women.

Benjamin Guggenheim, in evening clothes, smiles and says, "We've dressed up in our best and are prepared to go down like gentlemen."

1:40 A.M. Boat 14 is clear, and then 13, 16, 15 and C. The lights still shine, but the *Baltic* hears the blue spark say, "Engine-room getting flooded."

The *Olympic* signals. "Am lighting up all possible boilers as fast as can."

Major Butt helps women into the last boats and waves good-by to them. Mrs. Straus puts her foot on the gunwale of a lifeboat, then she draws back and goes to her husband: "We have been together many years; where you go I will go." Colonel John Jacob Astor puts his young wife in a lifeboat, steps back, taps cigarette on fingernail: "Good-by, dearie; I'll join you later."

1:45 A.M. The foredeck is under water, the fo'c'sle head almost awash; the great stern is lifted high toward the bright stars; and still the band plays. Mr. and Mrs. Harris approach a lifeboat arm in arm.

Officer: "Ladies first, please."

Harris bows, smiles, steps back: "Of course, certainly; ladies first."

Boxhall fires the last rocket, then leaves in charge of boat No. 2.

2:00 A.M. She is dying now; her bow goes deeper, her stern higher. But there must be steam. Below in the stokeholds the sweaty firemen keep steam up for the flaring lights and the dancing spark. The glowing coals slide and tumble over the slanted grate bars; the sea pounds behind that yielding bulkhead. But the spark dances on.

The *Asian* hears Phillips try the new signal—SOS.

Boat No. 4 has left now; boat D leaves ten minutes later. Jacques Futrelle clasps his wife: "For God's sake, go! It's your last chance; go!" Madame Futrelle is half-forced into the boat. It clears the side.

There are about 660 people in the boats, and 1,500 still on the sinking *Titanic*.

On top of the officers' quarters men work frantically to get the two collapsibles stowed there over the side. Water is over the forward part of A deck now; it surges up the companionways toward the boat deck. In the radio shack, Bride has slipped a coat and lifejacket about Phillips as the first operator sits hunched over his key, sending—still sending— "41-46 N.; 50-14 W. CQD—CQD—SOS—SOS—"

The Captain's tired white face appears at the radio-room door: "Men, you have done your full duty. You can do no more. Now, it's every man for himself." The Captain disappears—back to his sinking bridge, where Painter, his personal steward, stands quietly waiting for orders. The spark dances on. Bride turns his back and goes into the inner cabin. As he does so, a stoker, grimed with coal, mad with fear, steals into the shack and reaches for the lifejacket on Phillips' back. Bride wheels about and brains him with a wrench.

2:10 A.M. Below decks the steam is still holding, though the pressure is falling—rapidly. In the gymnasium on the boat deck the athletic instructor watches quietly as two gentlemen ride the bicycles and another swings casually at the punching bag. Mail clerks stagger up the boat-deck stairways, dragging soaked mail sacks. The spark still dances. The band still plays—but not ragtime:

> "Nearer my God to Thee,
> Nearer to Thee . . ."

A few men take up the refrain; others kneel on the slanting decks to pray. Many run and scramble aft, where hundreds are clinging above the silent screws on the great uptilted stern. The spark still dances and the lights still flare; the engineers are on the job. The hymn comes to its close. Bandmaster Hartley, Yorkshireman violinist, taps his bow against a bulkhead, calls for "Autumn" as the water curls about his feet, and the eight musicians brace themselves against the ship's slant. People are leaping from the decks into the nearby water—the icy water. A woman cries, "Oh, save me, save me!" A man answers, "Good lady, save yourself. Only God can save you now." The band plays "Autumn":

> "God of Mercy and Compassion!
> Look with pity on my pain . . ."

The water creeps over the bridge where the *Titanic's* master stands; heavily he steps out to meet it.

2:17 A.M. "CQ—" The *Virginian* hears a ragged, blurred CQ, then an abrupt stop. The blue spark dances no more. The lights flicker out; the engineers have lost their battle.

2:18 A.M. Men run about blackened decks; leap into the night; are swept into the sea by the curling wave which licks up the *Titanic's* length. Lightoller does not leave the ship; the ship leaves him; there are hundreds like him, but only a few who live to tell of it. The funnels still swim above the water, but the ship is climbing to the perpendicular; the bridge is under and most of the foremast; the great stern rises like a squat leviathan. Men swim away from the sinking ship; others drop from the stern.

The band plays in the darkness, the water lapping upwards:

> "Hold me up in mighty waters,
> Keep my eyes on things above,
> Righteousness, divine atonement,
> Peace and everlas . . ."

The forward funnel snaps and crashes into the sea; its steel tons hammer out of existence swimmers struggling in the freezing water. Streams of sparks, of smoke and steam, burst from the after funnels. The ship upends to 50—to 60 degrees.

Down in the black abyss of the stokeholds, of the engine-rooms, where the dynamos have whirred at long last to a stop, the stokers and the engineers are reeling against hot metal, the rising water clutching at their knees. The boilers, the engine cylinders, rip from their bed plates; crash through bulkheads; rumble—steel against steel.

The *Titanic* stands on end, poised briefly for the plunge. Slowly she slides to her grave—slowly at first, and then more quickly—quickly—quickly.

2:20 A.M. The greatest ship in the world has sunk. From the calm, dark waters, where the floating lifeboats move, there goes up, in the white wake of her passing, "one long continuous moan."

III

The boats that the *Titanic* had launched pulled safely away from the slight suction of the sinking ship, pulled away from the screams that came from the lips of the freezing men and women in the water. The boats were poorly manned and badly equipped, and they had been unevenly loaded. Some carried so

R. M. S. TITANIC *by HANSON W. BALDWIN* 505

few seamen that women bent to the oars. Mrs. Astor tugged at an oar handle; the Countess of Rothes took a tiller. Shivering stokers in sweaty, coal-blackened singlets and light trousers steered in some boats; stewards in white coats rowed in others. Ismay was in the last boat that left the ship from the starboard side; with Mr. Carter of Philadelphia and two seamen he tugged at the oars. In one of the lifeboats an Italian with a broken wrist—disguised in a woman's shawl and hat—huddled on the floor boards, ashamed now that fear had left him. In another rode the only baggage saved from the *Titanic*—the carry-all of Samuel L. Goldenberg, one of the rescued passengers.

There were only a few boats that were heavily loaded; most of those that were half empty made but perfunctory efforts to pick up the moaning swimmers, their officers and crew fearing they would endanger the living if they pulled back into the midst of the dying. Some boats beat off the freezing victims; fear-crazed men and women struck with oars at the heads of swimmers. One woman drove her fist into the face of a half-dead man as he tried feebly to climb over the gunwale. Two other women helped him in and stanched the flow of blood from the ring-cuts on his face.

One of the collapsible boats, which had floated off the top of the officers' quarters when the *Titanic* sank, was an icy haven for thirty or forty men. The boat had capsized as the ship sank; men swam to it, clung to it, climbed upon its slippery bottom, stood knee-deep in water in the freezing air. Chunks of ice swirled about their legs; their soaked clothing clutched their bodies in icy folds. Colonel Archibald Gracie was cast up there, Gracie who had leaped from the stern as the *Titanic* sank; young Thayer who had seen his father die; Lightoller who had twice been sucked down with the ship and twice blown to the surface by a belch of air; Bride, the second operator, and Phillips, the first. There were many stokers, half-naked; it was a shivering company. They stood there in the icy sea, under the far stars, and sang and prayed—the Lord's Prayer. After a while a lifeboat came and picked them off, but Phillips was dead then or died soon afterward in the boat.

Only a few of the boats had lights; only one—No. 2 —had a light that was of any use to the *Carpathia*, twisting through the ice-field to the rescue. Other ships were "coming hard" too; one, the *Californian*, was still dead to opportunity.

The blue sparks still danced, but not the *Titanic's*. *La Provence* to *Celtic*: "Nobody has heard the *Titanic* for about two hours."

It was 2:40 when the *Carpathia* first sighted the green light from No. 2 boat; it was 4:10 when she picked up the first boat and learned that the *Titanic* had foundered. The last of the moaning cries had just died away then.

Captain Rostron took the survivors aboard, boatload by boatload. He was ready for them, but only a small minority of them required much medical attention. Bride's feet were twisted and frozen; others were suffering from exposure; one died, and seven were dead when taken from the boats, and were buried at sea.

It was then that the fleet of racing ships learned they were too late; the *Parisian* heard the weak signals of *MPA*, the *Carpathia*, report the death of the *Titanic*. It was then—or soon afterward, when her radio operator put on his ear-phones—that the *Californian*, the ship that had been within sight as the *Titanic* was sinking, first learned of the disaster.

And it was then, in all its white-green majesty, that the *Titanic's* survivors saw the iceberg, tinted with the sunrise, floating idly, pack-ice jammed about its base, other bergs heaving slowly nearby on the blue breast of the sea.

IV

But it was not until later that the world knew, for wireless then was not what wireless is to-day, and garbled messages had nourished a hope that all of the *Titanic's* company were safe. Not until Monday evening, when P. A. S. Franklin, Vice-President of the International Mercantile Marine Company, received relayed messages in New York that left little hope, did the full extent of the disaster begin to be known. Partial and garbled lists of the survivors; rumors of heroism and cowardice; stories spun out of newspaper imagination, based on a few bare facts and many false reports, misled the world, terrified and frightened it. It was not until Thursday night, when the *Carpathia* steamed into the North River, that the full truth was pieced together.

Flashlights flared on the black river when the *Carpathia* stood up to her dock. Tugs nosed about her; shunted her toward Pier 54. Thirty thousand people jammed the streets; ambulances and stretchers stood on the pier; coroners and physicians waited.

In mid-stream the Cunarder dropped over the *Titanic's* lifeboats; then she headed toward the dock. Beneath the customs letters on the pier stood relatives of the 711 survivors, relatives of the missing—hoping against hope. The *Carpathia* cast her lines ashore; stevedores looped them over bollards. The dense throngs stood quiet as the first survivor stepped down the gangway. The woman half-staggered—led by customs guards—beneath her letter. A "low wailing" moan came from the crowd; fell, grew in volume, and dropped again.

Thus ended the maiden voyage of the *Titanic*. The lifeboats brought to New York by the *Carpathia*, a few deck chairs and gratings awash in the ice-field off the Grand Banks 800 miles from shore, were all that was left of the world's greatest ship.

V

The aftermath of weeping and regret, of recriminations and investigations, dragged on for weeks. Charges and countercharges were hurled about; the White Star line was bitterly criticized; Ismay was denounced on the floor of the Senate as a coward, but was defended by those who had been with him on the sinking *Titanic* and by the Board of Trade investigation in England.

It was not until weeks later, when the hastily convened Senate investigation in the United States and the Board of Trade report in England had been completed, that the whole story was told. The Senate investigating committee, under the chairmanship of Senator Smith, who was attacked in both the American and British press as a "backwoods politician," brought out numerous pertinent facts, though its proceedings verged at times on the farcical. Senator Smith was ridiculed for his lack of knowledge of the sea when he asked witnesses, "Of what is an iceberg composed?" and "Did any of the passengers take refuge in the water-tight compartments?" The Senator seemed particularly interested in the marital status of Fleet, the lookout, who was saved. Fleet, puzzled, growled aside, "Wot questions they're arskin' me!"

The report of Lord Mersey, Wreck Commissioner in the British Board of Trade's investigation, was tersely damning.

The *Titanic* had carried boats enough for 1,178 persons, only one-third of her capacity. Her sixteen boats and four collapsibles had saved but 711 persons; 400 people had needlessly lost their lives. The boats had been but partly loaded; officers in charge of launching them had been afraid the falls would break or the boats buckle under their rated loads; boat crews had been slow in reaching their stations; launching arrangements were confused because no boat drill had been held; passengers were loaded into the boats haphazardly because no boat assignments had been made.

But that was not all. Lord Mersey found that sufficient warnings of ice on the steamer track had reached the *Titanic*, that her speed of 22 knots was "excessive under the circumstances," that "in view of the high speed at which the vessel was running it is not considered that the lookout was sufficient," and that her master made "a very grievous mistake"—but should not be blamed for negligence. Captain Rostron of the *Carpathia* was highly praised. "He did the very best that could be done." The *Californian* was damned. The testimony of her master, officers, and crew showed that she was not, at the most, more than nineteen miles away from the sinking *Titanic* and probably no more than five to ten miles distant. She had seen the *Titanic's* lights; she had seen the rockets; she had not received the CQD calls because her radio operator was asleep. She had attempted to get in communication with the ship she had sighted by flashing a light, but vainly.

"The night was clear," reported Lord Mersey, "and the sea was smooth. When she first saw the rockets the *Californian* could have pushed through the ice to the open water without any serious risk and so have come to the assistance of the *Titanic*. Had she done so she might have saved many if not all of the lives that were lost.

"She made no attempt."

WIND AND WATER

RACHEL CARSON

RACHEL CARSON (1907–   ) was born in Springfield, Pennsylvania. At Pennsylvania College for Women she first specialized in English composition, but increasing interest in the natural world turned her attention to special study of biology and zoology. In 1932 she received a Master's degree in zoology from Johns Hopkins University. After a brief period of teaching at the University of Maryland, Miss Carson served for many years as a marine biologist for the United States government, resigning in 1952 to devote her entire time to writing. She has received many awards for accomplishment in her professional field of marine biology and also for her gifted scientific writing. In 1953 she was elected to the National Institute of Arts and Letters, the first science writer elected to the group in thirteen years. She is the author of *Under the Sea Wind* (1941), *The Sea Around Us* (1951), *The Edge of the Sea* (1955), and *Silent Spring* (1962).

The wind's feet shine along the sea.
SWINBURNE

AS the waves roll in toward Lands End on the westernmost tip of England they bring the feel of the distant places of the Atlantic. Moving shoreward above the steeply rising floor of the deep sea, from dark blue water into troubled green, they pass the edge of 'soundings' and roll up over the continental shelf in confused ripplings and turbulence. Over the shoaling bottom they sweep landward, breaking on the Seven Stones of the channel between the Scilly Isles and Lands End, coming in over the sunken ledges and the rocks that roll out their glistening backs at low water. As they approach the rocky tip of Lands End, they pass over a strange instrument lying on the sea bottom. By the fluctuating pressure of their rise and fall they tell this instrument many things of the distant Atlantic waters from which they have come, and their messages are translated by its mechanisms into symbols understandable to the human mind.

If you visited this place and talked to the meteorologist in charge, he could tell you the life histories of the waves that are rolling in, minute by minute and hour after hour, bringing their messages of far-off places. He could tell you where the waves were created by the action of wind on water, the strength of the winds that produced them, how fast the storm

From *The Sea Around Us* by Rachel L. Carson. Copyright 1951 by Rachel L. Carson. Used by permission of Oxford University Press, Inc.

is moving, and how soon, if at all, it will become necessary to raise storm warnings along the coast of England. Most of the waves that roll over the recorder at Lands End, he would tell you, are born in the stormy North Atlantic eastward from Newfoundland and south of Greenland. Some can be traced to tropical storms on the opposite side of the Atlantic, moving through the West Indies and along the coast of Florida, A few have rolled up from the southernmost part of the world, taking a great-circle course all the way from Cape Horn to Lands End, a journey of 6000 miles.

On the coast of California wave recorders have detected swell from as great a distance, for some of the surf that breaks on that coast in summer is born in the west-wind belt of the Southern Hemisphere. The Cornwall recorders and those in California, as well as a few on the east coast of America, have been in use since the end of the Second World War. These experiments have several objects, among them the development of a new kind of weather forecasting. In the countries bordering the North Atlantic there is no practical need to turn to the waves for weather information because meteorological stations are numerous and strategically placed. The areas in which the wave recorders are presently used have served rather as a testing laboratory to develop the method. It will soon be ready for use in other parts of the world, for which there are no meteorological data except those the waves bring. Especially in the Southern Hemisphere, many coasts are washed by waves that have come from lonely, unvisited parts of the ocean, seldom crossed by vessels, off the normal routes of the air lines. Storms may develop in these remote places, unobserved, and sweep down suddenly on mid-ocean islands or exposed coasts. Over the millions of years the waves, running ahead of the storms, have been crying a warning, but only now are we learning to read their language. Or only now, at least, are we learning to do so scientifically. There is a basis in folklore for these modern achievements in wave research. To generations of Pacific Island natives, a certain kind of swell has signaled the approach of a typhoon. And centuries ago, when peasants on the lonely shores of Ireland saw the long swells that herald a storm rolling in upon their coasts, they shuddered and talked of death waves.

Now our study of waves has come of age, and on all sides we can find evidence that modern man is turning to the waves of the sea for practical purposes. Off the Fishing Pier at Long Branch, New Jersey, at the end of a quarter-mile pipeline on the bed of the ocean, a wave-recording instrument silently and continuously takes note of the arrival of waves from the open Atlantic. By electric impulses transmitted through the pipeline, the height of each wave and the interval between succeeding crests are transmitted to a shore station and automatically recorded as a graph. These records are carefully studied by the Beach Erosion Board of the Army Corps of Engineers, which is concerned about the rate of erosion along the New Jersey coast.

Off the coast of Africa, high-flying planes recently took a series of overlapping photographs of the surf and the areas immediately offshore. From these photographs trained men determined the speed of the waves moving in toward the shore. Then they applied a mathematical formula that relates the behavior of waves advancing into shallow water to the depths beneath them. All this information provided the British government with usable surveys of the depths off the coast of an almost inaccessible part of its empire, which could have been sounded in the ordinary way only at great expense and with endless difficulty. Like much of our new knowledge of waves, this practical method was born of wartime necessity.

Forecasts of the state of the sea and particularly the height of the surf became regular preliminaries to invasion in the second World War, especially on the exposed beaches of Europe and Africa. But application of theory to practical conditions was at first difficult; so was the interpretation of the actual effect of any predicted height of surf or roughness of sea surface on the transfer of men and supplies between boats or from boats to beaches. This first attempt at practical military oceanography was, as one naval

officer put it, a 'most frightening lesson' concerning the 'almost desperate lack of basic information on the fundamentals of the nature of the sea.'

As long as there has been an earth, the moving masses of air that we call winds have swept back and forth across its surface. And as long as there has been an ocean, its waters have stirred to the passage of the winds. Most waves are the result of the action of wind on water. There are exceptions, such as the tidal waves sometimes produced by earthquakes under the sea. But the waves most of us know best are wind waves.

It is a confused pattern that the waves make in the open sea—a mixture of countless different wave trains, intermingling, overtaking, passing, or sometimes engulfing one another; each group differing from the others in the place and manner of its origin, in its speed, its direction of movement; some doomed never to reach any shore, others destined to roll across half an ocean before they dissolve in thunder on a distant beach.

Out of such seemingly hopeless confusion the patient study of many men over many years has brought a surprising amount of order. While there is still much to be learned about waves, and much to be done to apply what is known to man's advantage, there is a solid basis of fact on which to reconstruct the life history of a wave, predict its behavior under all the changing circumstances of its life, and foretell its effect on human affairs.

Before constructing an imaginary life history of a typical wave, we need to become familiar with some of its physical characteristics. A wave has height, from trough to crest. It has length, the distance from its crest to that of the following wave. The period of the wave refers to the time required for succeeding crests to pass a fixed point. None of these dimensions is static; all change, but bear definite relations to the wind, the depth of the water, and many other matters. Furthermore, the water that composes a wave does not advance with it across the sea; each water particle describes a circular or elliptical orbit with the passage of the wave form, but returns very nearly to its original position. And it is fortunate that this is so, for if the huge masses of water that comprise a wave actually moved across the sea, navigation would be impossible. Those who deal professionally in the lore of waves make frequent use of a picturesque expression—the 'length of fetch.' The 'fetch' is the distance that the waves have run, under the drive of a wind blowing in a constant direction, without obstruction. The greater the fetch, the higher the waves. Really large waves cannot be generated within the confined space of a bay or a small sea. A fetch of perhaps 600 to 800 miles, with winds of gale velocity, is required to get up the largest ocean waves.

Now let us suppose that, after a period of calm, a storm develops far out in the Atlantic, perhaps a thousand miles from the New Jersey coast where we are spending a summer holiday. Its winds blow irregularly, with sudden gusts, shifting direction but in general blowing shoreward. The sheet of water under the wind responds to the changing pressures. It is no longer a level surface; it becomes furrowed with alternating troughs and ridges. The waves move toward the coast, and the wind that created them controls their destiny. As the storm continues and the waves move shoreward, they receive energy from the wind and increase in height. Up to a point they will continue to take to themselves the fierce energy of the wind, growing in height as the strength of the gale is absorbed, but when a wave becomes about a seventh as high from trough to crest as the distance to the next crest, it will begin to topple in foaming whitecaps. Winds of hurricane force often blow the tops off the waves by their sheer violence; in such a storm the highest waves may develop after the wind has begun to subside.

But to return to our typical wave, born of wind and water far out in the Atlantic, grown to its full height on the energy of the winds, with its fellow waves forming a confused, irregular pattern known as a 'sea.' As the waves gradually pass out of the storm area their height diminishes, the distance between successive crests increases, and the 'sea' becomes a 'swell,' moving at an average speed of about 15 miles an hour. Near the coast a pattern of long, regular swells is substituted for the turbulence of open ocean. But as the swell enters shallow water a startling transformation takes place. For the first time in its existence, the wave feels the drag of shoaling bottom. Its speed slackens, crests of following waves crowd in toward it, abruptly its height increases and the wave form steepens. Then with a spilling, tumbling rush of water falling down into its trough, it dissolves in a seething confusion of foam.

An observer sitting on a beach can make at least an intelligent guess whether the surf spilling out onto the sand before him has been produced by a gale close offshore or by a distant storm. Young waves, only recently shaped by the wind, have a steep, peaked shape even well out at sea. From far out on the horizon you can see them forming whitecaps as they come in; bits of foam are spilling down their fronts and boiling and bubbling over the advancing face, and the final breaking of the wave is a prolonged and deliberate process. But if a wave, on coming into the surf zone, rears high as though gathering all its strength for the final act of its life, if the

crest forms all along its advancing front and then begins to curl forward, if the whole mass of water plunges suddenly with a booming roar into its trough —then you may take it that these waves are visitors from some very distant part of the ocean, that they have traveled long and far before their final dissolution at your feet.

What is true of the Atlantic wave we have followed is true, in general, of wind waves the world over. The incidents in the life of a wave are many. How long it will live, how far it will travel, to what manner of end it will come are all determined, in large measure, by the conditions it meets in its progression across the face of the sea. For the one essential quality of a wave is that it moves; anything that retards or stops its motion dooms it to dissolution and death.

Forces within the sea itself may affect a wave most profoundly. Some of the most terrible furies of the ocean are unleashed when tidal currents cross the path of the waves or move in direct opposition to them. This is the cause of the famous 'roosts' of Scotland, like the one off Sumburgh Head, at the southernmost tip of the Shetland Islands. During northeasterly winds the roost is quiescent, but when the wind-born waves roll in from any other quarter they encounter the tidal currents, either streaming shoreward in flood or seaward on the ebb. It is like the meeting of two wild beasts. The battle of the waves and tides is fought over an area of sea that may be three miles wide when the tides are running at full strength, first off Sumburgh Head, then gradually shifting seaward, subsiding only with the temporary slackening of the tide. 'In this confused, tumbling, and bursting sea, vessels often become entirely unmanageable and sometimes founder,' says the *British Islands Pilot*, 'while others have been tossed about for days together.' Such dangerous waters have been personified in many parts of the world by names that are handed down through generations of seafaring men. As in the time of our grandfathers and of their grandfathers, the Bore of Duncansby and the Merry Men of Mey rage at opposite ends of the Pentland Firth. The sailing directions for the Firth in the *North Sea Pilot* for 1875 contained a warning to mariners, which is repeated verbatim in the modern *Pilot:*

'Before entering the Pentland Firth all vessels should be prepared to batten down, and the hatches of small vessels ought to be secured even in the finest weather, as it is difficult to see what may be going on in the distance, and the transition from smooth water to a broken sea is so sudden that no time is given for making arrangements.'

Both roosts are caused by the meeting of swells

from the open ocean and opposing tidal currents, so that at the east end of the Firth the Bore of Duncansby is to be feared with easterly swells and a flood tide, and at the west end the Merry Men of Mey stake their revelries with the ebb tides and a westerly swell. Then, according to the *Pilot,* 'a sea is raised which cannot be imagined by those who have never experienced it.'

Such a rip may offer protection to the near-by coast by the very fury and uncompromisingness of the struggle between waves and tide. Thomas Stevenson long ago observed that as long as the Sumburgh roost was breaking and cresting heavily off the Head there was little surf on shore; once the strength of the tide was spent and it could no longer run down the seas a heavy surf rolled in against the coast and rose to great heights on the cliffs. And in the western Atlantic, the confused and swiftly running tidal currents at the mouth of the Bay of Fundy offer such strong opposition to waves approaching from any quarter from southwest to southeast that such surf as develops within the Bay is almost entirely local in its origin.

Out in the open sea, a train of waves encountering a hostile wind may be rapidly destroyed, for the power that created a wave may also destroy it. So a fresh trade wind in the Atlantic has often flattened out the swells as they rolled down from Iceland toward Africa. Or a friendly wind, suddenly springing up to blow in the direction the waves are moving, may cause their height to increase at the rate of a foot or two per minute. Once a group of moving ridges has been created, the wind has only to fall into the troughs between them to push up their crests rapidly.

Rocky ledges, shoals of sand or clay or rock, and coastal islands in the mouths of bays all play their part in the fate of the waves that advance toward shore. The long swells that roll from the open ocean toward the shores of northern New England seldom reach it in full strength. Their energy is spent in passing over that great submerged highland known as Georges Bank, the crests of whose highest hills approach the surface over the Cultivator Shoals. The hindrance of these submarine hills, and of the tidal currents that swirl around and across them, robs the long ocean swells of their power. Or islands scattered within a bay or about its mouth may so absorb the strength of the waves that the head of the bay is free from surf. Even scattered reefs off a coast may offer it great protection, by causing the highest waves to break there, so that they never reach the shore.

Ice, snow, rain—all are enemies of the waves and under proper conditions may knock down a sea or cushion the force of surf on a beach. Within loose pack ice a vessel may count on smooth seas even if a gale is raging and surf is breaking heavily about the edges of the pack. Ice crystals forming in the sea will smooth the waves by increasing the friction between water particles; even the delicate, crystalline form of a snow flake has such an effect on a smaller scale. A hail storm will knock down a rough sea, and even a sudden downpour of rain may often turn the surface of the ocean to oiled-silk smoothness, rippling to the passage of the swells.

The divers of ancient times who carried oil in their mouths to release beneath the surface when rough water made their work difficult were applying what every seaman today knows—that oil appears to have a calming effect on the free waves of the open ocean. Instructions for the use of oil in emergencies at sea are carried by most official sailing directions of maritime nations. Oil has little effect on surf, however, once the dissolution of the wave form has begun.

In the Southern Ocean where the waves are not destroyed by breaking on any beach, the great swells produced by the westerly winds roll around and around the world. Here the longest waves, and those with the greatest sidewise expanse of crest, are formed. Here, it might be supposed, the highest waves would also be found. Yet there is no evidence that the waves of the Southern Ocean surpass the giants of any other ocean. A long series of reports culled from the publications of engineers and ships' officers show that waves higher than 25 feet from trough to crest are rare in all oceans. Storm waves may grow twice as high, and if a full gale blows long enough in one direction to have a fetch of 600 to 800 miles, the resulting waves may be even higher. The greatest possible height of storm waves at sea is a much debated question, with most textbooks citing a conservative 60 feet, and mariners stubbornly describing much higher waves. Throughout the century that has followed the report of Dumont d'Urville that he encountered a wave 100 feet high off the Cape of Good Hope, science generally has viewed such figures with skepticism. Yet there is one record of a giant wave which, because of the method of measurement, seems to be accepted as reliable.

In February 1933 the U.S.S. *Ramapo*, while proceeding from Manila to San Diego, encountered seven days of stormy weather. The storm was part of a weather disturbance that extended all the way from Kamchatka to New York and permitted the winds an unbroken fetch of thousands of miles. During the height of the storm the *Ramapo* maintained a course running down the wind and with the sea. On 6 February the gale reached its fiercest intensity. Winds of 68 knots came in gusts and squalls, and the seas reached mountainous height. While standing watch on the bridge during the early hours of that day, one of the officers of the *Ramapo* saw, in the moonlight, a great sea rising astern to a level above an iron strap on the crow's nest of the mainmast. The *Ramapo* was on even keel and her stern was in the trough of the sea. These circumstances made possible an exact line of sight from the bridge to the crest of the wave, and simple mathematical calculations based on the dimensions of the ship gave the height of the wave. It was 112 feet.

Waves have taken their toll of shipping and of human life on the open sea, but it is around the shorelines of the world that they are most destructive. Whatever the height of storm waves at sea, there is abundant evidence, as some of the case histories that follow will show, that breaking surf and the upward-leaping water masses from thundering breakers may engulf lighthouses, shatter buildings, and hurl stones through lighthouse windows anywhere from 100 to 300 feet above the sea. Before the power of such surf, piers and breakwaters and other shore installations are fragile as a child's toys.

Almost every coast of the world is visited periodically by violent storm surf, but there are some that have never known the sea in its milder moods. 'There is not in the world a coast more terrible than this!' exclaimed Lord Bryce of Tierra del Fuego, where the breakers roar in upon the coast with a voice that, according to report, can be heard 20 miles inland on a still night. 'The sight of such a coast,' Darwin had written in his diary, 'is enough to make a landsman dream for a week about death, peril, and shipwreck.'

Others claim that the Pacific coast of the United States from northern California to the Straits of Juan de Fuca has a surf as heavy as any in the world. But it seems unlikely that any coast is visited more wrathfully by the sea's waves than the Shetlands and the Orkneys, in the path of the cyclonic storms that pass eastward between Iceland and the British Isles. All the feeling and the fury of such a storm, couched almost in Conradian prose, are contained in the usually prosaic *British Islands Pilot:*

'In the terrific gales which usually occur four or five times in every year all distinction between air and water is lost, the nearest objects are obscured by spray, and everything seems enveloped in a thick smoke; upon the open coast the sea rises at once, and striking upon the rocky shores rises in foam for several hundred feet and spreads over the whole country.

'The sea, however, is not so heavy in the violent gales of short continuance as when an ordinary gale has been blowing for many days; the whole force of the Atlantic is then beating against the shores of the Orkneys, rocks of many tons in weight are lifted from their beds, and the roar of the surge may be heard for twenty miles; the breakers rise to the height of 60 feet, and the broken sea on the North Shoal, which lies 12 miles northwestward of Costa Head, is visible at Skail and Birsay.'

The first man who ever measured the force of an ocean wave was Thomas Stevenson, father of Robert Louis. Stevenson developed the instrument known as a wave dynamometer and with it studied the waves that battered the coast of his native Scotland. He found that in winter gales the force of a wave might be as great as 6,000 pounds to the square foot. Perhaps it was waves of this strength that destroyed the breakwater at Wick on the coast of Scotland in a December storm in 1872. The seaward end of the Wick breakwater consisted of a block of concrete weighing more than 800 tons, bound solidly with iron rods to underlying blocks of stone. During the height of this winter gale the resident engineer watched the onslaught of the waves from a point on the cliff above the breakwater. Before his incredulous eyes, the block of concrete was lifted up and swept shoreward. After the storm had subsided divers investigated the wreckage. They found that not only the concrete monolith but the stones it was attached to had been carried away. The waves had torn loose, lifted, and bodily moved a mass weighing not less than 1,350 tons or 2,700,000 pounds. Five years later it became clear that this feat had been a mere dress rehearsal, for the new pier, weighing about 2,600 tons, was then carried away in another storm.

A list of the perverse and freakish doings of the sea can easily be compiled from the records of the keepers of lights on lonely ledges at sea, or on rocky headlands exposed to the full strength of storm surf. At Unst, the most northern of the Shetland Islands, a door in the lighthouse was broken open 195 feet above the sea. At the Bishop Rock Light, on the English Channel, a bell was torn away from its place of attachment 100 feet above high water during a winter gale. About the Bell Rock Light on the coast of Scotland one November day a heavy ground swell was running, although there was no wind. Suddenly one of the swells rose about the tower, mounted to the gilded ball atop the lantern, 117 feet above the rock, and tore away a ladder that was attached to the tower 86 feet above the water. There have been happenings that, to some minds, are tinged with the supernatural, like that at the Eddystone Light in 1840. The entrance door of the tower had been made fast by strong bolts, as usual. During a night of heavy seas the door was broken open *from within*, and all its iron bolts and hinges were torn loose. Engineers say that such a thing happens as a result of pneumatic action—the sudden back draught created by the recession of a heavy wave combined with an abrupt release of pressure on the outside of the door.

On the Atlantic coast of the United States, the 97-foot tower on Minot's Ledge in Massachusetts is often completely enveloped by masses of water from breaking surf, and an earlier light on this ledge was swept away in 1851. Then there is the often quoted story of the December storm at Trinidad Head Light on the coast of northern California. As the keeper watched the storm from his lantern 196 feet above high water, he could see the near-by Pilot Rock engulfed again and again by waves that swept over its hundred-foot crest. Then a wave, larger than the rest, struck the cliffs at the base of the light. It seemed to rise in a solid wall of water to the level of the lantern, and it hurled its spray completely over the tower. The shock of the blow stopped the revolving of the light.

Along a rocky coast, the waves of a severe storm are likely to be armed with stones and rock fragments, which greatly increase their destructive power. Once a rock weighing 135 pounds was hurled high above the lightkeeper's house on Tillanook Rock on the coast of Oregon, 100 feet above sea level. In falling, it tore a 20-foot hole through the roof. The same day showers of smaller rocks broke many panes of glass in the lantern, 132 feet above the sea. The most amazing of such stories concerns the lighthouse at Dunnet Head, which stands on the summit of a 300-foot cliff at the southwestern entrance to Pentland Firth. The windows of this light have been broken repeatedly by stones swept from the cliff and tossed aloft by waves.

For millennia beyond computation, the sea's waves have battered the coastlines of the world with erosive effect, here cutting back a cliff, there stripping away tons of sand from a beach, and yet again, in a reversal of their destructiveness, building up a bar or a small island. Unlike the slow geologic changes that bring about the flooding of half a continent, the work of the waves is attuned to the brief span of human life, and so the sculpturing of the continent's edge is something each of us can see for ourselves.

The high clay cliff of Cape Cod, rising at Eastham and running north until it is lost in the sand dunes near Peaked Hill, is wearing back so fast that half of the ten acres which the Government acquired as a site for the Highland Light has disappeared, and the cliffs are said to be receding about three feet a year. Cape Cod is not old, in geologic terms, being the product of the glaciers of the most recent ice age, but apparently the waves have cut away, since its formation, a strip of land some two miles wide. At the present rate of erosion, the disappearance of the outer cape is foredoomed; it will presumably occur in another 4000 or 5000 years.

The sea's method on a rocky coast is to wear it down by grinding, to chisel out and wrench away fragments of rock, each of which becomes a tool to wear away the cliff. And as masses of rock are undercut, a whole huge mass will fall into the sea, there to be ground in the mill of the surf and to contribute more weapons for the attack. On a rocky shore this grinding and polishing of rocks and fragments of rocks goes on incessantly and audibly, for the breakers on such a coast have a different sound from those that have only sand to work with—a deep-toned mutter and rumble not easily forgotten, even by one who strolls casually along such a beach. Few people have heard the sounds of the surf mill practically from within the sea, as described by Henwood after his visit to a British mine extending out under the ocean:

'When standing beneath the base of the cliff, and in that part of the mine where but nine feet of rock stood between us and the ocean, the heavy roll of the larger boulders, the ceaseless grinding of the pebbles, the fierce thundering of the billows, with the crackling and boiling as they rebounded, placed a tempest in its most appalling form too vividly before me ever to be forgotten. More than once doubting the protection of our rocky shield we retreated in affright; and it was only after repeated trials that we had confidence to pursue our investigations.' *

Great Britain, an island, has always been conscious of that 'powerful marine gnawing' by which her coasts are eaten away. An old map dated 1786 and prepared by the county surveyor, John Tuke, gives a long list of lost towns and villages on the Holderness Coast. Among them are notations of Hornsea Burton, Hornsea Beck, and Hartburn—'washed away by the sea'; of Ancient Withernsea, Hyde, or Hythe—'lost by the sea.' Many other old records allow comparison of present shorelines with former ones and show astonishing annual rates of cliff erosion on many parts of the coast—up to 15 feet at Holderness, 19 feet between Cromer and Mundesley, and 15 to 45 feet at Southwold. 'The configuration of the coastline of Great Britain,' one of her present engineers writes, 'is not the same for two consecutive days.'

And yet we owe some of the most beautiful and interesting shoreline scenery to the sculpturing effect of moving water. Sea caves are almost literally blasted out of the cliffs by waves, which pour into crevices in the rocks and force them apart by hydraulic pressure. Over the years the widening of fissures and the steady removal of fine rock particles in infinite number result in the excavation of a cave. Within

* From *Transactions*, Geol. Soc. Cornwall, vol. v, 1843.

such a cavern the weight of incoming water and the strange suctions and pressures caused by the movements of water in an enclosed space may continue the excavation upward. The roofs of such caves (and of overhanging cliffs) are subjected to blows like those from a battering ram as the water from a breaking wave is hurled upward, most of the energy of the wave passing into this smaller mass of water. Eventually a hole is torn through the roof of the cave, to form a spouting horn. Or, on a narrow promontory, what began as a cave may be cut through from side to side, so that a natural bridge is formed. Later, after years of erosion, the arch may fall, leaving the seaward mass of rock to stand alone—one of the strange, chimneylike formations known as a stack.

The sea waves that have fixed themselves most firmly in the human imagination are the so-called 'tidal waves.' The term is popularly applied to two very different kinds of waves, neither of which has any relation to the tide. One is a seismic sea wave produced by undersea earthquakes; the other is an exceptionally vast wind or storm wave—an immense mass of water driven by winds of hurricane force far above the normal high-water line.

Most of the seismic sea waves, now called 'tsunamis,' are born in the deepest trenches of the ocean floor. The Japanese, Aleutian and Atacama trenches have each produced waves that claimed many human lives. Such a trench is, by its very nature, a breeder of earthquakes, being a place of disturbed and uneasy equilibrium, of buckling and warping downward of the sea floor to form the deepest pits of all the earth's surface. From the historic records of the ancients down to the modern newspaper, the writings of man contain frequent mention of the devastation of coastal settlements by these great waves that suddenly rise out of the sea. One of the earliest of record rose along the eastern shores of the Mediterranean in A.D. 358, passing completely over islands and low-lying shores, leaving boats on the housetops of Alexandria, and drowning thousands of people. After the Lisbon earthquake of 1755, the coast at Cadiz was visited by a wave said to have been 50 feet higher than the highest tide. This came about an hour after the earthquake. The waves from this same disturbance traveled across the Atlantic and reached the West Indies in 9½ hours. In 1868, a stretch of nearly 3000 miles of the western coast of South America was shaken by earthquakes. Shortly after the most violent shocks, the sea receded from the shore, leaving ships that had been anchored in 40 feet of water stranded in mud; then the water returned in a great wave, and boats were carried a quarter of a mile inland.

This ominous withdrawal of the sea from its normal stand is often the first warning of the approach

of seismic sea waves. Natives on the beaches of Hawaii on the first of April 1946 were alarmed when the accustomed voice of the breakers was suddenly stilled, leaving a strange quiet. They could not know that this recession of the waves from the reefs and the shallow coastal waters was the sea's response to an earthquake on the steep slopes of a deep trench off the island of Unimak in the Aleutian chain, more than 2000 miles away; or that in a matter of moments the water would rise rapidly, as though the tide were coming in much too fast, but without surf. The rise carried the ocean waters 25 feet or more above the normal levels of the tide. According to an eyewitness account:

'The waves of the tsunami swept toward shore with steep fronts and great turbulence . . . Between crests the water withdrew from shore, exposing reefs, coastal mud-flats, and harbor bottoms for distances up to 500 feet or more from the normal strand-line. The outflow of the water was rapid and turbulent, making a loud hissing, roaring, and rattling noise. At several places houses were carried out to sea, and in some areas even large rocks and blocks of concrete were carried out onto the reefs . . . People and their belongings were swept to sea, some being rescued hours later by boats and life rafts dropped from planes.' *

In the open ocean the waves produced by the Aleutian quake were only about a foot or two high and would not be noticed from vessels. Their length, however, was enormous, with a distance of about 90 miles between succeeding crests. It took the waves less than 5 hours to reach the Hawaiian chain, 2300 miles distant, so they must have moved at an average speed of about 470 miles per hour. Along eastern Pacific shores, they were recorded as far into the Southern Hemisphere as Valparaiso, Chile, the distance of 8066 miles from the epicenter being covered by the waves in about 18 hours.

This particular occurrence of seismic sea waves had one result that distinguished it from all its predecessors. It set people to thinking that perhaps we now know enough about such waves and how they behave that a warning system could be devised which would rob them of the terror of the unexpected. Seismologists and specialists on waves and tides co-operated, and now such a system has been established to protect the Hawaiian Islands. A network of stations equipped with special instruments is scattered over the Pacific from Kodiak to Pago Pago and from Balboa to Palau. There are two phases of the warning system. One is based on a new audible alarm at seismograph stations operated by the United States Coast and Geodetic Survey, which calls instant attention to the fact that

* From *Annual Rept.*, Smithsonian Inst., 1947.

an earthquake has occurred. If it is found that the epicenter of the quake is under the ocean and so might produce seismic sea waves, a warning is sent to observers at selected tide stations to watch their gauges for evidence of the passage of the racing tsunamis. (Even a very small seismic sea wave can be identified by its peculiar period, and though it may be small at one place, it may reach dangerous heights at another.) When seismologists in Honolulu are notified that an undersea earthquake has occurred and that its waves have actually been recorded at certain stations, they can calculate when the waves will arrive at any point between the epicenter of the quake and the Hawaiian Islands. They can then issue warnings for the evacuation of beaches and waterfront areas. And so, for the first time in history, there is an organized effort to prevent these ominous waves from racing undetected over the empty spaces of the Pacific, to roar up suddenly on some inhabited shore.

The storm waves that sometimes rise over low-lying coast lands in hurricane zones belong in the class of wind waves, but unlike the waves of ordinary winds and storms, they are accompanied by a rise of the general water level, called a storm tide. The rise of water is often so sudden that it leaves no possibility of escape. Such storm waves claim about three-fourths of the lives lost by tropical hurricanes. The most notable disasters from storm waves in the United States have been those at Galveston, Texas, on 8 September, 1900, on the lower Florida Keys on 2 and 3 September, 1935, and the catastrophic rise of water accompanying the New England hurricane of 21 September, 1938. The most fearful destruction by hurricane waves within historic time occurred in the Bay of Bengal on 7 October, 1737, when 20,000 boats were destroyed and 300,000 people drowned.

There are other great waves, usually called 'rollers,' that periodically rise on certain coasts and batter them for days with damaging surf. These, too, are wind waves, but they are related to changes in barometric pressure over the ocean, perhaps several thousand miles distant from the beaches on which the waves eventually arrive. Low-pressure areas—like the one south of Iceland—are notorious storm breeders, their winds lashing the sea into great waves. After the waves leave the storm area they tend to become lower and longer and after perhaps thousands of miles of travel across the sea they become transformed into the undulations known as a ground swell. These swells are so regular and so low that often they are unnoticed as they pass through the short, choppy, new-formed waves of other areas. But when a swell approaches a coast and feels beneath it the gradually shoaling bottom, it begins to 'peak up' into a high, steep wave; within the surf zone the steepening be-

comes abruptly accentuated, a crest forms, breaks, and a great mass of water plunges downward.

Winter swell on the west coast of North America is the product of storms that travel south of the Aleutians into the Gulf of Alaska. Swell reaching this same coast during the summer has been traced back to its origin in the Southern Hemisphere belt of the 'roaring forties,' several thousand miles south of the equator. Because of the direction of the prevailing winds, the American east coast and the Gulf of Mexico do not receive the swell from far distant storms.

The coast of Morocco has always been particularly at the mercy of swell, for there is no protected harbor from the Strait of Gibraltar southward for some 500 miles. The rollers that visit the Atlantic islands of Ascension, St. Helena, South Trinidad, and Fernando de Noronha are historic. Apparently the same sort of waves occur on the South American coast near Rio de Janeiro, where they are known as *resacas*; others of kindred nature, having run their course from storms in the westwind belt of the South Pacific, attack the shores of the Paumotos Islands; still others have been responsible for the well-known 'surf days' that plague the Pacific coast of South America. According to Robert Cushman Murphy, it was formerly the custom of shipmasters in the guano trade to demand a special allowance for a certain number of days during which the loading of their vessels would be interrupted by the swell. On such surf days 'mighty rollers come pouring over the sea wall, and have been known to carry away forty-ton freight cars, to uproot concrete piers, and to twist iron rails like wire.'

The slow progression of swell from its place of origin made it possible for the Moroccan Protectorate to establish a service for the prediction of the state of the sea. This was done in 1921, after long and troublesome experience with wrecked vessels and wharves. Daily telegraphic reports of the condition of the sea give advance notice of troublesome surf days. Warned of the approach of swells, ships in port may seek safety in the open sea. Before this service was established, the port of Casablanca had once been paralyzed for seven months, and St. Helena had seen the wreckage of practically all the ships in her harbor on one or more occasions. Modern wave-recording instruments like those now being tested in England and the United States will soon provide even greater security for all such shores.

It is always the unseen that most deeply stirs our imagination, and so it is with waves. The largest and most awe-inspiring waves of the ocean are invisible; they move on their mysterious courses far down in the hidden depths of the sea, rolling ponderously and unceasingly. For many years it was known that the vessels of Arctic expeditions often became almost trapped and made headway only with difficulty in what was called 'dead water'—now recognized as internal waves at the boundary between a thin surface layer of fresh water and the underlying salt water. In the early 1900's several Scandinavian hydrographers called attention to the existence of submarine waves, but another generation was to elapse before science had the instruments to study them thoroughly.

Now, even though mystery still surrounds the causes of these great waves that rise and fall, far below the surface, their ocean-wide occurrence is well established. Down in deep water they toss submarines about, just as their surface counterparts set ships to rolling. They seem to break against the Gulf Stream and other strong currents in a deep-sea version of the dramatic meeting of surface waves and opposing tidal currents. Probably internal waves occur wherever there is a boundary between layers of dissimilar water, just as the waves we see occur at the boundary between air and sea. But these are waves such as never moved at the surface of the ocean. The water masses involved are unthinkably great, some of the waves being as high as 300 feet.

Of their effect on fishes and other life of the deep sea we have only the faintest conception. Swedish scientists say that the herring are carried or drawn into some of the fiords of Sweden when the deep internal waves roll over the submerged sills and into the fiords. In the open ocean, we know that the boundary between water masses of different temperatures or salinities is often a barrier that may not be passed by living creatures, delicately adjusted to certain conditions. Do these creatures themselves then move up and down with the roll of the deep waves? And what happens to the bottom fauna of the continental slope, adjusted, it may be, to water of unchanging warmth? What is their fate when the waves move in from a region of arctic cold, rolling like a storm surf against those deep, dark slopes? At present we do not know. We can only sense that in the deep and turbulent recesses of the sea are hidden mysteries far greater than any we have solved.

ROCKET SHOOT AT WHITE SANDS

JONATHAN NORTON LEONARD

JONATHAN NORTON LEONARD (1903–   ) was born in Somerville, Massachusetts, and attended Harvard University. For many years he was a free-lance writer, then became the Latin-American editor of *Time* magazine in 1943, and since 1945 has been the science editor of *Time*. Among his many books on popular science are: *Loki: the Life of Charles Proteus Steinmetz* (1929), *Tools of Tomorrow* (1935), *Flight into Space: the Facts, Fancies and Philosophy* (1953), and *Exploring Science* (1959).

A ROCKET SHOOT at White Sands Proving Ground is more than interesting, more than beautiful, more than exciting It is inspiring in a way that is equaled by few sights on earth.

Behind the austere buildings of the military post rise the spectacular Organ Mountains of New Mexico, with a fringe of dark pine trees climbing to their highest ridges. An uninhabited wilderness presses from all sides upon this isolated outpost of technological man. Jack rabbits bounce among the cactus and yucca. Deer dance down from the mountains at night to browse on the post's garbage, and sometimes mountain lions follow to browse on the deer.

In front, for forty miles, sweeps the gray-green

From *Flight into Space* by Jonathan Leonard, copyright 1953 by Jonathan Norton Leonard. Reprinted by permission of Random House, Inc.

desert of the Tularosa Basin. Dust devils swirl across it like yellow tornadoes, and sometimes great sand storms blot out the sun. But much of the time the air is as clear as a vacuum, showing a rim of distant mountains around the flat desert floor. A person standing in the center beyond where the rockets fly can easily imagine himself in one of the Moon's great craters with the jagged rampart circling the horizon.

The works of man seen from a distance look small in this setting, but some of them are startling when seen from close by. On a steep mountain slope perches a massive concrete structure that has the soaring aloofness of a Tibetan monastery. This is a test-stand where the biggest rocket motors are put through their flaming paces. It really looks like an adjunct for a flight to the Moon.

Far out on the desert stands an even weirder

structure—a peaked concrete igloo with walls and roof as solid as the stone of a pyramid. This "blockhouse" has narrow slits for windows with glass many inches thick. Its strength is a prudent precaution against the possibility that a rebellious rocket may turn on its creators and rend them to smoking shreds.

Near this modern donjon keep gather strange auxiliaries: tomblike underground storage places for violent chemical fuels; lacy steelwork towers; a forest of poles and spiderweb of wires. The desert for miles around is dotted with grotesque instruments. Radars sweep the sky with their pulsed electronic beams. The wide glassy eyes of cameras and theodolites stare at the launching site. Far off on the mountain rim great telescopes with forty-inch mirrors wait to follow the rockets on their flights into space.

There are ghosts in this desert too. The hollows between the mesquite hummocks close to the launching site are sprinkled with fragments of brilliantly painted pottery. Long ago, when the Tularosa Basin was a fertile valley, it supported a dense population of Indians, whose burial grounds and building foundations can still be traced among the thorny scrub.

No one knows what happened to these ancient people. Perhaps the climate grew drier; perhaps some river changed its course or sank into the sand. At any rate they are gone. They lacked the knowledge and resourcefulness to deal with such changes of environment. They left their dead and their pottery shards and the flint fragments of their poor, weak weapons. Amateur archaeologists from the Proving Ground sometimes dig in the sand close by the launching site and find their crouched skeletons, each with a painted pot inverted over its skull.

II

Space enthusiasts who speak lightly about flights to the Moon or Mars should be privileged to see what happens at White Sands. It would give them a sobering glimpse of difficulties ahead. The rockets that roar into the New Mexico desert are primitive things compared with what real space vehicles must be. They rise only a few hundred miles at most, and their speed is hardly one-tenth of the speed that would be needed to blast them free of the earth. They carry no human crews, and they all crash to utter ruin.

But these crude "beasts" (some rocket-men call them "beasts"; others call them "birds") are the best that space-striving man has to offer at present. To White Sands come the highest products of technological achievement: strange metals with treated surfaces to resist the white-hot scour of racing gases; electronic brains packed with transistors or tiny vacuum tubes and finished as precisely as microscope lenses; pumps no bigger than coffee cups that can push corrosive fuels as fast as the massive flow of irrigation canals.

Marching into White Sands comes a continuous parade of new and incredible instruments—those thousands of specialized senses with which man must augment the senses built into his body. They take their stations in the central laboratories, in the blockhouse, or in solid little huts dotted over the desert. There they get busily to work flashing their impressions on fast-flowing strips of photographic film or scribbling with delicate pens on streams of paper like quick-fingered stenographers writing a strange shorthand.

The men who govern the instruments are as skilled as they. To White Sands come top experts on electronics, optics, solid state physics, chemistry, metallurgy, mathematics, and astronomy. Some of them stay for years; others stay only long enough to make specific contributions to this remote deposit of technical virtuosity.

What these experts do is mostly secret. White Sands, officially, is an Army Ordnance center for the development and testing of new weapons—intelligent and terrible weapons. Some of them are mechanical falcons that scream into the air at a human command and run down and destroy anything flying there. Others are avenging angels designed to fly over continents, steering by the stars, and strike down offending cities in the flash of a nuclear explosion.

The men of White Sands do not talk lightly about these fearful projects. They know that they are necessary and will always be necessary so long as mankind is committed to a course of mutual destruction. But when the quiet of night has crept over the desert and the brilliant, many-colored stars flash in the clear sky, the men of White Sands like to turn their thoughts, half apologetically, toward a more peaceful project—the conquest and occupation of the vacuum above their heads.

Even the enlisted men—some of them learned GIs who play hot chess in the crowded barracks and chat in the chow lines about quantum mechanics—realize that they are working at the closest place on earth to space. They appreciate both the accomplishments of man on his march toward space and the enormous difficulties that still lie in his path. They know, for instance, that rockets are as temperamental as the graceful, smooth-flanked dancers that they so strangely resemble.

In the early days when Americans were first learning to fly captured German V-2 rockets, one of these flaming monsters rose from the launching site with a mutinous plot in its gyroscopic brain. Instead of rising vertically, as a good rocket should, it veered toward the south. Its launchers—both Americans and Germans—stared after it helplessly. There was nothing that they could do.

Across the Rio Grande fifty miles away, the city of Juarez, Mexico, was having a fiesta. Its wide garish main street at the end of the bridge from El Paso was packed with a gay crowd. Bands were playing, and fireworks cracked overhead. Slanting down from the north at three thousand miles per hour came the rebellious V-2. It shot across the crowd and buried itself with a vast concussion in a hillside cemetery just outside the celebrating city.

The Mexicans rather enjoyed this super-firework; they are friends of death when it comes in heroic form. But the authorities at White Sands are still acutely conscious of what that V-2 might have done if its rebellious brain had chosen a slightly different course.

One result of this international incident, which almost produced a catastrophe, was an elaborate safety system. Another was the construction of the massive blockhouse. Not long after it was completed, a second V-2 rebelled, made a great loop in the air and screamed within six hundred feet of it, trailing its tail of flame.

The captured V-2s were tamed at last, but all rockets, especially the new ones, contain within them the seeds of possible disaster. To make sure that they will perform as expected, they are sometimes given static tests while held securely to the ground. Even this sort of test, intended to forestall disaster, may go wrong in spectacular ways.

Not long ago, one of the biggest rockets was being tested statically. It stood on its tail, screaming, while floods of flame and smoke shot out of its shackled motor. Then it began to struggle fiercely like a captive wild animal suddenly conscious of its bonds. The hold-downs broke. The rocket soared upward and hid behind the blue sky.

A panicky pulse of alarm swept across White Sands. The many-eyed net of instruments had not been watching, but the radars sprang to attention in seconds and swept the echoing sky. Telescopes groped for the fugitive rocket. Radio beams raced after it like lariats flung into space. No one knew where it had gone, and it had enough range at worst to fall as far north as Santa Fe or as far south as Chihuahua in Mexico.

The men of White Sands will give few details about the rocket that got away. They will not tell —or perhaps they do not know—whether their electronic lariats caught it and controlled it before it

climbed out of the atmosphere. At any rate it fell in an uninhabited spot and did not dig its great crater in the plaza of Santa Fe.

* * * * *

III

On the day of a major shoot at White Sands the whole great apparatus spreading over the desert for hundreds of miles springs into tense activity. From the metal throats of invisible loud-speakers comes a slow throbbing sound. This is a half-second beat that binds all activities to the grid of time. Jeeps and trucks scurry across the desert, raising feathers of dust. The non-human eyes of the radars wing toward the launching site, where men swarm over the steel framework that surrounds the beautiful shape of the readied rocket.

Some of the rocket's attendants are muffled from head to foot, like Arabian women, in enveloping plastic garments to protect their skins from corrosive chemicals. Others wear earphones or carry walkie-talkie radios. They pump the rocket full of fuel, quiz its electronic brains, probe its valves and pumps with sensitive instruments. They are like midget masseurs grooming a tall and graceful ballerina for her first and last appearance on the stage of a great auditorium.

Inside the massive blockhouse, which feels part like a mine, part like a radio station, part like the bridge of a battleship going into action, is a hum of tense activity and purposeful running-around. Each man has a special duty, usually connected in some electronic way with the web of instruments spread over the desert. Squawking voices speak tersely with metallic tongues; vivid green lines zigzag across the faces of oscilloscopes.

On a long control panel under a slit window glows a line of little red lights. When one of them goes out, it means that some circuit is completed, some instrument far away has declared itself alert and ready. The half-second beat throbs on like a steady pulse.

Then a solemn, echoing voice comes over the loud-speaker. It says, "Zero minus thirty minutes."

This means that thirty minutes remain before the hour, the minute, and the second when the rocket will fly. The men in the blockhouse, climbing over the rocket or watching across the desert become a little more tense. Their blood runs a little faster. The moment is coming.

The little red lights on the control panel wink out one by one. Voices report trouble, then trouble overcome. "Zero minus twenty minutes," chants the loud-speaker.

Trucks and jeeps loaded with men dart away from

the danger area. Gates are being closed; chains are being drawn taut across distant highways. The men on the framework around the rocket are administering to it a kind of extreme unction. They check its intricate instruments for the last time and close the flush-fitting doors that cover access ports. They climb down reluctantly, and the steel framework is wheeled away, revealing the graceful shape of the doomed rocket. At this moment of unveiling, it looks like the most beautiful thing that has ever been built by man.

"Zero minus ten minutes," chants the loud-speaker.

Now a solemn hush spreads across the desert. No men are in sight. They have all fled away or gone inside the blockhouse like ants going underground ahead of an approaching shower. Only a few red lights still show on the control panel. Scientists who have worked for years on the rocket's burden of instruments are muttering over and over their profane technological prayers. Some of them finger incongruous rabbits' feet; some keep their fingers crossed like children in primary school.

"Zero minus one minute," chants the loud-speaker.

Now the impersonal voice of the unseen microphone shares the growing excitement. "Zero minus forty-five seconds," it chants in a higher key. Then, "Zero minus thirty seconds."

The last of the little red lights is gone from the control panel, leaving nothing between the rocket and its moment of glory. It stands naked and alone like a human sacrifice watched by a thousand priests. A plume of brilliant red smoke spurts from the ground beside it and drifts across the desert. This is a final visual warning to men, instruments, and airplanes with no electronic ears.

"Zero minus five seconds," chants the loud-speaker. Now its words come faster. "Four—three—two—one—ZERO!"

In the tense, hushed blockhouse, the firing officer throws a switch. A stab of yellow flame and a dense white cloud of smoke burst from the tail of the rocket, and a screaming roar rolls across the desert. The rocket rises slowly at first as if an invisible hoist were drawing it upward. It wobbles a little, standing on its tail of flame. Then it gains confidence, gathers speed, and shoots up toward space like a bellowing arrow. In a few seconds it is gone, leaving only a trail of smoke like a chalk mark against the blue sky.

For human eyes the flight is over, but instrument eyes are watching. The dish antennas of distant radars turn upward after the rocket. Cameras and theodolites crane upward their jointed necks. Down from the rocket, over a sheaf of radio channels, comes a flood of information for instruments below to gather and cherish.

The nose of the rocket is packed with delicate, specialized senses. They feel the air as it rushes past, measuring its temperature, its density, its motion. Spectrographs analyze the sunlight, which grows brighter as altitude increases. Geiger-tubes count the cosmic-ray particles striking fiercely out of space, and photon-counters feel for X-rays flooding out of the sun.

Some of their findings are recorded on photographic films that wind into steel cylinders that are strong enough to survive the final crash of the rocket. Other findings are radioed to earth, where skilled instrument-stenographers take them down on paper as swiftly waving lines.

Sometimes the information comes in the form of audible notes that sound for all the world like a small child playing a piano. The pitch of each note varies with the instruments' readings and can be analyzed by appropriate devices. This eerie music, which is to be inscribed on magnetic tape, tells the whole tale of the rocket's effort, of its triumph above the atmosphere, and of its ultimate death.

While the rocket is waiting on its launching platform, the singing instruments in its nose play a gentle, monotonous tune. Some of the tones are continuous, like the drones of a bagpipe. Others are "sampled" periodically so that they sound like piano notes. As the rocket rises, some of the tones remain steady; others vary in pitch in a strange modernistic way. The tinkling tune continues, but it becomes irregular, as if the child that is touching the keys were growing tired or frightened. As the rocket roars up toward space, it sends down groaning, quavering sounds. These record vibration, its struggle with the atmosphere. Long, low wails mean that the rocket is yawing or rolling. The tinkling music of the sampled tones plays on bravely above this background of discord, but the child at the piano sounds desperate now. The rocket is close to the peak of its speeds and struggling fiercely against the buffeting air.

As the rocket soars out of the atmosphere, the discords gradually die away. It is moving through space now, serene as an asteroid cruising around the sun, and the child at the piano plays his tinkling tune with confidence and skill.

His moment of peace in space does not last for long. The rocket reaches the top of its flight and then turns downward, tumbling over and over, toward the fringe of the atmosphere. When the air strikes it, the rocket straightens out, nose down, and points toward the spot on the desert where it will die. Vibration and yaw build up again, and discordant sounds obscure the tinkling tune. Louder and louder they grow as the rocket darts toward earth.

Radars and telescopes miles below slant downward

gradually as the rocket falls. They are judging coldly just where its death will occur. The child at the piano continues his tinkling tune, now almost blotted out by warning screams from the instruments. The hard, unyielding earth rushes upward at three thousand miles per hour.

Then, without warning, the music stops. The rocket has come to its death on the desert, digging a great hole. Nothing is left but crumpled metal and a few photographic films inscribed with precious information. The child at the piano will never play another tune.

THE WORK OF MANY PEOPLE

EDWARD TELLER

EDWARD TELLER (1908–   ) is a Hungarian-born physicist. He studied at the Institute of Technology at Karlsruhe, Germany, at Leipzig, and at Yale. Since 1935, he has taught physics at several American universities, and was concerned in the early planning and prediction of the function of the atomic bomb. He is the co-author of *The Structure of Matter* (1948), *Our Nuclear Future* (1958), and *Legacy of Hiroshima* (1962).

A MODERN technical and scientific development is rightly considered a wonderfully complex and difficult undertaking. The final intricate product has evidently required the greatest refinements of the art of engineering. The engineering phase has to be preceded by an experimental period of trials and adjustments, and even the very conception and theory of the device are rooted in many scientific thoughts and a mass of detailed calculations. Hundreds of ideas and thousands of technical skills are required for success. The hydrogen bomb is an achievement of this kind. It is the work of many excellent people who had to give their best abilities for years and who were all essential for the final outcome.

The story that is often presented to the public is quite different. One hears of a brilliant idea and only too often the name of a single individual is mentioned. This picture is both untrue and unjust. If one emphasizes the interaction of many different minds, one comes closer to the real life and the real excitement of exploration.

THE SUN AND OTHER STARS

George Gamow escaped from Soviet Russia in 1933 and came to George Washington University in 1934. He had many interesting stories to tell. One of them is the following.

Six years before his arrival in the United States, he reported in the U.S.S.R. Academy of Sciences a paper by the British physicist, Atkinson, and the

From *Science*, February 25, 1955. Reprinted by permission of the author.

German physicist, Houtermans. They suggested that the apparently inexhaustible store of energy radiated by the sun and by other stars is due to reactions between atomic nuclei. These particles, tiny even compared with atoms, are known to contain an energy a million times greater than that released in chemical reactions or explosions. Yet they are able to release this energy only when they come in contact with each other. Their electric charges usually prevent contact between them and thus the energy that they have been carrying for billions of years is preserved. In the deep interior of the stars, however, exceedingly high temperatures exist. Owing to the thermal agitation, occasional collisions between the nuclei do occur, and these nuclear reactions ultimately give rise to the brilliance of the stars and to the radiation of our sun.

After Gamow finished his lecture he was approached by a very high Soviet official, Bukharin. By that time Bukharin had lost his real influence and had the job of keeping an eye on scientific developments. A few years later he was to be executed. After the lecture he asked Gamow whether nuclear processes similar to those occurring in the sun could be harnessed to some direct application here on earth. He offered to turn over to Gamow the Electric Works of Leningrad for a few hours at nighttime if that would help in the job. Gamow said that the practical job could not be done, but he remembered this occurrence and he kept his interest in the question of stellar energies.

Of course, we possess no direct knowledge about the interior of stars. Yet astrophysicists, starting with Eddington, had a pretty accurate knowledge of the conditions in those completely inaccessible regions. It may be puzzling to hear that science, which is practically unable to predict properties of matter in its common form encountered on earth, should be able to state with high accuracy how matter behaves inside the stars. The reason is a simple one. At the relatively low temperatures prevailing around us, the properties of materials are determined by a sensitive balance between the attractions of the constituents of atoms and the energy of motion of these same particles. In the stellar interiors the temperatures are extremely high and the balance is destroyed. The atomic constituents—that is, the electrons and the nuclei—rush around at high velocities along straight lines, and the forces between these particles have little effect upon their motion. Thus matter, which in our common experience has many intricate and varied appearances and properties, behaves in a uniform and predictable manner in the inside of the hot gas balls which we call the stars.

The stars lose energy continuously and this energy must be replenished. Atkinson and Houtermans merely pointed out that the most probable source of this energy is the atomic nucleus itself. It was as yet unclear which of the great many possible reactions between nuclei give rise to the solar and stellar energy.

Gamow, with his wonderful sense for interesting problems, and with his contagious curiosity about the structure of the universe, stirred up quite a few of the physicists who had previously considered the interior of stars a too remote question. This soon led to the exploration of thermonuclear reactions, a long word which now has become quite familiar and which means the reaction of nuclei occurring at high temperatures. At that time, the late 1930's, the discussions and work were carried on with no idea of any practical applications. It was done merely to satisfy what to many would appear idle curiosity.

The first candidate for any thermonuclear reaction was the lightest of elements, hydrogen. In the sun and the stars this element appears to be by far the most abundant. Nuclei of hydrogen, by fusing into bigger nuclei, could release energies that are rather big even when compared with energies of most nuclear reactions. What is most important, hydrogen nuclei carry less charge than any other nucleus and therefore can approach each other more easily. Under the influence of Gamow's prodding, a small group of physicists and astronomers met at George Washington University and the Carnegie Institution in Washington in the spring of 1938. We had one of those disorganized discussions that we call a conference, which seem to lead nowhere but which often in the past had a great influence upon the development of science.

The conference did little more than pose the problems with some clarity, but the solution followed within the next few months. Hans Bethe, Charles Critchfield, and Gamow succeeded, not only in determining what reactions keep the stars going, but also in reconstructing how stars develop, change their appearance, and finally exhaust their sources of energy. The most remarkable part of this job was done by Bethe, who made a systematic study of all conceivable thermonuclear reactions, cataloging all the relatively meager experimental data of that day and supplementing them by wonderfully enlightened guesses about all the relevant nuclear reactions not yet experimentally explored. He found that, in addition to the possibility of hydrogen nuclei reacting with each other, one has to consider the reactions between hydrogen and carbon nuclei. His treatment of these reactions was so complete that in the next decade nothing useful could be added to his enumeration. Gamow had invented a new kind of game for the physicists, and Bethe proved to be the champion at it.

CONCEPTION OF THE SUPER

No one expected to be able to approach the conditions of the solar interior in any of our experiments. No container would have withstood the temperatures; no familiar source could deliver the energy in the necessary concentrated form. Then, in December 1938, Otto Hahn and Lise Meitner discovered fission.

It is now well known how fission releases energy. The neutron, a nuclear particle that carries no charge, can approach any nucleus even when no high temperatures are present. Some of the heaviest nuclei split under the impact of a neutron and produce more neutrons in the process. Thus a chain of reactions results, and the immense temperature and pressure of an atomic bomb can be produced.

Several years before Hiroshima, scientists started to wonder whether the high temperatures that were expected to occur in an atomic bomb could be utilized to start reactions similar to those that are proceeding within the sun. To me, this idea was first mentioned with some emphasis by Enrico Fermi. He proposed, in particular, to consider the reactions of heavy hydrogen rather than the reaction of the normal abundant light hydrogen. This heavy hydrogen, or deuterium, is present in ordinary hydrogen in the amount of 1 part in 5000, but it can be separated from the light hydrogen by some processes that are not altogether too costly. Furthermore it was known that the heavy hydrogen nuclei react with each other much more easily than those of light hydrogen. Therefore, the substitution of deuterium for hydrogen would be a long step toward realizing thermonuclear reactions under experimental conditions.

At that time, in the spring of 1942, both Fermi and I were at Columbia University. Physics had moved closer to the grim realities of war. Many of us had started to work on the fission bombs. It had become clear that these atomic bombs would be powerful but expensive. If deuterium could be ignited, it would give a much less expensive fuel.

After a few weeks of hard thought, I decided that deuterium could not be ignited by atomic bombs. I reported my results to Fermi and proceeded to forget about it.

In the early summer I found myself at the Metallurgical Laboratory of Chicago and in the company of Emil Konopinski, another physicist who had started to work on atomic energy. In the bustling laboratory of Chicago we were newcomers and at least for a few days we had no concrete job. I suggested that we go over my arguments about the thermonuclear reactions and that we make a conclusive written report that heavy hydrogen would be of no use in bombs. The more we tried, the harder it seemed to arrive at a definite conclusion. In fact, within a few days we found some loopholes that seemed to indicate that deuterium could be ignited, after all.

In the meantime, Robert Oppenheimer gathered around himself in Berkeley a small group of theoretical physicists for the purpose of investigating the properties and behavior of atomic bombs. This group included Van Vleck, Felix Bloch, Stanley Frankel, Bethe, and Robert Serber. Konopinski and I joined the group when it was just being formed, and all of us were soon engaged in the distant but absorbing question of whether deuterium could be exploded.

It is hard to describe the intensity and the fascination of the discussion that followed. We were again dealing with conditions of high temperature completely unknown to experiment but open to theoretical predictions because of the very simplicity of the types of motion occurring under those conditions. The experience proved perhaps even more challenging than the previous discussion about the interior of the sun. Here we were not bound by the known conditions in a given star but we were free within considerable limits to choose our own conditions. We were embarking on astrophysical engineering.

As fact after fact emerged and was clarified, the prospects changed. One day the job looked hopeless, the next day it seemed easy, only to turn out again

to be practically impossible on account of some considerations that had not been previously included. All of us contributed to the discussion, but without Konopinski and Bethe no real progress would have been made. I remember particularly the suggestion of Konopinski that the reactions of tritium should be investigated. At that time it was a mere guess. It turned out to be an inspired one. Bethe subjected all the relevant factors to the same kind of exhaustive scrutiny by which he had clarified the thermonuclear reactions occurring in the stars. By the middle of the summer of 1942, we were all convinced that the job could be done and that it would be relatively easy.

The spirit of spontaneity, adventure, and surprise of those weeks in Berkeley was never recaptured for me in the many years of hard work in which atomic bombs were developed. As the problems inevitably grew, as they came closer to the realities of engineering and hardware, exploration had to be replaced by schedule and spontaneous exchange of ideas by organization. I am sure that all the participants in those discussions still remember vividly the days when we thought that the atomic bomb could be easily used for a stepping-stone toward a thermonuclear explosion, which we called a "Super" bomb.

CERTAINLY DIFFICULT, PERHAPS POSSIBLE

When Los Alamos was established in the spring of 1943, the exploration of the Super was among its objectives. Within a year, however, the picture changed completely. This was due to the fact that both the atomic bomb and the Super bomb proved to be more difficult than had been expected. Our discussion of the thermonuclear reactions proved to be incomplete, and it became clear that to make a Super would be difficult, if not impossible. At the same time, it became clear that the construction of the A-bomb was a much bigger job than we anticipated, and yet this had to be done before our enemies could do it. That it was done in time to have an influence upon the war was to a great extent due to the leadership of our director, Oppenheimer. He knew what was going on in every corner of the big laboratory and was prompt both in his understanding and in his encouragement. In his office there was a poster with Lincoln's picture, carrying the modified quotation, "This world cannot exist half slave and half free." It was hardly necessary, and yet helpful to remind everybody in the laboratory of this fact. We had to win the war and there was no time for the Super.

In spite of the urgency of the situation, Oppenheimer did not lose sight of the more distant possibilities. He continued to urge me with detailed and helpful advice to keep exploring what lay beyond the immediate aims of the laboratory. This was not easy advice to give, nor was it easy to take. It is easier to participate in the work of the scientific community, particularly when a goal of the highest interest and urgency has been clearly defined. Every one of us considered the present war and the completion of the A-bomb as the problems to which we wanted to contribute most. Nevertheless, Oppenheimer, Fermi, and many of the most prominent men in the laboratory continued to say that the job at Los Alamos would not be complete if we should remain in doubt whether or not a thermonuclear bomb was feasible. Furthermore, the purely scientific aspects of the Super were so fascinating that the problem continued to attract attention even in the hectic days in which our efforts on the atomic bomb approached completion and success. Thus in early 1945 a small but very able group started to concentrate its efforts on the thermonuclear bombs.

Most of this work continued to be pure theory, but there was less discovery and more quantitative evaluation. A number of talented young people joined our group. One of Bethe's students, Henry Hurwitz, proved that he had learned from his professor how to be systematic and ingenious. Two students from George Washington University, Geoffrey Chew and Harold Argo, interrupted their studies and came to Los Alamos to help us. Anthony Turkevich from Chicago contributed his knowledge of the theory of chemical reactions. Rolf Landshoff, a refugee from Germany, was the only one of the group who was going to stay at Los Alamos uninterruptedly from those days up to the present time. Two mathematicians, Stan Ulam and Jack Calkin, started to make calculations which even to a theorist seemed abstract. Nicholas Metropolis became interested in the use of computing machines, which in the later development turned out to be of great importance.

The experimental approach was not completely neglected. Early measurements by John Manley, Elizabeth Graves, Marshall Holloway, and Charles Baker were continued by Egon Bretscher and other members of the British contingent. They, as well as our other British friends, participated without any restrictions in our great common work at Los Alamos.

Some of the most famous men in the laboratory kept in very close touch with our work and helped with frequent suggestions and criticism. One was Fermi, a physicist equally eminent in theory and experiment, the other was John von Neumann, one of the rare mathematicians who can descend to the level of a physicist.

In spite of all these contributions, no definite answer was reached. As the months went by, we still did not know whether the job could be done. But, paradoxical as this may seem, our very lack of certainty was based on a broader and more secure foundation. At the same time, all these people became acquainted with the increasingly complex arguments, and thus many of them could prepare themselves for further contributions in the future.

The most important part of all this work, however, was focused on one man, Konopinski. It was he who brought newcomers up to date, who made sure that none of the questions of which we were aware should go unexplored, and who finally made sure that our accumulating knowledge was preserved in clear and usable documents. Together with a young physicist, Cloyd Marvin, Jr., he also completed a strange and important task. He proved that a thermonuclear reaction, even if initiated on the earth, could not spread under any circumstances. It was necessary to prove, and he did prove, that the Super bomb could not ignite the atmosphere or the ocean. Later, his work was reviewed by one of the most conscientious, meticulous and painstaking physicists, Gregory Breit. It was clearly necessary to prove this point beyond the shadow of any doubt and it was so proved.

Then, in the summer of 1945, the work of the laboratory culminated in complete and terrifying success. The war was ended and the temper of the country and of the physicists seemed to preclude any further great efforts on the thermonuclear bomb. Some members of the wartime group, however, stayed on to prepare a summary review of the possibilities. It was Frankel and Metropolis who worked hardest and longest in preparing this report on the feasibility of the Super. The verdict was: Difficult, but with hard work, hopeful.

HIBERNATION

For several months after the end of the war it seemed likely that the Los Alamos Laboratory would be discontinued. Such an event would have been most dangerous for the security of the United States. That it did not happen was due to the effort of a few determined people who considered it their duty to try to keep Los Alamos alive, whatever the odds might be. The man whose leadership was crucial in those days was the new director, Norris Bradbury.

To keep Los Alamos alive was an uphill fight which remains clear in the memory of both those who stayed and those who left. One nontechnical event of great importance which all of us remember was the water shortage. In the fall of 1945 the snowfall came late, but frost came early. The water pipes froze and soon water had to be brought up the hill in trucks. We lacked ample water, one of the vital elements of civilization; this great discomfort continued into Christmas of 1945 and beyond. Los Alamos was a town of young people and there were many babies. Mothers started to wonder about dangers of epidemics, which fortunately never materialized. Many who had hesitated decided to leave Los Alamos. I recall one detail that may seem insignificant. During the war I developed, somewhat to my own surprise, two affections: a liking for strangers and the love of green grass. Both were in short supply. In the water shortage of 1945 the grass was dying.

Throughout all these difficulties Bradbury stayed on, kept smiling and encouraged others to stay with the job. Without his dedicated work the Russians would now be ahead of us in the atomic race.

I was one of the majority who returned at that time to academic work. The very success of the atomic bomb had raised some obstacles to the continuation of work on the thermonuclear weapon. There were those who felt that it would take a lifetime before the brilliant achievements of the war work could be improved. Of our thermonuclear group, only Landshoff remained, and most of his work was required for more immediate problems. Ulam left the laboratory for a short period and then returned to develop the Monte Carlo method, a highly successful procedure to deal with statistical problems by investigating individual happenings rather than the mass of the data. This fine work, however, was unrelated to the work on the Super. Ulam's contributions in that field came later. Thus, of the small group of experts whose skill was developed during the war, not one continued to devote his full time and energy to the next big problem in atomic weapons.

However, the idea of the Super bomb survived as a challenge and as a future task for Los Alamos. An exceedingly small group, headed by Robert Richtmyer, started to take over where others left off. They kept the spark alive, and their work should therefore be particularly remembered. In the following years I made many visits to Los Alamos and kept in close touch with the work of these people. From the very beginning this work had assumed a new direction and acquired a new style.

In the development of the atomic bomb, use of automatic computing machines had played an important role. It was essential that atomic bombs should be available without a lengthy preliminary period of experimentation. Furthermore, small-scale experimentation, similar in function to that of a pilot plant in industry, was out of the question in connection with atomic bombs: If you try to make a small atomic explosion you are likely to get no atomic explosion. Therefore, theoretical predictions

had to be particularly well considered and carried out in meticulous detail. This would have been most difficult without the extensive use of big computing devices. In the postwar period the theorists of the Super bomb turned their interest toward the most advanced computing machines.

In the months following the explosion of the first atomic weapons, Frankel and Metropolis started work on the new fast electronic computer in Philadelphia, the ENIAC. Their work was soon taken over by Richtmyer, Foster and Cerda Evans, and a few others. At the same time von Neumann, together with many excellent people throughout the country, was working hard at further plans and improvements of the fast electronic computers. After an absence of more than a year, Metropolis rejoined Los Alamos and started to build the MANIAC (which is supposed to mean Mathematical Analyzer Numerical Integrator And Computer). Richtmyer became interested in these computational methods and became one of the real masters in handling the machines.

A fast computer, while very efficient, needs detailed instructions, and it is quite an art to transform a mathematical problem into a set of symbols that will make the machine operate properly. Furthermore, this set of symbols is hardly ever free from errors, so that after a problem is fed into the machine the first set of answers usually makes no sense. There must follow a period of "debugging" in which the very answers obtained lead to the discovery of mistakes in the original instructions. To make matters worse, the machine itself makes occasional mistakes and these may get confused with errors in the instructions.

In the normal course of operating a computing machine, several people cooperate: the physicist who sets up the problem, the mathematician who provides the rigorous formulation, the coder who "explains" the problem to the machine, the machine operator who straightens out the errors, and then the physicist again who uses the answers to set up the next problem. Richtmyer argued that all these operations can be performed by a single man more efficiently, and he proceeded to demonstrate that this could be done. This style of computation is practiced at present by many able people.

Work on a difficult subject such as a Super bomb depends on the mutual help and encouragement of at least a few people. When the group is small there is danger that the effort will cease altogether; but in the case of the thermonuclear effort the small group of people kept on increasing, even though the increase was slow. The evident importance and scientific interest of the problem caught and held the imagination of additional workers. Frank Hoyt, a professor at the University of Chicago, visited from time to time to help out. Later he joined Los Alamos on a permanent basis. His quiet and devoted work contributed much to the sustained effort. Some of my students at Chicago also became interested and joined the laboratory after completing their graduate work. Harris Mayer and John Reitz were to make lasting contributions, and Marshall Rosenbluth eventually became one of the key men who carried the calculations to their successful conclusion.

I particularly remember a short visit from Lothar Nordheim from Duke University. He is a man who is likely to sit through a dinner among friends without participating in the conversation and who is likely to come up toward the end with just one remark. Later it turns out that one can recall, of the whole evening, only Nordheim's comment. His work proved to be of the same quality. He started it in the lean years. Later he joined Los Alamos for an extended period, always working inconspicuously either alone or with very few people. In the beginning his effort did not seem to amount to much. In the end it turned out to be one of the really significant contributions.

In the middle of 1949 I went back to Los Alamos to spend a considerable length of time there. In the preceding 3 years the laboratory had recovered to a remarkable extent. We had lost somewhat in competence as compared with the high-powered crew that was available at the end of the war, but we had progressed in some ideas, and the technique of big-scale computations had been developed. Then the Soviet bomb brought the realization that the arms race was no longer a possibility but a frightening reality.

THE CRISIS

It is clear that the hydrogen bomb would not have been built except for the efforts of a considerable number of people whose contributions ranged from political decisions to organization and on into the scientific work. My knowledge and appreciation are, of course, greatest in connection with this last phase, which is closest to my own interests. I shall talk only about the work that concerned equations and atoms and will stop short of blueprints and bombs. About the latter I do not know enough to give a just description. About the political decisions that had to be made after the explosion of the Soviet bomb, I know even less. My direct experience is limited to the few occasions when I was asked to give my opinion on technical possibilities and probabilities; but I feel that great gratitude is due to the men who in those difficult weeks arrived at the correct conclusions.

The decision concerning how to respond to the threat of a Soviet bomb was not an easy one. At Los Alamos there was a widespread feeling that the laboratory should turn to the development of the hydrogen bomb. During the war it had been understood that this possibility must be explored. Many people felt that the time for this had come. In the administration of the laboratory the first to make a concrete and determined effort toward planning a big-scale approach was Darol Froman. A 6-day work week was adopted upon the urging of Holloway and others.

However, the center of the hydrogen bomb activity remained for some time in the theoretical group on which plans had to depend. This group, although small, was of high quality and expanded rapidly. Much of the credit for its build-up and successful activity must go to its able organizer and leader, Carson Mark.

Frederic de Hoffmann had joined the laboratory in the early part of 1949. Even before the Soviet explosion he felt that the hydrogen bomb must be our main task. Now he acted like a man who has been freed from a terrible restriction. He was the kind of associate who would never let me forget the importance of the job that we were doing, and I am sure that my own effectiveness depended greatly on his skill, devotion, and example. Nordheim joined the laboratory to explore further the consequence of his earlier work. John Wheeler from Princeton interrupted a well-deserved sabbatical leave in Europe and, together with some of his students, plunged into furious and effective activity. Roy Goranson helped to maintain contact between the theory and the practical execution. James Tuck shelved his greatest interest, peacetime applications of atomic energy, and devoted himself to the urgent phase of the program. Together with a group of able experimental physicists, he made some measurements of vital interest to the thermonuclear program. Von Neumann and Fermi helped, if less frequently, no less effectively than during the war.

Our most urgent task was to reconsider with the greatest possible rigor the favored design of the hydrogen bomb. We intended to do this with the help of the high-speed computing machines. The best of these, however, were not yet operating at the time, and the calculation was set up on the ENIAC, which in the intervening years had been moved to the Aberdeen Proving Grounds. Ulam, with the able help of another mathematician, Cornelius Everett, undertook to execute the same job by straightforward hand computation. The next few months saw an amazing competition between the tortoise and the (electronic) hare.

The big modern computing machines open up possibilities of complex calculations which seemed to be beyond our reach only a few years ago, but real mathematical ingenuity, coupled with hard work, can on some occasions overcome computational difficulties with even greater success than the best apparatus so far invented. This is precisely what happened in the case of Ulam's calculation. It proceeded with a speed that surpassed all expectations. Results were available even before the lengthy instructions to the machines had been completed. Those who like to contrast ingenuity and endurance of the human brain with the lightning speed of standard operations on a machine will be able to conclude: In a real emergency the mathematician still wins—if he is really good.

Ulam's first partial results were disquieting; the more complete answers, most discouraging. I felt at the time that these calculations, which seemed to be in conflict with earlier results obtained on machines, were hard to believe. In actual fact they were correct, and they served a most important purpose in alerting us at an early date to the difficulties that we were facing. A few weeks later, when the more detailed and accurate results from the machine were in, it became completely clear that the plans which we had considered most hopeful had to be revised.

The probable success of a radically new device such as the hydrogen bomb is not likely to depend on one particular line of approach. Real progress depends on the compete understanding of the field and on the efficiency of methods that apply this understanding to detailed designs. It furthermore depends on experiments and tests to compare the theoretical knowledge with reality. The work of the years that had passed since 1942 had left us with a great store of knowledge of the principles and methods, but the calculations of Ulam and Everett deprived us of the best example of a device to which we could point and say: This is how we actually want to do it.

It is clear that there had to be discouragement. The remarkable thing is that the majority of the people engaged in the work at Los Alamos kept on working hard and with a good spirit. This included almost all the theorists who had been working on the project.

The plan for a complex apparatus like a hydrogen bomb is not tied to one single design. There are many possibilities and each possibility can be handled in many different ways. In early 1950 we had 8 years of fantasies, theories, and calculations behind us. We also had some significant measurements performed in the laboratories on the basic process, but we had no experience whatsoever that would tell us whether or not our assumptions and general ideas had anything to do with the behavior of real objects. It had become most urgent to come back to solid ground by establishing a connection between theory and practice. In

other words, we needed a significant test. Without such a test no one of us could have had the confidence to proceed further along speculations, inventions, and the difficult choice of the most promising possibility. This test was to play the role of a pilot plant in our development.

The first immediate job was, therefore, to make detailed calculations concerning the test. Because of the shortage of high-speed computing equipment, much of this arduous work still had to be carried out by hand. Under the supervision of Wheeler, Landshoff, Richtmyer, and some new recruits among whom were Conrad Longmire, Rosenbluth, and Burton Freeman, an incredible amount of numerical data was turned out by the untiring work of the people in the Los Alamos computing division. Thus, the comparison between the results of the test and the theory of thermonuclear burning could be anticipated with some measure of confidence.

In the second half of 1950 and in early 1951, the most complex kind of apparatus was being built in order to observe the results of the test. It is impossible for me to describe the excellent effort that went into this work. The device we were building was going to function for a minute fraction of a second. The observing equipment was going to be destroyed by the test explosion, yet delicate effects had to be recorded before the test apparatus was vaporized. We had to find out not only what actually happened in this test but also which were the best observational tools to be used in future tests.

Under the direction of Alvin Graves, Frederick Reines, Jack Clark, William Ogle, and others, an intricate laboratory was built on Eniwetok. The Los Alamos effort was augmented by excellent crews from the Naval Research Laboratory and from the Radiation Laboratory of the University of California. Never before have so many experimental scientists believed in such a mass of complex calculations not as yet compared with any process in the real world.

During most of these preparations plans for an eventually successful device had to take a low priority. The most important thing was the test, which required such a great effort and which was to confirm or disprove our ideas. We had to establish beyond a doubt that thermonuclear burning was possible. The question whether it could be used in an economically designed weapon had to wait for many months. Yet, it would be a mistake to believe that in this period plans were not maturing. The most fruitful suggestions often occur when one is occupied with a different and urgent project, and many of the hardworking physicists contributed in offhand discussions their ideas, sometimes fantastic, sometimes practical, to what might in the end become a usable device.

526   PROSE

However, the immediate thing ahead of us in the spring of 1951 was the test in the Pacific: Greenhouse. I do not know how many scientific experiments have been made under conditions as exotic or in a place as beautiful as was the setting for the first thermonuclear experiment. There must have been other events as strange, exciting, and unforgettable. What remains most clear in my mind is the contrast between the spectacular explosion, which in itself meant nothing, and the small piece of paper handed to me by my good friend, Louis Rosen, which showed that the experiment was a success. The test gave us the assurance that we needed. Our detailed calculations agreed remarkably well with the results of the test.

SUCCESS

All of us knew that after Greenhouse we faced the real decision: can a usable device be constructed or not? All of us worried about this question. Some made very specific plans. Wheeler set up a group in Princeton which was preparing for the long hard pull in the calculations that were to decide the issue. But the essential parts of the decision started to come faster than had been expected by anybody.

A few months before the Greenhouse test all calculations had to be completed, and at that time it became possible for many of us to devote our full attention to the problems of the construction of an actual bomb. This time the challenge found our group in Los Alamos fully prepared. Calculational techniques were developed to a high pitch. Half-examined ideas were lying around by the score. They had to be shoved aside for the sake of more immediate calculations. Now we had the opportunity to look at them in detail. A year had passed since the decision to go ahead at the fastest possible rate with the hydrogen program, and everyone was eager and anxious to come to grips with the real problem. Two signs of hope came within a few weeks: one sign was an imaginative suggestion by Ulam; the other sign was a fine calculation by de Hoffmann.

I cannot refrain from mentioning one particularly human detail in de Hoffmann's work. Since I had made the suggestion that led to his calculation, I expected that we would jointly sign the report containing the results. Freddie, however, had other plans. He signed the report with my name only and argued that the suggestion counted for everything and the execution for nothing. I still feel ashamed that I consented.

Even before the Greenhouse test it became evident to a small group of people in Los Alamos that a thermonuclear bomb might be constructed in a compara-

tively easy manner. To many who were not closely connected with our work this has appeared as a particularly unexpected and ingenious development. In actual fact this too was the result of hard work and hard thought by many people. The thoughts were incomplete, but all the fruitful elements were present, and it was clearly a question of only a short period until the ideas and suggestions were to crystallize into something concrete and provable. Both Los Alamos and the newly formed group in Princeton immediately started calculations on this new approach.

The calculations on the new plans, though still crude, were presented at a meeting in Princeton to the Atomic Energy Commission and its advisers shortly after the Greenhouse test. Even while this meeting was in session, fresh results from Wheeler's group were being brought in. This group, which was organized in a period of uncertainty, was gaining remarkable momentum and hope and their mood was contagious. In the Princeton meeting everyone clearly recognized that with a little luck, only a great deal of hard work stood between us and final success.

Now at last the high-speed computing machines started to play the significant role that had been foreseen a few years earlier. A somewhat modest but very efficient machine, the SEAC, was in operation at the National Bureau of Standards, and the director, Edward Condon, invited us to make use of it. With the help of this facility, initial details of the plans were ironed out in a few weeks rather than in tedious months. Soon even faster machines, including particularly the Los Alamos MANIAC, helped to speed our work, so that the calculations on the design could be carried through more thoroughly and in shorter time than anyone could have expected. The art of machine calculations was now shared by many of the leading theorists in Los Alamos. In the hands of Rosenbluth, Longmire, Nordheim, Freeman, and many others, speculations hardened into complete specifications. Wheeler's group at Princeton developed similar expert knowledge in an amazingly short time. John Toll, Kenneth Ford, and others not only helped to make sure of the success of the immediate plans but started to contribute toward designs that were to bear fruit only in the more distant future.

In the fall of 1951 I left Los Alamos. I felt sure that everything was going to be done to construct a thermonuclear bomb with the greatest possible care and precision. The theoretical division under Carson Mark had grown into a most able outfit, which was to be joined for the critical months by Bethe. All of us felt that his presence would make sure that nothing would be forgotten in the preparations. Yet people kept worrying about possible difficulties, even dreaming about them, up to the time of the final test explosion. Thus, with Los Alamos furnishing the solid foundation and Princeton much of the drive and optimism, one could look with confidence into the future.

It was a great disappointment to me that I could not participate in the final phases of this magnificent undertaking. The main reason that persuaded me to leave Los Alamos was a conviction that this was an opportune time in which to start plans for a second weapons laboratory. Science, as well as any kind of technical work, thrives on friendly competition, on the fostering of different points of view, and on the exchange of ideas developed in various surroundings. It is only too easy for a single group to become fascinated by some special aspects of a development and to neglect other hopeful approaches. I felt that the safety of our country could not be entrusted to a single laboratory, even though that laboratory were as excellent as Los Alamos.

In the course of time this second laboratory was established at the Livermore site of the Radiation Laboratory of the University of California under the directorship of Herbert York. Its work so far has been mostly that of learning the difficult art of inventing and making nuclear weapons. All the magnificent achievements that have become in the meantime known to the world have been accomplished by Los Alamos. But in the intervening years a group of young experts has grown up in Livermore. The more they see that Los Alamos is a long distance ahead of them, the more eager they are to catch up. Having had the privilege of being associated with this young and vigorous group, I feel sure that the work at Los Alamos and Livermore will be mutually helpful to the two laboratories and will be of the greatest importance to the country as a whole. It is of no interest which of the two laboratories will be able to accomplish the most in the future. The only important thing is that each of them should do what it can and that together they should do what is enough.

The difficulties of the task of a weapons laboratory could be no more clearly illustrated than by describing the work of the last year that preceded the explosion of the first successful hydrogen bomb in Eniwetok. My knowledge of the details of this undertaking is not good enough, however, to justify any description or evaluation of the great work of this year, but I would like to mention the kind of difficulties that had to be faced.

Traditional engineering is thoroughly empirical. The usual sound practice is to make progress in small steps. A big plant is preceded by a small pilot plant. A full-scale device is not started until details have

been checked on models. Work on atomic bombs makes it necessary to change this conservative practice. The final device is put together without any significant model experimentation. Tests, such as Greenhouse, can give guidance to the theorists, but they give little concrete support to the engineers. Dimensions, tolerances, strange materials go into the final design which would leave traditional engineers bewildered and helpless. Los Alamos had developed in the experience of many hard years an effective method of dealing with these grotesque difficulties of hardware. I can only guess how great these actual difficulties are, but I suspect that the greatest achievement in the production of the hydrogen bomb was not the conception or the invention but the execution. The man who was in charge of this undertaking was Marshall Holloway. I hope that at some time the story of this phase of the undertaking can be told, but the most important fact is this simple one: It was difficult and it was completely successful.

In October 1952 I was kindly invited to attend the explosion of the first full-scale device called "Mike." I would have liked to go, but it was clear that I would not have been of any concrete use in the Pacific. At the same time Livermore, only a few weeks old, was requiring the fullest attention of all of its members, so I chose the second best solution, which was much less expensive in money, effort, and time. I attended the first hydrogen shot by watching the sensitive seismograph in Berkeley.

In the morning of 1 November 1952 I was shown into the basement where the seismograph was operating. This seismograph is a recording instrument that writes with the help of a fine beam of light on a photographic film. The room was completely dark except for the tiny luminous spot that the pencil of light threw on the photographic paper. After my eyes became accustomed to the darkness, I noticed that the spot seemed quite unsteady. Clearly this was more than what could be due to the continuous trembling of the earth, to the "microseisms" that are caused by the pounding of the ocean waves on the shores of the continent. It was due to the movements of my own eyes, which in the darkness were not steadied by the surrounding picture of solid objects. Soon the luminous point gave me the feeling of being aboard a gently and irregularly moving vessel, so I braced a pencil on a piece of the apparatus and held it close to the luminous point. Now the point seemed steady, and I felt as if I had come back to solid ground again. This was about the time of the actual shot. Nothing happened or could have happened. About a quarter of an hour was required for the shock to travel, deep under the Pacific basin, to the

California coast. I waited with little patience, the seismograph making at each minute a clearly visible vibration which served as a time signal. At last the time signal came that had to be followed by the shock from the explosion and there it seemed to be: the luminous point appeared to dance wildly and irregularly. Was it only that the pencil which I held as a marker trembled in my hand? I waited for many more minutes to be sure that the record did not miss any of the shocks that might follow the first. Then finally the film was taken off and developed. By that time I had almost convinced myself that I must have been mistaken and that what I saw was the motion of my own hand rather than the signal from the first hydrogen bomb. Then the trace appeared on the photographic plate. It was clear and big and unmistakable. It had been made by the wave of compression that had traveled for thousands of miles and brought the positive assurance that "Mike" was a success.

WHAT NEXT?

I believe that everyone who has worked on the hydrogen bomb was appalled by the success and by its possible consequences. I also believe that everyone who was closely or distantly connected with the effort and who made any contribution, great or small, had a clear feeling that the work was necessary in the interest of the safety of our country. To that extent I feel that all of us had an equal sense of satisfaction in the final success on 1 November 1952 at Eniwetok in the Marshall Islands.

In the whole development I want to claim credit in one respect only. I believed and continued to believe in the possibility and the necessity of developing the thermonuclear bomb. I feel that it was a great privilege that I could stay with it until a time at which the successful conclusion was in sight.

At the present time I find myself unhappily in a situation of being given certainly too much credit and perhaps too much blame for what has happened. Yet, I feel that the development of the hydrogen bomb should not divide those who in the past have argued about it but rather should unite all of us who in a close or distant way, by work or by criticism, have contributed toward its completion. Disunity of the scientists is one of the greatest dangers for our country.

The very size of our progress has opened up other dangers. We may be led to think that this accomplishment is something ultimate. I do not believe that this is so. Where the next steps will lead, I do not know. It is not likely that it will be just bigger bombs again. The world is full of surprises, and great developments rarely go along straight lines. But the skills and the knowledge that developed the A-bomb and the H-bomb can undoubtedly be turned to new directions, and we shall fail if we rest upon our accomplishments.

The greatest and most obvious danger of the hydrogen bomb is its destructive power. Some may think that it would have been better never to develop this instrument. I respect their opinion and I understand their feelings. There can be nothing more strong and definite than our desire for peace and I am sure that those who were most closely connected with the development of the new destructive weapons feel this at least as strongly as anyone else. But I also believe that we would be unfaithful to the tradition of Western civilization if we were to shy away from exploring the limits of human achievement. It is our specific duty as scientists to explore and to explain. Beyond that our responsibilities cannot be any greater than those of any other citizen of our democratic society.

It is clear and it is true that atomic bombs and hydrogen bombs are terrible and unprecedented, but so have been many other developments that past generations have faced. The construction of the thermonuclear weapon was a great challenge to the technical people of this country. To be in possession of this instrument is an even great challenge to the free community in which we live. I am confident that, whatever the scientists are able to discover or invent, the people will be good enough and wise enough to control it for the ultimate benefit of everyone.

THE STRANGE DEATH
OF LOUIS SLOTIN

STEWART ALSOP AND RALPH E. LAPP

STEWART ALSOP (1914–   ) was born in New York City and attended Yale University. He worked as editor for a New York publishing house, and after seeing action in World War II, joined with his brother, Joseph Alsop, to write the column, "Matter of Fact," for the New York Herald Tribune Syndicate. He is co-author (with Joseph Alsop) of *We Accuse* (1954), *Reporter's Trade* (1958), and *Nixon and Rockefeller* (1960).
R. E. LAPP (1917–   ) was born in Buffalo, New York, and educated at the University of Chicago. Since 1943 he has been working in nuclear physics research for the government. He is the author of *Must We Hide?* (1949), *The New Force* (1953), *Nuclear Radiation Physics* (1954), *Man and Space: The Next Decade* (1961), and *Kill and Overkill* (1962).

D R. LOUIS SLOTIN, a young and brilliant atomic scientist, began to die at precisely twenty minutes past three o'clock, on the afternoon of May 21, 1946. The story of how he began to die, and of what happened afterward—which can only now be fully told—is in some ways a rather horrible story. Yet, if only because it helps strip the mystery from the most terrifying effect of atomic weapons—the invisible killer, nuclear radiation—Louis Slotin's story is worth telling all the same.

The place where Louis Slotin began to die was a laboratory in a canyon near Los Alamos, the war-built town in New Mexico where the world's first atomic bomb was made. A few minutes after he began to die, Doctor Slotin, with the precision of a trained scientist, drew a careful chart of this laboratory, showing the exact location of its occupants at the time. From this chart, and from the accounts of those who were present and survived, it is possible accurately to reconstruct the scene.

Visualize, then, a large, oblong, white-painted room, unfurnished except for a metal desk near the center, and a table against one wall, bearing the complicated equipment of the atom-bomb-maker's trade. The spring sunshine floods obliquely through the single large window. There are eight people in the room. Their silence is broken only by the staccato clicking of a Geiger counter, as all attention is focused on a short figure standing over the metal desk.

This is Louis Slotin, thirty-four years old, five feet six inches in height, slender, wiry, his face heavily bronzed by the New Mexico sun, his black hair already graying a little at the temples. He is wearing

Copyright, 1954, by the Curtis Publishing Company. Reprinted by permission of the authors.

an open sports shirt, a rather gaudy Mexican belt and khaki trousers tucked into cowboy boots. Through thick, horn-rimmed spectacles—which betray the scientist and the intellectual, despite the cowboy boots—he is peering intently at certain objects on the desk.

These are two hollow, silvery-gray half globes of metal, which Slotin is deliberately manipulating closer to each other, using an ordinary screw driver as a lever. These hunks of metal are the guts of an atomic bomb.

Standing behind Slotin is a fellow scientist—Scientist X, we shall call him—a quiet-mannered, pleasant-faced man, also thirty-four years old. Scientist X has his hand resting casually on Slotin's shoulder, and he is leaning forward with intense interest—he has never seen this experiment before.

The six other people in the room are laboratory assistants, technicians and others gathered more or less by chance to watch the experiment. Two are standing in front of the desk, at a distance of about six feet. The four others are grouped behind the desk, at a distance of eight feet or more. The scene is a casual one. Like Slotin, the others are dressed informally, in open shirts or sweaters. Slotin himself appears confident, almost gay. He loves this experiment—"tickling the dragon's tail," he calls it—and he has already performed it at least forty times. Even so, there is a certain tension in the room. Those present are aware that manipulating the guts of an atomic bomb is no child's play.

Slotin has his ear cocked to the click of the Geiger counter, and he also glances frequently at an instrument called a "neutron monitor," which is recording on a roll of paper, in a thin, wavy line of red ink, the radiation emitted by the lumps of metal. As Slotin slowly moves the lumps, the red line staggers upward and the Geiger counter clicks erratically, always a little faster, like a deranged clock.

Suddenly the Geiger counter begins to click insanely, and then stops dead. All in a moment, the people in the room sense rather than see a strange blue glow, stronger than the spring sunlight. Instantly, Slotin throws himself forward, thrusting the half globes of deadly metal apart with his naked hands. Then he stands up, his face a chalky white beneath the tan.

In a concerted, instinctive, almost somnambulistic movement, the eight people file quickly from the room, without speaking. Some of them are aware of a dry, prickly, sour sensation on their tongues—a sign of excessive radiation. Some of them are no doubt also aware of a little flicker of fear in their hearts. Yet aside from the sour taste, they feel nothing else at all—not even Louis Slotin, who has already begun to die.

To understand what happened, and why, and what it means, it is necessary to know something about Louis Slotin, and the reason he tickled the dragon's tail. The bare facts of Slotin's thirty-four years can be quickly recited.

He was born, Louis Alexander Slotin, in 1912, of prosperous Jewish parents in Winnipeg, Canada. At the tender age of fifteen, he entered Winnipeg's University of Manitoba, and received his master-of-science degree at the equally tender age of twenty-one. He studied physics for four years at the University of London, and got his Ph.D. in 1936.

In 1937 he was in Chicago, apparently on his way home to Winnipeg, when he ran into Prof. William D. Harkins, pioneer atomic chemist of the University of Chicago. Harkins remarked that he badly needed an assistant for cyclotron work, but he had no money to pay an assistant. Slotin immediately went to work for nothing a week—a salary for which he worked for almost two years.

His work at Chicago University led him directly into the Manhattan District, the supersecret wartime atomic project. He worked for a time in Chicago, then at Indiana University, and later at Oak Ridge. In late 1943, Slotin came to Los Alamos, when the job of actually putting the atomic bomb together was started, and there he began to tickle the dragon's tail.

So much for the bare facts. The bare facts, of course, do not answer the question: What kind of man was Louis Alexander Slotin?

"No man," John Donne wrote, "is an island unto himself." Yet Louis Slotin was more nearly an island unto himself than most men. He was extraordinarily reserved. "Louis was a sweet kind of guy," one of his former colleagues has remarked, "but no one ever got to know him really well."

Even so, certain well-marked characteristics of the man emerge through the mists of time. In the first place, Slotin was a brave man—but brave in an odd sort of way. "Slotin had a positive hankering for danger," another of those who knew him says. "He seemed to be suffering from some sort of inner tension, and he was always very quiet. But he was downright gay when he was doing something dangerous."

This hankering for danger led Slotin to pester the Manhattan District authorities to allow him to accompany the first atomic bombs to their Japanese targets, as a scientific observer. When the authorities refused, Slotin was deeply depressed for weeks. And the same strange hankering no doubt also led Slotin to become the Manhattan District's chief practitioner of the art of tickling the dragon's tail.

This experiment, it must be understood, was not a kind of scientific Russian roulette which Slotin and the other young physicists at Los Alamos thought up to relieve their boredom. It was a vitally important experiment, absolutely essential to the bomb-making process—and, indeed, it is still essential today.

Fissionable material—uranium 235 and plutonium—is queer stuff. Below a certain size and weight, a lump of this very heavy, greasy-gray metal is no more dangerous than a lump of lead. But it has one special characteristic which may one day destroy civilization as we know it. For if a certain amount of this metal is brought together all in one place, a chain reaction starts within the mass of metal. It is the chain reaction, of course, which lends to the atomic bomb the power to blast and sear a whole city. The amount of the metal required for the chain reaction to start is called a "critical mass"—a "crit," to use the physicists' shorthand.

But how much is a crit? There were and are ways of calculating theoretically the amount of fissionable material required to form a critical mass. But such calculations can never be wholly precise. Moreover, in order to achieve "optimum efficiency"—for which read killing power—in an atomic bomb, the size of the crit had to be determined—and still must—under various conditions.

Even today, for reasons of security, it is necessary to be a little imprecise about the experiment which Louis Slotin performed that May day in 1946—and which his successors are still performing under very different conditions. But it can be said, accurately though unscientifically, that the idea was to shove together lumps of fissionable material in such quantities, and in such a geometric relationship to each other, that the whole amount *just* went critical. In other words, a chain reaction was permitted to begin —thus establishing the crit—but it was stopped before the material became dangerously over-critical. The problem, of course, was to know when to stop.

No one at Los Alamos had any illusions about the danger involved. There was, to be sure, no danger that Los Alamos might be blown off the face of the map if something went wrong. In order to generate true explosive power, the critical mass must somehow be held together by an outside force—this is called "maintaining assembly." Otherwise the power of the chain reaction automatically "disassembles the crit." In the meantime, however, if a true chain reaction is permitted really to get under way, the critical mass of fissionable material becomes briefly but intensely radioactive. It sends out precisely the same lethal radioactive rays as an atomic bomb does when it explodes over a city.

Slotin particularly had good reason to be aware of this danger. Before the day when Slotin tickled the dragon's tail for the last time, at least three people at Los Alamos had fallen victim to the invisible killer. One of these was Slotin's friend and laboratory assistant, Harry Daglian. Slotin spent many hours at his assistant's bedside, during the month that it took Daglian to die.

Particularly after Daglian died, those in authority at Los Alamos worried about the radiation danger. One Nobel Prize winner told Slotin, "I predict you won't last a year if you keep on doing that experiment." But Slotin happily carried on.

"Sure, it's dangerous," Slotin remarked to one colleague, "but it has to be that way." One suspects that Slotin, perhaps unconsciously, wanted it to be that way.

Ironically, on May 21, 1946, Slotin was performing his beloved experiment for what he knew to be the last time. For more than two years he had performed the experiment again and again in different ways and under various conditions. He was particularly proud of the fact that he had been chosen to test the criticality of the world's first atomic bomb—he cherished the receipt for this bomb which he got when he returned it to be exploded at Alamogordo, after having tickled its tail. Now he had been ordered to Bikini, to participate in the bomb tests there. He was eager to be off—when final orders came to perform the experiment just once more, for the benefit of Scientist X. So Slotin tickled the dragon's tail just once more—and the dragon lashed back to destroy him.

What went wrong? Part of the answer may no doubt be found in Slotin's hankering for danger— such a man may always be tempted to go too far. But part of the answer is also certainly found in the fact that Slotin, at the age of thirty-four, was already an old-fashioned scientist.

Slotin received his whole training as a physicist in the '30's, before the time when national survival depended on the special skills of his kind. It was quite typical of those days that a brilliantly qualified physicist like Slotin should work for nothing a year. In the '30's physicists led a hand-to-mouth existence, dependent for their equipment, their experiments and their livelihood, not on an anxious and munificent Government, but on the sometimes capricious generosity of a few great universities.

In those years physicists learned to perform their experiments with whatever came to hand—even an ordinary screw driver. This cavalier attitude carried over into the well-financed period of the Manhattan District, and men like Slotin had a certain pride in their own casual approach to the great and mysterious forces locked up in matter. After Daglian died, for example, a rather simple spring-actuated safety device was designed, to push the lumps of fissionable material apart as soon as they threatened to become dangerously radioactive.

Slotin would have none of it. He had, he said proudly, "a feeling for the experiment," and besides, he argued, such devices would cause accidents rather than prevent them—the experimenter would come to rely on the safety devices rather than on his own judgment.

Certain photographs which the Atomic Energy Commission recently released provide a striking contrast between present and past. These pictures show two insanely complicated "critical assembly machines"—one is rather coyly called "Topsy" and the other "Godiva" because the assembly is allowed to become only "barely" critical. There is another photograph, of the remote-control panel used to work these machines. It is straight out of George Orwell's "1984"—complete with levers, knobs, three television screens and a blond lady in an asceptic white blouse. The blond lady is, according to the AEC release, "controlling the assembly of Godiva"— at a distance of a quarter of a mile.

In other words, the blond lady is manipulating the guts of an atomic bomb, just as Louis Slotin was doing that day in May when the nuclear age was still young. But in his case, the deadly stuff was right under his nose, and he had no levers, no knobs, no television screens, no remote-control panels. He had his Geiger counter, his neutron monitor, his skill and experience—and his screw driver.

There is no doubt about what happened that day in May or about when it happened. The record of the neutron monitor which Slotin used has been preserved. A thin red-ink line mounts gradually across the paper, showing the amount of radiation emitted by the lumps of metal at each given moment. At precisely 3:20 P.M., the line simply disappears. At this precise point the radiation became so intense that the instrument was forced right off scale.

As for why it happened, no one, not even Slotin himself, was entirely sure. The experiment was almost finished—it was a matter of manipulating one last piece of metal an eighth of an inch from the rest of the assembly. "When the point of criticality was almost reached," one of those present writes, "the piece somehow slipped and the gap was closed." The "somehow" is still unexplained. But the best explanation combines the overconfidence of an over-brave man with Slotin's casual use of an ordinary screw driver to lever the deadly hunks of metal. In a word, the screw driver slipped.

At any rate, Slotin knew instantly what had happened, and his reaction was instantaneous. When he lunged forward and pulled the chunks of metal apart, he "disassembled the critical mass." If he had not done so, if he had instantly ducked away from the table, he might conceivably have saved himself. It is far more probable that he would have condemned others in the room to death.

"It is unquestionably true," Scientist X has written, "that I and perhaps others of those present owe our lives to his action. I do not know whether this is heroism or not. I suspect that Louis would have objected to such a term."

To understand the meaning of Slotin's action, it is necessary to understand something of the nature of the invisible killer. The gamma rays emitted by a chain reaction penetrate into the body of anyone sufficiently exposed, and kill individual cells deep within the body. A grim peculiarity of radiation injury is that there is a latent period before this killing of the cells becomes apparent. This is because the cells do not die until the periodic cell division—a process which is going on all the time in everyone's body—takes place. Thus in a sense, radiation injury is the opposite of cancer. Cancer kills when the cells divide and reproduce themselves too rapidly. Nuclear radiation kills when the cells fail to divide and do not reproduce themselves at all.

But, even more than in the case of cancer, it is important for all of us who live in the age of nuclear war to understand that nuclear radiation need not be fatal. Everything depends on the size of the "dose." The "dose" is measured in r's, or roentgens, of radiation. When a person receives a radiation injury, the first thing the doctors want to know is whether he has received "LD/50." This is medical shorthand for a "median lethal dose," which causes a 50 per cent average death rate.

LD/50 has never been precisely determined, simply because there have not been many human guinea pigs on whom to test the human body's resistance to radiation injury. At the time of the accident, it was thought that LD/50 was in the neighborhood of 400 roentgens. The best estimates now place LD/50 at 525 roentgens, plus or minus 75.

The number of roentgens of radiation a person receives depends principally on the power of the radiation source and the time of exposure. When Slotin lunged forward to disperse the critical assembly and break the chain reaction, he sharply reduced the danger to the other people in the room, by reducing both the power of the radiation and the time of exposure of the others. He also, of course, exposed himself to actual physical contact with the lumps of fissionable material at the very moment the chain reaction was taking place.

Within an hour of the accident, all the eight people in the laboratory were taken to the Los Alamos hospital—a temporary, wartime, shacklike, wooden structure—and placed under close observation. Other than Scientist X, the man who had been closest to Slotin was an unmarried fifty-four-year-old technician, who was standing about six feet in front of the metal desk. He was kept in the hospital for two weeks, and he showed certain symptoms of radiation injury, including measurable radio-sodium and radio-phosphorus in his urine. But he felt quite well—and six weeks later this man, who was something of an athlete, was happily hiking six miles in one day without ill effect.

Others who were standing somewhat farther away had even less reason to complain, although everyone in the room had taken a dose of radiation. So much nonsense has been spread abroad about the silent nuclear killer that many people have come to feel that it is absolutely lethal at almost any range. Actually, the athletic technician took a dose of about 100 roentgens, according to later calculations—the same dose he would have taken if he had been wholly exposed to the radiation effect of a modern, 100-kiloton atom bomb exploding at a distance of 6500 feet.

Despite the technician's rapid and complete recovery, a dose of 100 roentgens is no laughing matter. If Slotin had not reacted so quickly, if the technician had been exposed a little longer, the technician would certainly have suffered as Scientist X suffered—and he might well have died.

Scientist X, remember, was standing with his hand on Louis Slotin's shoulder, watching intently the experiment which he himself would have to perform later, when the accident happened. According to later calculations, he took a dose of about 180 roentgens. This is still well under LD/50, but it is nevertheless in the danger area. It is the same dose he would have taken if he had been about 6000 feet from a modern atomic bomb, only a few hundred feet less than the athletic technician. Where nuclear radiation is concerned, short distances can make an enormous difference.

A courageous and unexcitable man by nature, Scientist X was calm and made no complaints when he was admitted to the hospital. Shortly after being admitted, he vomited once. The feeling of nausea passed away in about ten hours, leaving Scientist X feeling weak and tired, with little appetite, but otherwise well enough. He continued thus for about five days. On the fifth day the delayed effect of the gamma rays on his cell tissue began to make itself felt. His temperature climbed close to 103 degrees, and two blood transfusions were required. For some time he felt terribly drowsy and highly irritable, but his temperature fell gradually, and after the fifteenth day he was well enough to be sent home to rest.

But the gamma rays were not yet through with him. He had lost ten pounds, and for some weeks he tired very easily, and spent upward of sixteen hours in bed each day. On the seventeenth day after the accident an unpleasant experience, which Scientist X had known enough to expect, began. On that day the skin on his left temple and on the left side of his head—which had been most exposed—began to feel sensitive. In the two following days this sensitive feeling increased to the point of acute pain. On the twentieth day Scientist X was combing his hair, and found large tufts coming out in the comb.

Thereafter, his hair came out easily by the handful. He lost almost all the hair on the left side of his head, and his beard also stopped growing over most of his left cheek. He also became temporarily sterile, according to the AEC report on the case—a normal and expected symptom of radiation damage. But the point to emphasize is that such symptoms were wholly temporary.

The only permanent aftereffect which Scientist X has suffered is a moderate radiation cataract in the left eye, which reduces his vision from 20/20 to 20/40. The fact that he has suffered no other ill effect is underscored by his brilliant subsequent contributions to our atomic-energy program, notably in the development of that most terrible of weapons, the hydrogen bomb.

In short, a man can survive even a vicious attack by the silent radiation killer on his living cell tissue. But Scientist X unquestionably had a close brush with death. Of Louis Slotin, to whom, as he says, he owes his life, Scientist X has written:

"I can perhaps tell you as much about his per-

sonality and character as I could in very many words if I merely quote to you his first statement to me when we were alone together in a hospital room. He said, 'I'm sorry I got you into this. I am afraid I have less than a fifty-fifty chance of living. I hope you have better than that.' My own estimate of our chances coincided pretty well with his. I felt I had a pretty good chance. I only hoped he had."

For some days there seemed reason for hope. Slotin vomited twice before he got to the hospital, and in the first twelve hours thereafter he continued to vomit repeatedly. But he, too, like Scientist X, recovered from his initial nausea, and his only other immediate general symptoms were a slight temperature and feeling of tiredness.

His hands of course, had taken a terrible dose, since he had used them to shove the metal apart and break the chain reaction. Within three hours Slotin's left hand became very red, swollen and bluish under the nails. Twenty-eight hours after the accident this hand began to blister painfully, and the symptoms spread to his right hand and both arms. From this time on, both arms were packed in ice, to reduce the swelling and the pain. His lower abdomen also became red and tender, and this spread gradually and became more intense.

Yet aside from these local symptoms, Slotin's general condition seemed greatly to improve after the first twenty-four hours. What had happened quickly became known throughout the Manhattan District, and everything possible was done to help him. No fewer than ten doctors were called in to consult on his case. Maj. Gen. Leslie Groves wrote to him: "I have nothing but admiration for your heroic actions. . . . Your quick reactions and disregard for the danger to yourself undoubtedly prevented a much more serious accident."

Groves' letter cheered Slotin and he was cheered more when Groves ordered a special Army plane to bring his mother and father from Winnipeg to his bedside. When they arrived, they found their son normal, composed and even downright cheerful, despite the pain in his arms. When friends and colleagues came to visit him, he would introduce them to his parents, and then ask, half jokingly, the crucial question: "Well, what's the dose?"

For five days no one knew. But on the fifth day the answer became tragically obvious—the dose was more than LD/50. That morning Slotin had a new complaint—his tongue was sore opposite a tooth which had a gold inlay. The doctors found a small whitish ulceration on his tongue, and immediately suspected the cause. The gold in his tooth was heavily radioactive. The inlay was capped with gold foil and the pain eased. But this was a bad sign.

There was a worse sign on the same day, when Anna May Dickey, then a nurse in the Los Alamos hospital, took Slotin's blood count. When she looked at the results, she began to weep. She knew the meaning of the sudden, precipitous fall in the leucocyte, or white-blood-cell, count. The silent killer was at work on Louis Slotin's blood, and the life-saving white blood cells were failing to reproduce themselves.

On this same day Slotin's pulse rate rose very rapidly. Thereafter he could eat nothing, and visibly lost weight. On the seventh day his mind began to fail, and he had long periods of mental confusion, in which he could not recognize his parents or colleagues. Gradually, he sank into a coma. Early in the morning of the ninth day, May 30, 1946, Louis Slotin quietly died.

That is about the end of Louis Slotin's story. His parents flew back to Winnipeg with his corpse, and scientists and others from all over the United States and Canada attended his funeral. His parents offered a last sacrifice to the cause of science, when they permitted an autopsy to be performed on his body, although this was against the tenets of their religion. It was later estimated, according to the Atomic Energy Commission's recently declassified report on his case, that Slotin had taken about 880 roentgens of nuclear radiation. This was as though he had been fully exposed to the explosion of a modern atomic bomb at a distance of 4800 feet. Nothing could have saved him.

Louis Slotin was not a great or famous man, and he has been in his grave now for almost eight years. Yet his story has seemed worth telling, and not only because nuclear radiation, which kills without being seen or felt, is more terrifying than need be, just because it is so mysterious. It has seemed worth telling also because it is a story of human bravery and sacrifice, qualities which may yet save a civilization threatened with destruction by the very weapons Louis Slotin helped to make.

IN BACK OF MAN,
A WORLD OF NATURE

JOSEPH WOOD KRUTCH

JOSEPH WOOD KRUTCH (1893–   ) was born in Knoxville, Tennessee, and educated at the University of Tennessee and Columbia University. He has been a professor of English since 1917, teaching and lecturing at Columbia and other universities. He was for many years drama critic and associate editor of *The Nation,* and in 1940 he became a member of the New York Drama Critics Circle. Among his many books we note: *The Modern Temper* (1929; see selection on page 539); *Living Philosophies* (1931); *Samuel Johnson* (1944); *Henry David Thoreau* (1948); *The Desert Year* (1952); *The Measure of Man* (1954), recipient of the National Book Award; and *Human Nature and the Human Condition* (1959).

IN one of Aldous Huxley's early novels a very sophisticated young man tries to explain to a naïve one why a modern poet who talks about "dreams" is doing something which simply "isn't done" any more. On his premise a modern poet must also be at least a little careful about making any reference to "Nature's soothing presence." In the halls of Congress a favorite quotation may still be "To him, who in the love of Nature, holds communion with her visible forms—" but "Thanatopsis" is not exactly a much-used model among the more esteemed contemporary poets.

On the other hand, "Nature writing" as a separate department of literature flourishes vigorously. Indeed, it is largely a phenomenon of the nineteenth and twentieth centuries. Yet it remains a thing apart, something addressed to a special group of readers called "nature lovers" who are not infrequently referred to by outsiders in the same condescending tone they would use in speaking of prohibitionists, diet cranks, Holy Rollers and the followers, if there still are any, of the late M. Coué.

Those of us who do read "nature writing" and are glad to see it flourish wonder sometimes whether its

Reprinted from *Highlights of Modern Literature* by permission of the author and The New American Library of World Literature, Inc. Copyright, 1949, 1950, 1951, 1952, 1953, 1954, by The New York Times Company.

very importance as a "department" of literature does not mean that what was once an almost inevitable motif in most imaginative writing has become something recognizably special, simply because the writers of novels and poems and plays no longer find the contemplation of nature relevant to their purposes, at least to the same extent that they once did. And we wonder whether this seeming fact is merely the result of urban living or whether "merely" is not the wrong term to use in reference to a phenomenon which may mean much more than the mere disappearance from fiction of apostrophes to the mountains.

A generation ago the first page of the epoch-making "Cambridge History of English Literature" listed among the enduring characteristics of the English people, "Love of Nature." That phrase covers something which has meant a good many different things at different times. Still, would it have suggested itself to a critic who was concerned only with the most esteemed English or American books of our time? Is there any "Love of Nature"—as distinguished from an intellectual approval of the processes of biology—in Shaw? Does T. S. Eliot find much gladness in contemplating her? Does James Joyce's apostrophe to a river count; and is Hemingway's enthusiasm for the slaughter of animals really a modern expression of that devotion to blood sports which, undoubtedly, is a rather incongruous aspect of the English race's "Love of Nature"? In America Robert Frost is almost the only poet universally recognized as of major importance in whom the loving contemplation of the natural world seems the central activity from which the poetry springs.

All this is probably the result of something more than mere fashion. Ridicule of merely conventional description in fiction has long been familiar, and Mark Twain once tested his theory that readers skip it by inserting a paragraph which told how a solitary esophagus might have been seen winging its way across the sunset. On the other hand, observations of natural phenomenon do still get into fiction. Thus "The Grapes of Wrath" begins with the symbolical use of a turtle crossing the highway, and nearly everyone knows by now that at least one tree did grow in Brooklyn. Nevertheless and somewhere along the road, most modern writers have lost the sense that Nature is the most meaningful background of human life. They see their characters as part of society or, more specifically, as part of some profession or industry, or of some "class" rather than as part of Nature. Neither her appearance nor her ways any longer seem —to use a favorite contemporary term—as "relevant" as they once did. She is not often, nowadays, invoked to furnish the resolution of an emotional problem.

Whistler was probably the first English-speaking writer ever to say flatly: "Nature is usually wrong." Of course, he meant to be shocking and he also meant, "artistically wrong"—unpictorially or badly composed. Certainly most contemporary painting and sculpture are the products of hearty agreement with this dictum. Either natural objects are so distorted in the effort to correct Nature's wrongness that they are just barely recognizable, or the artist, refusing to look at Nature at all, plays at being God by attempting to create a whole new universe of man-made shapes. In either case the assumption is that modern man feels more at home, and gets more emotional satisfaction, in this world of his own making than in the world which Nature gave him.

Only the most extreme forms of "experimental" writing go anything like so far. Only the poets of dadaism produce literary analogues to "abstract" painting. Yet without being for the most part even aware of a theory about what they are doing, many novelists and poets have obviously ceased to feel either that the most meaningful physical setting for their characters is the fields and woods—or that the most meaningful intellectual and emotional context of their difficulties and problems is the natural world, rather than the world of exclusively human concepts.

This amounts to much more than a mere loss of faith in the dogma, "Nature never did betray the heart that loved her." It amounts also to more than the somewhat romantic Victorian distress in the face of the red tooth and red claw. It means that such writers find neither God dwelling in the light of setting suns nor even a very important aspect of the problem of evil in Nature's often careless cruelty. Faced with either the beauty or the ruthlessness of Nature their reactions seem to be rather a mere "So what?" Their own achievements and difficulties seem to them to lie in a different realm.

It is against this attitude that the nature writer is protesting, sometimes consciously and sometimes not. Thoreau is the founder as well as the most important member of the school because he so successfully combined a deep personal relationship to Nature with a clear sense of the meaning of the issue between him and those who did not feel that Nature was "relevant."

The nineteenth century invented the phrase "man's place in Nature" and Thoreau made it his business ceaselessly to insist that the phrase had much more than a merely scientific implication. It did not imply merely, or even most importantly, that, for example, man was descended from the apes and therefore still ape-like in many of his characteristics—a theory, by the way, of which he had only heard vaguely just before he died. What it really meant was that Nature supplied the inescapable context of man's life, physically and spiritually; that he could not, without unhappiness and ultimate disaster, cut himself off completely from either her sights and sounds or from the sense that he and she were part of a large enterprise together.

Nothing is more obvious than the fact that modern literature is among the most unhappy which the whole art of imaginative writing has ever produced or that it is unhappiest when, as in Kafka, the natural world does not appear in it. Thoreau, on the other hand, is nearly unique as a man who, insistently and persistently, proclaimed his own felicity. "I have heard," he wrote once, "no bad news." No doubt it would be dangerous to conclude too much from these facts. Yet, on the whole, "nature writing" is happy writing and, on the whole, the novelists and the poets in whose work Nature plays a large part have been those who found human life most acceptable.

Though many nowadays find the world which man has made predominantly ugly, the natural world is nearly always beautiful. It does not seem that it should be too hard to make out a case for the contention that an unhappy generation might do well to contemplate that natural world more frequently and with greater interest.

TRAGEDY AND THE COMMON MAN

ARTHUR MILLER

For a note on Arthur Miller, see page 374.

IN this age few tragedies are written. It has often been held that the lack is due to a paucity of heroes among us, or else that modern man has had the blood drawn out of his organs of belief by the skepticism of science, and the heroic attack on life cannot feed on an attitude of reserve and circumspection. For one reason or another, we are often held to be below tragedy—or tragedy above us. The inevitable conclusion is, of course, that the tragic mode is archaic, fit only for the very highly placed, the kings or the kingly, and where this admission is not made in so many words it is most often implied.

I believe that the common man is as apt a subject for tragedy in its highest sense as kings were. On the face of it this ought to be obvious in the light of modern psychiatry, which bases its analysis upon classic formulations, such as the Oedipus and Orestes complexes, for instances, which were enacted by royal beings, but which apply to everyone in similar emotional situations.

More simply, when the question of tragedy in art is not at issue, we never hesitate to attribute to the well-placed and the exalted the very same mental processes as the lowly. And finally, if the exaltation of tragic action were truly a property of the high-bred character alone, it is inconceivable that the mass of mankind should cherish tragedy above all other forms, let alone be capable of understanding it.

As a general rule, to which there may be exceptions unknown to me, I think the tragic feeling is evoked in us when we are in the presence of a character who is ready to lay down his life, if need be, to secure one thing—his sense of personal dignity. From Orestes to Hamlet, Medea to Macbeth, the underlying struggle is that of the individual attempting to gain his "rightful" position in his society.

Sometimes he is one who has been displaced from it, sometimes one who seeks to attain it for the first time, but the fateful wound from which the inevitable events spiral is the wound of indignity, and its dominant force is indignation. Tragedy, then, is the consequence of a man's total compulsion to evaluate himself justly.

Copyright © *The New York Times,* 1949; reprinted by permission of the author.

In the sense of having been initiated by the hero himself, the tale always reveals what has been called his "tragic flaw," a failing that is not peculiar to grand or elevated characters. Nor is it necessarily a weakness. The flaw, or crack in the character, is really nothing—and need be nothing, but his inherent unwillingness to remain passive in the face of what he conceives to be a challenge to his dignity, his image of his rightful status. Only the passive, only those who accept their lot without active retaliation, are "flawless." Most of us are in that category.

But there are among us today, as there always have been, those who act against the scheme of things that degrades them, and in the process of action everything we have accepted out of fear or insensitivity or ignorance is shaken before us and examined, and from this total onslaught by an individual against the seemingly stable cosmos surrounding us—from this total examination of the "unchangeable" environment—comes the terror and the fear that is classically associated with tragedy.

More important, from this total questioning of what has previously been unquestioned, we learn. And such a process is not beyond the common man. In revolutions around the world, these past thirty years, he has demonstrated again and again this inner dynamic of all tragedy.

Insistence upon the rank of the tragic hero, or the so-called nobility of his character, is really but a clinging to the outward forms of tragedy. If rank or nobility of character was indispensable, then it would follow that the problems of those with rank were the particular problems of tragedy. But surely the right of one monarch to capture the domain from another no longer raises our passions, nor are our concepts of justice what they were to the mind of an Elizabethan king.

The quality in such plays that does shake us, however, derives from the underlying fear of being displaced, the disaster inherent in being torn away from our chosen image of what and who we are in this world. Among us today this fear is as strong, and perhaps stronger, than it ever was. In fact, it is the common man who knows this fear best.

Now, if it is true that tragedy is the consequence of a man's total compulsion to evaluate himself justly, his destruction in the attempt posits a wrong or an evil in his environment. And this is precisely the morality of tragedy and its lesson. The discovery of the moral law, which is what the enlightenment of tragedy consists of, is not the discovery of some abstract or metaphysical quantity.

The tragic right is a condition of life, a condition in which the human personality is able to flower and realize itself. The wrong is the condition which suppresses man, perverts the flowing out of his love and creative instinct. Tragedy enlightens—and it must, in that it points the heroic finger at the enemy of man's freedom. The thrust for freedom is the quality in tragedy which exalts. The revolutionary questioning of the stable environment is what terrifies. In no way is the common man debarred from such thoughts or such actions.

Seen in this light, our lack of tragedy may be partially accounted for by the turn which modern literature has taken toward the purely psychiatric view of life, or the purely sociological. If all our miseries, our indignities, are born and bred within our minds, then all action, let alone the heroic action, is obviously impossible.

And if society alone is responsible for the cramping of our lives, then the protagonist must needs be so pure and faultless as to force us to deny his validity as a character. From neither of these views can tragedy derive, simply because neither represents a balanced concept of life. Above all else, tragedy requires the finest appreciation by the writer of cause and effect.

No tragedy can therefore come about when its author fears to question absolutely everything, when he regards any institution, habit or custom as being either everlasting, immutable or inevitable. In the tragic view the need of man to wholly realize himself is the only fixed star, and whatever it is that hedges his nature and lowers it is ripe for attack and examination. Which is not to say that tragedy must preach revolution.

The Greeks could probe the very heavenly origin of their ways and return to confirm the rightness of laws. And Job could face God in anger, demanding his right and end in submission. But for a moment everything is in suspension, nothing is accepted, and in this stretching and tearing apart of the cosmos, in the very action of so doing, the character gains "size," the tragic stature which is spuriously attached to the royal or the high-born in our minds. The commonest of men may take on that stature to the extent of his willingness to throw all he has into the contest, the battle to secure his rightful place in his world.

There is a misconception of tragedy with which I have been struck in review after review, and in many conversations with writers and readers alike. It is the idea that tragedy is of necessity allied to pessimism. Even the dictionary says nothing more about the word than that it means a story with a sad or unhappy ending. This impression is so firmly fixed that I almost hesitate to claim that in truth tragedy implies more optimism in its author than does comedy, and that its final result ought to be the reinforcement of the onlooker's brightest opinions of the human animal.

For, if it is true to say that in essence the tragic hero is intent upon claiming his whole due as a personality, and if this struggle must be total and without reservation, then it automatically demonstrates the indestructible will of man to achieve his humanity.

The possibility of victory must be there in tragedy. Where pathos rules, where pathos is finally derived, a character has fought a battle he could not possibly have won. The pathetic is achieved when the protagonist is, by virtue of his witlessness, his insensitivity or the very air he gives off, incapable of grappling with a much superior force.

Pathos truly is the mode for the pessimist. But tragedy requires a nicer balance between what is possible and what is impossible. And it is curious, although edifying, that the plays we revere, century after century, are the tragedies. In them, and in them alone, lies the belief—optimistic, if you will, in the perfectibility of man.

It is time, I think, that we who are without kings, took up this bright thread of our history and followed it to the only place it can possibly lead in our time—the heart and spirit of the average man.

THE TRAGIC FALLACY

JOSEPH WOOD KRUTCH

For a note on Joseph Wood Krutch, see page 534.

THROUGH the legacy of their art the great ages have transmitted to us a dim image of their glorious vitality. When we turn the pages of a Sophoclean or a Shakespearean tragedy we participate faintly in the experience which created it and we sometimes presumptuously say that we "understand" the spirit of these works. But the truth is that we see them, even at best and in the moments when our souls expand most nearly to their dimensions, through a glass darkly.

It is so much easier to appreciate than to create that an age too feeble to reach the heights achieved by the members of a preceding one can still see those heights towering above its impotence, and so it is that, when we perceive a Sophocles or a Shakespeare soaring in an air which we can never hope to breathe, we say that we can "appreciate" them. But what we mean is that we are just able to wonder, and we can never hope to participate in the glorious vision of human life out of which they were created —not even to the extent of those humbler persons for whom they were written; for while to us the triumphant voices come from far away and tell of a heroic world which no longer exists, to them they spoke of immediate realities and revealed the inner meaning of events amidst which they still lived.

When the life has entirely gone out of a work of art come down to us from the past, when we read it without any emotional comprehension whatsoever and can no longer even imagine why the people for whom it was intended found it absorbing and satisfying, then, of course, it has ceased to be a work of art at all and has dwindled into one of those deceptive "documents" from which we get a false sense of comprehending through the intellect things which cannot be comprehended at all except by means of a kinship of feeling. And though all works from a past age have begun in this way to fade there are some, like the great Greek or Elizabethan tragedies, which are still halfway between the work of art and the document. They no longer can have for us the im-

From *The Modern Temper* by Joseph Wood Krutch, copyright, 1929, by Harcourt, Brace & World, Inc.; renewed, 1957, by Joseph Wood Krutch. Reprinted by permission of the publishers.

mediacy which they had for those to whom they originally belonged, but they have not yet eluded us entirely. We no longer live in the world which they represent, but we can half imagine it and we can measure the distance which we have moved away. We write no tragedies today, but we can still talk about the tragic spirit of which we would, perhaps, have no conception were it not for the works in question.

An age which could really "appreciate" Shakespeare or Sophocles would have something comparable to put beside them—something like them, not necessarily in form, or spirit, but at least in magnitude—some vision of life which would be, however different, equally ample and passionate. But when we move to put a modern masterpiece beside them, when we seek to compare them with, let us say, a *Ghosts* or a *Weavers,* we shrink as from the impulse to commit some folly and we feel as though we were about to superimpose Bowling Green upon the Great Prairies in order to ascertain which is the larger. The question, we see, is not primarily one of art but of the two worlds which two minds inhabited. No increased powers of expression, no greater gift for words, could have transformed Ibsen into Shakespeare. The materials out of which the latter created his works—his conception of human dignity, his sense of the importance of human passions, his vision of the amplitude of human life—simply did not and could not exist for Ibsen, as they did not and could not exist for his contemporaries. God and Man and Nature had all somehow dwindled in the course of the intervening centuries, not because the realistic creed of modern art led us to seek out mean people, but because this meanness of human life was somehow thrust upon us by the operation of that same process which led to the development of realistic theories of art by which our vision could be justified.

Hence, though we still apply, sometimes, the adjective "tragic" to one or another of those modern works of literature which describe human misery and which end more sadly even than they begin, the term is a misnomer since it is obvious that the works in question have nothing in common with the classical examples of the genre and produce in the reader a sense of depression which is the exact opposite of that elation generated when the spirit of a Shakespeare rises joyously superior to the outward calamities which he recounts and celebrates the greatness of the human spirit whose travail he describes. Tragedies, in that only sense of the word which has any distinctive meaning, are no longer written in either the dramatic or any other form and the fact is not to be accounted for in any merely literary terms. It is not the result of any fashion in literature or of any deliberation to write about human nature or character under different aspects, any more than it is of either any greater sensitiveness of feeling which would make us shrink from the contemplation of the suffering of Medea or Othello or of any greater optimism which would make us more likely to see life in more cheerful terms. It is, on the contrary, the result of one of those enfeeblements of the human spirit not unlike that described in the previous chapter of this essay, and a further illustration of that gradual weakening of man's confidence in his ability to impose upon the phenomenon of life an interpretation acceptable to his desires which is the subject of the whole of the present discussion.

To explain that fact and to make clear how the creation of classical tragedy did consist in the successful effort to impose such a satisfactory interpretation will require, perhaps, the special section which follows, although the truth of the fact that it does impose such an interpretation must be evident to any one who has ever risen from the reading of *Oedipus* or *Lear* with that feeling of exultation which comes when we have been able, by rare good fortune, to enter into its spirit as completely as it is possible for us of a remoter and emotionally enfeebled age to enter it. Meanwhile one anticipatory remark may be ventured. If the plays and the novels of today deal with littler people and less mighty emotions it is not because we have become interested in commonplace souls and their unglamorous adventures but because we have come, willy-nilly, to see the soul of man as commonplace and its emotions as mean.

II

Tragedy, said Aristotle, is the "imitation of noble actions," and though it is some twenty-five hundred years since the dictum was uttered there is only one respect in which we are inclined to modify it. To us "imitation" seems a rather naïve word to apply to that process by which observation is turned into art, and we seek one which would define or at least imply the nature of that interposition of the personality of the artist between the object and the be-

holder which constitutes his function and by means of which he transmits a modified version, rather than a mere imitation, of the thing which he has contemplated.

In the search for this word the estheticians of romanticism invented the term "expression" to describe the artistic purpose to which apparent imitation was subservient. Psychologists, on the other hand, feeling that the artistic process was primarily one by which reality is modified in such a way as to render it more acceptable to the desires of the artists, employed various terms in the effort to describe that distortion which the wish may produce in vision. And though many of the newer critics reject both romanticism and psychology, even they insist upon the fundamental fact that in art we are concerned, not with mere imitation, but with the imposition of some form upon the material which it would not have if it were merely copied as a camera copies.

Tragedy is not, then, as Aristotle said, the *imitation* of noble actions, for, indeed, no one knows what a *noble* action is or whether or not such a thing as nobility exists in nature apart from the mind of man. Certainly the action of Achilles in dragging the dead body of Hector around the walls of Troy and under the eyes of Andromache, who had begged to be allowed to give it decent burial, is not to us a noble action, though it was such to Homer, who made it the subject of a noble passage in a noble poem. Certainly, too, the same action might conceivably be made the subject of a tragedy and the subject of a farce, depending upon the way in which it was treated; so that to say that tragedy is the *imitation* of a *noble* action is to be guilty of assuming, first, that art and photography are the same, and, second, that there may be something inherently noble in an act as distinguished from the motives which prompted it or from the point of view from which it is regarded.

And yet, nevertheless, the idea of nobility is inseparable from the idea of tragedy, which cannot exist without it. If tragedy is not the imitation or even the modified representation of noble actions it is certainly a representation of actions *considered* as noble, and herein lies its essential nature, since no man can conceive it unless he is capable of believing in the greatness and importance of man. Its action is usually, if not always, calamitous, because it is only in calamity that the human spirit has the opportunity to reveal itself triumphant over the outward universe which fails to conquer it; but this calamity in tragedy is only a means to an end and the essential thing which distinguishes real tragedy from those distressing modern works sometimes called by its name is the fact that it is in the former alone that the artist has found himself capable of considering and of making us consider that his people and his actions have that amplitude and importance which make them noble. Tragedy arises then when, as in Periclean Greece or Elizabethan England, a people fully aware of the calamities of life is nevertheless serenely confident of the greatness of man, whose mighty passions and supreme fortitude are revealed when one of these calamities overtakes him.

To those who mistakenly think of it as something gloomy or depressing, who are incapable of recognizing the elation which its celebration of human greatness inspires, and who, therefore, confuse it with things merely miserable or pathetic, it must be a paradox that the happiest, most vigorous, and most confident ages which the world has ever known—the Periclean and the Elizabethan—should be exactly those which created and which most relished the mightiest tragedies; but the paradox is, of course, resolved by the fact that tragedy is essentially an expression, not of despair, but of the triumph over despair and of confidence in the value of human life. If Shakespeare himself ever had that "dark period" which his critics and biographers have imagined for him, it was at least no darkness like that bleak and arid despair which sometimes settles over modern spirits. In the midst of it he created both the elemental grandeur of Othello and the pensive majesty of Hamlet and, holding them up to his contemporaries, he said in the words of his own Miranda, "Oh, rare new world that hath *such* creatures in it."

All works of art which deserve their name have a happy end. This is indeed the thing which constitutes them art and through which they perform their function. Whatever the character of the events, fortunate or unfortunate, which they recount, they so mold or arrange or interpret them that we accept gladly the conclusion which they reach and would not have it otherwise. They may conduct us into the realm of pure fancy where wish and fact are identical and the world is remade exactly after the fashion of the heart's desire or they may yield some greater or less allegiance to fact; but they must always reconcile us in one way or another to the representation which they make and the distinctions between the genres are simply the distinctions between the means by which this reconciliation is effected.

Comedy laughs the minor mishaps of its characters away; drama solves all the difficulties which it allows to arise; and melodrama, separating good from evil by simple lines, distributes its rewards and punishments in accordance with the principles of a naïve justice which satisfies the simple souls of its audience, which are neither philosophical enough to

question its primitive ethics nor critical enough to object to the way in which its neat events violate the laws of probability. Tragedy, the greatest and the most difficult of the arts, can adopt none of these methods; and yet it must reach its own happy end in its own way. Though its conclusions must be, by its premise, outwardly calamitous, though it must speak to those who know that the good man is cut off and that the fairest things are the first to perish, yet it must leave them, as *Othello* does, content that this is so. We must be and we are glad that Juliet dies and glad that Lear is turned out into the storm.

Milton set out, he said, to justify the ways of God to man, and his phrase, if it be interpreted broadly enough, may be taken as describing the function of all art, which must, in some way or other, make the life which it seems to represent satisfactory to those who see its reflection in the magic mirror, and it must gratify or at least reconcile the desires of the beholder, not necessarily, as the naïve exponents of Freudian psychology maintain, by gratifying individual and often eccentric wishes, but at least by satisfying the universally human desire to find in the world some justice, some meaning, or, at the very least, some recognizable order. Hence it is that every real tragedy, however tremendous it may be, is an affirmation of faith in life, a declaration that even if God is not in his Heaven, then at least Man is in his world.

We accept gladly the outward defeats which it describes for the sake of the inward victories which it reveals. Juliet died, but not before she had shown how great and resplendent a thing love could be; Othello plunged the dagger into his own breast, but not before he had revealed that greatness of soul which makes his death seem unimportant. Had he died in the instant when he struck the blow, had he perished still believing that the world was as completely black as he saw it before the innocence of Desdemona was revealed to him, then, for him at least, the world would have been merely damnable, but Shakespeare kept him alive long enough to allow him to learn his error and hence to die, not in despair, but in the full acceptance of the tragic reconciliation to life. Perhaps it would be pleasanter if men could believe what the child is taught—that the good are happy and that things turn out as they should—but it is far more important to be able to believe, as Shakespeare did, that however much things in the outward world may go awry, man has, nevertheless, splendors of his own and that, in a word, Love and Honor and Glory are not words but realities.

Thus for the great ages tragedy is not an expression of despair but the means by which they saved themselves from it. It is a profession of faith, and a sort of religion; a way of looking at life by virtue of which it is robbed of its pain. The sturdy soul of the tragic author seizes upon suffering and uses it only as a means by which joy may be wrung out of existence, but it is not to be forgotten that he is enabled to do so only because of his belief in the greatness of human nature and because, though he has lost the child's faith in life, he has not lost his far more important faith in human nature. A tragic writer does not have to believe in God, but he must believe in man.

And if, then, the Tragic Spirit is in reality the product of a religious faith in which, sometimes at least, faith in the greatness of God is replaced by faith in the greatness of man, it serves, of course, to perform the function of religion, to make life tolerable for those who participate in its beneficent illusion. It purges the souls of those who might otherwise despair and it makes endurable the realization that the events of the outward world do not correspond with the desires of the heart, and thus, in its own particular way, it does what all religions do, for it gives a rationality, a meaning, and a justification to the universe. But if it has the strength it has also the weakness of all faiths, since it may—nay, it must—be ultimately lost as reality, encroaching further and further into the realm of imagination, leaves less and less room in which that imagination can build its refuge.

III

It is, indeed, only at a certain stage in the development of the realistic intelligence of a people that the tragic faith can exist. A naïver people may have, as the ancient men of the north had, a body of legends which are essentially tragic, or it may have only (and need only) its happy and childlike mythology which arrives inevitably at its happy end, where the only ones who suffer "deserve" to do so and in which, therefore, life is represented as directly and easily acceptable. A too sophisticated society on the other hand—one which, like ours, has outgrown not merely the simple optimism of the child but also that vigorous, one might almost say adolescent, faith in the nobility of man which marks a Sophocles or a Shakespeare, has neither fairy tales to assure it that all is always right in the end nor tragedies to make it believe that it rises superior in soul to the outward calamities which befall it.

Distrusting its thought, despising its passions, realizing its impotent unimportance in the universe, it can tell itself no stories except those which make it still more acutely aware of its trivial miseries. When

its heroes (sad misnomer for the pitiful creatures who people contemporary fiction) are struck down it is not, like Oedipus, by the gods that they are struck but only, like Oswald Alving, by syphilis, for they know that the gods, even if they existed, would not trouble with them, and they cannot attribute to themselves in art an importance in which they do not believe. Their so-called tragedies do not and cannot end with one of those splendid calamities which in Shakespeare seem to reverberate through the universe, because they cannot believe that the universe trembles when their love is, like Romeo's, cut off or when the place where they (small as they are) have gathered up their trivial treasure is, like Othello's sanctuary, defiled. Instead, mean misery piles on mean misery, petty misfortune follows petty misfortune, and despair becomes intolerable because it is no longer even significant or important.

Ibsen once made one of his characters say that he did not read much because he found reading "irrelevant," and the adjective was brilliantly chosen because it held implications even beyond those of which Ibsen was consciously aware. What is it that made the classics irrelevant to him and to us? Is it not just exactly those to him impossible premises which make tragedy what it is, those assumptions that the soul of man is great, that the universe (together with whatever gods may be) concerns itself with him and that he is, in a word, noble? Ibsen turned to village politics for exactly the same reason that his contemporaries and his successors have, each in his own way, sought out some aspect of the common man and his common life—because, that is to say, here was at least something small enough for him to be able to believe.

Bearing this fact in mind, let us compare a modern "tragedy" with one of the great works of a happy age, not in order to judge of their relative technical merits but in order to determine to what extent the former deserves its name by achieving a tragic solution capable of purging the soul or of reconciling the emotions to the life which it pictures. And in order to make the comparison as fruitful as possible let us choose *Hamlet* on the one hand and on the other a play like *Ghosts* which was not only written by perhaps the most powerful as well as the most typical of modern writers but which is, in addition, the one of his works which seems most nearly to escape that triviality which cannot be entirely escaped by any one who feels, as all contemporary minds do, that man is relatively trivial.

In *Hamlet* a prince ("in understanding, how like a god!") has thrust upon him from the unseen world a duty to redress a wrong which concerns not merely him, his mother, and his uncle, but the moral order of the universe. Erasing all trivial fond records from his mind, abandoning at once both his studies and his romance because it has been his good fortune to be called upon to take part in an action of cosmic importance, he plunges (at first) not into action but into thought, weighing the claims which are made upon him and contemplating the grandiose complexities of the universe. And when the time comes at last for him to die he dies, not as a failure, but as a success. Not only has the universe regained the balance which had been upset by what *seemed* the monstrous crime of the guilty pair ("there is nothing either good nor ill but thinking makes it so"), but in the process by which that readjustment is made a mighty mind has been given the opportunity, first to contemplate the magnificent scheme of which it is a part, and then to demonstrate the greatness of its spirit by playing a role in the grand style which is called for. We do not need to despair in *such* a world if it has *such* creatures in it.

Turn now to *Ghosts*—look upon this picture and upon that. A young man has inherited syphilis from his father. Struck by a to him mysterious malady he returns to his northern village, learns the hopeless truth about himself, and persuades his mother to poison him. The incidents prove, perhaps, that pastors should not endeavor to keep a husband and wife together unless they know what they are doing. But what a world is this in which a great writer can deduce nothing more than that from his greatest work and how are we to be purged or reconciled when we see it acted? Not only is the failure utter, but it is trivial and meaningless as well.

Yet the journey from Elsinore to Skien is precisely the journey which the human spirit has made, exchanging in the process princes for invalids and gods for disease. We say, as Ibsen would say, that the problems of Oswald Alving are more "relevant" to our life than the problems of Hamlet, that the play in which he appears is more "real" than the other more glamorous one, but it is exactly because we find it so that we are condemned. We can believe in Oswald but we cannot believe in Hamlet, and a light has gone out in the universe. Shakespeare justifies the ways of God to man, but in Ibsen there is no such happy end and with him tragedy, so called, has become merely an expression of our despair at finding that such justification is no longer possible.

Modern critics have sometimes been puzzled to account for the fact that the concern of ancient tragedy is almost exclusively with kings and courts. They have been tempted to accuse even Aristotle of a certain naïveté in assuming (as he seems to assume) that the "nobility" of which he speaks as

necessary to a tragedy implies a nobility of rank as well as of soul, and they have sometimes regretted that Shakespeare did not devote himself more than he did to the serious consideration of those common woes of the common man which subsequent writers have exploited with increasing pertinacity. Yet the tendency to lay the scene of a tragedy at the court of a king is not the result of any arbitrary convention but of the fact that the tragic writers believed easily in greatness just as we believe easily in meanness. To Shakespeare, robes and crowns and jewels are the garments most appropriate to man because they are the fitting outward manifestation of his inward majesty, but to us they seem absurd because the man who bears them has, in our estimation, so pitifully shrunk. We do not write about kings because we do not believe that any man is worthy to be one and we do not write about courts because hovels seem to us to be dwellings more appropriate to the creatures who inhabit them. Any modern attempt to dress characters in robes ends only by making us aware of a comic incongruity and any modern attempt to furnish them with a language resplendent like Shakespeare's ends only in bombast.

True tragedy capable of performing its function and of purging the soul by reconciling man to his woes can exist only by virtue of a certain pathetic fallacy far more inclusive than that to which the name is commonly given. The romantics, feeble descendants of the tragic writers to whom they are linked by their effort to see life and nature in grandiose terms, loved to imagine that the sea or the sky had a way of according itself with their moods, of storming when they stormed and smiling when they smiled. But the tragic spirit sustains itself by an assumption much more far-reaching and no more justified. Man as it sees him lives in a world which he may not dominate but which is always aware of him. Occupying the exact center of a universe which would have no meaning except for him and being so little below the angels that, if he believes in God, he has no hesitation in imagining Him formed as he is formed and crowned with a crown like that which he or one of his fellows wears, he assumes that each of his acts reverberates through the universe. His passions are important to him because he believes them important throughout all time and all space; the very fact that he can sin (no modern can) means that this universe is watching his acts; and though he may perish, a God leans out from infinity to strike him down. And it is exactly because an Ibsen cannot think of man in any such terms as these that his persons have so shrunk and that his "tragedy" has lost that power which real tragedy always has of making that infinitely ambitious creature called man content to accept his misery if only he can be made to feel great enough and important enough. An Oswald is not a Hamlet chiefly because he has lost that tie with the natural and supernatural world which the latter had. No ghost will leave the other world to warn or encourage him, there is no virtue and no vice which he can possibly have which can be really important, and when he dies neither his death nor the manner of it will be, outside the circle of two or three people as unnecessary as himself, any more important than that of a rat behind the arras.

Perhaps we may dub the illusion upon which the tragic spirit is nourished the Tragic, as opposed to the Pathetic, Fallacy, but fallacy though it is, upon its existence depends not merely the writing of tragedy but the existence of that religious feeling of which tragedy is an expression and by means of which a people aware of the dissonances of life manages nevertheless to hear them as harmony. Without it neither man nor his passions can seem great enough or important enough to justify the sufferings which they entail, and literature, expressing the mood of a people, begins to despair where once it had exulted. Like the belief in love and like most of the other mighty illusions by means of which human life has been given a value, the Tragic Fallacy depends ultimately upon the assumption which man so readily makes that something outside his own being, some "spirit not himself"—be it God, Nature, or that still vaguer thing called a Moral Order—joins him in the emphasis which he places upon this or that and confirms him in his feeling that his passions and his opinions are important. When his instinctive faith in that correspondence between the outer and the inner world fades, his grasp upon the faith that sustained him fades also, and Love or Tragedy or what not ceases to be the reality which it was because he is never strong enough in his own insignificant self to stand alone in a universe which snubs him with its indifference.

In both the modern and the ancient worlds tragedy was dead long before writers were aware of the fact. Seneca wrote his frigid melodramas under the impression that he was following in the footsteps of Sophocles, and Dryden probably thought that his All for Love was an improvement upon Shakespeare, but in time we awoke to the fact that no amount of rhetorical bombast could conceal the fact that grandeur was not to be counterfeited when the belief in its possibility was dead, and turning from the hero to the common man, we inaugurated the era of realism. For us no choice remains except that between mere rhetoric and the frank consideration of our fellow men, who may be the highest of the anthropoids but who are certainly too far below the

angels to imagine either that these angels can concern themselves with them or that they can catch any glimpse of even the soles of angelic feet. We can no longer tell tales of the fall of noble men because we do not believe that noble men exist. The best that we can achieve is pathos and the most that we can do is to feel sorry for ourselves. Man has put off his royal robes and it is only in sceptered pomp that tragedy can come sweeping by.

IV

Nietzsche was the last of the great philosophers to attempt a tragic justification of life. His central and famous dogma—"Life is good because it is painful"—sums up in a few words the desperate and almost meaningless paradox to which he was driven in his effort to reduce to rational terms the far more imaginative conception which is everywhere present but everywhere unanalyzed in a Sophocles or a Shakespeare and by means of which they rise triumphant over the manifold miseries of life. But the very fact that Nietzsche could not even attempt to state in any except intellectual terms an attitude which is primarily unintellectual and to which, indeed, intellectual analysis is inevitably fatal, is proof of the distance which he had been carried (by the rationalizing tendencies of the human mind) from the possibility of the tragic solution which he sought; and the confused, half-insane violence of his work will reveal, by the contrast which it affords with the serenity of the tragic writers whom he admired, how great was his failure.

Fundamentally this failure was, moreover, conditioned by exactly the same thing which has conditioned the failure of all modern attempts to achieve what he attempted—by the fact, that is to say, that tragedy must have a hero if it is not to be merely an accusation against, instead of a justification of, the world in which it occurs. Tragedy is, as Aristotle said, an imitation of noble actions, and Nietzsche, for all his enthusiasm for the Greek tragic writers, was palsied by the universally modern incapacity to conceive man as noble. Out of this dilemma, out of his need to find a hero who could give to life as he saw it the only possible justification, was born the idea of the Superman, but the Superman is, after all, only a hypothetical being, destined to become what man actually was in the eyes of the great tragic writers—a creature (as Hamlet said) "how infinite in capacities, in understanding how like a god." Thus Nietzsche lived half in the past through his literary enthusiasms and half in the future through his grandiose dreams, but for all his professed determination to justify existence he was no more able than the rest of us to find the present acceptable. Life, he said in effect, is not a Tragedy now but perhaps it will be when the Ape-man has been transformed into a hero (the Übermensch), and trying to find that sufficient, he went mad.

He failed, as all moderns must fail when they attempt, like him, to embrace the tragic spirit as a religious faith, because the resurgence of that faith is not an intellectual but a vital phenomenon, something not achieved by taking thought but born, on the contrary, out of an instinctive confidence in life which is nearer to the animal's unquestioning allegiance to the scheme of nature than it is to that critical intelligence characteristic of a fully developed humanism. And like other faiths it is not to be recaptured merely by reaching an intellectual conviction that it would be desirable to do so.

Modern psychology has discovered (or at least strongly emphasized) the fact that under certain conditions desire produces belief, and having discovered also that the more primitive a given mentality the more completely are its opinions determined by its wishes, modern psychology has concluded that the best mind is that which most resists the tendency to believe a thing simply because it would be pleasant or advantageous to do so. But justified as this conclusion may be from the intellectual point of view, it fails to take into account the fact that in a universe as badly adapted as this one to human as distinguished from animal needs this ability to will a belief may bestow an enormous vital advantage as it did, for instance, in the case at present under discussion where it made possible for Shakespeare the compensations of a tragic faith completely inaccessible to Nietzsche. Pure intelligence, incapable of being influenced by desire and therefore also incapable of choosing one opinion rather than another simply because the one chosen is the more fruitful or beneficent, is doubtless a relatively perfect instrument for the pursuit of truth, but the question (likely, it would seem, to be answered in the negative) is simply whether or not the spirit of man can endure the literal and inhuman truth.

Certain ages and simple people have conceived of the action which passes upon the stage of the universe as of something in the nature of a Divine Comedy, as something, that is to say, which will reach its end with the words "and they lived happily ever after." Others, less naïve and therefore more aware of those maladjustments whose reality, at least

so far as outward events are concerned, they could not escape, have imposed upon it another artistic form and called it a Divine Tragedy, accepting its catastrophe as we accept the catastrophe of an *Othello,* because of its grandeur. But a Tragedy, Divine or otherwise, must, it may again be repeated, have a hero, and from the universe as we see it both the Glory of God and the Glory of Man have departed. Our cosmos may be farcical or it may be pathetic but it has not the dignity of tragedy and we cannot accept it as such.

Yet our need for the consolations of tragedy has not passed with the passing of our ability to conceive it. Indeed, the dissonances which it was tragedy's function to resolve grow more insistent instead of diminishing. Our passions, our disappointments, and our sufferings remain important to us though important to nothing else and they thrust themselves upon us with an urgency which makes it impossible for us to dismiss them as the mere trivialities which, so our intellects tell us, they are. And yet, in the absence of tragic faith or the possibility of achieving it, we have no way in which we may succeed in giving them the dignity which would not only render them tolerable but transform them as they were transformed by the great ages into joys. The death of tragedy is, like the death of love, one of those emotional fatalities as the result of which the human as distinguished from the natural world grows more and more a desert.

Poetry, said Santayana in his famous phrase, is "religion which is no longer believed," but it depends, nevertheless, upon its power to revive in us a sort of temporary or provisional credence and the nearer it can come to producing an illusion of belief the greater is its power as poetry. Once the Tragic Spirit was a living faith and out of it tragedies were written. Today these great expressions of a great faith have declined, not merely into poetry, but into a kind of poetry whose premises are so far from any we can really accept that we can only partially and dimly grasp its meaning.

We read but we do not write tragedies. The tragic solution of the problem of existence, the reconciliation to life by means of the tragic spirit is, that is to say, now only a fiction surviving in art. When that art itself has become, as it probably will, completely meaningless, when we have ceased not only to write but to *read* tragic works, then it will be lost and in all real senses forgotten, since the devolution from Religion to Art to Document will be complete.

THE AGE OF CRITICISM

RANDALL JARRELL

For a note on Randall Jarrell and examples of his poetry, see page 470. This selection, a humorous critique of the modern literary critic and his overwhelming influence, is taken from a collection of Jarrell's critical essays titled *Poetry and the Age* (1953).

THERE is a subject that I cannot do justice to, but would like to treat even unjustly—a subject readers and novelists and poets often talk about, but almost never write about: our age of criticism. Perhaps I ought only to talk or, at most, write a verse satire about it; one can say anything in verse and no one will mind. I wish that you would treat what I am going to write as if it were verse or talk, a conversation-with-no-one about our age of criticism. It is only a complaint, perhaps more false than true —partial, and full of exaggerations and general impressions; but it is a complaint that people do make, and may at least relieve their feelings and mine. And I will try to spare other people's by using no names at all.

The common reader does not know that it is an age of criticism, and for him it is not. He reads (seldomer and seldomer now) historical novels, the memoirs of generals, whatever is successful; good books, sometimes—good books too are successful. He cannot tell the book editor of the Chicago *Tribune* from Samuel Johnson, and is neither helped nor hindered by criticism—to him a critic is a best-seller list, only less so. Such a reader lives in a pleasant, anarchic, oblivious world, a world as democratic, almost, as the warm dark depths below, where nobody reads anything but newspapers and drugstore-books and comic-books and the *Reader's Digest* at the dentist's. This common reader knows what he likes, but is uncomfortable when other people do not read it or do not like it—for what people read and like is good: that is what *good* means.

On the slopes above (as a fabulist might put it) live many races of animals: the most numerous are the members of Book Clubs and the dwellers in the Land of Book Reviews. These find out from their leaders weekly, monthly, what they ought to read, what they ought to like; and since, thank goodness,

From *Poetry and the Age* by Randall Jarrell. Copyright 1953 by Randall Jarrell. Reprinted from the Vintage Books Edition by special arrangement with Alfred A. Knopf, Inc.

that is almost always what they would have read and liked anyway, without the help of the reviewers, they all live in unity and amity. It is the country of King Log, the fabulist would say: thousands of logs lie booming on the hillside, while their subjects croak around them; if you shut your eyes it is hard to tell who reads, who writes, and who reviews. . . . Nearby one finds readers of scholarly journals, readers of magazines of experiment, readers of magazines of verse. But highest of all, in crevices of the naked rock, cowering beneath the keen bills of the industrious storks, dwell our most conscious and, perhaps, most troubled readers; and for these—cultivated or academic folk, intellectuals, "serious readers," the leaven of our queer half-risen loaf—this is truly an age of criticism. It is about them and their Stork-Kings that I am going to talk for the rest of this article.

Four times a year (six if they read *Partisan Review*) these people read or try to read or wish that they had read large magazines called literary quarterlies. Each of these contains several poems and a piece of fiction—sometimes two pieces; the rest is criticism.

The rest is criticism. The words have a dull uneasy sound; they lie on the spirit with a heavy weight. There has never been an age in which so much good criticism has been written—or so *much* bad; and both of them have become, among "serious readers," astonishingly or appallingly influential. I am talking as a reader of the criticism of the last few years to other readers of it, and am assuming that we recognize its merits and services, which are great; I myself can and do read the magazines that I have been talking about, and they seem to me the best magazines that we have—the magazines which enjoy attacking them are almost ludicrously inferior to them. But, I think, they print far too much criticism, and far too much of the criticism that they print is of a kind that is more attractive to critics and to lovers of criticism than it is to poets and fiction-writers and to lovers of poetry and fiction. Criticism *does* exist, doesn't it, for the sake of the plays and stories and poems it criticizes? Much of this criticism does not; much of it gives a false idea of the nature and use of criticism, a false idea of the variety and importance of critics.

Some of this criticism is as good as anyone could wish; several of the best critics alive print most of their work in such magazines as these. Some more of this criticism is intelligent and useful—it sounds as if it had been written by a reader for readers, by a human being for human beings. But a great deal of this criticism might just as well have been written by a syndicate of encyclopedias for an audience of International Business Machines. It is not only bad or mediocre, it is *dull;* it is, often, an astonishingly graceless, joyless, humorless, long-winded, niggling, blinkered, methodical, self-important, cliché-ridden, prestige-obsessed, almost-autonomous criticism. Who *can* believe that either readers or writers are helped by most of the great leaden articles on Great or currently fashionable writers—always the same fifteen or twenty, if the critic can manage it—which encounter us as regularly as the equinoxes and the solstices? I have heard intelligent and cultivated people complain more times than I can remember, "I can hardly *read* the quarterlies any more"; and I once heard Elizabeth Bishop say, "After I go through one of the literary quarterlies I don't feel like reading a poem for a week, much less like writing one." Many other people have felt so; and for weeks or months or years afterwards they have neither read poems nor written them, but have criticized. For—one begins to see—an age of criticism is not an age of writing, nor an age of reading: it is an age of criticism. People still read, still write—and well; but for many of them it is the act of criticism which has become the representative or Archetypal act of the intellectual.

Critics may still be rather negligible figures in comparison to the composers and painters they write about; but when they write about writers, what a difference! A novelist, a friend of mine, one year went to a Writers' Conference; all the other teachers were critics, and each teacher had to give a formal public lecture. My friend went to the critics' lectures, but the critics didn't go to his; he wasn't surprised; as he said, "You could tell they knew I wasn't really literary like them." Recently I went to a meeting at which a number of critics discussed what Wordsworth had said about writing poetry. It was interesting to me to see how consciously or unconsciously patronizing they were—to poor Wordsworth, I almost wrote. They could see what he had meant, confused as he was, layman that he was; and because he had been, they supposed they must admit, a great poet, it did give what he had to say a wonderful documentary interest, like Nelson's remarks at Trafalgar. But the critics could not help being conscious of the difference between themselves, and Wordsworth, and my friend: *they* knew how poems and novels are put together, and Wordsworth and my friend didn't, but had just put them together. In the same way, if a pig wandered up to you during a bacon-judging contest, you would say impatiently, "Go away, pig! What do you know about bacon?"

It is no wonder that, in some of the places where critics are most concentrated, and their influence most overpowering, people write less and less. (By *write* I mean *write stories, poems, or plays.*) Some boys at a large and quite literary college I visited were telling me how much trouble they have getting poems and stories for the college's magazine. "There are only four or five we can depend on much," the editor said sadly; "everybody else that's any good writes criticism." I suppose I should have said to him, "Make the magazine criticism"; after all, isn't that the way you run a literary magazine?—but I hadn't the heart to.

These days, when an ambitious young intellectual finishes college, he buys himself a new typewriter, rents himself a room, and settles down to write . . . book reviews, long critical articles, explications. "As for living, our servants can do that for us," said Villiers de l'Isle Adam; and in the long run this gets said not only of living but also of writing stories and poems, which is almost as difficult and helpless and risky as living. Why stick one's neck out so far for so little? It is hard to write even a competent naturalistic story, and when you have written it what happens?—someone calls it a competent naturalistic story. Write another "Horatian Ode," and you will be praised as "one of the finest of our minor poets." No, as anyone can see, it is hardly worthwhile being a writer unless you can be a great one; better not sell your soul to the Muse till she has shown you the critical articles of 2100. Unless you are one of a dozen or so writers you will have a life like Trigorin's; he said that they would put on his tombstone that he had been a fine writer, *but not so good as Turgenev*—and sure enough, if you go and look on his tombstone that is what is there. Our Trigorins can hardly fail to see that, in serious critical circles, the very recognition of their merit dismisses it and them; there is written on their hearts in little red letters, "It's only me." I never remember hearing *anybody* say of a critic, "He's all right, but he's no Saint-Beuve"; but substitute *Dante* or some such O. K. name for *Saint-Beuve,* and there are very few writers about whom the statement hasn't been made.

When the first book of one of best of living poets was published, one of the best of living critics said about it only that it was "grating," and lacked the sweetness of the *Divine Comedy*. So it did; the poet might have replied with the same truth that his critic lacked Matthew Arnold's yellow kid gloves.

Critics can easily infect their readers (though usually less by precept than example) with the contempt or fretful tolerance which they feel for "minor" works of art. If you work away, with sober, methodical, and industrious complication, at the masterpieces of a few great or fashionable writers, you after a while begin to identify yourself with these men; your manner takes on the authority your subject matter has unwittingly delegated to you, and when—returned from the peaks you have spent your life among, picking a reluctant way over those Parnassian or Castalian foothills along whose slopes herdboys sit playing combs—you are required to judge the competitions of such artists, you do so with a certain reluctance. Everybody has observed this in scholars, who feel that live authors, as such, are self-evidently inferior to dead ones; though a broad-minded scholar will look like an X-ray machine at such a writer as Thomas Mann, and feel, relenting: "He's as good as dead." This sort of thing helps to make serious criticism as attractive as it is to critics: they live among the great, and some of the greatness comes off on them. No wonder poor poets become poor critics, and count themselves blest in their bargain; no wonder young intellectuals become critics before, and not after, they have failed as artists. And sometimes—who knows?—they might not have failed; besides, to have failed as an artist may be a respectable and valuable thing.

Some of us write less; all of us, almost, read less—the child at his television set, the critic or novelist in the viewplate of the set, grayly answering questions on topics of general interest. Children have fewer and fewer empty hours, and the eight-year-old is discouraged from filling them with the books written for his brother of ten; nor is anyone at his school surprised when he does not read very much or very well—it is only "born readers" who do that.

But if we read less and less—by *we*, this time, I mean the cultivated minority—a greater and greater proportion of what we read is criticism. Many a man last read *Moby Dick* in the eleventh grade, *The Brothers Karamazov* in his freshman year in college; but think of all the articles about them he's read since! It is no use to tell such a reader, "Go read *Moby Dick*"; he would only answer, "I've read it," and start out on the latest book about Melville. And imagine how he would look at you if you told him to read, say, *Kim*. In such a case, whether he has or

hasn't read it doesn't matter: he knows that he doesn't need to. It is criticism, after all, which protects us from the bad or unimportant books that we would otherwise have to read; and during the time we have saved we can read more of the criticism which protects us. I imagine, in gray hours, a generation which will have read a few masterpieces, a few thousand criticisms of these, and almost nothing else but—as the generation will say apologetically—"trash." It is an Alexandrian notion, but in many ways we *are* Alexandrian; and we do not grow less so with the years. I was told recently two awful and delightful instances of the specialization, the dividing into categories, of people's unlucky lives. A student at Harvard, taking his final examinations for a Ph.D. in English, was asked to make a short criticism of some contemporary book he had read and liked. This was the first question to give him any trouble—he had been particularly good on Middle English; he said after a while, "I don't believe I've read any contemporary books—at least not since I've been in college." Another student, taking *his* final examinations at Princeton, was asked to summarize Tennyson's "Ulysses." He did. "How does this treatment of Ulysses compare with that in the *Divine Comedy?*" someone asked. The student said that he didn't know, he hadn't read the *Divine Comedy*. "How does Tennyson's Ulysses compare with the one in the *Odyssey?*" someone else asked. The student said that he didn't know, he hadn't read the *Odyssey*. Both students were scolded and passed, and their professors came home to tell me the stories.

These men were indeed specialists in English. And yet, reader, aren't many intellectuals almost as great specialists in Important—that is to say, currently fashionable—books? Many of the intellectuals whom one hears discussing books certainly do not seem to have read widely or enthusiastically. Talking with an excellent critic and historian of ideas—a professor, too, *à la* Matthew Arnold—I asked him whether his students read much. He said, "My students! I can't get my colleagues to read anything!" Of course he was exaggerating; I felt that he was exaggerating very much; but it troubled me to remember the conversation at the literary parties at which he and I had occasionally met. Here people talked about few books, perhaps, but the books they talked about were the same: it was like the Middle Ages. And—this was like the Middle Ages too—they seemed more interested in the books' commentators than in the books; though when the books were Great, this was not always so. If you talked about the writings of some minor American novelist or short-story writer or poet—by *minor*, here, I mean anybody but the immediately fashionable six or eight—your hearer's eyes began to tap their feet almost before you had finished a sentence. (I have to admit that if you talked about such writers' unfortunate lives, and not their unfortunate writings, this didn't happen: lives, however minor, keep their primitive appeal.) But if you talked about what the ten-thousandth best critic in the country had just written, in the last magazine, about the next-worse critic's analysis of *The Ambassadors*, their eyes shone, they did not even interrupt you. There are few things more interesting to people of this sort than what a bad critic says of a bad criticism of a fashionable writer; what a good critic says of good criticism of him is equally interesting, if it is equally difficult, complicated, or novel.

If, at such parties, you wanted to talk about *Ulysses* or *The Castle* or *The Brothers Karamazov* or *The Great Gatsby* or Graham Greene's last novel —Important books—you were at the right place. (Though you weren't so well off if you wanted to talk about *Remembrance of Things Past*. Important, but too long.) But if you wanted to talk about Turgenev's novelettes, or *The House of the Dead*, or *Lavengro*, or *Life on the Mississippi*, or *The Old Wives' Tale*, or *The Golovlyov Family*, or Cunningham-Grahame's stories, or Saint-Simon's memoirs, or *Lost Illusions*, or *The Beggar's Opera*, or *Eugen Onegin*, or *Little Dorrit*, or the *Burnt Njal Saga*, or *Persuasion*, or *The Inspector-General*, or *Oblomov*, or *Peer Gynt*, or *Far from the Madding Crowd*, or *Out of Africa*, or the *Parallel Lives*, or *A Dreary Story*, or *Debits and Credits*, or *Arabia Deserta*, or *Elective Affinities*, or *Schweik*, or—or any of a thousand good or interesting but Unimportant books, you couldn't expect a very ready knowledge or sympathy from most of the readers there. They had looked at the big sights, the current sights, hard, with guides and glasses; and those walks in the country, over unfrequented or thrice-familiar territory, all alone— those walks from which most of the joy and good of reading come—were walks that they hadn't gone on very often. And unless they were poets or poetry-critics, or of the minority that still is fond of poems, they weren't likely to know much poetry. Nothing would surprise the readers of another age more than the fact that to most of us literature is primarily fiction. It still surprises visitors from another culture: a Colombian student of mine, marvelling at it, said, "In my country business men, quite a good many of them, write poetry; and when the maid cleans my room, she often picks up one of my poetry books and reads in it." When he said this I remembered that the critic and historian of ideas I spoke of had said to me, in a tone he would not have used for prose: "Now about *Paterson*—what do you think of it? Is it really much good?" I amused myself by trying to imagine Dr. Johnson asking Christopher Smart this about Gray's *Elegy*.

Many of the critics one reads or meets make an odd impression about reading, one that might be given this exaggerated emblematic form: "Good Lord, you don't think I *like* to read, do you? Reading is serious business, not something you fool around with in your spare time." Such critics read, pencil in hand, the books they have to read for an article, have to read for basic literary conversation—although most of these last, they are glad to think, they got through long ago. Readers, real readers, are almost as wild a species as writers; most critics are so domesticated as to seem institutions—as they stand there between reader and writer, so different from either, they remind one of the Wall standing between Pyramus and Thisbe. And some of *their* constant readers are so serious, responsible, and timid about reading a great work that they start out on it with a white hunter, native bearers, and a $10,000 policy they bought from the insurance-machine at the airport. The critics got back, but who knows whether they will be able to?

To the question "Have you read *Gerontion*?"—or some other poem that may seem difficult to people —I've several times heard people reply: "Well, not really—I've *read* it, but I've never read a thorough analysis of it, or really gone through it systematically." And one critic will say of another critic's analysis of a book like *Moby Dick*: "Mr. Something has given us the first thorough reading of *Moby Dick* that we have had." After people had leafed through it for so long, it's at last been read! Yet, often, how plain and actual the poem or story itself seems, compared to those shifting and contradictory and all-too-systematic "readings" that veil it as clouds veil the rocks of a mountain. Luckily, we can always seek refuge from the analyses in the poem itself—*if we like poems better than we like analyses*. But poems, stories, new-made works of art, are coming to seem rather less congenial and important than they once did, both to literary and not-so-literary readers. So far as the last are concerned, look at the lists of best-sellers, the contents of popular magazines—notice how cheerful and beefy *Time* is when it's reviewing a biography, how grumpy and demanding it gets as soon as it's reviewing a serious novel. And look at the literary quarterlies, listen to the conversation of literary people: how much of it is criticism of criticism, talk about talk about books!

People realize that almost all fiction or poetry is bad or mediocre—it's the nature of things. Almost all criticism is bad or mediocre too, but it's harder for people to tell; and even commonplace criticism can seem interesting or important simply because of its subject matter. An English statesman said that he liked the Order of the Garter because there was *no damned merit involved;* there is no damned inspiration involved in the writing of criticism, generally, and that is what the literary magazines like about it —there is an inexhaustible, unexceptionable, indistinguishable supply. They are not interested in being wildcat drillers for oil, but had rather have a hydroelectric plant at Niagara Falls. This was always the policy of the *Criterion,* their immediate ancestor: it gave a bare token representation to the literature of the '20's and '30's, and used up its space on criticism, much of it by J. Middleton Murry, John Gould Fletcher, and other Faithful Contributors.

A friend said to me one day, after he had opened his mail: "Whenever I have a story published, I get two or three letters asking me to write reviews." It isn't any different with poets. A young critic—one who makes his living by teaching, as most serious young critics do—could say in a practical justification of his work: "If you're a critic the magazines *want* you to write for them, they *ask* you to write for them —there's all that space just waiting to be filled with big articles, long reviews. Look at this quarterly: 2½ pages of poems, 11 of a story, 134 of criticism. My job depends on my getting things printed. What chance have *I* got to get in those 13½ pages? Me for the 134!" So he might speak. But the chances are that it has never even occurred to the young critic to write a story or a poem. New critic is but old scholar writ large, as a general thing: the same gifts which used to go into proving that the Wife of Bath was really an aunt of Chaucer's named Alys Persë now go into proving that all of Henry James's work is really a Swedenborgian allegory. Criticism will soon have reached the state of scholarship, and the most obviously absurd theory—if it is maintained intensively, exhaustively, and professionally—will do the theorist no harm in the eyes of his colleagues.

But one must remember (or remain a child where criticism is concerned) that a great deal of the best and most sensible criticism of any age is *necessarily absurd.* Hundreds of examples will occur to anybody: Goethe and Schiller thought so little of Hölderlin that after a while they wouldn't even answer his letters. "Ah, but *we* wouldn't have been so foolish as Goethe and Schiller," we always feel; "you won't catch us making that mistake." And you don't: we love Hölderlin. But some duckling we have never spared a smile for is *our* Hölderlin, and half the swans we spent our Sundays feeding bread-crumbs to will turn out to have been Southeys. And just as we will have been wrong about such people, so all of our critics will have been wrong: it's their *métier,* isn't it?—it always has been. It is easy to nod to all

this as a truism, but it is hard to feel it as a truth. To feel it is to be fortified in the independence and humility that we as readers ought to have.

Once critics wrote as best they could, like anybody else—they knew no better; but today many of them have a language and style as institutionalized as those of sociologists. They have managed to develop this style in fifteen or twenty years—one finds only its crude beginnings in the *Hound and Horn* and the *Dial;* the critics of those days may have sounded superior and difficult to the readers of those days, but to us, now, they seem endearingly amateurish and human and informal, so that one looks at some essay and thinks, smiling, "That was certainly the *Paul et Virginie* stage of Kenneth Burke." Who had perfected, then, that strange sort of Law French which the critic now can set up like a Chinese Wall between himself and the lay (i.e., boreable) reader? The first generation wrote distinguishably well; the second writes indistinguishably ill; who knows how the third will write? Academic or scholarly writing has some bad qualities, and the writing of Superior Intellectuals has others: the style that I am describing almost combines the two. It is a style, a tone, that is hard to picture: if the two bears that ate the forty-two little children who said to Elisha, "Go up, thou baldhead"—if they, after getting their Ph.D.'s from the University of Göttingen, had retired to Atta Troll's Castle and written a book called *A Prolegomena to Every Future Criticism of Finnegans Wake,* they might have written so.

This style partly is a result of the difficult or once-difficult position of such critics (and of such intellectuals in general) in both our universities and our general literary culture. Sociologists went in for jargon, psychologists for graphs and statistics, mostly because they knew that physicists and chemists and biologists did not think sociology and psychology sciences; English professors did the same thing for the same reason; and the critics in the universities probably felt a similar need to show the scholars who looked down on them that criticism is just as difficult and just as much of a science as "English." But the literary quarterlies are also "little magazines," revolutionary organs of an oppressed or neglected class; their contributors, by using a style which insists upon their superiority to the society that disregards them, both protect themselves and punish their society.

One can understand why so many critics find it necessary to worry and weary their readers to death, in the most impressive way possible; if they themselves understood, they might no longer find it necessary. Or so one thinks—but one is naive to think it: this style or tone of theirs is a spiritual necessity, and how can they give it up without finding something to put in its place? What began in need has been kept and elaborated in love. And I don't want them put out of their misery, I am only crying to them out of mine. May one of them say to the others, soon: "Brothers, *do* we want to sound like the *Publications of the Modern Language Association,* only worse? If we don't set things straight for ourselves, others will set them straight for us—or worse still, others won't, and things will go on as they are going on until one day even you and I won't be able to read each other, for sheer boredom."

Of course I do not mean that critics should all go out and try to have Styles, or that we should judge them by the way they write—though an absolutely bad writer is at least relatively incapable of distinguishing between good and bad in the writing that he criticizes. It is his reading that we judge a critic by, not his writing. The most impressive thing about the good critic is the fact that he *does* respond to the true nature and qualities of a work of art—not always, but often. But to be impressed by this you must be able to see these qualities when they are pointed out to you: that is, you have to be under favorable circumstances almost as good a reader as the critic is under less favorable ones. Similarly, the most impressive thing about the bad critic is his methodical and oblivious contempt for unfashionable masterpieces, his methodical and superstitious veneration for fashionable masterpieces and their reflections; but to be properly impressed with this you must have responded to the works themselves, and not to their reputations. There is a Critical Dilemma which might be put in this form: To be able to tell which critics are reliable guides to literature, you must know enough about literature not to need guides. (This is a less-than-half-truth, but a neglected one.) What we need, it might seem, is somebody who can tell us not which are the good and bad writers, but which are the good and bad critics; and half the critics I know are also trying to supply this need. In literature it is not that we have a labyrinth without a clue; the clues themselves have become a worse labyrinth, a perfect Navy Yard of great coiling hawsers which we are supposed to play out behind us on our way into the darkness of—oh, "To His Coy Mistress," or whatever it is we're reading.

It is easier for the ordinary reader to judge among poems or stories or plays than it is for him to judge among pieces of criticism. Many bad or commonplace works of art never even succeed in getting him to notice them, and there are masterpieces which can shake even the Fat Boy awake. Good critics necessarily disagree with some of the reader's dearest convictions—unless he is a Reader among readers—and they are likely to seem offensive in doing so. But the bad or commonplace critic can learn very easily (as easily as a preacher or politician, almost) which are the right people to look down on or up to, and what are the right things to write for any occasion, the things his readers will admire and agree with almost before he has written them. And he can write in an impressive and authoritative way; can use a definitive tone, big words, great weighty sentences, Clinching References—the plagues of Egypt couldn't equal all the references to Freud and Jung and Marx and myths and existentialism and neo-Calvinism and Aristotle and St. Thomas that you'll sometimes see in one commonplace article. ("If he knows all these things how can he be wrong about a little thing like a poem?" the reader may well feel.) It is perpetually tempting to the critic to make his style and method so imposing to everyone that nobody will notice or care when he is wrong. And if the critic is detailedly and solemnly enthusiastic about the great, and rather silent and condescending about the small, how *can* he go very badly wrong? make a complete fool of himself? But taking the chance of making a complete fool of himself—and, sometimes, doing so—is the first demand that is made upon any real critic: he *must* stick his neck out just as the artist does, if he is to be of any real use to art. . . .

"INVICTUS": A REGURGITATION

IRA WALLACH

IRA WALLACH (1913–   ), well-known American humorist, was born in New York City. His works include *The Horn and the Roses* (1947); a collection of literary parodies, *Hopalong-Freud* (1951); *Gutenberg's Golly* (1954); *The Absence of a Cello* (1960); and the plays *Horatio* (1954) and *Smiling, the Boy Fell Dead* (1961). The parody that follows shows how a "new critic" might approach an old poem.

INVICTUS
By William Ernest Henley

Out of the night that covers me,
    Black as the Pit from pole to pole,
I thank whatever gods may be
    For my unconquerable soul.

In the fell clutch of circumstance
    I have not winced or cried aloud.
Under the bludgeonings of chance
    My head is bloody, but unbowed.

Beyond this place of wrath and tears
    Looms but the Horror of the shade,
And yet the menace of the years
    Finds, and shall find, me unafraid.

It matters not how strait the gate,
    How charged with punishments the scroll,
I am the master of my fate:
    I am the captain of my soul.

INVICTUS describes man's reaction to life, and gives the poet's conclusions in terms of self-reliance. Night, he tells us, is "black as the Pit," but since he does not qualify the word "Pit," he makes subtle use of at least four of the currently available ambiguities. What kind of "Pit"—peach, orchestra, William? We can eliminate William since he has two t's. But what of that kind of pit which we associate with a declivity? The reader, as the poet intends, assumes the latter.

The affective significance of the words, in Stanza One, "from pole to pole," is heightened by the intertwining of two nouns with two prepositions, both

Reprinted from *Hopalong Freud and Other Modern Literary Characters*, by Ira Wallach. By permission of Abelard-Schuman Ltd. All rights reserved. Copyright 1951.

nouns ("pole") being the same. This use of the homonym is given both life and motion by the use of two different prepositions, "from," and "to," the "from" significantly preceding, rather than following, the "to."

Lines three and four of Stanza One are purely conative, and show an almost overeager emotive use of language. Again the poet employs ambiguities (this time three out of a possible seven) in speaking of "whatever gods may be," rather than employing specific terms such as Baal, Hermes, Gog, or Di Maggio.

The first stanzaic division leads us directly to Stanza Two which is based on the poet's fundamental acceptance of the doctrine of logical irrelevance, as evidenced in the first two lines. What is the "fell clutch"? What made the clutch fall? Did the clutch fall or did it slip? If the clutch slipped why did not the poet have it repaired? Has he been riding the clutch? Is there grease in his crankcase?

In Stanza Three the nonexistent plot enters the structure of the poem. Here the poet informs us that beyond a certain place, characterized by "wrath and tears," there is considerable shade. This creates tension since the poet has just come "out of the night that covers me." Despite this, he would still seek the shade were the shade not horrible. In fact, he refers to it as a "Horror" which does not fall gently, like other horrors, but "looms." This is a highly revealing example of the poet's mordant use of the double mood.

Up to this point the poet has suffered considerable discomfort. He has been submerged in pitch blackness. His clutch has slipped. Chance has bludgeoned him. His head is bloody and he has lost his bow tie. No sooner does he escape the Horror of the shade than the years menace him. Then he discovers that the scroll charges him with various punishments. (*Cf. Adam, Abou Ben*).

Here we come to the nexus of the poem, which

552

may be found primarily in its nonexistent symbolic value. The poet is telling us that despite the buffeting of fate ("bludgeonings of chance"), he remains the "master" of his destiny, the "captain" of his soul, terms which unite both ancient and modern sailing patois. As both "master" and "captain," he guides his vessel, which is himself, through the night, the Pit, and the horror of the shade.

He might have avoided all this if he had repaired his clutch.

CHRONOLOGY OF "INVICTUS"

8:30 a.m.	Poet arises. (This is an assumption, yet it is given credence by a recent New Critics Survey, *Rising Hour of British Poets, 1775–1925*).
8:45 a.m.	Discovers that night covers him. Confused, since clock indicates it is morning.
8:47 a.m.	Gives thanks to whatever gods may be.
9:00 a.m.	Breakfast.
9:15 a.m.	Clutch slips.
10:46 a.m.	Neither winces nor cries aloud.
11:00 a.m.	Low tea.
11:15 a.m.	Ends period of neither wincing nor crying aloud.
1:48 p.m.	Chance arrives, bloodies poet's head.
4:15 p.m.	High tea.
5:41 p.m.	Poet places cold towel on bloodied head.
7:34 p.m.	Horror of the shade looms.
8:00 p.m.	Dinner.
11:17 p.m.	Poet unlatches gate.
11:39 p.m.	Poet reads scroll, calls lawyer.
11:45 p.m.	Poet sleeps.
8:30 a.m.	Poet arises. (Cf. New Critics Survey, *Rising Hour of British Poets, 1775–1925*).
9:23 a.m.	Poet goes to Bureau of Licenses to apply for master's and captain's papers.
6 Months Later	Poet receives master's and captain's papers. Immediately commences to guide fate and soul.
11:00 a.m.	Low tea.

ON THE SIDEWALK

JOHN UPDIKE

JOHN UPDIKE (1932–   ) was born in Shillington, Pennsylvania, and educated at Harvard University and Oxford's Ruskin School of Drawing and Fine Art. He has been highly praised by critics, who single out particularly the precision and elegance of his diction. Among his books are a collection of poems, *The Carpentered Hen* (1958); the novels *The Poorhouse Fair* (1959) and *The Centaur* (1963); and *Pigeon Feathers and Other Stories* (1962). Updike's feeling for language is apparent in his parody of *On the Road* by Jack Kerouac.

I WAS just thinking around in my sad backyard, looking at those little drab careless starshaped clumps of crabgrass and beautiful chunks of some old bicycle crying out without words of the American Noon and half a newspaper with an ad about a lotion for people with dry skins and dry souls, when my mother opened our frantic banging screendoor and shouted, "Gogi Himmelman's here." She might have shouted the Archangel Gabriel was here, or Captain Easy or Baron Charlus in Proust's great book: Gogi Himmelman of the tattered old greenasgrass knickers and wild teeth and the vastiest, most vortical, most insatiable wonderfilled eyes I have

ever known. "Let's go, Lee," he sang out, and I could see he looked sadder than ever, his nose all rubbed raw by a cheap handkerchief and a dreary Bandaid unravelling off his thumb. "I know the WAY!" That was Gogi's inimitable unintellectual method of putting it that he was on fire with the esoteric paradoxical Tao and there was no holding him when he was in that mood. I said, "I'm going, Mom," and she said, "O.K.," and when I looked back at her hesitant in the pearly mystical UnitedStateshome light I felt absolutely sad, thinking of all the times she had vacuumed the same carpets.

His scooter was out front, the selfsame, the nonpareil, with its paint scabbing off intricately and its scratchedon dirty words and its nuts and bolts chattering with fear, and I got my tricycle out of

Reprinted by permission; © 1959 The New Yorker Magazine, Inc.

the garage, and he was off, his left foot kicking with that same insuperable energy or even better. I said, "Hey wait," and wondered if I could keep up and probably couldn't have if my beltbuckle hadn't got involved with his rear fender. That was IT. We scuttered down our drive and right over Mrs. Cacciatore's rock garden with the tiny castles made out of plaster that always made me sad when I looked at them alone. With Gogi it was different; he just kept right on going, his foot kicking with that delirious thirty-revolutionsasecond frenzy, right over the top of the biggest, a Blenheim six feet tall at the turrets; and suddenly I saw it the way he saw it, embracing everything with his unfluctuating generosity, imbecile saint of our fudging age, a mad desperado in our Twentieth Century Northern Hemisphere Nirvana deserts.

We rattled on down through her iris bed and broke into the wide shimmering pavement. "Contemplate those holy hydrants," he shouted back at me through the wind. "Get a load of those petulant operable latches; catch the magic of those pickets standing up proud and sequential like the arguments in Immanuel Kant; boom, boom, bitty-boom BOOM!" and it was true.

"What happens when we're dead?" I asked.

"The infinite never-to-be-defiled subtlety of the late Big Sid Catlett on the hushed trap drums," he continued, mad with his own dreams, imitating the whisks, "Swish, swish, swishy-swish SWOOSH!"

The sun was breaking over the tops of Mr. Linderman's privet hedge, little rows of leaves set in there delicate and justso like mints in a Howard Johnson's roadside eatery. Mitzi Leggett came out of the house, and Gogi stopped the scooter, and put his hands on her. "The virginal starchblue fabric; printed with stylized kittens and puppies," Gogi explained in his curiously beseechingly transcendent accents. "The searing incredible *innocence!* Oh! Oh! Oh!" His eyes poured water down his face like broken blisters.

"Take me along," Mitzi said openly to me, right with Gogi there and hearing every word, alive to every meaning, his nervous essence making his freckles tremble like a field of Iowa windblown nochaff barley.

"I want to," I told her, and tried to, but I couldn't, not there. I didn't have the stomach for it. She pretended to care. She was a lovely beauty. I felt my spokes snap under me; Gogi was going again, his eyes tightshut in ecstasy, his foot kicking so the hole in his shoesole showed every time, a tiny chronic rent in the iridescent miasmal veil that Intrinsic Mind tries to hide behind.

Wow! Dr. Fairweather's house came up on the left, delicious stucco like piecrust in the type of joints that attract truckers, and then the place of the beautiful Mrs. Mertz, with her *canny* deep-rooted husband bringing up glorious heartbreaking tabourets and knickknacks from his workshop in the basement, a betooled woodshavingsmelling fantasy worthy of Bruegel or Hegel or a seagull. Vistas! Old Miss Hooper raced into her yard and make a grab for us, and Gogi Himmelman, the excruciating superbo, shifted to the other foot and laughed at her careworn face. Then the breathless agape green space of the Princeling mansion, with its rich calm and potted Tropic of Cancer plants. Then it was over.

Gogi and I went limp at the corner under a sign saying ELM STREET with irony because all the elms had been cut down so they wouldn't get the blight, sad stumps diminishing down the American perspective whisperingly.

"My spokes are gone," I told him.

"Friend—ahem—*zip, zip*—parting a relative concept—Bergson's invaluable marvelchocked work—tch, tch." He stood there, desperately wanting to do the right thing, yet always lacking with an indistinguishable grandeur that petty ability.

"Go," I told him. He was already halfway back, a flurrying spark, to where Mitzi waited with irrepressible womanwarmth.

Well. In landsend despair I stood there stranded. Across the asphalt that was sufficiently semifluid to receive and embalm millions of starsharp stones and bravely gay candywrappers a drugstore twinkled artificial enticement. But I was not allowed to cross the street. I stood on the gray curb thinking, They said I could cross it when I grew up, but what do they mean grown up? I'm thirty-nine now, and felt sad.

READINGS FROM THE LIVES
OF THE SAINTS

MALCOLM COWLEY

MALCOLM COWLEY (1898–   ) was born in Belsano, Pennsylvania, and educated at Harvard University. In the 1920's he was a member of the American expatriate colony in Paris; and Exile's Return (1934), from which this selection is taken, describes the attitudes of the group during that period. He has written two volumes of poetry, Blue Juniata (1929) and Dry Season (1941), but is best known for his criticism, especially After the Genteel Tradition; American Writers since 1910 (1937) and The Literary Situation (1954).

TO American writers of my own age, or at any rate to those who went abroad in 1921, the author who seemed nearest to themselves was T. S. Eliot. Essentially the picture he presented was that of the local-boy-makes-good. He was born in St. Louis; he was in the class of 1910 at Harvard, where he took courses that any of us might have taken and belonged to three or four undistinguished clubs; he continued his studies at a French provincial university and got a job in London. Now, ten years after leaving Cambridge, he was winding himself in a slow cocoon of glory. But his glory, his making good, was not in the vulgar sense of making money, making a popular reputation: in 1921 the newspapers had never heard of this clerk in Barclay's Bank. His achievement was the writing of perfect poems, poems in which we could not find a line that betrayed immaturity, awkwardness, provincialism or platitude. Might a Midwestern boy become a flawless poet?— this was a question with which we could not fail to be preoccupied.

But it was not the only question that Eliot answered, or the only door by which he entered our secret minds. His early critical writings were concerned in large part with the dispute between form and matter, and he aligned himself with what we had learned to call our side of it. He effectively defended the intellect as against the emotions, and the conscious mind as against the libido, the dark Freudian wish. His poems, from the first, were admirably constructed. He seemed to regard them, moreover, as intellectual problems—having solved one problem, he devoted himself to another. From his early sketches in free verse, he moved on to "Portrait of a Lady" and "Prufrock"; thence he moved on to his Sweeney poems, thence to "Gerontion"; and it was

From *Exile's Return* by Malcolm Cowley. Copyright 1951 by Malcolm Cowley. Reprinted by permission of The Viking Press, Inc.

certain that his new ambitious work soon to be published in the *Dial* would mark another departure. For he never repeated himself and never, in those days, persisted in any attitude or technique: once having suggested its possibilities, he moved on.

Eliot, of course, did not originate the idea of "moving on." It was part of the general literary atmosphere, part of a long tradition—for example, it closely resembled the "theory of convolutions" that developed among my high-school friends. But Eliot's influence had the effect of making the idea vastly popular among young writers. They began to picture the ideal poet as an explorer, a buffalo hunter pressing westward toward new frontiers—from the Shenandoah he marches into unknown Tennessee, thence into the Blue Grass, thence into Missouri, always leaving the land untilled behind him, but who cares? —there will be disciples to follow the plow. No other American poet had so many disciples as Eliot, in so many stages of his career. Until 1925 his influence seemed omnipresent, and it continued to be important in the years that followed. But in 1922, at the moment when he was least known to the general public and most fervently worshiped by young poets, there was a sudden crisis. More than half of his disciples began slowly to drop away.

When *The Waste Land* first appeared, we were confronted with a dilemma. Here was a poem that agreed with all our recipes and prescriptions of what a great modern poem should be. Its form was not only perfect but was far richer musically and architecturally than that of Eliot's earlier verse. Its diction was superb. It employed in a magisterial fashion the technical discoveries made by the French writers who followed Baudelaire. Strangeness, abstractness, simplification, respect for literature as an art with traditions—it had all the qualities demanded in our slogans. We were prepared fervently to defend it against the attacks of the people who didn't understand what Eliot was trying to do—but we made private reservations. The poem had forced us into a false position, had brought our consciously adopted principles into conflict with our instincts. At heart—not intellectually, but in a purely emotional fashion—we didn't like it. We didn't agree with what we regarded as the principal idea that the poem set forth.

The idea was a simple one. Beneath the rich symbolism of *The Waste Land*, the wide learning expressed in seven languages, the actions conducted on three planes, the musical episodes, the geometrical structure—beneath and by means of all this, we felt the poet was saying that the present is inferior to the past. The past was dignified; the present is barren of emotion. The past was a landscape nourished by living fountains; now the fountains of spiritual grace are dry. . . . Often in his earlier poems Eliot had suggested this idea; he had used such symbols of dead glory as the Roman eagles and trumpets or the Lion of St. Mark's to emphasize the vulgarities of the present. In those early poems, however, the present was his real subject. Even though he seemed to abhor it, even though he thought "of all the hands that are raising dingy shades in a thousand furnished rooms" and was continually "aware of the damp souls of housemaids sprouting despondently at area gates," still he was writing about the life that all of us knew—and more than that, he was endowing our daily life with distinctions by means of the same distinguished metaphors in which he decried and belittled it. *The Waste Land* marked a real change. This time he not only expressed the idea with all his mature resources but carried it to a new extreme. He not only abused the present but robbed it of vitality. It was as if he were saying, this time, that our age was prematurely senile and could not even find words of its own in which to bewail its impotence; that it was forever condemned to borrow and patch together the songs of dead poets.

The seven-page appendix to *The Waste Land*, in which Eliot paraded his scholarship and explained the Elizabethan or Italian sources of what had seemed to be his most personal phrases, was a painful dose for us to swallow. But the truth was that the poet had not changed so much as his younger readers. We were becoming less preoccupied with technique and were looking for poems that portrayed our own picture of the world. As for the question proposed to us by Eliot, whether the values of past ages were superior or inferior to present values, we could bring no objective evidence to bear on it. Values are created by living men. If they believe—if their manner of life induces them to believe—that greatness died with Virgil or Dante or Napoleon, who can change their opinion or teach them new values? It

happened that we were excited by the adventure of living in the present. The famous "postwar mood of aristocratic disillusionment" was a mood we had never really shared. It happened that Eliot's subjective truth was not our own.

I say "it happened" although, as a matter of fact, our beliefs grew out of the lives we had led. I say "we" although I can refer only to a majority, perhaps two-thirds, of those already influenced by Eliot's poems. When *The Waste Land* was published it revealed a social division among writers that was not a division between rich and poor or—in the Marxian terms that would later be popular—between capitalist and proletarian.[1] Not many of the younger writers belonged to either the top or the bottom layer of society. Some of them, it is true, were the children of factory workers or tenant farmers, but even those few had received the education of the middle class and had for the most part adopted its standards. The middle class had come to dominate the world of letters; the dominant educational background was that of the public high school and the big Midwestern university. And the writers of this class—roughly corresponding to Marx's petty bourgeoisie—were those who began to ask where Eliot was leading and whether they should follow.

But there were also many young writers who had been sent to good preparatory schools, usually Episcopalian, before they went on to Yale, Harvard, Princeton, Williams or Dartmouth. Whether rich or poor, they had received the training and acquired the standards of the small but powerful class in American society that might be described as the bourgeoisie proper. These, in general, were the "young poets old before their time" who not only admired *The Waste Land* but insisted on dwelling there in spirit; as Edmund Wilson said, they "took to inhabiting exclusively barren beaches, cactus-

[1] It seems to me now that the division was more a matter of temperament, and less a result of social background, than I believed in 1934. The division was real, however, and it reflected attitudes toward life in our own time. When *The Waste Land* appeared, complete with notes, E. E. Cummings asked me why Eliot couldn't write his own lines instead of borrowing from dead poets. In his remarks I sensed a feeling almost of betrayal. Hemingway said in the *Transatlantic Review*, "If I knew that by grinding Mr. Eliot into a fine dry powder and sprinkling that powder over Mr. Conrad's grave Mr. Conrad would shortly appear, looking very annoyed at the forced return, and commence writing, I would leave for London early tomorrow with a sausage grinder." On the other hand John Peale Bishop, of Princeton, who was also in Paris at the time, told me that he was studying Italian so that he could get the full force of the quotations from Dante identified in Eliot's notes.

grown deserts and dusty attics overrun with rats." Their special education, their social environment and also, I think, their feeling of mingled privilege and insecurity had prepared them to follow Eliot in his desert pilgrimage toward the shrines of tradition and authority.

There were exceptions in both groups, and Eliot continued to be recited and praised behind the dingy shades of a thousand furnished rooms, but most of the struggling middle-class writers were beginning to look for other patterns of literary conduct. We were new men, without inherited traditions, and we were entering a new world of art that did not impress us as being a spiritual desert. Although we did not see our own path, we instinctively rejected Eliot's. In the future we should still honor his poems and the clearness and integrity of his prose, but the Eliot picture had ceased to be our guide.

James Joyce also presented us with a picture of the writer who never repeats himself. From *Chamber Music* through *Dubliners* and *A Portrait of the Artist as a Young Man,* each of his books had approached a new problem and had definitely ended a stage of his career. *Ulysses,* published in Paris in the winter of 1921–22, marked yet another stage. Although we had not time in the busy year that followed to read it carefully or digest more than a tenth of it, still we were certain of one thing: it was a book that without abusing the word could be called "great."

Thus we learned to couple Joyce and Eliot in a second fashion. Joyce, too, had become a success picture to fire the imagination of young writers, even though the success was on a different plane. He was another local-boy-makes-good, but not a St. Louis boy or a Harvard boy. His birthplace was the lower middle class; his home, above which he seemed to have soared, was the twentieth century. Can a writer of our own time produce a masterpiece fit to compare with those of other ages? Joyce was the first indication that there was another answer to this question than the one we were taught in school.

But—here were more difficult questions—what were the methods by and the motives for which he had written his indubitably great work? Had he set an example we should try to follow?

It seemed that from all his books three values disengaged themselves, three qualities of the man himself: his pride, his contempt for others, his ambition. Toward the end of *A Portrait of the Artist* they stood forth most clearly. The hero, Stephen Dedalus, was lonely and overweening in his pride; he despised the rabble of his richer schoolmates for being his inferiors in sensibility and intellect; and he set for himself the ambition, not of becoming a mere bishop, judge or general, but of pressing into his arms "the loveliness that has not yet come into the world." He would be the spiritual leader standing alone; he was leaving Ireland "to forge in the smithy of my soul the uncreated conscience of my race." Stephen Dedalus was obviously a more or less accurate picture of Joyce himself; but in life the author had chosen a still lonelier ambition. As he wandered through Italy, Austria, Switzerland and France, he continued to write about the Dublin of his youth and remembered the sound of Irish voices, but he half forgot that Irish race whose conscience was being forged in the smithy of revolution. He had chosen another destiny. Like Napoleon landing from Corsica, like Cortés or Pizarro marching into the highlands, he set himself a task of self-aggrandizement: he would be a genius!—he would carve out an empire, create a work of genius.

The intellectual resources at his command were not superhuman, and material resources were almost totally absent. He came of a family that had decayed with Ireland; all during his young manhood he was poor, desperately poor and unpopular. He was unusually sensitive, but no more so than half a dozen other Irish poets; he had a mind equaled in nimbleness by some of his Jesuit instructors; he had great learning of a type not impossible for any diligent student to acquire. But he was patient, obstinate—having chosen a goal he was willing to disregard all difficulties; he was a foreigner, penniless, in frail health; Europe was crumbling about his ears, thirteen million men died in the trenches, empires toppled over; he shut his window and worked on, sixteen hours a day, seven days a week, writing, polishing, elaborating. And it seemed to us that there was nothing mysterious in what he had accomplished. He had pride, contempt, ambition—and those were the qualities that continued to stand forth clearly from *Ulysses.* Here once more was the pride of Stephen Dedalus that raised itself above the Dublin public and especially above the Dublin intellectual public as represented by Buck Mulligan; here was the author's contempt for the world and for his readers—like a host being deliberately rude to his guests, he made no concession to their capacity for attention or their power of understanding; and here was an ambition willing to measure itself, not against any novelist of its age, not against any writer belonging to a modern national literature, but with the father of all the Western literatures, the archpoet of the European race.

And now this poor boy from the twentieth century had conquered his Peru and created his work of genius. We were not among the enthusiasts who placed him beside Homer, but this at least was certain: except possibly for Marcel Proust, there was no living author to be compared with him in depth, richness, complexity or scope. His achievement was there to urge us ahead; his ambition dignified our lesser ambitions. But obviously he had written *Ulysses* at a price—just how much had he paid in terms of bread and laughter? How did a man live who had written a masterpiece?

We fitted together passages from his books with sometimes erroneous information collected from magazine articles about him, bits of café gossip and the remarks of people allowed to meet him. The resulting picture, the Joyce picture of 1923, was not wholly pleasant. The great man lived in a cheap hotel, not picturesquely sordid, but cluttered and depressing. He was threatened with Homeric blindness, and much of his meager income was spent on doctors, for the disease from which he suffered was aggravated by hypochondria. He had no companions of his own intellectual stature and associated either with family friends or else with admiring disciples. Except in matters concerning literature and the opera, his opinions were those of a fourth or fifth-rate mind. It was as if he had starved everything else in his life to feed his ambition. It was as if he had made an inverted Faust's bargain, selling youth, riches and part of his common humanity to advance his pride of soul.

Having been granted an interview, I went to his hotel. He was waiting for me in a room that looked sour and moldy, as if the red-plush furniture had fermented in the twilight behind closed shutters. I saw a tall, emaciated man with a very high white forehead and smoked glasses; on his thin mouth and at the puckered corners of his eyes was a look of suffering so plainly marked that I forgot the questions with which I had come prepared. I was simply a younger person meeting an older person who needed help.

"Is there anything I can do for you, Mr. Joyce?" I said.

Yes, there was something I could do: he had no stamps, he didn't feel well enough to go out and there was nobody to run errands for him. I went out to buy stamps, with a sense of relief as I stepped into the street. He had achieved genius, I thought, but there was something about the genius as cold as the touch at parting of his long, smooth, cold, wet-marble fingers.

Ezra Pound presented a less intimidating picture, since he was known not so much for his own creations as for his advocacy of other writers and his sallies against the stupid public. His function seemed to be that of a schoolmaster, in a double sense of the word. He schooled the public in scolding it; he was always presenting it with new authors to admire, new readings of the classics, new and stricter rules for judging poetry. It was Gertrude Stein who said that he was "a village explainer, excellent if you were a village, but if you were not, not." Miss Stein herself seldom bothered to explain, although she liked to have young men sit at her feet and was not above being jealous of Pound's influence on the younger writers. The influence was extensive and well earned. He not only gave the best of advice to writers but often tried to organize them into groups or schools, each with its own manifesto and its own magazine; that is the second sense in which he might have been called schoolmaster.

In London he had started the Imagiste school and then, after relinquishing the name to Amy Lowell (who had dropped the "e" from it, together with most of the principles on which the group was founded), had assembled the Vorticists, who survived as a group until most of the members were called into military service. Besides these formal groups that Pound inspired he also had a circle of friends that included some of the greatest poets of our time. They deferred to Pound because they felt that he had shown an unselfish devotion to literature. He had fought to win recognition for the work of other writers at a time when much of his own work was going unpublished, and he had obtained financial support for others that he could as easily have had for himself. During most of his career he had earned hardly more than the wages of an English day laborer. "If I accept more than I need," he used to say, "I at once become a sponger."

He was in somewhat better financial circumstances in 1921, when he left London for Paris. During the next two years I went to see him several times, but the visit I remember is the last, in the summer of 1923. Pound was then living in the *pavillon*, or summer house, that stood in the courtyard of 70*bis*, rue Notre-Dames-des-Champs, near the Luxembourg Gardens. A big young man with intent eyes and a toothbrush mustache was there when I arrived, and Pound introduced him as Ernest Hemingway; I said that I had heard about him. Hemingway gave a slow Midwestern grin. He was then working for the International News Service, but there were rumors that he had stories in manuscript and that Pound had spoken of them as being something new in American literature. He didn't talk about the stories that afternoon; he listened as if with his eyes while Pound discussed the literary world. Very soon he rose, made a date with Pound for tennis the following day and went out the door, walking on the balls of his feet like a boxer. Pound continued his monologue.

"I've found the lowdown on the Elizabethan drama," he said as he vanished beard-first into the rear of the pavilion; he was always finding the lowdown, the inside story and the simple reason why. A moment later he returned with a worm-eaten leatherbound folio. "It's all in here," he said, tapping the volume. "The whole business is cribbed from these Italian state papers."

The remark seemed so disproportionate that I let it go unchallenged, out of politeness. "What about your own work?" I asked.

Pound laid the book on a table piled with other books. "I try not to repeat myself," he said. He began walking back and forth in his red dressing gown, while his red beard jutted out like that of an archaic Greek soldier (or, as I afterward thought, like a fox's muzzle). There was no attempt to play the great man of letters. With an engaging lack of pretense to dignity he launched into the story of his writing life.

At the age of twenty-two he had written a poem, the "Ballad of the Goodly Fere," that had been widely discussed and had even been reprinted in the *International Sunday School*. It was the first of the masculine ballads in the genre that Masefield would afterward exploit, and Pound might have exploited it himself—"Having written this ballad about Christ," he said, "I had only to write similar ballads about James, Matthew, Mark, Luke and John and my fortune was made." If he had missed falling into the gulf of standardization it was partly because he didn't see it was there. Instead he had gone to England in 1908 and started a new career.

He was still convinced that he had been right to leave America. America was England thirty years before. America was England without the fifty most intelligent men. America didn't print his poems in magazines until they had been collected into books in England. Perhaps he had been misled by the early recognition he received there; perhaps it had made him willing for a time to write the sort of poems that friendly critics expected him to write. He had spent three years studying Oxford English before he learned that he was wasting his efforts; that English is not Latin and must be written as one speaks it.

He had lost many of his English readers when he published *Ripostes* in 1912. The public doesn't like to be surprised and the new poems had been surprising, even a little shocking; they had proved that Pound wasn't merely an author of masculine ballads or a new Browning who brought medieval characters to life in medieval phrases. Still more of his readers had dropped away when he published *Lustra* in 1916; they hadn't liked his use of colloquial language or the frankness with which he described the feelings of *l'homme moyen sensuel*. It was the same when he published the *Mauberley* poems and the first of the *Cantos:* with each successive book he lost old readers and, after a time, gained some new ones, who disappeared in their turn; he had always outdistanced his audience.

Pound talked about some of his associates. Gaudier-Brzeska, killed at the front in 1916, had been the most gifted of the new sculptors; Pound had helped to keep him alive when he was starving in London. Wyndham Lewis was the real Vorticist, a man of amazing intellectual force. Lewis had visited New York in the spring of 1917 and two weeks later —Pound paused for emphasis—the United States had declared war on the Central Powers. In earlier days Pound had worked to gain recognition for Lewis, just as he had worked for Joyce, Eliot and dozens of gifted writers. Now he was thirty-seven years old and it was time for him to stop doing so much for other men and for literature in general, stop trying to educate the public and simply write. It would take years for him to finish the *Cantos;* he wanted to write an opera and he had other plans. To carry them out it might be best for him to leave Paris and live on the Mediterranean, far from distractions, in a little town he had discovered when he was in *villeggiatura.* . . .

I went back to Giverny, the village about sixty miles from Paris where I was living that year (not in *villeggiatura*), and re-read all of Pound's poems that I had been able to collect in their English editions. I liked them better than on first reading and was less irritated by their parade of eccentric scholarship. What impressed me now was their new phrases, new rhythms, new images, and their resolute omission of every word that he might have requisitioned from the stockroom of poetry. I could see how much Eliot had learned from them (although I didn't know at the time that he had sent the manuscript of *The Waste Land* to Pound for criticism and had accepted almost all the changes that Pound advised). I could also see that E. E. Cummings had used *Hugh Selwyn Mauberley* as a model in writing his own satirical poems and I could trace other derivations as well. Pound deserved the credit for discoveries which other poets were using, yet it seemed to me that some of the others—notably Eliot and Cummings—had a great deal more to say. For all his newness of phrase Pound kept making statements that were simply the commonplaces of the art-for-art's-sake tradition, when they did not belong to the older tradition of the tavern minstrel. He kept repeating that the public was stupid, that the poet was happier living in a garret, that he wrote to shock the public and that his songs would live when his readers were dead:

> Go, little naked and impudent songs,
> Go with a light foot!
> (Or with two light feet, if it please you!)
> Go and dance shamelessly!
> Go with an impertinent frolic!
>
> . . .
>
> Ruffle the skirts of prudes,
>   speak of their knees and ankles.
> But, above all, go to practical people—
>   go! jangle their door-bells!
> Say that you do no work
>   and that you will live forever.

In poems like this he was affronting the conventions in a fashion that was badly needed at the time and he was writing a declaration of independence for poets—but how could the songs live forever when they had so little fresh blood in their arteries? There was, moreover, another weakness in Pound's poetry that had been impressed on me by his remark about outdistancing his readers. He kept moving ahead into unexplored territory, like Eliot and Joyce, but it seemed to me that his motive was different. From his early ballads to *Ripostes*, to *Lustra*, to *Mauberley*, his poetic career might be explained, not as a search for something, but rather as a frantic effort to escape. I pictured him as a red fox pursued by the pack of his admirers; he led them through brambles and into marshes; some of them gave up the chase but others joined in. At present, in the *Cantos,* he had fled into high and rocky ground where the scent was lost and the hounds would cut their feet if they tried to follow, yet I felt that they would eventually find him even there and would crowd around muzzle to muzzle, not for the kill, but merely for the privilege of baying his praises. Then, with his weakness for defying the crowd, for finding crazily simple explanations and for holding eccentric opinions, to what new corner would the fox escape?

In November 1922 we heard that Marcel Proust had died, and it seemed that his death was the completion of a symbol. He represented an entirely different ambition from that of Pound or Joyce, for he strove neither to outdistance the public nor to create a work of genius by force of will. In Joyce the will had developed immoderately; in Proust it seemed almost to be atrophied. Not only his passions but his merest whims were stronger than his desire to control them, and he dispassionately watched himself doing silly things—it was almost as if the living Marcel Proust were an unpleasant but fascinating visitor in the house of his mind. Nevertheless, he had set himself a task and had carried it through.

He had determined to take the living Marcel Proust that was weak and fickle and transform it, transform himself, into an enduring work of art.

Eager to execute this project while he still had strength for it, he shut himself off from friendships, public life, the world in general, spending most of his time in bed in a room hermetically sealed to prevent drafts—they say he would feel and suffer from a breath of fresh air three rooms away. Flowers, even, were prohibited, because they brought on his asthma. He rarely saw daylight. Sometimes very late in the evening, wrapped to the ears in a fur-lined overcoat, he attended a reception in the Faubourg St. Germain; but usually he spent his nights writing hurriedly in a study that was completely lined with cork in order to shut out the street noises. He was racing against time, his enemy. Here in seclusion he was trying to recapture and preserve his past in the moment before it vanished, like a mollusk making its shell before it dies. And his death, I wrote in an essay published at the time, "was only a process of externalization; he had turned himself inside out like an orange and sucked it dry, or inscribed himself on a monument; his observation, his sensibility, his affectations, everything about him that was weak or strong had passed into the created characters of his novel."

When I came to read the last section of his book, which was not published until the end of the decade, I found that Proust had expressed the same idea about himself in different words. "Let us allow our body to disintegrate, since each fresh particle that breaks off, now luminous and decipherable, comes and adds itself to our work to complete it at the cost of suffering superfluous to others more gifted, and to make it more and more substantial as emotions gradually chip away our life." The passage must have been written only a few weeks before his final illness. By then his life was almost wholly chipped away and all its luminous particles were added to his work, which, in the process, had become the longest novel that had been written. Dying at a moment when *Remembrance of Things Past* was practically completed (only two sections remained to be revised), Proust had become for us a symbol of fulfilled ambition. And yet the symbol was too cold and distant to touch us closely. We had neither the wish nor the financial nor yet the intellectual resources to shut ourselves in cork-lined chambers and examine our memories. And Proust, moreover, had closed a path to us merely by choosing it for himself. He had accomplished his task so thoroughly that it would never have to be done again.

In 1921 Paul Valéry was fifty years old and had

recently entered his second literary career, which in a short time would carry him to the French Academy. His first career had begun some thirty years before; it had been brilliant and very brief. And it was his abandoning of that career, it was his deliberate, twenty-year-long refusal to write for publication, that impressed us even more than the high poems and the noble essays he had printed since consenting once more to become a writer like anybody else.

He had come to Paris in the autumn of 1892, a boy from the provinces with his road to make. Soon he attached himself to the circle of Symbolist poets surrounding Stéphane Mallarmé. Writing of that time he later said, "There was a certain austerity about the new generation of poets. . . . In the profound and scrupulous worship of all the arts, they thought to have found a discipline, and perhaps a truth, beyond the reach of doubt. A kind of religion was very nearly established." And again: "It was a time of theories, curiosity, glosses and passionate explanation. . . . More fervor, courage and learning, more researches into theory, more disputes and a more pious attention have rarely been devoted, in so short a time, to the problem of pure beauty. One might say that the problem was attacked from all sides."

Valéry himself chose the intellectual side. His ambition resembled that of T. S. Eliot's early days: he was obsessed by the idea of always moving through and "going beyond." Each poem could be translated into a problem capable of solution, capable of supplying a principle which could then be applied to the writing of other poems. But why bother to write them? "From the moment a principle has been recognized and grasped by someone," Valéry says that he said to himself, "it is quite useless to waste one's time applying it." Thus, he was always driven further, to attack new problems, discover new principles, until it became evident at a certain point in the process that literature itself was a problem capable of solution, and therefore was only an intermediate goal, a stage to be passed through and gone beyond. The poet was free to abandon poetry and devote himself to more essential aims.

For a young man of twenty-five, Valéry had won an enviable position; he had become a favorite disciple of Mallarmé and a leader among the younger Symbolists. His future seemed assured, and he abandoned it almost overnight. This deliberate choice, this apostasy, one might almost call it, exerted a powerful influence on the young French writers who followed him. Suddenly their highest value had been called into question, and not by the stupid public. Suddenly it seemed that the highest ambition might not be the writing of a great novel or poetic drama or the creation of any work of genius whatsoever. Apollo, after all, might be only a minor deity.

Valéry himself found his arguments so cogent that he had a hard time explaining, twenty years later, why he had once more begun writing essays and poems. He justified himself by saying on several occasions that literature was an *exercise,* a game worth playing for the same reasons that one plays tennis or chess or bridge. All these have difficult and arbitrary rules, but we observe them for the sake of the game; and the arbitrary and far more difficult conventions of classical poetry may be observed for the same reasons. One might even assert that these laws and constant requirements are the true object of the poem. "It is indeed an exercise—intended as such, and worked and reworked: a production entirely of deliberate effort; and then of a second deliberate effort, whose hard task is to conceal the first. He who knows how to read me will read an autobiography, in the form. The *matter* is of small importance."—His justification would have been more accurate, I think, if he had admitted from the first that the sport of writing was not altogether non-professional: that he derived pleasure from the praise his poems received, and wrote his essays for magazine editors who ordered and paid well for them. But always, in reading Valéry, one must learn to expect a certain high pretentiousness that accompanies and dilutes and sometimes conceals his real acuteness.

Whether the new essays that he began to publish after 1917 were written for sport or hire, they contained a valuable record of his thoughts during the years of silence.

It seems that the starting point of his researches, his first great problem outside the field of poetry, was to re-create the mind of "the universal man," to discover the *method* that unified the extremely varied accomplishments in science, warfare, mechanics and the arts of a genius like Leonardo da Vinci. His essay on Leonardo, written two or three years before the great renunciation, is a magnificent defense of the conscious mind, and of "the poet of the hypothesis" as against the specialized poet of quatrains or the patient accumulator of facts. It also proposes a new type of ambition. Might we not, by discovering his method, produce a new Leonardo, able to work freely with the infinitely rich materials of the present? But Valéry rejected the idea and seems to say that it would be useless to put the method into action. *To act,* for any individual of the first magnitude, is only an exercise, and one that may end by impoverishing the mind, since it is equivalent to choosing a single possibility and rejecting all the others with which the mind is teeming. Even "the universal man" becomes a problem capable of being reduced to a principle, to something that "it is quite useless to waste one's time applying."

Once more Valéry moved on, and this time to a problem he now regarded as the most far-reaching and difficult of all, "the study of the self for its own sake, the understanding of that attention itself, and the desire to trace clearly for oneself the nature of one's own existence." But it soon became evident that even this problem was capable of further refinement. Within the "self," what is the universal and changeless principle? It cannot be the body, which changes daily, or the senses, which tempt and deceive, or the mind, in which memories fade and ideas are dissipated; it cannot even be our *personality*, which we thoughtlessly mistake for our inmost characteristic—even the personality is only a *thing* that can be observed and reduced to tables and statistics. No, underneath all these is something else, the *I*, the naked ego, an essence that can finally be reduced to consciousness alone, to consciousness in its most abstract state. "This profound *tone* of our existence, as soon as it is heard, dominates all the complicated conditions and varieties of existence. To isolate this substantial attention from the strife of ordinary verities—is this not the ultimate and hidden task of the man with the greatest mind?"

Again he says:

Everything yields before the pure universality, the insurmountable generality, that consciousness feels itself to be. . . . It dares to consider its "body" and its "world" as almost arbitrary restrictions imposed upon the extent of its functions . . . and this attention to its external circumstances cannot react upon itself, so far has it drawn aside from all things, so great are the pains it has taken *never to be a part of anything it might conceive or do*. It is reduced to a black mass that absorbs all light and gives nothing back.

And still again:

Carried away by his ambition to be unique, guided by his ardor for omnipotence, the man of great mind has gone beyond all creations, all works, even his own lofty designs; while at the same time he has abandoned all tenderness for himself and all preference for his own wishes. In an instant he immolates his individuality. . . . To this point its pride has led the mind, and here pride is consumed. This directing pride abandons it, astonished, bare, infinitely simple, on the pole of its treasures.

This was the cheerless ambition, this was the path and the goal that Paul Valéry was proposing to the young writers who followed him after an interval of thirty years. They should regard poetry only as a beginning: from this they should move on to the methods of poetry, thence to methods in general (and in particular the methods of genius), thence to the universal self that determines all methods, and thence to mere consciousness, which is the only unchanging element in the self. Having reached this point, still undeterred by the bleakness of the way, they will discover that consciousness itself is a perpetual process of detachment from all things, from all emotions and sensations. Then, lest they still persist, Valéry paints an image to drive them back: "The man who is led by the demands of the indefatigable mind to this contact with living shadows and this extreme of pure presence, perceives himself as destitute and bare, reduced to the supreme poverty of being a force without an object. . . . He exists without instincts, almost without images; and he no longer has an aim. He resembles nothing. I say *man*, and I say *he*, by analogy and through lack of words." The supreme genius has ceased even to be human.

But the perfected consciousness, which "differs from nothingness by the smallest possible of margins," is not merely a goal and an abstraction. Like all ideals, it is something to be embodied in a man who eats, lives and suffers. In *An Evening with M. Teste*, almost the only work he wrote for publication during his long retirement, Valéry performs this labor of incarnation. M. Teste, "Mr. Head," is the thinking man, the modern Leonardo, and he is an almost wholly dehumanized creature. He does nothing, desires nothing, occupies no position, is almost completely cut off from society (which nevertheless continues to nourish him). He looks at people as if they did not exist. At night, when he retires to his chamber, he is left alone with three realities: thought, sleeplessness and migraine. He suffers from incurable headaches.—And why, we asked ourselves when reading the story, does genius lead to this inhuman state in which suffering is the only reality? Why does it seem to exist in the atmosphere of a closed room, a sickroom, where the blinds are always drawn to exclude the movement and sunlight of the streets and where there is nothing living, not even a red geranium in a pot? Everything seemed to point in the same direction, James Joyce's blindness, Proust's asthma (no less real for being half imaginary), even Eliot's reiterated complaint of being devitalized, "an old man in a dry season"—all these seemed to possess the same symbolic value, as if life were taking revenge on these men for being eliminated from their calculations. These were the great literary men of our age and they resembled one another in proposing a future as cold as the touch of cold hands.

Without losing our admiration for them, we turned aside to wonder what the writers of our own age were doing in France. They might have no genius, but they were younger certainly, and might be warmer and nearer to ourselves.

ON THE FUNCTION
OF THE NOVELIST

JOYCE CARY

JOYCE CARY (1888–1957) was born in Ireland and educated at Oxford. He studied art, history and law unsuccessfully, although he had long before determined to be a writer. His experiences in the Balkan War of 1912–13, with the West African Frontier Force during the First World War, and later with the Nigerian Political Service in Africa provided the background for some of his novels. *Aissa Saved* (1932) was the first of many books to establish his reputation as a superb craftsman and storyteller of great vigor and imagination. Among his many works are *Mister Johnson* (1939), *Herself Surprised* (1941), *The Horse's Mouth* (1944), *A Fearful Joy* (1949), *A House of Children* (1951), *Prisoner of Grace* (1952), *Except the Lord* (1953), and *Not Honour More* (1955).

IT has been said of Trollope that you can walk about in his books with your hat on. The notion is that his world is more real than that of Dickens. He thought so himself, and so misled a great many innocents, who concluded that a writer's job was to copy life, and got nowhere. For to copy life would be to produce nonsense.

Trollope found in life what we all find, a mass of detail without meaning, of useless cruelty, stupid evil, blind fate, fools doing accidental good and well-meaning saints doing immense evil; what he did was what every writer does, even those modest writers who frankly work for the pay: he created a work of art to give a certain kind of experience.

He said in effect: "This is the shape of things under the confusion of appearance; these are the forces which really move people to action." His whole story, however complex, was designed to illustrate and develop a theme. His essential task was the same as that of Dickens; he used only a different method.

As it is a philosopher's job to make sense of life to the mind, to present it as a rational unity, so it is a novelist's job to make sense of it to the feelings. And this means that we must have a consistent point of view. For it is only from one point of view that experience, like landscape, can be ranged in any kind of order.

It is dangerous perhaps to say that a book must have a moral, so let us call it a meaning. What, then, does "Tristram Shandy" mean? To read it is an event, like the first hearing of Stravinsky's "Petrouchka," and it remains a memory, as of a single experience, like a meeting of which one says, "That meant a lot

Reprinted from *Highlights of Modern Literature* by permission of the author. Copyright © 1949 by The New York Times Company.

to me." We can't define the effect in words, but we know that it was definite and lasting.

The objection, in fact, even to books that convey morals is not really to a form of art, but to bad art. Critics who find fault with Zola in his "Nana" for moralizing and driving his moral home with crude means should have protested against a crude moral. If Zola's forte was in brass, he had every right to compose for brass, but not, after he had stunned his audience into attention, to offer them a platitude or a fraud.

When at the end of the fable Nana dies of what Zola calls the small, but was, I fancy, originally the great pox, just as the French mob of the Second Empire is shouting in the streets "*à Berlin*," we are revolted by the cheapness of a device which suggests that there is anything in common between the dissolution of a harlot and the crisis of an empire. We see behind it the vulgar illusions, or suspect, what is worse, the claptrap, or a mind fed on party politics.

Zola was not a time-server. He fought for justice in the Dreyfus case at the risk of his life. But he was not a profound writer. He made a world rich in characters, but they moved on a surface. He was blind to all the large dimensions of history or morality. He could add intensity to old impressions, but he did not give a new intuition, much less a great one, if we mean by great rich in scope.

A great writer in this sense, whether poet, historian or novelist, is one whose world of organized experience harmonizes into one coherent impression the largest area of actual confusion. Tolstoy's "War and Peace" is a deliberate attempt to make sense, both to mind and feeling, of the whole realm of human action and inhuman fate. He did not succeed. For various reasons, both technical and real, no one is likely to succeed. But "War and Peace" is still one of the great achievements of art. And men live by art, greatly in great arts or cheaply in small arts.

Yet writers who, like Zola, give intensity to a common and superficial idea of the world are doing a useful work. The reason is that a very large number of people cease when quite young to add anything to a limited stock of judgments. After a certain age, say 25, they consider that their education is finished.

It is perhaps natural that having passed through that painful and boring process, called expressly education, they should suppose it over, and that they are equipped for life to label every event as it occurs and drop it into its given pigeonhole. But one who has a label ready for everything does not bother to observe any more, even such ordinary happenings as he has observed for himself, with attention, before he went to school. He merely acts and reacts.

For people who have stopped noticing, the only possible new or renewed experience, and, therefore, new knowledge, is from a work of art. Because that is the only kind of experience which they are prepared to receive on its own terms, they will come out from their shells and expose themselves to music, to a play, to a book, because it is the accepted method of enjoying such things. True, even to plays and books they may bring artistic prejudices which prevent them from seeing *that* play or comprehending *that* book. Their artistic sensibilities may be as crusted over as their minds.

But it is part of an artist's job to break crusts, or let us say rather that artists who work for the public and not merely for themselves are interested in breaking crusts because they want to communicate their intuitions.

Painters, for instance, had used impressionism in their sketches, made only for their private record and pleasure, during hundreds of years before Turner and Constable in England, Monet and his school in France, seized upon the sketch technique as a means to convey their new intuition, or vision, of nature as a play of light.

Of course, since they were born into a world which was accustomed to see nature as classical landscape, poetical objects composed in formal recession, they were not understood. They were labeled ignorant daubers or mountebanks, because these were the only pigeonholes then available for them. There was as yet no impressionist pigeonhole into which new and often original painting could be thrown and forgotten.

But the new school was resolved to be understood. It insisted on exhibiting its work. And since it had a brilliant technique and bold invention, since, too, it early attracted young and independent minds as well as smart dealers, it did finally break through the crust and give to the world a new and rich experience of permanent value, a new realm of ideal appreciation.

Great writers have done this over and over again. Richardson astonished Europe with his new world of sentiment; Rousseau followed hard upon him with his Emile and the Savoyard Vicar, and the crust which they broke was the crust of the feudal society. Its foundations were washed away—chiefly by sentimental tears.

Rousseau and Tolstoy have had direct revolutionary effect on history. But I am not proposing them as great artists only on that account. All art makes history but most of it by indirect and obscure means. Jane Austen was a great artist, and she is more read now than any writer of her time.

Her influence on minds has been enormous but subtle. It springs not from the novelty but the comprehension and balance of her idea of life and the technical power with which she conveys it. Her world is limited in surface but deep in content and, as far as it goes, more self-consistent than either Rousseau's or Tolstoy's. And she breaks the crust of a dry imagination not by a violent assault but by a series of light taps.

It is her style, her humor, that penetrate. And this, of course, is the means appropriate to her purpose. She was not going to open a tea party with a maroon or a blast of trumpets. She had too much of what Henry James called taste, meaning sense of proportion, both esthetic and moral. Much of her greatness as a novelist is precisely in her clear understanding of her job, which was to make a complete thing and have it felt. The function of the novel, in short, is to make the world contemplate and understand itself, not only as rational being but as experience of value, as a complete thing.

PAINTING AS A PASTIME

WINSTON S. CHURCHILL

SIR WINSTON CHURCHILL, K. G. (1874–   ), son of Lord Randolph Churchill, was educated at Harrow and Sandhurst. His brilliant career as soldier, journalist, biographer, historian, and statesman needs no comment in this place. He is the author, among many other books, of *The World Crisis* (1923–1929), *Marlborough, His Life and Times* (1933–1938), and *The Second World War* (1948–1953), for which he was awarded the Nobel Prize for Literature. The present selection from his work illustrates how a great mind can unbend and enjoy itself.

TO have reached the age of forty without ever handling a brush or fiddling with a pencil, to have regarded with mature eye the painting of pictures of any kind as a mystery, to have stood agape before the chalk of the pavement artist, and then suddenly to find oneself plunged in the middle of a new and intense form of interest and action with paints and palettes and canvases, and not to be discouraged by results, is an astonishing and enriching experience. I hope it may be shared by others. I should be glad if these lines induced others to try the experiment which I have tried, and if some at least were to find themselves dowered with an absorbing new amusement delightful to themselves, and at any rate not violently harmful to man or beast.

I hope this is modest enough: because there is no subject on which I feel more humble or yet at the same time more natural. I do not presume to explain how to paint, but only how to get enjoyment. Do not turn the superior eye of critical passivity upon these efforts. Buy a paint-box and have a try. If you need something to occupy your leisure, to divert your mind from the daily round, to illuminate your holidays, do not be too ready to believe that you cannot find what you want here. Even at the advanced age of forty! It would be a sad pity to shuffle or scramble along through one's playtime with golf and bridge, pottering, loitering, shifting from one heel to the other, wondering what on earth to do—as perhaps is the fate of some unhappy beings—when all the while, if you only knew, there is close at hand a wonderful new world of thought and craft, a sunlit garden gleaming with light and colour of which you have the key in your waistcoat-pocket. Inexpensive independence, a mobile and perennial pleasure apparatus, new mental food and exercise, the old harmonies and symmetries in an entirely different language, an added interest to every common scene, an occupation for every idle hour, an unceasing voyage of entrancing discovery—these are high prizes. Make quite sure they are not yours. After all, if you try, and fail, there is not much harm done. The nursery will grab what the studio has rejected. And then you can always go out and kill some animal, humiliate some rival on the links, or despoil some friend across the green table. You will not be worse off in any way. In fact you will be better off. You will know 'beyond a peradventure,' to quote a phrase disagreeably reminiscent, that that is really what you were meant to do in your hours of relaxation.

But if, on the contrary, you are inclined—late in life though it be—to reconnoitre a foreign sphere of limitless extent, then be persuaded that the first quality that is needed is Audacity. There really is no time for the deliberate approach. Two years of drawing-lessons, three years of copying woodcuts, five years of plaster casts—these are for the young. They have enough to bear. And this thorough grounding is for those who, hearing the call in the morning of their days, are able to make painting their paramount lifelong vocation. The truth and beauty of line and form which by the slightest touch or twist of the brush a real artist imparts to every feature of his design must be founded on long, hard, persevering apprenticeship and a practice so habitual that it has become instinctive. We must not be too ambitious. We cannot aspire to masterpieces. We may content ourselves with a joy ride in a paint-box. And for this Audacity is the only ticket.

I shall now relate my personal experience. When I left the Admiralty at the end of May, 1915, I still remained a member of the Cabinet and of the War Council. In this position I knew everything and could do nothing. The change from the intense executive activities of each day's work at the Admiralty to the narrowly-measured duties of a counsellor left me gasping. Like a sea-beast fished up from the depths,

From *Amid These Storms* by Winston Churchill; copyright 1932 by Charles Scribner's Sons and reprinted with their permission.

565

or a diver too suddenly hoisted, my veins threatened to burst from the fall in pressure. I had great anxiety and no means of relieving it; I had vehement convictions and small power to give effect to them. I had to watch the unhappy casting-away of great opportunities, and the feeble execution of plans which I had launched and in which I heartily believed. I had long hours of utterly unwonted leisure in which to contemplate the frightful unfolding of the War. At a moment when every fibre of my being was inflamed to action, I was forced to remain a spectator of the tragedy, placed cruelly in a front seat. And then it was that the Muse of Painting came to my rescue—out of charity and out of chivalry, because after all she had nothing to do with me—and said, 'Are these toys any good to you? They amuse some people.'

Some experiments one Sunday in the country with the children's paint-box led me to procure the next morning a complete outfit for painting in oils.

Having bought the colours, an easel, and a canvas, the next step was *to begin*. But what a step to take! The palette gleamed with beads of colour; fair and white rose the canvas; the empty brush hung poised, heavy with destiny, irresolute in the air. My hand seemed arrested by a silent veto. But after all the sky on this occasion was unquestionably blue, and a pale blue at that. There could be no doubt that blue paint mixed with white should be put on the top part of the canvas. One really does not need to have had an artist's training to see that. It is a starting-point open to all. So very gingerly I mixed a little blue paint on the palette with a very small brush, and then with infinite precaution made a mark about as big as a bean upon the affronted snow-white shield. It was a challenge, a deliberate challenge; but so subdued, so halting, indeed so cataleptic, that it deserved no response. At that moment the loud approaching sound of a motor-car was heard in the drive. From this chariot there stepped swiftly and lightly none other than the gifted wife of Sir John Lavery. 'Painting! But what are you hesitating about? Let me have a brush—the big one.' Splash into the turpentine, wallop into the blue and the white, frantic flourish on the palette—clean no longer—and then several large, fierce strokes and slashes of blue on the absolutely cowering canvas. Anyone could see that it could not hit back. No evil fate avenged the jaunty violence. The canvas grinned in helplessness before me. The spell was broken. The sickly inhibitions rolled away. I seized the largest brush and fell upon my victim with Berserk fury. I have never felt any awe of a canvas since.

Everyone knows the feelings with which one stands shivering on a spring-board, the shock when a friendly foe steals up behind and hurls you into the flood, and the ardent glow which thrills you as you emerge breathless from the plunge.

This beginning with Audacity, or being thrown into the middle of it, is already a very great part of the art of painting. But there is more in it than that.

> La peinture à l'huile
> Est bien difficile,
> Mais c'est beaucoup plus beau
> Que la peinture à l'eau.

I write no word in disparagement of water-colours. But there really is nothing like oils. You have a medium at your disposal which offers real power, if you only can find out how to use it. Moreover, it is easier to get a certain distance along the road by its means than by water-colour. First of all, you can correct mistakes much more easily. One sweep of the palette-knife 'lifts' the blood and tears of a morning from the canvas and enables a fresh start to be made; indeed the canvas is all the better for past impressions. Secondly, you can approach your problem from any direction. You need not build downwards awkwardly from white paper to your darkest dark. You may strike where you please, beginning if you will with a moderate central arrangement of middle tones, and then hurling in the extremes when the psychological moment comes. Lastly, the pigment itself is such nice stuff to handle (if it does not retaliate). You can build it on layer after layer if you like. You can keep on experimenting. You can change your plan to meet the exigencies of time or weather. And always remember you can scrape it all away.

Just to paint is great fun. The colours are lovely to look at and delicious to squeeze out. Matching them, however crudely, with what you see is fascinating and absolutely absorbing. Try it if you have not done so—before you die. As one slowly begins to escape from the difficulties of choosing the right colours and laying them on in the right places and in the right way, wider considerations come into view. One begins to see, for instance, that painting a picture is like fighting a battle; and trying to paint a picture is, I suppose, like trying to fight a battle. It is, if anything, more exciting than fighting it successfully. But the principle is the same. It is the same kind of problem, as unfolding a long, sustained, interlocked argument. It is a proposition which, whether of few or numberless parts, is commanded by a single unity of conception. And we think—though I cannot tell—that painting a great picture must require an intellect on the grand scale. There must be that all-embracing view which presents the beginning and the end, the whole and each part, as one instantaneous impression retentively and untiringly held in the mind. When we look at the larger Turners—canvases yards wide and tall—and observe that they are all done in one piece and represent one single second of time, and that every innumerable detail, however small, however distant, however subordinate, is set forth naturally and in its true proportion and relation, without effort, without failure, we must feel in presence of an intellectual manifestation the equal in quality and intensity of the finest achievements of warlike action, of forensic argument, or of scientific or philosophical adjudication.

In all battles two things are usually required of the Commander-in-Chief: to make a good plan for his army and, secondly, to keep a strong reserve. Both these are also obligatory upon the painter. To make a plan, thorough reconnaissance of the country where the battle is to be fought is needed. Its fields, its mountains, its rivers, its bridges, its trees, its flowers, its atmosphere—all require and repay attentive observation from a special point of view. One is quite astonished to find how many things there are in the landscape, and in every object in it, one never noticed before. And this is a tremendous new pleasure and interest which invests every walk or drive with an added object. So many colours on the hillside, each different in shadow and in sunlight; such brilliant reflections in the pool, each a key lower than what they repeat; such lovely lights gilding or silvering surface or outline, all tinted exquisitely with pale colour, rose, orange, green, or violet. I found myself instinctively as I walked noting the tint and character of a leaf, the dreamy purple shades of mountains, the exquisite lacery of winter branches, the dim pale silhouettes of far horizons. And I had lived for over forty years without ever noticing any of them except in a general way, as one might look at a crowd and say, 'What a lot of people!'

I think this heightened sense of observation of Nature is one of the chief delights that have come to me through trying to paint. No doubt many people who are lovers of art have acquired it in a high degree without actually practising. But I expect that nothing will make one observe more quickly or more thoroughly than having to face the difficulty of representing the thing observed. And mind you, if you do observe accurately and with refinement, and if you do record what you have seen with tolerable correspondence, the result follows on the canvas with startling obedience. Even if only four or five main features are seized and truly recorded, these by themselves will carry a lot of ill-success or half-success. Answer five big questions out of all the hundreds in the examination paper correctly and well, and though you may not win a prize, at any rate you will not be absolutely ploughed.

But in order to make his plan, the General must not only reconnoitre the battle-ground, he must also study the achievements of the great Captains of the past. He must bring the observations he has collected in the field into comparison with the treatment of similar incidents by famous chiefs. Then the galleries of Europe take on a new—and to me at least a severely practical—interest. 'This, then, is how —— painted a cataract. Exactly, and there is that same light I noticed last week in the waterfall at——.' And so on. You see the difficulty that baffled you yesterday; and you see how easily it has been overcome by a great or even by a skilful painter. Not only is your observation of Nature sensibly improved and developed, but you look at the masterpieces of art with an analysing and a comprehending eye.

The whole world is open with all its treasures. The simplest objects have their beauty. Every garden presents innumerable fascinating problems. Every land, every parish, has its own tale to tell. And there are many lands differing from each other in countless ways, and each presenting delicious variants of colour, light, form, and definition. Obviously, then, armed with a paint-box, one cannot be bored, one cannot be left at a loose end, one cannot 'have several days on one's hands.' Good gracious! what there is to admire and how little time there is to see it in! For the first time one begins to envy Methuselah. No doubt he made a very indifferent use of his opportunities.

But it is in the use and withholding of their reserves that the great commanders have generally excelled. After all, when once the last reserve has been thrown in, the commander's part is played. If that does not win the battle, he has nothing else to give. The event must be left to luck and to the fighting troops. But these last, in the absence of high direction, are apt to get into sad confusion, all mixed together in a nasty mess, without order or plan—and consequently without effect. Mere masses count no more. The largest brush, the brightest colours cannot even make an impression. The pictorial battlefield becomes a sea of mud mercifully veiled by the fog of war. It is evident there has been a serious defeat. Even though the General plunges in himself and emerges bespattered, as he sometimes does, he will not retrieve the day.

In painting, the reserves consist in Proportion or Relation. And it is here that the art of the painter marches along the road which is traversed by all the greatest harmonies in thought. At one side of the palette there is white, at the other black; and neither is ever used 'neat.' Between these two rigid limits all the action must lie, all the power required must be generated. Black and white themselves placed in juxtaposition make no great impression; and yet they are the most that you can do in pure contrast. It is wonderful—after one has tried and failed often—to see how easily and surely the true artist is able to produce every effect of light and shade, of sunshine and shadow, of distance or nearness, simply by expressing justly the relations between the different planes and surfaces with which he is dealing. We think that this is founded upon a sense of proportion, trained no doubt by practice, but which in its essence is a frigid manifestation of mental power and size. We think that the same mind's eye that can justly survey and appraise and prescribe beforehand the values of a truly great picture in one all-embracing regard, in one flash of simultaneous and homogeneous comprehension, would also with a certain acquaintance with the special technique be able to pronounce with sureness upon any other high activity of the human intellect. This was certainly true of the great Italians.

I have written in this way to show how varied are the delights which may be gained by those who enter hopefully and thoughtfully upon the pathway of painting; how enriched they will be in their daily vision, how fortified in their independence, how happy in their leisure. Whether you feel that your soul is pleased by the conception or contemplation of harmonies, or that your mind is stimulated by the aspect of magnificent problems, or whether you are content to find fun in trying to observe and depict the jolly things you see, the vistas of possibility are limited only by the shortness of life. Every day you may make progress. Every step may be fruitful. Yet there will stretch out before you an ever-lengthening, ever-ascending, ever-improving path. You know you will never get to the end of the journey. But this, so far from discouraging, only adds to the joy and glory of the climb.

Try it, then, before it is too late and before you mock at me. Try it while there is time to overcome the preliminary difficulties. Learn enough of the language in your prime to open this new literature to your age. Plant a garden in which you can sit when digging days are done. It may be only a small garden, but you will see it grow. Year by year it will bloom and ripen. Year by year it will be better cultivated. The weeds will be cast out. The fruit-trees will be pruned and trained. The flowers will bloom in more beautiful combinations. There will be sunshine there even in the winter-time, and cool shade, and the play of shadow on the pathway in the shining days of June.

I must say I like bright colours. I agree with Ruskin in his denunciation of that school of painting who 'eat slate-pencil and chalk, and assure every-body that they are nicer and purer than strawberries and plums.' I cannot pretend to feel impartial about the colours. I rejoice with the brilliant ones, and am genuinely sorry for the poor browns. When I get to heaven I mean to spend a considerable portion of my first million years in painting, and so get to the bottom of the subject. But then I shall require a still gayer palette than I get here below. I expect orange and vermilion will be the darkest, dullest colours upon it, and beyond them there will be a whole range of wonderful new colours which will delight the celestial eye.

Chance led me one autumn to a secluded nook on the Côte d'Azur, between Marseilles and Toulon, and there I fell in with one or two painters who revelled in the methods of the modern French school. These were disciples of Cézanne. They view Nature as a mass of shimmering light in which forms and surfaces are comparatively unimportant, indeed hardly visible, but which gleams and glows with beautiful harmonies and contrasts of colour. Certainly it was of great interest to me to come suddenly in contact with this entirely different way of looking at things. I had hitherto painted the sea flat, with long, smooth strokes of mixed pigment in which the tints varied only by gradations. Now I must try to represent it by innumerable small separate lozenge-shaped points and patches of colour—often pure colour—so that it looked more like a tessellated pavement than a marine picture. It sounds curious. All the same, do not be in a hurry to reject the method. Go back a few yards and survey the result. Each of these little points of colour is now playing his part in the general effect. Individually invisible, he sets up a strong radiation, of which the eye is conscious without detecting the cause. Look also at the blue of the Mediterranean. How can you depict and record it? Certainly not by any single colour that was ever manufactured. The only way in which that luminous intensity of blue can be simulated is by this multitude of tiny points of varied colour all in true relation to the rest of the scheme. Difficult? Fascinating!

Nature presents itself to the eye through the agency of these individual points of light, each of which sets up the vibrations peculiar to its colour. The brilliancy of a picture must therefore depend partly upon the frequency with which these points are found on any given area of the canvas, and partly on their just relation to one another. Ruskin says in his *Elements of Drawing*, from which I have already quoted, 'You will not, in Turner's largest oil pictures, perhaps six or seven feet long by four or five high, find one spot of colour as large as a grain of wheat ungraded.' But the gradations of Turner differ from those of the modern French school by being gently and almost imperceptibly evolved one from another instead of being bodily and even roughly separated; and the brush of Turner followed the form of the objects he depicted, while our French friends often seem to take a pride in directly opposing it. For instance, they would prefer to paint a sea with up and down strokes rather than with horizontal; or a tree-trunk from right to left rather than up and down. This, I expect, is due to falling in love with one's theories, and making sacrifices of truth to them in order to demonstrate fidelity and admiration.

But surely we owe a debt to those who have so wonderfully vivified, brightened, and illuminated modern landscape painting. Have not Manet and Monet, Cézanne and Matisse, rendered to painting something of the same service which Keats and Shelley gave to poetry after the solemn and ceremonious literary perfections of the eighteenth century? They have brought back to the pictorial art a new draught of *joie de vivre*; and the beauty of their work is instinct with gaiety, and floats in sparkling air.

I do not expect these masters would particularly appreciate my defence, but I must avow an increasing attraction to their work. Lucid and exact expression is one of the characteristics of the French mind. The French language has been made the instrument of the admirable gift. Frenchmen talk and write just as well about painting as they have done about love, about war, about diplomacy, or cooking. Their terminology is precise and complete. They are therefore admirably equipped to be teachers in the theory of any of these arts. Their critical faculty is so powerfully developed that it is perhaps some restraint upon achievement. But it is a wonderful corrective to others as well as to themselves.

My French friend, for instance, after looking at some of my daubs, took me round the galleries of Paris, pausing here and there. Wherever he paused I found myself before a picture which I particularly admired. He then explained that it was quite easy to tell, from the kind of things I had been trying to do, what were the things I liked. Never having taken any interest in pictures till I tried to paint, I had no preconceived opinions. I just felt, for reasons I could not fathom, that I liked some much more than others. I was astonished that anyone else should, on the most cursory observation of my work, be able so surely to divine a taste which I had never consciously formed. My friend said that it is not a bad thing to know nothing at all about pictures, but to have a matured mind trained in other things and a new strong interest for painting. The elements are there from which a true taste in art can be formed with time and guidance, and there are no obstacles or imperfect conceptions in the way. I hope this is true. Certainly the last part is true.

Once you begin to study it, all Nature is equally interesting and equally charged with beauty. I was shown a picture by Cézanne of a blank wall of a house, which he had made instinct with the most delicate lights and colours. Now I often amuse myself when I am looking at a wall or a flat surface of any kind by trying to distinguish all the different colours and tints which can be discerned upon it, and considering whether these arise from reflections or from natural hue. You would be astonished the first time you tried this to see how many and what beautiful colours there are even in the most commonplace objects, and the more carefully and frequently you look the more variations do you perceive.

But these are no reasons for limiting oneself to the plainest and most ordinary objects and scenes. Mere prettiness of scene, to be sure, is not needed for a beautiful picture. In fact, artificially-made pretty places are very often a hindrance to a good picture. Nature will hardly stand a double process of beautification: one layer of idealism on top of another is too much of a good thing. But a vivid scene, a brilliant atmosphere, novel and charming lights, impressive contrasts, if they strike the eye all at once, arouse an interest and an ardour which will certainly be reflected in the work which you try to do, and will make it seem easier.

It would be interesting if some real authority investigated carefully the part which memory plays in painting. We look at the object with an intent regard, then at the palette, and thirdly at the canvas. The canvas receives a message dispatched usually a few seconds before from the natural object. But it has come through a post-office *en route*. It has been transmitted in code. It has been turned from light into paint. It reaches the canvas a cryptogram. Not until it has been placed in its correct relation to everything else that is on the canvas can it be deciphered, is its meaning apparent, is it translated once again from mere pigment into light. And the light this time is not of Nature but of Art. The whole of this considerable process is carried through on the wings or the wheels of memory. In most cases we think it is the wings—airy and quick like a butterfly from flower to flower. But all heavy traffic and all that has to go a long journey must travel on wheels.

In painting in the open air the sequence of actions is so rapid that the process of translation into and out of pigment may seem to be unconscious. But all the greatest landscapes have been painted indoors, and often long after the first impressions were gathered. In a dim cellar the Dutch or Italian master recreated the gleaming ice of a Netherlands carnival or the lustrous sunshine of Venice or the Campagna. Here, then, is required a formidable memory of the visual kind. Not only do we develop our powers of observation, but also those of carrying the record—of carrying it through an extraneous medium and of reproducing it, hours, days, or even months after the scene has vanished or the sunlight died.

I was told by a friend that when Whistler guided a school in Paris he made his pupils observe their model on the ground floor, and then run upstairs and paint their picture piece by piece on the floor above. As they became more proficient he put their easels up a storey higher, till at last the *élite* were scampering with their decision up six flights into the attic—praying it would not evaporate on the way. This is, perhaps, only a tale. But it shows effectively of what enormous importance a trained, accurate, retentive memory must be to an artist; and conversely what a useful exercise painting may be for the development of an accurate and retentive memory.

There is no better exercise for the would-be artist than to study and devour a picture, and then, without looking at it again, to attempt the next day to reproduce it. Nothing can more exactly measure the progress both of observation and memory. It is still harder to compose out of many separate, well-retained impressions, aided though they be by sketches and colour notes, a new complete conception. But this is the only way in which great landscapes have been painted—or can be painted. The size of the canvas alone precludes its being handled out of doors. The fleeting light imposes a rigid time-limit. The same light never returns. One cannot go back day after day without the picture getting stale. The painter must choose between a rapid impression, fresh and warm and living, but probably deserving only of a short life, and the cold, profound, intense effort of memory, knowledge, and will-power, prolonged perhaps for weeks, from which a masterpiece can alone result. It is much better not to fret too much about the latter. Leave to the masters of art trained by a lifetime of devotion the wonderful process of picture-building and picture-creation. Go out into the sunlight and be happy with what you see.

Painting is complete as a distraction. I know of nothing which, without exhausting the body, more entirely absorbs the mind. Whatever the worries of the hour or the threats of the future, once the picture has begun to flow along, there is no room for them in the mental screen. They pass out into shadow and darkness. All one's mental light, such as it is, becomes concentrated on the task. Time stands

respectfully aside, and it is only after many hesitations that luncheon knocks gruffly at the door. When I have had to stand up on parade, or even, I regret to say, in church, for half an hour at a time, I have always felt that the erect position is not natural to man, has only been painfully acquired, and is only with fatigue and difficulty maintained. But no one who is fond of painting finds the slightest inconvenience, as long as the interest holds, in standing to paint for three or four hours at a stretch.

Lastly, let me say a word on painting as a spur to travel. There is really nothing like it. Every day and all day is provided with its expedition and its occupation—cheap, attainable, innocent, absorbing, recuperative. The vain racket of the tourist gives place to the calm enjoyment of the philosopher intensified by an enthralling sense of action and endeavour. Every country where the sun shines and every district in it has a theme of its own. The lights, the atmosphere, the aspect, the spirit, are all different; but each has its native charm. Even if you are only a poor painter you can feel the influence of the scene, guiding your brush, selecting the tubes you squeeze on to the palette. Even if you cannot portray it as you see it, you feel it, you know it, and you admire it for ever. When people rush about Europe in the train from one glittering centre of work or pleasure to another, passing—at enormous expense—through a series of mammoth hotels and blatant carnivals, they little know what they are missing, and how cheaply priceless things can be obtained. The painter wanders and loiters contentedly from place to place, always on the look out for some brilliant butterfly of a picture which can be caught and set up and carried safely home.

Now I am learning to like painting even on dull days. But in my hot youth I demanded sunshine. Sir William Orpen advised me to visit Avignon on account of its wonderful light, and certainly there is no more delightful centre for a would-be painter's activities: then Egypt, fierce and brilliant, presenting in infinite variety the single triplex theme of the Nile, the desert, and the sun; or Palestine, a land of rare beauty—the beauty of the turquoise and the opal—which well deserves the attention of some real artist, and has never been portrayed to the extent that is its due. And what of India? Who has ever interpreted its lurid splendours? But after all, if only the sun will shine, one does not need to go beyond one's own country. There is nothing more intense than the burnished steel and gold of a Highland stream; and at the beginning and close of almost every day the Thames displays to the citizens of London glories and delights which one must travel far to rival.

A CHILD'S CHRISTMAS
IN WALES

DYLAN THOMAS

For a note on Dylan Thomas and examples of his poetry, see page 466. Although principally known for his poetry, Thomas produced a substantial body of prose during his brief lifetime, prose which displays the same gifts of language, imagery, and exuberance that are to be found in his poetry. His prose works include the semi-autobiographical *Portrait of the Artist as a Young Dog* (1940) and *Adventures in the Skin Trade and Other Stories* (1955); a collection of broadcast scripts, *Quite Early One Morning* (1954), from which the present selection is taken; and *Under Milk Wood* (1959), a dramatized chronicle of life in a Welsh village.

ONE Christmas was so much like another, in those years around the sea-town corner now and out of all sound except the distant speaking of the voices I sometimes hear a moment before sleep, that I can never remember whether it snowed for six days and six nights when I was twelve or whether it snowed for twelve days and twelve nights when I was six. All the Christmases roll down toward the two-tongued sea, like a cold and headlong moon bundling down the sky that was our street; and they stop at the rim of the ice-edged, fish-freezing waves, and I plunge my hands in the snow and bring out whatever I can find. In goes my hand into that wool-white bell-tongued ball of holidays resting at the rim of the carol-singing sea, and out comes Mrs. Prothero and the firemen.

It was on the afternoon of the day of Christmas Eve, and I was in Mrs. Prothero's garden, waiting for cats, with her son Jim. It was snowing. It was always snowing at Christmas. December, in my memory, is white as Lapland, though there were no reindeers. But there were cats. Patient, cold and callous, our hands wrapped in socks, we waited to snowball the cats. Sleek and long as jaguars and horrible-whiskered, spitting and snarling, they would slink and sidle over the white back-garden walls, and the lynx-eyed hunters, Jim and I, fur-capped and moccasined trappers from Hudson Bay, off Mumbles Road, would hurl our deadly snowballs at the green of their eyes. The wise cats never appeared. We were so still, Eskimo-footed arctic marksmen in the muffling silence of the eternal snows—eternal, ever since

Reprinted from *Quite Early One Morning* by Dylan Thomas. Copyright 1954 by New Directions and reprinted with their permission.

Wednesday—that we never heard Mrs. Prothero's first cry from her igloo at the bottom of the garden. Or, if we heard it at all, it was, to us, like the far-off challenge of our enemy and prey, the neighbour's polar cat. But soon the voice grew louder.

"Fire!" cried Mrs. Prothero, and she beat the dinner-gong.

And we ran down the garden, with the snowballs in our arms, toward the house; and smoke, indeed, was pouring out of the dining-room, and the gong was bombilating, and Mrs. Prothero was announcing ruin like a town crier in Pompeii. This was better than all the cats in Wales standing on the wall in a row. We bounded into the house, laden with snowballs, and stopped at the open door of the smoke-filled room. Something was burning all right; perhaps it was Mr. Prothero, who always slept there after midday dinner with a newspaper over his face. But he was standing in the middle of the room, saying, "A fine Christmas!" and smacking at the smoke with a slipper.

"Call the fire brigade," cried Mrs. Prothero as she beat the gong.

"They won't be there," said Mr. Prothero, "it's Christmas."

There was no fire to be seen, only clouds of smoke and Mr. Prothero standing in the middle of them, waving his slipper as though he were conducting.

"Do something," he said.

And we threw all our snowballs into the smoke—I think we missed Mr. Prothero—and ran out of the house to the telephone box.

"Let's call the police as well," Jim said.

"And the ambulance."

"And Ernie Jenkins, he likes fires."

But we only called the fire brigade, and soon the fire engine came and three tall men in helmets brought a hose into the house and Mr. Prothero got out just in time before they turned it on. Nobody could have had a noisier Christmas Eve. And when the firemen turned off the hose and were standing in the wet, smoky room, Jim's aunt, Miss Prothero, came downstairs and peered in at them. Jim and I waited, very quietly, to hear what she would say to them. She said the right thing, always. She looked at the three tall firemen in their shining helmets, standing among the smoke and cinders and dissolving snowballs, and she said: "Would you like anything to read?"

Years and years and years ago, when I was a boy, when there were wolves in Wales, and birds the color of red-flannel petticoats whisked past the harp-shaped hills, when we sang and wallowed all night and day in caves that smelt like Sunday afternoons in damp front farmhouse parlors, and we chased, with the jawbones of deacons, the English and the bears, before the motor car, before the wheel, before the duchess-faced horse, when we rode the daft and happy hills bareback, it snowed and it snowed. But here a small boy says: "It snowed last year, too. I made a snowman and my brother knocked it down and I knocked my brother down and then we had tea."

"But that was not the same snow," I say. "Our snow was not only shaken from whitewash buckets down the sky, it came shawling out of the ground and swam and drifted out of the arms and hands and bodies of the trees; snow grew overnight on the roofs of the houses like a pure and grandfather moss, minutely white-ivied the walls and settled on the postman, opening the gate, like a dumb, numb thunderstorm of white, torn Christmas cards."

"Were there postmen then, too?"

"With sprinkling eyes and wind-cherried noses, on spread, frozen feet they crunched up to the doors and mittened on them manfully. But all that the children could hear was a ringing of bells."

"You mean that the postman went rat-a-tat-tat and the doors rang?"

"I mean that the bells that the children could hear were inside them."

"I only hear thunder sometimes, never bells."

"There were church bells, too."

"Inside them?"

"No, no, no, in the bat-black, snow-white belfries, tugged by bishops and storks. And they rang their tidings over the bandaged town, over the frozen foam of the powder and ice-cream hills, over the crackling sea. It seemed that all the churches boomed for joy under my window; and the weathercocks crew for Christmas, on our fence."

"Get back to the postmen."

"They were just ordinary postmen, fond of walking and dogs and Christmas and the snow. They knocked on the doors with blue knuckles. . . ."

"Ours has got a black knocker. . . ."

"And then they stood on the white Welcome mat in the little, drifted porches and huffed and puffed, making ghosts with their breath, and jogged from foot to foot like small boys wanting to go out."

"And then the Presents?"

"And then the Presents, after the Christmas box. And the cold postman, with a rose on his button-nose, tingled down the tea-tray-slithered run of the chilly glinting hill. He went in his ice-bound boots like a man on fishmonger's slabs. He wagged his bag like a frozen camel's hump, dizzily turned the corner on one foot, and, by God, he was gone."

"Get back to the Presents."

"There were the Useful Presents: engulfing mufflers of the old coach days, and mittens made for giant sloths; zebra scarfs of a substance like silky gum that could be tug-o'-warred down to the galoshes; blinding tam-o'-shanters like patchwork tea cozies and bunny-suited busbies and balaclavas for victims of head-shrinking tribes; from aunts who always wore wool next to the skin there were mustached and rasping vests that made you wonder why the aunts had any skin left at all; and once I had a little crocheted nose bag from an aunt now, alas, no longer whinnying with us. And pictureless books in which small boys, though warned with quotations not to, *would* skate on Farmer Giles' pond and did and drowned; and books that told me everything about the wasp, except why."

"Go on to the Useless Presents."

"Bags of moist and many-colored jelly babies and a folded flag and a false nose and a tram-conductor's cap and a machine that punched tickets and rang a bell; never a catapult; once, by mistake that no one could explain, a little hatchet; and a celluloid duck that made, when you pressed it, a most unducklike sound, a mewing moo that an ambitious cat might make who wished to be a cow; and a painting book in which I could make the grass, the trees, the sea and the animals any color I pleased, and still the dazzling sky-blue sheep are grazing in the red field under the rainbow-billed and pea-green birds. Hard-boileds, toffee, fudge and allsorts, crunches, cracknels, humbugs, glaciers, marzipan, and butterwelsh for the Welsh. And troops of bright tin soldiers who, if they could not fight, could always run. And Snakes-and-Families and Happy Ladders. And Easy Hobbi-

Games for Little Engineers, complete with instructions. Oh, easy for Leonardo! And a whistle to make the dogs bark to wake up the old man next door to make him beat on the wall with his stick to shake our picture off the wall. And a packet of cigarettes: you put one in your mouth and you stood at the corner of the street and you waited for hours, in vain, for an old lady to scold you for smoking a cigarette, and then with a smirk you ate it. And then it was breakfast under the balloons."

"Were there Uncles, like in our house?"

"There are always Uncles at Christmas. The same Uncles. And on Christmas mornings, with dog-disturbing whistle and sugar fags, I would scour the swatched town for the news of the little world, and find always a dead bird by the white Post Office or by the deserted swings; perhaps a robin, all but one of his fires out. Men and women wading or scooping back from chapel, with taproom noses and wind-bussed cheeks, all albinos, huddled their stiff black jarring feathers against the irreligious snow. Mistletoe hung from the gas brackets in all the front parlors; there was sherry and walnuts and bottled beer and crackers by the dessertspoons; and cats in their fur-abouts watched the fires; and the high-heaped fire spat, all ready for the chestnuts and the mulling pokers. Some few large men sat in the front parlors, without their collars. Uncles almost certainly, trying their new cigars, holding them out judiciously at arms' length, returning them to their mouths, coughing, then holding them out again as though waiting for the explosion; and some few small aunts, not wanted in the kitchen, nor anywhere else for that matter, sat on the very edges of their chairs, poised and brittle, afraid to break, like faded cups and saucers."

Not many those mornings trod the piling streets: an old man always, fawn-bowlered, yellow-gloved and, at this time of year, with spats of snow, would take his constitutional to the white bowling green and back, as he would take it wet or fire on Christmas Day or Doomsday; sometimes two hale young men, with big pipes blazing, no overcoats and wind-blown scarfs, would trudge, unspeaking, down to the forlorn sea, to work up an appetite, to blow away the fumes, who knows, to walk into the waves until nothing of them was left but the two curling smoke clouds of their inextinguishable briars. Then I would be slap-dashing home, the gravy smell of the dinners of others, the bird smell, the brandy, the pudding and mince, coiling up to my nostrils, when out of a snow-clogged side lane would come a boy the spit of myself, with a pink-tipped cigarette and the violet past of a black eye, cocky as a bullfinch, leering all

to himself. I hated him on sight and sound, and would be about to put my dog whistle to my lips and blow him off the face of Christmas when suddenly he, with a violet wink, put *his* whistle to *his* lips and blew so stridently, so high, so exquisitely loud, that gobbling faces, their cheeks bulged with goose, would press against their tinseled windows, the whole length of the white echoing street. For dinner we had turkey and blazing pudding, and after dinner the Uncles sat in front of the fire, loosened all buttons, put their large moist hands over their watch chains, groaned a little and slept. Mothers, aunts and sisters scuttled to and fro, bearing tureens. Auntie Bessie, who had already been frightened, twice, by a clock-work mouse, whimpered at the sideboard and had some elderberry wine. The dog was sick, Auntie Dosie had to have three aspirins, but Auntie Hannah, who liked port, stood in the middle of the snowbound back yard, singing like a big-bosomed thrush. I would blow up balloons to see how big they would blow up to; and, when they burst, which they all did, the Uncles jumped and rumbled. In the rich and heavy afternoon, the Uncles breathing like dolphins and the snow descending, I would sit among festoons and Chinese lanterns and nibble dates and try to make a model man-o'-war, following the Instructions for Little Engineers, and produce what might be mistaken for a sea-going tramcar. Or I would go out, my bright new boots squeaking, into the white world, on to the seaward hill, to call on Jim and Dan and Jack and to pad through the still streets, leaving huge deep footprints on the hidden pavements.

"I bet people will think there's been hippos."

"What would you do if you saw a hippo coming down our street?"

"I'd go like this, bang! I'd throw him over the railings and roll him down the hill and then I'd tickle him under the ear and he'd wag his tail."

"What would you do if you saw *two* hippos?"

Iron-flanked and bellowing he-hippos clanked and battered through the scudding snow toward us as we passed Mr. Daniel's house.

"Let's post Mr. Daniel a snowball through his letter box."

"Let's write things in the snow."

"Let's write, 'Mr. Daniel looks like a spaniel' all over his lawn."

Or we walked on the white shore. "Can the fishes see it's snowing?"

The silent one-clouded heavens drifted on to the sea. Now we were snow-blind travelers lost on the north hills, and vast dewlapped dogs, with flasks round their necks, ambled and shambled up to us, baying "Excelsior." We returned home through the poor streets where only a few children fumbled with bare red fingers in the wheel-rutted snow and cat-called after us, their voices fading away, as we trudged uphill, into the cries of the dock birds and the hooting of ships out in the whirling bay. And then, at tea the recovered Uncles would be jolly; and the ice cake loomed in the center of the table like a marble grave. Auntie Hannah laced her tea with rum, because it was only once a year.

Bring out the tall tales now that we told by the fire as the gaslight bubbled like a diver. Ghosts whooed like owls in the long nights when I dared not look over my shoulder; animals lurked in the cubby-hole under the stairs where the gas meter ticked. And I remember that we went singing carols once, when there wasn't the shaving of a moon to light the flying streets. At the end of a long road was a drive that led to a large house, and we stumbled up the darkness of the drive that night, each one of us afraid, each one holding a stone in his hand in case, and all of us too brave to say a word. The wind through the trees made noises as of old and unpleasant and maybe webfooted men wheezing in caves. We reached the black bulk of the house.

"What shall we give them? Hark the Herald?"

"No," Jack said, "Good King Wenceslas. I'll count three."

One, two, three, and we began to sing, our voices high and seemingly distant in the snow-felted dark-ness round the house that was occupied by nobody we knew. We stood close together, near the dark door.

Good King Wenceslas looked out
On the Feast of Stephen . . .

And then a small, dry voice, like the voice of some-one who has not spoken for a long time, joined our singing: a small, dry, eggshell voice from the other side of the door: a small dry voice through the key-hole. And when we stopped running we were outside *our* house; the front room was lovely; balloons floated under the hot-water-bottle-gulping gas; everything was good again and shone over the town.

"Perhaps it was a ghost," Jim said.

"Perhaps it was trolls," Dan said, who was always reading.

"Let's go in and see if there's any jelly left," Jack said. And we did that.

Always on Christmas night there was music. An uncle played the fiddle, a cousin sang "Cherry Ripe," and another uncle sang "Drake's Drum." It was very warm in the little house. Auntie Hannah, who had got on to the parsnip wine, sang a song about Bleeding Hearts and Death, and then another in which she said her heart was like a Bird's Nest; and then everybody laughed again; and then I went to bed. Looking through my bedroom window, out into the moonlight and the unending smoke-colored snow, I could see the lights in the windows of all the other houses on our hill and hear the music rising from them up the long, steadily falling night. I turned the gas down, I got into bed. I said some words to the close and holy darkness, and then I slept.

LETTER TO HIS DAUGHTER

F. SCOTT FITZGERALD

For a note on F. Scott Fitzgerald, see page 212.

August 8, 1933
La Paix, Rodgers' Forge,
Towson, Maryland

Dear Pie:

I feel very strongly about you doing duty. Would you give me a little more documentation about your reading in French? I am glad you are happy—but I never believe much in happiness. I never believe in misery either. Those are things you see on the stage

Reprinted from *The Crack-up* by F. Scott Fitzgerald by permission of New Directions. Copyright 1945 by New Directions.

or the screen or the printed page, they never really happen to you in life.

All I believe in in life is the rewards for virtue (according to your talents) and the *punishments* for not fulfilling your duties, which are doubly costly. If there is such a volume in the camp library, will you ask Mrs. Tyson to let you look up a sonnet of Shake-speare's in which the line occurs *Lilies that fester smell far worse than weeds.*

Have had no thoughts today, life seems composed of getting up a *Saturday Evening Post* story. I think of you, and always pleasantly; but if you call me

"Pappy" again I am going to take the White Cat out and beat his bottom *hard, six times for every time you are impertinent.* Do you react to that?

I will arrange the camp bill.

Half-wit, I will conclude. Things to worry about:

Worry about courage
Worry about cleanliness
Worry about efficiency
Worry about horsemanship . . .
   Things not to worry about:
Don't worry about popular opinion
Don't worry about dolls
Don't worry about the past
Don't worry about the future
Don't worry about growing up
Don't worry about anybody getting ahead of you
Don't worry about triumph
Don't worry about failure unless it comes through

your own fault
Don't worry about mosquitoes
Don't worry about flies
Don't worry about insects in general
Don't worry about parents
Don't worry about boys
Don't worry about disappointments
Don't worry about pleasures
Don't worry about satisfactions
   Things to think about:
What am I really aiming at?
How good am I really in comparison to my contemporaries in regard to:
   (a) Scholarship
   (b) Do I really understand about people and am I able to get along with them?
   (c) Am I trying to make my body a useful instrument or am I neglecting it?

                With dearest love,

FAMILY LIFE IN AMERICA

ROBERT BENCHLEY

ROBERT BENCHLEY (1889–1945) was born in Worcester, Massachusetts, and educated at Harvard University. He was well known as an actor as well as being a humorist and dramatic critic. His sketches of the average man fumbling his way through the activities of daily life are collected in *Of All Things* (1921), *Love Conquers All* (1922), *Pluck and Luck* (1925), *The Early Worm* (1927), *Twenty Thousand Leagues Under the Sea; or, David Copperfield* (1928), *My Ten Years in a Quandary* (1936), and *After 1903—What?* (1938).

I

THE naturalistic literature of this country has reached such a state that no family of characters is considered true to life which does not include at least two hypochondriacs, one sadist, and one old man who spills food down the front of his vest. If this school progresses, the following is what we may expect in our national literature in a year or so.

The living room in the Twillys' house was so damp that thick, soppy moss grew all over the walls. It dripped on the picture of Grandfather Twilly that hung over the melodeon, making streaks down the

"Family Life in America" by Robert Benchley from *The Benchley Roundup,* selected by Nathaniel Benchley. Copyright 1922 by Harper & Brothers, renewed 1950 by Gertrude Benchley. Reprinted with the permission of Harper & Row, Publishers, Incorporated,

dirty glass like sweat on the old man's face. It was a mean face. Grandfather Twilly had been a mean man and had little spots of soup on the lapel of his coat. All his children were mean and had soup spots on their clothes.

Grandma Twilly sat in the rocker over by the window, and as she rocked the chair snapped. It sounded like Grandma Twilly's knees snapping as they did whenever she stooped over to pull the wings off a fly. She was a mean old thing. Her knuckles were grimy and she chewed crumbs that she found in the bottom of her reticule. You would have hated her. She hated herself. But most of all she hated Grandfather Twilly.

"I certainly hope you're frying good," she muttered as she looked up at his picture.

"Hasn't the undertaker come yet, Ma?" asked young Mrs. Wilbur Twilly petulantly. She was boiling water on the oil-heater and every now and again would spill a little of the steaming liquid on the baby who was playing on the floor. She hated the baby because it looked like her father. The hot water raised little white blisters on the baby's red neck and Mabel Twilly felt short, sharp twinges of pleasure at the sight. It was the only pleasure she had had for four months.

"Why don't you kill yourself, Ma?" she continued. "You're only in the way here and you know it. It's just because you're a mean old woman and want to make trouble for us that you hang on."

Grandma Twilly shot a dirty look at her daughter-in-law. She had always hated her. Stringy hair, Mabel had. Dank, stringy hair. Grandma Twilly thought how it would look hanging at an Indian's belt. But all that she did was to place her tongue against her two front teeth and make a noise like the bathroom faucet.

Wilbur Twilly was reading the paper by the oil lamp. Wilbur had watery blue eyes and cigar ashes all over his knees. The third and fourth buttons of his vest were undone. It was too hideous.

He was conscious of his family seated in chairs about him. His mother, chewing crumbs. His wife Mabel, with her stringy hair, reading. His sister Bernice, with projecting front teeth, who sat thinking of the man who came every day to take away the waste paper. Bernice was wondering how long it would be before her family would discover that she had been married to this man for three years.

How Wilbur hated them all. It didn't seem as if he could stand it any longer. He wanted to scream and stick pins into every one of them and then rush out and see the girl who worked in his office snapping rubber bands all day. He hated her too, but she wore side-combs.

II

The street was covered with slimy mud. It oozed out from under Bernice's rubbers in unpleasant bubbles until it seemed to her as if she must kill herself. Hot air coming out from a steam laundry. Hot, stifling air. Bernice didn't work in the laundry but she wished that she did so that the hot air would kill her. She wanted to be stifled. She needed torture

to be happy. She also needed a good swift clout on the side of the face.

A drunken man lurched out from a doorway and flung his arms about her. It was only her husband. She loved her husband. She loved him so much that, as she pushed him away and into the gutter, she stuck her little finger into his eye. She also untied his necktie. It was a bow necktie, with white, dirty spots on it and it was wet with gin. It didn't seem as if Bernice could stand it any longer. All the repressions of nineteen sordid years behind protruding teeth surged through her untidy soul. She wanted love. But it was not her husband that she loved so fiercely. It was old Grandfather Twilly. And he was too dead.

III

In the dining room of the Twillys' house everything was very quiet. Even the vinegar cruet which was covered with fly specks. Grandma Twilly lay with her head in the baked potatoes, poisoned by Mabel, who, in her turn, had been poisoned by her husband and sprawled in an odd posture over the china closet. Wilbur and his sister Bernice had just finished choking each other to death and between them completely covered the carpet in that corner of the room where the worn spot showed the bare boards beneath, like ribs on a chicken carcass.

Only the baby survived. She had a mean face and had great spillings of Imperial Granum down her bib. As she looked about her at her family, a great hate surged through her tiny body and her eyes snapped viciously. She wanted to get down from her highchair and show them all how much she hated them.

Bernice's husband, the man who came after the waste paper, staggered into the room. The tips were off both his shoe-lacings. The baby experienced a voluptuous sense of futility at the sight of the tipless lacings and leered suggestively at her uncle-in-law.

"We must get the roof fixed," said the man, very quietly. "It lets the sun in."

MY OWN TEN RULES
FOR A HAPPY MARRIAGE

JAMES THURBER

JAMES THURBER (1894–1961) was born in Columbus, Ohio, and studied at Ohio State University. Until 1927, when he joined the staff of *The New Yorker,* he worked as a newspaper reporter in Columbus, Paris, and New York. For more than thirty years he was a regular contributor of line drawings and "light pieces running from one thousand to two thousand words" to *The New Yorker.* His books include *My Life and Hard Times* (1933), *Let Your Mind Alone* (1937), *The Beast in Me, and Other Animals* (1948), *Thurber Country* (1953), and *The Years with Ross* (1959). He was the co-author (with Elliot Nugent) of the play *The Male Animal.*

NOBODY, I hasten to announce, has asked me to formulate a set of rules for the perpetuation of marital bliss and the preservation of the tranquil American boudoir and inglenook. The idea just came to me one day, when I watched a couple in an apartment across the court from mine gesturing and banging tables and throwing *objets d'art* at each other. I couldn't hear what they were saying, but it was obvious, as the shot-put followed the hammer throw, that he and/or she (as the lawyers would put it) had deeply offended her and/or him.

Their apartment, before they began to take it apart, had been quietly and tastefully arranged, but it was a little hard to believe this now, as he stood there by the fireplace, using an andiron to bat back the Royal Doulton figurines she was curving at him from her strongly entrenched position behind the davenport. I wondered what had started the exciting but costly battle, and, brooding on the general subject of Husbands and Wives, I found myself compiling my own Ten Rules for a Happy Marriage.

I have avoided the timeworn admonitions, such as "Praise her new hat," "Share his hobbies," "Be a sweetheart as well as a wife," and "Don't keep a blonde in the guest room," not only because they are threadbare from repetition, but also because they don't seem to have accomplished their purpose. Maybe what we need is a brand-new set of rules. Anyway, ready or not, here they come, the result of fifty years (I began as a little boy) spent in studying the nature and behavior, mistakes and misunderstandings, of the American Male (*homo Americansis*) and his Mate.

RULE ONE: Neither party to a sacred union should run down, disparage or badmouth the other's former girls or beaux, as the case may be. The tendency to

Reprinted from *Cosmopolitan,* November, 1948, by permission of the author and *Cosmopolitan* magazine.

attack the character, looks, intelligence, capability and achievements of one's mate's former friends of the opposite sex is a common cause of domestic discontent. Sweetheart-slurring, as we will call this deplorable practice, is encouraged by a long spell of gloomy weather, too many highballs, hang-overs, and the suspicion that one's spouse is hiding, and finding, letters in a hollow tree, or is intercepting the postman, or putting in secret phone calls from the corner drugstore. These fears almost always turn out to be unfounded, but the unfounded fear, as we all know, is worse than the founded.

Aspersions, insinuations, reflections or just plain cracks about old boy friends and girl friends should be avoided at all times. Here are some of the expressions that should be especially eschewed: "That waffle-fingered, minor-league third baseman you latched onto at Cornell"; "You know the girl I mean —the one with the hips who couldn't read"; "That old flame of yours with the vocabulary of a hoot owl"; and "You remember her—that old bat who chewed gum and dressed like Daniel Boone."

This kind of derogatory remark, if persisted in by one or both parties to a marriage, will surely lead to divorce or, at best, a blow on the head with a glass ashtray.

RULE TWO: A man should make an honest effort to get the names of his wife's friends right. This is not easy. The average wife who was graduated from college at any time during the past thirty years keeps in close touch with at least seven old classmates. These ladies, known as "the girls," are named, respectively: Mary, Marian, Melissa, Marjorie, Maribel, Madeleine and Miriam; and all of them are called Myrtle by the careless husband we are talking about. Furthermore, he gets their nicknames wrong. This, to be sure, is understandable, since their nicknames are, respectively: Molly, Muffy, Missy, Midge,

Mabby, Maddy and Mims. The careless husband, out of thoughtlessness or pure cussedness, calls them all Mugs, or, when he is feeling particularly brutal, Mucky.

All the girls are married, one of them to a Ben Tompkins, and as this is the only one he can remember, our hero calls all the husbands Ben, or Tompkins, adding to the general annoyance and confusion.

If you are married to a college graduate, then, try to get the names of her girl friends and their husbands straight. This will prevent some of those interminable arguments that begin after Midge and Harry (not Mucky and Ben) have said a stiff good night and gone home.

RULE THREE: A husband should not insult his wife publicly, at parties. He should insult her in the privacy of the home. Thus, if a man thinks the soufflés his wife makes are as tough as an outfielder's glove, he should tell her so when they are at home, not when they are out at a formal dinner party where a perfect soufflé has just been served. The same rule applies to the wife. She should not regale his men friends, or women friends, with hilarious accounts of her husband's clumsiness, remarking that he dances like a 1907 Pope Hartford, or that he locked himself in the children's rabbit pen and couldn't get out. All parties must end finally, and the husband or wife who has revealed all may find that there is hell to pay in the taxi going home.

RULE FOUR: The wife who keeps saying, "Isn't that just like a man?" and the husband who keeps saying, "Oh, well, you know how women are," are likely to grow farther apart through the years. These famous generalizations have the effect of reducing an individual to the anonymous status of a mere unit in a mass. The wife who, just in time, comes upon her husband about to fry an egg in a dry skillet should not classify him with all the other males but should give him the accolade of a special distinction. She might say, for example, "George, no other man in the world would try to do a thing like that." Similarly, a husband watching his wife laboring to start the car without turning on the ignition should not say to the gardener or a passer-by, "Oh, well, you know, etc." Instead, he should remark to his wife, "I've seen a lot of women in my life, Nellie, but I've never seen one who could touch you."

Certain critics of this rule will point out that the specific comments I would substitute for the old familiar generalities do not solve the problem. They will maintain that the husband and wife will be sore and sulky for several days, no matter what is said. One wife, reading Rule Four over my shoulder, ex-

claimed, "Isn't that just like a man?" This brings us right back where we started. Oh, well, you know how women are!

RULE FIVE: When a husband is reading aloud, a wife should sit quietly in her chair, relaxed but attentive. If he has decided to read the Republican platform, an article on elm blight, or a blow-by-blow account of a prize fight, it is not going to be easy, but she should at least pretend to be interested. She should not keep swinging one foot, start to wind her wrist watch, file her fingernails, or clap her hands in an effort to catch a mosquito. The good wife allows the mosquito to bite her when her husband is reading aloud.

She should not break in to correct her husband's pronunciation, or to tell him one of his socks is wrong side out. When the husband has finished, the wife should not lunge instantly into some irrelevant subject. It's wiser to exclaim, "How interesting!" or, at the very least, "Well, well!" She might even compliment him on his diction and his grasp of politics, elm blight or boxing. If he should ask some shrewd question to test her attention, she can cry "Good heavens!" leap up, and rush out to the kitchen on some urgent fictitious errand. This may fool him, or it may not. I hope, for her sake—and his—that it does.

RULE SIX: A husband should try to remember where things are around the house so that he does not have to wait for his wife to get home from the hairdresser's before he can put his hands on what he wants. Among the things a husband is usually unable to locate are the iodine, the aspirin, the nail file, the French vermouth, his cuff links, studs, black silk socks and evening shirts, the snapshots taken at Nantucket last summer, his favorite recording of "Kentucky Babe," the borrowed copy of *My Cousin Rachel*, the garage key, his own towel, the last bill from Brooks Bros., his pipe cleaners, the poker chips, crackers, cheese, the whetstone, his new raincoat and the screens for the upstairs windows.

I don't really know the solution to this problem, but one should be found. Perhaps every wife should draw for her husband a detailed map of the house, showing clearly the location of everything he might need. Trouble is, I suppose, he would lay the map down somewhere and not be able to find it until his wife got home.

RULE SEVEN: If a husband is not listening to what his wife is saying, he should not grunt, "Okay" or "Yeah, sure," or make little affirmative noises. A husband lost in thought or worry is likely not to take in the sense of such a statement as this: "We're going to the Gordons' for dinner tonight, John, so I'm letting the servants off. Don't come home from the office first. Remember, we both have to be at the dentist's at five, and I'll pick you up there with the car." Now, an "Okay" or a "Yeah, sure" at this point can raise havoc if the husband hasn't really been listening. As usual, he goes all the way out to his home in Glenville—thirteen miles from the dentist's office and seventeen miles from the Gordons' house—and he can't find his wife. He can't find the servants. His wife can't get him on the phone because all she gets is the busy buzz. John is calling everybody he can think of except, of course, in his characteristic way, the dentist and the Gordons. At last he hangs up, exhausted and enraged. Then the phone rings. It is his wife. And here let us leave them.

RULE EIGHT: If your husband ceases to call you "Sugarfoot" or "Candy Eyes" or "Cutie Fudge Pie" during the first year of your marriage, it is not necessarily a sign that he has come to take you for granted or that he no longer cares. It is probably an indication that he has recovered his normal perspective. Many a young husband who once called his wife "Tender Mittens" or "Taffy Ears" or "Rose Lips" has become austere or important, like a Common Pleas Judge, and he wouldn't want reports of his youthful frivolity to get around. If he doesn't call you Dagmar when your name is Daisy, you are sitting pretty.

RULE NINE: For those whose husbands insist on pitching for the Married Men against the Single Men at the Fourth-of-July picnic of the First M. E. Church, I have the following suggestion: don't sit on the sidelines and watch him. Get lost. George is sure to be struck out by a fourteen-year-old boy, pull up with a charley horse running to first, and get his teeth knocked out by an easy grounder to the mound. When you see him after the game, tell him everybody knew the little boy was throwing illegal spitballs, everybody saw the first baseman spike George, and everybody said that grounder took such a nasty bounce even Phil Rizzuto couldn't have fielded it.

Remember, most middle-aged husbands get to sleep at night by imagining they are striking out the entire batting order of the Yankees.

RULE TEN: A wife's dressing table should be inviolable. It is the one place in the house a husband should get away from and stay away from. And yet, the average husband is drawn to it as by a magnet, especially when he is carrying something wet, oily, greasy or sticky, such as a universal joint, a hub cap, or the blades of a lawn mower. His excuse for bringing these alien objects into his wife's bedroom in the first place is that he is looking for "an old rag" with which to wipe them off. There are no old rags in a lady's boudoir, but husbands never seem to learn this. They search hampers, closets and bureau drawers, expecting to find a suitable piece of cloth, but first they set the greasy object on the dressing table. The aggrieved wife may be tempted, following this kind of vandalism, to lock her bedroom door and kick her husband out for good. I suggest, however, a less stringent punishment. Put a turtle in his bed. The wife who is afraid to pick up a turtle should ask Junior to help her. Junior will love it.

Now I realize, in glancing back over these rules, that some of my solutions to marital problems may seem a little untidy; that I have, indeed, left a number of loose ends here and there. For example, if the husbands are going to mislay their detailed maps of household objects, I have accomplished nothing except to add one item for the distraught gentleman to lose.

Then, there is that turtle. Captious critics will point out that a turtle in a husband's bed is not a valid solution to anything, but merely a further provocation. The outraged husband will deliberately trip his wife during their next mixed-doubles match. She will thereupon retaliate by putting salt in his breakfast coffee. . . .

Let somebody else try to figure out what to do about the Running Feud in marriage. The Williamses are coming to dinner tonight, and I promised to put the white wine on the ice at three o'clock. It is now six-thirty. After all, I have my own problems.

A SLIGHT SOUND AT EVENING
(ALLEN COVE, SUMMER 1954)

E. B. WHITE

E. B. WHITE (1899–   ) was born in Mount Vernon, New York, graduated from Cornell in 1921, and worked for a while as reporter and free-lance writer. He conducted a department, "One Man's Meat," in *Harper's Magazine*, 1938–43. He has worked most with *The New Yorker*, as contributor and editor. His pieces have been gathered in a number of volumes, including *Is Sex Necessary?*, with James Thurber (1929), *Every Day is Saturday* (1934), *One Man's Meat* (1942), *The Wild Flag* (1946), *The Second Tree from the Corner* (1953), and *The Points of My Compass* (1962).

IN HIS journal for July 10–12, 1841, Thoreau wrote: "A slight sound at evening lifts me up by the ears, and makes life seem inexpressibly serene and grand. It may be in Uranus, or it may be in the shutter." The book into which he later managed to pack both Uranus and the shutter was published in 1854, and now, a hundred years having gone by, *Walden*, its serenity and grandeur unimpaired, still lifts us up by the ears, still translates for us that language we are in danger of forgetting, "which all things and events speak without metaphor, which alone is copious and standard."

Walden is an oddity in American letters. It may very well be the oddest of our distinguished oddities. For many it is a great deal too odd, and for many it is a particular bore. I have not found it to be a well-liked book among my acquaintants, although usually spoken of with respect, and one literary critic for whom I have the highest regard can find no reason why anyone gives *Walden* a second thought. To admire the book is, in fact, something of an embarrassment, for the mass of men have an indistinct notion that its author was a sort of Nature Boy.

I think it is of some advantage to encounter the book at a period in one's life when the normal anxieties and enthusiasms and rebellions of youth closely resemble those of Thoreau in that spring of 1845 when he borrowed an axe, went out to the woods, and began to whack down some trees for timber. Received at such a juncture, the book is like an invitation to life's dance, assuring the troubled recipient that no matter what befalls him in the way of success or failure he will always be welcome at the party—that the music is played for him, too, if he will but listen and move his feet. In effect, that is what the book is—an invitation, unengraved; and it stirs one as a young girl is stirred by her first big party bid. Many think it a sermon; many set it down as an attempt to rearrange society; some think it an exercise in nature-loving; some find it a rather irritating collection of inspirational puffballs by an eccentric show-off. I think it none of these. It still seems to me the best youth's companion yet written by an American, for it carries a solemn warning against the loss of one's valuables, it advances a good argument for traveling light and trying new adventures, it rings with the power of positive adoration, it contains religious feeling without religious images, and it steadfastly refuses to record bad news. Even its pantheistic note is so pure as to be noncorrupting—pure as the flute-note blown across the pond on those faraway summer nights. If our colleges and universities were alert, they would present a cheap pocket edition of the book to every senior upon graduating, along with his sheepskin, or instead of it. Even if some senior were to take it literally and start felling trees, there could be worse mishaps: the axe is older than the Dictaphone and it is just as well for a young man to see what kind of chips he leaves before listening to the sound of his own voice. And even if some were to get no farther than the table of contents, they would learn how to name eighteen chapters by the use of only thirty-nine words and would see how sweet are the uses of brevity.

If Thoreau had merely left us an account of a man's life in the woods, or if he had simply retreated to the woods and there recorded his complaints about society, or even if he had contrived to include both

"A Slight Sound at Evening (Allen Cove, Summer 1954)" from *The Points of My Compass* by E. B. White. Copyright 1954 by E. B. White. Originally appeared in *The Yale Review* under the title "Walden—1954" and reprinted with the permission of Harper & Row, Publishers, Incorporated.

records in one essay, *Walden* would probably not have lived a hundred years. As things turned out, Thoreau, very likely without knowing quite what he was up to, took man's relation to nature and man's dilemma in society and man's capacity for elevating his spirit and he beat all these matters together, in a wild free interval of self-justification and delight, and produced an original omelette from which people can draw nourishment in a hungry day. *Walden* is one of the first of the vitamin-enriched American dishes. If it were a little less good than it is, or even a little less queer, it would be an abominable book. Even as it is, it will continue to baffle and annoy the literal mind and all those who are unable to stomach its caprices and imbibe its theme. Certainly the plodding economist will continue to have rough going if he hopes to emerge from the book with a clear system of economic thought. Thoreau's assault on the Concord society of the mid-nineteenth century has the quality of a modern Western: he rides into the subject at top speed, shooting in all directions. Many of his shots ricochet and nick him on the rebound, and throughout the melee there is a horrendous cloud of inconsistencies and contradictions, and when the shooting dies down and the air clears, one is impressed chiefly by the courage of the rider and by how splendid it was that somebody should have ridden in there and raised all that ruckus.

When he went to the pond, Thoreau struck an attitude and did so deliberately, but his posturing was not to draw the attention of others to him but rather to draw his own attention more closely to himself. "I learned this at least by my experiment: that if one advances confidently in the direction of his dreams, and endeavors to live the life which he has imagined, he will meet with a success unexpected in common hours." The sentence has the power to resuscitate the youth drowning in his sea of doubt. I recall my exhilaration upon reading it, many years ago, in a time of hesitation and despair. It restored me to health. And now in 1954 when I salute Henry Thoreau on the hundredth birthday of his book, I am merely paying off an old score—or an installment on it.

In his journal for May 3–4, 1838—Boston to Portland—he wrote: "Midnight—head over the boat's side —between sleeping and waking—with glimpses of one or more lights in the vicinity of Cape Ann. Bright moonlight—the effect heightened by seasickness." The entry illuminates the man, as the moon the sea on that night in May. In Thoreau the natural scene was heightened, not depressed, by a disturbance of the stomach, and nausea met its match at last. There was a steadiness in at least one passenger if there was none in the boat. Such steadiness (which in some would be called intoxication) is at the heart of *Walden*—confidence, faith, the discipline of looking always at what is to be seen, undeviating gratitude for the life-everlasting that he found growing in his front yard. "There is nowhere recorded a simple and irrepressible satisfaction with the gift of life, any memorable praise of God." He worked to correct that deficiency. *Walden* is his acknowledgment of the gift of life. It is the testament of a man in a high state of indignation because (it seemed to him) so few ears heard the uninterrupted poem of creation, the morning wind that forever blows. If the man sometimes wrote as though all his readers were male, unmarried, and well-connected, it is because he gave his testimony during the callow years, and, for that matter, never really grew up. To reject the book because of the immaturity of the author and the bugs in the logic is to throw away a bottle of good wine because it contains bits of the cork.

Thoreau said he required of every writer, first and last, a simple and sincere account of his own life. Having delivered himself of this chesty dictum, he proceeded to ignore it. In his books and even in his enormous journal, he withheld or disguised most of the facts from which an understanding of his life could be drawn. *Walden,* subtitled "Life in the Woods," is not a simple and sincere account of a man's life, either in or out of the woods; it is an account of a man's journey into the mind, a toot on the trumpet to alert the neighbors. Thoreau was well aware that no one can alert his neighbors who is not wide awake himself, and he went to the woods (among other reasons) to make sure that he would stay awake during his broadcast. What actually took place during the years 1845–47 is largely unrecorded, and the reader is excluded from the private life of the author, who supplies almost no gossip about himself, a great deal about his neighbors and about the universe.

As for me, I cannot in this short ramble give a simple and sincere account of my own life, but I think Thoreau might find it instructive to know that this memorial essay is being written in a house that, through no intent on my part, is the same size and shape as his own domicile on the pond—about ten by fifteen, tight, plainly finished, and at a little distance from my Concord. The house in which I sit this morning was built to accommodate a boat, not a man, but by long experience I have learned that in most respects it shelters me better than the larger dwelling where my bed is, and which, by design, is a manhouse not a boathouse. Here in the boathouse I am a wilder and, it would appear, a healthier man, by a safe margin. I have a chair, a bench, a table, and I can walk into the water if I tire of the land. My house fronts a cove. Two fishermen have just arrived to spot fish from the air—an osprey and a man in a small yellow plane who works for the fish company. The man, I have noticed, is less well equipped than the hawk, who can dive directly on his fish and carry it away, without telephoning. A mouse and a squirrel share the house with me. The building is, in fact, a multiple dwelling, a semidetached affair. It is because I am semidetached while here that I find it possible to transact this private business with the fewest obstacles.

There is also a woodchuck here, living forty feet away under the wharf. When the wind is right, he can smell my house; and when the wind is contrary, I can smell his. We both use the wharf for sunning, taking turns, each adjusting his schedule to the other's convenience. Thoreau once ate a woodchuck. I think he felt he owed it to his readers, and that it was little enough, considering the indignities they were suffering at his hands and the dressing-down they were taking. (Parts of *Walden* are pure scold.) Or perhaps he ate the woodchuck because he believed every man should acquire strict business habits, and the woodchuck was destroying his market beans. I do not know. Thoreau had a strong experimental streak in him. It is probably no harder to eat a woodchuck than to construct a sentence that lasts a hundred years. At any rate, Thoreau is the only writer I know who prepared himself for his great ordeal by eating a woodchuck; also the only one who got a hangover from drinking too much water. (He was drunk the whole time, though he seldom touched wine or coffee or tea.)

Here in this compact house where I would spend one day as deliberately as Nature if I were not being pressed by *The Yale Review,* and with a woodchuck (as yet uneaten) for neighbor, I can feel the companionship of the occupant of the pondside cabin in Walden woods, a mile from the village, near the Fitchburg right of way. Even my immediate business is no barrier between us: Thoreau occasionally batted out a magazine piece, but was always suspicious of any sort of purposeful work that cut into his time. A man, he said, should take care not to be thrown off the track by every nutshell and mosquito's wing that falls on the rails.

There has been much guessing as to why he went to the pond. To set it down to escapism is, of course, to misconstrue what happened. Henry went forth to battle when he took to the woods, and *Walden* is the report of a man torn by two powerful and opposing drives—the desire to enjoy the world (and not be derailed by a mosquito wing) and the urge to set the world straight. One cannot join these two suc-

cessfully, but sometimes, in rare cases, something good or even great results from the attempt of the tormented spirit to reconcile them. Henry went forth to battle, and if he set the stage himself, if he fought on his own terms and with his own weapons, it was because it was his nature to do things differently from most men, and to act in a cocky fashion. If the pond and the woods seemed a more plausible site for a house than an in-town location, it was because a cowbell made for him a sweeter sound than a churchbell. *Walden,* the book, makes the sound of the cowbell, more than a churchbell, and proves the point, although both sounds are in it, and both remarkably clear and sweet. He simply preferred his churchbell at a little distance.

I think one reason he went to the woods was a perfectly simple and commonplace one—and apparently he thought so, too. "At a certain season of our life," he wrote, "we are accustomed to consider every spot as the possible site of a house." There spoke the young man, a few years out of college, who had not yet broken away from home. He hadn't married, and he had found no job that measured up to his rigid standards of employment, and like any young man, or young animal, he felt uneasy and on the defensive until he had fixed himself a den. Most young men, of course, casting about for a site, are content merely to draw apart from their kinfolks. Thoreau, convinced that the greater part of what his neighbors called good was bad, withdrew from a great deal more than family: he pulled out of everything for a while, to serve everybody right for being so stuffy, and to try his own prejudices on the dog.

The house-hunting sentence above, which starts the Chapter called "Where I Lived, and What I Lived For," is followed by another passage that is worth quoting here because it so beautifully illustrates the offbeat prose that Thoreau was master of, a prose at once strictly disciplined and wildly abandoned. "I have surveyed the country on every side within a dozen miles of where I live," continued this delirious young man. "In imagination I have bought all the farms in succession, for all were to be bought, and I knew their price. I walked over each farmer's premises, tasted his wild apples, discoursed on husbandry with him, took his farm at his price, at any price, mortgaging it to him in my mind; even put a higher price on it—took everything but a deed of it— took his word for his deed, for I dearly love to talk —cultivated it, and him too to some extent, I trust, and withdrew when I had enjoyed it long enough, leaving him to carry it on." A copydesk man would get a double hernia trying to clean up that sentence for the management, but the sentence needs no fixing, for it perfectly captures the meaning of the writer and the quality of the ramble.

"Wherever I sat, there I might live, and the landscape radiated from me accordingly." Thoreau, the home-seeker, sitting on his hummock with the entire State of Massachusetts radiating from him, is to me the most humorous of the New England figures, and *Walden* the most humorous of the books, though its humor is almost continuously subsurface and there is nothing funny anywhere, except a few weak jokes and bad puns that rise to the surface like a perch in the pond that rose to the sound of the maestro's flute. Thoreau tended to write in sentences, a feat not every writer is capable of, and *Walden* is, rhetorically speaking, a collection of certified sentences, some of them, it would now appear, as indestructible as they are errant. The book is distilled from the vast journals, and this accounts for its intensity: he picked out bright particles that pleased his eye, whirled them in the kaleidoscope of his content, and produced the pattern that has endured—the color, the form, the light.

On this its hundredth birthday, Thoreau's *Walden* is pertinent and timely. In our uneasy season, when all men unconsciously seek a retreat from a world that has got almost completely out of hand, his house in the Concord woods is a haven. In our culture of gadgetry and the multiplicity of convenience, his cry "Simplicity, simplicity, simplicity!" has the insistence of a fire alarm. In the brooding atmosphere of war and the gathering radioactive storm, the innocence and serenity of his summer afternoons are enough to burst the remembering heart, and one gazes back upon that pleasing interlude—its confidence, its purity, its deliberateness—with awe and wonder, as one would look upon the face of a child asleep.

"This small lake was of most value as a neighbor in the intervals of a gentle rain-storm in August, when, both air and water being perfectly still, but the sky overcast, midafternoon had all the serenity of evening, and the wood-thrush sang around, and was heard from shore to shore." Now, in the perpetual overcast in which our days are spent, we hear with extra perception and deep gratitude that song, tying century to century.

I sometimes amuse myself by bringing Henry Thoreau back to life and showing him the sights. I escort him into a phone booth and let him dial Weather. "This is a delicious evening," the girl's voice says, "when the whole body is one sense, and imbibes delight through every pore." I show him the spot in the Pacific where an island used to be, before some magician made it vanish. "We know not where we are," I murmur. "The light which puts out our eyes

is darkness to us. Only that day dawns to which we are awake." I thumb through the latest copy of *Vogue* with him. "Of two patterns which differ only by a few threads more or less of a particular color," I read, "the one will be sold readily, the other lie on the shelf, though it frequently happens that, after the lapse of a season, the latter becomes the most fashionable." Together we go outboarding on the Assabet, looking for what we've lost—a hound, a bay horse, a turtledove. I show him a distracted farmer who is trying to repair a hay baler before the thunder shower breaks. "This farmer," I remark, "is endeavoring to solve the problem of a livelihood by a formula more complicated than the problem itself. To get his shoe strings he speculates in herds of cattle."

I take the celebrated author to Twenty-One for lunch, so the waiters may study his shoes. The proprietor welcomes us. "The gross feeder," remarks the proprietor, sweeping the room with his arm, "is a man in the larva stage." After lunch we visit a classroom in one of those schools conducted by big corporations to teach their superannuated executives how to retire from business without serious injury to their health. (The shock to men's systems these days when relieved of the exacting routine of amassing wealth is very great and must be cushioned.) "It is not necessary," says the teacher to his pupils, "that a man should earn his living by the sweat of his brow, unless he sweats easier than I do. We are determined to be starved before we are hungry."

I turn on the radio and let Thoreau hear Winchell beat the red hand around the clock. "Time is but the stream I go a-fishing in," shouts Mr. Winchell, rattling his telegraph key. "Hardly a man takes a half hour's nap after dinner, but when he wakes he holds up his head and asks, 'What's the news?' If we read of one man robbed, or murdered, or killed by accident, or one house burned, or one vessel wrecked, or one steamboat blown up, or one cow run over on the Western Railroad, or one mad dog killed, or one lot of grasshoppers in the winter—we need never read of another. One is enough."

I doubt that Thoreau would be thrown off balance by the fantastic sights and sounds of the twentieth century. "The Concord nights," he once wrote, "are stranger than the Arabian nights." A four-engined air liner would merely serve to confirm his early views on travel. Everywhere he would observe, in new shapes and sizes, the old predicaments and follies of men—the desperation, the impedimenta, the meanness—along with the visible capacity for elevation of the mind and soul. "This curious world which we inhabit is more wonderful than it is convenient; more beautiful than it is useful; it is more to be admired and enjoyed than used." He would see that today ten thousand engineers are busy making sure that the world shall be convenient if they bust doing it, and others are determined to increase its usefulness even though its beauty is lost somewhere along the way.

At any rate, I'd like to stroll about the countryside in Thoreau's company for a day, observing the modern scene, inspecting today's snowstorm, pointing out the sights, and offering belated apologies for my sins. Thoreau is unique among writers in that those who admire him find him uncomfortable to live with—a regular hairshirt of a man. A little band of dedicated Thoreauvians would be a sorry sight indeed: fellows who hate compromise and have compromised, fellows who love wildness and have lived tamely, and at their side, censuring them and chiding them, the ghostly figure of this upright man, who long ago gave corroboration to impulses they perceived were right and issued warnings against the things they instinctively knew to be their enemies. I should hate to be called a Thoreauvian, yet I wince every time I walk into the barn I'm pushing before me, seventy-five feet by forty, and the author of *Walden* has served as my conscience through the long stretches of my trivial days.

Hairshirt or no, he is a better companion than most, and I would not swap him for a soberer or more reasonable friend even if I could. I can reread his famous invitation with undiminished excitement. The sad thing is that not more acceptances have been received, that so many decline for one reason or another, pleading some previous engagement or ill health. But the invitation stands. It will beckon as long as this remarkable book stays in print—which will be as long as there are August afternoons in the intervals of a gentle rainstorm, as long as there are ears to catch the faint sounds of the orchestra. I find it agreeable to sit here this morning, in a house of correct proportions, and hear across a century of time his flute, his frogs and his seductive summons to the wildest revels of them all.

CHANNELLED WHELK

ANNE MORROW LINDBERGH

ANNE M. LINDBERGH (1906–   ) was born in New York City and educated at Smith College. She is the wife of Charles Lindbergh and has received many awards for her own contributions to flying. She is the author among other books of *Listen, the Wind* (1938), *The Steep Ascent* (1944), *Gift from the Sea* (1955), and *Dearly Beloved* (1962).

THE shell in my hand is deserted. It once housed a whelk, a snail-like creature, and then temporarily, after the death of the first occupant, a little hermit crab, who has run away, leaving his tracks behind him like a delicate vine on the sand. He ran away, and left me his shell. It was once a protection to him. I turn the shell in my hand, gazing into the wide open door from which he made his exit. Had it become an encumbrance? Why did he run away? Did he hope to find a better home, a better mode of living? I too have run away, I realize, I have shed the shell of my life, for these few weeks of vacation.

But his shell—it is simple; it is bare, it is beautiful. Small, only the size of my thumb, its architecture is perfect, down to the finest detail. Its shape, swelling like a pear in the center, winds in a gentle spiral to the pointed apex. Its color, dull gold, is whitened by a wash of salt from the sea. Each whorl, each faint knob, each criss-cross vein in its egg-shell texture, is as clearly defined as on the day of creation. My eye follows with delight the outer circumference of that diminutive winding staircase up which this tenant used to travel.

My shell is not like this, I think. How untidy it has become! Blurred with moss, knobby with barnacles, its shape is hardly recognizable any more. Surely, it had a shape once. It has a shape still in my mind. What is the shape of my life?

The shape of my life today starts with a family. I have a husband, five children and a home just beyond the suburbs of New York. I have also a craft, writing, and therefore work I want to pursue. The shape of my life is, of course, determined by many other things; my background and childhood, my mind and its education, my conscience and its pressures, my heart and its desires. I want to give and take from my children and husband, to share with friends and community, to carry out my obliga-

From *Gift from the Sea*, by Anne Morrow Lindbergh. ⓒ Copyright 1955 by Anne Morrow Lindbergh. Reprinted by permission of Pantheon Books, a division of Random House, Inc.

tions to man and to the world, as a woman, as an artist, as a citizen.

But I want first of all—in fact, as an end to these other desires—to be at peace with myself. I want a singleness of eye, a purity of intention, a central core to my life that will enable me to carry out these obligations and activities as well as I can. I want, in fact—to borrow from the language of the saints—to live "in grace" as much of the time as possible. I am not using this term in a strictly theological sense. By grace I mean an inner harmony, essentially spiritual, which can be translated into outward harmony. I am seeking perhaps what Socrates asked for in the prayer from the *Phaedrus* when he said, "May the outward and inward man be at one." I would like to achieve a state of inner spiritual grace from which I could function and give as I was meant to in the eye of God.

Vague as this definition may be, I believe most people are aware of periods in their lives when they seem to be "in grace" and other periods when they feel "out of grace," even though they may use different words to describe these states. In the first happy condition, one seems to carry all one's tasks before one lightly, as if borne along on a great tide; and in the opposite state one can hardly tie a shoe-string. It is true that a large part of life consists in learning a technique of tying the shoe-string, whether one is in grace or not. But there are techniques of living too; there are even techniques in the search for grace. And techniques can be cultivated. I have learned by some experience, by many examples, and by the writings of countless others before me, also occupied in the search, that certain environments, certain modes of life, certain rules of conduct are more conducive to inner and outer harmony than others. There are, in fact, certain roads that one may follow. Simplification of life is one of them.

I mean to lead a simple life, to choose a simple shell I can carry easily—like a hermit crab. But I do not. I find that my frame of life does not foster simplicity. My husband and five children must make their way in the world. The life I have chosen as wife and mother entrains a whole caravan of complications. It involves a house in the suburbs and either household drudgery or household help which wavers between scarcity and non-existence for most of us. It involves food and shelter; meals, planning, marketing, bills, and making the ends meet in a thousand ways. It involves not only the butcher, the baker, the candlestickmaker but countless other experts to keep my modern house with its modern "simplifications" (electricity, plumbing, refrigerator, gas-stove, oil-burner, dish-washer, radios, car, and numerous other

labor-saving devices) functioning properly. It involves health; doctors, dentists, appointments, medicine, cod-liver oil, vitamins, trips to the drugstore. It involves education, spiritual, intellectual, physical; schools, school conferences, car-pools, extra trips for basket-ball or orchestra practice; tutoring; camps, camp equipment and transportation. It involves clothes, shopping, laundry, cleaning, mending, letting skirts down and sewing buttons on, or finding someone else to do it. It involves friends, my husband's, my children's, my own, and endless arrangements to get together; letters, invitations, telephone calls and transportation hither and yon.

For life today in America is based on the premise of ever-widening circles of contact and communication. It involves not only family demands, but community demands, national demands, international demands on the good citizen, through social and cultural pressures, through newspapers, magazines, radio programs, political drives, charitable appeals, and so on. My mind reels with it. What a circus act we women perform every day of our lives. It puts the trapeze artist to shame. Look at us. We run a tight rope daily, balancing a pile of books on the head. Baby-carriage, parasol, kitchen chair, still under control. Steady now!

This is not the life of simplicity but the life of multiplicity that the wise men warn us of. It leads not to unification but to fragmentation. It does not bring grace; it destroys the soul. And this is not only true of my life, I am forced to conclude; it is the life of millions of women in America. I stress America, because today, the American woman more than any other has the privilege of choosing such a life. Woman in large parts of the civilized world has been forced back by war, by poverty, by collapse, by the sheer struggle to survive, into a smaller circle of immediate time and space, immediate family life, immediate problems of existence. The American woman is still relatively free to choose the wider life. How long she will hold this enviable and precarious position no one knows. But her particular situation has a significance far above its apparent economic, national or even sex limitations.

For the problem of the multiplicity of life not only confronts the American woman, but also the American man. And it is not merely the concern of the American as such, but of our whole modern civilization, since life in America today is held up as the ideal of a large part of the rest of the world. And finally, it is not limited to our present civilization, though we are faced with it now in an exaggerated form. It has always been one of the pitfalls of mankind. Plotinus was preaching the dangers of multiplicity of the world back in the third century. Yet, the problem is particularly and essentially woman's. Distraction is, always has been, and probably always will be, inherent in woman's life.

For to be a woman is to have interests and duties, raying out in all directions from the central mother-core, like spokes from the hub of a wheel. The pattern of our lives is essentially circular. We must be open to all points of the compass; husband, children, friends, home, community; stretched out, exposed, sensitive like a spider's web to each breeze that blows, to each call that comes. How difficult for us, then, to achieve a balance in the midst of these contradictory tensions, and yet how necessary for the proper functioning of our lives. How much we need, and how arduous of attainment is that steadiness preached in all rules for holy living. How desirable and how distant is the ideal of the contemplative, artist, or saint—the inner inviolable core, the single eye.

With a new awareness, both painful and humorous, I begin to understand why the saints were rarely married women. I am convinced it has nothing inherently to do, as I once supposed, with chastity or children. It has to do primarily with distractions. The bearing, rearing, feeding and educating of children; the running of a house with its thousand details; human relationships with their myriad pulls—woman's normal occupations in general run counter to creative life, or contemplative life, or saintly life. The problem is not merely one of *Woman and Career, Woman and the Home, Woman and Independence.* It is more basically: how to remain whole in the midst of the distractions of life; how to remain balanced, no matter what centrifugal forces tend to pull one off center; how to remain strong, no matter what shocks come in at the periphery and tend to crack the hub of the wheel.

What is the answer? There is no easy answer, no complete answer. I have only clues, shells from the sea. The bare beauty of the channelled whelk tells me that one answer, and perhaps a first step, is in simplification of life, in cutting out some of the distractions. But how? Total retirement is not possible. I cannot shed my responsibilities. I cannot permanently inhabit a desert island. I cannot be a nun in the midst of family life. I would not want to be. The solution for me, surely, is neither in total renunciation of the world, nor in total acceptance of it. I must find a balance somewhere, or an alternating rhythm between these two extremes; a swinging of the pendulum between solitude and communion, between retreat and return. In my periods of retreat, perhaps I can learn something to carry back into my worldly life. I can at least practice for these two weeks the simplification of outward life, as a beginning. I can follow this superficial clue, and see where it leads. Here, in beach living, I can try.

One learns first of all in beach living the art of shedding; how little one can get along with, not how much. Physical shedding to begin with, which then mysteriously spreads into other fields. Clothes, first. Of course, one needs less in the sun. But one needs less anyway, one finds suddenly. One does not need a closet-full, only a small suitcase-full. And what a relief it is! Less taking up and down of hems, less mending, and—best of all—less worry about what to wear. One finds one is shedding not only clothes—but vanity.

Next, shelter. One does not need the airtight shelter one has in winter in the North. Here I live in a bare sea-shell of a cottage. No heat, no telephone, no plumbing to speak of, no hot water, a two-burner oil stove, no gadgets to go wrong. No rugs. There were some, but I rolled them up the first day; it is easier to sweep the sand off a bare floor. But I find I don't bustle about with unnecessary sweeping and cleaning here. I am no longer aware of the dust. I have shed my Puritan conscience about absolute tidiness and cleanliness. Is it possible that, too, is a material burden? No curtains. I do not need them for privacy; the pines around my house are enough protection. I want the windows open all the time, and I don't want to worry about rain. I begin to shed my Martha-like anxiety about many things. Washable slipcovers, faded and old—I hardly see them; I don't worry about the impression they make on other people. I am shedding pride. As little furniture as possible; I shall not need much. I shall ask into my shell only those friends with whom I can be completely honest. I find I am shedding hypocrisy in human relationships. What a rest that will be! The most exhausting thing in life, I have discovered, is being insincere. That is why so much of social life is exhausting; one is wearing a mask. I have shed my mask.

I find I live quite happily without those things I think necessary in winter in the North. And as I write these words, I remember, with some shock at the disparity in our lives, a similar statement made by a friend of mine in France who spent three years in a German prison camp. Of course, he said, qualifying his remark, they did not get enough to eat, they were sometimes atrociously treated, they had little physical freedom. And yet, prison life taught him how little one can get along with, and what extraordinary spiritual freedom and peace such simplification can bring. I remember again, ironically, that today more of us in America than anywhere else in the world have the luxury of choice between simplicity and complication of life. And for the most part, we, who could choose simplicity, choose complication. War, prison, survival periods, enforce a form of simplicity on man. The monk and the nun choose it of their own free will. But if one accidentally finds it, as I have for a few days, one finds also the serenity it brings.

Is it not rather ugly, one may ask? One collects material possessions not only for security, comfort or vanity, but for beauty as well. Is your sea-shell house not ugly and bare? No, it is beautiful, my house. It is bare, of course, but the wind, the sun, the smell of the pines blow through its bareness. The unfinished beams in the roof are veiled by cobwebs. They are lovely, I think, gazing up at them with new eyes; they soften the hard lines of the rafters as grey hairs soften the lines on a middle-aged face. I no longer pull out grey hairs or sweep down cobwebs. As for the walls, it is true they looked forbidding at first. I felt cramped and enclosed by their blank faces. I wanted to knock holes in them, to give them another dimension with pictures or windows. So I dragged home from the beach grey arms of driftwood, worn satin-smooth by wind and sand. I gathered trailing green vines with floppy red-tipped leaves. I picked up the whitened skeletons of conch-shells, their curious hollowed-out shapes faintly reminiscent of abstract sculpture. With these tacked to walls and propped up in corners, I am satisfied. I have a periscope out to the world. I have a window, a view, a point of flight from my sedentary base.

I am content. I sit down at my desk, a bare kitchen table with a blotter, a bottle of ink, a sand dollar to weight down one corner, a clam shell for a pen tray, the broken tip of a conch, pink-tinged, to finger, and a row of shells to set my thoughts spinning.

I love my sea-shell of a house. I wish I could live in it always. I wish I could transport it home. But I cannot. It will not hold a husband, five children and the necessities and trappings of daily life. I can only carry back my little channelled whelk. It will sit on my desk in Connecticut, to remind me of the ideal of a simplified life, to encourage me in the game I played on the beach. To ask how little, not how much, can I get along with. To say—is it necessary?—when I am tempted to add one more accumulation to my life, when I am pulled toward one more centrifugal activity.

Simplification of outward life is not enough. It is merely the outside. But I am starting with the outside. I am looking at the outside of a shell, the outside of my life—the shell. The complete answer is not to be found on the outside, in an outward mode of living. This is only a technique, a road to grace. The final answer, I know, is always inside. But the outside can give a clue, can help one to find the inside answer. One is free, like the hermit crab, to change one's shell.

Channelled whelk, I put you down again, but you have set my mind on a journey, up an inwardly winding spiral staircase of thought.

ONE VOTE FOR THIS AGE OF ANXIETY

MARGARET MEAD

MARGARET MEAD (1901–   ) was born in Philadelphia and educated at De Pauw, Barnard and Columbia Universities. In 1926, she became assistant curator of ethnology at the American Museum of Natural History, associate curator in 1942. Her work as an anthropologist has taken her on expeditions to Samoa, New Guinea, and the Admiralty Islands. She has contributed much, through her books and lectures, to bring about a more intelligent, widespread understanding of individual and social growth. Among her books are *Coming of Age in Samoa* (1928), *Growing Up in New Guinea* (1930), *Male and Female* (1948), *New Lives for Old* (1956), and *An Anthropologist at Work* (1959).

WHEN critics wish to repudiate the world in which we live today, one of their familiar ways of doing it is to castigate modern man because anxiety is his chief problem. This, they say, in W. H. Auden's phrase, is the age of anxiety. This is what we

Reprinted from *The New York Times Magazine*, May 20, 1956, by permission of the author.

have arrived at with all our vaunted progress, our great technological advances, our great wealth—everyone goes about with a burden of anxiety so enormous that, in the end, our stomachs and our arteries and our skins express the tension under which we live. Americans who have lived in Europe come back to comment on our favorite farewell which, instead of the old goodbye (God be with you), is now "Take it easy," each American admonishing the other not to break down from the tension and strain of modern life.

Whenever an age is characterized by a phrase, it is presumably in contrast to other ages. If we are the age of anxiety, what were other ages? And here the critics and carpers do a very amusing thing. First, they give us lists of the opposites of anxiety: security, trust, self-confidence, self-direction. Then, without much further discussion, they let us assume that other ages, other periods of history, were somehow the ages of trust or confident direction.

The savage who, on his South Sea island, simply sat and let bread fruit fall into his lap, the simple peasant, at one with the fields he ploughed and the beasts he tended, the craftsman busy with his tools and lost in the fulfillment of the instinct of workmanship—these are the counter-images conjured up by descriptions of the strain under which men live today. But no one who lived in those days has returned to testify how paradisiacal they really were.

Certainly if we observe and question the savages or simple peasants in the world today, we find something quite different. The untouched savage in the middle of New Guinea isn't anxious; he is seriously and continually *frightened*—of black magic, of enemies with spears who may kill him or his wives and children at any moment, while they stoop to drink from a spring, or climb a palm tree for a coconut. He goes warily, day and night, taut and fearful.

As for the peasant populations of a great part of the world, they aren't so much anxious as hungry. They aren't anxious about whether they will get a salary raise, or which of the three colleges of their choice they will be admitted to, or whether to buy a Ford or Cadillac, or whether the kind of TV set they want is too expensive. They are hungry, cold and, in many parts of the world, they dread that local warfare, bandits, political coups may endanger their homes, their meager livelihoods and their lives. But surely they are not anxious.

For anxiety, as we have come to use it to describe our characteristic state of mind, can be contrasted with the active fear of hunger, loss, violence and death. Anxiety is the appropriate emotion when the immediate personal terror—of a volcano, an arrow, the sorcerer's spell, a stab in the back and other calamities, all directed against one's self—disappears.

This is not to say that there isn't plenty to worry about in our world of today. The explosion of a bomb in the streets of a city whose name no one had ever heard before may set in motion forces which end up

by ruining one's carefully planned education in law school, half a world away. But there is still not the personal, immediate, active sense of impending disaster that the savage knows. There is rather the vague anxiety, the sense that the future is unmanageable.

The kind of world that produces anxiety is actually a world of relative safety, a world in which no one feels that he himself is facing sudden death. Possibly sudden death may strike a certain number of unidentified other people—but not him. The anxiety exists as an uneasy state of mind, in which one has a feeling that something unspecified and undeterminable may go wrong. If the world seems to be going well, this produces anxiety—for good times may end. If the world is going badly—it may get worse. Anxiety tends to be without locus; the anxious person doesn't know whether to blame himself or other people. He isn't sure whether it is 1956 or the Administration or a change in climate or the atom bomb that is to blame for this undefined sense of unease.

It is clear that we have developed a society which depends on having the *right* amount of anxiety to make it work. Psychiatrists have been heard to say, "He didn't have enough anxiety to get well," indicating that, while we agree that too much anxiety is inimical to mental health, we have come to rely on anxiety to push and prod us into seeing a doctor about a symptom which may indicate cancer, into checking up on that old life insurance policy which may have out-of-date clauses in it, into having a conference with Billy's teacher even though his report card looks all right.

People who are anxious enough keep their car insurance up, have the brakes checked, don't take a second drink when they have to drive, are careful where they go and with whom they drive on holidays. People who are too anxious either refuse to go into cars at all—and so complicate the ordinary course of life—or drive so tensely and overcautiously that they help cause accidents. People who aren't anxious enough take chance after chance, which increases the terrible death toll of the roads.

On balance, our age of anxiety represents a large advance over savage and peasant cultures. Out of a productive system of technology drawing upon enormous resources, we have created a nation in which anxiety has replaced terror and despair, for all except the severely disturbed. The specter of hunger means something only to those Americans who can identify themselves with the millions of hungry people on other continents. The specter of terror may still be roused in some by a knock at the door in a few parts of the South, or in those who have just escaped from a totalitarian regime or who have kin still behind the Curtains.

But in this twilight world which is neither at peace nor at war, and where there is insurance against certain immediate, downright, personal disasters, for most Americans there remains only anxiety over what may happen, might happen, could happen.

This is the world out of which grows the hope, for the first time in history, of a society where there will be freedom from want and freedom from fear. Our very anxiety is born of our knowledge of what is now possible for each and for all. The number of people who consult psychiatrists today is not, as is sometimes felt, a symptom of increasing mental ill health, but rather the precursor of a world in which the hope of genuine mental health will be open to everyone, a world in which no individual feels that he need be hopelessly brokenhearted, a failure, a menace to others or a traitor to himself.

But if, then, our anxieties are actually signs of hope, why is there such a voice of discontent abroad in the land? I think this comes perhaps because our anxiety exists without an accompanying recognition of the tragedy which will always be inherent in human life, however well we build our world. We may banish hunger, and fear of sorcery, violence or secret police; we may bring up children who have learned to trust life and who have the spontaneity and curiosity necessary to devise ways of making trips to the moon; we cannot—as we have tried to do —banish death itself.

Americans who stem from generations which left their old people behind and never closed their parents' eyelids in death, and who have experienced the additional distance from death provided by two world wars fought far from our shores are today pushing away from them both a recognition of death and a recognition of the tremendous significance—for the future—of the way we live our lives. Acceptance of the inevitability of death, which, when faced, can give dignity to life, and acceptance of our inescapable role in the modern world, might transmute our anxiety about making the right choices, taking the right precautions, and the right risks into the sterner stuff of responsibility, which ennobles the whole face rather than furrowing the forehead with the little anxious wrinkles of worry.

Worry in an empty context means that men die daily little deaths. But good anxiety—not about the things that were left undone long ago, but return to haunt and harry men's minds, but active, vivid anxiety about what must be done and that quickly— binds men to life with an intense concern.

This is still a world in which too many of the wrong things happen somewhere. But this is a world in which we now have the means to make a great many more of the right things happen everywhere. For Americans, the generalization which a Swedish social scientist made about our attitudes on race relations is true in many other fields: anticipated change which we feel is right and necessary but difficult makes us unduly anxious and apprehensive, but such change, once consummated, brings a glow of relief. We are still a people who—in the literal sense— believe in making good.

WHAT I BELIEVE

E. M. FORSTER

EDWARD MORGAN FORSTER (1879–   ) was born in England and educated at King's College, Cambridge. He lived for a time in Italy and India, the scenes of some of his novels. In England he did reviewing and served as literary editor of the Labour *Daily Herald;* he also lectured on literature at Cambridge and other universities. He is known chiefly for a group of novels: *Where Angels Fear to Tread* (1905), *The Longest Journey* (1907), *A Room with a View* (1908), *Howard's End* (1910), and *A Passage to India* (1924). He has two volumes of collected stories, *The Celestial Omnibus* (1911), and *The Eternal Moment* (1928); a volume of literary papers, *Abinger Harvest* (1926); critical lectures entitled *Aspects of the Novel* (1927); also, *Two Cheers for Democracy* (1951), and *The Hill of Devi* (1953).

"I Believe" is an example of skill in stating precisely but with humanity and naturalness the basis of a man's thought.

I DO not believe in belief. But this is an age of faith, where one is surrounded by so many militant creeds that, in self-defense, one has to formulate a creed of one's own. Tolerance, good temper, and sympathy are no longer enough in a world which is rent by religious and racial persecution, in a world where ignorance rules, and science, who ought to have ruled, plays the subservient pimp. Tolerance, good temper, and sympathy—well, they are what matter really, and if the human race is not to collapse they must come to the front before long. But for the moment they don't seem enough, their action is no stronger than a flower, battered beneath a military jack boot. They want stiffening, even if the process coarsens them. Faith, to my mind, is a stiffening process, a sort of mental starch, which ought to be applied as sparingly as possible. I dislike the stuff. I do not believe in it, for its own sake, at all. Herein I probably differ from most of the contributors to this volume, who believe in belief, and are only sorry they can't swallow even more than they do. My lawgivers are Erasmus and Montaigne, not Moses and St. Paul. My temple stands not upon Mount Moriah but in the Elysian Field where even the immoral are admitted. My motto is "Lord, I disbelieve—help thou my unbelief."

I have, however, to live in an age of Faith—the sort of thing I used to hear praised and recommended when I was a boy. It is damned unpleasant, really. It is bloody in every sense of the word. And I have to keep my end up in it. Where do I start?

With personal relationships. Here is something comparatively solid in a world full of violence and cruelty. Not absolutely solid, for psychology has split

From *Two Cheers for Democracy*. Copyright, 1951, by E. M. Forster. Reprinted by permission of Harcourt, Brace & World, Inc. and Edward Arnold (Publishers) Ltd.

and shattered the idea of a "person," and has shown that there is something incalculable in each of us, which may at any moment rise to the surface and destroy our normal balance. We don't know what we're like. We can't know what other people are like. How then can we put any trust in personal relationships, or cling to them in the gathering political storm? In theory we can't. But in practice we can and do. Though A isn't unchangeably A or B unchangeably B, there can still be love and loyalty between the two. For the purpose of living one has to assume that the personality is solid, and the "self" is an entity, and to ignore all contrary evidence. And since to ignore evidence is one of the characteristics of faith, I certainly can proclaim that I believe in personal relationships.

Starting from them, I get a little order into the contemporary chaos. One must be fond of people and trust them if one isn't to make a mess of life, and it is therefore essential that they shouldn't let one down. They often do. The moral of which is that I must myself be as reliable as possible, and this I try to be. But reliability isn't a matter of contract—that is the main difference between the world of personal relationships and the world of business relationships. It is a matter for the heart, which signs no documents. In other words, reliability is impossible unless there is a natural warmth. Most men possess this warmth, though they often have bad luck and get chilled. Most of them, even when they are politicians, *want* to keep faith. And one can, at all events, show one's own little light here, one's own poor little trembling flame, with the knowledge that it's not the only light that is shining in the darkness, and not the only one which the darkness doesn't comprehend. Personal relations are despised today. They are regarded as bourgeois luxuries, as products of a time of fair weather which has now passed, and we are urged to get rid of them, and to dedicate ourselves to some movement or cause instead. I hate the idea of dying for a cause, and if I had to choose between betraying my country and betraying my friend, I hope I should have the guts to betray my country. Such a choice may scandalize the modern reader, and he may stretch out his patriotic hand to the telephone at once, and ring up the police. It wouldn't have shocked Dante, though. Dante places Brutus and Cassius in the lowest circle of Hell because they had chosen to betray their friend Julius Caesar rather than their country Rome. Probably one won't be asked to make such an agonizing choice. Still there lies at the back of every creed something terrible and hard for which the worshiper may one day be required to suffer, and there is even a terror and a hardness in this creed of personal relationships, urbane and mild though it sounds. Love and loyalty to an individual can run counter to the claims of the state. When they do—down with the state, say I, which means that the state will down me.

This brings me along to democracy, "even Love, the Beloved Republic, which feeds upon Freedom and lives." Democracy isn't a beloved republic really, and never will be. But it is less hateful than other contemporary forms of government, and to that extent it deserves our support. It does start from the assumption that the individual is important, and that all types are needed to make a civilization. It doesn't divide its citizens into the bossers and the bossed, as an efficiency regime tends to do. The people I admire most are those who are sensitive and want to create something or discover something, and don't see life in terms of power, and such people get more of a chance under a democracy than elsewhere. They found religions, great or small, or they produce literature and art, or they do disinterested scientific research, or they may be what is called "ordinary people," who are creative in their private lives, bring up their children decently, for instance, or help their neighbors. All these people need to express themselves, they can't do so unless society allows them liberty to do so, and the society which allows them most liberty is a democracy.

Democracy has another merit. It allows criticism, and if there isn't public criticism there are bound to be hushed up scandals. That is why I believe in the press, despite all its lies and vulgarity, and why I believe in Parliament. The British Parliament is often sneered at because it's a talking shop. Well, I believe in it because it is a talking shop. I believe in the private member who makes himself a nuisance. He gets snubbed and is told that he is cranky or ill-informed, but he exposes abuses which would otherwise never have been mentioned, and very often an abuse gets put right just by being mentioned. Occasionally, too, in my country, a well-meaning public official loses his head in the cause of efficiency, and thinks himself God Almighty. Such officials are particularly frequent in the Home Office. Well, there will be questions about them in Parliament sooner or later, and then they'll have to mend their steps. Whether Parliament is either a representative body or an efficient one is very doubtful, but I value it because it criticizes and talks, and because its chatter gets widely reported.

So two cheers for democracy: one because it admits variety and two because it permits criticism. Two cheers are quite enough: there is no occasion to give three. Only Love, the Beloved Republic deserves that.

What about force, though? While we are trying to be sensitive and advanced and affectionate and tolerant, an unpleasant question pops up: Doesn't all society rest upon force? If a government can't count upon the police and the army, how can it hope to rule? And if an individual gets knocked on the head or sent to a labor camp, of what significance are his opinions?

This dilemma doesn't worry me as much as it does some. I realize that all society rests upon force. But all the great creative actions, all the decent human relations, occur during the intervals when force has not managed to come to the front. These intervals are what matter. I want them to be as frequent and as lengthy as possible and I call them "civilization." Some people idealize force and pull it into the foreground and worship it, instead of keeping it in the background as long as possible. I think they make a mistake, and I think that their opposites, the mystics, err even more when they declare that force doesn't exist. I believe that it does exist, and that one of our jobs is to prevent it from getting out of its box. It gets out sooner or later, and then it destroys us and all the lovely things which we have made. But it isn't out all the time, for the fortunate reason that the strong are so stupid. Consider their conduct for a moment in the Nibelung's *Ring*. The giants there have the guns, or in other words the gold; but they do nothing with it, they do not realize that they are all-powerful, with the result that the catastrophe is delayed and the castle of Walhalla, insecure but glorious, fronts the storms for generations. Fafnir, coiled around his hoard, grumbles and grunts; we can hear him under Europe today; the leaves of the wood already tremble, and the Bird calls its warnings uselessly. Fafnir will destroy us, but by a blessed dispensation he is stupid and slow, and creation goes on just outside the poisonous blast of his breath. The Nietzschean would hurry the monster up, the mystic would say he didn't exist, but Wotan, wiser than either, hastens to create warriors before doom declares itself. The Valkyries are symbols not only of courage but of intelligence; they represent the human spirit snatching its opportunity while the going is good, and one of them even finds time to love. Brunhilde's last song hymns the recurrence of love, and since it is the privilege of art to exaggerate she goes even further, and proclaims the love which is eternally triumphant and feeds upon freedom, and lives.

So that is what I feel about force and violence. It is, alas! the ultimate reality, on this earth, but—hooray!—it doesn't always get to the front. Some people call its absences "decadence"; I call them "civilization" and find in such interludes the chief justification for the human experiment. I look the other way until fate strikes me. Whether this is due to courage or to cowardice in my own case I cannot be sure. But I know that if men hadn't looked the other way in the past nothing of any value would survive. The people I respect most behave as if they were immortal and as if society were eternal. Both assumptions are false: both of them must be accepted as true if we are to go on eating and working and loving, and are to keep open a few breathing holes for the human spirit. No millennium seems likely to descend upon humanity; no better and stronger League of Nations will be instituted; no form of Christianity and no alternative to Christianity will bring peace to the world or integrity to the individual; no "change of heart" will occur. And yet we needn't despair, indeed we cannot despair; the evidence of history shows us that men have always insisted on behaving creatively under the shadow of the sword; that they have done their artistic and scientific and domestic stuff for the sake of doing it, and that we had better follow their example under the shadow of the airplanes. Others, with more vision or courage than myself, see the salvation of humanity ahead, and will dismiss my conception of civilization as paltry, a sort of tip-and-run game. Certainly it is presumptuous to say that we *can't* improve, and that man, who has only been in power for a few thousand years, will never learn to make use of his power. All I mean is that, if people continue to kill one another at the rate they do, the world cannot get better than it is, and that since there are more people than formerly, and their means for destroying one another more diabolic, the world may well get worse. What's good in people—and consequently in the world—is their insistence on creation, their belief in friendship, in loyalty, for its own sake; and though violence remains and is indeed the major partner in this muddled establishment, I believe that creativeness re-

mains too, and will always assume direction when violence sleeps. So, though I am not an optimist, I cannot agree with Sophocles that it were better never to have been born. And although I see no evidence that each batch of births is superior to the last, I leave the field open for this happier view. This is such a difficult time to live in, especially for a European, one can't help getting gloomy and also a bit rattled.

There is of course hero worship, fervently recommended as a panacea in some quarters. But here we shall get no help. Hero worship is a dangerous vice, and one of the minor merits of a democracy is that it does not encourage it, or produce that unmanageable type of citizen known as the Great Man. It produces instead different kinds of small men, and that's a much finer achievement. But people who can't get interested in the variety of life and can't make up their own minds get discontented over this, and they long for a hero to bow down before and to follow blindly. It's significant that a hero is an integral part of the authoritarian stock in trade today. An efficiency regime can't be run without a few heroes stuck about to carry off the dullness—much as plums have to be put into a bad pudding to make it palatable. One hero at the top and a smaller one each side of him is a favorite arrangement, and the timid and the bored are comforted by such a trinity, and, bowing down, feel exalted by it.

No, I distrust Great Men. They produce a desert of uniformity around them and often a pool of blood, too, and I always feel a little man's pleasure when they come a cropper. Every now and then one reads in the newspapers some such statement as, "The *coup d'etat* appears to have failed, and Admiral Boga's whereabouts is at present unknown." Admiral Boga had probably every qualification for being a great man—an iron will, personal magnetism, dash, flair—but fate was against him, so he retires to unknown whereabouts instead of parading history with his peers. He fails with a completeness that no artist and no lover can experience, because with them the process of creation is itself an achievement, whereas with him the only possible achievement is success. I believe in aristocracy though—if that's the right word, and if a democrat may use it. Not an aristocracy of power, based upon rank and influence, but an aristocracy of the sensitive, the considerate, and the plucky. Its members are to be found in all nations and classes, and all through the ages, and there is a secret understanding between them when they meet. They represent the true human tradition, the one permanent victory of our queer race over cruelty and chaos. Thousands of them perish in obscurity; a few are great names. They are sensitive for others as well as for themselves, they are considerate without being fussy, their pluck is not swankiness but the power to endure, and they can take a joke. I give no examples —it is risky to do that—but the reader may as well consider whether this is the type of person he would like to meet and to be, and whether (going further with me) he would prefer that the type should *not* be an ascetic one. I'm against asceticism myself. I'm with the old Scotchman who wanted less chastity and more delicacy. I don't feel that my aristocrats are a real aristocracy if they thwart their bodies, since bodies are the instruments through which we register and enjoy the world. Still, I don't insist here. This isn't a major point. It's clearly possible to be sensitive, considerate, and plucky and yet be an ascetic too, and if anyone possesses the first three qualities, I'll let him in! On they go—an invincible army, yet not a victorious one. The aristocrats, the elect, the chosen, the best people—all the words that describe them are false, and all attempts to organize them fail. Again and again authority, seeing their value, has tried to net them and to utilize them as the Egyptian priesthood or the Christian Church or the Chinese civil service or the Group Movement, or some other worthy stunt. But they slip through the net and are gone; when the door is shut they are no longer in the room; their temple, as one of them remarked, is the holiness of the heart's imagination, and their kingdom, though they never possess it, is the wide open world.

With this type of person knocking about, and constantly crossing one's path if one has eyes to see or hands to feel, the experiment of earthly life cannot be dismissed as a failure. But it may well be hailed as a tragedy, the tragedy being that no device has been found by which these private decencies can be transferred to public affairs. As soon as people have power they go crooked and sometimes dotty, too, because the possession of power lifts them into a region where normal honesty never pays. For instance, the man who is selling newspapers outside the Houses of Parliament can safely leave his papers to go for a drink, and his cap beside them: anyone who takes a paper is sure to drop a copper into the cap. But the men who are inside the Houses of Parliament—they can't trust one another like that; still less can the government they compose trust other governments. No caps upon the pavement here, but suspicion, treachery, and armaments. The more highly public life is organized the lower does its morality sink; the nations of today behave to each other worse than they ever did in the past, they cheat, rob, bully, and bluff, make war without notice, and kill as many women and children as possible; whereas primitive tribes were at all events restrained by taboos. It's a humili-

ating outlook—though the greater the darkness, the brighter shine the little lights, reassuring one another, signaling, "Well, at all events I'm still here. I don't like it very much, but how are you?" Unquenchable lights of my aristocracy! Signals of the invincible army! "Come along—anyway let's have a good time while we can." I think they signal that too.

The savior of the future—if ever he comes—will not preach a new gospel. He will merely utilize my aristocracy; he will make effective the good will and the good temper which are already existing. In other words he will introduce a new technique. In economics, we are told that if there was a new technique of distribution, there need be no poverty, and people would not starve in one place while crops were dug under in another. A similar change is needed in the sphere of morals and politics. The desire for it is by no means new; it was expressed, for example, in theological terms by Jacopone da Todi over six hundred years ago. *"Ordina questo amore, O tu che m'ami,"* he said. "O thou who lovest me—set this love in order." His prayer was not granted and I do not myself believe that it ever will be, but here, and not through a change of heart, is our probable route. Not by becoming better, but by ordering and distributing his native goodness, will man shut up force into his box, and so gain time to explore the universe and to set his mark upon it worthily. At present he only explores it at odd moments, when force is looking the other way, and his divine creativeness appears as a trivial by-product, to be scrapped as soon as the drums beat and the bombers hum.

Such a change, claim the orthodox, can only be made by Christianity, and will be made by it in God's good time: man always has failed and always will fail to organize his own goodness, and it is presumptuous of him to try. This claim—solemn as it is —leaves me cold. I cannot believe that Christianity will ever cope with the present world-wide mess, and I think that such influence as it retains in modern society is due to its financial backing rather than to its spiritual appeal. It was a spiritual force once, but the indwelling spirit will have to be restated if it is to calm the waters again, and probably restated in a non-Christian form. Naturally a great many people, and people who are not only good but able and intelligent, will disagree with me here; they will vehemently deny that Christianity has failed, or they will argue that its failure proceeds from the wickedness of men, and really proves its ultimate success. They have Faith, with a large F. My faith has a very small one, and I only bring it into the open because these are strenuous and serious days, and one likes to say what one thinks while speech is still free: it may not be free much longer.

These are the reflections of an individualist and a liberal who has found his liberalism crumbling beneath him and at first felt ashamed. Then, looking around, he decided there was no special reason for shame, since other people, whatever they felt, were equally insecure. And as for individualism—there seems no way out of this, even if one wants to find one. The dictator-hero can grind down his citizens till they are all alike, but he can't melt them into a single man. That is beyond his power. He can order them to merge, he can incite them to mass antics, but they are obliged to be born separately and to die separately and, owing to these unavoidable termini, will always be running off the totalitarian rails. The memory of birth and the expectation of death always lurk within the human being, making him separate from his fellows and consequently capable of intercourse with them. Naked I came into the world, naked I shall go out of it! And a very good thing too, for it reminds me that I am naked under my shirt. Until psychologists and biologists have done much more tinkering than seems likely, the individual remains firm and each of us must consent to be one, and to make the best of the difficult job.

CLIMATES OF OPINION

CARL L. BECKER

CARL L. BECKER (1873–1945) was born in Iowa, studied at Cornell College, the University of Wisconsin, and Columbia, and taught history at Pennsylvania State College, Dartmouth, the Universities of Kansas and Minnesota, and after 1917 at Cornell University. He wrote on various phases of United States history (*Beginnings of the American People*, 1915; *The Declaration of Independence*, 1922) and on various aspects of the life of his own time. A collection of his shorter papers was published in 1935 with the title of one of his best-known essays, *Everyman His Own Historian*.

    "Climates of Opinion" was the introductory lecture in a series Professor Becker gave at Yale in 1931, published as *The Heavenly City of the Eighteenth-Century Philosophers* (1932). It furnishes in a historical perspective an introduction to the ways of speculation and belief today.

Superstition, like many other fancies, very easily loses its power when, instead of flattering our vanity, it stands in the way of it.

                         GOETHE

I

LIKE most men I hold certain cherished beliefs which I think valid because they follow logically from known and obvious facts. It often distresses me to find that an intimate friend of mine rejects one or other of these beliefs, even after I have laid before him all the relevant facts and have repeatedly retraced for his benefit the logical steps that ought to convince a reasonable mind. It may happen (is almost sure to, in fact) that he cannot refute my argument. No matter. Convinced against his will, he is of the same opinion still; and I realize at last that his mind is, unfortunately, not entirely open. Some perverse emotion, some deep-seated prejudice or unexamined preconception blinds him to the truth.

From *The Heavenly City of the Eighteenth-Century Philosophers*, 1932. By permission of the publishers, Yale University Press, New Haven.

The disturbing prejudice which leads my friend to wrong conclusions I readily forgive because I understand it. It is a minor error into which I myself, but for the grace of some happy chance, might have fallen. In major matters we agree well enough, for it happens that we are both professors. Our experience and our interests are much the same. The facts that appear relevant and the deductions that win assent are, generally speaking, the same for him as for me. Most of our premises, and the phrases we employ without analysis, are those familiar in the schools. Agreeing so well in fundamentals, we may argue copiously throughout the night, except in opinion, as Carlyle said, not being divided.

It is less easy for us, two professors, to argue throughout the night with men of another way of life —with, let us say, politicians or preachers. The argument soon falters for want of agreement. Facts which they accept as relevant we question or regard as negligible. Processes of reasoning which bring conviction to us they dismiss with perverse and casual levity as academic. Before the night is well begun the discussion peters out. We see that it is useless to go on because their thought is vitiated, not merely on the surface by prejudices peculiar to them as individuals, but fundamentally by unconscious preconceptions that are common to all men of their profession.

Nevertheless, great as our differences are, all of us—professors, politicians, preachers—would no doubt find that we had much in common after all if it were possible to meet in the flesh some distinguished representatives of a former age. Let us for the moment give way to fantasy and suppose that we could, by rubbing a Mazda lamp, bring Dante and Thomas Aquinas before us. Since it would be a waste of precious time to discuss the weather, we might ask St. Thomas to define for us the concept of natural law, a phrase as much used in his time as it is in ours. Always apt at definition, St. Thomas would not hesitate. He would say:

Since all things subject to Divine providence are ruled and measured by the eternal law . . . ; it is evident that all things partake somewhat of the eternal law, in so far as, namely, from its being imprinted on them, they derive their respective inclinations to their proper acts and ends. Now among all others, the rational creature is subject to Divine providence in the most excellent way, in so far as it partakes of a share of providence, by being provident both for itself and for others. Wherefore it has a share of the Eternal Reason, whereby it has a natural inclination to its proper act and end: and this participation of the eternal law in the rational creature is called the natural law.[1]

Having listened to this concise definition we might decide that after all a less academic subject would be better, for example, the League of Nations, something on which Dante had much to say under the caption of *De monarchia*. Being in favor of the League, Dante might support his position by the following argument:

Mankind is a whole with relation to certain parts, and is a part with relation to a certain whole. It is a whole, of course, with relation to particular kingdoms and nations, as was shown above, and it is a part with relation to the whole universe, as is self-evident. Therefore, in the manner in which the constituent parts of . . . humanity correspond to humanity as a whole, so, we say, . . . humanity corresponds as a part to its larger whole. That the constituent parts of . . . humanity correspond to humanity as a whole through the one only principle of submission to a single Prince, can be easily gathered from what has gone before. And therefore humanity corresponds to the universe itself, or to its Prince, who is God, . . . simply through one only principle, namely, the submis-

sion to a single Prince. We conclude from this that Monarchy [League of Nations] is necessary to the world for its well-being.[1]

After this the discussion would no doubt drag heavily. For what could any of us say in reply to either Dante or St. Thomas? Whatever we might say, on one side or the other, it is unlikely that either of them would find it strictly relevant, or even understand which side of the argument we were espousing. One thing only would be clear to us, namely, that the two men employed the same technique for achieving obscurity. Perhaps our first impulse would be to concede charitably that the distinguished guests were not at their best; our second, to mutter that, with all due respect, they were paying us with nonsensical rigmaroles. It may be so; to the modern mind, indeed, it is so; and it would clearly be unwise, for example, to reprint the *De monarchia* as a League of Nations propagandist tract. Nevertheless, what troubles me is that I cannot dismiss Dante or St. Thomas as unintelligent men. The judgment of posterity has placed them among the lordly ones of the earth; and if their arguments are unintelligible to us the fact cannot be attributed to lack of intelligence in them. They were at least as intelligent and learned as many who in our time have argued for or against the League of Nations—as intelligent perhaps as Clémenceau, as learned as Wilson.

Professor Whitehead has recently restored to circulation a seventeenth-century phrase—"climate of opinion." The phrase is much needed. Whether arguments command assent or not depends less upon the logic that conveys them than upon the climate of opinion in which they are sustained. What renders Dante's argument or St. Thomas' definition meaningless to us is not bad logic or want of intelligence, but the medieval climate of opinion—those instinctively held preconceptions in the broad sense, that *Weltanschauung* or world pattern—which imposed upon Dante and St. Thomas a peculiar use of the intelligence and a special type of logic. To understand why we cannot easily follow Dante or St. Thomas it is necessary to understand (as well as may be) the nature of this climate of opinion.

It is well known that the medieval world pattern, deriving from Greek logic and the Christian story, was fashioned by the church which for centuries imposed its authority upon the isolated and anarchic society of western Europe. The modern mind, which curiously notes and carefully describes everything, can indeed describe this climate of opinion although it cannot live in it. In this climate of opinion it was

---

[1] *Summa theologica*, Part II (First Part), Q. XCI, art. ii.

[1] *De monarchia* (English ed., 1904), Bk. I, chap. vii, pp. 24–25.

an unquestioned fact that the world and man in it had been created in six days by God the Father, an omniscient and benevolent intelligence, for an ultimate if inscrutable purpose. Although created perfect, man had through disobedience fallen from grace into sin and error, thereby incurring the penalty of eternal damnation. Yet happily a way of atonement and salvation had been provided through the propitiatory sacrifice of God's only begotten son. Helpless in themselves to avert the just wrath of God, men were yet to be permitted, through his mercy, and by humility and obedience to his will, to obtain pardon for sin and error. Life on earth was but a means to this desired end, a temporary probation for the testing of God's children. In God's appointed time, the Earthly City would come to an end, the earth itself be swallowed up in flames. On that last day good and evil men would be finally separated. For the recalcitrant there was reserved a place of everlasting punishment; but the faithful would be gathered with God in the Heavenly City, there in perfection and felicity to dwell forever.

Existence was thus regarded by the medieval man as a cosmic drama, composed by the master dramatist according to a central theme and on a rational plan. Finished in idea before it was enacted in fact, before the world began written down to the last syllable of recorded time, the drama was unalterable either for good or evil. There it was, precisely defined, to be understood as far as might be, but at all events to be remorselessly played out to its appointed end. The duty of man was to accept the drama as written, since he could not alter it; his function, to play the rôle assigned. That he might play his rôle according to the divine text, subordinate authorities—church and state—deriving their just powers from the will of God, were instituted among men to dispose them to submission and to instruct them in their proper lines. Intelligence was essential, since God had endowed men with it. But the function of intelligence was strictly limited. Useless to inquire curiously into the origin or final state of existence, since both had been divinely determined and sufficiently revealed. Useless, even impious, to inquire into its ultimate meaning, since God alone could fully understand it. The function of intelligence was therefore to demonstrate the truth of revealed knowledge, to reconcile diverse and pragmatic experience with the rational pattern of the world as given in faith.

Under the bracing influence of this climate of opinion the best thought of the time assumed a thoroughly rationalistic form. I know it is the custom to call the thirteenth century an age of faith, and to contrast it with the eighteenth century, which is thought to be preeminently the age of reason. In a sense the distinction is true enough, for the word "reason," like other words, has many meanings. Since eighteenth-century writers employed reason to discredit Christian dogma, a "rationalist" in common parlance came to mean an "unbeliever," one who denied the truth of Christianity. In this sense Voltaire was a rationalist, St. Thomas a man of faith. But this use of the word is unfortunate, since it obscures the fact that reason may be employed to support faith as well as to destroy it. There were, certainly, many differences between Voltaire and St. Thomas, but the two men had much in common for all that. What they had in common was the profound conviction that their beliefs could be reasonably demonstrated. In a very real sense it may be said of the eighteenth century that it was an age of faith as well as of reason, and of the thirteenth century that it was an age of reason as well as of faith.

This is not a paradox. On the contrary, passionate faith and an expert rationalism are apt to be united. Most men (of course I need parentheses here to take care of simple-minded folk and the genuine mystics) —most intelligent men who believe passionately that God's in his heaven and all's right with the world— feel the need of good and sufficient reasons for their faith, all the more so if a few disturbing doubts have crept in to make them uneasy. This is perhaps one of the reasons why the thought of Dante's time was so remorselessly rationalistic. The faith was still intact, surely; but it was just ceasing to be instinctively held —its ablest adherents just becoming conscious that it was held as faith. All the more need, therefore, for proving it up to the hilt. It was precisely because St. Thomas believed in a divinely ordered world that he needed, for his own peace of mind, an impregnable rational proof of a divinely ordered world. He could never have said, with Tertullian, "I believe that which is absurd." He could easily have said, with St. Anselm, "I believe in order that I may know." He might well have added, "I should be distressed indeed if I could not find a rational demonstration of what I know."

To reconcile diverse and pragmatic experience with a rational pattern of the world is a sufficiently difficult task, even if experience be limited and knowledge not too great—an impossible task unless logic proves amenable to the reasons of the heart which reason knows not of. And so the men of Dante's time found it. To devise a highly intricate dialectic was, of course, essential, but the least of their difficulties; for even with the aid of Aristotle's logic it was still not always possible to press what William James called the "irreducible brute facts" into the neat categories prescribed by the faith. It was therefore necessary, in emergencies, to seek, beneath the literal significance of authoritative texts, hidden meanings which could be elicited only by the aid of a symbolical interpretation. *Litera gesta docet; quid credas, allegoria; moralis quid agas; quo tendas, anagogia*—so runs the famous formula which the schoolmen devised for use in the schools, a formula which might be freely rendered:

> The letter teaches what we know,
> Anagogia what we hope is so;
> Faith's confirmed by allegories,
> Conduct's shaped by moral stories.

Thus it was possible for the thirteenth century, employing a highly intricate dialectic supported on occasion by a symbolical interpretation, to justify the ways of God to man. Paradise lost and paradise regained—such was the theme of the drama of existence as understood in that age; and all the best minds of the time were devoted to its explication. Theology related and expounded the history of the world. Philosophy was the science that rationalized and reconciled nature and history. Logic provided both theology and philosophy with an adequate methodology. As a result we have, among innumerable other works, the *Summa theologica*, surely one of the most amazing and stupendous products of the human mind. It is safe to say that never before or since has the wide world been so neatly boxed and compassed, so completely and confidently understood, every known detail of it fitted, with such subtle and loving precision, into a consistent and convincing whole.

We have now remained in the medieval climate of opinion as long as it is perhaps quite safe to do. Let us then descend from the peaks of the thirteenth to the lower levels of the twentieth century—to an atmosphere in which, since it is charged with a richer factual content, we can breathe with greater ease and comfort.

II

What then can we—scientists, historians, philosophers of the twentieth century—make of the theology-history, the philosophy-science, the dialectic-methodology of the thirteenth century? We can—must, indeed, since that is our habit—peruse with infinite attention and indifference the serried, weighty folios of the *Summa* and such works now carefully preserved in libraries. We can perhaps wonder a little —although, since nothing is alien to us, we are rarely caught wondering—at the unfailing zest, the infinite patience, the extraordinary ingenuity and acumen therein displayed. We can even understand what is

therein recorded well enough to translate it clumsily into modern terms. The one thing we cannot do with the *Summa* of St. Thomas is to meet its arguments on their own ground. We can neither assent to them nor refute them. It does not even occur to us to make the effort, since we instinctively feel that in the climate of opinion which sustains such arguments we could only gasp for breath. Its conclusions seem to us neither true nor false, but only irrelevant; and they seem irrelevant because the world pattern into which they are so dexterously woven is no longer capable of eliciting from us either an emotional or an æsthetic response.

With the best will in the world it is quite impossible for us to conceive of existence as a divinely ordered drama, the beginning and end of which is known, the significance of which has once for all been revealed. For good or ill we must regard the world as a continuous flux, a ceaseless and infinitely complicated process of waste and repair, so that "all things and principles of things" are to be regarded as no more than "inconstant modes or fashions," as the "concurrence, renewed from moment to moment, of forces parting sooner or later on their way." The beginning of this continuous process of change is shrouded in impenetrable mist; the end seems more certain, but even less engaging. According to J. H. Jeans:

Everything points with overwhelming force to a definite event, or series of events, of creation at some time or times, not infinitely remote. The universe cannot have originated by chance out of its present ingredients, and neither can it have been always the same as now. For in either of these events no atoms would be left save such as are incapable of dissolving into radiation; there would be neither sunlight nor starlight but only a cool glow of radiation uniformly diffused through space. This is, indeed, so far as present-day science can see, the final end towards which all creation moves, and at which it must at long last arrive.[1]

We need not, of course, make immediate preparation for that far-off, portentous event; the universe is still a going concern and will outlast our time. But we may be reasonably curious about the relation of man to this inevitable running down of the universe. How did man enter this galley, and what is he doing in it? According to Professor Dampier-Whetham, science offers two possible answers:

Life . . . may be regarded either as a negligible accident in a bye-product of the cosmic process, or as the

---

[1] *Eos, or the Wider Aspects of Cosmogony*, p. 55; quoted in Dampier-Whetham, *A History of Science*, p. 483.

supreme manifestation of the high effort of creative evolution, for which the Earth alone, in the chances of time and space, have given a fitting home.[1]

Between these alternatives there is little enough to choose, since in either case man must be regarded as part of the cosmic process, fated to extinction with it. Let us listen to Bertrand Russell:

That man is the product of causes which had no pre-vision of the end they were achieving; that his origin, his growth, his hopes and fears, his loves and his beliefs, are but the outcome of accidental collocations of atoms; that no fire, no heroism, no intensity of thought and feeling can preserve an individual life beyond the grave; that all the labours of all the ages, all the devotion, all the in-spiration, all the noonday brightness of human genius are destined to extinction in the vast death of the solar sys-tem, and that the whole temple of man's achievement must inevitably be buried beneath the debris of a uni-verse in ruins—all these things, if not quite beyond dis-pute, are yet so nearly certain that no philosophy which rejects them can hope to stand.[2]

Edit and interpret the conclusions of modern science as tenderly as we like, it is still quite impos-sible for us to regard man as the child of God for whom the earth was created as a temporary habita-tion. Rather must we regard him as little more than a chance deposit on the surface of the world, carelessly thrown up between two ice ages by the same forces that rust iron and ripen corn, a sentient organism endowed by some happy or unhappy accident with intelligence indeed, but with an intelligence that is conditioned by the very forces that it seeks to under-stand and to control. The ultimate cause of this cosmic process of which man is a part, whether God or electricity or a "stress in the ether," we know not. Whatever it may be, if indeed it be anything more than a necessary postulate of thought, it ap-pears in its effects as neither benevolent nor malevo-lent, as neither kind nor unkind, but merely as in-different to us. What is man that the electron should be mindful of him! Man is but a foundling in the cosmos, abandoned by the forces that created him. Unparented, unassisted and undirected by om-niscient or benevolent authority, he must fend for himself, and with the aid of his own limited in-telligence find his way about in an indifferent uni-verse.

Such is the world pattern that determines the character and direction of modern thinking. The pattern has been a long time in the weaving. It has

[1] *A History of Science*, p. 482.

[2] *Mysticism and Logic*, p. 47; quoted in Dampier-Whetham, *A History of Science*, p. 487.

taken eight centuries to replace the conception of existence as divinely composed and purposeful drama by the conception of existence as a blindly running flux of disintegrating energy. But there are signs that the substitution is now fully accomplished; and if we wished to reduce eight centuries of intellectual history to an epigram, we could not do better than to borrow the words of Aristophanes, "Whirl is king, having deposed Zeus."

Perhaps the most important consequence of this revolution is that we look about in vain for any semblance of the old authority, the old absolute, for any stable foothold from which to get a running start. Zeus, having been deposed, can no longer serve as a first premise of thought. It is true we may still be-lieve in Zeus; many people do. Even scientists, his-torians, philosophers still accord him the customary worship. But this is no more than a personal privi-lege, to be exercised in private, as formerly, in Prot-estant countries, Papists were sometimes permitted to celebrate mass in private chapels. No serious scholar would now postulate the existence and good-ness of God as a point of departure for explaining the quantum theory or the French Revolution. If I should venture, as certain historians once did, to ex-pound the thought of the eighteenth century as having been foreordained by God for the punishment of a perverse and stiff-necked generation, you would shift uneasily in your chairs, you would "register" embarrassment, and even blush a little to think that a trusted colleague should exhibit such bad taste. The fact is that we have no first premise. Since Whirl is king, we must start with the whirl, the mess of things as presented in experience. We start with the irreducible brute fact, and we must take it as we find it, since it is no longer permitted to coax or cajole it, hoping to fit it into some or other category of thought on the assumption that the pattern of the world is a logical one. Accepting the fact as given, we observe it, experiment with it, verify it, measure it if possible, and reason about it as little as may be. The questions we ask are "What?" and "How?" What are the facts and how are they related? If sometimes in a moment of absent-mindedness or idle diversion, we ask the question "Why?" the answer escapes us. Our supreme object is to measure and master the world rather than to understand it.

Since our supreme object is to measure and mas-ter the world, we can make relatively little use of theology, philosophy, and deductive logic—the three stately entrance ways to knowledge erected in the Middle Ages. In the course of eight centuries these disciplines have fallen from their high estate, and in their place we have enthroned history, science, and the technique of observation and measurement.

Theology, or something that goes under that name, is still kept alive by the faithful, but only by artificial respiration. Its functions, the services it rendered in the time of St. Thomas, have been taken over, not as is often supposed by philosophy, but by history—the study of man and his world in the time sequence. Theology in the thirteenth century presented the story of man and the world according to the divine plan of salvation. It provided the men of that age with an authentic philosophy of history, and they could afford to ignore the factual experience of mankind since they were so well assured of its ultimate cause and significance. But in the succeeding centuries men turned more and more to an investigation of the recorded story of mankind, bringing to that enterprise a remarkable attention to detail, an ever greater preoccupation with the factual event. In the light of the mass of irreducible brute facts thus accumulated, the theological vision of man and his world faded into a pale replica of the original picture. In the eighteenth century the clear-cut theological philosophy of history had degenerated into an amiable and gentlemanly "philosophy teaching by example." In the early nineteenth century, history could still be regarded as the Transcendent Idea realizing itself in the actual. In our time, history is nothing but history, the notation of what has occured, just as it happened. The object of history, according to Santayana, is quite simply "to fix the order of events throughout past times in all places." No respectable historian any longer harbors ulterior motives; and one who should surreptitiously introduce the gloss of a transcendent interpretation into the human story would deserve to be called a philosopher and straightway lose his reputation as a scholar.

I am, of course, using the word "history" in the broad sense. It is to be understood as a method of approach rather than as a special field of study. Literature and language, government and law, economics, science and mathematics, love and sport—what is there that has not in our time been studied historically? Much of what is called science is properly history, the history of biological or physical phenomena. The geologist gives us the history of the earth; the botanist relates the life history of plants. Professor Whitehead has recently illuminated physics by tracing the history of physical concepts. To regard all things in their historical setting appears, indeed, to be an instructive procedure of the modern mind. We do it without thinking, because we can scarcely think at all without doing it. The modern climate of opinion is such that we cannot seemingly understand our world unless we regard it as a going concern. We cannot properly know things as they are unless

we know "how they came to be what they are." Nor is it merely, or chiefly, the succession of external events that engages our attention. No doubt St. Thomas was aware that one thing follows another. What is peculiar to the modern mind is the disposition and the determination to regard ideas and concepts, the truth of things as well as the things themselves, as changing entities, the character and significance of which at any given time can be fully grasped only by regarding them as points in an endless process of differentiation, of unfolding, of waste and repair. Let St. Thomas ask *us* to define anything —for example, the natural law—let him ask us to tell him what it *is*. We cannot do it. But, given time enough, we can relate for him its history. We can tell him what varied forms the natural law has assumed up to now. Historical-mindedness is so much a preconception of modern thought that we can identify a particular thing only by pointing to the various things it successively was before it became that particular thing which it will presently cease to be.

Besides the historical approach to knowledge we have another to which we are even more committed —the scientific. As history has gradually replaced theology, so science has replaced philosophy. Philosophy, it is true, has managed, much better than theology, to keep up appearances in the modern world, and at the present moment signs are not wanting of refurbishings going on in its ancient and somewhat dilapidated dwelling. Yet, it is obvious that the undisputed sway which it formerly exercised has long been usurped by natural science. In the hands of St. Thomas, philosophy, with "deductive" logic as its instrument of precision, was a method of building a rational world, its aim being to reconcile experience with revealed truth. But the influences which disposed succeeding generations to examine the facts of human history, induced them also to examine the facts of natural phenomena. The rise of history and of science were but two results of a single impulse, two aspects of the trend of modern thought away from an overdone rationalization of the facts to a more careful and disinterested examination of the facts themselves.

Galileo, for example (not that he was the first by any means), did not ask what Aristotle had said about falling bodies, or whether it was reasonable to suppose that a ten-pound weight would fall to the ground more quickly than a one-pound weight. He applied to this problem the scientific method. He dropped two weights, differing as ten to one, from the leaning tower, and noted the fact that both weights reached the ground at the same time. In such a world as this, he said in effect, this is the way falling bodies behave. If that is not possible in a rational world, then the world we live in is not a rational one. Facts are primary and what chiefly concern us; they are stubborn and irreducible and we cannot get around them. They may be in accord with reason, let us hope that they are; but whether they are so or not is only a question of fact to be determined like any other.

This subtle shift in the point of view was perhaps the most important event in the intellectual history of modern times, but its implications were not at once understood. Philosophy continued to reign, and when in the eighteenth century she added a new word to her title (calling herself natural philosophy), no one noted the fact as ominous. Galileo and his successors were philosophers too, preëminently so, since their marvelous discoveries, based upon observation and experiment, uncovered so many secret places in the world, and by promising to banish mystery from the universe seemed to leave it more obviously rational than they found it. The laws of nature and nature's God appeared henceforth to be one and the same thing, and since every part of God's handiwork could all in good time be reasonably demonstrated, the intelligent man could very well do with a minimum of faith—except, of course (the exception was tremendous but scarcely noticed at the time), faith in the uniform behavior of nature and in the capacity of reason to discover its *modus operandi*.

In the course of the nineteenth century this optimistic outlook became overcast. The marriage of fact and reason, of science and the universal laws of nature, proved to be somewhat irksome, and in the twentieth century it was, not without distress, altogether dissolved. Natural philosophy was transformed into natural science. Natural science became science, and scientists rejected, as a personal affront, the title of philosopher, which formerly they had been proud to bear. The vision of man and his world as a neat and efficient machine, designed by an intelligent Author of the Universe, gradually faded away. Professors of science ceased to speak with any assurance of the laws of nature, and were content to pursue, with unabated ardor, but without any teleological implications whatever, their proper business of observing and experimenting with the something which is the stuff of the universe, of measuring and mastering its stress and movement. "Science," said Lloyd Morgan, "deals exclusively with changes of configuration, and traces the accelerations which are observed to occur, leaving to metaphysics to deal with the underlying agency, if it exists." [1]

It is well known that the result of pursuing this restricted aim (the scientific method reduced to its

[1] *Interpretation of Nature*, p. 58.

lowest terms) has been astounding. It is needless to say that we live in a machine age, that the art of inventing is the greatest of our inventions, or that within a brief space of fifty years the outward conditions of life have been transformed. It is less well understood that this bewildering experience has given a new slant to our minds. Fresh discoveries and new inventions are no longer the result of fortunate accidents which we are expected to note with awe. They are all a part of the day's work, anticipated, deliberately intended, and brought to pass according to schedule. Novelty has ceased to excite wonder because it has ceased to be novelty; on the contrary, the strange, so habituated have we become to it, is of the very essence of the customary. There is nothing new in heaven or earth not dreamt of in our laboratories; and we should be amazed indeed if tomorrow and tomorrow and tomorrow failed to offer us something new to challenge our capacity for readjustment. Science has taught us the futility of troubling to understand the "underlying agency" of the things we use. We have found that we can drive an automobile without knowing how the carburetor works, and listen to a radio without mastering the secret of radiation. We really haven't time to stand amazed, either at the starry firmament above or the Freudian complexes within us. The multiplicity of things to manipulate and make use of so fully engages our attention that we have neither the leisure nor the inclination to seek a rational explanation of the force that makes them function so efficiently.

In dismissing the underlying agency with a casual shrug, we are in good company. The high priest of science, even more than the common man, is a past master of this art. It is one of the engaging ironies of modern thought that the scientific method, which it was once fondly hoped would banish mystery from the world, leaves it every day more inexplicable. Physics, which it was thought had dispensed with the need of metaphysics, has been transformed by its own proper researches into the most metaphysical of disciplines. The more attentively the physicist looks at the material stuff of the world the less there is to see. Under his expert treatment the substantial world of Newtonian physics has been dissolved into a complex of radiant energies. No efficient engineer or Prime Mover could have designed the world, since it can no longer be fully understood in terms of mechanics. "What is the sense of talking about a mechanical explanation," asks Professor Whitehead, "when you do not know what you mean by mechanics?" [1] We are told that if we ascribe position to anything it ceases to have determinable velocity; if we ascertain its velocity it ceases to have deter-

[1] *Science and the Modern World*, p. 24.

minable position. The universe is said to be composed of atoms, an atom is said to be composed of a nucleus around which electrons revolve in determinable orbits; but experiments seem to show that an electron may, for reasons best known to itself, be moving in two orbits at the same time. To this point Galileo's common-sense method of noting the behavior of things, of sticking close to the observable facts, has brought us: it has at last presented us with a fact that common sense repudiates.

What can we do? Reason and logic cry out in pain no doubt; but we have long since learned not to bother overmuch with reason and logic. Logic was formerly visualized as something outside us, something existing independently which, if we were willing, could take us by the hand and lead us into the paths of truth. We now suspect that it is something the mind has created to conceal its timidity and keep up its courage, a hocus-pocus designed to give formal validity to conclusions we are willing to accept if everybody else in our set will too. If all men are mortal (an assumption), and if Socrates was a man (in the sense assumed), no doubt Socrates must have been mortal; but we suspect that we somehow knew all this before it was submitted to the test of a syllogism. Logics have a way of multiplying in response to the changes in point of view. First there was one logic, then there were two, then there were several; so that now, according to one authority (if a contributor to the *Encyclopædia Britannica* who ventures to employ humor can be an authority), the state of logic is "that of Israel under the Judges, every man doeth that which is right in his own eyes." With all due allowance made for mathematical logic (which has to do with concepts, not with facts), and for the logic of probability (which Mr. Keynes assures us has a probable validity), the secure foundations of deductive and inductive logic have been battered to pieces by the ascertainable facts, so that we really have no choice; we must cling to the ascertainable facts though they slay us.

Physicists, therefore, stick to the ascertainable facts. If logic presumes to protest in the name of the law, they know how to square it, so that it complaisantly looks the other way while they go on with illicit enterprises—with the business, for example (it is Sir William Bragg who vouches for it), of teaching "the wave theory of light on Monday, Wednesday, and Friday, and the quantum theory on Tuesday, Thursday, and Saturday." It need not surprise us, then, to learn that physicists make nothing, when it suits their convenience, of regarding nucleus and electron, not as substances, but only as radiations—thus, casually dissolving the substantial world into a congeries of repellent and attractive velocities which we are invited to believe in because they can be mathematically identified and made use of. Perhaps, as Professor Jeans suggests, the world we live in was designed by a mathematician. Why not, indeed, if it can be most easily understood in terms of mathematical formulas? We know that two apples plus two apples make four apples. We have always taken it for granted that the apples exist, but we can very well understand that even if no apples are anywhere found it still remains true that two plus two make four. The mathematician gets on just as well without the apples, better indeed, since the apples have other attributes besides number. When sufficiently hard pressed, therefore, the physicist solves his difficulties by turning mathematician. As mathematician he can calculate the velocities that are observed to occur, meantime assuring us that the velocities could readily be attributed to substantial electrons, provided substantial electrons with such velocities should ever turn up. There is really no occasion for despair: our world can be computed even if it doesn't exist.

Perhaps I have said enough to suggest that the essential quality of the modern climate of opinion is factual rather than rational. The atmosphere which sustains our thought is so saturated with the actual that we can easily do with a minimum of the theoretical. We necessarily look at our world from the point of view of history and from the point of view of science. Viewed historically, it appears to be something in the making, something which can at best be only tentatively understood since it is not yet finished. Viewed scientifically, it appears as something to be accepted, something to be manipulated and mastered, something to adjust ourselves to with the least possible stress. So long as we can make efficient use of things, we feel no irresistible need to understand them. No doubt it is for this reason chiefly that the modern mind can be so wonderfully at ease in a mysterious universe.

INDEX TO AUTHORS

INDEX TO AUTHORS